DATE DUE

Play from Birth to Twelve
and Beyond

GARLAND REFERENCE LIBRARY OF SOCIAL SCIENCE (VOLUME 970)

Play from Birth to Twelve and Beyond

Contexts, Perspectives, and Meanings

Editors
Doris Pronin Fromberg
Doris Bergen

GARLAND PUBLISHING, INC.
A member of the Taylor & Francis Group
New York & London
1998

We dedicate this book to the Dorises' husbands, Mel Fromberg and Joel Fink, who endured many hours of free-play time alone and many piles of papers in their homes while their wives were working at playing.

Library of Congress Cataloging-in-Publication Data

Play from birth to twelve and beyond : contexts, perspectives, and meanings /
    editors, Doris Pronin Fromberg, Doris Bergen.
        p.   cm. — (Garland reference library of social science ; v. 970)
    Includes bibliographical references and index.
    ISBN 0-8153-1745-X (alk. paper)
    1. Play. 2. Child development. 3. Play—Social aspects. I. Fromberg,
Doris Pronin, 1937– . II. Bergen, Doris. III. Series.
LB1137.P5545 1998
155.4'18—dc21   97-45203
                                                CIP

Cover photograph by Werner Bokelberg, The Image Bank, NY
Cover design by Robert Vankeirsbilck

Printed on acid-free, 250-year-life paper
Manufactured in the United States of America

Contents

xi   Preface

xv   Introduction
Doris Pronin Fromberg and Doris Bergen

1   **Section I. Contexts, Perspectives, and Meanings of Play**

3   **Contexts for Play**

5   Play in Historical Contexts
Donna R. Barnes

14   Play in the Context of Life-Span Human Development
Valeria J. Freysinger

23   Diversity and Play: Influences of Race, Culture, Class, and Gender
Patricia G. Ramsey

35   **Perspectives on Play**

37   Play as Children See It
Greta G. Fein and Nancy W. Wiltz

50   Play: A Medium for Literacy Development
James F. Christie

56   Play and Its Influence on the Development of Young Children's
Mathematical Thinking
Ranald H. Jarrell

68   Dabbling, Discovery, and Dragonflies: Scientific Inquiry
and Exploratory Representational Play
Christopher R. Wolfe, R. Hays Cummins, and Christopher A. Myers

77   Clinical Perspectives on Play
Karen Gitlin-Weiner

93 Play and Technology: Revised Realities and Potential Perspectives
Yasmin Bettina Kafai

101 **Meanings of Play**

103 The Meaning of Play as a Human Experience
Myrdene Anderson

109 No Learning by Coercion: *Paidia* and *Paideia* in Platonic Philosophy
Stephen R. Morris

119 Play, Proteus, and Paradox: Education for a Chaotic and
Supersymmetric World
Karen VanderVen

133 **Section II. Perspectives on Play Development**

135 **General Play Development**

137 Play Development from Birth to Age Four
Barbara P. Garner

146 Play Development from Ages Four to Eight
James E. Johnson

154 Play Development from Ages Eight to Twelve
M. Lee Manning

163 **Language Development and Play**

165 Play and Language: Individual Differences as Evidence of Development
and Style
Cecilia Shore

175 Language and Play: Natural Partners
Jane Ilene Freeman Davidson

185 **Social and Emotional Development and Play**

187 Gender Identity and Play
Beverly I. Fagot and Leslie Leve

193 Play as the Language of Children's Feelings
Garry Landreth and Linda Homeyer

199 **Play as a Developmental Tool**

201 The Role of Play in Assessment
Rebecca Fewell and Michelle Glick

208 Can I Play Too? Reflections on the Issues for Children with Disabilities
Gayle Mindes

215 Section III. Physical and Social Contexts of Play

217 Physical Settings for Play

219 City Play
Amanda Dargan and Steve Zeitlin

225 Children's Outdoor Play: An Endangered Activity
Mary S. Rivkin

232 Perspectives on Play in Playgrounds
Joe L. Frost and Irma C. Woods

241 School-Based Play and Social Interactions: Opportunities and Limitations
Jeffrey Trawick-Smith

248 Play as Ritual in Health Care Settings
Laura Gaynard

257 Play and Social Interactions

259 Adult Direct and Indirect Influences on Play
Wendy Haight

266 Peer and Sibling Influences on Play
Sherri Oden and Jennifer A. Hall

277 Adult Influences on Play: The Vygotskian Approach
Elena Bodrova and Deborah J. Leong

283 Intergenerational Play: Parents and Children
Mary Martin Patton

290 Play between Generations: Grandparents and Children
Carol Seefeldt

301 Section IV. Particular Meanings Embedded in Playful Experiences

303 Games, Achievement, and the Mastery of Social Skills
Peter J. Freitag

313 Fantasy and Imagination
Dorothy G. Singer and Jerome L. Singer

319 Challenge and Risk-Taking in Play
Tom Jambor

324 Play as a Context for Humor Development
Doris Bergen

338 Sociocultural Influences on Gender-Role Behaviors in Children's Play
Alice Sterling Honig

348 Play with Violence: Understanding and Responding Effectively
Diane Levin

357   Section V. Structuring the Study of Play

359   The Meanings in Play with Objects
      Shirley K. Morgenthaler

368   Social Play
      Robert J. Coplan and Kenneth H. Rubin

378   Sociodramatic Play: Pretending Together
      Patricia Monighan Nourot

392   Constructive Play
      George Forman

401   Rough-and-Tumble Play from Childhood through Adolescence:
      Differing Perspectives
      Anthony D. Pellegrini

409   Games with Rules
      Rheta DeVries

416   Sport as Play (and Work)
      Dan C. Hilliard

425   Section VI. Play in the Disciplines and Professions

427   The Arts and Humanities

429   Transcendence in the Play of Remembrance
      William R. Myers

435   Play in the Visual Arts: One Photographer's Way-of-Working
      Hilary A. Johnson

442   The Playful Ways of the Performing Artist
      Anne L. Wennerstrand

449   The Natural and Social Sciences

451   At Play in the Field of Archaeology
      Susan S. Lukesh

455   Playfulness in the Biological Sciences
      Roger Ganschow with Leonore Ganschow

461   Sociologists and Play Research
      Donald E. Lytle

468   Chemists and Play
      Elizabeth Kean

473   The Playful Ways of Mathematicians' Work
      Sharon Whitton

483   Business, Education, Journalism, the Law, and Medicine

485   Mixing Business with Pleasure: Play in the World of Work
       Lynette Unger

493   Play among Education Professionals
       Joan P. Isenberg

499   Play by Newspaper Journalists and Editors
       Ellen C. Creager

504   Use of Play in the Law
       Christopher E. Mengel

507   Playfulness in Medicine: A Pediatric Perspective
       Debra Esernio-Jenssen and Victor Turow

511   Section VII. The Present and Future of Play

513   Electronically Mediated Playscapes
       Eugene F. Provenzo Jr.

519   Advocacy for the Child's Right to Play
       Marcy Guddemi, Tom Jambor, and Robin Moore

530   Educational Implications of Play with Computers
       Steven B. Silvern

537   Emerging and Future Contexts, Perspectives, and Meanings of Play
       Doris Bergen and Doris Pronin Fromberg

543   Contributors

555   Index

Preface

Play is pervasive, infusing human activity throughout the life span. In particular, it serves to characterize childhood, the period from birth to age twelve. Within the past twenty years, many additions to the knowledge base on childhood play have been published in popular and scholarly literature. This literature has documented the study of play in varied contexts, explored it from numerous perspectives, and imbued it with a range of meanings. This book assembles and integrates this information, discusses disparate and diverse components, highlights the underlying dynamic processes of play, and provides a forum from which new questions may emerge and new methods of inquiry may develop. The place of new technologies and the future of play in the context of contemporary society also are discussed.

To accomplish this intellectually challenging task, a distinguished group of authors who have made strong scholarly contributions to the study of play from a range of perspectives join a group of distinguished professionals from a range of fields who have thought about the relationship of their work to play for the first time. Each contributor has prepared an original essay addressing a topic relevant to play.

This work can serve as a resource for students or teachers of the arts and humanities, social sciences, and various professional fields. Anthropologists, child development specialists, educators, psychologists, sociologists, community planners, play advocates, communication specialists, and human service professionals will all find this book to be useful. Beyond illuminating the meanings of play from these various perspectives, there is information that can serve to legitimize and advocate for play throughout childhood and the life span. Interested individuals who may have no specific link to play in their professional lives but who are players in their personal lives will find support for their playful selves. If they can learn about the value of play and consider the contexts in which it takes place, the perspectives on its qualities, and the meanings embedded in its practice, their lives will also be enriched, as will those of the children with whom they share their life space.

There is validity in taking play seriously (and playfully) as an intellectual construct. Moreover, there are important social, emotional, aesthetic, and cultural meanings embedded in play. This exploration of the knowledge base about play reconceptualizes the construct as one that is connected and integrated with its past, its present, and its future.

This book began to take shape outdoors on a paper napkin as the editors began to play with its possibilities. That napkin, however, represents the confluence of a strong oral and sociocultural tradition out of which the editors grew. Each in her own way had become seduced by the elusive and essential power of play in her own life as well as attracted to play as a subject of study.

As a child growing up in New York City, Doris Fromberg remembers social group play as a cement sidewalk activity with other children, an indoor activity with one or two children, and as a solitary activity. Ball games on the city street stand out as an involving, highly self-motivated, time-consuming, repetitive, skill-building process. She remembers stoop ball, in which she could gain points by bouncing the ball against the edge of the cement step, avoiding the riser. She remembers Chinese handball, in which the brick wall of a small apartment building served as a target surface and the cement sidewalk panels served as each player's separate area. She remembers lots of games of potsie or hopscotch or skelly, in which chalk-marked sections of sidewalk served as the playing field for tossing or flicking bottle caps or other markers into successive squares. Endless hours of playing cards began at four years of age with such games as war, casino, slapjack, rummy, gin rummy, poker, canasta, and an irretrievable version of bridge. Checkers at four years of age, chess at five, Monopoly at six, Sorry, Ouija, and other board games followed. All of these games included an element of competition.

With those boys who had train sets, she spent time setting up the terrain and mostly watching the repetitive circuits. In middle childhood, she occasionally played marbles and territory with the boys. "Territory," in retrospect, was practice in knife-throwing, and the game of marbles was practice in aiming (as were ball games in general).

Throughout childhood, there were also girl-owned dolls and playing house, often with elaborate props and fantasies that created an empowered world in which children alone could function without adults, a sort of country idyll, similar to the Catskill bungalow colonies that some children visited in the summer. Another fantasy-based activity took place in the backyards of houses that children annexed as their private thoroughfare. Small groups of children imagined adventures that included punishing and tying up the children who lived around the corner ("the enemy"). These adventures were born and died in the realm of imagination. In middle childhood, children would take long excursions in which they explored empty lots and watched the action at the car barns of the trolley/bus company depot while spinning stories about other times and places. They watched insects, mostly ants and earthworms, and built barriers and habitats for them. Both boys and girls engaged in these games, the boys during middle childhood moving away from the chalk-marked games into roadway-sited punchball or stickball.

Solitary play extended the doll-play fantasy with props, including building a bomb shelter under the kitchen table, building with small wooden blocks and Lincoln Logs, playing with plasticene, drawing and painting, knitting with a "horse rein," and sitting on the windowsill while watching the traffic and imagining herself in other times and places. Although adults might classify some of these activities as arts and crafts or sports, they felt like play because they were self-chosen, self-paced, absorbing, and satisfying. These were activities in which, without reflecting about the feelings, she felt competent or reasonably challenged. They transcended the moment and felt timeless rather than rushed.

As a child, she never reflected on her play. She just filled her time with it. She began to distinguish play from work when she was required to follow the kindergarten teacher's model of drawing a person and acquiesced to her mother's exhortation to practice the piano.

The play experiences of Doris Bergen occurred in a range of contexts. As a child, she lived in two midwestern cities (St. Louis and Cleveland), a southern rural setting (near Jackson, Mississippi), and a small town in Ohio. Her city play included many of those ball and rule games described by her coeditor, and she especially recalls using the steps and walls for ball playing and the street games such as kick-the-can, usually played in the evening with all the neighborhood. Her favorite recess game was colored eggs, in which the pavement depressions around the fenced-in schoolyard served as the "nests." It was in the city where she first learned to ride a two-wheeled bike, without her parents' knowledge, and she remembers how pleased she was when she could show them that she was ready to get a bike of her own.

The move to the South provided a whole new set of play experiences, including the chance to get the bike that she could ride on the country roads. She recalls her paper-doll play with the one girl who lived close enough to come over to play and such outdoor activities as swinging in the yard and exploring. She also got her first pet playmates: chickens and a dog. (In recently conducted interviews with adults who had lived on farms as children, she learned that pet playmates are common among children living in rural areas.)

She remembers her shock upon moving to the small Ohio town to find that, although the children played some games with names similar to those she played in the city, the rules were often different. For example, the game of marbles in the city was played on pavement and the point of the game was to knock one's own marbles out of the circle drawn on the pavement. In the small town, the game was played on the grass and the point was to throw your marble to hit the other player's marble. What a surprise!

One of her favorite play experiences during her small-town life was the cooperative digging of a large hole in the dirt of the lot between her house and the next one. With the child who lived in the other house (and occasionally other neighborhood children), she and her brother spent hours digging this gigantic hole, which became a house, a fort, a dugout, and a battlefield shelter at various times in its existence. She now wonders at the tolerance of the adults in the neighborhood, who allowed this unsightly hole to exist for a few years while it enriched their children's play lives.

Her indoor play consisted of much building with blocks, making structures such as a drive-in movie theater into which many small cars could drive, and schools and houses. These scenarios were played in many elaborate forms. The fact that she played quite often with her younger brother may have influenced her play, which had an extensive spatial component. She still loves to play with blocks!

Board games of many types were also favorites, most of which were played by her whole family. Both of her parents provided good models of play, and she recalls many happy times playing games with them. She recalls very little play going on in school, however. The one kind of "play" at school she remembers (which she detested and now categorizes as "work disguised as play") was academic "games"" she was forced to "play" in class. The one she hated most was the arithmetic competition game, in which two people had to compete at the chalkboard to see who could get the right answer the fastest. She still panics when she has to do a timed math problem. Such is the influence of early experiences!

The play experiences described by the editors may sound familiar to the reader, although translated into distinctive games, terrain, and opportunities. The contexts, perspectives, and meanings of play to be discussed in this book are presented with the hope that readers may better understand their own play experiences and link them to those of children.

We acknowledge the enthusiastic vision, style, and wisdom of Garland editor Marie Ellen Larcarda, who offered us essential support. When we began work on this book, we did not realize that we would learn so much from the authors who wrote from the perspectives of different disciplines; thus, we also thank the authors who dared to take up the challenge, to think about play in new ways, and to write about how play enriches not only children's lives but their own lives. We feel privileged to have worked on the project.

Introduction

Doris Pronin Fromberg
Doris Bergen

Contexts

Regardless of city, suburban, or rural settings throughout the world, children play. If they grow up in an agrarian economy and accompany their mothers into the fields, they find ways to play within that environment, and there are reports that mothers who work in such settings also find ways to make the time with their children pass in playful ways (Whiting & Edwards, 1988). Although the adults in their lives may supply them with toys that seem to direct a single-purpose use or engage them in multi-age observations and metaphorical group narratives (Heath, 1983), children find ways to extend their sense of power and possibilities through play. Whether their imagined adventures take them onto a stage with rock stars or into the adventures of Superman, Ninja Turtles, or Power Rangers; whether their rough-and-tumble activities are more or less forceful; whether they are building with commercial blocklike materials, rocks and twigs, or discarded boxes, children find ways to imagine, construct, and negotiate with one another. The surface forms of play appear to conform to some powerful underlying patterns. It is these underlying dynamic patterns that make play appear to be self-evident.

Play is a condition that changes in relation to different contexts. The contexts of play are simultaneously influenced by historical events, cultural variations, and personal possibilities. Play can take place in any context and at just about any time. Although opportunities available within different sociocultural contexts may offer different data for the development of event knowledge, the underlying "grammar" of play contributes to each child's integration of particular experiences. Consideration of context makes evident the relativity of play, in that contextual influences often determine whether participants in a culture consider certain behaviors play or not-play. Contexts also have a role in determining who is entitled to play, in that different cultures at certain time periods and in varied settings permit different age, gender, or status groups to play; contexts also provide a basis for judging certain types of play as acceptable or not acceptable.

Relativity

Play may be relatively present in different forms because it functions differently in different contexts; thus, the context codes the activity as play or not-play. Some societies, at different historical periods, for example, permit behaviors often characterized as play only within religious practice. Activities associated with religious rituals and ceremonies, which were performed by religious leaders, priests, or priestesses at an earlier time or in one location, may be recognized as play in other times, places, or cultures (Geertz, 1976; Schechner, 1985).

Some research suggests that children realize the contextual elements that determine play/not-play at an early age. When kindergarten children are able to choose an activity, for example, they code it as play, whereas they code as work the same activity when it is selected for them by an adult (King, 1987). Recent research indicates that children of this age are able to make quite fine distinctions between contextual elements that determine whether an activity would be called work, play, or learning (Marshall, 1994; Polito, 1994).

Play may also become transformed from the predominance of observation or physical involvement into verbal interaction. Play forms become transformed throughout childhood as the forms are socially redefined as other than play, becoming "recreation" or the "leisure-time activity" of adults. Verbalizations and physical action increasingly become internalized, and some types of play become more serious and competitive rather than playful (Bergen, 1988).

Entitlements

Historically, questions and issues have surfaced that concern who could play what activities and what forms of play were acceptable. Riding to hounds, for example, may appear to be leisure activity and the province of the wealthy, whereas using a farmhorse to plow has another connotation. With income that exceeds a subsistence level, many who are present-day "royalty" can afford similar leisure activities. Tennis, for example, once the game of kings, has become a gender-neutral activity within the middle class. Adults join a variety of groups, teams, and networks to engage in ball games, card games, bowling leagues, and other such play activities.

At the present, there is a burgeoning of play among adults. Velcro playroom walls against which adults in velcro suits can fling themselves and each other; indoor rock climbing sites; gentrified pool halls (billiard parlors); Roller Blading; the Society for Creative Anachronism (medieval jousting); and TV gladiators are some of the costly forms that adult play takes. With virtual reality technology, it is possible to simulate physically the experience of combat by using an electronic helmet and gloves. Observation at martial arts events, including the recently publicized no-holds-barred fights, is still another form of leisure activity, if not an active form of personal play. It is worth wondering how such experiences might affect real-life encounters and whether the expansion of adult opportunities to play can make play better or worse for children. For example, adults who will not vote for additional funding for education will pay to play bingo or a lottery; when the proceeds support education, adult play serves children.

One of the difficulties in studying play is that, because it is generated within particular contexts, even subtle changes in context can transform play into not-play.

Context-based questions include:

Who is playing?
With whom are they playing?
Who decides on the course of events?
How are participants engaged in play?
What is happening?
Why may they or may they not play?
When is play taking place?

Over time documented changes have occurred that indicate how styles of clothing, duration of the workday, and proportion of time for activities that support subsistence or leisure have facilitated or hindered play (see essays by Barnes, Freysinger, Hilliard, and Unger in this volume).

Manifestations of play, such as the size of gestures, the volume of speech or laughter, and the pace of activity have more or less acceptability in various national cultures, geographic locations within particular cultures, socioeconomic status levels, and times of day and year. Sanctions according to age, gender, class, ethnic group, and race are also apparent within the forms and expressions of play that are permitted within particular cultures. It might be considered childlike behavior in some cultures or economic groups for older children or adults to engage in rough-and-tumble play, for example, while in others it would be permitted or even encouraged (e.g., adult "show" wrestling). Context, of course, has an influence on the perspectives of those whose discipline involves the study of play.

Perspectives

Various theorists and researchers have interpreted play from different perspectives and used a range of definitional categories. Psychologists and educators usually have focused on individual aspects of play, such as the relationship of play to children's cognitive, linguistic, social, and creative (associative fluency and imagery) development (Garvey, 1977; Piaget, 1962; Smilansky, 1968). Anthropologists, folklorists, and sociolinguists have been more interested in sociocultural aspects of play, such as the communicative meaning of play within varied contexts (Huizinga, 1955; Schechner, 1985; Schwartzman, 1978; Slaughter & Dombrowski, 1989; Sutton-Smith, 1971, 1979). In investigations of naturally occurring play among animals as well as human beings, ethologists have focused on both the content of play and why play occurs (Ellis, 1973; Fagen, 1995; Smith, 1995).

Whether play represents an individual or a social phenomenon may be a less important distinction for understanding it than considering its permeable nature. In effect, play interacts with, parallels, represents, and integrates physical, social, emotional, aesthetic, and cognitive experiences. From a developmental viewpoint, play increases in complexity within these integrated developmental domain perspectives. Social play, for example, becomes more complex, less prop-dependent, more varied and verbal. From a physical domain perspective, skills increasingly become more complex, and the line between play and not-play becomes more clearly defined in an activity such as rough-and-tumble play. Similarly, the relationships among fantasy, creativity, and irrationality become more clearly defined. Regardless of the developmental perspective, the meanings of play remain fluid and shift in relation to particular perspectives for viewing the play and the situational contexts in which players find themselves.

When analyses are set aside, play is a self-evident activity to most people. In particular, it serves to characterize childhood, the period from birth to age twelve. But although usually associated with childhood, it is pervasive throughout the life span. Studied from the perspectives of many disciplines, play does not end at a particular age but continues to emerge, and occasionally erupt, in shifting forms throughout the life span. Therefore, there are two strands from which to consider play: First, students of different disciplines view play from their respective perches, such as historical, philosophical, sociological, psychological, or artistic. While sociologists might document how societies at different times view and participate in play, psychologists might focus on the individual's development of play and artists might be concerned with the creative forces unleashed in playful approaches to representation of the world. Second, on the surface, although adult behavior takes on many playful forms within the arena of particular professional perspectives, it is apparent that the underlying heuristics and dynamics of childhood play continue into adult roles in transformed ways. By identifying some of the ways in which different disciplinary specialists both conceptually define and engage in play, the relative value of play may become apparent.

Definitions

Those who have studied play from many perspectives offer a variety of ways to define play. The difficulty lies in the use of the term *play* as both a noun and a verb. As the discussion of context pointed out, play is a *relative* activity. The shifting functions in different settings contribute to researchers' problems in defining play. One definition for example, drawn from a review of research on play in early childhood, states that young children's play is:

Symbolic, in that it represents reality in "as-if" or "what-if" terms
Meaningful, in that it connects or relates experiences
Active, in that children are doing things (including imagining)
Pleasurable, even when children are engaged seriously in activity
Voluntary and *intrinsically motivated,* whether the motives are curiosity, mastery, affiliation, or others
Rule-governed, whether implicitly or explicitly expressed
Episodic, characterized by emerging and shifting goals that children develop spontaneously. (Fromberg, 1992)

Play has variously been considered a "medium" for learning (Bergen, 1988) and a "condition" (among others) for learning (Fromberg, 1995). Possibly the overriding attribute that is so gratifying and addictive about play is that it is intrinsically motivated, satisfying, and empowering. The experience of "flow," an "optimal" experience, is a compatible image (Csikszentmihalyi & Csikszentmihalyi, 1988). As a dynamic and integrative human activity, it is apparent that play is not at all a simple matter.

The perspectives concerning play in contemporary life take added significance from some of the principles of chaos and complexity theory. As a context-based phenomenon, play is sensitively dependent on initial conditions. This means that chance encounters and brief events, when influenced by the ongoing complexity and volume of daily experiences, can evolve into unrecognizable forms. To this extent, play is also a self-organizing system: when children interact with one another, they influence each other's development, thus creating new renditions of self-organized systems.

Within the broadly based literature of humanistic, scientific, artistic, and professional fields, discussions of play can serve as a way to develop the perspectives included in this volume; these various perspectives serve to bracket a definition of play. This book documents, therefore, an emergent, richly textured definition of play that reflects the broad range of meanings that play has in childhood (and in adult) experiences.

Meanings

The various perspectives from which scholars have studied play and how human beings engage in and experience play suggest that each player constructs different meanings that reflect particular contexts. Scientists and social scientists have variously defined meaning as "shared awareness" (Penrose, 1994, p. 53) and "isomorphism" (Hofstadter, 1985, p. 445). "Central to the development of the meaning system is the event representation (or script), which generalizes from experience of events to provide an interpretation of context" (Nelson, 1985, p. 9). In the children's play described in the preface, some universal themes of bipolar friends and enemies, dealing with fear or risk, escape to other times and places, and empowerment through community building are examples of children's event knowledge that has been built through play.

Meaning as a context-based subject of study is vast, beyond the scope of any one volume. The notion of a recursive process that provides an interplay between the meanings for each child (whose personal content base is in the form of event knowledge) and the shared negotiations with other children (who use their own event knowledge) makes possible the synergistic development of sociodramatic play episodes. With respect to play as a skill-building experience, moreover, it is the case that children's development takes place in social negotiation and competence skills, as well as cognitive expansion, elaboration, or flexibility, and/or physical game playing. Meaning, from these perspectives, therefore, includes both conceptual content and a degree of complexity tempered by commitment and caring. Commitment and caring relate to the self-motivational dynamic of play. Three themes that are evident in meaning-making are exploration, power and personal meaning, and imagery.

Exploration Contrasted with Play

Power is the central distinction between exploration and play, although both experiences may look playful to an observer. A widely held view (Hutt, 1976, p. 211) suggests that exploration deals with how objects or interpersonal situations function (What can it/they do?). Play, in contrast, deals with what the player can do (What can I do?). A related interpretation is that exploration is an opportunity to learn about perceptual properties, whereas play is an occasion for learning about the functional properties of objects (Collard, 1979, p. 52). Children at play have the power to control a situation in proactive ways.

Power and Personal Meaning

The personal experience of play as a creative force in human life takes on added significance in contemporary life. The end of the twentieth century in the United States provides a context that includes new technologies and theories that are shifting human paradigms for understanding the world. Complexity and chaos theories, for example, are contemporary ways of looking at knowledge and experience in general as dynamic, complex, and predictably unpredictable in wholesomely chaotic ways. Human beings who can be flexible connection makers can function more comfortably within such a worldview than can linear thinkers. Mirroring aspects of social pretend play, such contemporary theories add credence to the importance of play in human experience.

There are, therefore, both personal and cultural meanings that reflect play. It is important to look at issues concerning the respective personal meanings that boys and girls take out of and bring to play activities. It is also important to look at the personal meanings that children who have specific learning challenges take out of and bring to play activities. Within this discussion of power and personal meanings surfaces the nature of competition and losing. What is the point, for example, at which competition *sours* play or success *sweetens* play? Framed in this way, this issue represents a look at a *phase transition* between one state and another. From the perspective of complexity theory, learning takes place at the point of transformation from one phase to another.

Personal meanings may relate to the different perspectives from which each player perceives the experience. For some girls, for example, joy from winning may be tempered by the empathy they feel for a disappointed loser. Affiliative motives may also come into play in another way. In public winning, there may be some degree of feeling separated from others. Some boys in the United States, in contrast, may learn a societal message that winning, with its accompanying destruction of others or a sense of being set apart, is preferable. Other cultures create games in which the difficulty lies in avoiding winning by assuring that all participants finish on an equal footing (Bruner, 1980).

What, one might ask, does the child gambler, who continues to lose more than win, learn? Consider the continuum of covarying empowerment experiences in relation to the development of self-motivated play skills:

Power	In control	Loss of control
Practice	Perseverance	Obsession

This continuum between the self-motivated power to choose and the loss of control parallels the continuum between engaging in the practice of play and the loss of personal control.

These kinds of issues may, in part, tie the personal meanings of this empowerment continuum with sociocultural and political influences. Within sociodramatic play or other forms of fantasy play, for example, girls may be able to be more competitive even if they are the target of attention as a winner, because they are protected by the play frame from social isolation or marginalization. Sociodramatic play also is a collaborative, small-group activity.

Ethnic distinctions may also confound the inclusion-exclusion issue. These relative meanings also emerge out of particular sociocultural contexts and values. Although people of color and girls in competitive sports or professions, for example, have become more prevalent in the United States in recent years, a fully egalitarian transformation awaits the future. For a child who also carries a physical or verbal challenge into the play arena, the sense of inclusion or exclusion also has important personal connotations (see essay by Mindes in this volume).

Imagery

For the excluded child, imagination also is an important support system. It can transport the child to other times and places that may be happy, vengeful, or comforting. For the child who has physical challenges, imagery can serve as a vehicle for transcending, even alleviating, the challenging or difficult moment.

Besides contributing to success in games and pretending within a play framework, the personal use of imagery can act as a social commodity for any child. In physical activity, for example, winning athletes, performers, and visual artists are able to "psyche themselves" into a state of fluent imagery that helps them perform. In sociodramatic activity, children extend the richness of their play through imagery building and sharing the evolution of script building with other children. In both instances, there is an intensity of interest and a submersion within the rules of the game. Imagery and self-concept, within these contexts, together influence the development of the play and, in turn, become confirmed or disconfirmed. Play, therefore, serves not only to use event knowledge but offers an opportunity to add to the players' repertoire of event knowledge and new meanings.

Overview of the Book

The book is organized into seven sections. Section I, "Contexts, Perspectives, and Meanings of Play" includes essays that consider a variety of contexts, perspectives, and meanings of play. These synoptic essays cut across temporal, spatial, technological, and disciplinary boundaries.

Section II, "Perspectives on Play Development," looks at the development of play behaviors and experiences across childhood and considers various influences on that development. This section also includes discussion of issues surrounding the nature of intervention, individual needs, and assessment.

Section III, "Physical and Social Contexts of Play," looks at the various physical, personal, and social settings in which childhood play takes place. Essays in this section also discuss the relative roles of adults in these settings.

Section IV, "Particular Meanings Embedded in Playful Experiences," considers the role of imagination, exploration, challenge, humor, and sexuality in childhood play.

Section V, "Structuring the Study of Play," shares varied perspectives from which scholars have structured the study of play. There is a discussion of additional issues concerning the implications of such study for provisions that adults might make to improve the quality of children's lives.

Section VI, "Play in the Disciplines and Professions," offers views of specialists from various disciplines concerning play within the contexts of their respective domains. The editorial assumption that play is a valuable lifelong human activity worthy of recognition and nurture draws support from the multiple perspectives and variety of ways in which adults continue to be playful and generative in their work.

Section VII, "The Present and Future of Play," looks at the future of play in a postmodern world in which roles, agents, relationships, functions, and advocates may become delineated in fresh ways. The place of technology is a significant influence on trends in play and issues of advocacy concerning children's play.

The reader who dips into this book will develop a personal imagery. There are different textures to touch, savor, reject, and play with.

Bibliography

Bergen, D. (1988). *Play: A medium for learning and development*. Portsmouth, NH: Heinemann.

Bruner, J. S. (1980). *Under five in Britain*. Ypsilanti, MI: High/Scope.

Collard, R. R. (1979). Exploration and play. In B. Sutton-Smith (Ed.), *Play and learning* (pp. 45–68). New York: Gardner.

Csikszentmihalyi, M., & Csikszentmihalyi, I. S. (1988). (Eds.). *Optimal experience: Psychological studies in flow consciousness*. New York: Cambridge University Press.

Ellis, M. J. (1973). *Why people play*. Englewood Cliffs, NJ: Prentice-Hall.

Fagen, R. (1995). Animal play, games of angels, biology, and Brian. In A. D. Pellegrini (Ed.), *The future of play theory* (pp. 23–44). Albany: State University of New York Press.

Fromberg, D. P. (1992). A review of research on play. In C. Seefeldt (Ed.), *The early childhood curriculum: A review of current research* (2nd ed., pp. 42–84). New York: Teachers College Press.

Fromberg, D. P. (1995). *The full-day kindergarten: Planning and practicing a dynamic themes curriculum* (2nd ed.). New York: Teachers College Press.

Garvey, C. (1977). *Play*. Cambridge, MA: Harvard University Press.

Geertz, C. (1976). Deep play: A description of the Balinese cockfight. In J. S. Bruner, A. Jolly, & and K. Sylva (Eds.), *Play—Its role in development and evolution* (pp. 656–674). New York: Basic Books.

Heath, S. B. (1983). *Ways with words: Language, life, and work in communities and classrooms*. New York: Cambridge University Press.

Hofstadter, D. R. (1985). *Metamagical themas: Questing for the essence: Mind and pattern*. New York: Basic Books.

Huizinga, J. (1955). *Homo ludens: A study of the play elements of culture*. Boston: Beacon.

Hutt, C. (1976). Exploration and play in children. In J. S. Bruner, A. Jolly, & K. Sylva (Eds.), *Play—Its role in development and evolution* (pp. 202–215). New York: Basic Books.

King, N. R. (1987). Elementary school play: Theory and research. In J. H. Block & N. R. King (Eds.), *School play* (pp. 143–165). New York: Garland.

Marshall, H. H. (1994). Children's understanding of academic tasks: Work, play or learning. *Journal of Research in Childhood Education, 9*(1), 35–46.

Nelson, K. (1985). *Making sense: The acquisition of shared meaning*. New York: Academic.

Penrose, R. (1994). *Shadows of the mind: A search for the missing science of consciousness*. New York: Oxford University Press.

Piaget, J. (1962). *Play, dreams, and imitation in childhood* (C. Gattegno & M. F. Hodgson, Trans.). New York: W. W. Norton.

Polito, T. (1994). How play and work are organized in a kindergarten classroom. *Journal of Research in Childhood Education, 9*(1), 47–57.

Schechner, R. (1985). *Between theater and anthropology*. Philadelphia: University of Pennsylvania Press.

Schwartzman, H. (1978). *Transformations: The anthropology of children's play*. New York: Plenum.

Slaughter, D., & Dombrowski, J. (1989). Cultural continuities and discontinuities: Impact on social and pretend play. In M. N. Bloch & A. D. Pellegrini (Eds.), *The ecological context of children's play* (pp. 282–310). Norwood, NJ: Ablex.

Smilansky, S. (1968). *The effects of sociodramatic play on disadvantaged preschool children*. New York: John Wiley.

Smith, P. K. (1995). Play, ethology, and education: A personal account. In A. D. Pellegrini (Ed.), *The future of play theory* (pp. 3–22). Albany: State University of New York Press.

Sutton-Smith, B. (1971). A syntax for play and games. In R. E. Herron & B. Sutton-Smith (Eds.), *Child's play* (pp. 298–307). New York: Wiley.

Sutton-Smith, B. (Ed.) (1979). *Play and learning*. New York: Gardner.

Whiting, B. B., & Edwards, C. P. (1988). *Children of different worlds: The formation of social behavior.* Cambridge, MA: Harvard University Press.

Contexts, Perspectives, and Meanings of Play

Introduction

The essays in this section cover a variety of contexts, perspectives, and meanings of play. As an integrative activity in human life, play is an experience in simultaneity and immediacy. It is at once lymphatic and discontinuous, predictably unpredictable, and self-organizing in sometimes episodic ways. In these ways, it is both dynamic and paradoxical. This section contrasts with the sections that follow, which focus on particular processes and components of play rather than the simultaneity of the activity. Because the process of delineating such specialized views occasionally can have the effect of dismantling the uniqueness of play as a dynamic paradox, this integrative section is provided first.

The opening synoptic essays explore in turn the changing historical contexts as well as the multiple cultural contexts of play within the total life span of human development. While children's perspectives of play are a central and ongoing feature of play, adults' perspectives can either limit or extend the scope of children's experiences. Essay authors consider how children engage in and understand play, as well as how play interfaces with their literacy and conceptual learning. From the perspective of technological developments in contemporary life, it may be possible to revise some historical realities and expectancies concerning children's play. Technology, for example, offers the potential for either sharpening or dulling children's playful perspectives.

The meaning of play in human life is still another integrative issue to study. A teacher might assume, for example, that children are "only" playing if they do not appear to be paying attention to assigned tasks. An outside observer, however, might hear the children talking about the assigned task in a lively, relevant exchange (Dyson, 1988). The children themselves might perceive that they are working at the assigned activity, in this case, the children do not perceive that they are playing.

The personal experience of play varies for each individual. Each brings idiosyncratic meanings to play and constructs personal meanings from play. Social interaction transforms the nature of performances and the children's meanings through the ways that children engage in group play. Within sociodramatic play episodes, for example, children may scaffold each other's participation within a shared script. In a parallel way, play offers the potential to create instant community among former strangers or enhance the experience of community among friends. These meaningful potentials for play in human life touch on what it means to be a human being in the world.

The personal meanings that children bring to sociodramatic and pretend play also serve as a lymphatic system that integrates children's diverse experiences, whether linguistic, social, cognitive, or creative (Fromberg, 1992). Within the relatively new paradigms of chaos and complexity theory, there is discussion of the place of play as a present-time human experience and its implications for future generativity and creativity. From the various visions that each essay offers, the coherence and integration of play in human life stand out as significant.

Bibliography

Dyson, A. H. (1988). The value of "time off task": Young children's spontaneous talk and deliberate text. *Harvard Educational Review, 57,* 396–420.

Fromberg, D. P. (1992). A review of research on play. In C. Seefeldt (Ed.), *The early childhood curriculum: A review of current research* (2nd ed., pp. 42–84). New York: Teachers College Press.

Contexts for Play

Play in Historical Contexts

Donna R. Barnes

From the beginning of history, children have played. They have played alone or with other people, sometimes with adults, more often with other children. They have played with toys, games, animals, and found objects. They have engaged in both indoor and outdoor sports activities. They have invented or learned and recited rhymes, songs, verse; they have collected and traded objects that they prize; and they have joined in festivals and special celebrations. Play activities, sometimes varying from culture to culture, are often a function of a child's age, gender, and socioeconomic position, but can be seen as the "natural right" of childhood.

Through play, the serious "work of childhood" occurs. In play activity, children learn to test their strength, their agility, their determination, their capacities to cooperate and to compete, their speed, their cunning, their skills, their gracefulness, their memories, and their imaginative abilities. Of course, usually children do not realize that they are testing themselves in these ways; rather they think only of the activity and not the larger meaning of the activity.

Parents and child care providers obviously are interested in the play of children. Educators, librarians, social workers, and pediatricians have professional interests in children's play. Among the academicians, philosophers, psychologists, sociologists, cultural anthropologists, archaeologists, historians, art historians, theologians, ethicists, and folklorists focus attention on children and their behaviors. Manufacturers of children's clothing, toys, sporting equipment, playground equipment, and furnishings; authors, illustrators, and book publishers; song writers and musicians; computer program designers; television producers, dramatists, and filmmakers; advertising agents; recreational facilities owners, resort managers, travel agents, and coaches—all have an interest in what children do, what they need and want, and what they can be persuaded to acquire or use. Often, those who have a commercial interest direct their attention to play that is culturally sanctioned by gender.

The Play of Boys

Ask the Haitian child playing marbles what he is doing and he might tell you that boys (but not girls) compete to win marbles by well-aimed shots and by wagering. This boy might reveal some of the rules used by other players to decide which shot is best. Perhaps he might also describe the procedure for a boy who has lost his marbles but wants to stay in the game by playing "bokies"; wagering his ability to withstand pain he places his hands in the ring for others to shoot marbles at his knuckles.

The boy would probably not tell you that boys of different social backgrounds can play marbles together, crossing over social barriers that prevent their interactions on most other occasions. Nor is it likely that the marble player would explain that the verbal exchanges, sometimes encouraging and often jocularly insulting, among the male players is a pattern of male interaction that will last through adulthood. Nor would the boy reveal that Haitians believe it good for boys to spend time with other boys in activities that exclude the participation of girls, just as later in life he will spend time with grown men in relaxing activities that exclude adult women. The boy is playing marbles, and to him, that is the significance of the activity; he is playing to win and he is playing because it is fun.

In Attic Greece, through training programs in the open-air stadiums and arenas, boys learned to wrestle, run, throw the javelin, and jump. Stripped, their bodies oiled and coated with sand or soil, they worked out to develop bodily strengths. These skills would serve them well in their eventual adult roles as men who defended their own city-states when these came under enemy attack. Manhood was proven on the battlefield and in athletic competitions. Excellence, honor, and glory—all the rewards of *arete*—were celebrated in Homeric verse, in drama, and in olympiads.

Even if a boy was not destined to compete athletically at major contests, his physical training was thought to be important. Partly because of the Greek ideal of building sound bodies in which to house sound minds, and partly because adult warfare required men from the ages of fifteen to sixty-five to be prepared to fight, these programs of physical activity were important. Teenage boys were trained rigorously for military service, building upon the physical capacities already developed in childhood. Greek vase paintings show boys with wheeled carts, and scholarship reveals that "Boys played with model warships and were also encouraged to build their own toy boats and carts as well as model horses" (King, 1979, p. 8).

Part of the Greek ideal for education included the importance of athletic games and training (Jaeger, 1939/1960; Kitto, 1951/1962; Marrou, 1964). Similarly, the virtues of courage that physical training was meant to instill are celebrated in Greek mythology and drama (see Kingsley, 1855). Comparable patterns of training in weaponry and horsemanship persisted in medieval Europe for boys who were being groomed for knighthood. Competitions, jousts, and other games in the tiltyard served as means for chivalric education and displays of trained competence and courage.

The Play of Girls

In ancient Greece, little girls often learned to dance and run races, activities thought appropriate for them before they entered puberty. Once reaching early adolescence, however, greater modesty was demanded of them. Embedded in many childhood activities are preparations for later adult roles. Around the world and throughout many historical eras girls have played with miniature pots and pans and

spoons. Whether made of pottery, wood, metal, porcelain, glazed ceramic, or plastic, these toys have allowed girls to imaginatively use implements typical of household domestic utensils and to imitate the behaviors of adult women. Miniaturized pots have been excavated from ancient Egyptian tombs and archaeological sites in Crete. No doubt girls planned imaginary meals featuring olives, dates, bread, and honey more than thirty centuries ago.

Tea sets were popular toys for girls in England and the United States during the nineteenth and early twentieth centuries. Pretending to cook and serve food and drink allowed girls to practice behaviors eventually expected of them as homemakers and hostesses. Bread and jam, crumpets and fruitcake, tea with milk or lemon: these were what the young hostess offered her guests, whether dolls, teddy bears, or an occasional child or adult. Not just food preparation and serving but table manners and the rules governing hospitality were learned as miniature meals were envisioned. Tea sets for girls were manufactured in Europe during the eighteenth century (since the tea had been imported from India and China into Europe from the seventeenth century onward) and flourished in the nineteenth century (King, 1979). Not only basic tea sets with teacups and saucers, coffee cups, teapots, sugar bowls, bread and butter plates, and milk mugs, but entire dinner services with gravy boats, serving platters, vegetable bowls, dinner plates, soup bowls, covered soup tureens, and dessert plates were made in England and Germany. Colored patterns, for example, paralleled adult models of the Davenport company. Sometimes porcelain tea sets were illustrated with engraved images from nursery stories such as "Cinderella." "The toy tea-set could be used to instruct girls in the elements of social behaviour and the number of surviving sets suggests their play was often supervised. Production of . . . very well made sets appears to have declined in the early twentieth century, possibly because unsupervised play was becoming more common" (King, 1979, p. 191).

Similar sets of miniature tableware were produced in limited quantities in Holland during the seventeenth century and later mass-produced for that country's children in the eighteenth and nineteenth centuries. The Museum Boymans-van Beuningen in Rotterdam displayed such a collection of children's tableware in its *poppen-goed* exhibition, organized by the decorative arts department's curator. Similar collections can be found in the Rotterdam Historical Museum, the West Fries Museum in Hoorn, and the Mr. Simon van Gijn Museum in Dordrecht. A seventeenth-century Dutch etching depicting children at play shows a group of young girls with their miniature cookware. The elaborate seventeenth-century dolls' houses located in the Rijksmuseum in Amsterdam were not meant for children, but were created for a very few wealthy women. However, the creation of miniature tableware displayed in these dolls' houses also reflects the popularity of dishware items for children. By the late nineteenth and early twentieth centuries, dollhouses were common as girls played out domestic chores and imaginatively tried their hands at home decoration and furnishing.

The chores connected to kitchen work were also envisioned for the nineteenth-century British girl who played with a miniature kitchen range heated by methylated spirits. The child was expected to spend hours polishing the stove and its equipment. There is a photograph documenting such a stove (King, 1979, p. 175), as well as documentation of the sentiments concerning domestic chores (Davidson, 1982; Strasser, 1982).

Gender-Neutral Play

In the past thirty years in the United States and other industrialized Western nations attention has been on children's toys and activities that are not gender-restrictive. Often at the urging of feminists, child development specialists, and early childhood educators (Greenberg, 1978), boys have been encouraged to play in the miniaturized kitchens, learning to wash dishes or set tables or serve food; to push replicas of vacuum cleaners and small brooms and mops across the floor; and to play at shopping for household foodstuffs in child-sized supermarkets.

The recently opened Museum for Children in Old San Juan (Museo de los Niños) features just such a *supermercado* for youngsters, who push small shopping carts through the aisles as they make selections from well-known brands of canned beans, milk, juices, and cereals, and plastic oranges, bananas, and coconuts. Some children play the part of supermarket checker, ringing up purchases on a cash register at the check out area. These activities mirror the experiences of the adult world's markets and encourage boys and girls to try out adult roles.

Children were provided with similar opportunities to practice consumerism by role playing in the Edwardian grocer's shop with goods on display from the early days of the twentieth century or by playing with the model of an English butcher shop replete with cuts of beef, pork, and lamb fashioned from plaster-soaked fabric over wire netting and featuring three butchers dressing and selling meats, now at the Bethnal Children's Museum in London (King, 1979, pp. 188–189).

The hope has been that boys would learn that homemaking chores are not restricted to women and girls, that they, too, have roles to play in acquiring and preparing foodstuffs and keeping the family living quarters neat and clean. Montessori nursery schools in Europe and the United States, for example, have long operated on the principle that it was educationally sound for both boys and girls to keep their classroom tidy, but seldom has that "work" been seen as a form of "play," nor was the lesson typically expanded to males assuming responsibility for household domestic cleaning.

Girls, previously excluded from the block corners by the boys in their nursery schools, have been encouraged to build ramps and bridges with blocks; to put pilots' caps on their heads and pedal-drive mock airplanes and helicopters in the schoolyard; and to pick up stethoscopes and announce, "The doctor is in." Here the hope is that girls will not have their adult career options limited to the more traditional roles of mother, nurse, and schoolteacher but will think of engineering, architecture, technology, aeronautics, and medicine as possibilities for them in the twenty-first century.

For both boys and girls, the aim recently has been to enlarge children's eventual adult options by expanding the range of toys played with in childhood. Clearly not all parents and not all children respond enthusiastically to these gender-free efforts. Barbie doll sales are on the rise, for example, and they are not sold to or for boys. Ken, presumably her masculine counterpart, is not offered to boys, but rather is a doll partner for Barbie. The young girls who cherish their Barbies can arrange dates, slumber parties, and weddings for Barbie and Ken. They can pay attention to Ken's costume and fashionability, but he is an "accessory" to Barbie, just as her shoes, muff, and skis are. On the other hand, the "anatomically correct" G. I. Joe and other "action heroes" are geared for boys; girls are not expected to play with them.

Playthings

Dolls and Toys

Dolls are among the oldest known toys for children. Early earthenware examples from ancient Greece indicate attention to hairstyles, breasts, and buttocks, suggesting that the dolls were probably meant as playthings for girls. "The earthenware dolls of the Greeks have survived in some quantity; they were very simply shaped and limbs were articulated by cords at the shoulders and thighs"(King, 1979, p. 8).

But dolls were not the only toys available to children. Wheeled carts, toy boats, and model horses have already been mentioned. In addition, balls were tossed or rolled by children. Around the world, balls have been made of wood, leather, cloth, wool yarn, baked clay, polished stone, rubber, and plastic. Closely related to balls are the balloons made from inflatable latex rubber. Prior to the use of rubber, children would blow up, tie, and toss pig bladders, as evidenced in numerous seventeenth century Dutch genre prints and paintings. Chinese and Japanese children have long played with inflated tissue-paper "balloons." Balloons are often tossed, sometimes attached to a string and allowed to rise on the currents of moving air, and frequently broken with a loud pop. Fragile tubular rubber balloons have been twisted into animal shapes. Twentieth-century children in the United States have also come to enjoy helium-filled plastic balloons, often printed with greetings and messages.

Rattles appear in virtually all cultures. Native American peoples made their children rattles of dried gourds or turtle shells. During the time of the pharaohs Egyptians made rattles of clay. Chinese and Japanese youngsters had rattles made from hollow bamboo tubes whose heads were covered with paper or thin sheets of wood. Silversmiths working in Holland, Germany, and France during the sixteenth and seventeenth centuries created engraved silver rattles, sometimes enriched with pieces of coral, for the amusement and pleasure of children from well-to-do families.

Children in Africa, Asia, Europe, and the Americas have delighted in drums fashioned out of wood, tin, or pottery drum bodies and covered with tautly drawn animal skin, leather, or paper. Children have also found that hollow logs or cooking pots turned upside down can be beaten with a stick or spoon to make drumlike noises.

Among the very early toys in Europe were hobbyhorses. A wooden pole with the shape of a horse's head affixed to the top—perhaps the head carved in realistic bas-relief, or painted simply on a flat outline with a string, yarn, bristle, or fur mane attached—provided a reliable mount for children to imagine themselves riding across the fields, chasing enemies, or racing with friends in moments of derring-do. It is not surprising that hobbyhorses were popular in equestrian-based societies of Europe, when warfare was conducted by foot soldiers and mounted knights and warriors. While girls might have occasionally played with these hobbyhorses, they were much more often the toys of boys. Seventeenth-century prints from Holland depict boys with hobbyhorses and boys accompanying their mothers to market toy stands that sold hobbyhorses along with drums and dolls. Interestingly, horses remain popular toys for young children, even in twentieth-century highly industrialized societies where a child is unlikely to ride a horse for transportation or in war.

Besides hobbyhorses, rocking horses became popular with children in Europe and the United States in the nineteenth and twentieth centuries. These nursery steeds provide kinesthetic pleasure in their rocking movements and also serve to stimulate imaginary rides into terrains remote from home. Toy horses have an even older history. Some have been made of wood, like a painted horse from Benares decorated with calligraphy; a modern version of that horse was displayed in 1956 at the Museum of International Folk Art in Santa Fe, New Mexico, as part of its special exhibition, *Decorative Arts of India*. Another Indian horse, made of cast bronze with wheels, is characterized as having "all the requirements for a good toy: simple, sturdy, bright, and moveable" (Museum of International Folk Art, 1956, p. 24).

Brightly painted blue and red wooden horses are part of Swedish folk art traditions. Others have been made of metal, like the numerous tin horses made in Germany, England, and the United States in the nineteenth and twentieth centuries.

Tin began to assume importance as a toy-making material for mass production early in the nineteenth century, and model horses were quick favorites. The makers of tin flats in the eighteenth century had created a number of scenes and situations in which the horse was the most important creature, such as the *Boar*

Hunt made by the Hilperts of Nuremberg in 1770 that showed typically stylized horses. Johann Friedrich Ramm of Luneberg made a number of hunting scenes and menageries, while horse-drawn, transport was a specialty of Georg Spenkuch of Nuremberg. The early tin fire engines were, of course, horse-drawn, and some continued to be made this way until 1920. The amazing variety of late nineteenth-century horse-drawn transport can be witnessed in the London Museum's famous collection of "penny toys," most of which originated in France and Germany, though some were made in England (King, 1979, p. 42). Splendid examples of metal horses pulling fire engines, sales carts, and carriages can also be found in the Rotterdam Historical Museum in Holland as well as the collections of the Museum of the City of New York and the Shelburne Museum in Vermont.

Cards and Board Games

Children devise games for themselves or play games taught to them by adults or older children. Sometimes these are card games or board games in which either chance or strategy comes to the forefront. Among the oldest is chess, a strategic war game, that goes back to the seventh century A.D. but is within the tradition of board games, some of which were played in ancient Egypt and Sumeria.

Game boards and pieces have been preserved from the early Sumerian and Egyptian civilizations, as well as pictures of games being played. A wall painting in the Tombs of the Queens in Upper Egypt shows Queen Nefertari (the queen of Ramses II, reigned 1304–1237 B.C.) playing the board game *senet*: an Egyptian papyrus of about 1000 B.C. shows a seated gazelle and a lion engaged in the same pastime (Dennis & Wilkinson, 1968, p. viii).

Other favorite international games include checkers, parchesi, dominoes, mah jong, and backgammon. Backgammon was immortalized as *tric trac* by seventeenth-century Dutch genre painters such as Jan Steen, who show the game being played in homes and taverns.

Playing cards were printed from wood blocks during the medieval period; by the seventeenth century the Dutch were printing playing cards that were shipped to England, France, Poland, and Scandinavia. Images of card players can be found in Dutch art from the time period, and at least one painting by Frans Hals shows children playing cards. Despite the fact that moralizing writers warned parents against permitting children to play cards or play with dice, various games of chance were popular with Dutch children.

Later card games for children during the Victorian era tended to be more educational, with information about authors, rulers, countries, or trades rather than the spades, hearts, clubs, and diamonds used by adult players. But children have enjoyed matching images, besting one another with dares and bets, and playing for points in many card games. Solitaire is an option when there is no one to play with; Go Fish! is a way for the youngest children to begin matching images; cards with different designs and images printed on their backs have been traded and collected by children in the United States; and, when all else fails, playing cards can be balanced into towers and castles.

Construction Activities

Construction activities with such materials as blocks, Lincoln Logs, Erector sets, and Lego reflect a major genre of playthings. All are used to construct buildings, roadways, and machines. Children have long found ways of stretching a blanket or piece of fabric between the backs of chairs or over fenceposts and tree branches to form temporary castles, caves, hideaways, and tents. In these settings, children become warriors, explorers, prospectors, pirates, and other adventurers. More elaborate building schemes have been launched by those who build tree houses in the woods or in the backyard. Sometimes children use found objects to create settings for imaginative play. Discarded wine barrels become hiding places, or steeds from upon which to have mock battles. An abandoned automobile can become a space shuttle, racing car, submarine, tank, or airplane cockpit, depending upon the playfulness of its occupant(s). Teaching youngsters to play with machines was typical of industrialized societies. Toy manufacturers in Europe and the United States during the late nineteenth and early twentieth centuries reflected the growth of industrialization occurring in England, France, Germany, and the United States. Models of steam engines were meant to be instructive, not merely diversionary, for boys. Principles of leverage, balance, and gravity were inherent in many toys.

Communications Technology and Imagination

Child versions of typewriters and printing presses were intended to promote literacy while teaching about equipment used in business offices. Late in the twentieth century, children in the United States, Canada, Japan, and Europe have entered the computer and electronic age, playing with toys and computer games, such as Nintendo, that hone their computer literacy skills. Television programming for children, taking over the role previously served by radio, stereopticons, films, and magic lanterns, has expanded youngsters' knowledge of the world and exposed them to cartoon figures' antics and mayhem. Many children know how to turn on and turn off television sets and VCRs by the time they are two. They are part of the communication revolution.

Even small children learn how to answer the telephone through imitation and the use of small plastic toy versions. Some parents view such play as encouraging mannerly communication; for children, the early childhood fascination with the telephone is connected to its sound, the fact that using a real telephone seems like such an adult thing to do, and the mystery of hearing the voice of someone you know but cannot see. Sometimes children invent people to talk with on the telephone, just as they relish the opportunities to play make-believe and dress-up and wear costumes.

Animals as Playthings and Playmates

Live animals have also served children as both playthings and playmates. The Puerto Rican boy who carefully measures out feed and water for his rooster, for example, may view the cock as a pet who can be carried around from time to time by tucking the bird under the boy's arm. Perhaps the rooster will be trained by the boy to participate in cockfights, with metal spurs attached to his legs to slash away at competitors. Or perhaps the boy views the rooster as livestock that will mate with the hens to produce eggs and more chicks and that will eventually end his days in the stock pot for *caldo de pollo*. Caring for the rooster is both a form of work, which, with its routine of feeding and watering, requires careful attention to the health and condition of the animal, and a form of play, particularly if the boy talks to the bird, strokes its feathers, imitates its crowing sounds, or chases it around the pen.

Caring for animals—whether sled dogs in Alaska, caged crickets in China, pigeons on the rooftops of tenements in Brooklyn, horses in Khazhakstan, milk cows in Holland, golden carp in Japan, llamas in Peru, elephants in India, reindeer in Lapland, or cats in London—is an activity for children around the world. It is a way to learn responsibility and a source of pleasure for children. Images of children enjoying their play with animals are found on ancient Greek vase paintings; a sculpture from ancient Rome, now housed in the Vatican Museum, depicts a young boy with his goose. Medieval European sculpture and paintings from time to time show the infant Christ child playing with a bird. The artistic and literary traditions of children playing with pets are old ones.

Animals are a source of transport, and fun, to the children who grow up with them. Bedouin boys learn to saddle, cajole, and race camels across the desert, sampling victory and savoring the hot burning sun that casts shadows across the sand. Indian boys learn to drive elephants and decorate them with magnificently ornamented *howdah* and blankets for ceremonial procession in honor of earthly princes and the elephant-headed god Ganesha or various incarnations of Lord Vishnu. Asian youngsters in the rice paddies learn to ride the backs of water buffaloes.

Children sometimes interact with animals out of curiosity or out of cruelty. Chasing butterflies with a net, trapping small silvery fish by damming up a rushing stream with rocks, collecting glowing fireflies in a glass jar, following the hare's footprints in the snow, picking lizards from the swaying branch of the hibiscus plant, quietly staring at the redheaded woodpecker making holes in the trunk of a tree, rolling acorns in the direction of a squirrel, and following the swarming bees back to the hive may all be the result of curiosity. Such activities have occurred since time immemorial because children are interested in the natural world. There is literature that advises adults who wish to introduce children to nature, whether through the crashing waves at the beach during a powerful storm or the tiny seeds that sprout among the mosses in the woods (Carson, 1965). Publications for children, such as *Ranger Rick* (National Wildlife Federation), color photographs in the *National Geographic,* and public television broadcasts, such as *Nature,* have also prompted children's interest in birds, mammals, insects, and reptiles. Attendance figures at the

American Museum of Natural History in New York City, the British Museum of Natural History in London, and zoos throughout the world also bespeak children's curiosity about the lives of creatures in the animal world.

Many children respond to creatures of the natural world as playthings and playmates; some are tormenters of animals. They squash frogs, tease dogs by attaching metal cans to their tails, steal blue-shelled eggs from the robin's nest, throw sharp-edged rocks at snakes, or hurl cats and mice down a well. But whether responsible caretakers, curious investigators, or cruel tormenters, children play with animals. Much of that play is modeled on their observations and dramatizations of adult behaviors.

Imagination and Dramatization

Through observation, Greek children learned to participate in religious rites and joined other families attending festivals and games. They also had ample opportunities for the rich, imaginative recreation of the adventures and exploits of heroic gods and goddesses, warriors, kings, and queens during play activities in their own homes and among their friends. Imagining oneself the slayer of sea monsters or the ruler of a rich kingdom might have been enhanced by a wooden sword or old piece of cloth used as a royal robe. But, even without such props, Greek children could project themselves onto center stage, given the stories they had heard and the dramas they had seen.

Jewish children, on the contrary, were not encouraged to display the athleticism characteristic of the Greeks. Modesty ruled against nude wrestling and dancing. However, stories celebrating the courage of the Maccabees, the skill of David in his encounter with Goliath, and the cleverness of Esther in her dispute with the treacherous Hamen all played a part in the imaginative life of the children of Israel wherever they were found. Music, song, and dramatic storytelling were among their pleasures. Biblical approval had been granted to timbrels, strings, pipes, cymbals, lyres, harps, tambourines, and castenets. Ancient Hebrew peoples also taught their children to play the flute, trumpet, and oboe as well as to enjoy the pleasures of song and dance. Dramatizations through music, song, and dance were part of the celebratory holiday experiences of Jewish children as they grew up in Canaan, Egypt, and

Mesopotamia (America-Israel Culture Foundation, 1968). Storytelling and dramatizations among the people of Canaan formed and kept alive religious convictions. It was essential that children hear the dramatic stories that in the hands of biblical writers were spare of narrative details, arousing listeners' sense of wonder, curiosity, and imagination. Both biblical writers and those dealing with the ancient Greeks have documented storytelling devices that touch on the listeners' imagination and lead to dramatization (Chase, 1955/1962).

Children everywhere also enjoy hearing about fairies, leprechauns, ghosts, witches, elves, monsters, and spirit figures. For some children, these creatures are introduced in books, films, and videos. For others, they are the characters in tales told by storytellers or in puppet shows. Puppetry has been a source of delight for children in India, Indonesia, Japan, England, France, Italy, and the United States for many years. Whether puppets are made of paper, papier-mâché, wood, leather, fur, fabric, or plastic, they are granted a reality and life by child audiences. Imaginary beings also appear as masked figures in dramas, parades, and festivals. At the end of September in Ghana's city of Odumasi-Krobo, for example, the seven-day Nmayem festival is held to thank the gods who have provided millet. Talking drums, parading celebrants carrying carved statuettes that illustrate local legends, banners, brilliantly colored clothing and parasols are all part of the festival, which attracts, and enchants, children and adults (van der Post, 1970, pp. 78–81).

Symbolic Representations

Children around the world represent their play in a variety of forms, including singing and making music, dancing, making up stories, engaging in sociodramatic play, role-playing, laughing at the antics of puppets and clowns, and drawing with pencils, charcoal, crayons, paints, and other media. Perhaps what is most striking is that this impulse to play and draw finds expression even in the harshest of environments, for instance, children produced drawings in the Nazi concentration camps, some of which are on display at the Holocaust Museum in Washington, D.C.

Navajo children have made drawings with colored sands; colored peas and lentils are used in India; brilliantly colored bird feathers are used by children from New Guinea. Some children draw on eggshells, using dyes and wax, as the children of Poland have done for traditional Easter celebrations. Some draw on their own faces and bodies using dyes, paints, nail polishes, powders, or inks. Some color the skin of their companions. During the Holi festival in Bombay, India, which commemorates the triumph of Lord Krishna over the wicked Holika, youngsters squirt each other with colored water and dust-colored powders (Rau, 1969, p. 103). Revelers at Mardi Gras in New Orleans frequently paint their faces; children at city street fairs in the United States often pay small sums to have their faces painted like clowns; and Halloween costuming for small children has often included smudgy beards and moustaches drawn with burnt corks.

Rituals and Ceremonies

A night of feasting culminates the ten-day Ganesha's festival celebrated throughout India in the fall. Spectacular elephant parades in Mysore precede entertainment by traveling performers, professional storytellers, and puppeteers (Rau, 1969).

Children are often trained to participate in highly ritualized cultural ceremonies. These activities are not so much "play" as instances of instilling cultural values in aesthetically satisfying behaviors. Yet just such rituals are also part of the human capacity for play (Brown, 1963; Huizinga, 1950). Some Japanese girls, for example, are trained in the rituals of the tea ceremony (Steinberg, 1969, pp. 136–150), which takes years of study; others learn about the art of flower arrangement, or *ikebana*. Balinese youngsters, wearing elaborate headdresses, are taught to dance with stylized movements and play finger cymbals. Balinese girls in Serongga learn to balance on their heads towering food offerings, known as *bebanten*, of fruits, cakes, and rice balls decorated with flowers and carved palm fronds. The teenage girls carry these to the shrine of Batari Durga, the goddess of death. Once presented there, the delicacies will be returned to the families who have donated them for consumption at a ceremonial feast (Steinberg, 1970, p. 86–87). Training to balance these offerings begins at an early age.

Play in Natural Environments

In contrast with elaborate ritualized dramatizations are children's imaginative pursuits in natural environments. Children often treat as dramatic adventures the search for edible bounties. They often treat as "play" rather than "work" the acquisition of foods obtained as supplemental treats, those not the mainstays of the family diet.

Many children around the world are taught by older siblings or adults how to pick seasonal fruits, nuts, and edible mushrooms or seaweed that grow in the wild. Czech, Polish, and Russian youngsters search out mushrooms in the forests; when these are brought home they are cooked in simmering butter or sour cream, treats for the entire family. Micmac children in Maine picked huckleberries long before white settlers arrived in New England. Scotch-Irish youngsters in Appalachia know where the wild blackberries grow and how to avoid the snakes that frequently make their homes amidst the brambles. Caribbean island boys are often adept at scaling the trunks of coconut palms to bring down the ripe fruits. Irish children have gathered seaweed used to thicken puddings.

Similarly, children pick wildflowers and vines which they weave into wreaths or garlands, fashion into daisy chains, or bunch together into bouquets to give as gifts or use decoratively. They view these activities as a form of play.

Athletic events and childhood games based on physical prowess and skill have been a part of many societies. Ball courts, found among the ruins of the Taino peoples in Puerto Rico and the Mayan people of Mexico, illustrate the widespread popularity of ball games. Throwing balls, kicking balls, tossing balls, catching balls in wooden cups or woven baskets, or hitting them with bats, clubs, rackets, paddles, mallets, or pool cues are activities found in many societies throughout history. Children around the world have used balls and balloons in imaginative ways. Perishable mud balls and snowballs have also had short but dramatic lives in the experiences of many children. Sometimes there are elaborate rules governing the games which must be mastered by players; sometimes the rules are made up on the spot by the ball players, who agree to designate what will serve as "home" and where the "goal" will be.

Pieter Bruegel's paintings *Children's Games* and *Battle between Carnival and Lent* document the play of sixteenth-century children. While he might have meant to satirize adult behaviors, he provided a splendid compendium of more than a hundred different ways that Flemish children played and amused themselves.

Among other activities, children walk on stilts, whip tops, shoot marbles, duel on piggyback, play leapfrog, ride hobbyhorses, beat on drums, make mud pies, stand on their heads, swing on a rail, and play dice or jacks (see Foot, 1968, especially the chapter "Low Life in High Art").

African American children who jump rope in double Dutch patterns or who "do the dozens" with each other, British children who play May I? and Statues, and children who play hide-and-seek and tag and hop scotch are resorting to old games requiring minimal or no equipment. The persistence of these games, like the persistence of dolls and whistles and toy horses, speaks eloquently of the ability of children to amuse themselves in traditional ways.

Traditional play activities with natural props have also been present in varied forms. Children roll large snowballs into snowmen or flop into the snow with their arms outstretched to create angels. Children who splash and play in streams of rushing water in Cambodia, Spain, or Ecuador, or swim in the Dead Sea or the Ganges, or fish in Canadian trout streams or in the Yellow River are also carrying out time-honored behaviors that delight and amuse them.

Children have an astonishing capacity for play and for learning vitally important skills, values, attitudes, and information through play activities. All the more astonishing is the fact that children embrace this learning as part of play, not a product of work.

Learning to be a person in the world is a fundamental task for *every* human being, and a lifelong process that begins at birth. Infants and children must learn to find places for themselves in the natural world they inhabit and in the social milieus of their cultural group. Changing economic conditions, technological developments, ideological commitments, political organization, and religious beliefs might all impact on children's specific tasks, but one historical pattern is strikingly clear: Children have always learned and created places for themselves through play.

Bibliography

America-Israel Culture Foundation, Inc. (1968). *From the lands of the Bible: Art and artifacts* [Catalog]. New York: Author.

Brown, I. C. (1963). *Understanding other cultures*. Englewood Cliffs, NJ: Prentice-Hall.

Carson, R. (1965). *The sense of wonder.* New York: Harper & Row.

Chase, J. E. (1962). *Life and language of the Old Testament.* New York: Norton. (Original work published 1955)

Davidson, C. (1982). *A woman's work is never done: A history of housework in the British Isles, 1650–1950.* London: Chatto and Windus.

Dennis, J. M., & Wilkinson, C. K. (1968). *Chess: East and west, past and present.* New York: Metropolitan Museum of Art.

Foot, T. (1968). *The world of Bruegel, c. 1525–1569.* New York: Time-Life.

Greenberg, S. (1978). *Right from the start: A nonsexist guide to child-rearing.* Boston: Houghton-Mifflin.

Huizinga, J. (1950). *Homo ludens: A study of the play element in culture.* Boston: Beacon.

Jaeger, W. (1960). *Paideia: The ideals of Greek culture.* New York: Oxford University Press. (Original work published 1939)

King, C. E. (1979). *Antique toys and dolls.* New York: Rizzoli.

Kingsley, C. (1855). *The heroes of Greek fairy tales for my children.* Chicago: Donohue and Henneberry.

Kitto, H. D. F. (1962). *The Greeks.* Baltimore: Penguin. (Original work published 1951)

Marrou, H. I. (1964). *A history of education in antiquity.* New York: Mentor.

Museum of International Folk Art. (1956). *Decorative arts of India* [Exhibit catalog]. Santa Fe: Author.

Rau, S. R. (1969). *The cooking of India.* New York: Time-Life.

Steinberg, R. (1969). *The cooking of Japan.* New York: Time-Life.

Steinberg, R. (1970). *Pacific and Southeast Asian cooking.* New York: Time-Life.

Strasser, S. (1982). *Never done: A history of American housework.* New York: Pantheon.

van der Post, L. (1970). *African cooking.* New York: Time-Life.

Play in the Context of Life-Span Human Development

Valeria J. Freysinger

While theories of human development across the life span have roots in several different models or philosophies of human growth and behavior, such as mechanistic, organismic, and contextual (Cavanaugh, 1990), a number of assumptions are common to life-span perspectives. Two of these assumptions are of special interest: (1) Development occurs continually from conception to death, and (2) development occurs in the interaction of internal (biological and psychological) and external (sociocultural and historical) factors and forces. Situating play in the context of life-span human development suggests that the forms and meanings of, and opportunities for, play must be conceptualized as dynamic. Play changes across time(s) as individuals construct or produce and interact within their society, culture, and historical context.

Development as a Lifelong Process

The idea that development continues beyond the years of childhood and adolescence became central to the thinking of psychologists and sociologists in the United States in the mid-twentieth century. During this time, increased longevity led to older adults comprising a greater proportion of the population. The evidence from longitudinal studies suggested that adulthood was not simply a continuation or expansion of the same abilities and issues of childhood and youth (Featherman, 1983); rather, investigators identified developmental issues, changes, and tasks unique to the adult years and observed increasing differentiation within and heterogeneity among individuals.

The belief that development is a lifelong process raises a number of conceptual and philosophical issues. One of these is: Where is development anchored? To put the question in the context of this essay: Does play in childhood or in end-of-life leisure primarily influence development and construction of meaning? What a life-span perspective suggests is that both early and later play shape development. The so-called stages of life are not discrete periods; rather, the developmental tasks and changes at any given point in life are influenced by experiences of the past, shaped by present experiences, and responsive to the future normative expectations of every age.

Development as an Interactive Process

The interactive process of growth is a second assumption common to life-span perspectives. As a greater proportion of individuals survived into the sixth and seventh decades, longitudinal studies became available. More sophisticated data analysis technologies evolved and scholars recognized that it was no longer appropriate to describe development solely in terms of internal processes or social forces. Rather, a life-span perspective required scholars to situate the active individual in sociocultural and historical contexts and to see human beings as both shaped by and shapers of their contexts. In addition, in order to understand development, researchers had to take into account both internal and external factors that suggested consideration of multiple types of time, including chronological age, historical time, and time of measurement (Schaie, 1983).

Chronological Age

Chronological age, or years since birth, represents an individual's capabilities or level of functioning. Chronological age marks maturation or the internal readiness of the individual to engage in activities, for example, to run, skip, communicate verbally, kick a ball, and understand riddles. Because there is the belief that chronological age is a marker of ability, it is also the standard for granting rights and privileges (both formal and informal) and assigning expectations and responsibilities. Chronological age is used as a marker, for example, when an individual tries to join a youth sports league; when others expect that one should share toys; or when others state that one is "too old" to play. There are those, however, who question whether chronological age should be a marker of adult development (Giele, 1980) and whether patterns of age-related change can even be identified (Riegel, 1976). Today there is increasing flexibility in individual lives, for example, in decisions concerning if, when, and how work, spousal, and parental roles are taken on. This flexibility grows out of the increasing complexity and differentiation in society (e.g., in occupational roles because of economic and technological development; in family roles because of the availability of birth control). Hence, development across adulthood is much less ordered and age-related than it once was (Giele, 1980). In fact, one psychologist maintains that development is not predictable and, at most, is probabilistic (Reigel, 1976).

Historical Time

Chronological age also indicates the birth cohort to which an individual belongs. The birth cohort represents historical time. It signifies when an individual is born and at what age individual members of the cohort group might experience various social events, changes, and opportunities. Researchers continue to document the importance of this factor for patterns of growth and development (e.g., Elder, Modell, & Parke, 1993). A woman who was born and went through school before Title IX, for example, is less likely to play sports or be involved in physical activities as an adult: lack of opportunity in childhood to develop needed motor skills during crucial developmental stages and attitudes against females' involvement in such activity would have kept her away from sports. Conversely, girls who entered school after Title IX was implemented in 1972 had new opportunities for play, growth, and development.

Measurement Time

The time of measurement is the third type of time to consider from a life-span perspective. Time of measurement refers to current or contemporary time; that is, what is happening in the environment of an individual at the time a behavior or activity is observed or measured that may have an impact on the behavior. Media coverage of eating disorders among girls involved in gymnastics, for example, may cause some parents to discourage their daughters' pursuit of this sport, which subsequently affects girls' physical skill development and opportunity structure.

In sum, considering play in the context of life-span human development includes examining the influence of dynamic and interactive dimensions. This dynamism, however, does not mean that there is no continuity in development. In fact, recent scholarship suggests tremendous consistency in activities, identity, and personality across adulthood (Atchley, 1993; McCrae & Costa, 1988). One explanation for such continuity is that with advancing age individuals are increasingly aware of who they are and who they want to be, and of their likes and dislikes, strengths, and abilities. The play and leisure activities in which people engage provide both a statement of and feedback for the self. While being expansive or experimenting with many different activities allows individuals to "figure out" and construct an identity, narrowing one's focus and sticking with familiar activities or experiences allows individuals to maintain a valued identity in the face of the changing abilities and opportunity structures that accompany aging. Hence, continuity is a means of adaptation. Further, there is an environmental pressure for consistency in self-presentation. People expect continuity from one another, because continuity of self helps others maintain their self-integrity (Atchley, 1993). In addition, some see too much change as an indication of an unstable, weak, or ill personality—a sign that the individual may need clinical treatment.

When looking at play in the context of life-span development, therefore, both change and continuity take place and influence its meanings, motivations, forms, and opportunities. While every age has its own lucid meanings and forms, some meanings and characteristics of play transcend age (Sutton-Smith, Roberts, & Kozelka, 1969).

Change and Continuity in Play's Meanings across the Life Span

Those practices or activities that people commonly call play in childhood and youth, they typically refer to as leisure in adulthood. Many contend that this is an arbitrary distinction, as play and leisure share, or are defined by, several common dimensions. These dimensions include voluntariness, lack of necessity, or freedom of choice; personal expression or engagement; and motivation that is more intrinsic than extrinsic. In addition, individuals experience both play and leisure as enjoyable or pleasurable (Barnett, 1987; Kelly, 1996). These commonalities suggest that play and leisure are qualities of action, defined by how people do something rather than what they do or the time in which they do it.

There is no agreement, however, on the comparability of play and leisure. Conceiving of leisure as a relational practice, there are those who contend that the play of children and the leisure of adults cannot be compared and, in fact, exist in opposition to each other (Rojek, 1985). Behind this contention is a notion of the self as a construct of socialization; that is, the self develops in interactions with both specific (e.g., mother, father) and generalized (e.g., social institutions, such as school, work; social norms) others at a given time in history. Many adults assume that children's play is selfless because children are selves in the making; openness, unpredictability, and volatility characterize children's play. According to this view, "Children can find literally anything to play with, and they return to it afresh again and again. This inventiveness is the inventiveness of selflessness. Under it, the whole world can inspire dizzy pleasure one moment, and harbour hectic anxiety the next" (Rojek, 1985, p. 174). While society allows children such license, there are expectations that adults highly monitor and control their play, and that it is thoroughly self-conscious or self-constructed. This view states that, in fact, adult leisure is organized

> to exclude the distinctive features of the child's play world (formlessness, frankness, lack of seriousness, and irrationality) or, instead, to tolerate them only in their mi-

metic forms. The private self, which dominates modern leisure relations, engages in communal pursuits as a participant or a spectator. He [*sic*] always acts as an individual body, who is separate and distinct from others, with a life outside the leisure life. In the development of the self, the play world, with its exaggerated emotional polarities and pervasive sense of boundless immediacy is left behind. (Rojek, 1985, p. 174–175)

That is, because adults are enculturated beings, selflessness is not possible in adulthood. The "play" of adults must be legitimated or permissible fun and pleasure (Freud, 1979). And yet, "some of the most exciting and dangerous situations in adult leisure occur when social controls and discipline break down" (Freud, 1979, p. 180), that is, when individuals manipulate or defy social rules so that selflessness may re-emerge. This is consistent with studies of leisure meaning, which have found that high self-expression and low role constraint, or intrinsic motivation and a perception of freedom of choice, distinguish this type of leisure that is high in joy, pleasure, or positive affect. Scholars have labeled this type of experience "pure leisure" (Neulinger, 1981; Samdahl, 1988). It is pure, perhaps, because it comes closest to recapturing the selflessness of childhood play.

Change and Continuity in Life-Span Motivations for Play

Stability and change in motivations for play or leisure across the life span have been the focus of much research. A life-span perspective reveals that motivations are constructed in the interaction of the individual and her or his sociocultural and historical context. According to one viewpoint, as human societies become more civilized, life becomes increasingly routinized and predictable relative to the past (Elias & Dunning, 1969). Further, civilized societies expect humans to control the expression of strong, passionate emotions in everyday life, particularly in public settings, though others would argue that such control extends into the private realms of life as well (Foucault, 1983). Lack of spontaneity in emotional expression results in feelings of monotony and leads to a sense of staleness or lifelessness. To restore "mental tonus" or vitality, adults need to experience and release strong, passionate emotions, and society needs them to do so in safe and nondestructive ways. Within this context, "mimetic" leisure has developed as an outlet for the expression of excitement (Elias & Dunning, 1969). Rock concerts, spectator sports, theater, and Mardi Gras serve as examples of public contexts within which people can play and safely generate, experience, and resolve emotional tension or excitement.

Emotional Expression in Play

The control of emotional expression is very much age-related. In fact, it seems that one of the indicators of maturity or "being adult" is self-control. Self-control may well be antithetical to play and leisure, as both require an ability and willingness to step back or disengage from everyday reality in terms of social norms and expectations in order to express the self fully (Kleiber, 1985; Samdahl, 1988).

Other authors conceptualize leisure as varying according to the intensity of expressive involvement, with solitude being very low in expressive involvement and sexual activity and competitive games and sports very high in expressive involvement (Gordon, Gaitz, & Scott, 1976). Their view is represented in Figure 1. The social context sanctions the intensity of emotional expression and leisure motivations in terms of the attainment of goals or value themes, such as achievement, acceptance, compliance, and self-control. These value themes emerge out of a complex of culturally defined, idealized aspects of human life and social interaction.

FIGURE 1. QUALITATIVELY VARYING FORMS OF LEISURE ACTIVITY (EXPRESSIVE PRIMACY IN PERSONAL ACTIVITY), ACCORDING TO INTENSITY OF EXPRESSIVE INVOLVEMENT

FORMS OF LEISURE ACTIVITY

INTENSITY OF EXPRESSIVE INVOLVEMENT (Cognitive, Emotional, and Physical)			Forms
Very High	SENSUAL TRANSCENDENCE		SEXUAL ACTIVITY PSYCHO-ACTIVE CHEMICAL USE ECSTATIC RELIGIOUS EXPERIENCE AGGRESSION, "ACTION" (physical fighting, defense or attack, verbal fighting) HIGHLY COMPETITIVE GAMES AND SPORTS INTENSE AND RHYTHMIC DANCING
Medium High	CREATIVITY		CREATIVE ACTIVITIES (artistic, literary, musical, etc.) NURTURANCE, ALTRUISM SERIOUS DISCUSSION, ANALYSIS EMBELLISHMENT OF INSTRUMENTAL (art or play in work)
Medium	DEVELOPMENTAL		PHYSICAL EXERCISE AND INDIVIDUAL SPORTS COGNITIVE ACQUISITION (serious reading, disciplined learning) BEAUTY APPRECIATION, ATTENDANCE AT CULTURAL EVENTS (galleries, museums, etc.) ORGANIZATIONAL PARTICIPATION (clubs, interest groups) SIGHT-SEEING, TRAVEL SPECIAL LEARNING GAMES AND TOYS
Medium Low	DIVERSION		SOCIALIZING, ENTERTAINING SPECTATOR SPORTS GAMES, TOYS OF MOST KINDS, PLAY LIGHT CONVERSATION HOBBIES READING PASSIVE ENTERTAINMENT (as in mass media usage)
Very Low	RELAXATION		SOLITUDE QUIET RESTING SLEEPING

Reprinted with permission from "Leisure and Lives: Personal Expressivity across the Lifespan," by C. Gordon, C. M. Gaitz, and J. Scott, 1976. In R. H. Binstock and E. Shanas (Eds.), *Handbook of Aging and the Social Sciences*, New York: Van Nostrand-Reinhold.

Value themes intersect with stages of life, which emerge from the interaction of physical maturation, cognitive elaboration, social-role acquisitions and relinquishments, and economic resources across the life span. Cross-sectional research with adults twenty to ninety-four years of age, for example, indicates that age is inversely related to general level of leisure activity, to type of leisure involvement, and to leisure pleasure (Gordon et al., 1976). Specifically, engagement in highly expressive leisure activities declines with age. However, while involvement in external (to the home), high-intensity activities ("sensual transcendence") decreased with age, participation in homebound, moderate-level activities, such as creative and developmental activity, remained stable across the age groups (Gordon et al., 1976). The cross-sectional design of this research and the point in time at which it took place (1969–1970) cautions application of the findings to today's adults. At the same time, it suggests the need for research that considers the historical embeddedness of play and leisure. Such a contextual approach to research has rarely been incorporated into the work of psychologists and sociologists in North America.

Age-Related and Gender Forces in Emotional Expression

A number of age-related forces may influence an individual's ability and willingness to engage in highly expressive leisure. On the individual level, there is the belief that a sense of basic trust in self and others lays the groundwork for security in self-expression (Erikson, 1963). An individual who has feelings of shame or inferiority that lead to exaggerated feelings of self-consciousness is likely to have a limited capacity for self-expression. In addition, on the social level, there are very real consequences for ignoring both formal and informal sanctions that control affective expression and behavior. For instance, there are formal laws defining what is a disturbance of the peace, as well as gender and age norms regarding appropriate emotional expression for females and males, the young and the old. Age, for example, is often a stronger basis for perceived acceptability of participation in a physical activity than skill, interest, or ability (Ostrow & Dzewaltowski, 1986). Therefore, expectations that older adults have of themselves (because of social norms during childhood as well as current attitudes and media images) and that others have of them influence both opportunity for and interest in participation in highly expressive leisure.

The intrinsic motivation possible for players is also age-related. Specifically, younger and single adults have reported that daily life is more dominated by extrinsically motivated experiences, while older, family-oriented adults, report feeling more intrinsically motivated (Graef, Csikszentmihalyi, & Giannino, 1983). According to Kleiber (1985), there are both emergent and continuing motivational influences on the leisure chosen by individuals. The two are related because emergent motivation is often the source of continuing motivation. Emergent motivation is important up through young adulthood and evolves out of new environmental interaction. Continuing motivation develops out of interests that are pursued beyond those circumstances within which they were extrinsically rewarded. Thus, continuing motivation becomes progressively more important with age. A life-span perspective on human development offers some explanations for this difference in motivational orientation.

Both internal processes in the form of changing ego issues or psychosocial crises (Erikson, 1963) and external forces in the form of a sequence of age-related social roles (Riley, Johnson, & Foner, 1972) influence development. Many social roles (e.g., student, worker) function within a system of external sanctions and rewards that regulate entry into, performance in, and movement onto other social roles. The expectations attached to social roles may well mitigate against freedom of choice, spontaneity, and creativity; that is, against play and playfulness. Being a "good parent," for example, requires the ability to provide for the basic economic needs of the family and to defer gratification. To acquire and maintain employment, employers expect an individual to be predictable, responsible, and compliant. That is, to prepare for adulthood and establish themselves as adults, individuals enact social roles that emphasize extrinsic rewards. Research has found, however, that emphasis on extrinsic motivators decreases intrinsic motivation, which subsequently negatively affects feelings of competence and psychological well-being or happiness. Investigators confirm, for example, that entry into school brings a decrease in creativity among children (Graef, Csikszentmihalyi, & Giannino, 1983). As children progress through the educational system, motivation becomes increasingly extrinsic (Harter, 1981; Maehr, 1983). Hence, the challenge becomes "how to integrate deeply rewarding enjoyable feelings which usually are experienced in leisure settings into the fabric of everyday life" so that life is not "split into useless play and senseless work" (Maehr, 1983, p. 167).

Social roles are not the only factor shaping play or leisure and development across the life span. Psychosocial or ego development also influences this development. Given that the psychosocial issue of young adulthood is intimacy versus isolation (Erikson, 1963), for example, leisure interests are likely to include forms and contexts that are conducive to the establishment and maintenance of an intimate relationship with a significant other (Kelly & Godbey, 1992; Osgood & Howe, 1984). Research with adults has found that affiliative or relational needs are central motivators for, and meanings of, leisure among adults thirty-six to forty-three years of age (Freysinger, 1995).

There is a reorientation of motivation in middle and later adulthood that parallels the psychosocial crises of generativity versus stagnation and integrity versus despair (Erikson, 1963; Kleiber, 1985), as well as a greater tendency toward interiority (Neugarten, 1977). Extrinsic rewards, competitiveness, and a future orientation do not enhance successful adaptation in adulthood, as such motivations are antithetical to the development of generativity, integrity, and interiority. Leisure, however, may support such development. One definition of leisure describes processes of subjective disengagement and engagement; that is, a stepping back from arbitrary and/or external demands, an opening up to possibility, and an engagement in more personally meaningful activity (Kleiber, 1985). Adults, for example, may be employed in routine, repetitive work with little responsibility. They may be highly dissatisfied with this situation but stay with it because they do not perceive that other options are available and they need the income to support a family. While finding little joy in their employment, they may develop and pursue an avocation that provides opportunities for creativity, personal expression, and a sense of competence and mastery (Freysinger, 1995). A father, for example, may find himself in middle adulthood estranged from his teenage son because he spent most of his time when he was younger working overtime or at two jobs in order to support his family; leisure then becomes a way to establish a relationship with his son because it is a context for sharing interests (Freysinger, 1995). Therefore, leisure potentially has developmental value because it is both a means of adjusting to life as it is and a context for self-enhancement through the facilitation of intrinsic motivation or the realization of developmental issues (Kleiber, 1985).

Research on leisure motivations and satisfactions in adulthood reveal two continuous themes: affiliation or community and agency or self-determination (Freysinger, 1995; Kelly, Steinkamp, & Kelly, 1986). The theme of affiliation includes issues of social integration (e.g., development and maintenance of friendships), family affirmation and satisfaction, and development of children. Agency includes motivations for self-expression, learning and development, challenge and accomplishment, and recognition and credibility. Feeling connected with others and gaining and maintaining a sense of mastery and competence are not motivations exclusive to adulthood. They appear to be basic human motivations that are central motivations for play and leisure across the life span. However, the types or forms of activity individuals pursue to realize these motivations are likely to change across the course of life; the forms of play are also powerfully shaped by gender, race/ethnicity, and social class as well as age.

Change and Continuity in Play across the Life Span

In forms of play across the life span change and continuity are often difficult to identify because the form of activity may remain the same while the type of engagement and satisfactions sought in and motivations for the activity change. A young child, for example, may engage in sports for the fun of bodily movement and physical expression (Harris, 1994). With age, motivations may change to emulation of sports stars the child sees on cereal boxes and television commercials. In high school, motivation for participation in sports may be to gain status among peers and popularity with the opposite sex (Kelly, 1996). In college, sports are a source of scholarships and prestige. In young adulthood the individual may join a recreational sports league to meet others in the new city where she or he moved for a first job. Parents may find that their children's involvement in sports may motivate their own continued involvement (Unkel, 1981). In later life, participation may continue through Senior Olympics and master's games, which provide a sense of competence and mastery as well as social integration (Schreck, 1990). That is, one can maintain engagement in the same form of play or leisure, but how and why one participates may change.

Nonetheless, reiterating the theme of continuity and change, Kelly (1983) has proposed a core-and-balance model of leisure activity. His research suggests that a core of activities that remain fairly stable or consistent across the course of life characterizes individuals' leisure. Such activities tend to be convenient and inexpensive (e.g., reading the newspaper, watching television) and family and friend oriented (e.g., sex and intimacy, socializing). At the same time, individuals report a balance of activities that change across the life span as time, interests, and abilities change because of shifting social roles, opportunities, developmental orientations, and physical aging. That is, change in forms of play and participation with age varies in relation to the type of activity. Research indicates that involvement in activities requiring physical skill and exertion (e.g., competitive and outdoor sports) levels off and then shows a gradual decline with age. It is not until late old age (over seventy-five years), though, that a marked decline is visible. Other research has found little difference or even increased involvement in certain types of activity with age (Freysinger & Ray, 1994; Smale & Dupuis, 1993). The cross-sectional design of most of this research makes any definite statements about change in level of activity participation impossible. It is clear, however, that certain factors influence change in the forms of play in which individuals engage across the course of life.

Health is an important factor shaping type and level of activity involvement. Health, not chronological age, is the key factor in physical activity participation across the life span (Kelly et al., 1986). Previous experience also influences subsequent participation; that is, if individuals pursued a hobby as children, they are more likely to participate in that activity as adults. Most importantly, examining age within the context of other factors adds to an understanding of activity participation across the life span. In a longitudinal study of predictors of activity involvement in young and middle adulthood, for example, researchers found that previous involvement, such as high school activity, was not a significant predictor of activity participa-

tion for either women or men in young adulthood, but young adulthood activity involvement was a significant predictor of women's (but not men's) activity participation in middle adulthood (Freysinger & Ray, 1994).

In fact, research consistently has found that gender shapes forms of play and leisure in which individuals engage. There is disagreement as to why such differences exist. One explanation is that play and leisure differ by gender because the distribution of opportunities and power at all levels of society varies systematically by gender (Henderson, Bialeschki, Shaw, & Freysinger, 1996). This power differential leads to different experiences of self and social roles. In the family context, for example, while both women and men may be parents, gender influences how they enact the parental role and how they experience leisure. Mothers, for example, more than fathers play with their children regardless of age of the children and their own employment status (Horna, 1989); and fathers report a gain in parental satisfaction from sharing their leisure with children, while mothers do not (Freysinger, 1994). At the same time, fathers also report greater dissatisfaction with having their leisure constricted by parental obligations than do mothers (Wearing & McArthur, 1988).

This research makes apparent that gender constructs individuals' sense of themselves and their play and leisure interests, skills, motivations, and satisfactions or benefits (Henderson et al., 1996). Similarly, race/ethnicity and social class shape power and social relations, the experience of age, and individual development, and thus interest in, and opportunities for, play and leisure (Freysinger, 1993). Individuals, however, are not passive receptacles for social forces. Play and leisure are also contexts in which individuals challenge and sometimes transform age, gender, race, and class norms (Freysinger & Flannery, 1992; Wearing, 1990). While life-span perspectives on play require researchers and practitioners to understand the complexity of play and development, an awareness that age and play are "political" issues is, for the most part, missing from life-span research.

Thinking about play in the context of life-span human development requires one to examine play not only in childhood and adolescence but throughout adulthood as well. Although scholars disagree on whether the play of children and leisure of adults have the same meanings, and, hence, whether they can even be compared, a life-span perspective would suggest that childhood play shapes later-life leisure and later-life leisure shapes childhood play. A life-span perspective also suggests that play's meanings, motivations, and forms are grounded within the context of the interaction of internal (biological and psychological) and external (social and cultural) factors and forces that change across time and with historical events. There is both continuity and change in the motivations for and forms of play across the life span that emerge out of such interaction. Research design, such as cross-sectional versus longitudinal, and the focus of analysis—for example, general activity or specific forms of play and leisure—influence the conclusions that researchers have made. Play across the life span is very much situated in a specific historical time and the economic, political, religious, and social reality of the day. Finally, in North America, play and leisure have rarely been examined as practices constructed in social relations. Looking at play and leisure in this way not only provides insight into these concepts but into the meaning of age and development as well.

Bibliography

Atchley, R. C. (1993). Continuity theory and the evolution of activity in later life. In J. R. Kelly (Ed.), *Activity and aging* (pp. 5–16). Thousand Oaks, CA: Sage.

Barnett, L. A. (1987). Play. In A. Graefe & S. Parker (Eds.), *Recreation and leisure: An introductory handbook* (pp. 131–136). State College, PA: Venture Publishing.

Cavanaugh, J. C. (1990). *Adult development and aging.* Belmont, CA: Wadsworth.

Elder, G. H., Modell, J., & Parke, R. D. (1993). *Children in time and place: Developmental and historical insights.* New York: Cambridge University Press.

Elias, N., & Dunning, E. (1969). The quest for excitement in leisure. *Society and Leisure, 2,* 50–85.

Erikson, E. H. (1963). *Childhood and society.* New York: Norton.

Featherman, D. (1983). The lifespan perspective and social science research. In P. O. Baltes & O. G. Brim (Eds.), *Life-span development and behavior* (pp. 237–251). New York: Academic.

Foucault, M. (1983). The subject and power. In H. Dreyfus and P. Rabinow (Eds.), *Michel Foucault: Beyond structuralism and hermeneutics* (pp. 208–220). Chicago: University of Chicago Press.

Freud, S. (1979). *Civilization and its discontents* (J. Riviere, Trans.). London: Hogarth.

Freysinger, V. J. (1993). The community, programs, and opportunities: Population diversity. In J. R. Kelly (Ed.), *Activity and Aging* (pp. 211–230). Newbury Park, CA: Sage.

Freysinger, V. J. (1994). Leisure with children and parental satisfaction: Further evidence of a sex difference in the experience of adult roles and leisure. *Journal of Leisure Research, 26,* 212–226.

Freysinger, V. J. (1995). The dialectics of leisure and development for women and men in mid-life: An interpretive study. *Journal of Leisure Research, 27,* 61–84.

Freysinger, V. J., & Flannery, D. (1992). Women's leisure: Affiliation, self-determination, empowerment and resistance. *Society and Leisure, 15* (1), 303–322.

Freysinger, V. J., & Ray, R. O. (1994). The activity involvement of women and men in young and middle adulthood: A panel study. *Leisure Sciences, 16,* 193–217.

Giele, J. Z. (1980). Adulthood as a transcendence of age and sex. In N. J. Smelser & E. H. Erikson (Eds.), *Themes of work and love in adulthood* (pp. 151–173). Cambridge, MA: Harvard University Press.

Gordon, C., Gaitz, C. M., & Scott, J. (1976). Leisure and lives: Personal expressivity across the lifespan. In R. H. Binstock & E. Shanas (Eds.), *Handbook of aging and the social sciences* (pp. 310–341). New York: Van Nostrand-Reinhold.

Graef, R., Csikszentmihalyi, M., & Giannino, S. (1983). Measuring intrinsic motivation in everyday life. *Leisure Studies, 2,* 155–168.

Harris, A. R. (1994). *Children's perceptions of fun in organized youth sport settings.* Unpublished master's thesis, Miami University, Oxford, OH.

Harter, S. (1981). The development of competence motivation in the mastery of cognitive and physical skills: Is there still a place for joy? In G. Roberts & D. Landers (Eds.), *Psychology of motor behavior and sport* (pp. 3–29). Champaign, IL: Human Kinetics.

Henderson, K. A., Bialeschki, M. D., Shaw, S. M., & Freysinger, V. J. (1996). *Both gains and gaps: Feminist perspectives on women's leisure*. State College, PA: Venture Publishing.

Horna, J. L. (1989). The leisure component of the parental role. *Journal of Leisure Research, 21,* 228–241.

Kelly, J. R. (1983). *Leisure identities and interactions.* London: George Allen and Unwin.

Kelly, J. R. (1996). *Leisure.* Boston: Allyn and Bacon.

Kelly, J. R., & Godbey, G. (1992). *The sociology of leisure.* State College, PA: Venture Publishing.

Kelly, J. R., Steinkamp, M. W., & Kelly, J. R. (1986). Later life leisure: How they play in Peoria. *Gerontologist, 26,* 531–537.

Kleiber, D. A. (1985). Motivational reorientation in adulthood and the resource of leisure. In D. A. Kleiber & M. Maehr (Eds.), *Motivation in adulthood* (pp. 217–250). Greenwich, CT: JAI.

Maehr, M. L. (1983). On doing well in science: Why Johnny no longer excels, why Sarah never did. In S. Paris, G. Olson, & H. Stevenson (Eds.), *Learning and motivation in the classroom* (pp. 179–210). Hillsdale, NJ: Erlbaum.

McCrae, R. R., & Costa, P. T. (1988). Age, personality and spontaneous self-concept. *Journal of Gerontology, 43,* S177–S185.

Neugarten, B. L. (1977). Personality and aging. In J. E. Birren & K. W. Schaie (Eds.), *Handbook of the psychology of aging* (pp. 626–649). New York: Academic.

Neulinger, J. C. (1981). *The psychology of leisure* (2nd ed.). Springfield, IL: Charles C. Thomas.

Osgood, N. J., & Howe, C. Z. (1984). Psychological aspects of leisure: A life cycle developmental perspective. *Society and Leisure, 7,* 175–195.

Ostrow, A. C., & Dzewaltowski, D. A. (1986). Older adults' perceptions of physical activity participation based on age-role and sex-role appropriateness. *Research Quarterly for Exercise and Sport, 57,* 286–295.

Riegel, K. (1976, October). The dialectics of human development. *Developmental Psychology, 31* (10), 689–700.

Riley, M. W., Johnson, M., & Foner, A. (1972). *Aging and society: Vol. 3. A sociology of age stratification.* New York: Russell Sage Foundation.

Rojek, C. (1985). *Capitalism and leisure theory.* London: Tavistock.

Samdahl, D. (1988). A symbolic interactionist model of leisure: Theoretical and empirical support. *Leisure Sciences, 10,* 27–39.

Schaie, K. W. (1983). A general model for the study of developmental problems. *Psychological Bulletin, 64* (2), 92–107.

Schreck, M. A. (1990). *Factors influencing participation in Senior Olympic competition.* Unpublished master's thesis, Miami University, Oxford, OH.

Smale, B. J. A., & Dupuis, S. L. (1993). The relationships between leisure activity participation and psychological well-being across the lifespan. *Journal of Applied Recreation, 44,* 948–967.

Sutton-Smith, B., Roberts, J. M., & Kozelka, R. M. (1969). Game involvement in adults. In J. W. Loy & G. S. Kenyon (Eds.), *Sport, culture and society* (pp. 244–258). London: Macmillan.

Unkel, M. (1981). Physical recreation participation of females and males during the adult life cycle. *Leisure Sciences, 4,* 1–27.

Wearing, B. (1990). Beyond the ideology of motherhood: Leisure as resistance. *Australian and New Zealand Journal of Sociology, 26,* 36–58.

Wearing, B., & McArthur, M. (1988). The family that plays together stays together: Or does it? *Australian and New Zealand Journal of Sex, Marriage, and Family, 9,* 150–158.

Diversity and Play

Influences of Race, Culture, Class, and Gender

Patricia G. Ramsey

It is possible to infer from cross-cultural comparisons of children's play and research on children's cross-group attitudes and contact patterns how children from different racial, cultural, and social class backgrounds might play together. Research on cross-gender play is one example of how play interests and styles can potentially affect children's play. Given the prevalence of same-group preferences and the cross-group differences in play styles and interests, adults might expect that play between children of different groups would be less frequent and elaborate than that between children with similar backgrounds. At the same time, play is a vehicle for children to explore their differences and develop common themes that incorporate elements from many life experiences.

In a time when the population of the United States is becoming increasingly diverse and cross-group tensions are on the rise, it is important to understand how children from different racial, cultural, and class backgrounds play together. At this point, however, researchers know relatively little. Most studies on the effects of racial and ethnic differences focus on children's social contact patterns and attitudes rather than on the quality of their cross-group play. Researchers who do cross-cultural comparisons of children's play have identified play styles and rituals of specific groups but have not observed what occurs when children from different groups play together. One reason for these gaps in the research is that many children live in neighborhoods and attend schools that are ethnically and socioeconomically segregated. Even in schools that have more diverse populations, children often redivide themselves by race, culture, and social class, as well as by gender.

The sections that follow discuss how race, culture, social class, and gender potentially affect play styles and choice of play partners, and how these in turn may influence the play between members of diverse groups. Because of the limited information about what actually occurs in diverse settings, there is discussion of cross-sex play that considers the ways in which cultural and play style differences potentially affect cross-group play. The final section of this essay includes suggestions for using play to increase cross-group relationships. Because there is so little direct information about play in diverse settings, this review in many places is speculative, but might provide some incentives for future research.

Racial Differences

Race refers to groups that share visible physical attributes that traditionally are defined as *racial*. Although some people often use a biological distinction to denote race, it is, in fact, a socially constructed label, as is evident in the inconsistent and biased ways in which some people apply racial terms (Smedley, 1993). The contradictions of race have become even more apparent with increasing numbers of interracial births, transracial adoptions, and immigrants with mixed racial heritages (Root, 1992). At the same time, a person's race profoundly affects her or his status and prospects in this society (Ogbu, 1991) and, along with gender, is one of the ways that we systematically categorize people.

Despite (and possibly because of) these contradictions, children notice racial differences early in life; during their preschool and elementary school years, their perceptions and attitudes about race become more defined and elaborate. Katz (1976) postulated that children go through the following steps in their acquisition of racial attitudes: First, infants and toddlers seem to notice racial differences and often react with surprise when they see a racially unfamiliar person. By the ages of three and four, children have a rudimentary concept about race and can easily label and sort people by "racial" traits such as skin coloring and facial features. At this age they may begin to absorb and repeat evaluative comments about race, but not really understand their implications. The third stage is conceptual differentiation, when children elaborate and refine their concepts about race and clarify which characteristics are associated with particular racial groups. During the early elementary years, children learn that race is a permanent characteristic and distinct from temporary skin color changes caused by exposure to the sun. Concurrently, children develop more definite feelings and beliefs about different racial groups, which usually reflect the attitudes they have been exposed to in their communities. By around ten years of age, children's attitudes have crystallized and, from this point on, they are less open to changing their beliefs and perceptions.

Young children generally show a global preference for people "who are like me" over those "who are not like me" (Sigelman, Miller, & Whitworth, 1986). When they choose potential friends from pictures of unfamiliar peers, they usually select members of their own race (Fox & Jordan, 1973; Newman, Liss, & Sherman, 1983).

In real social situations, however, young children do not necessarily choose their friends by race. Because gender is a more reliable predictor of play style and activity preference, young children in racially mixed groups often form friendships based on gender rather than on race (Singleton & Asher, 1977, 1979). Ironically, gender segregation sometimes counteracts cross-racial avoidance. Same-race preference, however, has been observed in some racially mixed preschools and kindergartens, particularly on the part of white children (Finkelstein & Haskins, 1983; Ramsey & Myers, 1990). Several studies, reviewing the literature in cross-race friendship choices, pointed to a pattern of decreasing cross-race friendship choices during the elementary and secondary years (Epstein, 1986). In another study, however, third graders in a very racially diverse setting played more with their cross-ethnic peers than the kindergartners did, suggesting that a trajectory toward racial cleavage is not inevitable (Howes & Wu, 1990). As children get older, the effects of race may differ across boys' and girls' groups. A study of eight- and nine-year-olds in Britain, for example, noted that boys generally played large-group games, particularly soccer and chase games, which require more participants and little conversation (Boulton & Smith, 1993). Thus, although they may still prefer their same-race peers, boys may be more racially inclusive than girls, who function within their smaller and less physically active groups.

Given that racial differences such as skin color and physiognomy do not have any functional impact on children's interactions and play styles, why do children segregate themselves by race? This is a racially divided society and, throughout the history of the United States, race has determined a person's status and her or his access to opportunities and privileges (Gibbs, et al., 1989). According to one anthropologist, many groups of color in this country are treated as caste-like minorities (Ogbu, 1978, 1983); they are stigmatized and excluded from higher-status opportunities and roles and relegated to menial jobs and poor communities.

Thus, where and how people live, work, and go to school are largely dependent on their racial membership. Families usually live in racially segregated neighborhoods and socialize within their own racial groups, so that many young children have no cross-race friends either prior to coming to school or as neighborhood friends outside of school. White children, in particular, often have almost no different-race members of their immediate networks (Cochran & Riley, 1988). As children from more privileged groups develop their concepts about racial differences, they absorb the prevailing cultural images and attitudes of superiority and learn to associate the effects of poverty and discrimination with their images of people of color. Children who are the targets of discrimination, likewise, become increasingly frustrated by the barriers between their lives and the material success they see vividly portrayed in the media. Not surprisingly, many become increasingly alienated from the dominant group and refuse to "act white" (Ogbu, 1991). Thus, as children get older, the conflation of race and status seriously undermines cross-racial friendships.

Children also begin to notice differences in dress, interactive styles, and language that reflect the cultural heritages of specific racial groups. Lack of familiarity with particular childhood games and rituals may cause members from different groups to see each others' behaviors as strange and possibly threatening (Schofield, 1981) and to seek out same-race peers (Boulton & Smith, 1993). The following account (paraphrased from Beresin, 1994) of elementary school girls on a playground illustrates how the lack of shared rituals limits the roles and reciprocity of play:

> Five African American girls are playing double Dutch jump rope and chanting a popular rhyme that is a take-off on McDonald's menu. A Chinese immigrant child is trying to learn double Dutch and misses several times despite encouraging instructions from the other girls. A Polish American girl also enters, tries to jump, and also misses. One of her instructors shouts, "I told you not to come down!" At that point the bell rings to end recess and the children rush toward the door.

In this observation the children were trying to play together despite their lack of shared expertise in a particular game. The helpfulness of the African American girls and the willingness of the two outsiders to try an unfamiliar game suggests that children from different backgrounds are motivated to play together. At this point, however, each group is stuck in particular roles: the African American girls are instructors and the Chinese and Polish American girls are learners. Thus, the relationship is potentially unstable; over time, the outsiders may become embarrassed and intimidated if they continue to miss, and the patience of their instructors might wear thin. The next section discusses implications of these cultural differences.

Cultural Differences

Culture is both overt and covert (Garcia, 1990). Language, rituals, tools, edifices, artifacts, and arts are the external manifestations of particular cultures. These in turn reflect the beliefs, values, and orientations that are the covert aspects of a culture. In the United States, for example, shopping malls are common expressions of our culture's priorities of competition, con-sumption, newness, private property, and material success. Both these covert and overt aspects of culture are reflected in children's play, as seen in U.S. children's frequent enactments of "going shopping."

Young children cannot understand the concepts of culture or national origin because they do not yet grasp the significance of country or region (Lambert & Klineberg, 1967; Piaget & Weil, 1951). They do react, however, to the unfamiliar behavior, language, or dress of people from different cultural backgrounds. For example, children, frequently describe someone with an unfamiliar accent as "talking funny." Children who do not have the opportunity to become familiar with members of different cultural groups or to develop complementary themes and roles with peers from other groups may be wary of people from other cultures. This distance is reinforced when, as with racial differences, neighborhoods are segregated by ethnicity and parents socialize strictly within their own cultural groups. Some families, moreover, have their children attend after-school and weekend programs that emphasize the traditions and people from their home culture.

A study of Canadian classrooms containing both French- and English-speaking children, for example, found a striking degree of segregation between the two ethnolinguistic groups (Doyle, 1982). Moreover, same-group play lasted longer and involved more conversation and fantasy play than cross-group contacts did. Because many children were competent in both languages, the researcher concluded that the segregation was not simply a matter of fluency in the less familiar language. Rather, she attributed these patterns to the following cycle: children play less actively with dissimilar partners and do not develop common repertoires, which in turn means that their play is less engaging and active; children then gravitate more toward their familiar playmates, which precludes opportunities to create the same kind of shared repertoire with other children.

Even when children share a common ethnic background, differences in lifestyles and child-rearing priorities can create some social distance, as seen in the following observations:

> Karl lives in a household where there is no TV, and his parents go to considerable lengths to ensure that he does not watch any TV at other people's homes. One day in kindergarten, Karl is sitting next to

Glen, who tells him with great excitement that he is going to see a Goofy movie. With considerable animation, Karl answers, "I know what the word *goofy* means. It means silly. Goofy must be a silly person. I like silly things. Who is this Goofy person?" Glen looks puzzled, then annoyed, and begins to talk with another child.

Although the content and themes of play may differ across cultures, the type of play may not be that different. A comparison of children in Senegal and the United States found that the frequency and level of play in both groups was similar despite the difference in physical setting, interactions with adults, and the type of play objects that children used, including scrounged and handmade materials for the Senegalese children and manufactured ones for children in the United States (Bloch, 1989). In both groups, play was the dominant activity, and both engaged in similar types of play (functional, constructive, pretense, gross motor, and dance/music) for about the same percentage of time. The structure of play also may not be culturally specific. A comparison of three-year-olds in Mexico and in the United States found that the play themes mirrored the daily lives and activities of the children and therefore differed between the two groups (Farver, 1992). Both groups of children, however, constructed play sequences with spontaneous comments rather than explicit verbal negotiation or planned scripts.

Some types of play may be more vulnerable to cultural differences. Our family recently adopted Andrès, a three-year-old boy from Chile. Daniel, our six-year-old son, was adopted from Chile as an infant and is thoroughly assimilated into the peer culture of the United States. The following observations illustrate how some types of play are more affected by cultural differences than others:

Day 2 (Andrès had been with us for about forty-eight hours; we are in a park in Santiago, Chile.) Daniel calls to his brother, "Look at this, Andrès!" He then sings out, "Go, go, Power Rangers!" and leaps from a low brick wall. Andrès looks a little bewildered and turns away. "Donde esta la pelota? [Where is the ball?]," he asks and runs off. (Balls were one of the few toys that were available in the foster home where Andrès lived for three years.) Daniel

shouts again, "Look, Andrès!" and makes another leap. Meanwhile Andrès is looking under bushes trying to find the ball. Daniel looks down and walks away.

An hour later both boys are in the bathtub. They are blowing bubbles and pouring water over each other and laughing gleefully. Andrès sticks his head in the water and comes up with wet hair. Daniel follows suit and they both shriek with delight.

Play that is more sensory and motoric may be a better vehicle for stimulating cross-cultural (as well as cross-age) play than sociodramatic themes, which often require shared language or cultural knowledge.

Children are also learning culturally specific social conventions and priorities. A comparison of teacher interventions in Italy and the United States, for example, shows how the former reflect the priority of children's seeing themselves as members of the group and as contributors to the welfare of the group (Corsaro & Schwartz, 1991). In contrast, the suggestions and admonitions of the teacher in the United States emphasize the children's individual rights within the group.

Differences in social orientations and styles were vividly illustrated in a cross-ethnic and cross-social class comparison of children's social interactive styles (Rizzo & Corsaro, 1991). Children in a white middle-class preschool tended to be very concerned about the needs and feelings of others and were easily upset if peers threatened to deny them friendship. In general, their peer interactions and their feelings about them were fragile. The African American and Hispanic children in a Head Start program used a lot more teasing and oppositional and competitive talk with each other, but, unlike their middle-class counterparts, the Head Start children were not intimidated or upset by it. In fact, the authors felt that these playful exchanges helped the children create assertive friendships and a sense of group solidarity. If these two groups had been together, they might have misunderstood each other: the teasing and oppositional style of the Head Start children might have been perceived as aggressive and intimidating by the middle-class children; conversely, the Head Start children might have been bewildered at the fragility of the middle-class children's interactions and feelings.

Cultural differences also may be compounded by newcomer status. Children of recent immigrants to this country are likely to be intimidated by their unfamiliar surroundings and by trying to learn how to bridge the gap between their home culture and their new school culture (Igoa, 1995). A few studies have shown that these children engage in less social and pretend play than their culturally dominant peers (Child, 1983; Quisenberry & Christman, 1979; Robinson, 1978).

According to a critical review of the field, most studies of cultural differences in play have compared children across continuous cultures, where at least two generations have lived in the same culture (Slaughter & Dombrowski, 1989). Very few researchers have studied children in culturally discontinuous contexts, those in which the family has resided in the current setting for less than one generation. The studies of these latter children often simply compare the recent immigrants with their nonimmigrant peers in terms of the frequency of social and/or pretend play. They fail to consider the meaning of play in children's home cultures and how children's play reflects their attempts to accommodate to two (or more) cultural contexts. The reviewers argue for the need to study how children use play to adapt to multiple cultural contexts (Slaughter & Dombrowski, 1989). Moreover, there is a need to understand how play contributes to the development of attitudes of privilege and superiority on the part of children in the dominant cultures.

Socioeconomic Class Differences

As with cultural differences, young children are not consciously aware of social class (Naimark, 1983; Ramsey, 1991). Nevertheless, children often gravitate toward other children from similar socioeconomic (SES) backgrounds. Child-rearing goals and methods reflect the social and economic roles of specific groups (Ogbu, 1983) and, in turn, affect the behavioral goals and patterns of the children. Thus, themes and play styles may create some distance between children of different SES groups. Children from different SES groups may also be less familiar with each other because neighborhoods, social groups, and preschools are usually economically segregated. In one town, the kindergarten and first-grade teachers noticed that children (virtually all European American) often divided themselves along social class lines from the very beginning of school. Not only did the two groups come in with different home experiences, but many already knew members of their own SES group as a result of attending either a federally funded preschool program for low-income children or local tuition-based nursery schools and day care centers that served middle-income families. Different experiences that reflect SES can also make cross-group contacts more strained, as seen in the following observation:

> In a third-grade classroom, Andrea and Katy, both middle-SES, and Laurie, low-SES, are talking on the playground during recess. Andrea twirls around and says, "This is part of the recital." Katy smiles and says, "Yeah, we're doing that too," and twirls around. "It makes me dizzy, though. I hope that I don't fall down. Does it make you dizzy?" Andrea says, "No, not really," and she twirls around again. The two girls continue twirling and giggling. During this exchange, Laurie looks down at the ground.

Many of the researchers who study social class differences in play have concluded that low-income children engage in less sociodramatic play and are more often on the periphery of the play that occurs in socioeconomically integrated classrooms (Fein & Stork, 1981; Rubin, Maioni, & Hornung, 1976; Smilansky, 1968). These studies and findings have been criticized because the settings, observers, and assessment instruments potentially favor middle-class styles of play (McLoyd, 1982). The observation above illustrates how a middle-class bias in classroom props, books, and conversations could exclude low-SES children and in turn reduce their level of social involvement.

At the same time, we cannot diminish or ignore the devastating effects of poverty on all aspects of children's development, including their play. Behaviors and conditions often associated with poverty (school absences, frequent moves, poor health and nutrition) potentially impair students' social relationships and participation in play activities. A review of a number of recent studies consistently found that children from low-income homes are less popular than their middle-class peers (Patterson, Griesler, Vaden, & Kupersmidt, 1992). The reviewers speculate that severe economic stress influences family life and the child's feelings about herself or himself in ways that may interfere with forming positive peer relations and engaging in play.

Thus, although young children do not understand the concept of socioeconomic status, their play may be affected by it. Because schools are usually oriented to the values and subject matter of the middle class, low-income children may feel less at home and be more socially constrained than their middle-income peers. For example, role-play props and books that reflect more middle-class lifestyles create for middle-class children a more familiar context than for low-income children. Furthermore, teachers' reactions to children from different socioeconomic groups may imply that one group is smarter and more advanced than the other. These influences, combined with the lack of proximity and familiarity, may impede contact and play between children from different social class groups.

Gender Differences

As demonstrated in the previous sections, little is known about how children from different racial, cultural, and class backgrounds actually play together. In contrast, many researchers have studied cross-sex play, and these studies may shed some light on how differences that reflect race, culture, and class might affect children's play in mixed groups.

Same-sex preference dominates children's choices of friends at all grades in school. Cross-sex contacts, however, follow a curvilinear pattern: they decrease from preschool to middle school and then increase during adolescence (Epstein, 1986; Paley, 1984; Swadener & Johnson, 1989). Maccoby (1986) offers several reasons for this seemingly universal pattern of gender cleavage, two of which could apply to culture and/or SES. First, with early socialization, children learn to enjoy sex-typed activities and behaviors and are drawn to each other when they observe each other's play styles and activity preferences. Preschool girls typically tend to congregate in the art and housekeeping areas, and boys engage in more physically active play with blocks and trucks. In elementary schools, boys usually play vigorous physical contact games at recess, whereas many girls play games that require more precise physical skills and social coordination, such as jump rope. Second, Maccoby hypothesized that children are drawn to same-sex peers because they are more confident of what to expect. Conversely, they avoid cross-sex peers because they are unsure about how they will behave and are more uncertain of their own roles.

Researchers also have observed that girls and boys who play together in their neighborhoods frequently ignore their friends when they are in the public arena of school. Girls may learn to avoid their male classmates because when boys and girls do play or work together, the boys are often more assertive and dominate the interactions. During cross-gender entry attempts, for example, girls are more tentative with boys than they are with girls; boys, however, are more imperative with girls than with boys (Phinney & Rotheram, 1982). Sex-segregation increases during the elementary years and is reaffirmed by children's engagement in "borderwork" between the two groups (Thorne, 1986), such as cross-gender chasing games that sometimes include a threat of kissing or pollution rituals (for example, giving cooties to each other), and invasions in which one group (usually boys) disrupts the play of the other.

Regardless of its precise origin(s) or location, gender cleavage quickly becomes self-perpetuating. Children engage in sex-typed play, which brings them into more contact with same-sex peers. They also quickly learn that peer acceptance depends on conforming to sex-typed roles. One researcher observed six-year-old children's outrage at boys who played girl-type games (Damon, 1977). As children spend more time in segregated play, each group begins to form its own culture with clearly defined characteristics (Maccoby, 1986). With the increasing separation, those children who like members of the opposite sex find it increasingly difficult to maintain these friendships; children who cross the gender divide are often accused of "liking" someone of the opposite sex or being a member of that group (Thorne, 1986). Therefore, cross-gender friendships in childhood frequently "go underground."

Cross-racial, -cultural, and -SES contacts may go through a similar process. First, children are drawn to peers who are familiar in some way—appearance, language, activity preferences, and so forth. Second, they know what to expect from familiar peers and therefore feel more confident and comfortable and so stay with them. Third, as the groups congeal, they develop their own peer culture that reflects a merging of their home, community, and school cultures. Over time, group loyalty may make it more difficult for children to spend time with other groups, and so the divisions become more rigid.

Facilitating Cross-Group Play

Ironically, although these differences may interfere with intergroup play, play itself may be a means of encouraging cross-group contact. When children are engaged in true play—nonliteral, open-ended, and spontaneous play—they are creating their own world, which can potentially accommodate everyone. Yet how do we get children who regard each other as strangers to play with each other in the first place?

Teacher-facilitated groups is one possible strategy. A recent review of the effects of cooperative learning on cross-group relationships stated that cross-racial and cross-ethnic cooperative groups foster strong intergroup friendships as well as simply more amicable contacts (Slavin, 1995). Not only do children in the same cooperative groups become friends, but cross-ethnic friendships outside of the groups also increase. The reviewer speculates that once one cross-group friendship is formed, then friends of both parties get to know each other and in some cases become friends. Another researcher also observed that, when the teachers formed mixed-sex collaborative groups, boys and girls did become engaged in absorbing tasks (Thorne, 1986). Thus, group collaboration provides opportunities for children from different backgrounds to see each other, at least momentarily, as competent and familiar individuals and to develop some common ground. We do not know whether or not cooperative projects lead to more cross-group play, but the reviewer's description of cross-group friendships (Slavin, 1995) is encouraging since it implies that the relationships continue beyond the groups and presumably involve play and other recreational activities.

Teachers can also use the physical environment and materials to encourage children to play with a wider group of peers. One common technique is to arrange the room to bring groups of children who usually play separately into closer proximity. Two kindergarten teachers constructed an "Outer Space" center in what was formerly the housekeeping and block areas (Theokas, 1991). They found that the number of cross-sex contacts increased markedly during the period of time that the space center was available. Moreover, as they spent more time together, the boys and girls developed some common play themes and played together more cooperatively. In a less elaborate intervention, a teacher put a suitcase in the role-playing area. The children invented many travel themes that involved both girls and boys in a number of roles. Thus, the creation of an exciting but relatively gender-neutral area seems to increase children's willingness to play with opposite-sex peers. This same strategy might work with children from different racial, cultural, and socio-economic groups by including new props that would appeal to all groups.

A similar approach is to use some desirable activity to lure children into mixed-group situations. Novel toys in the sandbox, for example, might offer children a shared play medium that does not require a shared language. Likewise, the challenge of new computer games can be a vehicle to attract children to play together even if they do not have a lot of shared experiences and background knowledge in common. To make these kinds of interventions work, teachers may need to assign children to these activities so that they do not just gravitate to their usual friends. Moreover, they need to be sure that the materials do not favor one group over another. If some children, for example, have access to computers at home and others do not, then new computer games may widen the gap rather than bridge it.

Another strategy is to try to develop more common ground among children from different backgrounds. One kindergarten teacher noticed that her children from low-income families were sometimes left out of conversations that focused on the latest toy fads, such as mechanical gadgets or exotic dolls. She raised some money and bought a few of these toys for the classroom, so that all children could have access to them. Although this intervention did not address some of the more basic and long-lasting social class divisions, the teacher found that it did reduce the numbers of conversations divided by social class. In another classroom with three Cambodian children who were socially on the periphery, the teacher, with the help of the children and their parents, created a learning center with lots of books, pictures, art, and information about Cambodia. The Cambodian children introduced the area to their peers, became "experts" in the eyes of their peers, and enjoyed a great deal more social contact and visibility after that intervention. Moreover, some of the other children began to build "Cambodian houses" in blocks and cook "Cambodian food" in the role-play area, based on some of the photographs and books in the learning center. Thus, the center not only gave the Cambodian children a chance to become more socially active, it also served to create more potential play themes on the children's common ground.

Because play is spontaneous, fluid, and infinitely malleable, many cultural themes can be woven into it, as illustrated in the following observations of Daniel and Andrès, which the author calls "The Story of Qua qua and Karate."

Day 7. (Andrès has been with us for about a week; we are on a grassy area outside of our apartment in Santiago.) Daniel goes up to his brother and shouts, "Karate!" and starts "karate kicking" near Andrès. "Look at this, Andrès!" Daniel continues as he makes a spinning leap. Andrès looks a little bewildered and turns away. All of a sudden his eyes light up and he smiles broadly "Qua qua!" (a baby-talk version of the Chilean word for baby, "gua gua"), he crows and runs over to a family with a baby. (In his foster home, a number of babies either lived there or visited frequently, and playing with the babies was a focus for most of the older children.) Daniel looks surprised and then angry. "I don't want him for my brother!" he growls.

Day 9. (We are walking down the street.) Andrès suddenly shouts "Como Daniel! [Like Daniel!]" and thrusts his legs out in front of him in a wobbly version of Daniel's karate kicks.

Day 48. Andrès has developed a strong attachment to a small rubber baby doll whom he calls *Qua qua*. Since Andrès has taken up with Qua qua, Daniel has been doing a lot more dramatic play with his favorite teddy bear, Pooh, as exemplified by the following observations:

Daniel and Andrès have brought their pillows and blankets downstairs and are making elaborate beds for Pooh and Qua qua. They rearrange the bedding numerous

times and then kiss their two charges and say "Good night" and "Buenas noches." They then go through several rounds in which Pooh wakes up Qua qua and vice versa. Often the waking up process involves jumping on the other one. Pretty soon the two boys are rolling around on top of each other, laughing loudly and screaming "Wake-up!"

Day 54. Daniel and Andrès are riding large trucks around the kitchen, careening around corners and making lots of motor and crashing noises. Pooh is perched in front of Daniel's truck, and Qua qua is in exactly the same place on Andrès's.

Day 60. In the middle of trying to get the boys ready for bed, the phone rings and I am tied up for about ten minutes. Meanwhile the boys are giggling in the other room. They burst in and Andrès says "Mira, Mama! [Look, Mama]" and they hold up Andrès's sleeper pajamas with the heads of both Pooh and Qua qua sticking out of the neck.

Day 66. Andrès and Daniel are holding Qua qua and Pooh, respectively. Andrès shouts "Karate!" and Pooh and Qua qua begin to "karate kick" each other accompanied by the appropriate grunts and "Hiyahs!"

Later that day. We are eating supper and both Pooh and Qua qua are perched on the table. Daniel, in a squeaky "baby" voice, says, "Poohie hungry!" and "feeds" him some potatoes. Andrès in identical tones says, "Qua qua 'ungry!" and imitates Daniel's actions. This exchange continues for several rounds, with increasing volume and more elaborate gestures, until their father (who is watching the food begin to drop on the table) expresses concern that "Qua qua and Pooh will get sick if they eat too much."

These observations illustrate how children coming from different cultural and experiential backgrounds can weave together themes to create a shared play world. As one researcher also has found, the children developed and elaborated these themes and rituals (some of these episodes were repeated almost daily) spontaneously as they responded to each other and to different objects that happened to be available at the time, such as the pajamas (Farver, 1992). Although we cannot generalize too much from this example, it does show how quickly (and creatively) children can incorporate each other's play themes and rituals, despite different languages, cultures, life experiences, and ages. Thus, play has the potential of providing bridges between children from different groups. In many settings it is probably already happening; perhaps soon someone will provide the documentation.

Teachers who want to try to use play to facilitate cross-group contacts may need to set up particular situations (as described earlier in this section) or to assign children to areas in order to overcome their tendency to congregate with familiar peers. This does not mean that teachers then try to direct the play (assigning roles or suggesting themes). They can provide materials, props, and stories, along with some novel toys to attract attention, and let the children create their world and weave together themes as the play unfolds. Ultimately, however, children can create their own multicultural world, for example:

> I walked into a kindergarten classroom and two girls rushed over to me and said, "Look at our McDonald's!" They had set up a counter with a toy cash register and had laid out the food behind it—tacos, rice, grapes, salad, and several kinds of breads (now available from most early-childhood catalogues). On the two tables were chopsticks and forks. A stuffed dog had been squeezed into a coat hanger and was sticking out from the wall. I asked what it was and one of the girls cheerily answered, "The piñata for the birthday parties."

Teachers cannot ignore the segregation and inequities that prevail in the United States. Early in their lives, children learn to divide the world by race, culture, class, and gender; some experience the privileges and some the hardships of the status differences inherent in these divisions. These differences are often reflected in children's play and in their peer relationships, and societal divisions and hierarchies are often recreated in classrooms. Play, while it cannot change the external realities of children's lives, can be a vehicle for children to explore and enjoy their differences and similarities and to create, even for a brief time, a more just world where everyone is an equal and valued participant.

Bibliography

Beresin, A. R. (1994, April). *Until the bell rings: The play cultures at recess.* Paper presented at the annual meeting of the American Educational Research Association, New Orleans, LA.

Bloch, M. N. (1989). Young boys' and girls' play at home and in the community: A cultural-ecological framework. In M. N. Bloch & A. D. Pelligrini (Eds.), *The ecological context of children's play* (pp. 120–154). Norwood, NJ: Ablex.

Boulton, M. J., & Smith, P. K. (1993). Ethnic, gender partner, activity preference in mixed-race schools in the U. K.: Playground observations. In C. H. Hart (Ed.), *Children on playgrounds: Research perspectives and applications* (pp. 210–237). Albany: State University of New York Press.

Child, E. (1983). Play and culture: A study of English and Asian children. *Leisure Studies, 2,* 169–186.

Cochran, M., & Riley, D. (1988). Mother reports of children's personal networks: Antecedents, concomitants, and consequences. In S. Salzinger, J. Antrobus, & M. Hammer (Eds.), *Social networks of children, adolescents, and college students* (pp. 113–145). Hillsdale, NJ: Lawrence Erlbaum.

Corsaro, W. A., & Schwarz, K. (1991). Peer play and socialization in two cultures: Implications for research and practice. In B. Scales, M. Almy, A. Nicolopoulou, & S. Ervin-Tripp (Eds.), *Play and the social context of development in early care and education* (pp. 234–254). New York: Teachers College Press.

Damon, W. (1977). *The social world of the child.* San Francisco: Jossey-Bass.

Doyle, A. (1982). Friends, acquaintances, and strangers: The influence of familiarity and ethnolinguistic background on social interaction. In K. H. Rubin & H. S. Ross (Eds.), *Peer relationships and social skills in childhood* (pp. 229–252). New York: Springer-Verlag.

Epstein, J. L. (1986). Friendship selection: Developmental and environmental influences. In E. C. Mueller & C. R. Cooper

(Eds.), *Process and outcome in peer relationships* (pp. 129–160). New York: Academic.

Farver, J. M. (1992). An analysis of young American and Mexican children's play dialogues: Illustrative study no. 3. In C. Howes & C. C. Matheson (Eds.), *The collaborative construction of pretend* (pp. 55–63). Albany: State University of New York Press.

Fein, G. G., & Stork, L. (1981). Sociodramatic play: Social class effects in integrated preschool classrooms. *Journal of Applied Developmental Psychology, 2,* 267–279.

Finkelstein, N. W., & Haskins, R. (1983). Kindergarten children prefer same-color peers. *Child Development, 54,* 502–508.

Fox, D. J., & Jordan, V. B. (1973). Racial preference and identification of black, American Chinese, and white children. *Genetic Psychology Monographs, 88,* 229–286.

Garcia, R. L. (1990). *Teaching in a pluralistic society: Concepts, models, and strategies* (2nd ed.). New York: HarperCollins.

Gibbs, J. T., Huang, L. N., & Associates (1989). *Children of color: Psychological interventions with minority youth.* San Francisco: Jossey-Bass.

Howes, C., & Wu, F. (1990). Peer interactions and friendships in an ethnically diverse school setting. *Child Development, 61,* 537–541.

Igoa, C. (1995). *The inner world of the immigrant child.* New York: St. Martin's.

Katz, P. A. (1976). The acquisition of racial attitudes in children. In P. A. Katz (Ed.), *Towards the elimination of racism* (pp. 125–154). New York: Pergamon.

Lambert W. E., & Klineberg, O. (1967). *Children's views of foreign people.* New York: Appleton-Century-Crofts.

Maccoby, E. E. (1986). Social groupings in childhood: Their relationship to prosocial and antisocial behavior in boys and girls. In D. Olewus, J. Block, & M. Radke-Yarrow (Eds.), *Development of antisocial and prosocial behavior* (pp. 263–284). New York: Academic.

McLoyd, V. C. (1982). Social class differences in sociodramatic play: A critical review. *Developmental Review, 2,* 1–30.

Naimark, H. (1983). *Children's understanding of social class differences.* Paper presented at the biennial meeting of the Society for Research in Child Development, Detroit, MI.

Newman, M. A., Liss, M. B., & Sherman, F. (1983). Ethnic awareness in children: Not a unitary concept. *Journal of Genetic Psychology, 143,* 103–112.

Ogbu, J. U. (1978). *Minority education and caste.* New York: Academic.

Ogbu, J. U. (1983). Socialization: A cultural ecological approach. In K. M. Borman (Ed.), *The social life of children in a changing society* (pp. 253–267). Norwood, NJ: Ablex.

Ogbu, J. U. (1991). Immigrant and involuntary minorities in comparative perspective. In M. A. Gibson & J. U. Ogbu (Eds.), *Minority status and schooling: A comparative study of immigrant and involuntary minorities* (pp. 3–33). New York: Garland.

Paley, V. G. (1984). *Boys and girls: Superheroes in the doll corner.* Chicago: University of Chicago Press.

Patterson, C. J., Griesler, P. C., Vaden, N. A., & Kupersmidt, J. B. (1992). Family economic circumstances, life transitions, and children's peer relations. In R. D. Parke & G. W. Ladd (Eds.), *Family-peer relationships: Modes of linkage* (pp. 385–438). Hillsdale, NJ: Lawrence Erlbaum.

Phinney, J. S., & Rotheram, M. J. (1982). Sex differences in social overtures between same-sex and cross-sex preschool pairs. *Child Study Journal, 12,* 259–269.

Piaget, J., & Weil, A. M. (1951). The development in children of the idea of the homeland and of relations with other countries. *International Social Science Bulletin, 3,* 561–578.

Quisenberry, N. & Christman, M. (1979). A look at sociodramatic play among Mexican-American children. *Childhood Education, 56* (2), 106–110.

Ramsey, P. G. (1991). Young children's awareness and understanding of social class differences. *Journal of Genetic Psychology, 152,* 71–82.

Ramsey, P. G., & Myers, L. C. (1990). Salience of race in young children's cognitive, affective and behavioral responses to social environments. *Journal of Applied Developmental Psychology, 11,* 49–67.

Rizzo, W., & Corsaro, W. A. (1991, April). *Social support processes in early child-*

hood friendships. Paper presented at the biennial meeting of the Society for Research in Child Development, Seattle, WA.

Robinson, C. (1978). The uses of order and disorder in play: An analysis of Vietnamese refugee children's play. (ERIC No. ED 1153 944)

Root, M. P. (1992). *Racially mixed people in America*. Beverly Hills, CA: Sage.

Rubin, K. H., Maioni, T. L., & Hornung, M. (1976). Free play behaviors in middle- and lower-class preschoolers: Parten and Piaget revisited. *Child Development, 47,* 414–419.

Schofield, J. (1981). Complementary and conflicting identities: Images and interactions in an interracial school. In S. R. Asher & J. M. Gottman (Eds.), *The development of children's friendships (*pp. 53–90). New York: Cambridge University Press.

Sigelman, C. K., Miller, T .E., & Whitworth, L. A. (1986). The early development of stigmatizing reactions to physical differences. *Journal of Applied Developmental Psychology, 7,* 17–32.

Singleton L. C., & Asher, S. R. (1977). Peer preferences and social interaction among third-grade children in an integrated school district. *Journal of Educational Psychology, 69,* 330–336.

Singleton, L. C., & Asher, S. R. (1979). Racial integration and children's peer preferences: An investigation of developmental and cohort differences. *Child Development, 50,* 936–941.

Slaughter, D. Y., & Dombrowski, J. (1989). Cultural continuities and discontinuities: Impact on social and pretend play. In M. N. Bloch & A. D. Pellegrini (Eds.), *The ecological context of children's play* (pp. 282–309). Norwood, NJ: Ablex.

Slavin, R. E. (1995). Cooperative learning and intergroup relations. In J. A. Banks & C. A. M. Banks (Eds.), *Handbook of research on multicultural education* (pp. 628–634). New York: Macmillan.

Smedley, A. (1993). *Race in North America*. Boulder: Westview.

Smilansky, S. (1968). *The effects of sociodramatic play on disadvantaged preschool children*. New York: John Wiley.

Swadener, E. B., & Johnson, J. E. (1989). Play in diverse social contexts: Parent and teacher roles. In M. N. Bloch & A. D. Pellegrini (Eds.), *The ecological context of children's play* (pp. 214–244). Norwood, NJ: Ablex.

Theokas, C. (1991). *Modifying sex-typed behavior and contact patterns in a kindergarten classroom with an outer space intervention curriculum*. Unpublished master's thesis, Mount Holyoke College, South Hadley, MA.

Thorne, B. (1986). Girls and boys together . . . but mostly apart: Gender arrangements in elementary schools. In W. W. Hartup & Z. Rubin (Eds.), *Relationships and development* (pp. 167–184). Hillsdale, NJ: Lawrence Erlbaum.

Perspectives on Play

Play as Children See It

Greta G. Fein
Nancy W. Wiltz

Scholars have spent long hours, decades, and even centuries debating the definition of play. There are also those who bemoan the debate, as if a term for which there is no consensus should not be taken seriously (Berlyne, 1960). But the definitional status of play is no different from that of other terms that receive serious attention from scientists and educators. Terms like *aggression, love, teaching,* and *learning,* to name a few, also lack widely shared, rigorous definitions. Yet these terms signify large ideas that are understood in some fashion across cultures, across centuries, and by individuals of various statuses, ages, and experiences. Play is one of those large ideas that touch a strand of human experience beginning in childhood and, perhaps, in different forms, arc present throughout life. Formal definitional variations reflect scholarly discipline, ideology, and cultural preferences (Sutton-Smith, 1995).

As Sutton-Smith (1995) has argued so persuasively, folk ideas about play are richly laced with cultural "rhetorics" that reflect the preoccupations of a particular historical and social era. Play cannot be understood without regard to its ideological context, which then shades and shapes what an observer or participant sees and feels. It is even possible that these rhetorics change with age and vary with social status. If so, information about children's views of play might illuminate their appropriation of the values of their culture. However, it is only recently that investigators have asked what children, teachers, and parents mean when they use this term.

Definitions of play also have practical consequences. With the endorsement of Developmentally Appropriate Practices (DAP) by the National Association for the Education of Young Children (Bredekamp, 1987), play received formal professional recognition as a core component and educational tool in early childhood practice. Although not without its critics, DAP has received widespread approval from the field. Areas of disagreement have less to do with play per se than with matters such as the role of teacher-directed small-group activities (Fowell & Lawton, 1992). However, how play serves educational purposes will depend mightily on how it is used in the classroom. It is in this area that there may be major disagreements. Play in a general sense, as an underlying pedagogical attitude, has different implications from play in a particular sense, as a set of specific pedagogical strategies or curriculum plans.

The encouragement and cultivation of a child-centered play curriculum in preschools and kindergartens has several implications. Naïve observers easily agree on the occurrence of play even when they define it differently (Smith & Vollstedt, 1985). Some observers dismiss such a curriculum as just play, a way little ones keep busy. Better informed observers might see play as contributing primarily to children's social skills, especially their ability to function in a group. In either case, the contribution of play to intellectual competence is neglected. Although the contribution of play to aspects of development is an important issue, the second implication, which has received far too little attention, is that children also define and evaluate play.

How children themselves perceive the place of play in their homes and classrooms provides adults a context for viewing and evaluating the home and school experiences. At an early age children use the term *play* to describe their own and others' activities. What do they mean when they do so? Answers to this question have been explored in studies representing different theoretical traditions. Because these traditions have something useful to say about the meaning of play as viewed by players, they are reviewed in the following sections. The first section considers studies that ask children the seemingly simple question: What happens when you go to school? Of interest is whether play enters into children's school scripts and, if it does, where it goes. Do children's responses reveal their emotional and motivational judgments of school and, if so, how are these judgments expressed?

From script-oriented research, the second and third sections turn to studies that deal more specifically with the distinction between work and play. These studies view work and play as sociocultural concepts that children acquire at an early age. Studies of children's views of work and play examine the criteria children use to separate these concepts and how these criteria change with age. Finally, there is a summary of recent data about children's retrospective accounts of play, especially pretend play. What are the highlights of these memories? How are they organized? How do children of different ages remember their play as preschoolers?

Play in School: A Script Theory Perspective

One approach to understanding and documenting children's perspectives depends on the assumption that individuals create cognitive "scripts" to organize daily experiences (Nelson, 1978; Schank & Abelson, 1977). Scripts provide children with a way to remember and create meaning from daily events (King, 1979). They also provide a structure that guides behavior and shapes expectations (Nelson, 1978; Nelson & Gruendel, 1981). To create these scripts young children rely on linguistic skills as well as episodic memory, which involves remembering events as they are experienced.

According to script theory, children view what goes on at school, for example, as a series of events that make up the school day (Fivush, 1984; Garza, Briley, & Reifel, 1985; Nelson, 1978; Nelson & Gruendel, 1981). Play is simply one of those events organized in memory as a general event representation and then used to anticipate, understand, and interpret recurring events (Light, 1987; Mandler, 1983; Nelson & Gruendel, 1981; Schank & Abelson, 1977).

When young children answer a question about what happens at school, they tend to relate events in a series of fragmented, incoherent, and seemingly unrelated statements. In contrast, older children string multiple action sequences together into related episodes. The structural complexity of the narrative increases with age (Botwin & Sutton-Smith, 1977); as children get older, they are better able to describe the details of school activities (Garza et al., 1985; Reifel, 1988; Wiltz & Klein, 1994).

Each script has a skeletal sequential structure stored in long-term memory. This skeletal structure has slots reserved for the details of what happened, when, and to whom, which are filled as needed with appropriate information (Schank and Abelson, 1977). Children respond to questions about activities they engage in at school with general statements about playing, working, helping, making things, having lunch, taking naps, and going home. Some children mention some of these events and other children mention others; some children cite more and others cite fewer. Yet almost all children mention play.

In one of our studies of four-year-olds, we asked children "What happens when you come to school?" Here is a prototypical script theory response:

> *Ben:* I play. And I play with some toys and I play with my friends. Then we go outside and then we come in for snack. Then I wait for my mom and she picks me up.

It is not surprising that play figures prominently in preschoolers' accounts of what happens in school. Typical preschool classrooms provide areas and materials for various types of play (e.g., block centers, areas for manipulation of toys, housekeeping areas, large-motor play areas) and daily schedules provide significant periods of time for both indoor and outdoor play (Kantor, 1988). Physically and organizationally, support for play is evident in child care settings.

One investigator asked thirty kindergarten children on the second day, the second week, the fourth week, and the tenth week of school, "What happens when you go to school?" (Fivush, 1984). The interviewer also asked what had happened at school the previous day and mentioned specific events that had occurred. At all four interviews, the children answered other general school-day questions and specific memory questions. At the fourth and final interview, questioners asked the children to recall the first day of school. This investigator found that five-year-old children had a general representation of the kindergarten routine by the second day of school, which remained stable over time (Fivush, 1984). Even so, children had difficulty recalling specific episodes of the previous day. The content of children's reports changed over the semester, becoming more elaborate and incorporating more alternatives with increased experience. Whereas children in all interviews essentially reported lists of possible activities, the representation of specific events that occurred at a particular time and place in the routine became increasingly more complex. Listed activities showed remarkable consistency over time and some appeared more frequently than others.

These kindergartners mentioned play more than any other activity (Fivush, 1984). On the second day of school, 85 percent of the children talked about play, and by the tenth week, 100 percent did so. *Play* to them meant minigym, games, or children with whom they could play. Details of what constituted play were not explored, but play became a part of the kindergartners' script from the second day of school on. In a related study of younger preschoolers, the researchers claimed that children as young as two years of age remember novel events over periods longer than six months and can verbalize these memories (Nelson & Gruendel, 1981).

Beyond Script Theory

Script theorists agree that knowledge is organized around the structure and routine of daily activities, a process that begins at or near birth and continues throughout life. Several researchers have moved beyond this theory by examining how children organize different aspects of the school day. In these studies, sequence is less important than activity types.

One group of researchers asked fourteen three- to six-year-old preschool children in a full-day child care program, "Tell us what you do at school each day" (Garza et al., 1985; Reifel, 1988; Reifel, Briley, & Garza, 1986). Children listed a consistent core of classroom activities, including doing jobs, reading a story, lunching, napping, listening to music, going to the gym, going home, and playing. Even the youngest children included play as a part of

their overall structure of day care, using simple statements such as "We play" (Reifel et al., 1986, p. 85). Older children included riding scooters, playing outside, working on puzzles, playing with toys, playing games, and playing with mud in their responses. These researchers generated two main categories of play types that accounted for 93 percent of the responses: nonsocial play with materials included pretense (e.g., feeding dolls and playing house) and manipulation of materials (e.g., riding scooters); social play included dramatic play (e.g., make-believe or pretending) and games with rules (e.g., duck-duck-goose).

A more recent study (Wiltz & Klein, 1994) found that three-, four-, and five-year-old children reported a core of school activities consistent with previous research (Fivush, 1984; King, 1979; Klein, Kantor, & Fernie, 1988; Nelson, 1978; Reifel, 1988; Reifel et al., 1986; Takanishi & Spitzer, 1980; Tyler, 1986; Weinstein, 1983). These investigators, however, were interested in the distinction between teacher-controlled and child-controlled activities. School activities were divided into two broad categories: structured and unstructured. Structured activities were teacher controlled and were subdivided into three areas: curriculum, function, and construction. Curriculum activities related to the academic areas of school, were primarily teacher directed, and included such things as singing, reading, spelling, and math. Function activities involved routine tasks, such as eating lunch, doing jobs, watering plants, or taking a nap. Construction activities were primarily teacher guided and many involved making things. Lists of structured versus unstructured activities increased steadily with age, from 55 percent for the three-year-olds, to 61 percent for the four-year-olds, to 80 percent for the five-year-olds, and culminating at 90 percent for the six-year-olds. The most dramatic increases appeared in the curriculum category, where three-year-olds mentioned activities like writing stories and singing, while six-year-olds talked about doing math, reading, and taking spelling tests.

Unstructured activities fell into two main categories: creative play, which included activities such as outside play, dressing up, and playing house; and play with toys, which incorporated play with blocks, cars, trucks, and stuffed animals. In direct contrast to structured activities, both categories of play steadily declined with age, with a dramatic drop as children entered formal school. Three- and four-year-olds mentioned play more frequently than five-year-olds, and first-graders equated play at school only with recess. According to these children, a sharp curriculum shift occurs at five years of age.

Previous research supports several conclusions: First, even preschool children respond with an understanding of classroom activities beyond their mere sequencing. Second, older children relate school events in greater and more vivid detail than do younger ones (Fivush, 1984; Nelson, 1978, 1993; Nelson & Gruendel, 1981; Reifel et al., 1986; Wiltz & Klein, 1994). Third, children's reports accurately reflect the diminishing role of play in the kindergarten curriculum. Children's accounts of their school day reveal extensive substantive knowledge of the school world and the place of play within it (Corsaro, 1986).

How Children View Play: A Reflective Perspective

Script theory stresses the mental frame used to record daily events. In this view, play is of interest only because it is one of the events that children most frequently mention. A cited "activity" is taken as a given in the setting, and cited nonactivities (being happy, getting in trouble) are ignored. Script theory has little to say about how the school day gets segmented by the children; it provides few clues about the ways in which the emotional tone of events affects children's remembrances (Fein, 1987).

Other researchers have tried to investigate what the term *play* means to children. When children say they are playing, what do they think they are doing? Why do some children list going to the bathroom and time-out as school events, whereas others do not; why do some children talk about positive internal states, whereas others talk about negative ones? Script theory provides a structure to describe how children remember events, but it does not tell us why children remember this rather than that; it does not describe the motivational forces that cause children to evaluate these events.

Consider the following responses by four-year-olds to the question, "What happens when you go to school?"

Reb: You feel happy. (Pause. "What else?") Ohhh, you play a lot. If you need to, you can go to the bathroom.

Ant: I get in trouble. When I get in trouble when I play, I go in time-out . . .

Al: . . . sometimes I play with Dan when . . . when he's at school, and I play every single game he plays, and sometimes I don't and sometimes I do.

Ceci: Oh, we have to listen to the teacher's words and play . . .

Note that none of the five children quoted above used the term *play* in exactly the same way; all the children used the term, but its meaning shifted. To Reb, play involves autonomy and personal decision making ("If you need to . . . "); Ceci also sets up a strong contrast between play and what "we have to" do. To Ant it can be an occasion to get in trouble; for Al, play is being with a special friend. When children report school happenings, the same terms may not report exactly the same events.

In an effort to explain why children view play activities as they do, one must look further into their accounts of the play environment. In one of our studies, we asked twenty-six four-year-old children, "What happens when you come to school?" The children came from ten different community schools and child care centers. These results are shown separately for boys and girls in Table 1. Interestingly, only half the children offered a script that we defined as two or more distinctive activities regardless of accuracy of ordering. Far more children, 65 percent, mentioned play as one of the happenings, whether or not there were any others.

In our analysis of the children's responses, we also paid special attention to the emotional/

TABLE 1. Children's Responses to: What Happens When You Come to School?

	Girls (N=13)	Boys (N=13)
Scriptlike sequences	6	7
Play	9	8
Routines	6	8
Other activities (e.g., drawing)	2	4
Behavioral states	6	6
Linguistic forms reference		
I, we	8	10
You, they	5	3
Timeless verbs	12	13

motivational implications of what the children shared. The most provocative data come from what we call "behavior states," a category meant to gather children's observations about their own and others' mental and emotional states. We included in this category comments on desired behavior and disciplinary actions. Of the twelve children whose comments were scored in this category, only two made positive comments: "I feel happy" and "I give my mom a hug." For ten children, the report had a negative tone. Among the most poignant accounts was a child who reported, "When I get in trouble, I have to sit in the thinking chair." One child complained that the "Kids scream and shout." Another confessed, "Sometimes I forget;" and still another listed her faults; ". . . I don't listen, I don't come when I'm sick. I got paint on my dress . . . " And, of course, these comments were unrelated to whether the children listed play as a school activity. In itself, play in the preschool may not mean a positive learning environment.

Where these childhood concerns come from is not clear. Some parents may be anxious about the child's school behavior and overly stress faults and comportment. In some cases, the teachers might be critical and demanding. It is even possible that were we to observe these children, they would seem to be happy and comfortable but still talk about unpleasant moments in the school day. Several interpretations of these data are possible. In one, the children are veridical reporters of the emotional climate of the classroom. In another, the children reflect parental pressures to be mature and they try very hard to comply; their reports reflect strenuous efforts to follow their parent's wishes. In still another, the children's reports should be discounted because they simply reflect salient recent events rather than typical events: in most schools and homes, children are scolded and criticized, but these events are relatively infrequent and brief, even though they are unpleasant and likely to be remembered. Research in this area is much too new to evaluate the merits of these alternatives. Nevertheless, it is clear that children's reports of the school day provide provocative information about the context within which play occurs.

Another team of researchers asked fifty three- to six-year-olds, "Do you play at school?" (Wiltz & Klein, 1994). Eight of the nine three-year-olds agreed that they did. The four- and five-year-olds also acknowledged that they played at school, but they launched into narratives about experiences during play time or elaborated about what and how they played. The first-graders reported that play is something you only do at recess; when asked what they liked best about school, they replied either "lunch" or "recess." A different researcher also found that recess was the only sanctioned school activity that all school-age children agreed was play (King, 1983). The fact that recess is an activity normally done outside the classroom is one way that play is separated from the work of school.

Moreover, children as young as three have a mental picture of play as a part of their child care experience, but only five- and six-year-olds make references to games with rules as play (Reifel, 1988). Preschoolers also identified something as "just play" if they themselves decided on the activity and the ways in which to use materials, time, and space (Romero, 1989, 1991). "Learning play" existed in the nursery school only within adult-defined frameworks (Romero, 1989, 1991).

Preschoolers from five day care centers representing diverse programs responded to the Day Care Center Toy and Interview Questionnaire (Armstrong & Sugawara, 1989). A large majority of the three- to five-year-olds (76 percent) indicated that they preferred play activities to routines. The wide variety of play activities mentioned by the children was difficult to categorize. Some children just enjoyed playing while others enjoyed dramatic play, art, and physical activities. Still others preferred playing with materials like puzzles, trucks, and slides, or preferred playing with friends. Kindergartners told another investigator that play is noisier, more fun, and easier than work, and that it happens on the floor, when you move around, and when you do not have to obey the rules (LeCompte, 1980). In a cross-cultural study of fifty Chinese and fifty U.S. kindergartners, the investigators also confirmed that children in the United States focused on having fun at school while Chinese children were more concerned with learning (Zhang & Sigel, 1994). They discovered that the more children play, the more they want to play. Compared to their counterparts in the United States, Chinese children have much less time to play both inside and outside of school, yet only 8 percent of those questioned desired more play time; 33 percent of the youngsters in the United States longed to play more.

Work and Play

The normal, day-to-day sequence of events in the classrooms of young children includes not only the things children do, but also with whom they interact. The social dimensions of school also provide rules for the classroom and, in later life, rules for the workplace. Children's views of the distinction between work and play provide another way of understanding play's place in the world of childhood. In a series of studies, kindergarten children who responded to open-ended questions about experiences at school spontaneously used the categories of work and play to describe and define their daily classroom activities (King, 1979, 1990).

King (1979, 1990) studied four profoundly different kindergarten classrooms, two child-centered and two teacher-directed. Her study revealed that children describe most of their classroom experiences as work. Whereas the relationship between work and play in culture is not clear, anthropologists have begun to critically question the work/play dichotomy of Western societies. Recent ethnographic approaches to the study of these activities are intended to open the door to other kinds of characteristics (Schwartzman, 1978a, 1978b; Stevens, 1978).

In several studies of how children view school, the categories of work and play emerged as significant factors (Fein, 1985; King, 1979; LeCompte, 1980; Reifel, 1988; Wiltz, 1993a, 1993b). Prior to entry into kindergarten children view school as a place where they do what other people want them to do (LeCompte, 1980). Kindergartners associate learning, mandatory events, and teacher-controlled activities with work, while voluntary, self-chosen activities where the teacher is not involved are considered play (King, 1979). Kindergarten, first-, second-, and third-grade children state that work is extrinsically oriented and internally obligatory, while play is "fun" (Fein, 1985). The twenty-eight interviewees often provided instances of play with objects. For example, play happens "with a ball, with toys . . . [and] less often, with friends" (Fein, 1985, p. 47). Other researchers report that preschool children are able also to classify work and play activities (Fein, 1985; Hennessey & Berger, 1993; Romero, 1989, 1991). When asked, "Do you ever work at school?" three-year-olds unanimously agreed that they did not work at school, while four- and five-year-old children disagreed,

defining work as activities such as playing, coloring, drawing, and making pictures (Wiltz, 1993a). Romero (1989, 1991) asked four-year-old children whether they had played or worked in school the previous day; when given a list to choose from, these children classified more classroom activities as work than as play.

Hennessey and Berger (1993) used an innovative procedure to study children's notions of work and play. Twenty-seven children listened to stories that contrasted two activities that needed to be done, one "fun" and one "not-so-fun." Then the researcher showed them two paper dolls and asked them to decide which of the dolls was working and which was playing, and to award a sticker to the doll they believed deserved a reward. Most preschoolers awarded stickers to the doll they believed to be playing, and when asked which of the dolls really liked what she or he was doing, they were also significantly more apt to choose the doll that was playing. Chi-square analysis revealed that "not-so-fun" activities were consistently labeled as work. While these children were able to distinguish between work and play tasks, they saw no reason to reward the doll who was working over the doll who was playing.

The criteria children use to differentiate work from play change as children mature (King, 1979; Wiltz & Klein, 1994). Younger children focus on the social context of their activities and label all required activities work and all voluntary activities play. Repeated documentation indicates that four- and five-year-old children describe most of their classroom experiences as work, defining the activity as play only if it is voluntary, if there is an absence of obligation, if it is child controlled, and if the teacher is not involved (Fein, 1985; King, 1979; LeCompte, 1980). School-age children use the psychological context of activities as their primary criterion. Activities that are tedious or hard are called work while pleasurable activities are called play (King, 1982). Whereas kindergartners label as work activities that are not clearly play, as children move through the elementary grades, activities that are not clearly work are recategorized as play. First- and second-graders offer an interesting compromise by characterizing some activities as "in between" work and play (Wing, 1995).

In attempting to understand the relationships between work and play, one cannot assume that play is necessarily the opposite of work. There is discontinuity, however, between preschool, where play is emphasized, and public school kindergartens, where work is the major construct (Fernie, 1988). Children at younger and younger ages seem to be developing a sense of the differences between the two (Romero, 1989, 1991; Wiltz & Klein, 1994).

Play in the Elementary School

Based on observations and interviews, King (1982, 1983, 1986) posits three distinct types of play in the elementary school classroom: instrumental play, real play, and illicit play. Instrumental play includes activities that are required, controlled, and evaluated by the teacher, such as watching a movie, writing poems, listening to a story, doing a science experiment, and drawing a mural. Elementary school children enjoy these activities even though they are not voluntary and serve academic goals beyond the participants' pure enjoyment.

Real play includes voluntary and self-directed activities, such as during recess. All children say they like recess and many think it is the best part of school (King, 1983; Wiltz & Klein, 1994). As the major form of recreation in schools, recess provides children an opportunity to indulge in exuberant play, develop autonomy and self-expression, freely organize their time, choose their playmates, and plan, select, and carry out their own activities without adult intervention (King, 1983). Even in the preschool, children value outdoor play as a favorite activity (Cullen, 1993). Physical play accounted for the largest portion of children's time outdoors, followed by creative play. Boys engaged in significantly more physical play than girls. The majority of the children perceived outdoor play as something they did by themselves without the assistance of adults. All children identified activities they thought they were good at, as well as ones they enjoyed. Most of the children (82.5 percent) perceived outdoor play as a social activity (Cullen, 1993).

The third type of play, illicit play, is defined as unauthorized, surreptitious interactions during classroom events (King, 1982, 1983). It includes actions like whispering, passing notes, making faces, and giggling. Children are aware that this type of play is against the rules and are careful to conceal it and use it in nondisruptive ways. Illicit play not only provides children with a resistance to the dominant social structure, but allows them to develop autonomy within the classroom structure (King, 1983). Preschool children also engage in illicit play. During dramatic play periods, children enforced play rules when the teachers were nearby and disregarded these when teachers were not around (Romero, 1989, 1991).

Illicit play also occurs in the kindergarten during snack time. Interviews with twenty-one kindergartners during snack time revealed that play activities included "playing with your drink," "pretending," "telling a joke," "fooling around," and "goofing." Although "goofing" and "fooling around" were only recorded in 57 out of 386 episodes, these types of illicit play led to verbal reprimands from the teacher if children were caught in the act. These behaviors were exclusively performed by boys and, in fact, forty of the illicit play episodes were performed by five of the most popular boys in the class (Romero, 1989, 1991).

In the research discussed so far, investigators explored children's views of the distinction between work and play. If the children's views are lined up against Sutton-Smith's (1995) six rhetorics, how do the children come out? To the degree that the youngest children stress the obligatory nature of work and the voluntary nature of play, the children would seem to be operating within the *rhetoric of power*. Some children stress the social aspects of play: who one plays with rather than who controls the activity. These children operate within the *rhetoric of identity*. The oldest children pay more attention to the pleasures of play in a way similar to the *rhetoric of frivolity*. No child mentioned that play was good for children; that they played because it improved them in some way. Sutton-Smith's *rhetoric of power* has not influenced children of these ages. There appear to be no efforts to systematically analyze these relationships, but from a sociocultural perspective, one would expect that, as they get older, children will increasingly express the dominant rhetoric of their culture.

Children's Views of Pretend Play

From Piaget (1962) comes the idea that three different cognitive forms of play emerge during the first six years of life: "practice games, symbolic games, and games with rules, while constructional games constitute the transition from all three to adapted behaviours" (p. 110). What do children think is happening when they engage in one of these forms? Researchers have asked this question for only one of these forms: pretense.

There have been two ways of studying children's understanding of their own pretense, one drawn from theory of mind research, and the other from children's memories of their pretend play. One virtue of theory of mind research is that children are being queried directly. One problem is that the experimental paradigms used are highly constraining and depend on the child's understanding of the question that the experimenter is presenting. At issue is whether or not children can envision a mind—their own or others—capable of thinking about events that are not happening, may never have happened, and even may never happen. In the simplest case, how do children understand what happens mentally when someone pretends that a banana is a telephone? Most theorists assume that pretense involves a mental representation, or, perhaps, a "representation of a representation." When children talk into the tip of the banana, they are "thinking" of a telephone. Do children understand that pretense involves the mental representation of an object or event that is concurrently known not to be, in fact, present? Where children stand on this issue bears upon their "theory of mind."

Most of the research that deals with this issue presents children with hypothetical situations (Lillard, 1993). In one task, four- and five-year-olds were shown a troll doll and told, "This is Luna, and she's from the land of the trolls." Then the researcher posed the following premise: "Luna doesn't know what a rabbit is—she's never seen a rabbit before—but she's hopping up and down like a rabbit. Rabbits hop like that." To ensure that the children heard the premises the interviewer asked, "Does she know what a rabbit is?" and "Is she hopping like a rabbit?" If the children answered correctly, the third question was, "Would you say she's pretending to be a rabbit, or she's not pretending to be a rabbit?" Follow-up questions were "Why do you say that?" and "If you . . . said, 'ey, Luna! What are you doing?' what would she say?"

It is not surprising that preschoolers do poorly on this task. In fact, the premises are so intricate, it is conceivable that many adults would lose the subtle contrast between "like a rabbit" and "pretending to be a rabbit." In other words, the task requires a high level of comprehension monitoring in order to catch the shift from an observer's perspective ("like a rabbit") to a participant's perspective ("pretending to be a rabbit"). If one adopts the observer perspective throughout, there is no contradiction, because presumably one can observe someone doing something that the observer then characterizes as pretense. For the younger children, therefore, this may be a question about an observer's mind and not a question about Luna's mind.

A second problem comes from the supposition that these preschoolers are so sophisticated that they can imagine a creature from another universe who truly knows nothing about a familiar animal. They must be able to imagine such a mind for the task to make sense. If preschoolers can imagine such a naïve mind—a mind that does not know what the children themselves know—they will have a far greater appreciation of other minds than the task itself assesses. An "uninformed mind" task is used as the setting for a "pretend mind" task.

Custer (1996) designed a simpler task that investigated the question: Do three- and four-year- olds understand that mental representations are involved in pretense, memory, and false belief? In this task, the children might view a picture of a child who was pretending that a fish was hooked at the end of a fishing line, when there was actually a boot at the end of the line. The children first viewed the picture of the hooked boot and then viewed alternate "thought" pictures placed over the protagonist's head. One thought picture depicted the real situation (catching a boot), and the other depicted the pretend situation (catching a fish). The latter choice was the correct one because it depicted how the situation would be depicted if the protagonist were pretending. On this task, three-year-olds did extremely well, with eleven of the eighteen children correct on all trials. Thus, young children might understand the representational nature of pretense.

A somewhat different approach is to ask the children to reminisce about their own pretend behavior. Ultimately, one would want to ask three- and four-year-olds to explain how they play, but in one study we asked twenty-five five- to six-year olds (N=13 girls) and twenty-five seven- to eight-year-olds (N=12 girls) to tell us how they pretended when they were four and how they pretend now. Of course we cannot be sure that their accounts are accurate playbacks of what happened at four years of age; however, almost all children, regardless of age, recalled playing pretend games at age four. No child described pretend episodes that occurred in nursery school even though most children had attended. In fact, most of the play took place at home, in the yard or bedroom, away from adult scrutiny. Some of their accounts are so vivid that they convey the excitement and pleasure of the activity. Here is an especially vivid account of the pretense that a five-year-old claims to have played at the age of four:

> I played cops and robbers. My uncle James, we used to play cops and robbers. I was the little one and I used to go to the store and act like I be stealing something and he used to take my hands and put them behind me and tie something to the back of my hand and I couldn't break out. Then he used to tie me against the tree with a rope and I couldn't break out and then he be hitting me with sticks. Not that hard. Then he said he's going to do that again and I said no and then I go do it again and he can't catch me. I be hiding under the car.

Keep in mind that this five-year-old is offering a vivid account of a *pretend* scenario that happened sometime in the past. The scenario itself was represented in the present as a sequence of actual past events about pretend past events. The child is in the present, representing events about a previously represented event. Further, the events are "actlike." The narrator makes it clear that even being hit with sticks was "not hard." In pretense, children act, speak, dress up, and in as many other ways they can think of present themselves as the pretend characters they seek to be. However, these actions, statements, and clothing are not meant to be replicas of the real thing. They are exaggerations, abbreviations, and highlighted caricatures of whatever the children know and feel about what they are representing. To an adult, some childhood memories are unsettling. Why would children pretend that cops tied up robbers and beat them? Keep in mind, however, that the memories reveal what children play on their own time and in their own spaces. Another five-year-old described the following pretense:

> *Mar:* My brother keep making me wash the dishes, set the table, and my other brother telling me to wash the floor and wash the stairs.

> *Interviewer:* And what did you do?

> *Mar:* I done it all.

> *Interviewer:* In your game, what did you pretend to be?

> *Mar:* Cinderella.

Some memories of pretense reveal personal and painful pasts. A second-grader reported, "I pretend like when I lived with my grandparents again that I used to pretend that they were the bad guys . . . and we used to play that my parents and our grandparents were the robbers and we were the cops and we used to tie them up and everything." The interviewer asked, "Why did you play your grandparents were robbers?" The child answered, "Because [in real life] she was mean to our parents when they were our age, so we pretend like they're the bad guys."

Some children simply gave a popular label for the pretense theme (house, school), whereas others told the stories that they played. Some children described particular roles; one child described how she and her friend set out blankets to get a suntan: "We're pretending we are womens." Another said, "We pretend my sister is my sister and we go to school and that we have babies." Superheroes were overrepresented, but some children spontaneously described episodes of thematic fantasy play built around Jack the Giant-Killer, Hansel and Gretel, Pinocchio, and other characters.

Of the fifty children, all but six admitted to pretending when they were four, a figure that did not differ by age. A different picture, however, emerged in response to the question of whether they played pretense now. For the younger children, all but two said they did. But eight of the twenty-five older children denied playing pretend games, and of these, six were boys. One third-grader explained, "I'm too old to play like that . . . people say that pretend is baby stuff."

The proportion of children at each age level who mention roles and scenes is shown in Table 2. Five- and six-year-old boys are big role-players, and most of their roles are superhero or fantasy figures. When children talk about past self-directed pretense, they often describe scenes. This tendency shows a marked drop in accounts of their current play, which are fairly sophisticated accounts of mimed activity.

Some children describe object-substitution pretense, playing ball games such as football, kickball, or basketball without a ball. One third-grader described playing pretend kickball

TABLE 2. Memories of Pretense: Percentage of Children Who Mention Roles and Scenes

	Roles		Scenes	
	At 4	Now	At 4	Now
5–6-year-olds				
Girls	62	36	60	45
Boys	73	82	64	27
7–8-year-olds				
Girls	75	63	58	58
Boys	50	60	42	25

with his brother: "My brother was throwing the ball and I act like I kick it and ran to all the fake bases." One child pretended that he had a television in his room, another described running around the house as if he were riding a bike, and another talked about pretending that dolls were people.

What do these data tell us about children's understanding of pretense? A major theme in reminiscences of early play was the storylike character of the children's accounts. Many described enactments, theatrical renditions of stories, some conventional and some quite unique. In a sense, these enactments "represented" things, actions, and relationships. No child referred explicitly to a pretending mind; no child explicitly described pretense as an inner mental experience. They liberally used the terms *like*, *as if*, and *pretend* interchangeably, as if these terms adequately captured the phenomenon. As Lillard (1993) believes, children even at these ages might not consider pretense as a matter of "mental representations." Alternatively, this way of thinking about pretense might better characterize psychological theories than the theories of "folk" culture. One kindergarten child described playing with his dog: "We play going in the woods and we saw a fox. Casey grabbed it and pounced on it." Just think of the questions we would like to have asked, but did not. Does Casey know what a fox is? Did Casey really pounce on something? Did Casey think he was pouncing on a fox? Was he pretending? Such questions should be asked in the context of a reported scene. If Lillard is correct the child will answer yes to the last two questions. If Custer (1996) is correct, the child will answer no. We think that the child will find the questions puzzling because, after all, he said "we play." Perhaps it is only psychologists who think about representational minds; others may simply represent the representations of representations of others and themselves.

The Debate Continues

In Western culture, perceptions of play have been significantly influenced by attitudes about what play is not (Bowman, 1978; Schwartzman, 1978a). In apparent contradiction, play should be fun, active, spontaneous, free, unconstrained, self-initiated, and natural (Frost & Klein, 1979; Stevens, 1978); whereas at the same time, the seriousness, purposefulness, and intensity of play contribute to its role as a vehicle of learning during childhood. Play is a context or frame (Bateson, 1955), with an emphasis on process rather than goals. Play's major characteristics are active involvement, intrinsic motivation, attention to process rather than product, nonliterality, freedom from external rules, and self-reference rather than object-reference (Rubin, Fein, & Vandenberg, 1983).

Not everyone subscribes to the notion that play contributes to child development. For example, the value of play "in the life of the child . . . is perhaps something of little importance which he undertakes for the lack of something better to do" (Montessori, 1936/1956, p. 122). Another view holds that children, when left on their own, do not play, but work on social constructions that are evident in their social play activities (Denzin, 1977).

Some would argue that play provides children with opportunities to imitate and practice culturally appropriate adult roles (Schwartzman, 1978a). Others, however, argue that play involves social invention and therefore is a more original, creative process (Fein, 1987). Still another perspective takes the position that, during play, some children learn to create their own worlds within the adult-imposed physical and social world of school (Gracey, 1975). Kindergartners have said that "Play is at a different time; it is easy. Play is fun" (LeCompte, 1980, p. 123). Play episodes described in this way, as fun, spontaneous, and improvisational, suggest an apparent lack of externally imposed rules (Schwartzman, 1978b). Children seem to know what play is, and they know that "play is *not* working" (LeCompte, 1980, p. 123). "In the past, Westerners have assumed that work is painful and that play gives pleasure, when they actually should know that work is sometimes painful and sometimes gives pleasure, and play is sometimes pleasant and sometimes unpleasant" (Bohannan, 1963, p. 219).

The seeming dichotomy between work and play serves to help scientists synthesize, structure, and study society (Schwartzman, 1978b), while educators develop curricula that organize schools into routinized, controlled workplaces that serve society. Education, then, is a part of the socialization process that takes place in the school (Apple & King, 1978; Gracey, 1975; King, 1983). The dichotomy continues. Play complements and supports the work ethic of the school. Play activities provide a relief from the drudgery of work, and after periods of relaxation and/or physical exercise, adults expect children to return to work refreshed. Play serves as a reward, a prize, a compensation for those who are obedient, who complete assigned tasks, and who follow the rules. Likewise, the loss of recreational privileges serves to punish disruptive, disobedient children or those who do not finish their work (King, 1983).

Spontaneous, flowing play is not what one sees children do at school. Play at school is play in a workplace, confined to particular times, relegated to specific areas, limited to certain materials, and controlled by teachers. This is not memorable play and relatively few children mention it in their accounts. School play is not the play children describe with relish and delight many years later. Further, the play that matters in development may not be the play adults observe with their battery of videotapes and coding devices. Children's own accounts of the school day and their play are needed at this point in researchers' efforts to understand early schooling, play, and the role of each in development. Although these reminiscences may also be unreliable, they provide another source of information about how children perceive school and how they think about the play of childhood.

Bibliography

Apple, M. W., & King, N. R. (1978). What do schools teach? In G. Willis (Ed.), *Concepts and cases in curriculum criticism* (pp. 444–465). Berkeley, CA: McCutchan.

Armstrong, J., & Sugawara, A. (1989). Children's perceptions of their day care experience. *Early Child Development and Care, 49,* 1–15.

Bateson, G. (1955). A theory of play and fantasy. In N. S. Kline (Ed.), *Approaches to the study of human personality, Psychiatric Research Reports, 2* (pp. 39–51). Washington, DC: American Psychiatric Association.

Berlyne, D. (1960). *Conflict, arousal, and curiosity.* New York: McGraw-Hill.

Bohannan, P. (1963). *Social anthropology.* New York: Holt, Rinehart and Winston.

Botwin, G. J., & Sutton-Smith, B. (1977). The development of structural complexity in children's fantasy narratives. *Developmental Psychology, 12*(4), 377–388.

Bowman, J. (1978). The play context and message. In M. A. Salter (Ed.), *Play: Anthropological perspectives* (pp. 245–249). West Point, NY: Leisure Press.

Bredekamp, S. (1987). *Developmentally appropriate practice in programs serving children from birth through age eight.* Washington, DC: National Association for the Education of Young Children.

Corsaro, W. A. (1986). Discourse processes within peer culture: From a constructivist to an interpretive approach to childhood socialization. In P. A. Adler & P. Adler (Eds.), *Sociological studies of child development* (Vol. 1, pp. 81–101). Greenwich, CT: JAI.

Cullen, J. (1993). Preschool children's use and perceptions of outdoor play areas. *Early Child Development and Care, 89,* 45–56.

Custer, W. L. (1996). A comparison of young children's understanding of contradictory representations in pretense, memory, and belief. *Child Development, 67*(2), 678–688.

Denzin, N. K. (1977). *Childhood socialization.* San Francisco: Jossey-Bass.

Fein, G. G. (1985). Learning in play: Surface of thinking and feeling. In J. L. Frost & S. Sunderlin (Eds.), *When children play* (pp. 45–53). Wheaton, MD: Association for Childhood Education International.

Fein, G. G. (1987). Pretend play, creativity, and consciousness. In D. Gorlitz & J. Wohlwill (Eds.), *Curiosity, imagination, and play* (pp. 281–304). Hillsdale, NJ: Lawrence Erlbaum.

Fernie, D. E. (1988). Becoming a student: Messages from first settings. *Theory into Practice, 27* (1), 3–10.

Fivush, R. (1984). Learning about school: The development of kindergartners' school scripts. *Child Development, 55*(5), 1697–1709.

Fowell, N., & Lawton, J. (1992). An alternative view of appropriate practice in early childhood education. *Early Childhood Research Quarterly, 7,* 53–73.

Frost, J. L., & Klein, B. L. (1979). *Children's play and playgrounds.* Boston: Allyn and Bacon.

Garza, M., Briley, S., & Reifel, S. (1985). Children's views of play. In J. L. Frost & S. Sunderlin (Eds.), *When children play* (pp. 31–37). Wheaton, MD: Association for Childhood Education International.

Gracey, H. L. (1975). Learning the student role: Kindergarten as academic boot camp. In H. R. Stub (Ed.), *The sociology of education: A sourcebook* (3rd ed., pp. 82–95). Homewood, IL: Dorsey.

Hennessey, B. A., & Berger, A. R. (1993, March). *Children's conceptions of work and play: Exploring an alternative to the discounting principle.* Poster presented at the meeting of the Society for Research in Child Development, New Orleans, LA.

Holmes, R. (1992). Play during snacktime. *Play and Culture, 5,* 295–304.

Kantor, R. (1988). Creating school meaning in preschool curriculum. *Theory into Practice, 27* (1), 25–35.

King, N. R. (1979). Play: The kindergartner's perspective. *Elementary School Journal, 80* (2), 81–87.

King, N. R. (1982). Children's play as a form of resistance in the classroom. *Journal of Education, 164*(3), 320–329.

King, N. R. (1983). Play in the workplace. In M. W. Apple & L. Weiss (Eds.), *Ideology and practice in schooling* (pp. 262–280). Philadelphia: Temple University Press.

King, N. R. (1986). When educators study play in schools. *Journal of Curriculum and Supervision, 1*(3), 233–246.

King, N. R. (1990). Economics and control in everyday school life. In M. W. Apple (Ed.), *Ideology and curriculum* (pp. 43–60). Boston: Routledge and Kegan Paul.

Klein, E. L., Kantor, R., & Fernie, D. E. (1988). What do young children know about school? *Young Children, 43*(5), 32–39.

LeCompte, M. D. (1980). The civilizing of children: How young children learn to become students. *Journal of Thought, 15*(3), 105–127.

Light, P. (1987). Taking roles. In J. Bruner & H. Haste (Eds.), *Making sense: The child's constructions of the world* (pp. 41–61). London: Methuen.

Lillard, A. S. (1993). Young children's conceptualization of pretense: Action or mental representational state? *Child Development, 64,* 372–386.

Mandler, J. E. (1983). Structural invariants in development. In L. S. Liben (Ed.), *Piaget and the foundations of knowledge* (pp. 97–124). Hillsdale, NJ: Lawrence Erlbaum.

Montessori, M. (1956). *The child in the family.* New York: Avon. (Original work published 1936)

Nelson, K. (1978). How children represent knowledge of their world in and out of language: A preliminary report. In R. S. Siegler (Ed.), *Children's thinking: What develops?* (pp. 255–273). Hillsdale, NJ: Lawrence Erlbaum.

Nelson, K. (1993). Events, narrative, memory: What develops? In C. Nelson (Ed.), *Memory and affect in development: The Minnesota Symposia on Child Psychology* (Vol. 26, pp. 1–24). Hillsdale, NJ: Lawrence Erlbaum.

Nelson, K., & Gruendel, J. (1981). Generalized event representations: Basic building blocks of cognitive development. In M. E. Lamb & A. L. Brown (Eds.), *Advances in Developmental Psychology, 1* (pp. 131–158). Hillsdale, NJ: Lawrence Erlbaum.

Piaget, J. (1962). *Play, dreams, and imitation in childhood.* New York: Norton.

Reifel, S. (1988). Children's thinking about their early education experiences. *Theory into Practice, 27*(1), 62–66.

Reifel, S., Briley, S., & Garza, M. (1986). Play at child care: Event knowledge at ages three to six. In K. Blanchard (Ed.), *The many faces of play* (Vol. 9 pp. 80–91). Champaign, IL: Association for the Anthropological Study of Play: Human Kinetics.

Romero, M. (1989). Work and play in the nursery school. *Educational Policy, 3*(4), 401–419.

Romero, M. (1991). Work and play in the nursery school. In L. Weis, P. Altback, G. Kelly, & H. Petrie (Eds.), *Childhood education* (pp. 119–138). Albany: State University of New York Press.

Rubin, K., Fein, G., & Vandenberg, B. (1983). Play. In P. Mussen (Ed.), *Manual of child psychology* (Vol. 4, pp. 693–

774). New York: John Wiley.

Schank, R. C., & Abelson, R. P. (1977). *Scripts, plans, goals and understanding.* Hillsdale, NJ: Lawrence Erlbaum.

Schwartzman, H. B. (1978a). *Transformations: The anthropology of children's play.* New York: Plenum.

Schwartzman, H. B. (1978b). The dichotomy of work and play. In M. A. Salter (Ed.), *Play: Anthropological perspectives* (pp. 185–249). West Point, NY: Leisure Press.

Smith, P. K., & Vollstedt, R. (1985). On defining play: An empirical study of the relationship between play and various play criteria. *Child Development, 56,* 1042–1050.

Stevens, P. (1978). Play and work: A false dichotomy? In H. B. Schwartzman (Ed.), *Play and culture: 1978 proceedings of the Association for Anthropological Study of Play* (pp. 316–324). West Point, NY: Leisure Press.

Sutton-Smith, B. (1995). The persuasive rhetorics of play. In A. Pellegrini (Ed.), *The future of play theory: Essays in honor of Brian Sutton-Smith* (pp. 275–295). Albany: State University of New York Press.

Takanishi, R., & Spitzer, S. (1980). Children's perceptions of human resources in team-teaching classrooms. *Elementary School Journal, 80*(4), 203–212.

Tyler, L. (1986). Meaning and schooling. *Theory into Practice, 25*(1), 53–57.

Weinstein, R. S. (1983). Student perceptions of schooling. *Elementary School Journal, 83*(4), 287–312.

Wiltz, N. W. (1993a). *What children know about school: Interviews with young children.* Unpublished master's seminar paper, University of Maryland, College Park.

Wiltz, N. W. (1993b). *How preschool children in a Montessori school view work and play.* Unpublished manuscript.

Wiltz, N. W., & Klein, E. (1994). *What did you do at school today? Activities in child care from the child's point of view.* Paper presented at the annual meeting of the American Educational Research Association, New Orleans, LA.

Wing, L. A. (1995). Play is not the work of the child: Young children's perceptions of work and play. *Early Childhood Research Quarterly, 10*(2), 223–247.

Zhang, X., & Sigel, I. (1994, April). *Two kindergarten programs and children's perceptions of school—A cross-cultural study.* Paper presented at the annual meeting of the American Educational Research Association, New Orleans, LA.

Play as a Medium
for Literacy Development

James F. Christie

Current theories of literacy acquisition, including emergent literacy and critical theory, maintain that play can have an important role in early reading and writing development. There are links between play and literacy learning which have implications for education. These links suggest guidelines for setting up print-rich classroom play centers and for facilitative teacher involvement in play.

Emergent Literacy and Critical Theory

Beliefs and instructional practices connected with early literacy have changed dramatically over the past decade. Scholars used to believe that children learned very little about reading and writing until age five or six, when they entered school and began to receive formal instruction. They assumed that children waited for teachers to teach them how to read and write (Roskos, Vukelich, Christie, Enz, & Neuman, 1995). This instruction typically began with perceptual "readiness" activities, such as visual discrimination exercises, and then moved on to rote drill and worksheets focusing on letter-name recognition, handwriting, and letter-sound relationships. Schools delayed book reading and actual writing until children had mastered these prerequisite skills. Once children started doing "real" reading and writing, their teachers expected them to master conventional forms. During reading, children were supposed to accurately recognize all text items and accurately spell all words when writing.

This traditional view of literacy acquisition has been recently supplanted by two new perspectives: emergent literacy and critical theory.

The emergent literacy perspective maintains that children begin to learn about written language much earlier than had previously been believed. Infants and toddlers observe the literacy that surrounds them in everyday life—bedtime stories, environmental print (labels on cereal boxes, restaurant signs), and family literacy routines (looking up programs in *TV Guide,* writing down phone messages, making shopping lists)—and then begin to construct their own hypotheses about the function, structure, and conventions of print (Hall, 1987). In this process, young children invent their own "emergent" versions of reading and writing that initially have little resemblance to conventional forms: the story they "read" may be completely different than the one in the book and their writing may look like drawing or scribbles. As children have opportunities to use these emergent forms of literacy in meaningful social situations, their constructions become increasingly similar to conventional reading and writing (Sulzby & Teale, 1991).

Critical theory views literacy acquisition in the broader sociopolitical context of the children's culture (Solsken, 1993). It is concerned with how reading instruction affects the balance of power between different groups in society. According to this view, traditional textbook-based reading instruction benefits the upper classes by conditioning lower-class children to passively accept the status quo. Critical theorists believe that "schools should encourage and foster students' attempts to make sense of their immediate experience by establishing 'voices' that enable them to participate in control of their lives. . . . The goal . . . is to have students participate within the production of knowledge, culture, and society" (Shannon,

1990, p. 157). Critical theorists favor pedagogical approaches that give children control over their own literacy learning and that are closely linked to their own cultural experiences.

Early childhood educators who subscribe to these new perspectives believe that early childhood language arts programs should provide children with opportunities to construct their own knowledge about reading and writing. These programs feature print-rich classroom settings, daily storybook reading by the teacher, teacher modeling of the reading/writing process (e.g., language experience charts), and lots of opportunities for children to engage in meaningful reading and writing activities (Morrow, 1993). In addition, teachers try to connect these classroom activities with children's own cultural experiences outside of school.

Play and Literacy Connections

Sociodramatic play occurs when children take on roles and act out a situation or story. Several children, for example, might adopt the roles of family members and pretend to prepare and eat dinner. This type of play commonly takes place in classroom "housekeeping" or "theme" centers and can provide an ideal context for the types of literacy learning experiences advocated by these two new perspectives (Christie, 1991).

The following episode, which occurred in a university preschool classroom, is an example of how children can incorporate reading and writing into their sociodramatic play.

Several four-year-olds have agreed to take a make-believe train trip to France. They decide to use an elevated loft in the classroom as their train and begin moving chairs up the stairs to use as passenger seats. Two of the children go to an adjacent center and begin making tickets for the journey, using scribbles to represent writing. Once the tickets are made, they are distributed to every child and collected by the engineer as passengers enter the train. While the children wait for their teacher to finish packing his bag and join them on board, they lean over the loft railing and attempt to read signs that had been made earlier for the train, including "No Smoking," "No Drugs," and "No Ghosts." They have difficulty reading the prohibition against drugs and ask the teacher, "What's that say?" The teacher reads the sign out loud for the children and then climbs on board so that the journey can begin.

This vignette illustrates several ways in which sociodramatic play can promote literacy learning. First, the play scenario allowed children to demonstrate their emerging conceptions about the functional uses of print (Neuman & Roskos, 1989; Schrader, 1989). They knew that print communicates meaning (evident in the question, "What's that say?") and that it can be used to control behavior (prohibit smoking) and grant access to goods and services (via tickets). Second, the make-believe nature of the play provided an ideal context for experimenting with emergent forms of literacy (Christie, 1995; Morrow & Rand, 1991). It was perfectly acceptable to use scribble writing to produce tickets, and all of the players treated the pretend tickets as if they were real. Thus, play's fantasy component invited risk-taking while adding meaning and significance to children's attempts at reading and writing. Third, the play provided an opportunity for literacy-related social interactions with peers and with the teacher (Neuman & Roskos, 1991a; Roskos & Neuman, 1993). The children, for example, worked together to figure out the meaning of the train signs and also sought help from the teacher on the one sign they could not decipher on their own. In this instance, the teacher created what Vygotsky (1978) called a "zone of proximal development," allowing children to engage in a literacy activity (sign reading) that they could not do on their own.

This vignette also illustrates how sociodramatic play can provide links between classroom activities and children's cultural experiences outside of school. Two of the signs that the children had made for their train, "No Smoking" and "No Drugs," reflect community concern over passive smoke and substance abuse. The fact that these signs resemble real signs in the children's own neighborhoods makes them more salient and meaningful.

Educational Implications

Recent research has shed light on the conditions that encourage children to engage in this type of literacy-related play (Christie, 1994). First and foremost, play centers need to be equipped with relevant types of reading and writing materials. The second variable concerns how teachers interact with children during play. If teachers get involved in children's play in a facilitative manner, they can enrich the quality of the play and encourage the children to incorporate emergent forms of reading and writing into their dramatizations.

Literacy-Enriched Play Centers

Children are more likely to engage in play-related reading and writing activities if materials are present that invite these types of activities (Christie & Enz, 1992; Morrow & Rand, 1991; Neuman & Roskos, 1992; Vukelich, 1991). This "materials intervention" strategy involves making play areas resemble the literacy environments that children encounter at home and in their communities. The kitchen area of a home center, for example, might contain empty product containers (cereal boxes, soft drink cans, catsup bottles), cookbooks, a telephone directory, food coupons, message pads, and pencils. A restaurant center could be equipped with menus, wall signs, pencils, and notepads for taking food orders. These centers would then invite children to incorporate familiar literacy routines into their play.

Researchers have developed three criteria to assist teachers in selecting these literacy props: (a) *appropriateness:* the material is safe and easy for children to use; (b) *authenticity:* it is a literacy item that is used in real life; and (c) *utility:* the item serves a practical function in the children's play efforts (Neuman & Roskos, 1991b). One other criterion that can be added to this list is *cultural relevancy:* the materials should reflect the literacy environment of the children's own culture. One way to accomplish this is to ask parents and children to bring in reading and writing materials from their homes and neighborhoods (Roskos et al., 1995).

Table 1 presents examples of the literacy materials for a variety of sociodramatic play settings. Note that these props meet the three criteria above and could be supplemented with literacy materials from children's homes and neighborhoods.

One additional resource is needed to make sure that children can take maximum advantage of these literacy-enriched play environments: an adequate amount of time for play (Christie & Wardle, 1992). Young children need considerable time to plan and act out a sustained play episode. They need to assign roles, make props,

TABLE 1. Props for Literacy-Enriched Play Centers

Home Center	*Business Office*
Pencils, pens, markers	Pencils, pens, markers
Notepads	Notepads
Post-it notes	Telephone message forms
Babysitter instruction forms	Calendar
	Typewriter
Telephone message pads	Stationery, envelopes
Message board	File folders
Children's books, magazines, newspapers	Wall signs ("Open/Closed")
Cookbooks, recipe box	Order forms
Product containers (cereal boxes, etc.)	

Restaurant	*Post Office*
Pencils	Pencils, pens, markers
Notepads	Stationery, envelopes
Menus	Stamps
Wall signs ("Deli")	Mailboxes
Bank checks	Address labels
Cookbooks	Wall signs
Product containers	("Line Starts Here")

Grocery Store	*Veterinarian's Office*
Pencils, pens, markers	Pencils, pens, markers
Notepads	Appointment book
Bank checks	Wall signs
Wall signs ("Supermarket")	("Waiting Room")
	Labels with pets' names
Shelf labels for store areas ("Meat")	Patient charts
Product containers	Prescription forms
	Magazines (in waiting room)

Airport/Airplane	*Library*
Pencils, pens, markers	Pencils
Tickets	Books
Bank checks	Shelf labels for books
Luggage tags	("ABCs," "Animals")
Magazines (onboard plane)	Wall signs ("Quiet")
Air sickness bags with printed instructions	Library cards
Maps	Checkout cards for books

Source: Based on "The Effects of Literacy Play Interventions on Preschoolers' Play Patterns and Literacy Development," by J. F. Christie and B. Enz, 1992, *Early Education and Development 3,* 211. Reprinted with permission.

organize the setting, solve social problems, and plan the story they are going to enact. In one incident witnessed by this author, a group of four-year-olds spent more than forty-five minutes preparing to play pizza parlor. They sorted pizza ingredients made of felt fabric into containers, rearranged the furniture in the play center, and made a variety of props, including signs and money. The actual making and eating of the pizza took less than ten minutes! Had the play period only been thirty minutes long, the children would have had to stop and clean up before their drama had even started, and many valuable literacy experiences (sign making, menu reading, and money counting) would have been missed.

Teacher Involvement in Play

Teacher involvement in play can have either positive or negative effects, depending upon timing and the role that the teacher assumes. On the one hand, the key element to successful involvement in play is sensitivity (Roskos et al., 1995). When teachers observe carefully and link their involvement with children's current play interests, they can enrich and extend play episodes (Schrader, 1990). They also can encourage children to incorporate relevant literacy activities into their ongoing play episodes (Christie & Enz, 1992; Morrow & Rand, 1991). On the other hand, if teachers take control of the play or try to redirect children toward unrelated literacy activities, the results can be disastrous. Children may begin to think of the activity as work rather than play (King, 1979), and play will often get disrupted (Schrader, 1990). In such situations, children often stop playing altogether.

Research has revealed that there is a continuum of teacher roles in play, ranging from complete noninvolvement to directing what children do during play (Enz & Christie, 1994; Jones & Reynolds, 1992; Roskos & Neuman, 1993; Schrader, 1990). The most effective teacher roles, both in terms of facilitating high-quality play and encouraging play-related literacy activity, lie between these two extremes. Some researchers have found that four teacher roles were effective in enhancing preschoolers' play and literacy activities:

- *Audience.* The teacher watches children as they play, demonstrating that play is an important and worthwhile classroom activity. The teacher also subtly provides support by nodding in approval, verbalizing praise, and making brief comments designed to encourage children to continue their play activities. For example, if the teacher observes that children are using an emergent form of writing (scribbles, letterlike forms, or random strings of letters) in connection with a pretend trip to a store, she or he might compliment their efforts ("That's a nice shopping list that you've written"). This role is most appropriate when children are engrossed in rich, sustained play.

- *Stage Manager.* The teacher supports children's play by responding to their requests for materials, by helping them construct costumes and props, and by assisting in organizing the play set. In the vignette above, the teacher engaged in this role when he helped the children make the regulatory signs for their make-believe train. A stage manager may also make theme-related script suggestions to extend the children's ongoing dramatic play ("Why don't you make tickets for the train? Then you can give them to the conductor when you get on board"). As in the audience role, the teacher remains on the sidelines and does not join in the children's play. The stage manager role is often used at the beginning of play periods and during transitions when children are switching to new play themes and activities.

- *Coplayer.* In the coplayer role, the teacher accepts an invitation to play and actually becomes an actor in the children's dramatizations. As a coplayer, the teacher takes a minor role and carefully follows the children's lead, letting them make all the major decisions. For example, the teacher might take the role of a customer in a store dramatization. In this role, the teacher could model using a shopping list, reading product labels, and paying for purchases with a check, provided that these literacy activities fit in with the ongoing play.

- *Play Leader.* Like the coplayer, the play leader joins in and becomes the children's play partner. However, play leaders take a more active role and attempt to alter the course of the play by introducing new elements or plot conflicts. If a grocery store dramatization, for example, is growing stale and boring, the teacher might adopt the role of a customer and exclaim, "It's awfully hard to find anything in this store! The shelves need to be labeled so that we know where things are." Or the teacher might mention to a pretend family member, "I think I hear our baby crying. He must be hungry. We'd better finish shopping and hurry home." (Enz & Christie, 1994)

Flexibility is a key element in successful teacher involvement in play. Researchers found, for example, that experienced preschool teachers did not exhibit a dominant play interaction style (Roskos & Neuman, 1993). Instead, these veteran teachers adopted a variety of *extending-style* roles—onlooker, coplayer, and play leader—depending on the children who were playing and type of play that was occurring. They concluded that the teacher's ability to switch roles to fit the children's "play agenda" was as important as the interaction styles they used (Roskos & Neuman, 1993). Ideally, teachers should have a repertoire of play interaction styles and know when it is appropriate to use each one.

Sociodramatic play can be an excellent means for providing children with the types of literacy learning experiences advocated by emergent literacy and critical theory perspectives. Play can give meaning and significance to children's early attempts at literacy, and its "low-risk" atmosphere encourages experimentation with emergent forms of reading and writing. Play can also provide valuable social interactions connected with literacy, both with teachers and peers. It also presents opportunities for bringing culturally relevant literacy materials into the classroom.

For play to live up to this potential, teachers need to provide three things: (a) literacy-enriched play settings, (b) ample time for play, and (c) appropriate adult involvement in play. These prerequisites present varying levels of challenge. Converting traditional play areas into "literate" play centers is relatively simple. The reader will note that the literacy materials listed in Table 1 are inexpensive and easy to obtain. Finding adequate time for play can be more difficult because of competition from other areas of the early childhood curriculum and mounting pressure from parents to provide structured, formal instruction on the "basics." Strategies for overcoming these obstacles have been suggested elsewhere (See Christie & Wardle, 1992).

Providing appropriate teacher involvement in play presents a special challenge. Teachers not only need to have a repertoire of effective play interaction roles, they also need to be flexible, matching their role with the children's current play needs. Fortunately, new in-service education materials (see Roskos et al., 1995) are becoming available to help teachers acquire these play interaction skills.

When these three prerequisites—literacy-enriched settings, adequate time, and facilitative teacher involvement—are in place, sociodramatic play can function as an ideal medium for children to construct their own knowledge about reading and writing. Play makes literacy learning fun and enjoyable, and it guarantees that children's early attempts at reading and writing will be successful. Play also presents teachers with opportunities for "authentic" assessment by allowing children to demonstrate their growing knowledge about the forms and functions of print (Vukelich, 1991). For these reasons, literacy-related play deserves a central role in early childhood language arts programs.

Bibliography

Christie, J. F. (1991). *Play and early literacy development.* Albany: State University of New York Press.

Christie, J. F. (1994). Literacy play interventions: A review of empirical research. *Advances in Early Education and Day Care, 6,* 3–24.

Christie, J. F. (1995). Why play is important. In J. Christie, K. Roskos, B. Enz, C. Vukelich, & S. Neuman (Eds.), *Readings for linking literacy and play* (pp. 1–7). Newark, DE: International Reading Association.

Christie, J. F., & Enz, B. (1992). The effects of literacy play interventions on preschoolers' play patterns and literacy development. *Early Education and Development, 3,* 205–220.

Christie, J., & Wardle, F. (1992). How much time is needed for play? *Young Children, 47*(3), 28–32.

Enz, B., & Christie, J. F. (1994, December). *Ignore, play, or direct? The impact of adult play styles on preschoolers' language and literacy.* Paper presented at the meeting of the National Reading Conference, Coronado, CA.

Hall, N. (1987). *The emergence of literacy.* Portsmouth, NH: Heinemann.

Jones, E., & Reynolds, E. (1992). *The play's*

the thing: Teachers' roles in children's play. New York: Teachers College Press.

King, N. R. (1979). Play: The kindergartners' perspective. *Elementary School Journal, 80*, 81–87.

Morrow, L. M. (1993). *Literacy development in the early years* (2nd ed.). Boston: Allyn and Bacon.

Morrow, L. M., & Rand, M. K. (1991). Preparing the classroom environment to promote literacy during play. In J. F. Christie (Ed.), *Play and early literacy development* (pp. 141–165). Albany: State University of New York Press.

Neuman, S. B., & Roskos, K. (1989). Preschoolers' conceptions of literacy as reflected in their spontaneous play. In S. McCormick & J. Zutell (Eds.), *Cognitive and social perspectives for literacy research and instructions* (pp. 87–94). Chicago: National Reading Conference.

Neuman, S. B., & Roskos, K. (1991a). Peers as literacy informants: A description of young children's literacy conversations in play. *Early Childhood Research Quarterly, 6*, 233–248.

Neuman, S. B., & Roskos, K. (1991b). Play, print, and purpose: Enriching play environments for literacy development. *The Reading Teacher, 44*, 214–221.

Neuman, S. B., & Roskos, K. (1992). Literacy objects as cultural tools: Effects on children's literacy behaviors during play. *Reading Research Quarterly, 27*, 203–223.

Roskos, K., & Neuman, S. B. (1993). Descriptive observations of adults' facilitation of literacy in play. *Early Childhood Research Quarterly, 8*, 77–97.

Roskos, K., Vukelich, C., Christie, J., Enz, B., & Neuman, S. (1995). *Linking literacy and play: Facilitator's guide*. Newark, DE: International Reading Association.

Schrader, C. T. (1989). Written language use within the context of young children's symbolic play. *Early Childhood Research Quarterly, 4*, 225–244.

Schrader, C. T. (1990). Symbolic play as a curricular tool for early literacy development. *Early Childhood Research Quarterly, 5*, 79–103.

Shannon, P. (1990). *The struggle to continue: Progressive reading instruction in the United States*. Portsmouth, NH: Heinemann.

Solsken, J. (1993). *Literacy, gender, and work in families and in school*. Norwood, NJ: Ablex.

Sulzby, E., & Teale, W. (1991). Emergent literacy. In R. Barr, M. Kamil, P. Mosenthal, & P. D. Pearson (Eds.), *Handbook of reading research* (Vol. 2, pp. 727–757). New York: Longman.

Vukelich, C. (1991, December). *Learning about the functions of writing: The effects of three play interventions on children's development and knowledge about writing*. Paper presented at the meeting of the National Reading Conference, Palm Springs, CA.

Vygotsky, L. S. (1978). *Mind in society: The development of psychological processes*. Cambridge, MA: Harvard University Press.

Play and Its Influence on the Development of Young Children's Mathematical Thinking

Ranald H. Jarrell

Play is vital to the development of children's mathematical thinking. Unlike some forms of knowledge, mathematical knowledge, which deals with relationships between and among things, cannot be learned by children's hearing adults talk about it. Experimental research on play shows a strong relationship between play, the growth of mathematical understanding, and improved mathematical performance. This essay discusses the types of play and mathematics processes that children investigate, the nature of mathematical thinking in children, and how adults can assist children in this development.

It would be fair to say that without play, as it is described below, children's powers of mathematical reasoning would be seriously underdeveloped. Furthermore, when adults finally grasp the importance of play in mathematics development, they become absolutely committed to providing and protecting children's play as a matter of necessity and to learning how they can better design and facilitate play experiences to encourage children's natural mathematical investigations.

Adults are often surprised when they learn about the nature of mathematical thinking in young children and how children's play helps them build their mathematical understanding. When adults use these insights to help children build their own deeper, richer vision of mathematics and enhance their relationship to it, it is a source of joy both for children and for the adults who work with them.

The Nature of Mathematical Thinking

Have you known classmates who were brilliant in verbal areas such as English literature or po-etry analysis but seemed totally inept at the simplest algebra? Or have you known the fine mathematics or engineering student who could barely write an intelligible sentence? How could the smartest in the class in one subject be at the bottom in another? The reason is that mathematics and verbal subjects require entirely different kinds of thinking which develop in different ways.

Many verbal disciplines, such as linguistics and history, can be learned reasonably well by having the learner listen to an adult talk about them, then organize and memorize the lecture content and restate the presented content on tests. After children learn to read, adults can also give them printed material that conveys the content. When children understand linguistically based content through this process, they are learning by social transmission (Piaget, 1952).

Many teachers, for example, use the process of social transmission to teach spelling, the scientific names for particular plants, and the names of the state capitals. Because socially transmitted information is arbitrary—that is, the "correct" information may differ in various cultures—it must be conveyed by human beings who are familiar with the cultural context. Mathematical knowledge is fundamentally different, however, and must be learned in another way. Mathematical thinking arises when children work firsthand with objects, put them into relationships, and think about those relationships at their own pace during play. Mathematical understanding is based on conclusions a child reaches after much mathematical thinking.

Mathematics involves putting two or more things into a relationship and focusing one's thinking on the relationship, not on the things themselves (Piaget, 1952). Consider, for example, the series of dots that follow inside these parentheses:

(. . .)

If asked how many dots are shown, most people would say three, but they would have difficulty telling where, exactly, is the three or the "threeness" of this group of dots. Is it in the middle dot? No. Is it in the left dot? Again, no. The "threeness" of this group of dots exists only because the dots are arranged together as if they were related to each other, and they are then described in this relationship as "three." There is nothing within the dots themselves to make the mathematical relationship of three. All that is needed to alter this relationship is either to take a dot away

(. .)

or to add another dot

(. . . .)

In either case the pattern of the dots now conveys a different relationship, so different, in fact, that the set has a new name (twoness or fourness). The key is that when a person sees the dots as related to each other and describes that relationship with a number word, he or she is engaging in a mental act that each person looking at the dots must do for himself or herself (Piaget, 1973). Children can construct this kind of knowledge by making logical-mathematical relationships (Piaget, 1973). It cannot, however, be communicated through social transmission.

Consider one more example:

3 × 4.

This describes a relationship of four groups of three or

(... ... ...)

Not only are the dots related to each other in little groups of three, but a group of three is one of four groups with that same relationship. Take away even one dot and the relationship is changed dramatically and, again, must be renamed.

How Children Learn Mathematical Relationships

The words adults use to describe the mathematical relationships that they themselves have built and understand are not helpful to young children. Every child must personally put the dots or marbles or buttons or plastic chips or fingers together into groups in order to understand these relationships. The best way for children to build an understanding of mathematical relationships is through physically making such groups with their own hands many times and observing the similarity of results across many experiences (Baroody, 1987).

For the uninformed adult, a child's putting dried beans or plastic chips into little families of three for pleasure may be described as "just wasting time in harmless play." From the standpoint of mathematics development, however, the child is engaged in a highly fruitful exploration and investigation of mathematical relationships. The difference between social knowledge and mathematical knowledge is that mathematical relationships must be investigated firsthand by the child and cannot be short-circuited by the good intentions of adults who try to use words to pass on the discoveries they have earlier made about mathematical relationships. Key relationship words such as *equals, more than, seven, heavier than, take away,* and *times* must be constructed inside the learner's head after many experiences of handling and seeing the concrete physical relationships that these terms verbally represent.

The mere fact that adults cannot directly teach fundamental mathematical concepts to children does not mean, however, that they cannot help children to develop mathematically (Copeland, 1984). In fact, there are wonderful strategies available for those who understand the major processes of mathematics in which children can engage and the ways in which adults can encourage children to use those processes.

Key Mathematics Processes Children Use

What exactly is the mathematics that young children engage in? A close study of early childhood texts will show that they usually describe the following mathematics processes as appropriate for children to investigate: counting, measurement, patterns, computation, logical thinking, geometry, and the concept of number. Note that adults are comfortable with these examples of mathematical thinking because it looks like the mathematics they experienced. More important, however, is the fact that these processes are mathematical because they involve putting things into a relationship and focusing on that relationship. There is no substitute for a child's personal experiences of counting, measuring, finding and making patterns, and otherwise working with (thinking about) groups of objects. From having these experiences and reflecting on them, children reach the conclusions we call mathematical knowledge. A concrete example is that when children add together 3 and 2, the answer, 5, is larger than either of the components; this conclusion is essential to an understanding of addition, and without a child's knowing it, no addition is possible (Copeland, 1984).

If one has any doubt that mathematical thinking is putting two or more things together in a relationship and focusing attention on that relationship, that doubt is swept aside when considering the most fundamental terms used in early mathematics (Ginsberg, 1982). Consider the nature of the concept *equals* (=). When children must decide if two things are equal, they must take the mental steps of moving the two things beside each other and then comparing them to each other to see if one is bigger, longer, heavier, or more numerous than the other.

Other fundamental concepts in early childhood mathematics unavoidably involve making comparisons; that is, children must make judgments about the relationship of one thing to another or one group to another. The question, "Does Max have *more than* Nina?" (whether more money or jelly beans is immaterial), for example, is asking for a comparison of their quantities and a label of that relationship as *more* or *less*, if not equal. "Is Matthew's shoe *heavier than* Alexandra's?" focuses on the relationship between the shoes, not on the shoes themselves. "My pencil is *longer than* yours" states a conclusion based on the mental or physical act of placing two pencils beside each other and considering how their lengths are related.

When children have the opportunity to group things into a relationship and consider the properties of that relationship, they are engaging in mathematical thinking (Forman & Kuschner, 1983). From those efforts children reach conclusions that 7 is more than 5, that one big block weighs as much as several little ones, that a part is less than a whole, and many other basic facts upon which they can base a sound understanding of formal mathematics. Play offers a unique opportunity for children to investigate mathematical relationships closely. There is, in fact, considerable research evidence that cognitively rich play can improve children's mathematical abilities even if the play does not relate directly to anything mathematical.

Research on Play and Mathematical Thinking

A number of experimental studies on the effects of play on mathematical thinking support this relationship. Using a classic design, one researcher randomly assigned five-year-olds to experimental treatment and control groups (Yawkey, 1981). In small groups the children in the treatment group engaged in thematic sociodramatic play (Smilansky, 1968) for fifteen minutes during each kindergarten day for seven consecutive months. In contrast, the children in the control group spent the equivalent time block in a range of art activities. At the end of seven months, all of the children were given the same mathematics readiness test administered at the outset. The gains of the play treatment group were significantly greater than those of the control group. Especially interesting was the finding that children in the sociodramatic play group whose pretest scores had been particularly low made the greatest gains. The answer to the provocative question of whether even greater gains in mathematical learning would result if children engaged in a substantially longer block of time in sociodramatic play each day must await further research.

Children's understanding of formal mathematical concepts has also improved through carefully designed boisterous games (Rogers & Miller, 1984). Researchers designed a cops-and-robbers jailbreak game that required factoring, a difficult concept for the eight-year-old subjects they studied. Each child wore a T-shirt bearing a number from 1 to 10. The teacher began the game by announcing her own number, for example 18, and then saying she was going to chase and catch children wearing some numbers but not others. She then caught children wearing factors of her number, for example the child wearing 3 and then the child wearing 6, followed by 2 and 9. Each child caught was put in "jail." Then she wrote on the blackboard those numbers caught and her own number: 3, 6 / 2, 9 / 18. All of the uncaught numbers were written on another line some distance from the first. In a discussion that followed, the children quickly identified how the pairs of numbers were factors of the number 18. The children then played the game with two additional rules: (a) If one factor, such as 2, is in jail, the child wearing the related factor (9) could free that captive by running to the jail and touching 2; (b) the children with numbers that were not factors of 18 could block the chaser to prevent another factor's being caught.

To determine the effectiveness of the play on children's mathematical development, the researchers administered four tests: a pretest, a posttest, a "retention test" six weeks after the posttest, and a "transfer test" to see if the children could apply the same mathematical concept to more difficult but structurally similar problems. The reseachers found significant improvement in the children's performance from pretest to posttest. The lowest-performing students, based on their pretest and posttest, who also took part in five additional game sessions in which they were game leaders, showed a higher retention test score than pretest score (not seen in the other subjects). Although this subgroup's posttest performance was below that of the other children, their retention test scores were significantly higher than those of the other children; that is, with extra play sessions as the only added intervention, the initially poorest-performing students as a group outperformed all of the remaining students. Surprisingly, the transfer test scores of this group were also significantly higher than those scores for other children, thus giving weight to the view that exposure of underperforming children to extra sessions of play that embodies fundamental mathematics concepts can offset at least some earlier underachievement.

This research was extended by investigating the question of whether lower-performing children's understanding of the concept of factoring might be greater than their ability to express it on a paper- and pencil test (Rogers, 1989). Several subgroups of lower-performing children were identified on the paper-and-pencil test of factoring. Each of these subgroups showed significant improvement in performance on a play test using the same factoring problems. These results make a powerful argument that low mathematics performance for many children may arise not from their inability to understand concepts but from difficulty understanding how mathematical concepts are represented on paper-and-pencil tests. Thus, play offers the opportunity for children to learn mathematical concepts more effectively and also to demonstrate what they know more powerfully.

Other reseachers examined how children can transfer to more formal mathematical problems those mathematical processes that are embedded and practiced in play (Zammarelli & Bolton, 1977). To test this notion, researchers designed a toy so that play with it required use of a particular mathematical concept. The researchers exposed three groups of children (ten to twelve years of age) to the toy in different ways. One group (the "play group") played freely with the toy; the second group (the "yoked group") watched another child play with the toy; and the third group (the "control group") only looked at the toy while it was out of reach. All of the children took the same pretest and posttest that involved the mathematical concept embedded in play with the toy. None of the groups differed significantly on the pretest, but the play group's posttest performance was significantly higher than that of the other groups. Zammarelli and Bolton (1977) concluded, "These results provide a striking confirmation of the hypothesis that play with a specifically designed toy can lead to greater understanding of the rules involved in a mathematical concept . . . than can be provided by observation of the same stimuli but without manipulation" (p. 160).

The benefits of play on mathematical performance are not restricted to young children. Researchers also investigated the effects of computer play on eighth-grade inner-city students' learning of algebra concepts (Allen & Ross, 1977). Five groups of students participated in different learning experiences. The most play-oriented treatment group spent two years with a self-paced mathematics program entitled "Equations" and two weeks with a computer "math play kit" that addressed twenty-one concepts tested on the posttest. The most traditional treatment involved no exposure to either the computer play program or "Equations" and included only direct teacher instruction. Among the five treatment groups, students who played with the math play kits showed gains from pretest to posttest that were highly significant in comparison to all other groups. The authors concluded, "the results show that a combination of playing Equations over a two-year period and then working intensively with the [math play] kits for two weeks enables students to apply mathematical ideas better than any of the other four sets of conditions do . . . and . . . [their performance was] . . . better in each case by a highly conservative test at the extreme level of significance (.0001)" (Allen & Ross, 1977, p. 266).

There is still much research to be done concerning how and which types of play advance children's mathematical understanding. The research that does exist, however, is almost uniform in its finding that play engaging children's higher-order thinking has an important and positive impact on their mathematical thinking. What are some of the reasons why play seems to have this powerful influence?

For all of the differences between children's developing their ability to walk and developing their ability to think mathematically, there are two fundamental similarities. First, in both cases, children have to learn the task through direct personal experience; no amount of adult words is an adequate substitute for young children's practice at coordinating their steps to maintain balance or for their practice at putting things into relationships and reflecting on the nature of those relationships (Kamii, 1985). Second, both walking and the understanding of mathematical relationships vastly improve with the playful practice that children undertake voluntarily.

Mathematical Thinking as a Natural Outgrowth of Play

As children hold, look at, arrange, and rearrange physical objects, that is, when they voluntarily "play" with them, they inevitably consider many questions that are mathematical in nature. In examining a new toy such as pattern blocks, for example, a child's play involves an investigation to find out how many blocks there are, how many of each color, and how thick, heavy, wide, thin, strong, and hard they are. The child's hands, eyes, and ears are all engaged in answering these questions, and the answers all involve mathematical conclusions (Piaget, 1973).

Furthermore, as a child compares different objects to determine which of two or more objects is longer than, stronger than, weaker than, heavier than, slower than, faster than, bigger than, more than, or higher than another, that child is putting objects into relationships, even if the child does not yet know names for those relationships. When children try to find out what happens if they add more clay to the clay ball in their hand, cut it into pieces, take some away, double it, or hit it with a hammer to flatten it, they compare the appearance of the clay before they act on it with its appearance afterward. Such comparisons are essential to developing understanding of number, quantity, and other mathematical concepts (Ginsberg & Opper, 1988).

A child during playtime, for example, puts a group of white Lego pieces end-to-end in a line and calls them a train. Eventually the child counts them and finds that there are six train cars; then the child decides to add a red caboose. When the child counts the blocks again, he or she realizes that by adding the extra block at the end, several relationships have changed: the new train is longer than the old, there are more cars by number, and there are now different colors as well. Children build mathematical knowledge of the world slowly as they examine relationships, reflect on those relationships, alter objects, and, after further reflection, realize that the relationship is now a different one with different properties and frequently different descriptive names.

In middle childhood, children's mathematical thinking differs from that of younger children in two major ways. First, if they have played with physical objects and thought about them long enough, they have a much better understanding of the relationships between objects (Kamii, 1993). Second, they can use that knowledge to solve quickly more complex problems (Baroody, 1987). Their symbolic understanding has also developed so that they can make the connection between these relationships and the abstract symbols used to represent the relationships (Piaget, 1952).

Typical Play That Fosters Mathematical Understanding

If mathematics involves counting, measuring, classifying, geometry, patterns, and computation, do children actually use these processes in their play? In response to this question, this section examines several instances of ordinary play with ordinary materials.

Water Play

Imagine a child playing at a water table, dipping a four-ounce clear plastic cup under water and pouring its contents into a sixteen-ounce glass. What kinds of mathematical processes might be developing in this play episode? First, the child can work on understanding whole-part relationships; when all of the water is poured from the small cup into the big one, the child learns that the amount only partially fills the larger. Work on such whole-part relationships is crucial to understanding both fractions and many other forms of measurement and addition (Copeland, 1984). Second, the child can discover through many pouring experiences that it takes four of the full little cups to fill the big one. Such efforts also involve counting and understanding the concept of number. Third, in measuring the water, the child can learn about the effect that volume has on weight; for example, four cups of water in the big glass are much heavier than the contents of any one glass of water. Fourth, having several cups for children to use adds another way to explore counting insights and the concept of the constancy of number. If the child uses several four-ounce glasses, he or she will learn over several experiences that the last number word spoken, *four* is the same as the number of cups that it takes to fill the big glass. This is obvious to adults, but that is because they have had dozens of similar experiences in their own play experiences.

Block Play

A girl of four is playing with wooden blocks. From the earlier examples, what kind of mathematical understandings would you imagine she might be developing? You probably will identify opportunities for counting and the investigation of whole-part relationships (Leeb-Lundberg, 1984). Notice the similarity between "four cups fill up the big glass" and "eight little blocks laid end-to-end make as much road as one long big block." As the child holds the blocks and builds with them, he or she learns that some are heavier than others (measurement by weight) and that there is a relationship between the length of a block and its weight; this mathematical relationship of proportions is understood through computation and logical thinking (Hamilton-Speer, 1986). As the child builds the block structure higher, he or she becomes increasingly challenged by the concept of balance; if the child puts a block on one end of the tower, he or she must put one of the same size on the other or the whole structure will fall down. The thinking done here concerns both geometry—thinking of the positioning in space of one thing in relation to another—and applied mathematical computation. The most complex equations in mathematics are based on exactly the same kind of balance; that is, if you add something to one side you have to add the same to the other.

Sorting Play

Recently, the author observed a five-year-old boy and a five-year-old girl at the art table of their preschool who had decided to put all of the art supplies into "families that belong together." They found two empty boxes that the class used for storing art supplies. The art supplies on the table consisted of glue sticks, felt markers, colored paper clips, crayons, a stapler, paint brushes, cans of sparkle, pastel pencils, and buttons. If they had been given eight containers, they might well have put all of the markers in one container, the glue sticks in another, and so on. However, with only two containers available, the children had to fashion a classification system that placed together different kinds of objects that still shared some common characteristic. After some discussion, they decided to put the pencils, markers, sparkle, and crayons in one container because, they said, "These color our paper." They then put the stapler and paper clips in the second container, saying, "These hold paper together." Then they got into an argument over whether the white glue sticks belonged with the crayons group (because the glue made paper white when it was applied) or belonged with the paper clips group (because the glue kept things together).

Their remarkable discussion shows how children can classify objects by forging a relationship between them and defining that relationship. A child who can group some things together into a category is using the same "grouping process" as the more advanced mathematician who groups part of a formula on one side of an equation and then moves it to the other side, a vital step in mathematical problem solving. Long after the children have forgotten about their particular grouping, they will be able to transfer the insight to group other objects and situations. Once children group objects into smaller "families," as these children did, they soon begin to compare the quantities in the various families they have created to see which family is *bigger* or has *more*. These questions create the need to quantify the groups by counting and comparing them, an act at the heart of mathematics. It is true that the numbers these five-year-old children explored were relatively small, but their questions were highly mathematical and arose entirely from their own effort to make sense of the physical objects available to them. It really does not matter whether the children grouped the art supplies in the same way adults might. The important fact is that during their play they approached a group of objects with a mathematical question and formulated their own way of answering it mathematically. This is typical of the way young children in play strive to impose their own logical order on their environment (Kamii, 1985).

Constructive Play

As children build with blocks or other materials, they invariably measure their progress using a variety of other mathematical processes. They count the number of layers high they can build their structure before it falls. They count how many blocks high they can place blocks end-to-end and still maintain balance. They also find other ways to measure their progress and compare it to that of others. The episode that follows reveals how the disagreements that occur during play often require children to argue, problem solve, or negotiate. These play-based disagreements do much to help children sharpen their grasp of mathematical understandings (Kamii, 1985).

A wonderful mathematical argument recently took place between two children five or six years of age who were competing to see who could build the taller tower with wooden blocks. Child A said, "When I put my arm straight up in the air, my block tower comes up to my elbow. My tower is bigger than yours" (clearly a mathematical conclusion). Child B then said, "I put my arm straight up too, and my tower goes all the way up to my wrist. So my tower is bigger than yours." Child A then said, in a breathtaking display of mathematical insight, "Yes, but you are a lot shorter than me so the tower comes up on your arm more than on my arm. My tower is still taller than yours."

Consider what remarkable mathematical relationships Child A had to take into account to make that statement. She had to reason that a shorter person (Child B) would have a comparatively shorter upward reach (a mathematical relationship in itself). She also concluded that any measure of the comparative heights of the two towers would require using the same standard of comparison. The two children continued to argue until Child A finally insisted that Child B hold up his arm beside both towers; B found that his own tower stopped at his upraised wrist. B then found that A's tower soared a half inch above the end of his outstretched fingertips. B then said after further argument, "Yours is bigger, but mine is a prettier tower than yours." Even in his sense of defeat, which he expressed in mathematical terms, B put the two towers in a second math-

ematical relationship, albeit with an aesthetic twist.

Games with Rules

Much of the play of children in the late primary and elementary years focuses on games with highly structured rules that require children to pit their individual strategies and thinking processes against that of opponents. As children develop during the early and middle childhood years, they come to enjoy the challenge of playing with other children so much that they will suffer the risk and face defeat for the sake of the greater joy of continuing the play. Many of the games played by children in middle childhood draw upon specific mathematics processes, such as counting money, estimating probabilities, and organizing spatial categories.

How Adults Can Foster Mathematical Development during Play

Perhaps one reason play contributes so much to children's mathematical development, as opposed to some forms of adult-centered drill and practice, is that children at play are free to select their own ways of investigating the objects in the environment. Human beings have a remarkable tendency to be fascinated by the actions that are just beyond what they can do well at that moment (Kamii, 1985). The eagerness to investigate and practice what they are just learning ensures that their skills will advance quickly. Children, therefore, usually choose to investigate objects and practice actions that are just beyond what they already fully understand. These choices also require them to coordinate and integrate what they already can do (Kamii, 1989). Thus, children's most effective learning mode requires that they have some freedom to choose what they will investigate. That freedom must extend beyond the choice of materials; it must include selecting the way in which to investigate things. Play is the unique time when freedom to investigate and high-level learning merge; it is no wonder that children are willing to play with mathematical relationships. The remaining question is what adults can do to encourage children's mathematical thinking to develop fully during their daily play.

Although adults cannot directly teach children mathematical understanding, they can employ critical strategies during children's play that will have a major impact on mathematical thinking and development. The research studies discussed earlier show how children can increase their mathematical skills by having experiences of these types. As these studies demonstrate, the adult's role in fostering children's mathematical development through play is best described as one that allows children to operate in their "zone of proximal development" (Vygotsky, 1978). This means that adults support children's mathematical problem-solving efforts in ways that encourage the children to operate at higher thinking levels with adult support than they could independently. Three effective strategies are (1) arranging the physical environment to make high-level mathematical thinking readily possible, (2) asking questions that encourage children to think mathematically during play, and (3) playing with children games that have mathematical thinking embedded in them.

Arranging and Enriching the Physical Environment

First, adults can place in young children's play environment objects that lend themselves to being put into relationships by young children. Some examples of objects that fit this description are:

1. a water table with clear plastic cups and bowls of different sizes
2. blocks of all sorts for building, measuring, and counting
3. a sand table with clear plastic vessels
4. trains and track for planning, building, counting, and hauling
5. large assortments of different kinds of buttons, beans, pebbles, dried pasta, leaves, and old shoes to compare, sort, stack, group, and count
6. snacks and napkins for children to count, arrange, and distribute
7. recipes to follow as children measure, weigh, mix, and distribute
8. fruit to count, slice, distribute, and eat

Given the similarities and differences in the objects children handle and study in their play, they will naturally compare those objects and place them in relationships, think about those relationships, and thereby engage in mathematical thinking. For older children, environments that call upon more complex mathematical understanding can be similarly arranged.

Posing Questions Requiring Mathematical Thinking

Adults can encourage children's mathematical thinking by asking questions that are answerable only by placing things into relationships and considering the nature of these relationships (Copeland, 1984).

Examples of Mathematical Questions

Three examples of such questions to young children while they are playing are:

1. Which of these two piles of jelly beans do you think has more? (Later) How can you find out?

The first question asks the child to relate one group of jelly beans to another and to define their relationship quantitatively with an answer such as "This group has more jelly beans." By asking the second question, adults invite children to explore and play with strategies to find out or to confirm the original conclusion.

2. Which of these balls of clay do you think is bigger? (Later) How can you make the smaller one the same size as the other one?

The first question asks the child to put the uneven balls of clay into a relationship based on volume and to describe that relationship; for example, "This red one is bigger." The second, more interesting, question opens the way for the child to alter the facts mathematically, and the child may do this in a variety of ways. A very young child, for example, may just flatten the smaller ball slightly so that it covers about the same area as the larger one and then declare the balls to be the same size. This shows that the child's view of *same size* is limited to the square inches something covers on a table. This answer, which is perfectly normal for a young child, is different from what adults mean by the question and from the answer adults would give. A more advanced mathematical thinker will either (a) stick some more clay onto the smaller ball (an act of addition), (b) take some clay away from the larger ball (an act of subtraction), or (c) do a combination of these, taking a little from the larger ball and adding it to the smaller. It is worth noting that children can engage in this mathematical thinking long before adults try to "teach" them arithmetic. Children develop these insights naturally if they are given appropriate materials and enough time to investigate them, which is an adult act of greater importance in the long run than any questions that are fashioned. This time for exploration during which to raise open-ended questions is also extremely important for older children.

3.   Here is a big glass bowl and here are some little glass cups. If you use these little cups to fill the big bowl with water, how many little cups of water will fill the big bowl? How can you find out?

To answer the first question the child has to engage in some very interesting mental acts. He or she has to imagine combining the water from several cups and then compare that imaginary total with the volume in the larger bowl. For the child merely to give a considered answer to this multistep question, whether remotely close to accurate or not, requires a display of very complex mathematical thinking. Whether or not there is even a response to the first question, the second question is a more approachable one because it involves what children often do at water tables and in bathtubs: they fill the little containers and pour them into the big one. That act, regardless of the level of mathematical reasoning the child has reached, also involves counting and thinking about part-whole relationships, fractions, and the uniformity of measurement.

Asking a child of any age a question such as "How can you find out?" invites the child to develop a plan of investigation, execute the plan, draw his or her own informed conclusions, and describe the results. Consider that scientists who have won the Nobel prize go through exactly the same steps. The question that asks a child to *find out*, therefore, invites the child to walk in the footprints of giants.

Cautions about Questioning

There are some cautions about when and how to use such questions. Adults must remember to focus on what the primary goals of engaging a child in mathematical thinking should be: (a) to give the child an opportunity to think mathematically in ways that are currently within his or her reach, and (b) to provide experiences through which the child will feel more competent and successful as a learner. If the question poses a problem that is completely beyond the children's current level of reasoning, and if adults continue to press them to perform what they cannot yet do, they will feel like failures.

There are four safeguards for questioning that will help children view mathematical thinking as a natural, enjoyable part of play.

1.   The questions must relate to the child's immediate play. Mathematical-thinking questions should relate to what the child is playing at that moment. That puts mathematical thinking into the authentic context of actual play. Children experience as contrived and intrusive questions that disrupt their play. The questions above, about the length of blocks, for example, are addressed to children already involved in using the blocks to make roads and fences.

2.   Questions should be posed with a light touch. If, after posing what seems to be a highly relevant mathematical question to a child, the adult sees that the child does not understand it, he or she should try to rephrase the question only one more time. If the child does not understand the second attempted question, the adult should change the subject or walk away. The child probably has not yet developed the insights needed to understand the problem; therefore, it is better to abandon that particular question for a while rather than try to force the child's thinking in the direction the adult had in mind.

3.   After posing the question, adults should let the child own the effort to solve it and its proof. Well-meaning adults often ask important questions, but, if there is any hesitancy on the child's part, they too quickly help to answer the question. In an effort to help, such adults may take control of the inquiry and reduce the child to little more than a passive bystander. If advancing children's insights and self-confidence is the goal, then it follows that every effort should focus on the child in the role of playful problem solver.

4.   When children reach a conclusion that is incorrect, even after they have worked on a way to find out, adults should let the incorrect answer stand. Adults have a passion for correcting young children's conclusions and thereby communicating that they do not value children's thinking. This can reduce children's sense of self-confidence and belief that they can solve mathematical problems. Instead, children need opportunities to encounter the prob-

lem again at another time, play with the possibilities for solutions, and rethink their answer when they are ready to do so.

A wonderful example of allowing children to do their own problem solving comes from an incident where some four- and five-year-old children had heard the story "Stone Soup" and were actually making their version of the soup. After all the ingredients were boiling, a boy pulled his favorite granite rock out of his pocket to be dropped into the broth. He announced, "Now you just watch. This here rock of mine is gonna melt some and get littler in the soup."

At this point the teacher had two choices. The first was to dismiss the child's belief in the melting rock. Teachers do this in a wide range of subtle and not-so-subtle ways. Some say the child's prediction is nonsense. Others hammer away with questions as penetrating and sharp as those of Socrates until the child collapses and says he was wrong. Others take a poll of the other children and, by majority rule, declare that the boy is wrong. Now, if the content under consideration were crucial to the immediate safety and health of the children, where errors in conclusions could endanger them in some way, then teachers have an absolute duty to make their health and safety paramount. Whether a stone melts at 212 degrees, however, is not one of those cases.

The teacher, therefore, thought again about what the purpose of the dramatic reenactment of the "Stone Soup" story was. Her purpose was to have children repeat the story's dynamics and observe the changes in substances when they are heated, all matters of mathematical and scientific inquiry. One goal for the children was to consider the interaction of hot water and things put into it. Another goal was for the children to feel competent as investigators. The teacher's effort to make the child change his prediction would have furthered neither of those goals. Instead, this very competent teacher said, "Oh, Jack, I think you have just made a prediction. Now, how could you find out for sure if your rock gets smaller in our soup?" Jack tested his prediction and later explained his findings to his classmates. Whether or not Jack's method of testing his prediction was scientifically adequate is unimportant. What is important is that he remained in charge and engaged in the mathematical act of comparing his rock's size before and after its journey into the boiling soup.

Initiating High-Level Mathematics in Game Play

The third strategy adults can employ is to encourage the playing of games that have a rich array of mathematical problems embedded in them. Many games require mathematical reasoning as the key to effective play. Whether these games are commercially made or homemade is immaterial; however, they can be of the greatest benefit in terms of children's mathematical thinking and learning if adults also play with the children and encourage them to think about the mathematical questions the games pose.

Each game described below requires the player to solve a range of logico-mathematical problems. The major mathematical processes required in the game are identified.

Jacks

As children throw the small rubber ball into the air, they must pick up a specific number of small metal jacks. For the child whose grasp of small numbers is highly developed, jacks offers little, but to the playmate whose understanding is not yet developed, jacks provides the concrete experiences of counting and grouping. From a scattered array of jacks the player must impose order by putting them into a relationship of equally related groups. In light of the rules that the exact number must be picked up and that in picking up a group of jacks the others may not be touched, each player watches the other's movements closely; that focused attention helps younger children build a more stable concept of number.

"War" with Playing Cards

This card game is best played by younger children by first removing all face cards so that the only cards remaining contain numbers and a group of pictures equal in number to the numeral in the corner of the card. In each round the players place a card face up between them, and the player with the higher number card takes the other player's card. Each player accumulates cards throughout the hand. When all cards are played, each player counts the number of cards accumulated, and the player who accumulated more cards wins. Kindergarten children have had wonderful arguments over the issue of whether six or eight is the larger number. When such disputes arise, they can use the number of symbols on the card to compare quantities. Comparing the number of accumulated cards at the end gives the children the opportunity to count relatively large numbers. Children who could not yet count past nine have compared much larger accumulations of cards by making little groups of two, one card from each opponent, until one player's supply of accumulated cards was exhausted; they then concluded that the player with cards remaining must have had more and was, therefore, the winner.

Connect Four

In this game children try to put four round chips into a straight line relationship—horizontally, vertically, or diagonally—to win. Players must not only make a plan to place four of their own chips in an acceptable line to win; they must also constantly imagine that they are playing the other player's chips. That is, they must anticipate the pattern of four planned by the other player and block it with their own chip to stave off defeat. Relatively young children enjoy this game as soon as they understand the concept of a number as large as four.

Checkers

Checkers, like Connect Four, requires Player A to try to figure out how to use Player B's checkers to A's advantage and how Player B's checkers can pose a threat. A player must constantly create relationships between his or her own checkers, the board, and the opponent's checkers. Player A can advantageously act on some of these relationships; other actions can cause A to lose checkers. When A is surprised and loses a checker to B, it is usually because a potential relationship existed that A had not seen until it was too late to stop it. This is high-level computation indeed.

Other Strategy Games

Some commercially made games that require thinking about relationships include Othello, Battleship, Jenga, Mastermind, Stratego, and the most relationship-rich game of all, chess. The strength of virtually all of these games is that children can play them all the way through middle childhood, and chess, of course, continues to entertain well after that period. Younger children begin playing each of these games by focusing exclusively on their own positions. That strategy quickly and consistently leads to losing. In time, children come to see that they must carefully relate their own play to their opponent's play if they are to have a chance to win.

As children's reasoning begins to become more logical, between six and eight years of age, they begin to see their own position in the game in relation to that of the other player, and begin altering what they otherwise might do by what they think their opponent will do. In checkers, for example, the child begins to think, "If I jump his checker, he can double-jump two of mine and his piece will be made a king. So, I don't think I am going to jump that one." This form of strategic thinking is highly logical-mathematical and leads to the ability to play such games as chess. Chess is best introduced to children after they have had extensive success playing with the other types of games mentioned here; further, it is probably better introduced by one child to another.

Complex Strategy Development

Children continue to play many high-level mathematical thinking games through the primary- and middle-school years. It is not the specific games or rules that keep attracting them to play but the advancing, increasingly complex strategies that their opponents bring to their play. After introducing Mancala and playing it with two dozen first-graders for a month, this author was surprised when one of the eighth-grade mentors, Nadine, invited him to play it with her. No adult in the Western world has ever been slaughtered by such a wide range of compelling strategies as Nadine used. Hoping to console and to coach the author after his fifth straight loss to her, she said, "I've noticed, Ran, that one's play becomes more powerful if one integrates several variables into the same move." Sounding more like a statistics professor than an eighth-grader, she noted that her own game improved greatly when she began to think two to three moves ahead, and she suggested that he do the same. Indeed. Most of the games discussed here (and many others) have the ability to grow in complexity as children's thinking becomes more abstract and complex across the years of childhood.

Niels Bohr, winner of the Nobel prize in physics and a mentor to many brilliant young physicists earlier in this century, had a lifelong reputation for playing and joking while in his physics lab in Copenhagen. One of his more serious-minded students protested one day, asking Bohr why it was necessary for him to play so much. Bohr replied that their work in nuclear physics was so serious that they could not afford not to play while engaged in it (Rhodes, 1985). Mathematical understanding is of enormous importance to children's future lives. How remarkable it is that they can build their most fundamental understandings of mathematical relationships while engaged in play. Adults can serve these purposes by providing children with the materials they need for play, encouragement through relevant questions, and a willingness to play with them. The task of nurturing children's mathematical development is so serious that adults, in the spirit modeled by Niels Bohr, cannot afford not to play while engaged in it.

Bibliography

Allen, L. E., & Ross, J. (1977). Improving skill in applying mathematical ideas: A preliminary report on the instructional gaming program at Pelham Middle School in Detroit. *Alberta Journal of Educational Research, 23,* 257–267.

Baroody, A. J. (1987). *Children's mathematical thinking: A developmental framework for preschool, primary, and special education teachers.* New York: Teachers College Press.

Copeland, R. W. (1984). *How children learn mathematics: Teaching implications of Piaget's research.* New York: Macmillan.

Forman, G. E., & Kuschner, D. S. (1983). *The child's construction of knowledge: Piaget for teaching children.* Washington, DC: National Association for the Education of Young Children.

Ginsberg, H. P. (1982). *Children's mathematics: How they learn it and how they teach it.* Austin: Proed.

Ginsberg, H. P., & Opper, S. (1988). *Piaget's theory of intellectual development* (2nd ed.). Englewood Cliffs, NJ: Prentice-Hall.

Hamilton-Speer, P. (1986). *Block building art.* Philadelphia: Please Touch Museum.

Kamii, C. K. (1985). *Children reinvent arithmetic: Implications of Piaget's theory.* New York: Teachers College Press.

Kamii, C. K. (1989). *Children continue to reinvent arithmetic: Second grade: Implications of Piaget's theory.* New York: Teachers College Press.

Kamii, C. K. (1993). *Children continue to reinvent arithmetic: Third grade: Implications of Piaget's theory.* New York: Teachers College Press.

Leeb-Lundberg, K. (1984). The block builder mathematician. In E. H. Hirsch (Ed.), *The block book* (pp. 30–51). Washington, DC: National Association for the Education of Young Children.

Piaget, J. (1952). *The child's conception of number.* New York: Humanities Press.

Piaget, J. (1973). *To understand is to invent.* New York: Grossman.

Rhodes, R. (1985). *The making of the atomic bomb.* New York: Random House.

Rogers, P. J. (1989). Teaching mathematics through play to primary school children. *Educational Studies, 15,* 37–52.

Rogers, P. J., & Miller, V. (1984). Playway mathematics: Theory, practice and some results. *Educational Research, 26,* 200–207.

Smilansky, S. (1968). *The effect of sociodramatic play on disadvantaged preschool children.* New York: John Wiley.

Vygotsky, L. S. (1978). *Mind in society.* Cambridge, MA: Harvard University Press.

Yawkey, T. D. (1981). Sociodramatic play effects on mathematical learning and adult ratings of playfulness in five-year-olds. *Journal of Research and Development in Education, 14,* 30–39.

Zammarelli, J., & Bolton, N. (1977). The effects of play on mathematical concept formation. *British Journal of Educational Psychology, 47,* 155–161.

Dabbling, Discovery, and Dragonflies

Scientific Inquiry and Exploratory Representational Play

Christopher R. Wolfe
R. Hays Cummins
Christopher A. Myers

At first blush, it may appear that science and play represent two extremes of a continuum. Science, for example, is often characterized by precision of measurement, rigorous methods, mathematical formulations, and skepticism. Play, on the other hand, is typically regarded as carefree, spontaneous, and fun. Upon reflection, however, one soon discovers many relationships between play and science. As readers of these pages will surely recognize, both play and science are complex, multifaceted human activities incorporating sociocultural, cognitive, kinesthetic, and affective dimensions. The sciences address phenomena as different in scale and substance as astronomy, psychology, and atomic physics. Scientists employ a range of research methods including dissection, field observation, and laboratory experimentation; they construct scientific theories ranging from mathematical models to reliable qualitative generalizations.

In a similar vein, play includes games with rules, sociocultural-dramatic make-believe, and "roughhousing." More than identifying and cataloguing the web of connections between various aspects of science and play, the authors of this essay argue that shared systematic inquiry is the heart of science, and that exploratory representational play in middle childhood has an important role in the making of a scientist. Toward this end they speculate about the relationship between scientific inquiry and exploratory representational play from a number of theoretical perspectives, share the musing of an active scientist, and describe the principles underlying *Dragonfly,* an inquiry-based scientific journal for children.

Of Play and Science

The literature on play and science is both varied and interesting. It includes reports of "basic" research and descriptions of application to educational practice.

Research on Play and Science

One of the "basic" research issues studied is the relationship of aspects of play to performance on scientific achievement tests and other tasks (Cooper & Robinson, 1989). Researchers have found, for example, that four-year-olds who had opportunities to play with materials and those who were given direct instruction using those materials produced approximately equivalent direct transfer in a standard transfer task (Smith & Dutton, 1979). Children who had play opportunities were faster and needed fewer hints, however, than those with direct training in learning an innovative task.

A study of kindergarten children found that children who engaged in free play and make-believe play yielded more divergent thinking than a control group of children when they worked on a task requiring the generation of alternative uses for a paper clip (Li, 1978). In a transfer task, make-believe play produced more divergent thinking than free play of other types. Another study compared the effects of children's playing with convergent and divergent materials (form boards and puzzles) on subsequent convergent and divergent problem solving (Pepler & Ross, 1981). This study found that the divergent play group performed better on divergent tasks, and the convergent play group employed more strategy-based moves in solving convergent problems.

A thoughtful review of the literature on the

relationship between spatial abilities, scientific achievement, toy playing habits, and gender roles found indirect evidence that socially stereotyped "boy toys" may promote spatial abilities, which are employed extensively in some kinds of scientific thinking (Tracy, 1987). In subsequent research, the investigator found a positive correlation between spatial ability and science achievement scores (Tracy, 1990). She failed, however, to find the hypothesized relationships between science achievement and gender, sex-role orientation, or toy-playing habits. Thus, although there appears to be a "logical relationship" between gender, toy playing, and science achievement, an empirical relationship has not yet been adequately demonstrated.

Taken collectively, these studies suggest a relationship between play, problem solving, and science achievement. While educators must be careful to avoid promoting sex-stereotyped toy-playing habits, there are strong reasons to believe that play is a powerful and underutilized vehicle in elementary science education.

Applying Play to Science Education

The body of "applied" literature addresses play-oriented curriculum reforms in kindergarten and elementary science education (Fine & Josephson, 1984; von Aufshnaiter & Schwedes, 1989). Moreover, in a review of the literature on play and science, other authors argue that, "When teachers incorporate guided play into science activities, children develop fluent and flexible problem solving skills. In addition, playful learning also tends to increase creativity and general cognitive achievement, and improves aptitude scores" (Severeide & Pizzini, 1984, p. 60). A similar argument contends that learning science and mathematics through play promotes curiosity, motivation to learn, and divergent thinking (Henniger, 1987).

Play is an important feature of a play-debrief-replay model of elementary science education (Wassermann, 1988). The first stage is *play*, during which the teacher creates the conditions for focused scientific inquiry. Teachers provide materials conducive to hands-on investigations and try to create an atmosphere that promotes the generation and testing of hypotheses, observation, recording of findings, and evaluation of results. The next stage is *debriefing*, in which children and teachers reflect on their experience. "The purpose of debriefing is to *help pupils extract meaning from their experiences*"

(Wassermann, 1988 p. 233). Finally, students *replay* with the same materials to extend their initial inquiries and replicate earlier discoveries. While not a panacea, the play-debrief-replay curriculum model captures one of the key elements of science: the spirit of inquiry.

The Spirit of Inquiry

Shared systematic inquiry is at the heart of the scientific endeavor. Scientific inquiry is systematic in the sense that it is well planned and well reasoned, and shared in that it occurs in a highly refined social context. Although science is often a solitary (even lonely) enterprise, the "rules of evidence" of the scientific community, rather than the whims of the individual scientist, guide scientific inquiry. Moreover, presenting one's results and interpretations to the scientific community is always an important part of the process. Shared systematic inquiry is central to domains as diverse as theoretical physics and experimental psychology. The spirit of inquiry places curiosity and questioning at the heart of what it means to be a scientist. Although scientists spend a great deal of time studying the work of others, a distinguishing characteristic of science is asking questions to which no one has the definitive answer. For a scientist, inquiry means asking questions about nature and getting answers from empirical evidence.

Exploratory Representational Play

Play is a construct that subsumes a wide range of behaviors. Others have provided thoughtful definitions of play (see Rubin, Fein, & Vandenberg, 1983). For present purposes, it is sufficient to say that the term *play* describes activities that are internally motivated, self-directed, spirited, and characterized by some degree of divergent "as-if" thinking (Spodek & Saracho, 1988). Although sports, board games, and make-believe may exercise some role in the development of a scientist, science is a process of shared systematic inquiry that leads to *exploratory representational play* in the latency years (roughly eight- to twelve-year-olds), a pivotal experience in the development of a scientist.

Defining Exploratory Representational Play

It has been said that psychologists would rather use each other's toothbrushes than use each other's terminology. This essay adds to the fracas by coining the term *exploratory representational play (ERP)*. ERP means intrinsically motivated, self-directed explorations with a significant symbolic or representational dimension. In considering the meaning of ERP, it is useful to distinguish it from related concepts. Exploratory representational play is not identical to exploration. Children and adults often engage in explorations that are serious, extrinsically motivated, other-directed, or otherwise outside of play. As discussed in the context of the journal *Dragonfly*, eight- to twelve-year-old children are capable of engaging in the shared systematic inquiry that is science. Such shared systematic inquiry, however, need not be "play" in any of the ways described above. Exploratory representational play can also be distinguished from the exploratory play common among infants and toddlers. Exploratory representational play is primarily goal-directed and cognitive, rather than kinesthetic in nature. Exploratory representational play consists of mental representations that are personally meaningful to the individual, and may or may not manifest themselves as drawings or stories.

Christopher Wolfe remembers an afternoon when he was nine years old that provides an example of ERP. His cousin and he had been collecting butterflies for some time and got the notion that they would like to find the chrysalis of a monarch butterfly. Considering what they knew about the monarch's habits, they explored unfamiliar woods and fields asking themselves, "What do we know about monarchs?" They recalled that the monarchs make their chrysalis on milkweed plants, so they first learned to identify milkweed by breaking the leaves of a likely suspect (the sap looks and feels like Elmer's glue—great fun. From there, they could easily identify milkweed at a distance by the leaves and pods; they then limited their search to fields. They spent hours looking for chrysalises and found two. They became completely absorbed in the hunt, losing awareness of themselves as self or ego. Although the goal of finding a chrysalis guided their actions that afternoon, their selection and maintenance of that goal was playful. It may seem paradoxical to adults, but although the goal was at the forefront of their thinking, and directed their actions and conversations, the goal itself was less important than the process. Indeed, had the goal not sustained their play, they probably would have found another, and may have clung to it just as earnestly. Moreover, if someone else had fulfilled the goal for them by handing them a chrysalis, they probably would have been disappointed.

Exploratory representational play need not take the form of play-in-the-woods (although those were important experiences for these authors). Richard Feynman, the Nobel prize winning physicist, writes of the laboratory he set up when he was eleven or twelve, made from an old wooden packaging box. There he would create electric lamp banks, fix broken radios, and dabble with electrical gadgets. He recalls spending an afternoon trying to find a burned-out resistor in his mother's friend's radio and notes, "I finally fixed it because I had, and still have, persistence. Once I get on a puzzle, I can't get off. If my mother's friend had said, 'Never mind, it's too much work,' I'd have blown my top, because I wanted to beat this damn thing, as long as I've gone this far" (Feynman, 1985, p. 9). As the authors argue below, Feynman's persistence is an element of ERP as well as a handy quality of radio repairers.

Theoretical Perspectives on ERP

Exploratory representational play is not the predominant mode of play for older children (see Bergen, 1988, p. 64, for a clear portrait of developmental trends in play); however, it does play a key role in the development of a scientist. Several theoretical perspectives, including Piagetian theory, constructivism, fuzzy-trace theory, Vygotsky's theory, and Csikszentmihalyi's notion of flow, provide useful lenses through which to view the relationship between the exploratory representational play of children and the shared systematic inquiry of adults.

Piagetian Theory

Assimilation and accommodation are the "twin engines" of intellectual development from a Piagetian perspective. Assimilation refers to processes of incorporating experiences into existing mental frameworks (schemata); accommodation refers to processes of refining schemata to suit experiences that do not easily fit into existing schemata. Although most of the exploratory play of infants and toddlers consists of assimilation (Piaget, 1962), ERP is, for the most part, play with accommodation. Exploratory representational play changes one's representation of the world. One author describes scientists, for example, as "people who play with ideas in order to change the complex into the simple" (Trumbull, 1990, cited in Goldhaber, 1994, p. 26). Much the same could be said of ERP. While some Piagetians might argue that ERP is not play at all, the authors of this essay argue that the *play* comes from playfully selecting goals that challenge existing schemata, and from the joy of exploration.

Constructivism

The perspective of constructivism represents another useful theoretical lens. From a constructivist perspective, people build mental representations of the world that serve as the bases for beliefs and actions. Learning is thus a process of constructing mental frameworks rather than recording facts. A psychologist argues that "effective learning depends on the intentions, self-monitoring, elaborations, and constructions of the individual learner" (Resnick, 1989, p. 2). With the possible exception of self-monitoring, these elements are characteristics of ERP. In ERP, the child constructs and elaborates cognitive structures through the process of exploration. Indeed, ERP is no fun if everything is known or readily knowable. A child engaged in the exploratory representational play of hunting for snakes, for example, may prefer looking in new places, or for new species, once she or he has reliably mastered a particular situation. These same tendencies are the mental habits of a scientist.

This relationship between scientific inquiry and ERP highlights weaknesses in traditional methods of instruction and indicates the importance of discovery-oriented learning in science education (Bruner, 1966; Cummins & Myers, 1992). The authors agree with Einstein that "it is in fact nothing short of a miracle that modern methods of instruction have not entirely strangled the holy curiosity of inquiry. . . . It is a very grave mistake to think that the enjoyment of seeing and searching can be promoted by means of coercion and a sense of duty" (cited in Henniger, 1987, p. 169).

Fuzzy-Trace Theory

This theory emphasizes the importance of "getting the gist of it." A relatively new perspective, fuzzy-trace theory has important ramifications for cognitive processes such as learning, reasoning, and memory, and enjoys strong empirical support (Brainerd & Reyna, 1990a, 1990b; Reyna, 1991; Reyna & Brainerd, 1989; Wolfe, 1995).

The basic claim is that when information is encoded, global gist-like patterns, impressions, and essences are encoded along with verbatim information. The result is a multifaceted fuzzy-to-verbatim representation of information. Individual knowledge items are represented along a continuum such that vague, fuzzy-traces coexist with more precise verbatim representations. Moreover, people exhibit a strong preference to reason with the vaguest gist-like representations allowable for a given task. (Wolfe, 1995, p. 86)

Research on cognitive development suggests that young children initially reason with verbatim representations; as they develop, they gain an ability to reason with increasingly fuzzy representations (Brainerd & Reyna, 1990a, 1990b). From a fuzzy-trace perspective, it is likely that ERP facilitates the encoding of useful and meaningful gist by creating tasks with "the right mix" of familiar and novel components. ERP seems ideally suited for creating and refining intuitions (gist) because it puts children into playful positions of attempting tasks where existing intuitions and verbatim representations are inadequate. Although science is a matter of precision, scientific insight and understanding require the development of useful and appropriate intuitions.

Vygotskian Theory

In recent years, developmental theories constructed by the Russian psychologist Lev Vygotsky in the 1930s have become increasingly influential in the United States. "A basic premise of Vygotsky's theory is that all uniquely human, higher forms of mental activity are jointly constructed and transferred to children through dialogues with other people" (Beck, 1994, p. 30). A key concept in Vygotsky's theory is the "zone of proximal development," which refers to the set of cognitive tasks a child cannot yet perform alone, but which the child can complete with a little help from adults or older children (Vygotsky, 1962). By working on tasks in the zone of proximal development with older children and adults, children create a "cognitive scaffolding" that enables learning and development to take place. In a similar way, ERP is often, although not always, an activity shared with others. It is possible to speculate, therefore, that ERP creates cognitive scaffolding, because it is generally conducted in a zone of proximal development. Although some Vygotskians may disagree, it is conceivable that ERP encourages children to play at tasks at the edges of their current competencies, and thus promotes development even in the absence of interactions with older peers.

Theory of Flow

Thus far, ERP has been discussed primarily in cognitive terms. But ERP is also a strong feeling in childhood, accompanied by a raw sense of wonder and a deep connection to nature and exploration. Sadly, this feeling of connection is difficult to reproduce in adulthood. On occasion, however, scientists do feel immersed in the process of discovery. "Flow" is one way to characterize this feeling (Csikszentmihalyi, 1979). Flow is a condition in which task and talent are in harmony. People experiencing flow find that their work "takes their full concentration, they feel in control, they lack self-consciousness, and they have goals that lead to immediate feedback" (Bergen, 1988, p. 57).

It is interesting to note that immediate feedback and the same feelings of concentration, control, and lack of self-consciousness also characterize the feeling of ERP. These feelings in ERP may motivate children to become scientists. Experiencing the feeling of flow in childhood ERP also may be a necessary prerequisite for experiencing flow in adult scientific inquiry. The joy in matching talent to task may well be born of childhood experience. Just as the spirit of inquiry is at the heart of science, it may be that flow is at the heart of the spirit of inquiry.

This section has briefly described ERP and considered it from a number of theoretical perspectives. The section that follows shares the reflections of a scientist on the role of play in his development, with the hope that these reflections will provide some insight on the natural development of ERP in scientists.

On Play, Science, and Salvation: Dr. Cummins Reflects

I grew up in a troubled home. My parents eventually divorced, but only after many years of intense struggle and pain. It is in this context that I found my love for science and nature. As I look back, I am convinced that this connection saved my spiritual life and helped in my search for personal identity.

When I was thirteen years old, I told my parents I was going to the city park to look for turtles. They didn't want me going to the place I really intended to go, the place I needed to be—the extensive woods in eastern Orleans parish, my own private rain forest full of oak trees hundreds of years old, thick carpets of ferns, and spooky, dense swamps. Here my adrenaline flowed to the max and I experienced real fear and respect for what I was about to do and see.

My friend Eddie met me at the bus stop, as we had planned. It took about twenty minutes for me to calm down as I stepped from the bus and walked into the woods. I focused my fear and used it to connect me with the creatures I was trying to find. I stopped. What was that I heard? Sssh . . . Ten feet away, under the ferns, a box turtle withdrew into its shell. Somehow, I heard the turtle. I found it. It was all that mattered to me. On a good day I might find ten turtles this way.

I relished the images of swamps, primeval in their splendor, moss draped across cypress limbs, bayous meandering through the submerged jungle, and majestic blue herons, alligators, and marshes. I was up at dawn, bonded with my friend, and excited by the day. I explored prehistoric Indian sites. I loved it! Nighttime images included indigo-ink darkness, being knee-deep in water; I walked through a different world. I listened to the calling of tree frogs; the sound was deafening. Something very special was happening. Even then, before I had ever heard the term *ecology*, I recognized that each species had a different role, a unique call, a special place to be. I used the flashlight to locate the source of the sounds, amazed by just how swollen their vocal sacs were. I wondered how they produced that sound and why they were so focused.

I felt danger. Was it genetic memory? Copperheads, water moccasins, pygmy and canebrake rattlesnakes were here, under a bush or beside a tree. I wanted to see them, find them, fascinated by their beauty and danger.

I could not believe it. A massive canebrake rattlesnake lay on the ground before me. There it was, over six and a half feet of reptilian splendor with fangs about an inch long. Its head was bigger than my fist and the rattles were over three inches long. It showed no fear. As I admired the snake, it slowly crawled away. I called Eddie to come see it. The snake had almost disappeared into the brush when Eddie, for some reason known only to him, grabbed the reptile by the tail. A trophy. About twenty rattles detached as the snake disappeared into the woods.

Later, we caught a magnificent king snake. These constrictors make wonderful pets and we were proud to have found it. I could not wait to bring him home and add him to my ever growing collection of herps.

My mother was a saint. She hated reptiles, but I guess she loved me. By the time I was thirteen, my entire backyard was turned into a herpetarium. Cages were full of snakes while the fenced-in yard held upwards of a hundred box turtles. My only real problem was the high escape rate of my captive reptiles. Turtles were easy to recapture in neighbor's yards. But once loose, snakes presented numerous logistical problems. Most were never seen again. A few were spotted by anxious folk who rushed to my home for me to save them from the snakes.

Full of sacred images of my youth, the outdoors were my intellectual playground and focused my curiosity. I found a tremendous source of identity in my connection with nature, and fuel for the fire of my creativity as an adult. Frankly, my early schooling had little to do with my development as a scientist. It was these free explorations that led me to where I am today. Science was the only career choice for me. As a child, my connection to nature seemed complete, more fun, more true than it does today. I still feel the excitement while doing research in a tropical lagoon, or while exploring the rain forest, or snorkeling over coral reefs. Teaching is special as well. Yet my enthusiasm has been tempered by life's many demands and responsibilities. As a kid, I was one with nature. As an adult, I only get to visit now and then. I miss it.

The experiences of this scientist point to a question that must be addressed in science education. If science and play hold in common a sense of wonder and a passion for discovery, why is science education often perceived as tedious and dehumanizing? The next section tells of a project designed to connect science and play.

Project Dragonfly

Based on the earlier discussions of ERP, should not scientists and science students feel blessed by the uncommon opportunity to shape their lives around their own questions? In the ideal world, scientists would employ many elements of play. Even the rules of research seem to support fun, just as the rules children create for themselves make their games more satisfying. For many, however, play and science exist in separate worlds. Without a sense of play, science may no longer seem worth doing. It is a matter of concern when practicing scientists become disenchanted. It is even worse when children lose heart. How can science regain and retain its sense of play?

In order for science education to harness the power of play, it must, to some extent, be internally motivated, characterized by a degree of "as-if" thinking, and personally meaningful—the same characteristics that define ERP. But there are three related characteristics of science education that often undermine play. These three characteristics are intriguing, for they may be healthy, even essential, for science in low doses, but they become drawbacks when they dominate the spirit of inquiry. These obstructions to the flow of play are labeled *clogs*.

Clogs in Science Education

1. *Duty and Other Extrinsic Expectations.* When external demands become too great, internal motivation is compromised and play becomes work. For science students, duty includes homework that is not personally relevant, rigid expectations from parents and teachers, and grades. Memorizing the bones of the body or the periodic table of the elements, for example, is a meaningless experience for most children if taught without regard for their own interests and understandings. Adults too often ask young investigators to sacrifice the spirit of inquiry to externally imposed requirements.

2. *Overspecialization and Isolation.* Over time, the topics of science have grown

narrower and the possibility of meaningful exchanges between professionals, even in related subdisciplines, has grown more remote. This overspecialization has, unfortunately, spilled over into elementary science education. Human beings construct personal meaning from a full spectrum of experience. Overspecialization and isolation, therefore, can make it difficult for children to connect their own questions and interests with the curriculum. Addressing the question of why the grass is green and the sky blue, for example, requires children to draw upon and integrate a range of scientific disciplines, including physics, biochemistry, and the psychology of perception. Overspecialization thus shuts off a wide range of questions that children might wish to explore. When the sciences are taught in isolation, the spirit of inquiry may be compromised.

3. *Objectivism.* Without adequate outlets for subjective exploration, science becomes a poor vehicle for play. Children who are taught that science is purely objective might reasonably conclude that science has limited ability to inform their lives. This problem is particularly apparent among children who are not part of mainstream culture (Cajete, 1995). When teachers ask children to write lab reports that must exclude motivations and feelings, for example, this can undermine children's enthusiasm for the spirit of inquiry. Objectivism can reduce science to a collection of uninteresting, unconnected facts rather than a fully human process of creating knowledge.

Antidotes for Clogs

To focus on inquiry as the basis for ERP and the remedy for the clogs of science education, colleagues at Miami University and the National Science Teachers Association have initiated an experiment in educational media, Project Dragonfly. Project Dragonfly is producing a new journal for children, *Dragonfly*, a teacher's companion, a parent's companion, and supporting computer list and World Wide Web services. *Dragonfly* will provide a national outlet for the first-person investigations and creative expressions of children and scientists. By giving children more voice in their own investigations in ways exemplified by this project, educators can reap the benefits of ERP—increased internal motivation, divergent thinking, and personally meaningful explorations—which are critical for healthy science education.

Existing "objective" science texts rarely include the voices of real scientists and real children, so the process and intrigue of investigation are lost. Project Dragonfly offers an alternative vision of science as a community of investigators. It will publish articles by children and practicing research scientists, and provide support and guidance for children conducting their own scientific investigations.

When scientists report first-person research, including the affective aspects of their experience, children can see science as a creative, human endeavor. Scientists reporting their own work can communicate directly the habits of mind used in scientific research. Scientists focus on questions and on process. They become frustrated and elated. They wrestle with different methods to address research problems. They consider factors that influence their observations and interpretations. They do not always come up with the "right" answers, and they generate a variety of alternative explanations. Scientists experience uncertainty, which is vital to science as a creative (and playful) pursuit (Rutherford & Ahlgren, 1989).

Even more important for creating an environment that supports ERP is to allow children to pursue and communicate their own investigations. Children naturally wonder about such questions as where rainbows come from and what smoke is made of. They ask great questions, yet until their questions and investigations are given respect, children will not perceive themselves as part of the community of science. By writing to their peers about their inquiries, explorations, and affective experiences, children come to see themselves as fellow investigators, challenging the traditional role of the scientist as a distant source of facts. Peer and adult modeling fosters children's self-confidence and their disposition to be self-initiating problem posers and problem solvers (Brooks & Brooks, 1993). Internally motivated exploratory representations can be personally motivated and externally validated.

In short, the purpose of Dragonfly is to provide teachers with a set of tools for facilitating their students' spirit of inquiry and harnessing the power of ERP. In cooperation with teachers and children across the United States, this project and the ongoing assessment of this approach to science education is getting underway. Collecting both qualitative and quantitative data will help to refine present understandings of ERP and continuously improve Dragonfly. This project is one way to enhance the link between play and science. Its goal is to bring back to students and to science professionals the spirit of inquiry that young children have in abundance.

This essay began by asserting that the spirit of inquiry is central to science, and that exploratory representational play in childhood lays the foundations for adult scientific inquiry. In the reverie, however, something may have been lost. Science is not always true to the spirit of inquiry. Flow is sometimes blocked. Rather than placing science on a pedestal, the authors feel a longing for the playfulness of those early explorations. It does not have to be this way! Dragonfly is a hopeful step toward a more playful community of inquiry, a place of dabbling, discovery, and Dragonflies. As Rachel Carson (1956) stated so eloquently:

A child's world is fresh and new and beautiful, full of wonder and excitement. It is our misfortune that for most of us that clear-eyed vision, that true instinct for what is beautiful and awe-inspiring, is dimmed and even lost before we reach adulthood. If I had influence with the good fairy who is supposed to preside over the christening of all children, I should ask that her gift to each child in the world be a sense of wonder so indestructible that it would last throughout life, as an unfailing antidote against the boredom and disenchantments of later years, the sterile preoccupation with things that are artificial, the alienation from the sources of our strength. (pp. 42–43)

Bibliography

Beck, L. E. (1994). Vygotsky's theory: The importance of make-believe play. *Young Children, 49,* 30–39.

Bergen, D. (1988). Stages of play development. In D. Bergen (Ed.) *Play as a medium for learning and development: A handbook of theory and practice.* (p. 444) Portsmouth, NH: Heinemann.

Brainerd, C. J., and Reyna, V. F. (1990a).

Gist is the grist: Fuzzy-trace theory and the new intuitionism. *Developmental Review, 10,* 3–47.

Brainerd, C. J., & Reyna, V. F. (1990b). Inclusion illusions: Fuzzy-trace theory and perceptual salience effects in cognitive development. *Developmental Review, 10,* 365–403.

Brooks, J. G., & Brooks, M. G. (1993). *In search of understanding: The case for constructivist classrooms.* Alexandria, VA: Association for Supervision and Curriculum Development.

Bruner, J. S. (1966). *Toward a theory of instruction.* Cambridge, MA: Harvard University Press.

Cajete, G. (1995). *Look to the mountain: An ecology of indigenous education.* Durango, CO: Kidaki.

Carson, R. (1956). *The sense of wonder.* New York: Harper & Row.

Cooper, S. E., & Robinson, D. A. G. (1989). Childhood play activities of women and men entering engineering and science careers. *School Counselor, 36,* 338–341.

Csikszentmihalyi, M. (1979). The concept of flow. In B. Sutton-Smith (Ed.), *Play and learning* (pp. 257–274). New York: Gardner.

Cummins, R. H., & Myers, C. A. (1992). Incorporating sciences in a liberal arts education. *National Honors Report, 13,* 2–5.

Feynman, R. P. (1985). *Surely you're joking, Mr. Feynman.* New York: Bantam.

Fine, E. H., & Josephson, J. P. (1984). Footprints, fireflies, and flight: Primary science magic. *Childhood Education, 61,* 23–29.

Goldhaber, J. (1994). If we call it science, then can we let the children play? *Childhood Education, 71,* 24–27.

Henniger, M. L. (1987). Learning mathematics and science through play. *Childhood Education, 64,* 167–171.

Li, A. K. F. (1978). Effects of play on novel responses in kindergarten children. *Alberta Journal of Educational Research, 24,* 31–36.

Pepler, D. J., & Ross, H. S. (1981). The effects of play on convergent and divergent problem solving. *Child Development, 52,* 1202–1210.

Piaget, J. (1962). *Play, dreams, and imitation in childhood.* New York: Norton.

Resnick, L. B. (1989). Introduction. In L. B. Resnick (Ed.), *Knowing, learning, and instruction: Essays in honor of Robert Glaser* (pp. 1–24). Hillside, NJ: Lawrence Erlbaum.

Reyna, V. F. (1991). Class inclusion, the conjunction fallacy, and other cognitive illusions. *Developmental Review, 11,* 317–336.

Reyna, V. F., & Brainerd, C. J. (1989). Output interference, generic resources, and cognitive development. *Journal of Experimental Child Psychology, 47,* 42–46.

Rubin, K. N., Fein, G. G., & Vandenberg, B. (1983). Play. In E. M. Hetherington (Ed.) & P. H. Mussen (Series Ed.), *Handbook of child psychology: Vol. 4. Socialization, personality, and social development* (pp. 698–774). New York: John Wiley.

Rutherford, F. J., & Ahlgren, A. (1989). *Science for all Americans.* New York: Oxford University Press.

Severeide, R. C., & Pizzini, E. L. (1984). The role of play in science. *Science and Children, 2,* 58–61.

Smith, P. K., & Dutton, S. (1979). Play and training in direct and innovative problem solving. *Child Development, 50,* 830–836.

Spodek, B., & Saracho, O. N. (1988). The challenge of educational play. In D. Bergen (Ed.), *Play as a medium for learning and development: A handbook of theory and practice* (pp. 9–26). Portsmouth, NH: Heinemann.

Tracy, D. M. (1987). Toys, spatial ability, and science and mathematics achievement: Are they related? *Sex Roles, 17,* 115–138.

Tracy, D. M. (1990). Toy-playing behavior, sex-role orientation, spatial ability, and science achievement. *Journal of Research in Science Teaching, 27,* 637–649.

Trumbull, D. (1990). Introduction. In E. Duckworth, J. Easley, D. Hawkins, & J. K. Smith (Eds.), *Science education: A minds-on approach for the elementary years* (pp. 1–20). Hillside, NJ: Lawrence Erlbaum.

von Aufshnaiter, S., & Schwedes, H. (1989). Play orientation in physics education. *Science Education, 73,* 467–479.

Vygotsky, L. (1962). *Thought and language.* Cambridge, MA: MIT Press.

Wassermann, S. (1988). Play-debrief-replay: An instructional model for science. *Childhood Education, 2,* 232–234.

Wolfe, C. R. (1995). Information seeking on Bayesian conditional probability problems: A fuzzy-trace theory account. *Journal of Behavioral Decision Making, 8,* 85–108.

Clinical Perspectives on Play

Karen Gitlin-Weiner

In the interest of exploring "normal" and pathological behavior, the field of psychology has gone through many changes in the conceptualization of developmental functioning throughout the life span. Until fairly recently, psychological theorists had limited understanding of the usefulness and applicability of play and the methods by which play could be used in therapy. Although interest in play began during the 1920s, the significance of the potential power of play as a change agent in treatment was underestimated and not fully examined for decades. Even within the various theories of personality development, scholars discussed the issue of play only in relation to a small fraction of human behavior.

Lacking a focused direction and innovative thinking about play, clinicians' interest in it as a method of treatment diminished substantially during the 1960s, 1970s, and first half of the 1980s. In the past ten years, however, clinicians have significantly expanded their play-related theoretical ideas, treatment techniques, and assessment tools. Play is currently recognized as a distinct and valid treatment modality that facilitates adaptive functioning in a variety of areas, such as social, emotional, cognitive, and personality development. Because it is a central experience for children as well as a natural form of communication for them, play provides a unique opportunity to step into their world, as well as to have a positive and direct influence on their adaptive functioning.

Understanding Play

Although play is an essential activity that serves many unique purposes during the life span, the disparity of viewpoints about its meaning has impeded the development of a unanimously accepted definition. Many descriptions of play are too broad or too narrow to be functional or discriminative. Perhaps the concept of play is too complex, diffuse, expansive, and dynamic to allow a singular explanation of its distinctive characteristics and components. Yet researchers continue their efforts to grasp the special elements of play that make it different from other human activities.

Common and Uncommon Definitions of Play

Some of the more common features that adults have associated with play suggest that it is pleasurable, the antithesis of work, free of extrinsic goals, an absorbing process involving the temporary loss of awareness of one's surroundings, nonliteral (having an "as-if" quality), spontaneous, an opportunity to bestow novel meanings onto objects, and an overt expression of wishes and hopes (Cattanach, 1992, 1994; DeMaria & Cowden, 1992; Garvey, 1977; Schaefer, 1993). These aspects are certainly relevant to the play of well-adapted individuals.

Psychologists who have observed the play behaviors of children with emotional disabilities, however, have challenged many of these commonly accepted defining characteristics of play. Children whose functioning has been compromised in other areas may show a variety of features in their play that are not similar to those generally stated, such as inflexibility, concreteness, constrictedness, impulsivity, irrationality, unreliability, inability to engage in or sustain imaginative play, and inability to use play to gain some distance from previously experienced negative and painful emotions

(Hellendoorn et al., 1994; O'Connor, 1991). Although the quality of their play is often significantly different from those whose developmental course is on target, these children cannot be described as being unable to "play." For, indeed, their type and quality of play are important keys to understanding the difficulties therapists need to address in assisting the children to return to more appropriate developmental growth patterns.

Functions of Play

In response to this dilemma, some authors suggest that it is more useful for mental health workers to focus on the role of play rather than on its definition (Neubauer, 1987; Solnit, 1987). From this perspective, play therapists assess whether or not their use of play in treatment would serve a specific purpose, rather than assessing whether or not a child was actually engaging in "play" behaviors. This focus becomes even more important when the clinician understands that play alone does not create an effective therapeutic intervention. It is the pairing of the therapist's responses and the quality of the therapeutic relationship with play that promotes change.

There are four primary functions of play: biological, interpersonal, sociocultural, and intrapersonal (O'Connor, 1991). The biological functions include learning basic skills, expending energy, and experiencing kinesthetic stimulation. Practicing and achieving the separation-individuation phase of development and acquiring social behaviors are the categories incorporated under interpersonal functions. Exploring cultural roles and rehearsing individual ones are associated with the sociocultural domain. Especially important to psychological treatment is the intrapersonal function of play, which encompasses mastering of conflicts, learning to negotiate external situations, and meeting a basic need to "do something" instead of remaining idle.

Other authors who have further delineated the intrapersonal and interpersonal functions of play suggest that play promotes the development of problem-solving skills (Knell, 1993; White, 1966), is a source of self-esteem (Lewis, 1993), facilitates the definition of personal boundaries (Lewis, 1993), provides opportunities to become exonerated from guilt feelings (Downey, 1987), and assists in the development of a working understanding of cause-effect relationships, predictions, and consequences (Bretherton, 1984).

Developmental Theories of "Normal" and "Abnormal" Play

Play skills are similar to social and cognitive skills, in that they follow a fairly specific normative pattern of development that moves along a continuum ranging from basic to very complex actions. At each stage, play is essential to the acquisition and mastery of multiple developmental tasks. This information is especially important when working with emotionally challenged individuals. Therapists must have a solid understanding of typical age-appropriate play behaviors in order to identify delays, deviations, fixations, or precocities, as well as to plan and implement effective treatment interventions. Therapists' understanding of how play competencies are achieved permits them to establish realistic expectations for the content of play, choice of play activities, types of toys, continuity of play, ability to differentiate reality and fantasy, and degree of interaction with the therapist. The use of play in treatment is most effective when the type of challenge the therapist presents matches the individual's skills and developmental level of functioning.

The most noted and relevant theories of play development are those of Piaget (1951, 1969), Peller (1954), Anna Freud (1965), Erikson (1977), Ekstein (1966), and Jennings (1990). Piaget's conceptualizaton of play is based on his more elaborate theory of cognitive development; that is, play is viewed as a forerunner to logical thought processes. With regard to play development, he suggests that there are three primary phases: practice/mastery or sensorimotor play (through eighteen- to twenty-four months); symbolic, representational, or pretend play (two to six years); and game play with rules (six years and older). During practice play, the primary focus of activities is on reflex actions, imitation of simple and complex behaviors, and the ability to modify the behaviors being imitated. The goal is to gain mastery over movements. Symbolic play begins when a sense of make-believe becomes part of the child's play at a conscious as well as unconscious level. The child's primary objective, at this point, is to be able to encode experiences into images that she or he can recall and combine. Finally, game play requires the development of concrete operational cognitive skills as well as a number of social skills. The goal is to be able to play cooperatively as well as competitively while thinking more objectively. Play, in each of these phases, assists in the process of assimilating and accommodating new information and experiences. Piaget suggests that, through play, children can "mentally digest" and better understand personal experiences and, therefore, make use of such developments to progress. Of particular significance to psychological treatment is Piaget's implied notion that therapists need to match clients' cognitive level to the play therapy techniques they employ in order to have a positive outcome.

Instead of relating play to cognitive development, Peller (1954) describes how the various phases are indicative of an individual's attempts to master specific intrapsychic conflicts. She suggests that the first phase (through twelve months) is associated with mastery of anxieties about the body; the second (twelve to twenty-four months) with anxieties about the loss of significant others; the third (three to five years) with anxieties about the loss of love; and the fourth (above five years) with anxieties about peer relationships as well as those stemming from the superego. As the child progresses through these stages, the content and style of play will reflect these themes. Play observations provide clues as to how the individual is reacting to and conquering these critical issues. Peller's contribution to the understanding of play development has provided an initial conceptual framework for using play to gain insight into the inner emotional world of the child.

Rather than focusing on inner discord, Anna Freud (1965) describes the role of play in fulfilling a positive need for pleasure. She suggests that children obtain gratification from various sources during development. In the beginning, infants derive pleasure from their own bodies and from their nurturers. By one year of age, the focal point becomes a specific "transitional object," followed by an indiscriminate liking for various toys at age two. Toys become less prominent after age three and fantasy becomes more significant. Finally, children begin to gain satisfaction in seeing the end product of a task. From this point forward, play behaviors dwindle as children delegate their energies to work and gain pleasure through internal constructs, such as the superego and ego ideal, instead of through extrinsic sources. Anna Freud's ideas provide the foundation for the under-

standing that play is not only an expression of inner conflicts but also serves a positive adaptive function.

Extending his theory of psychosocial development, Erikson (1977) provides a formulation of play development as it relates to how people interact with their external environment. His view outlines stages through which play proceeds, including the "autocosmos" (the world of self), which begins with the infant concentrating on her or his own body, and ends with an interest in playing with the mother's body. The next stage is the "microsphere" (miniature world) in which play includes a limited number of toys that children employ in contact with a small world of significant others. Finally, there is the "macrosphere" (shared world), when play actions involve a cooperative effort with a larger group of people. Erikson's work focuses the therapist's attention on the influence that interactions with others through play have on personal development. Extending his theory to treatment issues, he suggests that within each stage, play can also reflect an individual's attempts to understand and adjust to the effects of traumatic experiences. An important notion discussed by Erikson is that of play disruption. He indicates that when a child is unable to cope with internal stresses, play activities that touch upon these sensitive issues will be stopped and remain unfinished until the child achieves a resolution.

Ekstein's (1966) work brings forth yet another perspective. It describes play development as a process involving "deneutralization" of inner energy and an effort to gain the ability to delay impulses while finding adaptive solutions to problems. "Action without delay" (through twelve months) is the first phase and is characterized by immediate satisfaction through impulsive efforts, especially in the mother-infant relationship. Although play continues to be ruled by primary-process thinking in phase two, "play action" (through twenty-four months), children begin to use language to mediate between the desire for immediate gratification of needs and their actions. The third phase, identified as "fantasy play" (three to five years), results in children's thoughts becoming more functional as substitutes for behaviors; thus, the ability to use internal sources to meet certain emotional needs becomes available. Finally, in "play acting" (five years and older), children show the first signs of attempts to solve problems in various ways by trying them out in role-playing. They continue to improve in their ability to delay impulses and to seek alternative solutions in more complex and refined ways through play.

The three developmental stages of play described by Jennings (1990) include embodiment play, projective play, and role play. Embodiment play describes the sensory exploration by the infant of her or his environment. Stories and narrations are associated with further investigation of objects in projective play, Dramatic play, in which the players restructure life events to gain a better understanding of the self and the world, occurs in the role play phase. During the second two stages, characteristics of the earlier one(s) may be evident. This is a particularly important point that is applicable to all of the theories. Therapists' understanding of this idea is essential for accurate assessment of functioning levels and progress in treatment. Without this knowledge, therapists might mistakenly conclude that temporary regressions are more serious developmental delays.

Evaluating "Normal" and "Abnormal" Play

When evaluating and treating children, therapists must have a practical understanding of normal, deviant, delayed, and precocious development in all areas of child functioning, including play. The theories of play development provide general guidelines, but they lack the specificity therapists need for implementing effective interventions. A wide variety of play assessment tools is now available to delineate details of normative behaviors at different ages; however, these still require study and investigation in relation to children in clinical care.

The current literature regarding normal development indicates that play serves multiple purposes in the growth process, in particular to help children seek adaptive defenses; acquire skills; cope with conflicts, deprivations, or environmental demands; understand the self and the world; learn how to become active in shaping experiences; explore alternatives and possibilities before choosing a solution to a problem; and develop the capacity for relatedness. Children typically exhibit each of these behaviors at different levels of sophistication in various age groups (Cattanach, 1992; Fall, 1994; Gil, 1991; Hellendoorn et al., 1994; Knell, 1993; O'Connor, 1991; Plaut, 1979). Psychologically

healthy children spontaneously use such age-appropriate play behaviors in promoting their interpersonal and intrapersonal growth.

Children whose development is problematic, however, may have compromised abilities to spontaneously use these growth-promoting aspects of play. Their attempts to use play in a normative pattern often result in failure and reflect their deficiencies, delays, deviations, or excesses. Therapists can use play observations to identify children who are temporarily having difficulty negotiating a specific developmental task and design play interventions that help these children reestablish their normal course of development.

Therapists who use play as an intervention with children who have serious emotional and social impairments have a goal of assisting them in acquiring the highest possible level of functioning given their existing limitations, rather than having them achieve age-appropriate functioning. Because play reflects symptom patterns, these children often come to treatment with a history of ineffective and dysfunctional play behaviors. Children diagnosed as obsessive-compulsive, for example, may spend so much time setting up a game or play activity that they have little time left to play. Those children who have attention deficit disorders may begin multiple activities without completing any. Children with conduct disorders may directly express themes of power, sadism, or uncontrolled anger, and show little ability to use fantasy or verbalizations to mediate the intensity of these feelings. Those with borderline personality disorders may show magical thinking, narcissistic themes, fear of annihilation, and splitting of the good and bad characters. Children diagnosed as psychotic may have such chaotic play that it is difficult to follow and interpret; these children are often especially unable to use play spontaneously to master conflicts, achieve developmental milestones, or gain understanding of themselves and significant others. Therapists, therefore, need to choose carefully the play techniques and treatment goals that meet the children's current level of functioning and projected potential for change.

Play Theories and Play Therapies

Therapists who employ psychological treatment interventions use a number of theories that provide frameworks from which they may develop strategies, techniques, goals, and progress evaluations. These theoretical perspectives have grown out of clinical individual observations of adults that therapists have subsequently applied to children. Scholars have proposed modification of traditional theories and developed new theories as their understanding of human behavior has increased but, within each orientation, the global perspectives of a particular set of theoretical assumptions affect the functions they attribute to play.

With regard to treatment intervention, traditional modalities have focused on exposing and resolving troublesome feelings, conflicts, and traumas. More modern treatments have additionally concentrated on promoting positive growth in personal, family, and social domains; therapists have used play in treatment as a powerful instrument for addressing a wide variety of developmental issues and psychological problems.

The major theories are reviewed here in a simplified format, in which only the significant aspects pertaining to play are described. All of these orientations share the belief that play provides a fundamental forum for connecting with the child in a collaborative effort to resolve the presenting difficulties.

Over numerous sessions, play themes unfold and gradually form into a "play narrative" that describes the child's unique life story. In the play therapy process, the individual learns to develop new "scripts" or knowledge structures for use in diminishing confusions, ambiguities, and overwhelming emotions, and to gain a sense of self-control and a more realistic sense of self. One of the most important features of play use in treatment is that clients can do in therapy what they cannot do outside the therapeutic setting. Children who are overly controlled, for instance, can be spontaneous and free of inhibitions; chronically sad children can experience periods of delight and joy. Another reason why play is such an effective treatment modality is that it is a mental process, in which clients can experience thinking, imagining, pretending, planning, wondering, doubting, remembering, guessing, hoping, experimenting, revising, and working through (Mayes & Cohen, 1993).

Psychoanalytic Theory and Play Therapy

The oldest comprehensive personality theory in psychology, psychoanalytic theory, is based on Sigmund Freud's (1953) instinct theory, which posits that the underlying force motivating behaviors is an innate state of excitation seeking tension release. Healthy development occurs when an individual maintains appropriate expression of this tension through the counterbalancing functions of the three structures of the psyche: the id (irrational, impulsive, instinctive features), the ego (rational component), and the superego (moral aspects, conscience). The central goal in this type of treatment is to help an individual gain insight into unconscious conflicts (obstacles that impede development) through the use of interpretation and working through (changing defensive strategies) in order to enable a higher level of adaptive functioning. When working with children, therapists use play activities to provide the opportunity to accomplish this. For each play action, there are multiple levels of meaning that the therapist needs to understand and reconfigure to support positive emotional growth. Each action also plays a part in reconstructing the past by recovering repressed memories associated with intrapsychic conflicts. To this end, the therapist uses play to observe the child, gain information, develop communication, and assist the child in expressing feelings.

Because play is seen as a means of gaining mastery, the child's tendency to repeatedly reenact difficult or traumatic experiences in play ("repetition compulsion") is a spontaneous and healthy effort to gain a sense of inner control. While the psychoanalytic therapist thinks of play as a way to assist the individual in the pursuit of the "road to reality" (serving the needs of the ego), play is also understood to be guided by the "pleasure principle" (serving the needs of the id).

Anna Freud (1928, 1946, 1965) and Melanie Klein (1932) both believed that play provided a greater opportunity to understand and communicate with children. Freud was more conservative, however, believing that play was an indispensable means for developing a positive therapeutic relationship that could help the therapist connect with the healthier aspects of the child client. Of primary importance was the collection of material concerning unconscious themes as well as the discovery of how the client tended to manage conflicts (defense mechanisms); however, the focus of therapy moved from play to talking as soon as possible.

Klein's premise was that, for the young client, play was a natural substitute for verbalizations; she viewed the process of free association (used with adults) and free play as equivalent. The content of the play itself rather than the verbalizations that accompanied the play was the primary focus of diagnosis, interpretations, and therapeutic change.

Many other clinicians have furthered the understanding of play within the psychoanalytic orientation, from its traditional as well as more modern perspectives. One theorist suggested that, in addition to being an expression of inner tension, play may be used by clients as a source of wish-fulfillment and need-gratification, as an attempt to imitate others in order to explore new possibilities, and as a process of diminishing the negative impact of unpleasant external situations and traumas (Waelder, 1933). Another stressed the cathartic function of play because unvented feelings can safely be purged through the actions of fantasy characters (Greenacre, 1959). Describing play as intermediary "space" providing a bridge between the child's inner and outer worlds, another theorist stated that play is not only symbolic but also provides a very "real" and creative experience that is essential to emotional development (Winnicott, 1951, 1968, 1971). Through play, the child may obtain from others or achieve within the self what she or he had not acquired. Play also provides an opportunity to gain a different perspective on past events by reexperiencing what had previously been too painful to absorb. This therapeutic play occurs when both the client and the therapist are prepared to enter into the play as fully as possible in a cooperative effort to help the child find a way out of her or his problems (Winnicott, 1951, 1968, 1971).

In play, employment of "projection" allows the child to cast negative or unwanted self-attributes onto the inanimate therapeutic materials. The child is then able to gain some distance from the problem, reconsider it from different points of view, and achieve some sense of self-assurance that it is a manageable issue and not overwhelming. Because puppet figures, and not the child, can express a fear of monsters, for example, the child is able to take on the role of problem solver (instead of victim) and help the puppets learn to cope with and conquer this feeling in various ways (Lowenfeld, 1939, 1967). A method based on projection, called "the world technique," allows children to play out experiences, thoughts, and feelings through miniaturized figures, thus

broadening their self-understanding while working through difficulties that may be impeding healthy development. The creation of the play world provides the opportunity for the child to reveal the "forgotten self": "Play . . . expresses a child's relation to himself and his [sic] environment and, without adequate opportunity for play, normal and satisfactory emotional development is not possible . . . play [is] an essential function of the passage from immaturity to emotional maturity . . . any individual in whose early life these necessary opportunities for adequate play have been lacking will inevitably go on seeking them in the stuff of adult life" (Lowenfeld, 1967, p. 321).

Proponents of ego psychology (Cangelosi, 1995) add that the relationship between therapist and patient, through play, is of critical importance, because it can provide a "corrective emotional experience" as well as support the more adaptive functioning of the individual.

Humanistic, Existential, and Gestalt Theory and Play Therapy

Humanistic, existential, and Gestalt theories view the individual as an integrated whole and each individual as capable of having a basically good, creative, purposeful, and trustworthy core self. Thus, the therapy focuses on enhancing psychological health rather than on correcting pathology. Transforming the basic belief system of humanistic psychology into practice, Carl Rogers (1951) developed client-centered therapy, a nondirective approach to working primarily with individual adults. The fundamental supposition underlying his work is the notion that there exists a universal and innate need for "self-actualization." If there is an imbalance between an individual's functioning level and environmental demands that prevent the gratification of this drive, inaccurate attitudes about the self, others, and the environment will evolve. Therefore, the goal of treatment is to provide the opportunity for clients to modify perceptions, replace symptomatic behaviors with self-acceptance, and achieve a more mature level of emotional development. Therapists with this view provide a nonjudgmental relationship within a permissive setting, expecting clients to use their intrinsic ability to heal themselves.

Virginia Axline (1947) adopted the rationale of client-centered therapy and modified it for work with children. Her framework stresses that the natural activity of play encourages self-expression as well as communication. Play provides a "holding environment" in which children are able to use optimally their internal resources toward positive growth. The therapist reacts to the play in a reflective manner to empower the child with a greater understanding of the barriers preventing progress. Thus, the process of play itself is a therapeutic intervention, not merely an adjunct to another form of treatment (Kranz & Lund, 1993).

Another therapist suggested that the actual experiencing of the "sense of relatedness" during the therapeutic process is necessary for growth to occur (Moustakas, 1953, 1955, 1959). The security experienced within the alliance between therapist and client is the key component to a successful intervention, and their interaction during the play process is where this happens most effectively in the treatment of children.

This perspective describes four stages of change in observable emotional expression during the therapeutic process. The diffuse negative feelings of the first phase emerge into intensely hostile attitudes directed at specific individuals or events in the second phase. Through the experience of understanding and acceptance in the client-therapist relationship, these powerful emotions become less frenzied in the third phase and, at this point, positive emotions begin to emerge with the negative. In the final phase, there is an appropriate balance in feelings that leads to a more accurate perception of the self and the world.

Another perspective emphasizes the potential role of the birth trauma in preventing an individual from developing adequate interactions with others (Allen, 1942; Taft, 1933). Play during therapy assists the child to feel safe enough to experience an intense relationship with the therapist, allowing previous anxieties and fears to diminish and not continue to hinder future relationships with significant others.

Gestalt play therapy is a process that provides activities and experiences to assist the child in strengthening the positive aspects of the self that have been suppressed, restricted, and/or lost (Oaklander, 1993, 1994). Play furnishes a secure setting in which the child is able to establish an adequate level of self-regulation. Positive changes are more likely to occur by heightening the therapist's as well as the individual's awareness of what she or he is doing and how it is being done.

Cognitive-Behavior Theory and Play Therapy

Cognitive-behavior therapy is derived from behavior and cognitive therapies, which developed separately before being united. Behaviorism (Bandura, 1969; Skinner, 1938; Wolpe, 1958) is based on the contention that behavior is lawfully determined, predictable, and environmentally controlled. Interventions are directed toward enabling new learning to take place or helping the client unlearn maladaptive habits through the use of reinforcement. Cognitive theory (Beck, 1963; Beck et al., 1979; Ellis, 1962; Kelly, 1963) focuses on internal thought processes (beliefs, assumptions, interpretations, logical distortions, imagery, and attitudes) and how these affect emotional experience, behavior, and personality development. Cognitive therapy aims to alter the underlying assumptions that dictate the client's perceptual views that have led to negative automatic thoughts. These theories have promoted the creation of multiple interventions designed to enhance self-management and self-regulation. Treatment is systematic and goal-directed, and it requires the client to be an active participant.

In cognitive-behavioral play therapy, the therapist is actively involved in selecting the direction of the play by introducing themes and toys in a specific manner that directly addresses the presenting problem(s) (Knell, 1993). The play, therefore, takes on an educational role in that specific skills, different problem-solving strategies, and alternative cognitions or behaviors are modeled as well as practiced. For instance, the act of playing may serve to relax an overly anxious child while the therapist gradually presents the child with the source of the phobia through a systematic desensitization hierarchy. In a less direct approach, puppets may model appropriate behaviors or coping self-statements to a child who has been socially unsuccessful because of difficulties controlling anger. Through fantasy storytelling, repetitive nonproductive interactions between parent and child may be successfully resolved by developing more adaptive response patterns. In this way, the child client can replace maladaptive thoughts, feelings, and behaviors with more functional and age-appropriate ones. Play provides the child client with the opportunity to try out new ideas through role-playing or to participate indirectly by acting out the alternatives through play characters, such as puppets, dolls, and story figures. In effect, the play acts as a scientific experiment in which the client is able to identify a problem, look at the evidence, test alternatives, examine the consequences, and make choices for personal change by reenacting critical situations in a variety of ways.

Other Theories and Play Therapies

Some play therapy theories and approaches focus on the individual child client, as do those previously discussed. Others treat the child within a group-focused context.

Individual Child-Focused Approaches

The beliefs of Jungian play therapy (Allen & Levin, 1993; DeDomenico, 1994; McCalla, 1994) fall between the psychoanalytic and client-centered approaches. This theory emphasizes the importance of the unconscious belief in development as destiny that moves forward by the search for "wholeness and completion." This theory also views personality as both the product and container of ancestral history (individuals are molded by the cumulative experiences of past generations). Within this framework, play is an important medium in which child clients can gain an understanding of the central theoretical suppositions while transforming their painful selves into healthier ones. Therapists observe children's patterns of play, which reflect such difficulties as emotional chaos and ineffective conflict resolutions, and use this information to help child clients gain a higher level of functioning. The therapists impose very few limits because they assume that individuals will automatically choose play activities that are relevant to their personal struggles and developmental concerns. Sand play and play with miniature figures, however, are especially important to this form of treatment. In addition to the standard therapeutic toys, Jungian play therapists provide many unique items that hold ancestral symbolic meaning.

The first structured therapeutic use of play was based on the principles of release therapy (Levy, 1938). This work evolved from work with children suffering from night terrors and posttraumatic stress disorders. Treatment involves repeatedly re-creating the traumatic experience within a secure and supportive environment until the associated negative thoughts and feelings diminish and become assimilated into nondestructive functioning. The introduction of structure in the play assists the client in managing overwhelming stress and provides

time to recover when the client becomes over-stimulated.

Another structured approach encourages repeated expressions of powerful, negative emotions such as fear and rage without any negative consequences (Solomon, 1938). Equally important to a successful outcome is the redirection of this excessive emotional energy to more appropriate play behaviors. A version of this approach, structured play therapy, focuses the child client on a specific play situation, in which the goal is for the child to work through the specific critical issue being presented (Hambridge, 1955). There are eleven play situations used, which address common conflicts, including sibling rivalry, release of repressed aggression/hostility, peer attack, punishment or control by elders, separation, genital difference, invisible child in the bedroom of parents, birth of a baby, acting out a dream, other individualized play, and testing play (Solomon, 1938).

Limit-setting therapy (Bixler, 1949; Ginott, 1959, 1961) suggests that the process of limit setting is actually a principal means of effecting change. Maladaptive behaviors are seen as the result of a lack of trust in adults to provide consistency and protection. With limits, the child is able to learn to express intense feelings in more appropriate ways that have positive rather than negative consequences. Play involves having many rules concerning the use of toys, such as not destroying property, not throwing toys (unless made for this purpose), and not removing toys from the room. Because the child clients cannot express hostile feelings through the destruction of materials, therapists encourage them to use the toys in more acceptable ways to express the same feelings.

Adlerian play therapists (Kottman, 1993, 1994) believe that there is a basic striving to gain a sense of "connectedness" with others as well as an underlying capacity to make choices and compensate for weaknesses. This form of treatment is based on Alfred Adler's (1927) holistic theory that depicts the individual as indivisible, self-consistent, self-determined, and unified, yet embedded in a social context. Play is used to establish a social interest in others through the relationship with the therapist, to understand inaccurate belief systems and inappropriate attitudes toward the self and others, to teach the individual to be responsible for setting and achieving goals (making unrealistic goals conscious), to encourage acceptance of strengths and weaknesses (bringing into awareness feelings of inferiority and compensatory superiority originating in the infantile experience of being powerless and helpless), and to convey a sense of hope and encouragement. This theory stresses the importance of working with family members as well as peers within the play context, instead of working alone with the child, because the child constructs and modifies attitudes and behaviors within these relationships.

Involvement of others in play sessions is also part of filial therapy (B. Guerney et al., 1966). The therapist supervises play interchanges among family members instead of directly engaging in play activities with the child. After parents have practiced the nondirective play therapy techniques, the therapist provides instruction in basic behavioral procedures to enhance child management. This approach is multifaceted and serves as a therapeutic medium for the child, a learning laboratory for the parents, and a means of improving parent-child relationships.

Theraplay (Jernberg, 1976; Jernberg & Jernberg, 1993) is a treatment modality based on the belief that a deficiency in emotionally positive sensory experiences during infancy has the potential for resulting in psychological difficulties in later life. Theraplay techniques are primarily nonverbal, direct, and physical, with play activities focusing on primitive and nurturing interactions such as feeding, dressing, structuring, challenging, and intruding. The therapist conveys an atmosphere of optimism with an emphasis on development of healthy relationships through lighthearted, empathic, and playful exchanges. Growth is an outcome of having an adult directly attend to the child's narcissistic needs while providing the developmentally appropriate amount of discomfort (frustration) necessary to remind the child of reality limitations. The goal of this type of treatment is to provide an intense bonding experience, which did not adequately occur in early developmental years. It is particularly successful with children who are autistic or have other developmental delays that make them less responsive to more traditional play therapy approaches.

One of the more recent interventions is ecosystemic play therapy, which is a "hybrid model that derives from an integration of biological science concepts, multiple models of child psychotherapy, and developmental theory" (O'Connor, 1994, p. 61). This form of therapy sees children's functioning as a reflection of their interpersonal interactions with various systems such as family, school, peer, cultural, legal, or medical. Play develops during the six phases of treatment—introduction, exploration, tentative acceptance, negative reaction, growing and trusting, and termination—to promote healthy development in the biological, interpersonal, intrapersonal, and sociocultural spheres. This method attempts to combine and integrate the various functions of play into one inclusive treatment approach.

Group-Focused Approaches

Although many theories and interventions primarily focus on the treatment of the individual child client, each modality also has the potential to be practiced with groups, including family groups. Adaptations of some of these models have resulted in a variety of methods that are specifically applicable to the group play therapy process. This approach focuses on the patterns of interpersonal behaviors between participants and group leaders, with individual needs addressed only as related to the group (O'Connor, 1991; Rothenberg & Schiffer, 1976; Semonsky & Zicht, 1976; Slavson, 1976; Van de Putte, 1994). The therapist directs attention to common treatment goals surrounding specific issues such as socialization skills, coping with divorce, surviving abuse, or managing chronic illnesses. The child clients feel supported and understood because they learn that they are not the only one who is suffering with their problems. Group dynamics may show supportive responses, catalytic reactions, or even collective negative responses in which the members unwittingly reinforce the pathology of each other.

The central objective of the majority of group play activities, which include role-playing, structured games, and collaborative art work, is to assist members in developing age-appropriate interpersonal skills. Therapists have gleaned multiple therapeutic effects from this form of play therapy. For instance, children who lack social skills may be able to learn how their individual problem behaviors have an impact on their relationships with others. The children can practice corrective modifications of maladaptive interpersonal behaviors. They can acquire some essential skills, such as selecting and attending to relevant stimuli, remembering those stimuli, sequencing stimuli or events, predicting logical sequences, anticipating consequences of actions, appreciating feelings, managing frustration, inhibiting actions, and learning to relax (O'Connor, 1991, p. 324).

Play-related child groups allow children to have experiences in the play group that are similar to those they might encounter elsewhere, but the safety and structure of the group enable them to be more productive in learning how to handle problems. That is, the children can test effects of acquired behavioral changes in the controlled environment where they can receive constructive feedback. Because these new skills have developed from direct experience, they are more likely to generalize to situations outside of treatment.

Children's play in the context of family therapy can be useful in uncovering and differentiating between dysfunctional and functional familial patterns (Ariel, 1992; Gil, 1994; B. Guerney et al., 1966; L. Guerney & Welsh, 1993; Schaefer & Carey, 1994; Van Fleet, 1994). Observations of play interactions among family members provide rich information on overt and covert communication patterns, individual and group expectations, and the multiple roles each member plays. Therapists can directly observe and treat attitudes, alliances, underlying feelings, nonverbal family functioning, goal-achievement processes, and problem-solving methods. Play interventions with families may take on a variety of formats, ranging from teaching the parents to serve as change agents as in filial therapy (B. Guerney et al., 1966; L. Guerney & Welsh, 1993; Van Fleet, 1994) to having the therapist play a more traditional role in helping all of the family members work together to change the family system (Ariel, 1992; Gil, 1994; Schaefer & Carey, 1994). In either case, there is an underlying assumption that the child's symptoms express the family's difficulties. Therapists' interpretations of play behaviors facilitate the understanding of how each member of the family contributes to the presenting problem.

The play environment provides a supportive place to test the limits and meanings of family relationships as well as to reenact current conflictual patterns at conscious and unconscious levels. Through play, the child becomes a productive and active member of the treatment team who is directly able to contribute to the process of change. Because the play activities provide an indirect method of communication through the use of metaphors, the child feels less intimidated in confronting the parents. On the one hand, the child can challenge previously undisclosed issues (family secrets) and resolve them with less anxiety. On the other hand, the parents have the opportunity, often for the first time, to see the issues from the child's perspective. Additionally, the parents are able to experience the problem as being part of a shared systemic development rather than feeling as if they have been the sole source of blame for what has occurred.

Because children's comfort with the play format is usually greater than the parents', children are able to take the lead in helping the family become psychologically available to therapeutic intervention. As therapy progresses, the once difficult child can become the family hero. Over the course of treatment, the family is able to learn and practice more productive communication patterns as well as coping strategies through playful experimentation. They eventually establish more appropriate lines of authority, thereby decreasing destructive power struggles. Since change occurs through the use of play, and play is a natural activity of childhood, the changes that occur in treatment are likely to be maintained at home, where family members can easily replicate these skills.

The Therapeutic Functions of Play

In the past fifteen years, a variety of formal and informal diagnostic techniques has incorporated play activities and observations. Therapists generally use these procedures as an adjunct to more traditional investigative methods, such as interviews, questionnaires, and standardized testing. Although many of the techniques do not yet have accompanying normative data, the information they glean from the tasks can be vital to confirming or disproving hypotheses about the presenting difficulties. Additionally, play provides the opportunity to assess many factors that are not included in other assessment procedures. Some of the advantages of using play in the assessment process include the ability to detect emerging skills that occur at a low frequency, observe problem-solving skills in action, observe the spontaneous use and integration of acquired skills, determine motivational factors, determine self-regulation and arousal levels, and repeat testing without a learning effect.

Although therapists have realized the importance of play in the therapeutic process, they have rarely identified the actual curative elements that are brought forth through the use of play. In general, they acknowledge that play provides an opportunity for child clients to come to a new level of awareness of their individual situation, to experience the self as having choices and being able to try out new behaviors, and to explore the value of making changes. The question remains, however, about what specifically makes play so special in comparison to other forms of child treatment. That is, what are the unique characteristics of play that result in its being such a powerful change agent? Two authors have recently proposed some initial answers to this question.

Change as a Function of the Nature of Symbolic Play

Ariel (1992) focuses on the structural and psychosocial properties of make-believe play. This perspective views symbolic play as a mechanism for regulating the level of emotional arousal when confronting sensitive issues that bring forth intense and potentially overwhelming feelings such as fear, anger, joy, and sadness. Play not only enables child clients to address their problems but also provides the framework for repairing inaccurate perceptions or conclusions that they may have developed. These changes occur through a sequence of events. First, the child expresses the problem through play themes that elicit varying levels of arousal. When overstimulation begins to occur, children can spontaneously and immediately change play characters and themes to introduce more soothing components. Once they obtain relief and diminish the threat of feeling out of control, they can return to the original problem. In this way, children can safely replay negative themes until they no longer elicit powerful feelings. Each time they reenact the themes, the children make progress toward their goal(s), using the processes of habituation (emotions become numbed), cognitive restructuring (less threatening perceptions and cognitions associated with the problem replace original ones), deconditioning (associating a negative theme with pleasant stimuli), and mastery (gaining control by combining two themes, reversing frightening situations, or introducing new and protective elements) (Ariel, 1992).

In addition to the function of regulating emotions, there are seven other important properties of symbolic play that make it such an effective treatment tool:

1. *Play framing,* in which the theraeutic process challenges and weakens invalid and unconscious attitudes that maintain inappropriate behaviors

2. *Owning and disowning the content of play,* which allow the child to reconsider and eventually abandon inaccurate convictions about self and others in which she or he has become invested

3. *Basic duality,* in which the child plays two roles, both controlling the play acts and observing them, thereby allowing the child to safely recognize the conflict between what she or he admits to and denies doing

4. *Symbolism or "arbitrariness of the signifier,"* in which discretionary assignment of symbols to play items signifies something else that has little similarity to the real object (e.g., a crayon or stick may be a sibling)

5. *Covert communication,* which provides an indirect way for the therapist and child to exchange messages, thereby detouring resistance to the therapeutic process

6. *Symbolic coding,* in which participants use representational language instead of objects to safely express painful messages

7. *Possible worlds,* in which clients can explore formerly unrealized conceivable ways of understanding their situation, whether they are actual potentials, unlikely possibilities, or improbable scenarios (Ariel, 1992).

Change as a Function of General Play Factors

Schaefer's (1993) consideration of the aspects of play that make it therapeutically valuable is not limited to make-believe activities. This author delineates fourteen essential curative play factors; these are only preliminary, because further inquiry is expected to reveal other components.

1. *Overcoming resistance* is a factor specific to play because it is an interesting and natural activity for children. By virtue of the fact that young clients are more comfortable with this format than sitting and talking, a working alliance is easier to establish. In play, they are less likely to act out their defiance in a disruptive and direct manner. Instead, they may express through play figures such resistant themes

as fear of new encounters, fear of further victimization, loyalty issues, and lack of motivation to own the presenting problems. As a result, the children are more likely to be responsive to interventions that will help them conquer these issues. With a greater level of receptivity to the therapeutic process, they tend to accept an active role in striving for positive change.

2. *Communication* through play leads to an increased understanding of the self as well as others. Play is a unique type of interchange because it is nonverbal and drive-dominated. It allows children to express conscious and unconscious thoughts and feelings that they cannot express in words. Because children are able to explain themselves in play in any way that is personally effective, there is an increased probability of revealing critical issues within the context of the total individual.

3. *Mastery or competence* is the element in play that assists the child in reaching functional levels of self-esteem because it promotes proficiency in all areas of development. In this sense, play is a "self-motivated activity" that produces a sense of effectiveness in being able to have an impact on the environment. Through play activities, children can practice appropriate interactions with significant others and adaptive responses to the demands of the immediate world. As children gain a sense of inner control and begin to believe in their own power and ability, they feel less vulnerable and are more likely to take responsibility for their own actions.

4. *Creative thinking* is an essential element for effective problem-solving skills. Through playing out their situations, children are able to consider multiple possible alternative responses and their consequences before choosing those they will actually implement. In this way, they are able to experience successful solutions repeatedly, which will, in turn, support positive emotional growth. Because children are able to acquire the knowledge and experience necessary to develop divergent thinking in a hands-on experience, Schaefer thinks that play is superior to direct verbal instruction when

children need to enhance their problem-solving skills.

5. *Catharsis* provides an opportunity for the safe discharge of emotional tension onto the play materials. The resulting sense of relief stems from the motoric expression of intense feelings such as anger, grief, or anxiety. Additionally, the processing of the personal meaning of these feelings to the individual increases the understanding of her or his own emotional energies. Prior to release, pent-up feelings tend to interfere with development. Once children begin to express them, the intensity of the feelings decreases, making the children more likely to move forward in their ability to successfully function in their environment.

6. *Abreaction* involves an intense discharge of affects associated with past stressful life events. Through this property of play, children are able to use the materials to replay traumas until they accomplish mastery. Because they are in control of the reexperiencing of the event, the associated anxiety can decrease. As a result, they can become receptive to a different perspective on the situation. They are then able to imagine a more positive outcome to their problem.

7. *Role-play* allows children to try out new behaviors and different emotions. Additionally, it encourages a better understanding of the perspectives of others and how these differ from the children's own views. The identity of the self as a separate entity, the experience of empathy, and the development of prosocial behaviors are just a few of the advantages of this property of play.

8. *Fantasy* helps children gain a sense of control and compensate for unmet emotional needs and/or weaknesses in general functioning, such as impulsivity or poor organization. Through fantasy, children are able to safely explore repressed ideas, feelings, and memories; resolve conflicts; and practice different coping techniques. Additionally, fantasy can be a source of pleasure and, therefore, promote healthier levels of functioning. With an active imagination, a child has a limitless potential to enhance emotional development while overcoming delays and/or deviations.

9. *Metaphoric teaching* occurs when children act out play themes through miniature play figures, role-playing, or storytelling characters. As the therapist develops an understanding of the child's issues that interfere with functioning and further development, the therapist has the opportunity to enter the play in order to provide alternative ways of conceptualizing the child's situation as well as more productive ways of solving problems. Additionally, the therapist can present various attitudes and belief systems as a model for the child to adapt, replacing the dysfunctional ones the child has developed. The therapeutic process can help play characters to control impulses, reduce excessive negative feelings, and express their conflicts in nondestructive ways. The child attains a sense of hope and collaborative work with the therapist as she or he begins to identify with these figures and repeatedly experiences a positive ending to the stories.

10. *Corrective emotional experience* allows for the development of an accepting sense of self and pleasure, in relationships.

11. *Attachment formation* through play facilitates a bond between the child and therapist.

12. *Relationship enhancement* involves a bond that is not only a working relationship, but one that is warm, respectful, and connected by mutual feelings of liking each other. These three together (10, 11, 12) are essential to the development of the positive, loving self and also important in minimizing the child's vulnerability to the potentially devastating effects of traumas.

13. *Positive emotion* is "the most apparent and fundamental aspect of play" (Schaefer, 1993 p. 12). As such, it contributes to the child's sense of well-being and is able to counteract the effects of stressful experiences. This aspect of play provides emotional relief and restores the energy as well as the persistence that children need to face and resolve problems. The pleasure and enjoyment associated with play can, additionally, assist in the process of "mastering developmental fears." Through play, the child comes to understand that many people share common fears (strangers, the dark, monsters, robbers) and minimize the associated anxiety so that it does not impede functioning.

14. *Game play* is a facilitator of social, emotional, and cognitive development. In learning to follow the rules of games, children experience impulse control, emotional regulation, competitive behaviors, and cooperative interactional skills. Additionally, game play enhances other aspects of play such as the therapeutic alliance, communication, fantasy, catharsis, sublimation, insight, reality testing, ego enhancement, recuperation, and adaptive expression of intense emotions (Reid, 1993).

Psychological interest in play has included a focus on descriptions of normal as well as pathological play development; on the role of play in personality development; on the use of play as an assessment tool; and on the therapeutic value of play in treating children with emotional disabilities and their families. Although play itself is difficult to define, many scholars recognize that play, in many variations, has an essential and universal role in the evolution of a well-adjusted and emotionally stable individual.

Although many acknowledge play's healing powers, those who engage in the play therapy process are aware that there still remain many gaps in our understanding of why and how play works. The presently existing theoretical base of information has only limited supporting empirical data. Even so, play has survived as a vital method of understanding and treating children; in fact, in the past ten years, there has been a resurgence of interest in it, which has resulted in a proliferation of new ideas, techniques, and procedures. Further exploration of uses of play in therapy is likely to confirm what therapists already know, expand their understanding, and extend their ability to implement playful therapeutic techniques.

Bibliography

Adler, A. (1927). *The practice and theory of individual psychology.* New York: Harcourt, Brace and World.

Allen, F. (1942). *Psychotherapy with children.* New York: Norton.

Allen, J., & Levin, S. (1993). "Born on my bum": Jungian play therapy. In T. Kottman & C. Schaefer (Eds.), *Play therapy in action* (pp. 209–244). Northvale, NJ: Jason Aronson.

Ariel, S. (1992). *Strategic family play therapy.* New York: John Wiley.

Axline, V. (1947). *Play therapy.* New York: Ballantine.

Bandura, A. (1969). *Principles of behavior modification.* New York: Holt, Rinehart, and Winston.

Beck, A. (1963). Thinking and depression. *Archives of General Psychiatry, 9,* 324–333.

Beck, A., Rush, A. J., Shaw, B. F., & Emery, G. (1979). *Cognitive therapy of depression.* New York: Guilford.

Bixler, R. (1949). Limits are therapy. *Journal of Consulting Psychology, 13,* 1–11.

Bretherton, I. (1984). Representing the social world. In I. Bretherton (Ed.), *Symbolic play: Reality and fantasy* (pp. 3–41). New York: Academic.

Cangelosi, D. (1995). Psychodynamic play therapy. In A. Eisen, C. A. Kearney, & C. Schaefer (Eds.), *Clinical handbook of anxiety disorders in children and adolescents* (pp. 439–460). Northvale, NJ: Jason Aronson.

Cattanach, A. (1992). *Play therapy with abused children.* Philadelphia: Jessica Kingsley.

Cattanach, A. (1994). *Play therapy: Where the sky meets the underworld.* Philadelphia: Jessica Kingsley.

DeDomenico, G. (1994). Jungian play therapy techniques. In K. O'Connor & C. Schaefer (Eds.), *Handbook of play therapy: Advances and innovations* (pp. 253–282). New York: John Wiley.

DeMaria, M., & Cowden, S. T. (1992). The effects of client-centered group play therapy on self concept. *International Journal of Play Therapy, 1*(1), 53–68.

Downey, T. (1987). Notes on play and guilt in child analysis. *Psychoanalytic Study of the Child, 42,* 105–126.

Ekstein, R. (1966). *Children of time and space, of action and impulse.* New York: Appleton-Century-Crofts.

Ellis, A. (1962). *Reason and emotion in psychotherapy.* New York: Lyle Stuart.

Erikson, E. (1977). *Toys and reason.* New York: Norton.

Fall, M. (1994). Self-efficacy: An additional dimension in play therapy. *International Journal of Play Therapy, 3* (2), 21–32.

Freud, A. (1928). Introduction to the techniques of child analysis. *Nervous and Mental Disease Monograph, 48.*

Freud, A. (1946). *The psychoanalytical treatment of children.* London: Imago.

Freud, A. (1965). *Normality and pathology in childhood: Assessments of development.* New York: International Universities Press.

Freud, S. (1953). *The standard edition of the complete psychological works.* (J. Strachey, Ed. and Trans.) London: Hogarth.

Garvey, C. (1977). *Play.* Cambridge, MA: Harvard University Press.

Gil, E. (1991). *The healing power of play: Working with abused children.* New York: Guilford.

Gil, E. (1994). *Play in family therapy.* New York: Guilford.

Ginott, H. (1959). The theory and practice of therapeutic intervention in child treatment. *Journal of Consulting Psychology, 23,* 160–166.

Ginott, H. (1961). *Group psychotherapy with children.* New York: McGraw-Hill.

Greenacre, P. (1959). Play in relation to creative imagination. *Psychoanalytic Study of the Child, 14,* 61–80.

Guerney, B., Guerney, L. & Andronico, M. (1966). Filial therapy. *Yale Scientific Magazine, 40,* 6–14.

Guerney, L., & Welsh, A. (1993). Two by two: A filial therapy case study. In T. Kottman & C. Schaefer (Eds.), *Play therapy in action* (pp. 561–588). Northvale, NJ: Jason Aronson.

Hambridge, G. (1955). Structured play therapy. *American Journal of Orthopsychiatry, 25,* 601–617.

Hellendoorn, J., van der Kooij, R., & Sutton-Smith, B. (Eds.) (1994). *Play and intervention.* Albany: State University of New York Press.

Hug-Hellmuth, H. (1921). On the technique of child-analysis. *International Journal of Psycho-Analysis, 2,* 287–305.

Irwin, E., & Curry, N. (1993). Role play. In C. Schaefer (Ed.), *The therapeutic powers of play* (pp. 167–187). Northvale, NJ: Jason Aronson.

Jennings, S. (1990). *Dramatherapy with families, groups and individuals, waiting in the wings.* London: Jessica Kingsley.

Jernberg, A. (1976). Theraplay technique. In C. Schaefer (Ed.), *Therapeutic use of child's play* (pp. 345–350). Northvale, NJ: Jason Aronson.

Jernberg, A., & Jernberg, E. (1993). Family theraplay for the family tyrant. In T. Kottman & C. Schaefer (Eds.), *Play therapy in action* (pp. 45–96). Northvale, NJ: Jason Aronson.

Kelly, G. (1963). *A theory of personality*. New York: Norton.

Klein, M. (1932). *The psychoanalysis of children*. London: Hogarth.

Knell, S. M. (1993). *Cognitive-behavioral play therapy*. Northvale, NJ: Jason Aronson.

Kottman, T. (1993). The king of rock and roll: An application of Adlerian play therapy. In T. Kottman & C. Schaefer (Eds.), *Play therapy in action* (pp. 133–168). Northvale, NJ: Jason Aronson.

Kottman, T. (1994). Adlerian play therapy. In K. O'Connor & C. Schaefer (Eds.), *Handbook of play therapy: Advances and innovations* (pp. 3–26). New York: John Wiley.

Kranz, P., & Lund, N. (1993). 1993: Axline's eight principles of play therapy revisited. *International Journal of Play Therapy, 2*(2), 53–60.

Landreth, G. (1993). Self-expressive communication. In C. Schaefer (Ed.), *The therapeutic power of play* (pp. 41–64). Northvale, NJ: Jason Aronson.

Levy, D. (1938). Release therapy in young children. *Psychiatry, 1*, 387–439.

Lewis, J. M. (1993). Childhood play in normality, pathology, and therapy. *American Journal of Orthopsychiatry, 63*(1), 6–15.

Lowenfeld, M. (1939). The world pictures of children: A method of recording and studying them. *British Journal of Medical Psychology, 18*, 65–101.

Lowenfeld, M. (1967). *Play in childhood*. New York: John Wiley. Mayes, L., & Cohen, D. (1993). Playing and therapeutic action in child analysis. *International Journal of Psycho-Analysis, 74*, 1235–1244.

Mayes, L., & Cohen, D. (1993). Playing and therapeutic action in child analysis. *International Journal of Psycho-Analysis. 74*, 1235–1244.

McCalla, C. L. (1994). A comparison of three play therapy theories: Psychoanalytic, Jungian, and client-centered. *International Journal of Play Therapy, 3*(1), 1–10.

Moustakas, C. (1953). *Children in play therapy*. New York: McGraw-Hill.

Moustakas, C. (1955). The frequency and intensity of negative attitudes expressed in play therapy. *Journal of Genetic Psychology, 86*, 301–325.

Moustakas, C. (1959). *Psychotherapy with children*. New York: Harper & Row.

Neubauer, P. D. (1987). The many meanings of play: Introduction. *Psychoanalytic Study of the Child, 42*, 3–10.

Oaklander, V. (1993). From meek to bold: A case study of Gestalt play therapy. In T. Kottman & C. Schaefer (Eds.), *Play therapy in action* (pp. 281–300). Northvale, NJ: Jason Aronson.

Oaklander, V. (1994). Gestalt play therapy. In K. O'Connor & C. Schaefer (Eds.), *Handbook of play therapy: Advances and innovations* (pp. 143–156). New York: John Wiley.

O'Connor, K. (1991). *The play therapy primer*. New York: John Wiley.

O'Connor, K. (1994). Ecosystemic play therapy. In K. O'Connor & C. Schaefer (Eds.), *Handbook of play therapy: Advances and innovations* (pp. 61–84). New York: John Wiley.

Peller, L. E. (1954). Libidinal phases, ego development and play. *Psychoanalytic Study of the Child, 9,* 178–198.

Phillips, R. (1994). A developmental perspective. *International Journal of Play Therapy, 3*(2), 1–20.

Piaget, J. (1951). *Play, dreams and imitation in childhood*. New York: Norton.

Piaget, J. (1969). *The mechanisms of perception*. New York: Basic Books.

Plaut, E. A. (1979). Play and adaptation. *Psychoanalytic Study of the Child, 34*, 217–232.

Reid, S. (1993). Game play. In C. Schaefer (Ed.), *The therapeutic powers of play* (pp. 323–348). Northvale, NJ: Jason Aronson.

Rogers, C. (1951). *Client-centered therapy*. New York: Houghton Mifflin.

Rothenberg, L., & Schiffer, M. (1976). The therapeutic play group: A case study. In C. Schaefer (Ed.), *The therapeutic use of child's play* (pp. 569–576). Northvale, NJ: Jason Aronson.

Schaefer, C. (Ed.). (1993). *The therapeutic powers of play*. Northvale, NJ: Jason Aronson.

Schaefer, C., & Carey, L. (1994) *Family play therapy*. Northvale, NJ: Jason Aronson.

Semonsky, C., & Zicht, G. (1976). Activity group parameters. In C. Schaefer (Ed.), *The therapeutic use of child's play* (pp. 591–606). Northvale, NJ: Jason Aronson.

Skinner, B. F. (1938). *The behavior of organisms*. New York: Appleton Century.

Slavson, S. (1976). Activity group therapy. In C. Schaefer (Ed.), *The therapeutic use of child's play* (pp. 577–590). Northvale, NJ: Jason Aronson.

Solnit, A. J. (1987). A psychoanalytic view of play. *Psychoanalytic Study of the Child, 42,* 205–219.

Solomon, J. (1938). Active play therapy. *American Journal of Orthopsychiatry, 8,* 479–498.

Taft, J. (1933). *The dynamics of therapy in a controlled relationship*. New York: Macmillan.

Van de Putte, S. (1994). A structured activities group for sexually abused children. In K. O'Connor & C. Schaefer (Eds.), *Handbook of play therapy: Advances and innovations* (pp. 409–428). New York: John Wiley.

Van Fleet, R. (1994). Filial therapy with children of alcoholics and addicts. In K. O'Connor & C. Schaefer (Eds.), *Handbook of play therapy: Advances and innovations* (pp. 371–386). New York: John Wiley.

Waelder, R. (1933). The psychoanalytic theory of play. *Psychoanalytic Quarterly, 2,* 208–224.

White, R. (1966). *Lives in progress*. New York: Holt, Rinehart and Winston.

Winnicott, D. W. (1951). Transitional objects and transitional phenomena. In D. W. Winnicott, *Collected papers* (pp. 29–242). New York: Basic Books.

Winnicott, D. W. (1968). Playing: Its theoretical status in the clinical situation. *International Journal of Psychoanalysis, 49,* 591–599.

Winnicott, D. W. (1971). *Playing and reality*. London: Tavistock.

Wolpe, J. (1958). *Psychotherapy by reciprocal inhibition*. Palo Alto, CA: Stanford University Press.

Play and Technology

Revised Realities and Potential Perspectives

Yasmin Bettina Kafai

Video games present virtual worlds in which children can control and interact with fantasy figures. Interactive technologies such as video games have become a significant part of children's play culture in the late twentieth century. Many computer toys now provide feedback responses tailored to children's interactions. Feedback and control are two important features of the interactive play technologies not previously available. A quick look at the current generation of electronic toys and video games with animated graphics, sound effects, and control devices confirms apparent differences when compared to more traditional toys and games for children.

If the nature of the play devices and environments themselves has changed considerably, the growing immersion of interactive technologies in children's living conditions is another important factor. Interaction with technological devices is not as new an experience for children as it is for most adults. Also, in contrast to most adults, children do not feel threatened by computational media and other programmable devices; they enjoy explorations of and interactions with them. For young children growing up today, technology is part of the fabric of their everyday life.

With these changes in living conditions and play devices it is worthwhile examining to what extent interactive technologies have changed the realities of play for children and what potentials they offer. The following sections present selected research on video games as a case in point for the revised realities of children's play. The social, cognitive, and motivational aspects of video game playing then are examined more closely by looking at the nature of games and their relevance to children's development. The potential of interactive technologies also is discussed by considering constructive aspects of play; one example is children's engagements in making games by using technological support. The potential perspectives of interactive play environments then are explored by looking at the next generation of electronic building blocks and virtual playgrounds.

Revised Realities of Play: Video Games as the New Electronic Playground

More than any other form of interactive technology, video games have entered children's homes and hearts and have received an enthusiastic reception. The number of hours spent in front of video screens must be in the order of hundreds of millions. Not only the time spent, but also the energy displayed in playing these games has initiated many discussions among parents, practitioners, and researchers about the impact on children's well-being. To understand the impact of video games it is worthwhile to analyze their particular nature in relation to other games that children play.

The psychologist Jean Piaget (1951) offered a classification of game playing that reflected children's various developmental needs. According to Piaget, most games can be classified as games of practice, symbolic games, rule-governed games, or games of construction. Children in early infancy engage mostly in games of practice to gain mastery over motor movements. Symbolic play enters at a later age in which "as if" plays a crucial role. In this context, children build their understanding of the world by reenacting situations and telling stories until they feel secure in the mastery of them. The next level are rule-governed games, where children play according to a finite set of rules (often set by others). At this level, children enjoy exploring and discovering a set structure that they can intentionally modify; that is, the rules are negotiable to make the game more enjoyable. Piaget considered games of construction to be the highest form of game playing because they require children to build representations of the world according to their understanding of it.

Even though Piaget's classification system was developed well before video games entered the playroom, it seems evident that video games combine three different forms of game playing: practice, symbolic, and rule-governed. Playing video games requires a great amount of practice before the player gains mastery and can advance to the next level. Video games are a stellar example of the central "as-if" quality of play: they allow children to be engaged in fantasy worlds and to accomplish incredible feats, such as fighting monsters, on the screen. In addition, each video game is set up as a world governed by a set of rules that the player has to uncover to win the game. It is the convergence of these three forms of game playing that makes video games different from traditional toys and games. The mastery of all three levels provides young players with an experience of control and competence previously not available.

This unique combination of features in video games might explain their motivational, cognitive, and social appeal to children. When one researcher observed several video game players and analyzed their interests in games, she identified features of role-playing, fantasy, and rule systems as responsible for the games' "holding power" (Turkle, 1984). Video games respond to children's developmental need to interact with well-defined rule systems. A further insight of her analysis was that playing video games resonated with different aspects of the players' personalities. Whereas some players were attracted to the fantasy aspects, for others the uncovering of principles designed by someone else or the perfection of performance were the most compelling aspects of video game play (Turkle, 1984). Other researchers confirmed this analysis by having students play a number of different computer games, rate the games according to attractiveness, and then name their outstanding features (Malone & Lepper, 1987). They found that players rated factors such as challenge, fantasy, curiosity, and control as the main attracting features of games.

Video games appeal on a motivational level and also provide cognitive challenges. Sensorimotor skills such as hand-eye coordination are a prerequisite to successful video game play and require hours of practice. There is an abundance of research documenting the spatial reasoning involved in video game playing (Gagnon, 1985; Greenfield, Brannon, & Lohr, 1994; McClurg & Chaille, 1987). Most games are large environments with complicated spatial arrangements not entirely visible on the screen. To successfully move through the different levels, the player needs to build a "mental map" of the video game world—something that takes hours of exploration.

One factor that clearly appeals to video game players is the uncovering of the rules that govern the screen world. Most of these rules are unknown and not apparent at the beginning of play; many of them also change as the player progresses to higher game levels. A number of cognitive processes are involved in the course of rule detection: trial and error, pattern generation, hypothesis testing, generalization, estimation, and organization of information (Loftus & Loftus, 1983). As players move through the game, they are engaged in analyzing their experiences and the ways they contribute to the mastery of the game. Players might decide to change responses in given situations to develop more successful strategies. Furthermore, many players are not satisfied with finding just one right way to achieve the final game level; instead, many pride themselves on knowing alternative routes or shortcuts to the next level. It is clear that to achieve the final level of a video game requires a great many skills and much investigation on the part of the player. Deserving of further consideration is that many of these processes are happening simultaneously; as players are mapping out the layout of the video world, they are also uncovering hidden principles and interacting with other game players (Greenfield, 1984).

The high concentration and coordination required for successful video game playing supports a commonly held notion of the antisocial nature of the players. Instead of playing with other children, the new generation of toys requires children to engage in solitary play against themselves (Sutton-Smith, 1986). One could characterize video game playing as a solitary activity because the player is interacting alone with the machine. This view, however, neglects to take into account that video games support a whole culture consisting of movies, magazines, fan clubs, and competitions. In fact, most video games are played in groups, where players exchange tricks and strategies for advancing in the game. Also, most machine setups allow for two players to compete against each other. Competition and cooperation are other features that make video games attractive for players (Malone & Lepper, 1987).

One of the most distinctive features of the video game culture is that the majority of game players are boys (Provenzo, 1991). There is a consistent pattern of gender differences in interest and achievement in video game playing; few girls play video games, and their performance lags behind that of boys (Gailey, 1992; Provenzo, 1991). One explanation lies in the spatial skills that are crucial to successful video game play. New research (Subrahmanyan & Greenfield, 1994), however, points out that these observed gender differences disappear after extended exposure. The violent themes and gender stereotypes provided in video games offer a more compelling explanation. One commentator argued that the values embedded in movies, toys, television, and video games are powerful stereotypes for children's thinking (Kinder, 1991). In many commercial video games, the main game figure is usually a male hero whose function is to save a female or obtain a treasure (Kinder, 1991). Many video games take the eternal conflict between evil and good as their main theme. Children find the theme compelling because it supports their need to understand their own position and place in the social context. Some researchers have speculated that boys are drawn to identify with the characters in video games, whereas girls prefer to interact with the figures. This might provide an explanation for why boys take so easily to video games.

Gailey (1992) has questioned to what extent children experience violence and gender stereotyping. She analyzed what values video games convey, how child players interpret the play process, and what children get out of the games. One of her findings is that children do not accept the universals provided in video games; instead they make up their own descriptions. Irrespective of the considerable gender stereotyping found in many video games (portraying women as victims or prizes), girls seem to resolve the dilemma by redefining their roles—placing themselves in managerial roles.

It is clear that video game playing offers children an engagement that challenges them at various levels, including the cognitive, motivational, and social. Video games are the new playground that can provide entrance into a fantasy world in which children can experience control and competence. Children have always been able to create their own fantasy worlds by playing with traditional toys and games. What is new is that this generation of games and toys can "talk back," responding in sophisticated ways to children's interactions, and that players are able to control the flow of the game by their own interventions. It is apparent that the design of characters and themes in many video games replicates gender preferences found for traditional toys. After all, video game worlds— their figures, actions, and contents—are environments constructed by others, by game designers. In general, players have very few opportunities to change the features of a purchased video game. Therefore, it is worthwhile to investigate another variant of interactive technologies: constructive play. The idea of using technology to make video games and further game technology developments is presented in the following section.

Potential Perspectives of Play: Electronic Play as Constructive Activity

While video games in their current form provide children with new playgrounds, the potential of interactive technologies to provide construction material for play has received far less attention. We know that, as much as children enjoy playing games according to given rules, they are also constantly modifying rules and inventing their own. Piaget (1951) claimed that these modifications reflected children's growing understanding of the world. The process of game construction represented for Piaget the ultimate efforts by children to master their environment by creating external representations of the world. Researchers in the digital domain, however, have not considered extensively this constructive aspect of children's play. They have seen the difficulties associated with learning programming, the language of construction for computers, as a major obstacle. It is only in the last decade that some have considered programming computers an appropriate and feasible activity for children (see Papert, 1980, 1993).

Turkle (1984) has pointed out an interesting parallel between the attractions of playing games and programming computers. She sees programming as a way for children to build their own worlds. Within this context, children can determine the rules and boundaries governing the game world and become the makers and players of their own games. In contrast, when children play a video game, they are always playing a game programmed by someone else; they are always exploring someone else's world and deciphering someone else's mystery. Turkle concludes that what she calls the holding power of playing purchased video games can be applied to the making or programming of video games.

This parallel provided the rationale for investigating game making as a new avenue for children's play with interactive technologies. In one study, which may serve as an example for this kind of effort (Kafai, 1995), a group of ten-year-old children made their own video games. The children met every day over a period of six months to design their own games, creating all their own characters, story lines, game themes, and interactions. It is worthwhile to take a closer look at the video games that the students created and to what extent they represent play preferences known from other games and toys (Kafai, 1996).

All the games include sophisticated graphics, animation, and interaction in their programming. The most distinctive feature, however, is the degree to which gender differences permeate nearly all aspects of game design. Almost all of the boys, for example, created adventure hunts and explorations, whereas the girls' games were more evenly divided among adventure, skill/sport, and teaching. The sports theme was selected by a few students who focused on skill aspects, such as navigating a maze or spider web or dunking basketballs. Only two students (girls) chose an educational format, a teaching game, to incorporate the content to be learned. One of the sharpest thematic differences between boys and girls concerned the morality issue of the contest between good and evil, in which one good player fights off the bad guys to achieve a goal. In the boys' games the goal is to recover objects to defeat evil creatures and receive a prize. Not one girl incorporated the conquest of good versus evil in her game, whereas five boys chose to do so.

The diversity of genre and gender differences was also reflected in the design of the game world. All game designs centered around the construction of physical spaces. In many instances, game worlds could be described as fantasy places because they were imaginary worlds for the younger players. The majority of boys created fantasy places such as imaginary cities, islands, or countries. Most girls confined their game places and worlds to real-life settings, whereas only one boy did so.

The places or worlds in which the games were situated were populated with an interesting cast of characters. One group contained the game character assigned to the player, the other the supporting cast of game actors. Nearly all the boys chose fantasy figures or assigned a specific gender to the player. Most of the boys also assumed that the player would be male. Some of them had fantasy names by which the gender was more difficult to detect. In contrast, most girls left the player's gender or age open. They addressed the player simply as a generic "you" without any further specifications. One might interpret this choice as involving a more personal identification between the player and the character. The cast of supporting game actors emphasized this result even more; most boys created several characters with fantasy names for the game world in which the player had to interact. Most girls chose one or two figures for their supporting cast. It is apparent in this comparison that the girls had a significantly different take on the roles that the player and actors have in the game.

The feedback provided as a result of the interaction between the player and the game differed as well. Boys' feedback modes were overwhelmingly violent; girls' feedback modes were overwhelmingly nonviolent. In the case of a wrong answer, most boys chose to end the game in a violent fashion. Their game characters either lost their lives before the game was over or as a result of it. In contrast, almost all the girls programmed different kinds of feedback for a wrong answer. In case of a wrong answer, their player usually continued, but did not receive a reward (or punishment).

Most of the games' designers set all of the worlds, including characters and interactions, within a narrative context. As students made their games, they also created a story that situated the actors in a fantastic yet meaningful context. Students included additional scenes in which the different actors spoke to each other. The graphics were accompanied by text. A possible explanation for the popularity of the narrative game format is that it allowed students to incorporate fantasy and decorate their worlds in more attractive ways. This was also one of the features that other researchers identified as appealing to children in playing games (Malone & Lepper, 1987).

Making video games emphasized the gender differences found in playing purchased video games, but with an interesting difference: the stories, characters, and worlds of most of the girls differed in kind from those created by most of the boys. The influence of commercially available games was especially strong in the case of boys' games. Many game designers started out with ideas taken from popular video games such as "Super Mario Brothers" or "Pacman." Many of the boys' game implementations included violent aspects, as documented in the design of their feedback to player interactions. Violence is one of the most prominent features in commercial video games (Provenzo, 1991). Boys incorporate this violence into their own game designs; girls do not. In the commercial games female figures rarely are cast in the main role, and the thematic embedding of video games in hunts and adventures is not to many girls' tastes; they compensate for this by creating their own world in which they include familiar spaces and characters from their households.

The game design activity offered a framework in which both girls and boys could situate their preferred ideas and fantasies. In their choices of game themes and their programming of animation and interactions, the students offered a glimpse into what they found appealing and unappealing in the games and stories they experience through other media. Making a game and its rules allowed the game designers to be in charge and to determine the player's place and role in the world along with all the consequences. These results point toward the potential of new interactive play technologies that provide construction tools for making computational toys and games.

Programmable Building Blocks, Computational Games Tool Kits, and Virtual Playgrounds

There is a long tradition of construction tools and toys in children's play history, such as Froebelian blocks, Lincoln Logs, Tinker Toys, and Lego bricks. These tools offer children the opportunity to build structures they find in the real world and to populate them with their own figures and actions. Even though they are all categorized as construction tools and toys, each set offers distinct building possibilities that reflect technological advances in engineering. Whereas Lincoln Logs clearly favor building variations of wooden cabins, for example, Tinker Toys and Lego bricks allow for a much wider range of structures. The materials of physical construction tool kits define, to a certain extent, the objects to be built.

It is worthwhile to consider for a moment what the computational equivalents or extensions of the traditional building blocks could be. For that reason, the following sections contain some examples of computational construction building blocks and tool kits in different settings. The first section looks at a combination of traditional building blocks and control structures that merge the computational world with the physical world. The second examines a computational game tool kit. The last extends the settings to virtual playgrounds that allow children to bridge large distances to come together and play. These examples are only indicators of what is possible.

Programmable Building Blocks

A first step in the direction of computational construction tool kits is to combine the physical building blocks with computational control elements. Children would be able not only to build mechanical objects and structures but also to have ways of programming and controlling engines and sensors that allow for movements and interactions. Rather than just building architectural structures, children would also become involved in engineering. Lego bricks with sensors and motors that could be connected via wires and controlled through programs would provide such programmable building blocks (Resnick & Ocko, 1991). Further developments would provide bricks that contain all the computational power. An extension of computational Lego bricks, called the programmable brick (Sargent & Resnick, 1994), allows control of motors and sensors without being tethered to a personal computer. These programmable bricks would allow children to build computational objects that can interact independently with the world. In that sense, each playroom in a house could become a potential game environment with computational elements in it. Children could create a haunted house, for example, by attaching programmable bricks to doors that make creaking sounds when they open and drop spiders when people walk into the room. Children also could use programmable bricks to send secret messages via infrared beam to other children in the room. In addition, they could build creatures with sensors that explore the environment. A computational version of Mr. Potato Head might have eyes that move toward the light and a mouth that starts to talk when placed on a head.

Computational Game Tool Kits

This kind of tool kit would allow children to make their own software or video games. The Pinball Construction Set (Greenfield, 1984), for example, provides players with a blank board and all the necessary tools and parts to install flippers, backgrounds, and controllers for their own pinball game. The user can design innumerable versions, and he or she can play the game alone or with others. More generic computational tool kits would allow children to make any kind of game world, characters, and game rule. Children could be provided with primitive rules and actions and could change the parameters to fit the game's needs and children's desires. The sharing of ideas and strategies, already an essential part of the existing video game culture, could continue because children could invite each other to play the games they have designed.

Virtual Playgrounds

Video games are considered the new electronic playground in which children can control and interact with figures in a world. A step further would be to think about networked video games in which children could control characters that interact with those controlled by others. From the vision of one player with a machine, we would move into a world where the computer provides a platform to connect several players for a play experience; they then could interact with each other. Multi-user dungeons, or MUDs, are one example of networked environments that allow children to play with each other even though they are physically located at different places. MUDs are text-based virtual reality environments that are organized around metaphors of physical spaces such as space stations or buildings that users can access from all over the world (Curtis, 1992). Players

assume fantasy characters that explore the space provided and build new structures and objects for other players to find. Other examples of MUDs provide children with the beginning of a virtual city they can fill with images, text, sounds, and more buildings (Conn, 1994).

Programming is the initial problem that concerns the control of interaction in all kinds of computational environments. The potential of play in these environments is always defined by the extent to which children master the control language. Whereas Lego bricks and Lincoln Logs can be manipulated by hand, computational construction elements are manipulated through a command language that requires very specific directions. Here it is appropriate to point out one important difference between play in the physical world and play in the virtual world. In a miniature amusement park built out of Lego bricks, for example, the movement and energy used is constrained by physical laws. Cars cannot simply drive through houses; they have to drive around them to continue on their route. In a computational environment, however, objects that represent "cars" can easily drive through objects representing "houses"; furthermore, they do not need to respect gravity unless programmed to do so. Play in computational worlds is less constrained by the laws and limitations of the physical world. Instead, limitations of knowledge and command language impose constraints on the manipulation and construction of objects. It is unclear at this moment what impact these differences have on children's play behavior and development.

Video games and electronic toys are the new digital playground for children. Children's play is still the same, but their world and materials with which they grow up have changed. When compared to a set of toys developed by Friedrich Froebel over 150 years ago—woolen balls for toddlers to catch and throw, papers and sticks to be folded in intricate patterns, wooden blocks to create houses and buildings— it becomes clear that the nature of toys, and consequently, the interactions with them, have changed. But play with digital media and in virtual playgrounds can still have the features of make-believe and relate to children's experiences.

Parents, educators, and psychologists need to carefully consider interactive technologies' potential to be both ready-made play worlds provided by adults for children and the materials with which children can create their own worlds. The current reality of interactive technologies tends to undervalue the constructive aspects of play in which children have always engaged. However, electronic building blocks and virtual playgrounds are materials and places that should be as accepted as wooden blocks, bricks, and sandboxes.

Bibliography

Conn, C. (1994). Coco's channel: Connie Guglielmo. *Wired, 2*(4), 58–60.

Curtis, P. (1992). *Mudding: Social phenomena in text-based virtual realities.* Proceedings of Directions and Implications of Advanced Computing. Berkeley, CA: Available via anonymous ftp from parcftp.xerox.com in pub/MOO/papers/DIAC92.{ps,txt}.

Gagnon, D. (1985). Video games and spatial skills: An exploratory study. *Educational Communications and Technology Journal, 33,* 263–275.

Gailey, C. (1992). Mediated messages: Gender, class, and cosmos in home video games. *Journal of Popular Culture, 15*(2), 5–25.

Greenfield, P. M. (1984). *Mind and media: The effects of television, video games, and computers.* Cambridge, MA: Harvard University Press.

Greenfield, P. M., Brannon, C., & Lohr, D. (1994). Two-dimensional representations of movement through three-dimensional space: The role of video game expertise. *Journal of Applied Developmental Psychology, 15*(1), 87–104.

Greenfield, P. M., & Cocking, R. R. (Eds.) (1994). Effects of interactive entertainment technology on development. Special Issue. *Journal of Applied Developmental Psychology.*

Kafai, Y. (1995). *Minds in play: Computer game design as a context for children's learning.* Hillsdale, NJ: Lawrence Erlbaum.

Kafai, Y. (1996). Gender differences in children's construction of video games. In P. M. Greenfield & R. R. Cocking (Eds.), *Interacting with video* (pp. 39–66). Norwood, NJ: Ablex Publishing Corporation.

Kinder, M. (1991). *Playing with power.* Berkeley: University of California Press.

Loftus, G. R., & Loftus, E. F. (1983). *Minds at play: The psychology of video games.* New York: Basic Books.

Malone, T. W., & Lepper, M. R. (1987). Making learning fun: A taxonomy of intrinsic motivations for learning. In R. E. Snow & M. J. Farr (Eds.), *Aptitude, learning and instruction. Volume 3: Cognitive and affective process analyses* (pp. 223–253). Hillsdale, NJ: Lawrence Erlbaum.

McClurg, P. A., & Chaille, C. (1987). Computer games: Environments for developing spatial cognition? *Journal of Educational Computing Research, 3,* 95–111.

Papert, S. (1980). *Mindstorms.* New York: Basic Books.

Papert, S. (1993). *The children's machine.* New York: Basic Books.

Piaget, J. (1951). *Play, dreams, and imitation in childhood.* New York: Norton.

Provenzo, E. F. (1991). *Video kids: Making sense of Nintendo.* Cambridge, MA: Harvard University Press.

Resnick, M., & Ocko, S. (1991). LOGO: Learning though and about design. In I. Harel & S. Papert (Eds.), *Constructionism* (pp. 141–150). Norwood, NJ: Ablex.

Sargent, R., & Resnick, M. (1994). Programmable bricks: Ubiquitous computing for kids. In Y. Kafai & M. Resnick (Eds.), *Constructionism in practice* (pp. 101–108). Cambridge, MA: MIT Media Laboratory.

Subrahmanyan, K., & Greenfield, P. M. (1994). Effects of video game practice on spatial skills in girls and boys. *Journal of Applied Developmental Psychology, 15*(1), 13–32.

Sutton-Smith, B. (1986). *Toys as culture.* New York: Gardner.

Turkle, S. (1984). *The second self: Computers and the human spirit.* New York: Simon and Schuster.

Meanings of Play

The Meaning of Play
as a Human Experience

Myrdene Anderson

Culture, society, language, and biology conspire to render play significant in human experience. While play *shapes* the individual, it also *reflects* the individual, and that same reflexivity must be reserved for play, players, and playing vis-à-vis culture, society, language, biology, and any other conventional paradigms employed in our playful workplace jargon. Consequently, the notion of play figures in many contexts and at many levels, and its exploration invites parallel interrogation of what (all) play is, is not, might be, and should be: from the inside out, from the outside in, and from within the edge, as well as indoors, outdoors, alone, with familiars, with intimates locked into birth order, in confederation with relative strangers, in safe conditions and with risk, and when winning and losing. Play also exemplifies some dynamics of comedy and tragedy.

Evolutionary and Developmental Play

"Life, liberty, and the pursuit of happiness" sums up adults' idealistic image of childhood play. Adults consider play, even that silent, still, and solitary musing at any age, to be open-ended and dynamic. Healthy children have the energy to epitomize "life" that is endowed with just the degrees of freedom (within traditional settings, anyway) sufficient to indulge in "liberty" without endangering themselves. They also experience a medley of autotelic motivations yielding to "happiness," variously revealed as sheer joy, risk-taking, mastery, cooperation, dominance, and addiction.

Evolutionary Play

The most clearly *innovative* play is evolutionary in that it is open-ended, exploratory, unpredictable, unique, and "comedic" or imbued with "surprise" (following Salthe, 1991). From the *outside* looking in, adults might wonder at the reasons for such a wild, nonlinear, means-oriented autotelic activity (or inactivity), blooming in human beings and other species and persisting quite beyond childhood. Could it be a cog in cogniton, or practice in coping with the unanticipated, or the organism filling a vacuum with itself? Too often, this line of reasoning reduces, or inflates, play to practice work.

From *inside* the evolutionary play, however, there is little chance for the player to rationalize anything. The opportunity at once becomes the invitation that simultaneously turns into the self-fueled, synergistic, inherently rewarding, but not necessarily rewarded, process called play. The player, from habit more than from reflection, assumes an intrinsic win-win benefit to playing, summed up as its being "fun." This intrinsic motivation to play may precede birth, and scarcely lets up before death.

Developmental Play

Other forms of play with more *predictable structure,* such as sports and games, still allow some fluidity in turn-taking, role reversals, and repetitive rounds. Such relatively tame scenarios entrain the player, through socialization within the immediate setting and through enculturation in the deeper patterns apt to recur, with kinky, fascinating contradictions in other realms of daily life.

Sports, games, and other cultural pastimes have more predictable shape than the utterly open-ended evolutionary, comedic forms of play. From *inside* the play, sports and games follow an organismic, temporal logic of beginnings and ends, often aided and abetted by rules; they are "developmental," and have outcomes that may be "tragic" insofar as the players can anticipate them in "suspense" (following Salthe, 1991). Logic prescribes a digital win-lose grid on the round of play, but players may feel encouraged to find payoffs in losing as well, if only to justify another encounter.

Players *within* these developmental genres of play can be intently motivated, much as evolutionary players. Just as our individual neurological systems *evolve* unique habits and complex, provisional associations as they *develop* with age and growth, the individual player evolves unique meanings and motivations at the same time he or she falls into some developmental trajectory of maturation, socialization, and enculturation.

From *outside* the play, scorekeeping may extend beyond winning and losing in single encounters, such that individuals and teams come to have analogous statistical histories consumed by outsiders as well as insiders. Both insiders and outsiders may discursively replay the event, however. The viewing audience and remote consumers thereby play the game as well as the replayers, but in different roles, as in a leisure commodity. Sometimes wagering games can saprophytically bootstrap on lower-level sports and games. With or without wagering, players and scorekeepers can cheat. Meanings emerge dependently and independently in all these spheres. Analysts also distill their own meanings from the study of play.

From *without,* the student of childhood play may resort to finding meaning in function, displacing the significance of play to another place or time. Describing play enactment in sport and game settings, functionalistic theory points to the exercise of motor and social coordination, to the inculcation of skills preparatory to "work," and to accelerated opportunities for experiencing a range of outcomes for similar behaviors. Looking from the outside in onto either evolutionary or develop-

---

FIGURE 1. Outside and Inside Experiences of Evolutionary and Developmental Play

Features	*Evolutionary Play* Innovative, playful Informal, open-ended Surprising, comedic	*Developmental Play* Gaming, sporty Formal, scripted, scored Suspenseful, tragic
Meanings (at the time of play)	*From **Inside** the Play*	
	Individual Means-oriented Play for play's sake	Individual and group Means- and ends-oriented Play for play's sake and play for outcome's sake
	*From **Outside** the Play*	
	Attributed to individual and process: Context enables recognition of *spontaneity* and appreciation of the *serendipitous*	Attributed to all players as well as to process: Context plus intention foregrounds contingency in *decisions*
Meanings (at a later time) by players by observers by analysts	With the passage of time, there is a tendency to substitute a linear, logical, *developmental* rationale for any evolutionary nuances and indeterminancies. This leads analysts, especially, to reduce meaning to explanation or "cause," a favorite being functions deferred in time or displaced in space	

mental play, the tendency of analysts has been to ascribe some function to play. Play in this discourse joins many other processes deemed adaptive and selected for in cultural history. Function, however, will seldom be the meaning experienced, imagined, interpreted, or constructed by the player. Figure 1 shows some of these play dimensions.

Children as well as adults weave evolutionary and developmental playing into their daily existence. For some, there may seem no distinction between play and waking life. Young children at play are more apt to be in a labile evolutionary mood than in a developmental mood. Parents and other caregivers reminding a playing child of the exigencies of food, drink, clothing, sleep, or shelter often find their rhetoric shy of persuasive. As a child matures, play can also be used deliberately as insulation from other activities and states.

To say that a child is "in" play suggests its molar qualities, and also suggests that language may be a prism through which to profitably view play.

Language of, in, and for Play

Language behavior is often integral to play itself. The player thinks, sometimes in words, uses comments such as "oboy," "oh-oh," and "hmm," and speculates through evolutionary open-ended *what-if* and developmentally goal-oriented *if-then* scenarios. Some play entails vocal and verbal exchanges—to oneself, to other players, or to an audience. Sports in particular are choreographed as much through dialogue as through physical practice and then rescripted by players and audiences for other vicarious nonplayers. Storytelling obviously entails languaging. Because of this incorporation of language into the performance of play, cognitive and social development may be linked correlates of play. This is a realm particularly sensitive to social context, gender, and even birth order (Fein, 1995).

Before directing this linguistic stained-glass window onto the meanings of play, it is worth noting that human language and culture have encumbered as much as enlightened children with a tangle of doublets. "Right and wrong," "right and left," "back and forth," "black and white," "winning and losing," "sheep and goats" all figure in our practice of "play and work" with or without "toys and tools." Humans' anatomic bilateral near-symmetry, asymmetric upward growth, directed senses, and locomotion influenced but did not necessarily determine the sample linguistic habits discussed above.

One semantic triangulation test of any analytical domain, such as "play," brings to light how it is articulated in the spoken native language, as well as in other languages. The meaning or meanings of play derived in one language, however, while perhaps overlapping will not be coterminous with the meaning in another language. This suggests that it is useful to be cautious about universalizing and essentializing play. From language to language, cultural period to period, and context to context, definitions and meanings of such terms as *play, fun,* and *work* may wax and wane in regard to what the terms imply, infer, denote, connote, include, and exclude.

The English-language notion of *play* conventionally spars with *work.* Young and old in the United States enjoy the former, but only adults are burdened with the latter, which they do not expect to enjoy without the admission of the sins of the workaholic. The most afflicted workaholics confuse these dichotomies by finding the play in work that they experience as fun—the heady engagement. Work can include play, therefore, and, for some, play such as sports can be work. Children routinely hide behind play or any activity of their own volition to rebuff other demands on their time.

Meaning of Play in and for Society

As pointed out above, there exist many avenues for meanings of play. Most elementarily, there is the meaning for the player, at the time (impossible to access) or later on (at many moments). There also is the meaning assigned by an outside observer or analyst. In addition, there is the meaning for a coplayer, whose meanings will be even more complex when referenced to the focal player's, because the coplayer may have some kind of privileged knowledge by being simultaneously within and without the play.

Cultural Contexts of Meaning

Culture and society shape children's play enactment as much as language shapes its conceptualization. Small-scale societies dependent on hunting and gathering may not distinguish play and work as hermetically as technologically complex societies do. Work in hunting and gathering societies comes about through immersion in cultural life, not through instruction. The adults in such societies do not analytically decompose work tasks into units specifically for children's small fingers and naïve skills. Children may imitate adults and decide themselves when the facsimile work should figure as the real thing. Spontaneous play, imitation work, and genuine work appear, to observers, equally engaging. In this respect, their work may resemble play to an observer from the United States.

Adults in such small-scale societies differentially reward children, in play and in general, for their exercise of independence and innovation more than for obedience. This matches their egalitarian and heterarchic social organization (e.g., see Loy & Hesketh, 1995).

The Saami reindeer breeders of Lapland, studied by this author, exemplify such a small-scale society (Anderson, 1986). Although they are pastoralists rather than hunters and gatherers, each Saami child ripens in individual fashion and paces into a unique complement of adult capacities. Play may have an important role because formal instruction is absent. Adults casually monitor and note effort rather than success.

Saami children, as well as adults, are eager for all activities, not just play, to be "fun." Indeed, for Saami, play and work both tend to be spontaneous, unstructured, and imbued with "flow" (Csikszentmihalyi & Csikszentmihalyi, 1988). Commercial toys are becoming more popular, but children capably sculpt and script play situations with a minimum of props. Some children encounter toys for the first time when they enter school at age seven. From that age onward, the nation-state as much as the family shapes play. The school system even provides a long, potentially educational holiday so children may accompany their families on the spring reindeer migration. Certain activities that someone from the United States would see as recreation, such as skiing, are not optional pastimes but quotidian skills.

In the Saami case, gender figures minimally in either play or work, while birth order can be important in both contextualizing play and determining inheritance. The last-born offspring, regardless of gender, inherits both rights and responsibilities, and will remain in the natal family when grown up. This means that the parents, as long as they are fit, will buffer the youngest child's place in society. The youngest child may appear indulged in work as well as in play; every new child *is* that youngest potential heir, suitably spoiled, until displaced by the next born and more likely heir. Throughout Saami childhood and into adulthood, siblings and cousins are usually significant in number and proximity; generations are as integral to play as any family unit.

By way of contrast, Western society provides many contexts for childhood play, some of them highly structured and embellished with paraphernalia. Caregivers may indulge, and the media, particularly television, may stimulate younger children. In some families and communities near-aged children who could be potential playmates are scarce. To be successful in a complex society, children's play needs to be more than "fun" and more than "educational"; it needs to "pacify" them without leading them into trouble.

In these societies, children at play receive more explicit feedback from the play setting and from outsiders, to the extent that it is clear they are rewarded for respecting responsibility, obedience, and hierarchy. Gender roles anticipate those in adult society, and the media render gender even more indelible. Adults expect work to require explicit instruction and practice and to be at risk for being odious. Sometimes chores are parsed so that youngsters can master some segments. When this is done, children's work tasks may masquerade as play (although this disguise does not fool children) (see King, 1982). The predigesting of chores for children, whether premeditated as work inputs or pretended as play, calls for an investment by caregivers that simply may not be available in some contemporary families.

Historical Contexts of Meaning

If the significance of play varies from culture to culture, it also changes from time period to time period. A scant generation or two ago, most children in the United States grew up in or near a rural environment, constructed their own toys, explored the terrain, familiarized themselves with local animals and plants, and, while having to "be useful," also engaged in a lot of ad lib playing. They could value the rare commercial toy as an heirloom rather than plaything.

In contemporary U.S. society, scholars have described children as being as adultlike as adults are childlike (and childish) (Meyrowitz, 1984; Postman, 1982). Most children grow up in population centers, if not in dense urban settings, and such an environment is not uniformly sheltering of the young. In fact, many children have little space to play, even if they may have more time. Theoretically, they have more time free of chores, but less time for active play, given their routine devotion to television and other media, including computer games. The sports of greatest significance in the United States reflect the gradual exhaustion of the frontier (baseball), the foregrounding of military and commercial interests (football), and the adaptation to restricted space and constricted time (basketball) (Bjarkman, 1985).

Meanings of Play for the Players

According to historians, childhood is a recent invention (Ariès, 1962). Play obviously is not a recent invention, although it is reinvented with every pulse of culture (deMause, 1974). The toys of a particular period also strikingly reflect the era in both their appearance and their manner of engagement with children (Goldstein, 1994).

Before children experienced a childhood, adults perceived and treated children as miniature adults and valued their utility in concrete terms. Children had to earn or justify their keep, either at home or indentured outside the home. The few toys that existed reflected this lack of childhood years. Dolls, for instance, were not neotenic and cuddly, but were shaped with near-adult proportions, often with heads oddly smaller than we would expect.

In Western culture, there have been several watersheds for children's play. One of these was the Industrial Revolution; another was the successive demographic changes involving migration to cities. Provision of public education was another. Now economic and technological changes touching families on their own turf have made further impacts on play (Roopnarine & Johnson, 1994).

Children throughout these periods engaged in both evolutionary and developmental play. The open-ended informal play of premodern times now recurs in the form of computer video games, especially role-playing games at younger and younger ages. The experience of playing in such liminal space-time can be quite addictive; the absence of any precisely repeating contexts or contents precludes boredom (Laughlin, 1990; Sutton-Smith, 1995).

While the postmodern child amply experiences evolutionary play, much modernist developmental play remains in the form of sports and games with closure, resulting in winners and losers. The meaning to children in this type of play may vary in relation to their degree of success in the venture.

To children, play most often means an autotelic pastime wherein they clearly articulate their own preferences. Insofar as children may initiate play while alone, a sense of autonomy accompanies the evolutionary, exploratory grammar of free-form or imitative activities. When children play in company, such open-ended recreation involves negotiation around verbal and material fantasies, often via role-taking.

Other more structured forms of play have a repetitive or linear, developmental shape. Sometimes viewing serial bouts of creative, evolutionary play, an analyst can discern larger developmental patterns. Similarly, by unpacking the most rule-governed of developmental play, such as sports and games, the analyst finds the dynamic evolutionary moments making each encounter unique.

Play means a freedom to have fun, to tempt risks, to enter into a social relationship. In the culture and language of present-day United States, play also means not work. Contemporary society typically expects very little utility of children. To children, play amounts to an absorbing essential activity tucked between other pleasant ones, such as eating and sleeping, as well as a few unpleasant ones.

Later on, persons will remember their childhood play and construct new meanings for it. Like smells and tastes, memories of play and playthings can be enormously evocative (e.g., see Mergen, 1995). During childhood, however, play is the closest thing to a habit that humans of that age have. Eating and sleeping are mandated by biology, and maybe playing is too. Children foreground the options, uncertainties, infinite varieties, and surprise and suspense in play, making it our medium of encounter with the kin, culture, and cosmos.

Bibliography

Anderson, M. (1986). Continuity and change in Lapland. *Scandinavian Review, 74*(4), 23–30.

Ariès, P. (1962). *Centuries of childhood: A social history of family life.* New York: Vintage.

Bjarkman, P. C. (1985, February). *Baseball comic, football heroic, and the basketball dance: The use of myth and metaphor in the great American games.* Presentation at Charles Darwin Society and Purdue Linguistics Group, W. Lafayette, IN.

Csikszentmihalyi, M., & Csikszentmihalyi, I. S. (Eds.). (1988). *Optimal experience: Psychological studies in flow consciousness.* New York: Cambridge University Press.

deMause, L. (Ed.). (1974). *The history of childhood.* New York: Psychohistory Press.

Fein, G. G. (1995). Toys and stories. In A. D. Pellegrini (Ed.), *The future of play theory: A multidisciplinary inquiry into the contributions of Brian Sutton-Smith* (pp. 151–164). Albany: State University of New York Press.

Goldstein, J. H. (Ed.). (1994). *Toys, play, and child development.* Cambridge: Cambridge University Press.

King, N. (1982). Work and play in the classroom. *Social Education, 46*(2), 110–113.

Laughlin, C. D. (1990). At play in the fields of the lord: The role of metanoia in the development of consciousness. *Play and Culture, 3,* 173–192.

Loy, J. W., & Hesketh, G. L. (1995). Competitive play on the Plains: An analysis of games and warfare among Native American warrior societies, 1800–1850. In A. D. Pellegrini (Ed.), *The future of play theory: A multidisciplinary inquiry into the contributions of Brian Sutton-Smith* (pp. 3–106). Albany: State University of New York Press.

Mergen, B. (1995). Past play: Relics, memory, and history. In A. D. Pellegrini (Ed.), *The future of play theory: A multidisciplinary inquiry into the contributions of Brian Sutton-Smith* (pp. 257–274). Albany: State University of New York Press.

Meyrowitz, J. (1984). The adultlike child and the childlike adult: Socialization in an electronic age. *Daedalus, 113*(3), 19–48. Proceedings of the American Association of Arts and Sciences.

Postman, N. (1982). *The disappearance of childhood.* New York: Delacorte.

Roopnarine, J. L., & Johnson, J. E. (1994). The need to look at play in diverse cultural settings. In J. L. Roopnarine, J. Johnson, & F. H. Hooper (Eds.), *Children's play in diverse cultures* (pp. 1–8). Albany: State University of New York Press.

Salthe, S. N. (1991). *Development and evolution: Complexity and change in biological systems.* Cambridge, MA: MIT Press.

Sutton-Smith, B. (1995). Conclusion. The pervasive rhetorics of play. In A. D. Pellegrini (Ed.), *The future of play theory: A multidisciplinary inquiry into the contributions of Brian Sutton-Smith* (pp. 275–295). Albany: State University of New York Press.

No Learning by Coercion

Paidia and *Paideia* in Platonic Philosophy

Stephen R. Morris

The enigmatic fragment "Lifetime is a child at play, moving pieces in a game. Kingship belongs to the child" (Heraclitus, D.52, translated by Kahn, 1979, p. 71) expresses a commonplace view, which is the same one Shakespeare gives voice to in a well-known passage of *As You Like It* (Act II, scene 7, lines 137 ff.) This view asserts that all of human life, no matter how earnestly or gravely or seriously engaged, is but a game, no different in kind from child's play. The thought is a "cheap metaphor," besides being an extension of the concept of play, perhaps to the point of vacuity (Huizinga, 1955). Yet it is also, if properly constructed and arrived at, an important insight and a piece of wisdom. So Plato believed, and his belief has endured.

Plato's thinking about play may be viewed as an ambivalent gloss on Heraclitus's epigram, with which Plato was almost certainly familiar (Friedlander, 1973). Plato finally affirms it, in a distinctive formulation in his final dialogue, the *Laws,* after following a tortuous path, the retracing of which exposes some of the most fruitful tensions and problems of his philosophy. Specifically, Plato's theory of play cuts across three of the fundamental thematics of his thought: his critique of the rhetoricians (the Sophists); his critique of imitative art (the tragedians); and his development of the metaphysics of appearance and reality. Although this essay will only touch the surface of these broader thematics, they provide crucial contexts for understanding the Platonic dicta on play, by contrasting the Greek concepts of *paidia* (play) and *paideia* (the sum of all formative influences by which a person's habits are forged into character).

Plato's Theory of Play: Some First Principles

The English word *play* translates the Greek *paidia*, a word that wears on its face its cognate relation to the word *pais*, meaning "child." Thus, on the face of it, it is almost laughable to speak of something so grave as a "theory" of *paidia*. *Paidia* is simply childish play or harmless amusement (Liddell & Scott, 1925/1968). It is something characteristic of young children and of adults only by way of pastime. Plato himself offers this succinct definition, at *Laws* 667e[1]: "That which has neither utility nor truth nor likeness, nor yet, in its effects, is harmful, can best be judged by the criterion of the charm that is in it, and by the pleasure it affords. Such pleasure, entailing as it does no appreciable good or ill, is play—*paidia*" (translation by Huizinga, 1955, p. 160). *Paidia,* then, is a neutral category and a seemingly innocuous one.

Yet Plato's use of the word *paidia* is rarely innocuous; almost always it resonates with deeper theoretical concerns. These concerns, in turn, derive from two sources: first, from an ongoing polemic, aimed at distinguishing rightly structured and adequately conceived philosophical expressions of *paidia* from what imitative artists (tragedians) and dramatic speakers (Sophists) do, which looks similar but, Plato insists, is not; and second, an ongoing project of thinking through the links between play and the formation of character that is in Greek, between *paidia* and *paideia*. Like *paidia,* *paideia* derives from the Greek work for "child." It was commonly used to signify both the process of a child's rearing and training, and also the result of that process; that is, mental culture, learning, and education (Liddell & Scott, 1925/1950).

In book 3 of the *Republic,* early in his discussion of the education of the guardian class, Socrates[2] observes to an interlocutor, Adeimantus, "have you not noticed that imitations, if they last from youth for some time, become part of one's nature and settle into habits of gesture, voice, and thought?" (*Republic,* 395d). The principle here enunciated is the fundamental point of departure of Plato's theory of education. Education for Plato is the process of character building through habit-formation, the mechanism of which is imitation. Plato takes a special interest in the early stages of this process. Thus, at the base of the good city, he constructs a regime of "lawful play": "When children play the right games from the first, they absorb obedience to the law through their training in the arts, quite the opposite of what happens to those who play lawless games. This lawfulness follows them in everything, fosters their growth, and can correct anything that has gone wrong before in the city." (*Republic,* 425a). And compare *Laws:* "The correct way to bring up and educate a child is to use his playtime to imbue his soul with the greatest possible devotion to the occupation in which he will have to excel when he matures" (*Laws,* 643bc).

The emphasis on properly structured play derives from another Platonic principle of education: that *paidia* offers a natural medium for *paideia,* because it is at play that children reveal their innate dispositions. These dispositions in turn are the raw material of which the skilled educator must guide the developmental formation. But, Plato offers as a watchword, always instruct the children "in play, where you will see better what each of them is by nature fitted for" (*Republic,* 537a).

Suitable play, in turn, will consist for the most part in imitative activity tailored to the right forms. At least, that looks like the main strand of Plato's answer to the question of what "lawful-playing" children should play at. So, rightly conceived, imitative play should focus on "role models" (in present vernacular) of the "different forms of moderation and courage, of generosity and munificence, and the things kindred to them" (*Republic,* 402b).

But there is more to Plato's theory of the role of imitative play in education than the anodyne thought that children who imitate good people become good. Indeed, Plato himself explicitly draws a fracture line across that thought

in commenting on the type of imitations that good people of sound character will be ashamed to do. For, he writes, they "will resent shaping and moulding themselves after those worse than themselves . . . except perhaps for the sake of *paidia*" (*Republic,* 396e). Socrates' comment arises in the context of the *Republic'*s first discussion of imitation (beginning at 394d) and is particularly directed to the question of what kinds of imitations guardians of the good city will find edifying and enlightening. On its face, the exception made for *paidia* is perplexing. Plato's view is that children's play must be "law-abiding" to be truly edifying, and he identifies play as a particularly educable, therefore vulnerable condition. Given these premises, the proper Platonic inference would seem to be a ban against any form of improper imitation, whether undertaken in play or not. How, after all, could Plato justify allowing the depiction of cowardice or lust or lack of will power "for the sake of play"? Plato's answer is not that such play will allow children to learn what vice is without actually indulging it, since in fact the good, well-formed character only learns of injustice late, as something alien, and then only as something known or understood, not as something experienced (*Republic,* 409bc). Moreover, the imitation of wrongdoing and ugliness, at least when it takes the form of tragic imitation (of the sort purveyed at Athenian dramatic festivals by such as Sophocles and Euripides), is simply too powerful and too affecting to be trusted at all as a popular art form (much less as a suitable vehicle for moral object lessons) (see *Republic,* 605d ff.).

In truth, the exception made for play, unless we treat it as a careless afterthought, is a tiny, intriguing caesura in Plato's argument that points beyond its immediate context to other settings within his thought. To understand it, a review of the contexts of Plato's theory of *paidia* and in particular of influence exerted upon it by the Sophists and tragedians, is warranted. Further, the ambivalent figure of Socrates must be explored.

The Contexts of Plato's Theory of Play

Socrates flourished during the golden age of the sophistic movement, that is, the last half of the fifth century BCE. (For an introduction to this movement, see Guthrie, 1971, and Kerferd,

1981.) The Sophists were teachers and writers who converged upon Athens looking for lucrative fees from young men seeking training in the sophistic arts of rhetoric, argument, and persuasion. The Sophists became notoriously associated with a wide range of "radical" ideas—from relativism, to atheism and agnosticism, to theories of realpolitik. Several of Plato's dialogues, written, to be sure, well after Socrates' death in 399, are set as vivid encounters between Socrates and the great Sophists of his day. (For discussion of these issues see Kahn, 1996.) Tragedians do not usually appear in person, but in the *Laws,* and especially in the *Republic,* the art of tragedy as a whole is a central preoccupation.

Successful Sophists and tragedians were influential public figures in classical Athens; Sophists, by virtue of their status as teachers of rhetoric (the art of persuasion), were influential with the richest and most powerful politicians of the democracy. Tragedians, by virtue of their access to mass audiences at the public festivals where their works were produced and judged by popular vote, were influential among the general public. Plato was profoundly critical of both groups, and particularly of the role each played in public life (see Irwin, 1992).

The essence of Plato's criticism was simple: Rhetoric and tragedy alike, as practiced by the Sophists and tragedians of the day, rely for their appeal on the "mob impulse" of individual souls and within the body politic. Thus, orators are content (and successful) reciting and expatiating on popular prejudices, whether or not these coincide with what is in fact beneficial to the community. Moreover, orators are incapable of inquiring whether the feelings and impulses they arouse in their audiences are in accord with what individuals in those audiences really want. Plato's critique focuses on the mob impulse in its political dimension and its tacit metaphysical presumption: that a clear line can in principle be drawn between what appears good and what is so, since it is precisely this presumption that is at issue between Plato and the Sophists.

Whereas rhetoric has made a sycophant's art of tending to the whims of the "great beast" of the mob mentality of democratic rule (*Republic,* 493ad), tragedy has committed itself just as assiduously to feeding and fostering the irrational, heedlessly appetitive part of its audiences' souls (*Republic,* 595a–608b). The result, according to Plato, is a subtle corrosion of character and integrity, by which the souls of those trained by and habituated to the sensibilities of tragedy are made more susceptible to "injustice, license, cowardice, and ignorance" (*Republic,* 609d). Plato contends that, although Sophists and tragedians have made the manipulation of appetite and emotion their specialty, they are as ignorant about what really ought to be feared, pitied, desired, and admired as their audience is. Thus the habituating, cultivating influence their spectacles invariably exert is entirely haphazard. (Parallels between Plato's critique of tragedians and contemporary criticisms of mass media have been drawn by Nehamas, 1988.)

These concerns provide one of the primary contexts of Plato's theory of play. For, insofar as both sophistry and tragedy appeal to the irrational, frivolous, foolish sides of souls and polities alike, both can be said to engage in mere *paidia,* forsaking serious pursuits (such as philosophy). Thus, *paidia* is forced into a polarized semantic field, where it is defined in relation to its opposite, seriousness. For Plato, this polarization provides an opportunity to rethink the entire nature of play.

Plato's Polemic against the Sophists and Tragedians

The root of Plato's disdain for the Sophists and tragedians, and of his conviction that their spheres of activity are inferior and dangerous, is a belief that sophistry and tragedy make of human life a mere game. The irony of this observation, in Plato's voice, is that the same might well be said of Platonic philosophy, as Plato himself understood very well, but with this difference: for Plato, the game of philosophy is no "mere" game, but something profoundly serious. The difference is wholly valuative, of course, and Plato establishes it, therefore, to the extent that he does, by a moralizing polemic against his rival Sophists and tragedians, a polemic whose primary aim is to distinguish in moral terms what he does from what they do.

For their part, tragedians deal in images of images, "a third remove from the truth" (*Republic 10,* 602a ff.; Nehamas, 1982). They specialize in crafting appeals to the "inferior part" of the soul. Their skill lies in the manipulation of emotions, which it is best that reason should govern, but which, under the sway of tragic spectacle, become oblivious to reason. Even the best, most well-harmonized souls find themselves giving way to its seductive, yet subtly disintegrative ministrations, thus allowing impulses and dispositions "to be nurtured and watered, which ought to be left to wither" (*Republic,* 602a ff.). The upshot, notoriously, is that the tragic poets must be banished from the well-governed city, as their works must be shielded from well-governed souls. Plato vacillates then between seeming indifferent disdain and grave admonitions against tragedy's corrupting influence.

Plato shows the same authorial soul divided against itself in his analysis of sophistry. In the *Protagoras,* Socrates dismisses one of his Sophist interlocutor's primary areas of expertise—the interpretation of poetry—as "frivolous *paidia,*" which "men of *paideia* shun" (*Protagoras,* 347d). Socrates defends his harsh appraisal by pointing to the indeterminacy of poetic hermeneutics—the tendency of such conversation to degenerate into a trackless exchange of opinions, in which some say the poet's meaning is one thing and some another, and no conclusive argument is ever reached. Best, Socrates states confidently, to dismiss the poet, and "conduct the conversation on the basis of our own ideas."

Here the poets and Sophists are linked as fellow traffickers in the frivolous, in sharp contrast to "serious" philosophers. That contrast is the main theme and running joke of one of Plato's most entertaining dialogues, the *Euthydemus.* Euthydemus and his brother Dionysiodorus practice a kind of carny-barker's brand of sophistic (they are a far cry from the dignified figure presented by the *éminence grise* of the Sophists, Protagoras). Together they set out to befuddle a young protégé of Socrates', Clinias. They succeed, it would seem, but in the process they are held up to some intensive (Socratic) scrutiny themselves. When Socrates urges the brothers to get serious about the topics of the conversation—wisdom, virtue, education—and to stop "making these things into a joke," they show themselves oblivious to the distinction. They certainly do not recognize it in their own sophistic practice; as the dialogue makes amply clear, every topic, no matter how abstruse, is an occasion for jejune wordplay and penny-ante fallacy-mongering. Young Clinias might well have left their company thinking that the difference between *paideia* and *paidia* really is just a matter of naïve convention.

The two brothers represent one style of sophistic, which Plato depicts as a manic impulse to treat everything, without discrimination, as mere *paidia.* There are more sophisticated kinds of Sophists of course, and Plato

offers a comprehensive taxonomy of the species in his dialogue, the *Sophist.* In a wide-ranging discussion, where a playful "hunt" for "illusive quarry" gives way to a dense exploration of fundamental issues in Platonic ontology, Plato arrives at some interesting formulations for characterizing the essence of sophistic technique. After attributing to this technique a sort of "magical power," Plato identifies the source of this power as the Sophist's capacity to create a convincing impression of his (or her[3]) own omniscience. This illusion in turn works because of the Sophist's mastery of the variegated art of *mimesis* (imitation), "of all forms of *paidia,* the most skillful and amusing."

Plato's depiction recalls Huizinga's (1955) Sophist, imagined as a patchwork of archaic patterns ("prophet, medicine-man, seer, thaumaturge and poet, whose best designation is *vates*— . . . the possessed, the God-smitten, the raving one"). In fact, Plato associated god-smitten raving more with poets than with Sophists (*Ion; Apology,* 22bc; *Phaedrus,* 245a). As Protagoras himself claims, sophistry is an "ancient art" (*Protagoras,* 316d), and as such, it stands as the inheritor of certain culture functions made obsolete in their other manifestations by transformations of political economy. What remains constant across those transformations, Plato asserts, is the felt need within the culture for a "province of play," that is, the Sophist's province (*Sophist,* 235a; for an overview of the play element in Greek culture, see Spariosu, 1991).

Plato, however, is suspicious of felt needs. Human beings are easily deluded, and they are never more susceptible to delusion than when they are consulting their emotions and desires. Thus, the sophistic mastery of jokes, games, illusions, imitations, and disguises—of "mere play"—turns out to be pernicious if it is oriented only to a human standard (that is, if it is measured simply by what works on humans). "The true master imitators are the ones who tailor their imitations to what is permanent and real" (*Republic,* 500c, 540b). Such true imitators— philosophers—also work in the "province of play." But to make this claim understood, Plato redraws the bounds of that province.

Socratic *Paidia:* Play as Eccentricity
At a crucial juncture in his conversation with his lifelong friend Crito, which Plato has set in the prison cell where he awaits his death sentence,

Socrates urges Crito to take the same approach to the question of whether he should attempt to escape that he has always taken in thinking through problems. That is, to "heed only that argument which on reflection seems best" (*Crito,* 46b). To proceed otherwise, to abandon reflective argument in the face of circumstantial exigency, would be to proceed as if "what was said before was mere play" (46d).

There is irony here, as there often is with Socrates. (For a study of Socratic irony, see Vlastos, 1991.) Socrates himself had the reputation of being a man who had never grown up, that is, of a man who did not know how to take anything seriously. In the *Gorgias,* Callicles—a hard-headed political realist, Sophist-taught, and extremely ambitious—upbraids Socrates for persisting in childish pastimes. "Philosophy," he says, "is a delightful thing when touched in moderation at the right time of life." But that time is childhood. Thus, philosophy is something that serious-minded people grow out of, as they come to understand what being a free adult citizen is all about, namely, the pursuit of power through politics (*Gorgias,* 484c–485e).

According to his own telling in the *Apology,* Socrates stopped working for a living some time in his mid-forties. (For commentary on the *Apology,* see Reeve, 1989.) From that time until his trial at the age of seventy, he spent his days in the public squares and gymnasia, seeking out conversation with anyone he "happened to meet, young and old, citizen and stranger" (*Apology,* 30a). His usual audience was a crowd of idle youth, scions of the landed gentry, and the Sophists' most lucrative clients. They had leisure to wile away hours listening to Socrates confront the pillars of the democratic power structure: the poets, public craftsmen, and professional rhetors. (For a discussion of the political ramifications, see Stone, 1988.) They were also inclined by native disposition, stamped upon them through years of intensive conditioning at home, to respond favorably when democratic political eminence was brought low by the thousand cuts a thorough Socratic examination could inflict. As a group, the wealthy, landed families from which Socrates' young auditors came grew increasingly unfriendly to the democracy in the last half of the fifth century BCE. Athens became embroiled in a draining conflict with Sparta, the Peloponnesian War, that proved a particularly onerous burden for them. As debate over the war became more ideologically polarized between oligarchs and democrats, Socrates' critical mission became more controversial. Finally, the perception, misguided though it may have been, that Socrates was the avatar of a potential oligarchic junta landed him on trial for his life.

Socrates defended himself, in part, by urging his judges (i.e., the 501 jurors) to see that it is a basic misunderstanding of his life to regard it in political terms. It is true, Socrates concedes, that he has "meddled and interfered" in his fellow citizens' affairs; but he has deliberately avoided the political assemblies and law courts (*Apology,* 31c). He has acted, he says, out of interlocking concerns for the sanctity of the Oracle at Delphi and the good condition of his own soul. Both ends have impelled him to a public mission of constant engagement with his fellows as individuals, but not as a collective body. He is a "private busybody," a contradiction in terms in the contemporary conception of things.

This new orientation to public life and personal "soul therapy" (as Socrates calls it at *Apology,* 30b) was perhaps too subtle to convey to a courtroom packed with edgy democrats, freshly stirred by Socrates' prosecutors with visions of "Laconizing" (sympathetic to Sparta) cabals awaiting Socrates' signal before unleashing the final counterrevolution (see Ostwald, 1986). What was clearer to see was the influence Socrates manifestly exercised on a certain group of rich young men, including some of the most aggressive oligarchs of the day. Socrates is insouciant about the effects of his mission, however, because he does not regard himself as a teacher. He is merely a servant of the god of Delphi, tending above all to a pressing personal matter that necessitates his being in continual contact with his fellow citizens. If a few young men with time on their hands see fit to imitate him and his methods, that is their affair. If their parents and elders take offense, they should either answer the challenge put or reform their lives so as to make such answer more compelling. But it is evading the underlying problem to vent their resentment on him.

Socrates, then, was the consummately ironic teacher. That is, he taught what he did by not teaching, just as he was wise in the wisdom of his own ignorance. He calls his wisdom "peculiarly human," and sums it up in the observation that "human wisdom is worth little or nothing" (*Apology,* 20d, 23b). The hidden meanings in such ironic gestures can get lost on large crowds and in the brute judgments of public opinion. Yet Socrates refused simply to shun that forum and persisted to the end in trying to grapple and reckon within it with the prejudices against him. Ultimately he failed, and he paid for that failure with his life. In Plato's assessment well after the fact, Socrates should have foreseen as much. That he did not, pointed to two deep flaws in his philosophical persona.

Plato discusses these flaws by drawing explicit contrast between Socrates' "polypragmatism" and the conduct of the truly just person. Justice, Plato teaches, consists in understanding what one is fit by one's natural constitution to do, and simply doing that, "without meddling in the tasks of others" (*Republic*, 433a). Looking back, Plato seems to have concluded that Socrates' obdurate pursuit of open-ended engagement with his fellow citizens represented a certain restlessness of the soul, an unsettledness that reflected Socrates' failure to appreciate how profoundly his philosophical gift set him apart from the common run of humanity. As a result, Socrates developed the fractured soul of the "polypragmatist" meddler, rather than the perfect single-mindedness of the psychically harmonized philosopher, who knows the futility of political engagement in a corrupt city.

Plato offers a precaution to philosophic educators working with untested youth. In Plato's view, Socrates erred, and erred profoundly, when he allowed the youth of Athens indiscriminate access to himself. He simply failed to understand the power he had, the potency of the methods he was deploying, and the breadth of understanding he really possessed. Thus, he squandered it. Above all, he made of his work in philosophy something that could too easily be turned into mere *paidia* in the hands of fools and opportunists.

Socrates himself was sanguine at the prospect of young puppies imitating him. After all, such activity "is not unpleasant" (*Apology*, 33c). This reflected a playfulness in Socrates that was not so far removed from the sophistic play Plato derides. The key difference: Socratic play is ironic play, layered with meanings therefore that will resonate as a variant function of his auditors' attentiveness and capacities. That is to say that Socratic play is never "mere" play, because it is never "mere" anything (*Apology*, 30c). Nevertheless, for all its ironic wisdom, it does derive from a fundamental nonconformism, which Socrates' character epitomized. He did not, as the Platonic philosopher does, merely make the best of life in a corrupt city. He

flourished in that city, making himself into an eccentric exemplar of it. In the end, in Platonic hindsight, he was too much the individual and not enough the form; too much improvisation and not enough structure. In short, he was too playful, and his play was too free. He marked a clear progression beyond the Sophists but only, Plato wrote many years after Socrates' death, to the point of being a sort of "noble Sophist." True philosophy (and therefore also true play) lies beyond sophistry entirely. Socratic play, in the mature (critical) Platonic view, marks a development beyond the sophistic-tragic type, but it still lacks a certain metaphysical gravitas. Consequently, it is limited in precisely the way Socrates' method of open-ended inquiry from the standpoint of ironic ignorance is, in comparison with the mature Platonic method of synoptic dialectic.

The *Paidia/Paideia* Nexus

One of the reasons that Plato was reluctant either to dismiss the category of *paidia* as neutral and innocuous, or to relegate it to the negative pole of an axis governed by "serious philosophy" on its positive end, was his love of puns (e.g., *Apology*, 24d, 25c, 26a). That a word meaning trivial amusement—*paidia*—differed by only a single letter from a word signifying the sum of all formative influences by which a person's habits are forged into finished character—*paideia*—was, simply, too intriguing to leave unexplored. The question therefore posed itself: What is the link between *paidia* and *paideia*? Plato's answer, in short, is that it is a fundamental one, forged from two basic pedagogic principles. The first is that play is a medium of activity in which the player's natural underlying dispositions are revealed. (These in turn constrain, without determining, the cultivating influence of *paideia*.) The second is that play is the ideal medium of a child's *paideia*; that is, learning is most effective when play is its medium. There are a number of implications that can be drawn from these principles in regard to Plato's theory of development, as well as for his concept of fully actualized philosophic activity as a kind of perfectly realized play.

The Philosopher at Play

There are four settings in which to consider the broad range of activities befitting philosophical character as Plato models it, which Plato characterizes as "playful." The passage most resonant with these is *Laws,* 636e–674c, in which Plato furnishes the room left open for play at *Republic,* 396e, with a prescription for unconventional pedagogy.

It is early going in Plato's longest work, and the Athenian, speaking in the voice of Platonic doctrine, has dropped a provocative remark: Drinking parties, he says, when in the charge of a skilled "symposiarch," have a positive part to play in the education of young people. Of course his friends from Sparta and Crete, countries known for conservative social mores, are scandalized. For them, the very term "drinking party" (in Greek, *symposium*) connotes unrestrained revelry, the loss of self-control, and therefore, it seems to them, the antithesis of sound education. We have seen already that Plato recognizes in principle and theory the crucial formative role of play. Here, he evinces that recognition in an elaborate explanation for his suspicious companions. Drinking, Plato observes, elicits intense emotions, and makes such emotions easy to elicit. A well-run symposium will exploit this fact to promote sound habits, by testing drinkers under conditions far safer than those that actually have such impact. So, for example, instead of entering into an actual contract with someone with an overdeveloped inclination to cheat, it is less risky and more efficient to get him drunk and pretend to exchange promises with him. Plato calls this "examination through play," using the same Greek term, *elenchus,* that Socrates used as a general description of his method. (For discussion of the *elenchus,* see Robinson, 1953.)

The Socratic resonance of Plato's playful proposals calls attention to an important feature of them. They are *addressed to the paideia* of the philosopher, not to the philosopher fully formed. Like Socrates himself, the child at well-structured play has not yet reached the complete actualization of his or her potentialities for flourishing excellence (the ultimate end of a human life for all the classical philosophers). What role for play when this condition has been attained? To be sure, the "end" of good *paideia* is not an object, separate as such from the process of striving that brings it about. It is, rather, like health: realized precisely through engaging in the activities that produce it (Aristotle, 1094a 3–4, translated by Ostwald, 1962). But it is the full formation, the "perfection" (in the sense of "completion") of abilities and habits that are

still being shaped in the psyches of the young. Plato's theory of education is aimed at achieving such perfection in an entire city of citizens. So the question is: Does the fully formed philosopher still play, and if so, in what does his or her play consist?

There is considerable latitude within Plato's concept of the philosopher for the concept of play. And indeed, although the philosopher at play is revealed only in glimpses and asides here and there in the dialogues, there is enough in these scattered *aperçus* for a vivid collage.

Writing as Play

At *Phaedrus,* 276–278, toward the end of his strange, profound conversation with Phaedrus, Socrates takes up the nature of writing, after having devoted scrupulous and thorough attention to speech. The passage appears to be, and has been read as, an emphatic relegation of writing to inferior status within the storehouse of the philosopher's talents and abilities. But what Socrates actually says is subtler than a blunt ranking. The philosopher, he asserts, "writes, when he does, in *paidia,*" with an eye to years ahead when "age oblivious comes." When undertaken in the spirit of play, writing is an excellent pastime, surpassing almost any other. Of course, at its best, writing falls short still of dialectic, the art of conversation in its philosophic expression.

Ontology as Play

Plato says, at *Phaedrus,* 277e, that all writing necessarily contains "much *paidia.*" But he does not in this passage dismiss writing as "mere *paidia.*" As we have seen he reserves that attitude for the shenanigans of such as Euthydemus and Dionysiodorus. But the philosopher's activity is always different in kind from that of the Sophist—at least, so a basic premise of Platonic philosophy holds.

Writing, then, if not mere *paidia,* is nevertheless a form of philosopher's play. Thus, it is clear that *paidia* is within the philosopher's repertoire of activity. An aside in the *Parmenides* makes this clear. One of Plato's densest and least accessible works, it shows Plato deep within the puzzles and problems of the late metaphysical phase of his career (see Miller, 1986). The setting is a probably fictional meeting between the venerable founder of Greek metaphysics, Parmenides, and a young Socrates. After a complex round of preliminaries, Parmenides finally offers to initiate Socrates in the abstruse techniques of the dialectics of being and unity, the very heart of true philosophy, according to the *Phaedrus's* telling. The wording of Parmenides' offer is striking: "Would you like me, since we are committed to this laborious *paidia,* to begin the game with my own supposition, that there is a 'one'?" That Plato could call the succeeding thirty pages of intricate argumentation a game (literally, "gymnastic"), much less *paidia,* has caused some commentators consternation, even moving one or two to excuse themselves from the task of working through Parmenides' hypotheses with care and concentration (as if a well-played game did not often require exquisite care and concentration). A better reading sees in it another view of the philosopher at play.

Myth Creating as Play
Twice Plato refers to myth creating as a kind of play (Friedlander, 1973). In the *Phaedrus,* at 265c, Socrates refers to the magnificent rhetorical display he has just offered as "really just *paidia.*" He then proceeds to deconstruct it, by a reduction of its multifarious mythic dimensions, to a pair of powerful, if austere, metaphysical principles. Of course, the distinction at work here augurs the analogous one he draws a few pages after between writing and dialectic. Within that analogy writing and myth making both end up as kinds of play distinctively characteristic of the philosopher.

Again, in the *Statesman* (268de), Plato refers to a grand and gorgeous myth he has created as a "*paidia.*" But, the Eleatic Stranger (the teller of the myth) says to Socrates, "it is not so many years since you left off child's play." The Stranger turns to myth, he says, in seeking relief from the labor (that is, the "laborious play," as the *Parmenides* puts it) of dialectic. What follows is a wide-ranging story in which the evolution of the *polis* (the political community) is placed within the context of the cycles of cosmic generation and destruction. The result for the dialectical investigation is a sense of depth that it acquires in the wake and light of the myth, perhaps not unlike the ineffable resonance that the philosopher's technical prowess takes on when he or she engages in play.

Natural Science as Play
Finally, in the *Timaeus* (59d), Plato sets one more philosophical pastime under the broadening rubric of play, namely natural science (that is, what Plato calls "the study of the truths of generation"). Such study, he says, is "wise and

moderate *paidia.*" The "truths of generation," it should be said, mark a strange new metaphysical category for Plato, a new reconciliation of the ideas of truth and becoming that in earlier articulations of his metaphysics had been held to be flatly contradictory. The *Timaeus* is largely devoted to limning this reconciliation in detail. A consequence is the emergence of a theoretical prospect uncontemplated before: a Platonic science of the natural world.

Paidia as the Medium for Paideia
For Plato, play is at once the natural medium of formative *paideia* (the condition in which children take most readily to what they must learn), as well as the natural medium of the child's underlying dispositions of desire and appetite (the raw stuff that *paideia* seeks to train and channel). Play is something more to the mature philosopher, something that binds together myth creation, natural science, ontological gymnastic, and writing itself. Indeed, in view of the broad range of philosophical activity Plato is willing to label as play, it does not seem an exaggeration to say that *paidia* is a sort of unifying principle of Platonic philosophical praxis—a signature the philosopher's actions bear that marks them as distinctively philosophical. Plato himself says as much in the *Laws* (803d).

The passage concerns the "right use of leisure," that is, the right use of freedom. The core principle, the Athenian says, is sound habituation: to use our leisure well we must train our desires in such a way that what we end up wanting is just what conduces to flourishing leisure. (It might be said, in Platonic tenor, that one's leisure habits are one's most basic habits of character.)

At this point, however, the Athenian takes a peculiar turn from his earnest reflections: "Not that human affairs are worth taking very seriously—but take them seriously is just what we are compelled to do, alas."

He explains that, in fact, human beings are merely "a toy of God's," but that this is no mean station to occupy in the scheme of things. The imperative that rests on such creatures is simple: "Every man and every woman should play this part and spend life making our *paidia* as perfect as possible—admittedly an inversion of the prevailing view!" The prevailing view is that there is a clear line between play and seriousness, leisure and work, and that human beings engage in the latter for the sake of the former. In truth, however, "real leisure—that is, *paidia* in the true sense"—just is a life of sound *paideia*.

Of course, there is a certain circularity in Plato's beguiling formula: good *paideia,* he seems to say, is playing as one plays who has undergone good *paideia.* But this circle is the one in which the human condition is embedded, in Plato's view. We only come to know how to live through the formative influence of persons who had come to their understanding of how to live through having themselves been rightly formed. What these cycles end up being is *paideia;* but what moves them—the dynamic energy that actualizes what they are—is play.

Notes

1. The text citations are to the Stephanus numbers, appearing in the margins of most editions of Plato's works, and enabling easy cross-reference. This translation is Huizinga's, from *Homo Ludens* (1955), supra note 3, p. 160.
2. Here, and in the discussion that follows, "Socrates" refers to the main character of the Platonic dialogues. The *Apology* marks the limit of verisimilitude in Platonic depictions of Socrates. Everywhere else we encounter a character who has taken life in a philosophical-literary imagination made text by Plato.
3. I parenthesize the pro forma generic inclusion because Plato does. That is, alone among ancient thinkers we know of, Plato insists that women be trained alongside men, in the full range of vocations and skills for which they display natural aptitude (which, he believes, will describe the same range among women as a group as it does among men). Plato is still a sexist thinker, in the sense that he believes women as a class to be inferior to men as a class. What he disputes in the sexist ideology of his day is that women as a class are naturally fit for one function only, child rearing. Plato, then, was an equal opportunity sexist, which, in the context of his day, was a kind of feminist. See *Republic,* 451 ff., 466c ff., and *Laws,* 804e ff. Plato twice features women in important speaking roles in his dialogues: Aspasia (the mistress of Pericles, and a luminary of mid-fifth-century Athenian intellectual culture) in the *Menexenus,* and, more famously, the probably fictional (but still fascinating) Diotima, in the *Symposium.*

Bibliography

Friedlander, P. (1973). *Plato* (H. Meyerhoff, Trans.). Vols. 1–3. Bollingen Series 5a. Princeton, NJ: Princeton University Press.

Guthrie, W. K. C. (1971). *The Sophists.* Cambridge: Cambridge University Press.

Huizinga, J. (1955). *Homo ludens: A study of the play element in culture.* Boston: Beacon.

Irwin, T. H. (1992). Plato: The intellectual background. In R. Kraut (Ed.), *The Cambridge companion to Plato* (pp. 51–89). Cambridge: Cambridge University Press.

Kahn, C. H. (1979). *The art and thought of Heraclitus: An edition of the fragments with translation and commentary.* Cambridge: Cambridge University Press.

Kahn, C. H. (1996). *Plato and the Socratic dialogue.* Cambridge: Cambridge University Press.

Kerferd, G. B. (1981). *The sophistic movement.* Cambridge: Cambridge University Press.

Liddell, H. G., & Scott, R. (1925). Revised by H. S. Jones (1968). *A Greek-English Lexicon* (9th ed.). Oxford: Oxford University press.

Miller, M. H. (1986). *Plato's Parmenides: The conversion of the soul.* University Park: Pennsylvania State University Press.

Nehamas, A. (1982). Plato on imitation and poetry in Republic 10. In J. Moravcsik & P. Temko (Eds.), *Plato on beauty, wisdom, and the arts* (pp. 47–48). Totowa, NJ: Rowman and Littlefield.

Nehamas, A. (1988). Plato and the mass media. *The Monist, 71,* 214–234.

Ostwald, M. (1962). Trans. of Aristotle. *Nicomachean ethics.* The Library of the Liberal Arts. Indianapolis: Bobbs-Merrill.

Ostwald, M. (1986). *From popular sovereignty to the sovereignty of law: Law, society, and politics in fifth-century Athens.* Berkeley: University of California Press.

Reeve, C. D. C. (1989). *Socrates in the Apology: An essay on Plato's apology of Socrates.* Indianapolis: Hackett.

Robinson, R. (1953). *Plato's earlier dialectic* (2nd ed.). Oxford: Clarendon.

Shakespeare, W. (1986). *The complete works.* Oxford: Oxford University Press.

Spariosu, M. I. (1991). *God of many names: Play, poetry, and power in Helenic thought from Homer to Aristotle.* Durham, NC: Duke University Press.

Stone, I. F. (1988). *The trial of Socrates.* Boston: Little, Brown.

Vlastos, G. (1991). *Socrates, ironist and moral philosopher.* Ithaca, NY: Cornell University Press.

Play, Proteus, and Paradox

Education for a Chaotic and Supersymmetric World

Karen VanderVen

Utilizing a chaos theory rationale, this essay discusses how a mentally effective adult "Protean" self (adaptive and resilient) can develop through the childhood experience of play. Educators can use "Supersymmetry," which is a means of optimally combining chaotic (play) and linear (traditional) types of instruction, in order to pave the way toward the Protean self.

As the end of the twentieth century approaches, rapid change is the hallmark in all modes of human endeavor. Major institutions in society—family, work, community—have been transformed from earlier years. "The modern nuclear family is fast disappearing. In its stead we now have a new structure—the postmodern permeable family—that mirrors the openness, complexity, and diversity of our contemporary lifestyles" (Elkind, 1994, p. 1). Workers no longer can assume they will have just one employer and one career in a lifetime; they are urged to have portable skills, be prepared for frequent mobility, and anticipate several careers. Daily life is not bounded by just one's own community; global concerns touch everybody no matter where they live. A prominent futurist, predicting the global economy of the future, asserts that people will need to understand "global paradox:" the importance of small entities as others grow larger and larger (Naisbitt, 1994).

These radical changes not only govern how people live in the world today, but also how they view and make meaning of it. The perspective of "chaos theory" expresses and can help people understand and relate to these transformations in world changes and worldviews. (In this essay, the term "chaos theory" subsumes consideration of the term "complexity," which some consider to be part

of and others consider to be separate from, chaos theory.)

As new worldviews so often do, chaos theory emanates from conceptual and empirical advances in the physical sciences. Challenging the classical scientific view of the world as orderly, rational, predictable, and controllable, chaos theory is concerned with disequilibrium, complexity, and unpredictability. In fact, this transformed perspective is so compelling that it affects perception of the very nature of the change process. One theorist states that change is "not what it used to be" (Handy, 1989, p. 4). From this theoretical perspective, the reality of the world is essentially chaotic (Goerner, 1994). In fields such as health, economics, and industry, which are beginning to embrace chaos theory, it increasingly informs the perspectives of professionals in those fields.

Given this context, these questions arise: What kind of persons will be able to live successfully in "chaotic" times? How can educators and parents prepare children and youth to have the requisite attributes? In other words, how can children develop the "Protean" selves that will be needed for life in chaos? The concept of a Protean self, "embracing human resilience, is predicated on Proteus, the Greek sea god of many forms" (Lifton, 1993), who was able to be resilient and responsive because he could change (or adapt) his form to meet conditions. An appropriate metaphor to express the human qualities necessary for success is the "Protean self." Such a person is able to adapt readily to a rapidly changing, even confounding, context while still being able to maintain an internal sense of direction.

Helping children develop Protean selves is a daunting challenge to educational and developmental missions, philosophies, and practices. Despite the need to meet this challenge, however, professionals in the fields of early childhood and elementary education seem to be among the slowest in embracing the perspectives and practices derived from chaos theory. Traditional structures, teaching methods, and curriculum content continue to prevail. The reluctance of educators to change both their thinking and their practices, even in the face of compelling evidence to justify change, may be due to many factors, ranging from a resistance to the principles of chaos theory to an obliviousness concerning these tenets.

Play, affirmed for its dynamic qualities (Fromberg, 1995; Smilansky, 1990a, 1990b), is an ideal medium for providing an understanding of the world as chaotic. For this compelling reason, play should not only be accepted as a legitimate educational activity in the early childhood and elementary school grades, but also as a featured curricular component at all educational levels (appropriately in conjunction with other school instructional methods). For play to provide this most powerful impact and facilitate children's development of Protean selves, however, requires educators to pay special attention to the functions, characteristics, facilitation, and development of play that are relevant to chaos theory.

A salient example of the resistance to play and its role in the curriculum is that, despite a substantial literature describing play's power to positively affect young persons' development in all spheres (Fromberg, 1992; Smilansky, 1990a), many educators still view play as, at best, an activity to be tolerated and, at worst, a practice to be discouraged or eliminated in favor of formal academic instruction and drill in isolated subjects (Seefeldt, 1992; Smilansky, 1990a).

This essay focuses primarily on the role of play in fostering "Protean self-development" in children. It provides an overview of chaos theory and its basic tenets most relevant to child development and education; shows the relationship of these characteristics of play to chaotic phenomena and to the qualities that would characterize Protean selves; proposes a chaotically oriented educational approach that incorporates play in the curriculum; and looks beyond chaos theory to "supersymmetry" (balanced playful and academic activity) as an ultimate embracing paradigm that unifies both play and school instruction.

Chaos Theory

According to one theorist, "Where chaos begins, classical science stops" (Gleick, 1987, p. 3). Thus, it is perhaps easiest to understand chaos theory in contrast to the mechanistic worldview of classical theory in the physics of the sixteenth into the twentieth century in which lawfulness, precision, linearity, predictability, stasis, and reductionism held sway (Gleick, 1987; Goerner, 1994; Penrose, 1989). The advent of quantum theory, "a theory of uncertainty, indeterminism, and mystery" (Penrose, 1989, p. 150), ushered in a new worldview. Chaos theory, referring to the nonlinearity, interdependence, and unpredictability of dynamic systems (systems that move) (Goerner, 1994) expresses this new worldview.

Nonlinearity, Interdependence, and Unpredictability

Nonlinearity implies multiple causation and nonabsolute proportionality. Educators, however, frequently utilize linear thinking, in which one cause yields one effect. If Johnny is acting differently today, for example, the linear thinker might say that he is upset "because something is going on at home," rather than consider that he may be affected by multiple occurrences in home, school, and other settings such as the neighborhood. In contrast to the linear view, Johnny's behavior is not unidirectional; that is, these events do not just affect him. In turn, he would affect them as well, in an ever-evolving, transactional process. If he were upset because he had gotten in a fight, but had driven off the bullies, for example, his life in the neighborhood would be different from if he had been unsuccessful in challenging their aggression. His behavior at school would be different as well.

Similarly, in a nonlinear world, proportionality is not absolute or directly additive. "More is better" thinking (VanderVen, 1994), for example, would suggest that children will absolutely learn more in school if the school day is lengthened. Nonabsolute proportional thinking, however, might paradoxically suggest that children will learn less if they spend the additional time engaging in more drill work and other passive occupations, because then the children will become even more disengaged from learning.

Interdependence refers to the effect of

multiple variables of a system in interaction with each other. The ecological theory of child development (Bronfenbrenner, 1977) offers a powerful example of interdependence by seeing each child influenced by concentric circles of multi-directional systems that interact among each other. The power of each of these systems is partially related to their place in the total system but also to the salience of their characteristics in relation to the child's developmental and educational needs at any one time.

Unpredictability refers to the fact that in a "chaotic" world, even a very small single input may lead to an output that is unexpected or unpredictable. Practitioners of a behavior modification program, for example, might "take points away" from children who "misbehave" and expect that they will be able to control children's actions in a desired way. Imagine the consternation of those who utilize these practices if they find that the behavior is "worse" than ever and even harder to "control" (VanderVen, 1994). From the perspective of chaos theory, however, unpredictability is often reflected by novel, surprising, and paradoxical or unexpected occurrences. In fact, a relatively minor change in teacher or child behavior might result in a strong change in direction of the consequent behavior.

Complex Adaptive Systems

Systems that appear chaotic, as they evolve in time, establish a pattern of behavior that, although complex, is eventually recognizable and describable. This phenomenon leads to another tenet—that there is order in chaos (Goerner, 1994). As the systems access information from interactions with other systems in the environment, they feed this information back into the system of interest, thereby demonstrating "learning" and defining regularities or schemata. Based on these schemata, the chaotic systems then continue to act on the world in an "ordered" way (Gell-Mann, 1994). Complex adaptive systems thus are both emergent and evolutionary. One system may spawn a new one, which in turn evolves into a new, coherent, and complex form, and the cycle of creation and re-creation continues. Complex adaptive systems are present in all aspects of the world, animate and inanimate. The concept of complex adaptive systems is central to the rationale for the power and significance of play.

Other Concepts of Chaos Theory

There are other specific concepts describing chaotic phenomena that exist within dynamic systems. Those concepts that are most pertinent to play, education, and the goals and dynamics of human development are recursion, entrainment, disequilibrium, weak chaos, bifurcation, self-organization, fractal, attractor, sensitive dependence on initial conditions, entropy, dissipative system, determinism, phase portrait, and fuzzy logic. The concepts and their definitions are in Figure 1. They integrate earlier definitions described by VanderVen, 1994; and they draw from Gell-Mann, 1994; Gleick, 1987; Goerner, 1994; and Wheatley, 1992.

Integrating Play and the Concepts of Chaos Theory

The section that follows will offer a "chaotic" analysis of the functions, characteristics, facilitation, and development of play, integrating the concepts of chaos theory. This discussion is based on the following premises:

- Play itself is a significant complex adaptive system within human development, with chaotic aspects that embrace and generate within it other complex adaptive systems continuously representing and generating information. Play, then, can relate to and increase the effectiveness of learning.
- Play is necessary for young learners, not only in order to let them experience the pervasive characteristics of chaos, but also to help them gain a sense of themselves as complex adaptive systems and as continual learners in a lifetime of development into "Protean selves."

As one author remarks, "It seems that the very experiences these children seek out are ones we avoid: disequilibrium, novelty, loss of control, surprise. These make for a good playground . . ." (Wheatley, 1992, p. 75).

Functions of Play

When considering the significance of play in the development of the Protean self, its specific functions in development are key. A synthesis of research and scholarship on play (Fromberg, 1992; Smilansky 1990a, 1990b) suggests that

FIGURE 1. Concepts of Chaos Theory Relevant to Play

- *Recursion.* Information from a system is fed back on itself, thereby changing the nature of the system and affecting the initial condition. Often recursion effects are responsible for unanticipated or paradoxical outcomes.
- *Entrainment.* Two or more systems join to become a larger, synchronous system, effecting "the synchronization of two or more rhythmic systems into a single pulse" (Nachmanovitch, 1990, p. 99). Entrainment thus embraces a combinatory notion; that separate entities become juxtaposed or connected in ways that form new combinations and coherent patterns.
- *Disequilibrium.* A system that is in a state capable of change.
- *Weak chaos.* A small amount of chaos that may be introduced into a system to keep it dynamic.
- *Bifurcation.* A transformation can influence a system to re-organize or enter into a completely different, new state; a bifurcation may result in surprise, due to the rapidity and nature of the change.
- *Self-organization.* Characteristic of a complex adaptive system; the spontaneous reemergence of a turbulent, disequilibrious system into patterned, computational behavior that is purposeful.
- *Fractal.* Self-similarity, in which iteration reproduces the a self-similar pattern at different levels of scale, over and over.

- *Attractor.* A system that may appear to exist in apparent disorder may continue to refer, in its evolution, toward a certain "attracted" behavior or state of being.
- *Sensitive dependence on initial conditions.* A very small input into a system may yield widely disparate results, in both form and quantity.
- *Entropy.* "The inexorable tendency of the universe, and any isolated system within it, to slide toward a state of increasing disorder" (Gleick, 1987, p. 257).
- *Dissipative system.* An open, bounded system whose energy is given off to, or dissipated to, its surrounds; as contrasted to a tightly bounded "conservative system" (Goerner, 1994).
- *Determinism.* This refers to the paradoxical fact that language makes it possible to describe and prescribe the parameters and behavior of a system although it is not possible to linearly predict the form of its evolution over time.
- *Phase portrait.* Phase portraits or "phase space portraits" are the geometrical, topological representations of the dynamics of a system that enable the "mapping of possible states (the) system can go through" (Goerner, 1994, p. 206)
- *Fuzzy logic.* Reasoning with non-absolute or dichotomous quantities or concepts (Kosko, 1993); relates to the mental processes that enable human beings to understand chaos.

---

play promotes the following understandings, which are related in a later section to the attributes of the Protean self:

- *Representational/symbolic.* Play allows the player to let one thing stand for another. Players use symbols and represent their perceptions of the world through both the symbolic and nonsymbolic use of various media. Play is an ideal medium for representing, and hence experiencing, chaotic content and concepts.
- *Meaning making.* Through enabling the player to connect various elements of experience, play is personally meaningful and, in a constructivist context, enables players to make meaning out of their experience as they combine various aspects into larger configurations. The patterned aspect of a complex adaptive system is relevant here; the play enables

the player to gain an experiential sense of meaningful patterns.
- *Dynamic.* By its very nature play embraces continual change; it has an "oscillatory" quality in which themes and the use of materials shift from moment to moment (Fromberg, 1992). Children at play thus experience and learn from play's capacity to convey the dynamic aspects of a phenomenon or situation. Play develops and evolves in the growing human being.
- *Connectionist.* Play enables the players to make connections among themes, situations, and persons. The nature of "cooperative" play makes play an ideal medium in which to study interdependence. Indeed, as one author points out, a goal of the Education 2000 project has been to help children "develop a sense of the interdependence that char-

acterizes today's world" (Beane, 1995, p. 91).

- *Referential.* Play has a focus at all times. This focus may be in the form of a theme or a frame of reference that gives the play itself a purpose, thus encouraging goal-oriented or computational behavior.
- *Regulatory.* Play is a form of self-expression that enables the integration and mastery of diverse, and perhaps puzzling, experiences. In this way, play serves a major role in the development of self-regulation.
- *Creative.* Play, with its combinatory, integrative aspects, both developing and reflecting divergent thinking, enables creativity to take place in the construction of new patterns and configurations. In fact, children elaborate and modify the themes of their play. In these ways they are being creative in the essential sense of producing "variations on a theme" (Hofstadter, 1985, p. 232).
- *Informational.* As a dynamic system in constant evolution, play creates information, including the development of abstraction, knowledge of attributes of both objects and persons, and, through entrainment, the incorporation of new information into older constructs.

Chaotic Characteristics of Play

The characteristics of play that make it "playful" and reflect its chaotic capacities are described as follows:

- *Recursive.* Because it is constructivist, play is recursive; that is, it feeds back into itself information that it creates, and therefore changes the nature of the player(s) and the evolving nature of the play.
- *Entraining.* Playful activity is entraining by taking two disparate elements, combining them, and enabling them to function together integratively and harmoniously.
- *Disequilibrious.* Children initiate play as a result of an internal feeling of disequilibrium; the act of play is designed to modify that feeling. Disequilibrium is not always a negatively perceived situation to be quickly resolved; curiosity, for example, can create a sense of disequilib-

rium that engages children in enjoyable action. When a play episode results in a child's perception that inner equilibrium has been achieved, the child may become curious about another domain of knowledge and focus play in that area.

- *Fractal.* Many play materials have fractal qualities in that they are similar in form no matter what their size. Blocks are just one example. One of the fascinations for children in pattern building with blocks is the exploration of their fractal nature.
- *Sensitive to (dependent on) initial conditions.* In play, a minor or apparently insignificant occurrence can have extensive and influential outcomes. The simple, perhaps even casual act of suggesting that a certain object stand for a theme-related concept can initiate a dynamic and expansive play episode that may last for days, weeks, or months.
- *Attractor-driven.* The goal or theme of any particular play event serves as the attractor or driving point around the play as it revolves and evolves. The dynamic nature of play implies that goals and themes can shift and, as they do, so will the attractor. These changes may be gradual or transformational. Transformational changes are often governed by a periodic or even "strange" attractor.
- *Self-organizing.* As play evolves into a complex adaptive system, it is self-organizing, developing its own pattern of coherence. Each player must self-organize and make meaning of the experience.

Play Facilitation

Just as adults resist the idea that play is a legitimate educational component of the curriculum, they also resist the suggestion that teachers might have an active role in enabling good quality play to occur. Such intransigence persists despite research evidence that children with gaps in their development and experience need such activity, and that it results in higher-level play and developmental outcomes.

Among facilitation strategies are such adult actions such as suggesting a theme or a use for an object, taking on or assigning a role, adding a player, introducing a new object, and changing the physical environment (Smilanksy, 1990a). Creating a web, a strategy for bifurcating play into higher, more complex levels, takes on new significance in a chaos analysis. The issue of the adult role in encouraging quality play is the subject of debate, despite research (Smilansky, 1990b) contending that adult facilitation of play is crucial for children, particularly those with gaps in their earlier development or exposure to certain experiences. Several chaos concepts are particularly relevant to justify such play facilitation:

- *Determinism.* This paradoxical concept (i.e., that a system can be both determined *and* have unpredictable outcomes) is useful in play facilitation. Teachers need not view their play facilitation strategies, such as setting the stage for play or suggesting a theme, as "dampers" on children's creative use of play because the outcomes of these facilitations will not be totally predictable.
- *Weak chaos.* Any play facilitation action injects weak chaos (i.e., a change in the dynamic) into the system and keeps it dynamic, changing, moving, and evolving.
- *Bifurcation.* The facilitator, in order to extend play, may encourage a bifurcation, which is a transition into a new form or state. The Vygotskian concept of "scaffolding," for example, enables a child to move to higher levels of development that require a transitional period (Berk & Winsler, 1995). Scaffolding in this context is analogous to creating a bifurcation. Given "Sensitive Dependence on Initial Conditions," the theory implies that any facilitation can encourage such a bifurcation.
- *Attractor.* As play settles into a stable pattern and then begins to run down, adult facilitation may alter the attractor to reconfigure the play into a novel focus that engages the children's energy and attention. Adding slightly novel materials such as a "real" lunchbox or toolbox to a sociodramatic play center will enable children to reinvest in their play.
- *Phase portrait.* This term suggests a geometrical, topological representation of the dynamics of a system. Phase portraits or "phase space portraits" enable the "mapping of possible states [the] system can go through" (Goerner, 1994, p. 206). Although this is a simplification, the process of "webbing," which graphically maps the extensions, existing knowledge,

and related themes of a given concept, can be considered the childhood analogy of a phase portrait. Indeed, a well-done web, with its varied patterns and connections, is a dynamic representation.

Play Development and Human Development

Traditionally, play as a construct or phenomenon has been subsumed within the wider fields of human development. With a chaotic analysis of human development, therefore, both play and play facilitation take on even greater legitimacy. No longer is human development throughout the life span viewed as a sequence of invariant stages, in which the person moves linearly and sequentially from one to the next. Rather it is conceived as a recursive, dynamic process in which new, complex capacities emerge as a result of individuals making meaning of their experiences, and constructing a new sense of self in a constantly emergent and evolutionary process (Kegan, 1982). This shift in conceptualizaton of development "from entity to process, from static to dynamic, from dichotomous to dialectical," and as a lifelong process in which "evolution or adaptation is the master motion in personality" (Kegan, 1982, pp. 13, 113) has a strong flavor of chaos. This perspective would suggest support for the examination of more specific components of development such as play, so that they can be effectively integrated within the contemporary viewpoint.

Human development itself is like play, a complex adaptive system in which human beings take in experiences and integrate them with existing information, in effect, a process of "constructivism" (Kegan, 1982). This feedback process results in the formation of new internal schemata that become entrained with others. A developmental domain such as motor skills, which is a component of play, similarly has chaotic aspects. Complex coordinated movements that not only develop during childhood but also are essential for good functioning in later life have characteristics of "non-equilibrium dissipative systems" (Thelen, 1995, p. 83). Using the scalar concept of a fractal, a specific component of development such as motor capacity, a larger developmental construct such as play, and human development itself have fractal qualities. That is, the same chaotic processes occur in all of these in an integrating fashion. Like human development itself, play development has the characteristics of a complex adaptive system.

Play Development as a Complex Adaptive System

Play not only reflects the essential characteristics of chaos, including interdependence, nonlinearity, and unpredictability; play itself is a complex adaptive system that constantly evolves into more intricate forms and patterns. Play is open-ended, like a complex adaptive system, or more specifically, a dissipative system. Play may take multiple pathways, forms, and options or, in a chaos framework, become bifurcative, recursive, and hence unpredictable. It can go in one direction, or take another, at any time! In this way, of course, play encourages divergent thinking, the compiling of responses to a problem out of multiple sources rather than simply providing one answer, thereby bringing out and enabling the expression of creativity (Baer, 1993; Russ, 1993).

Chaotic Characteristics of Play Development

To show how play functions and develops as a complex adaptive system over time as children grow older, it is helpful to review some of the commonly recognized forms and developmental sequences of play. Sara Smilansky (1990a) provides a model in which there are five basic forms of play:

1. *Functional,* or exploratory play, is a sensorimotor approach in which a child learns the nature of his or her surroundings.
2. *Constructive* play describes children combining pieces or entities, such as blocks.
3. *Dramatic* play entails pretending.
4. *Sociodramatic* play is a form of dramatic play with more than one player interacting around a theme and a time trajectory over which the play continues and evolves.
5. *Games with rules* encompass cooperative play, often with winners and losers. These games are distinguished by child-controlled rules and thus are different from the competitive games usually called "sports."

As a child grows, functional play allows the importation of information into the child's mind and behavioral repertoire. When new forms of play emerge, this repertoire expands, and children select anew from their interaction with others and their physical environment. As children connect and then integrate these forms with each other through entrainment, or combine "individual action sequences into multischeme combinations" (Fromberg, 1992, p. 57), the play becomes more complex.

Sociodramatic play, particularly as it develops out of combinations of other forms of play, embraces interdependence and complexity. It may be the most "chaotic" of the established play forms because it has many of the elements identified in chaos theory.

As new themes emerge, perhaps with facilitation, previously combined forms may entrain again into more combinations. For example, as children add constructive play and other play forms to their sociodramatic play, "projects" emerge. In this process, not only may the play be bifurcative, moving into a transformed state, but it may also increase the number of connections among various aspects. This activates cooperative play, which is characterized by the ability to enable the formation and utilization of already existent connections with both objects and other persons. This is one of the most important functions of play.

The emergence of new forms of play, such as in the sequence proposed by Smilansky (1990a), is actually not a straight trajectory. Play development is more in line with chaos theory and the more contemporary theories of human development (Kegan, 1982). That is, it involves a recursive unfolding and regeneration. Precursor behaviors become entrained into more complex and synchronous forms, and then the form, like a fuzzy image becoming focused, surfaces visibly. Games can serve as an example. Game playing begins during infancy; such simple behaviors as "patty cake" and "peekaboo" promote the anticipation of another's actions. These early game forms might be called *games with implicit rules* since there is no order or pattern to the play. Although game playing is a primary form of play of elementary age children, it does not, therefore, suddenly emerge during the school years as *games with rules*. As children grow older, prior to the introduction of the more formal rules of many games, a somewhat more complex form of play emerges as, *games with informal rules*. These games are characterized by adapting one's own response to nominal guidelines, but with little or no emphasis on winning and losing.

Games with rules, which evolve from this dynamic sequence, often do include winning and losing. The dynamic aspect of games, in all forms, requires anticipation of others' moves, adaptation, and cooperation. Rule-bound games may be significant in preparing children for adult life and also for their ability to reflect dynamic, chaotic aspects of systems (Sigmund, 1993). In fact, this chaotic analysis suggests that teachers may appropriately use game activity in early childhood programs earlier, and more explicitly, than they do now. In order for the games to keep the dynamic and chaotic aspect, however, child control of rules (i.e., ability to adapt the rules to their needs) must be maintained.

Through their exposure to play and other forms of games throughout childhood, children develop the crucial quality of self-regulation (Berk & Winsler, 1995). Children also acquire information and make connections with others as they adapt to the parameters of evolving play scenarios. The experience with games and other forms of play embodies a strong developmental precursor to the adult Protean self. This step toward the Protean self develops as children engage in active play and begin to develop a sense of themselves as having multiple capacities applicable to different situations. Figure 2 provides a graphic representation of the development of play as an evolving complex adaptive system that continually promotes developmental capacities.

Representing Chaos in Play

If children are to embrace a chaotic worldview in adulthood, such learning appropriately begins in early childhood through actual representation. Children can use play materials, both highly structured and preformed ones, such as blocks and other manipulatives; and plastic media, such as clay and water, which must be shaped by an external element, to represent chaotic dynamics.

FIGURE 2. The Development of Play as a Complex Adaptive System

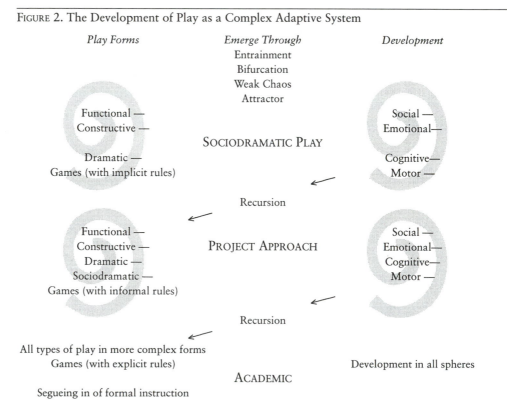

Play Forms *Emerge Through* *Development*

Entrainment
Bifurcation
Weak Chaos
Attractor

Functional —
Constructive —

SOCIODRAMATIC PLAY

Social —
Emotional—

Dramatic —
Games (with implicit rules)

Cognitive—
Motor —

Recursion

Functional —
Constructive —
Dramatic —
Sociodramatic —
Games (with informal rules)

PROJECT APPROACH

Social —
Emotional—
Cognitive—
Motor —

Recursion

All types of play in more complex forms
Games (with explicit rules)

Development in all spheres

ACADEMIC

Segueing in of formal instruction

Evolution of more complex forms of play continues. It may be integrated with formal instruction, which recursively enriches both play and the conceptual level of knowledge and understanding. Instruction may offer continued scaffolding toward higher levels of functioning.

Block forms, ranging from the simple to the extremely complex, allow the creation and representation of many chaotic patterns. Because blocks and many related manipulative materials have fractal properties, they are an ideal way for children to learn the notion of scale and self-similarity. Sequences of blocks from the "simple" squares and rectangles to the more complex varied geometric forms of parquetry, pentaminoes, tangrams, and the like, stopping perhaps just short of Penrose's (1989) tilings of complex but coherent patterns with unusual forms, show the fractal and combinatory range of this well-known play medium. Similarly, children can use three-dimensional blocks to represent the trajectory of complexity, beginning with a simple ordering of unit blocks to working toward the infinite patterns and combinations of Rubik's cubes. Playing with dominoes—doing the favorite childhood trick of setting them on edge, side by side, and then knocking over just one (a small input) and watching as the whole row falls in a flowing stream, one by one, gathering speed (amplification)—is not only a childhood tradition, but also an example of Sensitive Dependence on Initial Conditions.

Materials such as clay, water, paint, paper, and the like have less inherent structure. They can, however, represent combinatory, patterned, transformational aspects of chaos in numerous chaotic ways. Simply dropping paint in water and watching it disperse in the currents is a perfect example of entropy. The "tornado" or vortex created by connecting two large soda bottles at the lips and letting water from one flow into the other is an ideal illustration of creation of turbulence or disequilibrium.

Clay as well as paper can be used for topological representation. Putting a twist into the traditional paper chain, for example, results in a Möbius strip, a transformational change in the state of the paper.

Toward Implementing Play for a Chaotic and Complex Future World

Play may help children to develop the ability to meet the challenges of the chaotic and complex future world, for as one author suggests, "Games and plays help to explore the world and teach us how to come to grips with it" (Sigmund, 1993, p. 7).

Attaining the Protean Self through Play

Childhood experiences that include good quality and facilitated play that represents chaotic dynamics can contribute to the emergence of an adult thinker with the potential to become a creative member of society. Such a person would have the Protean capacities to:

- Self-regulate, to maintain one's center and focus in a shifting context
- Function as a contributing and adaptive member of an entrained, synchronized system
- Think systemically, to recognize interdependence among components of a situation or phenomenon
- Integrate, to see pattern across formally bounded situations and occurrences
- Improvise and create new combinations out of disparate elements or components
- Anticipate and respond flexibly to unpredictability, sudden change, and surprise
- Be reflexive, to be able to look at one's experience and utilize it in planning one's next actions
- See the possibility of paradox in the outcomes of apparently logical interventions into ordinary situations
- View phenomena and situations as emergent and evolutionary, changing in various ways over time
- Be proactive by constructing one's own life and meaning, thereby creating weak chaos and contributing to the continued evolution of humankind; and to see each human being, not only nature, as a vital player in determining what happens in the future (Darling, 1993)
- Utilize metacognition to become aware of one's own thinking processes and actions and to develop and apply them (Fromberg, 1995; Perkins, 1992).

There is a compelling argument for including play in educational settings that support the tenets of chaos. Play, when coupled with the need in society for persons who can relate productively to a chaotic world, can be a major force in creating these individuals. What provisions are necessary to encourage play in human service and educational programs that still seem so linear?

Two frameworks for generating an agenda, which reflect chaotic aspects, are discussed in this section. One is a combined vertical-and-horizontal approach; the other is an ecological approach to development. These two frameworks can aid in attaining the crucial and fractal quality (Perkins, 1992) that can bring coherence and effectiveness to schools and other educational and human service settings.

Vertical-and-Horizontal Integration
A chaos thread of interrelatedness and self-similarity is apparent in the concept of vertical-and-horizontal integration, which consists of connection and adaptation across and "up" and "down" a hierarchy of systems. The most coherent and effective systems will represent both.

In regard to both vertical and horizontal integration, however, the wider child care and education system is greatly fragmented and disconnected—a situation that has had a direct effect upon the integration of play and playfulness in both early childhood and elementary grade settings.

While early childhood programs usually allow—if not actively and richly facilitate—play, for example, their approach is usually quite

disconnected from the pedagogy of elementary education. Elementary education emphasizes a prescriptive curriculum of almost exclusively convergent thinking, memorization, linear and additive progression of bounded subject instruction, delivered within a rigid school bureaucracy. This abrupt transition in the boundary between early childhood and elementary education represents a lack of vertical integration and it constitutes a barrier to an integrated approach to using play in the curriculum. Rather than evolving along a continuum of greater complexity, pattern, and bifurcative aspects, subsequent schooling is thus dichotomized into "play" (in early years) and "work" (in later years).

Across the systems that support and educate young children there is also a lack of integration, which is exemplified in the myriad family structures, agency initiatives, and educational programs that address aspects of the care and education of children. These units often operate without collaboration or even knowledge of other systemic components, resulting in a lack of horizontal integration that affects the care and educational supports as well as the types of play settings available to young children.

Figure 3. Beyond Chaos to Supersymmetry: The Linear and Chaotic Microsytem

	Linearity -------- Chaos	
	Academic Instruction -------- *Play*	
	Less Playful -------- *Playful*	
Physical Environment	Limited options in defined context	Extended options in varied, unbounded contexts
Materials	Sequentially presented Limited	Randomly distributed Richly available
Content	Literal Realistic	Pretend, make believe Creating scenarios
Actions	Independent	Patterned, connected
Role of Adults	Directive Controlling	Facilitative Instructional
Schedule	Pre-set with invariant limits	Emergent Planned with flexibility
Guidelines/Rules	Specific/Prescriptive External organization	Self-organization Flexible Semi-permeable boundaries
Mental Processes	Convergent Memory only	Divergent, combinatory Memory/construction
	Either/or Dichotomous thinking	Fuzzy sets and logic
	Focus on "correct" or "right"	Risk taking Experimentation Learn through error

Ecological Approach to Development

Bronfenbrenner's ecological theory (1977), which posits four-tiered concentric circles of influences on children, consists of (1) the microsystem, the immediate setting containing a child; (2) the mesosystem, the connections among these settings; (3) the exosystem, the institutions of society; and (4) the macrosystem, the values that drive society and, in this case, notions of human development and education. This framework provides a systems-oriented, vertically and horizontally integrated model for considering ways to enhance the utilization of play.

Microsystem

Microsystems, the settings that actually contain children, such as classrooms, include a physical space, furnishings, a time frame, activities, participant roles, and implicit and explicit rules and guidelines for behavior. Figure 3 offers a model reflecting the notion that work and play are not dichotomous. In an educational context, academic instruction is the linear end of a continuum that has the potential to evolve into and resonate with chaotic play; both together can entrain into a powerful supersymmetric model.

Within this model, linear academic instruction—the "less" playful dimension—paradoxically is not inappropriate or of lesser value in developmentally sound education. In a synergistic fashion, both have a place in an evolving educational model not only for children but also persons throughout the life span. At certain times, for certain purposes, and in certain contexts, linear instruction or chaotic play may be the predominant, but not necessarily exclusive, approach. This entrained perspective, also paradoxically, may actually modify the more overt rejection or de-emphasizing of play by reframing the issue as one or both. The focus then changes from either/or, when, and how, depending on situation and context. This model also allows reframing the issue as one of oscillation and recursion in place of dichotomous, nonfuzzy thinking. Moving back and forth between the dimensions of playful and less playful, an emphasis on one approach may indeed fuel or feed into the other, allowing perhaps the most powerful approach of all.

Mesosystem

Within the mesosystem, the connections among immediate settings that contain a child, such as the school itself and its neighborhood, are influential. The nature of the school as an organization and of teacher preparation practices are two important components subsumed in the mesosystem as fundamental determinants of the school experience.

In recent years, there has been a growing literature on school-based management and school reform, referring basically to a restructuring of these traditionally hierarchical, bureaucratic, prescriptive, firmly bounded institutions that support rigid, primarily didactic, curricula. In fact, some formulations (e.g., Hargreaves, 1995) apply chaos theory to show how such a transformed worldview can best be applied to creating schools with fractal aspects such as participative management, systemwide learning, organizational evolution, and interdisciplinarity.

In a vertically integrated model of education that will utilize the power of play throughout the childhood years, these concepts have a great deal of promise for shaping the necessary transformed structures and themes. In a horizontally integrated model, the connections between play and traditional modes of teaching would result in a more coherent curriculum. A coherent curriculum (Beane, 1995) is systemic and fractal, crossing traditional disciplines and connecting common threads among them.

The chaos worldview, by the very fact of its complexity, provides compelling support for acting on the research showing that intelligent, highly educated practitioners are necessary to best meet the developmental and educational needs of children. However it is done, it is important to recruit the most intelligent, curious, well-educated, Protean people into the fields of early childhood and elementary education. One author says that to implement a play-based curriculum that reflects dynamic systems theory requires teachers who must "be expected to bring to bear their own intelligence, knowledge and feelings in their teaching. On the whole, however, they are not accorded this degree of professional respect . . . they are expected to . . . 'cut,' as it is, [the curriculum] into tiny pieces. It is clear . . . that youngsters will continue to be shortchanged in schools as long as this is the case" (Duckworth, 1987, p. xv).

To truly transform the educational system, to move it from its inexorable adherence to a linear model, the focal point, or "attractor," of this effort must be the workforce, including developmentalists, caregivers, teachers, supervisors, and administrators, whose preparation must include in-depth coverage of the following:

- Play—its functions, dynamic, and chaotic characteristics. Perhaps, most important, personnel need to be prepared to facilitate rich and dynamic play in all human service professional curricula;
- The nature of chaos—its historical evolution, definition, concepts, and applications;
- Humanities, physical sciences, and social sciences in forms that serve as a foundation for professional study involving overall breadth of understanding; and
- "Erodynamics," the emergent science that is concerned with utilizing complex dynamical systems theory for modeling social systems "which are usually too complicated to model without a theory that allows for chaos and bifurcation" (Abraham, 1994, p. 209), particularly for leaders and academics.

Exosystem

From the perspective of the exosystem, it is crucial to look at the educational system and all of those institutions that affect it, such as the economy, transportation, mass media, the legal system, and the like. The notion of the full-service school (Dryfoos, 1994), in which a multiplicity of services needed by child and family are located in the same setting is a chaotic social service model. The process involves evolution as a complex adaptive system with entrainment and the entire service system becoming more coherent—in effect, fractal.

This system increases accessibility and service integration. Within a total school program, various services can sponsor various playful activities that involve various age groups, thereby injecting another fractal and combinatory element.

Macrosystem

At the values level of the macrosystem, beliefs about the economic system and the work-play dichotomy need attention. Economic values govern the allocations of money. Society needs a brand new attractor that places high-quality education and child care as the focal point for adequate economic support. This is not likely to be achieved soon, given the current climate in the United States but it should be a goal for educators.

At the practice level, it is necessary to abandon the either/or notion that play is the opposite of work, and that since children need to work, their time spent on play must be limited. This widely held view represents the epitome of linear thinking. Within the perspective of a chaos model, the relationship between play and work would not be viewed as opposing concepts or even places on the same continuum. The relationship is fuzzy rather than absolute. It is interconnected and, in many ways, fractal or containing self-similar elements, as indicated in Figure 3.

Toward the Future:
Beyond Chaos to Supersymmetry

A futurist would ask the question, What will be the emergent worldview beyond chaos? It is important to ask this question in the context of an evolving worldview that proceeds from linear to chaotic perspectives. Evolutionary dynamics suggest that the current perspective is due for an inevitable transformation. As one author suggests, "A final theory will rest on principles of supersymmetry" (Weinberg, 1992, p. 212).

This essay playfully proposes that supersymmetry will be the new worldview beyond chaos. Some scientists already consider supersymmetry to be a significant scientific concept (Freedman, 1991; Weinberg, 1992), although not in any particular relationship to chaos theory. Symmetry itself implies similarity and balance; supersymmetry goes beyond these more orderly qualities to embrace chaotic qualities as well, and synthesizes them as a unity. The unity in supersymmetry is a connected, synergistic, recursive, and oscillatory entraining into an all-embracing dynamic. This concept of supersymmetry enables the consideration of *both* linear and chaotic approaches as a matter of relative emphasis in a particular context, rather than excluding one or the other as needed at a particular time.

The related image of the yin and yang diagram, a circle with a curved diametric line separating a dark half from a light half, each half containing an opposite-shaded smaller circle. The smaller circle shows that a component of an opposite quality always exists in any given entity, and that, in an ideal situation, nothing should be absolute. The curved line suggests dynamism, one entity gradually merging or shifting into another. This is more than a mere New Age symbol; it represents the notion that too much of an entity causes an opposing reaction from the opposite entity that is always there. There are pitfalls in pushing too hard with one approach, or absolute all-or-nothing thinking (Senge, 1990). A Nobel prize-winning physicist (Weinberg, 1992), for example, takes the position that there is danger in totally abandoning scientific reductionism.

Professionals in the current educational system, within the context of contemporary thinking about dynamic processes, need to place a much greater emphasis on play in a vertically and horizontally integrated way throughout early and elementary education. At the same time, instructional approaches that include labeling experiences can help children move toward developing metacognition, a knowledge of the strategies that help one to know what one knows. To be able to reason, even fuzzily, in any particular field, one must have core knowledge of its concepts and their characteristics as well as be able to use the language of that particular field. The issue is how clearly adults present and explain data so that they are "conceptually accurate, explicit, meaningful and sequenced" (Perkins, 1992, p. 46).

Another role of play or playful activities in the curriculum at any level is to provide the context for application, practice, and integration of all forms of knowledge which can then bifurcate into more complex forms. A supersymmetric world, in which linearity both maintains itself and merges, synchronizes, and oscillates with chaotic processes, such as play, will be the best of all worlds for empowering children and youth to be the effective Protean selves of the future.

Bibliography

Abraham, R. (1994). *Chaos, Gaia, Eros*. San Francisco: Harper.

Baer, J. (1993). *Creativity and divergent thinking: A task-specific approach*. Hillsdale, NJ: Lawrence Erlbaum.

Beane, J. (1995). *Toward a coherent curriculum*. Alexandria, VA: Association for Supervision and Curriculum Development.

Berk, L. & Winsler, A. (1995). *Scaffolding children's learning: Vygotsky and early childhood education*. Washington, DC: National Association for the Education of Young Children.

Bronfenbrenner, U. (1977). Towards an experimental ecology of human development. *American Psychologist, 33* (7), 513–532.

Brown, S. (1994, December). Animals at play. *National Geographic, 186*(6), 2–35.

Darling, D. (1993). *Equations of eternity*. New York: Hyperion.

Dryfoos, J. (1994). *Full-service schools. A revolution in health and social services for children, youth and families*. San Francisco: Jossey Bass.

Duckworth, E. (1987). *"The having of wonderful ideas" and other essays on teaching and learning*. New York: Teachers College Press.

Elkind, D. (1994). *Ties that stress*. Cambridge, MA: Harvard University Press.

Freedman, D. (1991, August). The new theory of everything. *Discover, 12*(8), 53–61.

Fromberg, D. (1992). A review of research on play. In C. Seefeldt (Ed.), *The early childhood curriculum: A review of current research* (2nd ed., pp. 42–84). New York: Teachers College Press.

Fromberg, D. (1995). *The full day kindergarten: Planning and practicing a dynamic themes curriculum* (2nd ed.). New York: Teachers College Press.

Gell-Mann, M. (1994). *The quark and the jaguar*. New York: W. T. Freeman.

Gleick, J. (1987). *Chaos*. New York: Viking.

Goerner, S. (1994). *Chaos and the evolving ecological universe*. Langhorne, PA: Gordon & Breach.

Handy, C. (1989). *The age of unreason*. Cambridge, MA: Harvard Business School Press.

Hargreaves, A. (1995, April). School renewal in the age of paradox. *Educational Leadership, 52*(7), 14–19.

Hofstadter, D. (1985). *Metamagical themas: Questing for the essence of mind and pattern*. New York: Basic Books.

Kegan, R. (1982). *The evolving self*. Cambridge, MA: Harvard University Press.

Kosko, B. (1993). *Fuzzy thinking*. New York: Hyperion.

Lifton, R. (1993). *The Protean self*. New York: Basic Books.

Nachmanovitch, S. (1990). *Free play*. Los Angeles: Tarcher.

Naisbitt, J. (1994). *Global Paradox*. New York: Avon.

Penrose, R. (1989). *The emperor's new mind*. New York: Oxford University Press.

Perkins, D. (1992). *Smart schools*. New York: Free Press.

Russ, S. (1993). *Affect and creativity: The role of affect and play in the creative process*. Hillsdale, NJ: Erlbaum.

Seefeldt, C. (1992). Preface. In C. Seefeldt (Ed.), *The early childhood curriculum: A review of current research* (2nd ed., pp. vii–ix). New York: Teachers College Press.

Senge, P. (1990). *The fifth discipline*. New York: Doubleday.

Sigmund, K. (1993). *Games of life*. New York: Oxford University Press.

Smilansky, S. (1990a). *Facilitating play: A medium for promoting cognitive, socio-emotional and academic development in young children*. Gaithersburg, MD: Psychological and Educational Publications.

Smilansky, S. (1990b). Significance of creative materials and "pretend" activities as a medium for the development of cognitive, academic and socio-emotional abilities and skills of young children. In B. Po-King Chan (Ed.), *Early childhood toward the 21st century: A worldwide perspective,* (pp. 295–310). Gaithersburg, MD: Yew Chung Education Publishing.

Thelen, E. (1995). Motor development: A new synthesis. *American Psychologist, 50*(2), 79–95.

VanderVen, K. (1994). Preventing second-generation child abuse: Applying chaos theory to reframe interventions. *The Child and Youth Care Administrator, 6*(1), 27–34.

Weinberg, S. (1992). *Dreams of a final theory*. New York: Pantheon.

Wheatley, M. (1992). *Leadership and the new science*. San Francisco: Berrett-Koehler.

Perspectives on Play Development

Introduction

Most observers of children would agree that the nature of play changes over the course of children's development and that these changes occur in orderly stages. The early theorists' categorizations of various types of play at different age levels formed the framework for the perception of play as a developmental phenomenon (Rubin, 1982). Early researchers categorized the play they observed in young children into age-related stages (e.g., Parten, 1932/1971). Later theorists described the stages of play development in specific domains (Erikson, 1976; Piaget, 1976; Vygotsky, 1976, 1978). Play development is related to cognitive and moral reasoning; language cognition and social understanding; and social-emotional mastery. Many researchers have attempted to verify the theoretical stages of play in precise and detailed studies. Although Erikson's stage theory, for example, has been influential in therapeutic practice, it has rarely been tested in empirical studies. Vygotsky's views, however, are the subject of much recent research.

The conceptualization of play as a developmental phenomenon has resulted in systematic study of trends in types of play exhibited at various ages, in diagnostic practices that identify developmental problems when these types of play do not occur as expected, and in recommendations for intervention to enhance play development (Bergen, 1988). The systematic study of play development has also made explicit individual and cultural differences that may occur in the sequence, transitions, and content of play. Apparently, the well-established landmarks that are considered developmentally typical in Western dominant cultures are not always manifest in other cultures (Roopnarine, Johnson, & Hooper, 1994).

Even in the dominant culture, a number of assumptions about the qualitative differences that occur in play at various ages and stages have recently been called into question. Pretend play, for example, has usually been characterized as a phenomenon primarily of early childhood. Retrospective self-reports by adults on the play in which they engaged during elementary-age years reveal that pretense is still a major type of play during that time (Bergen, Liu, & Liu, 1994). The settings in which it occurs (home, backyard) differ from the more public settings (preschool, school) of the early childhood years, however, and the activities are usually more private. Although solitary play has usually been characterized as a phenomenon of young children, this type of play seems to have a mature as well as an immature form (Rubin, Fein, & Vanderberg, 1983). Recent study of adult "leisure activities" shows that many of these activities have characteristics and purposes similar to children's play, even though they are not called by that name (Freysinger, 1994).

Nevertheless, a substantial body of literature supports the view that play development does occur across the life span and that it is possible to chart systematic and sequential trajectories for that development (Bergen, 1988). For most children, play is as effortless as breathing and as varied as the images in a kaleidoscope. Their development of proficient use of language, social competence, complex thinking, and creative problem solving seems to occur in parallel and integrative ways in concert with their play development.

There are some children, however, for whom both play development and progress in other developmental domains may be more costly acquisitions. If they have disabilities that hinder their active participation, or come from environments where adults do not encourage playful action, they may not have as much ease in meeting developmental challenges. Although most educators and psychologists are sensitive to the basic needs of such children, this sensitivity often has excluded their play lives, perhaps because learning the essential survival skills of daily life has such emphasis. The scholarship on play, however, suggests that all children can have optimal growth opportunities when play and playful learning approaches are integrated with their everyday lives.

The essays in this section describe the knowledge base that has been accumulated through the study of play development. The descriptions of the "typical" development of play during three age periods provide a basis for discussing specific developmental domain issues. The specific domains include cognitive and language facets of play development, and the connections between play, gender identity, and emotional development. The use of play in assessment and the role of play in the lives of children with disabilities are also sensitive issues that relate to the general sequences of play development.

Bibliography

Bergen, D. (1988). *Play as a medium for learning and development.* Portsmouth, NH: Heinemann.

Bergen, D., Liu, W., & Liu, G. (1994). *Chinese and American college students' memories of childhood play: A comparison.* Paper presented at the conference of the Association for the Study of Play, Atlanta, GA.

Erikson, E. (1976). Play and actuality. In J. S. Bruner, A. Jolly, & K. Sylva (Eds.), *Play: Its role in development and evolution* (pp. 688–703). New York: Basic Books.

Freysinger, V. J. (1994). Leisure with children and parental satisfaction: Further evidence of a sex difference in the experience of adult roles and leisure. *Journal of Leisure Research, 26,* 212–226.

Parten, M. (1971). Social play among preschool children. In R. E. Herron & B. Sutton-Smith (Eds.), *Child's play* (pp. 83–95). New York: John Wiley. (Original work published 1932)

Piaget, J. (1976). *The grasp of consciousness.* Cambridge, MA: Harvard University Press.

Roopnarine, J. L., Johnson, J. E., & Hooper, F. H. (Eds.). (1994). *Children's play in diverse cultures.* Albany: State University of New York Press.

Rubin, K. H. (1982). Non-social play in preschoolers: Necessary evil? *Child Development, 53,* 651–657.

Rubin, K. H., Fein, G. G., & Vanderberg, B. (1983). Play. In E. M. Hethington (Ed.), *Handbook of child psychology: Socialization, personality, and social development* (pp. 693–774). New York: Wiley.

Vygotsky, L. S. (1976). Play and its role in the mental development of the child. In J. S. Bruner, A. Jolly, & K. Sylva (Eds.), *Play: Its role in development and evolution* (pp. 537–554). New York: Basic Books.

Vygotsky, L. S. (1978). *Mind in society: The development of higher psychological processes* (M. Cole, V. John-Steiner, S. Scribner, & E. Souberman, Eds.). Cambridge, MA: Harvard University Press.

General Play Development

Play Development from Birth to Age Four

Barbara P. Garner

Play is a ubiquitous activity of young children. Exploratory and sensorimotor types of play are primary during the early infancy period, and during the first years of life symbolic play begins and reciprocal social games emerge. These early play behaviors form the basis for play throughout life (Bergen, 1988). As significant developmental changes occur during the first four years of age in children's social, emotional, physical, and cognitive domains, concomitant progressive changes occur in play.

Defining and Categorizing Infant Play

Many investigations into play have led to a variety of definitions and thus numerous problems in arriving at consensus regarding definitions, categories, and developmental progressions of play. Researchers' theoretical orientations to play often confound definitions and categories from one study to another. Whether or not researchers observe play in solitary or social contexts and whether or not they conduct research in a laboratory or a naturalistic setting may yield varying categories of play types. Definitions of play during infancy are often especially amorphous and flexible. One prevalent definition of play during early childhood, for example, holds that the activity is pleasurable and intrinsically motivated (Fromberg, 1992). Using this definition, it is possible to define as play many behaviors in which infants engage. For example, although adults might define as work infants' struggle to balance and begin to stand independently, infants experience intrinsic motivations for achieving these motor skills and do express pleasure in achieving them.

Thus, it is possible to include this motor practice as play, although scholars have not often defined it that way.

There are various categories that delineate infants' play. Researchers have fairly constantly observed object play, which they have variously called practice, exploratory, manipulative, or functional play. They have often investigated the category of social play under the rubrics of peer interactions and adult-child interactions. They have focused studies on the comparisons of social play with or without objects, and social play with familiar or unfamiliar objects or people, while giving little attention to motor practice play in infancy. There has been much research about the beginnings of pretend play, perhaps because researchers often link it to advances in cognitive development.

During infancy, however, categories of play frequently overlap. Children engaged in exploratory play, for example, may be practicing newly acquired motor skills in the presence of familiar peers. Similarly, when children imitate each other's motor behaviors, the activity may be either practice play or social play, and when infants are practicing emerging motor skills, the activity may be play, exploration, or work. Because infants are not able to label their play, it may be especially difficult to identify pretense when observing certain motor actions.

Throughout infancy, developmental changes in other domains encourage and change the kinds and levels of play. Changes in physical development, for example, result in changes in coordinated motor play. As children acquire gross motor skills that allow mobility, they can expand their exploration of the environment, and advanced fine motor skill promotes exploration through greater manipulation of objects.

As cognitive concepts develop, infants begin to see relations between individual action patterns; as they combine these, relational and functional play increases. When representational/symbolic thinking advances, pretense emerges and develops. As social development changes from a symbiotic view of self to recognition of a separate self, peer interactions in play begin and progress rapidly. In this discussion of types of infant and toddler play, therefore, two facts must be kept in mind: (1) the rapid developmental changes in other domains influence play development, and (2) it is often difficult to categorize play into discrete types in infancy.

Categorizing Infant and Toddler Play

Although there are many different types of infant and toddler play, scholars often categorize them as object play, motor play, social play, and symbolic/pretend play.

Play with Objects

Object play in the first few months of life is limited if not absent. Infants' reflexive grasp may permit a chance contact with an object that allows infants momentary exploration of the object, but this is fleeting and is certainly not the primary mode of play during the newborn period. Over the first few months of life, an infant's play consists of practice play that is focused on the body; that is, the body is the object of play. Infants repeat over and over again the motor behaviors that cause an interesting event to occur. Piaget (1962a, 1962b) called this period of development primary circular reactions.

By four months of age, infants' interests begin to shift away from the primary focus of the body to things external to the body, such as objects and people. Exploring objects is something that infants seem uniquely motivated to do. At first, they indiscriminately engage in mouthing, banging, and shaking objects, food, and people. Later in the first year, differentiation occurs, and infants shake rattles, bang toys, and mouth bottles and food (Uzgiris & Hunt, 1975). Between four and twelve months, many developmental milestones allow infants access to many more interesting events in their environment. With the ability to sit, infants are able to have visual guidance in reaching to grasp objects and bring their hands to midline for object exploration. Between seven and twelve months, infants' manipulative skill increases to the point that they can use both hands independently for exploring.

A review of research on object manipulation in infancy suggests that studies of manipulation have been conducted primarily to explore cognition or perceptual development, and not because of interest in the developmental trends of object manipulation itself (Lockman & McHale, 1989). Subsequent to these reviewers' call for more detailed research on manipulation, several researchers have investigated the developmental sequence involved in manipulating objects.

A group of researchers recently investigated the way infants explore objects (Baldwin, Markman, & Melartin, 1993). They indicate that patterns of exploratory play emerge between nine and sixteen months, which suggests that infants are capable of making inferences about novel objects based on very short exposures to an exemplar. When given similar objects with similar properties, infants immediately used similar patterns of exploration. The researchers found that infants were able to use visually available surface properties to infer the presence of underlying functional properties of the objects. If infants are capable of making such quick and correct inferences, this would help explain how infants' knowledge base expands so rapidly over this period. Knowing that objects have such an impact on infants' cognitive development provides support for the value of environments that are rich in the availability of a wide variety of objects for play.

Another research team explored how infants between seven and twelve months increase in manipulative skill to the point that both hands can manipulate an object independently of each other. Typically, one hand will stabilize an item and the dominant hand will manipulate the object. Simple independent use of both hands was observed as early as seven months. In this early time period, the specific properties of the object do not seem to matter. Infants will use each hand independently regardless of whether or not the object has movable parts. As infants' cognitive development advances, however, the property of the object comes into play. At this later stage, the object needs to have movable parts in order for infants to manipulate it. The manipulative skills develop as infants' concepts of causality and object properties, such as stability and movability, increase. (Kimmerle, Mick, & Michel, 1995).

Functional play (i.e., object play with relational goals) increases over a similar time span as infants become more able to combine action patterns. At first, infants will combine the action patterns indiscriminately: a comb may be placed in a bowl or a spoon on top of a truck. Later in this developmental stage, they will begin to combine items in typical relational patterns: they will place a spoon in a pot or a bowl, for example, and may place a lid on the top of a container. Before they are one year old, most infants will begin to put items into containers and, by the time they are one, many will have learned to dump items out of the container.

Although play changes during the second year, the major focus of play remains object-centered. Manipulative play with objects is the predominant activity during play sessions throughout the second year. Mouthing as a form of exploration decreases in frequency and is rarely seen after the second year (Mayes, Carter, & Stubbe, 1993). Infants between one and two years of age seem to ask, "What can I do with this object?" (Vondra & Belsky, 1989, p. 176). Now infants have entered the cognitive stage of tertiary circular reactions (Piaget, 1962a, 1962b), frequently referred to as the age of experimentation. Indeed, toddlers are like scientists experimenting with what objects can do and what they can do with the object. At this point some researchers say that the manipulative activity has changed from exploration to play (Hutt, 1979). Infants from twelve to eighteen months delight in toys that react to their actions: pop-up characters, activated by pressing buttons, jack in-the-boxes that pop out when someone pulls a string, and books that emit words or music when toddlers press a button are examples. Making a mark may also begin to be of interest at this time.

As children enter the third year of life, manipulative materials such as clay, fingerpaints, toys for water play, blocks, books, dolls, stuffed animals, and puzzles take on added importance. Young children's sense of mastery increases as they find more and more activities that can be under their control. Manipulative or practice play remains an important part of play for the three-year-old, but most play now is functional, that is, in the service of a goal, rather than simply exploration.

Motor Play

Few researchers have studied the sequence of motor play during infancy, although many have investigated motor activities in relation to physical development. The developmental psychology literature on play has focused more on the implications of social and cognitive development for early play. This is unfortunate because motor development is intimately tied to infants' play. "Enough research has been done to clearly show that the body plays a fundamental role . . . [in development and] . . . there is no such thing as a brain without a body" (Fischer & Hogan, 1989, p. 298). Indeed, as stated earlier, infants' practice play focused on the body makes up the majority of play activities over the first few months of life.

When infants discover that they can bring their hands and feet to their mouth, their manipulation of body parts increases. As infant motor skills are developing, practice of these skills takes precedence over all other activities. Although manipulation of objects and interactions with adults and peers increase dramatically during the first year, motor play continues to have an important presence.

Over the last quarter of the first year, a great deal of infant play relates to developing physical skills. Infants from nine to twelve months are learning to pull themselves up, cruise along furniture, stand alone, and many walk independently. Physiological factors such as body build and muscle tone, as well as genetic factors, affect the time that infants accomplish these milestones. Environmental factors, however, play a role as well. The age of onset of walking has decreased, perhaps due to parents' lessened use of playpens in recent decades. When infants have opportunities to explore, risk, and try again and again, in an environment that is safe but challenging, they can engage in motor practice play that leads to advanced physical abilities.

Two-year-old children are more physically active than at any other time of life. Interest in large motor activities increases as children's motor abilities improve. The availability of safe climbing structures enhances the opportunity for their gross motor play as well as advances in physical development. The two-year-old will climb, if not on safe equipment that adults provide, then on anything available, some of which may be dangerous. Toys that children can push and pull encourage practice play in the area of motor activities. Riding toys become important as infants reach the second and third year of life. By their second birthday, most children have developed motor skills to the point where they can run with ease and pleasure. Peers frequently practice running and make a game of imitation that looks like "Do what I do." When young children can jump off the ground with both feet, they regale everyone to "Watch me." Throughout this age period, practice of motor skills continues to be an important form of play.

As fine motor control develops, young children engage in activities that practice these newfound skills. When the well-defined pincer grasp develops, for example, a favorite activity is poking fingers into holes, picking up minuscule items from the floor, and using toys that they can activate by a poke. Most children over one year are interested in objects that make marks. Although they do not have the refined skills to allow them to have good control of marking instruments, they enjoy the practice of making marks and scribbles. By three years, many children have increased in fine motor skill activities and are beginning to cut, paste, and use varied kinds of art materials. They can, for example, use their advanced fine motor skills with clay and play dough. Children at this age are still primarily interested in the manipulation of and learning about the medium, however, and they will not yet initiate the creation of a product.

Social Play

Adults and children (both peers and siblings) act as play partners during this early age period. Each provides different kinds of interactive play experiences.

Social Play with Adults

Adults, in particular mothers and fathers, are infants' first play partners. During the first few months, adults initiate this play but infants quickly enter into it. Simple exchanges of vocalization are the first games babies play with parents. By six weeks infants respond to these overtures with smiles and coos. Adults' play with infants changes over the first year and infants' responses change as well. Initially, infants will respond to peekaboo games and tickle games with equal delight. By eight months, a tickle will not automatically produce laughter as it did previously. Pat-a-cake and peekaboo games increase, and tickle games begin to decrease. By twelve months, tickle games have almost disap-

peared, and give-and-take games, and point-and-name games have increased. Whatever the game, infants' attention and exploring increase by play with an adult (Lockman & McHale, 1989).

An early study found that more sustained and complex infant play with objects occurred when infants were playing with mothers than when they were playing alone (Escalona, 1968). Mothers seemed able to adjust their introduction of new toys to their infants' needs by offering new play activities and regulating the intensity of play. More recent research has supported these findings. When infants are engaged in object play, the quality of play and the sustained amount of play increase when playing with mothers over playing alone (Cielinski, Vaughn, Seifer, & Contresas, 1995; Stern, 1974).

Fathers also play with infants, but their interactions often start later. After the eighteen-month-old period, fathers initiate more play episodes with infants than do mothers (Clark-Stewart, 1977, cited in Bergen, 1988, p. 52). Fathers tend to engage in more physically rousing play, roughhousing, tossing infants in the air, and run-and-chase games than do mothers. Mothers' play tends to involve a teaching component and to be more verbal than fathers'. They spend more of this play time naming objects, labeling, and pointing than they do in physically active play (Hughes, 1991).

Because adult partners seem to offer the benefit of extending and enhancing the quality of infants' play, how mothers are able to scaffold play for their infant has been interesting for researchers' speculation. Mothers' views of play may motivate infants and have real consequences for social and cognitive development. A number of parenting behaviors seem to be intuitive. In terms of language development, for example, parents are adept at scaling their language just slightly above infants' capabilities and thus increase infant language competence (Papousek & Papousek, 1982). Mothers and fathers both seem to make adjustments in their play based on the developmental level of the infant. One group of researchers, in the interest of understanding what mothers actually believe about developmental levels of play, had mothers rate the difficulty of play behaviors (Tamis-LeMonda, Damast, & Bornstein, 1994). They found that mothers, based on these ratings, have an excellent concept of the developmental progression of play. The only responses that did not match the empirical ordering of play were for animate-directed pretense versus inanimate-directed pretense: mothers believed it was easier for children to pretend with an animate rather than an inanimate other.

Social Play with Peers

Initially, infants are unaware of self as distinct from others. However, very early in life, they seem to distinguish familiar adults from other infants. Infants exhibit behaviors that look very much like excitement when another infant is present (Fogel, 1979). When seated on their mothers' laps, for example, infants will lean forward and stare intently at other infants. These first social encounters are brief and unsophisticated. First exchanges are often simply looks, followed in a short while by smiles and vocalizations.

One line of research on peer interaction addresses whether or not toys or objects that are present increase infants' peer interaction. A number of researchers have data that support the hypothesis that infants under one year spend more time interacting when in a setting devoid of objects (Eckerman & Watley, 1977; Vandell & Mueller, 1980). In another study, this finding held true for children under one year, but a shift was evident at about fourteen months (Jacobson, 1981). At this time, longer interactions were present when infants were in settings with objects available.

Children's interest in peers increases throughout the second year. Early in this year interactions with peers remain largely looking, offering, and taking toys and objects. At fourteen months there is a shift in the role of objects and peer interactions. Objects now become important in lengthening the time of interactions. Although social interaction may not originate in an object-centered context, object-centered play seems to enhance infants' ability to engage in extended social interactions (Jacobson, 1981).

Children in the early toddler period are able to engage in complementary and reciprocal social interactions. They engage in complementary activities such as run-and-chase and give-and-take (Howes, 1987). Well-acquainted infants often engage in ritual-like interactions. These rituals may be similar to scripts that older preschool children use for social pretend play. The complementary and reciprocal nature of play during the early toddler period may be a prerequisite for children's being able to engage in cooperative social pretend play in the latter part of the toddler years (fifteen to thirty-six

months). Young children who are in play groups, and who have become familiar with the available peers, begin to show preferences for certain play partners. First friendships are formed, and many are stable into the preschool years (Howes, 1987; Howes & Matheson, 1992; Howes, Unger, & Seidner, 1989).

Symbolic/Pretend Play

Symbolic play is the category of play that scholars have most closely linked to early cognitive development. Very simple pretend play becomes evident at approximately one year of age. The onset of pretending appears to be sudden, is universal, and in its earliest form, infants direct it toward themselves (Fein, 1981). Infants may use a brush or comb on their hair, for example, or they may "drink" from a bottle or cup, or hold a play telephone to their ear. Although this type of actor-focused pretend play appears at about twelve months, pretense is not a predominant mode of play in the first year of life. Early pretending is a solitary play activity; social pretend play develops after the first twelve months (Howes & Matheson, 1992; Howes, Unger, & Seidner, 1989).

This dramatic change to pretense, which emerges and expands during the toddler years, is fleeting at first and accounts for a small percentage of the time that children spend in play (Vondra & Belsky, 1989). They may perform these pretend acts in the company of peers, however, making the activity social in nature. An initial social pretend activity may begin with eye contact with another peer, but the activity does not elicit a response in the peer: young children who make eye contact with another child may pretend to drink from a cup, but the activity does not elicit reciprocal imitation prior to fifteen to sixteen months. Between fifteen and twenty months, toddler peers will imitate the pretend acts and continue eye contact. Both may feed the baby a bottle, for example, rock the baby, or push the baby in a stroller. At about twenty to twenty-four months, they enhance these activities with social exchanges such as smiles, vocalizations, or offers of the doll to the peer. Between two and two-and-one-half years, children participate in the same theme but do not coordinate their activity in any way. Two toddlers may go to the grocery store, complete with shopping carts, dolls, and purses, but each pretends independently. They do recognize that their behaviors are appropriate to the theme, however, and the participants begin to be able to decide upon the theme rather than having the behavior decide the activity. In the age range of thirty to thirty-six months, children's increased awareness of social roles will shape their pretend play. At this point, role-taking becomes a part of social pretend play (Howes, Unger, & Seidner, 1989).

The ways children use objects in pretense changes as their level of pretend play advances. When infants are using objects in solitary pretending, with the initial pretending directed to self, for example, they may use a cloth to pretend to wash their own face. Pretending with the object gradually extends to other objects or people; for example, they may use the cloth to wash a doll's face or their mother's face. As toddlers approach the end of the second year, they make the dolls or stuffed animals assume roles, thus having the objects take an active part in the pretending; for example, they expect dolls to eat pretend food at a pretend birthday party. During the third year, their pretense becomes more elaborate, and dolls or other objects carry out longer scenarios, usually with familiar homelike themes (Hughes, 1991).

Pretend play also moves from a simple, one-action pattern to combining action patterns. As evidenced in play with objects, as infants move through the sensorimotor period of development, pretending combines action patterns, or sequences of actions, and more elaborate pretending is possible. Initially infants may comb the doll's hair; later they comb the doll's hair and wash the doll's face; still later, they comb the doll's hair and wash and dress the doll (Hughes, 1991).

By the time children are between three and four, they use replica objects as the actors in sequenced themes. A doll may get ready for a party that she is going to attend with her doll friends, for example, and they will ride in a car to the event, eat food and dance at the party, and return home. Several research studies have linked the ability to string pretend actions together to the advancement of language; for example, children who use two-word sentences typically also sequence two pretend actions (Fensen, 1984).

Realistic props enhance early pretending. Children will more readily use a realistic toy phone for pretending than the wooden block shaped vaguely like a phone. As children mature, they begin to use less realistic substitute objects. Children under three typically pretend

more readily if the substitute object has some resemblance to the real item. They may use a cloth as a pillow, but the two-year-old would have difficulty using a shoe as a pillow, for example, because shoes are for feet! Between three and four years, children can readily use even counterconventional substitute objects (Bretherton & Beeghly, 1989).

Adults' Effects on Pretend Play

Adult effects on pretend play are often indirect rather than direct. Although some mothers actively encourage pretend play (Miller & Garvey, 1984), there is wide variation in how actively parents engage in pretending with young children. Parents do, however, affect children's inclination toward pretending by allowing ample opportunities for practice play; their children also engage in pretending (Singer, Singer, Desmond, Hirsch, & Nocol, 1988). Parents who engage in discussion and storytelling allow children the opportunity to "frame complex events within organized structures" (Singer et al., 1988, p. 341). These children tend to spend a greater amount of time in fantasy or pretend play than do the children of parents whose interactions are predominantly prescription- and discipline-oriented. By tolerating pretending and providing materials and time for play, parents foster the development of pretending. When parents limit the amount of time young children spend viewing television, they also encourage the development of pretend play (Singer et al., 1988).

Aside from encouraging and providing materials for infants' pretend play, the attachment status of infants to a significant adult seems to have an influence on the amount and kind of play in which children engage (Roggman et al., 1990). Securely attached infants are more likely to explore the environment when in the presence of their mothers, are more sociable, and are more likely to engage in peer interactions. They also engage in more complex and sustained fantasy or pretend play (Hazen, 1989; Pepler & Ross, 1981; Singer, 1973; Sutton-Smith, 1979).

A recent investigation of differences between pretend play with a mother and with an older sibling among infants thirty-three to forty months old found that, on the whole, there were more pretend relationships between child and sibling than between mother and child (Youngblade & Dunn, 1995). Children in the study engaged in more role-play with their older siblings or with sibling and mother than they did with mother alone. The investigators found that early pretend play is related to "the child's developing understanding of others' beliefs and feelings" (p. 1488). Siblings may be instrumental in the development of "other minds" (p. 1486).

Effects of Gender on Infant and Toddler Play

Infants' play is quite similar for boys and girls, but by three years of age, play preferences are evident. Girls prefer play with dolls and household items, art activities, and dressing up, while boys play with transportation toys and blocks and engage in more large-group and aggressive play. Where these differences come from and when they begin is of interest to parents and researchers alike (Bergen, 1988). Adults' influence on children's sex-typed play is undoubtably both direct and indirect.

Although researchers find few actual gender-related differences among infants, parents tend to begin the socialization process into gender-stereotypic behaviors from birth. A direct impact on infant play is the fact that parents provide infants with sex-typed toys, thus beginning the process of gender-stereotypic activities. Parents also furnish young children's rooms, and those furnishings reflect differences based on gender-appropriate activities and materials (Reingold & Cook, 1975).

Parents also selected gender-stereotypic toys when researchers asked them to interact with their twelve- to twenty-four-month-old children (Eisenberg, Wolchick, Hernandez, & Pasternack, 1985). Infants as young as eighteen to twenty-three months have shown preferences for sex-typed toys (Caldera, Huston, & O'Brien, 1989): they were less involved with toys stereotyped for the opposite gender and preferred toys stereotyped for their own gender. Adults indirectly influence infants into gender-stereotypic play by reinforcing play the parents consider appropriate for their children. "Masculine" and "feminine" toys elicit different behaviors from infants and from adults interacting with infants and toys. "Masculine" toys tend to elicit low levels of teaching and low proximity between infants and parents; "feminine" toys elicit closer proximity and more verbal interactions between parents and infants (Caldera et al., 1989).

One study showed that differences in adults' interactions with infants in a classroom setting also occur (Fagot, Hagan, Leinbach, & Kronsberg, 1985). Although researchers initially found no differences in the kinds or frequency of interactions between twelve- to eighteen-month-old infants, the child's gender influenced adult interactions. For example, when boys hit, pushed, or grabbed a toy, the teacher responded to the behavior 41 percent of the time; the same behavior by a girl elicited a response from the teacher only 10 percent of the time. These percentages were basically reversed for communication, with teachers responding to verbalizations from girls at a higher rate than from boys. Approximately one year later, boys performed more aggressive acts, while girls spent more time talking and interacting with teachers (Fagot et al., 1985).

The question of whether children's playing with gender-stereotypic toys and actions is or is not a beneficial kind of play is inherent in a discussion of gender influences on play. The research on developing androgyny in children, which was prominent in the 1970s, suggested that children and adults need to be able to respond to a situation in adaptable, appropriate ways rather than in gender-stereotypic ways. This should be a topic of interest for further study.

Although it may be expedient to suggest that parental influence on children is the most salient reason that children play with gender-stereotypic materials, a cognitive dimension is also involved that must be taken into consideration. Young children have not arrived at gender constancy until they reach about six or seven years of age. These young children may well be using stereotypic play materials provided by their parents to arrive at gender constancy.

From the newborn period to the age of four, infants' play changes from that of experimenting with how body parts work to elaborate and highly complex pretend play. As these changes occur, there is also a complementary change in infants' development in other domains. Deciding whether play causes developmental changes or other developmental changes cause changes in play is rather like the chicken-and-egg debate or the nature-nurture controversy. Rather than spending time and energy debating the issue, the question to explore is how each of these, the other developmental domains and play development, interact to enhance both.

Infants' early play allows them to build schemata of what their movements might do to affect the environment, thus allowing infants to have a sense of efficacy. Play with objects encourages manipulative skills, and play with adults and peers encourages and enhances social development. Pretend play enhances cognitive development, increases social interactions, gives young children outlets for fears and frustrations, and provides a foundation for good mental health. Because play stays with individuals across the life span, the foundations for a life well lived are laid in the play of infants.

Bibliography

Baldwin, D. A., Markman, E. M., & Melartin, R. L. (1993). Infants' ability to draw inferences about nonobvious object properties: Evidence from exploratory play. *Child Development, 64,* 711–728.

Bergen, D. (1988). *Play as a medium of learning: A handbook of theory and practice.* Portsmouth, NH: Heinemann.

Bretherton, I., & Beeghly, M. (1989). Pretense: Acting "as if." In J. J. Lockman & N. L. Hazen (Eds.), *Action in social context: Perspectives on early development* (pp. 239–268). New York: Plenum.

Caldera, Y. M., Huston, A. C., & O'Brien, M. (1989). Social interactions and play patterns of parents and toddlers with feminine, masculine, and neutral toys. *Child Development, 60,* 70–76.

Cielinski, K. L., Vaughn, B. E., Seifer, R., & Contresas, J. (1995). Relations among sustained engagement during play, quality of play and mother-child interaction in samples of children with Downs syndrome and normally developing toddlers. *Infant Behavior and Development, 18,* 163–176.

Eckerman, C. O., & Watley, J. L. (1977). Toys and social interaction between infant peers. *Child Development, 48,* 1645–1656.

Eisenberg, N., Wolchick, S. A., Hernandez, R., & Pasternack, J. F. (1985). Parental socialization of young children's play. *Child Development, 56,* 1506–1513.

Escalona, S. (1968). *The roots of individuality.* Chicago: Aldine.

Fagot, B. I., Hagan, R., Leinbach, M. D., & Kronsberg, S. (1985). Differential reactions to assertive and communicative acts of toddler boys and girls. *Child Development, 56,* 1499–1505.

Fein, G. G. (1981). Pretend play in childhood: An integrative review. *Child Development, 52,* 1095–1118.

Fensen, L. (1984). Developmental trends for action and speech in pretend play. In I. Bretherton (Ed.), *Symbolic play: The development of social understanding* (pp. 249–270). New York: Academic.

Fischer, K. W., & Hogan, A. E. (1989). The big picture for infant development: Levels and variations. In J. J. Lockman & N. L. Hazen (Eds.), *Action in social context: Perspectives on early development* (pp. 275–300). New York: Plenum.

Fogel, A. (1979). Peer vs. mother directed behavior in 1- to 3-month-old infants. *Infant Behavior and Development, 2,* 215–226.

Fromberg, D. P. (1992). Play. In C. Seefeldt (Ed.), *Early childhood education: A review of research* (pp. 42–84). New York: Teachers College Press.

Hazen, N. (1989). Individual differences in environmental exploration and cognitive mapping skills: Early development in social contexts. In J. J. Lockman & N. L. Hazen (Eds.), *Action in social contexts: Perspectives on early development* (pp. 207–234). New York: Plenum.

Howes, C. (1987). Peer interaction of young children. *Monographs of the Society for Research in Child Development, 53*(1, Serial No. 217).

Howes, C., & Matheson, C. C. (1992). Sequences in the development of competent play with peers: Social and social pretend play. *Developmental Psychology, 28,* 961–974.

Howes, C., Unger, O., & Seidner, L. B. (1989). Social pretend play in toddlers: Parallels with social play and with solitary pretend. *Child Development, 60,* 77–84.

Hughes, F. P. (1991). *Children, play and development.* Boston: Allyn and Bacon.

Hutt, C. (1979). Exploration and play. In B. Sutton-Smith (Ed.), *Play and learning* (pp. 174–194). New York: Gardner.

Jacobson, J. L. (1981). The role of inanimate objects in early peer interaction. *Child Development, 52,* 618–626.

Kimmerle, M., Mick, L. A., & Michel, G. F. (1995). Bimanual role-differentiated toy play during infancy. *Infant Behavior and Development, 18,* 299–307.

Lockman, J. J., & McHale, J. P. (1989). Object manipulation in infancy: Developmental and contextual determinants. In J. J. Lockman & N. L. Hazen (Eds.), *Action in social context: Perspectives on early development* (pp. 129–167). New York: Plenum.

Mayes, L. C., Carter, A. S., & Stubbe, D. (1993). Individual differences in exploratory behavior in the second year of life. *Infant Behavior and Development, 16,* 269–284.

Miller, P., & Garvey, C. (1984). Mother-baby role play. In I. Bretherton (Ed.), *Symbolic play* (pp. 101–130). New York: Academic.

Mueller, E. C., & Brenner, J. (1977). The origins of social skills and interaction among playgroup toddlers. *Child Development, 48,* 854–861.

Papousek, H., & Papousek, M. (1982). Vocal imitations in mother-infant dialogues. *Infant Behavior, 5,* 176.

Pepler, D., & Ross, H. S. (1981). The effects of play on convergent and divergent problem-solving. *Child Development, 52,* 1202–1210.

Piaget, J. (1962a). *Play, dreams and imitation in childhood.* London: Routledge and Kegan Paul.

Piaget, J. (1962b). *The origins of intelligence in children.* New York: International Universities Press.

Reingold, H. L., & Cook, K. V. (1975). The contents of boys' and girls' rooms as an index of parents' behavior. *Child Development, 47,* 459–463.

Roggman, L. A., Carroll, K. A., Pippin, E. A., & McCool, D. E. (1990). *Toddler play in relation to social and cognitive competence.* (Report No. PS 018837) Little Rock: University of Arkansas. (ERIC Document Reproduction Service No. ED 320 664)

Singer, J. L. (1973). *The child's world of make-believe: Experimental studies of imaginative play.* New York: Academic.

Singer, J. L., & Singer, D. G. (1983). Psychologists look at television: Cognitive, developmental, personality and social policy implications. *American Psychologist, 38,* 826–834.

Singer, J. L., Singer, D. G., Desmond, R., Hirsch, B., & Nocol, A. (1988). Family mediation and children's cognition, aggression, and comprehension of television: A longitudinal study. *Journal of Applied Developmental Psychology, 9,* 329–347.

Stern, D. N. (1974). Mother and infant at play: The dyadic interaction involving facial, vocal and gaze behaviors. In M. Lewis & L. Rosenblum (Eds.), *The effect of the infant on its caregiver* (pp. 187–213). New York: John Wiley.

Sutton-Smith, B. (1979). *Play and learning.* New York: Gardner.

Tamis-LeMonda, C. S., Damast, A. M., & Bornstein M. H. (1994). What do mothers know about the developmental nature of play? *Infant Behavior and Development, 17,* 341–435.

Uzgiris, I., & Hunt, J. M. (1975). *Assessment in infancy.* Urbana: University of Illinois Press.

Vandell, D. L., & Mueller, E. C. (1980). Peer play and friendships during the first two years. In H. C. Foot, A. J. Chapman, & J. R. Smith (Eds.), *Friendships and social relations in children* (pp. 181–208). London: John Wiley.

Vondra J., & Belsky, J. (1989). Exploration and play in social context: Developments from infancy to early childhood. In J. J. Lockman & N. L. Hazen (Eds.), *Action in social context: Perspectives on early development* (pp. 173–203). New York: Plenum.

Youngblade, L. M., & Dunn, J. (1995). Individual differences in young children's pretend play with mother and sibling: Links to relationships and understanding of other people's feelings and beliefs. *Child Development, 66,* 1472–1492.

Play Development from Ages Four to Eight

James E. Johnson

Critical transformations occur in children's relationships to their social and physical world between four and eight years of age. Most four-year-olds possess considerable language mastery, an impressive array of social and physical concepts, and rudimentary and preoperational thinking skills. They have acquired sufficient levels of social competence and abilities to regulate attention, affect, and activity to sustain child-child social interactions, nurture budding friendships, and engage in prolonged play episodes alone or with others. Children gradually integrate the parent-child socialization system with the peer socialization system, and the social ecology of home and family increasingly meshes with the cultures of child care and school, neighborhood, and community.

Children at eight years of age have made gigantic developmental strides. They usually possess rather sophisticated communicative and social skills and often are members of various social groups. Their levels of social cognition enable them not only to perspective-take the perceptions, thoughts, intentions, and feelings of others, but also to coordinate diverse perspectives to construct elementary conceptions of social justice and group organization. Their knowledge base has expanded remarkably in four years. They are by now at least beginning, concrete-logical reasoners equipped with reversible thought operations and with a good elementary grasp of various symbolic notational systems. Basic literacy and numeracy as well as other academic attainments are the norm. Moreover, children have more differentiated self-concepts, higher levels of social competence, and more mature friendship relationships. Many children also have well-established impulse control and the ability to delay gratifi-

cation. Not surprisingly, then, eight-year-olds' play is quite different from that of four-year-olds.

Play Types and Development

The child development and early education literature has classified play forms in diverse ways. Researchers typically have recognized social, emotional, motor, and cognitive dimensions in their category systems and have given attention to play context and structural properties of play behavior and its functional or motivational characteristics (Bergen, 1988; Fein, 1975; Johnson, Christie, & Yawkey, 1987). Researchers have further noted that, although one can divide play into types and can attempt to calibrate behaviors in terms of levels of performance, or arrange play types hierarchically into developmental sequences (e.g., functional play, constructive play, dramatic play, and games with rules), play expression is actually more complex and classification somewhat artificial and limiting. Not only do play episodes demand description with multiple categories and subcategories to do justice to the phenomena (e.g., parallel-dramatic play with person and object transformations), there is the need for additional modifiers to capture something about play tempo, intensity, style, and other important qualities. There is also the need to note information about the play setting and context. Moreover, scholars also acknowledge that age-related developmental stages of play (e.g., solitary, parallel, associative, and cooperative) become less useful with older children and beg the question of how development unfolds within each play form. The parallel play or dramatic play of the toddler, for instance, is certainly different from the parallel play or dramatic play of the child who is six years old.

Descriptive and experimental studies of sequences and stages of play development, including observations and interviews with children between four and eight years of age, have yielded an abundance of evidence that significant changes in levels of performance do indeed occur within diverse play types, without necessarily suggesting *sequences* or stages of play development per se (see von Glasersfeld & Kelley, 1982, for a cogent discussion of differences among the terms *period, phase, stage,* and *level* in human development). Accordingly, the sections that follow represent a typology of play, but not necessarily a developmental hierarchy; this typology is based upon the Consumer Product Safety Commission's manual for making age specifications for toys (Goodson and Bronson, 1985). This typology organizes the play of children between four and eight years of age in a manner that usefully and comprehensively describes the age span under consideration.

The activities and behaviors described in one category of play sometimes overlap other sections. The discussion relaxes the distinction between play and work during this age span because it is less important to make this distinction, given that children are growing into what Erikson calls the age of industry versus inferiority, the beginning of the middle childhood years. With the end of the magic years of early childhood, during the span of years under discussion, definitions of play from the child's point of view shift from an external or sociological criterion to an internal or psychological criterion (King, 1982). One researcher demonstrated, for example, that whereas five-year-olds say something is work when an adult requires the activity, eight-year-olds judge the same activity to be play as long as they find it intrinsically satisfying, whether or not an adult mandates the behavior at the time (King, 1982).

Gross Motor/Active Play

Preschoolers from three or four years of age have progressed considerably in their physical and motor play development. They can walk and run easily, and tiptoe and balance themselves on one foot. They can throw and aim at short distances, putting a ball in a basket or box from five feet away. Climbing stairs to go up on lofts and other play structures or using the ladders of slides are common skills, as is the ability to ride tricycles and other simple vehicle toys. They can kick and catch a large ball thrown from short distances. Four-year-olds can make whole- and part-body responses to music, such as clapping, stamping, and simple dancing.

From four to five years and on to six years of age, children achieve further fine and gross motor mastery together with active play skill and dexterity, allowing for the emergence of newer and more variegated play forms. These children frequently engage in climbing, hopping, running, skipping (especially girls), and chasing (especially boys). Some children ride small bicycles, first with and then without supportive training wheels; many jump rope (primarily girls) and do acrobatics or trapeze tricks. The advance of their fine muscle development contributes to their ability to string beads, cut with scissors, paste, trace, draw, and color; they can also use a computer keyboard.

From six to eight years, children make further strides in physical and active play expression in accord with their growing physical prowess, the result of maturation and experience. They continue their interest and heightened proficiency in outdoor games and other physical play, including rough-and-tumble play. Daredevil play, roughhousing and risk-taking become more prevalent. Capture and escape, hide-and-seek, cops and robbers, tag, and "it" and its variants (dungeon tag, frozen tag) are commonplace. During these years of childhood, they engage in and improve their form in sports, athletics, Roller Blading, skateboarding, ice skating, swimming, aerobics, and acrobatics, as well as various forms of dance. Organized sports and adult-sponsored lessons in ballet or gymnastics, for example, are increasingly the norm.

In the domain of fine motor activity and accomplishment, children of six to eight years exhibit remarkable skill development, from hand games and snapping fingers to constructing model airplanes. This physical and motor development also facilitates other types of play such as collecting, building, and making various objects and structures.

Manipulative/Constructive Play

By four years of age most preschool children have reached many developmental milestones with respect to object play. Object play has progressed in terms of how many objects young children can incorporate into play, and how well children can use these objects. The play has progressed from the simple to the complex as children gain increasing ability to order objects and actions in time and space. As children develop they exhibit less manipulative or functional play that consists of using toys only in an "appropriate" (or expected) manner. There is more constructive play and organized goal-oriented play. Preschoolers become increasingly skilled in building complex structures and in producing recognizable products through drawing, painting, arranging designs, and making small constructions. By four years of age such constructive play is commonplace, often occupying over 50 percent of free play time in preschool settings, especially among girls (Rubin, Fein, & Vandenberg, 1983).

Five- and six-year-olds continue to engage in considerable amounts of constructive play, particularly in indoor play settings. Their constructive play is distinguished from the play of younger preschool children, however, by its enhanced elaborativeness and by the higher levels of social collaboration that often accompany it. Moreover, elements of pretense or dramatic play are more likely present. Kindergartners, compared to preschoolers, for instance, more often take to building props as a prelude to sociodramatic play, spending considerable time and showing good persistence and cooperation in setting the stage "just right" for playing grocery store or putting on a circus.

Seven- and eight-year-olds' forms of manipulative and constructive play continue to include blocks as a dominant play activity medium. As is the case with the preschool child, primary-grade school children enjoy (and have fully mastered) the use of Lego blocks, Lincoln Logs, and other assorted playthings that have fitted notches or interlocking pieces. Children of this age generally prefer construction sets with complex interlocking pieces. They also like models that result in detailed, realistic productions. Many enjoy using tiny screws, nuts and bolts, and even hooking up and using battery-powered construction sets (Goodson & Bronson, 1985). They also enjoy measuring and balancing objects, activities that reflect the emergence and consolidation of concrete operational thinking. Object manipulation, experimentation, and construction often occur in social commerce with peers and many times include pretense or game-like play qualities as well. Thus, while preschoolers enjoy matching and sorting objects, older children become increasingly scientific and experimental and engage in classification by using multiple criteria in combination.

Imitative/Imaginative/Dramatic Play

Make-believe or pretend play is a major play form during childhood, with its earliest emergence occurring usually in the second year of life as children's symbolic functioning develops. Pretense entails employing a transformational mode or an "as-if" stance toward ostensible reality. When pretending, children are assuming an identity in role enactment, they relate to other persons or objects as if they are other than themselves, or alter time and space in the form of situational transformations. Imitating, imagining, and dramatizing are all part of this kind of play as children represent and relive or reenact their actual experiences using the symbolic, language, and social skills available to them at a given developmental level. The expression and the theorized importance of pretense to the children's development and well-being change a great deal during the period between four and eight years of age.

By the age of four, the typical child is already quite accomplished at role enactment and the ability to do other-person, object, and situational transformations. It is not uncommon to see children at this age able to take on a whole host of pretend characters, ranging from the common familial and everyday occupational roles witnessed day in and day out, to the more far-fetched superhero and other fictional roles that children observe on television and in other media.

Role enactments frequently take place with other children and show a high degree of reciprocity, and social and verbal interaction, within the play frame. Fours and fives reach a high-water mark in the kind of overt make-believe of sociodramatic play (Smilansky, 1990) or collaborative pretense. Whether children are in such social groups or alone and playing independently, they display ease in using various props in support of play episodes. In addition to realistic props such as a toy telephone, children freely use substitute objects or invented or imagined objects in play, for example, a block for a telephone. Depending on the episode's play theme, the situational transformations also range considerably from the proximal to the distal. Their pretense, for example, ranges from a typical day at home or at the grocery store to being out in the forest in the middle of the night or traveling to a distant country.

Although declines occur in overt social make-believe play after age five or six years (at least in classroom or playground settings), children continue to exhibit a keen interest in it, even as other play forms gain in popularity. Generally speaking, older children's pretend play demonstrates richer texts, more contoured scripts, and more organized plots than the play of younger children. Play episodes of older children are more differentiated and elaborated, as seen, for example, when children put on a puppet show or a skit, or dramatize a circus, battle, or county fair. Six- to eight-year-olds, unlike fours and fives, are capable of a good deal more stage managing and directing or redirecting in their play when giving dramatic performances.

Although primary-grade school children often employ role-play materials appropriate for preschoolers, the older children can use a greater quantity of materials as well as more detailed equipment. Children within the four- to eight-year age span very much enjoy costumes and props, such as cash registers, play money, toy guns, and toy cameras, for a variety of dramatic play roles. They enjoy constructing and are able to make their own props out of blocks, cartons, and other manipulatives. Older children typically desire more detail and prefer more realism in their imaginative play props than do younger children, even though they have the cognitive ability to do without the real McCoy. Furthermore, play objects and materials of primary-grade children often become subjects of collections, crafts, or hobbies, in addition to functioning as props for playing library, store, and war games or taking trips.

Finally, pretense serves different purposes in development from four to eight years of age. For younger children, not only does pretense serve to strengthen various cognitive skills such as perspective taking, narrative competence, and decontextualization abilities, it also supports and promotes emotional and social development, particularly in the area of finding one's place or status in the peer group. Pretense helps children overcome fears and cope with these feelings as they make transitions from home to school; sharing fantasies also can be indispensably useful for making friends (Paley, 1988). With older primary-grade children, collaborative pretense continues to serve these purposes and becomes especially important for trust building and the formation of intimacy in friendship relationships (Howes et al., 1992).

Creative Play

Creative play in early and middle childhood develops and finds expression in various domains during the four- to eight-year age range. Typically, the laurel of "creative" describes children's play when it is a product of their directed thinking or self-regulated behavior, as opposed to nondirected or free-association-type thinking, or random or stimulus-dominated patterns of behavior (e.g., scribbling in which one mark on the page simply leads to another). Also, creative behavior usually implies original and aesthetically, or technically useful, expressions. Unlike creativity in adults, where a societal criterion is imposed, creativity for children usually means that the play or activity is original for this particular child, based on a personal or individual criterion. What is technically or aesthetically useful normally goes uninterpreted for younger children, but becomes more of an issue as children mature and can be expected to be judged according to social norms for creativity. Domains of creative play include arts and crafts, designing miniature play scenes (which may then result in imaginative play), and using musical instruments or audiovisual equipment.

Arts and Crafts

By four years of age, children's "creative" drawings and constructions already have moved beyond "acting-on-objects" and "exploration-of-the-medium" to a concern with the product (as opposed only to the process) for defining what is important to the child. Children at this age can usually make at least several color distinctions and possess the fine motor coordination needed to enjoy and create products with paints, finger paints, strings, beads, Magic Markers, scissors, large crayons, pencils, paste, and the like. Although four-year-olds can make representational products and are proud of them, five-year-olds' products are more realistic and elaborate. At this age, children can also more easily use watercolor paints, smaller crayons, coloring books, and simple weaving looms. Children who are six, seven, and eight years of age can make better use of all the materials and activities enjoyed by younger children in the sense of coming up with more skillful and more finished products. Primary-grade children can also sew and do woodworking and enjoy model building and craft kits involving leather work, papier-mâché, simple jewelry, and enameling.

Miniature Play Scenes

Creative play is apparent in the tabletop (or on a floor) microcosms young children recreate by constructing miniature worlds or designing play scenes involving various nonrealistic/unstructured (e.g., pipe cleaners, blocks) or realistic/structured (e.g., farm set) toys and other toys with small parts.

In imaginative or creative play with miniature worlds, children not only act on objects, and build and produce various configurations with the objects, they also often interject narratives or create stories about the play scenes, either in solitary play or as a form of collective, cooperative play. Children up to six years of age show peak interest in this form of imaginative play as they do for sociodramatic play. Preschool children enjoy both familiar play scenes such as garages and farms, and imaginary worlds such as space and military forts. By age five, children like to plan, construct, and play with miniature worlds, and they can show attention to detail, work various mechanisms, and use simple battery-powered accessories. As interest in sociodramatic play wanes, interest in creative play continues through the primary-grade years. Older children, however, prefer very detailed and realistic models in their play with miniature worlds or virtual realities (i.e., computer simulations), and they often combine this form of play with constructive play. Gender differences in the type of material and themes of miniature play, as is the case with sociodramatic play, are usually very pronounced; playing house, using dollhouses, and Barbie dolls are common for girls, for example, while playing with toy soldiers and playing superhero are common for boys.

Musical Instruments

Musical and rhythmic instruments are appropriate for children across a wide age range; and children are able to engage in expressive play with them. During the preschool years children's musical skill increases dramatically. Four-year-olds can carry a tune, recognize melodies, and even sing short, simple songs in their entirety. Language play during the preschool years includes inventing songs and rhymes. Children can keep time with music as they jump, gallop, and run—activities that lead to real dancing around five years of age. They experiment with rhythm instruments and can produce sounds with various musical instruments such as the harmonica, ocarina, horn, and simple recorder. They also use other musical instruments such as drums and xylophones. Primary-grade children begin to learn to play real instruments and read music. They show interest in group singing and can use their own song books. Children, especially girls, use their own records, CDs, or tape players, and begin to show interest in dance lessons. Hence, playful expression and more worklike craft and talent merge.

Cognitive Play

All types of play involve cognition but, as used in this section, this category label refers to games with rules, educational or skill-development toys, and books. Preschoolers and primary-grade children exhibit different types and levels of cognitive play.

Games with Rules

Most younger children cannot play games with rules, even with adult scaffolding. By four years of age, however, many children can play when the sit-down games have only a few simple rules, an easy scoring system, few if any reading requirements, and depend on simple chance but not skill or strategy. Preschool children enjoy matching and lotto-type games with pictures and colors, as well as simple letters and numbers when they are older. Younger preschool children find games with spinners or color cards easier than those that involve dice. Race games, in which the child only has to move the game piece along a preordained path without the option of blocking an opponent's piece, are age-appropriate. Preschoolers can also play games involving simple fine motor ability such as pick-up sticks. Interest in games increases during the primary-grade school years. For six- and seven-year-old children, games must remain rather simple and straightforward with few rules and with little skill or strategy required.

Around eight years of age, however, or when children reach the stage of concrete operations and are capable of formulating and carrying out a plan or strategy, they can enjoy a much wider array of games with rules, including rather sophisticated games based on fantasy or adventure themes. Genuine cooperation and competition then are possible and become important ingredients in games-with-rules play;

video and computer games generally are very popular among primary-grade school children.

Skill-Development Toys

Preschool and primary-grade children use educational toys and games, including electronic devices and computers, and literacy, mathematics, and science toys. Preschoolers enjoy cognitive play centered on naming and classifying the world around them. They enjoy performing copying, naming, matching, and sorting activities in their play. Skill-development materials include those that teach colors, shapes, and simple letter and number concepts. Among other materials, science toys for preschoolers include magnifying glasses, flashlights, prisms, magnets, color mixes, rock and shell collections, simple calculators, and see-through clocks. Many available computer software programs are educational in nature and are developmentally appropriate for preschoolers, eliciting various forms of cognitive (and social) play. By six years of age and throughout the primary-grade years, children play with many toys and materials that enhance specific skill development. Older children (six to eight years of age) are interested in their own anatomy and in the wider world around them, including other countries and times past. Among many other materials, they may enjoy microscopes, chemistry sets, field binoculars, and more complex software for computers. Electronic sports games are also highly popular around seven or eight years of age.

Books

Books elicit the cognitive play of preschoolers and primary-grade children. Preschoolers enjoy looking at books and love having adults read to them. Four-year-olds love ridiculous and silly stories; wild, dramatic, and fantastic stories (including fairy tales); animal books; verse; and stories about everyday life, including some factual books. Five-year-olds as well as six-year-olds generally prefer realistic and credible stories, poetry, holiday and seasonal stories, and comics. Six-year-olds also enjoy stories about fears and magic, nature, and the elements. By seven or eight years of age children can use a table of contents and an index. They also enjoy classics and books about travel, adventure, geography, primitive times, legions, and folktales. They continue to like newspaper comics and show an interest in magazines and store catalogues.

Individual and Group Variations in Play Development

Children around the world have a basic right to their childhood, and play is part of the magic of childhood. Quite remarkable strides in play expression between four and eight years of age occur in all five of the play categories described in this essay. Enormous differences and changes in various developmental domains characterize the growth of children between four and eight years of age. There is a qualitative difference, for example, in both the cognitive and social-cognitive ability of preoperational preschoolers as well as concrete-operational primary-grade school children.

Play developments, and development in such domains as physical and cognitive growth, take place in a dynamic, reciprocal relationship. Play both reflects children's developmental status and contributes to the same, either by consolidating developmental acquisitions or by serving generative functions in development. Although development is a major factor in play expression, however, and play expression is a major factor in development, these "main effects" enter into complex interactions with individual (gender, personality) and group (social-economic status, ethnicity/culture) differences among children, and with situational influences. Complex forces produce wide variations in the type and rate of play performance between four and eight years of age. The descriptive trends in play that this essay outlines reflect the interaction of these contexts and perspectives.

Individual Variation

Systematic individual differences exist in the expression of play between the ages of four and eight years that are related to the status of children's gender, personality, and special needs. In general, for example, boys are more likely to engage in rough-and-tumble play, superhero dramatic play, large block play, play themes that are active or adventuresome with pretend violence or aggression, and in various sports or organized athletic team activities. Girls usually prefer to play in smaller groups and show an interest in a greater variety of toys and play materials, including constructive play and other table activities. Games, crafts, and hobbies are acutely sex-typed during this stretch of ontogenesis, which overlaps with the Freudian latency period of psychosexual development and the Eriksonian stage of industry versus inferiority.

Personality further moderates play differences and may reflect age and gender. Some children prefer more reality-oriented play such as building models, doing puzzles, or reading realistic stories, while other children prefer more fantasy-oriented activity, as seen in their choice of toys, games, books, and dramatic play themes. Still other children are more object-centered, while some are more person-centered in their play. The former are more meticulous and fastidious in attending to the stimulus detail of play objects; the latter are more concerned with peer group reactions, adult attention, and social interaction.

Finally, the status of special needs has an impact on play development and expression during the four- to eight-year age spread. Although, in general, all children have similar interests and needs for play and peer relations, children who have special needs often possess a more limited repertoire of the social and cognitive skills needed for elaborative forms of independent and group play. The condition of special needs often adversely affects the rate and terminal level of development for children in relation to various categories of play. Such children may require interventions to prevent or remediate their situation.

Group Variation

Both social-economic status (SES) and cultural differences modulate patterns or regularities in play expressions and sequences from four to eight years of age. SES factors, such as low income or poverty, may set limits on availability and accessibility of high-quality play environments and expensive toys and equipment. Quality of play may suffer as a consequence. Lower levels of play (i.e., exploration, functional play) may predominate over higher forms of play (i.e., constructive, sociodramatic, and games with rules) when children lack experience with basic play materials, adult modeling, or encouragement (Smilansky, 1990).

Cultural factors further interact with SES and individual difference variables to produce variation in play behavior and development from four to eight years. Although structural features of play such as sociality of play, elaborativeness of language, and imagination may not differ across cultures, play themes and content are often culturally specific. Educa-tional or academic play, such as creative play and cognitive play, may show higher degrees of similarity across developed and developing countries than expressive or recreational play with games, books, sports, or dramatic play themes, which are more likely to retain the unique flavor of the specific individual cultures.

Play from four to eight is rich and multifarious and can serve as a window on the child's developmental status, personality, and emotional well-being. Play also promotes and reinforces the child's development in social and cognitive areas. Individual and group differences moderate the dynamic relation of play with development. Socialization agents do not always respect or value the importance of play for children who are making the transition from the preshool to the primary-grade school years. The societal push to rush children through their immaturity poses a threat to the optimization of the potential in play of four- to eight-year-old children. These attitudes are apparent in many school systems in the United States and in families where parents pressure children toward adult-defined group activities such as organizations, ball leagues, or lessons. Adult overmanagement of children's time and activities can also result in more passive, less robust play. Play, for example, has been eliminated or sharply curtailed when schools drop recess or neglect to provide interesting playground equipment. Perhaps the most serious threat to play during this age period, however, comes from the children themselves when adults do not check their notorious tendencies to reject peers and play in segregated groups.

Clearly, adults have a critical role to play to ensure that all children play up to potential during this age period. Providing quality physical environments is only part of the needed response. Adults must also value play and seek to create favorable, socially inclusive environments for all children that honor the right of each individual child to play. Curricular restructuring that leads to more play-oriented experience in the classrooms is another step in the right direction. Some adults view recess and playground time as outside extensions of sound, child-sensitive, activity-based educational programs. As more and more parents and teachers gain insight into the importance of play for children, and understand how adults are often implicated in threats to play, they may eliminate many of the barriers that now exist so that play can flourish for all children at every age.

Bibliography

Bergen, D. (1988). *Play as a medium for learning and development: A handbook of theory and practice*. Portsmouth, NH: Heinemann.

Erikson, E. (1977). *Childhood and society* (2nd ed.). New York: Norton (Original work published in 1963)

Fein, G. G. (1975). A transformational analysis of pretending. *Developmental Psychology, 11*, 291–296.

Freud, S. (1961). *Jokes and their relation to the unconscious*. New York: Norton (Original work published in 1960)

Goodson, B. D., & Bronson, M. B. (1985). *Guidelines for relating children's ages to toy characteristics* (Contract No. CPSC-85–1089). Washington, DC: U.S. Consumer Product Safety Commission.

Howes, C., Unger, O., & Matheson, C. (1992). *The collaborative construction of pretend: Social pretend play functions*. Albany: State University of New York Press.

Johnson, J. E., Christie, J., & Yawkey, T. D. (1987). *Play and early childhood development*. Glenview, IL: Scott, Foresman.

King, N. R. (1982). Work and play in the classroom. *Social Education, 46,* 110–113.

Paley, V. (1988). *The boy who would be a helicopter*. Cambridge, MA: Harvard University Press.

Piaget, J. (1962). *Play, dreams and imitation in childhood*. New York: Norton.

Rubin, K. H., Fein, G. G., & Vandenberg, B. (1983). Play. In P. H. Mussen (Ed.), *Handbook of child psychology: Vol. 4. Socialization, personality, and social development* (4th ed., pp. 693–774). New York: John Wiley.

Smilansky, S. (1990). Sociodramatic play: Its relevance to behavior and achievement in school. In E. Klugman & S. Smilansky (Eds.), *Children's play and learning: Perspectives and policy implications* (pp. 18–42). New York: Teachers College Press.

von Glasersfeld, E., & Kelley, M. F. (1982). On the concepts of period, phase, stage, and level. *Human Development, 25,* 152–160.

Play Development
from Ages Eight to Twelve

M. Lee Manning

Children's play has been a controversial topic for many years and has been neglected in many schools and homes. Controversy has centered around an appropriate definition, the belief that play contradicts our nation's work ethic, and the mindset that schools and learners, to achieve "excellence," require less play and more work. Some adults might even consider children between eight and twelve years of age too old to play. While a vast body of research has documented the contribution of play to younger children's cognitive and literacy development and to their social growth, less research and scholarly opinion has focused attention on the significance of play in the development of eight- to twelve-year-olds.

Many unanswered questions exist. Among them: What developmental sequences and experiences do eight- to twelve-year-olds undergo? How do gender, socioeconomic status, and attitudes of parents and educators affect play? Do eight- to twelve-year-olds even have a right to play? This essay examines the play of eight- to twelve-year-olds, looks at contexts and perspectives such as gender and adults' expectations, and recommends that schools, professional associations, parents, and children's advocacy groups take the stand that children have the right to play.

Definitions

Play means different things to different people. Various definitions (Bruce, 1993; Manning & Boals, 1987; Pellegrini & Galda, 1994), theories (Rubin & Coplan, 1994), and characteristics (Daiute, 1989; Rubin & Coplan, 1994) have been offered to explain play. Likewise, authors have examined play from historical and contemporary perspectives and in terms of its contributions to the developing child (Daiute, 1989; Manning & Boals, 1987; Rubin & Coplan, 1994). Rather than providing a detailed review of the accumulated literature, this section reviews several definitions of play that pertain to eight- to twelve-year-olds, identifies some characteristics of play in which eight- to twelve-year-olds might engage, and examines play from its historical and contemporary perspectives.

Among traditional definitions of play are those that consider play as a means of reducing energy (Spencer, 1860); as a preparation for life and for aesthetic appreciation (Groos, 1901); as a means of expressing oneself or to relieve anxieties and fears; and as a result of wish fulfillment (Rubin & Coplan, 1994). Some more contemporary definitions of play regard it as the purest form of assimilation (Piaget, 1952); as an essential link in the association of abstract meanings and associated concrete objects; and as an exploration of new combinations of behaviors and ideas within a psychologically safe milieu (Bruner, 1972).

Regardless of which definition one chooses, play among eight- to twelve-year-olds will likely be:

- *symbolic* of significant aspects of the child's life experiences
- *active* in the sense that it requires participation
- *voluntary and pleasurable* due to some sense of satisfaction or gratification
- *meaningful* from the perspective of the child's context (for example, eight- to twelve-year-olds might consider the play of three- and four-year-olds to be unfulfilling)

One view of play includes behaviors whereby one child influences or is influenced by another child (Garvey, 1974, 1990). Such a definition includes the ability of children to play with other children in a cooperative, socially acceptable manner while verbally and nonverbally sharing, taking turns, and responding. Examples of social, nonverbal communication include facial expressions, vocalizations, postures and movements, aggressive or nonaggressive behaviors, and social gestures. Still another characteristic of play among eight- to twelve-year-olds includes preparing for the future or attempting to reduce the worry and stress of an upcoming event.

Characteristics of Play among Eight- to Twelve-Year-Olds

Play is often experimental or exploratory; children try alternatives based on implicit principles of language, the social world, or some other phenomena. Eight- to twelve-year-olds, for example, might make up and repeat riddles or might experiment with natural phenomena such as gravity by trying various ways to roll a ball. Children also "play" with other linguistic and physical phenomena (Daiute, 1989).

Many characteristics of play could be listed, depending on one's definition of play and the age level or maturity of the child participating in the play activity. Characteristics of play in later elementary- and early middle-school-age children include intrinsic motivation, spontaneity, self-imposed goals, and active engagement rather than daydreaming and aimless loafing (Rubin, Fein, & Vandenberg, 1983). As children play, they create a safe context in which to master the communication of meaning, learn to compromise, and allow for exploring issues of trust (Howes, 1992).

Contextual Factors

Several contextual factors affect the play of eight- to twelve-year-old children. First, children's developmental maturity affects the types and purposes of their play. Second, socioeconomic status and gender also affect the type, amount, and reasons for play. A child from a more affluent socioeconomic group, for example, might engage in play that represents leisure pursuits, while a child from a less affluent socioeconomic group might engage in play related to everyday survival. Girls' play might differ dramatically from boys' play. Likewise, cultural backgrounds may affect children's play. Cultural differences in play have been exhibited by lower-class and middle-class Israeli children and in African American and Anglo-American children (McLoyd, 1982). Of course, one must be careful with such generalizations because acculturation differs and crossover might occur in relation to socioeconomic status, gender, or cultural heritage.

Historical Perspectives

Some teachers and parents have been reluctant to acknowledge the contribution of play to children's overall development or to regard it as a worthy part of the middle childhood years. The failure to encourage play at this age perhaps resulted from society's lack of understanding of children and the zealous commitment to the work ethic of our nation.

A historical look at play indicates that teachers and parents have intentionally neglected play as a vital entity in children's development (Sutton-Smith, 1967). During colonial times, adults considered children's play to be a sign of moral laxity and encouraged children to avoid the frivolity of play in favor of work and study (King, 1979). Those who gave top priority to the role of work in the increasingly industrialized society of the United States, while derogating recreation and leisure, did not recognize the importance and necessity of play. Continuing the play-versus-work argument, one commentator has suggested that there is an irreconcilable incompatibility between "child's play" and the characteristics of societal expectations (Vandenberg, 1986). The nation's pragmatic attitudes did not view play as having a payoff or a bottom-line gain and could not accept behaviors that did not provide easily observable benefits.

Today, those who favor an extreme emphasis on academic achievement might consider play to be frivolous, especially for eight- to twelve-year-olds in schools and homes. They would perceive an incompatibility between play, schoolwork, and academic achievement. They might also believe that eight- to twelve-year-olds, unlike their younger counterparts, are too old for "child's play." These views reflect a trend toward children's "growing up" at a rapid pace, thereby shortening the childhood years. Perceptive educators and parents with an understanding of child development readily recognize the fallacy of these beliefs. While the types and purposes of play change as children develop, there continues to be a powerful need for play in late childhood.

In fact, some early educators, such as Friedrich Froebel (1782–1852), did consider play to be important for children's development and, even more, the basis for all childhood education (Ransbury, 1982). Likewise, John Dewey (1916) supported play as a worthwhile educational endeavor. Much later, King (1979) summarized contemporary thought by stating that play was necessary for healthy mental, physical, and social development. In some situations, the concept of play appears to have come full circle from a time when adults admonished children to avoid the frivolity of play to a time when people consider play to be an essential aspect of the childhood years (King, 1979).

Manifestations of Play among Eight- to Twelve-Year-Olds

The physical, cognitive, and psychosocial development of later elementary and early middle school children results in different types of play than those play forms in which younger children engage.

The Public and the Private
Any legitimate discussion of play among eight- to twelve-year-olds must admit the possibility of a discrepancy between the public and the private. In effect, children's authentic play sometimes succumbs to factors beyond their control. Teachers and parents, for example, who fail to understand the value of play, may discourage play by calling it "babyish" and suggesting that the children engage in more "age-appropriate" activities. Therefore, "public" play in eight- to twelve-year-olds might be limited due to parents' and teachers' expectations, socioeconomic factors, and gender expectations.

Adults' memories of play indicate a difference between "public" play and "less noticeable" play during the eight- to twelve-year-old period. For example, while public play appears to decline, some of this play only becomes more private. Adults report that their play changed during this period, perhaps because other children urged them to "act their age" or because types of play for this age group develop a more private nature. Other adult memories include symbolic play becoming integrated into games with rules, such as competitive board games, and becoming more abstract by transformation into mental games and language play. Other play during this age period includes participation in verbal invention and verbal play such as inventing and participating in riddles, puns, tongue twisters, insults, chants, rhymes, and secret codes that might involve playing with syntax and semantics of language (Bergen, 1988).

Professionals who guide play activities attempt to look beyond physical appearances as they play with children. Considerable developmental diversity exists, after all, among ten- to twelve-year-olds, especially considering individual and gender differences, which affect the timing of growth spurts. With this caution firmly in mind, several aspects of play in eight- to twelve-year-olds can be explicated.

Gender-typed Play
As elementary-age children develop gender roles and gender-specific behaviors, they readily identify and show a preference for gender-typed play activities that are culturally sanctioned for their gender. At this age, boys typically involve themselves in physical and independent types of play, while girls choose less physical play types. Boys, more than girls, seem to be aware of gender differences and avoid playing with objects that might be labeled "feminine" (Turner & Helms, 1983). Girls participate in more varieties of play than boys. It is important to note, however, that the preference for gender-typed play activities might be changing. Increasingly, softball and soccer teams encourage girls to participate, either on their own teams or on mixed teams. Also, as schools provide gender-neutral activities, boys might perceive less stigma from participating in activities traditionally considered feminine.

Physical Play
Eight- to twelve-year-old children select increasingly demanding physical play, which gives them a greater opportunity to develop muscle control and coordination. At this age, boundless amounts of energy and enthusiasm appear to be hallmark characteristics as children enjoy running, tumbling, climbing on jungle gyms, and swinging. As children gain motor skills and confidence, they begin more advanced forms of

play such as roller skating, skipping rope, skate boarding, and throwing and catching (Turner & Helms, 1983). Children's increased physical abilities and improved coordination also allow participation in team sports and other organized activities whereby one's physical ability affects the outcome of the game.

Social Play

Ten- to twelve-year-old children, in particular, develop the social skills necessary to participate in complex, cooperative forms of play. The complexity and flexibility of their verbal as well as nonverbal communication contribute to this cooperative potential. They are also able to make friends, interact competently and confidently in social situations, and build on their increasing self-esteem (Manning, 1993). These enhanced social skills allow children to see others' perspectives and allow them to realize the benefits of playing socially and cooperatively. Actual play, which requires social skills, might consist of games, team sports, and organized activities.

A concern voiced over two decades ago held that schools often provided play activities that emphasize competition rather than cooperation (Ellis, 1973). This concern continues to be valid as the twenty-first century nears. Educators sometimes lose sight of play's contributions to learning the social skills necessary for everyday life. Instead, they emphasize competition, perhaps because determining winners and losers is easier than evaluating the improvement of social skills. Regardless of the reason, promoters and advocates of play understand that play for eight- to twelve-year-olds should place emphasis on cooperative behaviors rather than on competition. Also, competition may be inappropriate for the females, who often place a priority on cooperation and harmony rather than on competitive efforts.

Outdoor Play

Children, predominantly ten- to twelve-year-olds, shift allegiance from parents and teachers to peers and increasingly seek freedom and independence, which results in their playing away from home and, often, away from direct adult supervision. Children might visit ballfields, playgrounds, and recreation centers where others play or where special equipment is available.

Outdoor play has several advantages. Researchers have maintained that outdoor play can stimulate physical-motor development (Henniger, 1993–1994; Pellegrini, 1991), can serve as a positive setting for enhancing social interaction (Pellegrini & Perlmutter, 1988), and can stimulate a variety of play forms (Henniger, 1985).

Outdoor play should not be equated with the recess periods of younger children, which often results in little more than a break from classwork. Depending on the school and its ability to provide playground equipment, these breaks may provide little chance for children to learn social skills through games and to improve their physical skills through effective outdoor play environments.

Developers of well-planned and equipped playgrounds have viewed them primarily as an opportunity to develop physical skills through vigorous exercise and play (Henniger, 1993–1994). Educators consider the outdoor setting to be an extension of the classroom, with the same potential for enhancing development (Henniger, 1993–1994). In support of this goal, researchers have recommended that playgrounds include seven play zones: transitional, manipulative/creative, projective/fantasy, focal/social, social/dramatic, physical, and natural element (Esbensen, 1987; Henniger, 1993–1994). While all these play zones might not be appropriate for all eight- to twelve-year-olds, it is important that all learners have equal access to playground zones so that they can make their own choices.

Game Play

Children's increasing cognitive abilities allow more advanced forms of organized games and team activities where rules guide actual behaviors. Although younger children often play together (though, actually, they may only be playing near each other), they also often play alone. Eight- to twelve-year-olds might also play alone, either by choice or by necessity; however, their increasing cognitive abilities (especially in those ten to twelve years of age) allow them to play with others in situations requiring consistent, complex rules.

Depending on their popularity at the time, several types of games are prevalent: steady or constant games such as tag; recurrent or cyclical games such as marbles or hopscotch; and sporadic games such as hula hoop contests, which rise in popularity and then disappear. After twelve years of age, games decline in popularity and are replaced by unstructured play, conversations, and organized play (Bergen, 1988).

Most eight- to twelve-year-old children are able to engage in sustained cooperative and competitive social interactions, to plan and carry out longer and longer sequences of purposeful activities, and to exercise self-control and submit voluntarily to restrictions and conventions. These emerging capacities rest on the reciprocal interaction of children's experiences with their physical, cognitive, and psychosocial growth (Garvey, 1990).

Cognitive Play

The cognitive abilities of ten- to twelve-year-olds also allow for more advanced forms of play such as word games, riddles, and other literacy-related play. Other cognitive characteristics that contribute to their ability to participate in cognitive play include the ability to think hypothetically, reflectively, and abstractly; the ability to engage in propositional thought; and the ability to reason through more than one variable (Manning, 1993). These types of literacy play and play as thought particularly contribute to academic achievement, higher-order thinking skills, and other learning and writing activities (Daiute, 1989).

One researcher contends that play also offers a rich context for children's literacy learning (Vukelich, 1993). Such a contention is especially valid for eight- to twelve-year-olds who are experiencing rapid cognitive and psychosocial development. Play environments that foster children's engagement in literacy behaviors lead to significant increases in amounts of literacy activity during play; reading and writing behaviors become more purposeful in literacy-enriched play settings; and activities in literacy-enriched play become more connected. In concert, such literacy behaviors suggest that an enriching play environment provides children with a significant context for developing additional understandings about reading and writing (Vukelich, 1993).

Technological Play

Many technological advances allow new forms of play. Children can play a wide array of computer games either alone or with another youngster. Software, such as for chess, requires that children think and participate in actual decision making, while other software requires writing and complex thinking. As technological advances become commonplace in our society, children will have greater access to problem-solving programs, CD-ROMs, videodiscs, and simulation programs. Many eight- to twelve-year-old children who have benefited from computer use in schools are sufficiently computer literate to "play" with the many technological advances. They also have the cognitive and psychosocial capacity to work alone and to perform the thinking required to benefit from increasingly complex computer games.

Pretend Play

Although the pretend play of earlier years is not seen in school settings, children in this age range engage in much symbolic play at home and in other private or semiprivate environments. In fact, the most salient types of play remembered by many adults are pretend play and games with rules. Research also indicates that there are cross-cultural differences in types of play. Adults in the United States, for example, tend to remember more pretend play activities, while Chinese adults recall more examples of games with rules (Bergen, Liu, & Liu, 1994). The different types of pretend play include use of miniature objects to simulate real-life experiences, building forts and tree houses for various and changing purposes (e.g., a fort one day, a house the next), playing school and house (a favorite activity of eight- to nine-year-olds), and giving plays (more common in ten- to twelve-year-olds).

Perspectives on Play among Eight- to Twelve-Year-Olds

There are various sociocultural perspectives that can affect children's play. Educators and parents, for example, might encourage children to engage in specific play behaviors rather than allow children to choose for themselves. Educators and parents sometimes consider play the antithesis of work and learning. Sociocultural attitudes also can influence the relationship between play and gender; for example, children often select play activities that are culturally sanctioned for their gender. Adults who value, and provide for, well-planned outdoor play also can make a difference in children's play experiences.

Parents Encouraging Specific Play Behavior

Parents tend to reward gender-typical play in their children. Many parents, for example, support active large motor play in boys yet discourage such active play in girls. Some parents reward their daughters for playing with dollhouses and domestic toys but punish them for playing with military toys and vehicles. Some parents reward their sons for playing with military toys and vehicles but punish them for playing with dollhouses and domestic toys (Etaugh & Liss, 1992).

Through societal expectations, most eight- to twelve-year-old children acquire some idea of gender-role behaviors. These behaviors sometimes result from personal choice, but sometimes children feel pressured by adults and peers to engage in particular "boy" or "girl" behaviors. Societal and parental expectations can create powerful pressures for females and males to behave in "appropriate" ways and to play with "appropriate" toys. The nature of play as *voluntary, pleasurable,* and *meaningful* suggests that children should be allowed to choose the behaviors and toys they want. Enlightened parents encourage play in eight- to twelve-year-olds and encourage children to select behaviors and toys that have personal meaning and relevance.

Attitudes of Educators

Just as parents often encourage specific types of play, educators also, perhaps unknowingly, have a significant impact on children's play. Educators of preschool children, for example, usually encourage fantasy play by providing time, materials, and space for fantasy (Pellegrini & Galda, 1994); however, they may consider eight- to twelve-year-olds too old for fantasy or may consider that fantasy is unproductive play: in effect, play that does not contribute to academic growth. Some educators consider all play to be a poor expenditure of time or a waste of energy. Since play's benefits are usually not measurable with standardized tests, educators often feel that they should not allow too much time for play, especially when they perceive that it takes away from the kinds of study and other academic pursuits that prepare children for such tests. These harsh criticisms of play may grow more intense when reports suggest schools are failing in their academic mission and when achievement test scores decline. Perceptive educators and scholars acquainted with the benefits of play realize that play contributes to learning and academic achievement and is not a cause of their decline.

Gender and Culture

Societal expectations as well as parents' and educators' opinions influence the relationship of gender and play. There might be a fine line between children's actual choice of behaviors and those dictated by others.

Some research has documented gender differences in children's play behaviors (Bergen, 1994; Garvey, 1990; Pellegrini & Galda, 1994). As our schools become more gender-equitable and gender-conscious in the twenty-first century, educators need to understand the relationship between gender and play and, whenever possible, provide equitable play opportunities for both girls and boys. Since violent play themes and aggressive actions result in a more powerful person winning and a weaker person losing (Bergen, 1994), this type of competitive play favors boys, who tend to be physically stronger in this age group. A corollary message in this type of play is that males are more likely than females to accept violence as a means of solving problems. In fact, because parents and educators are more accepting of aggression in boys, when girls participate in aggressive behaviors they are more likely to be reprimanded.

Those who have studied rough-and-tumble play found that boys participate in such behaviors more than girls (Garvey, 1990; Pellegrini & Galda, 1994). These differences might result from hormonal and/or socialization factors. A cross-cultural study supports the finding that rough-and-tumble play reflects cultural differences. Boys among the Ilocano of Luzon, the Mixtecans of Mexico, and the Taira of Okinawa, for example, participate in more boisterous and rowdy play than girls (Garvey, 1990). But in other cultures, such as the Pilaga Indians, girls also often engage in rough play.

Culture, therefore, plays an important part in children's amount and selection of play behaviors. Among intracultural and generational differences, some Asian Americans, for example, might place priority on work over play and might be more insistent that children's behaviors be more gender-specific. Adopting the Confucian ideals of hard work and self-discipline (Feng, 1994), these parents and families might view play as unnecessary, especially when they do not understand its relationship to academic achievement.

Right to Play

While the literature has not focused extensively on children's having a "right to play," there has been a proposal that children have this basic right because it contributes to healthy development (Almy, 1984). Current emphasis on narrow perspectives of academic achievement has prohibited widespread acceptance of eight- to twelve-year-olds' right to play. The growing recognition, however, of the importance of play in children's general development as well as their academic achievement might underscore the position that play is a right of all children. Recognizing play as a basic right can be a major step toward recognizing play as valuable both in itself as well as because of its contributions to broad cognitive and social growth.

The benefits of play in the lives of eight- to twelve-year-old children are too significant to ignore. Play contributes to children's cognitive and psychosocial development, to academic achievement, and to a foundation for thinking, writing, and other forms of literacy. Although those who support the provision of opportunities for children to play have written extensively about children's need for play and its many contributions, a discrepancy continues to exist between "public play environments" and "private play environments." Children's play deserves greater respect. Now is the time for schools, professional associations, parents, and children's advocacy groups to take a stand for children's having a right to play.

Bibliography

Almy, M. (1984). A child's right to play. *Young Children, 39*(4), 80.

Bergen, D. (1988). Stages of play development. In D. Bergen (Ed.), *Play as a medium for learning and development* (pp. 49–66). Portsmouth, NH: Heinemann.

Bergen, D. (1994). Should teachers permit or discourage violent play themes? *Childhood Education, 70*(5), 300–301.

Bergen, D., Liu, W., & Liu, G. (1994). *Chinese and American college students' memories of childhood play: A comparison.* Paper presented at the conference of the Association for the Study of Play, Atlanta, GA.

Bruce, T. (1993). The role of play in children's lives. *Childhood Education, 69*(4), 237–238.

Bruner, J. S. (1972). Nature and uses of immaturity. *American Psychologist, 27*(8), 687–708.

Daiute, C. (1989). Play as thought: Thinking strategies of young writers. *Harvard Educational Review, 59*(1), 1–23.

Dewey, J. (1916). *Education and democracy.* New York: Macmillan.

Ellis, M. J. (1973). *Why people play.* Englewood Cliffs, NJ: Prentice-Hall.

Esbensen, S. (1987). *An outdoor classroom.* Ypsilanti, MI: High/Scope Press.

Etaugh, C., & Liss, M. B. (1992). Home, school and playroom: Training grounds for adult gender roles. *Sex Roles, 26*(3–4), 129–147.

Feng, J. (1994). Asian American children: What teachers should know. (Report No. EDO-PS-94-4). Washington, DC: Office of Educational Research and Improvement. (*ERIC Document Reproduction Service No E0369 577).*

Garvey, C. (1974). Some properties of social play. *Merrill-Palmer Quarterly, 20*(3), 163–180.

Garvey, C. (1990). *Play.* Cambridge, MA: Harvard University Press.

Groos, K. (1901). *The play of man.* New York: Appleton.

Henniger, M. L. (1985). Preschool children's play behaviors in an indoor and outdoor environment. In J. L. Frost & S. Sunderlin (Eds.), *When children play* (pp. 145–149). Wheaton, MD: Association for Childhood Education International.

Henniger, M. L. (1993–1994). Enriching the outdoor play experience. *Childhood Education, 70*(2), 87–90.

Howes, C. (1992). *The collaborative construction of pretend.* Albany: State University of New York Press.

King, N. R. (1979). Play: The kindergartener's perspective. *Elementary School Journal, 80*(3), 81–87.

Manning, M. L. (1993). *Developmentally appropriate middle level schools.* Wheaton, MD: Association for Childhood Education International.

Manning, M. L., & Boals, B. M. (1987). In defense of play. *Contemporary Education, 58*(4), 206–210.

McLoyd, V. (1982). Social class differences in sociodramatic play: A critical review. *Developmental Review, 2*(1), 1–30.

Pellegrini, A. (1991). Outdoor recess: Is it really necessary? *Principal, 71*(40), 23.

Pellegrini, A. D., & Galda, L. (1994). Play. In V. S. Ramachandran (Ed.), *Encyclopedia* of human behavior (pp. 535–543). New York: Academic.

Pellegrini, A., & Perlmutter, J. (1988). Rough and tumble play on the elementary school playground. *Young Children, 43*(2), 14–17.

Piaget, J. (1952). *The origins of intelligence in children*. New York: International University Press.

Ransbury, M. K. (1982). Friedrich Froebel 1782–1852: A reexamination of Froebel's principles of children's learning. *Childhood Education, 59*(2), 104–106.

Rubin, K. H., & Coplan, R. J. (1994). Play: Developmental stages, functions, and educational support. In T. Husen & T. Postlethwaite (Eds.), *The international encyclopedia of education* (2nd ed., Vol. 8, pp. 4536–4542). New York: Elsevier.

Rubin, K., Fein, G., & Vandenberg, B. (1983). Play. In E. M. Hetherington (Ed.), *Handbook of child psychology: Vol. 4. Socialization, personality, and social development* (pp. 693–774). New York: John Wiley.

Spencer, H. (1860). *Education: Intellectual, moral, and physical*. New York: A. L. Fowle.

Sutton-Smith, B. (1967). The role of play in cognitive development. *Young Children, 22*(6), 361–370.

Turner, J. S., & Helms, D. B. (1983). *Lifespan development*. New York: Holt, Rinehart and Winston.

Vandenberg, B. (1986). Mere child's play. In K. Blanchard (Ed.), *The many faces of play* (pp. 115–120). Champaign, IL: Human Kinetics.

Vukelich, C. (1993). Play: A context for exploring the functions, features, and meaning of writing with peers. *Language Arts, 70*(1), 386–391.

Language Development and Play

Play and Language

Individual Differences as Evidence of Development and Style

Cecilia Shore

Play and language, as two ways to represent the world, show lifelong interaction. Adults, for example, play games such as Monopoly and Diplomacy that represent events in the world through actions and language, and enact plays from Shakespeare. As early as the second year of life children begin to use play and language to represent objects and events in their lives (Piaget, 1962, p. 96). There are several different ways in which these two media intersect. First, language often serves as the material/medium for play, as in nursery rhyme games such as "This Little Piggy," sound games such as pig Latin, and verbal humor such as puns (Ferguson & Macken, 1983; Weeks, 1979). Second, language often accompanies play; children narrate their pretend activities and use language to negotiate the roles and action (Giffin, 1984; Nelson & Seidman, 1984; Schwartzman, 1978). Third, some theorists say that language and play share underlying cognitive skills, such as knowledge that one thing can symbolize something else. It is this linkage between language and play that will be the primary focus for this essay. It will focus on the early phases of gestural and verbal symbolization, and on early play that is representational (variously termed symbolic, pretend, or dramatic).

In these preschool years, the language and play of children within the same age group can differ dramatically from one another. Some differences between children may arise because one child is making more rapid progress down a developmental pathway. Children are "ahead" of their age-mates, for example, if they can sequence pretend actions, such as "pouring" pretend cereal into a bowl, "eating," and saying "yum," while others can only carry out one action at a time. In terms of language such differences might appear in the size of toddlers' vocabulary. Other differences between children appear to be a matter of style, content, or emphasis rather than developmental progress. Some children's early vocabularies, for example, emphasize nouns and object words, while others emphasize interpersonally useful phrases. In play, some children appear to focus on accurately representing objects and their relationships (e.g., using blocks to carefully depict a castle), while others emphasize characters and their interactions (e.g., using the blocks to represent the king and queen and having them "talk" to one another). This essay will focus primarily on these *stylistic* differences in play and language. It will briefly address developmental differences in play and language, describe differences in play and language styles, show possible linkages between these styles, and explore the origins and implications of stylistic differences.

Developmental Differences in Play and Links to Language

There are clearly characteristic age differences in play. In the first year play tends to be exploratory, but near the end of that year functional and spatial play and the beginnings of symbolic play appear. Over the second year, toddlers' symbolic play becomes more distanced from the self, more combinatorial of actions, and less dependent on the support of realistic objects. These latter trends continue into the preschool years, in that children's ability to use gesture to represent absent objects and to coordinate roles in pretend play tends to increase with age (Belsky & Most, 1981; Boyatzis & Watson,

1993; Fein, 1981; McCune-Nicolich, 1981; Watson, 1984). Although these age differences may appear on the average, there is some question about whether all individual children's play emerges in the same developmental sequence (Hoppe-Graff, 1993).

Correlational studies indicate that individual differences between toddlers in their developmental level of play may be related to three factors: exploratory competence, parental support, and representational competence (Tamis-LeMonda & Bornstein, 1993). First, exploratory competence generally involves visual attention and object manipulation. Infants as young as five months who were better able to sustain attention to examining objects and making them create effects (e.g., squeezing a squeaky toy) engaged in more symbolic play at thirteen months (Tamis-LeMonda & Bornstein, 1993).

Second, parents also provide support for their infants' play. Over the second year of life, parents tend to play with their babies in gradually more sophisticated ways, and infants' play tends to be more sophisticated with their mothers than when they play alone (e.g., O'Connell & Bretherton, 1984). Maternal participation is particularly helpful when the play is joint and reciprocal, rather than when the mother intrudes into the baby's activity (Fiese, 1990). For example, the child's "eating" pretend soup is more likely to occur in an episode in which the mother and toddler take turns "stirring" and "eating" than in an episode in which mother holds out a spoon to a child who is busy dumping blocks out of the pan. Reciprocity and positive affect appear to be particularly important in at-risk populations (see review by O'Reilly & Bornstein, 1993).

Third, representational competence is the ability to use one thing, such as a word or a gesture, to *stand for* or represent something else. Representational competence is important because researchers have found correlations between developmental levels in play and language (Shore, Bates, Bretherton, Beeghly, & O'Connell, 1990; Tamis-LeMonda, Kahana-Kalman, Damast, Baumwell, & Bornstein, 1992). These correlations tend to be *specific* to particular ages and particular aspects of play and language. At thirteen months of age, for example, infants who have many gestural "names" for objects (e.g., put cup to lips or comb to head as if to say "I know what this is") have a larger vocabulary of object words. At twenty months, children who can use substitute objects to enact a *sequence* of symbolic actions (e.g., "stir" in a bowl with a comb and then pretend to eat) tend to be producing longer strings of words in early sentences.

If language and symbolic play share underlying cognitive abilities, one would expect children with language delay to also show deficits in their symbolic play. A recent study indicates that toddlers with expressive specific language impairment were less able than their age-mates to apply pretend actions to a doll or other person, to put pretend actions into sequences, and to use substitute objects in pretense (Rescorla & Goossens, 1992; for other reviews, see Leonard, 1987; Sigman & Sena, 1993).

Stylistic Individual Differences in Play

Children's language or play may also differ *qualitatively*. That is, there may exist different patterns of behavior at the same developmental level, or alternative pathways of development. Such qualitative individual differences are thought of as "styles" of language or play development. If a behavior pattern is "stylistic," the child has other modes of acting but prefers this one. Second, a "style" is a generalized observable tendency that is apparent in a variety of behaviors; behaviors that are thought to represent this general tendency, therefore, should be correlated with one another. Third, styles are stable across time. Finally, as mentioned above, stylistic differences should not reflect developmental level (Wolf & Gardner, 1979; Wolf & Grollman, 1982).

The literature on play describes two major types of stylistic differences in children's play: patterners versus dramatists, and object versus social mastery motivation. This discussion will reveal that, though these different characterizations are distinct from one another, they share features in common.

Patterners vs. Dramatists

Patterners, according to the research, are skilled in fitting objects together to make a pattern. These children are curious—exploring, manipulating, and naming the object world—and fascinated by how things work. Patterners' language is heavily biased toward labels and descriptors. In play, they emphasize narration of actual objects and events and indulge in objective comparisons. Dramatists, however, are interested in thoughts, feelings, communication, and relationships. Dramatists' language focuses on names of people and social and emotional expressions. They use language to engage others in the play activity, and delight in "embroidering" the situation or narrative (Wolf & Gardner, 1979).

A description of a patterner's play follows:

The child (at 18.5 months) selects a toy teapot with which to play. She puts the lid on and off several times. After "pouring" it into a cup and taking a sip, she sets the cup down next to the pot. She then lines up all the cups and plates and puts a spoon in each cup. She picks up the teapot and goes down the row of items with it, using it to tap each of the items in turn. (Wolf & Gardner, 1979, p. 117)

By contrast, a description of a dramatist's play:

This child (at 16 months) selects a toy teapot and a doll. She "gives the doll a drink," making smacking noises. Then she puts the doll down and covers it with a towel, saying "night night." She does this twice, tenderly. Then she appears to use the toy spoon to "feed herself" from the teapot, "pours" from the teapot into a toy cup, and "drinks" from the cup. Then she says "baby," carries the cup over to the doll, and "gives the baby a drink." (Wolf & Gardner, 1979, p. 117)

The original description of these play styles is both qualitative and narrative. Other researchers have described efforts to express these tendencies in quantitative terms (Dixon & Shore, 1991).

Object vs. Social Mastery Motivation

Obtaining and retaining others' attention is typical evidence of social mastery motivation. One researcher has assessed social mastery motivation by observing the child's efforts to produce an effect with an object or to solve problems involving objects (Wachs, 1993). A study of more than sixty twelve-month-olds found that about 55 percent of the sample could be characterized as high on object orientation and low on social mastery, whereas the remaining 45 percent showed the opposite pattern (Wachs, 1993).

The researcher believes that his results are consistent with the "social" versus "object" flavor of patterner versus dramatist styles, even though the play criteria differed from that used in the patterner-dramatist study. One might expect that infants who had a patterner's symbolic play style would score high on object mastery motivation, since both of these seem to contain an element of object-centeredness. Similarly, one might expect dramatists to rank high on social mastery motivation, because these seem to share an interest in people. Another study, however, found the children's dramatist score to be *negatively* related to their social mastery score (Dixon, 1990). The author argues that task content and context influence play styles, and so it is not easy to tell whether the studies cited above (Wachs, 1993; Wolf & Gardner, 1979) are in fact measuring the same "social" versus "object" orientations (Dixon, 1990).

Stylistic Individual Differences in Language

Researchers in children's early language have also noticed differences between children in terms of their apparent object versus person orientation, or analytic versus holistic tendencies. The most common distinction is between "referential" and "expressive" styles, which are easiest to describe by exaggerating the differences. (It is important to realize that any one child's pattern of development will likely contain elements of *both* of these approaches.) The classic referential/analytic sequence of development involves single words, often nouns, giving way to multiword combinations and eventually "telegraphic" early sentences, such as "Baby cookie." The expressive/holistic pattern, by contrast, emphasizes phrases, generally of personal-social utility, such as, "Lemme see," from the beginning; children gradually come to recognize that the words that make up these phrases are separate. Early utterances may contain grammatical elements that are incompletely understood, such as the contracted verb in "Dat's mine." Sometimes highly "expressive" children focus on the overall intonation contour of sentences and produce partially unintelligible utterances rather than clear distinct words (Bloom, Lightbown, & Hood, 1975; Nelson, 1973, 1975; Peters, 1983).

Do Different "Styles" Mean Different "Types" of Children?

An important question is whether children belong to one or another category of language or play style. Typologies are problematic for several reasons. One is that many, perhaps most, children show some characteristics that are typical of *both* styles, changing with different situations or contexts, so drawing an either/or line between two groups is not easy. Also, whenever there are two categories, there is a temptation to ask Which one is better?, which may not be an appropriate way of thinking about alternative developmental pathways.

An alternative is to think of two *dimensions,* from very low object-oriented to very high object-oriented and from very low socially oriented, to very high socially oriented. This picture is more complicated than a typology, but has some advantages. In a multidimensional approach, each child could have *both* kinds of abilities, with a typical balance or preference between them, which could change as the situation required. Another advantage is that both of these dimensions are positive characteristics: more than one dimension makes it possible to be smart in different ways. Consequently, many descriptions of stylistic differences in language and play involve at least two dimensions of ability (Bates, Bretherton, & Snyder, 1988).

Relationships between Language Style and Play Style

Researchers often suspect that stylistic, qualitative differences in play are accompanied by differences in children's language. It is easy to see how one might expect a child who emphasizes patterner or object mastery aspects of play to also lean in a referential or analytic direction in language development. Similarly, dramatist or social mastery tendencies in play could be expected to coincide with an expressive/holistic bent in language.

Links between Language and Patterner/Dramatist

Researchers studied what would happen when they showed twenty-one-month-olds a familiar scenario, but enacted with inappropriate objects (e.g., pretending to eat cereal with a comb) (Dixon & Shore, 1991). Since dramatists show disregard for object characteristics, they might have expected the children who imitated these scenes to show more expressive language style characteristics. Instead, children who imitated play with inappropriate objects scored high on referential language. This relationship with analytic referential language makes sense if object substitutions involve a certain amount of analytic ability. That is, object substitutions require the child to distinguish the symbol (the comb) from what it stands for (a spoon) (Dixon & Shore, 1991).

A related question is whether overall patterner play characteristics would correlate with referential language, and whether dramatist play would coincide with expressive language. This was the case in one sample of twenty-one-month-olds; when this sample was combined with another to give a total of sixty children, patterner scores correlated with both types of language, but slightly more with the referential score (Dixon, 1990).

Links between Language and Mastery Motivation

There are some indications that referential language style may accompany an interest in object mastery, while less referential language may be related to more social motivation. In two studies, referential children showed more interest in exploratory, pretend, and problem-solving play with toys, while less referential children were more socially oriented, and their toy play was more varied but more conventional (Rescorla, 1984, p. 109; Rosenblatt, 1977). These studies, however, give little detail about the evidence for these conclusions.

Some studies have been unable to find a relationship between language style characteristics and object versus social orientations in play (Dixon, 1990; Goldfield, 1987). In one study, the referential child spent *less* time in toy play and exploration than any of the other children in the study (Goldfield, 1985–1986). The difference between referential and expressive children may not lie in the sheer amount of toy play or social interaction, but rather whether or not the parent and child use objects as a joint focus of attention. Children who had many referential words often used objects to engage their mothers' attention. Expressive children were just as interested in objects and people as referential children, but tended not to use objects as a joint focus of attention (Goldfield, 1985–1986, p. 130).

On the one hand, therefore, a straightforward link between mastery motivation and language style has not been demonstrated. On the other hand, the studies to date have focused on aspects of linguistic style that have to do with language *form,* such as preponderance of nouns and pronouns. Relationships between object versus social mastery motivation and language style might appear if studies focused on *functional* aspects of language, for example, the relative emphasis on informational versus interpersonal purposes.

Caveats Regarding the Links between Language and Play Styles

Strong empirical evidence does not support the idea that observable individual differences in play coincide with those in language. Issues of size of sample, method of study, and context of study may influence the interpretation of studies.

First, most of the studies in this area involve very few subjects, often fewer than twenty. In such small samples, researchers might miss some important relationships, while accidental associations of variables can appear (Hardy-Brown, 1983).

A second weakness is finding out *how* young children process information. The basic research strategy has been correlational: children who do well on aspects of language that researchers might have extracted by means of analytic processes are also likely to do well on play tasks that might also rely on analytic skills. Of course, it is possible to question assumptions about the underlying skills involved in the tasks.

A third concern comes from task variation in performance (Dixon, 1990). This raises issues about reliability of measures, but also indicates the importance of context. Whether a behavior should be considered "object-oriented" or "people-oriented" often depends on the situation and point of view. For example, labeling objects might be a very social activity (Bates et al., 1988, p. 52).

Sources of Individual Differences in Play and Language

Where do these individual differences in play and language come from? The explanations for language development styles range from broad environmental factors such as socioeconomic status all the way to rate of maturation of brain areas (Shore, 1995). Those explanations that apply to stylistic differences in *both* play and language and the linkage between them are discussed in the following section.

Focus on Object vs. Person Aspects of Symbol Use

Some theorists see both language and symbolic play as manifestations of the use of symbols (Piaget, 1962; Werner & Kaplan, 1963). In order to use a symbol to communicate with another person, four elements are related to one another: the self, the other person, the symbol (e.g., the word), and the referent (the thing the symbol represents) (Werner & Kaplan, 1963). For example, if I say the word "spoon" to you, you and I both know what spoons *are,* that the word "spoon" is used to *stand for* those objects, and that you and I can communicate with one another by means of this word "spoon." Children have to learn about all of these relationships, that the sounds people make are related to objects and events in the world, and that people use these sounds to *tell* each other things about the world and to *influence* each other. Words are not the only symbols that the child learns to use. Symbolic play activities in which one object stands for another—for example, pretending to lick a block as though it were an ice cream cone—are also thought to involve the same understanding of symbols. Consequently, since language and play involve the same skills, they should be linked to one another.

Language and play styles may also be a result of differences between what aspects of symbol use children best understand. This view argues that patterners emphasize the relations among the speaker, the word, and the *object,* while dramatists emphasize the relations among the speaker, the word, and the *other person* (Wolf & Gardner, 1979). In the example with the word "spoon," a child with a patterner style would be said to have a strong grasp of the idea that the word "spoon" is used to *stand for* the object, even though the word does not resemble the spoon itself, and that this word can be reminiscent of the spoon even in its absence. A child with a dramatist style would have a good understanding of the idea that by saying "spoon" the speaker can communicate information or requests to the other, because the other person also has access to the meaning of this symbol.

It is unclear how or why these differences arise or how flexible they are, though children's preferred modes might be overruled by social pressure (Wolf & Gardner, 1979, p. 134). Perhaps they originate in children's overall personalities and characteristic ways of selecting, organizing, and presenting information (Shotwell, Wolf, & Gardner, 1979, p. 133).

Analytic vs. Holistic Skills

A similar point of view is that language and symbolic play share cognitive abilities that make symbol use possible (Bates, 1979). One cognitive component is analysis, an ability to distinguish symbol and referent. But symbol use also involves some *rote* or holistic processes as well. Since the relationship between symbol and referent is arbitrary, the child has to be able to make this link by imitation and just memorize it; for example, "cow" means *cow,* no reason, it just does. Finally, to put these relations into practice, the child has to *intend to communicate* his or her meaning to others (Bates, 1979).

Analytic abilities and rote-holistic abilities may help account for individual differences in language and play (Bates et al., 1988). Toddlers who are particularly good at analyzing symbol-referent relations would be expected to do well at referential-analytic language. They may also substitute neutral or inappropriate objects in pretend play instead of the conventionally appropriate props, such as using a comb as a spoon. Toddlers who excel at rote-holistic processes would be expected to be outstanding in terms of expressive, personal-social, formulaic language. Their play would be expected to emphasize the reproduction of coherent, familiar event wholes, such as using realistic props to enact "having breakfast."

Focus on Object vs. Social-Formulaic Aspects of Events

Another view of the interaction of play and language gives central importance to the child's participation in familiar scripted events, such as lunch or bedtime, which are organized by social interactions (Nelson, 1985). By the end of the first year, infants have come to understand these daily events and the phrases that typically accompany them (e.g., baby crawls to high chair when parent says, "Do you want lunch?"). In the early part of the second year, the child begins to distinguish the separate aspects of these familiar events and relate words to these parts. Near the end of a meal, for example, the parent might ask, "Do you want more applesauce?" The child may focus on the fact that at different meals various foods appear on the tray, and realize that the last part of the parent's utterance varies with the different foods. Or the child may focus on the social realm, and realize that "Do you want more . . . ?" is an *offer* that occurs not only at meals, but also in other situations, such as "Do you want more piggyback ride?"

The children who emphasize the object realm would be expected to emphasize referential language; those who emphasize the personal-social formulas would be anticipated to have more expressive-style language. This preference for *informational* use of language versus *interpersonal* use of language could arise either because of the parent's tendency to emphasize that function or the child's predisposition to pay attention to that use of language.

This thinking can be extended to play as well. Social interactions and socially derived routines and scripts provide a foundation for the objects and events that the child uses in pretend play. Infants may differ in their focus on the objects that make up these scripts or the coherence of the sequence of events. The preference for one or the other could arise from either playing with caregivers who emphasize these different aspects of familiar events or tending to pay more attention in one kind of play interaction versus the other.

Social-interactionist theories would emphasize that the crucial element is the support that caregivers provide for infants' involvement in exchanges of meaning (e.g., Bruner, 1983; Show, 1989). Parent-infant dyads may prefer to interact in ways that focus around objects or in ways that focus on the participants' relationships. Some parents and infants, for example, may enjoy playing with toys such as blocks, whereas others may prefer non-object-oriented play such as chasing games. In such situations, children are not only learning different ways of playing, they are also likely to be exposed to different types of vocabulary and uses for language. One would expect that play with toys would foster the discovery that language conveys information, such as the names of objects; while nontoy play would support language that conveys interpersonal intentions: "I'm gonna get you!" Children might be expected to show stylistic facility with the type of play and language with which they are most familiar (Gold-field 1985–1986, 1987).

Future Directions and Applications

Envisioning the future of this field, one can speculate about new theoretical approaches and practical applications. In relation to developmental theory building, several new lines of thought are beginning to have an impact. One of these, nonlinear dynamic systems theory ("chaos" theory), assumes that multiple interacting factors are involved in causing an outcome, and links this to the idea that there may be individual differences in the outcomes. Individual differences, therefore, can point to the influences that are operating on a system (Thelen, 1990).

An application of this idea in language development is to think of analytic and holistic processes as two magnets that both pull on children's processing of utterances. It is possible to envision styles of language acquisition emerging that depend on the relative strength of these two attractors. Children for whom the analytic attractor is stronger might show a more noun-referential pattern of acquisition, while those for whom the holistic attractor is stonger might show a more phrasal-expressive pattern.

Representing experience in symbolic play typically involves using one or more objects to enact events, often in relation to a socially conventional script. Two ways to understand the objects and the actions during play are either as component processes or as the magnets that attract the child's play activity. Those for whom the "object" attractor is stronger may show patterner play styles, while those for whom the "narrative/event" attractor is stronger may show more dramatist tendencies.

What are the practical implications of stylistic differences? The most basic implication of these differences in play and language is that parents and caregivers may recognize that such differences between children do not necessarily mean that one child is more advanced than the other. Parental acceptance of the child's approach to language is supportive of language progress (Nelson, 1973); one would think that the same would hold true for play (Wachs, 1993, p. 50).

There are some tantalizing possibilities for application in education and intervention as well. At this time, these questions are speculative and need a more solid research foundation.

First of all, how generalizable are these stylistic approaches across different cultures and languages? The vast majority of the research on stylistic differences in language and play involves typical children acquiring English, mostly within a middle-socioeconomic status. Several investigators have pointed out cultural or subcultural variation in what aspects of language adults value, and in how families expect children to learn language (Lieven, Pine, & Barnes, 1992, p. 306; Peters, 1983). Another researcher has distinguished between "literal" and "nonliteral" parental play styles (Beizer, 1993): parents with "literal" style tend to enjoy play with blocks and rough-and-tumble games, whereas "nonliteral" parents engage in more pretense. These parental approaches may be related to children's development and preferences.

Second, are the stylistic differences that adults observe in toddlers' play and language predictive of children's approaches to later symbol-using tasks, such as reading? As children reach the end of the third year, their stylistic preferences may become less pronounced (Nelson, 1975; Wolf & Gardner, 1979). Traces of their original stylistic preference, however, might emerge when confronted with acquiring a new symbol-using skill. Researchers have observed stylistic differences, for example, in beginning readers (Bussis, Chittenden, Amarel, & Klausner, 1985). Some children skipped around on workbook pages, previewed text, and approximated or skipped over unknown words. Others worked carefully and methodically, recalled details of stories in sequence, and focused on faithfully translating written words into speech, rarely skipping, slurring, or guessing words (Bussis et al., 1985). It is worthwhile to wonder whether these reading styles are consistent with the children's early approach to spoken language.

It is also possible to speculate about applications to reading problems. Scholars sometimes see pathology as occupying the extremes of normal variation. It might be that some reading disorders represent the extremes of the holistic (expressive, phrasal) versus analytic (referential, individual word) dimensions noted in typical children. Researchers of dyslexia, for example, have distinguished between holistic and segment-based processes in dysphonetic versus dyseidetic early readers (Fried, Tanguay, Boder, Doubleday, & Greensite, 1981). They found that dysphonetic children have considerable difficulty "sounding out" words, making use of words' individual letters. By contrast, dyseidetic children have difficulties with remembering words and letters as a whole (Fried et al., 1981). Once again, it is worthwhile to wonder whether these difficulties with written language are consistent with the children's early language style.

Knowing that there are many ways to learn a language "should help us to think more creatively about therapy, intervention and education" (Goldfield & Snow, 1989, p. 32). The same is true of play. Not all children will benefit equally from the same classroom or therapeutic activities, and if one approach does not work, another approach might.

Bibliography

Bates, E. (1979). *The emergence of symbols.* New York: Academic.

Bates, E., Bretherton, I., & Snyder, L. (1988). *From first words to grammar: Individual differences and dissociable mechanisms.* Cambridge: Cambridge University Press.

Beizer, L. (1993, March). *Literal and nonliteral orientations in parent-infant play: Individual differences in parents: Goals and related play styles.* Paper presented at Society for Research in Child Development, New Orleans, LA.

Belsky, J., & Most, R. K. (1981). From exploration to play: A cross-sectional study of infant free play behavior. *Developmental Psychology, 17,* 630–639.

Bloom, L., Lightbown, P., & Hood, L. (1975). Structure and variation in child language. *Monographs of the Society for Research in Child Development, 40*(2, Serial No. 160), 1–78.

Boyatzis, C., & Watson, M. (1993). Preschool children's symbolic representation of objects through gestures. *Child Development, 64*(3), 729–735.

Bruner, J. (1983). *Child's talk: Learning to use language.* New York: Norton.

Bussis, A. M., Chittenden, E. A., Amarel, M., & Klausner, E. (1985). *Inquiry into meaning: An investigation of learning to read.* Hillsdale, NJ: Lawrence Erlbaum.

Dixon, W. E., Jr. (1990). *Individual differences in three domains of cognitive development.* Unpublished doctoral dissertation, Miami University, Oxford, OH.

Dixon, W. E., Jr., & Shore, C. (1991). Measuring symbolic play style in infancy: A methodological approach. *Journal of Genetic Psychology, 152*(2), 191–205.

Fein, G. (1981). Pretend play in childhood: An integrated review. *Child Development, 52,* 1095–1118.

Ferguson, C., & Macken, M. (1983). The role of play in phonological development. In K. E. Nelson (Ed.), *Children's language* (Vol. 4, pp. 231–254). Hillsdale, NJ: Lawrence Erlbaum.

Fiese, B. (1990). Playful relationships: A contextual analysis of mother-toddler interaction and symbolic play. *Child Development, 61,* 1648–1656.

Fried, E., Tanguay, P., Boder, E., Doubleday, C., & Greensite, M. (1981). Developmental dyslexia: Electrophysiological evidence of clinical subgroups. *Brain and Language, 12,* 14–22.

Giffin, H. (1984). The coordination of meaning in the creation of a shared make-believe reality. In I. Bretherton (Ed.), *Symbolic play: The development of social understanding* (pp. 73–100). Orlando, FL: Academic.

Goldfield, B. (1985–1986). Referential and expressive language: A study of two mother-child dyads. *First Language, 6,* 119–131.

Goldfield, B. (1987). The contributions of child and caregiver to referential and expressive language. *Applied Psycholinguistics, 8,* 267–280.

Goldfield, B., & Snow, C. (1989). Individual differences in language acquisition. In J. Berko Gleason (Ed.), *The development of language* (2nd ed.) (pp. 303–325). Columbus, OH: Merrill.

Hardy-Brown, K. (1983). Universals and individual differences: Disentangling two approaches to the study of language acquisition. *Developmental Psychology, 19,* 610–624.

Hoppe-Graff, S. (1993). Individual differences in the emergence of pretend play. In R. Case & W. Edelstein (Eds.), *The new structuralism in cognitive development: Theory and research on individual pathways* (Contributions to Human Development series, Vol. 23, pp. 57–70). Basel, Switzerland: Karger.

Leonard, L. (1987). Is specific language impairment a useful construct? In S.

Rosenberg (Ed.), *Advances in applied psycholinguistics* (Vol. 1, pp. 1–39). Cambridge: Cambridge University Press.

Lieven, E., Pine, J., & Barnes, H. (1992). Individual differences in early vocabulary development: Redefining the referential-expressive distinction. *Journal of Child Language, 19,* 287–310.

McCune-Nicolich, L. (1981). Toward symbolic functioning: Structure of early pretend games and potential parallels with language. *Child Development, 52,* 785–797.

Nelson, K. (1973). Structure and strategy in learning to talk. *Monographs of the Society for Research in Child Development, 38* (1–2, Serial No. 149).

Nelson, K. (1975). The nominal shift in semantic-syntactic development. *Cognitive Psychology, 7,* 461–479.

Nelson, K. (1985). *Making sense: The acquisition of shared meaning.* San Diego: Academic.

Nelson, K., & Seidman, S. (1984). Playing with scripts. In I. Bretherton (Ed.), *Symbolic play: The development of social understanding* (pp. 45–71). Orlando, FL: Academic.

O'Connell, B., & Bretherton, I. (1984). Toddlers' play, alone and with mother: The role of maternal guidance. In I. Bretherton (Ed.), *Symbolic play: The development of social understanding* (pp. 337–368). Orlando, FL: Academic.

O'Reilly, A., & Bornstein, M. (1993). Caregiver-child interaction in play. In M. Bornstein & A. O'Reilly (Eds.), *The role of play in the development of thought* (New Directions for Child Development series, Vol. 59, pp. 55–66). San Francisco: Jossey-Bass.

Peters, A. (1983). *The units of language acquisition.* Cambridge: Cambridge University Press.

Piaget, J. (1962). *Play, dreams and imitation in childhood.* New York: Norton.

Rescorla, L. (1984). Individual differences in early language development and their predictive significance. *Acta Paedologica, 1,* 97–116.

Rescorla, L., & Goossens, M. (1992). Symbolic play development in toddlers with expressive specific language impairment. *Journal of Speech and Hearing Research, 35,* 1290–1302.

Rosenblatt, D. (1977). Developmental trends in infant play. In B. Tizard & D. Harvey (Eds.), *Biology of play* (pp. 33–44). London: William Heineman Medical Books.

Schwartzman, H. B. (1978). *Transformations: The anthropology of children's play.* New York: Plenum.

Shore, C. (1995). *Individual differences in language development.* Thousand Oaks, CA: Sage.

Shore, C., Bates, E., Bretherton, I., Beeghly, M., & O'Connell, B. (1990). Vocal and gestural symbols: Similarities and differences from 13 to 28 months. In V. Volterra & C. J. Erting (Eds.), *From gesture to language in hearing and deaf children* (pp. 79–92). New York: Springer-Verlag.

Shore, C., & Bauer, P. (1984, April). *Language styles and symbolic play.* Paper presented at International Conference on Infant Studies, New York, NY.

Shotwell, J. M., Wolf, D., & Gardner, H. (1979). Exploring early symbolization: Styles of achievement. In B. Sutton-Smith (Ed.), *Play and learning* (pp. 127–156). New York: Gardner.

Show, C. (1989). Understanding social interaction and language acquisition: Sentences are not enough. In M. H. Bornstein & J. S. Bruner (Eds.), *Interaction in human development* (pp. 83–103). Hillsdale, NJ: Lawrence Erlbaum.

Sigman, M, & Sena, R. (1993). Pretend play in high-risk and developmentally delayed children. In M. Bornstein & A. O'Reilly (Eds.), *The role of play in the development of thought* (New Directions for Child Development series, Vol. 59, pp. 29–42). San Francisco: Jossey-Bass.

Tamis-LeMonda, C., & Bornstein, M. (1993). Play and its relations to other mental functions in the child. In M. Bornstein & A. O'Reilly (Eds.), *The role of play in the development of thought* (New Directions for Child Development series, Vol. 59, pp. 17–28). San Francisco: Jossey-Bass.

Tamis-LeMonda, C., Kahana-Kalman, R., Damast, A., Baumwell, L., & Bornstein, M. (1992, April). *Associations between patterns of language acquisition and symbolic play across the first two years.* Paper presented at the Conference on Human Development, Atlanta, GA.

Thelen, E. (1990). Dynamical systems and the generation of individual differences. In J. Colombo & J. Fagen (Eds.), *Individual differences in infancy: Reliability, stability, prediction* (pp. 19–44). Hillsdale, NJ: Lawrence Erlbaum.

Wachs, T. (1993). Multidimensional correlates of individual variability in play and exploration. In M. H. Bornstein & A. W. O'Reilly (Eds.), *The role of play in the development of thought* (New Directions for Child Development series, Vol. 59, pp. 43–53). San Francisco: Jossey-Bass.

Watson, M. (1984). Development of social role understanding. *Developmental Review, 4,* 192–213.

Weeks, T. E. (1979). *Born to talk.* Rowley, MA.: Newbury House.

Werner, H., & Kaplan, B. (1963). *Symbol formation.* New York: John Wiley.

Wolf, D., & Gardner, H. (1979). Style and sequence in symbolic play. In M. Franklin & N. Smith (Eds.), *Early symbolization* (pp. 117–138). Hillsdale, NJ: Lawrence Erlbaum.

Wolf, D., & Grollman, S. (1982). Ways of playing: Individual differences in imaginative style. In D. J. Pepler & K. H. Rubin (Eds.), *The play of children: Current theory and research* (Contributions to Human Development series, Vol. 6, pp. 46–63). Basel, Switzerland: Karger.

Language and Play

Natural Partners

Jane Ilene Freeman Davidson

What is the relationship between language and play? To answer this question, consider two examples of children playing.

> It is recess time in first grade. Andrew and Malcolm are sitting on the climber swapping jokes. It is Andrew's turn.
> "Knock, knock."
> "Who's there?" Malcolm answers.
> "Banana."
> "Banana who?"
> "Banana."
> "Banana who?"
> "Orange."
> "Orange who?"
> "Orange you glad I didn't say banana."
> Both boys burst into gales of laughter. The boys spend the rest of recess exchanging knock-knock jokes.

> Shakeeta and Carly, both four years old, are in the pretend house area of their child care center. Carly announces, "Sister, it's time to get dressed. We're going to the ball." They talk about what they will wear as they don frilly negligees, necklaces, and high heels. Yomi asks, "Can I come too?"
> "Yeah," says Shakeeta. "You have to get dressed up."
> "No!" corrects Carly. "She's Cinderella. She has to stay home."
> Yomi readily takes on the Cinderella role.
> "You need to yell at me to clean," she tells Shakeeta, "cause you're the mean stepsister."

Both of these examples show the relation between play and language. In the first the chil-dren are using language in a playful way: they are manipulating language to create a humorous pun which serves as the punch line for the joke. In the second example the children are using language to further their play: they use it both in the context of their pretend play—"Sister, it's time to get dressed"—and to plan their play—"You need to yell at me to clean." These examples show clearly the two distinct relationships that exist between language and play: (1) Children can play with the language itself; (2) children can use language as a tool in play. What is the nature of each of these relationships?

Playing with Language

Children play with all aspects of language, including its sound, meaning, form, and purpose. These aspects are discussed in turn.

Playing with Language Sounds

Children begin playing with language before they can speak. Babies delight in playing with sounds; by moving the tongue and lips and varying the air flow, they produce sounds and interesting vibrations and feelings in the mouth. As the child gets closer to talking, the verbal play will expand to explore the intonation and rhythm of language as well as the speech sounds. The babble of the nine-month-old will often replicate the intonation of adult speech, sounding like a question with a raised tone at the end or like a command with a quality of firmness, while the content is still gibberish. Although the baby explores language for the pleasure of the sounds and feelings, and for the social response it creates, this play with sounds also develops the muscles, vocal skills, and social interaction patterns that will form the basis for language.

Even after children begin to talk they still enjoy playing with the sounds of language. Toddlers and preschoolers will repeat intriguing words, frequently turning them into a chant, or varying the emphasis to create subtle differences. Harriet Johnson recorded the chant of a two-and-a-half-year-old after completing a block building:

> Now it's done un un
> Done un un un un. (Garvey, 1990, p. 62)

As children begin to interact with peers, their conversations will often involve this type of chant constructed in a turn-taking verbal interchange. Garvey (1984) recorded the following conversation of two-and-a-half-year-olds about the father of Judy's baby:

> *Judy:* Well, someday you can see dada, but not for a long time.
> *Tom:* I have a dada, too.
> *Judy:* I have a dada, too.
> *Tom:* I have a *real* dada.
> *Judy:* I have a special dada.
> *Tom:* I have a real dada.
> *Judy:* I do too.
> *Tom:* I do too.
> *Judy:* I have a special dada, too.
> *Tom:* I do too.
> *Judy:* I have a special dada doo. Da daaa (starts to chant). (pp. 160–161)

This playful rhythmic exchange involves a combination of repetition, slight modification, and expansion of one another's statements. As children get older the modifications may be greater from statement to statement, and the silliness often develops sooner and becomes more pronounced.

This type of jointly constructed wordplay is an important form of social interaction among young children. Once they develop a funny pattern they often will use it over and over again in the way that they repeat favorite rhymes.

Playing with the Meaning of Language

In addition to playing with the sounds of language, children will also experiment with the meaning, the structure, and the function of language. When they need to describe something new children will use old words in unique ways. Four-year-old Michael, for example, had been to Sleeping Bear sand dunes. He was impressed with the wave-like hills of rolling sand extending in every direction. A few weeks later he noticed a steep, grassy bank along the side of the road. "Look at the grass dune," he exclaimed. Anyone who has spent time with young children will hear examples of creative word use. A Russian poet similarly documented unique word uses among Russian children (Chukovsky, 1963).

This stretching of words to fit new contexts continues through elementary school as children try to make newly learned words their own, but often they use them in odd ways. An eight-year-old walking through a patch of seaweed along the shallows of a lake, for example, warns his brother, "Watch out for the allergy." He was looking for the word *algae*, but came up with a similar-sounding word that he also knew only slightly.

Playing with the Forms of Language

As children learn language they often invent new word forms. A four-year-old brags, "I runned up the slide." A two-year-old points out the "two snowmans." These children are subconsciously beginning to learn about past tense and plurals. They use this knowledge to create their own past tense form of *run* and to make *snowman* plural. These children will eventually learn the exceptions to the rules of forming past tense and plurals but, for now, playing with forms helps them to understand better how language works.

The above examples of language use are "play" because they are innovative, self-motivated, and satisfying. Children also construct language in this way. Such language construction, however, is not a conscious act. Michael, for example, does not think, "I wonder what new and interesting way I can describe the grassy bank." Nor did the child mentioned above think about how to say *run* in the past tense. These playful uses of language are natural and unconscious.

Purposeful Play with Language

Children also play with language in conscious, purposeful ways as they tell jokes, test limits, adapt rhymes, adapt language from books, and narrate stories. These playful ways are discussed in turn.

Joking Around
Children's first jokes are not the formal kind that we tell as adults but, instead, a purposeful misstatement of something they know:

> Two-year-old Adam is looking at a farm-yard picture with his dad. As Dad points to animals Adam makes the appropriate sounds. He now knows the sound of every animal in the picture. As Dad points to the dog, Adam gets a twinkle in his eye, pauses a minute, and says "Meow!" then begins to giggle. Adam continues to make the wrong sound for each animal and the giggles get louder and louder.

Adam is purposefully playing with language and the concepts behind the language. He is intentionally making the wrong sounds to create a humorous incongruity. Adam is in control of the language; he can play with it and change it to amuse himself. As with Adam, it is typical for children to play with parts of language they have recently mastered. They cement their new knowledge by being able to manipulate it at will.

An older child would not find it amusing to suggest that a dog says "meow!" What types of changes a child finds humorous are a good indication of what knowledge the child has just acquired. Children will play with those aspects of language they have just mastered:

> Monica, soon to be five, has been fascinated with names. She will introduce herself with her full name, Monica Rachel Hankins. One day when she enters the child care center she stands by the attendance chart watching the arriving children pick out their name cards and place them on the chart. She repeats the name as it is placed in the chart: Binta, Jackson, Julie. Because she knows Jason's full name she says "Jason Tenson" as he puts his name on the chart. She then tries Jason's last name on Darcy: "Darcy Tenson," she proclaims and giggles. Darcy looks a bit unsure, until Monica makes herself a new name, "Monica Rachel Tenson," then both girls laugh. They go around the class making all their peers into Tensons.

Monica has learned that people have more then one name, and the specific names belong to specific people. She has created incongruity by assigning the wrong names to the people around her. Darcy does not realize at first that Monica's errors are intentional; once she understands the game she quickly joins in. Playing with names is popular with children. Even in elementary school children delight in exchanging names with each other. Lily will become Crystal, and Crystal will be Lily. They will enjoy the confusion that is caused when they answer to each other's name.

The above examples show how children create their own jokes, but children also enjoy traditional jokes like the knock-knock joke at the beginning of this essay. When that joke is told by a four-year-old, rather than a seven-year-old, it sounds something like this:

> Knock knock.
> Who's there?
> Banana.
> Banana who?
> Banana.
> Banana who?
> Apple!! I didn't say Banana.

Other four-year-olds will then repeat the joke using other fruit, or putting in other words, such as "refrigerator." To an adult or an older child the original version is better; the incongruity in using *orange* to mean "aren't you" catches the listener off guard and creates the humor. Younger children, however, are not able to comprehend the double meaning of words (Shultz & Pilon, 1973). An orange is an orange and cannot be anything else. Younger children find both versions funny. To them the incongruity comes from having an orange, apple, or refrigerator at the door, rather than from the play on words. In effect, one researcher suggests, "although adults and older children find incongruity humor funny because it makes sense in some unexpected or improbable way, preschoolers find it funny because it *makes no sense*" (McGhee, 1984, p. 226).

At seven or eight years of age children begin to understand the dual meaning of words (McGhee, 1984; Shultz, 1972; Shultz & Horibe 1974). One author, for example, describes her confusion when her brother told her a moron joke when she was five (Geller, 1985). He asked, "Why did the moron tiptoe past the medicine cabinet?" and answered it by saying, "So he wouldn't wake the sleeping pills" (p. 1). A few years later while brushing her teeth, staring at the contents of the medicine cabinet, the double meaning came to her and she began laughing. Her enjoyment of the joke came as much from the thrill of now being able to see both sides as from the joke itself. Children delight in playing with their newly found ability to see multiple meanings.

Children from seven to ten years of age enjoy collecting and sharing jokes based on puns with their friends. The telling of jokes becomes an important social ritual. Swapping jokes often is an icebreaker with new acquaintances. Outsiders have few advantages when they enter an established play group, but knowing new jokes provides them with a special status and a way to become part of the group.

At this age it is the words in the joke that are most important, rather than the telling of the joke. By eleven years of age, jokes become more narrative. Tellers begin to play with the timing, characterizations, and general presentation style when performing the joke. Their jokes become more similar to those of adults, who not only must say the right words in order to have a good story, but must create an ambience that makes the words funny.

Testing the Limits: Is It All Right to Say That?
Not only are children gaining knowledge about the sounds, meaning, and form of language, they are also coming to understand what types of language are appropriate and when they are appropriate. Thus violating the rules of propriety becomes another common form of language play. A four-year-old might name her doll "Poopy-head" and laugh. The child knows that poopy is a naughty word, so the humor comes from using a word in a place in which it definitely does not belong. A group of preschoolers will find conversation seasoned with bathroom language hilarious.

Language can also allow children to try out unacceptable ideas, as in this description from a class of four-year-olds:

Colton, Wesley, and Ilana are filling containers at the water table. "I am making soup," Ilana explains.

"Yeah," says Wesley. "My soup is hot."

"I know," suggests Colton, "let's pretend it is poison soup." The others agree and work for a while cooking their poison soup. When Mr. Wilder, the teacher, comes over to see what they are doing, they giggle.

"We're making soup," says Colton.

"It's yummy," claims Wesley.

"It smells good," says Mr. Wilder.

"Would you like some?" asks Ilana. Mr. Wilder pretends to eat some. The children all begin to giggle. "You ate poison soup," they tell him.

Poisoning a teacher is a totally unacceptable action, but as children create pretend situations with language they can try it out in a harmless fashion. They have the power of imagining that they could care for themselves without a teacher, but know that in reality this will not happen.

As children get older they continue to push the limits of acceptability with their wordplay. They will use jokes as an excuse to try out "naughty" language and ideas. A first-grader might tell friends the following story:

A boy asked his teacher if he could go to the bathroom. The teacher asked the boy to recite the alphabet first.

"A B C D E F G H I J K L M N O Q R S T U V W X Y Z."

The teachers asks, "Where is the p?" The boy tells her, "It's running down my leg."

The joke offers an excuse for using an off-color word and discussing an unacceptable action. Children can strengthen their knowledge about what behaviors are acceptable by violating these expectations in a humorous way.

As children become older, exchanging witty insults becomes a form of competition, with each child seeing who can come up with a better zinger. The following playful insult was shared by a twelve-year-old: "Is that your face or did you just sneeze?" Insult creation becomes a contest of verbal agility. Playing "the dozens," an insult-trading dialogue begun by black teens, relies heavily on sexual insults and innuendo about the other person or the other person's family. "Talking trash" or using slang and bad language to insult your opponent is also a show of verbal agility that may be imitated by older elementary school children.

Playing with Rhymes

Young children are captivated by the lilting flow and rhythm of rhymes. There are differences between nursery rhymes and other chants (Geller, 1985). Nursery rhymes are a form of language play that parents introduce to their children. Parents might recite "This Little Piggie Went to Market" while washing their baby's toes; they may draw their young children into play with action rhymes such as "Pat-a-cake, Pat-a-cake, Baker's Man" (Geller, 1985). These rhymes are repeated from generation to generation because children delight in hearing them over and over. The repetition of words, the rhyming pattern, and the catchy rhythm draw children into reciting the rhymes with their parents and, when they are ready, chanting them on their own.

This enjoyment of rhymes remains as children get older, but beginning in about kindergarten, or earlier if the child has older siblings, the source of the rhymes becomes other children rather than adults; children then will learn a wide variety of rhymes. Opie and Opie (1959) have made an extensive collection of children's rhymes and other wordplay lore from the playgrounds of English schools. They have traced back many of the rhymes over two hundred years, although new groups of children often feel sure that the rhymes are fresh and new. The rhymes have many different purposes. Some rhymes are parts of games. Counting-out chants such as "Eenie Meanie, Minie Moe" are often used to decide who will go first. Jumping rope, ball bouncing, and clapping games also are often accompanied by rhyming chants.

Some chants have no purpose other than to amuse, as is the case of this tangle talk:

One fine day in the middle of the night,
Two dead men got up to fight,
Back to back they faced each other,
Drew their swords and shot each other.
A paralyzed donkey passing by
Kicked a blind man in the eye,
Knocked him through a nine-inch wall
Into a dry ditch and drowned them all.
(Opie & Opie, 1959, p. 25)

Rhymes also provide a forum for teasing and trying out off-color language. A group of children might chant the following:

I see London
I see France
I see someone's
Underpants.

In repeating a chant the child does not feel responsible for his or her action. The word *underpants,* which elementary children consider almost a swearword, is acceptable when said here because the rhyme demands it. Often other children will join in, turning the chant into a group action, thus seeming to absolve each child of individual responsibility. While children might not tease other children about seeing their underwear, the rhyme provides a socially accepted way of both using the "bad" language and engaging in teasing.

A whole group of children's chants make fun of, or challenge, people in authority. These are often parodies of other poems or songs, as in this grade-school version of "Deck the Halls."

Deck the halls with gasoline,
(chorus: Fa la la la la, la la la la)
Light a match and watch it gleam,
(chorus)
Watch the school burn down to ashes.
(chorus)
Aren't you glad you played with matches?
(chorus)

Rap is a form of rhyme that offers children both the chance to memorize and repeat more up-to-date, cool rhymes, and a format for creating their own rhymes. Children make up a rap for any number of reasons, such as to immortalize a special event, brag about a success, poke fun at something, or tell a story. When creating rap, children can play with words as well as add hand rhythms and sound effects; they can turn a rhyme into a performance.

Playing with Language from Books

Books provide wonderful language for children's play. Dr. Seuss books and other children's books with strong rhythms and rhymes draw children into chanting along. Some books that have favorite repetitive sections will become so much a part of the child's repertoire that the book's language will be used while playing.

Two-year-old Raymond loves the book *Good Night Moon* by Margaret Wise Brown (1947). The book describes the things in a bedroom, then says "Good night" to each thing. One day, when playing in the house area of his preschool, Raymond began walking around saying, "Good night, bed. Good night, table. Good night, shoe."

Raymond does not make his phrases rhyme as they do in the book, but he has used the repetition of "good night" that holds the rhyming phrases together.

Four-year-old Julieann often reads *Chicka Chicka Boom Boom* (Martin & Archambault, 1989), which is about a group of letters that climb up a coconut tree. It gets so crowded that they all fall down. While going down the slide she chants some favorite lines from the book: "I'll meet you at the top of the coconut tree. Will there be enough room? Chicka chicka BOOM BOOM." Sarah hears Julieann and joins in with the chicka chicka boom boom as she too goes down the slide. Eventually there is a group of four children repeating the phrase from the book as they slide.

The language play allows Julieann to add an extra dimension to her sliding, and it also creates a social event by drawing in her peers. Often, therefore, favorite books provide a body of shared rhymes and language play that a group of children can use as the basis for social interaction.

Playing with Storytelling
Language allows children to create incredible stories, in which they can play with absurd ideas and situations.

At group time in a preschool class, Miss Garica asks the children, "Where have you seen birds?" Most list the usual places you would expect, such as the sky, a tree, and the park.

But Julia, who is almost four years old, announces, "Last night an eagle flew into my house. It flew around, then it ate my dinner."

"What a wonderful story," said her teacher.

"No! It really happened!" Julia insisted.

Julia wants to make her story more real by having others believe that it really did happen. Usually children are willing to accept their inventions as stories, but it is still exciting to use words to make incredible things happen in these stories. Exchanging and building one another's tall tales is popular with children through first grade. As they get older, stretching reality through storytelling continues to be a part of the verbal interaction of children, but their greater skill with words will produce more refined stories. In the same way that the manner in which one tells a joke becomes more important around eleven years, the style of telling stories will also gain importance around this age.

Language as a Tool in Play

Not only do children play with language, they also use language as a tool in their play. When playing pretend, children use language to enact the role they have selected. The mother might say, "Don't bother me now! Can't you see I'm making dinner!?" The shopkeeper might inform the customer, "Those shoes are $200." The doctor might tell the patient, "You need a needle. It will hurt a little." Talking as the character is one way children define their role: by using motherlike language it is easier to become the mother. The character's conversation can also communicate to the other players how the play will go; in the extract at the beginning of this essay, Carly lets Shakeeta know what she wants to play by having her character say, "Sister, it is time to get dressed. We're going to the ball." A researcher discusses numerous techniques children have for setting the direction of the play while remaining in character (Giffin, 1984). For example, children will also step out of their pretend role to discuss what is happening in the play. In observing pretend play, one will hear children distributing roles: "I'm the mother and you're the sister." They also use language to describe and plan the play: "Let's play sea monster." "Yeah! It will chase us to the boat."

The joy of playing pretend pushes children to stretch their language skills in a number of ways. First, this shifting between contexts of talk takes sophisticated language skills. The requirements of talking effectively in each context are different. To be a character in the play one must use an appropriate tone of voice and the language that fits the role. When planning play it is important to use clear, persuasive language that will sway others to one's point of view.

Second, the language that children use in playing pretend is often similar to the language used in books. When children talk in the role of the play character, they use a more storylike language than when talking as themselves. The booklike nature of pretend play language is particularly obvious when you watch children narrating their play as they manipulate small toy figures. Many researchers feel that this type of play prepares children for understanding stories that are read to them, or that they are beginning to read themselves, and also prepares them to create their own written stories.

Third, dramatic play is one of the first forums in which children begin to talk about language itself. This knowledge about language is a sign of metalinguistic awareness. When Yomi tells Shakeeta, "You need to yell at me to clean, 'cause you're the mean stepsister," she is talking about the type of language that fits the role. She is demonstrating awareness of the tone and form of the language as well as its content.

In these ways, strong language skills enhance children's pretend play. Strong language skills are apparent as children show their ability to switch contexts, use story language, and talk about language itself. Playing pretend also provides a forum to develop and strengthen these skills. Strong language skills facilitate the play and play facilitates the development of language skills. Thus, language is a tool in play and play is a tool in the development of language.

Pretend Play in Elementary School

Investigators have written much about the pretend play of children through kindergarten age (Bergen, 1988; Davidson, 1996; Fein, 1981; Rogers & Sawyers, 1988). Little has been written, however, about the pretend play of children once they reach elementary school. Looking at what has been written one might erroneously assume that pretend play ends when children become seven years of age. In fact, pretend play is still important to elementary school children, it just becomes less visible to the adults around them, as evidenced by the following events:

Carla and Jane, both ten, are making the daily, mile-long walk to elementary school. They appear to be walking and talking. Each girl occasionally pats her own thigh, and their walking turns to a sort of galloping skip from time to time. These small actions are the only physical indication that they are pretending. Their conversation revolves around the pretend horses they are riding and the continuing imaginary story they have created around the horses. The horses live in the woods that border the road. The girls have developed elaborate stories around each horse's herd, history, and temperament. According to the narration, they have been taming the horses over the year. Now they are quite easy to ride on the way to school. At times the conversation turns to schoolwork or other matters, but the horse story is maintained with an occasional, "Whoa," or a mention of another horse glimpsed in the woods.

A casual observer might merely have seen two girls walking to school. The occasional pat to the thigh could be interpreted as checking to be sure lunch money was there and the gallop as just a need for physical activity. Unlike younger children these children do not "dress up" or use large overt actions to define their pretending. Their pretend play has become more verbal; it is language, not action, that defines the play of these older children. Planning the play becomes as important, or more important, than the actual enacting of the pretend events. The play story often continues to build from day to day over a period of weeks or months. This move to a more language-based play, with an emphasis on planning and a story line that continues across play periods, is also evident as these older children use Barbies, action figures, Legos, or other small toys to create imaginary stories.

At times the pretend stories of older children are solely a verbal creation. Children might create stories that link them with famous or admired people, perhaps inventing a family composed of television or movie actors and, of course, also including themselves and favored peers. Others might create the ideal sports team, pulling in players from everywhere, and often starring themselves as the quarterback or as the player that makes the incredible winning play. Their least liked peers are likely to drop the crucial pass or make some other game-losing error.

As in the above example, the language-play

stories become a part of everyday actions. These girls use language to create play about horses as they walk to school. Another child may use language to become Cinderella while making the bed or doing other tedious chores. Bad guy/good guy themes that include superheroes, soldiers, or aliens might be integrated into games of running and fort building. The fantasy sports teams that children create can enrich pickup ballgames.

In the elementary school years the difference between pretend play and storytelling becomes unclear. The planning of the pretending becomes longer and more involved, often itself becoming a form of storytelling. These children therefore are simultaneously playing with language (using language to create stories) and using it as a tool in their play (using language to further pretend play).

Integrating Language Play during Social Interactions

It is not just in pretend play that language and language play become a more integral part of older children's interactions. In elementary school language use, play takes on an important role in children's play in general and in their particular social interactions. While younger children enjoy just chanting favorite rhymes, elementary school children integrate rhymes into other play activities. Children chant rhymes as they jump rope. The text of the rhyme often dictates the jumper's actions, as in the following:

Teddy Bear Teddy Bear turn around
Teddy Bear Teddy Bear touch the ground
Teddy Bear Teddy Bear climb the stairs
Teddy Bear Teddy Bear say your prayers
Teddy Bear Teddy Bear say good night
Teddy Bear Teddy Bear turn out the light.

Other rhymes combine the action with a prediction for the future, as in the following:

Anna and Mark sitting under the tree
K - I - S - S - I - N - G.
First comes love, then comes marriage
Then comes Anna with a baby carriage.
How many babies will she have?
The players count how many fast jumps Anna can do; the number she reaches is the number of babies she will have. Similar rhymes predict such things as how many kisses the jumper will get or what letter of the alphabet begins the

name of the jumper's sweetheart. Children also often use rhymes of this type while on the see-saw or when playing hand-clapping games.

Rhymes also expedite games. Children often use counting-out rhymes like the following to select special roles in games:

One potato Two potato
Three potato Four
Five potato Six potato
Seven potato more.

The caller points to each child at each successive number. The child who is "more" stops playing. The chanting and counting continue until only one child remains; the child who remains is "It," goes first, or has some other special role in the play.

In many cultures, rhyming wordplay of this type infuses all parts of the social world in elementary school. Opie and Opie (1959) include a lengthy chapter, "Code of Oral Legislation," and explain that the schoolchild "conducts his [sic] business with his fellows by ritual declarations. His affidavits, promissory notes, claims, deeds of conveyance, receipts, and notices of resignation, are verbal, and are sealed by the utterance of ancient words which are recognized and considered binding by the whole community" (p. 121). Promises are sealed with words such as "Cross my heart and hope to die." Found treasures are claimed by declaring "Finders keepers, losers weepers." Children use other ritualized language to seal bargains, pledge friendship, claim the right to be first, or excuse themselves from volunteering for an unpleasant task.

Some language rituals, however, have no particular purpose. Seeing a blue Volkswagen Beetle might evoke the following words and accompanying action from one group of children:

Punch buggie blue (the chanter playfully
    punches his friend)
and no punches back.

Another group might have language rituals that are tied to the beginning of the month, the type of clothing someone is wearing, or some other prompt. These rituals have become an accepted part of the culture of that social group. Having these shared language rituals helps to confirm the cohesiveness of a social group: we belong together because we share the same verbal games.

Social groups use other forms of verbal play to reinforce their solidarity. Groups of children will often form clubs or gangs that have secret passwords or special phrases that only those in the group can understand. Elementary school children enjoy using "secret languages" with peers so others will not understand. These languages often involve complex manipulation of English; pig Latin is one of the most familiar of these secret languages. To speak pig Latin one must take the first consonant, or consonant blend, of the word, move it to the end of the word, and add "ay." This sentence in pig Latin would look like this: "Isthay entencesay inay igpay atinlay ouldway ooklay ikelay isthay." Other secret languages may involve saying parts of the word backwards or adding additional sounds to each syllable. To speak any of these languages requires a clear sense of how words are composed, then an ability to alter this composition to fit a new set of rules.

From infancy through school age, play and language create a natural partnership. Children play with language for the joy of it and as a way of strengthening what they know about language. The ways children play with language become more refined and elaborate as their language skills become more refined. Children also use language as a tool to further their play. As children become older, often the separation between playing with language and supporting play with language narrows. Children's language becomes more sophisticated and complex. Language play becomes an integral part of many forms of play and social interaction.

Bibliography

Bergen, D. (Ed.). (1988). *Play as a medium for learning and development: A handbook of theory and practice.* Portsmouth, NH: Heinemann.

Brown, M. W. (1947). *Good night moon.* New York: Harper & Row.

Chukovsky, K. (1963). *From two to five.* Berkeley: University of California Press.

Davidson, J. (1996). *Emergent literacy and dramatic play in early education.* Albany, NY: Delmar.

Fein, G. (1981). Pretend play: An integrative review. *Child Development, 52,* 1095–1118.

Garvey, C. (1984). *Children's talk.* Cambridge, MA: Harvard University Press.

Garvey, C. (1990). *Play.* Cambridge, MA: Harvard University Press.

Geller, L. (1985). *Wordplay and language learning for children.* Urbana, IL: National Council of Teachers of English.

Giffin, H. (1984). The coordination of meaning in the creation of shared make-believe reality. In I. Bretherton (Ed.), *Symbolic play: The development of social understanding* (pp. 73–100). Orlando, FL: Academic.

Martin, B., & Archambault, J. (1989). *Chicka chicka boom boom.* New York: Simon and Schuster.

McGhee, P. (1984). Play, incongruity, and humor. In T. Yawkey & A. Pellegrini (Eds.), *Child play: Developmental and applied* (pp. 217–234). Hillsdale, NY: Lawrence Erlbaum.

Opie, I., & Opie, P. (1959). *The lore and language of schoolchildren.* New York: Oxford University Press.

Rogers, C. S., & Sawyers, J. K. (1988). *Play in the lives of children.* Washington, DC: National Association for the Education of Young Children.

Shultz, T. R. (1972). A cognitive-developmental analysis of humor. In A. J. Chapman & H. C. Foot (Eds.), *Humour and laughter: Theory, research and applications* (pp. 11–54). Chichester, England: John Wiley.

Shultz, T. R., & Horibe, F. (1974). Development of the appreciation of verbal jokes. *Developmental Psychology, 10,* 13–20.

Shultz, T. R., & Pilon, R. (1973). Development of the ability to detect linguistic ambiguity. *Child Development, 44,* 728–733.

Social and Emotional Development and Play

Gender Identity and Play

Beverly I. Fagot
Leslie Leve

Gender differences in play are one aspect of gender identity. Research on the development of gender identity and its relation to the development of play offers evidence that preference for gender-typed toys occurs prior to gender identity, but is incorporated as part of the child's gender schema during the third year of life. These findings suggest implications for the development of gender-differentiated play in terms of long-term outcomes.

While children's maturing cognitive capacities influence their gender identity, environmental variables also affect the timing and intensity of preferences. Children's identification of themselves as boys or girls also has consequences for whom they play with (gender segregation), the types of play materials they choose, and the roles they take. Once children establish their gender identity, the nature of their play changes forever. The interaction of gender and play therefore influences the nature of a child's relationships with peers and teachers, a child's cognitive competencies, and a child's adoption of functional or dysfunctional behaviors.

Boys and girls tend to play more with same-gender peers and avoid opposite-gender peers (Maccoby, 1988). Across the world, children also engage in different kinds of gender-specific play activities (Whiting & Edwards, 1988). As children play, they develop distinct forms of sex-role socialization, although the structure of their play and the degree of their involvement with play partners may vary from culture to culture (Whiting & Edwards, 1988).

Sex differences in play begin to emerge early in the second year of life (Caldera, Huston, & O'Brien, 1989). When children acquire the ability to identify gender during their third year, the distinctive gender differences in their play become increasingly complex (Fagot & Leinbach, 1993). Researchers generally agree that three-year-olds have established their gender identity, as evidenced by their sex-differentiated play.[1]

This essay discusses, in turn, the processes that influence the development of such gender identity and early sex-differentiated play; some distinctive characteristics of boys' and girls' play; and then some of the typical behaviors that emerge later in childhood.

The Emergence of Gender Identity and Sex-Differentiated Play

Some researchers have found that children begin to engage in sex-differentiated play before they are able to use gender labels (Caldera, et al., 1989). Their findings suggest that children may only recognize their own boyness or girlness after integrating the cognitive and social information in their environment. Despite these observations, other researchers contend that, before two years of age, self-labeling is an early step toward knowing what it means to be male or female (Maccoby, 1980).

Indeed, a study of sixty-four two-year-olds showed that most of them had some ability to

---

Much of the research discussed was supported by grants to the first author from the National Institute of Child Health and Human Development, HD 19739; the National Science Foundation, BNS 8615868; and the National Institute of Mental Health, MH 38911.

accurately label the gender in matched photographs and to answer related questions (Fagot, 1985b). Both boys and girls were equally able to label male and female photographs, with 50 percent older than twenty-six months making accurate identifications, but only 8 percent of children younger than that age (Leinbach & Fagot, 1986). Children of both sexes who could label by gender were the same children who spent 80 percent of their time in same-sex groups, while those who could not label by gender spent half their time in same-sex groups. Boys who did not provide gender labels played with dolls at rates about equal to girls' rates, but boys who did provide gender labels almost never played with dolls.

Those children who accurately identified and labeled the gender of head-shot photographs played significantly more often with same-sex playmates than did children who were not able to label accurately (Fagot, Leinbach, & Hagan, 1986). Girls, moreover, who provided accurate labels were less aggressive than those who did not label accurately. Although boys more than girls avoided female-typed toys and played with male-typed toys for a significantly longer period of time, sex-typed toy choice was not related to gender labeling. Researchers suggest that the presence of older children, the environmental design, and the provision of sex-typed toys may affect children's play choices and patterns. It may be that additional research dealing with children's ongoing contact with members of their own sex will provide additional understanding of the possible relation of the ability to label gender and sex-typed play behavior.

A later longitudinal study of eighteen-through twenty-seven-month-olds suggests that it is not possible to predict later play patterns at eighteen months of age (Fagot & Leinbach, 1989). When half the children, at twenty-seven months of age, were able to label photographs by gender, there were distinct features in their play. These early labelers engaged in more sex-typed toy play, played with more sex-typical toys, and showed less aggression than later-labeling girls and less than either group of boys. Early labeling girls also communicated with adults more than did late labeling girls or either group of boys.

Inasmuch as parents contribute to their children's learning of gender labels and their sex-typed behavior, researchers (Fagot & Leinbach, 1989) have observed in home settings as well as used a professional instrument, the Sex Role Learning Index (Edelbrock & Sugawara, 1978). The study in home settings found that early and late labelers, when first observed at eighteen months of age, did not differ on behavior categories in which sex differences have often been found (large motor activity, male-typed toy play, communication behaviors, and aggression). By twenty-seven months, when half of the children could correctly provide gender labels, these two groups differed in the following ways: early labeling children engaged in more sex-typed toy play; early labeling girls were less aggressive than other boys and girls; and early labeling girls engaged in more communication with adults.

Parents' responses to their children's behavior clustered into three categories: instructional, negative, and positive. Parents of early labeling children provided more emotionally charged positive and negative reactions to eighteen-month-olds. By the time children were twenty-seven months of age, the parents of both early and late labeling children were similar in their approval of sex-typical play. Fathers of early labelers were particularly influential, as they provided more traditional responses that reflected traditional sex-role attitudes. At four years of age, early labelers knew more about gender categories, but they did not necessarily have stronger preferences for same-sex activities. This finding suggests to the researchers that preference tests may reflect the current socialization context rather than cognitive processing. It also suggests that early labelers have had a longer period of time to practice sex-typed behaviors and consolidate sex-typed knowledge and attitudes. While it is true that later labelers catch up, there is a need to investigate other possible cognitive and social correlates of early labeling.

The Developmental Sequence of Play and Gender Identity

This section examines how the sequence of play behaviors interacts with the child's developing gender identity. Smilansky (1968) suggested a very simple system for coding the developmental levels of play:

- *Functional play* involves repetitive muscle movements, where the main goal of play is the movement of the object

- *Constructive play* involves objects to make something
- *Dramatic play* involves role-playing or make-believe
- *Games with rules* involve the recognition and acceptance of and conformity with preestablished rules.

While there is little evidence for gender differences in functional play, all other types of play show the influence of children's developing gender identity. There is evidence that boys are more likely to engage in constructive play (Rubin, Watson, & Jambor, 1978), but that may be a function of the type of toys available to boys and girls in play settings. Dramatic play increases during the preschool years, with boys and girls taking on very different roles; in particular, girls tend to practice social roles more often, while boys are more likely to engage in mock battles (Johnson & Roopnarine, 1983). Throughout the preschool years, the cognitive level of boys and girls is not that different, but the content of their play becomes increasingly different.

Outcomes of the Gender-Identity Process

Gender Segregation

The separation of boys and girls into single-sex groups exists in most cultures throughout the elementary school years, although the timing of its occurrence differs across cultures. Many cultures maintain gender segregation through adult-directed separation of the sexes. In industrialized countries, however, preschools are rarely organized with the specific goal of promoting gender segregation. Thus, while gender segregation is often treated as an outcome of sex stereotyping, it could equally well be considered a cause, since it precedes the child's ability to accurately code gender (Maccoby, 1988).

Because gender segregation begins early and persists throughout the human life span, there is a great deal of speculation in the psychological literature concerning the origins of gender segregation. One theory has emerged to account for children's tendency to begin to sort themselves into gender-segregated play groups. LaFreniere, Strayer, and Gauthier (1984), for example, build upon a hypothesis termed *behavioral compatibility* (Goodenough, 1934), which suggests that children play in sex-segregated groups because of different interests and behavioral styles. While

boys and girls in preschool classrooms are equally active, boys spend more time in rough-and-tumble play (Maccoby, 1988).

Other researchers found that play in same-sex groups was more cooperative than in mixed-sex groups; that more socially skilled children chose to play with other socially skilled children regardless of sex; and that within same-sex groups, girls were more socially skilled than boys (Serbin, Moller, Powlishta & Gulko, 1991). They suggested that gender segregation is related to different behavioral styles but not to specific toy and activity preferences.

Gender segregation very likely occurs because of a number of factors. Children who are in the process of developing a gender schema, for example, use every cue available to adopt the culturally expected, appropriate behaviors. (Playing with those like yourself is a powerful indicator that you are, indeed, a boy or a girl.) Their knowledge of gender labels, according to a cross-sectional sampling study, is also related to gender segregation (Fagot, 1990; Fagot, Leinbach, & Hagan, 1986). They also sort themselves in terms of behavioral compatibility. Preschool-aged children respond and change their behaviors at the instigation of their own sex, but not at the instigation of the opposite sex (Fagot, 1985a).

There is a noticeable difference in peer group reactions to boys' and girls' cross-gender interactions. Girls who attempt to join male peer groups and participate in cross-sex behaviors are, at worst, ignored (Fagot, 1977; Maccoby, 1988). Boys who attempt to participate in female activities receive more negative feedback from peers, both boys and girls (Fagot, 1977, 1989). In a German sample, for example, boys did not value female activities and they disliked boys who did, whereas girls valued female activities but did not react negatively when other girls tried out male activities (Trautner, Helbing, & Sahm, 1985).

Gender and Aggression

Differences in the use of direct aggression, particularly physical aggression, remain one of the most consistent differences reported in boys and girls. Maccoby and Jacklin's (1974) review of observational studies of aggression found that boys were more aggressive than girls in 67 percent of the studies. Block (1976) later noted, however, that age strongly influences sex differences in aggression. Block reclassified into three age groups the studies that Maccoby and Jacklin had reviewed, as follows: infancy through age four, ages five to twelve, and age thirteen and older. In the youngest age group, Block noted that 37 percent of the studies revealed reliable sex differences; in grade-school children, 47 percent of the studies showed significant differences; and in the adolescent group, 57 percent of the studies showed significant differences.

An extensive study of cross-cultural differences in aggression also suggests that male aggression increased from infancy through school age (Whiting & Edwards, 1988). Cultures differ greatly in the level of aggression that children show, but in almost all cultures boys more than girls appear to use direct techniques to obtain their goals.

The cross-cultural studies tend to favor observations of children in peer settings, either in preschools or under the care of older siblings and peers. Even for young children, the male stereotype in the United States is heavily defined by aggressive props and activities. In attempting to develop a list of very sex-stereotyped activities or props among four-year-olds, one researcher found that five of the six most masculine items—such as guns, knives, fighting tools—involved aggression (Hort, 1989).

Studies also have shown that teachers perpetuate sex-stereotypic behavior in children. Researchers have found that teachers react differently to assertive and communicative behaviors of boys and girls, beginning when the children were fourteen months old (Fagot, Hagan, Leinbach, & Kronsberg, 1985). No differences were found in boys' and girls' attempts to communicate or to assert themselves at this young age, either in terms of frequency of occurrence or time spent in these activities. There were, however, very different patterns of responses from teachers. Teachers responded to girls' attempts to communicate much more often than to boys'. In addition, they responded when the girls made tentative attempts to communicate, whereas boys had to use more forceful approaches to get the teachers to respond. The teachers were more likely to respond to girls' attempts with a positive, supportive response, but they were more likely to respond to boys with a negative or diversionary response. Once they began to communicate, the interactions of girls and teachers lasted almost twice as long as the interactions between boys and teachers. The reactions of teachers to boys' and girls' assertive behaviors

were also different. Teachers responded to only 10 percent of girls' assertive behaviors but to 41 percent of boys'. When these same children were observed as toddlers, the children showed sex differences in their behavior, with girls communicating more with adults and boys being significantly more aggressive. Interestingly enough, teachers then were not responding differentially by sex of child but instead seemed more influenced by the type of behavior.

We see then that the environment gives children different messages concerning aggression, but that children also construct different cognitive schemata concerning the appropriateness of some behaviors. One consequence of this is that when boys and girls are engaging in fantasy, boys' play is more likely to have aggressive content, even when the style of play itself is cooperative.

Gender and Cognitive Competence

One of the questions concerning gender segregation and the resulting differences in activity choice concerns implications for cognitive skills. Block (1983) used Jean Piaget's (1947/1959) mechanism of adaptation to discuss the play of young children. Block suggested that boys engage in activities that require them to change their own structures. This researcher suggested that boys' toys and boys' activities allow them to solve problems in new and creative ways. Girls, on the other hand, were more likely to engage in activities that imitated life roles and that did not require them to change but allowed them to rehearse cultural roles; therefore, girls might actually know more about the expectations of the culture.

Is there support for Block's ideas that differences in intellect arise from these early differences in play and interactional styles? So far, the data are only correlational. The relation to intellectual development is not well documented, but girls who show extremely feminine play preferences are less likely to do well in math and science (Fagot & Littman, 1975). Other researchers showed that spatial abilities appeared to be related to practice with certain types of toys, almost all of them masculine-stereotyped (Connor, Schackman, & Serbin, 1978). With practice, however, girls quickly became as capable with such activities as boys.

Gender and Intimacy

One concern with gender segregation throughout childhood is that boys and girls will meet in adolescence virtually as strangers, having learned different styles of interaction and different coping styles (Leaper, 1994). In a longitudinal study, Fagot (1994) suggests that boys and girls interpret the same pattern of interactions in very different ways, with girls seeing negative interactions as meaning peers do not like them, but boys interpreting negative interactions as positive.

Another researcher points out that sociometric and observational data do not tell the entire story, for cross-sex friendships do exist throughout childhood, but after preschool they are hidden from the peer group at large (Gottman, 1994). Cross-sex friendships continue, but the children tend to interact within the confines of their homes and/or neighborhoods. Cross-sex friendships tend to be very intense emotional relationships and, while same-sex friendships can be used to work through difficulties, there is a different quality to discussions when a girl is present. Boy pairs appear to use mastery mediated through fantasy or humor to deal with fears, whereas with a girl present there is increased use of emotional support mediated through comfort, soothing, and love to combat fear. Girl pairs do not seem to discuss fear as much, in part because it is most often a boy who introduces the fearful topic. When girls do discuss fears together, they use reassurance to comfort each other.

We see that, for some children, childhood is not as gender-segregated as it appears from surveys of school data. Yet it really is unknown if children who have cross-sex friendships are more able to interact with the opposite sex throughout life. Given that boys, as early as preschool, discount the attempts of girls to interact with them and female teachers to control them (Fagot, 1985a), this is an area that needs additional study. Thus, the context and content of play appear to vary in important ways that influence how children develop their gender identity.

There appear to be long-term consequences to the different play styles that develop within boys' and girls' peer groups. As with many processes, it is difficult to untangle where the chain starts. Do boys and girls segregate because they prefer different styles of play, or does segregation cause the different styles? Does boys' aggression drive girls away and force them to separate? It is likely that all of the above explanations have some merit, but what we know for sure is that the process of gender schema development is intertwined with play and other forms of communication throughout childhood.

Note
1. A criterion in diagnosing gender deviance disorder, for example, includes a child's choice of play activities that the culture identifies as belonging with the "opposite sex" (Zucker & Green, 1992).

Bibliography
Block, J. H. (1976). Issues, problems, and pitfalls in assessing sex differences: A critical review of "The psychology of sex differences." *Merrill-Palmer Quarterly, 22,* 283–308.

Block, J. H. (1983). Differential premises arising from conjectures. *Child Development, 54,* 1335–1354.

Caldera, H. J., Huston, A. C., & O'Brien, M. (1989). Social interactions and play patterns of parents and toddlers with feminine, masculine, and neutral toys. *Child Development, 60,* 70–76.

Connor, J. M., Schackman, M., & Serbin, L. A. (1978). Sex-related differences to practice on a visual-spatial test and generalization to a related text. *Child Development, 49,* 20–24.

Edelbrock, C., & Sugawara, A. I. (1978). Acquisition of sex-typed preferences in preschool-aged children. *Developmental Psychology, 14,* 614–623.

Fagot, B. I. (1977). Consequences of moderate cross-gender behavior in preschool children. *Child Development, 48,* 902–907.

Fagot, B. I. (1985a). Beyond the reinforcement principle: Another step toward understanding sex roles. *Developmental Psychology, 21,* 1097–1104.

Fagot, B. I. (1985b). Changes in thinking about early sex role development. *Developmental Review, 5,* 83–89.

Fagot, B. I. (1989). Cross-gender behavior and its consequences for boys. *Italian Journal of Clinical and Cultural Psychology, 1,* 79–84.

Fagot, B. I. (1990, April). A longitudinal study of gender segregation: Infancy to preschool. In F. Strayer (Chair), *Determi-*

nants of gender differences in peer relations. Symposium, International Conference for Infant Studies, Montreal, Canada.

Fagot, B. I. (1994). Gender role learning and preschool education. In T. Husén & T. N. Postlewaite (Eds.), *International encyclopedia of education* (pp. 2449–2452). Oxford: Pergamon.

Fagot, B. I., Hagan, R., Leinbach, M. D., & Kronsberg, S. (1985). Differential reactions to assertive and communicative acts of toddler boys and girls. *Child Development, 56,* 1499–1505.

Fagot, B. I., & Leinbach, M. D. (1989). The young child's gender schema: Environmental input, internal organization. *Child Development, 60,* 663–672.

Fagot, B. I., & Leinbach, M. D. (1993). Gender-role development in young children: From discrimination to labeling. *Developmental Review, 13,* 203–224.

Fagot, B. I., Leinbach, M. D., & Hagan, R. (1986). Gender labeling and the adoption of sex-typed behaviors. *Developmental Psychology, 22,* 440–443.

Fagot, B. I., & Littman, I. (1975). Stability of sex role and play interests from preschool to elementary school. *Journal of Psychology, 89,* 285–292.

Goodenough, F. (1934). *Developmental psychology: An introduction to the study of human behavior.* New York: Appleton-Century.

Gottman, J. M. (1994). Why can't men and women get along? In D. Canary & L. Stafford (Eds.), *Communication and relational maintenance* (pp. 203–229). San Diego: Academic.

Hort, B. (1989). *Jane's gun and John's mascara: A difference in peer reactions to males and females who display cross-gender behaviors.* Unpublished doctoral dissertation, University of Oregon.

Johnson, J., & Roopnarine, J. (1983). The preschool classroom and sex differences in children's play. In M. Liss (Ed.), *Social and cognitive skills* (pp. 193–218). New York: Academic.

LaFreniere, P., Strayer, F. F., & Gauthier, R. (1984). The emergence of same-sex affiliative preferences among preschool peers: A developmental/ethological per-

spective. *Child Development, 55,* 1958–1965.

Leaper, C. (1994). Exploring the consequences of gender segregation on social relationships. In W. Damon (Series Ed.) and C. Leaper (Vol. Ed.), *New directions for child development: Child gender segregation: Causes and consequences* (No. 65, pp. 76–86). San Francisco: Jossey-Bass.

Leinbach, M. D., & Fagot, B. I. (1986). Acquisition of gender labeling: A test for toddlers. *Sex Roles, 15,* 655–666.

Maccoby, E. E. (1980). *Social development: Psychological growth and the parent-child relationship.* New York: Harcourt Brace.

Maccoby, E. E. (1988). Gender as a social category. *Developmental Psychology, 24,* 755–765.

Maccoby, E. E., & Jacklin, C. N. (1974). *The psychology of sex differences.* Stanford, CA: Stanford University Press.

Piaget, J. (1959). *The psychology of intelligence.* (M. Piercy & D. E. Berlyne, Trans.). London: Routledge and Kegan Paul. (Original work published 1947)

Rubin, K., Watson, K., & Jambor, T. (1978). Free-play behaviors in preschool and kindergarten children. *Child Development, 49,* 534–536.

Serbin, L. A., Moller, L., Powlishta, K., & Gulko, J. (1991, April). The emergence of gender segregation and behavioral compatibility in toddlers' peer preferences. In C. Leaper (Chair), *Gender differences in relationships.* Symposium at the Society for Research in Child Development, Seattle, WA.

Smilansky, S. (1968). *The effects of sociodramatic play on disadvantaged preschool children.* New York: John Wiley.

Trautner, H. M., Helbing, N., & Sahm, W. B. (1985). *Schlussbericht uber des VW-Projeckt "Geschlechtstypisierung."* Frankfurt: Munster.

Whiting, B. B., & Edwards, C. P. (1988). *Children of different worlds: The formation of social behavior.* Cambridge, MA: Harvard University Press.

Zucker, K. J., & Green, R. (1992). Psychosexual disorders in children and adolescents. *Journal of Child Psychology and Psychiatry, 33,* 107–151.

Play as the Language of Children's Feelings

Garry Landreth
Linda Homeyer

Children possess the capacity for experiencing emotions with great feeling and intensity. When they hurt, they hurt all over. When they are happy, they are completely happy. Children are not able, however, to use a verbal language to adequately express the depth or range of these feelings. Their natural language of communication is play and it is through this medium that they express their emotional reactions. Play is a form of self-expression and symbolic play is a vehicle for expressing feelings; humor also plays an important role in play. These expressions occur within the important limits and boundaries of play relationships. In many ways, therefore, the various dimensions of play also facilitate children's emotional growth and development.

Children are people too, and experience the same kinds of feelings as adults. The difference is in the way they express those feelings. Typically, children lack the verbal facility to adequately express the range of emotional reactions they experience. However, when provided the opportunity in a safe environment, they will communicate the depth of their feelings through play, which is the most natural thing children do. Children do not talk out their concerns and feelings; they play them out.

Play Is the Child's Self-Expression

When adults observe and clinically analyze children's behaviors, play emerges as the unique, singular, central activity of childhood, occurring at all times and in all places; it is the medium through which children project the dimensions of their personalities. The distinctive characteristics of play are described by Freud (1958): "every child at play behaves like an imaginative writer, in that he [sic] creates a world of his own or, more truly, he arranges the things of this world and orders it in a new way that pleases him better" (p. 45). Thus, through play, children express all parts of the self that exist and that they experience at the moment. Expression of only a part of the self would not be self-expression. Play enables children to express themselves completely, without reservation or fear of reprisal, because children at play feel safe. Nothing is held back. This total expression of self through play is described by Frank (1982) as a process in which children express emotions in play, express their thoughts in play, rehearse behaviors in play, exert their will in play, move through developmental stages with play, and learn with play.

Everything the child is, does, and becomes may at one time or another be demonstrated through play. Children use toys and materials to express what they cannot verbalize, do things they would otherwise feel uncomfortable doing, and express feelings they might be reprimanded for verbalizing. These expressions of self and the accompanying feelings are played out but not planned out by the child. They occur spontaneously and creatively as the child experiences the freedom inherent in play that is devoid of the trappings of adult-imposed structure. A child's play cannot always be understood on the basis of logic and reality. An educator observed that "the inner coherence of play is as often based on emotion, as it is on logic or action" (Biber, 1984, p. 191). Therefore, since play is the child's expression of self, the child's play must be understood from the child's frame of reference. Play represents the child's symbolic language of self-expression and can reveal the child's past experiences, reactions to those experiences, feelings about what was experienced, the child's wants and needs, and the child's perception of self (Landreth, 1991). Play can be viewed as the process through which the total self of the child is created, expressed, and recreated.

Symbolic Expression in Play

Play is the child's symbolic language of self-expression, and the symbolism represented in play can be likened to a container of the child's emotions. Piaget (1962) proposed that, through play, children deal in a sensorimotor way with concrete objects that are symbols for something else they have experienced directly or indirectly. Play represents the attempt of children to organize their experiences. According to Bettelheim (1987), inner processes motivate what a child chooses to play. When children encounter an insurmountable problem, they play it out in symbolic ways that they may not understand because they are reacting to inner processes whose origin may be buried deep in the unconscious.

Play gives concrete form and expression to the unverbalized inner world of children which may be too frightening for children to express directly. Therefore, a major function of play is the changing through symbolic representation of what may be unmanageable in reality to manageable situations. Telling adults about being abused or even using dolls to act out the abuse experience may be much too threatening to traumatized children. However, when children feel safe and when allowed to direct their own play, they will distance themselves from the frightening or threatening experience by selecting toys that symbolically represent the individuals in the real-life experience. Feelings associated with the experience can then safely emerge and be expressed through the play. This symbolic representation was observed in the case of five-year-old Jackie, who acted out his abuse and accompanying feelings of helplessness and anger by having an alligator puppet swallow a small child figure. He then smashed the alligator with a mallet many times with obvious anger, and gleefully buried the alligator in the sandbox, announcing, "There, that takes care of him!" In this acting-out process, toys are like the child's words and play is the language of expression. Thus Jackie expressed

a great deal more intensity of emotion than his words would indicate.

From a psychoanalytic perspective, authors describe play as reflecting inner life, tensions, and the child's response to life's challenges (Solnit, Cohen, & Neubauer, 1993). They view play as allowing children to review their current situation, explore new possibilities, experiment with new solutions, and develop new integrations. Play allows children to experience being in control of that which they may not be able to control in reality. "Since children do not easily express their emotions, play helps the child master the conflict, trauma, or anxious situation in his or her life through the act of repetition" (Bluestone, 1991, pp. 257–258).

The process of play provides healing for hurts, releases emotions, dissolves tension, and gives vent to pent-up urges toward self-expression. The activity of play is one of the most important ways in which children learn that they can safely express their feelings without reprisal or rejection from others (Cass, 1973). By acting out a frightening or traumatic experience or situation symbolically, releasing and expressing associated pent-up feelings, and by returning to that event again and again through play and perhaps changing or reversing the outcome in play activity, the child moves toward an inner resolution and then is better able to cope with or adjust to the problem. Through this process of self-expression in play, children resolve conflicts and liberate themselves from overwhelming feelings by reconstructing the conflictual experiences and expressing their feelings in symbolic play.

This process of symbolic representation was readily observed in the play of five-year-old Trisha, who witnessed her six-month-old baby brother stop breathing, turn blue, and die in her mother's arms. Following this experience, Trisha repeatedly placed her arm beside her mother's arm and compare their color, remarking, "I'm darker than you." Indeed, she was darker than her mother, having inherited the dark skin of a father she had never seen. This was Trisha's way of expressing her fear of dying, which was very real for her because her skin was darker than her mother's. In play therapy, Trisha repeatedly acted out a scene of an airplane crashing and burning, followed by her arranging small cars around a small box. Her words as she described her activity did not indicate any particular fear or anxiety, but her play behavior certainly did. To the play therapist, the airplane crashing and burning represented bodies burning, turning dark like Trisha's skin, and the cars arranged around the box represented Trisha's enactment of a funeral and a coffin. This was undoubtedly a scene of fear and anxiety. Such free play allows the expression of feelings and attitudes that have been waiting to be released. Once these feelings are expressed, children can deal with them in ways that are more emotionally healthy. Symbolic play provides a safe vehicle for children to express emotions, since the emotion itself or the target of the emotion is disguised through the symbolism.

How Children Express Feelings in Play

Children use play to express how they feel about themselves and their world, both their current perceptions and how they would like it to be. Children use play to relax tension and anxiety, discharge aggression, express conflict, and turn the unmanageable into the manageable (Hartley, Frank, & Goldenson, 1952; Schaefer, 1993). Play also expresses delight, joy, surprise, and contentment. This range of emotional experience is evident in three-year-old Jessie's play, as she sang her own delightful, lilting, made-up song about colors while she painted with reckless abandon at the easel. At this moment in time, she was happy with herself and in her world. At other times, Jessie placed all the toy animals in a circle around the spot where she buried the "scary man" in the sandbox. In a quiet, hopeful voice she said that the animals would "keep the people safe from the scary man." Other parts of Jessie's world were not as happy, nor as safe. The freedom to be oneself in play, expressing a wide range of feelings, is a freeing experience. Children are then able to be fully themselves (Moustakas, 1973).

As children play, they express and experience their emotions (Axline, 1947; Landreth, 1991; Oaklander, 1988). Children externalize their feelings through play, thus experiencing feelings in the more concrete form of the substance of play. As children control the substance and direction of their play, they develop a sense of mastery and control. In the above example, Jessie was able to express her happiness and delight while painting; she was also able to express her fear of "the scary man" and her hope

and need to feel safe through the use of the protecting animals. She may have also been expressing her view that the people in her world were not providing the care that she needed.

Children purposively select play media to express their feelings and emotions. For this reason it is appropriate for them to have access to a wide variety of toys. They can easily express nurturing play, for example, through the use of baby dolls, bottles, and blankets. Many children express nurturing toward self and others through cooking and feeding, so pots, pans, spoons, cups, plates, and the like are useful. Plastic food items are helpful, but not necessary; children thoroughly enjoy cooking with sand, water, or both, and serve the results with complete genuineness.

Many of these nurturing toys are useful for the child who needs to regress to an earlier age. Kevin, age three years, played out how he felt about his newly arrived baby brother. While cooking himself muffins of sand and water, Kevin sucked on a baby bottle. He was expressing his desire to be like a baby again, to receive special attention, and to have his every need met.

Children have expressed aggressive feelings through dinosaurs, wild animals, rubber knives, a bop bag, toy soldiers, and musical instruments. Cardboard blocks are also useful for this purpose. Building a tower and repeatedly knocking it over can be a very satisfying, and appropriate, way for an angry child to express self. As children use these toys to shoot, bite, hit, and stab, they can release their aggressive feelings, allowing the child to move toward more self-enhancing, positive feelings. Medical equipment with doctor and nurse figures allow children to confront fears and concerns about doctors, medical procedures, and hospitalizations. Children also use the doctor's medical kit for healing and nurturing play.

Children who have had the freedom to express strong negative emotions typically move on to express more positive feelings. This seems to be largely the result of feelings having become more clear after repeated expressions in play; subsequently, feelings of confidence and courage can emerge (Moustakas, 1959). Often the stressors in children's lives may not have changed, but when they experience the opportunity to express themselves through the natural medium of play communication, they are able to move on to other healthy and age-appropriate uses of play. Piers and Landau (1980) stated that children heal themselves of emotional injuries through the use of play. Without play, the emotional wounds might never heal, leaving the child with a lifetime of unresolved emotional conflicts. "If children did not play, they could not thrive, and they might not survive" (Piers & Landau, 1980, p. 16).

Sociodramatic Play

In sociodramatic play the child uses toys and other items as props to assist in the acting out of specific roles and a wide variety of experiences (Smilansky, 1990). Role-playing allows children to enter the world of the adult and portray situations that they may not completely understand. During sociodramatic play children are in control of the content, may assume any number of roles, and change the outcome, while simultaneously experiencing the various feelings attached to each. Roles that children select may be the opposite of their own personality. This allows children the opportunity to break out of the limitations that confine them in reality (Caplan & Caplan, 1973) and to experience the expression of a much wider range of feelings, as well as the accompanying intensity of those feelings. An aggressive child may take the part of a caring and gentle caretaker; a confident, outgoing child may play the role of a quiet, much younger child; a compliant child may take the role of a bossy older sibling. Such reversals are quite common in children's play. Role reversal allows the observer an open window into children's perception of their world. While children generally exaggerate personality characteristics during role reversal, they clearly communicate how they feel about that person (Hughes, 1991). Thus, one might observe in children's play a teacher who belittles or a parent who shames.

In addition to developmental purposes, sociodramatic play serves a major function in the emotional/feeling development of children. Research indicates that the benefits of role-playing for children include a greater sense of happiness, feelings of power over the environment, emotional awareness, and sensitivity (Singer & Singer, 1977). In the process of role-playing, preschoolers develop emotional strength and stability, and older children develop spontaneity, humor, and positive feelings about self (Piers & Landau, 1980).

Through the use of the language of pretense (Cohen & Stern, 1983), children unfamiliar with each other are able to interact. Sociodramatic pretending allows children to act out various relationship roles, switching easily from one role to another. Or, as children interact with assumed roles, they are able to experience emotional responses to each role and can decide to continue in that role, change the role, or select an entirely different role. This process also develops problem-solving skills as children review the current situation, explore other possibilities, try out new solutions, and select the one that fits best (Solnit et al., 1993).

Testing Limits as a Way of Expressing Feelings

An often misunderstood area of feeling expression in play is children's use of limit-testing behavior. The innate growth potential in children cannot be fully maximized in settings where children feel insecure. Limits on behavior provide a structure to the environment and the relationship in which children can feel secure. When there are no boundaries and limitations on behavior, children feel insecure and often experience feelings of anxiety; they feel neither safe nor accepted. Some children have difficulty controlling their own impulsiveness and so need the security of limits, which provide them with an opportunity to gain control of their own behavior and promote feelings of self-acceptance and adequacy. Limits, therefore, help to assure the emotional security of children. When children discover where the boundaries are in a relationship or setting and experience consistent adherence to those boundaries, they feel secure because there is predictability (Landreth, 1991).

When children push the boundaries or attempt to break established limits in a play relationship, they may, among other things, be expressing feelings of anxiety, fear, anger, insecurity, or in effect expressing a need for consistency and predictability in their lives. Another possibility is that they are expressing a need to feel accepted and are attempting to find out if the person they are is accepted in spite of their behavior. When viewed in this context, a child's attempt to shoot the adult with a dart gun or hit the adult with a block takes on an entirely new dimension, one that calls for the adult's understanding of the child's feeling rather than the typical attempt to stop the behavior. Some children can only be certain of the adult's unconditional acceptance by testing the adult with the most unacceptable aspects of their personality.

Humor in Play

Although some early work addressed humor (e.g., Freud, 1958, 1960), until recently children's humor was not a major area of study. However, research now indicates that children select various forms of humor according to their developmental level (Levine, 1977). Developmentally delayed children, for example, have difficulty enjoying humor and expressing feelings through humor. Children who are sick, or those who are frightened or bewildered, often will not play or smile (Garvey, 1977). Severely abused and neglected children often must be taught to play and do not use humor until later stages of therapy (Allan, 1988). Conversely, children who are more advanced in the development of humor have been found to be more talkative, have larger vocabularies, and have the ability to be more expressive (Cohen, 1987); thus, these children are more likely to express a wider range of feelings in their play. Some researchers have found that children's humor increased self-control, enabled children to indirectly deal with difficulties and feelings, maximized positive feelings, minimized negative feelings, and reduced anxiety and fear (Tower & Singer, 1980). These results are readily observable in children's play.

Children use humor in many of the same ways they use play and often in conjunction with play as a means through which to express other feelings. Children may use humor with others in the midst of play to provide a buffer between self and another person or experience they find uncomfortable or embarrassing. Aggressive humor is used in play by children to release tension and allow emotional relief, thus developing the ability to control aggressive impulses. Hostile humor is used to cope with destruction or suffering, or as a "disguised attack with the individual deriving gratification from this expression of aggression" (Biblow, 1973, p. 127).

Infectious laughter, group glee, and the spontaneous eruption of laughter among children at play are delightful to witness. Group glee may begin with one child or all the children at the same time. A wave of giggles, often accompanied by jumping up and down and hand clapping, usually lasts only nine or ten seconds (Garvey, 1977). This group experience of being in tune with each other and resonating with the same emotion provides children opportunities for expressing deep emotional satisfaction that comes from emotional identification with others.

The child's world is a world of great emotional intensity and diverse feelings that can only be fully expressed through children's spontaneously generated play. Left to their own devices, children will play, for that is their most natural form of intrinsic expression. Whether or not the meaning of their play is important is not dependent on the understanding of observers. When adults do not interfere, children play out feelings and reactions in the ways they choose. This playing out process is a natural coping mechanism for children, which allows them to release and explore emotions in a step-by-step process as they feel safe to do so. Therefore, not interfering with children's play is perhaps the most caring and sensitive thing adults can do.

Bibliography

Allan, J. (1988). *Inscapes of the child's world: Jungian counseling in schools and clinics.* Dallas, TX: Spring.

Axline, V. (1947). *Play therapy.* New York: Ballantine.

Bettelheim, B. (1987, March). The importance of play. *Atlantic Monthly, 35–46.*

Biber, B. (1984). *Early education and psychological development.* New Haven: Yale University Press.

Biblow, E. (1973). Imaginative play and the control of aggressive behavior. In J. Singer (Ed.), *The child's world of make-believe: Experimental studies of imaginative play* (pp. 104–128). New York: Academic.

Bluestone, J. (1991). School-based peer therapy to facilitate mourning in latency-age children following sudden parental death. In N. B. Webb (Ed.), *Play therapy with children in crisis: A casebook for practitioners* (pp. 254–275). New York: Guilford.

Caplan, F., & Caplan, T. (1973). *The power of play.* Garden City, NY: Anchor/Doubleday.

Cass, J. E. (1973). *Helping children grow through play.* New York: Schocken.

Cohen, D. (1987). *The development of play.* New York: New York University Press.

Cohen, D., & Stern, V. (1983). *Observing and recording the behavior of young children* (2nd ed.). New York: Teachers College Press.

Frank, L. (1982). Play in personality development. In G. Landreth (Ed.), *Play therapy: Dynamics of the process of counseling with children* (pp. 19–32). Springfield, IL: Charles C. Thomas.

Freud, S. (1958). The relation of the poet to daydreaming. In S. Freud (B. Nelson, Ed. and J. Riviere, Trans.), *On creativity and the unconscious* (pp. 44–54). New York: Harper & Row. (Originally published as Collected Papers IV, 1925)

Freud, S. (1960). *Jokes and their relation to the unconscious*. New York: Norton.

Garvey, C. (1977). *Play*. Cambridge, MA: Harvard University Press.

Hartley, R., Frank, L., & Goldenson, R. (1952). *Understanding children's play*. New York: Columbia University Press.

Hughes, F. P. (1991). *Children, play, and development*. Boston: Allyn and Bacon.

Landreth, G. (1991). *Play therapy: The art of the relationship*. Muncie, IN: Accelerated Development.

Levine, J. (1977). Humor as a form of therapy: Introduction to Symposium, the International Conferences on Humour and Laughter. In A. J. Chapman & H. C. Foot (Eds.), *It's a funny thing, humour* (pp. 127–137). Oxford: Pergamon.

Moustakas, C. (1959). *Psychotherapy with children*. New York: Harper & Row.

Moustakas, C. (1973). *Children in play therapy*. New York: McGraw-Hill.

Oaklander, V. (1988). *Windows to our children: A Gestalt therapy approach to children and adolescents*. Highland, NY: Center for Gestalt Development.

Piaget, J. (1962). *Play, dreams, and imitation in childhood*. New York: Routledge.

Piers, M. W., & Landau, G. M. (1980). *The gift of play*. New York: Walker.

Schaefer, C. (1993). *The therapeutic powers of play*. Northvale, NJ: Jason Aronson.

Singer, D., & Singer, J. (1977). *Partners in play: A step-by-step guide to imaginative play in children*. New York: Harper & Row.

Smilansky, S. (1990). Sociodramatic play: Its relevance to behavior and achievement in school. In E. Klugman & S. Smilansky (Eds.), *Children's play and learning: Perspectives and policy* (pp. 18–42). New York: Teachers College Press.

Solnit, A., Cohen, D., & Neubauer, P. (1993). Introduction. In A. Solnit, D. Cohen, & P. Neubauer (Eds.), *The many meanings of play: A psychoanalytic perspective* (pp. 1–5). New Haven: Yale University Press.

Tower, R. B., & Singer, J. L. (1980). Imagination, interest, and joy in early childhood: Some theoretical considerations and empirical findings. In P. E. McGee & A. J. Chapman (Eds.), *Children's humor* (pp. 27–58). New York: John Wiley.

Play as a Developmental Tool

The Role of Play in Assessment

Rebecca Fewell
Michelle Glick

There are differences between the goals and methods of appoaches that use play in the assessment of children's development. Two important approaches to the use of play in assessment are (1) the assessment of play as a developmental phenomenon and (2) the assessment of the development of language, problem-solving, motor, and social skills while children are playing. Videotaping can capture play behavior and assessors can code actions from the tape. To do so, however, they need to consider some key decisions when planning play assessment.

Jean Piaget (1962) offers an important theoretical perspective from which to examine the role of play in assessment. He saw children as active explorers and experimenters who use play to gain knowledge through a process of assimilation and accommodation. In so doing, children are able to organize their world and reflect their growing intellect. Piaget described three stages of play development: sensorimotor, symbolic and pretend, and games with rules. Through play, adults can observe these stages of the maturing intellect in much the same way as they observe the changing stages of language and motor behavior.

Psychologists and other professionals who have reported linkages and correlations between play behavior and skill development in such areas as language have broadened this Piagetian view of play (Beeghley, Hanrahan, Weiss, & Cicchetti, 1985; Casby & Corte, 1987; Finn & Fewell, 1994), social skills (Caster, 1984; Johnson, Christie, & Yawkey, 1987), and motor skills (Johnson, Christie, & Yawkey, 1987; Mullan, 1984). Their findings provide a strong reason to examine the development of children in the context of the joyful activity of play. The play environment is both a natural and a valid arena in which to see developing children exercise their play skills and other developmental attributes. This essay describes ways investigators can use play as a paradigm for assessing children's development, provides an overview of prevailing techniques, and discusses some critical points to consider when using play in assessment.

Observations of the Child at Play

Given the current state of technology, parents begin observing their infants long before they are born. These early observations are carefully analyzed to help parents and health care professionals understand the developing child. If health professionals note serious problems, they can address them immediately to minimize the effect on the maturing child. Observations of a child's actions are a source of important information to parents as they seek to understand their child's growth and development. With well-defined information on play development, therefore, professionals can exploit play observations, using them as the basis for assessing a child's development.

If play is to have a role in child assessment, then it is important for the examiners to be clear on how they will use play. Two approaches to play assessment are described in the professional literature; (1) play as a developmental phenomenon and (2) play as a context for observing the development of skills such as cognition, language, social, and motor behavior.

Play as a Developmental Phenomenon

To assess a child's play development as a developmental domain is to take the view that play has a discernible, sequential path of maturation. It is possible to assess play skills in ways that are comparable to those used in assessing other domains of development (Belsky & Most, 1981; Fenson, 1985; Hill & McCune-Nicolich, 1981; Piaget, 1962; Sheridan, Foley, & Radlinski, 1995). The scales of play development and the options for coding play described below, for example, are based on the premise that play is a viable phenomenon for understanding and interpreting the child's abilities.

Play as a Context for Observing Development

Play provides children with opportunities to express whatever they wish, whether through bodily movements, actions on objects, words, or simply facial expressions. Without constrictions on what they do or say, children can be themselves. It is in this context that the behaviors of children tell observers about development. The young girl who gets up from a grassy knoll to chase a butterfly demonstrates her agility and ability to move in space. The boy who picks up a cookie, feeds it to Barney, and says, "Barney cookie" tells the observer about his understanding of eating and food preferences, in addition to his understanding and use of language symbols and sequencing of words. These simple examples permit others to see the child's competence in many domains. There is no requirement that the child run a specified distance, at a given pace, within a predetermined period of time. Opportunities arise and children can decide how to confront them. Within the context of the play experience, observers can see how the child uses time and makes decisions, two important applied skills that are valid indicators of the intellect.

Play, while often associated with young children, is actually ageless. Senior citizens interacting in a game of bridge are engaged in a play act involving a game with rules. If we take a broad definition of play, including as play the early exchanges between parents and children and extending to the playful rhythms being tapped as an elderly man reminisces about earlier times when he played the drums, then we can view play as an opportunity to see what persons care to reveal about themselves at any age. For those who wish to use the play arena for observing children's developmental skills, some facilitations or manipulations might be useful to elicit the desired behavior. For ex-

ample, if one wishes to observe children's movements with balls or steps, placing these things in the environment are likely to elicit the behavior. It is quite natural to encourage the demonstration of skills without being intrusive. It is for this reason that play presents a potentially excellent environment for the assessment of children. It requires patience and a clinical knowledge of development, actually a more in-depth understanding of development than does traditional assessment. Play may not be a setting that can assure standard procedures, but it adds a dimension to testing that is seldom captured in traditional child assessment. Perhaps the time has come to recognize and value children's play and realize the opportunity it presents for understanding a child's development.

Assessment of Play Development

Investigators can assess play development, like the development of language, by taking a sample of behavior and analyzing that sample for indications of certain concepts. They also can measure it in more structured ways, such as giving children a specific toy or set of toys and then observing children's actions, looking for behaviors known to be associated with a particular toy or object.

Free-Play Coding Systems

Examiners may select one or more key elements they wish to code while children are playing. It may be necessary to determine the primary and secondary behaviors to code. One example of how a team worked through the complexities of coding play is an Oxfordshire study of 240 observations of children at play (Sylva, Roy, & Painter, 1980). The team described the action codes (pretend, gross motor, and manipulation); social codes (settings, positioning near others, interactions with others, and group size); language codes (number of utterances addressed to and emitted by the target child; types of utterances); and play bouts (longer periods of activity that capture unity across activities) that they used during the observations and later coded in analysis. They included the forms that are so often missing when journal articles describe procedures.

Rubin, Watson, and Jambor (1978) used a combination of the cognitive play categories of Smilansky (1968) and the social categories of

Parten (1932) in developing a coding system for use in a particular study. They demonstrated that, with minor adaptations in associative and cooperative play categories, they could use with both preschool and kindergarten-age children the coding system Rubin, Maioni, and Hornung (1976) used with preschool-age children.

Howes (1980) noted that researchers were challenging Parten's classic description of social play and needed other means of observing social interactive play. She described a five-level scale, the Peer Play Scale, that moves sequentially from parallel play to reciprocal social play involving contingent social behaviors and complementary actions. Other researchers have also developed systems for coding free play. Nicolich (1977), for example, described procedures for assessment of free play based on Piagetian stages of development. Still other authors have found it useful to analyze free play in their research (Belsky & Most, 1981; Gowen & Schoen, 1984; Lunzer, 1958).

Semistructured Procedures for Assessing Play

Researchers also have developed scales that are more quantifiable than the various free-play coding systems described above. These formats often meet a specific need, such as a way to compare a group of children with disabilities to children developing normally. One format is to present toys singly or in order and then rate the child's interactions (Largo & Howard, 1979). Another format uses structured observations and parent input to determine developmental scores in both play and language (Westby, 1980). A different set of procedures permits an examiner to give sets of toys to a child, observe and score the developmental sequences of play behavior, and then derive a play age score (Fewell, 1991). Because of the flexibility in the toys and timing, this scale has been used frequently with children under age three who have disabilities and others who respond poorly to standardized testing.

Assessment of Skill Development

In addition to assessing children's play competence one can use play as a medium for observing children's social, cognitive, communicative, and motoric development (McCune-Nicolich, 1980; Parten, 1932; Rogers, 1982). Information gained from observations during free play time can supplement test scores from standardized and structured assessments. Almost every area of development can be assessed through play observation.

Observation of Social Skills

Social skills are readily observable in a play setting. Observers can compare how children interact with parents, siblings, teachers, strangers, and peers. These observations can yield important information concerning a child's needs for intervention related to social interaction skills. After observations of mother-child play, for example, a team might suggest strategies for the mother to use to promote turn-taking with the child. Through peer play observations, teachers and other professionals can note whether a child needs to learn how to approach other children to join in their play.

Observation of Cognitive and Language Skills

Observing children during play also yields valuable information regarding cognitive and communication development. The cognitive skills of problem solving, mastery motivation, attention, classification, and sequencing, for example, are often observable during play (Linder, 1993). In the language domain, observers can notice children's spontaneous use of eye contact and gestures as well as vocalizations, words, and sentences during familiar and pleasurable activities. Ogura (1991) reports developmental correspondences between the onset of six language markers (first words, naming words, vocabulary spurts, word chains, nonproductive two-word utterances, and productive two-word utterances) and the onset of thirteen subcategories of play.

Observation of Motor Skills

Although observers can easily see both fine and gross motor skills, motor behavior during play is a neglected area of study. In a typical setting with object toys, children use their hands to grasp and pick up objects, put objects inside containers, or hold a crayon. Children sit, climb into chairs, and move from one place to another. A playground provides a perfect setting for observing gross motor skills that require larger spaces; one can observe walking, running, jumping, climbing, swinging, and throwing and catching balls. Researchers have begun to identify the motor skills of children on playgrounds and have used these observations to develop a Playground Skills Test for elementary school-age children (Butcher, 1991).

Observation of Informal Play

The current work of the essay's authors includes the beginning development of informal play procedures to observe the development of infants and toddlers with special needs. This paradigm is an attempt to avoid relying solely on traditional standardized measures to assess the children's progress in their early intervention program. A "videotesting" procedure involves videotaping the children interacting with the teaching assistant. Each session includes the following: gross motor observations of the child on the patio outside the classroom; fine motor and play observations while the child interacts with a set of toys; language observations as the child reads a book and interacts with others; and cognitive observations as the assistant or parent engages the child in tasks on a cognitive screening measure. Parents are included in the process so that the authors can observe parent-child interaction. The development and refinement of this videotesting model may serve to garner support for the idea that reliable and valid observations of a child in all domains can occur within an unstructured, play context.

Assessment Instruments

One question that arises is: How does one know what specific skills to look for in each developmental area during observation of a child at play? The answer to this question varies depending upon the purpose of the observations. A classroom teacher, for example, will want to observe play in order to adapt the curriculum to the needs of the children. An evaluation team, however, may need more specific information about the level of the child's functioning in each domain.

The Play Development Progress Scale may be useful for teachers (Johnson, Christie, & Yawkey, 1987). This scale sequences behaviors observable in a child's play from about birth to six years in the following areas: manipulative/constructive, symbolic, social, and physical. Skills are arranged on the scale according to the approximate age levels in which they occur.

Using the forms, the teacher can keep an account of the child's progress in dramatic play, social play, and motor development. Teachers may also wish to use a tool such as the Frost-Wortham Checklist, which is a guide for learning about play and individual children between the ages of three and five years (Frost, 1992).

Another approach to assessing multiple skills within the context of play is the use of curriculum-based assessment measures, which assess performance on goals and objectives used in teaching specific tasks. These have been used by teachers for many years with the teacher doing all the observations and assessments. One curriculum-based measure is the Hawaii Early Learning Profile (Furuno et al., 1984). A more recent curriculum-based measure that describes how to use the tool during play and other classroom activities to ascertain a child's functioning level is the Assessment, Evaluation, and Programming System (AEPS) Measurement for Birth to Three Years (Bricker, 1993).

Arena Assessment

As early childhood assessment and intervention teams have become transdisciplinary in nature and less discipline-specific, arena assessment has become a popular method (Foley, 1992). In arena assessment, professionals from different disciplines simultaneously assess the child. One team member typically acts as the facilitator and other team members observe the process live in the same room, live through an observation window, or later, while viewing a videotape.

Transdisciplinary teams are beginning to use play-based observational procedures as part of their arena assessments (Bergen, 1994). An example of a well-known procedure is Transdisciplinary Play-Based Assessment (TPBA). TPBA involves observing aspects of children's development as they interact in structured and unstructured play situations (Linder, 1993). The information collected can be used to identify the child's service needs, develop intervention plans, and evaluate progress. TPBA includes the following assessment situations: unstructured facilitation, child-child interaction, parent-child interaction, motor play, and snack. Thus, information can be collected in the areas of cognition, social-emotional, communication and language, and sensorimotor development. The TPBA provides guidelines with approximate age ranges for the observation of each area (Linder, 1993).

Decision Points

Before beginning observations of play for assessment purposes, investigators decide on the purposes of the observations and how they will be used. Those who evaluate children to decide on their eligibility for special services, for example, may need to collect different types of information and use different types of coding schemes than would classroom teachers or other early intervention team members who need to plan a child's intervention. Another decision is whether or not there is a need for more structured, formal assessment measures in addition to the play assessment. Play assessment yields valuable information, although examiners often consider it supplementary to traditional, standardized tests. The advantages of play assessment include an environment that is familiar to the child, the ability to adapt the situation to children with special needs, and the ability to reflect cultural and linguistic diversity. Until more is known about the validity and reliability of assessment during play, however, it is likely that standardized assessment will continue to be necessary and appropriate.

Investigators also must decide on the method of observation. Are videotaped interactions or live coded behavior more helpful? The use of videotape to assess play skills or other domains of development through play has become increasingly popular. Videotaping enables teachers, parents, and researchers to examine children's progress over time (Linder, 1993; Prizant & Wetherby, 1993). Individuals can visually and auditorily compare the children's behavior from one point in time to another, making it easier to detect subtle differences. In a transdisciplinary model, team members who are unable to complete their evaluations during the time of the assessment can refer to the videotape (Linder, 1993). Busy classroom teachers who do not have time to observe how children play during the day can videotape different areas of the classroom and then code the behaviors during a less hectic time (Johnson, Christie, & Yawkey, 1987). Videotaping enables the observation of detailed information that might not be possible during firsthand observation (Johnson et al., 1987). Although children often cannot be encouraged to repeat an unintelligible utterance or an unheard vocalization, the videotape of the session can be easily rewound.

Although videotaping is a useful tool, its disadvantages need to be considered. First, assessing a child and then scoring behavior from the videotapes is often time consuming. Second, some observational tools may not be appropriate to use when scored from a videotape. Researchers, for example, have found differences in the coding of live and taped observations with groups of children in a playgroup setting (Fagot & Hagan, 1988). Possible differences between the two methods of coding need further investigation. Another disadvantage to videotaping occurs when the camera is visible and novel to the children. The visibility may cause children to change their behavior; they may, for example, point to the camera or act shy. Last, the individual who does the videotaping needs to be trained to adequately capture what is needed on tape. It is necessary, therefore, to choose the observational tool in advance to plan the kinds of actions and behaviors that must be captured by the videotaping.

How to use and report findings depends on the purpose of the assessment. As mentioned earlier, play observations can be used in diagnosing children, making placement decisions, and also in planning children's intervention services. Play assessment data is often very valuable for researchers who are conducting program evaluations. While investigators often use standardized instruments, play assessment captures children's typical performance rather than their performance in a strange situation.

Children's play provides a delightful arena for viewing developmental skills in action. Today's assessment team members can capture the functional use of the skills of all domains as children use them while having fun. The opportunity that play provides through an informal process requires the assessor to have good clinical and observational skills and to make decisions about what should be done during the assessment process. Researchers are providing evidence that the play assessment process, both from the perspectives of assessing play as a domain and the assessing of other domains within the play context, is a valid and reliable way to capture and quantify children's developing skills.

Bibliography

Beeghley, M., Hanrahan, A., Weiss, B. W., & Cicchetti, D. (1985). *Development of communication competence in children with Down syndrome.* Paper presented at the biannual meeting of the Society for Research on Child Development, Toronto.

Belsky, J., & Most, R. K. (1981). From exploration to play: A cross-sectional study of infant free play behavior. *Developmental Psychology, 17*(5), 630–639.

Bergen, D. (1994). *Assessment methods for infants and toddlers.* New York: Teachers College Press.

Bricker, D. (1993). *Assessment, evaluation, and programming system (AEPS) for infants and children: Vol. 1. AEPS measurement for birth to three years.* Baltimore: Brookes.

Butcher, J. (1991). Development of a playground skills test. *Perceptual and Motor Skills, 72*(1), 259–266.

Casby, M. H., & Corte, M. D. (1987). Symbolic play performance and early language development. *Journal of Psycholinguistic Research, 16*(1), 21–42.

Caster, T. R. (1984). The young child's play and social and emotional development. In T. D. Yawkey & A. D. Pellegrini (Eds.), *Children's play and play therapy* (pp. 17–29). Lancaster, PA: Technomic.

Fagot, B., & Hagan, R. (1988). Is what we see what we get? Comparisons of taped and live observations. *Behavioral Assessment, 10*(4), 367–374.

Fenson, L. (1985). The developmental progression of exploration and play. In C. C. Brown & A. W. Gottfried (Eds.), *Play interactions: The role of toys in children's development* (pp. 31–38). Skillman, NJ: Johnson and Johnson.

Fewell, R. R. (1991). *Play assessment scale.* Unpublished manuscript, University of Miami School of Medicine.

Foley, G. M. (1992). Portrait of the arena evaluation: Assessment in the transdisciplinary approach. In E. D. Gibbs & D. M. Teti (Eds.), *Interdisciplinary assessment of infants: A guide for early intervention professionals* (pp. 271–286). Baltimore: Brookes.

Frost, J. L. (1992). *Play and playscapes.* Albany, NY: Delmar.

Furuno, S., O'Reilly, K. A., Hosaka, C. M., Inatsuka, T. T., Zeisloft-Falbey, B., & Allman, T. (1984). *HELP checklist.* Palo Alto, CA: Vort.

Gowen, J. W., & Schoen, D. (1984). *Levels of child object play.* Unpublished coding scheme manuscript, Carolina Institute

for Research on Early Education of the Handicapped, Frank Porter Graham Child Development Center, Chapel Hill, NC.

Hill, R. M., & McCune-Nicolich, L. (1981). Pretend play and patterns of cognition in Down's syndrome children. *Child Development, 52*(2), 611–617.

Howes, C. (1980). Peer Play Scale as an index of complexity of peer interaction. *Developmental Psychology, 16*(4), 371–372.

Johnson, J. E., Christie, J. F., & Yawkey, T. D. (1987). *Play and early childhood development.* Glenview, IL: Scott, Foresman.

Largo, R. H., & Howard, J. A. (1979). Developmental progression in play behavior of children between nine and thirty months. 1: Spontaneous play and imitation. *Developmental Medicine and Child Neurology, 21*(3), 299–310.

Linder, T. W. (1993). *Transdisciplinary play-based assessment: A functional approach to working with young children* (Rev. ed.). Baltimore: Brookes.

Lunzer, E. A. (1958). A scale of the organization of behavior for use in the study of play. *Educational Review, 11,* 205–217.

McCune-Nicolich, L. (1980). *A manual for analyzing free play.* New Brunswick, NJ: Rutgers University Press.

Mullan, M. R. (1984). Motor development and children's play. In T. D. Yawkey & A. D. Pellegrini (Eds.), *Children's play and play therapy* (pp. 7–15). Lancaster, PA: Technomic.

Nicolich, L. (1977). Beyond sensorimotor intelligence: Assessment of symbolic maturity through analysis of pretend play. *Merrill-Palmer Quarterly, 23*(2), 89–101.

Ogura, T. (1991). A longitudinal study of the relationship between early language development and play development. *Journal of Child Language, 18*(2), 273–294.

Parten, M. B. (1932). Social participation among pre-school children. *Journal of Abnormal and Social Psychology, 27,* 243–269.

Piaget, J. (1962). *Play, dreams, and imitation in childhood.* New York: Norton.

Prizant, B. M., & Wetherby, A. M. (1993). Communication and language assessment in young children. *Infants and Young Children, 5*(4), 20–34.

Rogers, S. J. (1982). Cognitive characteristics

of young children's play. In R. Peiz (Ed.), *Developmental and clinical aspects of young children's play* (pp. 1–13). Monmouth, OR: WESTAR.

Rubin, K. H., Maioni, T. L., & Hornung, M. (1976). Free play behaviors in middle- and lower-class preschoolers: Parten and Piaget revisited. *Child Development, 47*(2), 414–419.

Rubin, K. H., Watson, K. S., & Jambor, T. W. (1978). Free-play behaviors in preschool and kindergarten children. *Child Development, 49*(2), 534–536.

Sheridan, M. K., Foley, G. M., & Radlinski, S. H. (1995). *Using the supportive play model.* New York: Teachers College Press.

Smilansky, S. (1968). *The effects of socio-dramatic play in disadvantaged preschool children.* New York: John Wiley.

Sylva, K., Roy, C., & Painter, M. (1980). *Childwatching at playgroup and nursery school.* Ypsilanti: High/Scope.

Westby, C. E. (1980). Assessment of cognitive and language abilities through play. *Language, Speech and Hearing Services in the Schools, 11*(3), 154–168.

Can I Play Too?

Reflections on the Issues for Children with Disabilities

Gayle Mindes

Observers and participants ascribe various meanings to the phenomenon of play, the developmental benefit of play, the nature of disability, the intervention into the lives of children with special needs, and the nature of labels. On the one hand, a psychological perspective supports the idea of adult intervention in play to increase meaning for the player. On the other hand, the variables of mislabeling and sociocultural and environmental factors interfere with, and challenge, the notion of "normality." Also, the perspectives of the individual players' reflected meanings, significant others, culture, and the community at large must be considered. Overall, trying to understand the meaning of play and intervention for children with disabilities requires the simultaneous attention to multiple contexts and constructs. The thread to consider is: Is it real for the player, the other, and whose reality is it?

Memories of Childhood Play

Almost everyone can recall a play experience that was "not fun" or "not play." Whether a memory of not being chosen for the neighborhood baseball game, being unable to hit the hoop or the little white ball sitting on the little pin in the green grass, always missing the volley at the crucial moment, or maybe even being more interested in the flowers than the action around the soccer ball, the memory is bittersweet. In thinking about these "experiences" or family stories, the tendency is to shrug and say, "Oh well, it's just one of those things." So many more successful memories of "good play" crowd to the front of recollection. After all, the marvelous sculptures created from plasticine, the exquisite puns, clever

raps, the record-setting broad jump, or the story of being the "cutest" turkey in the play fill a reservoir of competence.

Nevertheless, what if "inept play" is a way of life? For children with real or labeled disabilities, this may often be the case, whether their own reflections ascribe ineptness or others react to them as if their play were "incompetent." Play is another failure, another instance of nonacceptance, shunning, or inadequacy. Issues worth struggling with thus include the developmental definitions of play, typical instances of successful play, definitions of disability, challenges for children with disabilities, interventions to support "better" play, another way to construct disability and play, and the implications of this alternative view in the age of inclusion in the mainstream of children with special needs.

Developmental Definitions of Play

Often the natural learning medium of the child is play. From a competence perspective,

> play is a complex process that involves social cognitive, emotional, and physical elements, and relates to an aspect of reality as not "serious" or "real." For the child this characterization makes it possible to relate to things that might otherwise be confusing, frightening, mysterious, strange, risky, or forbidden, and to develop appropriate competencies and defenses. The active solution of developmental conflicts through play thus enables the child to show and feel . . . competence. (Mindes, 1982, p. 40)

Typical children play, and they benefit developmentally, educationally, and personally. It is a "win-win" situation; they have fun and grow. Their play activity defines and sustains life (Csikszentmihalyi, 1975; Erikson, 1963; Freud, 1965). For the player the rewards are both immediate—an intrinsic joy—and long term—development. At play, whether at home, in the community, or at school, typical children grow and gain proficiency as they play alone, by themselves, in groups, or under the guidance of adults (Rubin, Fein, & Vandenberg, 1983).

Competencies Developed through Play
Child accomplishments developed through play include communication skills, physical agility, independence, social judgment, cooperation, and impulse control. Illustrations of the typical developmental sequence of play include the following: Babies coo, play with their toes, gaze at interesting patterns of light and color, and gradually begin to jiggle keys, drop rattles, and otherwise move into the world of toys. Toddlers show their growing competence by crawling, walking, using one- and two-word sentences, imitating the actions of significant people in their environment, and playing beside friends in water, soil, sand, and other environmental media. Preschoolers add fantasy to play through the imitation of the actions of the world around them, such as lunch at McDonald's and the actions of Power Rangers, Pocahontas, Mom, Dad, and the ever present Big Bird. With their greater social, emotional, cognitive, and physical competence, preschoolers enjoy many more options for play, such as table games, blocks, small toys, and rough-and-tumble activities.

Young children make choices based on interests, settings, and capabilities. They invent playtime for themselves. Older children enjoy games with rules that adults define, such as sports and board games, and those that they create, often including codes and special languages. During the period between six and twelve years, children enjoy painting, drawing, music, and acting out "real" plays of stories read and told. It is in this period that lifelong passions of rock collecting, chess, the violin, basketball, sculpting, and acting may begin (see Bergen, 1988).

By definition, children must internally control the limits and process of play activities. Choices of activity must be free for the child; otherwise the activity is not play. A parent who requires an hour of piano practice is creating work for the child; when the child sits at the piano for hours to enjoy the thrill of mastery of the keyboard and sounds created, it is play. Teachers creating work sheets of turtles marching to illustrate math facts are making material "play-like." Only the child who enjoys repetitive, rote demonstrations of competence, however, might consider this activity "play." For the player, the rewards must be inherent.

Environment shapes play opportunities and goals (see Hughes, 1995). Swinging on vines across creeks to play Tarzan and Jane characters is probably an option only for children living in exurbia. Skateboarding up and over trash cans is an option for city slickers. Sledding requires hills, snow, and equipment. Playing at home in front of the television or video game while Mom and Dad are at work may diminish choices and the development of artistic and sports ventures.

These aspects and variables of play are from the vantage point of typical children. For children with disabilities, these and other variables apply, depending on the nature and severity of the disability.

Defining Disability

Formal definitions of disabilities include symptoms of developmental differences in motor, language, cognitive, social, emotional, physical, and behavioral performance. These symptoms affect development in complex ways. Sometimes, children cannot produce typical behavior. Often, those who do not believe that the behavior is within the repertoire of a particular child foreshorten opportunities.

From birth, or at the age of the diagnosis of the special need, these are the children whose experiences will be "different" lifelong. They will face special challenges. Familial, cultural, social, and educational contexts will determine their opportunities for development, education, and personal growth. The severity, nature, and type of disability also will influence opportunity.

Trying to make things better for children with disabilities, parents, interventionists, and teachers place attention on helping the child with disabilities to blend or fit into the established definition of typical behavior; this practice permits and promotes acceptance by the majority. Children learn early that their disabilities create challenges for them to solve so that they may "fit in."

Play for Children with Atypical Development

Developmental challenges frequently begin at birth. Certainly, the severe and profound difficulties that might affect typical development are present at birth. Parents and others who encounter these babies may foreclose opportunities; they may not encourage play because they are worried about survival, the need for medical equipment, and the fragility of the baby with special needs. In turn, these perceptions may contribute to difficult feeding, sleeping, and self-help routines. Thus, in the earliest relationship, synchrony, contingency, play autonomy, and flexibility are missing (Zirpoli, 1995). Other challenges emerge that parents and diagnosticians find during the developmental period; some examples, discussed below, represent the impact of disability on play activities.

Receptive and Expressive Language Delays

Receptive and expressive language delays that make sociodramatic play difficult may cause young children not to play. Instead of playing, they may wander the schoolroom or playground aimlessly, rather than face the stress of competition or the frustration of being misunderstood when trying to communicate. They may skip the storytelling and sharing, active listening, acting, and role-playing at home or in preschool situations. During the school years, such children may develop defensive, aggressive, or passive actions to mask the pain of being forced to compete in verbal situations. If other play activity choices are not available, they may engage in disruptive behavior. Their peers and teachers may perceive them as babyish. These children may develop a reputation for not "going with the program," being out of sync with the rest of the class (see Fromberg, 1995).

Attentional Problems or Visual or Auditory Perceptual Difficulties

Attentional problems, or visual or auditory perceptual difficulties in children with learning disabilities, may contribute to "missed chances" for the players. That is, the children may not understand the goals of the play from the vantage of peers or the peers may misunderstand the children with learning disabilities. These children may leave the play, seemingly dissatisfied, destroy the group or individual product, or in another way become nonplayers. For these children, stacking blocks, putting together puzzles, remembering the rules to Monopoly, or focusing on one activity may create hair-pulling frustration. Such children may never complete model cars or airplanes because the small pieces dumped from the box are overwhelming, particularly when accompanied by the distraction of such everyday events as siblings playing or the television or radio being on.

Children with Emotional Disturbances or Unique Time or Space Perceptions

Children with emotional disturbances and those with unique time or space perceptions may face difficulty in any social context. Problems in making and keeping friends and sharing may diminish play opportunities for these children. Other children do not choose them or avoid them when they seek out playmates. Their disruptive behavior may be frightening to others. In school situations, teachers may devote so much time trying to control their behavior that both teacher and children are frustrated, locked into power struggles, and have feelings of failure. In the neighborhood, other children may not invite them to parties or neighborhood games and activities. Consequently, children with disabilities may be excluded from the typical play opportunities and options, further stunting their development as competent players.

Different Physical Capacities or Sensory Impairment

For those children with differences in physical capacities or sensory impairment, their limitations in the perceptions and realities of opportunities for play by themselves and with others are critical. Toys and materials may be unsuitable. Buttons, levers, and blocks may be too small or too close together. Access to some activities may be limited: shelves may be too high or pathways too narrow; playing fields may be too uneven for children in wheelchairs or those using walkers or crutches. Toys with only one purpose may lack attractiveness for the child who cannot see or hear. A toddler with sensory hypersensitivities and motor difficulties may find changes threatening, when touches and movements are unexpected. When such children do not enjoy roughhousing, this may lead to stress, overstimulation, and a cycle of miscommunication with the outer world of parents, siblings, and peers (Ensher & Clark, 1994). Children with severe disabilities may have diminished opportunities for play due to time in a hospital, overprotective parents and caretakers, or limitations of medical technology supporting life.

Cognitive Delays and Mental Retardation

Children with cognitive delays and mental retardation often do not "get" the joke or do not remember the words to plays and poems. They often enjoy activities that their friends have long since given up as babyish. Even at age seven, riding a bicycle may be daunting, since they may lack the coordination to succeed with this "typical" activity of childhood. In group activities, they may forget "the rules" or apply them rigidly when latitude is an implied norm for the group.

Interventions to Support Play

On a continuum from typical to atypical behavior, teachers, parents, and others may see some linguistic, physical, cognitive, social, and emotional difficulties in typical children. In typical settings, teachers, peers, siblings, and parents frequently intervene to help children bridge appropriately into an activity. The teacher, peer, and sibling, or parent observes a problem, tosses out one or more solutions, and moves on to let the child solve the problem, for example, asking "Why don't you try it this way?" and shifting a puzzle piece around. For children with special needs this approach may not be enough.

Children with disabilities may need more support and intervention in play if they are to be successful community members. They may even need technological assistance. The diagnosis of such children is based on individual performance and described in terms of deficits and strengths. Transdisciplinary staff plan interventions to "normalize" the behavior of the individual with special needs. A frequent consequence is that teachers, parents, peers, and others see children first through the lens of their

disabilities and second as children. Sometimes the behavior of the child with disabilities is frightening for siblings, parents, relatives, teachers, and others. Loud cries, self-abuse, kicking, screaming, and biting, for example, are behaviors that are difficult to overlook or understand. Many, therefore, avoid interactions with children who exhibit such behaviors.

It is too simple to say, "Well, let's forget the disability and let the child grow and evolve typically." By definition, this cannot happen. Thus, those involved in the lives of children with special needs must further hone the skills of intervention in children's play. For the children, the experience must be supported play. There is a continuum from intrusion and intervention to play for the player: intrusion . . . intervention . . . play . . . improved play. The result can be growth and enhanced personal development. For teachers, parents, and others, this means using all the tricks in the book, including being stage manager, mediator, player, scribe, assessor, and planner (Jones & Reynolds, 1992).

A mediator prepares a safe environment and helps with problem solving and conflict resolution. The mediator role may include physically positioning the child with cerebral palsy; providing structure for problem solving for the learner who does not learn "incidentally"; interpreting the ritualistic behavior of an autistic child; and setting up a structure for the child who flits.

Play facilitators can assist children with linguistic disabilities by the *selective use of language; mirroring,* reflecting a child's nonverbal expressions; *self-talk,* comment on one's own actions; *parallel talk,* or talk about the child's own actions; *imitating,* repeating the child's comments; *elaborating,* introducing new information to build on the child's words; *corroborating,* repeating correctly what the child has said in error; *expanding,* responding with a corrected or expanded version of the child's own words; and *modeling,* conversation without using the child's words (Linder, 1993).

Parents and teachers can support children in playing effectively if these adults sharpen their observational skills. Adults must focus on what is going well for the child with disabilities and then provide challenges, permit regression, interpret the child with special needs to siblings and peers, promote tolerance of individual difference, and otherwise employ a finely tuned assessment role. That is, parents and teachers as assessors must set the stage for play and then intervene when the child is unsuccessful. To intervene, parents and teachers must cultivate extended observational skills, such as functional assessment and task analysis (Mindes, Ireton, & Mardell-Czudnowski, 1995). Such skills are directed toward the maintenance of children with special needs in inclusive classrooms that support and encourage independence, creativity, problem-solving skills, mediation skills, and overall growth and development. It is not enough to return children with special needs to the mainstream. Teachers must devote careful planning and ongoing assessment to their adjustment so that children with special needs can flourish in the typical settings. Otherwise, teachers perpetuate negative stereotyping and isolation to the detriment of individual children who "fail" and to the typical mainstream children who persist in a narrow view of acceptable and "right" behavior.

Successful results for mainstreaming include the growth and enhanced personal development of all the children served. This is not a casual process for the parent or teacher in the assessor role. Overlapping symptoms, complex determinants of behavior, the nature of the child's developmental and sociocultural experience, and the social environments of the community and classroom all combine to require detailed parent, child, and teacher assessment.

An additional demand for the assessor is that parents, children, and teachers must accomplish all of this assessment and intervention without disturbing the play-based opportunities in the environment. That is, if the parent or teacher is directing the script, telling the child with special needs what to do and how to do it, it is not "play" but work disguised as play. Play requires internal control and self-determination of the activity agenda. If a teacher or parent says to Bobby, for example, "Let's play Legos," because this will be good for Bobby's fine motor development, it is not *play* unless Bobby agrees to play and continues on his own to play, elaborating on the prompt given by the parent or teacher. If Bobby says, "No, I want Play Doh," and the parent or teacher continues with Legos, the task has become work for Bobby. He is not having fun; he is doing what the adult wants, working on fine motor skills in an activity that is difficult and frustrating for him. With the proviso that the player is the determiner of the agenda, parents and teachers must search carefully in the natural environment to support and enhance the opportunity for successful play experiences for children with special needs (Division for Early Childhood, 1993; Mallory & New, 1994).

Constructing a Different Paradigm for Disability and Intervention

Successful individuals with disabilities are always those who defy the "handicap" label: Ray Charles, the Kennedy who skis with a prosthesis, deaf actor Marlee Maitlin, and a recent Miss America designee, Heather Whitestone, as well as those represented in contemporary films such as *My Left Foot, Children of a Lesser God, Rainman,* and *Mask.* The spirit and drive of these individuals may help people without known, visible disabilities to accept them, admire them, and expect everyone with disabilities to conform to a conventional and uniform definition of "right" behavior, without regard to prior knowledge of individual experience, cultural values, individual style, or other characteristics.

Flunking softball at home or school is not a joke for a child who has tried his or her best and still cannot see where the batter's box really is, judge how fast the ball is moving in order to catch it, or decide how far to throw it true-to-home. Individual reaction to this failure may be to forget it, to defy the teachers' or parents' definition of acceptable behavior, aggressively to become a nonparticipant, to throw sand in the eyes of others, or to laugh at oneself graciously while inwardly crying. Being labeled a klutz may be "okay" for a girl who accepts the conventional definition that girls are not supposed to be good at sports; for a boy, it may cost acceptance with the other guys or a loss of face.

At the heart of this issue is the definition of disability and "right" behavior in the home, community, and school situation. Individual maladjustment may occur when parents dream of watching their child compete successfully in competitive sports. The child, a chunky, uncoordinated twelve-year-old, may not consider the 6 A.M. run in the park a joyful experience. Exacerbating the parent-child reciprocal interaction is the feeling of failure on both sides. For the child, the failure is an inability to please the parent; for the parent, the failure is the inability to produce the ideal child.

People in different contexts and social situations define normal and typical differently.

"Rule breaking, rule breakers, and those who have considered it their responsibility to react against these have undergone many changes in the history of human societies . . . the powerful have always decided which behaviors and individuals were 'deviant'" (Suchar, 1978, p. 7). Definitions of deviance often make a difference in the lives of children and whether or not others regard them as successful players.

Racism enters the definitional picture for urban, poor children (Haymes, 1995). Some African American cultures, for example, value aspects of expressive, charismatic, and stylistic language more than vocabulary breadth; play includes verbal rituals, rap songs, and memorization of messages. When a white child cannot read, commentators often suggest that there is an inappropriate match between his or her level of development and the curriculum or instructional strategies. When a black child cannot read, commentators often suggest that he or she is culturally deprived and genetically inferior (Hale, 1994, p. 7).

Miscommunication between teacher and child begins with ability grouping and the child's response to it. If the teacher ascribes low ability to a child, the child either accepts the label and lives up to it, or fights it and becomes labeled aggressive. Neither is a successful adaptation to school life. If the label is based on soft signs, including academic achievement, it is a self-fulfilling prophecy. Sometimes, children get out of the system of nonachievement by investing energy in sports, an important marker of cultural success for some children. When sports success is limited, adults and children accept school nonsuccess. The school thereby has contributed in an institutionalized way to the perpetuation of an underclass (Hale, 1994).

School-age children with social, emotional, and learning disabilities who carry the labels of deviant or bad players have particularly painful community and school experiences. Classification manuals often use ambiguous language that may sound logical and rational, in order to define criteria and procedures (Kirk & Kutchins, 1992, p. 221). Consider, for example, what "often loses temper" means when deciding whether a child possesses a conduct disorder. How often is "often"? What does "temper" mean? How often do "ordinary" children lose their tempers? In another example, a discussion might occur between a chaplain and a juvenile court judge in a situation in which a child pulled a knife on a teacher. Adults might define the child as a "good kid" who made a mistake or as a "juvenile delinquent," a "bad kid" who challenged an established authority figure. The difference could result in either a reprimand or a jail term (Gubrium, Holstein, & Buckholdt, 1994, p. 188). These examples illustrate that the lens applied to the label and the road taken to the label may be culturally biased, and that school failure still creates the problem of play failure for large numbers of urban children.

"The practical solution . . . may be to embrace ambiguity fully: . . . to view the human plenitude without fixed ideational or material goods, evils, heroes, or villains, either to glorify or blame. Whatever else freedom can mean, it must include action to explore, affirm, confront, and transform. . . . [there are multiple truths and an] endless play of difference" (Luske, 1990, p. 118). If adults define disabilities in culturally rooted and, often, school-based terms (see Gliedman and Roth, 1980), there is always the risk that there will be rare times when children have an opportunity to play, enjoy, and march to their own drum. When others try to shape, mold, and "adjust" children, they will heighten the pain of those who fail to attain the label of "acceptable" or "typical" or "normal"; they are not respecting or noticing the importance of difference. This is a critical issue in the culture of the United States at this juncture, as are the issues of race, class, gender, and ethnicity. These issues challenge and have an impact on concepts of acceptable and typical. If a society values true acceptance and promotion of individual growth and personal responsibility, then there must be opportunity for children to play and to enjoy, and for peers to expand their understanding of what is typical and usual. Such changed perceptions may relieve the pain that has prevailed for many children with disabilities.

In one group, the teacher and children were developing a play based on the story of Cinderella (Fulghum, 1991). One boy, who was frequently "not chosen," convinced the teacher that he should be "the pig" who interprets Cinderella. Do we have room for the pigs in our lives? Or must we rely on traditional, conventional definitions of acceptable behavior that is tolerable only to some people in some circumstances?

To ignore these issues in defining and thinking about disabilities and play is to condemn large numbers of children to lives of pain and isolation. The question "Can I play too?" needs an affirmative answer. Thoughtful and caring people must broaden the boundaries to their constructs, enrich the opportunities for individuals, intervene with skill and sensitivity, and consider which sociocultural lenses will describe reality. The answers must be affirmatively kaleidoscopic.

Bibliography

Bergen, D. M. (Ed.). (1988). *Play as a medium for growth and development: A handbook of theory and practice.* Portsmouth, NH: Heinemann.

Csikszentmihalyi, M. (1975). *Beyond boredom and anxiety.* San Francisco: Jossey-Bass.

Division for Early Childhood. (1993). *DEC recommended practices: Indicators of quality in programs for infants and young children with special needs and their families.* Pittsburgh: Author.

Ensher, G., & Clark, D. (1994). *Newborns at risk: Medical care and psychoeducational intervention* (2nd ed.). Rockville, MD: Aspen.

Erikson, E. (1963). *Childhood and society.* New York: Norton.

Freud, A. (1965). *Normality and pathology in childhood: Assessment of development.* New York: International Universities Press.

Fromberg, D. P. (1995). *The full-day kindergarten: Planning and practicing a dynamic themes curriculum* (2nd ed.). New York: Teachers College Press.

Fulghum, R. (1991). *Uh-oh: Some observations from both sides of the refrigerator door.* New York: Ivy.

Gliedman, J., & Roth, W. (1980). *The unexpected minority: Handicapped children in America.* New York: Harcourt.

Gubrium, J. F., Holstein, J. A., & Buckholdt, D. R. (1994). *Constructing the life course.* Dix Hills, NY: General Hall.

Hale, J. E. (1994). *Unbank the fire: Visions for the education of African American children.* Baltimore: Johns Hopkins University Press.

Haymes, S. N. (1995). *Race, culture, and the city: A pedagogy for Black urban struggle.* Albany: State University of New York Press.

Hughes, F. P. (1995). *Children, play and development* (2nd ed.). Boston: Allyn and Bacon.

Jones, E., & Reynolds, G. (1992). *The play's the thing: Teachers' roles in children's play.* New York: Teachers College Press.

Kirk, S. A., & Kutchins, H. (1992). *The selling of DSM: The rhetoric of science in psychiatry.* New York: Aldine DeGruyter.

Linder, T. W. (1993). *Transdisciplinary play-based intervention.* Baltimore: Brookes.

Luske, B. (1990). *Mirrors of madness: Patrolling the psychic borders.* New York: Aldine DeGruyter.

Mallory, B. L., & New, R. S. (Eds.). (1994). *Diversity and developmentally appropriate practice.* New York: Teachers College Press.

Mindes, G. (1982). Social and cognitive aspects of play in young handicapped children. *Topics of Early Childhood Special Education, 2,* 14.

Mindes, G., Ireton, H., & Mardell-Czudnowski, C. (1995). *Assessing young children.* Albany, NY: Delmar.

Rubin, K. H., Fein, G. G., & Vandenberg, B. (1983). Play. In P. H. Mussen (Ed.), *Handbook of child psychology* (4th ed., pp. 693–744). New York: John Wiley.

Suchar, C. S. (1978). *Social deviance: Perspectives and prospects.* New York: Holt.

Zirpoli, T. J. (1995). *Understanding and affecting the behavior of young children.* Englewood Cliffs, NJ: Merrill.

Physical and Social Contexts of Play

Introduction

Because play has a quality of extreme sensitivity to environmental factors, any analysis of play quality must consider the physical and social contexts in which play occurs. The physical factors in the environment include the materials and equipment available, the spatial arrangement and dimensions, the organization of time, and the presence of a range of sensory experiences such as texture, color, and sound. The broader ecological environment, such as an urban or rural community or the presence of natural or artificial features, also influence the quality of play. The social environment consists of child-adult and child-peer interactions within the contexts of family, school, community, religious, and other settings. It also includes influences from media, from ethnic and cultural messages, and from the values promoted by all of the social, economic, and political forces in the broader society.

Children are likely to play in any environment, whether or not it is physically safe or culturally circumscribed. The nature of their play, however, will be different if the environment lacks play materials or is emotionally risky. If adults want to facilitate play, they can be models of playfulness and provide interesting and challenging spaces for play. Many environments are conducive to high-quality play because they are designed especially to enhance play development. Natural environments also provide many opportunities for play if children can be safe. Traumatic environments, however, may prevent play or cause it to be minimal or distorted. Without question, play helps children to engage in the outside worlds of people and resources. These interactions have a profound impact on their capacity to cope with challenges and problems as well as successes that occur within or beyond play events.

The physical settings the essayists discuss in this section include play locations found by children in cities; outdoor play in unplanned, natural settings; and park and playground play specifically designed for children. Other authors discuss play at school and in the potentially traumatic setting of hospitals and clinics. In regard to social contexts, the essayists examine the influences of adults on the play of children in both early and middle childhood. These adult-child interactions can occur with parents, grandparents, and other family members, as well as with caregivers and teachers. Important social play interactions also occur with siblings and peers. The distinctive confluence of who plays, where and when they play, how they play, and their motives for play contributes in complex ways to the children's experiences.

Physical Settings for Play

City Play

Amanda Dargan
Steve Zeitlin

When John Jacob Raskob and his partners transformed the New York skyline by erecting the Empire State Building, they probably never considered that beneath the tower's express elevators the old Sunfish Creek had once formed a natural swimming hole; nor did they imagine that across the East River in Queens, children would use the switching on of the building's lights to tell the time for coming in from play. Indeed, the architects of cities in the United States did not design stoops for ball games or sidewalks for jumping rope, and no one considered the hazard to kites when they put up telephone wires. As a result of countless design decisions like these, however, a young person's experience of New York gradually changed as streets were paved, buildings grew upward, cars pushed children from the streets, row houses filled once vacant lots, and the increasing density led to rooftop games and cellar clubs.

It is possible to understand an urban setting, such as New York City, by exploring the traditional activities that give it meaning. The tradition of childhood play can imbue harsh and imposing city objects, often made of metal and concrete, with human values, associations, and memories. Play is one of the ways in which children develop a sense of neighborhood in a large city. Play is one of the ways a city street can become "our block."

Barging out of doors with play on their minds, city children confront stoops, hydrants, telephone poles, lampposts, automobiles, brick walls, concrete sidewalks, and asphalt streets. Children leaping from the doorways as He-Man and Sheera, Captain Blood, Superman, or the Knights of the Round Table have at their disposal an array of swords and shields that, to the uninitiated, more closely resemble dented garbage can lids and discarded umbrellas. For the would-be circus performer or ballet dancer, the stoop provides the perfect stage. Those with ball in hand have sewer covers, automobiles, hydrants, and lampposts to define a playing field. Jumping off ledges, using discarded mattresses and box springs as trampolines, or riding bikes up ramps made from scrap wood, children enjoy the dizzying thrills of vertigo. Each element of play—vertigo, mimicry, chance, physical skill, and strategy—has its own city settings and variants (see Callois, 1961; Roberts, Arth, & Busch, 1959).

Play as Transformation

In the crowded, paved-over city, urban dwellers joyfully locate play by incorporating features of the urban landscape into their games. They transform the detritus of urban life into homemade playthings and costumes, and they exert control over their environment by creating and passionately defending private spaces.

The rules of playful transformation, a focused interaction, tell players how the real world will be modified inside the encounter (Goffman, 1961). With the outside world held at bay, players create a new world within. A kind of "membrane" forms around them (Goffman, 1961). They often experience a sense of intimacy, the closeness of sharing a world apart.

Certain kinds of action outside the games, such as an ambulance going by or a building manager yelling out the window, can cause the play scene to "flood out," bursting the membrane (Goffman, 1961). Playing fields exist in such identifiable forms as diamonds, gridirons, courts, and playgrounds, but a playing field can, in fact, be anywhere. It is more akin to an energy field that repels forces outside its domain of interest and envelops the players with a force as powerful as their concentration.

Within play worlds, time has its own measures: "We played until it was too dark to see," many people have recalled. Children play while the last reflection of twilight in the sky still dimly silhouettes a flying ball; they will play while hunger is still possible to ignore. "The heat of the day, the chill of rain, even the pangs of hunger are not sufficient to intrude on the absorption of a child at play" (Biber, n.d., p. 1). Play time often goes by in a split second, metered by the turning of a rope or the rhythm of a rhyme: "Doctor, doctor will I die?/ Yes, my child, and so will I/ How many moments will I live?/ One, two, three, four . . . "

In play, the players themselves define rules and boundaries, such as "This is first base," and so it is. This sidewalk square is jail, this broken antenna is a ray gun, and, through the magic of play, they are. Transformation is the process of recasting the rules, the boundaries, the images, and the characters of the real world within the boundaries of play. Taking a space or an object and devising a new use for it, thereby making it one's own, is at the heart of play.

As they transform the city for play, children manifest a remarkable imagination. A playful order prevails. Hydrants, curbs, and cornices of the city become a game board. The castoffs of city living, such as bottlecaps, broomsticks, and tin cans, become playing pieces. Growing up in an East Harlem tenement, one New Yorker recalls: "The older kids taught the younger ones the arts and crafts of the street. . . . [A]shcan covers were converted into Roman shields, oatmeal boxes into telephones, combs covered with tissue paper into kazoos . . . a chicken gullet into Robin Hood's horn, candlesticks into trumpets, orange crates into store counters, peanuts into earrings, hatboxes into drums, clothespins into pistols, and lumps of sugar into dice" (Levenson, 1967, p. 83).

Street toys are not found objects; children need to *search* for them. A great deal of effort often goes into locating and shaping precisely the right object for play. In Bedford-Stuyvesant, for instance, children filed down a Moosehead Ale bottleneck on the curb to produce a glass ring smooth enough to slide along concrete and serve as a prized cap for the sidewalk game of skelly. In Astoria, the best skelly pieces were the plastic caps from the feet of school desks.

Neighborhoods provide different raw materials. In Chinatown, parents who work in the garment industry provide sought-after items: jacks are often made from buttons, each "button jack" consisting of a set of five or six buttons sewn together. Children use rubberbands hooked together to create a "Chinese jump rope." The elastic is stretched between the feet of two girls while a third does cat's-cradle-like stunts with her legs. Sometimes, the ropes are fashioned from white elastic bands parents bring home from the factories.

"Play is an arena of choice in many contexts where life options are limited" (Kirshenblatt-Gimblett, 1989). In a crowded city with its contested arenas, the freedom to play is hardly regarded as a basic human right. In some parts of the city where space is uncontested, a child can mark the boundaries of a play space with a piece of chalk, and nothing more is needed; children can "frame" their play space with boundaries based on mutual agreement. More often, however, the task of establishing play spaces takes on a different character as young and old battle for autonomy and control. Perhaps the toughness sometimes perceived in city children comes from the human battles they fight to earn and maintain the right to playfully and autonomously transform some space in the city. Through it all, children strive to gain control over their play worlds (see Dargan & Zeitlin, 1990). As Alissa Duffy (personal communication, 1985) chanted as she and a friend jumped up and down on a discarded refrigerator box, "We're just kids! I am five and he is three and we rule everything!"

Folklore Study of Childhood Play

The scholarly interest in children's folklore in the United States dates from the work of William Wells Newell (1883/1963), who helped found the American Folklore Society in 1988. Like many of the scholars who documented children's games after him, Newell was primarily interested in traditional games and rhymes that had survived across generations of children. Collecting from both adults and children in Boston, New York, and Philadelphia, Newell believed that "quaint" rhymes of children were "survivals" and "relics" of ancient songs and poetry.

Contemporary folklorists believe that children's rhymes and games are interesting because of the way they comment on the present rather than the past. Nonetheless, through a century of collecting, scholars have emphasized traditional rhymes and games, transmitted through the generations in fixed phrases. The rhymes and games gathered in these works echo one another, and their texts affirm a conservative side of children, who pass on rhymes with small variations from one generation to the next. In New York some of the rhymes have a distinctive urban flavor:

> I won't go to Macy's any more, more,
>   more,
> There's a big fat policeman at the door,
>   door, door.
> He'll grab you by the collar and make
>   you pay a dollar.
> I won't go to Macy's any more, more,
>   more.[1]

> I should worry, I should care,
> I should marry a millionaire.
> He should die, I should cry,
> I should marry another guy.
>   (L. Senhouse, personal
>   communication, 1987)

> Flat to rent, inquire within,
> A lady got put out for drinking gin,
> If she promises to drink no more
> Here's the key to the front door.
>   (M. Brirenfeld, personal
>   communication, 1986)

Changes in Urban Play

In the 1930s and 1940s, Oscar and Ethel Hale compiled a single-spaced, thousand-page manuscript titled, *From Sidewalk, Gutter, and Stoop,* about traditional games on the streets of New York. They documented hundreds of different games and hundreds of variations of each of those games. They include not only double Dutch, but also double Irish, double dodge, French fried, French Dutch, and double Jewish (Hale & Hale, 1938, p. 77).

Half a century later, researchers did not find anywhere near the number or variety of games played out of doors (Dargan & Zeitlin, 1990). In the 1980s, far fewer blocks preserved that confluence of lifestyle and urban geography that sustains the traditional games and outdoor play. The photographs of Martha Cooper taken on the Lower East Side in the 1970s reveal a life very different from the Leipzig photographs

from the 1940s, where Red Rover, ring-a-leavio, and Johnny-on-the-pony were played by large groups of children on the sidewalks and street. Her photographs do not document large groups of children choosing up sides and organizing traditional games. Instead, her pictures have one, two, and sometimes three children on their own in empty lots or on broken sidewalks (see Dargan & Zeitlin, 1990).

In the poorer neighborhoods Cooper visited in Harlem and the Lower East Side, children continue to play outdoors and creatively manipulate their environment. In these neighborhoods, interiors are smaller, less comfortable, and often unairconditioned; the street offers open space and fresh air. There is also the concentration of children necessary for group activities. In some neighborhoods, such as Bedford-Stuyvesant's Marcy projects, half a dozen ropes still turn on a hot day. Groups of five or six girls perform cheers, a chanted dance ensemble piece with hand clapping and improvised (often sexual) verses. Groups of girls rehearse in private so that rival groups will not "steal" their cheers, and sometimes they try out their chants on the roaring subways where they can sing at the top of their lungs and hardly disturb their fellow riders.

The changes in city play over the past one hundred years are tied to the changes in city life over the past few generations. In his book, *A History of Children's Play,* Brian Sutton-Smith (1981) offers an extraordinary analysis of some of the complex changes affecting play. Partly because of what he regards as his own optimistic outlook, this New Zealand–born scholar sees many of the changes in play for the better. He suggests that the contemporary forms of play with electronic toys and television are less physically violent than the earlier outdoor games; although the fantasies on television and in video games are all about war, children are not actually bullying each other, as they do on the playground.

These electronic diversions and creative playthings, he suggests, also provide the kind of training that children need today for the world they will inherit. The manual world of the nineteenth century has been replaced by a world of signs and symbols, in which information systems, particularly television, play a major role. "It is necessary," Sutton-Smith (1981) writes, "to produce generations of children who can be innovative, not in killing birds with catapults but in ideas for use in mass media, advertising, selling, bureaucratizing, computing, education and so on" (p. 288).

Today, when children gather after school and face the recurrent question of what to do, street games are only one possibility that must compete with a range of organized sports and commercial amusements as well as television and radio.

> When life is full of . . . an ever-changing round of "fads and fancies," ranging from a new record album which one "simply must have," to the reincarnation of Batman at the local movie theater . . . unrewarded perseverance at the old traditional games may seem pointless. . . . Sports and modern entertainment bring in their train adult interest and encouragement. Traditional games whose only incentive is the enjoyment of playing them cannot compete with these influences. That any such games still persist is testament to the intrinsic importance and meaningfulness of those games to the players. (Sutton-Smith, 1981, p. 249)

Many of the new games that have flourished on the streets of New York bear this out; some, like double Dutch, thrive partly in competitive, adult-run forums such as the annual double Dutch competition at Lincoln Center; even the ghetto-fostered style of gymnastics performed on discarded mattresses and box springs has become a formal adult-sponsored performance with groups such as the Flip Boys. Other activities, deliberately antagonistic to public, polite adult society, thrive on the streets, but have as their purpose engaging the interest and attention, and sometimes the rage, of the adult world. Graffiti, which may appear to be a kind of random vandalism to the uninitiated, is, from the perspective of the graffiti writers, a game played for the "fame" that comes from having one's code name read all over the city by one's peers. Breakdancing, while it has some roots in mock fighting, is largely a performance, played for recognition, for prizes, for prestige, for the money that can come from street performance, and for a ticket out of the ghetto; it is a long way from marbles or skelly played to wile away an afternoon. Similarly, rapping, a street tradition of competitive verbal artistry fostered originally at block and playground parties in black neighborhoods, is now intimately tied to the recording industry that promotes and markets the music.

To a certain extent, Sutton-Smith is correct in his optimism. Children's games and toys, though store-bought, are often creative, and they are well suited to the current time; the same is true of many television programs. However, although bought toys, television, and video games may encourage certain kinds of individual play, they do not create communities. They are placeless; the world they create is on the screen, in the mind, and not on the block. With television, people do not necessarily live where they are (M. Hufford, personal communication, 1988).

The media cannot replace the real experiences of growing up and getting to know a city street; they cannot create a sense of place. In the television-soaked contemporary United States, young people become frustrated with communities and relationships that have none of the glamour of the world depicted on television; advertisements remind them constantly of what they do not have. Ironically, the fear of crime keeps many city residents locked in their apartments, allowing in nothing except television. Thus, local communities become devalued while the constant barrage of the media emphasizes success stories and celebrities.

Children whose lives really turn on the city block draw the most minute distinction in their environment; Hamilton Fish Armstrong (1963) writes about roller skating down his Sixth Avenue block and knowing who lived in each house without looking up; he could tell by the particular buzz created by the pavement on his feet. Other children distinguished between "kite hill" and "vulture's hill" and "dead man's curve," and knew such exotic places as the Casbah, which was a nickname for the railing (the "caz-bar") leading up to the entrance of P.S. 1 in Long Island City, Queens (Armstrong, 1963, p. 76). The block was a place to be from.

The children who play on the streets of New York not only play together, they often see each other every day in many contexts. They learn how to share spaces together and build relationships and bonds in their neighborhood. Their communities do not revolve around a single interest, such as Little League or bingo. When social interaction moves beyond a single interest, and people become involved in a multiplicity of ways, communities are born; relationships move beyond a simple use and exchange and take on new meaning. As one New York taxi driver put it, a real neighborhood is where the butcher comes to your funeral.

Both adults and children are involved on a day-to-day basis on a patch of urban turf that they come to think of as their own. While there may be an invisible membrane that forms around players intent upon their game (Goffman, 1961), there is another kind of membrane that pulls across the block, that contains the varied groups of children of different ages at their play. It is a membrane created by the adults, a safety net, a web of sociability and unobtrusive vigilance that enables children to create secret societies and play worlds that swell and burst out of harm's way.

The true measure of any city is the degree to which it can nurture and protect this core activity of play. "We must make the streets of our city safe for children because streets that are safe for children are [also] safe for adults" (Edelman, 1987). The quality of playfulness must be cared for, protected, and nurtured. Children and adults need both physical and emotional space to play, to develop their own indigenous arrangements and solutions, and to give their imagination free rein. Sutton-Smith (1981) comments on the "right of free play": "the present record of children's play makes the point that children no less than adults live in order to live vividly, and that their play—and I would add their art—is at the center of such vividness. It seems absurd to me to contrive any future playground or any school or any society in which the pursuit of such vividness is not a major focus of that construction" (p. 297).

Improvisation and Play

Although scholars and laypeople have a long-standing interest in the conservatism of traditional rhymes and games, improvisation has always played a major role in children's play. There is an "apparently paradoxical co-existence of rules and innovation within play" (Hawes, 1974, p. 13). One observer reported that a children's game whose object was to step on all the sidewalk cracks was an exact inversion of another popular neighborhood game, "Step on a crack, break your mother's back" (Hawes, 1974, p. 16). She suggests that "only these cultural items which are susceptible to variation have much chance of survival" (p. 16). Although scholars have noted the improvisatory quality in children's lore, this kind of play has rarely been thoroughly documented, nor

has it received the kind of attention paid to traditional children's games.

The research of this essay's authors (Dargan & Zeitlin, 1990) emphasizes the improvisatory side of children's lore; children may be jumping to the same rhymes and playing the same games, but they are improvising with the materials, negotiating the rules, and imaginatively fitting them into various city spaces. After all, before they can play a game, the players must agree upon the rules; in the city, deciding just how an abstract set of regulations will play in this space at this moment is as important as the game itself. Traditional games and rhymes are testaments to the conservatism of children; but the ways in which they actually play the games at any given moment, the ways they adapt the games to particular urban settings, and the ways they improvise upon them reveals a creativity that is no less important to the legacy. In a similar vein,

> Play as a medium of adventure infuses all aspects of city life. . . . As "poets of their own acts," players in the city occupy space temporarily; they seize the moment to play as the opportunity arises, inserting the game into the interstices of the city's grid and schedule. . . . While lacking the kinds of institutions and spaces controlled by the powers that be, players transform the mundane into an adventure by means of a rope, a ball, a dance or a haircut in spaces occupied for the moment. Those adventures lead in many directions. (Kirshenblatt-Gimblett, 1990, p. 194)

The memories of many New Yorkers and other city dwellers, taken together, present a case for the role of play in building multifaceted communities rooted in place; street games contributed to a neighborhood life that made growing up and living in the city memorable. It is probably not possible or relevant to reintroduce games from past times. At the same time, it is probably not productive to simply curse the modern world and paint television and organized games and sports as ogres that would eat children. It may be possible, however, to prevent these forms from becoming the predominant influence on young people. Ultimately, it makes sense to find ways to learn from the indigenous adaptations and transformations of children and adults at play; teachers must learn to encourage free play on school playgrounds; urban planners must learn to build cities that children and adults can use for both work and leisure; and parents must understand the importance of safe havens for play. The current context demands the conscious efforts of individuals, as members of communities, neighborhoods, cities, and nations, to understand what was and is meaningful about their communities, and what about them they can conserve in a changing world.

Note

1. This traditional rhyme is still remembered by many New Yorkers who grew up in the city in the 1930s and 1940s.

Bibliography

Armstrong, H. F. (1963). *Those days*. New York: Harper & Row.

Biber, B. (n.d.). *What play means to your child*. Unpublished manuscript.

Callois, R. (1961). *Man, play and games*. New York: Free Press.

Dargan, A., & Zeitlin, S. (1990). *City play*. New Brunswick, NJ: Rutgers University Press.

Edelman, M. W. (1987). Sermon at the Unitarian Church of all Souls, Manhattan, New York. Unpublished talk.

Goffman, E. (1961). Fun in games: Two studies in the sociology of interaction. In E. Goffman (Ed.), *Encounters* (pp. 15–81). Indianapolis: Bobbs-Merrill.

Hale, E., & Hale, O. (1938). *From sidewalk, gutter and stoop: Being a chronicle of children's play and game activity*. New York Public Library: Unpublished manuscript, 2 packages.

Hawes, B. L. (1974). Law and order on the playground. In L. M. Shears & E. M. Bower (Eds.), *Games in education and development* (pp. 12–22). Springfield, IL: Charles M. Thomas.

Kirshenblatt-Gimblett, B. (1989). *Urban play*. Unpublished manuscript.

Kirshenblatt-Gimblett, B. (1990). Afterword: Other places, other times. In A. Dargan & S. Zeitlin, *City play* (pp. 175–194). New Brunswick, NJ: Rutgers University Press.

Levenson, S. (1967). *Everything but money*. New York: Pocket.

Newell, W. W. (1963). *Games and songs of American children*. New York: Dover. (Original work published 1883)

Roberts, J. M., Arth, M. J., & Busch, R. R. (1959). Games in culture. *American Anthropologist, 61*, 597–605.

Sutton-Smith, B. (1981). *A history of children's play: The New Zealand playground, 1840–1950*. Philadelphia: University of Pennsylvania Press.

Children's Outdoor Play

An Endangered Activity

Mary S. Rivkin

Think for a moment of your favorite places to play when you were a child. Chances are, one of them was outside. If you went there today, would the place be the same or would it have been altered so that no child could play there?

Throughout the industrialized world, circumstances have combined in this century to deprive children of safe, accessible, outdoor play spaces. No one planned that this should happen, yet from this end-of-century perspective, it clearly has. Two major phenomena have occurred: loss of habitat for children's play and loss of access to those habitats that do exist.

Loss of Habitat

Although the extent of natural habitat for outdoor activity varies in different regions of the United States and throughout the world, overall there has been a strong trend toward loss of such habitat during the past fifty years. The loss of habitat has three main causes: the dominance of automotive vehicles; the growth in population; and pollution.

Automobiles and Roads

The dominance of the automobile is a major contributor to loss of habitat. Industrialization has increased the dependence of the economy on roads connecting all parts of the landscape, which is unfavorable for children's access to the outdoors. Roads crisscross the landscape, creating barriers to the free ranging of small, slow, vulnerable creatures such as children. In England, special tunnels are built under roads for toads so they may have access to their usual habitats. In the United States, a few communi-

ties have tunnels under roads for pedestrians, including children, but by and large, children's movements are heavily restricted by the presence of roads.

What is wrong with roads? While concrete and asphalt roads provide children with areas for certain kinds of play such as stickball, bicycling, and hopscotch, they also prevent the kind of play that needs space for playhouses, hiding places, and nature-based activities, such as climbing trees and playing in streams. The building of roads eliminates natural, playworthy features of the landscape.

The most deadly aspect of roads, however, is the presence of cars and other motorized vehicles, which overpower and endanger children. When vehicles are moving, they can injure or kill children; when they are parked along a street, they block a child's view of danger and conceal children from motorists. One is hard-pressed to imagine an invention more unfriendly toward the development of children. While the very young, "knee" and "yard" children, need constant adult supervision, "neighborhood" children (Whiting & Edwards, 1988) ought to be out and about exploring their neighborhood and mentally mapping their home terrain (Moore, 1990). Cars severely inhibit the completion of this developmental task.

Population Increase

More people means less land for children to play on. Land has been turned into roads, houses, parking lots, shopping centers, and other buildings. Vacant lots have been built on or fenced off; streams have been channeled into culverts and vanish from view. In the United States, aided and abetted by a tax code that encourages single-family dwellings, suburban sprawl has minced and privatized the land, restricting and isolating children from access to communal outdoor play spaces. In the world as a whole, population growth has resulted in the transformation of natural land areas into housing and other facilities to support the increased population.

Pollution

Aside from population growth and heedless land use, enormous damage has been done to the landscape by resource depletion and inadequate waste management, further reducing children's access to good outdoor play. Streams and rivers are dirty, the air causes breathing problems, and the ozone layer, thinned in part by modern effluents, no longer protects people from ultraviolet rays. In Australia, children routinely wear hats and sunscreen when they go outside to play. Soon sunscreen will be as common in U.S. preschools as milk and juice, and all children will have to use it.

Children from low-income households suffer environmental neglect disproportionately. A recent study by the United Church of Christ indicated that three of five African American and Hispanic American children in the United States live in communities with toxic-waste sites. Furthermore, lead poisoning is endemic in many communities: 55 percent of African American children from low-income households have toxic blood-lead levels (Commission for Racial Justice, 1987). Lead from car exhaust, paint, and manufacturing lingers in the soil of long-populated cities, never chemically decaying, always poisonous to children playing in the dirt. One of the consequences when cities repair their old bridges, tunnels, and elevated roadways is the release of even more lead into the environment; land near bridges being repainted is particularly hazardous (Levy, 1993).

Reduced Access to Habitat

Children have lost access to outdoor play in their neighborhoods even when habitats for play, such as parks or open, connecting yards unthreatened by busy streets, do exist. Five interrelated factors are at work here: the institutionalization of children, an economy requiring most adults to work away from home, an increase in negative social conditions, communi-

cations technologies, and, particularly in the United States, a litigiousness that sees children as liabilities to be guarded against.

Institutionalization of Children

As schooling became compulsory for all children over the past century, children gained access to a wider world of knowledge but lost access to their immediate neighborhoods. The institutionalization of children—in child care, schools, sports, lessons, and camps—has reduced their time to play outside. Furthermore, simply getting to these various institutions has further restricted children's independent mobility. A recent study in Great Britain showed that, while in 1971 80 percent of seven- and eight-year-olds walked or biked to school, in 1990 less than 9 percent got themselves to school (Hillman, Adams, & Whitelegg, 1990). Children go from building to building confined in vehicles, and are usually kept almost motionless by mandatory seatbelts, which while necessary, reduce independent mobility.

Homes without Adults Present

Institutionalization has been partly a result of another late-century phenomenon of parents, especially mothers, working away from home. This phenomenon has other consequences for children's outdoor play; for example, because parents are not in the neighborhood to supervise or rescue, many children are not allowed out of doors after coming home from school. In addition, many neighborhoods are perceived as dangerous. Indeed, as contemporary chroniclers (e.g., Kozol, 1995) and the urban daily newspapers attest, inner-city neighborhoods, in particular, often *are* dangerous. A child advocate has stated, "At least 13 children die daily from guns, and at least 30 others are injured every day" (Edelman, 1994, p. 21). The gun epidemic is ten times worse than the polio epidemic at its height (Christoffel, 1995). Many children believe they will not grow up; many even plan their own funerals.

Negative Social Conditions

Even designated public play spaces such as parks are, with justification, perceived as unsafe for play. Drug trafficking, vagrancy, and homelessness, combined with shrunken budgets for upkeep and supervision, contribute to a climate of danger for children, as well as adults. An inducement to inhabitants of some New York City apartments, in fact, is the presence of indoor playrooms for their children, so that families can avoid the problems of outdoor parks. Fear of crime and lack of "neighborly" involvement of other adults in children's activities also add to concerns about giving children free rein in outdoor environments.

Communication Technologies

Television, computers, and, to a lesser extent, electronic games have also eroded the traditional lure of the outdoors for children. Numerous commentators have attested to the deleterious effect of much of television on children. Contemporary parents in the United States "speak often, and sometimes defensively, of this strange divorce between children and the outdoors" (Louv, 1990, p. 176): "It's all this watching. We've become a more sedentary society as a whole. VCRs, videos—all these machines the kids sit and watch. When I was a kid growing up in Detroit, we were always outdoors. The kids indoors were the odd ones. We didn't have any wide open spaces, but we were outdoors on the streets, in the vacant lots, playing baseball, hopscotch. We were out there playing, even after we got older" (p. 176). There is an apt adjective for such consequences of television and related technologies: *iatrogenic,* unintended but nonetheless bad.

Legal Suits

Finally, the fear of and fondness for lawsuits, along with a desire for privacy, has caused many landowners in the United States to fence property or otherwise restrict children from access to "attractive nuisances" such as ponds, highly educative though they are. Fear of lawsuits has also led parks and schools to remove equipment that might cause injury. Although a wholesome degree of risk-taking is desirable for children, the line between risk and hazard is not always clear and depends on a particular child's age and ability. A flowing stream that could safely delight an eight-year-old is of course extremely hazardous to an unsupervised toddler. The usual response is to cover the stream and channel its flow underground. Trees that children might have climbed are removed as hazardous and replaced with climbing equipment. Too often, however, the resilient surfaces that would

cushion falls are not installed, or if installed are not well maintained; then using the equipment becomes dangerous, so the equipment is removed. At the present time, New York City is completing the removal of all its metal pipe jungle gyms, due to perceived hazards (Martin, 1996).

The Importance of Outdoor Play

Arguments for the importance of outdoor play come from the perspectives of evolution, of human knowledge, of human development, and of cultural transmission.

Children—An Endangered Species?

An axiom of environmental science is that the main cause of species extinction is habitat loss. Human beings may as well consider themselves a species no less on the defensive than the spotted owl or snail darter and regard anxiously the decline of their habitat, particularly for their young. As Darwin observed, humans are an undomesticated species, accustomed to roam at will wherever they consider "home." The human species evolved in the outdoors; senses developed in daylight and moonlight, not electric light; body rhythms are like those of other animals, dependent on light and temperature and other factors only partly understood. Perhaps for fully grown humans, life without much exposure to the outdoors is acceptable, even desirable to some, but is evolution being disturbed when children grow and develop with minimal involvement in the outdoor world?

The "biophilia hypothesis," offered by sociobiologist Edwin O. Wilson, suggests "a human *need,* fired in the crucible of evolutionary development, for deep and intimate association with the natural environment, particularly its living biota," and that nature not only supplies material needs but also "aesthetic, intellectual, cognitive, and even spiritual meaning and satisfaction" (cited in Kellert, 1993, pp. 20–21). Humans and nature are linked. Technology cannot replace but only atrophy these links, creating children somehow crippled or limited (Wilson, 1993, pp. 31–32).

The Knowledge Loss

When children are not outdoors, they fail to learn about the outdoors. A recent study of families from Anglo, Native American, and Hispanic groups indicated that all children knew far less about nature than the adults, and what they did know they tended to get from television and schoolbooks rather than direct experience (Nabhan & St. Antoine, 1993). Furthermore, they didn't know the cultural meanings of the living things in their own locales, such as myths, legends, medicinal or food uses. Unfortunately, when such knowledge is embedded in nontelevision and nonschool sources and conveyed through indigenous languages, it vanishes when the speakers of these languages pass away (Nabhan & St. Antoine, 1993).

Furthermore, children learn through television and books by using only the senses of sight and hearing. Such knowledge is pallid compared to that gained through multisensory encounters. Imagine what it would be like only to see pictures of snow, never feel it melt or squeezed into a snowball, or hear its quietness, taste its delicate chill, or roll in its cold softness. Many children experience snow as a major phenomenon, but there are countless smaller phenomena unregarded and hence unknown by contemporary children.

Developmental Issues

No one knows if this generation of children who lack outdoor play will develop "normally," but there are suggestions that certain positive developmental characteristics may be related to outdoor play (Dovey, 1984; Moore, 1990). Thus, an important question is whether children's confinement to buildings and vehicles may be distorting their development.

One area of concern may be children's ability to map out their environment mentally. If children cannot physically explore, at their own pace, how can they grasp the topography of their neighborhoods and, by extension, the rest of the earth's surface? Studies of children's interpretation of space revealed how personal and idiosyncratic children's internal maps are (Hart, 1979; Moore, 1990). Humans are perhaps as territorial as any other species (consider fights over parking spaces!), but how do humans learn about the nature of territories without exploring them?

Another concern is an affliction of the late twentieth century: many children (especially boys) are being judged as too active.[1] This "epidemic" could be partly a cultural disease, evident particularly in indoor settings such as homes and schools (Angier, 1994). Outside, where there are fewer restrictions, children's movement and noise are less disruptive because vigorous activity is the norm. An environmental designer concludes from her work on the relationship between space and well-being that many adults are bothered by children's movements and thus restrict them (Olds, 1980). She asserts that such restrictions "that limit opportunities for movement and active engagement contribute substantially to, if not actually cause, many so-called behavioral and learning difficulties" (p. 24).

Another developmental issue is that of satisfactory separation from family, which occurs in late adolescence. Ability to separate appropriately might be related to childhood hut building. Research in the United States, England, and the West Indies indicates that fort or hut building is a consistent behavior of six- to eleven-year-olds (Sobel, 1993). The researcher theorizes that it occurs because children need to practice their eventual separation from family (Sobel, 1993). An account of an Australian private school that allowed hut building in a section of its play yard underscores the centrality of such constructions to children (Dovey, 1984). While children usually favor natural areas, recent evidence from observation of their behavior in cities indicates that children, like nesting birds, seek shelter spots everywhere imaginable (Dargan & Zeitlin, 1990). They need time, space, and materials, however, for their constructions.

Finally, there is the question of how children acquire a sense of stewardship for the land if they do not have direct experience with the land as they are growing up. Although it is not well understood how children acquire environmental values (Moore, 1990), interviews with environmental activists in Norway and the United States revealed that these persons ascribed their activism to childhood experiences in natural areas and to the examples of family members (Chawla, 1995). The researcher states, "the two most salient influences, in terms of mention rate, were rooted in childhood" (p. 4). In another study, of eight hundred eight- to ten-year-olds in Great Britain, experience with vegetation (including playing, eating, mowing the lawn, gardening, hiking, camping, and being allergic to it) was positively correlated with intellectual and aesthetic appreciation of the natural environment (Harvey, 1989). In arguing for children's "need of wild places," one author asserts, "We need to return to learning about the land by being *on* the land, or better, being *in* the thick of it. That is the best way we can stay in touch with the fates of its creatures, its indigenous cultures, its earthbound wisdom. That is the best way we can be in touch with ourselves" (Nabhan, 1994, p. 107).

Knowledge of the natural world can lead to both environmental activism and knowledge of oneself as a part of nature. Thus, a major question is: How can we get children back "in the thick of it"?

Restoring Children's Habitat

A hundred years ago, children made up a third of the population in the United States. They were highly visible. Major cities such as New York and Boston planned playgrounds and play programs. Now children are less than a fifth of the U.S. population. It is hard to argue their needs over those of adults who have cars, jobs, and commutes.

Hence, for the short term, the most practical course of action to get children "back in the thick of it" is to rebuild habitats at the one institution dedicated to children, their schools. Movements in Canada, Great Britain, and a few parts of the United States are underway. But for a more substantial restoration of habitats, agencies other than schools must contribute. Both public and governmental cooperation are needed to redirect transportation, housing, recreation, and land-use policies to provide for children's outdoor experiences. In an era of reduced faith in public policy and shrinking budgets for innovation, this is, of course, difficult. Nonetheless, there are notable efforts in such a direction.

Habitat Restoration in the Schoolyard

Most schoolyards are bleakly devoid of good play opportunities. Adults appear to value the ease of maintenance offered by asphalt and mown grass over the play value of woods, meadows, and wetlands. Playground equipment has frequently been imagined as providing primarily gross motor activity, although many newer structures do accommodate social and dramatic play as well. Too often, though, such equipment serves only a fraction of the children on a playground at a time. School recesses, for example, are typified by large num-

bers of children, a small amount of equipment, and the minimum of adult interaction of the sort that might foster good play.

A notable exception has been the Washington Environmental Yard, at a public school in Berkeley, California. In its prime years it offered children some asphalt for ball games and hopscotch, but also a wooded area with a hill, streams and ponds where there were fish to try to catch, bushes to shelter under, plants such as willow to cut and make things with, and wildflowers to pick and arrange (Moore & Wong, 1996).

A recent movement in Great Britain has succeeded in inspiring more than a third of all British elementary schools to undertake schoolyard renovation. While each school has different possibilities and needs, the basics include trees for shade, shelter, and structure, water, places to sit, native plants, and accessibility (Lucas, 1994). A key to the strength of the project has been its tight link to Britain's national curriculum, Learning Through Landscapes. A series of attractive, explicit guides to teaching content such as English, math, science (geology, entomology, beekeeping, botany), as well as videos and teacher training have assured teachers and parents that being outdoors can be highly educative, and in fact that some curriculum is best learned in a well-developed outdoor environment.[2]

One of the most child-oriented schoolyards in Britain, Coombes Infant School, began its transformation from bleakness long before the current movement. The asphalt here has been painted with math games, and there are a rowboat for dramatic play, long logs on the edge for climbing and experiencing wood's aging into decay, tunnels for hiding away, and a dense border of bushes that attracts birds and other wildlife. Beyond the border lies a broad paved path where lunches are eaten every dry day, bordered by more bushes; interspersed are four ponds of various types, with lilies, frogs, and fish. Beyond this are fruit and nut orchards and a willow maze, and wildflower borders. Every year children help decide on a new major project, and every year every child plants a tree. Children do whatever work they can, and the work that only adults can accomplish (e.g., repairing the roof) is closely observed by children. The library has books with stories, photos, and pictures documenting the events. The result is a densely alive and changing environment to which children feel a commitment. Coombes is an important example of a principal and staff persisting in steadily improving their outdoor environment in the interests of children's pleasure and learning (Humphries & Rowe, 1994).

The Evergreen Foundation in Canada has recently undertaken a School Grounds Naturalization initiative. Several hundred schools have had projects to add wildlife habitats to their grounds.[3] In the United States, several states have wildlife habitat programs, including New Hampshire, Florida, New York, and Maryland among the most developed. Interestingly, the effort in most instances originates in departments of natural resources rather than in departments of education. The concept of habitat, now familiar in our thinking about animals, is entering the environments of children if not yet the discourse on children.

Other Habitats for Consideration

The recent increase in greenways will help bring play spaces to children. Some envision connecting all schools with greenways, providing pathways for children and small animals for daily intimate use (Lusk, 1994). Efforts to "calm traffic" will also help children play safely. Reducing speeds, adding speed bumps, narrowing passages, and restricting hours all contribute to safer streets. In Northern Europe the practice of creating residential streets, called "*Woonerven* in Germany," in the place of traffic streets provides children with areas where cars are slowed to walking speed, and plantings, bollards, benches, and no curbs increases playability and livability. One study of two German streets before and after becoming *Woonerven* showed that children played more outside, interacted more with one another and with objects, rode wheel-toys more, and engaged in more fantasy play, music making, and dancing (Eubank-Ahrens, 1984–1985).

Finally, while many neighborhoods do not support children's play, some progressive communities have planned for children's needs; in the East, Columbia, Maryland, and Reston, Virginia are notable (Francis, 1984–1985). Too often, however, adults verbalize but do not actualize the resources for children's needs: one distinctive development in the mid-Atlantic region trumpets its commitment to "community" and front-porchy friendliness, but its main playground is a barren tract ringed by a four-lane road. So much for community! The message conveyed is "Stand in your tiny fenced front yard (every house has one), but do not go to play anywhere else." If children's needs are to be served, adult home buyers must insist that developers provide for children as well as adults.

Lewis Thomas (1975) wrote that if humans would regard themselves as "truly indispensable elements of nature" they would no doubt worry about themselves even more than the rest of the environment. He argued that, if humans did see themselves as part of nature, "movements might start up for the protection of ourselves as valuable, endangered species" (p. 125). Such a movement should start first for the most vulnerable ones in the human species, the children, to restore to them an ancient and indisputable part of their natural habitat, the outdoors.

Notes

1. "There is now an attempt to pathologize what was once considered the normal range of behavior of boys. . . . today Tom Sawyer and Huck Finn surely would have been diagnosed with both conduct disorder and ADHD," according to M. Konner, Emory University professor of anthropology and psychiatry (quoted in Angier, 1994).

2. For further information, contact Learning Through Landscapes, Winchester, Hants, UK.

3. For further information, contact The Evergreen Foundation, 355 Adelaide Street West, Suite 5A, Toronto, Ontario, M5V 1S3, Canada.

Bibliography

Angier, N. (1994, July 24). The debilitating malady called boyhood. *New York Times* (northeast ed.), sec. 4, 1.

Chawla, L. (1995). *Life paths into effective environmental action.* Paper presented at the annual conference of the North American Association of Environmental Education, Portland, ME.

Christoffel, K. K. (1995). Handguns and the environments of children. *Children's Environments, 12*(1), 39–48.

Commission for Racial Justice, United Church of Christ. (1987). *Toxic wastes and race in the United States: A national report on the racial and socio-economic characteristics of communities with hazardous waste sites, 14,* New York: Commission for Racial Justice.

Dargan, A., & Zeitlin, S. (1990). *City play.* New Brunswick, NJ: Rutgers University Press.

Dovey, K. (1984). The creation of a sense of place: The case of Preshil. *Places, 1*(2), 32–40.

Edelman, M. W. (1994, Autumn). Cease fire! Stopping the war against children. *Harvard Medical Alumni Bulletin, 68*(2), 18–23.

Eubank-Ahrens, B. (1984–1985, Winter). The impact of *Woonerven* on children's behavior. *Children's Environments Quarterly, 1,* 39–45.

Francis, M. (1984–1985, Winter). Children's use of open space in village homes. *Children's Environments Quarterly, 1,* 36–38.

Hart, R. (1979). *Children's experience of place.* New York: Ivington.

Harvey, M. R. (1989, Spring). Children's experiences with vegetation. *Children's Environments Quarterly, 6,* 36–43.

Hillman, M., Adams, J., & Whitelegg, J. (1990). *One false move . . . : A study of children's independent mobility.* London: Policy Studies Institute.

Humphries, S., & Rowe, S. (1994). The biggest classroom. In P. Blatchford & S. Sharp (Eds.), *Breaktime and the school: Understanding and changing playground behaviour* (pp. 107–117). London: Routledge.

Kellert, S. R. (1993). Introduction. In S. R. Kellert & E. O. Wilson (Eds.), *The biophilia hypothesis* (pp. 20–21). Washington, DC: Island Press/Shearwater.

Kozol, J. (1995). *Amazing grace: The lives of children and the conscience of a nation.* New York: Crown.

Levy, C. J. (1993, June 12). Lead levels force closing of parts of two parks. *New York Times,* pp. 23, 25.

Louv, R. (1990). *Childhood's future.* Boston: Houghton Mifflin.

Lucas, B. (1994, August). *Grounds for change: The British example.* Presentation at Out of the Classroom . . . Into the Garden: International Symposium on the Prepared Learning Environment, the Montessori Foundation and the American Horticultural Society, Arlington, VA.

Lusk, A. (1994, July). Let's build 108,000 new garden classrooms for children. *American Horticulturalist* (Proceedings from AHS National Symposium), 34–35.

Martin, D. (1996, April 11). That upside-down high will be only a memory. *New York Times* (northeast ed.), B1, 4.

Moore, R. C. (1990). *Childhood's domain.* (Reprint, Berkeley, CA: MIG Communication).

Moore, R. C., & Wong, H. (1996). *A natural way of learning: The experience of the Washington Environmental Yard.* Berkeley, CA: MIG Communication.

Nabhan, G. P. (1994). Children in touch, creatures in story. In G. P. Nabhan & S. Trimble (Coauthors), *The Geography of Childhood* (p. 107). Boston: Beacon.

Nabhan, G. P., & St. Antoine, S. (1993). The loss of floral and faunal story: The extinction of experience. In S. R. Kellert & E. O. Wilson (Eds.), *The biophilia hypothesis* (pp. 229–250). Washington, DC: Island Press/Shearwater.

Olds, A. (1980, Winter). From cartwheels to caterpillars: The child's need for motion outdoors. *Human Ecology Forum, 10,* 24.

Sobel, D. (1993). *Children's special places: Exploring the role of forts, dens, and bush houses in middle childhood.* Tucson, AZ: Zephyr.

Thomas, L. (1975). *Lives of a cell.* New York: Bantam.

Whiting, B. B., & Edwards, C. P. (1988). *Children of different worlds.* Cambridge, MA: Harvard University Press.

Wilson, E. O. (1993). Biophilia and the conservation ethic. In S. R. Kellert & E. O. Wilson (Eds.), *The biophilia hypothesis* (pp. 31–32). Washington, DC: Island Press/Shearwater.

Perspectives on Play in Playgrounds

Joe L. Frost
Irma C. Woods

Organized playgrounds for older children in the United States originated with the outdoor gymnasiums of Massachusetts in 1821 and with the sand gardens of Boston for younger children in 1887. Thereafter, public school and public park playgrounds followed a physical fitness and recreation tradition while preschool playgrounds followed a developmental emphasis. During the twentieth century, playgrounds evolved from a traditional pattern of standard equipment, such as merry-go-rounds, seesaws, swings, and jungle gyms, spaced around open fields, to novelty, adventure, designer, creative, and vest-pocket types. Reflecting concerns for child safety, indoor pay-for-play entertainment centers have now begun to supplement or replace outdoor play environments, raising concerns about opportunities for child development through creative play. Issues in playground design and use include safety, developmental appropriateness, provisions for inclusiveness, play leadership, and accessibility. The best playgrounds are never finished but evolve to meet children's changing needs.

Playgrounds for children in a wide variety of settings are a common sight in the United States. They are found in community parks, child care facilities, hotels, hospitals, fast food restaurants, elementary schools and, of course, backyards. Regardless of the setting, playgrounds are designed to support play and development. The discussion that follows begins with historical perspectives on the development of playgrounds in the United States, describes the existing types of playgrounds, considers issues in playground design, and concludes with perspectives on the future of playgrounds.

History of Playgrounds

The gymnasiums founded in Massachusetts in the 1820s were the forerunners of the playground movement. Based on the physical fitness philosophy of Friedrich Jahn from Germany, the first private gymnasium was founded in 1821 at the Latin School in Salem, Massachusetts (Mero, 1908). The focus of the gymnasiums was not on play or group games, but on individual exercise to keep the body fit and to promote "moral purity" (Cavallo, 1981, p. 19). Following the establishment of the first public gymnasium in the United States in 1826, interest in gymnasiums waned, and the next fifty years was a dormant period in the playground movement.

In the 1880s, a political leader, Von Schenckendorff, developed play areas in Berlin that consisted of piles of sand bordered by wooden squares called sand gardens (Sapora & Mitchell, 1948). During a visit to Berlin, Dr. Marie Zakrzewska from the United States observed the sand gardens and proposed that they be established in Boston to alleviate the slum conditions for children of the poor (Cavallo, 1981; Mero, 1908). Boston city officials responded and constructed ten sand gardens in the city's poorest districts in 1887. Trained kindergarten teachers provided supervision (Cavallo, 1981; Mero, 1908). Thus began the first supervised playgrounds in the United States for young children and the true beginning of the playground movement.

During the late 1800s, vacation schools, housed in public school buildings, led to summer school playgrounds and to year-round play modeled after the school playgrounds of Gary, Indiana (Cavallo, 1981; Frost, 1992a). The principal aim of these early playgrounds was to "overcome lawless tendencies acquired in the street and crowded tenement life" (Mero, 1908, p. 122). Playgrounds were also established to serve as agents of Americanization for the large number of immigrants, especially in the industrial Northeast and in Chicago (Cavallo, 1981).

By 1905 the playground movement began to lose support. Communities used their limited resources for other urban reforms. The lack of a well-defined theory of play on the value of playgrounds for the growth and development of children led to the establishment of the Playground Association of America (PAA) in 1906 (Cavallo, 1981). The work of John Dewey and Friedrich Froebel convinced advocates of younger children's play that playground experiences were a means to help children develop cognitive skills, moral tendencies, and social values (Cavallo, 1981; Frost, 1992a). Many reformers, however, held to the belief that the point of organized play was to coordinate the child's psychological and physical apparatus as efficiently as possible (De Groot, 1914). The recapitulation theory of G. Stanley Hall promoted this belief by advocating that morality or strength of character was a direct result of physical fitness (Cavallo, 1981).

From 1906 to 1920 the PAA was responsible for the amazing growth of public and private playgrounds. By 1917, 481 cities operated 3,940 playgrounds and employed 8,748 directors (Cavallo, 1981). These golden years, however, were short-lived. Efforts to broaden its appeal led to changing the name of the association in 1911 to the Playground and Recreation Association of America (Cavallo, 1981; Frost, 1992a). In 1930 the name of the association was changed again to the National Recreation Association and later to the National Recreation and Park Association, which exists today. The removal of the word *playground* in essence ended the association's active advocacy for children's playgrounds and influenced the physical fitness/recreation emphasis of public school and public park playgrounds to the present time. Preschool playgrounds nevertheless evolved from a developmental emphasis dating back to Froebel and Dewey, and this tradition has remained in place.

The United States' entry into World War I saw organized play pass primarily to the public school systems because material to build equipment was no longer available. Following the war, four types of playgrounds were devel- oped: traditional, designer or contemporary, adventure, and creative (Frost, 1985). Presently, indoor and outdoor pay-for-play playgrounds and entertainment centers are rapidly emerging, supplementing or supplanting the traditional community and city public playground concept.

Playground Types

Although a number of playground types exist, the designations or terms used to categorize playgrounds are largely arbitrary. Differences in playgrounds continue to expand and change according to types and varieties of equipment and materials, natural elements, age groups served, and supplementary areas provided, such as nature areas, gardens, and other forms, as well as their ongoing modifications.

Traditional Playgrounds

Traditional playgrounds grew out of the early playground movement with its emphasis on exercise and physical fitness. The traditional playground is generally flat with fixed equipment set in concrete, asphalt, or hard, compacted dirt. Equipment on a traditional playground includes steel structures such as swing sets, slides, merry-go-rounds, seesaws, and climbers. The message of traditional playgrounds is clear: There is one way to use the equipment for the single purpose of exercise. Many playgrounds today are representative of this type, including most elementary school playgrounds. The lack of variety and challenge in such traditional playgrounds leads to boredom with the equipment and influences children to experiment (Hudson, 1989). Experimentation on traditional playgrounds by children who may lack the necessary skills and experience often leads to playground injuries (Ward, 1987).

Adventure Playgrounds

In contrast, the emphasis of the adventure playground is on construction play using a wide variety of manipulative materials. Adventure playgrounds are available to children only when play leaders are present to provide supervision (Vance, 1982). The first adventure playground was developed in 1943 by C. Th. Sorensen in Emdrup, outside Copenhagen, Denmark. "Often referred to as a junk playground, the adventure playground is a place where children of all ages, with trained play leaders, are free to do many things they can no longer do in crowded urban society: building huts, walls, forts, dens, tree houses, lighting fires and cooking . . . or doing nothing" (Michaelis, cited in Brett, Moore, & Provenzo, 1993, p. 26). "The point of Emdrup is that it was not 'provided' for children. They were allowed to make it themselves" (Lambert, 1992, p. 13). Its developer, the architect Sorensen, upon a visit to the site stated, "Of all the things I have helped to realize, the adventure playground is probably the ugliest: yet for me it is the best and most beautiful of my works" (cited in Lambert, 1992, p. 13).

Adventure playgrounds never gained much popularity in the United States, largely because of their unsightliness, concerns with safety, and lack of well-trained play leaders. Nevertheless, the Houston Adventure Play Association in Houston, Texas, currently sponsors three adventure playgrounds in the city, and California has three association branches (Shell, 1994).

Designer Playgrounds

The goal of designer playgrounds was to provide experiences not found in traditional playgrounds and to stimulate fantasy play. Professional architects, designers, sculptors, and general handymen developed designer playgrounds in the 1950s and 1960s. They used metal and concrete sculptures, timbers, ropes, and tunnels to create opportunities for children to use their imagination. Their creations frequently resembled animals, spaceships, and so forth. Consequently, they are sometimes called novelty playgrounds. Over time, manufacturers developed modular equipment and linked components to provide children with a wider variety of movement and experiences (Brett et al., 1993).

Creative Playgrounds

The term *creative playground* (Frost, 1978) was coined in response to the need to integrate elements of adventure playgrounds into contemporary settings where adults resisted efforts to develop "junk" playgrounds because of perceived safety and appearance factors. The creative playground is a semiformal environment containing commercial equipment typical of traditional playgrounds and loose materials characteristic of adventure playgrounds. The loose parts usually consist of tools, tires, cable spools, building materials, and other scrounged materials. Promoted in the late 1970s and the 1980s, creative playgrounds offer parents, teachers, children, and community leaders opportunities to work together in building a unique playground that is both aesthetically pleasing and developmentally rich.

Vest-Pocket Playgrounds

Developed in the 1970s, primarily in large urban cities, vest-pocket playgrounds utilized unused building sites in old city areas. Many functioned much like adventure playgrounds. Built on empty lots where two or three dilapidated buildings not worth saving had been removed, vest-pocket playgrounds were usually bordered by one or two buildings, thus the name (Rouard & Simon, 1977). The vest-pocket playground (Bengtsson, 1970) was short-lived and has all but disappeared in communities across the United States.

Pay-for-Play Playgrounds and Entertainment Centers

Playgrounds at fast food restaurants have expanded rapidly in recent years. They were originally miniature replicas of public playgrounds with modifications for color and appeal. Following a pattern of injuries and litigation, sponsors are replacing original equipment with "soft play" equipment, intended to be ultra safe, yet appealing for large motor activity, follow-the-leader, and chase games. Studies by operators show that these play areas quickly compensate for their cost through customer attraction. The developmental benefits for children are limited, but these play areas help to compensate for the absence of neighborhood play places.

Indoor pay-for-play centers are now expanding across the country. They respond to growing concerns about safety, violence, and deprivation of play opportunities for children (Frost & Jacobs, 1995). Parents are increasingly restricting children from playing in public playgrounds, particularly inner-city playgrounds, because of the threat of drugs, kidnapping, drive-by shootings, and violence in general. Television and video games have become the entertainment of choice and necessity, thereby restricting active, creative play and, consequently, depriving children of social, intellectual, and physical development as well as therapeutic play.

Much of the activity at pay-for-play centers, however, is not play. Junk food parties, violent video games, and games of chance in noisy, crowded clusters are essentially *entertainment,* which deprives children of time for creative play and constructive time with parents. Such activities, furthermore, appear to be guilt-reduction devices for absent fathers who assume the roles of "Disney Dads," ostensibly fulfilling their fathering responsibilities by annual trips to theme parks with their children or an occasional weekend trip to the local pay-for-play entertainment center.

Issues in Playground Design and Use

The issues in playground design and use are much more complex now than even a decade ago. The growing tendency of people in the United States to resolve their problems through lawsuits has heightened public awareness of playground injuries and safety. The growth of violence in inner cities has made many public playgrounds unsafe for children's play and has spurred the development of alternative play places. Accelerating interest in play and play environments among researchers and professionals across the behavioral sciences has heightened awareness and knowledge of the developmental benefits of play and has led to greater interest in playground design and function. The Americans with Disabilities Act of 1990 (PL 101–336) influenced, indeed required, that children's public playgrounds be accessible for all children and has stimulated intense study of appropriate means for inclusion.

Playground Safety

Beginning in the mid-1970s the U.S. Consumer Product Safety Commission (CPSC) began to consider the issue of playground safety. This concern was influenced by petitions from citizens, injury data from the newly formed National Electronic Surveillance System, and an increase in playground injury lawsuits. Following several years of study, the *Handbook for Public Playground Safety* was published by the CPSC in 1981. Further study led to the publication of a revised handbook in 1991. The American Society for Testing and Materials (ASTM) approved the *Standard Specification for Impact Attenuation of Surface Systems Under and Around Playground Equipment* in 1991. In 1993 the ASTM published the *Standard Consumer Safety Performance Specification for Playground Equipment for Public Use.* The 1991 CPSC guidelines were developed for the consumer and the manufacturer, but the more technical 1993 ASTM standards were addressed to the manufacturer. Both sets of standards are voluntary, but they are now recognized as the national standard of care and tend to prevail in litigation.

Child care center playgrounds are regulated by state departments of human services or their equivalent agencies throughout the United States. Most states, however, have very weak regulations that place child care center operators at risk in litigation. A number of professional organizations and agencies have also published weak guidelines or standards that contribute to this problem. Most state education agencies, while responsible for regulating public schools, have no regulations or guidelines for school playgrounds. None has guidelines equivalent in quality to the CPSC guidelines or the ASTM standards. In the absence of mandatory safety standards for community playgrounds, parents, teachers, and other individuals in each community need to demand safer playgrounds (Hendricks, 1993).

How serious is the playground safety issue? Two reasons for unsafe play equipment and playgrounds are lack of consumer interest and traditional equipment left unreplaced for decades (Ward, 1987). According to recent statistics, over 200,000 injuries occur on playgrounds each year (Frost, 1992b). Most injuries and some fatalities on playgrounds are the result of falls from equipment onto hard surfaces (Frost, 1990; Tinsworth & Kramer, 1990; U.S. Consumer Product Safety Commission, 1991). A fundamental tenet that is widely accepted for adults has yet to be understood or accepted for children. That is: accidents are not merely a natural consequence of growing up; accidents can be prevented.

The extent of hazards on playgrounds has been documented in five national surveys (of public schools, community parks, and preschools), three published by the American Alliance for Health, Physical Education, Recreation, and Dance (AAHPERD) (Bruya & Langendorfer, 1988; Thompson & Bowers, 1989; Wortham & Frost, 1990) and two by the Consumer Federation of America (Sikes, Fise, & Morrison, 1992; Wood, Fise, & Morrison, 1994).

The AAHPERD surveys revealed that among public school, community park, and preschool playgrounds, public schools were the most hazardous. Generally, playgrounds in all three surveys were antiquated, hazardous, and unfit for children's play. Maintenance was slipshod or nonexistent. The national survey of preschool playgrounds (Wortham & Frost, 1990) was conducted by 62 trained volunteers in 31 states and included 349 preschools. The most common equipment, in order of most to least frequency was swings, slides, balance beams, overhead ladders, rocking apparatus, tire/net climbers, firefighters' poles, trapeze bars, suspended bridges, seesaws, merry-go-rounds, geodesic domes, and monkey bars. Portable materials in order were tricycles, loose tires, sand, wagons, barrels, loose boards, water, wheelbarrows, building materials, gardening tools, art materials, and carpentry tools. The only equipment and portable materials averaging more than one item per center were swings, slides, tricycles, and loose tires. In general, the center playgrounds were very poorly equipped.

As examples of safety findings, the height of climbing equipment ranged up to twelve feet, with one-fourth over seven feet tall. Over half the climbing equipment had no approved protective surfacing, such as sand, pea gravel, mulch, or commercial matting, and most of this was not properly installed or maintained.

The AAHPERD study of community park playgrounds (Thompson & Bowers, 1989) showed that these playgrounds were in poorer condition than preschool playgrounds. Climbers, swings, and slides accounted for 63 percent of all playground equipment, and 57 percent of the playgrounds did not separate large and small equipment on the playground. Over one-fourth of the swing seats were made of metal or wood. Wallach (1989) addressed special needs: sand play areas were not common in park playgrounds, with only 15 percent of the playgrounds providing sand play areas; only 3 percent of the park playgrounds had wading pools or water play. Instructional signs, though a new concept on playgrounds, serve as reasonable or "due care," and the study shows very little use of signs at play areas.

A growing number of states have passed or are considering legislation on playground safety. They include California, Oklahoma, Arkansas, Texas, and Pennsylvania. A prevailing issue is whether mandating safety will have detrimental effects on creativity in design and use of play-ground equipment. Clearly, design of equipment is only one important factor in ensuring reasonably safe play places for children. Other important considerations are installation of equipment, maintenance and supervision of playgrounds, and the promoting of cognitive and motor skills for children who use playgrounds. Children with poorly developed perceptual-motor skills are at risk on any playground. Making children safe for playgrounds may be as important as making playgrounds safe for children (Frost & Henniger, 1979).

Developmentally Appropriate Playgrounds

The evidence that play is a primary vehicle for development, indeed that play enhances development, is now clearly documented. Extensive reviews of research show that play promotes cognitive development (discovery, verbal judgment, reasoning, memory, divergent production), language, social maturity, and motor abilities (Berk, 1994; Frost, 1992a; Rubin, Fein, & Vandenberg, 1983). In addition, play has therapeutic power, allowing children to express and explore feelings, thoughts, and experiences and, consequently, to overcome anxiety and fear (Axline, 1947; Erikson, 1950; Landreth, 1991). Time for play and rich materials for play are essential for optimal development.

The national AAHPERD studies of community parks reveal that most community park playgrounds and public school playgrounds can still be classified as traditional playgrounds. These are designed for limited functions, particularly exercise activity and organized games, while providing little or no material support for make-believe or dramatic play, construction play, play with natural elements, such as sand and water, or work-play in gardens or nature areas. Further, no distinction is made for different developmental or age groups. This requires children of all ages to adapt to standard-sized, frequently oversized, equipment, thereby reducing opportunities for creative play and increasing the likelihood of inappropriate behavior and injury.

The developmentally appropriate playground is designed to match the developmental levels of child users. Keen observers of children and consumers of research on play know that the best cues for selecting equipment and materials for play environments and for creating play zones are the play behaviors of children who use the play environment (Fantuzzo et al., 1995).

Infants and early toddlers, for example, need a wide range of sensory and exploratory opportunities. As they develop into the preschool years, they need playgrounds that provide exercise areas, such as climbers and swings; make-believe or dramatic play areas, such as wheeled vehicles, cars, boats, and play houses; and areas for constructing, stacking, and digging that include tools, dirt, water, and sand. As they approach kindergarten age, an additional element—flat, grassy areas for organized games—often is added, and equipment must be more complex and challenging. Storage facilities on the playground are required to house the 101 loose parts that support play and work-play areas, such as gardens, nature areas, orchards, and so forth.

There is a growing body of research that points to the need of children to interact with the environment in diverse and complex ways (Beckwith, 1982; Frost, 1986a, 1992b). Play environments for young children, therefore, need to contain fixed and complex equipment that offers different levels of challenges. Children need to experience raw materials found in nature, such as sand, water, rocks, and soil. Having trees, plants, gardens, and shrubs in the environment can teach children to see living things as an integral part of the environment and help them to understand how nature supports their lives (Talbot, 1985). Plants also help to create soothing experiences in playgrounds and provide a wide range of sensory experiences (Talbot & Frost, 1990). "Play environments must be powerful enough to sustain children's activity without constant motivational and/or directional assistance from non-players, especially adults" (Gehlbach, 1991, p. 138). Finally, play environments can be beautiful as well as functional.

Playgrounds for All Children: Inclusion

The Americans with Disabilities Act mandates that playgrounds be inclusive, that is, that they be accessible to all children, regardless of disability. One of the criteria for selecting playground equipment is the play value of the equipment or the degree to which the equipment matches the developmental needs of the child (Frost, 1992b). This criterion includes equipment for children with special needs. Playgrounds need to provide for mobility, accessibility, play options, proximity, sensory-rich materials, and challenges for all children (Arroyo, 1990; Esbensen, 1991; Frost, 1992a; Moore, Goltsman, & Iacofano, 1987). One of the most challenging playground design provisions is to offer accessibility to children who need wheelchairs. Three major means are now being used, including ramps for gaining access onto play equipment without leaving the wheelchair; transfer stations (special deck/handloop access) for leaving the wheelchair to gain access onto play equipment; and specially sized equipment at ground level for play without leaving the wheelchair. Manufactured surfacing materials or special wood mulch surfacing facilitates wheelchair access to equipment. Loose materials such as sand and pea gravel do not allow wheelchair movement.

Children with disabilities need to have the same opportunities as other children to interact with the environment through direct experiences with materials and equipment. Inclusive playgrounds need to provide for interactions among children of all mental and physical capabilities (Arroyo, 1990). Some of the developmental delays in visually impaired children can be attributed to lack of experience, especially in gross motor interactions with the environment (Schneekloth, 1989).

All children have an inherent right to play and to those experiences necessary for their development. Observations of children with disabilities at play indicate that most adults underestimate children's abilities to engage in ever more complex play and to learn from their play. Children with disabilities can learn and want to learn.

Play Leadership

Perspectives for the future include the training of play leaders. The best play leadership training is modeled after that of the Scandinavian adventure playground movement. With all the social issues facing the United States today, play leaders can take a very important role in supporting the play of children in playgrounds. It is not enough for play leaders to be good supervisors. Effective play leaders need to possess technical expertise and creative curiosity, knowledge of children, a sense of humor, leadership capability, and community involvement skills (Barnet, 1969; Vance, 1982). They need to know the basic principles of affirming children's play.

A long-time play leader in London described the proper role of a play leader as a person who learns from children, who listens to them, and who understands what they are saying (Lambert, 1992). The attitude must be, "Let's find out!" It is as though the play leader is discovering what it is like to be a child the second time around. One must be willing to relate to children as one would with any other person, to engage in the adventure of play, and to make available to children the materials and tools that they need. The responsibility for the playground must be a shared one, then maintenance and potential vandalism become less of a problem and more of a challenge.

Alternative Playgrounds

Threats of violence in community parks, absent or working parents, and the poor quality of many existing playgrounds are creating the need for alternative playgrounds, particularly in cities. Educators have proposed a new type of playground for the future, the safe-haven playground (Brett et al., 1993). The safe-haven playground would be supervised by a play specialist, be available year-round from early morning until dark, and provide a wide variety of activities through an informal educational process. The adventure playgrounds for the after-school play of latchkey children, sponsored by the Houston Adventure Playground Association, are yet another successful venture for children.

The children's museums now located in cities throughout the nation are shining examples of positive, wholesome approaches to alternative places for children's play and learning. They are a far cry indeed from the pay-for-play entertainment complexes at theme parks, gambling casinos, and strip shopping malls.

Play specialists have proposed the concept of a temporary playground (Brett et al., 1993; Poole & Poole, 1982). A mobile play unit would take "the playground" to the children. This concept appears ideal for taking raw materials, such as sand and water activities, to playgrounds that lack these opportunities. In England, surplus double-decker buses are used for this purpose. The London Handicapped Adventure Playground Association uses small buses to transport children from all over London to three specially designed adventure playgrounds that employ trained play leaders, provide special safety features, and offer a wealth of challenges for children with disabilities.

A play and playgrounds revolution is underway in the United States. Not since the first decade of the twentieth century has so much playground development been evident. More, and generally better, is being done in several areas: most manufacturers are designing safer and more challenging play equipment; a growing number of cities and schools are scrapping their old, antiquated equipment and developing new play environments; some are adding complementary elements of sand, water, storage, portable materials, gardens, nature areas, and separate areas for younger and older children; and most new playgrounds include some adaptations for children with disabilities.

In addition, special playgrounds are being developed at special places. Growing awareness of the therapeutic qualities of play has influenced hospitals to complement indoor play rooms with outdoor playgrounds. Research confirmation that play promotes learning and development has led to the integration of play materials and spaces at children's museums across the country. Further, commercial agencies are developing pay-for-play places at an unprecedented rate. A number of negative features of these commercial play places must be resolved, however, if they are to win the support of professionals who work closely with children.

Finally, examination of perspectives on play and playgrounds leads one to the conclusion that playgrounds should promote learning and development for all children and that good playgrounds are never finished (Frost, 1986b). Because "childhood is the great unexplored land, greater than any continent" (Larsson, 1965, p. 10) playgrounds must continue to evolve.

Bibliography
Arroyo, F. (1990). Designing play for all. *Parks and Recreation, 25*(8), 40–43.
Axline, V. (1947). *Play therapy.* Boston: Houghton-Mifflin.
Barnet, D. (1969). Staffing for socio-educative activities for children. *International Playground Association, 3*(6), 23–25.
Beckwith, J. (1982). It's time for creative play. *Parks and Recreation, 17*(9), 58–62.
Bengtsson, A. (1970). Impressions from a trip to the USA. *International Playground Association, 4*(5), 20–22.

Berk, L. E. (1994). Vygotsky's theory: The importance of make-believe play. *Young Children, 50*(1), 30–39.

Brett, A., Moore, R. C., & Provenzo, E. F. (1993). *The complete playground book.* Syracuse, NY: Syracuse University Press.

Bruya, L. D., & Langendorfer, S. J. (Eds.). (1988). *Where our children play: Elementary school playground equipment.* Reston, VA: American Alliance for Health, Physical Education, Recreation, and Dance.

Cavallo, D. (1981). *Muscles and morals: Organized playgrounds and urban reform, 1800–1920.* Philadelphia: University of Pennsylvania Press.

De Groot, E. B. (1914). Playground equipment. *Playground, 7,* 439–445.

Erikson, E. H. (1950). *Childhood and society.* New York: Norton.

Esbensen, S. B. (1991, November). *Playground design and mainstreaming issues: Beyond ramps.* Paper presented at the annual conference of the National Association for the Education of Young Children, Denver, CO.

Fantuzzo, J., Sutton-Smith, B., Coolahan, K. C., Manz, P. H., Canning, S., & Debnam, D. (1995). Assessment of preschool play interaction behaviors in young low-income children: Penn interactive peer play scale. *Early Childhood Research Quarterly, 10*(1), 105–120.

Frost, J. L. (1985). The American playground movement. In J. L. Frost & S. Sunderlin (Eds.), *When children play* (pp. 165–170). Wheaton, MD: Association for Childhood Education International.

Frost, J. L. (1986a). Children's playgrounds: Research and practice. In G. Fein & M. Rivkin (Eds.), *The young child at play* (pp. 195–211). Washington, DC: National Association for the Education of Young Children.

Frost, J. L. (1986b). Planning and using children's playgrounds. In J. S. McKee (Ed.), *Play: Working partner of growth* (pp. 61–67). Wheaton, MD: Association for Childhood Education International.

Frost, J. L. (1990). Young children and playground safety. In S. C. Wortham & J. L. Frost (Eds.), *Playgrounds for young children: National survey and perspectives* (pp. 29–48). Reston, VA: American Alliance for Health, Physical Education, Recreation, and Dance.

Frost, J. L. (1992a). *Play and playscapes.* Albany, NY: Delmar.

Frost, J. L. (1992b). *Playground guidelines for school systems* (Report No. PS-021–083). Austin: University of Texas at Austin. (ERIC Document Reproduction Service No. ED 353–082)

Frost, J. L., & Henniger, M. L. (1979). Making playgrounds safe for children and children safe for playgrounds. *Young Children, 34*(5), 23–30.

Frost, J. L., & Jacobs, P. J. (1995). Play deprivation and juvenile violence. *Dimensions, 23*(3), 14–20, 39.

Gehlbach, R. D. (1991). Play, Piaget, and creativity: The promise of design. *Journal of Creative Behavior, 25,* 137–144.

Hendricks, C. (1993). *Safer playgrounds for young children* (Report No. EDO-SP-925). Washington, DC: Office of Educational Research and Improvement. (ERIC Document Reproduction Service No. ED 355–206)

Hudson, S. (1989). Location, accessibility, and equipment on park playgrounds. In D. Thompson & L. Bowers (Eds.), *Where our children play: Community park playground equipment* (pp. 27–35). Reston, VA: American Alliance for Health, Physical Education, Recreation, and Dance.

Lambert, J. (1992). *Adventure playgrounds.* (Available from "Out of Order Books" 24 High Street, Winchendon, MA, 01475. 508-297-3729).

Landreth, G. L. (1991). *Play therapy: The art of the relationship.* Muncie, IN: Accelerated Development.

Larsson, L. (1965). Children aren't just small people. *International Playground Association, 2*(5), 9–10.

Mero, E. B. (1908). *American playgrounds: Their construction, equipment, maintenance, and utility.* Boston: American-Gymnasia Co.

Moore, R. C., Goltsman, S. M., & Iacofano, D. S. (Eds.). (1987). *Play for all guidelines: Planning, design, and management of outdoor play settings for all children.* Berkeley, CA: MIG Communications.

Poole, G. S., & Poole, B. L. (1982). Parks and playgrounds as adjunct classrooms. *Parks and Recreation, 17*(9), 63–66.

Rouard, M., & Simon, J. (1977). *Children's play spaces: From sandbox to adventure playground.* Woodstock, NY: Overlook.

Rubin, K. H., Fein, G. G., & Vandenberg, B. (1983). Play. In P. H. Mussen (Ed.), *Handbook of child psychology* (Vol. 4, pp. 693–774). New York: John Wiley.

Sapora, A. V., & Mitchell, E. D. (1948). *The theory of play and recreation.* New York: Ronald Press.

Schneekloth, L. H. (1989). Play environments for visually impaired children. *Journal of Visual Impairment and Blindness, 83,* 196–201.

Shell, E. R. (1994). Kids don't need equipment, they need opportunity. *Smithsonian, 25*(4), 79–86.

Sikes, L., Fise, M. E., & Morrison, M. L. (1992). *Playing it safe: A nationwide survey of public playgrounds.* Washington, DC: Consumer Federation of America.

Talbot, J. (1985). Plants in children's outdoor environments. In J. L. Frost & S. Sunderlin (Eds.), *When children play* (pp. 243–251). Wheaton, MD: Association for Childhood Education International.

Talbot, J., & Frost, J. L. (1990). Magical playscapes. In S. C. Wortham & J. L. Frost (Eds.), *Playgrounds for young children: National survey and perspectives* (pp. 215–234). Reston, VA: American Alliance for Health, Physical Education, Recreation, and Dance.

Thompson, D., & Bowers, L. (Eds.). (1989). *Where our children play: Community park playground equipment.* Reston, VA: American Alliance for Health, Physical

Education, Recreation and Dance.

Tinsworth, D. K., & Kramer, J. T. (1990). *Playground equipment-related injuries and deaths.* Washington, DC: U.S. Consumer Product Safety Commission.

U.S. Consumer Product Safety Commission. (1991). *Handbook for public playground safety.* Washington, DC: U.S. Government Printing Office.

Vance, B. (1982). Adventure playgrounds: An American experience. *Parks and Recreation, 17*(9), 67–70.

Wallach, F. (1989). Sand play containers, wading pools, signs, trees, and pathways. In D. Thompson & L. Bowers (Eds.), *Where our children play: Community park playground equipment* (pp. 61–71). Reston, VA: American Alliance for Health, Physical Education, Recreation, and Dance.

Wallach, F. (1990). Playground safety update. *Parks and Recreation, 25*(8), 46–50.

Ward, A. (1987). Are playground injuries inevitable? *Physician and Sportsmedicine, 15*(4), 162–168.

Wood, B., Fise, M. E., & Morrison, M. L. (1994). *Playing it safe: A second nationwide safety survey of public playgrounds.* Washington, DC: Consumer Federation of America.

Wortham, S. C., & Frost, J. L. (Eds.). (1990). *Playgrounds for young children: National survey and perspectives.* Reston, VA: American Alliance for Health, Physical Education, Recreation and Dance.

School-Based Play and Social Interactions

Opportunities and Limitations

Jeffrey Trawick-Smith

Play is an ideal context for acquiring social skills and language. Play at home and in the neighborhood is sufficiently open-ended and child-directed to allow opportunities for social learning; children can choose when and what to play and with whom, and they can terminate play interactions with peers if they wish. School-based play, however, is more limited, and there are several distinct features of school play that can limit social and play development. Adults need to plan with children to emancipate play in school so that children can realize its full potential for enhancing social competence.

An appreciation of the social benefits of play has led teachers to plan play experiences in classrooms. Play is common in preschools and kindergartens, less so in elementary school programs. Typical classrooms for older children do include group games, open-ended cooperative learning experiences, and outdoor playground activities, which may rightfully be considered play. Classroom play provides opportunities for social experience, but the manner in which play is structured in typical schools in the United States can also limit play development. It is worthwhile, therefore, to consider the relationship of play and social competence.

Play and Social Competence

A four-year-old in preschool is pretending to drive a car constructed from large hollow blocks; another child sits next to her in the passenger seat. "We're going to drive to New York City," she announces. Her playmate disagrees: "Oh, no. It's too crowded there today. Let's go to McDonald's instead."

"Well, okay," the first child responds. "We'll go to McDonald's. Then we'll go to New York for the show." Her playmate seems satisfied with this plan; they set out on their pretend trip.

Play has been viewed as an ideal context for the acquisition of social skills and language competence, partly because of its symbolic and nonliteral qualities. As illustrated in the above example, children must regularly negotiate shared symbolic meanings and coordinate ideas and intentions in play (Fein & Schwartz, 1986; Garvey, 1977; Rubin, 1980). In preschool symbolic play, for example, children coordinate ambiguous personal symbols. When they announce make-believe actions ("We're driving to New York"), they must be ready to explain and defend these representations. Peers may affirm such play suggestions or offer alternative symbolizations ("Let's go to McDonald's instead"). Original proposals for make-believe may need to be modified to satisfy all players ("We'll go to McDonald's. Then we'll go to New York"). In any case, intricate conversations and negotiations take place as children attempt to reconcile their personal symbolic meanings with those of others. The ambiguous, nonliteral quality of play leads, then, to an inordinate amount of complex interaction and verbalization (Fein & Schwartz, 1986; Trawick-Smith, 1993).

As children negotiate in play, specific sociolinguistic competencies are acquired. These include play group entry skills that children utilize to gain admission into games or play enactments already in progress (Corsaro, 1985). Research suggests that some entry strategies are likely to succeed (e.g., joining a play group unobtrusively and performing an interesting action); others are rarely successful (e.g., asking, "Can I play?"). Children also learn to persuade peers in play (Trawick-Smith, 1993). They may discover that with certain playmates one type of persuasive behavior is more effective than another. When playing with bullies, for example, friendly requests work better than aggressive demands. Conflict resolution abilities are also acquired in play (Hartup, French, Laursen, Johnston, & Ogawa, 1993). Play disputes provide an optimal context for learning to compromise, be tactful, and avoid violence (Hazen, Black, & Fleming-Johnson, 1984; Trawick-Smith, 1993). One commentator has suggested that arguing *about* play may be more valuable for children than play itself (Rubin, 1980).

Acquiring these sociolinguistic competencies through play interactions can result in acceptance by peers and the formation of reciprocal friendships (Hartup & Moore, 1990). Skilled players are often better liked and have more friends; such positive peer relationships have been found to predict long-range positive social development and mental health (Hartup & Sancilio, 1986).

Some Unique Features of School-Based Play

School-based play differs markedly from play at home or in the neighborhood. It has a different structure and interpersonal dynamic. It involves distinct play skills. Adults and sometimes children adopt unique goals for classroom play. These differences can lead to social outcomes that contrast sharply with those of open-ended free play outside of school.

Open- Versus Closed-Field Play

Hartup and colleagues (1993) have distinguished between open- and closed-field play. Open-field play takes place in relatively unrestricted social contexts; examples include spontaneous interactions in the neighborhood, where children are free to choose when to play and with whom. Closed-field play is socially confined or controlled. School-based cooperative learning groups, competitive games, or teacher-assigned dramatic play activities are examples; in these settings children may be unable to choose their playmates or to terminate play interchanges.

Differences between home and school play can be observed most clearly in children's arguments. The *neighborhood-based* narrative in Example 1 illustrates the social interactions in open-field play.

Example 1
Two seven-year-old children are climbing into a cardboard box and rolling down a hill in their neighborhood. An argument erupts.

Child A: Let's say this is our cave and we have to hide in it. Hunters are coming, all right? And so we have to hide.
Child B: No! Let's just play. (Climbs into the box and rolls down the hill alone)
Child A: Jamal! No! Don't roll down! This is the cave, all right?
Child B: (Ignores Child A; drags the box back up to the top of the hill)
Child A: I'm not going to play. I don't want you to roll it down. (Begins to walk away)
Child B: We could say it's a cave that can roll down, all right, Alonzo? (Laughs) It could be a cave that rolls down.
Child A: (Laughs) That's pretty funny. Caves rolling down. It'll be a rolling cave. Come on. (Climbs into the box with Child B and continues to play)

Open-field play, as represented in this example, can be discontinued suddenly, at any time, by any participant. When conflicts become too strong, an individual player can separate from play interactions. Since children are usually committed to maintaining play in progress, they will make efforts to assure that activities do not dissolve in conflict. Child B, sensing that his playmate will leave because of an argument, initiates a carefully-crafted compromise to keep the play alive ("it's a cave that can roll down . . ."). It may be hypothesized that in open-field play children are more likely to be persuasive rather than demanding, to compromise, and to resolve disputes without aggression. They are apt to adopt positive peer-group entry strategies rather than barging in; there is a possibility of not being admitted in an open-field context. Generally, children in open-field play will seek to "manage their conflicts in ways that minimize risk to their interactions" (Hartup et al., 1993, p. 446). So, open-field play affords rich opportunities to exercise interpersonal skills.

The social interactions in the following *school-based* play narrative in Example 2 contrast with those in Example 1.

Example 2

The teacher has assigned two five-year-old children to the dramatic play area during their kindergarten center time. Following a field trip to a local medical facility, the teacher had created a pretend hospital in this space. The children are dressing dolls; one suggests a new medical-related play theme.

Child C: Our babies are sick, all right, Cheryl? So, we need to drive them to the hospital now.

Child D: They're not sick. They're just . . . um . . . they're sleeping.

Child C (in a loud, angry tone): Cheryl! These babies go to the doctor! We need to take them! This is the hospital, see? Hurry! Before snack! (Snatches the doll out of Child D's hands)

Child D: No, Samantha! Give it to me! (Turns and shouts across the room to a teacher) Mrs. DeSoto! Samantha took my doll!

Teacher (moving over quickly): Cheryl, you seem very angry!

Child D (in a loud voice): Samantha took my doll!

Child C (in a loud voice): We need to take the babies to the hospital!

Teacher: Let's calm down a minute and talk in quieter voices. What can we do about this problem?

Child D: I want my doll.

Teacher: Okay. Samantha, you shouldn't just grab Cheryl's doll. Can you give it back to her please?

Child C (hands Child D the doll): Okay, but I want to play the babies are sick.

Teacher: You could pretend that you each take your own baby to the hospital. I could play the doctor, if you want. (Begins to play out a hospital theme)

In the context of the school-based, closed-field play of Example 2, the children engaged in a limited exercise of interpersonal skills. Their school-based setting was more thematically, temporally, and interpersonally bound; how and what they played, with whom, and for how long were regulated. These limitations may restrict play development and hamper positive peer interactions. In contrast, play at home, illustrated in Example 1, is relatively unbound; children in the neighborhood are free to choose playmates and play themes. They may play as long as they wish (or at least until dinner); they can opt to stop playing altogether if conflicts become too intense.

Such is not the case in closed-field interactions. Children need not work as hard in these contexts to maintain play. Child C in Example 2 is not required to soften her demands to preserve interactions. Her playmate must remain in the area and at her disposal; thus, snatching a toy carries less interpersonal risk.

Research supports the thesis that closed-field play involves less positive social interaction. Some researchers have found that pairs of school-aged friends—who in open-field settings had displayed remarkable conflict resolution abilities—argued more frequently and more intensely in play settings that were closed (Hartup et al., 1993). These authors concluded that in closed-field play children have less to lose by being bossy, aggressive, or otherwise aversive.

It is possible to represent openness and closedness as a continuum. A neighborhood game can be relatively closed (e.g., a parent may insist that a child play with a younger sibling); school play can be comparatively open (e.g., a teacher might provide pure free choice of activities and play partners within a preschool). It is proposed here, however, that typical school-based play is relatively closed, when compared with other play contexts. Children in classrooms are often confined in their choice of play partners to a small, finite group of peers with whom they are expected to play and get along.

The narrowness of playmate choices is exacerbated by three common classroom practices:

1. Teachers will sometimes assign children to particular centers and certain groups of peers during free play or center time. This "assign and rotate" system of managing free play has come under recent criticism, but is nonetheless common in kindergartens and primary-grade classrooms (Trawick-Smith, 1994).

2. Teachers will set a policy that all children must include all other children in

play groups; the "You can't say you can't play" rule advocated by Paley (1992) is an example. In this case there is no freedom to terminate interactions.

3. Teachers implement "match-making" strategies to bring less socially competent children together with prosocial models. An example would be assigning a withdrawn child and an outgoing child to play together in the class library. Here, children's play partners are selected by adults. These efforts have clear benefits; their cost, however, is interpersonal restriction.

Time-Bound Classroom Play

Play in school is distinctly time-bound. There is usually a designated period for play activities in classrooms; in kindergartens and elementary schools play time is being threatened by growing expectations for teacher-directed academic instruction. Some kindergarten teachers have reported, for example, providing ten minutes or less of free choice time in school (Hatch & Freeman, 1988). Such temporal restraints on play are problematic for several reasons. Play, like art or writing, cannot be performed on demand; children play when the time is right. (Can play that is required at the wrong time still be considered play?) Play themes take time. Games, pretend enactments, even rough-and-tumble activities are complex. They progress in stages; these include planning, implementation, and closure (Garvey, 1977).

Of concern in this essay is the effect of time constraint on social interactions. Play takes longer if it is to be socially meaningful and useful. Children spend an inordinate amount of time engaged in joint planning for play (Forbes, Katz, Paul, & Lubin, 1982; Garvey, 1977). In preschool symbolic play, for example, children must create together their make-believe themes and roles; they must decide which peers get to play along. For this reason, it has been recommended that blocks of thirty to fifty minutes be allowed for play in school (Johnson, Christie, & Yawkey, 1987); yet even this may not be enough. One study found that five-year-olds who were afforded adequate play time spent an average of thirty minutes just setting up for and organizing pretend play themes before actually playing (Trawick-Smith, 1993).

Conflicts in play take time to resolve. Several researchers have documented long chains of arguments and counterarguments that occur in disputes (Forbes et al., 1982; Markell & Asher, 1984). Prosocial resolutions may take longer than less positive ones. Angry hitting or screaming are delivered more quickly than elaborate persuasive behaviors, for example (Trawick-Smith, 1992). In Example 2 above, temporal urgency may have caused Child C's harsh demands. She likely felt compelled to rush her play demands without the usual negotiation and planning, since play time would soon end ("Hurry! Before snack!") It is possible that she would have used more elaborate and positive persuasive strategies if time had permitted.

Thematically Bound Classroom Play

With threats to play coming on every side and a movement in American education toward "cognitive child labor" (Sutton-Smith, 1983, p. 13), teachers have been driven to make outrageous claims about play's contributions to academic achievement. There is great pressure to make play something that it is not. One approach has been to make play part of the content of the curriculum; all classroom play spaces are designed, in this method, around central educational themes. When preschool children are taught about transportation, for example, the dramatic play center is transformed into a train station, the block area is filled with toy vehicles. In another effort to legitimize play, all playful experiences are recast as literacy events (Christie, 1991). Every play space, for example, is saturated with books and writing implements. If play helps children to read and write, surely play detractors will be silenced.

The net effect of these strategies is to distract children from the important "work" of play. The imaginative qualities and interpersonal meanings of play are threatened in such thematically bound contexts. A child who has been spanked with a belt by his mother on a particular morning may need to play something other than train engineer in the dramatic play center. Another child with ego needs for feelings of power and mastery may do better playing a magical princess, rather than a customer trying to decode print on a pretend train schedule. Adult-devised play themes may dissuade children from pursuing their own play needs.

A question of interest is how thematically bound play influences peer relations. Teachers create thematic play experiences by using a preponderance of realistic props and materials; to elicit children's grocery store play, for example, shopping lists, cash registers, and empty food containers are provided. This realism tends to limit interpersonal interaction. The uses of realistic props do not require as much explanation or justification, do not demand the same level of agreement among players. The forms and functions of a shopping list or a grocery cart are obvious; no ongoing negotiations are needed about what these represent. In contrast, transforming a wooden rod into a fire hose requires some debate, since so many alternative symbolizations can be imagined. One child may propose that the object is a hose, another may suggest a magic wand; these personal symbols must be reconciled if cooperative play is to continue.

Research verifies that toy realism can be socially limiting; one study found that children verbalized and interacted far less when playing with realistic than with nonrealistic materials (Trawick-Smith, 1993). These limiting effects are apparent in Example 2 above, as Child C confines her play pursuits to themes suggested by teacher-selected play props. Her rigid insistence on hospital play leads to hopeless conflict. Would she have been more likely to compromise or negotiate had expectations for hospital play not been so fully dictated by the play environment? In contrast, the cardboard box in Example 1 lends itself to multiple representations, so negotiation is possible. In fact, lack of realism allows the children to integrate two seemingly disparate play interests: a pretend cave theme and a hill-rolling game.

Adult-Facilitated Classroom Play

Play is the one arena where children have a modicum of control over their lives. In play children run the show; they are powerful and free of adult regulation. This is especially true in neighborhood or home play, perhaps less so in school. Teachers will often facilitate play; this is justified by a growing body of research suggesting that some children need support in play and that intervention can lead to positive developmental outcomes (Smilansky, 1968). There is a fine line, however, between facilitating and managing play; teachers have been found to be sometimes heavy-handed in their interventions (Trawick-Smith, 1994). In an effort to assure that play yields cognitive benefits, teachers will occasionally interrupt play themes with educative questions, directives, or praise statements that are incongruous with activities in progress.

For example, they may ask, "What shape is that pan you're cooking with?" or "What is the name of that vegetable you are putting in your soup?" Teachers often issue admonishments against loud and active play or reminders that only certain numbers of children are allowed in particular areas. One study observed that the vast majority of teacher interactions in play involved terminating or quieting children's activities (Trawick-Smith, 1987).

This heavy-handedness is a particular problem in social interactions. Adults usually wish to structure activities and environments for children so as to avoid conflict and assure peaceful peer relations. Teachers may intervene too quickly and intensively, then, when play arguments erupt. They may impose adult solutions to social problems. They may, for example, mandate timed sharing arrangements in disputes over toys, such as "Alonzo can have the big wheel for five minutes, then Hanna can have it for five minutes." They may quickly separate children when they are arguing by stating, "Sarah, you can't play nicely with Lawanda right now; why don't you come over with me and read a book." These tend to be adult solutions. Would children, left to their own devices, resolve disputes in these ways?

Example 2 shows how teachers can impose adult resolutions to conflict. This kindergarten teacher insists that children "calm down and talk in quiet voices." Anyone who is familiar with children's conflict knows that loud expressions of anger are fundamental (though perhaps unpleasant) aspects of resolving play disputes. Like adults, children may need to speak their minds and show their intense feelings before moving on to reconcile disagreements. In the neighborhood, children would not hesitate to argue things out.

The teacher of Example 2 imposes a solution to the conflict ("pretend you each take your own baby to the hospital"), rather than allowing the children to do so. Here she may have deprived students of an opportunity to generate and test their own alternative social strategies. Decision making and problem solving are critical features of overall social competence; children must read social situations, scan their own repertoire of available strategies, and choose those that match the demands of a particular circumstance (Crick & Ladd, 1987; Trawick-Smith, 1992). The imposing interventions of this kindergarten teacher may have obstructed this process.

Children need to get into arguments to learn how to resolve them; they must be excluded from groups to learn play group entry skills. They must play with disagreeable peers and bullies to broaden their repertoire of social strategies. They must have play ideas rejected so they can learn to become persuasive. When adults intervene too quickly in conflict, these opportunities are lost.

Classroom Play in Primary and Middle Grades

Classroom play in the elementary or middle school years—or what passes for play at these grade levels—is even more closed, time-bound, and teacher-directed. Elementary teachers often provide "play centers" that line the periphery of their classrooms; however, these are used rarely. Children sit at their desks in the middle of the room and complete math problems or reading assignments; they may also use the centers when the "important work of school" is finished. Outdoor play is a reward for work completion. So, children in most need of a break from the rigors of academic work, those with a high preference for movement, or who have attentional challenges, for example, are regularly deprived of playground time. Play, when it occurs, is overmanaged; children are given play assignments (an oxymoron?) or rigid time limits for play. Noise and social interaction are usually not tolerated.

By middle school, even the appearance of play has vanished. Recess is a thing of the past at this age group in most countries of the world. Teachers might initiate cooperative learning groups or engage students in active debate or discussion, but nothing approaching the open-ended, socially active quality of early free play may be observed in the modern middle school. Play, then, in the elementary and middle school years must go underground. It becomes illicit. Elementary school children create imaginative doodles on paper or notebooks during work time. Cuisenaire rods are transformed into rocket ships during math lessons. Adolescents create elaborate fantasy worlds during algebra class. Teachers cannot prevent children from playing in these ways, although they sometimes make them feel guilty for doing so.

What can be concluded about school-based play? Typical play in school is more bound than play at home; it can and should be emancipated. Four recommendations for emancipating play in school are:

1. Children should be given the chance to play with whomever they choose during at least a portion of the school day, because such open-field play allows greater opportunity to exercise positive social skills.
2. Play time should be lengthened, because positive interactions in play take longer than negative ones. It may not be enough to make time in school for play; play may need to become a focus of school!
3. Open-ended raw materials should be provided in school because realistic props and curriculum-bound play themes can restrict conversation and debate. A move to generic play contexts, where children can invent what they will do, may better allow pursuit of personally felt play needs.
4. Teachers should avoid intervening too quickly in play disputes and give over to children the regulation of social interchange. Certainly a degree of intervention is warranted; some children will need support if they are to engage in play at all. Heavy-handed interventions or those not related to play in progress, however, will distract children from the very important work of play.

Bibliography

Christie, J. F. (Ed.) (1991). *Play and early literacy development*. Albany: State University of New York Press.

Corsaro, W. A. (1985). Friendship and social integration in peer culture. In W. A. Corsaro (Ed.), *Friendship and peer culture in the early years* (pp. 121–170). Norwood, NJ: Ablex.

Crick, N. R., & Ladd, G. W. (1987, April). *Children's perceptions of the consequences of aggressive behavior: Do the ends justify the means?* Paper presented at the biennial meeting of the Society for Research in Child Development, Baltimore, MD.

Fein, G. G., & Schwartz, S. S. (1986). The social coordination of pretense in preschool children. In G. Fein & M. Rivkin (Eds.), *The young child at play: Reviews of research* (Vol. 4, pp. 95–111). Washington, DC: National Association for the Education of Young Children.

Forbes, D. L., Katz, M. M., Paul, B., & Lubin, D. (1982). Children's plans for joining play: An analysis of structure and function. In D. L. Forbes & M. T. Greenberg (Eds.), *Children's planning strategies* (pp. 61–79). San Francisco: Jossey-Bass.

Garvey, C. (1977). *Play.* Cambridge, MA: Harvard University Press.

Hartup, W. W., French, D. C., Laursen, B., Johnston, M. K., & Ogawa, J. R. (1993). Conflict and friendship relations in middle childhood: Behavior in a closed-field setting. *Child Development, 64,* 445–454.

Hartup, W. W., & Moore, S. G. (1990). Early peer relations: Developmental significance and prognostic implications. *Early Childhood Research Quarterly, 5,* 1–17.

Hartup, W. W., & Sancilio, M. F. (1986). Children's friendships. In E. Schopler & G. B. Mesibov (Eds.), *Social behavior in autism* (pp. 61–79). New York: Plenum.

Hatch, J. A., & Freeman, E. B. (1988). Kindergarten philosophies and practices: Perspectives of teachers, principals, and supervisors. *Early Childhood Research Quarterly, 3,* 151–166.

Hazen, N., Black, B., & Fleming-Johnson, F. (1984). Social acceptance: Strategies children use and how teachers can help learn them. *Young Children, 39*(3), 26–36.

Johnson, J. E., Christie , J. F., & Yawkey, T. D. (1987). *Play and early development.* Glenview, IL: Scott, Foresman.

Markell, R. A., & Asher, S. R. (1984). Children's interactions in dyads: Interpersonal influence and sociometric status. *Child Development, 55,* 1412–1424.

Paley, V. (1992). *You can't say you can't play.* Cambridge, MA: Harvard University Press.

Rubin, K. H. (1980). Fantasy play: Its role in the development of social skills and social cognition. In K. H. Rubin (Ed.), *Children's play* (pp. 69–84). San Francisco: Jossey-Bass.

Smilansky, S. (1968). *The effects of sociodramatic play on disadvantaged preschool children.* New York: John Wiley.

Sutton-Smith, B. (1983). One hundred years of change in play research. *Association for the Anthropological Study of Play Newsletter, 9*(2), 13–17.

Trawick-Smith, J. (1987). *The validity and reliability of an instrument to measure the dramatic play behavior of young children.* (ERIC Document #1 Reproduction Service No. ED 286 654)

Trawick-Smith, J. W. (1992). A descriptive study of persuasive preschool children: How they get others to do what they want. *Early Childhood Research Quarterly, 7, 95*–115.

Trawick-Smith, J. (1993, April). *Effects of realistic, nonrealistic, and mixed realism play environments on young children's symbolization, verbalization, and social interaction.* Paper presented at the annual meeting of the American Educational Research Association, Atlanta, GA.

Trawick-Smith, J. (1994). *Interactions in the classroom: Facilitating play in the early years.* Columbus, OH: Merrill.

Play as Ritual in Health Care Settings

Laura Gaynard

Children confronted with chronic illness, disabilities, and intense or repeated health care experiences face unique physical, emotional, and mental challenges. From a social-emotional perspective, the process of becoming a hospital patient involves:

- Mortifying experiences involving loss of self integrity
- Traumatic separation from family, home, and community
- Loss of bodily comforts
- Exposure to an overwhelming array of strangers
- Introduction to a foreign and threatening environment.
  (Beuf, 1989; Goffman, 1961)

This process is frightening and disconcerting for individuals of any age. It is especially difficult for children due to their limited life experience and the immaturity of their information-processing abilities (Beuf, 1989; McCollum, 1980; Thompson, 1985; Vernon, Schulman, Foley, Sipowicz, & Schulman 1965).

The Value of Play in Health Care Settings

To reduce the potential developmental disruption created by childhood hospitalization, hospital personnel have implemented and researched the effectiveness of various interventions. Among these interventions are programs centered around play. As the most natural activity of childhood, play in health care environments is an essential element in reducing the degree of threat perceived by children in the new and unfamiliar surroundings (Bolig, 1984; Thompson, 1989). Play in health care settings functions to optimize children's development, facilitate learning, and promote the expression of feelings. Various forms of play activities can provide young patients with diversion from discomfort, boredom, and pain; support continued development in all domains; promote peer interactions; motivate children to comply with health care regimes; soothe and comfort young patients; and help children cope effectively with their health care experiences (Bergen, Gaynard, & Hausslein, 1988; James, 1989; Petrillo & Sanger, 1980; Thompson & Stanford, 1981).

The health care professionals who most often facilitate play with children in health care settings are the child life specialists, who are certified members of the pediatric health care team. A central goal of child life programming is to enhance children's ability to cope and feel competent in health care environments, not only to minimize the stresses of illness, injury, and treatment, but ideally to make it a positive, growth-enhancing experience (Child Life Council, 1995; Gaynard, Wolfer, et al., 1990).

In addition to the benefits of play cited above, it is possible that the play of young patients may serve an additional purpose. Young patients may seek out, and become involved in, play for *ritualistic benefits*. It makes sense that the loss of control and the accompanying stress that young patients experience when confronted with health care challenges, compel them to play in ritualistic ways. Thus, one value of play for young patients is the provision of ritualized behavior that

- Is self-comforting
- Increases their perceived sense of control over illness, disability, institutionaliza-

tion, and their subsequent physical and emotional responses
- Helps prepare them for impending medical procedures

Ritual, in the play of young patients, can ameliorate the trauma of health care experiences.

The Value of Ritual

Scholars define the term *ritual* as both "an established form of conducting a religious rite" and as "any practice or behavior repeated in a prescribed manner"; *rite* refers to "a ceremonial act or procedure" (Flexner, Stein, & Su, 1980). Ritual behaviors sometimes may be ceremonial or connected with religious experiences. The term *ritual* can be applied to individual behaviors as well as group experiences (Homans, 1972; Malinowski, 1972; Miracle, 1986; Radcliffe-Brown, 1972).

Ritual behaviors are peculiar to humans, a universal characteristic of the human animal, and one that has allowed the individuals who performed rituals to survive better than those who did not. In fact, in human evolution the imperative to establish ritual has been more pressing and immediate than the need to produce tools. Yet, the way human behavior manifests rituals is directly related to culture; that is, they learn specific ritual behaviors. Humans perform ritual and ceremonies deliberately, not instinctively. But, beneath the performance of ritual, some scholars maintain there lies an innate human behavioral tendency that aids survival (Dissanayake, 1992).

Although rituals vary in form from one society to another, they occur in response to strikingly similar circumstances. All societies observe "rites of passage," which are states of transition between one significant state and another (e.g., birth, puberty, marriage, death). Additionally, people perform rites to assure prosperity or good fortune in such contexts as hunting, raising crops, curing illness, obtaining absolution, achieving reunification and mediation, and proclaiming allegiances. They also perform rituals to mark significant transitions between seasons, sickness and health, discord and concord, and so forth (Dissanayake, 1992). Ritualistic behavior, in whatever form, is a coping mechanism that humans usually practice to deal with uncontrollable situations.

In circumstances that they perceive as threatening, troubling, or uncertain, where strong emotions are stirred up, humans have the tendency not just to fight, flee, or wait, as other animals might, but "to *do* something." One scholar has referred to this quality as "the imperative to act" (Lopreato, 1984, p. 299).

More than any other living creature, humans deliberately try to do something to affect their own welfare, to influence, forestall, transform, or otherwise *control;* to bring extreme or untrustworthy situations under control by extraordinary intervention. *Control* is regarded here as influencing, harnessing, or bringing oneself into alignment with the powers of nature. What is controlled, then, in these situations, is oneself. By controlling one's behavior one can feel, by analogy, that the provoking situation is also under control. One is "doing something" about the situation. Malinowski (1922), for example, describes how, during a terrifying storm, a group of Trobriand Islanders with whom he lived chanted charms together in a singsong voice. Whether or not the gale subsided, the measured rhythm of the chanting and the sense of unity it provided was more soothing than uncoordinated, fearful reactions (Dissanayake, 1992).

Thus, in uncertain circumstances, following the "imperative to act," things are done to bring about desired results and to deal with feelings of anxiety. The effect of ritual actions is surely to make people feel better. Indeed, one might suggest that humans do not so much expect ritual practices to work—though people certainly hope that they will—as to deliver them from anxiety (Devlin, 1987).

Ritual and Play

Numerous scholars assert that play and ritual serve similar needs in cultural contexts. As previously stated, ritual behaviors are universal, found in every human society, as are play behaviors. The purpose of rituals includes stating and publicly reinforcing the values of a group of people; uniting a group in common purpose and belief; explaining the inexplicable, such as birth, death, illness, or natural disaster; and attempting to control life and make it bearable. People play for similar reasons (Abrahams, 1986; Dissanayake, 1992; Norbeck, 1971).

As is true of ritual, play includes a special order, realm, mood, or state of being. The penchant for acknowledging an extraordinary realm is inherent in the behavior of both play and ritual, where actions are "not for real." Ritual and play are set off from real or ordinary life. Play is preceded by the acknowledgment that it is "framed"; that is, there is an indication that the player(s) recognize it as an extra-ordinary dimension of experience. This is also true of rituals, which, by their very nature, are either exceptional kinds of experiences or acts outside the daily routine. Rituals make common occasions more significant or special, such as prayer at mealtime or storytelling before bedtime (Dissanayake, 1992).

Both ritual and play use various means to arouse, capture, and hold attention. Both can serve as a "container" for, and molder of, feelings. Moreover, in both play and ritual the player can manipulate responses. The rhythm and form of play can expand, contract, excite, calm, and release feelings of the involved players (Allan, 1980; Axline, 1969; Erikson, 1950; Esman, 1983; Guerney, 1983). Ritual also tends to have a similar emotional climate for those involved. In both play and ritual, one or more of the "players" control the script and can manipulate the outcome according to their desires.

Play for Young Patients

The self-comforting aspect of ritualized play can be very important to young patients. Humans share with other animals a preference for order rather than disorder. Regularity and predictability are the ways we make sense of our world; understanding or interpreting anything means recognizing its structure or order. A major source of anxiety for children coping with chronic illness and frequent health care procedures is that they feel little control over their lives. It is often difficult or impossible, for example, to predict exacerbations or relapses of illness. Normal daily routines are frequently interrupted for the child and family by treatments, clinic visits, hospitalizations, symptoms from the illness itself, and side effects of medications.

When hospitalized, children experience even less predictability about their lives. It is usually impossible to know when procedures and tests will take place, and hospitalized children are forced to interact with an overwhelming number of staff, many of whom are strangers. Young patients are often unable to predict who will come to visit and when. They may be unable to control what and when they will eat or drink, and, in some situations, children even lose control of bowel and bladder due to illness and treatment. In sum, child patients struggle, on a daily basis, with a continual lack of control that is exacerbated by regular clinic visits and unpredictable admissions to the hospital. This often results in considerable anxiety.

Ritual Play for Self-Comfort

The literature on ritual behaviors for humans points out that action, which for children usually takes the form of play, is soothing and can be a stress reducer (Malinowski, 1948). It gives one something to do rather than merely waiting passively for events to happen, and health care settings are notorious for making people wait. Activity that is deliberately, or actively, shaped feels more effective and soothing than uncontrolled random flailing about, and it is a more effective coping behavior. Even nonhuman animals tend to use action to shape feelings of anxiety or despair. Caged animals sometimes move repetitively in formalized obsessional movements. Male chimpanzees, for example, may rhythmically run about, slap the ground, and vocalize during thunderstorms. This rhythmic mode is also sometimes present in human behavior. We rhythmically tap toes, drum fingers, and wiggle various body parts as ways of relieving impatience, boredom, or worry.

In health care settings, the simple, familiar action of play is comforting in itself to both child and parents. Play reduces anxiety because it is a child's familiar medium. Additionally, it allows children to engage actively in interaction or activity that they can control, which is often a rare experience for young patients. Within the hospital setting, for example, children are able to choose where they want to play, who they will play with, what they will play, and for how long. Play is the only activity in the hospital over which children can exercise control, and one of the only experiences to which children can say "No."

During play interactions young patients are able to express energy and anxiety through a multitude of acceptable, fun activities. As is often the case with ritual behaviors, such expressive play helps children shape and channel feelings via a safe, familiar, and soothing behavior that becomes a container for the fear, anxiety, and frustration hospitalized children typically experience. Parents, too, tend to experience a decrease in distress as they observe their child engaging in a "normal" activity such as play. As parents and family members are able to interact with their children through the familiar medium of play, they are reassured to see normal play behaviors while rituals diminish since their child's admission to the hospital. This often leads to decreased distress and an increase in effective coping abilities and feelings of control for both young patients and their parents.

Rhythm and Repetition for Self-Comfort and Self-Control

Rhythm and repetition alone are positively enjoyable and have anxiety-reducing, self-comforting properties. Rhythm is the inevitable result of repetition and is a most pervasive environmental fact. In brain waves and circadian rhythms, in lunar and solar cycles, repetition and rhythm characterize animate and inanimate nature. Breathing, sucking, and crying—the infant's earliest repertoire—are all performed rhythmically. Older infants and children, healthy or compromised, respond to both stress and joy by rhythmic, repetitive action, from head banging and rocking to spoon banging and marching. A steady rhythm seems to establish and sustain a predictable ground or "frame" that helps individuals cope more easily with, or even ignore, disturbances caused by the pain and discomfort of illness, injury, and health care (Dissanayake, 1992).

Repetition and rhythm also give shape to time and can increase children's perceived control of time. There is comfort in simply repeating an action. This process explains how humans can transform obsessional or soothing actions into the movements, chants, and gestures of ritual ceremonies. The repeated individual displacement activities, or "comfort movements" provoked by personal uncertainty and stress, often become ritualized behaviors that reduce distress created in perilous or confusing circumstances (Dissanayake, 1992).

Hospitalized children frequently engage in "ticlike," self comforting behaviors that appear to stem from anxiety (Freud, 1952). Children will pick their noses or their skin, pull out eyebrows or eyelashes, incessantly scratch and rub various parts of their bodies. Other children will rock in their beds or cribs for long periods of time, or cry in a rhythmic manner (Bowlby, Robertson, & Rosenbluth, 1952; Freud, 1952; Thompson, 1985). Although some of these ac-

tions can be considered self-mutilating, they tend to comfort young patients who are observed to engage spontaneously in these ritualized behaviors in a repetitive manner with considerable compulsion.

Young patients sometimes utilize rhythm and repetition to cope with health care experiences during invasive procedures. For example:

Anne is a renal patient who has needed hemodialysis for most of her eleven years. At the beginning of each dialysis session (three and one-half hours, three times a week) nurses need to place two very large needles in a vein and an artery. Several years ago, Anne spontaneously began blowing in a rhythmic manner during needle insertions. Just prior to these invasive experiences Anne closes her eyes, "thinks happy thoughts," and begins slow rhythmic blowing. When Anne feels the prick of the needle her blowing becomes faster but still maintains a repetitive rhythm. As the pain subsides Anne's blowing slows, and as the tape is positioned she takes several deep breaths and relaxes. Anne tells me that her blowing helps her cope effectively with the invasive health care procedures she frequently experiences, and she often requests music (via a personal stereo) with a strong beat which, she reports, "helps me, even more, through the hard part."

Another example of a young patient who frequently uses rhythm and repetition to cope with health care experiences is Cindy, an eight-year-old dialysis patient.

Cindy enjoys art activities a great deal and is particularly attracted to this type of play. When Cindy is hospitalized, she receives hemodialysis in her room, which means she remains in bed for three and one-half hours. Child life staff provide play interactions with Cindy during her dialysis time to enhance her coping skills. The staff members have noted that Cindy's play takes on increased intensity and is more repetitive and rhythmic during dialysis. During these times, Cindy draws only scribbles or doodles and becomes totally engrossed in the pulsating beat she creates with her strokes. Cindy repeatedly draws one symbol, totally covering a piece of paper, then moves to another page without missing a "beat." When Cindy begins a new page she draws a different symbol, and she repeats the pattern, rhythmically covering the page, then moving on to the next. Staff note that when Cindy is drawing in this manner she appears more calm and relaxed than when observed in other play interactions during hospitalizations.

Whether children transform anxiety into repetitive, patterned art movements or ritualized "ticlike" behaviors, rhythmic movement appears to help young patients feel control over their feelings of distress associated with health care. Repetitive play often has a major role in this self-comforting ritual and adults can facilitate its beneficial functions.

Adult-Guided Play with Young Patients

Historically, play theorists have expressed concern that adult-guided play is a contradictory term, that adult-guided interactions and activities cannot be considered true play. Child life professionals, however, have asserted that the treatment-focused play that characterizes many child life programs provides benefits for young patients struggling to make sense of health care experiences. Research regarding the value of adult-guided play with young patients shows that this form of play assists the coping and well-being of children in health care settings (Gaynard et al., 1990; Thompson, 1985; Wolfer et al., 1988; Wolfer & Visintainer, 1975). What is most important is that young patients have opportunities to experience a variety of forms of play while in hospitals, including both spontaneous and adult-guided forms, and that the play adults facilitate has children's voluntary participation and includes children's intrinsic objectives as well as adult extrinsic objectives.

Preparation Play and Ritual

Because a major source of distress for young patients is the lack of knowledge and understanding about impending medical procedures, many child life programs include psychological preparation through which children and their families are introduced to the circumstances and procedures they will encounter. The value of these programs in reducing emotional disturbance in hospitalized children is well docu-

mented in the literature (Thompson, 1985, 1989; Wolfer et al., 1988).

Psychological preparation usually takes the form of adult-guided play within which the child life professional provides information of importance to the child and family in a manner that is comprehensible and age appropriate. The child life specialist, for example, often engages young patients in doll play to show them what they will see, hear, taste, smell, and feel during a procedure, and to demonstrate how the medical equipment will be used. The adult then encourages the young patients to play through that procedure on the doll to help them gain a greater understanding and knowledge of forthcoming events (Gaynard, Goldberger, & Laidley, 1991).

Adult goals in facilitating these play interactions include:

1. Increasing young patients' sense of predictability regarding a specific procedure or health care experience
2. Increasing perceived sense of control
3. Reducing distress from unrealistic fantasies about the procedure
4. Increasing effective coping
5. Dispelling confusion and misconceptions.
     (Gaynard et al., 1990;
     Goldberger, Gaynard, & Wolfer, 1990;
     Thompson, 1989; Wolfer et al., 1988)

In addition to achieving these goals, however, preparation play may also provide ritualistic benefits. In general, the practice of preparation rituals marks transitions, assures good fortune or prosperity, satisfies the "imperative to act" when faced with a threatening situation, and/or increases a sense of control about specific situations. Many children in the United States, for example, leave an offering of cookies and milk for Santa on Christmas Eve in hopes that he will leave many gifts. Similarly, children in Nepal routinely light special devotional lamps that represent the Hindu god Narayana in hopes that their household will be protected (Dissanayake, 1992).

Thus the goals of preparation rituals are similar to the goals of all preparation play: control, safety, and mental preparation for an uncertain event. Through this play, young patients can help to shape and understand the information regarding the upcoming medical event that has created anxiety. The events become comprehensible and structured—in other words, ritualized, thus becoming less distressing (Dissanayake, 1992).

For young patients with chronic illnesses who experience a multitude of health care procedures, preparation play often becomes ritualistically repetitive in idiosyncratic ways. For example:

Tyler was a seven-year-old boy with leukemia who was admitted to the hospital every six weeks for chemotherapy and a spinal tap. Tyler typically arrived at the hospital on a Thursday evening, was admitted, and had intravenous (IV) medications started Thursday night. A spinal tap was routinely performed the next morning. Tyler's IV medication was completed by Saturday morning, and he was typically discharged home by the next Friday afternoon.

I would usually meet Tyler on admission to the hospital on Thursday afternoons. He always brought his spelling list with him; so, during the placement of the IV catheter in his arm, I could distract him by quizzing him on his spelling homework. Subsequent to the start of his IV medicine Tyler would announce to me that he needed to perform a spinal tap on his doll in the treatment room. Using actual medical equipment Tyler and I would enact the procedure on his doll in preparation for Tyler's spinal tap the following morning. As is typical of many chronically ill patients, Tyler was meticulous during the preparation play, being very careful to include every detail of the procedure. He would also be very vocal when I would do something "wrong" in my role-play as the "nurse."

I observed that, with each admission, the preparation play became increasingly ritualistic. The play always had to be done in the treatment room, with a doll as a patient, on the evening of Tyler's admission, and with the use of actual medical equipment. Tyler monitored our play so that it included every detail of the actual lumbar puncture, and he protested any variation. Furthermore, Tyler was adamant that he "needed" to play through the lumbar puncture with the doll only once each admission, whereas many other children want to engage in endless preparation play.

Many pediatric health care professionals have similar anecdotes of young patients' ritualized preparation play behavior. The children have unique play rituals that are most supportive for them in preparing for, and coping with, procedures. What all of these child patients share, however, is the tendency to seek out health care play that is repetitive and ritualistic in their own meticulously similar manner.

The Extra-Ordinary Realm of Preparation Play

Another ritualistic benefit of preparation play may result from the special realm, or mood, created between the child life specialist and the young child. Child patients enact both play and ritual in an extra-ordinary realm set off from "real" or ordinary life. They are both compelling in nature and involve various means of arousing, capturing, and holding the participants' attention. Hospitalization itself is set off from normal life and tends to heighten and sharpen young patients' attention and emotions. Their health care crises and concerns about impending medical procedures keep patients in a hypervigilant state in which they are constantly on guard and aware of all that happens around them; emotions, especially anxiety and fear, are heightened and easily triggered.

In the midst of this frightening hospital regimen, which has triggered the child's hypervigilant state, the child life professional engages the child in preparation play that appears to be soothing and self-comforting. The child experiences, sometimes for the first time since admission, an individual who obviously enjoys and easily connects with children. The child life specialist facilitates playful interactions that include valuable information about forthcoming medical events presented in a way the child can comprehend. As preparation play unfolds, the rhythm and form of play calm and facilitate the release of feelings in a pleasurable and acceptable way, helping the child feel more in control.

Thus, as in other preparation rituals, the play interaction is set off from both "real" life and hospital life. The child's already heightened emotional state, combined with the age-appropriate information assimilated in the process of play, makes this form of play interaction so powerfully helpful that the observer can easily perceive the special realm created between the young patient and the child life specialist. The research data, which indicate that psychological preparation play increases coping and decreases distress of young patients, suggest that this extraordinary dimension of care is highly beneficial (Gaynard, Wolfer, et al., 1990; Thompson, 1985; Wolfer et al., 1988; Wolfer & Visintainer, 1975).

Separation Play and Ritual

A significant portion of the trauma involved in the process of becoming a patient can be attributed to separation of the patient from home, family, and community. The child is taken out of the home, sometimes due to traumatic circumstances, and delivered to an institution that imposes a whole new set of rules and a standard "patient identity." In the absence of family members, hospitalized children may feel abandoned and experience significant difficulties as they attempt to understand what is happening to them in the hospital and why it is happening (Thompson, 1985; Wolfer & Visintainer, 1975).

Although recent hospital policies typically allow twenty-four hour visitation for parents, they are usually not able to stay with their child twenty-four hours a day due to obligations at home or work. Single parents are especially challenged, as are families with numerous siblings as well as those with little or no extended family in the vicinity of the hospital. Many children hospitalized in large medical centers come from long distances and are especially disconnected from their home and community.

Even in situations where parents and other caregivers are readily available to the child, the child patient typically experiences the most significant stress points (during procedures, in the recovery room, during induction for surgery) without parents present (Gaynard et al., 1990; Goldberger, 1988; Wolfer & Visintainer, 1975). Thus, the experience of separation is inherent in the process of hospitalization.

Many hospital play programs provide opportunities for children to engage in separation play to help reduce anxiety. Play that addresses separation includes:

- Reading to children stories with a separation theme
- Facilitating symbolic play such as peekaboo and going-and-coming-back-again games with bubbles, balls, cars
- Hiding-and-finding games, such as finding shapes inside a sorting toy
- Using dramatic play with family/animal figures to address separation issues. (Gaynard et al., 1990)

Separation play is one form of expression that tends to become very ritualized in the repetitive manner that young patients play. Individual play with family figure dolls is an example of one form of separation play common to many hospital play programs. When introducing the family dolls, child life specialists often initiate a separation theme that young patients may pick up and elaborate upon. With little or no prompting by adults, children sometimes will initiate their own separation themes using the family dolls.

Carrie, a three-year-old girl who was scheduled to be in traction for three weeks, was offered the family dolls by a child life specialist on Carrie's second day in the hospital. As the specialist held up each doll, Carrie quickly assigned names and roles to each figure, including Mommy and Daddy, sister, and brothers (Carrie had three brothers at home). Then the child life specialist picked up the sister doll and said "I think she's crying. Why do you think she's crying?" Carrie explained that the little girl was lost and couldn't find her family. Using the dolls, Carrie acted out the story, describing how the family was searching for the little girl who was "lost." She described in detail the parents' feelings of concern and sadness. In the process of play, Carrie directed the specialist to perform various acts with one or more of the dolls while she manipulated the other figures. After much searching, the parents finally found the girl amidst hugging, kissing and laughter. . . . (This all took place on Carrie's traction bed.) Carrie played out this separation story via the family figures several times in the 30-minute play session with the specialist.

(Gaynard et al., 1990, p. 87)

What is particularly impressive about this form of play is that patients who are six years of age or younger typically seek out separation play opportunities over other types of play (Gaynard & Bergen, 1986). In the case above, the child would greet the author (the child life specialist) each day and ask, "Do we get to play with the family dolls today?" Carrie would then play out this theme of getting lost and being found for thirty minutes or more. Furthermore, Carrie would play out this theme with meticulous attention to detail, repeating the play sequence each day in the same manner, with the same story line that she reenacted every day. If the author added or changed details, Carrie was quick to correct her: "No. That's not the way it goes."

As is true in preparation play, children vary in the unique, idiosyncratic details of the separation themes played out. The play takes on a ritualistic characteristic in the compulsion young patients seem to have to repeat this form of play over and over. Separation play also becomes ritualized in the way child patients recreate the play in exactly the same fashion, time and time again. It appears that children find ritualized separation play, in and of itself, calming and soothing.

In addition to providing other benefits for hospitalized children, play seems to fulfill their psychobiological propensity to engage in ritualistic behaviors. Psychologists usually explain that play can be of therapeutic value in that it allows for sublimation and self-expression (Axline, 1969; Erikson, 1950; Freud, 1952; Kranz & Lund, 1993). The reason such play is comforting and healing for child patients, however, has much to do with the fact that play allows them to order, shape, and control a small piece of their world. To repeat and pattern sounds, movements, and events seem to be innate tendencies in humans that provide pleasurable feelings of mastery, security, and relief from anxiety (Dissanayake, 1992).

It is likely that the play of young patients is a ritualistic coping mechanism similar to many other ritualistic behaviors universally practiced by humans during other times of crisis. As described in this essay, such health care play can be spontaneous or adults can facilitate it to enhance effective coping responses of young patients. As is true in any environment where children play, however, the opportunities for child patients to control their lives as much as possible is of primary importance. Play and ritual often combine to help them do that.

Bibliography

Abrahams, R. (1986). Play in the face of death: Transgression and inversion in a West Indian wake. In K. Blanchard, W. Anderson, G. Chick, & E. Johnsen, (Eds.), *The many faces of play* (pp. 29–44). Champagne, IL: Human Kinetics.

Allan, J. (1980). *Inscapes of the child's world*. Dallas, TX: Spring.

Axline, V. (1969). *Play therapy* (Rev. ed.). New York: Ballantine.

Bergen, D., Gaynard, L., & Hausslein, E. (1988). Designing special play environments. In D. Bergen (Ed.), *Play as a medium for learning and development* (pp. 275–297). Portsmouth, NH: Heinemann.

Beuf, A. (1989). *Biting off the bracelet*. Philadelphia: University of Pennsylvania Press.

Bolig, R. (1984). Play in hospital settings. In T. Yawkey & A. Pellegrini (Eds.), *Child's play: Developmental and applied* (pp. 323–345). Hillsdale, NJ: Lawrence Erlbaum.

Bowlby, J., Robertson, J., & Rosenbluth, D. (1952). A two-year-old goes to the hospital. *Psychoanalytic Study of the Child, 7*, 82–94.

Child Life Council. (1995). *Child life position statement*. Rockville, MD: Author.

Devlin, J. (1987). *The superstitious mind: French peasants and the supernatural in the nineteenth century*. New Haven: Yale University Press.

Dissanayake, E. (1992). *Homo aestheticus: Where art comes from and why*. New York: Macmillan.

Erikson, E. (1950). *Childhood and society*. New York: Norton.

Esman, A. (1983). Psychoanalytic play therapy. In C. Schaefer & K. O'Connor (Eds.), *Handbook of play therapy* (pp. 11–20). New York: John Wiley.

Flexner, S., Stein, J., & Su, P. (Eds.). (1980). *The Random House Dictionary*. New York: Random House.

Freud, A. (1952). The role of bodily illness in the mental life of children. In R. Eissler, A. Freud, H. Hartmann & E. Kris (Eds.), *The psychoanalytic study of the child* (Vol. 8, pp. 69–81). New York: International Universities Press.

Gaynard, L., & Bergen, D. (1986, March). *Young children's discovery of humorous incongruity in a hospital setting*. Paper presented at the annual conference of the Association for the Study of Play, Tempe, AZ.

Gaynard, L, Goldberger, J., & Laidley, L. N. (1991). The use of personalized dolls with hospitalized children: Techniques and benefits. *Children's Health Care, 20*(4), 216–224.

Gaynard, L., Wolfer, J., Goldberger, J., Thompson, R., Redburn, L., & Laidley,

L. (1990). *Psychosocial care of children in hospitals*. Washington, DC: Association for the Care of Children's Health.

Goffman, E. (1961). *Asylums*. Garden City, NY: Anchor.

Goldberger, J. (1988). Issue-specific play with infants and toddlers in hospitals: Rationale and intervention. *Children's Health Care, 16*(3), 134–141.

Goldberger, J., Gaynard, L., & Wolfer, J. (1990). Helping children cope with health-care procedures. *Contemporary Pediatrics, 1*(3), 141.

Guerney, F. (1983). Client-centered (nondirective) play therapy. In C. Schaefer & K. O'Connor (Eds.), *Handbook of play therapy* (pp. 11–20). New York: John Wiley.

Homans, G. (1972). Anxiety and ritual: The theories of Malinowski and Radcliffe-Brown. In W. A. Lessa & E. Z. Vogt (Eds.), *Reader in comparative religion: An anthropological approach* (3rd ed., pp. 83–88). New York: Harper & Row.

James, B. (1989). *Treating traumatized children: New insights and creative interventions*. Lexington, MA: Lexington Books.

Kranz, P. L., & Lund, N. L. (1993). Axline's eight principles of play therapy revisited. *International Journal of Play Therapy, 2*(2) 53–60.

Lopreato, J. (1984). *Human nature and biocultural evolution*. Boston: Allen and Unwin.

Malinowski, B. (1922). *Argonauts of the western Pacific*. London: Routledge and Kegan Paul.

Malinowski, B. (1948). *Magic, science, and religion*. Boston: Beacon.

Malinowski, B. (1972). The role of magic and religion. In W. A. Lessa & E. Z. Vogt (Eds.), *Reader in comparative religion: An anthropological approach* (3rd ed.,

pp. 63–72). New York: Harper & Row.

McCollum, A.T. (1980). *The chronically ill child*. Springfield, IL: Charles C. Thomas.

Miracle, A. (1986). Voluntary ritual as recreational therapy: A study of the baths at Hot Springs, Arkansas. In K. Blanchard, W. Anderson, G. Chick, & E. Johnsen, (Eds.), *The many faces of play* (pp. 164–171). Champagne, IL: Human Kinetics.

Norbeck, E. (1971, December). Man at play. *Natural History Magazine*, 48–53.

Petrillo, M., & Sanger, S. (1980). *Emotional care of hospitalized children*. Philadelphia: Lippincott.

Radcliffe-Brown, A. R. (1972). Taboo. In W. A. Lessa & E. Z. Vogt (Eds.), *Reader in comparative religion: An anthropological approach* (3rd ed., pp. 72–83). New York: Harper & Row.

Thompson, R. (1985). *Psychosocial research on pediatric hospitalization and health care: A review of the literature*. Springfield, IL: Charles C. Thomas.

Thompson, R. (1989, July). Child life programs in pediatric settings. *Infants and Young Children*, 76–81.

Thompson, R., & Stanford, G. (1981). *Child life in hospitals: Theory and practice*. Springfield, IL: Charles C. Thomas.

Vernon, D., Schulman, J., Foley, J., & Sipowicz, R. (1965). *The psychological responses of children to hospitalization and illness*. Springfield, IL: Charles C. Thomas.

Wolfer, J., Gaynard, L., Goldberger, J., Laidley, L., & Thompson, R. (1988). An experimental evaluation of a model child life program. *Children's Health Care, 16*(4), 244–254.

Wolfer, J., & Visintainer, M. (1975). Pediatric surgical patients' and parents' stress responses and adjustment. *Nursing Research, 24*, 244–255.

Play and Social Interactions

Adult Direct and Indirect Influences on Play

Wendy Haight

Parents have long been intrigued by observing playful transformations that provide a glimpse into their child's inner life, and by the opportunity to participate within that world, for example, when children transform the parent into a baby and themselves into the parent. Consider a mother discussing the spontaneous pretend play between herself and her three-year-old daughter:

> I have a tendency of watching how she's pretending . . . to see if she is having any anxieties or worries of . . . happiness that she wants to share with me that maybe she—at her age—isn't able to come right out and say "I'm scared about this.". . . I feel like it's important for me to see what's on her mind. . . . When they pretend you can pick up on what they're feeling and kind of what direction you might need to go in to help them. (Haight, Parke, & Black, in preparation)

Many parents are similarly extensively involved in the play of their young children at home (Garvey, 1990). Although Piaget (1962) characterized pretend play as a solitary activity in late infancy, developmental psychologists (e.g., Howes, 1992), early childhood educators (e.g., Paley, 1984), play therapists (e.g., see Hellendoorn, van der Kooij, & Sutton-Smith, 1994), and, more recently, early interventionists (Sheridan, Foley, & Radlinski, 1995) have considered pretend play as a context that both reflects and facilitates development, and adult-child play as a means through which adults may support children's emotional, social, and cognitive development (see Rubin, Fein, & Vandenberg, 1983).

This essay first considers the developmental significance of parent-child pretend play from a sociocultural perspective. Next, there is a discussion of the ways in which parents directly and indirectly facilitate children's pretend play. Finally, the discussion considers sources of individual and cross-cultural variability in the extent and quality of parent-child pretend play.

The Significance of Parent-Child Pretend Play from a Sociocultural Perspective

Increasingly, scholars from different disciplines consider pretend play to be a potentially rich context for the creation and re-creation of cultural meanings (Haight & Miller, 1993; Schwartzman, 1978; Singer & Singer, 1990). In a classic essay on play, a psychologist discussed two little sisters who pretended to be sisters (Vygotsky, 1978). He noted that in a literal context, children behave without thinking about their role relationships; but in pretending, for example, to be sisters, their actions must conform to the cultural "rules" of sisterly behavior. Thus, "What passes unnoticed by the child in real life becomes a rule of behavior in play" (Vygotsky, 1978, p. 95).

In addition to re-creating existing cultural meanings, however, innovation, creativity, and variability are essential components of play from the earliest parent-infant play (Fogel, Nwokah, & Karns, 1993) to the most elaborate social pretend play in middle childhood (Schwartzman, 1978; Sutton-Smith, 1993). In pretending with particular meanings, for example, of parent-child relations, children not only become more deeply rooted in a system of meanings, they also alter, comment upon, and reinterpret meaning (Schwartzman, 1978). One view argues: "The tension between the myths imposed from without and the exertion of personal control in shaping one's interpretation and use of myths reflects the poles of a dialectic relationship between the individual and his culture. Through play, the child is socialized into a general cultural framework while developing a unique individuality with a distinctly personal matrix of life history and lived meanings" (Vandenberg, 1986, p. 8). A similar perspective characterizes pretend play as a context in which young children negotiate meanings through borrowing, expressing, and inventing meanings from available social and cultural materials (Slade & Wolfe, 1994). Thus, pretend play is a preface to the ongoing and vital cultural activity of making and remaking meaning.

That play may assist in the transmission (Smith, 1994; Trudye, Lee, & Putnam, 1995) and creation of cultural meanings suggests a greatly increased role for adult-child play. During parent-child pretend play, children interact with partners who are more experienced and share an intimate knowledge of their lives. Indeed, play is one of the few contexts in which typically powerless children interact with their parents on a relatively equal footing around emotionally significant topics of mutual concern such as anger and aggression (Haight & Sachs, 1995). Such interactions can be instrumental in negotiating various cultural meanings, including harmonious interpersonal interactions (Haight, Masiello, Dickson, Huckeby, & Black, 1994), the interpretation and display of emotion (Haight & Sachs, 1995), and literacy (Lightfoot & Valsiner, 1992; Whiting & Edwards, 1988). In the words of one father, "I think it's [pretend play] a good way to . . . stay in close touch with your 2-year-old . . ." (Haight, Parke, & Black, 1997).

How Parents Facilitate Children's Play

Given the developmental significance of pretend play, as well as its basically social nature, it is important to consider the ways parents facilitate their children's developing pretend play through teaching them how to pretend and inspiring within them a love of play.

Teaching Children to Pretend

Several parents during interviews (Haight, Parke, & Black, 1997) spontaneously mentioned that parent-child pretending is important for teaching their two-year-olds to pretend. In the words of one father, "it's fun to teach him to pretend in different ways, like with the farm . . . or that he can be a fireman, or he can go to work today. . . . I like to give him ideas that he wouldn't think of. . . . " Like this father, many parents spontaneously support their young children's developing pretend play through a variety of direct and indirect methods.

Direct Methods of Parental Facilitation of Pretend Play

First, parents can introduce the nonliteral, pretend frame to their older infants (Beizer, 1991; Haight & Miller, 1992). In a longitudinal, observational study, one researcher documented mothers' spontaneous introduction of pretend play to their infants, even though the infants did not pretend independently, during daily routines in the home (Beizer, 1991). A mother might, for example, animate the peas during feeding, making them greet her eight-month-old.

Second, parents can prompt their young children to pretend. Another longitudinal, observational study reported that, during everyday routines in their homes, mothers typically prompted their children to pretend (Haight & Miller, 1993). A twelve-month-old, for example, vocalized to her teddy bear and her mother prompted, "Say, 'Hi, Teddy-Tie!'"

Third, parents can elaborate upon their toddlers' forays into pretend play. Mothers commonly extended their young children's pretending by adding new material that was thematically relevant (Haight & Miller, 1992). For example, a twenty-four-month-old child pointed a straw at her mother, waved it, and commented, "Magic." Her mother elaborated, "Oh! You turned me into a frog!"

Consistent with Vygotsky's zone of proximal development (Sutton-Smith, 1993), recent research suggests that parents' direct involvement with their young children facilitates pretending. Children's pretend play with mothers is more sustained (Dunn & Wooding, 1977; Haight and Miller, 1992; Slade, 1987), complex (Fiese, 1987; Slade, 1987), and diverse (O'Connell & Bretherton, 1984) than their solo pretending, and young children incorporate their mothers' pretend talk into their own subsequent pretending (Haight & Miller, 1992).

Although research has focused on mother-child pretend play, recent observations suggest that fathers also support their toddlers' pretending (Farver & Wimbarti, 1995; Haight, Parke, & Black, 1997).

Indirect Methods of Parental Facilitation of Pretend Play

Parents also may exert a powerful indirect influence on the development of pretending through their arrangement of the physical and social contexts to provide children with ample space, objects, and stimulating partners for play (Haight & Miller, 1992). There is considerable agreement in the literature that objects affect children's pretend play. Authors, for example, describe toys as the "pegs on which to hang our play," and suggest that "because the human imagination is so extensive and complex . . . children seem to look for solid tangible reference points, as it were, from which to range more freely. Just as language makes subtle and complicated thought possible, perhaps toys do the same for play" (Newson & Newson, 1979, p. 12). By providing their children with replica toys suggestive of particular play themes, for example, baby dolls, tea sets, miniature cars, and action figures, parents may indirectly shape their young children's play.

Recent empirical evidence, however, suggests considerable cultural variation in the extent to which parents provide their children with replica objects. One study found that the pretend play of North American, middle-class toddlers and preschoolers revolved around replica toys (Haight & Miller, 1993). In Taipei, however, a sizable proportion of children's pretend play involved no objects at all, but frequently did involve the enactment of social routines such as formally greeting a teacher (Haight et al., 1995). Perhaps children in less materialistic communities "hang" their pretend play on other types of "pegs" such as social routines, or elaborate upon other forms of play such as physical or language play (Edwards & Whiting, 1993).

Inspiring a Love of Pretend Play

As fascinating as pretend play is for a child, an enthusiastic partner who offers appealing ideas and can put to words the child's depicted actions must inspire pretending (Garvey, 1990). In the words of the mother of a prolific and inspired two-year-old player (Haight, Parke, & Black, 1997), "I love to pretend play! I mean Frank [husband] has told me that I only had a child so I could have a playmate. . . . I played with baby dolls up until I was 16 or 17 years old. . . . " During interviews, one quarter of parents spontaneously cited encouragement of pretend play in explaining why parent-child pretending is important (Haight, Parke, & Black, 1997). In the words of one father, "I want to show her a love for it [pretending]."

In the explorations of adults' memories of childhood play, researchers stress the importance of a key person in the child's life who "inspires and sanctions play and accepts the child's inventions with respect and delight" (Singer & Singer 1990, p. 4). A. A. Milne, for example, credited his parents, who sanctioned his childhood play, in the creation of his imaginary forest. Vyvyan Holland remembered his father, Oscar Wilde, as a playmate who would go down on all fours and become "a lion, a wolf, a horse" (Singer & Singer, 1990, p. 10).

Indeed, many parents and children apparently derive great pleasure from their joint pretend play. Parent-child play typically is affectively positive (see MacDonald, 1993; Singer, 1994) and associated with secure attachment (see Sutton-Smith, 1993). By the time children are fluent pretenders in their third year of life, both children and parents actively initiate pretending with one another (Dunn & Wooding, 1977; Haight & Miller, 1992) and generally are responsive to the others' initiations (Haight & Miller, 1993). Interviews of children aged six to twelve years revealed that even in middle childhood, many children desire opportunities for pretending with their parents (Otto & Riemann, 1990, as cited in Sutton-Smith, 1993).

Accounting for Variation in the Quantity and Quality of Parent-Child Pretend Play

Naturalistic evidence suggests that although parental participation in young children's pretending is relatively widespread, it is by no means universal (e.g., Goncu & Mosier, 1991; Haight, Wang, et al., 1995; Miller & Garvey, 1984). The potential significance of parent-child pretend play raises the question of how to interpret individual and cross-cultural variability in the extent and quality of parents' participation in their young children's pretending.

Undoubtedly, some variability in parent-child pretend play is related to social and economic factors influencing child care and work patterns (see Edwards & Whiting, 1993).

Work requirements and/or explicit sanctions against playing are evident in communities in Kenya, Israel, the Andes, and Central America (Sutton-Smith, 1993). Some variability in the development and sharing of pretend play will be related to a handicapping condition such as hearing impairment (Sheridan et al., 1995). Variability also will be related to adult status, such as maternal depression (Cohn, 1993).

Accounting for cross-cultural and individual variation in parent-child pretend play also requires attention to the meaning of play in various communities and for various individuals. Parental beliefs, for example, provide a frame of reference within which parents interpret experience and formulate goals and strategies for socializing their children (Harkness & Super, 1992). Their beliefs concerning the relevance of pretense to the development of skills and qualities that parents perceive as necessary for success in their particular communities, and their views concerning the appropriateness of adult participation in children's play, would influence their support of their children's pretend play in complex and possibly indirect ways.

Ethnographic research suggests that middle-class parents in the United States (Goncu & Mosier, 1991; Haight, Parke, & Black, 1997), Turkey (Goncu & Mosier, 1991), and China (Haight, Wang, et al., 1995) generally view play as significant to young children's development, and view themselves as appropriate play partners for their children. The increasing emphasis in Japanese preschools on pretend play (Takeuchi, 1994), for example, has been attributed, in part, to exposure to beliefs in the United States about the importance of play to development. In contrast, Mexican (Farver, 1993) and Italian (New, 1994) mothers do not view play as particularly significant to children's development, and Mayan and tribal Indians (Goncu & Mosier, 1991) think of play as the child's domain and judge adult participation to be inappropriate. Consistent with these beliefs, naturalistic observations reveal that Turkish, Chinese, and U.S. parents participate in pretend play with their young children, while Mayan, Mexican, Italian, and tribal Indians engaged in relatively little or no pretending.

There also is some evidence that parents' beliefs may account for some of the variation in the quantity and quality of parents' participation in young children's pretending within communities, although such relations are complex and not well understood. European American, middle-class mothers and fathers who did not differ in the extent and quality of their pretend play, or in their beliefs about pretend play, did differ in the relationships between their beliefs and behaviors (Haight, Parke, & Black, 1997). Fathers who pretended relatively frequently with their children viewed pretend play as enjoyable. Mothers who pretended relatively frequently, however, viewed pretend play as a developmentally significant activity and their own participation as important. The extent to which mothers viewed pretend play as an enjoyable activity was related to the quality of their participation; for example, mothers who enjoyed pretending typically elaborated upon children's initiations of pretending. These findings suggest that the extent and quality of parents' pretend play is related not only to their beliefs about play per se, but to broader networks of practices and beliefs such as the role of mothers and fathers in the care and development of young children (Haight, Parke, & Black, 1997).

Parent-child pretend play is a potentially rich context for the socialization and acquisition of cultural meanings. Parents may facilitate their children's pretending by teaching them to pretend, introducing the pretend mode to older infants; elaborating upon their toddlers' early forays into the nonliteral; and encouraging an enthusiasm for pretend play. Given the significance of pretend play to children's development, and of parents' contribution to the development of pretend play, recent advocacy that parent-child play should be encouraged (Sutton-Smith, 1993) seems sound. However, available evidence of cross-cultural and within-cultural variation in the extent and quality of parents' participation in children's pretend play suggests that these activities are complexly related to other systems of practices, for example, the role of mother versus others in the care and development of young children; as well as specific beliefs about and individual preferences for pretend play. Thus, before advocating parent-child play, practitioners must consider the cultural appropriateness of adult-child play, adults' own preferences for interaction with children, as well as other play and nonplay contexts that may promote similar developmental outcomes. After all, the unique benefits of adult-child play can accrue only if the activity truly is play, embedded within a climate of spontaneity and fun (Levenstein & O'Hara, 1993).

Bibliography

Beizer, L. (1991). *Preverbal precursors of pretend play: Developmental and cultural dimensions*. Paper presented at the biannual meeting of the Society for Research in Child Development, Seattle, WA.

Cohn, J. (1993). Mother-infant play and maternal depression. In K. MacDonald (Ed.), *Parent-child play: Descriptions and implications* (pp. 239–256). Albany: State University of New York Press.

Dunn, J., & Wooding, C. (1977). Play in the home and its implications for learning. In B. Tizard & D. Harvey (Eds.), *Biology of play* (pp. 45–58). London: Heinemann.

Edwards, C., & Whiting, B. (1993). "Mother, older sibling and me": The overlapping roles of caregivers and companions in the social world of two- to three-year-olds in Ngeca, Kenya. In K. MacDonald (Ed.), *Parent-child play: Descriptions and implications* (pp. 305–329). Albany: State University of New York Press.

Farver, J. (1993). Cultural differences in scaffolding pretend play: A comparison of American and Mexican American mother-child and sibling-child pairs. In K. MacDonald (Ed.), *Parent-child play: Descriptions and implications* (pp. 349–366). Albany: State University of New York Press.

Farver, J., & Wimbarti, S. (1995). Paternal participation in toddlers' pretend play. *Social Development, 4,* 17–31.

Fiese, B. (1987, April). Mother-infant interaction and symbolic play in the second year of life: A contextual analysis. Paper presented at the meeting of the Society for Research in Child Development, Baltimore, MD.

Fogel, A., Nwokah, E., & Karns, J. (1993). Parent-infant games as dynamic social systems. In K. MacDonald (Ed.), *Parent-child play: Descriptions and implications* (pp. 43–70). Albany: State University of New York Press.

Garvey, C. (1990). *Play*. Cambridge, MA: Harvard University Press.

Goncu, A., & Mosier, C. (1991). *Cultural variations in the play of toddlers*. Paper presented at the biannual meeting of the Society for Research in Child Development, Seattle, WA.

Haight, W., Masiello, T., Dickson, L., Huckeby, E., & Black, J. (1994). The everyday contexts and social functions of spontaneous mother-child play in the home. *Merrill-Palmer Quarterly, 40,* 509–533.

Haight, W., & Miller, P. (1992). The development of everyday pretend play: A longitudinal study of mothers' participation. *Merrill-Palmer Quarterly, 38,* 331–349.

Haight, W., & Miller, P. (1993). *Pretending at home: Development in sociocultural context*. Albany: State University of New York Press.

Haight, W., Parke, R., & Black, J. (1997). Mothers' and fathers' beliefs about and spontaneous participation in their toddler's pretend play. *Merrill-Palmer Quarterly, 43,* 271–290.

Haight, W., & Sachs, K. (1995). A longitudinal study of the enactment of negative emotion during mother-child pretend play from 1–4 years. In L. Sperry & P. Smiley (Eds.) & W. Damon (Series Ed.), *New directions in child development: Developmental dimensions of self and other* (pp. 33–46). San Francisco: Jossey-Bass.

Haight, W., Wang, X., Fung, H., Williams, K., & Mintz, J. (1995). *The ecology of everyday pretending in three cultural communities*. Paper presented at the biannual meeting of the Society for Research in Child Development, Indianapolis, IN.

Harkness, S., & Super, C. (1992). Parental ethnotheories in action. In I. Sigel, A. McGillicuddy-DeLisi, & J. Goodnow (Eds.), *Parental belief systems: The psychological consequences for children* (pp. 373–391). Hillsdale, NJ: Lawrence Erlbaum.

Hellendoorn, J., van der Kooij, R., & Sutton-Smith, B. (Eds.). (1994). *Play and intervention*. Albany: State University of New York Press.

Howes, C. (1992). Introduction. In C. Howes (Ed.), *The collaborative construction of pretend: Social pretend play functions* (pp. 1–12). Albany: State University of New York Press.

Levenstein, P., & O'Hara, J. (1993). The necessary lightness of mother-child play. In K. MacDonald (Ed.), *Parent-child play: Descriptions and implications* (pp. 221–237). Albany: State University of New York Press.

Lightfoot, C., & Valsiner, J. (1992). Parental belief systems under the influence: Social guidance of the construction of personal cultures. In I. Sigel, A. McGillicuddy-DeLisi, & J. Goodnow (Eds.), *Parental belief systems: The psychological consequences for children* (pp. 393–414). Hillsdale, NJ: Lawrence Erlbaum.

MacDonald, K. (1993). Parent-child play: An evolutionary perspective. In K. MacDonald (Ed.), *Parent-child play: Descriptions and implications* (pp. 113–143). Albany: State University of New York Press.

Miller, P., & Garvey, C. (1984). Mother-baby role play: Its origins in social support. In I. Bretherton (Ed.), *Symbolic play: The development of social understanding* (pp. 101–130). Orlando, FL: Academic.

New, R. (1994). Child's play—una cosa naturale: An Italian perspective. In J. L. Roopnarine, J. E. Johnson, & F. H. Hooper (Eds.), *Children's play in diverse cultures* (pp. 123–147). Albany: State University of New York Press.

Newson, J., & Newson, E. (1979). *Toys and playthings*. New York: Pantheon.

O'Connell, B., & Bretherton, I. (1984). Toddler's play alone and with mother: The role of maternal guidance. In I. Bretherton (Ed.), *Symbolic play: The development of social understanding* (pp. 337–368). Orlando, FL: Academic.

Otto, K. & Riemann, S. (1990). *Zur specifik der besiehungen zwischen kindern und erschenen im spiel*. Paper presented at the bienniel meeting of the International Council of Children's Play, Andreasburg, Germany.

Paley, V. (1984). *Boys and girls: Superheroes in the doll corner*. Chicago: University of Chicago Press.

Piaget, J. (1962). *Play, dreams and imitation in childhood*. New York: Norton.

Rubin, K. H., Fein, G. G., & Vandenberg, B. (1983). Play. In E. M. Hetherington (Ed.), *Handbook of child psychology: Socialization, personality, and social development* (Vol. 4, pp. 693–774). New York: John Wiley.

Schwartzman, H. B. (1978). *Transformations: The anthropology of children's play*. New York: Plenum.

Sheridan, M., Foley, G., & Radlinski, S. (1995). *Using the supportive play model: Individualized intervention in early childhood practice*. New York: Teachers College Press.

Singer, D., & Singer, J. (1990). *The house of make-believe*. Cambridge, MA: Harvard University Press.

Singer, J. (1994). The scientific foundations of play therapy. In J. Hellendoorn, R. van der Kooij, & B. Sutton-Smith, (Eds.), *Play and intervention* (pp. 27–38). Albany: State University of New York Press.

Slade, A. (1987). A longitudinal study of maternal involvement and symbolic play during the toddler period. *Child Development, 58*, 647–675.

Slade, A., & Wolfe, D. (1994). Preface. In A. Slade & D. Wolfe (Eds.), *Children at play: Clinical and developmental approaches to meaning and representation* (pp. v–viii). Oxford: Oxford University Press.

Smith, P. K. (1994). Play training: An overview. In J. Hellendoorn, R. van der Kooij, & B. Sutton-Smith (Eds.), *Play and intervention* (pp. 185–194). Albany: State University of New York Press.

Soto, L., & Negron, L. (1994). Mainland Puerto Rican children. In J. L. Roopnarine, J. E. Johnson, & F. H. Hooper (Eds.), *Children's play in diverse cultures* (pp. 104–122). Albany: State University of New York Press.

Sutton-Smith, B. (1993). Dilemmas in adult play with children. In K. MacDonald (Ed.), *Parent-child play: Descriptions and implications* (pp. 15–40). Albany: State University of New York Press.

Takeuchi, M. (1994). Children's play in Japan. In J. L. Roopnarine, J. E. Johnson, & F. H. Hooper (Eds.), *Children's play in diverse cultures* (pp. 51–72). Albany: State University of New York Press.

Trudye, J., Lee, S., & Putnam, S. (1995). *Young children's play in socio-cultural context: Examples from South Korea and North America*. Paper presented at the biennial meeting of the Society for Research in Child Development, Indianapolis, IN.

Vandenberg, B. (1986). Beyond the ethology of play. In A. Gottfried & C. Brown (Eds.), *Play interactions: The contribution of play materials and parental involvement to children's development* (pp. 3–11). Lexington, MA: Lexington Books.

Vygotsky, L. S. (1978). *Mind in society: The development of higher mental processes.* Cambridge, MA: Harvard University Press.

Whiting, B., & Edwards, C. (1988). *Children of different worlds: The formation of social behavior.* Cambridge, MA: Harvard University Press.

Peer and Sibling Influences on Play

Sherri Oden
Jennifer A. Hall

Parents and educators often express curiosity or concern about the influences of siblings and peers on children's development. Are the children learning to express and develop their individuality as they learn to get along? Are they enjoying positive, constructive relations with their siblings and peers? Parents and educators are often somewhat unsure of their own roles. While sibling and peer play is interesting, fun, and compelling, it is also sometimes frustrating to contend with or even just to behold. Yet developmental and educational psychologists purport that peer and sibling play can make important contributions to children's development, and that parents and educators should help support children's relationships with other children.

Over the past twenty-five years, researchers and educators have come to realize that siblings and peers together construct their own versions of reality and challenge each other's conceptions of reality. They construct and assume social roles in fantasy play, such as police officer, teacher, doctor, or parent. They also routinely enact their own versions of the social roles of helper, friend, collaborator, and competitor. They stimulate each other's language and social development as well as their emotional expression, perspective taking, and physical coordination.

When children play together, many factors potentially influence the nature of their play, its focus, content, roles, and processes. Various influences on children's play can be conducive or detrimental to how constructively children will influence each other as they play together.

Researchers have found that during peer and sibling play children make mutual contributions to each other's development in many settings, such as their homes, yards, neighborhoods, playgrounds, recreational centers, schools, and places of worship. Such settings provide myriad opportunities for a variety of peer relationships that include friends, acquaintances, peer groups, activity partners, and siblings. Each setting and relationship provides different developmental challenges and opportunities. Except for first or only children, siblings are often children's earliest peer influence, and sibling play is likely to have a unique and powerful impact on children's development.

Influences in Sibling Play

Children's relationships with their siblings tend to be qualitatively distinct from relationships with their parents or peers. Unlike friends, siblings do not choose one another, and therein may lie some of the challenges, limitations, and unique sources of influence. While sibling relationships may be exceptionally close, they may also be fraught with conflict; most typically, sibling play includes both intensely positive and intensely negative elements. It is easy to observe or recall two siblings trying to establish who is the rightful proprietor of a game or toy, or who will be in charge of an activity.

Researchers have examined many factors thought to influence the quality and quantity of siblings' play. We begin with a focus on developmental progression, age-related factors, birth order, and gender (sometimes called structural variables or influences). Unlike peer interactions, where children typically choose same-gender and similar-age peer playmates, sibling choices for play partners are limited. Insights from sibling research may generalize somewhat to peer play, but caution should be used. Even when peers differ in age or developmental level (e.g., cognitive or social maturity), the differences loom less large in peer play than when siblings play together. Perhaps the strong impact of age and gender among siblings is due to the tendency of family members to attach privileges and responsibilities to children's age, birth order, and gender. Several studies support the contention that children's developmental level, birth order, and gender predict the types of play activities chosen by siblings and the roles they assume as they play together.

Developmental Factors in Sibling Play

The nature and intensity of sibling relationships change in the course of children's development, as do aspects of their play. Infants and toddlers, for example, engaged in more functional play, according to researchers, while their preschool-aged siblings engaged in more games, construction, and fantasy play (Stevenson, Leavitt, Thompson, & Roach, 1988). These researchers found that, compared to older children, preschool-aged children were less likely to adjust their own play style to that of their sibling, although they would make adjustments when they played with their parents.

The relative age of siblings exerts a strong influence on the roles each assumes in play, with the older child generally being more directive and controlling. (See Boer & Dunn, 1992, for a thorough discussion of developmental issues in sibling relationships.) Somewhere between ages three and four, the younger sibling becomes more able to cooperate and contribute in joint play with the older sibling (Dunn, 1992; Munn & Dunn, 1989). Both cooperative play and conflict between siblings may increase at this time, reflecting the ambivalence that so often characterizes sibling relationships (Dunn, 1983; Dunn & Munn, 1986).

Is the nature of sibling relationships stable? That is, is there reason to expect that siblings who are very close when they are young will continue to be close into their adolescence? And will siblings embroiled in conflict continue to have difficulty getting along? Longitudinal research has shown that a fair amount of stability exists in both the positive and negative aspects of sibling relationships (Dunn, 1992; Munn & Dunn, 1989). A study of pairs of siblings between preschool and early adolescence confirms these findings, especially after the youngest sibling turned five years of age (Dunn, Slomkowski, & Beardsall, 1994). This eight-year study assessed sibling interactions through observation and mothers' and siblings' reports concerning positive interactions and hostile behavior such as hitting, teasing, and so on. These findings may be both encouraging and discouraging to parents.

Combined Influences

birth Order

Researchers have found that first-born siblings were more likely to assume dominant roles, such as teacher and manager, when playing with a second-born sibling (Stoneman, Brody, & MacKinnon, 1984, 1986). The younger sibling, in turn, was more likely to accept the teaching and managing attempts of the older sibling.

Gender

Male dyads more often played competitive games outdoors, and female dyads more often played fewer competitive games indoors (Stoneman et al., 1984). Thus, not only can an observer expect play roles to differ for older and younger siblings, but such differences are likely to be further affected by the gender of the children involved. Another study, for example, found that same-sex sibling dyads, when compared to opposite-sex sibling dyads, were more likely to engage in both more competitive physical play activities and in more gender-stereotypical play activities (Stoneman et al., 1986). These researchers further found that an older sister was more likely than an older brother to manage the play with a younger sibling. This asymmetrical pattern may be a function of typical roles into which girls are socialized as nurturers or helpers.

Structure of Play Situations

Just as there are research findings that children's play with peers outside the family can facilitate children's social and cognitive development, sibling play also can enhance the benefits of play for siblings. Different types of sibling play may be more or less conducive to various aspects of development. An observational study of sibling pairs, for example, found that unstructured play in a card-toss game that imposed few rules and some flexibility was associated with more positive interactions between siblings (MacKinnon, 1989). In comparison, the structured play of sibling pairs in a game with many rules and clear expectations involved more teaching and helping behaviors, which may more directly facilitate cognitive and social development (MacKinnon, 1989). Another study found that older siblings provided opportunities for their younger siblings to join play during activities that included problem solving, artistic skill mastery, social play, and motor experience, however found no correlation between this type of sibling play and the younger sibling's cognitive development (Teti, Bond, & Gibbs, 1988). Nonetheless, on the whole, the body of research suggests that sibling play does offer opportunities for social, cognitive, and language development (Dunn, 1983).

As parents likely know only too well, while factors such as developmental level, birth order, and gender do appear to influence the types of play children choose, they will not neatly predict how well a given pair of siblings will get along and play together in general, from hour to hour or from day to day. Other factors, such as temperament and social factors in the family, divorce, and socioeconomic factors, affect the tone of sibling play. The tone of sibling play, its positivity or negativity, and the overall ratio of positive to conflictual play can vary.

Individual Temperament

Children's temperaments are important in influencing the type or quality of interactions and affect both sibling and peer play. Among sibling pairs, for example, one study found that mothers' ratings of their children's temperaments were more predictive of both the siblings' play and conflict than was their gender or age (Munn & Dunn, 1989). They also found that the larger the difference between the temperaments of the two children, the more conflict occurred.

Family Influences

Social Factors

Social factors in the family may influence children's peer interactions in complex or different ways. It is interesting, however, to consider the effects that such factors may have on sibling pairs who, unlike their unrelated peers, are experiencing the same family environment. Some studies, for example, have found that di-

vorce is often associated with changes in children's peer relationships (Hetherington, Cox, & Cox, 1979). Only recently have researchers begun to examine whether divorce affects sibling interactions. Researchers who observed sibling pairs from both married and divorced parent families in a free play situation found no significant differences in any of the various types of play they examined (Kier & Fouts, 1989). Another study, however, found that siblings from divorced parent families, compared to siblings from married parent families, engaged in fewer positive play interactions (MacKinnon, 1989).

Socioeconomic Status

Because the effect of divorce on sibling play is unclear, additional factors need to be considered, such as socioeconomic status, paternal involvement with the children, and parents' reactions to sibling conflict (Herzberger & Hall, 1993). Low family socioeconomic status, independent of divorce, correlated with more negativity during sibling play (MacKinnon, 1989). Other researchers also found that low socioeconomic status is associated with fewer positive sibling interactions, although only for older children (Dunn, Slomkowski, & Beardsall, 1994). The relatively few studies on family factors, however, warrant only the conclusion that such factors are likely to have some influence on siblings' play, yet the nature and direction of the influence are also likely to be complicated.

The Continuity of Influences from Sibling to Peer Play

Another issue concerns the continuity between children's sibling play and their peer play. As they increasingly interact and establish relationships with their unrelated peers, children experience many of the same types of influence as they do with their siblings. Thus, sibling experiences can provide some degree of structure or predisposition for how children will interact with their peers. Furthermore, the additional and different influences of peer interactions should both challenge and expand the children's experiences with siblings and other children. There are some major understandings about various sources of influence on peer play, including who plays with whom and the quality of the interactions. (For more extensive discussions of the peer social development research, see Bergen & Oden 1988; Oden & Ramsey, 1993; and Ramsey, 1991.)

Developmental Factors and Progression

During the early childhood years, most children increasingly play with their peers and form relationships as activity partners or friends while their play roles emerge in peer dyads, triads, and groups within growing peer cultures (Oden, 1988). The patterns and content of play do change as children develop. Older friends in upper elementary school, for example, become increasingly focused on sharing their inner selves through secrets, and personal feelings, whereas preschoolers and primary school-age children are focused more on activity play and sharing materials, or fantasy role-playing.

Peer Play

Early individual differences in children's responsiveness to peers may predispose a child to potentially long-lasting peer interaction tendencies or patterns (Kagan, Reznick, & Gibbons, 1989). From early peer contacts in the toddler years through the preschool years, most children's peer interactions become more frequent and more complex (Howes, 1987, 1988). By the elementary school years, a child's peer status becomes a marker of the child's short-term social adjustment and may predict future social competence and even poor mental health (Parker & Asher, 1987).

Gender-Specific Play

Gender-specific play begins before preschool and increases throughout the childhood years. Around their fourth year of age, children's preferences for same-gender peers increases dramatically (Ramsey, 1989). As children spend more time in same-gender play, according to Maccoby (1986), each group begins to form its own culture. Among peers, boys play in larger groups, often outdoors and involving rough-and-tumble or aggressive play that focuses on competition for dominance. Girls tend to play indoors, in smaller groups, and focus on forming close friendships. Because children readily divide themselves by gender, parents and educators may unintentionally support and reinforce this tendency. There is evidence that while preschool boys and girls do play together when specifically reinforced for doing so, they are likely to revert to same-gender patterns when reinforcement stops (Serbin, Tonick, & Sternglanz, 1977). One study showed a more lasting effect for cross-gender interaction when kindergarten boys and girls participated in role-play activities that the children found to be especially interesting or engaging (Ramsey & Theokas, 1993).

Mixed-Age Play

The content of mixed-age peer and sibling play appears to share many features. Older peers or siblings, for example, will accommodate to the toys, activity interests, and linguistic capabilities of the younger child, perhaps to get or keep the younger child engaged in playing. Thus, on the one hand, the older child may be more authoritative or even controlling, but on the other hand, the older child will compromise and accommodate to what the younger child is capable of playing. Over time, therefore, younger siblings have an increasing influence over what will be played and how it will be played as they play with their older siblings, thus increasing their ability to interact in peer relationships.

Expanding Influences on Peer Play

The contexts of peer play influence the course of events. Cultural and socioeconomic factors generally affect the nature of play and children's choices of peers. The educational settings in which children find themselves also affect opportunities for children to play. Children's perceptions of the distinctive characteristics of other children can also influence their choice of playmates.

Cultural, Socioeconomic, and School Influences

Experiences with peers, rather than siblings who usually share familial experiences, are likely to both challenge and broaden children's play experience. Community or societal attitudes about race, culture, and social class influence how peers perceive each other and with which peers children elect to play. Preschool children's play relations with peers shift frequently, and children tend to select friends on the basis of proximity and easily observable characteristics. Thus, as some researchers have pointed out, children who live in the same neighborhood are likely to be from the same social groups and participate in many of the same types of activities, such as music lessons, soccer, and basketball, both in school and out of school (Ramsey, 1991).

The more frequent play that is readily observable between toddler and preschool peers of the same race or ethnic/cultural background also reflects the racial or ethnic patterns in society. Children notice racial differences early in their preschool years, but it is in their early childhood and elementary school years that their perceptions and attitudes about race become more defined (Finkelstein & Haskins, 1983; Ramsey & Myers, 1990). While preschoolers usually select same-race, unfamiliar peers for potential friends while engaged in research tasks (Newman, Liss, & Sherman, 1983), in actual practice they do not necessarily choose their friends according to race. In racially mixed groups, elementary school children, for example, have formed friendships based on gender rather than race (Singleton & Asher, 1977, 1979).

Compared to children and youths in the upper grade levels, preschool and primary school-age children do not yet grasp the significance of nationality backgrounds, but they notice differences associated with a cultural background that differs from their own, such as unfamiliar dialects, interactive styles, dress, and social customs. Cultural customs may influence how a child greets peers, tries to gain entry to a peer group's play activity, and expresses interest in, or familiarity with, certain play activities and experiences, such as specific childhood rhymes, songs, sayings, or story or video characters (Doyle, 1982; Ramsey, 1991).

Children with Learning Differences

Familiarity gained from playing with peers of different gender, age, race, or cultural backgrounds can foster children's playing together. Differences, however, may interfere with communication and cooperative play in areas such as social ability, physical handicaps, and learning styles, and may require further attention. In some ways, the differences in competence between siblings can be a preparation (positive or negative) for interacting with peers who have different learning styles, social and cognitive abilities, and physical competence. More experiences with peers who have a greater diversity in adeptness or adaptiveness have the potential to expand children's social development.

Social Competence

Socially competent children, even in preschool, are generally considered by their peers to be friendly, cooperative, attractive, capable, and confident, making them appealing playmates, friends, peer group members, and leaders. Other children have persistent problems with peer social ability. During the elementary school years, more extreme, persistent difficulties result in children being rejected for play because they are considered too aggressive, inappropriate, or unengaging. Overly aggressive children, for example, re-create their negative peer status across time and peer groups (Coie & Kupersmidt, 1983).

Similarly, over the years, highly unengaged children may enter a cycle of withdrawal and rejection (Rubin, Hymel, & Mills, 1989); thus, they fail to get the social experience they need for social play and peer relationships. Some children are just less socially adept or not well known to their peers; they may operate on the sidelines and draw little concern or interest from their peers or teachers. As they tend to pursue their own interests or play alone with some measure of contentment, they may rarely be considered for peer inclusion in activities. Yet these children may be operating less out of choice, perhaps viewing themselves as lacking the ability to hold their own in social relationships, or they may be feeling lonely (Asher & Wheeler, 1985). Other peers have a mixture of both positive and negative peer relations. Studies show, however, that effectively conducted guidance or coaching of children about peers' norms and expectations, helping them to think through the consequences of their actions for others, or altering situations to increase their likelihood of positive play inclusion can offset patterns of peer exclusion or neglect (Ladd, 1981; Mize & Ladd, 1990; Oden, 1986; Oden & Asher, 1977).

Children with Learning Disabilities

Children with differences in their learning approaches or abilities often behave somewhat differently from their peers. Their peers, therefore, may reject or avoid playing with them, although this is less true for younger children. Preschool and primary school-age children tend to be more accepting of classmates with disabilities than are older children (Goodman, Gottlieb, & Harrison, 1972). Because young children are less cognitively sophisticated and less socially experienced, they are less likely to stigmatize their peers or to assign fixed reputations to peers. Their process-oriented play projects are also less likely to highlight children's differences in ability.

Teachers in the intermediate grades often report frustration with "mainstreaming" or "inclusion" when it does not automatically result in peers playing together (Iano, Ayers, Heller, McGettigan, & Walker, 1974; Taylor, Asher, & Williams, 1987). The extent or type of a child's disability or a child's general developmental level, compared to peers, may figure into how well others will accept the child as a play partner. There is evidence, however, that over the course of the school year, the peer status of children with and without disabilities becomes more similar as children in groups became more familiar with each other (Dunlop, Stoneman, & Cantrell, 1980).

The Influences of Educational Environment on Peer Play

As peer groups engage in the activities of an educational environment, the teacher, the emerging peer culture, and factors in the setting coalesce to influence young children's early peer interactions (Corsaro, 1985; Fernie & DeVries, 1990; Kantor, Elgas, & Fernie, 1989; Rizzo, 1989). Although there are few studies on the educational environment's influence on children's peer group status and relationships, the existing studies provide some suggestive information with respect to program philosophy, adult roles, physical environment, daily schedule, and activity structure.

Program Philosophy

Some children in Montessori schools, for example, engage in more constructive play but less dramatic role-play than children in more traditional preschools (Rubin, 1977). In a comparison of several curricular models, researchers found that constructivist, child-centered approaches, compared to other curriculum approaches, fostered greater cooperative peer play and positive conflict resolution (DeVries, Haney, & Zan, 1991). Some specific curriculum models include the High/Scope approach, which encourages children to plan, take initiative, and carry out activities individually and in peer dyads and peer groups (Hohmann, 1989). Another curriculum model is the project approach, in which children pursue their interests and collaborate in sustained projects (Katz & Chard, 1989). In such approaches, the sociomoral atmosphere supports children's reasoning about social relations such as conflict resolution. In contrast to controlling or discouraging

children's actions by giving attention to rules, these approaches emphasize growth in children's knowledge, understanding, and experiences, thus supporting or fostering their peer social development.

Teachers' Roles

Teachers' roles and philosophical orientations about how involved they should be with children's social development in the classroom vary greatly. On the one hand, when adults over-control and provide too little constructive input into activities, children may spend more time in onlooking and unoccupied behaviors and engage in fewer cooperative interactions (Pellegrini, 1984). Adults who hover may provide instructions, direct activities, or reprimand children for misbehavior. Such actions are not compatible with constructive or cooperative play among peers. But adults can also facilitate children's play. In a study of the year-long evolution of "circle time," preschool teachers effectively used both modeling and direct instructions to guide children in taking turns and responding meaningfully to each other in conversations (Kantor, Elgas, & Fernie, 1989).

Physical Environment

Physical environmental features such as size, design, structure, and available materials can influence the size of peer groups and the type of peer play. Large areas designed for gross motor play, for example, usually attract groups of four or more children (Vandenberg, 1981). In enclosed spaces, children are more likely to engage in cooperative play, but these places may also stimulate more territorial disputes (Ramsey, 1986). In lofts and other single-entrance spaces, children tend to cooperate in repelling the advances of peers who might try to enter. Complex materials and well-defined role-play areas usually promote more interactive and imaginative peer play. In art activities, for example, children usually engage in parallel and constructive play; in block activities they also play constructively, but are more likely to interact (Pellegrini, 1984). With intermediate-age children, open, flexible physical environmental arrangements that foster group interactive learning and problem solving are especially appropriate, as are activities that extend to other areas of the school and community (Bergen & Oden, 1988).

Schedule

The daily schedule also can affect children's social participation. After ten or more minutes, children's play becomes more complex. Thus, preschool programs with play periods of thirty minutes or more are most conducive to young children's cooperative play (Tegano & Parsons, 1989). In contrast to the more fluid preschool context, the elementary school schedule often limits children's opportunities to interact. As a result, children may engage in less spontaneous peer interactions and may decide ahead of time with which specific peers they will play, even during unstructured activities such as recess (Rizzo, 1989).

Classroom Grouping

The structure of the classroom also influences children's peer contacts and play. First-grade children in one study, for example, were aware of which peers were in the higher and lower reading groups (Rizzo, 1989). These children also played more often with classmates at their own reading levels and tended to tease or reject peers in the lower reading groups. There is some evidence that children in classrooms structured so that they play in "interest groups" are more likely to make friends with children of a wider range of performance levels than children in more competitive classrooms that are structured around academic competition and ability groups (Bossert, 1979). A great deal of research has shown that carefully planned, well-run, cooperative activity groups can increase children's academic achievement as well as foster their positive peer relationships (Sapon-Shevin, 1986; Slavin, 1988) and increase the numbers of other-race and mixed-ability peer play partners (Slavin, 1988).

Summary of Key Influences

The examination of research above indicates that siblings provide opportunities for children to:

- Learn how to lead, compromise, and accommodate
- Experience a close relationship
- Experience constructing play in a family context
- Experience challenge and resolve conflicts
- Share and develop individuality
- Learn to contend with differences in age, gender, and other factors

Children's interactions and relationships with their peers offer opportunities to:

- Learn about different cultural and family backgrounds
- Broaden their experience with a diversity of peers
- Broaden their experience in constructing play activities
- Develop friendships and other peer relationships
- Develop individuality apart from siblings and family
- Engage in different social roles in various play activities

Guidelines for Parents and Educators

Parents often wonder what they can do to promote positive sibling interactions, including play. More often, they are really interested in how to discourage sibling conflict. Primarily, parents should understand that sibling conflict, while irritating, is normal and to be expected. Because so many types of variables influence sibling play and conflict, there is a limited amount that parents can reasonably do to affect the nature of their children's interactions. They can, for example, provide good models for perspective taking, conflict resolution, and imaginative involvement. Beyond that, they need to set limits around sibling conflict so that the children do not harm one another. It is generally considered unrealistic and unwise for parents to involve themselves in all instances of sibling conflict, because doing so may prevent the development of conflict resolution skills in the children. Putting these cautions aside, there are many things that parents can do to support the constructive social development of their children, such as:

- Give attention to each sibling to lessen the tendency for children to compete for attention
- Provide opportunities for siblings to play in structured and unstructured activities in the home
- Observe a sibling or peer conflict, allow the children the opportunity to determine the pathways to resolve the conflicts, and intervene only when there appears to be danger of harm to a child

- Create opportunities for each child to express and develop individual interests and personalities, thus lessening some children's tendencies to either dominate or accommodate to their siblings or peers
- Construct occasions for their children to play with other peers to help siblings not get "locked" into roles

Educators might consider that children may carry play roles from their sibling play into their play with classroom peers. They need to design educational experiences, therefore to expand children's social roles and experiences. Although there needs to be more research, educators face numerous challenges as they help children to construct positive peer relationships (see Oden & Ramsey, 1993, for recommended research directions). One main challenge for educators is to help those children who lack social skills learn to join a group, form friendships, and resolve conflicts without antisocial aggression. When educators encourage children to develop and express their individual interests, they also help the children to constructively attract peer interest and learn more from, and about, each other. Another main challenge for educators is to set up activities that discourage the stigmatization of children who are different in various ways, such as their ethnic or economic background, language, gender, and social or other skill differences. Furthermore, while educators should discourage exclusive friendships by providing activities that mix peers together, children should have times in the daily schedule to play and converse with peers to form and sustain friendships and activity partnerships. Through creative planning of activities and situations, educators can develop many approaches to support and facilitate positive and constructive peer interactions and relationships. Educators can:

- Create interesting activities to help children get to know each other in a variety of peer relationships through friendships and activity partners
- Encourage reticent or quieter children to enter peer activities and converse with peers by coaching them in communication and cooperation skills for resolving conflicts
- Help children who are locked into a conflict or are becoming harmful to others by asking each child to take the other's perspective, propose solutions, compromises, or accommodations that allow each child to benefit
- Structure learning situations to offset tendencies for peer stigmatization due to differences in race or ethnicity, social class, gender, or learning styles or skills
- Structure learning situations to encourage children to play a variety of social roles, including leader, helper, friend, and activity collaborator

Peers and siblings will have conflicts but will also enjoy each other, play creatively, and form unique relationships that allow for individuality. Their play offers major opportunities for children's social development. Siblings, for example, can prepare each other for current and subsequent peer interactions; thus, they may enrich or restrict peer social development. While both sibling and peer interaction can be conflictual, the conflict is a further opportunity to learn about individual differences and to learn to construct a balance between cooperation and compromise, while taking individual desires into consideration. Sibling relationships, somewhat like best friendships, can provide a secure basis for learning about another person with room for individual expression. These relationships, however, can also be too exclusive and limiting. Parents and educators, therefore, must endeavor to be creative in their planning of activities and situations that foster and support their children's development of constructive, enriching peer and sibling interactions and relationships.

Bibliography

Asher, S. R., & Wheeler, V. A. (1985). Children's loneliness: A comparison of rejected and neglected peer status. *Journal of Consulting and Clinical Psychology, 53,* 500–505.

Bergen, D., & Oden, S. (1988). Designing play environments for elementary age children. In D. Bergen (Ed.), *Play as a medium for learning and development* (pp. 245–269). Portsmouth, NH: Heinemann.

Boer, F., & Dunn, J. (Eds.). (1992). *Children's sibling relationships: Developmental and clinical issues.* Hillsdale, NJ: Lawrence Erlbaum.

Bossert, S. T. (1979). *Tasks and social relationships in classrooms: A study of instructional organization and its consequences.* New York: Cambridge University Press.

Coie, J. D., & Kupersmidt, J. B. (1983). A behavioral analysis of emerging social status in boys' groups. *Child Development, 54,* 1400–1416.

Corsaro, W. A. (1985). *Friendship and peer culture in the early years.* Norwood, NJ: Ablex.

DeVries, R., Haney, J. P., & Zan, B. (1991). Sociomoral atmosphere in direct-instruction, eclectic, and constructivist kindergartens: A study of teachers' enacted interpersonal understanding. *Early Childhood Research Quarterly, 6,* 449–471.

Doyle, A. (1982). Friends, acquaintances, and strangers: The influence of family and ethnolinguistic background on social interaction. In K. H. Rubin & H. S. Ross (Eds.), *Peer relationships and social skills in childhood* (pp. 229–252). New York: Springer-Verlag.

Dunlop, K. H., Stoneman, Z., & Cantrell, M. L. (1980). Social interaction of exceptional and other children in mainstreamed preschool children. *Exceptional Children, 47*(2), 132–141.

Dunn, J. (1983). Sibling relationships in early childhood. *Child Development, 54,* 787–811.

Dunn, J. (1992). Sisters and brothers: Current issues in developmental research. In F. Boer & J. Dunn (Eds.), *Children's sibling relationships: Developmental and clinical issues* (pp. 1–17). Hillsdale, NJ: Lawrence Erlbaum.

Dunn, J., & Munn, P. (1986). Siblings and the development of prosocial behavior. *International Journal of Behavioral Development, 9,* 265–284.

Dunn, J., Slomkowski, C., & Beardsall, L. (1994). Sibling relationships from the pre-school period through middle childhood and early adolescence. *Developmental Psychology, 30,* 315–324.

Fernie, D. E., & DeVries, R. (1990). Young children's reasoning in games of nonsocial and social logic: "Tic Tac Toe" and a "Guessing Game." *Early Childhood Research Quarterly, 5,* 445–460.

Finkelstein, N. W., & Haskins, R. (1983). Kindergarten children prefer same-color peers. *Child Development, 54,* 502–508.

Goodman, H., Gottlieb, J., & Harrison, R. H. (1972). Social acceptance of EMRs integrated into a non-graded elementary school. *American Journal of Mental Deficiency, 76,* 412–417.

Herzberger, S. D., & Hall, J. A. (1993). Consequences of retaliatory aggression against siblings and peers: Urban minority children's expectations. *Child Development, 64,* 1773–1785.

Hetherington, E. M., Cox, M., & Cox, R. (1979). Play and social interaction in children following divorce. *Journal of Social Issues, 35,* 126–149.

Hohmann, M. (1989, September). Social and emotional development in the High/Scope approach. *Extensions, 4*(1), 1–4. Ypsilanti, MI: High/Scope Press.

Howes, C. (1987). Social competence with peers and young children. *Developmental Review, 7,* 252–272.

Howes, C. (1988). Peer interactions of young children. Monographs of the *Society for Research in Child Development, 53*(1, Serial No. 217).

Iano, R. P., Ayers, D., Heller, H. B., McGettigan, F. J., & Walker, V. S. (1974). Sociometric status of retarded children in an integrative program. *Exceptional Children, 40*(4), 267–271.

Kagan, J., Reznick, J. S., & Gibbons, J. (1989). Inhibited and uninhibited types of children. *Child Development, 60,* 838–845.

Kantor, R. Elgas, P. M., & Fernie, D. E. (1989). First the look and then the sound: Creating conversations at circle time. *Early Childhood Research Quarterly, 4,* 433–448.

Katz, L. G., & Chard, S. C. (1989). *Engaging children's minds.* Norwood, NJ: Ablex.

Kier, C. A., & Fouts, G. T. (1989). Sibling play in divorced and married-parent families. *Journal of Reproductive and Infant Psychology, 7,* 139–146.

Ladd, G. (1981). Effectiveness of a social learning method for enhancing children's social interaction and peer acceptance. *Child Development, 52,* 171–178.

Maccoby, E. E. (1986). Social groupings in childhood: Their relationship to prosocial and antisocial behavior in boys and girls. In D. Olewus, J. Block, & M. Radke-Yarrow (Eds.), *Development of antisocial and prosocial development* (pp. 263–284). New York: Academic.

MacKinnon, C. E. (1989). Sibling interactions in married and divorced families: Influence of ordinal position, socioeconomic status, and play context. *Journal of Divorce, 12,* 221–234.

Mize, J., & Ladd, G. W. (1990). A cognitive-social learning approach to social skill training with low-status preschool children. *Developmental Psychology, 26*(3), 388–397.

Munn, P., & Dunn, J. (1989). Temperament and the developing relationship between siblings. *International Journal of Behavioral Development, 12,* 433–451.

Newman, M. A., Liss, M. B., & Sherman, F. (1983). Ethnic awareness in children: Not a unitary concept. *Journal of Genetic Psychology, 143,* 103–112.

Oden, S. (1986). Developing social skills instruction for peer interaction and relationships. In G. Carledge & J. F. Milburn (Eds.), *Teaching social skills to children* (2nd ed., pp. 246–269). New York: Pergamon.

Oden, S. (1988). Alternative perspective on children's peer relationships. In T. D. Yawkey & J. E. Johnson (Eds.), *Integrative processes and socialization: Early to middle childhood* (pp. 139–166). Hillsdale, NJ: Lawrence Erlbaum.

Oden, S., & Asher, S. R. (1977). Coaching children in social skills for friendship making. *Child Development, 48,* 495–506.

Oden, S., & Ramsey, P. G. (1993). Implementing research on children's social competence: What do teachers and researchers need to learn? *Exceptionality Education Canada, 3*(1 and 2), 209–232.

Parker, J. G., & Asher, S. R. (1987). Peer relations and later adjustment: Are low-accepted children "at risk"? *Psychological Bulletin, 102,* 357–389.

Pellegrini, A. D. (1984). The social cognitive ecology of preschool classrooms: Contextual relations revisited. *International Journal of Behavioral Development, 7,* 321–332.

Ramsey, P. G. (1986). Possession disputes in preschool classrooms. *Child Study Journal, 16,* 173–181.

Ramsey, P. G. (1989, April). *Friendships, groups, and: Changing social dynamics in early childhood classrooms.* Paper presented at the biennial meeting of the Society for Research in Child Development, Kansas City, MO.

Ramsey, P. G. (1991). *Making friends in school: Promoting peer relationships in early childhood.* New York: Teachers College Press.

Ramsey, P. G., & Myers, L. C. (1990). Salience of race in young children's cognitive, affective, and behavioral responses to social environments. *Journal of Applied Developmental Psychology, 11,* 49–67.

Ramsey, P. G., & Theokas, C. (1993, March). *The effects of classroom interventions on young children's cross-sex contacts and perceptions.* Paper presented at the biennial meeting of the Society for Research in Child Development, New Orleans, LA.

Rizzo, T. A. (1989). *Friendship development among children in school.* Norwood, NJ: Ablex.

Rubin, K. H. (1977). Play behaviors of young children. *Young Children, 32,* 16–24.

Rubin, K. H., Hymel, S., & Mills, S. L. (1989). Sociability and social withdrawal in childhood: Stability and outcomes. *Journal of Personality, 57*(2), 237–255.

Sapon-Shevin, M. (1986). Teaching cooperation. In G. Cartledge & J. M. Milburn (Eds.), *Teaching social skills to children* (2nd ed., pp. 270–302). New York: Pergamon.

Serbin, L. A., Tonick, I. J., & Sternglanz, S. H. (1977). Shaping cooperative cross-sex play. *Child Development, 48,* 924–929.

Singleton L. C., & Asher, S. R. (1977). Peer preferences and social interaction among third-grade children in an integrated school district. *Journal of Educational Psychology, 69,* 330–336.

Singleton, L. C., & Asher, S. R. (1979). Racial integration and children's peer preferences: An investigation of developmental and cohort differences. *Child Development, 50,* 936–941.

Slavin, R. E. (1988). *Student team learning: An overview and practical guide.* Washington, DC: National Education Association.

Stevenson, M. B., Leavitt, L. A., Thompson, R. H., & Roach, M. A. (1988). A social relations model analysis of parent and child play. *Developmental Psychology, 24,* 101–108.

Stoneman, Z., Brody, G. H., & MacKinnon, C. (1984). Naturalistic observations of children's activities with their siblings and friends. *Child Development, 55,* 617–627.

Stoneman, Z., Brody, G. H., & MacKinnon, C. (1986). Same-sex and cross-sex siblings: Activity choices, roles, behaviors, and gender stereotypes. *Sex Roles, 15,* 495–511.

Taylor, A. R., Asher, S. R., & Williams, G. A. (1987). The social adaptation of mainstreamed mildly retarded children. *Child Development, 58,* 1321–1334.

Tegano, D., & Parsons, M. (1989, April). *The effects of structure and play period duration on preschoolers' play.* Paper presented at the biennial meeting of the Society for Research in Child Development, Kansas City, MO.

Teti, D. M., Bond, L. A., & Gibbs, E. D. (1988). Mothers, fathers, and siblings: A comparison of play styles and their influence upon infant cognitive level. *International Journal of Behavioral Development, 11,* 415–432.

Vandenberg, B. (1981). Environmental and cognitive factors in social play. *Journal of Experimental Child Psychology, 31,* 169–175.

Adult Influences on Play

The Vygotskian Approach

Elena Bodrova
Deborah J. Leong

Contexts for Play

In the cultural-historical approach developed by Vygotsky and his colleagues and students, "play" as currently understood is a relatively late phenomenon in human history (Elkonin, 1978). In primitive societies, when children functioned as equals with adults in such tasks as helping to gather food or tend animals, modern play did not exist. Play at that time was primarily pragmatic in that it sharpened needed skills and could not be differentiated from the actual adult activities. Children made things with carpentry tools, for example, and hunted with miniature bows and arrows.

Modern play is nonpragmatic in that it does not prepare the child for specific skills or activities, but prepares the child's mind for the learning tasks of today as well as future tasks that humans cannot yet imagine. Modern play emerged as society evolved, as professional skills required more and more training, and as the information to be learned became more complicated and demanding. Not only does the modern training process take more time, but it is also based on more advanced psychological abilities. Until children develop sufficient underlying skills and abilities, they will not be able to acquire the knowledge base and skills necessary for this highly industrialized and technical society. Children who are seven years of age, for example, cannot be taught how to program a computer system even by the most gifted teacher unless the child has an extensive background of numerical skills and the logical understandings that are the prerequisites for understanding programming.

Vygotskians argue that, while formal schooling provides the training for these advanced psychological processes, play produces important prerequisites for them (Vygotsky, 1966/1977). Children's observable play provides the means for acquiring and practicing underlying skills in preparation for learning the more advanced and technical ones later. Much human learning, for example, requires literacy. Play prepares the child for literacy by providing practice and opportunities to master the making and manipulation of symbols and representations. Until children can think and draw using symbols, they will not be able to learn to read.

Nonpragmatic play gives children very broad and general experience that prepares the mind for later learning. It helps children to develop social skills, to regulate emotional reactions, and to master cognitive skills. Since social skills have been the focus of much Western research, there are aspects of Vygotskian theory that expand and enrich this understanding of how children develop self-regulation and cognitive abilities in play.

As is true of other mental processes in the Vygotskian approach, play is something that is coconstructed and not invented by the child alone (Vygotsky, 1930/1978). Coconstruction involves interaction with another person, either another child or an adult. Adults historically have supported play in different ways depending on whether play was pragmatic. In addition, the adult role in play depends on the child's age, play stage, and the abilities of other children. When children are younger, the older person takes on a larger role in the play, for example, labeling what the child is doing. As the child matures, the adult will be a coequal in developing the plot or may follow the child's lead, responding to the child's directives.

The Definition of Play
in the Vygotskian Approach

For behavior to be classified as "play," it must have specific characteristics that include creating an imaginary situation having defined roles with implicit rules, and using language.

First, play must create an imaginary situation in which children pretend "as if." As children mature, these imaginary situations become more elaborate and are shared between partners. You can tell if this imaginary situation has emerged when children play with objects in novel, unconventional ways or use language to change the function of an object, for example, "Let's pretend the spoon is a magic wand."

Play's second characteristic is that it has defined roles with implicit rules for acting in each role. A child will play being the teacher, which implies that he or she must act in a specific way that is different from when he or she is acting as the student. The role is identified aloud to the other participants in the play. The rules for acting out the role are not necessarily spelled out, but can be seen when a child violates them. When the "teacher" brings a "baby" to school, for example, other children will protest that the teacher doesn't have a baby. Only when the "teacher" says "I'm a mommy and a teacher" would this violation be allowed. Children can adjust their roles or take another role that implies that the rules have also changed.

Finally, play must involve language. The child must be able to label the role and describe the imaginary situation. The child is either talking to other children, negotiating roles and the imaginary situation, or the child can be engaged in self-directed speech. Children use language to help create and maintain the play. Thus a child who is trying on hats would not necessarily be considered "playing" unless the child says or can explain, "I'm playing hat store and I'm going to buy myself a nice hat to go to a party." Without the language, the child is only exploring the material, not playing. Both language and the contents of children's play offer observable opportunities to assess the developmental level of play.

The Importance of Play
in Development

The Zone of Proximal Development
Vygotskians define development with two levels on which a child can perform at any given

time (Vygotsky, 1966/1977). The lower level is what the child can do independently, without help from anyone. The upper level of the child's ability is what that same child can do with assistance from another person either directly or indirectly. The zone of proximal development (ZPD) is the distance between the lower and upper levels. It defines where the child's learning happens. The ZPD is a dynamic structure because as the child masters skills that were previously assisted, new skills emerge at the upper level of the zone. Most of the examples of the ZPD given in Western literature show adults or peers in the classroom providing assistance. For Vygotsky, however, the ZPD extends to informal settings, such as play interactions with adults, siblings, and peers.

For many behaviors, play provides support at the highest levels of the ZPD. The same five-year-old, for example, who cannot stop interrupting the teacher and talks during group time, when playing school with another child can hold up his or her hand and pretend to be a "model student." As the child's self-regulatory skills develop through play, it is possible to expect that in the future this child will be able to stop interrupting during group time.

Play facilitates the transition to more mature functioning in the following ways: (1) It forces children to renounce reactive behavior (2) promotes symbolic thinking, and (3) provides a context to practice planning and self-regulation.

Setting Limits on Behavior
One of the distinctive features of the Vygotskian approach to play is the belief that the play situation actually sets limits on a child's behavior instead of setting the child "free" or promoting totally spontaneous behavior (Berk, 1995; Berk & Winsler, 1995). To engage in play, children must act in a specific way that is agreed upon by other children. If the children are playing bus, for example, there is a driver and passengers. Not everyone can be a bus driver, and all of the participants have specific behaviors they perform. The driver, for example, announces the stops, opens the door, takes tickets, and drives; the passengers enter and leave from a specific place, buy tickets, give the tickets to the driver, and sit down. The "passenger" who starts opening the bus door or pretends to drive will be chastised by the

other children, who will note, "You can't do that. You aren't the driver."

For Vygotsky, therefore, play has very specific roles and rules (Vygotsky, 1966/1977). To be "in" the play you must renounce your immediate spontaneous wishes and conform to the way you are supposed to act and play. Children, however, change and renegotiate these roles and rules, so play does not become a rigid script that the actors follow. Neither is it a mosaic of unrelated actions and episodes with each child's spontaneous interests acted out without any coordination. So strong is the desire to integrate each child's separate actions into a whole that preschool children will assign a special role to a younger child who is not able to invent his or her own. This allows the little one to participate without disrupting the play of others.

Promoting Symbolic Thinking

Another feature of play is that it facilitates the separation of thought from actions and objects (Vygotsky, 1934/1962, 1930/1978). Children act in accordance with internal ideas or symbols rather than external reality. They pretend that the wooden block is a telephone or a boat; they are not dependent on having the actual object. In the early stages of play, children will treat the block in the same way they would a telephone. As children's play matures, they use language to substitute for action; it is enough, for example, to say, "Let's pretend that this is the phone." Overt actions become more and more abbreviated, and symbolic thought in the form of language begins to represent the constellation of actions and behaviors associated with a specific role.

Children create a fantasy world that may have objects that do not exist in reality. Through language they create a shared fantasy with another child and act out their fantasy. This ability to depart from reality and function in a world of imagination and symbols is the first step toward the development of abstract symbolic thought.

Practicing Planning and Self-Regulation

Another important aspect of self-regulation in play is the ability to plan, monitor, and reflect on one's own behavior (Elkonin, 1978). These regulatory skills set the stage for the later development of metacognitive skills when children plan, monitor, and reflect on thinking. For Vygotskians, children who do not practice planning, monitoring, and reflecting on their overt behaviors will not be able to use these processes in their mental actions.

In play, children must reflect on their own plans—what they want to do—and think about how to make these plans merge with the themes and plans of the other partners. For example, David wants to be the garage mechanic, but his friend Linda has already started playing hospital with another child. David has to revise his initial idea of the garage and his role of mechanic into becoming the ambulance driver so he can still wear the tool belt, fix the car, drive, and yet keep interacting with his friends.

The Role of Adults in the Development of Play

Adults influence child play in both an indirect and a direct way. Adults influence play indirectly by setting up the environment, choosing toys and props, and encouraging children to play together: "Why don't you play with Susan?" Adults also provide experiences that become the fodder for play themes. For example, a field trip or book about zoo animals leads to playing zoo.

For Vygotskians, adults may also directly influence child play, particularly in the case of toddlers and young preschoolers who may lack necessary skills. Teachers may model, for example, how to play with a toy, take turns, settle disputes, and then describe to a partner what one is going to do: "I'm going to be the zebra and you are the lion." As a rule, as children progress toward more advanced levels of play, the need for adult intervention decreases.

Infants and Toddlers: Preparation for Play

Vygotskians do not use the word play to describe many of the interactions infants and toddlers have with objects and people. This is different from Western views, where the word play is used more broadly. Because infants explore objects using sensorimotor actions, not involving any symbolic representation, Vygotskians do not consider this to be play. Infants can use objects in a nonconventional way, not because they are pretending, but because they do not know how to use the object.

Preparation for play occurs in infancy. The most important thing about the interactions that occur in infancy is the establishment of a warm, caring relationship with a caregiver. This attachment becomes the foundation of all later learning, which for Vygotskians always takes place in a social context. Thus, the baby learns how to use objects as well as how to interact with others. Learning to manipulate objects and to interact with others about these objects are precursors to being able to use objects in pretend play. In addition, infants acquire language, which is the third characteristic of play through interaction with others.

The role of adults during infancy is to establish the attachment and to interact with the baby using toys, books, and other objects. But adults should not rely on objects alone as the primary way to stimulate development: without interaction with another person around these objects, the infant will not acquire mature levels of play later on. It would be better, therefore, to have fewer toys but more interaction with people who demonstrate various ways to use those toys.

Toddlerhood is the period when the first elements of play emerge in the child's behavior, but these elements are not organized into a structure as they are at the preschool ages. Toddlers start using objects in a pretend way, although most of their play is determined by the conventional use of objects. The toddler will also take on some roles, but these are usually determined by the characteristics of the objects. Putting on an apron, for example, makes you "Mommy," but this role is not elaborated with speech and action; the apron is enough. Finally, toddlers are in the process of mastering language and they begin to use it to label what they are doing.

The adult role when interacting with toddlers is to help the child see the potential imaginary situation, the roles and implicit rules, the uses of language to describe action, and the ways to facilitate social interaction with peers. The teacher, for example, sees the toddler wearing the apron and says, "Oh, I see you are cooking something. Can I have a piece of pie?" Toddlers may need help using objects in an unconventional way. The teacher might say, "We can pretend there is a pie here." Teachers facilitate social interaction with others by indicating how another child's play can be incorporated into the situation. The teacher might say to a toddler playing alone, "Josh, I see you're driving a truck. Could you drive to the store to get some more flour and milk, and help us make more pies?"

Play in Preschool

During the preschool years, play evolves into its most mature form. By the time they are four and five years of age, children learn to create elaborate imaginary play situations that involve complex roles and extended scenarios. Play themes are begun one day and reworked the next. Preschoolers are able to negotiate roles so that the ideas of a number of partners can be integrated into the whole theme. They use language to describe the actions and roles to be played out. These are discussed in detail, and the actual playing out of the actions and roles begins to take a secondary role to the planning and discussion that precedes it. By the time children are six years of age, the actual overt actions can become abbreviated, with the discussion and preparation to play occupying most of the children's time.

Play as a coconstructed activity is not meant to imply that all of the partners must be physically present. Vygotskians describe a special kind of play, "director's play," when the child pretends alone, playing all of the parts as if there were other people involved. The preschooler plays as if there are imaginary partners there. For example, Joan is having a tea party all by herself. She talks to the animals and then runs to an empty chair and pretends to talk to Joan, the hostess. She changes her voice when she is the visitor and then jumps up and pretends she is the hostess again. She is engaged in what some psychologists would call solitary play (e.g., Parten, 1932), but all the signs of mature play are actually present. Vygotskians consider this play on a par with mature play with others.

For Vygotskians, movement to this mature level of play does not happen naturally when a child turns five or six years of age. Preschoolers learn from others how to play at this mature level. When children interact in mixed-age groups with older children who have mature play, the social context will scaffold the play of the younger children. Playing with an older sibling, an older neighborhood friend, or more mature schoolmate, therefore, will provide the ZPD necessary for development. When children do not have these older children to play with, adults may have to provide the missing scaffolding. This does not mean that the teacher should play in the playhouse like a child, but rather that the teacher should make suggestions or organize activities so that the more mature behavior can emerge.

When a child's play is at the immature level, such as putting shoes in and out of a cupboard, teachers take a more active role by labeling the child's actions and helping the child to define a role. If a child flits from play area to play area without becoming engaged in play, the teacher must find ways to help this child maintain interest to engage in an extended role for longer and longer periods of time. When a child cannot interact with others without fighting, the teacher must intervene to facilitate that child's as well as the other children's interactions.

For Vygotskians, the most beneficial times for teachers to facilitate and scaffold play is during the planning stages and at the end of the play time, when children will plan for the next day's play. Adult monitoring during the entire play time may only be necessary for specific children or groups of children who are having trouble sustaining their interactions. As children begin, the teacher's presence can prompt more discussion and richness of possible roles than the children may be able to initiate on their own. Sensitivity is needed because the teacher will not want to direct the children's play, but just make suggestions that will expand and encourage more pretending. Teachers may have to explain how different people's ideas can be woven into the same play. This planning is not rigid and, as the play evolves, children need to know that they can modify and change their plans.

The ending of a play period is as important as the beginning for Vygotskians. By planning the next day's play, children begin to learn the self-regulation skills necessary for later development. Teachers can facilitate this development by eliciting plans, setting aside props for the next day, or making notes on paper with the children so they can have a reminder of what they wanted to do. This becomes the basis of the next day's discussion. Once again, the teacher should make clear to the children that these are just ideas that they are free to change and modify on the next day. This extended play provides more opportunities to create more complete mental images and to use more complex mental processes.

Play in Elementary School

The fantasy play that emerges in preschool does not die in elementary school, but loses its leading role in cognitive and social development. Vygotskians believe that children still engage in fantasy play well through the elementary grades.

During elementary school, games, another type of play, become the more dominant type of interaction. Like Piaget (1932), Vygotsky believed that rules govern games. For Piaget, games emerge as children lose their egocentrism and become more realistic in their orientation (Smilansky & Shefatya, 1990). For Vygotsky, the existence of rules in fantasy play indicates that the child is not egocentric to begin with and, furthermore, that games are a natural extension of the earlier types of play. In games, the imaginary situation is hidden, and the rules are explicit: "For example, playing chess creates an imaginary situation. Why? Because the knight, king, queen, and so forth can only move in a specified way; because covering and taking pieces are purely chess concepts. Although in the chess game there is no direct substitute for real-life relationships, it is a kind of imaginary situation nevertheless" (Vygotsky, 1930/1978, p. 95).

Games are the context in which children learn more about rules: how to follow the rules, negotiate rules, and reestablish rules. This means that children continue to practice self-regulation in this naturally motivating context. Children can only learn self-regulation by practicing regulating themselves and others, just as they did in fantasy play.

Adults should take a minor role in the children's game playing during the elementary grades. An appropriate role, for example, would include clarifying rules or giving written rules for such games as chess and checkers. Children today too often engage in sports and games such as Little League and team soccer that are completely dominated by adults. Instead of children's learning how to negotiate rules and face the consequences, adults act as referees. If these are the only circumstances in which children play games, then they are robbed of important and necessary practice at self-regulation. Just as in the case of play in the preschool years, children learn games by interacting with peers who are slightly older or more mature.

In the Vygotskian paradigm, play has a unique place in a child's development. Play is not something that all children develop spontaneously. It is learned through interactions with others in a social context. For play to promote the development of cognitive abilities and self-regulation, adults must plan for interactions that are most beneficial and relevant to the child's age and level of play.

Bibliography

Berk, L. E. (1995). Vygotsky's theory: The importance of make-believe play. *Young Children, 50*(1), 30–39.

Berk, L., & Winsler, A. (1995). *Scaffolding children's learning: Vygotsky and early childhood education.* Washington, DC: National Association for the Education of Young Children.

Elkonin, D. (1978). *Psikhologija igry* [The psychology of play]. Moscow: Pedagogika.

Parten, M. B. (1932). Social participation among preschool children. *Journal of Abnormal and Social Psychology, 27,* 243–269.

Piaget, J. (1932). *The moral judgement of the child* (M. Gabain, Trans.). New York: Harcourt, Brace and World.

Smilansky, S., & Shefatya, L. (1990). *Facilitating play: A medium for promoting cognitive, socio-emotional, and academic development in young children.* Gaithersburg, MD: Psychological Educational Publications.

Vygotsky, L. S. (1962). *Thought and language* (E. Hanfmann & Gertude Vakar, Trans.). Cambridge, MA: MIT Press. (Original work published 1934)

Vygotsky, L. S. (1977). Play and its role in the mental development of the child. In M. Cole (Ed.), *Soviet developmental psychology* (pp. 76–99). White Plains, NY: M. E. Sharpe. (Original work published 1966)

Vygotsky, L. S. (1978). *Mind and society: The development of higher mental processes.* Cambridge, MA: Harvard University Press. (Original work published 1930)

Intergenerational Play

Parents and Children

Mary Martin Patton

The mass media is replete with commentaries on the demise of the traditional family in the United States. Clearly the stereotypic *Leave It to Beaver* family is no longer characteristic of most children and their families. Changing family structures and lifestyles have resulted in the fragmentation of the extended family, the elimination of the neighborhood as a social entity, and an emphasis on age-segregated programs such as elder care and child care (Powell & Arquitt, 1978). Concerns about the effects of intergenerational isolation have prompted research and writing about programs that bring adults and children together (e.g., Aday, Sims, McDuffie, & Evans, 1996).

Many children spend the majority of their days with same-age peers in care and educational settings for young children where they have few opportunities for close, personal, sustained adult-child experiences. In addition, the "hurried child" syndrome (Elkind, 1988) has parents rushing their children to same-age activities, such as dance, Scouts, and soccer after school or child care, leaving little time for parent-child play and sibling play. Educators and psychologists, recognizing the value of intergenerational experiences for children, as well as for socially isolated adults, have implemented various innovations in an effort to bridge the intergenerational gap. The most frequent references in the literature are to intergenerational programs for older adults and children in collaborative elder care/child care settings (Chamberlain, 1994; Powell & Arquitt, 1978) and family literacy programs (Paratore, 1992).

Research on intergenerational play is emerging, however, as researchers focus on the changing families in our contemporary so-ciety (Swick, 1993). The discussion that follows addresses a number of issues concerning the intergenerational play between parents and children.

Parent-Child Play

The phenomenon of play has been studied extensively (Bergen, 1988; Fromberg, 1992); researchers from diverse disciplines have examined play from many perspectives and contexts, including that of adult-child interaction. Adult-child interaction in play is a key factor in helping (or hindering) children to scaffold their learning. The adult as the "expert" play partner guides and, in the best of play interactions, leads development (Berk & Winsler, 1995). While there are few observational studies of parent-child play interactions with school-age children (Bergen, 1988), existing studies show that the most "effective" parent-child play appears to rely on the parent's playfulness rather than directiveness (Levenstein & O'Hara, 1993). Historically the notion of the "playful" adult has captured the interest of many who study the development of children. Researchers support the belief that playful interactions are as beneficial for the adult as for the child. As one researcher says, "The adult who remains aloof from play misses opportunities for engaging with and learning from children" (Frost, 1992, p. 336).

The early play of mothers and their children is well documented in the play literature (Bretherton, 1984). Many investigators have found that infant and toddler play is more sophisticated with adult play partners (Escalona, 1968; Power & Parke, 1980; Stevenson,

Leavitt, Thompson, & Roach, 1988). Similarly, studies of children four to eleven years old indicate a strong correlation between the imaginative life of the parents and that of their children (Singer & Singer, 1990). Parents of highly imaginative children engage in playful interactions through storytelling, reading, and fantasy games, and they restrict television watching. In turn, imaginative children consistently exhibit improved cognitive performance, less aggression, and less restlessness (Singer & Singer, 1988). Parents who attach importance to play provide a large number of toys, set aside space for play, join in the play of their children (Smilansky, 1968), and bring a "lightness" to the play relationship that supports optimal cognitive and social-emotional development (Levenstein & O'Hara, 1993, p. 234).

Numerous studies have examined the ways adults step in and out of play and the roles they assume when interacting with children (Johnson, Christie, & Yawkey, 1987). Including adults (caregivers and parents) in play with children as a means of enhancing children's development (Graul & Zeece, 1992) is consistently documented as an effective way to promote higher levels of social and cognitive play, but always with the caveat that inclusion of adults must not be "too intrusive, overpowering, or one-sided" (Sutton-Smith, 1993, p. 24). Adult education models that teach caregivers and parents to assume play roles of parallel player, coplayer, play tutor, and spokesperson for reality have demonstrated success in fostering children's cognitive and social growth (Johnson, Christie, & Yawkey, 1987; Smilansky, 1968). The Mother-Child Home Program (Levenstein & O'Hara, 1993), for example, introduces mothers of at-risk preschoolers to toys and books to use in fun rather than encouraging didactic interactions with their children. Follow-up studies of the children who participated indicate lasting gains in academic achievement. Researchers attribute these findings to the program mothers' increased ability to stimulate verbal behaviors in their children by responding in warm conversational ways that supported play dialogues (Levenstein & O'Hara, 1993). The data on the importance of parent-child play are compelling and have generated "considerable confidence . . . that the parent's play with the child makes a difference in the child's playfulness and in the child's competence as measured both cognitively and socially" (Sutton-Smith, 1993, p. 20).

Modern Influences That Decrease Intergenerational Play

Those who study play lament and deplore the decline of play opportunities for children. Increased work demands for dual-working and single-income families, coupled with formalized activities for children, have resulted in a loss of time available for family interaction. By some estimates family time has shrunk by ten to twelve hours a week since 1960 (Fuchs, 1988). What, then, are families doing with the remaining time? The technology explosion has had a dramatic impact on family interaction. Children are spending more hours watching television, playing on computers, and using video games than ever before (Guddemi & Jambor, 1993). Many children have televisions, video games, and stereos in their bedrooms, ensuring that from a very young age they can "disappear" for hours on end to engage in solitary recreation. This effectively robs families of the little time they do have together.

One author laments the shrinking of indoor and outdoor spaces designed and provisioned with children in mind (Elkind, 1994). In homes, the game room space that used to be set aside for children has given way to in-home offices and workout rooms for adults. Contemporary development of indoor playgrounds encages children with untrained young adults who supervise while parents go off to soundproof rooms to read, exercise, or watch television. Outdoor playground designs often manifest little thought to supporting intergenerational play; in fact, by their very design they encourage parents to stand back and watch (Boyer, 1991).

Families often are unaware of the importance of parent-child play. They need access to the information on the importance of family play time and specific suggestions for managing passive television viewing and solitary video game playing. Most importantly, they need viable alternatives to these very seductive pastimes. Recently, educators and designers have shifted from bemoaning the "families in demise" to making a proactive commitment to helping contemporary families make the transition into new interactive structures that may better serve children. They have designed various innovative intergenerational play spaces that encourage family experiences. Although they hold promise, there is a need for research on the effectiveness of such approaches.

Designing Intergenerational Play Spaces and Experiences for Families

A recent trend toward more inclusionary play settings has resulted in a number of innovative designs. Some of these are commercially implemented while others are public programs.

Commercial Initiatives

The Richard Scarry "Busytown" exhibit touring the country, for example, is a hands-on science and technology play environment for children and parents. The construction, exploration, and sociodramatic play opportunities are accessible to both parents and children. Each station has explanations in English and Spanish of what children might be learning as they play, and suggests questioning and extension strategies for parents. Another innovation is "Sesame Place" in Langhorne, Pennsylvania, a family-oriented physical play park specifically designed to provide a variety of play experiences that appeal to both adults and children (Clements, 1995). It provides families with nine acres of mazes, climbing structures, water tubes and slides, performers, and creative picnic areas. The goal of the developers is to promote intergenerational socialization and education. Parents have the opportunity to participate in demonstrations on ways to provide play activities and environments at home. McDonald's has developed a pay-to-play environment that is also designed to encourage families to play together (Boyer, 1991). This environment, called "Leaps and Bounds," offers parents and children forty different play possibilities organized by age in an eleven-thousand-square-foot playground (Boyer, 1991 p. 103).

Public Parks and Recreation Facilities

Parks and recreation programs around the country are also addressing the need for intergenerational play in response to "a decade marred by television addiction, poor fitness, high blood pressure, tension headaches and drug abuse" (Brock, 1994, p. 65). Tips for involving families include "generation mixing," accommodating family schedules, and teaching recreational skills to both parents and children rather than focusing exclusively on competitive spectator sports. At the same time, recreation specialists are cautioned not to assume that parents and children know how to share a rec-

reational experience, as "they may have never participated in something really fun together before" (Brock, 1994 p. 65).

Museums

Museums have become the single most popular out-of-home family activity in the United States (Dierking & Falk, 1994). Over four hundred children's museums have been developed since the 1970s (Boyer, 1991). The Fort Worth Museum of Science and History boasts several family attractions, including "DinoDig," "KIDSPACE," and the "Hands-on Science" exhibits where children and parents can dig for dinosaur bones, build houses, play at the water station, dismantle machines at the take-apart table, and explore aerodynamics at the air table. The possibilities for informal science through play are limitless.

Toy Libraries

Toy libraries are another response to the need to promote family play. They have toy collections ranging from fifty to five thousand toys in more than five hundred programs around the United States (Iacuzzi, 1995–1996). While toy libraries function in a variety of ways around the world, they share a common purpose of promoting shared play and the loan of toys (Brodin & Bjorck-Akesson, 1992). Toy libraries have played an especially important role for families with disabled children by providing specially adapted toys that activate with minimal pressure, voice commands, or light (Jackson, Robey, Watjust & Chadwick, 1991). The Maryland Department of Education provided funds for ten counties in the state to establish Activity, Book, and Toy Libraries (Weiss, 1995). They are administered through the public school system and are housed in elementary schools. At the ABT Libraries parents can check out simple kits containing a book, a toy, and instructions for an activity.

Community Initiatives

All children and families need access to intergenerational play opportunities. Museums, pay-to-play environments, and recreational programs often are not an option for low-income families who do not have the resources to get to the site or pay to play. Communities must take back their neighborhoods for families. Safe, attractive neighborhoods promote more positive and nurturing interactions among families (Popenoe, 1988); active, supportive family involvement in social settings is correlated with low crime rates (Wilson & Herrnstein, 1985). Communities across the country are beginning to turn vacant lots and vacant buildings into places for families to play. The definition of neighborhoods is becoming broadened to include outdoor and indoor parks; street playgrounds in urban areas; libraries, museums, and zoos; and shopping malls that incorporate play areas (Boyer, 1991). A specialist suggests that "Neighborhoods for Learning" should reclaim neighborhoods for families by making them safe, friendly places "with open spaces that invite play and spark the imagination" (Boyer, 1991, p. 91). The problem of staffing such sites might be solved by service corps of high school and college students who would volunteer to serve as play leaders.

There is no lack of innovation in creating intergenerational play spaces, only lack of time, commitment, and resources. Intergenerational play opportunities need to become commonplace in every community. This can happen only through the collaborative efforts of schools, communities, and business and industry working together with the common commitment to develop programs that support families.

Research on Parent-Child Play

There is presently a strong need for systematic research about play between parents and children, especially in these specially designed intergenerational play environments. These environments appear to be appropriate ways to support greater parent-child play opportunities. There is presently little research, however, to support that assumption. In fact, at least one study has called the assumption into question.

A recent study of parents and children examined patterns of interaction in a hands-on museum exhibit designed to support playful adult-child interactions (Wigington, 1995). Thirty hours of observation and a thematic analysis of interactions yielded descriptors of parents as nonplayers and players.

This study categorized *nonplayer* parents as onlookers, "teachers," disrupters, and stiflers. Typical behaviors observed in these parents were interacting in a manner aloof from the play and exploration of the child, standing back and watching, repeatedly interrupting to "teach," or denigrating the child's play attempts. A child, for example, who was stacking magnets upright and parallel excitedly yelled out, "Hey, Mom, look! It sticks standing up!" The mother, in a monotonal tone of voice, replied, "Yeah, it's a magnet," and walked away (Wigington, 1995, p. 14). While these parents apparently valued museum experiences for their children, having brought them to this setting, they seemed unaware of the impact their interactions would have on the exploration and play of their children, and they did not recognize the opportunity for intergenerational play and learning.

The *player* parents in the study were described as coplayers, parallel players, and solitary players. They seemed to enjoy engaging in play and learning with their children, beside them, or even alone. One example is of a mother and daughter playing with doodle tops:

> The mother let the top go into a spin, and the daughter moved the tray controlling the top as her mother had done. When it fell the daughter said through exhausting giggles and a smile, "Oh, it fell. Ohhh, but look at what it made though!" as she pointed at the design. "Yeah," replied her mother, "That's neat!" "Okay Mom, let's do the same thing. You know, I make it go all over the paper when I move like this (as she demonstrates holding the empty tray at angles) but, then, you make it go in the air and try to keep it spinning when it comes back! Okay, okay?" the young girl hurriedly said almost out of breath. "Well, we can try," commented her mother as she twisted the top into another spin, but this time after the top began to spin, she hit the bottom of the tray with her finger making the top hop a few times before it landed on its side and slid off into the mother's hands. Laughingly, the mother caught it. (Wigington, 1995, p. 23)

This study supports the contention of other researchers that environment alone does not support children's play. The play must be elaborated and extended through playful *inter*action.

In an ongoing study on intergenerational play, this author is examining the responses of parents and children to take-home "play centers" that promote playful parent-child interaction with hands-on, open-ended materials and toys (Patton, in preparation). The study draws on the intergenerational literacy research by including a strong shared-reading component but goes further by focusing on play as a vehicle for learning. Preliminary findings indicate that parents welcome suggestions for family play time and express an increased awareness of its value.

One author points out how intergenerational play in the home promotes strong links between such play and children's humor, cognitive, and creative development (Bergen, 1989a). For these interactions to occur, however, families must have time to spend together. Educators often encourage parents to monitor their children's homework but do little to support playful family time. Research on the benefits of homework monitoring is inconclusive, but there is evidence that it adds to the stress of hurried families (Kokoski & Patton, in press). "Assigning" family time by asking parents to turn off the television and play games, go for walks, and read with their children would be an easy way for teachers to encourage family time; this could be implemented as a schoolwide strategy. If children made a record, such as a graph or chart, of the amount of family time each day, they would not only reinforce their mathematics skills but also heighten family awareness of the importance of this intergenerational playtime. There are many resources that educators could make available to parents to give them ideas for family time. The book *Playing Smart* (Perry, 1990) has chapters on "Instant Fun," "Mind Snacks: Recipes for Kitchen Learning," and a most unlikely chapter entitled "Learning Comes Alive at the Cemetery!" Instead of dealing with children's tears over spelling lists, parents could be laughing, playing, and learning together with their children.

Current research on family play will determine the future development of environments and programs for children and families. This requires ongoing inquiry into effective school-home programs, community-based recreation programs, business and industry family support programs, and environments for family play. A network of interdisciplinary researchers could define a diverse agenda centered around questions in common that might include a focus on family literacy, family recreation, intergenerational care, and intergenerational play. If researchers developed a collaborative agenda of this nature to address the dynamics of intergenerational play in contemporary families, then parents, children, and educators would benefit. One author suggested a research network approach to the study of play and offered to coordinate such a network (Bergen, 1989b). In this author's view, research on intergenerational play, especially parent-child play, needs such a network.

In his book on childrearing, a noted psychiatrist stated: "The parent who fully participates in his [sic] child's activity because of personal involvement has a perfect understanding of how important it [play] is—and this participatory attitude is very different from being involved only as a parent" (Bettelheim, 1987, p. 229).

The family in the United States is shifting and redefining itself. Educators and lawmakers are in agreement that the best interventions for young children involve the entire family unit (Swick, 1993). This requires a national effort to define an agenda that supports intergenerational programming for all families and provides the leadership and resources to make it happen. The crises affecting families in the United States have been studied in depth, and many models for improving families have been suggested. Some of these strongly support emphasizing intergenerational play between parents and children. It is time for action on this agenda. Professionals committed to encouraging play in the lives of children can do these children a great service by leading community efforts to provide more family play opportunities and helping parents rediscover family playfulness. It is an opportune time for research, education, and advocacy for intergenerational play.

Bibliography

Aday, R. H., Sims, C. R., McDuffie, W., & Evans, E. (1996). Changing children's attitudes toward the elderly: The longitudinal effects of an intergenerational partners program. *Journal of Research in Childhood Education, 10*(3), 143–151.

Bergen, D. (1988). *Play as a medium for learning and development: A handbook of theory and practice*. Portsmouth, NH: Heinemann.

Bergen, D. (1989a). Intergenerational play: Influences on creativity throughout the life span. *Creative Child and Adult Quarterly, 14,* 231–237.

Bergen, D. (1989b). *Methods of studying play in early childhood: Reviewing the "state of the art" and planning future directions.* (ERIC Document Reproduction Service No. ED 305 182)

Berk, L. E., & Winsler, A. (1995). *Scaffolding children's learning: Vygotsky on early childhood education.* Washington, DC: National Association for the Education of Young Children.

Bettelheim, B. (1987). *A good enough parent: A book on child-rearing.* New York: Knopf.

Boyer, E. L. (1991). *Ready to learn: A mandate for the nation.* Lawrenceville, NJ: Princeton University Press.

Bretherton, I. (Ed.). (1984). *Symbolic play: The development of social understanding.* New York: Academic.

Brock, B. J. (1994). Recreation programming for the '90s family: Demographics and discoveries. *Journal of Physical Education, Recreation & Dance, 65,* 64–67.

Brodin, J., & Bjorck-Akesson, E. (1992). Toy libraries/Lekoteks in an international perspective. *EuroRehab, 2,* 97–102.

Chamberlain, V. M. (1994). Innovation in elder and child care: An intergenerational experience. *Educational Gerontology, 20,* 193–204.

Clements, R. (1995, February). Intergenerational play experiences in '95. *IPA Newsletter, 39,* pp. 5, 10.

Dierking, L. D., & Falk, J. H. (1994). Family behavior and learning in informal science: A review of the research. *Science Education, 78*(1), 57–72.

Elkind, D. (1988). *The hurried child: Growing up too fast too soon.* Reading, MA: Addison-Wesley.

Elkind, D. (1994). *Ties that stress: The new family imbalance.* Cambridge, MA: Harvard University Press.

Escalona, S. (1968). *The roots of individuality.* Chicago: Aldine.

Fromberg, D. (1992). A review of research on play. In C. Seefeldt (Ed.), *The early childhood curriculum: A review of current research* (pp. 42–84). New York: Teachers College Press.

Frost, J. (1992). *Play and playscapes.* Albany, NY: Delmar.

Fuchs, V. (1988). *Women's quest for economic equality.* Cambridge, MA: Harvard University Press.

Graul, S. K., & Zeece, P. D. (1992). Helping adults learn the importance of play: The partners in play training model. *Dimensions, 20,* 18–24.

Guddemi, M., & Jambor, T. (Eds.). (1993). *A right to play.* Little Rock, AR: Southern Early Childhood Association.

Iacuzzi, J. Q. (1995–1996). *Directory of toy lending libraries in the United States.* Evanston, IL: USA Toy Library Association.

Jackson, S., Robey, L., Watjust, M., & Chadwick, E. (1991). Play for all children: The toy library solution. *Childhood Education, 68,* 27–30.

Johnson, J. E., Christie, J. F., & Yawkey, T. D. (1987). *Play and early childhood development.* Glenview, IL: Scott Foresman.

Kokoski, T. M., & Patton, M. M. (in press). *Beyond homework: Science and mathematics backpacks: Extending science/ mathematics learning through school-home connections.* Manuscript submitted for publication.

Levenstein, P., & O'Hara, J. (1993). The necessary lightness of mother-child play. In K. MacDonald (Ed.), *Parent-child play: Descriptions and implications* (pp. 221–237). Albany: State University of New York Press.

Paratore, J. R. (1992, December). *An intergenerational approach to literacy: Effects of literacy learning of adults on the practice of family literacy.* Paper presented at the meeting of the National Reading Conference, San Antonio, TX.

Patton, M. M. (1997, May). *Backpacks: Families Learning and Playing Together.* Presented at First Impressions Early Childhood Institute, sponsored by the Fort Worth Independent School District, Fort Worth, TX.

Perry, S. (1990). *Playing smart: A parent's guide to enriching, offbeat learning activities for ages 4–14.* Minneapolis, MN: Free Spirit.

Popenoe, D. (1988). *Disturbing the nest: Family change and decline in modern societies.* New York: Aldine de Gruyter.

Powell, J. A., & Arquitt, G. E. (1978). Getting the generations back together: A rationale for development of community based intergenerational interaction programs. *Family Coordinator, 27,* 421–426.

Power, T. G., & Parke, R. D. (1980). Play as a

context for early learning: Lab and home analyses. In I. E. Sigel & L. J. Laosa (Eds.), *The family as a learning environment* (pp. 147–178). New York: Plenum.

Singer, J. L., & Singer, D. G. (1988). Imaginative play and human development: Schemas, scripts, and possibilities. In D. Bergen (Ed.), *Play as a medium for learning and development: A handbook of theory and practice* (pp. 75–79). Portsmouth, NH: Heinemann.

Singer, J. L., & Singer, D. (1990). *The house of make-believe.* Cambridge, MA: Harvard University Press.

Smilansky, S. (1968). *The effects of sociodramatic play on disadvantaged preschool children.* New York: John Wiley.

Stevenson, M. B., Leavitt, L. A., Thompson, R. H., & Roach, M. A. (1988). A social relations model analysis of parent and child play. *Developmental Psychology, 24,* 101–108.

Sutton-Smith, B. (1993). Dilemmas in adult play with children. In K. MacDonald (Ed.), *Parent-child play: Descriptions and implications* (pp. 15–40). Albany: State University of New York Press.

Swick, K. J. (1993). *Strengthening parents and families during the early childhood years.* Champaign, IL: Stipes.

Weiss, S. (1995). *Raising our future: Families, schools and communities joining together.* Cambridge, MA: Harvard Family Research Project.

Wigington, H. (1995). *Intergenerational play: Playing to learn, learning to play.* Unpublished master's thesis, Texas Christian University, Fort Worth, TX.

Wilson, J., & Herrnstein, R. (1985). *Crime and human nature.* New York: Simon and Schuster.

Play between Generations

Grandparents and Children

Carol Seefeldt

When children and their elders play together, each can gain a measure of stability and security that serves them well in the presently rapidly changing world. As one woman remarked,

> In the summer when I was a child, just as the dusk was about to turn to night, my grandmother and I would sit under the large maple trees in the backyard and wait for the first star of the evening to appear. We would talk about what we would wish for when we saw that first star. My grandmother never laughed at my wishes, and never made me feel guilty if I wished for something foolish. She loved me so, and I'll always remember how secure I felt when I was with her. Nothing could hurt me; I knew I was loved.

Is there any doubt that the young and old should share a similarly special bond in the rapidly changing future as well? Elders who are free of the responsibility of raising their own children can shower the young with unconditional love. Receiving the unconditional love of an older adult, children can gain a feeling of security. When they can experience the undivided attention of an elder who has time to spend with them and who enjoys playing with them, children know for sure they are valued. Is this close tie through playful interaction still possible to achieve in present day society?

Changing Cultural Context for Child-Grandparent Relationships

Exempt from the emotional intensity characterizing the parent-child relationship, many older people take great joy in being with and playing with children (Seefeldt, Jantz, Serock, & Bredekamp, 1982). Not only is the connection between old and young emotionally powerful, but it was once critical for the continuation of society. In the slowly changing societies of the past, in which life stayed essentially the same from generation to generation, the continuity of culture depended on the living presence of at least three generations (Mead, 1970). In earlier times a grandparent holding a newly born grandchild could not conceive of a future for the child different from his or her own past life. In the postfigural societies of the past, the transmission of the culture, and often of life itself, was dependent on the old. The expectations of the old, the wisdom of the old, were necessary to inform the young. Only the old could teach the young how to fish, where to look for deer, how to rear children, which gestures to use to communicate pleasure or displeasure, how to play, and how to irritate or appease the gods.

Today, however, rapidly changing technological societies do not depend on the old. It is no longer the old who teach the young the "shoulds" and "should nots" nor is it the old who engage them in play. Today's elders, who have never been young in the present world, are "pioneers, immigrants in time, who have left behind their familiar worlds to live in a new age under conditions that are different from any they have known" (Mead, 1970, p. 57). As immigrants in time, elders today are no longer the repositories of knowledge and wisdom, nor do they even serve as family historians (Neugarten & Weinstein, 1964).

More likely, today it is the children who serve to inform their elders of the culture. Accustomed to living in a world their elders have never experienced, children become the experts on society's expectations and how to function in the technological world; for example, children are the teachers when playing computer games with adults. It is natural that in a society characterized by rapid change, the bonds between young and old will also change. Researchers have documented play and interaction between young and old within these changing contexts. To prevent the bond between old and young from breaking, a number of programs have been implemented to bring young and old together. The research on grandparent and child relationships and implementation of programs promoting their interaction suggest some implications for practice and research.

Elders' Perceptions of Play Interactions with Children

In present day society, those elders who are financially stable are free to enjoy being with and playing with children, especially their own grandchildren. Financial stability, even for those elders who themselves have divorced and remarried, and whose children are single parents or remarried, seems to be related to enjoyable, playful interactions with children. Elders who are financially well off affirm this perception. In one study of grandchildren/grandparent interaction, elders who were classified as wealthy told about how much they enjoyed traveling with grandchildren, taking them on cruises, camping trips, or trips to other countries (Beck, 1990).

With the proviso that they can be in control of the interaction, today's elders, regardless of financial stability, report that they enjoyed being and playing with children. Nearly half of a nationwide sample of almost 1,000 elders said they interacted with children at least once a week, with another fourth saying that they had contact with children at least several times a month. Even elders who lived far from grandchildren, nieces, or nephews, and who reported seeing those children only once or twice a year, were found to spend time with children. These visits generally extended over several weeks or months (Seefeldt et al., 1982, p. 122).

Elders said that children were "fun to be with," and would "make good friends for old people" (Seefeldt, Jantz, et al., 1982, p. 74). Studies suggest that older people enjoy a variety of activities when with children. Among the most frequently mentioned interactions were card and board games. Elders talked about the enjoyment they gained from teaching the young games they had played as children. One grandmother, as she was being interviewed, recalled teaching her grandchildren to play the game Cootie, tossing dice and then drawing the cootie (an insect) instead of assembling it from the plastic parts in their purchased game. The children were entranced with the idea of drawing their own outrageous cooties. Comparing the virtues of their grandmother's way of playing the game and their current game, the children reached the conclusion, "You were just like us when you were little, but we have plastic cooties and you didn't."

Talking with children and watching television with them were the next most frequent activities. Taking walks, going shopping, and sewing, knitting, and cooking with children were also mentioned. Grandparents spoke with emotion especially of the pleasures of being with grandchildren, reading aloud to them, and playing games (Silvey, 1994). A smaller number reported more physically active interactions with children. These elders said they liked to take children to museums, zoos, or concerts, attend sports events, sail, play ball, or camp with them (Seefeldt et al., 1982).

In general, the higher the level of education of the elders, the more frequent were the contacts with children under the age of twelve years. Greater knowledge of children, their growth and development, was also associated with education, and females indicated greater contact with children than did males. Attitudes toward children, as well, were related to educational level of the elders. The elders with higher educational levels were less likely to say, "Children ask too many questions" and "Children should be less demanding," and to disagree with statements: "Adults should never give in to children," "Children who receive a lot of attention turn out to be spoiled," and "Children deserve what they get" (Seefeldt et al., 1982, p. 80).

The elders were very clear, however, that they wanted to determine when they would play with children, what they would play, and when they would end the interaction. Women, especially, expressed the need to be in control of any interaction they had with their own grandchildren or children not a part of their family. Women expressed this need forcefully, saying things like "I did all, everything I was supposed to do—quit school to get married, raised children. Now it's my turn to enjoy life. Someone else can take care of, and play with children, not me—I'm off to my golf game!"

Rapid social change has not totally broken the bond between the old and young children, however. The old continue to serve as play models and companions for children under the age of ten or eleven. Young children continue to bask in playing or just being with elders, especially with their grandparents (Fintushel, 1993; Kornhaber & Forsyth, 1994; Seefeldt & Tafoya, 1981). Although in a study conducted thirty years ago, nearly a third of grandparents interviewed expressed discomfort in their role as grandparent (Neugarten & Weinstein, 1964), most elders in a recent study seemed to enjoy being and playing with their younger grandchildren (Seefeldt et al., 1982). One reason older people seem to prefer being with younger children is that, "Once they get over 10 or 11 years old, they're too smart aleck," as one elder in this nationwide study explained (Seefeldt et al., 1982, p. 75).

Age of the elder is another salient variable in the functioning of intergenerational play. In this early study of seventy grandparent pairs, the younger the grandparents, the more time they spent in play and fun with grandchildren (Neugarten & Weinstein, 1964). The grandparents over the age of sixty-five were more likely to exhibit grandparenting behaviors that were categorized as "formal." When with their grandchildren, this group emphasized "proper" roles and behavior; they wanted to be somewhat aloof from their grandchildren and maintain their dignity as an elder. These grandparents, while interested in and somewhat involved with their grandchildren wanted to leave childrearing and active play and interaction up to the children's parents.

Grandparents who were in the younger group, under sixty-five, professed to be more fun-loving when with grandchildren. They were not at all concerned with being authority figures in their grandchildren's lives. Overall, about a third of the grandparents in the study reported being "distant" from their grandchildren. Other interactions were reported as being fleeting and infrequent. This group reported that being a grandparent had relatively little effect on their own lives and perceived the grandparenting role as empty of meaning. They did, however, expect that their relationship with their grandchildren would develop more fully as the children aged.

The grandparents in 1964 would probably be astonished at the complexities of being a grandparent today. Many grandparents in contemporary society have little choice in their roles. Instead of seeing grandchildren only on holidays for parties or taking grandchildren on cruises or to Disneyland, for example, the changes in family structure in present-day culture in the United States may require close and highly intimate involvement of grandparents in the caregiving of their grandchildren. The fact that nearly half of all children are likely to live in a single parent family at some time in their lives has changed many grandparents' role of playmate to one of childrearer. Many grandparents, therefore, for reasons that transcend race and economics, may be involved in caring for grandchildren on a daily basis (Jendrek, 1994). Such factors as the high divorce rate, high remarriage rate, and adolescent motherhood have also influenced the grandparent role, making many grandparents ambivalent about the role they should take.

In blended families, for example, grandparents may question their role with their step-grandchildren. One grandparent remarked, "This was the first Christmas Albert and Allan, Joe's second wife's children from her first marriage, were with us for Christmas. We hope we made them feel included, but we just haven't gotten to know them very well." Without the biological bond tying grandparent and child together, along with the ambivalent feelings accompanying divorce and remarriage, relationships between grandparents and grandchildren may be strained.

Other grandparents find themselves negotiating the grandparent role in gay or lesbian families (Seligmann, 1990). "Her new partner's daughter is delightful, but I don't know if I should act like her grandmother, aunt, or what," said one grandmother. (Seligmann, 1990, p. 38). Instead of playing with grandchildren or taking them on cruises, many grandmothers find themselves caring for grandchildren whose parents have died of AIDS (Lee, 1994), are crack addicted (Minkler, Roe, & Robertson-Beckley, 1994), are divorced, or are young and unmarried (Chase-Lansdale, Brooks-Gunn, & Zamsky, 1994; Pearson et al., 1990).

Children's Perspectives on Play with Grandparents and Other Elders

As one author asserts, "Societies' attitude toward the old is always deeply ambivalent" (de

Beauvoir, 1973, p. 9). The rapidly changing nature of knowledge, and the fact that the old no longer serve as reservoirs of wisdom, may be threats to the historical and traditional bond between old and young. This is illustrated in a study of Native Alaskan children's attitudes toward the elderly (Seefeldt & Tafoya, 1981). In the Lake and Peninsular District of Alaska, as everywhere else on this earth, rapid change is taking place. In this area of Alaska, elders may still hunt, fish, and trap, but they also travel to Anchorage on a 737 jet to buy supplies, see a movie, and visit "town" relatives. A child may wake in the morning, collect firewood, then go to school on a snowmobile to study, play, and learn by using a microcomputer and interactive television.

When asked how they felt about old people, children spoke lovingly of their grandparents and their enjoyment of being with them. One child reports, "I like to hear my auntie [grandmother] when she talks native and tells me about the olden days (Seefeldt & Tafoya, 1981, p. 16)." Other children also spoke of the thrill of doing things with their elders. Regardless of their deep affection for their own grandparents, however, these same children exhibited highly negative attitudes toward the elderly in general, and they greatly feared their own aging. The Native Alaskan children rated young people significantly more positively than the old. Their ratings of old people were significantly more negative than those of children in other cultures, including mainland United States (Galper et al., 1981), Paraguay (Seefeldt, 1982), Korea (Seefeldt, 1990), and Thailand (Seefeldt, 1986). When asked to describe old people, the Native Alaskan children said their elders were "old and stiff," "couldn't do anything, because they get tired too fast," and "are wrinkled all over and look really ugly" (Seefeldt & Tafoya, 1981, p. 16). It was unclear from this study whether these negative views of the elderly were related to technological advances.

Another researcher, however, has documented the effects of rapid change on the bond between grandparents and children. In a study of Jewish-Oriental grandparent and child relationships, an investigator postulated that rapid change served to deteriorate this bond (Stahl, 1993). He concluded that as the power and status of older people eroded through continual, rapid change, the young exhibited attitudes of disrespect and physical neglect even of their own grandparents.

Other studies of children's attitudes toward the elderly seem to support this conclusion. Children generally hold deep affection for their own grandparents and believe that old people are very good. At the same time, however, they do not want to grow old themselves, view the physical characteristics of older people with outspoken horror, and deny and dread their own aging (Seefeldt & Warman, 1990). The younger the children, the more negative are their attitudes toward age and the elderly in general. One study showed that children in preschool through second grade indicated their preference to be with or play with younger rather than older people. "They're good [younger people], and they can do things with you. Old people can't play." (Jantz et al., 1977, p. 94).

Even though children under the age of eleven or twelve years are believed incapable of understanding the finality of death, the three- and four-year-olds in one study appeared to associate aging with death (Galper et al., 1981). "You don't want to grow old," said a four-year-old, "because you have a better chance of living if you're brand new." "I'll feel terrible when I get old," said many others; "all you can do when you're old is wait to die" (p. 96).

Although four- and five-year-olds love grandparents and can name an older person they play with and enjoy being with, they just don't want to look and be like them. They seem appalled by the thought of aging and abhor the physical characteristics of age. "All old people do is look for glasses all day," explained a five-year-old when asked why she did not want to play with older people [excluding her grandparents] (Galper et al., 1981, p. 98). When the research pointed out that she too was wearing glasses and she was only five, she refused to change her views, explaining, "Old people are just too ugly to be with" (Galper et al., 1981, p. 102). Wrinkles, losing hair, and the loss of mobility were also cited by five-year-olds as reasons for not wanting to interact with older persons. A number of children were concerned that if they touched an older person they too would get wrinkles. "Do you think wrinkles hurt?" asked one (p. 98).

Children in the primary grades do not perceive being old as anything positive, but they are less negative than preschoolers in their general attitudes toward the elderly. The fact that some of the elderly are among the wealthiest group in the nation (AARP, 1986) has not escaped children. "I like to be with Nama," explained a first grader; "she has lots, and lots of money and can take me neat places and buy me neat things" (Jantz et al., 1977, p. 98). Primary grade children still express negative attitudes about their own aging, however. As preschoolers do, primary-age children say they prefer to be with younger people because they can do more interesting, active things than older people, including their grandparents.

Older children, in the third through fifth grades, have somewhat more positive attitudes toward the old. Significantly more of the nine- to eleven-year-olds selected an older person as opposed to a younger one to play with. This selection, however, was based either on the older person's being wealthier than the younger or for an altruistic reason. When third- and fifth-graders who said they preferred to be with an older person were asked to justify their choice, they did so on the basis of wealth or for altruistic reasons. "They [old people] have money and can take you to Six Flags," said one, and another said, "You see, young people don't have enough money, and then you can't do anything with them. If people are old, then they have money, and they like to spend it on you" (Jantz et al., 1977, p. 100). "I don't like old people," a fifth grader said, "but it's good to do something nice for them" and "It makes you feel good to play with an old person, they're so lonely and old, they need someone" (Galper et al., 1981, p. 100).

Some researchers attribute children's negative attitudes to lack of contact between children and elders, to the culture in the United States that values youth over age, or to the materialistic nature of the culture. Yet many children in the United States do have frequent contact with their grandparents and other elders, and their attitudes toward the elderly are significantly more positive than those of children in other countries where such attitudes have been studied, such as Paraguay, Korea, and Thailand (Seefeldt, 1982, 1986, 1990).

Whatever the cause, stereotypic negative attitudes by children toward the elderly and by the elderly toward children may be potentially harmful. Like any bias, they limit thinking and, often, behavior. Children who perceive the old as sick, unable to do anything, and in the least productive time of life, dread their own aging. Elders who see children as too demanding, "spoiled," or "smart aleck" are also not likely to enjoy playful interactions with them. The voluntary nature of play means that playful interactions will find scant space to root within the context of such negative perceptions.

A Remedy: Intergenerational Programs

Recognizing that the traditional bond between young and old is being stretched thinner and thinner, and that the young and old are ambivalent toward each other, a number of intergenerational programs have been created to remedy the situation. Theory holds that both elders and children will benefit if they are brought together and have opportunities to play. Based on the hypothesis (Amir, 1969)—that children who know and have contact with elders who are healthy and active will not be able to stereotype the old as ugly, sick, and tired—a number of intergenerational programs have been implemented with the goal of fostering children's positive attitudes toward the elderly. Research offers some support for a contact theory. Children who know elders and who have contact with their grandparents seem less likely to stereotype the old (Goyer, 1995). With the goals of changing children's attitudes toward the elderly, helping children understand and accept their own aging, providing children with accurate information about aging, and fostering more positive attitudes between children and the elderly, a plethora of diverse intergenerational programs are currently taking place in the United States. These programs are based upon the belief that they will benefit both elders and children; elders benefit from giving their experience and serving others, and children from seeing first-hand that older people can be active, contributing members of society who can play with them.

Intergenerational Program Models
Different models of intergenerational programs are in place. One model is programming that involves elders as volunteers in children's classrooms, such as the National Retired Teachers Association and the Older American Volunteers Program. These programs support teachers' work as well as offering elders opportunities to play with children. Elder volunteers also work in libraries, museums, child care centers, and clubs and groups such as Boy Scouts and Girl Scouts. Another model involves programs that operate in child care centers within nursing homes, such as the Generations Day Care. Another model, FOXFIRE, consists of old and young sharing experiences such as singing, making crafts, and dancing. A number of programs of this type revolve around different ac-

tivities. One involves elders and children fishing together, another reading books, and still another has older persons sharing history through photographs. Still another model has programs that take children, including the very young, to visit infirm elders in nursing homes.

The Facilitating Mutually Supportive Linkages between Generations model seeks to facilitate healthier intergenerational contact and understanding through programs of cross-age tutoring, daycare and nursing home exchange programs, support groups, and the development of educational materials for children, youth, and older persons. Elders participating in Project Caressing soothe, rock, cuddle, and play with infants from two months to two years of age in a room in their nursing home. The Retirement with Enrichment program integrates arts into the education of disabled children. The major purpose of this program is to bring the Very Special Arts Festival to disabled persons in all fifty states, the District of Columbia, and Puerto Rico.

Foster Grandparents assigns elders to children from birth to six years of age in Head Start centers and home programs; Generations Together requires ten visits between an older person and child age four to ten years. Their exchanges center around issues of friendship and affection, conflicts, generosity, play, family, and heritage. Elders Adopt Tiny Tots invites children from a nearby child care center to visit with residents at their nursing home one day a month. During the visits, children and elders eat lunch together, work on activities such as kite making, play, and watch puppet shows.

Nearly every community and school system across the United States has some form of intergenerational program in operation. Some are small and informal, involving one or two elder volunteers; others are more extensive. Manuals, publications, and other materials containing lesson and activity plans or step-by-step procedures that foster intergenerational play are readily available.

Documentation of Effectiveness of Intergenerational Play Programs

There is a great deal of anecdotal evidence supporting the concept that programs such as these will actually improve intergenerational attitudes. Children are reported saying to elder volunteers in their school, "I like it when you come to school" and "You make me feel good

inside" (Newmann, 1985, p. 23). Elders report enjoying their experiences in school: "At 65 my life has new meaning. I wake each day full of enthusiasm and excitement knowing I will be of some value to a child" (p. 23).

Highly personal interactions between elders and children in a foster grandparent program were reported as proof that intergenerational contact leads to positive outcomes (Saltz, 1985). One child in the program was heard referring to her foster grandparent as "her grandma," and another would threaten children by saying, "I'm going to tell my grandpa on you" (Saltz, 1985, p. 22). The grandparent volunteers also exhibited possessive feelings toward the children they worked and played with, referring to "my Nancy," or "my Billy."

One school program, in which healthy, active older people worked as volunteers in third- and fifth-grade classrooms over a school year, resulted in children's being less likely to stereotype the old as a group. After the program, when asked to reveal their attitudes about "old people," children responded that one would have to specify which older person they were to describe, because they could not give adjectives that would adequately address all old people: "They're all too different, you see," said one (Saltz, 1985, p. 23).

At the same time, children in this group continued to express dread and fear of their own aging. Research findings indicate that some children who have visited nursing homes have their stereotypic views of the elderly as sick, ugly, and tired reinforced (Seefeldt, 1987). Another study concluded that increasing the intergenerational interaction between elder volunteers and 120 elementary school children increased the negativity of children's unfavorable attitudes toward the old (Immorlica, 1980).

Other questions, therefore, arise. How can showing children an extremely small sample of infirm elders in nursing homes that are unrepresentative of the total population of the elderly positively change their attitudes? Would not visits to "play with" infirm elders in nursing homes only serve to support their stereotypic views and confirm for them that growing old is something to be avoided?

Implications for Research and Practice

In this rapidly changing technologically based world, the adult-remembered or child-longed-for interactions and play with grandparents, beloved elderly aunts, uncles, cousins, or friends and neighbors, may offer children a measure of security and stability. For those who recall the undivided attention and unconditional love of an elder and for those who only longed for this love and attention, the memory of or idealized hope of being cared for, played with, and loved unconditionally by someone older and wiser is comforting.

Nevertheless, the realities of today challenge this image. The picture painted by researchers, dependent on societal and economic conditions, is a great deal less comforting. This is sometimes a picture of elders who live in poverty, are ill, or are the sole caregivers of grandchildren of single parents or unmarried teen mothers. The changed role of women has also added to the picture. Many older women, who believed they had few choices when young, resent being asked to spend their remaining years interacting or playing with children. The increased wealth of many of the elderly and their longer period of good health, however, may increase their willingness to engage in playful interactions with children.

These conditions point to the fact that the old cannot be stereotyped, but are as individual and diverse as any other group. There are elders, just as there are parents, who do not enjoy being with children, especially children who are very young and demand constant care or children who are older and striving for independence. Simply being old does not mean a person will be loving toward and playful with children. Just as there are young people who are addicted to drugs or alcohol or who, never having experienced love and security themselves, are unable to give love to or play with others, there are elders who are rejecting or abusive to children. Accepting the fact that the elderly population is comprised of individuals with diverse needs, backgrounds of experience, and desires, it would follow that not all elders want to play with children. Even the elders who do enjoy the company of children require a measure of control and choice over the interaction.

Just as the group called "the old" are individuals, so are children. It is incorrect to stereotype children as always wanting to be with or play with grandparents or other elders, and just as incorrect to think all children hold negative and unfavorable attitudes toward older people or that they will be troublesome and annoying. Children, too, must have a choice in when they will play with elders, what the play will consist of, and how long they will interact.

Advocates for intergenerational play must also consider the cohort effect. It is common, for example, for people of the same age to want to be and play with each other because humans are held together by what they have in common. Age-homogeneous friendships also serve as an integrative force for elders and for children. Besides sharing similar experiences and roles at the same period in history, elders also group themselves with those who are similar to themselves in status characteristics and age because these often signal mutuality of experiences, tastes, or values (Hess, 1972). Such preference for homogeneous age-mates is shared by children, especially adolescents, who need the support of others of the same age to make successful transitions to adulthood.

This does not mean, however, that children and elders cannot share special moments together and enjoy playing with one another. When barriers of age integration have been overcome, perhaps through the implementation of intergenerational programs in schools, then old and young have become friends and can maintain these friendships over time (Struntz & Reville, 1985). Further, familial ties that bind together people of different generations are strong and naturally bring young and old together in shared play and productive activities.

It may be that the drive to bring together young and old in play is based on an image or myth. There seems to be a prevailing belief that the youth-oriented culture of the United States teaches people to devalue age and the elderly. Extending this concept, some believe that if the young could know elderly persons, play with them, and form friendships, people in this society would learn to value age and elders. Research, however, negates this premise. First, the research indicates that the old in numerous other cultures are more negatively evaluated, treated less well, and rejected to a significantly greater degree than the old in the United States (Arnoff, Leon, & Lorge, 1964), especially if they live in poverty (Amos & Harrell, 1981). Such research, therefore, suggesting that contact does not automatically result in positive intergenerational attitudes or to valuing of age, is worth considering.

Nevertheless, play between young and old, whether artificially arranged through intergenerational programs or naturally occurring in the home and family, should continue to be encouraged, if for no other reason than for children to experience the continuity of life. If by playing and being with each other, both the young and old experience and come to know the fact that life continues and extends beyond the individual, then intergenerational contact is of value.

For this contact to be productive and satisfying for both old and young players, a number of criteria must be met. First, as is true for all types of play, both old and young must have a choice of when they interact, for how long, and what they will do. Next, when interacting, whether in an intergenerational, community-based program, or at home, old and young must be able to maintain dignity and respect. The very premise that old and young will interact positively when together because they are both childlike demeans and negates the dignity of both. "You see," explained one director of an intergenerational program who was encouraging a child to make the "choice" of going to a nursing home, "old grandma is just like you: she has accidents in her pants, and spills her food too." Giving a child such a viewpoint will not increase acceptance of the old.

The interaction must be without frustration for both child and elder and also be pleasant and rewarding. Understanding the individuality of elder and child helps to reduce frustration when interacting together. Just because an elder enjoys boating, quilting, hiking, or cooking does not mean that the children will appreciate or enjoy these activities. Likewise, simply because a child wants to listen to rock music or play computer games does not mean that the elder, to be loving and caring, must do the same.

In order for contact not to lead to additional stereotyping between groups, there must be equal status between the members of both groups (Amir, 1969). This would seem difficult to overcome in intergenerational contact. Children are given low status in the United States, and the elderly, the most powerful political group, are of relatively high status, that is, unless the elders are infirm, without wealth, or power, when the reverse might be true.

Despite the large body of literature on intergenerational programs, there is limited information on how old and young play with each other. While there is self-report information on the activities elders and children enjoy together, data on what intergenerational play consists of, how old and young play with each other, where they play, and what they play are so limited as

to be almost nonexistent. There appears to be a desperate need for observational research to describe the nature of interactions between young and old. Who initiates the contact? What do the old and young say to each other? What is the nature of this communication? Because most of the research and literature on old and young together involves grandmothers playing with or interacting with grandchildren, the role of older males and how they interact and play with children must also receive attention.

As the citizens of this country step across the threshold into the twenty-first century, will they be able to keep the emotional bond between young and old as strong and healthy as it has been in the past? Of course they will. Society has always changed and will continue to do so. Despite continual and even dramatic changes, the bonds of love and caring between generations will remain. The lessons of history suggest that humans have survived, to their betterment, by accommodating to and using whatever changes have occurred. Just as there will always be a future, there will always be children and elders, especially grandparents and grandchildren who love and enjoy playing with each other. Even though the way children and the old interact will certainly change, the bonds between old and young can remain strong, especially when they are strengthened by playing together.

If this society values having young and old play together in ways that are beneficial to both groups, then the process must begin with today's children. Research is clear that it is only when children have had the chance to be born safely, to be nurtured and cared for during infancy, and to have the chance to play and learn during childhood that they will be able to accept each stage of life, and glory in each day of life, regardless of their age. Only when each has tasted all the life cycle has to offer will each, in turn, be able to care for and play with others.

Bibliography

American Association of Retired Persons (AARP). (1986). *Truth about aging*. Washington, DC: Author.

Amir, T. (1969). Contact hypothesis in ethnic relations. *Psychological Bulletin, 71*, 319–342.

Amos, P. T., & Harrell, S. (1981). *Other ways of growing old*. Stanford, CA: Stanford University Press.

Arnoff, F. N., Leon, H. V., & Lorge, I. (1964). Cross-cultural acceptance of stereotypes toward aging. *Journal of Social Psychology, 5,* 41–58.

Beck, M. (1990). Travels with Grandpa: Seeing the world. *Newsweek, 116(5),* 48.

Chase-Lansdale, P. L., Brooks-Gunn, J., & Zamsky, E. S. (1994). Young African American multigenerational families in poverty: Quality of mothering and grandmothering. *Child Development, 65,* 373–393.

de Beauvoir, S. (1973). *Coming of age.* New York: Warner.

Fintushel, N. (1993). The grandparent bond: Why kids need it. *Parents' Magazine, 68(8),* 160–165.

Galper, A., Jantz, R. K., Seefeldt, C., & Serock, K. (1981). The child's concept of age and aging. *International Journal of Aging and Human Development, 12,* 340–356.

Goyer, A. (1995). Image is everything. *Modern Maturity, 38(3),* 90.

Hess, B. (1972). Friendship. In M. W. Riley, M. Johnson, & A. Foner (Eds.), *Aging and society* (pp. 357–377). New York: Russell Sage Foundation.

Immorlica, A. C. (1980). The effect of intergenerational contact on children's perceptions of old people (Doctoral dissertation, University of South Carolina). *Dissertation Abstracts International, 40,* 5621B.

Jantz, R. K., Seefeldt, C., Serock, K., & Galper, A. (1977). *Children's attitudes toward the elderly.* College Park: University of Maryland. (ERIC Document Reproduction Service No. ED 142 860)

Jendrek, M. P. (1994). Grandparents who parent their grandchildren: Circumstances and decisions. *The Gerontologist, 34(2),* 206–211.

Kornhaber, A., & Forsyth, S. (1994). *Grandparent power.* New York: Random.

Lee, F. (1994, November 21). AIDS toll on elderly: Dying grandchildren. *New York Times,* p. A5.

Mead, M. (1970). *Culture and commitment.* New York: Doubleday.

Minkler, M., Roe, K., & Robertson-Beckley, R. (1994). Raising grandchildren from crack-cocaine households: Effects on family and friendship ties of African American women. *American Journal of Orthopsychiatry, 64(1),* 20–30.

Neugarten, B., & Weinstein, J. (1964). The changing American grandparent. *Journal of Marriage and the Family, 26,* 199–204.

Newmann, S. (1985). The impact of intergenerational programs on children's growth and older persons' life satisfaction. In K. A. Struntz & S. Reville (Eds.), *Growing together: An intergenerational sourcebook* (pp. 22–24). Washington, DC: American Association of Retired Persons.

Pearson, J. L., Hunter, A. G., Ensminger, M. E., & Kellam, S. G. (1990). Black grandmothers in multigenerational households: Diversity of family structure and parenting involvement in the Woodlawn community. *Child Development, 61,* 434–442.

Saltz, R. (1985). We help each other: The U.S. foster grandparent program. In K. A. Struntz & S. Reville (Eds.), *Growing together: An intergenerational sourcebook,* (pp. 22–28). Washington, DC: American Association of Retired Persons.

Seefeldt, C. (1982). Children's attitudes toward the elderly in Paraguay. *International Journal of Comparative Sociology, 23(3),* 40–53.

Seefeldt, C. (1986). Children's attitudes toward the elderly in Thailand and the United States. *International Journal of Comparative Sociology, 26,* 226–232.

Seefeldt, C. (1987). The effects of preschoolers' visits to infirm elders in a nursing home. *The Gerontologist, 27,* 228–232.

Seefeldt, C. (1990). Children's attitudes toward the elderly in Korea and the United States. *International Journal of Comparative Sociology, 31(3 and 4),* 343–350.

Seefeldt, C., Jantz, R. K., Serock, K., & Bredekamp, S. (1982). Elderly persons' attitudes toward the elderly. *Educational Gerontologist, 60(2),* 74–86.

Seefeldt, C., & Tafoya, E. (1981). Children's attitudes toward the elderly: Native Alaskan and mainland United States. *International Journal of Marriage and the Family, 11(1),* 15–24.

Seefeldt, C., & Warman, B. (1990). *Young and old together.* Washington, DC: National Association for the Education of Young Children.

Seligmann, J. (1990). Variations on a theme: Gays, single mothers and grandparents challenge the definitions of what is a family. *Newsweek, 114*(27), 38.

Silvey, A. (1994). A legacy for our children. *The Horn Book, 70*(4), 389–391.

Stahl, A. (1993). Changing attitudes toward the old in Oriental families in Israel. *International Journal of Aging and Human Development, 37,* 261–269.

Struntz, K. A., & Reville, S. (1985). *Growing together: An intergenerational sourcebook.* Washington, DC: American Association of Retired Persons.

Particular Meanings Embedded in Playful Experiences

Introduction

All play represents meanings that grow out of children's experiences. There are a variety of representational forms that embody varying intensities of play. Among the forms in which children represent their play are imagination, creativity, challenge, humor, and sexuality. Exploration, in contrast, is a step that precedes play. This section focuses attention on some of these forms that represent particular strands contributing to children's play experiences.

Children at play, for example, may exhibit humor and whimsy or engage in sexual play. Constrained by their event knowledge and the context of a particular setting, their representations will be more or less accurate and accessible. Their humor, for example, provides an important window into their understanding of concepts and language, permits them to express their exuberance in glee and their hostility in insults, and helps them learn the pragmatics of community-appropriate social interaction. Their playing with sexual content or issues dealing with bodily functions may have considerably less (or more) meaning than an observing adult might infer.

Other representational forms, such as exploration, creativity, and challenge, while encompassing playful elements, are not play per se, but may reflect proximity to the *phase transitions* that have the potential to easily transform into play. They might be considered mind-sets or approaches to life events. Humor, for example, is a type of mind-set, but it requires a playful frame of mind. In contrast, play might be humorous or whimsical, but it might also be serious. Exploration, from one perspective, is when children attempt to find out what something can do or how it works, whereas play is their proactive attempt to see what they can do with it (Hutt, 1976).

Fantasy, imagination, and risk-taking share with play a sense of empowerment and control. Although play and creativity share the possibility for children to make connections and have some elements of problem solving in common, adults might judge a phenomenon as creative only when a connection or solution is original, elaborative, or useful (Torrance, 1962). For a child, a new connection or solution to a problem may be new or original only to her or him.

Sexual play represents children's particular event knowledge, as well as an opportunity to control potentially unacceptable or dangerous ideas in a safe context. It might also be a way to predictably control adult and peer behavior when the child perceives that the meanings will engender negative attention.

When children engage in sociodramatic play, the meanings that exist in their event knowledge undergo development within the collaborative scripts, a form of oral playwriting, in which they engage with other children. Preschool and primary-age children play out scripts as varied as weddings, street violence that they have witnessed or heard about, and funerals; superheroes, heroines, and other media adventurers; and hospital, housekeeping, and storekeeping play. They include gestures, intonations, and practices that represent their multicultural experiences.

These reflections on the meaning of play to children suggest that meanings are specific to a particular personal and social context for each child. To help children feel increasingly competent and supported, adults who have contact with them have a challenging responsibility to continuously learn about the alternative perspectives and meanings that children bring to their play. Some of these understandings can occur when adults study the contexts from which children take their meanings, reserve judgments during sensitive observations, and attempt to try supportive alternative and adaptive responses, while continuing to care about children's meanings.

Bibliography

Hutt, C. (1976). Exploration and play in children. In J. S. Bruner, A. Jolly, & K. Sylva (Eds.), *Play—Its role in development and evolution* (pp. 202–215). New York: Basic Books.

Torrance, E. P. (1962). *Guiding creative talent.* Englewood Cliffs, NJ: Prentice-Hall.

Games, Achievement, and the Mastery of Social Skills

Peter J. Freitag

It is worthwhile to consider an anthropologist's premise that "toys are matters of considerable cultural importance, not just something that children play with" (Sutton-Smith, 1986, p. 12). Specifically, the premise is that, since the late nineteenth century, children's games have both reflected and promoted the views of success predominant in the culture of the United States. In this view, games become mirrors of society or, in the words of a cultural critic, games are "semantic maps, symbolic representations of the real world" (Canary, 1968, p. 427). Thus, they provide children with messages about achievement and the mastery of social skills necessary to be successful in their society.

This is not to argue that games are *designed* to teach children how to succeed or that this is their stated purpose. Of course, adults have used games and toys to educate children. Play is a means by which human beings gain skills and knowledge, and adults have often used them deliberately as a pedagogical device. It is important to note, however, that the teaching and learning about success that result from playing games may be unintentional. The goal of game manufacturers is to sell games. The goal of children in playing games is to have fun. In the process, however, a "hidden curriculum" may be in operation as children learn values, attitudes, and beliefs compatible with the society in which they live. Whether or not the teaching is by design or the learning is conscious, games help children to form expectations and define meaning. As one sociologist puts it, game playing is an "*activity* of socialization" through which children "learn the complex role-playing skills relevant to later life" (Lever, 1976, p. 478).

Success as Moral Virtue

The late eighteenth and early nineteenth century marked the introduction of board games to the United States. By and large, such games were produced in England and exported to this country. During this period, the educational purpose of children's games, particularly their usefulness in teaching moral values, was manifest. The object of the game The Mansion of Bliss, invented by Thomas Newton and published by William Darton in 1822, for example, was "to promote the progressive improvement of the juvenile mind and to deter them from pursuing the dangerous paths of vice" (cited in Goodfellow, 1991, p. 55).

The New Game of Human Life, published in 1790 by John Wallis and Elizabeth Newberry of London, was a path game in which players advanced from infancy to immortality in eighty-four stages, each representing a "character" corresponding to a year in the life of a human being. Parents were directed to "take upon themselves the pleasing Task of Instructing their Children" by offering "a few moral and judicious observations, explanatory of each Character as they proceed & contrast the happiness of a Virtuous & well spent life with the fatal consequences arising from Vicious & Immoral Pursuits" (from the directions on the game board).

In the game, the player "passes through life in a variety of situations which are here arranged in the order they generally succeed each other." These situations result in rewards and penalties, depending on their nature. "The Studious Boy at 7" and "The Assiduous Youth at 15," for example, receive stakes and advance on the path, while "The Prodigal at 30" and "The

Drunkard at 63" pay stakes and are sent back to the beginning spaces of the board. The rules of the game state that "[t]he Immortal man, who has existed 84 years, seems worthy by his Talents and Merit to become a Model for the Close of Life which can end only by Eternity."

In similar games, published first in England (e.g., The Reward of Merit, John Harris and John Wallis, 1801, and Virtue Rewarded and Vice Punished, William Darton, 1818) and later in the United States (e.g., The Mansion of Happiness, W. and S. B. Ives, 1843), the values of Christianity were stated forthrightly. Through them, children were taught to live a life of virtue. They learned, for example, that it was right to be generous, wrong to be miserly; good to be forgiving, bad to be vindictive; proper to be moderate, disgraceful to be profligate; and smart to be patient, ignorant to be hasty (for details see Goodfellow, 1991, pp. 48–55, 119). The successful life ended in a peaceful death and the immortality of heaven.

While such games continued to be produced and reissued until the end of the 1800s, their popularity began to slip by mid-century. According to writers on the subject: "by the 1850s one can detect a certain 'despiritualization of life' in American culture. It is reasonable to expect that this decline in the influence of Protestant ideology should have a corresponding impact on how Americans defined success" (Higham, quoted in Adams & Edmonds, 1977, p. 361). It was not that Christian values were being rejected at this time; it was that virtue was no longer its own reward. Rather, upholding a belief in such values became a requisite of worldly success. Living a life of virtue was no longer an end in itself but a requirement for advancement in the emerging industrial society. As one author put it: "[S]ociety itself becomes industrialized. It develops its own ideals of life and puts its high stamp of approval on such virtues as working efficiency, special working ability, industry, thrift and sobriety. Respect and honor are paid to the principles of industrialism, and reverence is offered its founders and leaders" (Nystrom, cited in Ewen, 1976, pp. 52–52).

This conjunction of spritual values and worldly achievement was illustrated in the first game developed by Milton Bradley, The Checkered Game of Life (1860). While emphasis continued to be placed on vice and virtue, the reason for embracing the former and eschewing the latter had changed and was redefined in utili-tarian terms. "The successful individual realizes . . . that behaviors that lead to rewards are as important as directly rewarding behaviors" (Burns, 1978, p. 60). Moreover, the values themselves were beginning to change. Unlike the earlier games of morality, players were exhorted to be ambitious to achieve fame, to be industrious to achieve wealth, and to pursue a career in politics to achieve a position of power. While Bradley's game endorsed the "values, ideals and attributes of the Christian ethic" (Burns, 1978, p. 62), the idea of success moved away from that of religious salvation. Virtue had become secularized.

Success as Hard Work and Sacrifice

The period from 1875 to 1900 was a time in which Horatio Alger published stories of men who had made it from rags-to-riches, promoting the myth that with a little luck and a lot of hard work and determination, anyone could rise from poverty to wealth, from obscurity to fame. This motif was a popular one in board games as well. In fact, some authors argue that games were better suited to that theme than Alger's books because "the dice provided the lucky break, the stroke of divine intervention" (Adams & Edmonds, 1977, p. 380). From about 1880 until the end of the century, U.S. manufacturers introduced a large number of games that suggested the possibility of upward mobility, a possibility more easily realized in the fiction of the novel and the play world than in fact. In these games, one advanced from a lowly position as a youth, such as a messenger boy, to success as an adult, such as the president of the firm. This theme of advancement was echoed in hundreds of games published from the 1880s through the first decade of the twentieth century.[1] All of them focused exclusively on boys moving up the career ladder. No such games were directed toward girls: in this way, the world of these games mirrored the real world, which excluded women from the public arena and opportunities for accomplishment outside the home.

One of the earliest variations on the success theme was H. B. Chaffee's From Log Cabin to White House (New York, ca. 1880). Players followed a spiral path of sixty-four spaces from the periphery to the center of the board, moving to increasingly higher positions of political power. One began as a messenger for the Common Council, advanced to various municipal offices (e.g., health commissioner) through a series of state posts (e.g., lieutenant governor) to national office (e.g., U.S. senator), ambassadorial positions (e.g., minister to Great Britain), cabinet posts (e.g., attorney general) and, finally, to the presidency. Along the way one risked losing elections or, worse yet, demotion as a result of personal failure such as negligence, incompetence, or embezzlement. But through perseverance one could reach the top. Character and success were tied together; without the former one could not achieve the latter.

While the manner in which people played the game did not suggest how advancement was to take place, the illustrations bordering the game board made things clear. Men were depicted in various occupations, such as trappers, bargemen, lumberjacks, and farmers. The games showed a boy reading the law and two scenes of men serving their country during times of war. Simply, if one wished to succeed, the price to be paid was hard work and sacrifice.

This combination formed the central premise of many games of this type. In The Errand Boy (McLoughlin Brothers, New York, 1891), for example, a child, still in knickers, enters the employ of a merchant. Through a series of steps, determined by the turns of a spinner, he advances to salesman, then head of department, and then manager. He is admitted to the firm, becomes its president, amasses great wealth, then retires from the mercantile business with $5 million and a new career in banking. The game ends when one of the competitors lands on the forty-fourth square, having become "an honorable & respected banker and a good citizen."

The box cover of the game depicts two young men, apparently both working as errand boys. One boy has been entrusted to carry a parcel labeled, "IMPORTANT DELIVER AT ONCE." He is neatly attired, looking in the direction in which he is heading, the package tucked securely under his arm. He appears to be heading somewhere, both literally and figuratively. The other boy has been distracted from his work by a group of younger children. A cigarette dangles from his mouth while he tugs at the ear of one of the schoolboys. His preoccupation with the child has caused him to lose his grip on the bundle of boxes he is delivering; they tumble to the ground, opening and spilling their contents. His "inattention," one of the penalty spaces on

the board, will no doubt cause him to be disciplined and, in the game, to lose a turn.

The picture that dominates the center of the game board offers a similar story of two contrasting characters. A well-dressed young man walks briskly to his destination. He carries a large package marked "IMPORTANT DELIVERY" and a smaller box. He has a look of determination on his face; his eyes appear to be focused not only on his immediate goal but on his future. He passes by a fellow errand boy who leans against a fence, gazing toward the sky, lost in reverie as he puffs away on a cigarette. The latter boy's hands are in the pockets of his stained trousers, which have a patch on the right knee; his vest is ill-fitting and unbuttoned.

The message on the box cover and on the game board is clear. Here are two young men: Which one is more likely to succeed? Which one would the child choose to be? One is a person on the move, going places; one day he will be the head of firm and then "an honorable & respected banker and a good citizen." The other will flounder as an errand boy and, if one were to hazard a guess, amount to nothing.

While the illustrations of the games depicted the qualities necessary for success, the spaces on the game boards stated quite clearly which traits of character led to approbation and advancement and which to condemnation and decline. Thus, in the 1886 Game of the District Messenger Boy (McLoughlin Brothers, New York), for example, landing on the space marked "Intelligence" helps the player advance to the position of "Sergeant" in the messenger firm. "Promptness" meant a promotion to "Clerk," and so on. Neatness, integrity, accuracy, ambition, and affability were all approved attributes resulting in one's forward progress in the game, as in life. There were, however, more flaws than merits indicated, despite the game's subtitle of "Merit Rewarded." "Inattention" meant moving backward to a space marked "Discipline." "Impertinence" caused one to retreat to "Rebuke." "Drowsiness" resulted in "Reprimand." Other sins to be avoided included carelessness, stupidity, laziness, loitering, untidiness, and error. The game's greatest disapproval was reserved for "Theft," which sent one to an area of the board marked "Prison," in which the player would have to wait until all others had passed the space labeled "Approval." After that, the penalized player would begin the game again at the starting point. There would appear to be here a clear relationship between conduct and success: One's character is one's destiny, the game seemed to say.

In sum, then, the games of the late nineteenth and early twentieth century marked a shift in U.S. attitudes toward success. Whereas in the early part of the nineteenth century games defined success in moral terms, the later games abandoned the idea that virtue was its own reward. In contrast, the "rags-to-riches" games suggested that, to be successful, one needed to advance within organizations and to achieve great wealth. It is not that virtue dropped out of the picture; simply, now, spiritual values were integrally tied to one's hopes for worldly accomplishment. Positive and negative character traits continued to be depicted, as they were in the earlier games of virtue, but now they were embraced as a means to an end rather than ends in themselves.[2]

The common feature of all such games was that one started with little or nothing. All that one had, in effect, was the hope of success through advancement. Through one's employment in the firm, promotion was possible and was gained by living a decent life and avoiding temptation. But the realities of life in the twentieth-century United States may have made it difficult for most people to continue to believe in that version of the American Dream. One of the lessons of the Great Depression was that one could work hard, be honest, embrace morality, and still lose one's shirt. The tie between success and virtue was severed, and what emerged was a new vision of what it meant to be successful and how to achieve it.

Success as the Pursuit of Wealth

The games of the 1930s did not even hint at the need for work, or character, for that matter, as a means of making it. The late depression era spawned a number of games that stressed not the attainment of a respectable position but the accumulation of wealth. In these games, success and dollars were synonymous, not surprising since, before the onset of the recovery, money had been sorely lacking for much of the population. The period gave rise to Monopoly, the most popular and best-selling game in history. Its theme was that, through the buying, selling, and renting of real estate or other enterprises, one could become enormously wealthy.

Monopoly had, in fact, originated thirty years before it emerged on the national scene.

Contrary to popular belief, which attributes the game to an unemployed salesman who created it at his kitchen table, it had been invented in 1904 as The Landlord's Game. The game's originator, Lizzie J. Magie, designed it to instruct people in the virtues of Henry George's "single-tax theory." The first part of the game, similar to the current one, was supplemented by a second part that "employs the same capitalist principles, but mixes them with a healthy dose of tax reform to prevent the evils of monopolistic ownership and thus transform all the players into enlightened winners" (McFarland, 1993, p. 51). In its 1930s incarnation, monopoly was not a vice but a virtue. The acquisition of wealth theme was echoed in many other games of the same period. In fact, some of them were so similar to Magie's original game that they shared the same patent number. The idea of Parker Brothers' (Salem, MA) 1935 version of the game "is to BUY and RENT or SELL properties so profitably that one becomes the wealthiest player and eventual MONOPOLIST." This description was altered in subsequent editions by replacing the word "MONOPOLIST" with "WINNER."

In a different way than in the earlier era, the games of the late depression reflected the tenor of the times. While writers of proletarian novels turned their attention to those who suffered and government redefined its role to encompass social welfare, game manufacturers provided an escape from harsh economic realities. Sitting around a table, people could pretend to have amassed the wealth they dreamed about. They could hold in their hands ersatz dollar bills. While, in society, wild speculation in securities had sparked the financial panic that led to the depression years, in Monopoly, careful planning, sound investment, and a little luck could bring the player large sums of money.

Unlike the games of the late nineteenth century, there was no concern with moral behavior, no penalty for malfeasance except for paying an occasional parking fine. In fact, one received money as a result of a "bank error" instead of being rewarded for honesty in returning it. Success was achieved not only through the unbridled pursuit of mammon but heightened by one's ability to wipe out one's opponents. There was no room for kindness, mercy, or generosity if one wanted to win.

Success, as defined in the earlier games, meant a climb from the bottom to the top; they paid homage to the value of hard work and to an honest life. Success, as defined in the later games, meant beginning with a stake that one parlayed into larger sums of money. They did not concern themselves with moral behavior or hard work; rather, through investment, luck, and cutthroat competition, one would remain the only survivor, a wealthy one.

The game of Easy Money (Milton Bradley, New York, 1936) is described as "The Game of Modern Business!" The directions reveal that it involves "Buying and Selling—Building, Borrowing—Banking and Trading." Players travel around the board, stopping at various locations, buying rental property or paying rent, purchasing utilities, or paying for their services, collecting a $250 bonus for each circuit of the board. The goal of the game is to accumulate the most cash and property by the end. The game board consists of forty-nine spaces representing roads and streets ready for development, utilities (e.g., a telephone company and a transit company), public buildings (e.g., hospital and hotel), and various opportunities for profit or loss. Its center consists of a line drawing of a building labeled "Bank," with coins bordering it on the bottom right and left. That is the game's only illustration.

There are no cautionary tales or pledges of future success, only the promise of money. Looking at the board as symbolic, the player is left largely uninformed. The player gains no understanding of what it takes to reach the end, only that cash is of obvious importance. The aim is only to win, and winning is defined not in terms of work or of character but simply as accumulating more than anyone else. People having been deprived of money for so long, it should come as no surprise that they would be drawn to games such as this one, in which success was interpreted not as *doing* but as *having*.

In fact, money appears almost miraculously. One does nothing to earn directly much of what one gets. It is only through the buying and selling of property and the collection of rents and fares that a player actually "makes" any money. Houses are erected on properties simply by paying cash; they come into existence without anyone's sawing a piece of wood or lifting a hammer. Here, what the game omits is more important than what it includes. The playing of the game suggests that the relationship between work and reward has been severed. No longer were the "captains of industry" the role models of society; instead, players came to revere the landlords whose role they assumed in

the game. This may have been for good reason since the rent was due no matter whether one had lost one's job.

The depression-era games also contained rewards and penalties, but these were less tied to anything that a player had achieved or at which she or he had failed. In Monopoly, winning second prize in a beauty contest did not suggest virtue, nor did paying a doctor's fee suggest vice. Even the "Go to Jail" space gave no indication of what one might have done to deserve that penalty. The 1936 game Big Business (Transogram, New York) made use of charts linked to dice rolls to determine gains and losses. Each player was designated a member of the President's Cabinet, given a stake of $100,000, a salary of $15,000, and encouraged to travel around the country seeking business opportunities. (Apparently, the principle of conflict of interest had not yet been developed.) Referring to the charts upon landing in designated spaces, a player would be directed to pay or collect money. One reads, "Shipping your mother-in-law in a wooden box across the State line without a trucking permit is considered Interstate Commerce. Pay a fine of $5000." Another says simply, "Mazie gets a court decision against you. Pay $7000." Rewards were based on similarly silly scenarios. For example, "Burp-Up Beer has been declared non-alcoholic and good for the whole family. Go ahead and endorse it and get paid $6000," and "Uncle Sourpuss mentioned you in his will. You get $3000."

These examples that show the difference between these games and the earlier ones illustrate three messages. First, rewards and penalties are now determined by events depicted in a humorous manner. Play is no longer viewed as a time for providing serious moral lessons; it is simply for fun. Second, one's achievements and failures are now the result of fortuitous or insignificant events. Even the few serious or likely occurrences, such as violating the antitrust law or receiving an income tax refund, are reduced in importance because they are seen as equivalent to paying for Aunt Agatha's new wooden leg or selling the "Combination Knife, Fork, Spoon and Safety Razor" one has invented. Third, every reward or penalty has been given a monetary equivalent. Vice and virtue have been rendered commodities, for sale, in effect, on the open market.

For much of the twentieth century, manufactured children's games were ungendered, except that the packaging usually pictured males. To be more accurate, games simply assumed a male audience. In both the "messenger boy" games of the early era and the games of finance of the later era, male images predominated. The emphasis in these games was on competition and achieving success in a male-dominated world. By mid-century, however, a new phenomenon arose with games designed specifically for girls, which emphasized a different type of success path.

Different Paths to Success for Boys and Girls

In a mass market book on board games of the 1950s and 1960s, the authors write: "Let's face it: when we were growing up, games about teen life catered almost exclusively to girls. Mystery Date, Miss Popularity, and other games were designed to fuel a teenage girl's social fantasies, but there was nothing quite the same for boys, who were too busy destroying battleships and performing other intrepid deeds while playing games" (Polizzi & Schaefer, 1991, p. 68). The emphasis in boys' games became increasingly focused on competitiveness and combativeness. Men were depicted as always on the go, fighting one another on the playing field or the battlefield, while women were portrayed largely as passive, except in their pursuit of a "dream date" or "perfect wedding."

The jobs of men were highlighted in games about such careers as milkmen, firemen, police officers, newspaper reporters, and photographers (The Merry Milkman, Fearless Fireman, and Police Patrol, all by Hasbro, 1955; Star Reporter, Parker Brothers, 1960; and Flash, Selchow and Righter, 1956), but women's work, even in the traditional roles of housewife and mother, was not the subject of games. Perhaps such activities were seen as unworthy of imitation. Perhaps they were viewed as distasteful. Perhaps they were considered simply boring. This omission of traditional women's roles in the home leads to an interesting situation, in that, with the exception of their position as shoppers, women were depicted neither in the public sphere nor the private sphere. Where then did they appear? In what ways did games portray women?

For girls, the world of games defined success in terms of popularity, particularly being popular with boys. Such was the case with

Dream Date (Transogram, 1963) and Mystery Date (Milton Bradley, 1965). The object of the former, subtitled "The Game Where Girl Meets Boy," was "to attract the boy of your choice. Pick up a friendship ring . . . and go out on a date to the movies . . . beach . . . prom . . . or picnic." In the latter, girls tried to assemble the right wardrobe so as to be ready for a date when they opened the mystery door in the center of the playing board. "The first girl to open the door and find the proper 'DATE' for which she is 'READY,' is the lucky winner."

One writer states that "one may view social play as a form of practice—a means by which the organism 'tests' different behavioural patterns and learns to integrate its behaviour with that of other members of its species" (Einon, 1980, p. 24). What then are children to make of a game like Mystery Date? What social learning is going on here "for girls 8 to 14" years of age? First, it reinforces the idea that success for a young woman is to be discovered in finding the "right" young man. Second, preparation for interaction with a man consists of wearing the right clothes, thus highlighting again the importance of appearance. A match between a boy and a girl in this game is established when their outfits correspond. Happiness is thus defined, not in terms of one's actions or accomplishments, but by the way one looks and the possessions one has.

For girls growing up in the United States in the past thirty-five years, the symbol of female popularity has not been a real person but a doll, Barbie. Introduced as a toy in 1959, she has spawned several spin-off games, including The Barbie "Queen of the Prom" Game (Mattel, 1960), Barbie's Keys to Fame Game (Mattel, 1963), Barbie's Little Sister Skipper Game (Mattel, 1964), and, for a new generation of her fans, The Barbie Game (Golden, 1980) and Barbie Charms the World Game (Mattel, 1986). What draws these games together is a concern with personal appearance, and a shapely figure,[3] beautiful hair, fashionable clothes, and expensive possessions. These are presented as the keys to popularity, the way to attract the man of one's dreams.

What is perhaps most surprising about the games of the late twentieth century is that, for the most part, they have continued to reinforce the gender roles and perceptions of the 1950s and 1960s. At the present time, the keys to success for young women are portrayed as not much different from the make-believe world of

Barbie, nor are they different from the 1961 Miss Popularity Game (Transogram). The 1988 Miss America Pageant Game (NALPAC Corporation) was produced at a time when one might expect heightened awareness of women's issues, yet there is little evidence that women in the game are anything more than "window dressing." The stand-up doll tokens are wearing swimsuits, and each has a nine-piece wardrobe ranging from casual wear to a formal gown. To advance to different stages of the competition, players must collect cards (each picturing and including information about real competitors) in the categories of talent, scholarship, appearance, personality, and character. These cards identify the qualities, it seems, that make young women popular, desirable, and worthy of emulation.

In a game version of marriage, however, material possessions are at the core; the theme of acquisition as the central focus of getting married is echoed in the 1993 game called Perfect Wedding (Cadaco). Players travel around the board purchasing the things they need to have the "perfect wedding." Every element (reception, honeymoon, rings, tuxedo, bridal gown, flowers, music, and cake) has a dollar amount, although the instructions hasten to point out that "[s]ince this is a fantasy wedding, costs of the items in PERFECT WEDDING are for game play only, and do not reflect actual costs!!!"

If the symbol of femininity in the girl's world of toys and games has been Barbie, then the symbol of masculinity in the boy's world of toys and games has been G.I. Joe.[4] Like its Barbie doll predecessor, the action figure was followed by several games after its release in 1964, including G.I. Joe Combat Infantry Game (Hasbro, 1964), G.I. Joe Marine Paratroop! Game (Hasbro, 1960s), G.I. Joe Navy Frogman Game (Hasbro, 1964), G.I. Joe Adventure Board Game (Hasbro, 1982), and G.I. Joe Commando Attack Game (Milton Bradley, 1985). In comparing boys' games and girls' games, it is apparent that men are typically portrayed in action while women are posed for a picture. In the G.I. Joe Navy Frogman Game, the character is swimming underwater with an attack knife in his right hand and a clenched left fist, with which he appears to be ready to strike the mine that he has discovered on the ocean floor. The aim of this game is not accumulation but destruction: as the cover says, "Destroy the Enemy Shore Installations." In reality, there is not much difference in the way this game and the earlier Barbie Game are played, but, for boys, it appears there must be at least the suggestion of danger, aggression, and feats of physical strength, which also sends a message about what brings success!

There are countless military games that have been produced during times of war (beginning, in the United States, with the Spanish-American War) and during times of peace. Perhaps even more popular than war games have been sports games. All dimensions of sports activity have been replicated in games, in hundreds of variations. As in the G.I. Joe games, the motif usually involves action. In some cases, sports heroes sit posed for a photograph or drawing, but, for the most part, the boys or men are actively engaged in their sport.

While the games in which girls are involved are typically as competitive as boys' games (the idea is to be the first one to reach the end, whether it be as Miss America or as the successful defender of the fleet), the aspect of competition is more often highlighted in the latter than in the former. The goal in the boys' games is often to wipe out an enemy or defeat an opponent, not simply to be the fastest to finish the race.

When one walks through the aisles of a toy store today, it is apparent that contemporary games for boys differ little from their 1960s' counterparts. It is as if the progress of the movement toward gender equality and androgyny stalled. Boys, for example, may choose from among Battleship, Battle Dome, Cross-Fire, Flying Thunder, Pirates Gold, Weapons and Warriors, and X-Men Alert. The male role continues to be defined largely in terms of action, adventure, and war.

How do contemporary U.S. board games depict success? Although girls are not now overlooked as game players, as they were in earlier times, since the mid-century game ideas of success have been gendered, suggesting different paths for men and women. It would seem that to be a successful woman, one engages in acquiring goods (particularly those that enhance one's attractiveness), becoming popular, and, ultimately, being a bride (not a wife or mother or independent woman). In the world of games, women are at one and the same time amassing possessions and becoming a possession. They are continuously on display, showing off the beauty that has been enhanced by what they have purchased. To be a successful man, one must compete vigorously, trying to destroy the competition. According to game values, men must be on the move, searching for adventure. One must prove one's heroism, particularly during combat. In the world of games, machismo is still very much the norm. It is no surprise to find that the games of the 1960s portrayed women as passive and men as active. More surprising is that such games continued (and still continue!) to be produced after the mid-1970s, when the women's movement in the United States had already made substantial gains, and feminist ideas were achieving wider acceptance by both men and women. Perhaps they suggest that gender-bound stereotypes are more difficult to overcome than many believed. Do game makers reflect or create the models of success that are portrayed in games for boys and girls? What is the future for games in this society?

Looking toward the Future

As the turn of the twenty-first century approaches, there is speculation about the direction in which games are headed. Certainly, the nature of the game industry has changed. Advances in information technology have led to the computerization of games and the decline of many of the board games that were popular not too long ago. Rather than disappearing, however, many of these games have simply been electronically enhanced or computerized. And while the introduction and proliferation of video games and computer games constitute a change in technological sophistication, it is doubtful that they signal a change in attitudes toward success. The fantasy world into which children now enter when they play games may seem different because it leaves less to the imagination, but the themes and messages presented there will, in all likelihood, remain very much the same.

Video games for boys seem to focus on the same themes that are found in board games. Sports themes and situations involving combat continue to dominate. For the most part, manufacturers have directed the computerized games toward boys. Board games directed to girls suggest an even more striking continuity. Barbie Dream Date and Barbie Queen of the Prom are still on the shelves, joined by variations on already familiar themes, such as Mall Madness, Party Mania, Pretty Pretty Princess, and Enchanted Palace. There seems to be little, if any, change on the horizon.

In fact, perhaps the changes in the society of the future will bring about, in the world of games, a strengthening of the values of the past. Just as the games of the early twentieth century stressed the possibility of moving from rags to riches while, in fact, chances for rapid upward mobility were limited, and just as the games of the depression era reinforced rather than challenged the virtues of capitalism, so may the games of the future continue to separate fantasy from reality. If gender roles become less well-defined, games may enhance the differences between men and women. If downsizing of business enterprise continues, games may suggest the importance of making it in the corporate world. If the threat of war is lessened, games may become increasingly violent. Simply stated, perhaps the uncertainties wrought by change in the real world call forth a need for stability in the fantasy world of games.

One of the great thinkers of this age has said: "With their simple and unequivocal rules, [games] are like so many islands of order in the vague untidy chaos of experience. In games one passes from the incomprehensible universe of given reality into a neat little man-made [sic] world where everything is clear, purposive and easy to understand" (Huxley, cited in Brady, 1974, pp. 32–33). If Huxley is right, then games constitute a world in microcosm, a miniature version of society and its values. In particular, children's games may reveal changing notions of success and how players can achieve it.

Perhaps the games of each era gave people what they wanted most. The games of the early to mid-nineteenth century extolled the importance of living the good life, and virtue and morality defined success. People sought assurance that the reward for goodness rested in heaven. Success was synonymous with immortality. The games of the late nineteenth and early twentieth century extolled hard work, a life of virtue, and a steady progression up the corporate ladder as the keys to success. The games of the mid-twentieth century stressed investment, competition, and making a fortune. They defined success in terms of money, which was in such short supply. People dreamed of a time when they would not have to worry about the vicissitudes of the economy.

The games of the late twentieth century suggest differing paths to success for boys and girls. Boys succeed through action, aggression, and competition. Girls succeed through beauty, popularity, and the acquisition of material goods. If, as one author has suggested, "[h]ow and what we play defines our character" (Mergen, 1982, p. 418), then the games of these eras may indicate a shift in the national temperament. They may also be reminders of the importance of play and contemporary games in reflecting the nature of today's society and its values. It is often through popular culture and play that children become socialized. They learn the values that they will adopt as adults in a manner that is largely unconscious and undeliberate.

Play has the potential to be many things. Game playing may provide a clue to understanding the way children are socialized at the present time. Games have the potential to be forces of both stability and change. They help children to anticipate and adapt to the expectations that will be placed upon them as adults. More often than not, it seems, games have been a conservative element, mirroring traditional values and supporting stereotypes, even after they have outlived their usefulness. Within them, however, also lies the possibility for contributing to progressive change. As one writer says: "Games are not haphazard invention. They illuminate the preoccupations and problems of growing up, and ease the long journey from infancy to adulthood. They teach the child things it may not think it has to learn and has no recollection of ever learning, and provide it with a diversity of experiences that would be hard to get in any other way" (Cherfas, 1980, p. 67).

Perhaps the games for the future still need to be invented!

Notes

1. They also included the following: Telegraph Boy (McLoughlin Brothers, 1888) Office Boy and Soldier Boy (both by Parker Brothers, 1889), Sailor Boy (J. H. Singer, 1889), Messenger Boy, Shop Boy, Telegraph Messenger (all by J. H. Singer, 1890s), Business: Going to Work (Parker Brothers, 1895), Postal Telegraph Boy (E. O. Clark, 1900), and The Little Soldier (United Games, ca. 1900).
2. It is interesting to note that, while such games were not abandoned entirely, their meaning certainly changed. As late as 1963, for example, Milton Bradley produced a game based on the Broadway musical, *How to Succeed in Business Without Really Trying*. Like the earlier games, its object was "to become CHAIRMAN of the BOARD. Players move by throws of the dice from WINDOW WASHER through the various offices and rooms, advancing to higher positions in the business organization." Unlike the earlier versions, however, players are cautioned at the outset that "the game should be played STRICTLY FOR FUN. It is a spoof on big business and an exaggeration of people found in almost every organization."
3. It has been reported that if the dimensions of a Barbie doll were translated into real human terms she would stand over seven feet tall, have a bust measurement of better than 40 inches, a waist of about 15 inches, and hips measuring about 38 inches. Rather than representing an image of femininity and beauty, these figures suggest that Barbie is, in fact, outside the realm of human potential.
4. Polizzi and Schaefer (1991) claim that "[t]he G.I. Joe action figure was originally inspired by the main character of a television show about the United States Marines, 'The Lieutenant,' but Hasbro was hesitant to wed the proposed toy with a fleeting television series. It wanted to create its own character, one it would have complete control over" (p. 49).

Bibliography

Adams, D. W., & Edmonds, V. (1977). Making your move: The educational significance of the American board game, 1832 to 1904. *History of Education Quarterly, 17,* 359–383.

Brady, M. (1974). *The Monopoly book.* New York: David McKay.

Burns, T. A. (1978). The game of Life: Idealism, reality and fantasy in the nineteenth- and twentieth-century versions of a Milton Bradley game. *The Canadian Review of American Studies, 9,* 50–83.

Canary, R. H. (1968). Playing the game of Life. *Journal of Popular Culture, 1,* 427–432.

Cherfas, J. (1980). It's only a game. In J. Cherfas & R. Lewin (Eds.), *Not work alone* (pp. 45–67). London: Temple Smith.

Einon, D. (1980). The purpose of play. In J. Cherfas & R. Lewin (Eds.), *Not work alone* (pp. 21–32). London: Temple Smith.

Ewen, S. (1976). *Captains of consciousness.* New York: McGraw-Hill.

Goodfellow, C. (1991). *A collector's guide to games and puzzles*. Secaucus, NJ: Chartwell.

Lever, J. (1976). Sex differences in the games children play. *Social Problems, 23,* 478–487.

McFarland, P. (1993). The woman behind Monopoly. *Audacity, 2,* 51.

Mergen, B. (1982). The discovery of children's play. *American Quarterly, 27,* 399–420.

Polizzi, R., & Schaefer, F. (1991). *Spin again: Board games from the fifties and sixties*. San Francisco: Chronicle.

Sutton-Smith, B. (1986). *Toys as culture*. New York: Gardner.

Fantasy and Imagination

Dorothy G. Singer
Jerome L. Singer

Fantasy and imagination are two of the most powerful components of human experience. There are various definitions and theories of imagery (Bruner, 1964; Horowitz, 1978), computer models (e.g., Kosslyn, Margolis, Barret, Goldknopf, & Daly, 1990), and pioneering experiments on the delay of gratification (Mischel, Ebbeson, & Zeiss, 1972). Within these contexts, it is worthwhile to consider the origins of imagination and fantasy, moving from Piaget's sensorimotor stage to the concrete stage of operations, when the overt pretend behavior and symbolic play of the young child take the form of covert speech and more private imagery. Such observable play has helped scholars to assess imagination and consider the constructive uses of imaginative processes.

What Is Fantasy and Imagination?

When does the capacity for fantasy and imagination begin? One view suggests that four-year-olds are aware of the power of images and thought: "My four-year-old son and I play a game, naming the parts of each other's bodies we like the most. . . . 'Mama, the part of everyone's body I like the most is their head, what's inside their head—because that's how you think'" (Brickman, 1995, p. 14).

How we think, plan, daydream, imagine, fantasize—all of these processes have intrigued scientists and laypersons alike. One definition of imagery focuses on mental stimulation, or "the capacity to rehearse actions and activities, to explore the possible outcomes of these in the real world. . . . [I]magery functions in all areas of mental and physical life where adaptation and change are necessary or where there is a need better to understand existing states of affairs" (Marks, 1990, p. 7). Theorists have attempted to discover such origins through both physiological and psychological tests.

Images, according to brain researchers, appear to be associated with the right hemisphere of the brain and its functions, which include visual and auditory imagery, spatial representation, pure melodic thought, fantasy, and emotional components of ongoing thought (J. L. Singer & Pope, 1978). Different components of mental imagery ability, furthermore, might have different neuroanatomic loci (Farah, 1984). One study identified a number of case reports of adult patients who lacked the ability to visualize a mental image from stored long-term visual memory information (Farah, 1984). These patients evidenced damage in the left quadrant of the brain close to the posterior language centers of the left hemisphere. Many of the patients who manifested this particular lesion were unable to communicate their loss of imagery. Image generation per se, according to this study, appears to be a left hemisphere function, while spatial ability and higher visual processing may be a right hemisphere function.

Components of imagery such as kinesthetic/sensory, perceptual or structural, affective, and cognitive may all play a role in the forms of imagery expression. Jerome Bruner (1964) conceptualized three modes of representation of images: the *enactive* mode, which reflects events through motor responses (a baby waves "bye bye" without the words); the *iconic* mode, which selectively organizes individual perceptions and images (games such as playing space people); and finally, the *symbolic* mode, which transforms experience into abstract and complex methods of representation (the words used to describe an image without the physical representation).

Expanding on Bruner's model, Horowitz (1978) conceptualized a system of *enactive, image,* and *lexical* representations of conscious expression. Enactive representation is based on memories of motor actions and the retention of imitative behavior of another person's actions. Enactive thought is thinking in action with the tensing of different muscle groups that may signify covert trial actions; both skeletal musculature and visceral neuromusculature are involved. Images, according to Horowitz, are based on perceptions, memories, and fantasies, and are especially effective in yielding information about spatial relationships and forms. Emotional response may be incorporated into images. When human beings inhibit or block image formation, associated emotions may also be delayed. Finally, the lexical mode is the rational one dealing with abstraction and conceptualization.

Computer models of image formation have been proposed that suggest that images are similar to displays on a computer screen (Kosslyn, 1983). In this way, we can generate pictures whenever we wish and manipulate them as easily in our minds as when we manipulate information on computers. Researchers suggest further, in a highly technical paper, that subsystems are involved in image formation (Kosslyn et al., 1990). Images are evoked when stored information is activated through input of a particular object. Information is either ignored or selected for further processing through an "attention window."

To test image generation, image maintenance, image scanning, and image rotation, these researchers compared the performance of five-year-olds, eight-year-olds, fourteen-year-olds, and adults on four imagery tasks utilizing those processes that are commonly used in visual thinking (Kosslyn et al., 1990). They found that older subjects were able to *scan and rotate* images better than younger subjects, and older subjects were better at generating images. There were no differences in *maintaining image* based upon age. Females, however, were generally superior in generating and maintaining images, but among the eight-year-old group, the males were faster than females in an image maintenance test. These researchers found no evidence to suggest that younger children have fewer processing components; the very youngest are relatively poor at scanning, rotating, and generating objects, but relatively good at maintaining images. Their findings seem to confirm that children are capable of eidetic imagery and can keep these images over time.

Eidetic images, related to photographic memory, are usually under voluntary control of the imager. They are almost as vivid as a perception, can be scanned, may be spontaneous or produced, are externally localized, and may persist for weeks or even years. Whether or not all children have eidetic imagery is still an open question, but most reviews of the literature indicate that about 10 to 15 percent of children are true eidetics (Morris & Hampson, 1983).

Researchers engaged in psychological rather than physiological studies of image-producing capacity found that the delay of gratification was facilitated when children were able to "think fun," thereby using pleasant cognitive distractions to postpone the receiving of a reward (Mischel, Ebbeson, & Zeiss, 1972). However, when children thought "sad thoughts" or thought about the rewards themselves, the delay time was shorter. If we accept these findings, it would appear that babies thinking about the mother would *increase* tension and shorten the ability to delay gratification. This is in contrast to Sigmund Freud's notion of delay developing as a result of primary process images. An additional step must be taken before delay is established. The ego must direct energy away from the "mother" image to other images of a pleasant nature less associated with milk, or to some instrumental activity, such as playing with a mobile or rattle or sucking on fingers while awaiting the reward of the milk (Freud, 1911/1962; J. L. Singer, 1955).

Developmental Aspects of Fantasy and Imagination

It is difficult to test Freud's assumption that the baby begins to image the mother's face and, through this capacity for imaging and delay of gratification, can move from primary process or id functioning to secondary process or ego functioning. And yet the contours of the caregiver's face must leave an impression quite early in life, as demonstrated by the infant's smile of recognition at about six weeks. It is true that the mother or caregiver's odor, touch, and voice also can evoke the smile of the infant, but think how much more effective is the animated face of the adult in achieving the smile response and accompanying global movements.

Developmental psychologists, particularly Jean Piaget, believed that images, the precursors of memory, begin to form in the later part of the sensorimotor period of life, eighteen- to twenty-four months of age, at about the time that object permanency develops (D. G. Singer & Revenson, 1996). The baby now can search for objects he or she drops or be upset if the mother leaves the room, because the child's cognitive capacity has matured beyond the perspective that "out of sight" is "out of mind." During this stage of life and perhaps earlier, infants were able to imitate movements of others without seeing the movement on their own bodies, such as opening and closing of eyes and mouth (Meltzoff & Moore, 1983). Infants as young as nine months manifested a phenomenon of "deferred imitation," in effect, observing an action television one day and then directing their behavior accordingly on another day (Meltzoff, 1988).

Related to these findings was the observation of infants during the second half of their first year who could find an object hidden in an unfamiliar location after a twenty-four-hour delay (Ashmead & Perlmutter, 1980). There is also the record of a six-month-old who would kick in her crib when exposed to a toy across the room, acting as if she remembered kicking at this toy when it was actually in her crib (Piaget, 1952). There is additional support for the notion that eight-month-olds are able to remember an object that was hidden and how tall it was (Baillargeon, 1987). It has also been reported that infants whose parents use sign language with them can use conventional signs at around six or seven months (Mandler, 1990).

Thus, the power of imagery may begin earlier than we had believed during the past two decades. Actually, as one-and-a-half- to two-year-olds become more mobile and begin to use language, they manifest the capacity for symbolic thinking through play, their main mode of activity during the preoperational stage of development, between two and four years of age.

Gradually, material gets organized into more complex structures and hierarchies through the processes of assimilation and accommodation. If all basic needs are met, an innate curiosity of children motivates them to explore their environment and form scripts or schemata that may or may not be accurate representations. We may laugh at some of the toddlers' antics or mistakes, or remark that what they do is cute or quaint. From the children's perspectives, their responses seem logical and correct. As they develop and gain more control over the complex stimuli that surround them, they begin to reproduce their ideas, thoughts, and experiences through play and imagination. This symbolic representation is what Piaget calls the child's "self-assertion for the pleasure of exercising his powers and recapturing fleeting experience" (1962, p. 131).

As the two- to seven-year-olds move into the stage of concrete operations, where logical thinking prevails, they still draw on fantasy and imagination, but make-believe goes on privately through imagery and covert speech (Luria, 1932). During and beyond early adolescence, children continue to use their imagination to pretend to be sports heroes in their athletic play, write poetry or short stories, and paint or use photography to express their imaginative capacity. Some children join dramatic clubs and write plays for their peers at school. Others enjoy computer or video games as part of their imaginative or fantasy experience. Cognitive psychologists have traced the origins of video games to their earliest prototypes, war and athletic contests, and to their most recent forebears, the mechanical games found in arcades that mirror sports and war scenes, gambling, and fortune-telling (Loftus & Loftus, 1983).

Because of the increased complexity of cognitive development, especially the ability to conceptualize, children may begin to play chess, fantasy games such as Dungeons and Dragons, or advanced CD-ROM computer games such as Myst. Children also may manifest creative expression in serious science experiments or in more frivolous activities such as outrageous hair styles, nail polish (each fingernail a different color), wearing funky clothing, or even body piercing, if a parent permits a twelve-year-old to emulate a more adventuresome teenager.

Measures of Fantasy and Imagination

There are numerous ways to measure a person's capacity for imagination or ability to fantasize. One informal test of visual spatial ability is actually quite simple. Imagine a letter B, turn it on its side so the vertical line is now horizontal; remove the horizontal line and report the name of the letter, which is now W (Finke, 1990). Standardized tests, such as the Bender-Gestalt Visual Motor Test or the Benton Test of Visual

Memory (Benton, 1963), enable the examiner to determine an individual's ability to transform information from the visual modality to a motor one.

Observing children in their play, and rating them on a scale of imaginative production, is useful in attempting to assess preschool children's fantasy productions (J. L. Singer & D. G. Singer, 1981; D. G. Singer & J. L. Singer, 1990). Self-report measures such as journals, diaries, interviews, storytelling, and naturalistic reports also yield information about types and styles of fantasy production. Another form for assessment is a fantasy questionnaire consisting of forty-five items that has good validity based on a large sample of first- and third-grade children (Rosenfeld, Huesmann, Eron, and Torney-Puta, 1982). A modification of this measure tested fantasy production of first-graders to assess the relationship between television viewing and imaginal activity (McIlwraith & Schallow, 1982–1983).

Researchers and therapists have used projective techniques in clinical and school settings to assess thoughts and fantasies related to conflict or motives that may not emerge during play therapy, interviews, or observations. These measures include word-association tasks, sentence-completion tests, and tests of storytelling, like the Children's Apperception Test, the Rorschach inkblots, and drawings of one's family.

Clinicians are trained to note changes in facial expression, breathing, muscle tone, and eye movements when clients are engaged in fantasy reports. Researchers have carried out physiological measures of children's imagery, however, mainly in laboratory experiments, but only rarely. The area of physiological measurement in children needs to be more thoroughly studied. With additional insights, older children and adolescents might learn, then, to become more aware of changes in their physiological state, attach a cognitive label to such changes, and thereby perhaps enable them to lower blood pressure, reduce heart rate, and relax muscle tension.

Constructive Uses of Fantasy and Imagination

Parents need to provide the external conditions of psychological safety and freedom for children to thrive in a creative environment. Children experience psychological safety when they are accepted unconditionally and treated with empathy (Rogers, 1954); they experience psychological freedom when caregivers allow them to express themselves symbolically and with few restraints. When children play in ways that are silly or unrealistic, therefore, parents must not tease or laugh at them. One educational researcher finds that "children are experts on the meaning of their play" (King, 1986, p. 30). Many educators believe that school experiences can foster creativity and imagination, and they have carried out experiments to demonstrate how imagination training can increase children's cognitive and social skills. (For a review, see D. G. Singer & J. L. Singer, 1990.)

In addition to the pretend play of younger children, older children can pass the time through fantasy or daydreaming when they need to wait in places such as airports and doctors' offices. They can also learn to use fantasy to help change their moods and to work out disagreeable encounters with their peers to avoid physical or verbal confrontations. Psychotherapists using relaxation techniques with clients ask them to imagine pleasant scenes as part of sensitivity training or relaxation therapy (D. G. Singer, 1993). Studies of pain similarly indicate that making up a mental story of being in another place at another time is one of the most useful and effective procedures in achieving relief. Coping with fear through the use of narrative thought or imagery is a successful way to alleviate anxiety about such dangers as flying during a storm, being stranded in a snowstorm, and being lost on a mountain trail.

Play therapists have acknowledged the importance of arts and crafts and puppet play as part of their regimen in working with children. Some teachers have been pioneers in helping young people develop imagery skills. These programs are spelled out in step-by-step fashion and use few props and sometimes only imagery methods, movement, and music (Bonny & Savary, 1973; De Mille, 1973; McCaslin, 1984; Rosenberg, 1987; D. G. Singer, 1986).

Finally, fantasy and imagination help children project their thoughts into the future. Their imagination allows them to think about a variety of possibilities for themselves. Children can play out the notions of "What if?" or "Who can I be?" in internal scripts as a rehearsal for later avocations and even careers. Trying out an occupation in one's mind can convey some semblance of what an actual experience might offer. In a similar way, many athletes use imagery as part of their training; although there is no substitute for the necessary physical practice, fantasy rehearsal of a particular athletic setting or competitive event seems to give an edge to those athletes who use these methods (Sheikh & Korn, 1984).

Fantasy and imagination fostered through play can be useful to all persons. While fantasy and imagery exploration flourish before puberty, and may well reach their peak by adolescence, this gift continues throughout human life. Through reading, music, education, peer interaction, and television, as well as an awareness of adult occupation and role models, preadolescents and adolescents are able to envision a vast range of possible futures and possible selves. The seeds of imagination are found in early childhood, when children engage in make-believe play. Through caregivers' acceptance and nurturance of play and fantasy, children may enter the fascinating realm of *possibility*.

Bibliography

Ashmead, D. H., & Perlmutter, M. (1980). Infant memory in everyday life. In M. Perlmutter (Ed.), *New directions for child development. Vol. 10: Children's memory* (pp. 1–16). New York: Jossey-Bass.

Baillargeon, R. (1987). Object permanence in 3.5- and 4.5-month-old infants. *Developmental Psychology, 23,* 655–664.

Benton, A. L. (1963). *Revised visual retention test: Manual.* New York: Psychological Corporation.

Bonny, H., & Savary, L. (1973). *Music and your mind.* New York: Harper & Row.

Brickman, H. (1995, July 2). Live and let die (Hers Column). *New York Times,* p. 14.

Bruner, J. S. (1964). The course of cognitive growth. *American Psychologist, 19,* 1–15.

De Mille, R. (1973). *Put your mother on the ceiling.* New York: Viking.

Farah, M. J. (1984). The neurological basis of mental imagery: A componential analysis. *Cognition, 18,* 245–272.

Finke, R. A. (1990). *Creative imagery: Discoveries and inventions in visualization.* Hillsdale, NJ: Lawrence Erlbaum.

Freud, S. (1962). Formulations on two principles of mental functioning. In J. Strachey (Ed.), *The standard edition of the complete psychological works of Sigmund Freud* (Vol. 2, pp. 213–226). London: Hogarth. (Original work published 1911)

Horowitz, M. J. (1978). *Image formation and cognition.* New York: Appleton-Century-Crofts.

King, N. (1986). Play and the culture of childhood. In G. Fein & M. Rivkin (Eds.), *The young child at play* (pp. 29–41). Washington, DC: National Association for the Education of Young Children.

Kosslyn, S. M. (1983). *Ghosts in the mind's machine.* New York: Norton.

Kosslyn, S. M., Margolis, J. A., Barret, A. M., Goldknopf, E. J., & Daly, P. F. (1990). Age differences in imagery abilities. *Child Development, 61,* 995–1010.

Loftus, G. R., & Loftus, E. F. (1983). *Mind at play.* New York: Basic Books.

Luria, A. S. (1932). *The nature of human conflicts.* New York: Liveright.

Mandler, J. M. (1990). A new perspective on cognitive development in infancy. *American Scientist, 78,* 236–243.

Marks, D. F. (1990). On the relationship between imagery, body and mind. In P. J. Hampson, D. F. Marks, & J. T. Richardson (Eds.), *Imagery: Current developments* (pp. 1–38). London: Routledge.

McCaslin, N. (1984). *Creative drama in the classroom.* New York: Longman.

McIlwraith, R. D., & Schallow, J. R. (1982–1983). Television viewing and styles of children's fantasy. *Imagination, Cognition and Personality, 2,* 323–331.

Meltzoff, A. N. (1988). Imitation of televised models by infants. *Child Development, 59,* 1221–1229.

Meltzoff, A., & Moore, M. K. (1983). Newborn infants imitate adult facial gestures. *Child Development, 54,* 702–709.

Mischel, W., Ebbeson, E. B., & Zeiss, A. R. (1972). Cognitive attentional mechanisms in delay and gratification. *Journal of Personality and Social Psychology, 21,* 204–218.

Morris, P. E., & Hampson, P. J. (1983). *Imagery and consciousness.* New York: Academic.

Piaget, J. (1952). *The origins of intelligence in children* (M. Cook, Trans.). New York: International Universities Press.

Piaget, J. (1962). *Play, dreams and imitation in childhood.* New York: Norton.

Rogers, C. R. (1954). Towards a theory of creativity. *ETC: A Review of General Semantics, 11,* 249–260.

Rosenberg, H. S. (1987). *Creative drama and imagination.* New York: Holt, Rinehart and Winston.

Rosenfeld, E., Huesmann, L. R., Eron, L., & Torney-Puta, J. V. (1982). Measuring patterns of fantasy behavior in children. *Journal of Personality and Social Psychology, 42,* 347–366.

Sheikh, A. A., & Korn, E. R. (Eds.). (1984). *Imagery in sports and physical performance.* New York: Baywood.

Singer, D. G. (1986). Encouraging children's imaginative play: Suggestions for parents and teachers. In R. van der Kooij & J. Hellendorn (Eds.), *Play—play therapy—play research* (pp. 89–99). Amsterdam: Swets and Zeitlinger.

Singer, D. G. (1993). *Playing for their lives: Helping troubled children through play therapy.* New York: Free Press.

Singer, D. G., & Revenson, T. (1996). *A Piaget primer: How a child thinks* (Rev. ed.). New York: Plume.

Singer, D. G., & Singer, J. L. (1990). *The house of make-believe: Play and the developing imagination.* Cambridge, MA: Harvard University Press.

Singer, J. L. (1955). Delayed gratification and ego-development: Implications for clinical and experimental research. *Journal of Consulting Psychology, 19,* 259–266.

Singer, J. L., & Pope, K. S. (Eds.). (1978). *The power of human imagination: New methods in psychotherapy.* New York: Plenum.

Singer, J. L., & Singer, D. G. (1981). *Television, imagination & aggression: A study of preschoolers.* Hillsdale, NJ: Lawrence Erlbaum.

Challenge and Risk-Taking in Play

Tom Jambor

In the present age of lawsuits and litigation, references to challenge and risk-taking in children's play get one's attention, particularly with regard to outdoor environments. While the terms *challenge* and *risk-taking* have been part of the time-honored vocabulary used to describe children's natural reactions while at play, they often elicit a variety of both negative and positive emotions and responses from adults. Parents and other monitoring adults generally consider challenge a positive characteristic of play, because it incorporates skill development and competency attainment. Risk, on the other hand, usually carries negative connotations, such as its potential for accident and injury. How does one separate the two? Or are they, in reality, a blended necessity for normal growth, development, and learning? Both children's developmental needs and adults' concern for safe play environments are important perspectives.

Challenge and Risk as Testing Grounds for Development

An important element of play for all children is seeking excitement through challenge or risk-taking. Observers report seeing risk-taking behavior in children's play throughout the world. Scholars have observed it in Norway (Jambor, 1986), England (Handicapped Adventure Playground Association, 1978), New Zealand (Croll, 1984), and Canada (Brink, 1983). In fact, it is hard to imagine trying to define play without including risk-taking behavior as part of the process. Learning to handle risk is part of a child's natural growth and development; it is part of growing up; it pervades most human

activities throughout life. As children play they "learn that becoming real [unlike being a stuffed toy animal] involves risk-taking and willingness to be hurt, get shabby, and become loose in the joints" (Bergen, 1988, p. 301). Children today, therefore, need the same natural, risk-taking, and consequential learning opportunities that were common to children of past generations. As a Danish play advocate put it, "the environment of my childhood remains the landscape of my soul . . . a beautiful reminder of the fact that childhood is about shaping and forming the platform from which we will explore life" (Jensen, 1990, p. 37).

During childhood the play environment becomes a testing ground for the development of decision-making skills, understanding social implications of decisions, and weighing those decisions based on risk factors. Within this sociophysical environment children need to take risks to explore their physical selves in the social context of their peers to find out what they can and cannot do. To meet this end, adults need to provide children with challenging opportunities and circumstances to explore, practice, and reach personal levels of competence. This applies to all children, including children with disabilities. Lady Allen Hurtswood of England (Handicapped Adventure Playground Association, 1978), an early play specialist, pointed out that children, especially those with mental and physical handicaps, build self-confidence and develop independence by challenging themselves to confront and overcome risks.

Children usually play at a level at which they will be able to meet their developmental needs. If adults are going to provide play environments that meet children's needs, these environments must contain "play value," offering elements of challenge and adventure. Environments with high play value have elements that draw children to them and keep children involved in the play process. If an environment is lacking in play value (i.e., if it is dull and unappealing), children will create their own challenging experiences within that environment. Some adults may view these attempts as opportunities for children to develop imagination and creative skills. Unfortunately, they may also create opportunities for children to use equipment in a dangerous manner. It is common to see children involved in adventurous, risky, and even frightening (to adults, that is) situations at local school or public park playgrounds. This risk-taking behavior is often the result of nonstimulating equipment that encourages the user to reassess its play value by finding new, adventurous ways to use it (Brink, 1983; Hazeltine, 1994; Hewes, 1974; Jambor, Chalmers, & O'Neill, 1994). That is, children create their own play value by inventing new play possibilities on boring equipment, which often leads to feats that increase the probability of injury. Fortunately, few children are without a strong sense of self-preservation; few attempt what they cannot achieve (Handicapped Adventure Playground Association, 1978).

Knowing one's own abilities and limitations plays a big part in developing a sense of self-preservation. Children construct this knowledge through the experiences of daily play encounters. Through trial and error during these play encounters, children become aware of their ability level and subsequent challenge level for interaction. As children rely on old skills to maintain play activity, they practice new skills that challenge them to take on the next level of participation.

As astute observers, children watch other children as they interact with playmates and the play environment and make decisions on entry points for participation. Children enter the action of play as social agents who become caught up in the interaction of peer play and to test their limitations within the framework of these play opportunities. Once children establish personal competence and a sense of security, they strive for more complex levels of play involvement. In a recurring pattern, when children obtain play competency and self-security at one level, they seek out and move on to the next level of challenge with its new confrontations, new uncertainties, and new contemplations for risk-taking.

Cautions in Challenge and Risk-Taking Play

In spite of the value of these play behaviors, there are also cautions. While middle-school-age and older children may be ready for this mode of behavior, preschool and many primary-school-age children may not yet be ready to engage in higher risk levels. Young children, who are egocentric in their thinking, who cannot predict accurately situational outcomes or are unable to accept the consequences of their intended actions, may be unable to evaluate a situation and determine undue risk-taking levels. Thus, adults who allow young children to challenge themselves within settings designed for older children must be aware of the younger child's incomplete understanding of play challenge outcomes. The challenge for adults, then, is to monitor and explain risk, design environments with appropriate levels of challenge, and supervise these play experiences carefully while allowing children to control their own play.

Toddlers, for example, have little, if any, understanding of potentially dangerous situations and must be closely monitored. Contoured grass hills of various sizes and pitches of slope bring challenge to this age child and offer a relatively safe, natural play space requiring minimal supervision. Climbing equipment, in contrast, must be low, with manageable exit routes and protective guard rails, and requires close supervision.

Preschoolers also need supervision as well as the opportunity to indulge in developmentally appropriate play actions and activities that lead to enhanced competency, an understanding of self, and progressions to higher levels of involvement. Sand and water combinations, loose parts, outdoor blocks for construction and manipulation, and tire combinations for climbing and movement experimentation all offer physical, social, and cognitive challenges (Kostelnik, Stein, Whiren, & Soderman, 1988).

Primary-age children become increasingly less dependent on adult guidance, and by age seven can independently evaluate risks involved in most play actions and activities. Games of chase and tag, involving movement through vertical mazes of tire walls, vertical and horizontal rope traverses, tunnels, and balance beams, prepare these children to explore levels of challenge and evaluate risk factors. They are unlikely to exceed their ability and take undue risk unless pressured by playmates or adults.

Children quite often assume, however, that what was an easy play action for them will also be an easy task for playmates (Kostelnik et al., 1988). In such a case, a child with more advanced physical skills and leadership capabilities may march playmates, like little lemmings, to potential danger. Adults, observing this circumstance, should provide the child with "guidance in recognizing the difference between being supportive to peers and challenging them to potentially dangerous activities" (Kostelnik et al., 1988, p. 147).

Individual Differences in Challenge and Risk-Taking

There are also biological differences in risk-taking. Some children are strong risk-takers at early ages. It appears that they may be born to take greater risks than others. This genetic factor is located in the enzyme monoamine oxidase (MAO), a brain chemical that is related to risk-taking (Buchsbaum & Haier, 1983; Donahue, 1986). Everyone has MAO—some have more, some less.

Those with high MAO levels are characteristically more sedate, do not like a lot of activity, are more shy, and avoid being participants in stimulating activities or actions. Those with low MAO levels, on the other hand, have a need for brain stimulation: they are risk-takers, with a chemical predisposition to desire thrilling experiences. Such sensation seekers seem to need to take physical and psychological risks. Children who have lower MAO, then, will seek out stronger physical, sensory, and cognitive challenges, demonstrate more risk-taking behavior throughout their childhood, and may carry these behaviors into adulthood. They may engage in fast driving, sky diving, bungee jumping, mountain climbing, or gambling. Adults who observe these youngsters engaging in acts that may seem developmentally advanced and somewhat dangerous may be alarmed. In reality, these children, like their peers, are perfecting skills, but at an accelerated pace because of this biologically induced need to stimulate the brain and satisfy their need for thrill and sensation. One perspective suggests that, for children with low MAO levels, "voluntary pursuit of dangerous activities is odd, anti-social, and even perverted . . . [but] . . . exactly like other games in their formal characteristics . . . voluntary, satisfying in and of themselves, and offer[ing]

the player a highly structured setting in which to control external forces" (Csikszentmihalyi, 1976, p. 484).

Risk-taking pervades most human activities from birth to death (Cohen & Hensel, 1976) and is necessary for normal development (Reynolds, 1990). There are two kinds of risk, one where the outcome is certain and known (e.g., crossing a new wooden suspension bridge between two platforms, riding a ski lift, taking an amusement park ride), and the other where the outcome is uncertain and unknown (e.g., taking a flying leap to a suspended vertical rope, slalom skiing, tailgating a car while on Roller Blades) (Brink, 1983).

It should be noted, however, that individuals select among available risk alternatives in such a way as to maximize expected outcomes (Davidson & Suppes, 1957). An alternative, for example, can be simply deciding whether or not to enter a game with other children. Risk is inherent in accepting the challenge presented by the elements of the game. Accepting the challenge may mean demonstrating failure. Entering the game at an appropriate capability level, and making spontaneous decisions regarding risk-taking alternatives to challenge oneself to a higher level of participation during the rigors of the play process, then, will determine level of success. "Thus, a game will present a meaningful challenge to the child only if the degree of skill and understanding required for playing it, or for fulfilling a certain role in it, is both within the child's capacities, and is at the same time such as not to predetermine completely the outcome of a particular round of the game" (Eifermann, 1971, p. 287).

The universal game of tag, for example, may take a child through a maze of alternative pathways to pursue or escape a tag. As the game moves through the trees and structures of the play environment, players must make quick decisions as to what route to take: the stone ledge or the hill path; the balance beam or the horizontal traverse ropes; the platform suspension bridge or the long vertical Tarzan rope. The simple game of tag has a continuum of skills and physical involvement (running, jumping, climbing, and eluding), which the players quickly set so as not to lose levels of challenge (Eifermann, 1972). The "it" and the "catch" have very clear roles associated with challenge and risk-taking. The person who is "it" has much latitude and freedom in setting the intensity level of the chase. On the one hand, the "it" must decide on the extent of immediate risk in not catching and tagging someone and, thus, must choose to go after either an easy or a difficult "catch." The "catch," on the other hand, tests abilities and skills by deciding how far away he or she must stay in order not to get caught. The player is trying to master the degree of challenge he or she is ready to take on in any given situation.

The concept of "flow" (Csikszentmihalyi, 1979) reinforces this position. Flow deals with the matching of challenge and skills. In play, then, the child's goal would be to create a balance between challenging experiences and personal skills. The play situation may also be "a simulation of a challenge-skill match which prepares the child for the flow of adult experiences . . . a training ground for the more adequate adult life of flow in any kind of experience (work or play)" (Sutton-Smith, 1979, p. 275). If this is the case, the provision of challenging play environments to meet all entry skill levels is of paramount importance to play providers and designers.

Do children, however, really understand the outcomes associated with their risk-taking behavior as they press for new levels of challenge? The cognitive task involved is to make an assessment of the presented risk, the reward for achievement, and the outcome with regard to probability of failure. Children learn these relationships, and their judgments improve with experience. Most children, though, do not have the experience to make judgments based on these factors. They do not know the outcome of specific actions. Even if children were to know the outcomes they may want to test them, learning through personal experience, for example, by jumping from varying heights or dodging cars crossing a busy street (Brink, 1983). The question is whether children can get the experience necessary to make judgments based on assessment of risk, and the achievement of rewards and failures within a play environment deemed safe by adult prescription.

Challenge, Risk-Taking, and Injury Control

There may be a fine line between what is safe and what is not; between what is undue risk-taking and what is developmentally challenging; between what is exciting and stimulating, and what is boring and stagnant. If adults are to encourage and promote children's cognitive, social, and physical development, the design of optimal outdoor, as well as indoor, play environments will need to include challenging opportunities. The purpose of play settings is to provide exciting places for children to congregate, play together, and be motivated to return because the challenge meets their level of competency. While this is the ultimate goal of designers and communities investing in play spaces, it is obvious that, as more children play in any given setting over a period of time, the likelihood is greater that an "accident" will occur. To construct the ultimate "accident-proof" play environment is probably impossible, and to try to do so may actually be a disservice to children's needs.

A more constructive effort is to differentiate between what is developmentally challenging and what is unnecessary risk. On the one hand, heavily worn S-hooks on a swing may hide injury potential because the player is not able to recognize or evaluate the problem; this presents the player with an unnecessary risk or a "hazard." On the other hand, swinging as high as possible is developmentally challenging but also risk-oriented; risk in this situation, though, lets the player identify the challenge, evaluate the challenge level, and decide on action alternatives (Wallach, 1992). The difference between the two terms, *risk* and *hazard,* is based on the player's opportunity to use judgment. Although injuries do occur because of poor judgment in risk-taking, hazards cause most injuries.

There are no easy procedures for putting optimal challenge and risk-taking into children's play while maintaining maximum injury control. Identifying hazard potential during the design process or during maintenance inspections, however, would be a good initial step in helping children and parents deal with fears of injury. If children are to have optimal play environments, providers must also strike a balance between national playground safety guidelines, such as those of the U.S. Consumer Product Safety Commission and American Society of Testing Materials, and the challenge and risk-taking needs of children.

Children's play needs have not changed over time. Children have always sought out challenging play experiences and have exhibited risk-taking behavior. The need for adventure and exhilaration within the play experience extends the play encounter and feeds growth, development, and learning. What has changed over time, however, is adults' perceptions of children's play needs and their provision of meaningful play environments. With increased restrictions on play spaces and their design, and reduced play opportunities, play value for children has plummeted. While safety concerns must be attended to, they must not stifle the play needs of children. The challenge to playground and play opportunity providers is to fulfill those needs. In a land saturated with liability concerns and litigation, this may indeed be the ultimate *adult* challenge and risk-taking action.

Bibliography

Bergen, D. (1988). Play, technology, and the authentic self. In D. Bergen (Ed.), *Play as a medium for learning and development: A handbook of theory and practice* (p. 299–301). Portsmouth, NH: Heinemann.

Brink, S. (1983). The dilemma of providing acceptable levels of risk and challenge in safe play environments for children. *IPA Newsletter, 8*(5), 4–5, 21.

Buchsbaum, M., & Haier, R. (1983). Psychopathology: Biological approaches. *Annual Review of Psychology, 34,* 401–430.

Cohen, J., & Hensel, M. (1956). *Risk and gambling: The study of subjective probability.* New York: Philosophical Library.

Croll, S. (1984). Teenagers at play: Secondary schools. *IPA Newsletter, 8*(9), 20.

Csikszentmihalyi, M. (1976). The Americanization of rock-climbing. In J. Bruner, A. Jolly, & K. Sylva (Eds.), *Play: Its role in development and evolution* (pp. 484–488). New York: Basic Books.

Csikszentmihalyi, M. (1979). The concept of flow. In B. Sutton-Smith (Ed.), *Play and learning* (pp. 357–394). New York: Gardner Press.

Davidson, D., & Suppes, P. (1957). *Decision making: An experience approach.* Stanford, CA: Stanford University Press.

Donahue, P. (Director/Producer) (1986). *The human animal: Nature and nurture* [video]. Princeton, NJ: Films for the Humanities and Sciences.

Eifermann, R. (1971). Social play in childhood. In R. Herron & B. Sutton-Smith (Eds.), *Child's play* (p. 270–297). New York: John Wiley.

Eifermann, R. (1972). It's child's play. In J. Bruner, A. Jolly, & K. Sylva (Eds.), *Play: Its role in development and evolution,* (pp. 442–455). New York: Basic Books.

Handicapped Adventure Playground Association (1978). *Adventure playgrounds for the handicapped.* London: Author.

Hazeltine, P. (1994). *A review of playground and related surveys and studies* (2nd Ed.). London: The Sports Council/National Play Information Centre.

Hewes, J. (1974). *Build your own playground!* Boston: Houghton Mifflin.

Jambor, T. (1986). Risk-taking needs in children: An accommodating play environment. *Children's Environments Quarterly, 3*(4), 22–25.

Jambor, T., Chalmers, D., & O'Neill, D. (1994). *The New Zealand Playground Safety Manual.* Wellington, New Zealand: Accident Rehabilitation and Compensation Insurance Corporation.

Jensen, M. (1990). Playground safety: Is it child's play? *Parks and Recreation, 25*(8), 36–38.

Kostelnik, M., Stein, L., Whiren, A., & Soderman, A. (1988). *Guiding children's social development.* Cincinnati, OH: South-Western.

Reynolds, E. (1990). *Guiding young children: A child centered approach.* Mountain View, CA: Mayfield.

Sutton-Smith, B. (1979). Overview: Play or flow; Introduction. In B. Sutton-Smith (Ed.), *Play and learning* (pp. 275–294). New York: Garner Press.

Wallach, F. (1992, April). What did we do wrong? *Parks and Recreation, 26*(4), 53–57, 83.

Play as a Context
for Humor Development

Doris Bergen

Although play and humor are closely connected conceptually, in that both are enjoyable, reality bending, and internally motivated and controlled, there has been only a small body of research that has looked at the ways they are related and the means by which playful contexts might facilitate humor development. Theories that attempt to explain humor development have described some connections between early play and humor and hypothesized that they arise from similar sources. A few researchers have identified qualities of humor in the personality construct of "playfulness." Others have described factors in play contexts that may affect humor expression and appreciation, including the influences of adult and peer interaction. As a consequence of these theories and research studies, they have also identified a number of strategies that adults can use to foster children's humor development during their play. Much still remains to be learned, however, about the important relationships between play and humor development.

Many researchers have studied how play can provide a context for the development of children's thinking and problem solving, social-moral interactions, emotional control, language, and motor coordination. Others have examined the relationship of play to the learning of literacy, math, science, and other academic content. Surprisingly, however, few of those interested in research on play have tried systematically to connect the development of children's sense of humor to the context in which it might be mostly likely to flower—that of play.

In general, the research literature has only snatches of information to report about the play-humor connection. Because researchers studying humor have often conducted their studies in play-oriented environments such as preschools and playgrounds, they have provided some insights into the social and environmental factors that are likely to be present when children express humor in their play. From this research, for example, one can make some inferences regarding the importance of the presence of playmates (peers or adults) in facilitating humor development. Researchers who are engaged in the study of play, however, usually have not examined the affective quality of the play events they study. They could provide useful additions to the knowledge base on children's humor development if they gave some systematic attention to the nature of children's humor that occurs in the play contexts they are observing. This information could add an important dimension to the existing research on children's humor.

Research on Humor Development

The study of children's humor has followed a pattern relatively similar to that of the study of play, in that there was an interest in this topic during the 1920s and 1930s, a dearth of studies for almost fifty years after that, and a resurgence of interest in the past twenty years. The overall number of studies of humor development has been small, however, in comparison to the many studies of play.

The early studies of humor (as well as the early studies of play) were primarily naturalistic ones conducted in university laboratory nursery environments (e.g., Brackett, 1934; Ding & Jersild, 1932; Gregg, 1928; Jones, 1926, Justin, 1932). Because the researchers used naturalistic observation of humor instances that occurred in the play-oriented environments of these nurseries, they typically described the play context when reporting their results. They explored questions such as what types of humor were observed during the children's play times, how often different manifestations of humor were observed at those times, and what factors in the setting influenced humorous expression. One researcher, for example, investigated the relationship of laughter to a number of other variables and found it was associated with active play situations, surprising events, and peer interactions (Justin, 1932). This researcher also found that girls' humor was more subdued than boys', with girls showing more smiling and boys more laughing, which she attributed to early socialization expectations. Another researcher found, however, that during play time laughter was exhibited about equally by boys and girls (Brackett, 1934).

During the 1970s and 1980s, studies of children's humor focused primarily on its relationship to cognitive development, especially perception of humorous incongruity, and on qualities of the social environment that might affect humor production or responsiveness, such as the effects of peer presence. Many of these studies were conducted in experimental settings, although some also used preschool or school classroom and playground environments. The study results indicate that typical types and stages of humor can be reliably observed; that the sequence of humor development shows relationships to that of other developmental domains; and that both the physical and social contexts affect the types and amount of humor expressed and appreciated.

Types of Humor Children Exhibit

A number of researchers have recorded and categorized the types of humor exhibited by children in home and school settings (e.g., Bergen, 1989, 1992; Bernstein, 1986; Bowes, 1981; Canzler, 1980; Frabrizi & Pollio, 1987; Groch, 1974; McGhee & Lloyd, 1982). Their research findings indicate that infants respond to humorous situations initiated by adults, and toddlers begin to initiate their own versions of humor. In fact, "the majority of toddler's humor is self-generated" (McGhee, 1979, p. 2). Even two-year-olds begin to show iconoclastic humor, which seems to be deliberately designed to gain some control in social interactions (Aimard, 1992). There is some progression in

types, with young children most enjoying the humor of unexpected actions and language, while children of seven or eight enjoy hearing and telling conventional riddles and jokes that convey a range of meanings. By age twelve, most children are able to comprehend and use jokes that convey complex meanings as long as the content is within their range of experience. Children enjoy types of humor that are also appreciated by adolescents and adults, although the sophistication of content and complexity of meaning are, of course, much greater at older ages. Table 1 gives examples of humor types found in the author's studies of children age two to twelve (Bergen, 1989, 1990, 1993; Bergen & Brown, 1994).

Researchers have used both experimental and observational methods to study particular types of humor (e.g., riddles or jokes), and have compared this development with cognitive or social factors. They have explored age level as well as gender differences.

Cognitive Aspects of Humor Development

Not surprisingly, researchers interested in cognitive dimensions note that older and younger subjects often find different types of humor funny and, within the same type of humor (e.g. riddles), researchers see some differences in level of understanding. They have been particularly interested in the development of riddles and jokes as indicators of children's understanding of incongruity humor, which is defined as "conflict between what a person expects and what is actually experienced" (Pien & Rothbart, 1976, p. 966). In general, older children show more ability to express and understand the complexities of humor. One study found, for example, that six-year-olds laugh at incongruity in jokes even if there is no resolution of the incongruity, but that older children enjoy jokes with resolvable incongruity more (Shultz & Horibe, 1974). This finding was disputed, however, when another study did not find an age difference in children's appreciation of incongruity resolution humor (Pien & Rothbart, 1976).

Before they master the riddle concept, children of five or six often tell and laugh at "preriddles," which have the form of riddles but not the incongruous point (Bernstein, 1986). One study suggests that children first comprehend conceptual-trick riddles (i.e., ones that

TABLE 1. Humor Types with Examples

Humor Category/Type	Examples
Expressed joy in mastery and movement play	Tickling games, tag or other chasing; trial-and-error actions/manipulative play
Clowning	Making faces, very exaggerated movements or voice, with child monitoring of "effect" on "audience"
Verbal/behavioral teasing, iconoclastic humor (mockery, resisting control)	Using provoking actions or words, such as calling sister "Baby, Baby," deliberately holding toy out of sibling's reach or dropping food from high chair and faking surprise to adult
Discovering incongruous objects/actions/events	Observing and reacting with surprise and laughter to a picture of a cat wearing a dress
Performing incongruous actions/pretend/fantasy	Putting boxes on feet and acting as if they are the shoes of a clown
Sound play	Chanting or singing nonsense words such as "ringo, dingo, bingo"
Reproduction/elaboration of story/song/poetry pattern	Repeating familiar song but changing words, such as "I hate you" instead of "I love you"
Word play with multiple meanings	Covering the dog with a blanket and saying, "Now he's a hot dog"
Describing impossible events or incongruities	Telling a "tall tale" about growing as tall as the ceiling and jumping over the house
Riddling patterns or "preriddles"	Asking "Why does the turtle cross the road? and answering "To go to bed"
Conventional riddling	Asking "What do you call a yo-yo that only goes up? and answering "A yo"
Joking or playing jokes	Putting "trick" candles (that won't go out) on a birthday cake
Self-disparagement/displacement	After making a mistake in a game, saying, "My brain must be on vacation"

violate knowledge of what the reality should be) and at later ages understand those based on language ambiguity and absurd situations (Yalisove, 1978). Another researcher found, however, that most riddles told by children are of only moderate complexity and those with lexical ambiguity are in the majority (70 percent), with jokes becoming the more popular type of verbal humor by age twelve (Bowes, 1981). In middle childhood, language play is a common vehicle for humor; children engage in gibberish rhymes, puns based on sound similarities, "catching" others with trick repetitive patterns, tangletalk, verbal duels, and tongue twisters (Kirschenblatt-Gimblett, 1979; Opie & Opie, 1959).

Other cognitive researchers have been interested in the relationship of stages of logical thought to humor understanding. One researcher studied children who varied in the length of time they had mastered the concept of conservation, for example, and found that those who most appreciated humor that violated this concept were those who had only recently mastered the concept (McGhee, 1976). Long-time conservers found the humor less funny, perhaps because it was no longer challenging to their understanding. Two other studies were less clear about the relationship of cognitive processes to humor. One researcher found that both conservers and nonconservers could understand the cognitive incongruity in a humor stimulus based on the concept of qualitative identity (Klein, 1985). Others were not able to demonstrate a straightforward relationship between conservation stage and humor, although at some ages and for certain types of riddles, conservation abilities and humor did seem to be related. (Whitt & Prentice, 1977) They concluded that "the role of logical thinking in the development of children's riddle enjoyment and comprehension was not clearly demonstrated" (p. 135). Thus, there is need for more study of the precise connections between humor and cognitive processes.

Social Aspects of Humor

Researchers interested in social aspects of humor have been most interested in the effects of same- and cross-gender peers on humor expression, although they have also looked at various other environmental effects. A series of experimental studies indicated that elementary-school-age children find humor funnier and laugh more when a peer is present (Chapman, 1975; Chapman & Chapman, 1974; Chapman and Wright, 1976). In some of these studies, there were gender differences, with girls more likely to be influenced by the social setting (e.g., Chapman, 1973). Another study showed that the models (laughing and nonlaughing) observed by preschool children in different social conditions also affect the amount of laughter they show (Brown, Wheeler, & Cash, 1980). Preschool boys also are more likely to enjoy aggressive humor than do girls (King & King, 1973).

Other indicators that the social situation facilitates humor come from naturalistic observations in elementary schools, which typically indicate that boys are more likely to express humor and girls to be responders to humor (Canzler, 1980; Masten, 1986). One age difference found in an observational study conducted in third-, seventh-, and eleventh-grade classrooms found that children were more likely to show disruptive humor at middle school age (Fabrizi & Pollio, 1987). Other observational studies with preschoolers indicated that 95 percent of humor occurred in the presence of peers or adults (Bainum, Lounsbury, & Pollio, 1984) and that the size and gender composition of groups affected the expression of group "glee" (Sherman, 1977). A "good" sense of humor may also be a facilitator of social acceptance. Fourth-grade children who rated their peers

high on sense of humor, for example, also rated those peers as less socially distant (Sherman, 1988).

Even though there are some typical cognitive-stage-based responses to humor, there are also indicators of individual differences in humor expression and appreciation levels among subjects of the same age, and these differences moderate the effects of social factors. One set of studies, for example, found differences in humor responsiveness both for social conditions and for individual conceptual tempo, with reflexive children showing more understanding than impulsive children, but impulsive children showing more intense appreciation (Brodzinsky & Rightmyer, 1980; Brodzinsky, Tew, & Palkovitz, 1979). Another study indicated that the communicative competence of the individuals was a major factor in amount of humor expression (Carson, Skarpness, Schultz, & McGhee, 1986). Thus, depending on cognitive and motivational characteristics, children of similar age may respond differently to varied themes of humor (Pinderhughes & Zigler, 1985).

Although many questions remain to be answered, overall the results of research on humor development suggest that there are three types of competence that may be related to its development: intellectual ability, social relations with peers, and mastery motivation (Masten, 1986; see Honig, 1988, for further review of humor development research).

Research on Play-Humor Connections

In the past twenty years there have been only a few researchers specifically intent on investigating the connections that might be found between humor and play. Some of them have studied the personality construct of *playfulness,* examining the extent that qualities of humor (e.g., manifest joy, sense of humor) relate to overall playfulness qualities (e.g., Barnett & Fiscella, 1985; Barnett & Kleiber, 1982; Leiberman, 1977; Steele, 1981). These researchers have found that the presence of these humor qualities is highly related to children's overall "playfulness" rating. There are also some gender differences, with adults rating boys as having more playful components (exuberance, teasing, clowning) than girls (Barnett & Fiscella, 1985).

A number of the researchers whose primary interest has been in social facilitation of humor but who conducted their studies in preschool and school settings (discussed earlier) also noted how characteristics of the setting related to play, such as presence of peers and adults as play facilitators and play group size factors (e.g., Bainum et al., 1984; Groch, 1974; Sherman, 1975). In general, however, present research provides only glimpses of how various play-related factors may affect humor development. A study based on longitudinal data collected from children in preschool and day camp settings showed, for example, that ratings of children who were high in creativity (partially based on their pretend play activity) in preschool did not predict their expression of humor in middle school, but that their ratings after the age of six years did predict their later humor initiation levels (McGhee, 1979). Play requiring gross motor skills, in comparison to fine motor play, was also related to later sense of humor. Both boys and girls "who were aggressive, dominating, and talkative" at younger ages showed a "most fully developed" sense of humor at later ages. Their early play, especially boys', was imitative of peers and more likely to be parallel rather than social. They apparently learned as they grew older that they could gain peer attention and approval "within the playful framework of humour" (McGhee, 1979, p. 233).

The patterns of adult attention and affection were complex, showing an early relationship between humor and mother acceptance and warmth but a later relationship to mother distance, especially for girls. In particular, girls with these family patterns showed higher humor levels in elementary school than girls with different patterns (McGhee, 1979). In contrast, two cross-sectional studies of children's sense of humor have suggested that the presence of interactive, playful adult models may encourage humor expression and appreciation in preschool- and elementary-age levels (Bergen, 1989; Bergen & Brown, 1996).

Although the existing body of *humor* research gives information on a few aspects of the play-humor connection, it is surprising that so few published studies in the research literature on *play* include information about the humor children expressed or responded to within the play contexts where the data were collected. Researchers on play rarely include humor as one of the behaviors coded in their play-based observations or experiments. They do not even report many incidentally observed humor instances when describing the results of studies conducted in home, classroom, or playground play settings. So little is humor mentioned in the play literature, in fact, that a thorough reader of this literature might conclude that humor is rarely evident during play! This is particularly strange because there is a strong theoretical link between humor and play as well as evidence that both teachers and parents are aware that much child humor is exhibited during play events with peers and with play-oriented adults (Bergen, 1989).

Play Connections to Theories of Humor Development

Theorists have explained humor development and its connections to play in a number of ways. While some of them have addressed the connection only incidentally, others have tried to explain how play and humor development are directly connected.

The Perspective of Psychoanalytic Theory

One theoretical explanation of the role of play in the course of humor development has come from psychoanalytic theory (Freud, 1960). Although this theory emphasizes adult use of jokes to express unconscious emotions and relieve tension, the theory also connects early emotional development to humor, particularly in regard to children's emerging ability to "joke." The theorist states, "Before there is such a thing as a joke, there is something we may describe as 'play' or as 'a jest'" (p. 156). In this view, there are two types of humor—verbal and conceptual—with verbal humor beginning earlier. In the first stage, called "play," young children of about age two begin "learning to make use of words and to put thought together . . . to practise their capacities" (p. 157). Their pleasure comes from repeating similar sounds, putting together strings of words, and performing repetitive acts with objects; that is, it is based on "the child's peculiar pleasure in constant repetition" (p. 281). Because early humor behaviors do not have the intent of communication of meaning, they are not the same as later expressions of humor; thus, they are "play." This definition of play is similar to the concept of "practice play" (Piaget, 1962).

From the psychoanalytic perspective, at about age four children begin to use humor to convey meaning. This occurs both because children's critical faculties have developed and because they have learned that "reasonableness" rather than "absurdity" is preferred by the adults in their lives. Thus, "jesting" becomes the primary humor mode. In jesting, children begin to use some joking techniques that convey meaning, but they are not conveying unique or even "new" meaning. Although "all the technical methods of jokes are already employed" (Freud, 1960, p. 158), the true joke, in which children of about age seven begin to display "sense in nonsense," must have meaning that is freshly enhanced by the use of a joke. "If what a jest says possesses substance and value, it turns into a joke" (p. 161).

Another psychoanalytically oriented theorist extended the theory to describe how children's developmental stages are reflected in their humor (Wolfenstein, 1954). Their humor serves to counter the general distress of being a child in a world of adults and to master the anxieties triggered at various developmental age levels. This view explains, for example, why toddlers find "wrong name" play humorous when they are establishing their own self-identity, why preschoolers engage in gender-reversal humor when their gender identity is being confirmed, and why elementary children use "dumb" jokes to show their achievement of learning competence.

Older children's humor is also related to the developmental themes of their lives, in particular to issues around aggression and sexuality. Many early jokes are crude because children have not yet learned the subtleties of humor expression, and they often seem cruel because they are not couched in the language of appropriate conventions. With increasing age, however, children become adept at disguising hostile and sexual elements within a "joke façade" (Wolfenstein, 1954).

During the age period from seven to eleven, children gain facility both in telling conventional riddles and jokes and in inventing their own spontaneous jokes. By age twelve, children have learned most humor conventions, which enable them to understand the socially shared emotional meanings and humorous intent of other joke tellers. This understanding of shared social intent results in ability to express "laughter not only at distortions of reality, but also at the derision of the social world" (Bariaud, 1989, p. 42) and marks their transition to the adult stage of humor. This transition to adultlike joke telling takes some time and during the transition children may tell jokelike

riddles unsuccessfully because they leave out some point that is essential to the joke's meaning. They also may be able to tell the riddle or joke correctly but cannot explain the socially derisive or sexual meaning. These examples, told by ten-year-olds (Bergen & Brown, 1994, 1996), show the transitional stage:

> Why did the elephant take toilet paper to the party?
> Because he was a party pooper.
> (Reason why it is funny: Because it's a joke.)

> How do you drown a blond?
> Throw a mirror down to the bottom of a pool.
> (Reason why it is funny: People think blonds are stupid; if they see their reflection, they think they're drowning.)

> Why is a pool table green?
> You would be green too if someone hit your balls around.
> (Reason why it is funny: It just made me laugh.)

This explanation of a hostile meaning conveyed effectively within a joke façade was told by a twelve-year-old in one of these studies:

> We think "insult" jokes are funny, like:

> Your mother's so dumb she tried to alphabetize M and M's.
> Your mother's so fat that you'd get lost trying to walk around her.
> Your mother's so dumb she tripped over the cordless phone. (And on and on . . .)
> (Reason why it is funny: It's stupid humor; you use it when you are trying to insult someone in a funny way.)

Thus, from the psychoanalytic viewpoint, a "good" sense of humor is one that can convey a range of emotions, including highly negative ones that could never be expressed directly. The ability to engage in joking that conveys complex, meaning-laden emotions is the end product of a process that begins with the exuberant, repetitive mastery play of young children. Perhaps these "unacceptable" meanings are allowed to be expressed in adult jokes because, at some level, they still connote the playful context from which they were initially generated.

The Perspectives of Sociological/ Anthropological, Communication, and Information Processing/Arousal Theory

Another theoretical perspective that connects humor with play initially arose from sociological/anthropological sources, but it has also been supported by communication and information processing/arousal theory. In this view, early adult-child interactions communicate shared cultural understandings and frames for appropriate behaviors. When adults interact with infants in a playful way, they signal "This is play" (Bateson, 1956). From early play, children learn what behaviors are to be exhibited when events occur within or outside of the "play frame" (Bateson, 1956). Thus, the play frame is the condition that marks the boundaries between play and not play, and it prescribes the role of each player. In addition to communicating what are appropriate roles, the play contains the metacommunication "that there is such a thing as a role" (p. 148). Engagement within a play frame is also necessary for humor expression because "Humor supposes this dual awareness . . . [and] transcends this awareness through its intent to amuse . . . it is only complete when it is set in social communication whose aim is to make others laugh" (Bariaud, 1989, p. 18). As with play, there must be communicative signals that invite the participants to take the incongruous aspects of the event in a playful, humorous way.

Children thus learn the cues for "This is humor" in the same manner that they learn the cues for "This is play," and often these cues are the same. Both come from early adult-initiated interactions with children that signal "This is play/This is humor." Parents signal both play and humor by giving infants cues such as exaggerated facial expressions, high-pitched and emphasized voice quality, intense play gazes, and smiles and laughter, for example, in social games such as peekaboo or "gonna get you" (Stern, 1974; Sutton-Smith, 1979). Infants of about four months are already able to distinguish playful modes used by adults from those that signal seriousness, and they respond with smiles, laughter, excitement, and other positive affect (Pien & Rothbart, 1980). In fact, "playful interpretation of incongruous events depends on the development of an infant's play capacity" (p. 5).

However, if the cues signaling that the interaction is nonliteral are difficult for the child to understand, if the adult increases the child's arousal level too quickly or intensely, or if the adult is an unfamiliar person, children may see these cues as fear-producing rather than as humorous (Sroufe & Wunsch, 1972). Research based in arousal theory has shown that children adjust their arousal level to meet the play context demands (Shultz, 1972); thus, when they are able to be in control of their humor response levels, they exhibit the most enjoyment. That is, humor is most evident when the challenge level is optimal for the child and there is a context that is both safe and playful.

From this theoretical perspective, children's ability to develop a good sense of humor is based on their early adult-child play experiences because these experiences transmit the essential metacommunication "This is humor." The implication of this view is that the human capacity to become socially skilled users of humor depends on their incorporation of this message.

The Perspective of Cognitive Theory

Another source of understanding of humor development is derived from Jean Piaget's (1962) cognitive theory. Although this theorist recorded instances of his own young children initiating humor-inducing actions, he did not address the play-humor connection in detail. Other theorists and researchers, however, have drawn upon cognitive theory and information processing theory to explore how children's humor arises from their increasing ability to perceive cognitive incongruities.

Reacting to incongruity is not the same as reacting to novelty. It is a more complex cognitive process "because an incongruous stimulus is *mis*expected . . . while a novel stimulus is *un*expected" (Pien & Rothbart, 1980, p. 3). Even young children have expectations of what *should* happen that conflict with what they experience. These authors make a strong case for adult-child social play during the first year of life because it is one way that children's initial understanding of incongruity can be facilitated. They argue that incongruity humor begins at about four months of age, before the development of symbolic play, and that it "involves only the recognition of incongruity and playful interpretation of incongruity" (p. 3).

Other theorists, however, have focused on the importance of symbolic play for humor development (e.g., McGhee, 1979; Tower &

Singer, 1980). Explanations for humor development from this perspective typically pinpoint humor as beginning when children are able to engage in pretend play. As children progress from sensorimotor to symbolic thinking, they become able to represent actions and thoughts in pretend play and to act "as if." This ability is seen as essential for humor development, as evidenced in these authors' view that the "most extensive and complex forms of humour development and humor appreciation may be related to the 'as if' and imaginative character of symbolic play" (Tower & Singer, 1980, p. 29). These authors speculate that "children who play at make-believe can later enjoy humour and express their joy" (p. 39).

Children's increasing cognitive ability to perceive incongruity is the basis of one Piagetian-based theory of humor development (McGhee, 1979). In this view, there are four stages of increasing sophistication in incongruity detection. In stage 1, beginning about age two, children find humor in observing incongruous actions of objects, people, or animals. For example, "face-making" or watching an animal character perform unusual physical actions on television is likely to make children laugh. They also perform such actions themselves by putting objects in unusual places (e.g., making a carrot their "nose"). Examples from one of the author's studies follow (Bergen, 1992):

> C., *age three:* He put a doll's baseball
>   cap on his head and laughed.
> R., *age two:* She laughed when her slipper
>   flew off her foot.

In stage 2, children of two to four typically find incongruous language and labeling of objects and events humorous, but there is variation in when this stage begins, depending on how well developed the child's language is. Adult-child games such as "Where's your . . ." suddenly become funny when the child points to the wrong place and laughs. The syntactic and semantic structures and rules of language are much used for humor; for example, two children may engage in turn-taking play, each saying a more preposterous sentence, such as "I'll eat a cookie; I'll eat a pie, I'll eat a house, I'll eat an elephant!"

During the preschool years, children need relatively broad cues to interpret the incongruous humor of others while they "know" the incongruity embedded in the humor they devise.

One author indicates that one of the best evidences that children really know information well is their ability to generate humor by giving "incorrect" responses to questions on well-known information (Chukovsky, 1963). Adults are sometimes surprised, for example, when young children say things such as "The cow says meow" or "The cat says moo" and then laugh heartily, or older children make up wordplay or parodies to songs or stories that they know well. The adults may not be aware that this behavior is evidence of children's increasing ability to devise incongruities to express humor. Another example illustrates this (Bergen, 1992):

> C, *age three:* When C. was finishing lunch, Mother said she was going to the store and he could come too. He said, "And C. can come too, and Dad can come too, and Fluffy can come too, and cheese can come too, and bread can come too . . . " (Many repetitions of pattern, with laughter).

Stage 3, humor derived from conceptual incongruity, becomes a major mode of humor by age six. Children often display this ability through the telling of riddles that have conceptual incongruities. The transitional stage, in which children use a riddling pattern without the conceptual meaning present, usually occurs at about age four to six. These "preriddles" (at which young children laugh "appropriately" at non-meaningful riddle patterns) show children's lack of understanding that conceptual incongruity is essential for this humor. One such example is the laughter of kindergarten children to the answer "To be a baby" when responding to a version of the riddle "Why did the chicken cross the road?" (Ramsey & Reid, 1988, p. 218). Another preriddle example is the following (Bergen & Brown, 1996):

> Why did the frog cross the road?
> To get to the pond.
> (Reason why it is funny: I made it up
>   and my mom laughs at it. Every
>   time I do it my mom laughs.)

Even when children laugh correctly at a riddle that has conceptual incongruity, however, they may not really understand its meaning, as shown in the explanations given by various children for why this set of riddle variations is funny (Bergen & Brown, 1996):

What is black and white and red all over?
A newspaper.
(Reason why it is funny: I don't know.)

A blushing penguin
(Reason why it is funny: Most people think the answer is a newspaper but this answer's different.)

A suntanned zebra.
(Reason why it is funny: Thinking about a zebra with a suntan makes me laugh.)

As children move toward formal reasoning and have expectations about what should happen logically, violations of these expectations appear humorous. Children who have multiple classification skills and ability to detect lexical ambiguity are adept users of conceptual incongruity and word play, as some of these examples show (Bergen & Brown, 1996):

Where are elephants found?
You can't find them because they never get lost.
(Reason why it is funny: Elephants are big; they can always be seen.)

What can be served but cannot be eaten?
A volleyball.
(Reason why it is funny: It sounds like you're serving food to eat but it tricks you.)

A boy's dad said, "Goodbye, I have to leave to catch a train."
The boy said, "Do you think you're strong enough?"
(Reason why it is funny: Nobody can really catch a train.)

This last stage of cognitive incongruity humor, wordplay with multiple meanings, begins about age seven, and is the primary mode of elementary-age children's humor (McGhee, 1979). Authors of humorous children's books are well aware of children's ability to understand conceptual incongruity and multiple meanings and they use that knowledge to create the humorous situations in their books. Elementary-age children can usually explain why riddles or jokes are funny by using explanations that correctly point out the wordplay—but not always, as the following examples show (Bergen & Brown, 1996):

Why are Saturday and Sunday strong days?
Because the rest are week days.
(Reason why it is funny: I don't know, it just is.)

Where do sick boats go?
To the dock.
(Reason why it is funny: The word's got two meanings.)

Elementary children's multiple meanings are often designed to be shocking, which gives support to the view that the "joke façade" permits such meanings to be expressed. These riddles provide examples (Bergen & Brown, 1996):

Why did the condom fly across the room?
Because it got pissed off.
(Reason why it is funny: It's just weird.)

What do you get when you cross a bull-dog and a Shitzu?
Bullshit.
(Reason why it is funny: The play on words is funny.)

One of the best ways for adults to learn what children really do understand is by seeing what types of humor are enjoyable to them. In particular, observing children's response to humor with conceptual incongruities and multiple meanings is an excellent way to determine their understanding of subtle information distinctions. This joke, for example, from a twelve-year-old, shows a more sophisticated level of understanding (Bergen & Brown, 1996):

A guy is driving a truck full of penguins to the zoo when his truck breaks down. He asks another guy, "Will you take these penguins to the zoo?" and he gives him twenty dollars. When the truck is fixed the guy goes to the zoo and sees the other guy leaving with the penguins still in the car. That guy says, "I had money left so now I'm taking them to the movies."
(Reason why it is funny: Because the guy who picked up the penguins thought that the first guy meant for him to take them to the zoo for pleasure, not to drop them off to stay.)

The cognitive-humor stage perspective shows the progress of children's humor from their enjoyment of incongruous actions and language within the play frames of their early childhood experience to the sophistication of the multiple meanings of wordplay. As one author states, "Humor is the logical result of an extension of playful forms of behavior to the more abstract intellectual sphere of ideas" (McGhee, 1979, p. 103).

Play and Humor as Separate Conceptual Entities

The theories discussed all suggest that play and humor seem to be closely connected behaviors originating from similar sources; however, the question remains as to how they become differentiated and varied in the nature of their connectedness. Young children's humor is closely connected not only to play, of course, but also to emotional growth, communicative and metacommunicative competence, and increasing ability to recognize incongruity. One hypothesis is that, although humor and play both originate at the time that children develop the capability for symbolic activity, they become differentiated as children's "as-if" abilities develop. Because both pretend play and humor require the ability to be free of reality and to act in an "as-if" mode, they are initially closely linked. One theorist states, "Humor develops as the child's playfulness extends to recently mastered ideas and images, as well as overt play with objects" (McGhee, 1979, p. 61). Not all play is connected to humor, however, because it requires the child to imagine that the objects he or she is playing with "do something that he knows is nonsense, absurd, or impossible" (p. 61). "In humor, as in pretend play, there is a certain 'distancing' from the norms of reality, and a combination of being fooled and complicity required from the other" (Bariaud, 1989, p. 21). That is, the "as-if" stance is evidenced in the ability of children to understand that incongruities expressed in humorous action are not "incorrect" but of a "pretend" nature.

Although humor may share a similar origination point with pretend play, one theorist says pretense becomes differentiated when it splits into two strands, which she called "serious" make-believe and "joking" make-believe (Wolfenstein, 1954). The difference is that serious pretend intends to create a world that differs from the children's actual world primarily because it is governed by children (as the actual

world is not). In joking pretend, on the other hand, children are not acting "as if" the pretend world is real, but rather, they deliberately continue to distort reality through "silliness" or "nonsense." Thus, in the "joking" pretend world, children emphasize incongruity, but in the "real" pretend world, they imagine that the world they have created makes sense. "Joking pretend play involves inventing fictitious deformations of the world, of others and of oneself. This fiction is not there for purposes of reverie, but to trigger laughter" (Bariaud, 1989, p. 23). This joking pretend is also the probable root of what adult humor researchers call "nonsense" humor (Ruch, 1993). Interestingly, the two major adult forms of humor that researchers have studied are "nonsense" and "incongruity" humor.

Observations of the humor of young children are rich with examples of joking pretend, which typically arise as children are playing together in a "real" pretend situation and something triggers a change to repetitive wordplay or sound play, "silly" and exaggerated actions, or deliberate distortions of meaning. One reason that humor may not be observed in many play situations in preschool or school may be that teachers encourage "serious" make-believe but discourage "joking" make-believe because they are concerned about its "out-of-bounds" nature (Bergen, 1992).

Playful Methods of Facilitating Children's Humor Development

Whether children initially learn that certain things they do are funny through solitary fantasy play (McGhee, 1979) or accidentally through social interactions with adults who "react" to their funny actions or words (Bariaud, 1989; Singer, 1973) is another question of interest. It is probable that internal cognitive processes and external interactions with the social world both contribute to humor development. The audience does seem to be essential, however, because "the feeling of funniness is more apparent when the child, using language, becomes able to exploit his personal incongruous invention to fool others and at the same time to lead them into an upsidedown world with their complicity" (Bariaud, 1989, p. 22).

For play and humor to develop optimally, an important message that adults must convey during play interactions with infants and young children is that the play frame is a safe environment. The cues that signal "This is play/This is humor" must clearly communicate that it is safe for children to exhibit a "what-if" attitude (i.e., behavior may be more unusual or risk-taking because there are no "real" consequences). The nature of adults' responses to children's humor attempts is also likely to have an influence on how much children engage in humorous behavior and the types of humor they express. The presence of "playfulness" in parents and teachers, for example, seems to be related to the children's expressions of humor (Bergen, 1989; Bergen & Brown, 1996).

Ways that adults facilitate humor in children include performing as models of humor (e.g., telling funny stories or using cues that help children know they are joking); selecting materials or activities that encourage humor appreciation (e.g., tapes of silly songs, sound-play games); eliciting humor expression from children (e.g., asking them if they know any riddles); and responding to children's humor attempts (e.g., laughing at riddles even if they have been heard numerous times). Most importantly, because humor initially arises from playful "as-if" situations, adult provision of a safe climate in which humor expression and appreciation are valued and welcome is essential for children at all age levels (Bergen, 1992).

Thus, although the research evidence is limited, whether humor development will flourish as an expanded part of children's behavioral repertoire does seem to depend partly on the facilitating actions of adults in the environment who give the cues that help children know the distinctions between what is real and what is a humorous contradiction to reality. Further, the evidence that, as they grow older, boys and girls are similar in their understanding of humor but increasingly differ in humor expression (with boys expressing more) suggests that adults also give "permission" for socially and culturally appropriate humor expression.

While the theoretical basis for connecting play and humor is not new, it is relatively strong. In contrast, research evidence regarding the nature of the play contexts that foster humor development is not yet extensive. Thus, the play-humor connection is a largely untapped area of research. The limited research base that does exist indicates that play-based social interactions, language and sound play, pretend play, and adult and peer models of playfulness all contribute to humor development. Cognitive, emotional, and social developmental domains, especially as expressed in early play behavior, appear to be related to the stages of humor development and its modes of expression and appreciation. It is also likely that there are personality variables that make both "playfulness" and a "sense of humor" more prevalent in some children and adults (Bergen, in press).

Both humor and play are pervasive parts of the human experience. They enhance the quality of life for adults as well as children, and they are present in rituals that ameliorate traumatic events. What is play without laughter, without joy? How can humor exist without playfulness? From personal experience, this author knows that the play-humor connection needs further exploration. Moreover, it is fun to explore!

Riddle: What is the difference between a researcher who studies play and one who studies humor?
Answer (choose one or make up your own): One finds the humor in play and one finds the play in humor.
One is full of play and the other is playful.
Nothing, both must be humored and played up to.

Riddle: How many researchers are needed to study the play-humor connection?
Answer (choose one or make up your own): One hundred: one to conduct the study and ninety-nine to convince Congress to fund it.
One, as long as the subject is taken seriously.

Bibliography

Aimard, P. (1992). Genese de l'humour. *Devenir, 4*(3), 27–40.

Bainum, C. K., Lounsbury, K. R., & Pollio, H. R. (1984). The development of laughing and smiling in nursery school children. *Child Development, 55,* 1946–1957.

Bariaud, F. (1989). Age differences in children's humor. *Journal of Children in Contemporary Society, 20*(1–2), 15–45.

Barnett, L. A., & Fiscella, J. (1985). A child by any other name . . . A comparison of the playfulness of gifted and nongifted children. *Gifted Child Quarterly, 29*(2), 61–66.

Barnett, M. A., & Kleiber, D. A. (1982). Playfulness and the early play environment. *Journal of Genetic Psychology, 144*(2), 153–164.

Bateson, G. (1956). The message "This is play." In B. Schaffner (Ed.), *Group processes: Transactions of the second conference* (pp. 145–241). New York: Josiah Macy, Jr. Foundation.

Bergen, D. (1989). An educology of children's humour: Characteristics of young children's expression of humour in home settings as observed by parents. *International Journal of Educology, 3, 2,* 124–135.

Bergen, D. (1990, August). *Young children's humor at home and school: Using parents and teachers as participant observers*. Paper presented at the International Humor Conference, Sheffield, England.

Bergen, D. (1992). Teaching strategies: Using humor to facilitate learning. *Childhood Education, 68*(4), 105–106.

Bergen, D. (1993, September). *Structures and strategies in humor expression: Changes in cognitive and social-emotional meaning from ages two to twelve*. Paper presented at the International Humor Conference. Luxembourg.

Bergen, D. (in press). Development of children's sense of humor. In W. Ruch (Ed.), *Measurement approaches to the sense of humor*. Berlin: Mouton deGruyter.

Bergen, D., & Brown, J. (1994, June). *Sense of humor of children at three age levels: 5–6, 8–9, and 11–12*. Paper presented at the International Humor Conference, Ithaca, NY.

Bergen, D., & Brown, J. (1996). *Sense of humor development: A longitudinal study*. (Manuscript in preparation.)

Bernstein, D. (1986). The development of humor: Implications for assessment and intervention. *Topics in Language Disorders, 6*(4), 65–71.

Bowes, J. (1981). Some cognitive and social correlates of children's fluency in riddle-telling. *Current Psychological Research, 1,* 9–19.

Brackett, C. W. (1934). Laughing and crying of preschool children. *Child Development Monographs, 14*.

Brodzinsky, D. M., & Rightmyer, J. (1980). Individual differences in children's humour development. In P. McGhee & A. Chapman (Eds.), *Children's humour*

(pp. 181–212). Chichester, England: John Wiley.

Brodzinsky, D. M., Tew, J. D., & Palkovitz, R. (1979). Control of humorous affect in relation to children's conceptual tempo. *Developmental Psychology, 15*(3), 275–279.

Brown, G. E., Wheeler, K. J., & Cash, M. (1980). The effects of a laughing versus a nonlaughing model on humor responses in preschool children. *Journal of Experimental Child Psychology, 29,* 334–339.

Canzler, L. (1980, April). *Humor and the primary child*. (ERIC Document Reproduction No. ED 191 583)

Carson, D. K., Skarpness, L. R., Schultz, N. W., & McGhee, P. E. (1986). Temperament and communicative competence as predictors of young children's humor. *Merrill-Palmer Quarterly, 32*(4), 415–426.

Chapman, A. J. (1973). Social facilitation of laughter in children. *Journal of Experimental Social Psychology, 9,* 528–541.

Chapman, A. J. (1975). Humorous laughter in children. *Journal of Personality and Social Psychology, 31*(1), 42–49.

Chapman, A. J., & Chapman, W. A. (1974). Responsiveness to humor: Its dependency upon a companion's humorous smiling and laughter. *Journal of Psychology, 88,* 245–252.

Chapman, A. J., & Wright, D. S. (1976). Social enhancement of laughter: An experimental analysis of some companion variables. *Journal of Experimental Child Psychology, 21,* 201–218.

Chukovsky, K. (1963). *From two to five*. Berkeley: University of California Press.

Ding, G. F., & Jersild, A. L. (1932). A study of the laughing and smiling of preschool children. *Journal of Genetic Psychology, 40,* 452–472.

Fabrizi, M. S., & Pollio, H. R. (1987). A naturalistic study of humorous activity in a third, seventh, and eleventh grade classroom. *Merrill-Palmer Quarterly, 33*(1), 107–128.

Freud, S. (1960). *Jokes and their relation to the unconscious*. New York: Norton.

Gregg, A. (1928). *An observational study of humor in three-year-olds*. Unpublished master's thesis, Columbia University, New York.

Groch, A. S. (1974). Joking and appreciation of humor in nursery school children.

Child Development, 45, 1098–1102.

Honig, A. (1988). Humor development in children. *Young Children, 43*(4), 60–73.

Jones, M. C. (1926). The development of early behavior patterns in young children. *Pedagogical Seminary, 33,* 537–585.

Justin, F. (1932). A genetic study of laughter-provoking stimuli. *Child Development, 3,* 114–136.

King, P. V., & King, J. F. (1973). A children's humor test. *Psychological Reports, 33,* 632.

Kirschenblatt-Gimblett, B. (1979). Speech play and verbal art. In B. Sutton-Smith (Ed.), *Play and learning* (pp. 219–238). New York: Gardner.

Klein, A. J. (1985). Humor comprehension and humor appreciation of cognitively oriented humor: A study of kindergarten children. *Child Development, 15*(4), 223–235.

Lieberman, J. N. (1977). *Playfulness: Its relationship to imagination and creativity.* New York: Academic.

Masten, A. S. (1986). Humor and competence in school-aged children. *Child Development, 57,* 461–473.

McGhee, P. (1971). Cognitive development and children's comprehension of humor. *Child Development, 42,* 123–138.

McGhee, P. (1976). Sex differences in children's humor. *Journal of Communication, 26,* 176–189.

McGhee, P. (1979). *Humor: Its origin and development.* San Francisco: Freeman.

McGhee, P. (1988). *Humor and children.* New York: Haworth.

McGhee, P., & Chapman, A. J. (Eds.). (1980). *Children's humour.* New York: John Wiley.

McGhee, P., & Lloyd, S. (1982). Behavioral characteristics associated with the development of humor in young children. *Journal of Genetic Psychology, 41,* 253–259.

Opie, I., & Opie, P. (1959). *The lore and language of school children.* London: Clarendon.

Piaget, J. (1962). *Play, dreams and imitation in childhood.* New York: Norton.

Pien, D., & Rothbart, M. K. (1976). Incongruity and resolution in children's humor: A reexamination. *Child Development, 47,* 966–971.

Pien, D., & Rothbart, M. (1980). Incongruity humour, play and self-regulation of arousal in young children. In P. McGhee & A. J. Chapman (Eds.), *Children's humour* (pp. 1–26). New York: John Wiley.

Pinderhughes, E. E., & Zigler, E. (1985). Cognitive and motivational determinants of children's humor responses. *Journal of Research in Personality, 19,* 185–196.

Ramsey, P., & Reid, R. (1988). Play environments for preschoolers and kindergarteners. In D. Bergen (Ed.), *Play as a medium for learning and development* (pp. 213–239). Portsmouth, NH: Heinemann.

Ruch, W. (1993). Exhilaration and humor. In M. Lewis & J. M. Haviland (Eds.), *The handbook of emotions* (pp. 605–616). New York: Guilford.

Sherman, L. S. (1975). An ecological study of glee in small groups of preschool children. *Child Development, 46,* 53–61.

Sherman, L. S. (1977). Ecological determinants of gleeful behaviours in two nursery school environments. In A. Chapman & H. Foot (Eds.), *It's a funny thing, humour* (pp. 357–360). New York: Pergamon.

Sherman, L. S. (1988). Humor and social distance in elementary school children. *Humor: International Journal of Humor Research 1,* 389–404.

Shultz, T. R. (1972). The role of incongruity and resolution in children's appreciation of cartoon humor. *Journal of Experimental Child Psychology, 13,* 456–477.

Shultz, T. R. (1974). Development of the appreciation of riddles. *Child Development, 45,* 100–105.

Shultz, T. R., & Horibe, F. (1974). Development of the appreciation of verbal jokes. *Developmental Psychology, 10,* 13–20.

Singer, J. L. (Ed.) 1973. *The child's world of make-believe.* New York: Academic Press.

Sroufe, L. A., & Wunsch, J. P. (1972). The development of laughter in the first year of life. *Child Development, 43,* 1326–1344.

Steele, C. (1981). Play variables as related to cognitive constructs in three- to six-year-olds. *Journal of Research and Development in Education, 14*(3), 58–72.

Stern, D. N. (1974). Mother and infant at play: The dyadic interaction involving facial, vocal, and gaze behaviors. In M. M. Lewis & I. Rosenblum (Eds.), *The effect of the infant on its caregiver* (pp. 187–213). New York: John Wiley.

Sutton-Smith, B. (1979). Epilogue: Play as performance. In B. Sutton-Smith (Ed.), *Play and learning* (pp. 295–322). New York: Gardner.

Tower, R. B., & Singer, J. L. (1980). Imagination, interest, and joy in early childhood: Some theoretical considerations and empirical findings. In P. McGhee & A. J. Chapman (Eds.), *Children's humour* (pp. 27–57). New York: John Wiley.

Whitt, J. K., & Prentice, N. M. (1977). Cognitive processes in the development of children's enjoyment and comprehension of joking riddles. *Developmental Psychology, 13*(2), 129–136.

Wolfenstein, M. (1954). *Children's humor: A psychological analysis*. Glencoe, IL: Free Press.

Yalisove, D. (1978). The effects of riddle structure on children's comprehension of riddles. *Developmental Psychology, 14,* 173–180.

Sociocultural Influences on Gender-Role Behaviors in Children's Play

Alice Sterling Honig

Gender Differences in Play Styles

Children from time immemorial have played. Many theories about play and the "reasons" investigators give for children's play have slighted sex or gender differences to focus on the linguistic/cognitive and social skill developmental advantages that play offers (Bergen, 1988). Play helps young children clarify and articulate similarities and differences in concepts and categories. Another major emphasis in studying play has been to observe how peers learn to resolve conflicts through play adjustment and how they learn to understand symbolic uses of materials and toys in creating sociodramatic play scenarios (Johnson, Christie, & Yawkey, 1987).

Psychodynamic theorists have indeed conceptualized play as a way for children to express emotional resonances in their lives. Play helps children express sorrow, anger, and fear. Play opens pathways for them to cope with stress and also serves as a medium to express different worldviews as a function of their gender. Psychoanalyst Erik Erikson (1963) studied dramatic scenes constructed by young children as they freely used blocks and toys. Boys and girls differed significantly in the toy configurations and scenarios they created and recounted. Boys tended to create stories full of bold actions and tall block constructions. Girls tended to create more peaceful, enclosed domestic scenes.

During play, children invent approaches and patterns of interrelating with other persons. They imbue activities and objects with values, and think and feel about them in ways that may differ strongly depending on child gender (Slade & Wolf, 1994). "By the time they enter school, children have long been aware of their basic gender identities, have acquired many stereotypes about how the sexes differ, and have come to prefer gender-appropriate activities and same-sex playmates. . . . During middle childhood . . . their behavior, especially if they are boys, becomes even more gender-typed" (Sigelman & Shaffer, 1995, p. 307).

A summary of two decades of play research notes that differences in play styles as a function of child gender have not changed over the years in the following ways: "Girls engage in more doll play and domestic rehearsal, more art activities, and dressing up. Boys play more with transportation toys, with blocks and with carpentry toys. Boys also engage in more aggressive activities and play more in larger peer groups. Girls spend more time talking and spend far more time with teachers than do boys" (Fagot, 1988, p. 134). Preferred play themes differ by gender. Boys have listed preferences for cowboys and soldiers; girls listed playing house and school (Sutton-Smith, Rosenberg, & Morgan, 1963).

Sex differences are not found in children's progressively more sophisticated *cognitive* understandings of gender identity (one is a male or a female), gender stability (gender identity is stable across time), and finally, gender constancy or consistency (one's sex cannot be altered by superficial situational changes such as cross-dressing). Boy and girl toddlers are equally able to label themselves as a boy or girl. Preschoolers may not understand that sex ascription is stable; many still believe that in the future they can carry out biological roles of the other sex.

Roy was visiting with Grandma and playing with his cuddly toy monkey while Mother was in the bedroom nursing the new baby. Roy lifted up his shirt and pretended peacefully to nurse his own furry monkey. Grandma remarked lovingly that his mama had nursed him too when he was a baby. She also explained that boys cannot grow up to make milk and nurse babies. Only girls can grow up to nurse a baby. "Oh yes I will too be able to nurse when I grow up!" Roy asserted indignantly.

Gender constancy does not develop until the later preschool years. By early school age, children across cultures understand that not only is gender classification stable across time, but also across situations (Archer, 1992). Gender will not change because a child wishes to be of a different sex or engages in cross-sex activities. A study of preschool children's gender understanding in divorced versus intact families in Taiwan revealed that in a culture that values males preferentially, older preschool boys in mother custody showed an increased awareness of gender constancy in comparison both with peers in intact families and with children in father custody (Honig & Su, 1995). Thus, family/cultural variables may hasten some young children's understanding that a person's sex does not change. Gender roles, of course, do change, depending on culture and personal choice.

Early Sex Differences in Play Partner Preference

Sex differences in interactive play styles begin to appear from ten to fourteen months of age and are well established by the time children are thirty-six months old (Fagot, 1988). The earliest studies of developmental changes in levels of play among preschoolers found that children in two-thirds of the play groups chose same-sex play partners, and their preferred favorite playmates were usually the same sex as the child (Parten, 1933). Almost a half century later, other investigators found similar behavior among the solitary and social play of pairs of thirty-three-month-olds in a laboratory playroom (Jacklin & Maccoby, 1978); male and female toddlers were twice as sociable with same-sex as with opposite-sex playmates.

Biological Explanations
Almost all reviews of sex differences emphasize that boys show a higher level of activity and engage in more physically vigorous play than girls, whether indoors or outdoors (Hoyenga & Hoyenga, 1979; Rubin, Fein, & Vandenberg, 1983).

Some young boys at play on my front lawn were engaged in fairly strong tussling and wrestling holds with each other. "Boys, if you need to fight, you will have to find a place at your own house," I called out. "We wasn't fighting. We was just wrestling!" explained one boy cheerfully as he disentangled from the pile of boy bodies thrashing vigorously around on the grass and stood up to explain boy play fighting.

Preschool boys engage in more rough-and-tumble play than do girls. This phenomenon has been found in six cultures among males from three to eleven years (Whiting & Edwards, 1973). When they are a few months shy of three years old, boy peers playing together are already more likely to play tug-of-war than girl peers playing together or girl-boy pairs who are playing (Jacklin & Maccoby, 1978).

Even in humorous interactions during play, boys' responses are more vigorous. Young school-age boys are more likely to laugh and initiate behavioral and verbal humor than girls. Boys are more likely to clown playfully and throw themselves on the floor (Honig, 1988). Indeed, many researchers hypothesize that the very early tendency of young children from three years onward to play in same-sex groups may be particularly attributed to different gender *styles* in play and, possibly, gender differences in fearfulness. There is a tendency for specific fears and phobias to be more frequent in girls at all ages from school entry onward. Feeling more fearful, girls may not be as likely to opt to play an outlaw fleeing a posse or an explorer facing a stampeding herd of wild animals. Since boys show higher levels of active, rough-and-tumble play, toddler females may prefer to play with other girls, whose styles are less bumptious. Thus, the basic biological primate pattern, that males are both more active and more aggressive than females, may in part be responsible for early choices for sex-segregated play.

Cognitive Developmental Explanations
Other theorists suggest that cognitive growth during the early years is deeply implicated in the marked separation by sex in play groups. Chil-

dren come to understand their own self-definition as a girl or boy as part of a growing ability and need to categorize persons to understand social relations. Adults are big and children are small. Some children are boys, some are girls. A researcher suggests that "these essentially oppositional categories form part of children's social reasoning from their earliest encounters in the public domain of the . . . nursery school" (Cook-Gumperz, 1991, p. 213).

Sex Stereotyping in Toy Preference

The kinds of toys that boys and girls play with differ in infancy, even prior to establishing clear identity as a male or female (Fagot & Leinbach, 1989). Toddlers start segregating themselves by toy preference, so that boys age fourteen to twenty-two months prefer to play with trucks and cars, while girls prefer soft toys and dolls (Huston, 1985; Smith & Daglish, 1977). Researchers have reported finding higher frequencies of preschooler play with same-sex than with cross-sex toys (Langlois & Downs, 1980).

Boys often prefer war toys, whereas many girls prefer Barbie dolls (Goldstein, 1994). As children move into the elementary school years, their preferences for toys, as expressed in letters written to Santa Claus, are even more gender stereotyped (Richardson & Simpson, 1982). Far more girls than boys asked for play items that were typed for the opposite sex. Almost 25 percent of the girls, for example, asked for baby dolls and only .6 percent of boys. About 15 percent of the girls and 25 percent of the boys asked for sports equipment or spatial toys, such as construction sets. Thus, the *breadth* of toy preference differs for males and females. Girls are far more likely to play with masculine toys than boys with feminine toys. Boys also avoid "girl" toys far more than girls avoid "boy" toys (Rubin, Fein, & Vandenberg, 1983). Such lopsided preference by girls for boys' toys in comparison with boys choosing girls' toys is consistently found by researchers (Etaugh & Liss, 1992).

Moral Development and Gender Differences in Play

Gender bias is not reflected in young children's responses to moral transgressions in play. Preschoolers, whether male or female, respond to violations of moral and ethical imperatives

(such as not pulling a child's hair) with explanations of injury or loss. They point to the hurt child's emotional reactions, such as crying.

Younger preschoolers are fairly flexible in moral judgments about socially appropriate gender roles. When one researcher asked four- to nine-year-olds about a little boy named George who insisted he wanted to play with dolls even though his parents told him that dolls are for girls, many of the youngest children believed that doll play and other cross-sex toy play was okay if that was what George wanted to do (Damon, 1977). By age six, however, their responses become far more rigid. Children react with intolerance toward those who violate traditional sex-role differences in play. They view transgressions against conventional sex-appropriate behaviors and use of toys very seriously (Nucci & Nucci, 1982). Children entering school affirm stringent beliefs, such as "Boys don't play with dolls. That's girls' stuff," and "Girls should never cuss!"

Thus, six-year-olds interpret the importance of adhering to gender stereotypes in play as if they are absolute moral imperatives (such as not injuring someone) rather than social conventions (such as wearing party shoes rather than sneakers to a fancy restaurant). Why is this so? A researcher suggests that young children must exaggerate gender roles to make them cognitively clear (Maccoby, 1990). At Piagetian late preoperational or early concrete operational levels of intellectual functioning, children may view any societal custom or rule as equivalent to a natural law, such as the law of gravity (Carter & Patterson, 1982).

By nine years of age, children are able to distinguish between moral rules that people must obey (such as not deliberately smashing a window) and traditional customs that children could choose to ignore (such as a boy's playing with dolls), but they usually do not, since other children would be mean to them (Damon, 1977).

Influence of Parents and Peers on Sex-Stereotyped Play

Peers are powerful influences. Whom children are with affects their willingness to play with cross-sex toys. When three- and four-year-old boys and girls were left alone with toys, they were more likely to play with cross-sex toys. The lowest probability of such play occurred when they were with an opposite-sex peer (Serbin, Connor, Burchardt, & Citron, 1979). Males particularly discourage cross-sex toy play for other males. They respond quite negatively to boys who choose cross-sex toys or choose to play with girls.

"Daniel, I hate girls! Do you hate girls?" inquired Christopher of his six-year-old peer who lived down the block and was visiting in Chris's yard. Anxious to please his friend, Daniel hesitantly answered, "Yes. All except Natalie." "Who is Natalie?" asked the frowning Chris. "She's my new baby sister," whispered Daniel bravely.

Male peers impose a more stringent and possibly even menacing meaning at any hint of male peer appreciation or enjoyment of activities and toys perceived as "female." Indeed, a researcher reports that boys tend to ignore teachers or other girls, but their male peers give them "constant feedback on both appropriate play styles and appropriate playmates" (Fagot, 1988, p. 135). Thus, the gender play preferences of females and their play interaction scenarios are perceived as a danger to be avoided by boys who want to be accepted into the world of male peer play.

This massive negative socialization toward activities, toys, and agents perceived as female is troubling. In conjunction with evidence of greater male infant/toddler vulnerability to lack of maternal warmth and support, this negative socialization may well account for later interpersonal difficulties that some males face. When they enter the school system, boys may not have had the wealth of opportunities to learn the sophisticated turn-taking, sharing, compromising, adjusting to others' needs, and other subtle socialization skills that females are learning as they play in more domestic spheres in the world of the preschool.

Parental expectations from birth onward provide powerful incentives, both as direct reinforcers and models, for sharply divergent gender-role behaviors (Honig, 1983; Schan, Kahn, Diepold, & Cherry, 1980). Fathers strenuously punish the non-gender-stereotyped play of both daughters and sons. Mothers, however, actively reward cross-gender play; they "interact with sons when playing with feminine-typed toys" (Golombok & Fivush, 1994, p. 116). Mothers are equally likely to engage in play with daughters *regardless* of which toy a girl chooses. Thus,

boys may be getting mixed and confusing messages from mothers and fathers.

As families join in and praise or else punish cross-sex play, the reinforcements for sexual meanings of play materials and activities are subtle and pervasive (Block, 1983). Parents encourage boys to find out how toys work and how to play in large groups with peers. Fathers of boys tend to play more physical games with infant sons. Fathers provide sons with more vehicles, construction materials, role-enactment toys (such as laser guns and light sabers), balls, and sports equipment, and with fewer dolls and domestic toys.

Families reward girls for learning interpersonal rules that make them easy to keep in close contact with adults. Girls, compared with boys, also engage in different kinds of pretend or sociodramatic role-play. Older sisters, therefore, "may be more likely to involve younger siblings in role play than are older brothers" (Ervin-Tripp, 1991, p. 87). Thus, the meaning of sex differences in play becomes profound for promoting divergence in developing interpersonal skills in contrast to skillful manipulation of objects in the physical world. Girls will tend to value and be more adept at the former; boys will value and become more adept at the latter. Parents and teachers endow boys' and girls' misbehavior during play with different meanings. Caregivers respond significantly more to noncompliant male preschooler responses, although both sexes tend to be mostly compliant with teacher requests (Wittmer & Honig, 1977).

Television's Influence on Sex Roles in Play

Many adults consider television an enlightening force for bringing new ideas to viewers about the range of life roles that men and women can assume. Women are portrayed as doctors as well as nurses, as police officers and business managers as well as secretaries. Research shows, nevertheless, that young children's television diet seems to be cementing even more rigid sex-role conceptions in recent years. In play groups, for example, males are more likely to enact fictional, superhero roles often portrayed on salient television shows (*He-Man, Ghostbusters,* or *Ninja Turtles,* for example), while females are more likely to portray familial characters.

In the 1990s particularly, salient television superheroes are the Power Rangers, who average more than two hundred acts of violence per hour, compared with one hundred for the Teenage Mutant Ninja Turtles. The *Power Rangers* show interduces footage of real-life actors and settings with special animation effects. This blurring of conceptually clear boundaries between real and film characters may heighten males' tendency to model the violent acts they view. Preschool teachers report that the Power Rangers "encourage more violent play, interfere with imaginative, cooperative play, and . . . squelch creativity in play" (Levin & Carlsson-Paige, 1995, p. 69). Young children regard the Power Rangers as powerful role models. Decades ago, researchers demonstrated that male preschoolers were far more likely than female preschoolers to imitate the aggressive acts of a powerful adult model, particularly an adult male (Bandura, Ross, & Ross, 1963). Thus, such television fare works toward widening differences between boy and girl play patterns in the direction of increasing male admiration, and acting out, of violent, antisocial behaviors.

The Effect of Play Situation on Sex Differences

Sex differences very evident in one setting may not be as noticeable in another setting. Situational factors are particularly evident in mixed-sex settings. Kindergarten and first-grade girls stay closer to an adult than do boys in mixed settings. The girls, however, are willing to go farther from an adult to play with peers when in an all-girl group (Maccoby, 1990).

Preschool teachers can use creativity in planning and organizing activities that will minimize strong differentiation in play patterns. Taking down barriers between the housekeeping corner and the block area may make it easier for boys and girls to use construction materials as well as kitchen make-believe appliances in playing "house." One author makes a passionate plea for preschool educators to sustain the "generative energy and transformational power" of children's creative sociodramatic play into the school years (Fromberg, 1990, p. 243). Indeed, her call for such teacher support promises a deeper understanding of all children:

> The content of sociodramatic play themes can help to illuminate individual children's development and how they experience contexts and relationships.
>
> As a type of syntax that generates changes over time, play has a surface structure and a deep structure. The surface structure consists of what appear to be topics and themes, such as superhero or family play. The deep structure touches on subjective experiences and relationships. (p. 243)

A teacher-researcher similarly urges teachers to allow young children to choose and elaborate on their preferred play themes (Paley, 1986). As they perceptively study the transformational themes in children's sociodramatic play, caregivers gain insights into how to facilitate learning, both in the classroom and in the emotional/social sphere that will enrich the repertoires of both boys and girls. Teachers can make a significant difference in enlarging the creative, imaginative scope of preschooler sociodramatic play (Smilansky & Shefataya, 1991). Research reveals that this active involvement in decreasing negative sexual meanings in play is urgently necessary. One study, for example, paired four-year-olds with a playmate of the same sex (Mathews, 1981). The children mostly enacted the roles of mother and father. Boys' playing wife roles suggested that wives are inept and helpless. As fathers, boys enacted leadership roles and did little participation in housekeeping. Girls, in contrast, role-played mothers as nurturant, generous, and highly managerial. They too, however, portrayed wives as helpless and incompetent! Children portray the role of mother as positive in play. The role of wife is not.

Sex Play

Sex play begins very early in infancy. The baby focuses the earliest sex play, as any other form of play, such as waving hands back and forth or kicking legs vigorously, on the baby's own body. Freed of his diaper on a changing table, a baby will often reach for his penis and caress it. Boy babies have erections very early. Little girls have a harder time finding the vulva or clitoris, but they too pat and feel their sexually pleasurable parts in early sex play with their own bodies. One psychiatrist reported that his nearly three-year-old daughter patted her vulva and shared confidentially as he was snuggling her in her crib at bed time, "Daddy, this is my best feeling part."

Sex play with others often begins as curiosity about the organs that other children have that are similar to or different from one's own.

> After toileting time among the three-year-olds, Jerry came over to Lana and lifted up her dress before she had pulled up her panties. The teacher was tense as she turned and saw this. She was sure that Jerry was going to inspect or touch the little girl's sexual parts. Instead he lifted the dress all the way up and gently touched Lana's belly button. Wondrous! She had one too—just like his!

Curiosity about body parts not only can lead to needless teacher tension but also can lead to some comic sequences in terms of sex part disclosures among three- and four-year-olds.

> Daisy came home from day care and informed her mother in no uncertain terms that she was tired of pulling down her panties in play with boys in her classroom. She had seen their penis enough and they had seen her "gina" (as she called her vagina) enough! Her mama empathized and suggested that she simply firmly tell the boys next time they started the game of "Let's show each other" that she had shown them enough and seen enough. Daisy agreed. She made her announcement with vigor next time the little boys in her play group wanted to engage in sex showing. Sex play of this mutual voyeuristic sort then stopped.

Sometimes, sex play does not represent simple curiosity about how boys and girls differ. Instead, it represents a need to engage in what the preschooler already feels is a "forbidden" play experience that must be hidden from adults.

> Mr. Stearns noted quietly that Davon and Leroy were always going into the bathroom together and trying to keep others out. Through the partly opened door, he noticed that their sex play involved taking down their pants, looking at and touching each other's genitals. Mr. Stearns walked into the bathroom with other preschoolers and announced cheerfully that if there was something interesting to see, then all the children wanted to see too! Davon and Leroy were surprised. They already had learned in their families that sex was "secret." This open approach to accepting that boys have testicles and penises and that girls have vulvas was not what they had in mind in their furtive play. Calm acknowledgment and open acceptance of sexual anatomy decreased the secretive nature of their sex play and they no longer sought to continue.

Many young boys enjoy the power of their ability to urinate over a distance and to urinate standing up. In play with girls, a boy may tease, "You can't pee standing up and I can!"

> Five-year-old Maida protested to the teacher, "I can so pee standing up!" The teacher agreed she surely could try, and after the little girl had straddled the toilet and heroically managed to urinate standing up, the teacher remarked, "Well, you sure showed Robert that you *can* pee standing up if you want to." The teacher further explained that it surely also felt more comfortable to pee sitting down. Maida could choose whichever way *she* felt like, not a way that a boy used or teased her about.

Sometimes, children whose parents have not been forthright about labeling sexual parts or matter-of-factly explaining that boys have certain sexual parts and girls have other sexual parts will move on during the early elementary years to sex play that involves mutual masturbation. Indeed, if sexuality has not been honestly and calmly dealt with in the family, some children seem at young ages to have an early feeling that sexual parts are "dirty" and "shameful." They "hide" sex games from adults. They will call out tauntingly if a child's pants slip down and sexual organs are bared.

Some caregivers bring their own sexual hangups into the classroom. A toddler teacher shakes her finger warningly and calls out, "Get your hand out of your pants" to a child masturbating dreamily under his blanket at nap time. By their own rejection of the naturalness of masturbation when a child is upset or getting calm at sleep times, some adults confirm lessons from home that sexuality is somehow "bad." Caregivers, of course, can mention that some places and situations (such as nap time) are far more appropriate than others for patting one's genitals. When self-stimulation occurs compulsively and pervasively, teachers will need to find out and ameliorate the source of the child's tensions and also work on increasing a child's feeling of security and interest in play domains.

Sexual play that involves dominating or assaulting another child must be firmly forbidden, discussed, and handled by adults who establish clear boundaries and keep children safe from hurt.

> A distraught mother came to consult about her son's weekend visits with his father under a joint custody divorce agreement. The father's girlfriend and children lived with the boy's dad. The older children tried to put sticks and did force pebbles into the six-year-old's anus. The boy was terrified. He cried and told his mother they had threatened to harm him if he told his dad. She called her ex-husband but he scoffed at her concerns. Since there was joint custody, the mother had been legally told that she and her ex-husband were to work out their own problems; the courts would not intervene. Professional help was urgently needed.

Strong, clear messages about appropriate touches and inappropriate touches need to be given by caregivers, teachers, and parents. Appropriate sexual touching of oneself is fine when a child is in a private space, such as crib or bed. Touching, poking, or hurting sexual parts of another child is *not* OK. Sexual parts are private. During play, children must not interfere with each other's private parts.

Caregivers can read books to children that help satisfy young children's curiosity about sexual differences (Gordon, 1974). A book that can help parents and teachers explain sexual puzzlements very simply to young children is *Did the Sun Shine Before You Were Born?* (Gordon & Gordon, 1977). The illustrations are gentle and support family closeness. Where children have been brought up with peaceful, matter-of-fact acknowledgment of all parts of the body, including sexual parts, early sex play is likely to be mostly to satisfy curiosity about differences. It does not develop into furtive, compulsive, or hurtful behaviors toward others. Indeed, under such rearing conditions, children take each other's differences for granted.

On the child care lawn, children of varied ages were pretending that the large cardboard carton they were playing in was a big boat and they were sailors. One of the younger boys had an itch. He took down his shorts and scratched vigorously under his testicles. None of the other playmates remarked on this, nor did they tease or pay much attention. When the boy finished attending to his itch, he picked up his pants and continued the pretend sailor game with his playmates.

Preschoolers often explore each other's genital and anal regions under the guise of "playing doctor." They may pretend they need to put a thermometer in another child's rectum. They may get another child to undress so they can use the toy stethoscope and get a leisurely inspection of nipples and belly buttons. When children are peaceably reared without shame for their bodies, adults can expect a certain amount of such "doctor play" among preschoolers. But adults must allow no hurting, furtiveness, or coercion. The more that adults accept the naturalness of sexual parts and functions, the more they answer children's sexual questions simply, the less coercive sex play is likely to be. Indeed, early acceptance of children's sensual and sexual selves often leads to their sharing their feelings quite naturally.

> Three-year-old Daniel had just urinated quite carefully into the toilet. "Daniel, you were really careful," remarked Grandma admiringly. "All your pee-pee went right into the toilet." "Want me to tell you how you do it, Grandma?" asked Daniel. "Sure, love," agreed Grandma. "Well, you hold your penis and point it straight down and you rest your testicles on the rim of the toilet, and then all the pee-pee goes straight into the toilet," explained Daniel, proud of his teaching ability and urinary dexterity. His Grandma was mighty impressed also!

The more deeply adults recognize that little children are sexual beings as well as social and physical and thinking beings, the more likely that sex play will involve simple curiosity and sensual self-stimulation for comfort, but not hurtfulness toward others.

Over the past decades, how have caregivers and social institutions fared in decreasing marked gender differences both in playmate choice and in creation of personal and social meanings through play scenarios?

In the 1970's there were concerted efforts by parents and educators to diminish the gender stereotypes promoted in children's literature, television, film, and children's toys. It was to some degree successful as girls, particularly, began to cross gender lines in their play (Liss, 1986). It became more acceptable for boys to be sensitive and nurturing and for girls to be assertive and independent. But in the 1980's much of this ground was lost as toy commercials specifically targeted children's interest in conforming to social perceptions of gender identity in order to sell more toys. (Van Hoorn, Nourot, Scales, & Alward, 1993, p. 178)

Preschool teachers have tried to encourage girls particularly to increase their command of spatial understandings through more construction activity and motoric play. Typically, girls have chosen activities such as dancing to develop bodily kinesthetic intelligence. Caregivers now encourage both girls and boys to develop fine and gross motor skills in a wider variety of play activities, including building space forts, for example, which formerly would have been predominantly a male play choice. Whether there have been equivalent active efforts by teachers to engage males in learning to articulate strong emotions rather than act them out, and in learning interpersonal conciliation and turn-taking skills, is a challenge for researchers to discover in the next decade.

The increase in single-parent, female-headed households, with fewer role models of males using negotiation and interpersonal cherishing of adult females and their viewpoints, means that young males have fewer opportunities to observe and internalize adult male roles that value the wifely role. Men's ongoing engagement in the interpersonal skills that enrich a marriage and provide powerful observational learning opportunities for young boys needs to be promoted more in families and in child care facilities.

The play world young children construct promotes rigid concepts of sexual differences in play and in the manner in which play activities are carried out. Present efforts to make little girls' play more like that of boys does not hold much promise for helping both boys and girls to become more skilled in empathy and nurturance, compromise and caring, as well as in motor skills and adventuresomeness in play scenarios. Caregivers and parents need to engage in more dialogue about how they can use play-space planning, role-playing, judicious adult participation, and scaffolding of sociodramatic scenarios to enhance play learning opportunities for children (Honig, 1982). Adults need also to accept deeply that children are sexual and sensual beings who will masturbate gently while listening intently to a long story. Sexual self-play even helps some young children concentrate better on listening to a story!

Children are often curious about sexual similarities and differences between boys and girls. Caregivers need to accept children's urge to know and understand differences and promote diversified play that includes domestic *as well as* adventurous, innovative *as well as* stereotypic themes. The adults will then promote increased imaginative play and more egalitarian opportunities in play. Adults will be helping young children to become creative and skilled at empathic sharing, kindness, intimacy, and win-win negotiations in play, as well as skilled in group teamwork, physical adventuring, and complex gross motor activities.

Bibliography

Archer, J. (1992). Childhood gender roles: Social context and organization. In H. McGurk (Ed.), *Childhood social development: Contemporary perspectives* (pp. 31–61). Hove, UK: Lawrence Erlbaum.

Bandura, A., Ross, D., & Ross, S. S. (1963). Imitation of film-mediated aggressive models. *Journal of Abnormal and Social Psychology, 66,* 3–11.

Bergen, D. (Ed.). (1988). *Play as a medium for learning and development: A handbook of theory and practice.* Portsmouth, NH: Heinemann.

Block, J. H. (1983). Differential premises arising from differential socialization of the sexes: Some conjectures. *Child Development, 54,* 1335–1354.

Carter, D. B., & Patterson, C. J. (1982). Sex roles as social conventions: The development of children's conceptions of sex-role stereotypes. *Developmental Psychology, 18,* 812–829.

Cook-Gumperz, J. (1991). Children's construction of "childness." In B. Scales., M. Almy, A. Nicolopoulou, & S. Ervin-Tripp (Eds.), *Play and the social context of development in early care and education* (pp. 207–298). New York: Teachers College Press.

Damon, W. (1977). *The social world of the child.* San Francisco: Jossey-Bass.

Erikson, E. (1963). *Childhood and society.* New York: Norton.

Ervin-Tripp, S. (1991). Play in language development. In B. Scales, M. Almy, A. Nicolopoulou, & S. Ervin-Tripp (Eds.), *Play and the social context of development in early care and education* (pp. 84–97). New York: Teachers College Press.

Etaugh, C., & Liss, M. B. (1992). Home, school, and playroom: Training grounds for adult gender roles. *Sex Roles, 26,* 639–648.

Fagot, B. I. (1988). Toddlers: Play and sex stereotyping. In D. Bergen (Ed.), *Play as a medium for learning and development: A handbook of theory and practice* (pp. 133–135). Portsmouth, NH: Heinemann.

Fagot, B. I., & Leinbach, M. D. (1989). The young child's gender scheme: Environmental input, internal organization. *Child Development, 60,* 663–672.

Fromberg, D. P. (1990). An agenda for research on play in early childhood education. In E. Klugman & S. Smilansky (Eds.), *Children's play and learning: Perspectives and policy implications* (pp. 235–249). New York: Teachers College Press.

Goldstein, J. H. (1994). *Toys, play, and child development.* New York: Cambridge University Press.

Golombok, S., & Fivush, R. (1994). *Gender development.* New York: Cambridge University Press.

Gordon, S. (1974). *Girls are girls and boys are boys.* New York: John Day.

Gordon, S., & Gordon, J. (1977). *Did the sun shine before you were born?* Syracuse, NY: Ed-U Press.

Honig, A. S. (1982). *Playtime learning games for young children.* Syracuse, NY: Syracuse University Press.

Honig, A. S. (1983). Research in review: Sex role socialization in young children. *Young Children, 38,* 57–70.

Honig, A. S. (1988). Research in review: Humor development in children. *Young*

Children, 43(4), 60–73.

Honig, A. S., & Su, P. (1995). *Mother vs. father custody for Taiwanese preschoolers.* Paper presented at the annual meeting of the American Psychological Association, New York, NY.

Hoyenga, K. B., & Hoyenga, K. T. (1979). *The question of sex differences: Psychological, cultural, and biological issues.* Boston: Little, Brown.

Huston, A. C. (1985). The development of sex typing: Themes from recent research. *Developmental Review, 5,* 1–17.

Jacklin, C., & Maccoby, E. (1978). Social behavior at thirty-three months in same-sex dyads. *Child Development, 49,* 557–569.

Johnson, J. E., Christie, J. F., & Yawkey, T. D. (1987). *Play and early childhood development.* Evanston, IL: Scott Foresman.

Langlois, J., & Downs, C. (1980). Mother, father, and peers as socialization agents of sex-typed play behaviors in young children. *Child Development, 51,* 1217–1247.

Levin, D. E., & Carlsson-Paige, N. (1995). The Mighty Morphin Power Rangers: Teachers voice concern. *Young Children, 50(6),* 67–74.

Liss, M. B. (1981). Patterns of toy play: An analysis of sex differences. *Sex Roles, 7,* 1143–1150.

Maccoby, E. E. (1990). Gender and relationships: A developmental account. *American Psychologist, 45,* 513–520.

Mathews, W. S. (1981). Sex role perception, portrayal, and preferences in the fantasy play of young children. *Sex Roles, 1(10),* 979–987.

Nucci, L., & Nucci, M. S. (1982). Children's social interactions in the context of moral and conventional transgressions. *Child Development, 53,* 403–412.

Paley, V. (1986). *Boys and girls: Superheroes in the doll corner.* Chicago: University of Chicago Press.

Parten, M. B. (1933). Social play among preschool children. *Journal of Abnormal and Social Psychology, 28,* 136–147.

Richardson, J. G., & Simpson, C. H. (1982). Children, gender, and social structure: An analysis of the contents of letters to Santa Claus. *Child Development, 52,* 429–436.

Rubin, K. H., Fein, G. G., & Vandenberg, B.

(1983). Play. In P. H. Mussen & E. M. Hetherington (Eds.), *Handbook of child psychology. Vol. 4: Socialization, personality, and social development* (pp. 693–774). New York: John Wiley.

Schan, C. G., Kahn, L., Diepold, J. H., & Cherry, F. (1980). The relationships of parental expectations and preschool children's verbal sex-typing to their sex-typed toy play behavior. *Child Development, 51,* 266–270.

Serbin, L. A., Connor, J. A., Burchardt, C. J., & Citron, C. C. (1979). Effects of peer presence on sex-typing of children's play behavior. *Journal of Experimental Child Psychology, 27,* 303–309.

Sigelman, C. K., & Shaffer, D. R. (1995). *Life-span human development* (2nd ed.). Pacific Grove, CA: Books/Cole.

Slade, A., & Wolf, D. P. (1994). *Children at play.* Oxford: Oxford University Press.

Smilansky, S., & Shefataya, L. (1991). *Facilitating play: A medium for promoting cognitive, socio-emotional and academic development in young children.* Gaithersburg, MD: Psychosocial and Educational Publications.

Smith, P. K., & Daglish, L. (1977). Sex differences in parent and infant behavior in the home. *Child Development, 46,* 1250–1254.

Sutton-Smith, B., Rosenberg, B. G., & Morgan, E. (1963). Development and sex differences in play during preadolescence. *Child Development, 34,* 119–126.

Van Hoorn, J., Nourot, P., Scales, B., & Alward, K. (1993). *Play at the center of the curriculum.* New York: Macmillan.

Whiting, J., & Edwards, C. P. (1973). A cross-cultural analysis of sex differences in the behavior of children aged three through 11. *Journal of Social Psychology, 91,* 171–188.

Wittmer, D. S., & Honig, A. S. (1977). Do boy toddlers bug teachers more? *Canadian Children, 12*(1), 21–27.

Play with Violence

Understanding and Responding Effectively

Diane Levin

The current violent environment in which children are growing up requires rethinking how adults look at, interpret, and respond to play with violence. Theorists and researchers have viewed play with violence most commonly through the two often opposing lenses of the developmental and sociopolitical perspectives. Using the two lenses together can help adults understand why all play with violence is not the same, and how the nature of the play influences what children learn and the degree to which their play meets their needs. This approach also points to why much of the play with violence today is the subject of frequent debate and concern. The combined lenses, nevertheless, can help adults develop informed and effective responses to children's involvement in play with violence.

> For the fourth time in twenty minutes, four-year-olds Wanda and Shelley have made a building with large hollow blocks. Wanda carefully crawls inside and Shelley starts to crash the building down with his fists and feet and yells, "Bang, Pow, Pow, Crash." As he continues kicking and shouting, Wanda, who is now buried under the blocks, yells, "Help me, I'm trapped. My house just blew up on me. I'm trapped. I can't move. Help, Help!" While the first three building demolitions ended with Wanda "dead" under the collapsed building, this time as she calls out for help, Shelley frantically starts pulling blocks off the pile and shouting, "Don't worry, here I come, here I come." Then he enthusiastically pulls a laughing Wanda out of the wreckage. Within minutes they begin rebuilding again.

> Jackson picks up his plastic Tyrannosaurus figure and crashes it into other toy dinosaurs, yelling, "I'm smashing your bones, I'm squishing your eyes, I'm gonna grind you up, I'm gonna suck your blood . . ." As the Tyrannosaurus continues the attack, Jackson frantically hands a dinosaur to a nearby adult, instructing, "Hold this and yell, 'Please don't kill me, I don't want to die.'" After several more attacks Jackson has the other dinosaurs capture the Tyrannosaurus in a bloody battle and puts a plastic box over it. Holding a Brontosaurus in his hand, he turns to the other dinosaurs and says, "There, we got it. It's in jail. It won't ever get out of there!" (Adapted from Carlsson-Paige & Levin, 1987, pp. 37–38)

> Four- and six-year-old Mighty Morphin Power Ranger fans Anton and Phil are sitting together on an imaginary airplane using a collection of Power Ranger action figures. They repeatedly push a button on the backs of the figures that "morphs" (transforms) their faces from those of regular high schoolers to Power Rangers wearing masks and back again. Next, the boys take Power Rangers in each hand and begin bumping them against the chairs in front of them with accompanying "Pow, Pow" sounds. Soon, they begin to playfully karate chop each other with the figures. As the figures are put away and the boys get off the plane, they begin using their own bodies to karate chop at each other, making the same "Pow, Pow" sounds.

The children in these three scenarios are involved in play with violent themes. The content from each scenario is in some way connected to violence the children have seen. Anton and Phil's grows out of their exposure to *Mighty Morphin Power Rangers,* a violent television show and movie that is marketed with a line of toys and other products. Jackson's play occurs soon after he has seen a cartoon about dinosaurs in which a Tyrannosaurus rex violently attacks, kills, and eats other dinosaurs. Shelley and Wanda's play, which occurs the day after the bombing of the federal building in Oklahoma City, seems to grow out of news they have heard about the bombing.

The documentation of and debates about children's involvement in play with violent themes, often called war play[1] have discussed the origins of such play in children, its role in development and learning, its relationship to violence in society, and how adults should respond to it (Baruch, 1942; Freud & Burlingham, 1943; Goldstein, 1994; Saki, 1914/1988). In recent years, especially as violence in society has increased dramatically and as many children seem increasingly involved in play with violent themes, efforts to resolve these issues have taken on a growing sense of importance and urgency (Carlsson-Paige & Levin, 1987, 1990; Kostelnik, Whiren, & Stein, 1986; Levin & Carlsson-Paige, 1995; Miedzian, 1991). Such efforts invariably lead to a conundrum of complexities, research, and theoretical and practical questions, which can make it extremely difficult to imagine integrating such issues into a coherent and comprehensive position.

Conventional Views of Play with Violence

Until recently, arguments about play with violent themes have tended to fall into two distinct camps (Carlsson-Paige & Levin, 1987). One, the developmental perspective, focuses primarily on children's individual needs and the role of play with violence in helping children meet their needs (Bettelheim, 1987; Freud & Burlingham, 1943; Groves & Mazur, 1995; Singer, 1993; Sutton-Smith, 1986). Adherents of this view have argued that play with violent themes or content helps children work through many important developmental issues, such as feelings of aggression and frustration, a need to feel powerful and strong, and an understanding of the violence they have heard about or experienced directly. Adherents also usually hold that children need to be in

charge of what they play; their choices reflect their experiences, needs, and interests. If children choose to engage in violent play, then they are showing us what they need to do. Therefore, from this point of view it is generally argued that play with violence is important, serves a useful purpose, and should be allowed.

The other dominant point of view, the sociopolitical perspective, has tended to focus more on what the content of play with violence might be teaching children and what messages they are learning about violence and about how people treat each other (Kuykendall, 1995; Miedzian, 1991). Adherents of this perspective argue that children learn antisocial messages and behaviors from engaging in war play and that adults, by allowing it, are tacitly condoning such behavior. They are also concerned that such play contributes to glorification of violence, desensitization to violence, and increases in overall levels of violence in individual children's behavior and, ultimately, in the broader society. Proponents of the sociopolitical perspective usually argue that, whenever possible, play with violent themes and aggressive toys should be strongly discouraged or banned.

Convincing arguments represent both sides of the debate over play with violent themes. Children do often bring to their play that which is important to them and what they want or need to work out and master. At the same time, as children play they are working out ideas, resolving issues, and learning (Berk, 1995; Levin, 1995). Thus, if children bring violent content to their play, one could argue that they are bringing it there because they need to. As they play with that violent content, however, they can be learning lessons about violence, potentially worrisome lessons (Carlsson-Paige & Levin, 1987; Levin, 1995).

We are left with a dilemma: How can the strong arguments of both perspectives be reconciled when both make good sense? How can we help children use their play to meet their developmental needs and work on the increasing amounts of violence they see, while at the same time promote nonviolence and positive social behaviors?

All Play with Violence Is Not the Same

Looking at the three episodes described above, using the perspectives represented by the two sides of the war play debate, can lead to a more coherent and comprehensive understanding of play with violence than when either side of the debate is viewed alone.

Working Out an Understanding of Real-World Violence

Shelley and Wanda's play grows out of what they have heard about people getting buried when the Oklahoma City federal building was bombed. They are using their block play to re-enact the event, including what happened to the people involved. In fact, they reenact the same situation several times. Finally, they change what they do so that, by the end, instead of the scenario ending with Wanda "dead"—one consequence of violence—they have finally figured out a way to have a positive effect: rescuing the victim and making sure she is safe.

From a *developmental perspective,* while the teacher might wish that these children had not heard about the bombing or brought what they heard to the classroom, the intensity of their involvement and the details of their play suggest that they are working on something that is vitally important to them. It seems that once they did hear about the bombing in Oklahoma City, their play became an important vehicle for working out their understanding, questions, and concerns, and thereby for reaching some degree of resolution and a renewed sense of safety after the bombing.

As Wanda and Shelley play, they focus on those aspects of what they heard that are most understandable at their level of development, the most graphic and concrete aspects of the situation: the people getting buried in the building when it collapses (Carlsson-Paige & Levin, 1985; Levin, 1994). They use what they already know—for instance, how it feels to be buried under a pile of blocks, what an explosion might be like, how a rescue operation works—as the starting point for working out their understanding. Their considerable skills in using blocks as a play material and in working out a shared play scenario contribute to their ability to use their play to work out the bombing in a meaningful way. Their play also provides adults with information about what the children have heard, how they understand what they have heard, and what else they may need in order to work through their concerns.

From a *sociopolitical perspective,* we need to ask what the children might be learning about violence and how people treat each other. The excitement of the early scenes seems to glorify and emphasize the violence as Shelley pretends to hurt Wanda while he knocks down the building. The play evolves so that Shelley also becomes the helper and rescuer. The children, therefore, are not left merely with a sense of the excitement that comes from the violence of knocking down a building with no awareness of the consequences that violence can have. Nor are they merely experiencing the sense of helplessness and fear that violence can often instill. Instead, they are working through an understanding of the effects of violence on people and objects, while directly experiencing the empowering and reassuring message that people can and do help in ways they can understand through their own actions. The children learn positive social messages that are meaningful in their own immediate world.

Working Out an Understanding of Entertainment Violence with Open-Ended Toys

As with Wanda and Shelley, Jackson's play seems to grow out of violence that has come from the media, but, in this case, it comes from entertainment violence (a claymation cartoon) rather than from television news reporting.

At the beginning of his play, Jackson uses his toy dinosaur figures to reenact (or imitate) the brutal attacks of the Tyrannosaurus on the other dinosaurs he saw in the cartoon. He uses very violent words and actions as he carries out the attacks. As he plays, things gradually evolve into a plot of his own making; he uses his largest dinosaur (the Brontosaurus) as the powerful hero who can rescue the victimized dinosaurs. First, he does this by violent means, "killing" (as he understands it) the Tyrannosaurus several times. By the end of the play, he has come up with a nonviolent solution that creates a safe world for all the dinosaurs by putting the bad Tyrannosaurus in a jail where he "can't ever get out."

From a *developmental perspective,* Jackson is bringing to his play the violence he has seen in entertainment media because he needs to work out some degree of mastery and control over it. He starts with those aspects of the cartoon that were most dramatic and probably troubling to him and finds a way to re-create them that is based on how he understands them. He then transforms them into something over which he can have control. He uses his collection of toy dinosaurs in the service of these efforts, and he is always in charge of what they do. He is the actor, scriptwriter, prop person, and director. We can learn a lot about him as we watch, including what is upsetting to him, how he understands death and violence, and what play skills he has.

Looking at Jackson from a *sociopolitical* point of view can lead to additional conclusions about the value and meaning of his play. As he starts out energetically recreating the violence he saw in the cartoon, it seems as if he is enjoying and glorifying the violence and destruction. In fact, when the adult observer was given the job of speaking for the dinosaur victims, she reports she was quite conflicted about whether to participate or try to stop the play because of the level of intensity and verbal brutality involved. As Jackson's play continues, he begins to work through and transform the violence he saw. He increasingly takes the point of view of the victims and even gives them a voice ("Please don't kill me . . ."). He creates a good-guy hero (the big Brontosaurus) who first uses violence and kills the Tyrannosaurus over and over again to keep the smaller victims safe. By the end of the play, the Brontosaurus has found a nonviolent solution, "a jail" made out of a box. The bad guy does not have to be hurt; he can be rendered harmless to never hurt again the other dinosaurs. In these ways, Jackson seems to have tamed the violence in the cartoon and restored the peace by creating a safe environment for his dinosaurs without having to hurt the villain anymore.

Imitating Entertainment Violence with Media-Linked Toys

Anton and Phil are playing with Power Ranger action figures that are highly realistic replicas of the characters on the popular *Mighty Morphin Power Ranger* television show (Levin & Carlsson-Paige, 1995). They are focusing on those actions that the toys were designed to perform: kicking, karate chopping, and "morphing" back and forth between high schoolers with faces like the actors who play their parts on the television show and Power Ranger superheroes with masked faces. As this scenario changes, it stays focused primarily on the fighting aspects of the Power Rangers; the figures fight with each other, then hit objects around them, and when the figures are put away the boys use their bodies to karate chop each other.

From a *developmental perspective,* since Anton and Phil are bringing to their play the karate-chopping action that they have seen the Power Rangers do on television, they must need to work it out and understand it in some way, to serve some developmentally useful function. The action figure toys, which are highly realistic replicas of the television characters, however, are used for one thing: fighting. Similar to the other two scenarios, this play begins with the boys imitating the most graphic and dramatic aspects of the violence. Now, however, the play stays focused on the violence from the Power Ranger television show—the karate chops and fighting—with little other content and with little evolution or resolution of the story or violence. As we observe the children's play, we learn little about what the violence means to them or what they are struggling to work out and understand. They seem to be taking a less active role than the previous children in their play or in using their creativity, imagination, and skills to transform the content they saw on television into something that is uniquely meaningful to them. Through this developmental lens we are led to question whether the boys' play is meeting their needs as fully as the play of the children in the two previous scenarios. If not, then there is cause for concern because the play is not truly serving their developmental interests.

Using a *sociopolitical* lens also leads to more worrisome conclusions than from the two previous episodes. Throughout their play, Phil and Anton focus on imitating the same violent actions of the Power Rangers over and over again. They do not seem to explore that violence, its effects on others, or alternatives to it. In this situation, it seems as if they are less likely to be learning the deeper lessons about violence and nonviolence that could counteract the glorification of the violence they saw on the screen.

The Functions and Value of Violence Play

Using developmental and sociopolitical lenses to look at these three play episodes points to fundamental differences in the nature and possible functions of the play. On the one hand, the play in the first two scenarios is probably serving the children's social, moral, and intellectual development in positive ways (especially given that the children were exposed to violence that they are trying to master). On the other hand, the play in the third episode points to different, potentially worrisome conclusions. Anton and Phil do not seem to be using their play in the service of their development, nor do they seem to working on any content that will move toward more positive social attitudes or behavior.

Anton and Phil's play with violence is similar to that described by many teachers and parents who have watched children's play in recent years. Teachers often say they are seeing much repetitive, unidimensional play with violence that is becoming harder and harder to limit or control. These kinds of concerns are expressed most often around play like Anton and Phil's, which is associated with television shows and the toys that accompany them, like the Power Rangers (Levin & Carlsson-Paige, 1995) and Teenage Mutant Ninja Turtles (Carlsson-Paige & Levin, 1992). But teachers also say that similar play often occurs around whatever violence children have seen (Carlsson-Paige & Levin, 1991). It seems that the functions and value of violence play lie in the nature of the play.

More Violence in Society

By any measure, the violence in the lives of children in the United States has increased dramatically in the past decade (Children's Defense Fund, 1995). In fact, the level of violence some children are exposed to on a regular basis has led some clinicians and researchers to compare growing up in the United States to growing up in a war zone (Garbarino, Dubrow, Kostelny, & Pardo, 1992; Garbarino, Kostelny, & Dubrow, 1991).Whether it be violent crime, domestic and child abuse, terrorism, or "just-for-fun" entertainment violence, children are exposed to more and more violence both directly and through the media.

Children now have more content of a violent nature to try to figure out and over which to develop some sense of mastery and control. They also have more models of violent behavior to try to incorporate into their play. Given this current climate, we would expect them to engage in more and more play of a violent nature. As children are increasingly exposed to violence and are bringing that violent content to their play, however, there are other factors that seem to be undermining their efforts.

Changes in Children's Media and Toys

What children play, how they play, and what they play with are increasingly influenced by media and popular culture. Young children watch an average of four hours of television a day. They will see an average of 8,000 killings and more than 100,000 other acts of violence by the time they finish elementary school, most of which will be entertainment violence (Diamant, 1994). When children are not watching television, much of their play time is taken up using toys that are highly realistic replicas of what they are seeing on children's television programs, many of which are violent.

Marketing whole lines of toys with children's programs is a relatively new phenomenon that began in 1984 when the Federal Communications Commission deregulated children's television. Within two years of deregulation nine of the ten best-selling toys had television shows and seven of those nine television-linked toys were violent (Carlsson-Paige & Levin, 1987, 1990). Once the marketing of violence to children through television and other forms of media (including movies, videotapes, and video games) became possible, one smash hit after another swept through the childhood play culture, including *Masters of the Universe, G.I. Joe, Transformers, Ghostbusters, Teenage Mutant Ninja Turtles,* and most recently *Mighty Morphin Power Rangers.* Each successive program has had more violence than the previous one. The *Ninja Turtles* averaged just over fifty acts of violence per half-hour episode, compared with the *Power Rangers* show, which has been clocked at just over one hundred per episode (Lisosky, 1995). The sale of products marketed with children's media also has continued to grow, with the Power Rangers reaching a record $1 billion in retail sales in 1994 (Levin & Carlsson-Paige, 1995). One recent survey of a mass market toy store by this author and her son found more than two hundred products with the Power Ranger logo.

Changes in the Quality and Quantity of Violence in Children's Play

Almost immediately after deregulation, teachers and parents began to report having problems with children's violent play and toys. The play of some children seemed to focus increasingly on violent themes and content. Children were pretending to fight and hurt each other more, and they were making more toy weapons. Teachers thought they were dealing with more instances where children used fighting to resolve their conflicts. They were also seeing more hurt children, which they thought was related to the increases in play fighting. Efforts to ban, limit, or redirect the play were getting more difficult, as adults often found themselves confronted with children who were sneaking around behind their backs and engaging in "guerrilla" wars (Carlsson-Paige & Levin, 1987, 1992).

Not only did teachers and parents report seeing increases in play with violence and having more difficulty managing it, they were also describing a particular kind of fighting play, similar to that we saw in Anton and Phil's Power Ranger play. It is narrow and repetitive, focusing on content and actions that involve fighting, often with children taking on the roles of good-guy television characters fighting the bad guys. In one study, after watching such characters on television children's play and interactions were significantly more aggressive than the play of children who did not recently see such a program (Boyatzis, Matillo & Nesbitt, in press). In addition, teachers often reported that the play did not develop or change much over time. One of the most striking aspects of accounts of such play from teachers all over the country was that it sounded pretty much the same everywhere. It did not have the rich variations of play like that of the children in the Oklahoma City bombing or dinosaur scenarios discussed above (Carlsson-Paige & Levin, 1987, 1992; Levin & Carlsson-Paige, 1995).

Creative versus Imitative Play

Play with violence, like Phil and Anton's, does not match common notions of play very well, where children are in control and shape what they do to fit their own needs and concerns at their own level of development (Carlsson-Paige & Levin, 1990; Levin, 1995). Phil and Anton's activity seems more like imitation (Piaget & Inhelder, 1969). In effect, they are replicating the fighting they saw among the Power Rangers. It looks as if they get stuck at that level of action without bringing in any of their own ideas, needs, or skills. Unlike the dinosaur and block play in the first two play scenarios, which the children use in the service of their evolving plot, the Power Rangers action figures seem to show the boys what to do and keep them focused on the fighting.

Play like Phil and Anton's is not what adherents to the developmental side of the debate refer to when they talk about war play that is meeting children's needs. If children are not working on their own ideas in playing about what they have seen, they are less likely to be successful in working out the issues they are bringing to their play in ways that serve their social, emotional, or intellectual development. It will probably be harder for them to resolve the content about violence so they can move on to new issues and content.

When children are primarily imitating the violence they see, as Phil and Anton do, rather than working it through in some more meaningful way, they run the risk of merely assimilating whatever violence they have seen without creating a more realistic view of that violence or transforming it into more positive social solutions. When that happens, they seem to fixate on the violent and aggressive aspects of what they have seen rather than use their play to develop a repertoire of positive, nonviolent responses to violence (Carlsson-Paige & Levin, 1990; Levin & Carlsson-Paige, 1989).

Reframing the Debate over Play with Violence

As adults have struggled to figure out how to respond to the changing nature of children's play with violence, many have relied on the old paradigm of the two sides of the debate. They are then often frustrated and worried by what might be the results. Parents, who worry what children learn about violence from their play with violence, have often tried to limit it. They usually report that they have either thrown up their hands in despair because their struggles feel ineffectual or they have converted to a developmental view and decided that it is just a normal part of children's growing up. Many teachers who find this play very hard to control, and worry that it promotes violence, report working harder and harder to try to limit or ban war play from the classroom. Some reluctantly allow it in a specially designated place like the playground and deal with the frequent problems that arise when children get hurt. Such responses are understandable within the context of the conflicting forces that seem to be influencing children's play with violence.

Using a lens that incorporates both the developmental and sociopolitical views, as illustrated in the three scenarios above, can help sort out the dilemma (Carlsson-Paige & Levin,

1990). On the one hand, it appears that simply allowing imitative play with violence leaves children in charge of the lessons they learn from their play with violence without the benefit of adult support and influence. Children also will be left to their own devices to engage in imitative play, without adult help in transforming it into creative, imaginative play that has the potential of meeting their developmental needs.

On the other hand, banning play with violence leaves children who are exposed to violence without some way to work it out. Unless adults find alternative channels for play that can help children work through the violence in their lives (Dyson, 1994), children will be denied an important vehicle for achieving some level of equilibrium and mastery of the violence they have seen. In addition, as many teachers and parents report, children will simply engage in violent play behind adults' backs, so the ban cuts off adults from influencing the play but has little impact on the influence the play is having on children.

Deciding on an Approach: Meeting the Needs of Children in Society

It is hard to imagine any perfect approach for dealing with children's play with violence in these times (Carlsson-Paige & Levin, 1995). This essay takes the position that the best approach would be to vastly reduce the amount of violence to which children are exposed. This would include limiting the marketing of violence to children through media and toys.

As long as children growing up today are seeing vast amounts of violence, however, they will continue to seem to have a greater need to use their play to work through it than children in the past. As they do, there is always the risk that they will learn messages that promote and glorify violence. This danger is heightened when children merely imitate what they have seen rather than work it through in creative and personally meaningful play. Even when children do succeed in working through the violence in their play, it continues to be difficult to understand what they are learning when so much of their play time and energy is devoted to such violent play.

Adults, therefore, need to develop responses that take into account both the multiple needs of children who are growing up in the midst of violence and the concerns of adults who worry about how play with violence might be contributing to the overall level of violence in society. A dynamic approach, which is forged to match the needs of specific children, families, and classrooms as well as the wider community, is presented here:

- Try to limit young children's exposure to violence of all types as much as possible, even though our best efforts will often feel ineffectual.

- Look for meaningful avenues that will allow children to work through the violence to which they are exposed. In addition to using their play, art, writing, and other forms of creative expression, they need to talk to caring adults who can help children tell their stories in ways that can promote growth and healing.

- Observe children as they engage in play with violence to learn more about what specific aspects of violence they have experienced or heard about, what aspects of it they may be working on and how, and what their particular needs may be. Use this information to decide how to help the children better use their play with violence in positive, growth-promoting ways.

- Try to limit children's use of highly realistic media-linked toys that help to keep play narrowly focused on violent content. When they do play with such toys, help them devise more creative and varied uses.

- Encourage the use of open-ended toys, which enhance rather than control play. Remember that children who use a lot of media-linked toys often need help learning how to use toys that do not show them exactly what to do.

- Help children become good dramatic players. Even though most adults trained to work with young children have been taught not to take an active role in children's dramatic play, many children engage in repetitive, imitative play with violence and need direct help from adults to move beyond that narrow focus (Jones & Reynolds, 1992; Smilansky & Shefataya, 1990). As children become better players, they are more likely to be able to work through the violence they encounter in their play.

- Develop strategies for counteracting the messages children may be learning that glorify and promote violence both in and out of their play, and teach them alternatives to that violence (Carlsson-Paige & Levin, 1992; Levin, 1994).

- Work in the wider community to change the conditions that are contributing to so much violence in children's lives.

Note

1. The terms *play with violence* or *violence play* are used to describe play that has at least some elements of children's pretending aggressively to hurt others or themselves. The terms used here are intended to more fully encompass the various forms of fighting and aggressive play children engage in than the more common term, *war play*.

   Focusing discussions of what to do about play with violence merely on whether to allow or ban such play fails to take into account children's needs, the societal context, or that all play with violence is not the same. What children are learning and how well their needs are being met will depend on their experience and the nature of their play. Therefore, adults' efforts to develop effective responses to play with violence need to take into account this growing understanding of the complexities of such play and the current societal context. This can best be done by using the combined lenses of the developmental and sociopolitical perspectives.

Bibliography

Baruch, D. W. (1942). *You, your children, and war.* New York: D. Appleton-Century.

Berk, L. (1995). Vygotsky's theory: The importance of make-believe play. *Young Children, 50*(1), 30–39.

Bettelheim, B. (1987, March). The importance of play. *The Atlantic, 259*(3), 35–46.

Boyatzis, C., Matillo, G., & Nesbitt, K. (in press). Effects of the "Mighty Morphin Power Rangers" on children's aggression with peers. *Child Study Journal.*

Carlsson-Paige, N., & Levin, D. E. (1985). *Helping young children understand peace, war and the nuclear threat.* Washington, DC: National Association for the Education of Young Children.

Carlsson-Paige, N., & Levin, D. E. (1987). *The war play dilemma: Balancing needs and values in the early childhood classroom.* New York: Teachers College Press.

Carlsson-Paige, N., & Levin, D. E. (1990). *Who's calling the shots: How to respond effectively to children's fascination with war play and war toys.* Philadelphia: New Society.

Carlsson-Paige, N., & Levin, D. E. (1991, March–April). Children and the crisis in the Persian Gulf. *Family Day Caring,* 4–5.

Carlsson-Paige, N., & Levin, D. E. (1992). The subversion of healthy development and play: Teachers' reactions to the Teenage Mutant Ninja Turtles. *Day Care and Early Education, 19*(2), 14–20.

Carlsson-Paige, N., & Levin, D. E. (1995). Can teachers resolve the war play dilemma? *Young Children, 50*(5), 62–63.

Children's Defense Fund. (1995). *The state of America's children yearbook.* Washington, DC: Author.

Diamant, A. (1994). Special report: Media violence. *Parents Magazine, 69*(10), 40–41, 45.

Dyson, A. H. (1994). The Ninjas, the X-Men, and the ladies: Playing with power and identity in an urban primary school. *Teachers College Record, 96*(2), 219–239.

Freud, A., & Burlingham, D. T. (1943). *Children and war.* New York: Ernst Willard.

Garbarino, J., Dubrow, N., Kostelny, K., & Pardo, C. (1992). *Children in danger: Dealing with the effects of community violence.* San Francisco: Jossey-Bass.

Garbarino, J., Kostelny, K., & Dubrow, N. (1991). *No place to be a child: Growing up in a war zone.* Lexington, MA: Lexington Books.

Goldstein, J. (Ed.). (1994). *Toys, play, and child development.* New York: Cambridge University Press.

Groves, B. M., & Mazur, S. (1995). Shelter from the storm: Using the classroom to help children cope with violence. *Child Care Information Exchange, 102,* 47–49.

Jones, E., & Reynolds, G. (1992). *The play's the thing: Teachers' roles in children's play.* New York: Teachers College Press.

Kostelnik, M. J., Whiren, A. P., & Stein, L. C. (1986). Living with He-Man: Managing superhero fantasy play. *Young Children, 41*(4), 3–9.

Kuykendall, J. (1995). Is gun play OK here? *Young Children, 50*(5), 56–59.

Levin, D. E. (1994). *Teaching young children in violent times: Building a peaceable classroom.* Cambridge, MA: Educators for Social Responsibility.

Levin, D. E. (1995). Media, culture and the undermining of play in the United States. In E. Klugman (Ed.), *Play, policy, and practice* (pp. 175–184). St. Paul, MN: Red Leaf.

Levin, D. E., and Carlsson-Paige, N. (1989). Piaget, war play and peace. *Genetic Epistemologist, 17*(3), 11–14.

Levin, D. E., & Carlsson-Paige, N. (1995). Mighty Morphin Power Rangers: Teachers voice concern. *Young Children, 50*(6), 67–72.

Lisosky, J. M. (1995, March 12–16). *Battling standards worldwide—"Mighty Morphin Power Rangers" fight for their lives.* Paper presented at the World Summit for Children and Television, Melbourne, Australia.

Miedzian, M. (1991). *Boys will be boys: Breaking the link between masculinity and violence.* New York: Doubleday.

Piaget, J., & Inhelder, B. (1969). *The psychology of the child.* New York: Basic Books.

Saki. (1988). Toys of peace. In *The complete works of Saki* (pp. 393–398). New York: Dorset. (Original work published 1914)

Singer, D. G. (1993). *Playing for their lives: Helping troubled children through play therapy.* New York: Free Press.

Smilansky, S., & Shefataya, L. (1990). *Facilitating play: A medium for promoting cognitive, socio-emotional and academic development in young children.* Gaithersburg, MD: Psychosocial and Educational Publications.

Sutton-Smith, B. (1986). *Toys as culture.* New York: Gardner.

Structuring the Study of Play

Introduction

During the past twenty years, the phenomenon of play has been a topic of great research interest. Researchers from a number of disciplines have conducted studies of play and based their work on diverse theories and a range of definitional categories. When researchers have looked at play as primarily an individual phenomenon they have structured their study very differently than when they have been interested in play as a cultural phenomenon (Sutton-Smith, 1981). Psychologists and educators, for example, have usually focused on individual aspects, such as the relationship between cognition and play or the adult-child or child-child interaction aspects of play. Anthropologists, sociologists, folklorists, and sociolinguists have been interested in sociocultural aspects, such as the communicative meaning of play within various cultural contexts.

Another difference in approaches to the study of play is whether the questions of interest are about what play is (content) or why it occurs (motive) (Ellis, 1973). If researchers are studying the content of play, they might use the observed category structures, such as the types and stages of sociodramatic play, in their analysis. If the processes of play are of most interest, investigators might structure the study to observe antecedents, sequences, contexts, and outcomes, such as how children initiate and conclude rough-and-tumble play.

It is apparent from the essays in this section that researchers have studied many forms of play that are accessible for observation. Study of play behaviors can serve as a lens through which to view children's motives and feelings and as an authentic way to assess their development.

This section describes the phenomenon of play as it has been studied from a variety of perspectives. Essay authors discuss the structural frameworks most useful for answering questions of interest, as well as the findings from these studies. Content areas discussed include the varied ways young children play with objects and with the individuals in their environments (peers and adults), and what they learn from this object and social play. The essays examine some influences of the social world on play, the way children combine symbolic play and social play in sociodramatic play, and the characteristics of constructive play. The essays also present perspectives on other play phenomena, such as rough-and-tumble play, games with rules, and sports.

Bibliography

Ellis, M. J. (1973). *Why people play.* Englewood Cliffs, NJ: Prentice-Hall.
Sutton-Smith, B. (1981). *A history of children's play.* Philadelphia: University of Pennsylvania Press.

The Meanings in Play with Objects

Shirley K. Morgenthaler

Play with objects is a pervasive activity of children from a very early age. This play involves objects of large and small size and of simple and complex character. Contexts also influence the types of object play that can be observed and the meanings children attribute to the play. Although the meanings of object play may differ among individual children, there are a number of age/stage differences in object play that have been observed.

Age-Related Characteristics of Object Play

The object play of infants and toddlers is of a different character than that of older children, although both manipulative and symbolic object play occur at every age. Numerous studies have documented the developmental stages of object play.

Children of Infant and Toddler Age

Object play of very young children is often solitary and imitative in nature, but it may engage the interest of an adult who will actively extend and expand that play. Infants use parts of their bodies, such as fingers, toes, or nose, as objects for their early play. With adult encouragement, this play is often elaborated and transformed into a social game, such as "Where's your nose (eye, toe)?"

Object play of toddlers is primarily exploratory and manipulative. Toddlers begin to include story-based or imaginative manipulation and imitation in their play, however, and to use props to imitate simple adult roles, such as Mommy, and daily activities, such as rocking baby. Props are usually quite realistic. Toddlers may find something to carry that represents a briefcase to play Mommy or Daddy, for example, or they may remove pots and pans from cabinets to play mealtime or cooking. Although most toddler object play has a realistic basis and is manipulative rather than symbolic, toddlers do begin to use objects symbolically in their play (Fenson, 1986). In so doing, they are building the foundation for symbolic functioning as a cognitive process.

During the second year of life, children are engaged in activities that move their play through a series of increasingly complex symbolic stages. These stages are called decentration, decontextualization, and integration (Fenson, 1986). In *decentration,* the toddler moves from self-focus in the use of objects toward a focus on the object as both the recipient and the initiator of make-believe actions. *Decontextualization* refers to the level of similarity between the play object and its make-believe function. At one year, there is a high degree of similarity between the object and its make-believe role, while by age two that similarity has usually diminished. With the stage of *integration,* children move from disconnected to interrelated themes in object play. This sequence demonstrates the age-level difference in the degree of relatedness between play themes and the objects used as symbolic tools.

Children Ages Three to Five

Children in the age range of three to five continue to use objects as symbolic tools, elaborating and extending that play into social contexts with playmates. Peer social play is initially turn-taking in nature, however, rather than being cooperative or collaborative play. Sociodramatic play, in which children use objects as props to develop story episodes that involve other children, is seen increasingly as the children progress through this age period. Children's elaborated play with blocks, in which they give each block structure a meaning and function, also becomes important at this age. Play with trucks, cars, dolls, and housekeeping materials may be solitary or social. If it is social, it will continue as long as each player agrees to the meanings assigned to the objects (Winnicott, 1982). Thus, this age period is the first in which children develop skills in sharing the meanings embedded in their object play.

During the preschool years, children's construction with objects begins to take on increasingly elaborate forms. This construction includes play with blocks (Hirsch, 1974) and other three-dimensional media such as clay, Play Doh, and collage materials. In this type of play with objects, the objects become elements in a larger whole toward which the child is building (Monighan-Nourot, Scales, & Van Hoorn, 1987).

Children Ages Six to Eight
Primary-age children (ages six to eight) are adept at cooperative play and skilled at negotiating the meanings and functions of play objects with other children to create shared meanings. As children use objects for group play, the objects still may be a manipulative resource, but the children use them primarily as props for story- or fantasy-based play. Miniature objects such as Barbie-like dolls (with girls) and action/adventure dolls (with boys) become the props for both story and fantasy play. As children manipulate these objects, they negotiate the story line for them (Winnicott, 1982). In the primary years children continue to use objects for individual play, either as fantasy materials or as props in manipulative play; however, small objects such as dollhouse figures, construction toys, stuffed animals, or even board game pieces become the material for story episodes in children's pretense. Because this play is often more internal (thinking about) than external (acting out), adults must engage in careful observation and sensitive interpretation if they are to understand the meanings of such play (Singer & Singer, 1990).

Children Ages Nine to Twelve
Intermediate-age children in the nine to twelve age range also use objects both manipulatively and dramatically. The dramatic or story-based play of these children becomes quite elaborate and intricate and the same theme may go on for days. Themes may be drawn from books, television, and movies, or from the everyday life of their expanded world. They may also engage in intricate play by having miniature replica objects taking the roles of the actors. In this type of play, children focus on the inherent properties of the objects and often attempt to create new structures and realities with combinations of objects. This play may also be with complex computer games, intricate board games, or action/adventure and Barbie-like doll play (Singer & Singer, 1990).

Theoretical Views of Play with Objects

The role of objects in shaping play has been discussed from a variety of theoretical perspectives. These include the psychoanalytic view, which focuses on the emotional or larger personal meanings of the objects and the play; the pragmatic view, in which objects are the means of meeting functional ends; the developmental/cognitive view, which focuses on ways play with objects fosters the reasoning, problem-solving, and other cognitive functioning of the child; and the sociocultural view, which examines the meanings embedded in social and cultural contexts of children's play with objects.

The Psychoanalytic View
Psychoanalytic theory views the object as a tool for the mastery of feelings and emotions. This perspective focuses on story-based play and the internal processes involved in such play. In addition, it stresses the study of the individual in the play, rather than on the social context and general meaning of such play. This psychoanalytic (or psychodynamic) view of play emphasizes the larger personal meaning of the play; the psychoanalyst attempts to draw conclusions about the child's emotional struggles from the emotional quality of the play. Erikson's (1977) analysis of play exemplifies this perspective.

From this viewpoint, children use objects in play to facilitate the mastery of emotions and feelings; this is regarded as personally therapeutic. It is the child, however, who must give meaning to the play. Children who engage in object play for the mastery of emotions often engage in what appears to be regressive play, that is, play that they may have mastered in a prior stage of development. This "regression" is viewed as a part of the therapeutic nature of such play (Axline, 1969). All parents of a second child have seen the older child engage in "baby" play, for example, taking on the actions and qualities of babyhood, often with the objects of babyhood, such as bottles, pacifiers, and blankets. This play can help the child master the emotional challenge of sharing parental attention with a sibling.

Play therapists observe object play in the counseling room and use their observations to interpret the meanings of such play in their therapy. This requires great skill; the play therapist avoids assigning meaning beyond the child's intent. That is not to say that children may not reveal meanings they do not yet understand through their object play, because that also occurs. The skilled therapist, however, is able to discern such meanings and help the child see them without projecting meanings beyond those present (Schaefer, 1985).

All children, from time to time, engage in play that has psychodynamic meanings. To ignore this perspective of object play would be a serious omission, but to imbue all forms of object play with psychodynamic meaning would be an error of overgeneralization (Hughes, 1995).

The Pragmatic View

The pragmatic view focuses on the outer activity and function of object play. For the most part, proponents of this view are not interested in the larger meanings of such play, but see the objects used in play as having a pragmatic function and purpose. In this view, objects are the means to functional ends. Thus, the game pieces of a popular board game, the sticks or other props of an active outdoor game, or the child-size cooking utensils of classroom or playroom housekeeping play are used in the ways that the characteristics of the objects "afford" (Wachs, 1985). That is, the attributes of the objects, such as responsivity to manipulation, influence the nature of children's object play. The combined set of stimulus properties that prompt positive levels of object interaction has been called "high affordance" (Wachs, 1985). From this perspective, children's interest in the object as play material depends upon its level of affordance. The materials designed and used by Montessori

(1973) are examples of object affordance because the object itself is supposed to elicit certain child actions. The Montessori environment provides many objects that children can use in functional ways; thus it is designed from a pragmatic perspective. Adult interactions with children are minimal in this environment because the objects themselves are expected to provide the stimuli for interaction.

The Developmental/Cognitive View

This perspective looks to play with objects as a means for fostering the cognitive functioning of children. It focuses on the cognitive mastery of reasoning and problem-solving strategies that are enhanced by object play. A developmental/cognitive perspective sees object play as helping the child to reach forward toward mental or developmental challenges that are not yet a part of the child's day-to-day repertoire. It is this perspective that Jean Piaget used in his analysis of the child's play with objects (1962; Flavell, 1985).

Children's play with parquetry blocks or tangrams exemplifies play with objects for the purpose of cognitive mastery. The manipulation of individual pieces to reproduce design patterns or to create original designs requires reasoning and problem-solving strategies to be employed and enhanced through play. Development of logical-mathematical and spatial reasoning, for example, could be furthered in this type of play. Adults' ability to observe and encourage without intruding on the reasoning aspect of this form of object play is crucial to children's development of internally based problem-solving strategies.

The Sociocultural View

The sociocultural view examines the social and cultural contexts of children's play with objects. From this perspective, play with objects takes on a shared meaning between players, imbuing it with social significance (Hughes, 1995). Make-believe play with simple props provides children the raw materials for social interactions and "group productivity" (Rosen, 1974). It is this perspective that Dewey (1966) held in his discussions of the child's entry into the culture through social play.

Children's dramatic play with dress-up and housekeeping objects and artifacts, for example, is most often carried out in a shared social setting. In this form of object play, children negotiate shared meanings through their questions, directives to fellow players, and ongoing dialogue (Rocissano, 1982). Adult provision of appropriate dramatic play props provides the "stage" for these shared meanings to be negotiated. Adult involvement beyond observation and awareness is usually not supportive of children's need for social negotiation of meaning with peers.

Although all of these theoretical perspectives view play with objects as having meanings, they differ in their emphasis on the domains of meaning and the importance of object play for symbolic development. Each perspective, however, has given rise to explorations of the structures and processes present in children's play with objects.

Structures and Processes of Object Play

Children's play with objects involves a variety of processes and structures the experiences of children. Children may use objects functionally or fantastically. Objects may support external or internal processes. They may be largely manipulative props, or they may be dramatic, story-based props. The size of objects and their inherent structures may also affect the processes of play. The objects used in play may be a variety of sizes, ranging from diminutive pieces that require mastery of fine motor skills to the larger-than-life objects of the playground, which stress the use of gross motor skills.

Functional or Dramatic

Object play may focus on the manipulation of the functions of the object. Children may repetitively use board game pieces, sorting and classification toys, blocks, or even computer-generated representational objects to master motor or cognitive functions (Mergen, 1982). Object play may also focus on the dramatic properties of objects, providing the vehicle for story-based play (Koste, 1995; Sies, 1922).

When children use the computer mouse to "paint" a picture, for example, they are manipulating the representation of a paintbrush to master the movements needed to satisfactorily complete a picture. When they manipulate blocks and small classification toys, they may be using the objects to master either the motoric

challenges involved or the cognitive challenges of space, pattern, and relationships. When children use objects as story vehicles in dramatic play, their use of the object becomes dramatic and they can transform the object into the story prop it represents.

Realistic or Imaginative

Object play may be realistic or imaginative. Children may focus on the real properties of the objects as they play or they may go beyond the literal qualities to assign imaginative properties and roles to objects. For the most part, very young children use objects realistically and literally (Fenson, 1986). As children's ability to pretend increases, they begin to assign imaginative roles and properties to objects in their play. Preschool and primary-age children readily engage in this type of imaginative object play. Simple objects may become spaceships, furniture, or people as children pretend.

Intermediate school-age children, on the other hand, may again prefer literal or realistic qualities of props in their play with objects (Hughes, 1995; Piaget, 1962). Detailed replica objects such as Barbie-like dolls and the action/adventure toys popular with intermediate boys fall into this category. That is, the figures must have clothes, furniture, vehicles, and equipment that are similar to the real objects. While there are imaginative themes expressed in this play, it requires these realistic aspects in order to be satisfying to the players. Replicas of transportation toys, for example, become the vehicles for space travel and dollhouses require intricate and realistic furniture. Doll players at this age level require many more props and changes of clothing than they needed at earlier ages. Action figure players have similar requirements for realistic props, such as replicas of actual gun or airplane models, to engage in hero or superhero activities. Often children of this age spend more time arranging and discussing the plans for the imaginary play than in actual pretend with them. They also especially enjoy computer simulations, such as "SimCity," that involve building their own "world."

There is wide difference in the imaginative quality of various children's play. Some of this is related to the ages of children, while some of the variation is related to children's play and intellectual interests (Singer & Singer, 1990). It may also be that some of the variation is due to the availability and complexity of play objects to support imaginative play (Rubin, 1977).

Internal and External Processes

Play with objects usually focuses on both internal and external processes. Adults are more likely to observe the external processes initially and may not be aware of the internal processes, especially when children are very young. There are almost always internal processes involved in play with objects, however, with the possible exception of manipulative play that has a very repetitive or "doodling" quality. Even then, children may be playing out internal themes. A child who is repeatedly practicing a basketball throw, for example, may be imagining a game in which he or she is the star. Similarly, a child who is manipulating small, doll-like figures may be creating an elaborate scenario for a family event, such as a birthday party or vacation trip. As children develop the ability to think logically and systematically in middle childhood, they also develop the ability for internal play (Singer & Singer, 1990). While objects may still be involved as catalysts for the play, more often they serve as the external stimuli for a primarily internal process.

Influence of Physical Size Characteristics

Objects of play come in varied sizes, ranging from life-size to minute. Large objects include the child-size objects of the housekeeping or block areas of preschool classrooms, the large beads or sandbox toys of toddler environments, and the larger-than-life-sized "stage coaches" or "ships" of the intermediate child's playground. These large objects may present physical challenges and encourage psychological victories as children use then to master, maneuver, and dominate materials that are and feel larger than life to them.

Play objects may also be very small, and children also love these. Smaller-than-life materials include the diminutive objects of dollhouse play, the table-sized objects of manipulative play, the miniature pieces of board games, and the accessories for Barbie-like dolls, action/adventure toys, and Transformers and robots. These objects enable children to focus on their emotional and cognitive mastery of the manipulation, allowing an intricacy of domination and a complexity of control not possible with larger objects. Very small cars and trucks, dollhouses, and the numerous "small worlds" (e.g., farm, zoo, shop, train sets) are examples of the inherent interest children have in miniature objects. Children's fascination with such miniatures and the duration of their play with them attest to the powerful appeal of these small objects. Symbolic play, in particular, becomes miniaturized as children grow older (Bergen, 1988).

Methods of Inquiry for Play with Objects

Although much has been studied about children's object play, there is still much to be learned. The challenge for adults interested in appreciating or guiding children's play with objects lies in the interpretation of the meanings of such play.

Direct questions often are not productive for gaining information, and adults must employ indirect (from the child's perspective) methods of inquiry. Thus, observations and subequent analysis of these may provide more objective data for study and interpretation than testing or experimentation. Several scales and observational inventories have been developed for this purpose (Johnson, Christie, & Yawkey, 1987). To learn more about children's play with objects, adults can use systematic observation and analysis of the play within the varied contexts in which it occurs.

Observation of children's activity is one method of inquiry that may be useful for understanding children's play with objects. To fully use this method, careful and intentional observation is required, and the adult must observe without intruding. When children are playing with objects, they may see mere awareness of an adult observer as an intrusion. To avoid this, the adult may concurrently engage in "adult" activities near where the child is playing; this legitimizes the adult's proximity to the play. However, systematic observations should only be conducted after receiving permission of the child's parents. Parents who wish to observe their child's play often engage in activities at home such as washing dishes, ironing, gardening, or caring for another child. Teachers may also do routine classroom activities as they focus their observations on particular children. The goal of nonparticipant observation is to observe the play without intruding, for an intrusion will change the nature of the play and not allow the results the observer desires.

Analysis of the observations can focus on the use of specific objects by children. This requires the adult to determine which structures and processes are being used by the children involved in object play. They can determine whether the play is function- or fantasy-based, assess whether the play is primarily manipulative or story-based/dramatic, ascertain to what extent the play involves the working out of internal processes, and how it is influenced by the physical characteristics of the objects.

Another method of inquiry is the extrapolation of the meanings of object play. That is, the adult can consider which of the various theoretical views of play with objects best helps in interpreting the meanings of the play. This is the approach used in the various forms of play therapy (Axline, 1969; Hughes, 1995). Each of the theoretical views of play with objects attaches different types of meanings to such play. As adult observers begin to understand those various theoretical perspectives, they can deepen their understanding of the meanings of a child's play with objects.

It is important to note, however, that any analysis of the meanings of object play also requires a knowledge of the child and of the context of the play. Parents may have the advantage in that they have the most information about the child's perspective on a day-to-day basis and can thereby postulate meaning more accurately than adults who have a more limited experience with the child. Educators and other adult professionals, however, may have a more detached perspective, which will be helpful in supporting and interpreting children's play in an objective and impartial manner, because they can look at the play from a broader range of theoretical perspectives in the context of development and learning.

Contexts for the Study of Play with Objects

Children's play with objects must be viewed in the larger context of their overall activities. Only as one begins to understand each child's activity holistically can the meanings of that child's play with objects be fully appreciated and understood. For the child, objects may function as inspiration for fantasy play or as touchstones back to reality during fantasy play. It is the adult's task to determine, as much as possible, the meanings of object play within the contexts of the child's life. To do so enriches the adult's understanding of the child as a whole, and supports the adult's interactions with the child in sympathetic and knowledgeable ways.

Although naturalistic observations give a broader contextual view, staged observations and interviews of children help to ascertain internal meanings. Including these methods in inquiry can help to more fully explore contextual influences on the meanings of play with objects.

Influences of Specific Contexts on Object Play

As with other types of research, the mere fact of study may influence the outcome. Even objectively oriented observers enter the observation with a sense of expected results, which may make them see what they want to see.

The type of setting in which the play is observed can also have a profound influence on the outcomes of this study. Staged settings, because of their selective nature, may produce results that inadvertently support the biases of the person setting the stage. Open-ended and naturalistic settings, on the other hand, provide the opportunity to observe children's object play in the context chosen by them, thus most closely honoring their perspective. These settings, because they are not completely controlled by the adult observer, add the challenge of unpredictability and novelty to the study. But because even natural settings have constraints designed by the adults in that setting (e.g., toys available, rules of behavior), researchers must always be careful about recording the setting characteristics and examining the results in the light of those characteristics (Fein & Rivkin, 1977).

Influences of Individual Learning Styles on Object Play

Important contributions to an understanding of the meanings of children's object play come from a variety of related fields, drawn from the various theoretical views discussed earlier. Others are inherent in an understanding of developmental issues and individual differences among children. Yet another important source is in the literature on learning styles and processes by which children acquire and utilize new information.

Children engage in play with objects in a variety of ways, somewhat dependent on development but also dependent on their learning styles and internal learning structures. While most of the information about learning styles focuses on intermediate children or older individuals, informed and careful observation and interpretation of children's play with objects can result in a better understanding of the learning styles of even very young children (Morgenthaler, 1989).

Children who will later be identified as visual learners tend, even as infants, to focus on the visual qualities of the objects of their play. Children who will later be called auditory learners are more likely to note the auditory or noise-making qualities of the objects of their play. Kinesthetic learners, on the other hand, tend to focus even as young children on the manipulative, the textural, or the movement options of objects. Already as infants, they may attempt to mouth or to bend objects as a part of their exploration of the objects. They may exhibit an early focus on the texture of play objects or on the movement of multipieced objects. It may also be that kinesthetic learners are the most engrossed with the pull and push toys of toddlerhood (Dunn & Dunn, 1992; Dunn, Dunn, & Perrin, 1994).

Assumptions That May Influence Interpretations of Play Meanings

One assumption that does not facilitate understanding of the meanings of object play is that the play adults observe accurately shows the level of maturity of the child's play. Sometimes, when children are engaged in simple experimentation and manipulation, adults assume that this is the highest level of play in which the child can engage. It may not be the case that the child is incapable of more mature play, but merely that the child's current activity is specific and literal, perhaps due to contextual influences at that time. Adults may make the faulty assumption that brief observation of object play can provide a window into the thinking and developmental level of the child. While this may be true at times, it is not always true. The adult must have an extensive observational base, understand the context, and have a base of knowledge of the individual child in order to draw such a conclusion.

Careful and informed observation of the object play is needed for adults to understand that play. If adults do not observe children's object play carefully, they may inappropriately interpret the play and assign maturity or inaccurate meaning that will not facilitate the adult's interactions with the child. The child may be manipulating materials from a board game, for example, creating patterns that appear intricate and complex to the adult. This complexity may be intended, but it may also be accidental and serendipitous at that moment. In fact, as the child discovers the pattern or complexity in the process of object manipulation, that meaning may be extended and elaborated. The adult needs to refrain from assigning intentionality to activity that is exploratory in nature.

The adult must determine whether the play in question is, in fact, cognitive play and be able to distinguish between play in which children are using objects primarily as psychodynamic tools for emotional resolution from that in which they are using objects for cognitive integration of ideas. These different uses are difficult to determine without knowing the child and being able to theorize a purpose for the play. Of course, both purposes may coexist as well.

Another assumption that does not facilitate understanding of play meaning is that observational data have a direct one-to-one correspondence with meanings. Rather, these observations must be informed by an understanding of the child, the context, and the various theoretical perspectives on play with objects.

A phenomenon that both facilitates and hinders understanding is the emphasis on object play as functionally related to its future utility. Object play is very often respected by adults because it is seen as a type of preparatory play that readies children for more abstract cognitive tasks. This is both helpful and problematic.

From one perspective, respecting object play as an important activity of children is always desirable. On the other hand, to respect object play only for its cognitive contributions is too narrow an approach. Play with objects often has emotional or psychological benefits, and it has social and cultural benefits as well, in addition to pragmatic benefits. To assign it primarily cognitive importance does not respect the other meanings that play with objects has for children at a given point in time. The full appreciation of the power of object play requires an awareness and understanding of all of its varied natures and meanings, as well as a willingness to take the time to understand the unique utilization that a particular child may be employing in a given play episode.

Adults can allow and facilitate play with

objects for primarily manipulative or pragmatic purposes. Adults need to be sensitive to children's simple, natural needs to experiment and to try activity at a variety of levels. Not all object play needs to be interpreted or analyzed for its larger meanings. Knowing that a range of potential meanings is possible, however, allows adults to appreciate and facilitate play in helpful ways, even if that facilitation is simply permission and/or encouragement of manipulation and experimentation.

The appreciation and understanding of children's play with objects are important ingredients in the comprehensive understanding of children's perspectives and developmental progress. Each of the views of the meanings of object play adds to an understanding of the child's use of objects to acquire meanings. Looking at the variety of structures and processes involved in the child's implementation of objects for play purposes aids the understanding of object play, and knowing which strategy or method of inquiry to employ for a given purpose is an important consideration for the full appreciation of that play.

Appreciating the impact of the child's learning style preferences will also affect adults' discernment of the nuances of children's play. Becoming aware of the power of both positive and negative assumptions on the comprehension of meanings of object play will guard against false conclusions in the actual attempt to understand that play. It is critical for adults to appreciate all of the ways in which children employ objects in their play. The ability of children to use objects in an array of ways for a variety of purposes enriches the impact of that play on their cognitive, physical, social, and emotional development. To allow or assume less is to limit the power of that play and our understanding of it. The ability of adults to appreciate play may also be related to their willingness to continue to play themselves. The preservation of playfulness is important for the awareness and understanding of children's play.

Bibliography

Axline, V. (1969). *Play therapy*. New York: Ballantine.

Bergen, D. (1988). Play development. In D. Bergen (Ed.), *Play as a medium for learning and development* (p. xxx). Portsmouth, NH: Heinemann.

Dewey, J. (1966). *Democracy and education*. New York: Free Press.

Dunn, R. S., & Dunn, K. J. (1992). *Teaching elementary students through their individual learning styles: Practical approaches for grades 3–6*. Boston: Allyn and Bacon.

Dunn, R. S., Dunn, K. J., & Perrin, J. (1994). *Teaching elementary students through their individual learning styles: Practical approaches for grades K–2*. Boston: Allyn and Bacon.

Erikson, E. H. (1977). *Toys and reason*. New York: Norton.

Fein, G., & Rivkin, M. (1977). *The young child at play: Reviews of research, Vol. 4*. Washington, DC: National Association for the Education of Young Children.

Fenson, L. (1986). The developmental progression of play. In A. W. Gottfried & C. W. Brown (Eds.), *The contribution of play materials and parental involvement to children's development* (pp. 53–66). Lexington, MA: Heath.

Flavell, J. H. (1985). *Cognitive development*. Englewood Cliffs, NJ: Prentice Hall.

Hirsch, E. S. (1974). *The block book*. Washington, DC: National Association for the Education of Young Children.

Hughes, F. P. (1995). *Children, play, and development*. Boston: Allyn and Bacon.

Johnson, J. E., Christie, J. F., & Yawkey, T. D. (1987). *Play and early childhood development*. New York: Harper Collins.

Koste, V. G. (1995). *Dramatic play in childhood: Rehearsal for life*. Portsmouth, NH: Heinemann.

Mergen, B. (1982). *Play and playthings: A reference guide*. Westport, CT: Greenwood.

Monighan-Nourot, P., Scales, B., & Van Hoorn, J. (1987). *Looking at children's play: A bridge between theory and practice*. New York: Teachers College Press.

Montessori, M. (1973). *The Montessori method*. Cambridge, MA: Bentley.

Morgenthaler, S. K. (1989). A question of answer-finding. *Lutheran Education, 129*, 83–86.

Piaget, J. (1962). *Play, dreams, and imitation*. New York: Norton.

Rocissano, L. (1982). The emergence of social conventional behavior: Evidence from early object play. *Social Cognition, 1* (1), 50–69.

Rosen, C. E. (1974). The effects of sociodramatic play on problem-solving behavior among culturally disadvantaged preschool children. *Child Development, 45,* 920–927.

Rubin, K. H. (1977). Play behaviors in young children. *Young children, 32*(6), 16–24.

Schaefer, C. E. (1985). Play therapy. *Early Child Development and Care, 19,* 95–108.

Sies, A. C. (1922). *Spontaneous and supervised play in childhood.* New York: Macmillan.

Singer, D. G., & Singer, J. L. (1990). *The house of make-believe: Children's play and the developing imagination.* Cambridge, MA: Harvard University Press.

Wachs, T. C. (1985). Home stimulation and cognitive development. In C. C. Brown & A. W. Gottfried (Eds.), *Play interactions: The role of toys and parental involvement in children's development* (pp. 142–152). Skillman, NJ: Johnson and Johnson.

Winnicott, D. W. (1982). *Playing and reality.* New York: Tavistock.

Social Play

Robert J. Coplan
Kenneth H. Rubin

The phenomenon of social play is the play activities that take place when two or more partners interact with one another. Social play provides a unique and important context for young children's social, social-cognitive, and emotional development. From a structural perspective, for example, researchers have distinguished between functional, constructive, and dramatic play activities (e.g., Piaget, 1962; Smilansky, 1968). These structural forms of play occur in a variety of social contexts; children's play behaviors vary along a number of important dimensions. Therefore, it is relevant to consider the following questions: (1) What is social play? (2) What are the methods used to assess social play? (3) Why is social play important in the lives of children? and (4) What are the predictors, concomitants, and outcomes associated with individual differences in social play?

What Is Social Play?

To state the obvious, the component that distinguishes *social* play from other forms of play involves the notion of *interaction with others*. Social play cannot exist without the presence of more than one child; as such, social play must be understood and assessed as a property of the dyad or group.

Social play occurs when the child (a) is motivated to engage others in playful activities; (b) is able to regulate emotional arousal; (c) possesses the skills necessary to initiate interac-

tions with another child, such that (d) the social overtures are accepted in kind. Accordingly, social play comprises the associated constructs of social participation, social competence, and sociability.

Social Participation

In the 1920s, several attempts were made to develop comprehensive taxonomies for describing children's social interactions with peers. Psychologists, for example, systematically observed nursery school children and created various categories of social and nonsocial play (Andrus, 1924; Verry, 1923). One psychologist categorized social attitudes such as "treating playmates as objects" and "cooperating with the group" (Verry, 1923). Another observer developed a coding scheme that included the category "occupied with other children" (Bott, 1928, p. 48). Within this category, the behaviors of talking, watching, interference, imitation, and cooperation were distinguished.

Parten's (1932) observational framework is perhaps the best known of the early social participation taxonomies. In her now classic study, she included six categories of social participation. The first four categories comprised nonsocial or "semi"-social play activities:

1. *Unoccupied behavior*—the demonstrated marked absence of focus or intent. For example, the unoccupied child may stare blankly into space or wander aimlessly.

Support for the writing of this chapter was provided by a Social Science and Humanities Research Council of Canada doctoral fellowship to author Coplan, and by an Ontario Mental Health Foundation Senior Research Fellowship to author Rubin.

2. *Onlooker behavior*—the observation of others' activities without an attempt to enter into the peers' activity.

3. *Solitary play*—playing apart from the other children at a distance greater than three feet, or with her or his back to other children. During solitary play, the child plays with toys that are different from those the other children are using. The focal child is centered on her or his own toys, and pays little or no attention to others in the area.

4. *Parallel play*—the child plays independently; however the activity often, though not necessarily, brings her or him within three feet of other children. The child plays *beside* or in the company of other children, but *not* with companions.

Parten (1932) also defined two categories of socially interactive play.

1. *Associative play*—the child interacts with other children and may be using similar materials: however, there is no real cooperation or division of labor.

2. *Cooperative play*—a group activity organized for the purpose of carrying out some plan of action or attaining some goal. Play partners coordinate their behaviors and take particular roles in pursuit of the common goal.

In studies postdating the 1970s, other researchers have combined both associative and cooperative play within social play (e.g., Rubin, Maioni, & Hornung, 1976; Rubin, Watson, & Jambor, 1978).

The legacy of Parten's (1932) taxonomy of social participation is that it continues to be used in studies that bear no resemblance to those originally published in the 1930s. Contemporary researchers have refined the original scale for purposes of examining developmental (Rubin, 1993) and individual differences (Coplan, Rubin, Fox, Calkins, & Stewart, 1994) in children's social and nonsocial play.

Methods of Assessing Social Play

There currently exist a plethora of measures designed to assess social play and its related constructs. These measures can be characterized in terms of the source of information regarding children's play behaviors: outside sources and direct observation.

Outside Source Assessments

Outside source assessment procedures involve asking "expert" informants, such as peers, parents, and teachers, to rate or nominate children's social participatory inclinations. There are several advantages to using paper-and-pencil rating scales or nomination techniques. To begin with, outside source assessment is comparatively quick and inexpensive. As well, parents, classmates, and teachers have the potential to observe children in many different circumstances and for long periods of time; thus, they can make inferences about specific children's "everyday" behaviors.

The disadvantages of outside source observation methods center on the use of untrained observers for the purpose of data collection. Because they are untrained, they may not be able to identify specific and detailed aspects of behaviors. There may also be some bias in their recall of the children's characteristic social behavior patterns.

There do not exist many rating scale measures designed to directly assess social play. Some components and related constructs are assessed by measures designed to examine children's social competence, personality, temperament, and classroom behaviors. These include peer rating scales and nomination techniques (e.g., the Revised Class Play, Masten, Morison, & Pellegrini, 1985), parent rating scales (e.g., the Colorado Child Temperament Inventory, Rowe & Plomin, 1977), and teacher rating scales (e.g., the Preschool SocioAffective Profile, La Freniere, Dumas, Capuano, & Dubeau, 1992; Preschool Play Behavior Scale, Coplan, 1995).

Direct Observations

Direct observation techniques involve the systematic recording of children's play behaviors. There are several advantages of observational techniques. First, the behaviors observed are "face valid." Second, "blind" observers reduce biases in the coding process; that is, coders are not influenced by their past knowledge of a child's behaviors. Third, coders can be trained to observe and record very specific and detailed behaviors.

Disadvantages of observational techniques include obvious costs in time and personnel.

Coders may be limited in the contexts, settings, and time frames within which they can observe behaviors. Methodological advances in both time and event-sampling techniques, however, have increased the generalizibility of direct observational techniques.

There currently exist several observational coding schemes designed to assess social play and its related constructs (see Bergen, 1988, for a review). The social aspects of children's play have been investigated using time sampling (e.g., Ladd & Price, 1993; Rubin, 1989); event samples (e.g., Pettit & Harrist, 1993); and scan samples (e.g., Hart, Dewolf, & Burts, 1993). These coding schemes have been employed to observe social play in the classroom (e.g., Rubin, 1982; Rubin, Watson, & Jambor, 1978), on the playground (e.g., see Hart, 1993), and in the home with adults (e.g., Pettit & Bates, 1990). In the authors' work, they have made frequent use of the Play Observation Scale (POS) (Rubin, 1989). This measure is described in more detail below.

Play Observation Scale

The POS (Rubin, 1989) is an observational taxonomy designed to assess the structural components of children's play *nested* within social participation categories. Accordingly, the POS employs a time sampling methodology within which ten-second segments are coded for both social participation (e.g., solitary, parallel, and group) and the cognitive quality of children's play (e.g., functional, sensorimotor, constructive, and dramatic). Several additional free play behaviors are assessed, including instances of unoccupied behavior, onlooking, exploration, peer conversation, anxious behaviors, hovering, transitional behavior, rough-and-tumble play, and aggression. The POS coding taxonomy is illustrated in Figure 1.

The use of the POS in the authors' laboratory (e.g., Coplan, Rubin, Fox, et al., 1994;

Rubin, Coplan, Fox, & Calkins, 1995) and in many others' (e.g., Baudonniere, 1988; Guralnick & Groom, 1987; Roopnarine & Johnson, 1987) has allowed for a clearer understanding not only of children's social play behaviors but also of developmental (e.g., Rubin, 1993), contextual (e.g., Einslein & Fein, 1981), gender (e.g., Johnson & Ershler, 1981), and individual differences (e.g., Coplan & Rubin, 1993) therein.

One important finding is that the *same* structural form of play can have very different "meanings" when displayed in different contexts. For example, sociodramatic play (group pretense) is generally viewed as an index of social competence and social adjustment (e.g., Howes, 1992). However, *solitary-dramatic,* in the presence of peers, appears to reflect impulsivity and social immaturity; it is also associated with externalizing (or acting-out) problems in early childhood (Coplan, 1995; Coplan, Rubin, Fox, Calkins, & Stewart, 1994; Rubin, 1982). Thus, it is the interaction between the structure of play and the type of social participation that best characterizes various forms of children's social and nonsocial free play behaviors (see Rubin & Coplan, in press, for a recent review).

Why Is Social Play of Developmental Significance?

For the young child, the peer group provides an important and unique context for the acquisition and manifestation of social skills. Theorists have been positing the developmental significance of peer interaction for over fifty years (See Parker, Rubin, Price, & Desrosiers, 1995, for a recent review).

Jean Piaget

Piaget (e.g., 1926, 1932) suggested that peer interaction provides children with an important

---

FIGURE 1. Behavioral Categories on the Play Observation Scale

Transitional
Unoccupied or onlooker
  Solitary: constructive exploratory, functional, dramatic, games
  Parallel: constructive exploratory, functional, dramatic, games
  Group: constructive exploratory, functional, dramatic, games
  Peer conversation:
        Double-coded behaviors: anxious behaviors, hovering, aggression, rough-and-tumble
        Time sample

---

and unique learning environment. In particular, exposure to seven instances of interpersonal differences of opinion and thought, and opportunities for discussion and negotiation about these differences, were viewed as aiding children in the acquisition and development of sensitive perspective-taking skills in interpersonal relationships. According to Piaget, a particularly important component of the peer group setting for social-cognitive learning was its symmetrical and egalitarian nature; in times of cognitive disequilibrium, children involved in interaction with adults would be more likely to unilaterally accept the conclusions of these higher status individuals. With peers, however, children would be more likely to confront their own interpersonal conflicting thoughts.

George Herbert Mead

Mead (1934) echoed Piaget's emphasis on the importance of the development of perspective taking through peer interaction. In addition, Mead stressed the significance of peer interaction in the development of the self-system. Mead believed that children experienced themselves indirectly through the responses of their peers. Thus, exchanges among peers, in the contexts of cooperation, competition, conflict, and friendly discussion, allowed the child to gain an understanding of the self as both subject and object. In this regard, Mead proposed that peer interactions were not only an important factor in the evolution of social perspective-taking skills, but also in the development of the self-system.

Harry Stack Sullivan

Sullivan (1953) proposed that the experience of peer relationships is essential for the child's development of the concepts of mutual respect, equality, and reciprocity. Moreover, he argued that the development of skills for cooperation, compromise, empathy, and altruism emerged from peer experiences during middle and late childhood. In particular, Sullivan emphasized the importance of "chumships," or special relationships, for the emergence of these concepts. Thus, for example, equality, mutuality, and reciprocity were acquired *between* special friends, and then these concepts were thought to be extended to other relationships.

In summary, early theorists postulated that the peer group provided children with a context to acquire, manifest, and practice important social skills. Moreover, through repeated interactions in the egalitarian milieu of the peer group, children learn important lessons about both themselves and others (see Hartrup, 1983, for similar contemporary views).

What Are the Predictors, Concomitants, and Outcomes Associated with Individual Differences in Social Play?

It is well documented that with increasing age, children are more likely to engage in social play (e.g., Rubin, Fein, & Vandenberg, 1983). However, there also exist marked individual differences in the degree to which children are socially initiative and willing to participate in peer play. Furthermore, sociability appears to be generally stable across time (Bronson, 1985; Kagan & Moss, 1962).

Although few researchers have directly examined the origins, correlates, and outcomes of social play behaviors in children, many have studied theoretically related and relevant variables. In this section, the authors briefly review the literature pertaining to children's sociability and social competence. This allows an initial picture to be drawn of those factors that may influence, and that are influenced by, individual differences in children's social and nonsocial play.

The Development of Social Play, Sociability, and Competence

Researchers have investigated many factors, both internal and external to the child, that are believed to influence the development of individual differences in social play, sociability, and competent social interaction.

Genetic Factors

There is growing evidence that sociability is influenced by genetic factors. Sociability is a personality/temperament factor that may influence social play initiations (see, e.g., Rubin & Coplan, in press). The heritability of sociability is evidenced through an examination of twin studies. For example, identical twins are more similar than fraternal twins in terms of sociability in early infancy (Freedman, 1974), toddlerhood (Matheny, 1983), and well into middle childhood (Scarr, 1968). Plomin and Daniels

(1986) reviewed eighteen twin studies and reported that, particularly among nine younger children, shyness and sociability were more highly associated in monozygotic twins than in dizygotic twins.

Temperament and Physiology

Researchers have also suggested that there exists a biological link with social play. This link can be accessed through the study of temperamental patterns that may be precursors to the development of social play. For example, Kagan (e.g., 1989; Kagan, Reznick, & Gibbons, 1989; Kagan, Reznick, & Snidman, 1988) has distinguished between *inhibited* and *uninhibited* children. The former group can be characterized as being quiet, vigilant, and restrained while they experience *novel* situations. The latter group, alternatively, reacts with spontaneity, as if they do not distinguish between novel and familiar situations. Inhibited children, compared to their uninhibited counterparts, have higher and more stable heart rates, larger pupil diameters, greater motor tension, and higher levels of morning cortisol (Garcia-Coll, Kagan, & Reznick, 1984; Kagan, Reznick, & Snidman, 1987, 1988). These data are viewed as supporting the notion that inhibited children have a biologically predispositioned low threshold for arousal in the face of novelty. A recent study found that uninhibited toddlers tend to become preschoolers who engage in a comparatively high frequency of social play (Calkins, Fox, Rubin, & Coplan, 1995).

Fox and colleagues (e.g., Fox & Calkins, 1993) have argued that physiological mechanisms of emotional regulation are important components of children's dispositions to engage others in interactions or to withdraw from them. These physiological mechanisms include patterns of hemispheric imbalance (as measured by EEG activation) and vagal tone (a measure of parasympathetic control over heart rate). For example, Fox, Rubin, et al. (in press) found that preschool children who engaged in more socially interactive behaviors and made and received more social initiations from peers during free play exhibited greater left frontal activation. Preschoolers who displayed more withdrawn and wary behaviors during free play sessions exhibited greater right frontal activation. As well, Fox and Field (1989) found that temperamentally active preschoolers with high vagal tone, as compared to their low vagal tone counterparts, demonstrated a greater increase in socially interactive play over the course of the first six weeks of preschool.

Parenting Behaviors

Another influence on children's inclinations to engage in social play is their parents. In this regard, researchers have focused on the constructs of parenting style or discipline techniques as well as on the quality of the parent-child attachment relationship.

Generally, authoritative parents (high in control and warmth) are likely to raise well-adjusted children who are socially responsible and competent, friendly, cooperative, and prosocial with peers (Baumrind, 1967, 1971; Hart et al., 1993). In contrast, parents who provide insufficient or imbalanced responsiveness and control (authoritarian, permissive, or uninvolved) are likely to have children who are socially incompetent, aggressive, and/or socially withdrawn (Baumrind, 1967, 1971, 1991; Dishion, 1990; Lamborn, Mounts, Steinberg, & Dornbusch, 1991).

Parent-Child Attachment Relationships

Social competence and social play are also predicted by the quality of the parent-child attachment relationship in infancy. For example, secure attachment status in infancy has been found to predict, at four years of age, more elaborate and flexible play styles and more positive social engagement than insecure attachment relationships (e.g., Sroufe, 1983). As well, securely attached four-year-olds are more likely to engage peers in social play than are their insecurely attached age-mates (Booth, Rose-Krasnor, McKinnon, & Rubin, 1994).

A Developmental Pathway Model to Social Play

The various factors described above are synthesized by Rubin and colleagues, who have described several pathways in which the *interplay* between physiology, parenting, and the environmental context result in the development of social play styles (e.g., Rubin, Lemare, & Lollis, 1990; Rubin, Stewart, & Coplan, 1995). Rubin and colleagues argue that the quality of children's interactions with peers is a function of social competence, which in turn is a function of the developmental interplay between intra-individual, interindividual, and macrosystemic forces. One pathway begins with an easy-tempered child, born into a family in which there are sensitive and responsive parents and a general lack of major stresses or crises. These starting points are viewed as providing an essential base for the establishment of a secure parent-child attachment relationship (Rubin & Lollis, 1988). A secure attachment relationship is caused and maintained, in part, by parents who are sensitive, responsive, and "in tune" with the child's behaviors (Isabella & Belsky, 1991; Spieker & Booth, 1988). In turn, secure primary relationships predict the development of social and emotional adaptation (Booth, Rose-Krasnor, & Rubin, 1991; Booth, Rose-Krasnor, McKinnon, et al., 1994; Sroufe, 1983).

Within the context of a secure relationship, the child comes to believe that parents are available to serve her or his needs. This allows the child to feel secure, confident, and self-assured when introduced to novel settings. Moreover, the internal working model of "felt security" fosters the child's active exploration of the social environment (Sroufe, 1983). In turn, exploration of the social environment allows the child to address a number of significant "other-directed" questions, such as "What are the properties of this other person?", "What is she or he like?", and "What can and does she or he do?" Once these exploratory questions are answered, the child can begin to address "self-directed" questions, such as "What can I do with this person?" Thus, felt security may have a central role in the enhancement of social exploration, and exploration may result in peer play (Rubin, Fein, et al., 1983).

Developmental Outcomes of Individual Differences in Social Play
Having established the importance of social play in children's social, social-cognitive, and emotional development, the question remains as to what "outcomes" are associated with individual differences in social play.

Waterloo Longitudinal Project
In actuality, there have been few follow-forward longitudinal studies of the developmental course of children's social and/or nonsocial play. We focus our attention on results from the Waterloo Longitudinal Project (WLP), initiated originally in 1980 to examine the stability and predictive "outcomes" of childhood social and nonsocial play (e.g., Rubin, 1982, 1985; Rubin, Chen, & Hymel, 1993; Rubin, Chen, McDougall, Bowker, & McKinnon, 1995; Rubin, Hymel, &

Mills, 1989; Rubin, Hymel, Mills, & Rose-Krasnor, 1991).

To begin with, results from the WLP have indicated that social play is relatively stable from preschool through to adolescence (e.g., Rubin, 1993; Rubin & Both, 1989; Rubin, Hymel, & Mills, 1989). Observed social play in early childhood is predictive of positive feelings of self-worth and *negatively* associated with feelings of loneliness in late childhood (e.g., Rubin, Hymel, & Mills, 1989). Moreover, in a recent study (Rubin, Chen, McDougall, et al., 1995), a sample of children from the WLP was followed into high school, at age fourteen years. Results indicated that an aggregate of observed social play and peer-rated social competence at age seven years significantly predicted higher self-regard and felt security in the peer group, and lower self-reported loneliness in adolescence.

Results from the WLP have also provided insights into the negative developmental outcomes associated with the display of *nonsocial* play in childhood. For example, longitudinal outcomes associated with social withdrawal include peer rejection, selected deficiencies in interpersonal problem solving, loneliness, depression, negative self-regard, and internalizing problems (Hymel, Rubin, Rowden, & Lemare, 1990; Rubin, 1993; Rubin, Chen, & Hymel, 1993; Rubin & Coplan, in press; Rubin, Hymel, & Mills, 1989; Rubin, Lemare, & Lollis, 1990; Rubin & Mills, 1988; Rubin & Rose-Krasnor, 1992). Findings like these have led some researchers to suggest models of psychopathology in which sociable and socially competent children are viewed as being buffered from maleveolent outcomes (e.g., Cole, 1991; Garmezy, Masten, Nordstrom, & Ferrarese, 1979).

A Caveat about Outcomes Associated with Social Play
Overall, social play is generally associated with social adjustment. However, results from a few recent studies from our laboratory suggest that the frequent display of social play, in and of itself, does not "guarantee" social adjustment. For example, Coplan and Rubin (1993) reported that an extreme group of sociable preschoolers were more likely than average children to display both rough-and-tumble play (an index of social competence; e.g., Pellegrini, 1988) and aggression during free play with peers. As well, Rubin, Coplan, Fox, and Calkins (1995) found that an extreme group of socially interactive preschoolers who were also emo-

tionally *dysregulated* (i.e., temperamentally highly reactive and difficult to soothe) were rated by mothers as having more externalizing problems than comparison groups of extremely socially interactive but *well-regulated* children and average children.

Thus, among preschoolers, children who frequently display social play may not represent a homogeneous group in terms of social competence. In particular, the ability to regulate emotions appears to be an important mediating variable. Moreover, researchers (Rubin, Chen, McDougall, et al., 1995) recently found that social play in early childhood was not only predictive of positive outcomes in adolescence, but also predicted deviant behaviors (i.e., drug and alcohol use). Thus, not *all* young children who display a high frequency of social play grow up to be competent, well-adjusted teenagers.

The goal of this essay was to explore the construct of children's social play within the context of peer interactions. Clearly, social play provides children with a unique and important environment for development. Through social play and associated interactions with peers, children are exposed to a domain where they can acquire important social-cognitive and interpersonal skills. Social play allows children to acquire an understanding of other children's perspectives and leads to a greater understanding of cooperation, negotiation, and conflict resolution. Moreover, children who experience a consistent impoverished quality of social play and social interactions are at risk for later social maladjustment. Thus, social play represents a safe haven for children to learn about themselves and others and to acquire skills and knowledge that will assist throughout their lifetime.

Bibliography

Andrus, R. (1924). *A tentative inventory of the habits of children from two to four years of age* (Contributions to Education No. 160). Columbia University, Teachers College.

Baudonniere, P. M. (1988). *L'evolution des competences a communiquer.* Paris: Press Universitaires de France.

Baumrind, D. (1967). Child care patterns anteceding three patterns of preschool behavior. *Genetic Psychology Monographs, 75,* 43–88.

Baumrind, D. (1971). Current patterns of parental authority. *Developmental Psychology Monographs, 4* (No. 1, Pt. 2).

Baumrind, D. (1991). To nurture nature. *Behavioral and Brain Sciences, 14,* 386.

Bergen, D. (1988). Methods of studying play. In D. Bergen (Ed.), *Play as a medium for learning and development* (pp. 27–44). Portsmouth, NH: Heinemann.

Booth, C. L., Rose-Krasnor, L., McKinnon, J., & Rubin, K. H. (1994). Predicting social adjustment in middle childhood: The role of preschool attachment security and maternal style. *Social Development, 3,* 189–204.

Booth, C. L., Rose-Krasnor, L., & Rubin, K. H. (1991). Relating preschoolers' social competence and their mothers' parenting behaviors to early attachment security and high risk status. *Journal of Social and Personal Relationships, 8,* 363–382.

Bott, H. (1928). Observation of play activities of three-year-old children. *Genetic Psychology Monographs, 4*(1), 1–88.

Bronson, W. C. (1985). Growth and organization of behavior over the second year of life. *Developmental Psychology, 21,* 108–117.

Calkins, S. D., Fox, N. A., Rubin, K. H., & Coplan, R. J. (1995). *Longitudinal outcomes of behavioral inhibition: Implications for behavior in a peer setting.* Unpublished manuscript.

Cole, D. A. (1991). Preliminary support for a competency-based model of depression in childhood. *Journal of Abnormal Psychology, 100,* 181–190.

Coplan, R. J. (1995, April). *Assessing multiple forms of nonsocial behaviors in a familiar setting: The development and validation of the Preschool Play Behavior Scale.* Poster presented at the biennial meetings of the Society for Research in Child Development, Indianapolis, IN.

Coplan, R. J., & Rubin, K. H. (1993, July). *Multiple forms of social withdrawal in young children: Reticence and solitary passive behaviors.* Paper presented at the biennial meetings of the International Society for the Study of Behavioral Development, Recife, Brazil.

Coplan, R. J., Rubin, K. H., Fox, N. A., Calkins, S. D., & Stewart, S. L. (1994). Being alone, playing alone, and acting alone: Distinguishing among reticence, and passive and active solitude in young children. *Child Development, 65,* 129–138.

Dishion, T. J. (1990). The family ecology of boys' peer relations in middle childhood. *Child Development, 61,* 874–892.

Einslein, J., & Fein, G. G. (1981). Temporal and cross-situational stability of children's social and play behavior. *Developmental Psychology, 17,* 760–761.

Fox, N. A., & Calkins, S. D. (1993). Pathways to aggression and social withdrawal: Interactions among temperament, attachment, and regulation. In K. H. Rubin & J. Asendorpf (Eds.), *Social withdrawal, inhibition, and shyness in childhood* (pp. 811–900). Hillsdale, NJ: Lawrence Erlbaum.

Fox, N. A., & Field, T. M. (1989). Individual differences in preschool entry behavior. *Journal of Applied Developmental Psychology, 10,* 527–540.

Fox, N. A., Rubin, K. H., Calkins, S. D., Marshall, T. R., Coplan, R. J., Porges, S. W., Long, J. M., & Stewart, S. L. (in press). Frontal activation asymmetry and social competence at four years of age: Left frontal hyper- and hypo-activation as correlates of social behavior in preschool children. *Child Development, 66,* 1770–1784.

Freedman, D. G. (1974). *Human infancy: An evolutionary perspective.* Hillsdale, NJ: Lawrence Erlbaum.

Garcia-Coll, C., Kagan, J., & Reznick, J. S. (1984). Behavioral inhibition in young children. *Child Development, 55,* 1005–1019.

Garmezy, N., Masten, A. S., Nordstrom, L., & Ferrarese, M. (1979). The nature of competence in normal and deviant children. In M. W. Kent & J. E. Rolf (Eds.), *Social competence in children* (pp. 23–43). Hanover, NH: University Press of New England.

Guralnick, M. H., & Groom, J. M. (1987). The peer relations of mildly delayed and nonhandicapped preschool children in mainstream playgroups. *Child Development, 58,* 1556–1572.

Hart, C. H. (1993). *Children on playgrounds: Research perspectives and applications.* Albany: State University of New York Press.

Hart, C. H., DeWolf, M., & Burts, D. C. (1993). Parental disciplinary strategies and preschoolers' play behavior in playground settings. In C. H. Hart (Ed.), *Children on playgrounds: Research perspectives and applications* (pp. 217–314). Albany: State University of New York Press.

Hartrup, W. W. (1983). Peer relations. In P. H. Mussen (Ed.), *Handbook of child psychology, Vol.4: Socialization personality, and social development* (pp. 103–196). New York: John Wiley.

Howes, C. (1992). *The collaborative construction of pretend.* Albany: State University of New York Press.

Hymel, S., Rubin, K. H., Rowden, L. & Lemare, L. (1990). A longitudinal study of sociometric status in middle and late childhood. *Child Development, 61,* 2004–2121.

Isabella, R. A., & Belsky, J. (1991). Interaction synchrony and the origins of infant-mother attachment: A replication study. *Child Development, 62,* 373–384.

Johnson, J. E., & Ershler, J. (1981). Developmental trends in preschool play as a function of classroom program and child gender. *Child Development, 52,* 995–1004.

Kagan J. (1989). Temperamental contributions to social behavior. *American Psychologist, 44*(4), 668–674.

Kagan, J., & Moss, H. A. (1962). *Birth to maturity: A study in psychosocial development.* New York: John Wiley.

Kagan J., Reznick, J. S., & Gibbons, J. (1989). Inhibited and uninhibited types of children. *Child Development, 60,* 838–845.

Kagan J., Reznick, J. S., & Snidman, N. (1987). The physiology and psychology of behavioral inhibition in children. *Child Development, 58,* 1459–1473.

Kagan J., Reznick, J. S., & Snidman, N. (1988). Biological basis of childhood shyness. *Science, 240,* 167–171.

Ladd, G. W., & Price, J. M. (1993). Play styles of peer-accepted and peer-rejected children on the playground. In C. H. Hart (Ed.), *Children on playgrounds: Research perspectives and applications* (pp. 130–161). Albany: State University of New York Press.

La Freniere, J., Dumas, J. E., Capuano, F., & Dubeau, D. (1992). Development and validation of the preschool socioaffective profile. *Psychological Assessment, 4,* 442–450.

Lamborn, S. D., Mounts, N. S., Steinberg, L., & Dornbusch, S. M. (1991). Patterns of competence and adjustment among adolescents from authoritative, authoritarian, indulgent and neglectful families. *Child Development, 62,* 1049–1065.

Masten, A. S., Morison, P., & Pellegrini, D. S. (1985). A revised class play method of peer assessment. *Developmental Psychology, 3,* 523–533.

Matheny, A. P. (1983). A longitudinal twin study of the stability of components of the Bailey's Infant Behavior Record. *Child Development, 54,* 356–360.

Mead, G. H. (1934). *Mind, self, and society.* Chicago: University of Chicago Press.

Parker, J., Rubin, K. H., Price, J., & Desrosiers, M. (1995). Peer relationships and developmental psychopathology. In D. Cicchetti & D. Cohen (Eds.), *Manual of 19 developmental psychopathology* (pp. 96–161). New York: John Wiley.

Parten, M. B. (1932). Social participation among preschool children. *Journal of Abnormal Psychology, 27,* 243–269.

Pellegrini, A. D. (1988). Rough-and-tumble play and social competence. *Developmental Psychology, 24,* 802–806.

Pettit, G. S., & Bates, J. E. (1990). Describing family interaction patterns in early childhood: A "social events" perspective. *Journal of Applied Developmental Psychology 11,* 395–418.

Pettit, G. S., & Harrist, A. W. (1993). Children's aggressive and socially unskilled playground behaviors with peers: Origins in early family relations. In C. H. Hart (Ed.), *Children on playgrounds: Research perspectives and applications* (pp. 240–270). Albany: State University of New York Press.

Piaget, J. (1926). *The language and thought of the child.* London: Routledge and Kegan Paul.

Piaget, J. (1932). *The moral judgment of the child.* Glencoe: Free Press.

Piaget, J. (1962). *Play, dreams, and imitation in childhood.* New York: Norton.

Plomin, R., & Daniels, D. (1986). Genetics and shyness. In W. H. Jones, J. M. Cheek, & S. R. Briggs (Eds.), *Shyness: Perspectives on research and treatment* (pp. 63–80). New York: Plenum.

Roopnarine, J., & Johnson, J. (1987). Approaches to early childhood education. New York: Merrill.

Rowe, D. C., & Plomin, R. (1977). Temperament in early childhood. *Journal of Personality Assessment, 41*(2) 150–156.

Rubin, K. H. (1982). Non-social play in preschoolers: Necessary evil? *Child Development, 53,* 651–657.

Rubin, K. H. (1985). Socially withdrawn children: An "at risk" population. In B. H. Schneider, K. H. Rubin, & J. E. Ledingham (Eds.), *Peer relations and social skills in childhood: Issues in assessment and training* (pp. 125–139). New York: Springer Verlag.

Rubin, K. H. (1989). *The Play Observation Scale (POS).* Ontario: University of Waterloo.

Rubin, K. H. (1993). The Waterloo Longitudinal Project: Correlates and consequences of social withdrawal from childhood to adolescence. In K. H. Rubin & J. Asendorpf (Eds.), *Social withdrawal, inhibition, and shyness in childhood* (pp. 291–314). Hillsdale, NJ: Lawrence Erlbaum.

Rubin, K. H., & Both, L. (1989). Iris pigmentation and sociability in childhood: A reexamination. *Developmental Psychology, 22,* 717–726.

Rubin, K. H., Chen, X., & Hymel, S. (1993). Socioemotional characteristics of withdrawn and aggressive children. *Merrill-Palmer Quarterly, 39,* 518–534.

Rubin, K. H., Chen, X., McDougall, P., Bowker, A., & McKinnon, J. (1995). The Waterloo Longitudinal Project: Predicting internalizing and externalizing problems in adolescence. *Development and Psychopathology, 7,* 751–764.

Rubin, K. H., & Coplan, R. J. (in press). Social and non-social play in early childhood: An individual differences perspective. In B. Spodek & O. N. Saracho (Eds.), *Play in early childhood education* Albany: State University of New York Press.

Rubin, K. H., Coplan, R. J., Fox, N. A., & Calkins, S. D. (1995). Emotionality, emotion regulation, and preschoolers' social adaptation. *Development and Psychopathology, 7,* 49–62.

Rubin, K. H., Fein, G., & Vandenberg, B. (1983). Play. In E. M. Hetherington (Ed.), *Handbook of child psychology,*

Vol 4: Socialization, personality, and social development (pp. 693–774). New York: John Wiley.

Rubin, K. H., Hymel, S., & Mills, R. S. L. (1989). Sociability and social withdrawal in childhood: Stability and outcomes. *Journal of Personality, 57,* 238–255.

Rubin, K. H., Hymel, S., Mills, R. S. L., & Rose-Krasnor, L. (1991). Conceptualizing different pathways to and from social isolation in childhood. In D. Cicchetti & S. Toth (Eds.), *The Rochester Symposium on Developmental Psychology, Vol. 2. Internalizing and externalizing expressions of dysfunction* (pp. 91–122). New York: Cambridge University Press.

Rubin, K. H., Lemare L. J., & Lollis, S. (1990). Social withdrawal in childhood: Developmental pathways to rejection. In S. R. Asher & J. D. Coie (Eds.), *Peer rejection in childhood* (pp. 217–249). New York: Cambridge University Press.

Rubin, K. H., & Lollis, S. (1988). Peer relationships, social skills, and infant attachment: A continuity model. In J. Belsky & T. Nezworski (Eds.), *Clinical implications of attachment* (pp. 219–252). Hillsdale, NJ: Lawrence Erlbaum.

Rubin, K. H., Maioni, T. L., & Hornung, M. (1976). Free play behaviors in middle and lower class preschoolers: Parten and Piaget revisited. *Child Development, 47,* 414–419.

Rubin, K. H., & Mills, R. S. L. (1988). The many faces of social isolation in childhood. *Journal of Consulting and Clinical Psychology, 6,* 916–924.

Rubin, K. H., & Rose-Krasnor, L. (1992). Interpersonal problem-solving and social competence in children. In V. B. van Hasselt & M. Hersen (Eds.), *Handbook of social development: A lifespan perspective* (pp. 283–323). New York: Plenum.

Rubin, K. H., Stewart, S. L., & Coplan, R. J. (1995). Social withdrawal in childhood: Conceptual and empirical perspectives. In T. Ollendick & R. Prinz (Eds.), *Advances in clinical child psychology* (Vol. 17, pp. 157–196). New York: Plenum.

Rubin, K. H., Watson, K. S., & Jambor, T. W. (1978). Free-play behaviors in preschool and kindergarten children. *Child Development, 49,* 534–536.

Scarr, S. (1968). Environment bias in twin studies. *Eugenics Quarterly, 15,* 34–40.

Smilansky, S. (1968). *The effects of sociodramatic play on disadvantaged preschool children.* New York: John Wiley.

Spieker, S. J., & Booth, C. L. (1988). Maternal antecedents of attachment quality. In J. Belsky & T. Nezworski (Eds.), *Clinical implications of attachment* (pp. 95–135). Hillsdale, NJ: Lawrence Erlbaum.

Sroufe, L. A. (1983). Infant-caregiver attachment and patterns of adaptation in preschool: The roots of maladaptation and competence. In M. Perlmutter (Ed.), *Minnesota Symposium in Child Psychology, 16* (pp. 41–76). Hillsdale, NJ: Lawrence Erlbaum.

Sullivan, H. S. (1953). *The interpersonal theory of psychiatry.* New York: Norton.

Verry, E. E. (1923). *A study of mental and social attitudes in the free play of preschool children.* Unpublished master's thesis, State University of Iowa.

Sociodramatic Play

Pretending Together

Patricia Monighan Nourot

When teachers of young children get together to tell stories about their work, the content of their talks is often anecdotes of children's socio-dramatic play. Adults marvel at the detail of the characters, settings, and action children derive from the "real" world, delight in the imaginative leaps and connections that define children's ongoing make-believe worlds, and both applaud and lament children's social negotiation techniques. These include collectively spinning a story and stopping along the way to adjust their "frame" or just to check in with one another. Adults watch, sometimes with held breath, as children make moral decisions about who does what and how ideas get to be played, and their hearts respond to the emotional power of the characters and stories that children evoke. Pretend dramatic play reveals the essence of early childhood and privileges those who teach young children to a bird's-eye view of the landscape of imagination created in the hearts and minds of those in their care.

Studying Sociodramatic Play

Researchers in early childhood education have long studied dramatic and sociodramatic play in the lives of young children and their teachers. Early research focused on the affective and psychodynamic aspects of such play, viewing it as a therapeutic tool for working through childhood fears and unconscious emotions, mastering conflict, and fulfilling wishes (Erikson, 1963/1977; Fraiberg, 1959; Gould, 1972; Hartley, Frank, & Goldenson, 1957; Isaacs, 1933). Some contemporary early childhood educators have continued this tradition, drawing on dramatic play to reveal the emotional lives of

young children they teach (Griffin, 1982; Paley, 1981, 1984, 1990, 1992, 1995).

Others examined sociodramatic play through cognitive lenses. Smilansky (1968) drew upon Piaget's (1962) descriptions of the interaction of imitation and play in children's construction of symbolic thought to devise a scheme for facilitating dramatic and socio-dramatic play. She defined two overarching characteristics of such play. The first element is play that children imitate from their experiences in the "real" world, such as a remembered setting, a character's expression or gestures, action, and talk. The second is imagination, or make-believe, which frames play in a pretend context. These two major dramatic play elements include:

1. *Role-Play,* imitating the action or verbalization of a character other than the self
2. *Pretending with objects,* using toys, unstructured materials (cloth, sticks, boxes), gesture, or verbal declaration to represent the object
3. *Pretend actions and situations,* using gesture or verbalization to represent actions and/or situations
4. *Persistence* within the imaginary play frame to create a play episode or event. (Smilansky, 1990)

For *socio*dramatic play Smilansky (1990) adds two additional criteria:

1. *Interaction* with one or more play partners
2. *Verbal communication* among play partners regarding the play event

Both dramatic and sociodramatic play encompass a broad range of physical, cognitive, social, emotional, and moral characteristics in the repertoires of children, and both include spontaneity and improvisation (Bergen, 1988; Fromberg, 1992; Garvey, 1977/1990; Jones & Reynolds, 1992; Van Hoorn, Nourot, Scales, & Alward, 1993).

Researchers in the last two decades have focused more closely on some of the components of sociodramatic play delineated by Smilansky. Script theory, for example, looks at the schemata children derive from their experiences that they bring to their dramatic play (Bretherton, 1984; Goncu & Kessel, 1984; Miller, 1982; Nelson & Seidman, 1984). Some of these scripts are characterized by the mundane: "event scripts" for bedtime rituals, mealtime routines, going to the doctor, going to church. Others express the social-emotional scripts of daily lives: Grandma's disciplinary techniques; baby sister's invasion of the play space; teenage laments about rules and responsibilities. Still other scripts may be derived from media or storybooks, with characters and plots shaped by children's interpretations of these outside story forms. These interpretations vary predictably by gender in ways that have been documented by researchers who have studied children's play and imagination (Black, 1989; Halliday & McNaughton, 1982; Liss, 1986; Nicolopoulou, Scales, & Weintraub, 1994). For example,

> Both the boys and the girls draw images from popular culture (including material transmitted by television, video, and children's books), but what is interesting is that they do so *selectively*. They have already developed a differential sensitivity and preference for the elements presented to them by their cultural environment; they appropriate different elements and find ways to weave them into distinctive imaginative styles. For example, whereas the girls are particularly fond of princes and princesses and other fairy-tale characters, the boys favor cartoon action heroes such as Superman, He-Man, Teenage Mutant Turtles and so on. (Nicolopoulou et al., 1994, p. 112)

As such, children play what they know, and fuse cognitive and affective dimensions of their lives using both imitated images and fantasy constructions.

Play Scripts

Children appear to become more skilled at detailed representations and the use of abstract symbols with their continued experience as dramatic players (Howes, Unger, & Matheson, 1992; Mann, 1984; Matthews, 1977; Rubin, Fein, & Vandenberg, 1983; Sachs, Goldman, & Chaille, 1984). They add the elements of make-believe to their "event scripts" through symbolic representation of objects, settings, and characters.

Imagination and make-believe are manifested in an even deeper way through the distortions and paradoxes evident in sociodramatic play events. From one viewpoint these represent children's evolving but "imperfect" understanding of the worlds they represent. From more interpretive viewpoints these distortions and paradoxes express children's propensity to construct mythic forms of meaning outside the boundaries of reality (Egan, 1988), or their selective interpretation and even parody of adult roles and behaviors (Gaskins, Miller, & Corsaro, 1992; Nicolopoulou et al., 1994). Adults may flatter themselves in assuming that children seek to emulate adult behavior when children may simply be making fun of what they observe adults do (Schwartzman, 1978). An example observed in a kindergarten classroom gives credence to this view:

> Mariana and Sally are playing "party." They have decorated their pretend home with flowers picked from their pretend garden, and have made peanut butter and jelly sandwiches to go with the "wine" they are serving. As their guests arrive, Mariana greets each one effusively in a loud high-pitched voice, "Oh, Amy, I'm sooo glad you could come," and she and Sally make kissing noises in the air next to their guests' cheeks.

Framing a Play Script

Metacommunication or metaplay takes place when players communicate to one another the message that "This is play," and then communicate about the content and flow of that play (Bateson, 1972). Much like the processes implicit in improvisational jazz (Oldfather & West, 1994), children signal and respond to one another that what they are doing (or planning to do) is not really what it appears to be, but is instead the delicious paradox humans frame as play. This process is illustrated in the following example, in which Emelia, Mark, and Ethan are playing with a castle they have built from blocks.

> Emelia (to Ethan): You be the crocodile and I'll be the prince.
> Mark: I'll be the guard.
> Ethan: Here's a net for them to climb up. (He places strands of string along the castle "wall.") Here's a higher part.
> Mark: He goes here, and then here, here, here (moving his toy figure up the wall of the castle).
> Emelia: I'll need this to climb up (pointing to the string "ladder"). I'll give it back as soon as I get to the top.
> Ethan: Here's the horse. The race can start now! Get the king!

Once this make-believe frame is cast around the "play world" (Huizinga, 1950) of children, the metacognitive processes in metaplay weave in and out of the play enactment. These negotiations may occur in both *directing* and *enacting* modes of play. Directing modes are more explicit: children step out of the play frame to make suggestions and elaborate on the ongoing script, frequently marking these negotiations with language such as tag questions to establish agreement (Corsaro, 1983, 1992). This process in sociodramatic play, called *intersubjectivity*, in which play partners adjust to the perspectives of one another, creates and sustains common ground for their play frame as it flows and expands (Goncu, 1993).

> Ellen and Marcus are playing camping out on the rug in the block area. They have constructed a tent and campfire from blocks and cloth, and have brought backpacks and pretend food from the playhouse area.
>
> Ellen: Let's pretend it started to rain, and we had to go into the tent, OK? (She covers her head with her hands and begins to rush toward the tent.)
> Marcus (agreeing): It started to rain real, real hard, and our boots got muddy. (He covers his head with his hands and begins to walk stiffly, as if sloshing through mud.)

Players might agree to reframe or elaborate a play script by simply repeating the statement or gesture, or extending the idea by adding a new element, as Marcus did. Countersuggestions may also follow a particular form in metaplay exchanges within playgroups. These forms may range from overt contradiction—"No, it's hot at our camping place"—to temporizing—"It was raining, but we were already in our tent 'cause it was night."

After these negotiations occur outside the play frame, children reenter their play worlds to enact the elaborated theme or plot. Similar negotiations might occur over character roles, possession of objects (both real and pretend), and the setting of the play (Black, 1989; Doyle & Connolly, 1989; Elgas, Klein, Kantor, & Fernie, 1988; Farver, 1992; Giffin, 1984; Goncu, 1993; Goncu & Kessel, 1984).

Metaplay in the enactment mode is more subtle than in the directing mode since children do not step out of the play frame to negotiate. In one sense this form of metaplay may be more sophisticated because it involves using the pretend character role to manipulate and control the play frame from within the script, requiring skill in representing the perspectives of others (Berk, 1994; Giffin, 1984).

Marney elaborates the flow of play within her role as the mother:

> Marney (to Elise, who is sitting at the housekeeping corner table): Now darling, it's time to get your coat and go to the bus.
> Ring, ring. Oh hello, teacher. (She picks up a block and holds it to her ear as a phone.)
> Elise (prompts sotto voce): Not teacher, *police*.
> Marney: Okay. Hello, is this the police? The bridge is flooded? So no school bus? Thank you. Goodbye.
> (to Elise) The river is flooded some more. We have to move our stuff upstairs. (She picks up a chair and makes stair-climbing movements with her feet.)
> Elise (imitates her action, and adds): How will we get food, Mommy?

Such metaplay choreography within the enactment mode draws upon the young child's skills at coordinating multiple perspectives. She represents not only her own perspective as a player in the flood drama, but that of her role as mother within the play, and then the complementary perspectives of both the police on the phone and her "daughter" Elise in relation to the requirements of her role. The children use symbolic representational skills to create a make-believe telephone and make-believe stairs through objects and gesture. The process of representing multiple selves in such play is a major contributor to the child's understanding of how roles and rules are coordinated in social contexts (Kohlberg & Fein, 1987; Mead, 1934; Monighan-Nourot, Scales, Van Hoorn, & Almy, 1987).

Play Script Strategies

There is a five-element continuum of verbal negotiation and coordination techniques that range from the overt proposals of the younger child's directing mode ("Let's pretend . . . ") to messages within the older child's enactment mode, such as Marney's messages about the flow of pretend action in the above example (Giffin, 1984). Make-believe orchestration strategies that vary in the degree to which players make the pretend frame explicit exist in between the out-of-frame and in-frame contexts (Giffin, 1984). These include:

1. *Implicit pretend,* in which players make proposals about actions or roles without prefacing them with "Let's pretend" or "Let's say" (a strategy occurring outside the pretend frame in the directing mode).
2. *Prompting,* which is a momentary "step" outside the play frame to prompt another player's performance in a pretend role. Elise's sotto voce correction of Marney's greeting from "teacher" to "police" is an example within this mode.
3. *Storytelling* is marked by a characteristic sing-song cadence and the word "and." It frequently gives background and detail to the characters and situation of the play worlds, interpreting motives or providing histories of the make-believe events, such as "And the mom and the dad had to leave the baby home."
4. *Underscoring* is verbal accompaniment to action, more like self-guiding speech than other-guiding speech, such as Mark's saying "He goes here, here, here" as he moves his toy figure up the wall of the pretend castle.
5. *Ulterior conversation* occurs fully in the enactment mode. Players intentionally propose new elements to the play action

not previously present by clarifying characters' histories or intentions within the pretend frame. Marney's comment to Elise, "It's time to get your coat and go to the bus," is an example of this orchestration strategy. Strategies within the enactment mode, in which the rules of pretend remain implicit and negotiation about play occurs within characters' roles, are characteristic of older children, who skillfully interweave rationales for action into the flow of pretend play.

Scaffolding Metaplay Negotiations

The shared histories of children who are frequent playmates may make negotiations about the play frame go more smoothly as they establish patterns of control, compromise, and reciprocity (Garvey, 1977/1990; Howes et al., 1992; Jones & Reynolds, 1992). Shared scripts may also come from events outside the microsphere of the classroom, such as the winter floods played out in the example above, or from powerful characters and action sequences derived from children's literature or media, thus ensuring that children's schemes for enactment have many qualities in common (Carlsson-Paige & Levin, 1990; Dyson, 1994; Nourot, Henry, & Scales, 1990; Van Hoorn et al., 1993). "Uneven" friendships between dominant and subordinate children, however, may leave little room for true negotiation, and may alert teachers to the need for their orchestration of particular aspects of sociodramatic play (Black, 1989; Howes et al., 1992; Paley, 1984, 1990, 1992, 1995; Rubin, 1980; Trawick-Smith, 1992, 1994).

Metaplay and Cognitive Development

Researchers have linked complex sociodramatic play with many other aspects of development and learning in early childhood, including the construction of creative ideas, language and literacy, abstract reasoning, memory, hypothesis formation, classification, problem solving, and narrative organization (Bergen, 1988; Eckler & Weininger, 1989; Fein, 1981; Fromberg, 1992; Golomb, Gowing, & Friedman, 1982; Johnson, Ershler, & Lawton, 1982; Smilansky, 1990; Van Hoorn, 1991).

Some researchers contend that the metaplay aspects of sociodramatic play are responsible for many of the cognitive advances associated with complex sociodramatic play reported in the research literature, rather than being due to the play enactment itself (Williamson & Silvern, 1992). It seems very difficult, however, to separate both the metaplay elaboration that occurs within play enactment from the flow of play itself, and the nonverbal from the verbal negotiation strategies that take place. The personal histories, linguistic backgrounds, roles, and power relationships within the play frames further contextualize and complicate the picture of metaplay (King, 1992; Meyer, Klein, & Genishi, 1994; Orellana, 1994; Schwartzman, 1978).

This discussion of *communication during play in the service of pretend* has focused on the complex social choreography that rests on the interaction of contextual elements. Some of this research described the instrumental value of communication within and about play for children's cognitive development.

The reverse of this relationship, *the role of pretend in the service of communication,* elucidates yet another perspective on the function of play and imagination in early childhood and the value of these human capacities for future development and learning, particularly in the ways that boys and girls play, which is discussed in a later section (Sheldon, 1992).

Finding the Story in Sociodramatic Play

Why is the appeal to mutual pretend or story making so powerful and effective for all children? One theorist makes a strong case for the power of imagination and fantasy play to lead the development of thought in early childhood, because they bring adults closer to the truly passionate concerns of young children (Egan, 1988). A teacher-researcher identifies fantasy, friendship, and fairness as the major concerns of preschool children (Paley, 1986). A psychological theorist also takes this position (Vygotsky, 1978). Three other aspects of the role of fantasy in early childhood illuminate aspects of sociodramatic play: (1) the oral nature of the peer culture in early childhood, (2) the importance of binary opposites in creating dramatic tension in play themes, and (3) the sense of magic and ecstasy revealed in social pretend play (Egan, 1988).

In contrast to the view that fantasy somehow undermines the "real purpose of education to create logical, rational thinkers," this view

states that fantasy in the play and story of early childhood is the element that "gives rationality life and energy" (Egan, 1988, p. 44). The aspect of sociodramatic play that extends characters, creatures, and events into the realm of the impossible is a primary form of logic that encompasses ambiguity and paradox, and stretches the landscape of the known world into new dimensions and possibilities.

"Mythic thinking," in which paradox and ambiguity are integral to making meaning in the world, forms the foundation for noncontradictory forms of logic that appear in middle childhood. Rather than beginning with the known world of the child's everyday life and gradually expanding horizons into the probable and then the fantastic, young children's grasp on reality begins by first exploring its outer limits (Egan, 1988). Therefore, sense and nonsense, the everyday and the fantastic, and the safe and the frightening form dramatic tensions that define the borders of physical, social, and emotional reality. These borders offer frames for children to find their own places, or their own selves, within the scope of their fantasy landscapes. Thought and feeling necessarily merge in these efforts to make sense of life through the stories that children compose and enact in sociodramatic play. Egan (1988) contends:

> Very generally we may say that young children's experiences of the world are such that they have very little sense of the limits, the boundaries, the contexts, in which much of their experience is meaningful. And they have an urge to make sense of their experience, asking endless questions, eager to learn. The story is the linguistic unit, that, as it were, brings its boundaries with it. Within the story, as within the game, the world is limited, the context is created and given and so the events of a story can be grasped and their meaning understood more readily than can the events in a less hospitable, imprecisely bounded world. Equally applicable to stories is Huizinga's observation about play and games, "each creates order, *is* order." (Huizinga, 1950, p. 29, 100)

This viewpoint is echoed by Bruner (1986, 1990) when he describes meaning-making as the essence of human mental activity and the ways in which narrative forms are intrinsic to the ordering and classification of experience.

These theorists all point to the affective quality of the "logic" of narrative and find its origin in the social nature of the construction of reality (Bakhtin, 1981; Bruner, 1990; Egan, 1988; Vygotsky, 1978).

An essential feature of the union of affect and cognition in early childhood is the oral nature of children's culture. There are parallels between cultures that depend on oral rather than literate communication, as does children's fantasy play: "We live in a world of nature, but have invented techniques, developed over uncounted millennia for stimulating a vivid mental life that draws members of a society together by strong affective bonds. For children in our society, too, these techniques create mental worlds distinct from the natural world around us, mental worlds charged with vividness and emotional intensity" (Egan, 1988, p. 85).

Dramatic play is the earliest form of oral storying, a linguistic form that comes fully equipped with its own context. As each aspect of the play-story unfolds, the players clarify and elaborate its meaning by its relationships to other parts. In dramatic play these stories are "told" to the self; in sociodramatic play meanings are situated, communicated, and negotiated in the peer culture (Corsaro, 1985, 1992; Paley, 1981). In doing so, children refine their memory skills, charged with emotion and cast in a story form; they explore metaphor and poetic representation; and they create the social bonds that give life and structure to the peer culture of childhood (Berk, 1994; Dyson, 1994; Paley, 1990, 1992).

The binary oppositions frequently noted in children's dramatic play themes (Bettelheim, 1976; Corsaro, 1985; Egan, 1988; Garvey, 1977/1990; Paley, 1988)—big/little; love/hate; good guy/bad guy; death/rebirth; threat/security; and lost/found—reflect a characteristic of children's early organization of meaning that helps them discriminate features of their physical and social worlds. Tensions between fantasy and reality mapped by children in their imaginative play contribute to a clarified sense of self, framing ideas of character, plot, and setting through bipolar opposition, and then mediating between these "poles" to enrichment and elaboration of story schemata. These bipolar tensions also support shared scripts and conceptions of roles, settings, and events that facilitate negotiation in sociodramatic play. Children want passionately for play to continue despite the potential pitfalls of differing ideas about characters or events in the play, and realize that shared understandings about the figures and dramas facilitate play's smooth progress (Bruner, 1986).

Play at the Leading Edge of Development

Play, particularly sociodramatic play, is the vehicle for young children to make sense of the world and their experiences, and to negotiate these meanings with others. But this is not the whole picture. The joyful engagement of children in social pretend play creates a kind of ecstasy that characterizes the creative process throughout life (Bohm, 1987; Csikszentmihalyi, 1993; Nachmanovitch, 1990). Social pretend play also evokes "magic," or the exploration of the borders of human experience that characterizes the probing of the mysteries of life found in intellectual and aesthetic disciplines (Kaku, 1994; Sutton-Smith, 1986, 1988; Zukav, 1979).

This reaching beyond the known in play calls forth theories about the importance of play in leading the development of thought in early childhood (Vygotsky, 1976, 1978). Play leads development in the early years because it creates the "zone of proximal development" (ZPD) in which children stretch beyond their usual level of functioning in play with their peers (Vygotsky, 1976). This developmental stretch occurs because of the power of relationship in sociodramatic play. The sense of ecstasy and magic that pervades the mutual exploration of the boundaries of possibility is a powerful motivator to move beyond one's own view to encompass the perspectives of others, a quality consistently found in descriptions of "master players" (Jones & Reynolds, 1992). In this way children develop self-regulation in concert with abstract thinking during pretend play.

(Kindergarten classroom. James and Nelson are playing in the kitchen of the playhouse. They have plastic fruit in their hands.)

J: No, you say, "Could I have a bite?"
N: Can I have a bite?
J: Now, it's my turn.
N: Let's be workmen. There's two hammers. Hurry!
J: Well, you get mine. (They begin to hammer plastic nails into the Playskool workbench.)

N: Who'll be the father?

J: How 'bout me. I'll be the father. I have to work. (He continues hammering.) I can't do mine. (He struggles to pull a nail out with the hammer claw, eventually succeeding. He repeats the hammering-and-pulling-out sequence four times.)

J (singing): I'm the dad. Hammer, hammer, La la la la. (His head moves back and forth as he hammers and sings. They both hammer together in rhythm to James's song. The tune becomes "If I had a hammer, I'd hammer in the morning . . ." as they sing loudly "I gotta nail . . . in the morning . . . ")

N: You wait for me.

J: I forget. Okay. I won't do it 'til you do. Wait! Now, you hammer. We'll both do it at the same time. Get ready. On you mark. Set. (They begin hammering in unison and resume their song, smiling as they sing loudly and make eye contact with one another.)

The Social Nature of All Play

All play is essentially social (Vygotsky, 1978). Even the Legos, blocks, sticks, toy vehicles, and character dolls used by solitary dramatic players encompass the social meanings of that child's culture. An imaginary interlocutor may be more agreeable to one's play agenda but contributes the development of perspective through role taking all the same (Kohlberg & Fein, 1987; Mead, 1934).

All play also has rules (Vygotsky, 1978), and the role of binary opposites in fantasy play may serve to scaffold these rules, as do the shared play events and personal histories, culture, and languages of pretend partners (Egan, 1988; Haight & Miller, 1993; Howes et al., 1992; King, 1992; Orellana, 1994). For example, knowing the characteristics of the Bad Guy and the Good Guy, the Lost and the Finders, the Princesses and the Princes as accepted within the classroom peer culture allows play to proceed with implicit rules (Nicolopoulou et al., 1994; Paley, 1995). When players violate these rules, enacted play may come to a halt and metaplay negotiation outside the play frame begin. For example:

Amy and Ruth are playing "Star Wars" on the climbing structure. Amy has taken the role of Princess Leia. Ruth wants to take the same role. Amy suggests that Ruth could be "Princess Leia's sister," and Ruth agrees. Ruth goes to the shelf and selects a large straw hat with ribbons that tie. She asks a participating parent, "Will you tie this on for me?" The adult ties the hat, and Ruth returns to the "spaceship." Amy turns and comments, "Princess Leia doesn't have a hat." "I *know,*" responds Ruth. "And neither does her sister!" retorts Amy. Ruth reluctantly takes off the hat and returns it to the shelf. She picks up an apron and holds it to her waist, commenting, "Princess Leia's sister needs this to cook!" (Monighan-Nourot et al., 1987, p. 82)

The reflection on rules encompassed in metaplay forms a bridge from the oral culture of early childhood to the oral-and-literate culture of middle childhood and later development (Egan, 1988). In play, too, the emphasis shifts from the implicit rules and explicit fantasy of sociodramatic play to the explicit rules and implicit fantasy of games with rules in middle childhood (Nicolopoulou, 1991; Vygotsky, 1976).

Personal Styles in Play

The rules for social behavior throughout development also govern the entry, exit, and production of play events that encompass the human issues of identity, status, power, and control. Sociocultural contexts influence rule-governed behavior by defining the relative roles of different groups.

Gender Influences on Sociodramatic Play

Gender is one important aspect of implicit rule making in the peer culture of children's play. Boys and girls have distinctive play styles characterized by particular roles, themes, and actions, and these differences are apparent early in the preschool years (Black, 1989; Carlsson-Paige & Levin, 1990; Halliday & McNaughton, 1982; Liss, 1986; Nicolopoulou et al., 1994; Pellegrini, 1989; Scales & Cook-Gumperz, 1993). In their research into story play, Nicolopoulou and colleagues (1994) found that girls structure ordered stories around social relationships, frequently family ones contextualizing characters in kinship relations and taking place in a home, echoing routines of family life. Even animals and exotic characters, such as witches and princesses, inhabit a stable world marked by order and family. Girls structure plots that maintain or restore order following a threat or destruction.

Boys' stories, in contrast, focus on disorder, unpredictability, and transitory relationships. While both boys and girls depict active violence, boys do so more often and in more detail than girls. A critical point is that both boys and girls encompass themes of danger and disorder but girls deal with these elements by neutralizing them, or downplaying their importance, while boys elaborate and intensify threatening elements.

Girls close the story play in a manner that restores order, while boys typically do not. In expressing these meanings boys and girls draw upon images of both the larger cultural context (Bronfenbrenner, 1979) and the immediate culture of the classroom to shape their identities as boys and girls. They are distinct from one another through the use of imaginative conventions. The bipolarity of the symbolic styles that emerge between groups of boys and girls through their play illustrates the view that a stable sense of self is framed by creating axes that explore the boundaries of the possible and locate the self within that range (Egan, 1988). The assertive language of preschool girls is in contrast to that of their male playmates. Sheldon (1992) characterizes the "directing" and assertive behavior of preschool girls as "double voice discourse," in which the perspective of the play partner is implicit in the language used to advance one's own agenda. Inviting the interlocutor into a pretense frame to gain one's position is a frequently effective strategy that meshes self-assertion with an appeal for reciprocity, cooperation, and solidarity, as this example demonstrates:

Lucy (4.9) picks up the phone, enthusiastically proposing a phone conversation. Karla (5.0) is busy driving the car.

Lucy: Hey, I think I'll call a party. Now 'tend you heard your telephone ring. Ding dong ding dong.
Karla: Pretend I wasn't there.
Lucy: All right—but you got your telephone anyway. All right?
Karla: Yeah.

Lucy: Ding dong. Ding dong. Ding dong. Ding dong.
Karla: (No response, continues to drive the car.)
Lucy (exasperated that Karla hasn't answered): Pretend you got it. Pretend you got it.
Karla: No, pretend I wasn't home.
Lucy: Pretend you were. (Tone of exasperation, pleading.)
Karla: Okay. (Leaves car with a sigh and picks up phone.) (p. 107)

Each play partner uses pretend to overcome her companion's resistance. Such a strategy furthers the movement of the play within the play frame and, at the same time, offers play partners the opportunity to present alternatives in a "Yes, but" format.

In contrast, single-voice discourse, used more frequently by boys than by girls, leaves the play partner with fewer options to maintain his or her power or control in the negotiation by demanding a unilateral voice.

Four players are playing with the toy plastic sea animals in the block corner. They range in age from 6.8 to 7.11 years old.

Brian: I want a squid.
Damon (to Brian): Let's put all these inside the cage.
(Amos leaves with two sea animals from the collection on the rug.)
Brian (taking what he wants from the collection): This, a squid, and a sperm whale.
Damon: Hey, guys, the animals need water right now . . .
Brian: Go make your own cage! Go make your own cage!
Damon: I thought we'd be together in one cage.
Brian: No. No! (Ritz, 1994, p. 44)

Ritz concludes that the double-voice strategy is both more effective in achieving one's goals and allows play to continue more harmoniously and for a longer time than the single-voice strategy because it interweaves self-interest and communal interest through shared make-believe. She draws parallels between this strategy that very young girls use effectively and the negotiation strategies labeled by Fisher & Ury as "soft" or "mutual gains approach" (1981).

Researchers who have studied the development of peer culture in classrooms with young children also identify the complex interactions that occur in children's efforts to gain access to play events and, conversely, to protect their "interactive space" from intruders (Corsaro, 1985, 1992; Elgas et al., 1988; Kantor, Elgas & Fernie, 1993; Paley, 1988, 1990, 1992).

Social status within the peer culture leads to disputes and bargaining over the possession of territory, such as blocks or the slide; materials, such as capes or sticks; and coveted roles. Metaplay negotiations within the play frame and out of the play frame center on these issues, and create the patterns of tensions, alliance, control, and exploitation that characterize the peer culture of any social group (Corsaro, 1985).

Teacher Influences on Sociodramatic Play

Play orchestration strategies that facilitate communication about access to play, turn-taking, and alternatives that may expand the borders of possibility in pretend frames are well described by teachers and researchers in the field (Isenberg & Jalongo, 1993; Jones and Reynolds, 1992; Trawick-Smith, 1992, 1994; Van Hoorn et al., 1993). Indirect scaffolds for play in the environment, such as providing adequate space, ample time, and the appropriate kinds and amounts of materials, form one level of orchestration (Christie & Wardle, 1992; Isenberg & Jalongo, 1993; Van Hoorn et al., 1993). More directly, teachers guide play enactments, help to elaborate fantasy, and help children negotiate "warrants" for play participation (Van Hoorn et al., 1993). Teachers' roles range from the stage manager to the very direct play tutoring advocated by Smilansky (1968) for children whose engagement in sociodramatic play is minimal. In all cases, teachers' skills as keen observers, and their respect for children's feelings, intellect, language, and culture, help them manage the complex choreography of both individuals and the group.

Vivian Paley (1992) brings to the forefront the powerful and controversial issues that situate sociodramatic play in the peer culture of the early childhood classroom. She believes that the patterns of inclusion and exclusion established early in children's lives have profound and lasting effects on their future development.

"Are you my friend?" the little ones ask in nursery school, not knowing. The responses are also questions. If yes, then what? And if I push you away, how does that feel?

By kindergarten, however, a structure begins to be revealed and will soon be carved in stone. Certain children will have the right to limit the social experiences of their classmates. Henceforth, a ruling class will notify others of their acceptability, and the outsiders learn to anticipate the sting of rejection. Long after hitting and name-calling have been outlawed by the teachers, a more damaging phenomenon is allowed to take root, spreading like a weed from grade to grade. (p. 3)

Permission to control, dominate, and exploit is implicit in the long-standing tradition of early childhood education that holds teachers apart from the dance of the peer culture expressed on the stage of dramatic play. Paley (1992) challenges teachers to imagine what would happen if they interrupted the forces that sanction insiders' exclusion of outsiders. In early childhood the trust and control of the boundaries of behavior are still within the hands of the teacher, and their influence is profound: "Equal participation is, of course, the cornerstone of most classrooms. This notion usually involves everything except free play, which is generally considered a private matter. Yet, in truth, free acceptance in play, partnerships, and teams is what matters most to any child" (p. 21). Paley's new social order, the classroom rule that states, "You can't say you can't play," is a courageous step on a path fraught with difficulty. Teachers who have experimented with the idea express mixed feelings. Like the idea of controlling war play and violence in sociodramatic play themes, the idea of leaving play frames open to all brings up fundamental questions about the traditional views of sanctity of imagination, fantasy, and social relationships in childhood. Such questions require a close look at sociodramatic play with full awareness of its richness and potential for human thinking, feeling, storying, and interacting with others.

As teachers carefully observe and interpret the play of children in their care, awareness of all facets of play events is paramount. As Paley reminds us, first and foremost are children's feelings about themselves as they play and negotiate with peers within and about play scripts and roles. Teachers may well ask themselves if strategies such as providing a well-chosen prop, suggesting an additional role, or helping sustain play by entering the pretend frame will foster a more inclusive play event. Alternatively, establishing a rule such as "You can't say you can't play" also requires the teacher to be a keen observer and active participant in helping children expand and elaborate their play scripts and in helping to sustain their play. Perhaps there are times when the highly engaged play of one group of children needs to be protected and would-be interlopers guided to create new play events. In each situation, the teacher's understanding of children's histories, the developing peer culture of the classroom, and children's feelings and ideas call for an interpretive stance. From this stance, decisions to participate or not to participate in orchestrating children's play are based on the particular children and particular context. The artistry of play orchestration is alive in each moment of its creation.

Sociodramatic play in early childhood is a rich, complex, and many-splendored phenomenon. It draws upon children's capacities for constructing meaning, framing stories, and making sense of their worlds in ways that enrich the development of the individual and the group simultaneously. Sociodramatic play provides the matrix for understanding and representing the perspectives of others and for opportunities to compromise and to stand firm in one's beliefs and intentions.

For teachers of young children, sociodramatic play offers a unique privilege and a formidable responsibility. The privilege is to enter the magical worlds that children create in their pretense together; the responsibility is to help each child reach his or her potential in the powerful realm of shared make-believe.

Bibliography

Bakhtin, M. (1981). Discourse in the novel. In M. Holquist (Ed.) and C. Emerson & M. Holquist (Trans.), *The dialogic imagination: Four essays by M. M. Bakhtin* (pp. 259–420). Austin: University of Texas Press. (Original work published 1934–1935)

Bateson, G. A. (1972). *Steps to an ecology of mind.* New York: Ballantine.

Bergen, D. (Ed.). (1988). *Play as a medium for learning and development: A handbook of theory and practice.* Portsmouth, NH: Heinemann.

Berk, L. (1994). Research in review: Vygotsky's theory: The importance of make-believe play. *Young Children, 50,*(1), 30–39.

Bettelheim, B. (1976). *The uses of enchantment: The meaning and importance of fairy tales.* New York: Knopf.

Black, B. (1989). Interactive pretense: Social and symbolic skills in preschool play groups. *Merrill-Palmer Quarterly, 35,* 379–397.

Bohm, D. (1987). Quantum theory as an indication of a new order in physics. Part B. Implicate and explicate order in physical law. *Foundations of Physics, 3,* 139–160.

Bretherton, I. (1984). *Symbolic play: The development of social understanding.* In I. Bretherton (Ed.), *Symbolic play: The development of social understanding* (pp. 1–44). New York: Academic.

Bronfenbrenner, U. (1979). *The ecology of human development: Experiments by nature and design.* Cambridge, MA: Harvard University Press.

Bruner, J. (1986). *Actual minds, possible worlds.* Cambridge, MA: Harvard University Press.

Carlsson-Paige, N., & Levin, D. (1990). *Who's calling the shots?* Santa Cruz, CA: New Society.

Christie, J., & Wardle, F. (1992). How much time is needed for play? *Young Children, 47*(3), 28–31.

Corsaro, W. (1983). Script recognition, articulation, and expansion in children's role play. *Discourse Processes, 6,* 1–19.

Corsaro, W. (1985). *Friendship and the peer culture in the early years.* Norwood, NJ: Ablex.

Corsaro, W. (1992). *Interpretive approaches to children's socialization.* San Francisco: Jossey-Bass.

Csikszentmihalyi, M. (1993). *The evolving self: A psychology for the third millennium.* New York: Harper Collins.

Doyle, A. B., & Connolly, J. (1989). Negotiation and enactment in social pretend play: Relations to social acceptance and social cognition. *Early Childhood Research Quarterly, 4,* 289–302.

Dyson, A. H. (1994). *The ninjas, the X-men, and the ladies: Playing with power and identity in an urban primary school* (Tech. Rep. No. 70). Berkeley: University of California, National Center for the Study of Writing.

Eckler, J. A., & Weininger, O. (1989). Structural parallels between pretend play and narratives. *Developmental Psychology, 25*(5), 736–743.

Egan, K. (1988). *Primary understanding: Education in early childhood.* New York: Routledge.

Elgas, P., Klein, E., Kantor, R., & Fernie, D. (1988). Play and the peer culture: Play styles and object use. *Journal of Research in Childhood Education, 3*(2) 142–153.

Erikson, E. (1977). *Childhood and society* (2nd ed). New York: Norton. (Original work published 1963)

Farver, J. (1992). Communicating shared meaning in social pretend play. *Early Childhood Research Quarterly, 7*(4), 501–516.

Fein, G. G. (1981). Pretend play in childhood: An integrative review. *Child Development, 52,* 1095–1118.

Fisher, R., & Ury, W. (1981). *Getting to yes: Negotiating agreement without giving in.* Boston: Houghton Mifflin.

Fraiberg, S. (1959). *The magic years: Understanding and handling the problems of early childhood.* New York: Charles Scribner's Sons.

Fromberg, D. (1992). A review of research on play. In C. Seefeldt (Ed.), *The early childhood curriculum: A review of current research* (2nd ed., pp. 42–84). New York: Teachers College Press.

Garvey, C. (1990). *Play.* Cambridge, MA: Harvard University Press. (Original work published 1977)

Gaskins, S., Miller, P., & Corsaro, W. (1992). Theoretical and methodological perspectives in the interpretive study of children. *New Directions in Child Development, 58,* 5–23.

Giffin, H. (1984). The coordination of meaning in the creation of a shared make-believe reality. In I. Bretherton (Ed.), *Symbolic play: The development of social understanding* (pp. 73–100). New York: Academic.

Golomb, C., Gowing, E. D., & Friedman, L. (1982). Play and cognition: Studies of pretense play and conservation of quality. *Journal of Experimental Child Psychology, 33,* 257–279.

Goncu, A. (1987). Toward an interactional model of developmental changes in social pretend play. In L. Katz (Ed.), *Current topics in early childhood education* (pp. 108–123). Norwood, NJ: Ablex.

Goncu, A. (1993). Development of intersubjectivity in the dyadic play of preschoolers. *Early Childhood Research Quarterly, 8,* 99–116.

Gould, R. (1972). *Child studies through fantasy.* New York: Quadrangle.

Griffin, E. (1982). *Island of childhood: Education in the special world of the nursery school.* New York: Teachers College Press.

Haight, W. L., & Miller, P. J. (1993). *Pretending at home: Early development in sociocultural context.* Albany: State University of New York Press.

Halliday, J., & McNaughton, S. (1982). Sex differences in play at kindergarten. *New Zealand Journal of Educational Studies, 17,* 161–170.

Hartley, R. E, Frank, L., & Goldenson, R. M. (1957). *The complete book of children's play.* New York: Crowell.

Howes, C., Unger, O., & Matheson, C. (1992). *The collaborative construction of pretend: Social pretend play functions.* Albany: State University of New York Press.

Huizinga, J. (1950). *Homo ludens: A study of the play element in culture.* London: Routledge and Kegan Paul.

Issacs, S. (1933). *Social development in young children.* London: Routledge and Kegan Paul.

Isenberg, J., & Jalongo, M. (1993). *Creative expression and play in early childhood curriculum*. Columbus, OH: Merrill.

Johnson, J. E., Ershler, J., & Lawton, J. (1982). Intellective correlates of preschoolers' spontaneous play. *Journal of General Psychology, 106,* 115–122.

Jones, E., & Reynolds, G. (1992). *The play's the thing: Teachers' roles in children's play.* New York: Teachers College Press.

Kaku, M. (1994). *Hyperspace: A scientific odyssey through parallel universes, time warps, and the 10th dimension.* New York: Doubleday.

Kantor, R., Elgas, P., & Fernie, D. (1993). Cultural knowledge and social competence within a preschool peer culture group. *Early Childhood Research Quarterly, 8*(2), 125–148.

King, N. (1992). The impact of context on the play of young children. In S. Kessler & B. Swadener (Eds.), *Reconceptualizing the early childhood curriculum* (pp. 43–61). New York: Teachers College Press.

Kohlberg, L., & Fein, G. (1987). Play and constructive work as contributors to development. In Kohlberg et al. (Eds.), *Child psychology and childhood education* (pp. 392–449). New York: Longman.

Liss, M. B. (1986). Play of boys and girls. In G. Fein & M. Rivkin (Eds.), *The young child at play: Reviews of research* (Vol. 4, pp. 127–140). Washington, DC: National Association for the Education of Young Children.

Mann, B. L. (1984). Effects of realistic and unrealistic props on symbolic play. In T. D. Yawkey & A. D. Pellegrini (Eds.), *Child's play: Developmental and applied* (pp. 359–376). Hillsdale, NJ: Lawrence Erlbaum.

Matthews, W. (1977). Modes of transformation in the initiation of fantasy play. *Developmental Psychology, 13,* 212–216.

Mead, G. H. (1934). *Mind, self and society.* Chicago: University of Chicago Press.

Meyer, C., Klein, E., & Genishi, C. (1994). Peer relationships among 4 preschool second language learners in "small-group time." *Early Childhood Research Quarterly, 9*(6), 1–85.

Miller, P. J. (1982). *Amy, Wendy, and Beth: Learning language in South Baltimore.* Austin: University of Texas Press.

Monighan-Nourot, P., Scales, B., Van Hoorn, J., & Almy, M. (1987). *Looking at children's play: The bridge between theory and practice.* New York: Teachers College Press.

Nachmanovitch, S. (1990). *Free play: The power of improvisation in life and the arts.* New York: Putnam.

Nelson, K., & Seidman, S. (1984). Playing with scripts. In I. Bretherton (Ed.), *Symbolic play: The development of social understanding* (pp. 45–71). New York: Academic.

Nicolopoulou, A. (1991). Play, cognitive development, and the social world: The research perspective. In B. Scales, M. Almy, A. Nicolopoulou, & S. Ervin-Tripp (Eds.), *Play and the social context of development in early care and education* (pp. 129–142). New York: Teachers College Press.

Nicolopoulou, A., Scales, B., & Weintraub, J. (1994). Gender differences and symbolic imagination in the stories of four-year-olds. In A. H. Dyson & C. Genishi (Eds.), *The need for story: Cultural diversity in classroom and community* (pp. 102–123). Urbana, IL: National Council of Teachers of English.

Nourot, P. M., Henry, J., & Scales, B. (1990). *A naturalistic study of story play in preschool and kindergarten.* Paper presented at the annual meeting of the American Educational Research Association, Boston, MA.

Oldfather, P., & West, J. (1994). Qualitative research as jazz. *Educational Researcher, 23*(8), 22–26.

Orellana, M. (1994). Appropriating the voice of the superheroes: Three preschoolers' bilingual language uses in play. *Early Childhood Research Quarterly, 9*(2), 171–193.

Paley, V. G. (1981). *Wally's stories.* Cambridge, MA: Harvard University Press.

Paley, V. G. (1984). *Boys and girls: Superheroes in the doll corner*. Chicago: University of Chicago Press.

Paley, V. G. (1986). *Mollie is three*. Chicago: University of Chicago Press.

Paley, V. G. (1988). *Bad guys don't have birthdays*. Chicago: University of Chicago Press.

Paley, V. G. (1990). *The boy who would be a helicopter: The uses of storytelling in the classroom*. Cambridge, MA: Harvard University Press.

Paley, V. G. (1992). *You can't say you can't play*. Cambridge, MA: Harvard University Press.

Paley, V. G. (1995). *Kwanzaa and me*. Cambridge, MA: Harvard University Press.

Pellegrini, A. D. (1989). Elementary school children's rough and tumble play. *Early Childhood Research Quarterly, 4*(2), 245–260.

Piaget, J. (1962). *Plays, dreams and imitation in childhood*. New York: Norton.

Ritz, K. (1994). *Peer conflict in a multi-age setting*. Unpublished master's thesis, Sonoma State University, Rohnert Park, CA.

Rubin, K. H. (1980). Fantasy play: Its role in the development of social skills and social cognition. In K. H. Rubin (Ed.), *Children's play* (pp. 69–84). San Francisco: Jossey-Bass.

Rubin, K., Fein, G., & Vandenberg, B. (1983). Play. In E. M. Hetherington & P. H. Mussen (Series Ed.) (Eds.), *Handbook of child psychology: Vol. 4. Socialization, personality, and social development* (pp. 698–774). New York: John Wiley.

Sachs, J., Goldman, J., & Chaille, C. (1984). Narratives in preschool sociodramatic play: The role of knowledge and communicative competence. In L. Golden & A. Pellegrini (Eds.), *Play, language, and stories: The development of children's literate behavior* (pp. 45–61). Norwood, NJ: Ablex.

Scales, B., & Cook-Gumperz, J. (1993). Gender in narrative and play: A view from the frontier. *Advances in Early Education and Day Care, 5,* 167–195.

Schwartzman, H. B. (1978). *Transformations: The anthropology of children's play*. New York: Plenum.

Sheldon, A. (1992). Conflict talk: Sociolinguistic challenges to self-assertion and how young girls meet them. *Merrill-Palmer Quarterly, 38*(1), 95–117.

Smilansky, S. (1968). *The effects of sociodramatic play on disadvantaged preschool children*. New York: John Wiley.

Smilansky, S. (1990). Sociodramatic play: Its relevance to behavior and achievement in school. In E. Klugman & S. Smilansky (Eds.), *Children's play and learning: Perspectives and policy implications* (pp. 18–42). New York: Teachers College Press.

Sutton-Smith, B. (1986). The spirit of play. In G. Fein & M. Rivkin (Eds.), *The young child at play: Review of the research* (Vol. 4, pp. 3–16). Washington, DC: National Association for the Education of Young Children.

Sutton-Smith, B. (1988). The struggle between sacred play and festive play. In D. Bergen (Ed.), *Play as a medium for learning and development* (pp. 45–48). Portsmouth, NH: Heinemann.

Trawick-Smith, J. (1992). A descriptive study of persuasive preschool children: How they get others to do what they want. *Early Childhood Research Quarterly, 7*(1), 95–114.

Trawick-Smith, J. (1994). *Interactions in the classroom: Facilitating play in the early years*. Columbus, OH: Merrill.

Van Hoorn, J. (1991). Research in review: Symbolic play in preschool and primary settings. *Young Children, 46*(6), 40–50.

Van Hoorn, J., Nourot, P. M., Scales, B., & Alward, K. (1993). *Play at the center of the curriculum*. Columbus, OH: Merrill.

Vygotsky, L. S. (1976). Play and its role in the mental development of the child. In J. S. Bruner, A. Jolly, & K. Sylva (Eds.), *Play: Its role in development and evolution* (pp. 537–554). New York: Basic Books.

Vygotsky, L. S. (1978). *Mind in society:*

Development of higher psychological processes. Cambridge, MA: Harvard University Press.

Williamson, P., & Silvern, S. (1992). "You can't be the grandma; you're a boy": Events within the thematic fantasy play context that contribute to story comprehension. *Early Childhood Research Quarterly, 7*(1), 75–94.

Zukav, G. (1979). *The dancing Wu Li masters: An overview of the new physics.* New York: Macmillan.

Constructive Play

George Forman

Children's play with construction materials can render patterns, objects, functional systems, and pretend sequences. Study of constructive play reveals a child's developmental level, how children learn, and the precursors to later cognitive structures. Methods of study should include a microanalysis of the process of play. Adults can support constructive play by protecting the time it takes, by asking children to design before they build, and by establishing a social dynamic that encourages risk-taking. Animated computer graphics have created microworlds that give children new methods to reflect on their constructive play. Children's museums also have provided new learning environments that enhance the educational value of constructive play. These new learning environments require their own forms of evaluation.

Constructive Play Defined

Researchers have studied play from many perspectives and have defined various categories, including constructive play. One way to look at constructive play is to think of it as a set of questions about the value of play materials that children use to build or construct something. These play materials include any elements that can be put together or shaped into structures, such as Lego bricks, Lasy blocks,[1] Constructo straws, clay, pipe cleaners, wooden blocks, and even natural objects such as blades of grass for weaving patterns and pebbles for making designs. We should also include electronic objects, such as movable icons that can be assembled on a computer screen (Bransford, Sherwood, & Hasselbring, 1988; Forman, 1985; Harel & Papert, 1991).

Construction itself has it own complex definitions. Fundamentally, the builder(s) construct from basic elements. These basic elements are reiterated in number, arranged in a plane, oriented at a point, and even sequenced across time to yield some product that embodies a goal of these processes. The constructions can be static or dynamic, that is, the construction can be a stationary product or an animated product. A block tower is static, for example, while an animated cartoon on a computer is dynamic.

Computer animation is an example of constructive play that does not employ three-dimensional objects. Psychologically, the cognitive demands and educational value of building a block tower with movable computer icons, given that the computer is programmed to make the tower fall when it violates the laws of physics, is eqivalent to an example of constructive play. Animating a sequence of wing positions that simulate bird flight when run in real time on a computer is also a case of construction.

Children engage in constructive play when they are trying to make something, from a drawing, to a Lasy system that works, to a mosaic pattern that appeals. It will be helpful, however, to distinguish between several types of products in constructive play: the pattern, the object, the system, and the sequence.

Patterns

Children can construct mosaic patterns with parquetry blocks or computer icons. These patterns may have no particular referent in the outside world. The goal is pure symmetry, variations on symmetry, repeated motifs, and other parameters of aesthetics. These are an important form of constructive play. As children mature, they translate their play with patterns into the notations of mathematics, music, and computer language (Forman, 1982a; Langer, 1982; Sinclair, Stambak, Lezine, Rayna, & Verba, 1989). Of particular note is that pattern construction seems to be emphasized when children play with computer graphics (Papert, 1993; Wright and Shade, 1994).

Constructive play with spatial patterns occurs when children focus on the spatial relationship of the medium's elements to each other, rather than to the semantic relationship of the elements to some imagined or sighted object outside the medium itself. The constructive play in this context looks more self-referential and nonsymbolic. The placement of one element is determined by the placement of a previous element. The child's objective is primarily the extension and elaboration of a spatial rule, such as play with jigsaw puzzles that do not make identifiable pictures (Forman, Laughlin, & Sweeney, 1971).

Objects

Children can build cars with plastic elements, birdhouses with wooden pieces, and miniature playground equipment with pipe cleaners and cardboard. These objects do have referents in the world outside the medium in which the children work. Object construction play gives observers insight into how children learn to represent and to make meanings (Reifel & Greenfield, 1982; Smith & Franklin, 1979).

Constructive play to make objects is determined by the child's reflective thinking about something external to the medium. Paradoxically, these objects may be patterns, such as a child trying to make a good-looking snowflake from parquetry blocks. It is the psychological stance toward the media elements that distinguishes play-to-construct-patterns from play-to-construct-objects. When constructing patterns, children are intrigued with the regularities, repetitions, and permutations of element relations, independent of what they represent. When constructing objects, children will correct an arrangement of elements if it does not look like the reference object, even if this correction yields an arrangement that violates patternlike rules of symmetry and motif (Forman, 1994).

Systems

Children can build working systems, such as a waterwheel that spins, a miniature Ferris wheel that allows the seats to remain upright, or a fanciful mousetrap that catches three mice at once. The cognitive demands of systems are greater than for the construction of most static objects. Building a clockwork with gears, for example, requires a great deal of thinking about patterns of reversed direction, spatial configuration, and relative size (Metz, 1985).

Constructive play to make systems adds the demand of building a working set of elements. Elements are not only attached, but also articulated (movable); the articulations often need to be constrained in definite ways. The system, such as a miniature machine, needs to stay intact while its parts move. Watching children build systems provides observers, therefore, with special insights into children's cognitive development, such as their increasing ability to deal with compound movement, gear ratios, principles of leverage, and torque (Forman, 1986).

Sequences

Children can design specific sequences of action that demonstrate and inform, such as drawing the various postures of a person making a broad jump (Forman, 1993), using the "Widget Workshop" computer program to make a whimsical device that sorts random objects into three piles according to height, or making a robot that intelligently navigates a maze using Lego/LOGO blocks (Granott, 1991).

Constructive play with a temporal sequence is somewhat new to the research literature, primarily because the best medium for this type of play, computer animation, is itself rather new. Constructing sequences requires that children go beyond what is possible and consider what is reasonable. A machine or cartoon might move in a well-oiled manner, but children need to ask if it performs the work in a sequence that guarantees the desired product or produces it in an efficient manner. The difference between a sequence and a system is really the difference between a general system (building a toy car that rolls) and a specific sequential application of a system that requires an ordered set of actions (driving the toy car through the miniature village from the train station to the town hall).

Children can approach all of these cases with a playful attitude. That is, they need not build something in a ritualized manner. They are not making their fortieth origami bird for the Christmas tree. They are varying the means, rearranging parts just to see how they look, and inventing new sequences to inspect and then to approve or reject. It is this element of variation during construction that makes it play. The children are taking a metacognitive attitude toward the process (see Fromberg, 1992). Rather than being worried about finishing the product, they have taken one step back and asked, "What is the form of the process?" In other words, during constructive play, as opposed to construction, the children are reflecting on the process and on their own assumptions about what processes are appropriate. It is in this category, constructive play, that observers most often confuse play and work. Placing elements together to get the job done is not play. Placing elements together to see if the arrangement might get the job done is play. The "what-if" attitude defines the act as play and places it in an entirely different epistemic stance to cognition and development (Hutt, 1976).

Why Look at Constructive Play?

Constructive play provides a window into children's thinking. A child trying to build a waterwheel might orient the paddle blades more like a ceiling fan (same plane as the hub) than like a paddle wheel (at right angles to the hub). When he or she plays with this construction in the water, however, he or she reorients the paddle blades. Therefore, constructive play, in this instance, can provide a window through which to watch the processes by which children learn to modify part of a structure they are using. The fact that this architectural problem arises in the context of self-regulated play provides observers with an authentic sighting of childhood thinking. The thinking is not mediated or scaffolded by adults in this instance; it bears witness to how children invent solutions based upon their own reflections on prior attempts.

In addition to solitary play with objects, observers can study constructive play in small group contexts and in the context of adult scaffolding. These kinds of studies answer the Vygotskian question of how specific learning with a more competent person can improve general development of the individual. No simple conclusions are possible regarding the quality of play with materials alone versus play with more competent peers. Both prepared environments and peers can provoke the indi-vidual child to engage an interesting problem. Both features bear the mark of a more competent peer, either in the sensitive way adults lay out materials to engage the child's mind or the sensitive way an adult asks the child to describe his or her play at a slightly higher level of abstraction (Pellegrini, 1986).

Shifts from Constructive Play to Construction

If a child becomes too goal-oriented, construction ceases to be play. A child trying to complete a bridge from Erector set pieces can become frustrated when the bridge falls down for the third time. His or her attitude can visibly shift from a lighthearted, "What if I do this?" attitude to a "Why won't it do that?" attitude. This shift from "I" to "it" is the death knell for constructive play (Forman & Hill, 1984). In other words, the playful child is content to change what he or she does, just to see what it yields. The task-oriented child is determined to achieve a particular goal.

There is a psychological difference between acting to make something happen and acting to see if something might happen. Play rides on the back of tentativeness. When children are tentative, they know that they do not know, but they have a theory about what might work. The tentative act is an attempt to find out, not an attempt to make something happen. This tentativeness is an essence of constructive play and distinguishes it from construction.

The playful child may keep the goal in mind, but not always in the foreground. The playful child understands that free-flowing exploration can be of great service to later success with the ultimate goal. This attitude toward construction requires a type of dual thinking. The playful period is not goal-directed now, but helpful to goal direction later. Finding the optimal balance between play and problem solving, therefore, places great cognitive demands on the player.

Factors That Support the Play Attitude toward Construction

As obvious as it might sound, the most essential condition to support constructive play is the child's sense of the schedule. Play does not survive when children feel rushed; constructive play must be nurtured by time. Children distracted by the minute hand on a clock will not allow themselves to become immersed in the autonomous flow of play. Teachers who value constructive play need to allow more time for it.

While longer periods are necessary for constructive play, they are not sufficient. Adults can support constructive play by asking children to design before they construct. Design, like play, is essentially a "what-if" proposition (Fromberg, 1992). During design, children can change their minds without suffering the consequences of making a system that does not physically work. The separation of performance from particular goal states is also an essential aspect of play.

The wrong social dynamic among children can also destroy a playful attitude toward construction. It is common, for example, for children to work in twos and threes when designing microworlds on the computer. If one member of the group, however, is both expert and condescending, the other children will back away from taking risks (see Wright & Shade, 1994). Risk-taking and the suspension of evaluation are critical to generative, constructive play.

Current Interest in Constructive Play

The interest in constructive play has derived in part from several findings in the child education and development literature. First, researchers have found a high level of thinking when children participate in rich problem-solving environments with minimal direct instruction from an adult (DeVries & Kohlberg, 1987). Second, problem solving requires a period of divergent in addition to convergent thinking in order to progress. Third, children learn more completely and with greater understanding when they engage in the design and construction of their own invented systems (Resnick & Ocko, 1991). Fourth, there has been a shift in educational objectives from learning facts to learning how to organize facts into personal systems of meaning (Turkle & Papert, 1991); this metacognitive attitude has more resemblance to playing around with relationships than it does with learning the elements themselves. Fifth, the school emphasis on intuitive theories has created a great interest in construction as a variation on science education. Today's teachers have developed academic rationales for the purchase of constructive material to build simple machines, computer simulations, ecosystems, and mathematical patterns. Their comfort with these academic rationales comes in part from their recognition of the logic and planning involved when children play with construction material (Forman & Hill, 1984).

The Developmental Importance of Constructive Play

The study of constructive play fits the Piagetian perspective that, generally speaking, cognitive development beyond age seven draws from constructive play before age seven. The logico-mathematical structures of cognition in middle childhood have their analogue in self-regulated play with objects in the first years of life (Forman, 1982b).

Suppose, for example, that a child is trying to construct a roof for a building where the supporting walls must be eighteen inches apart and the child only has six blocks, two long and four short (see Figure 1). The child tries to bridge the gap by placing the small blocks on the far edges of the long blocks (Scheme A in Figure 1). This scheme causes the long block to fall, so the child learns that small block on large block is a negative. Later, the child notices that when he or she slides the small block to the rear of the long block, the long block begins to stabilize. The assimilation of this move, however, is difficult because scheme A causes the child to read all placements of small on large as a negative. In essence, to solve the cantilever roof problem, the child has to negate the negative: in effect, avoid the avoidance and learn to unlearn. The demands of this construction are difficult, but, once the problems are solved, the child's success marks an advance in the child's ability to deal with the logic of negations (see Fosnot, Forman, Edwards, & Goldhaber, 1988).

Methods for Studying Constructive Play

Constructive play is a process, and should be studied as such. Category checklists for different levels of constructive play will too often miss the subtle framing that defines an act as playful. The checklist uses a definition for a category that is, of necessity, decontextualized from the manifest content. This definition is

Goal: Child trying to make a roof between two block
columns that are glued to the table surface.

Scheme A: Placing small blocks above
causes long block to fall down.

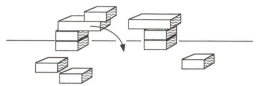

Figure 1A

Scheme A (1): Placing small blocks above
causes long block not to fall down.

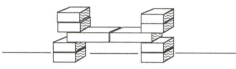

Figure 1B

*Figure 1. Constructive Play: How Children Learn
to Unlearn Previously Useful Schemes*

written to increase the agreement rate between
independent raters observing the same play
episode. This checklist, however, will overly
constrain the researcher's ability to understand
the relationship between behavior and thought.
Thinking invariably occurs in context and
should be studied in situ (see Turkle & Papert,
1991). A preferred approach to study, called
microanalysis, involves a careful documentation and subsequent analysis of the flow of behavioral acts.

In microanalysis the researcher first captures, in some form of notation, the sequence of
acts, verbalizations, changes of mind, and transformation of materials in a connected temporal
flow. The researcher then analyzes and rewrites
the construction process from the premises of
the theory that drove the analysis. In a study of
block play, for example, the author filmed children making spontaneous clusters with geometric blocks (Forman, 1982a). The notation system captured every placement, rotation, change
of position, and choice of block that the children made across time, and included a description of the block as a spatial array. From this
microanalysis the author discovered that the
nonstationary movements of blocks (banging
identical blocks together at the midline) presage
the stationary construction of blocks on the
table (two identical blocks placed side by side

on the table). The block constructions, even
without clear representational status for cars
and trains, therefore, are symbolic expressions
of the earlier gestures. The block structures are
a type of "atemporalization" of action and thus
are symbols. From these data, this author contends, as did Piaget (1954), that constructive
play with geometric objects provides an ana-
logical base for higher mathematics and logical
relations that are based on action units rather
than nominal categories.

Constructive Play in Small Groups

It is important to study the constructive play not
only of a lone child building a private structure,
but as a joint venture among several children.
The complexity of construction makes it a perfect medium in which to study collaboration
among children. In these contexts, constructive
play can encompass discourse analysis as well
as the arrangement of physical elements. During the process of constructing a complex objective, children will have to maintain their focus, divide labor, evaluate progress, share
perspectives, design additions, and engage in a
host of other issues that are inherently social.

Constructive Play in a Virtual World

As mentioned earlier, building virtual physical
systems on a computer screen has all the requisite attributes of construction and participants
can engage in a playful mode. The computer
can offer the user a virtual physical world to
explore when adults have it programmed to
treat object icons as physical objects that tilt and
fall, maintain their shape as users move them,
and conform to laws of friction, solid obstruc-
tion, elasticity, and so forth. Such electronic
worlds are called *microworlds* (Char &
Forman, 1994; Pea & Sheingold, 1987).

One of the first market successes was a
computer program called the Bill Budge Pinball Construction Kit by Electronic Arts. Children could design a pinball rolling board filled
with bumpers, magnets, drop holes, and flippers, then propel a virtual ball into this electronic space to watch the ball bounce, careen,
and be hit by flippers that the children activated. The children could change the Newton-
ian parameters of gravitation, kick, and elasticity to study the effects of these changes on
ball play.

Microworlds allow the child to predict a result during the design process and observe its effects when the ball is released. The computer allows the children to easily edit the space, stretch it, add bumpers, eliminate dead spaces that trap the ball, and so forth. Because the computer makes it so easy to vary the pinball rolling space, the children are free to play around with their creative ideas. If they had to physically build these spaces, the effort involved in making only one space would be so great that the children would not risk a playful stance toward the task. For constructive play to occur, players need to be able to easily vary the process. Otherwise, the players would have to plan and debug the plan from a more conceptual and analytical stance than from a "Let's see what happens" stance.

Herein lies the paradox. While it is important for children to play around, learning environments that make it easy to vary the process could encourage a type of mindless "push-and-see" attitude. If it takes no effort to make a change when one does not get the desired effect, then why not just start anywhere and, by the process of elimination, create the desired effect in time? How can scholars cite the value of constructive play in microworlds if the play is mindless? If it is too difficult to vary the process, however, children will become so premeditated and locked into one plan that they will not explore alternative solutions and expressions. The process seems to be caught between the fluidity of random play and the rigidity of premeditated plans. The study of constructive play, therefore, needs to establish the look and the source of a balance between these extremes.

Classroom use of computers provides a good site to study how educators provide this balance between playing and planning. The new use of LOGO in classrooms combines the open environment of turtle geometry with the structure of specified problems to solve. The work by Juda Schwartz (Harvard University) on the "Geometric Supposer" (Sunburst Software) is a case in point. The software asks children to derive the regularities that explain a certain set of geometric conditions, but they can easily vary angle, line, and relationship in a microworld that instantly draws upon their ideas. The educators require students to document their initial period of experimenting with options. The "play," therefore, becomes an object of reflection and, over time, becomes less random while

at the same time maintains fluidity. This is the stuff of expertise, which is the balance between planning and fluency.

The more advanced versions of microworlds, such as "Working Model" by Knowledge Revolution, produce mathematical equations for the physics involved in the movements of a simulated machine. This role of the computer, to take the child's constructions and translate them automatically into equations, rather than the other way round, is an advance in educational practice (see Forman, 1988a, 1988b). Children then can learn the formal notations of mathematics through spontaneous play on a computer screen, much as they learned their native language in a social context with adults.

Constructive Play in Children's Museums

Children's museums, as an industry, grow at the rate of twenty new museums a year (D. Kohl, personal communication, February 1995). This growth rate indicates that these centers fill a real community need for children to have a place in which to explore, discover, and construct. Given that children come voluntarily to the children's museum, the exhibits must elicit a playful attitude, otherwise the children will not interact with the exhibit and will not return. The best exhibits are hands-on, participatory, interactive exhibits that focus on some event that is interesting to children.

A good exhibit will have certain features in common. First, children of the age range for which it is designed are able to immediately discern its purpose. Second, children have some control over the events produced by the exhibit. Third, these changes are easily made by children in the age range for which the exhibit is designed. Fourth, the event is more than a single reaction to a simple act. Fifth, the exhibit leads children into problems they are interested in solving.

Figure 2 portrays an exhibit called the Gravity Wall (Loc Kits, Inc.), which manifests these attributes. First, children see a ball and criss-cross patterns of ramps on the wall. Children from age two upward immediately place the ball somewhere on the slanted ramp, ready to roll.

Second, the children can control the initial placement of the ball and which type of ball

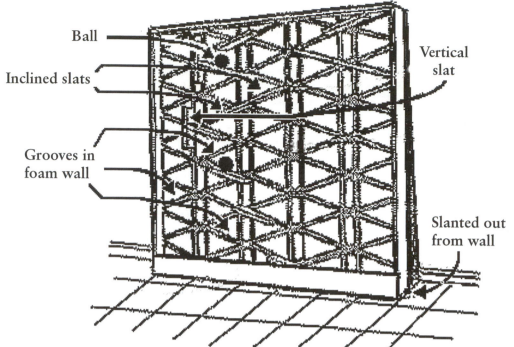

Ball

Inclined slats

Grooves in
foam wall

Vertical
slat

Slanted out
from wall

Figure 2. The Gravity Wall, by Loc-Kits, Inc., North Berwick, Maine.

they choose to use (Ping-Pong ball, golf ball, tennis ball), but more important, they can change the number, location, and spacing of the wooden slats by taking them out of the grooves in the foam wall. Third, removing and inserting the slat is simple, even for two-year-olds. Fourth, the path of the rolling balls can be simple or complex. Older children might design paths for two balls released at the same time so that one gets ahead of the other, or they create a syncopated rhythm as they clatter down the ramps. These reactions are not a simple output, but a complex pattern of variation. Fifth, in the course of play, children often confront solvable problems, such as a gap that drops the ball into an undesired location, a dead spot where the ball gets trapped, or a path that causes the ball to get to the bottom too soon. The Gravity Wall is a rich problem-solving environment suited for children from age two to adulthood.

It is interesting that so little research exists on the evaluation of constructive play within the context of children's museums. In general, museum exhibits typically are evaluated only by two or three criteria: safety, durability, and frequency of use. None of these criteria deals with the educational value of the exhibit. Given that both five-year-olds and twelve-year-olds spend an average of twenty minutes at the Gravity

Wall, for example, it is worth asking what concepts they are learning and how these concepts are appropriate to their developmental level. Answers to these questions, at a minimum, would require the exhibit evaluator to videotape the children's play. It is doubtful that an "exit interview" would yield much more than very general findings, and these would be impoverished by the verbal skills of the child. An analysis of video segments, however, could reveal the following: Five-year-olds experiment with the initial placement of the ball in an attempt to maximize the time it takes to complete the roll; twelve-year-olds experiment with paths that cause two balls to weave across each other's path without colliding. Thus, the five-year-olds are learning principles of space and distance, and the twelve-year-olds are learning about comparative velocities. A cataloguing of concepts that children spontaneously explore at different ages could help the museum designer preserve and enhance quality play with an exhibit.

Play with elements that players assemble into patterns, objects, systems, and sequences is an extremely rich source of information about children's development. Indeed, our everyday parlance alludes to the objects that children use in constructive play, such as in the phrase "DNA molecules are the building blocks of life." The architect Frank Lloyd Wright attested to the importance of a set of Froebel building blocks his aunt bought him at the Chicago World's Fair when he was young and their influence on his sense of design much later in life. Blocks, puzzles, and now computer constructions provide children with physical analogues to complex thoughts, a culture of mind embodied in the structure of these materials (Minsky, 1986). The fact that these materials lend themselves to a playful mode of exploration makes their value even greater.

Note

1. Lasy blocks are similar to Lego blocks but grip each other by a system of slots, giving the child an infinite number of positions for each combination of attached blocks.

Bibliography

Bransford, J., Sherwood, R., & Hasselbring, T. (1988). The video revolution: Some initial thoughts. In G. Forman & P. Pufall (Eds.), *Constructivism in the computer age* (pp. 173–201). Norwood, NJ: Ablex.

Char, C., & Forman, G. (1994). Interactive technology and the young child: A look to the future. In D. Shade & J. Wright (Eds.), *Technology and young children* (pp. 178–186). Washington, DC: National Association for the Education of Young Children.

DeVries, R., & Kohlberg, L. (1987). *Programs of early education: The constructivist view.* New York: Longman.

Forman, G. (1982a) A search for the origins of equivalence concepts through a microanalysis of block play. In G. Forman (Ed.), *Action and thought: From sensorimotor schemes to symbolic operations* (pp. 97–136). New York: Academic.

Forman, G. (Ed.). (1982b). *Action and thought: From sensorimotor schemes to symbolic operations.* New York: Academic.

Forman, G. (1985). The value of kinetic print in computer graphics for young children. In E. Klein (Ed.), *New dimensions for child development: No. 28. Children and computers* (pp. 61–75). San Francisco: Jossey-Bass.

Forman, G. (1986). Observations of young children solving problems with computers and robots. *Journal of Research in Childhood Education, 1*(2), 61–75.

Forman, G. (1988a). Making intuitive thoughts explicit through future technology. In G. Forman & P. Pufall (Eds.), *Constructivism in the computer age* (pp. 83–101). Norwood, NJ: Ablex.

Forman, G. (1988b). The importance of automatic translation for the representational development of young children: Get a code of my act. *Genetic Epistemologist, 21*(1), 5–10.

Forman, G. (1993). Multiple symbolization in the long jump project. In C. Edwards, L. Gandini, & G. Forman (Eds.), *The hundred languages of children: The Reggio Emilia approach to early childhood education (pp. 171–188).* Norwood, NJ: Ablex.

Forman, G. (1994). Different media, different languages. In L. Katz & B. Cesarone (Eds.), *Reflections on the Reggio Emilia approach* (pp. 41–54). Urbana, IL: ERIC Clearinghouse on Elementary and Early Childhood Education.

Forman, G., & Hill, F. (1984). *Constructive play: Applying Piaget in the preschool.* Menlo Park, CA : Addison-Wesley.

Forman, G., Laughlin, F., & Sweeney, M. (1971). The development of jigsaw puzzle solving in preschool children: An information processing approach. *DARCEE Papers and Reports, 5*(8), 38. Nashville: Kennedy Center for Research.

Fosnot, C., Forman, G., Edwards, C., & Goldhaber, J. (1988). The development of the balance concept and its enhancement through stopped action video feedback. *Journal of Applied Developmental Psychology, 9*(1), 1–26.

Fromberg, D. (1992) A review of research on play. In C. Seefeldt (Ed.), *The early childhood curriculum: A review of current research* (pp. 42–84). New York: Teachers College Press.

Granott, N. (1991). Puzzled minds and weird creatures: Phases in the spontaneous process of knowledge construction. In I. Harel & S. Papert (Eds.), *Constructionism* (pp. 295–310). Norwood, NJ: Ablex.

Harel, I., & Papert, S. (Eds.). (1991). *Constructionism. Norwood, NJ: Ablex.*

Hutt, C. (1976). Exploration and play in children. In J. S. Bruner, A. Jolly, & K. Sylva (Eds.), *Play: Its role in development and evolution* (pp. 202–215). New York: Basic Books.

Langer, J. (1982). From pre-representational to representational cognition. In G. Forman (Ed.), *Action and thought: From sensorimotor schemes to symbolic operations* (pp. 37–64). New York: Academic.

Metz, K. (1985). The development of children's problem solving in a gears task: A problem space perspective. *Cognitive Science, 9*(3), 431–471.

Minsky, M. (1986). *Society of mind.* New York: Simon and Schuster.

Papert, S. (1993). *The children's machine: Rethinking school in the age of the computer.* New York: Basic Books.

Pea, R. D., & Sheingold, K. (1987). *Mirrors of minds: Patterns of experience in educational computing.* Norwood, NJ: Ablex.

Pellegrini, A. D. (1986). The effect of play centers on preschoolers' explicit language. In G. Fein & M. Rivkin (Eds.), *The young child at play* (pp. 40–48). Washington, DC: National Association for the Education of Young Children.

Piaget, J. (1954). *The construction of reality in the child* (M. Cook, Trans). New York: Basic Books. (Originally Published in French in 1937)

Reifel, S., & Greenfield, P. (1982) Structural development in a symbolic medium: The representational use of block constructions. In G. Forman (Ed.), *Action and thought: From sensorimotor schemes to symbolic operations* (pp. 203–234). New York: Academic.

Resnick, M., & Ocko, S. (1991). Lego/LOGO: Learning through and about design. In I. Harel & S. Papert (Eds.), *Constructionism* (pp. 141–150). Norwood, NJ: Ablex.

Sinclair, H., Stambak, M., Lezine, I., Rayna, S., & Verba, M. (1989). *Infants and objects: The creativity of cognitive development.* New York: Academic.

Smith, M., & Franklin, M. B. (Eds.). (1979). *Symbolic functioning in childhood.* Hillsdale, NJ: Erlbaum.

Turkle, S., & Papert, S. (1991). Epistemological pluralism and the revaluation of the concrete. In I. Harel & S. Papert (Eds.), *Constructionism* (pp. 161–192). Norwood, NJ: Ablex.

Wright, J. L. (1994). Listen to the children: Observing young children's discoveries with the microcomputer. In J. L. Wright and D. D. Shade (Eds.), *Young children: Active learning in a technological age* (pp. 3–18). Washington, DC: National Association for the Education of Young Children.

Wright, J. L., & Shade, D. D. (Eds.). (1994). *Young children: Active learning in a technological age.* Washington, DC: National Association for the Education of Young Children.

Rough-and-Tumble Play from Childhood through Adolescence

Differing Perspectives

Anthony D. Pellegrini

The Controversy Surrounding Rough-and-Tumble Play

Educators and researchers often take for granted the value of play in the lives of children. Some educators view play as the quintessence of developmentally appropriate practice (Brede-kamp, 1987). Researchers, too, have treated play as a hallowed developmental process, essential to a variety of social and cognitive processes (see Bruner, Jolly, & Sylva, 1976; Pellegrini & Galda, 1993; Smith, 1982, 1988 for discussion). Both, however, view play as a natural process by which children come to know their worlds.

Recently, however, there has been some dissonance. First, the empirical record supporting the unequivocal value of play is weak (Smith, 1988). Second, some adults have voiced concern over the role of certain forms of play in children's lives. Specifically, children's play with "war toys" and their play fighting, or rough-and-tumble play (R-and-T), have been the subject of wide and heated debate. On the one hand, the "anti's" (those opposed to war toys and R-and-T) generally view these forms of play as encouraging children's antisocial behavior and advocate policies to discourage them. Supporters of these forms of play, on the other hand, see them as merely children's expression of fantasy that adults, particularly female teachers, do not understand (Sutton-Smith, 1988). A number of recent papers refer to war toys (Smith, 1994; Sutton-Smith, 1988; Wegener-Spohring, 1994). The related topic, R-and-T and its role in children's development, has also been a subject of research.

To understand the construct R-and-T properly, it is crucial to define it in relation to aggression. As part of this definition, the differing developmental trajectories of R-and-T and aggression will also be discussed. The following section will address the different ways in which R-and-T and aggression predict social-cognitive status in primary and middle school youngsters. As part of this discussion, there will be a discussion of a darker side to R-and-T, the ways in which some youngsters use R-and-T as an aggressive tactic to bully their classmates.

Defining R-and-T in Relation to Aggression

Often R-and-T is confused with aggression because at some levels they resemble each other. Upon close inspection, however, they are clearly different. (For a fuller discussion see Pellegrini, 1995.) Categories of behavior, like aggression and R-and-T, can be classified, or defined, along the following dimensions: individual behaviors, consequences, structure, and ecology.

Individual Behaviors
Beginning with individual behaviors, numerous factor analytic studies have differentiated R-and-T and aggression behaviorally (Blurton Jones, 1972; Smith & Connolly, 1972, 1980) in some reliable ways. The assumption here is that

Work on this chapter was supported by grants from the National Institutes of Health, the H. F. Guggenheim Foundation, and the Institute for Behavioral Research at the University of Georgia.

behaviors with similar meaning, for example, will reliably co-occur and form a meaningful whole, or category. R-and-T is composed of these behaviors: run, chase, flee, wrestle, and open-hand hit. Aggression, in contrast, is typified by a different set of behaviors: closed-hand hits, shoves, pushes, and kicks. R-and-T and aggression also differ in their expression of affect. Smiles generally accompany R-and-T while frowns, or crying, accompany aggression.

Consequences

Classes of behavior can also be differentiated in terms of consequences, or behaviors that follow those that are of interest. Behaviors that follow a focal behavior (in this case, the focal behavior is R-and-T) describe the function or meaning of the behavior. R-and-T and aggression are different because they have different consequences and functions. When R-and-T bouts end, for example, children often stay together and begin cooperative social games (Pellegrini, 1988). Aggression, on the other hand, usually leads to one of the participants trying to separate from the other (Humphreys & Smith, 1984). Thus, R-and-T may have a peer-affiliative function while aggression does not. Longer-term, or more distal, consequences of R-and-T and aggression are also evident. These will be discussed in the section on developmental trajectories.

Structure

The structure of R-and-T is also different from that of aggression (Humphreys & Smith, 1984). For example, the structure of roles that typify each class of behaviors differ. In R-and-T youngsters alternate roles, such as chaser and chasee. In some cases, stronger or bigger players "self-handicap" so as to sustain play. An older child, for example, may pretend to fall while trying to escape from a pursuer, thus enabling the younger child to "capture" him or her. Self-handicapping enables children of different levels of strength and physical prowess to play together.

Role alternation is a hallmark of other forms of play, such as dramatic play where children often change or negotiate roles repeatedly in the course of an episode (Garvey, 1990). Role alternation seems to play an important part in children's social perspective taking; taking different play roles, both in fantasy (Burns and

Brainerd, 1979) and R-and-T (Pellegrini, 1993), enables children to take different perspectives. Aggression, on the other hand, is typified by unilateral roles: aggressors do not switch roles with their victims. Thus, the social perspective-taking function is absent in aggression.

Ecology

Ecological factors also influence the expression of R-and-T. It tends to occur in spacious areas, such as the outdoors (Smith & Connolly, 1980), and on those parts of playgrounds with soft, grassy surfaces (Pellegrini 1989b). That R-and-T is physically vigorous and involves running, falling, and wrestling means that it is more likely to occur in areas that can support this sort of behavior, compared to more confined areas.

School policy variables, such as adult tolerance for R-and-T and the amount of time permitted between outdoor play breaks, also relate to the observed amount of physically vigorous behavior, including R-and-T. Some schools have an explicit policy forbidding children to engage in any form of play fighting, because adults typically (and incorrectly!) assume that it will escalate into "real" fighting.

School policy related to the timing of free play and recess periods affects R-and-T as well as other forms of physically vigorous behavior. When children spend longer rather than shorter periods indoors involved in sedentary activities before recess, their outdoor play is more physically active and socially interactive (Pellegrini, Huberty, & Jones, 1995; Pellegrini & Smith, 1993). Correspondingly, high levels of physical activity often lead to aggression (DeRossier, Cillessen, Coie, & Dodge, 1994). Thus, long confinement before recess probably has the effect of increasing both types of physical activity.

Aggression does not, however, vary according to playground location (Pellegrini, 1989a); it is likely to occur anywhere. Where toys and play are present, however, the cause of aggression often stems from children's disputes over objects (Smith & Connolly, 1980). As is the case with R-and-T, school policy can influence aggression to the extent that an explicit policy discouraging aggression and other forms of bullying does reduce aggression (Olweus, 1993; Smith & Thompson, 1991).

Although research has indicated that, under close scrutiny, it is evident that R-and-T and aggression are distinct constructs, many teachers and playground supervisors do not differentiate R-and-T from aggression but, rather, categorize all vigorous physical interaction as aggression. It may be necessary, from a policy perspective, to "educate" these caregivers about the difference between the two because, while R-and-T leads children into a very positive developmental trajectory, this is not the case for aggression.

Developmental Trajectories and Differences in Expression

The distinction between R-and-T and aggression is further evidenced by the fact that each has a different developmental trajectory. R-and-T, like other forms of play (Fagen, 1981), follows an inverted-U developmental function. It accounts for about 5 percent of the free play of preschoolers, increases to 10 to 17 percent of the play of elementary school children, and declines in middle school to about 5 percent (Humphreys & Smith, 1984; Pellegrini, 1989b). Aggression, on the other hand, is stable from childhood through adolescence (Olweus, 1979); the trajectory is flat.

Gender Differences

There are also differences in the individual expression of R-and-T and aggression, most notably in the differential expression of each by boys and girls. Boys exhibit both R-and-T and aggression more than girls do (Maccoby & Jacklin, 1974). These differences have been observed cross-culturally (Whiting & Edwards, 1973) and among most higher primates (Humphreys & Smith, 1984). These gender differences are not *individual* differences per se but are probably due to both hormonal and socialization events (Maccoby, 1986). Among the factors that may influence boys' expression of vigorous and rough play at higher rates than girls are hormonal events, such as higher levels of testosterone during the development of the fetus; socialization pressures, such as the selection of certain toys and games; and permission to engage in active play.

Individual Differences

There are, however, individual differences in the expression of R-and-T by children of the same sex. Primary school boys who are both sociometrically rejected by their peers (that is, they are rated as disliked by more of their peers than they are liked) and physically aggressive tend to engage in R-and-T at rates similar to other boys. Their R-and-T, however, co-occurs with aggression. That is, rates of aggression and R-and-T are significantly intercorrelated for rejected, physically aggressive boys (Pellegrini, 1988). Further, the R-and-T of these boys tends to escalate into aggression; that is, when an R-and-T bout ends, aggression is likely to follow (Pellegrini, 1988). Boys who are aggressive and rejected in the primary grades retain this status as they move into adolescence. In adolescence, however, these boys engage in a particularly rough form of R-and-T and tend to use R-and-T to bully their peers (Pellegrini, 1995). While rates of R-and-T decline markedly for most adolescent boys, the R-and-T of rejected boys remains relatively high and continues to relate to aggression (Pellegrini, 1995).

Attention Deficit Hyperactivity Disorder (ADHD) is another individual difference that relates to children's expression of aggression. ADHD is a commonly diagnosed (some would say too commonly diagnosed) syndrome where children (also mostly boys) exhibit high levels of physical activity and/or low levels of attention. (See Pellegrini & Horvat, 1995, for a critique of the ADHD literature.) These children often exhibit aggression as well as R-and-T.

This syndrome also seems to be exacerbated or inhibited by certain environments. It may be that in extreme cases, ADHD is primarily a biological problem, but in most cases it is probably the interaction between individual biological differences and environment. A moderately active kindergarten boy, for example, might be considered a problem in a classroom where adults expect children to sit quietly most of the day. In a classroom where the stress is on social interaction among peers, this same child would probably not be a problem.

Thus, for most children during middle childhood, especially boys, R-and-T is a playful construct, the exception being in rejected/aggressive boys. As most boys move into adolescence, R-and-T declines dramatically. Those boys who continue to engage in R-and-T, however, tend to be aggressive and to use R-and-T in antisocial ways. Thus, R-and-T relates to social-cognitive outcomes during childhood and early adolescence.

R-and-T as a Predictor of Social-Cognitive Status

Two separate two-year longitudinal studies offer data on some ways in which R-and-T predicts social-cognitive status during childhood and early adolescence. (A more thorough description is available in Pellegrini, 1995).

R-and-T in the Primary School Years

During the primary school years, the consequences of children's R-and-T depends on their sociometric status, or the degree to which they are liked and disliked by their peers. For popular boys, R-and-T predicts peer popularity, engagement in cooperative games, and social problem solving (Pellegrini, 1995). For boys rejected by their peers, R-and-T is correlated with aggression and does not predict positive social cognitive outcomes. During childhood for most boys, therefore, R-and-T is a positive predictor of social cognitive status. R-and-T does not have these positive benefits for rejected boys; indeed, it predicts antisocial behavior.

These results have important implications for school policy. They clearly suggest that the R-and-T of *most* boys does not escalate to aggression. Indeed, it is related to a number of positive outcomes. Thus, school policy that discourages R-and-T needs to be reconsidered. Of course, for those children who are rejected and aggressive, their aggression and associated behaviors cannot be tolerated. Numerous social skills training programs are available to help aggressive children (Coie & Koeppl, 1990).

R-and-T in Adolescence

Early adolescence witnesses a dramatic shift in the role of R-and-T: its rate decreases dramatically after the primary school years. This decrease probably reflects boys' increasing concerns with heterosexual relationships (Pellegrini, 1995). Whereas primary school boys play in groups composed predominantly of other boys, young adolescent boys spend more of their free time in groups composed of both boys and girls and, therefore, do not engage in activities such as R-and-T that do not include girls.

Those adolescent boys who continue to engage in R-and-T tend to be antisocial and unpopular with their peers (Pellegrini, 1995). It seems that these boys use R-and-T as an opportunity to target weaker boys and then "victim-

ize up." It may be the case that these "tough" boys, bullies, sample a variety of probable targets for their aggression through R-and-T overtures. When they find weaker boys who succumb to their aggression, they probably continue to victimize them. In this way, what starts off ostensibly as play typically ends with aggressive boys turning R-and-T into aggression, especially toward boys they consider to be weaker than they.

It is probably the case that these "bullies" are using R-and-T as a way to exhibit dominance to their peers. This explanation is supported by the observation that adolescence is a period during which dominance is in considerable flux (Fagen, 1981). As a result of rapid change in body size and changes in schools (from primary to secondary) and peer groups, youngsters must renegotiate their peer status. Bullies may be using physical aggression as a basis for peer affiliation, whereas other, well-adjusted boys, use other means, such as academics and sport.

It may be the case that most boys use R-and-T in childhood as a way to learn and practice social skills necessary for other sorts of cooperative interaction, such as social games. As they mature and the presence of R-and-T diminishes, they use those skills learned and practiced in R-and-T for other forms of interaction. The longitudinal relationship between R-and-T and cooperative games noted above illustrates this point. In effect, for many boys, R-and-T may be a bridge between the social fantasy play characteristic of preschool age and the social games with rules typical of middle childhood. They continue to structure their play with alternating roles and physically vigorous behaviors, while the goals of the play become subject to the rules that larger social groups enforce.

Asking Youngsters about R-and-T

Thus far, indirect methods of study have established the value, or function, of R-and-T in childhood and adolescence. Researchers have correlated one set of behaviors (R-and-T) with other behaviors, such as aggression, or related R-and-T behaviors to various tasks, such as sociometric nominations or contrived social problems, and then made inferences about the meaning of those relations. Interviewing children is a more direct method to assess the meaning and function of R-and-T. Questionnaires can ask about R-and-T in general, or children can view filmed episodes of R-and-T and aggressive bouts and then answer questions about those bouts. Researchers have used variants of both of these procedures.

Some researchers have used questionnaire procedures with children in the United Kingdom and Italy (Costabile et al, 1991; Smith, Smees, Pellegrini, & Menesini, 1993). They asked children a series of questions about their perceptions of R-and-T and aggression; for example, the frequency with which they engage in R-and-T, the identity of their partners in R-and-T, and their reasons for engaging in R-and-T. These studies, like the behavioral studies discussed above, clearly show that children differentiate R-and-T from aggression and can give reasons supporting their judgments. Generally, and not surprisingly, children say they engage in R-and-T because it is fun.

The videotape methodology has taken two forms. Children more commonly view videotapes of the R-and-T and aggression of unfamiliar children. In this case, again, children clearly differentiate R-and-T from aggression and can give numerous reasons for doing so (Pellegrini, 1989b).

It should be noted, however, that individual differences also crop up here. Rejected children, compared to popular children, neither are very accurate in their discriminations nor do they give as many reasons for their decisions. This difference may be due to a social information-processing deficit (Dodge & Frame, 1982). Briefly, these researchers have suggested that rejected children simply do not accurately process ambiguous, provocative interactions such as R-and-T (Dodge & Frame, 1982). When they see an ambiguous/provocative event that can be either playful or aggressive, they tend to attribute aggressive intent to it; thus, they see R-and-T as aggression.

There is another explanation for rejected children's poor performance on these discrimination tasks. It may be that these children, as general "problem children" in school (Parker & Asher, 1987), take on a negative stance when they are being interviewed. As a way to project this negative image to the interviewer, they label R-and-T bouts as aggressive (thus the aggressive bias) and minimally comply with requests to give reasons for their responses (thus the low number of attributes given to differentiate R-and-T from aggression). In short, their responses may be a way of expressing defiance/noncompliance to an adult in school.

This purposeful, rather than deficient, explanation is consistent with other research showing that rejected boys are also very purposeful in their choice of R-and-T partners. For a particularly rough variant of R-and-T, but not other forms of social interaction, rejected boys (who are also considered to be "tough" by their peers) initiate interaction with boys who are weaker than they; peers also consider these targets to be "victims." These R-and-T bouts typically escalate into aggression at a greater-than-chance probability (Pellegrini, 1995). Thus, "tough" boys may use R-and-T as a pretext for victimizing less dominant boys.

Another, less commonly used, videotape method involves showing children and their teachers aggressive and R-and-T bouts in which they and their classmates were participants (Smith, Smees, et al., 1993). Individual children who participated in the R-and-T bouts viewed the films on the same day as the bouts and again two weeks later; their classmates and teachers viewed the films at the same intervals. Researchers predicted that teachers' interpretations would be at odds with children's. From previous findings (Sutton-Smith, 1988), the researchers knew that teachers tended to be biased against R-and-T, considering it aggression.

Instead, researchers found that participants agreed with each other on the meaning of the event, in effect, whether it was R-and-T or aggression. This agreement was stable across a two-week period. Nonparticipating peers and teachers also agreed with each other, but their interpretations were significantly different from the participants.

What does this mean? At a very simple level it means that different people have different interpretations of the same ambiguous events. To understand ambiguous events, such as R-and-T, one may require a participant's point of view. Participant status, however, may be a proxy for something else. It may be the case that these participants are also friends and have a different sort of relationship between them than do nonparticipants. Friends tend to engage in R-and-T with each other more than with peers who are not friends (Humphreys & Smith, 1984). Friends also have a more accurate understanding of each other than do nonfriends (Hartup, 1983). Thus, it may be that R-and-T participants agree with each other because they are friends.

These results have very clear implications for both research and educational policy. Researchers should make provision for the differing interpretations of ambiguous provocation events, such as R-and-T, when they interview children. From a policy perspective, these results suggest that to understand potentially ambiguous forms of behavior, such as aggression and R-and-T, teachers and school administrators should interview participants and their friends and not rely on what bystanders say.

This essay outlined the ways in which one form of play, R-and-T, differs from aggression. As part of this exposition, the review of evidence showed that R-and-T and aggression have very different developmental histories and, consequently, very different impacts on children's social cognitive status. R-and-T is quite "normal" and actually a "good" form of play for young children, particularly prevalent among boys. R-and-T is "good" because it predicts cooperative interaction, popularity, and social problem solving. It may also be the case that engaging in R-and-T affords an opportunity to practice encoding and decoding social information. Further, the role alternation characteristic of R-and-T may be an important component in perspective taking. Skills learned and practiced in R-and-T play during childhood are then used during adolescence in other forms of reciprocal social interaction, such as cooperative games.

An interesting developmental shift occurs in adolescence. R-and-T no longer has positive implications for social cognitive development. During this period, R-and-T is used primarily by bullies victimizing their weaker peers. Thus, this is an interesting case of a set of behaviors serving different functions for different youngsters—rejected versus popular—at different periods—childhood versus adolescence. This form of play is not all good for all children.

Another important conclusion from this work is that not all children seem to need this specific form of play in order to develop. R-and-T is a particularly male phenomenon and many boys seem to use it in the service of their social cognitive development. Girls generally do not engage in R-and-T but also develop into well-functioning social beings. Girls use other strategies to become socially competent; they engage in social pretense play at high rates, compared to boys, which suggests that this form of play, not R-and-T, is important for their social cognitive development.

In short, not all children must travel the same developmental path to competence. This sort of behavioral flexibility seems crucial in light of the fact that children, as a species, are reared in a variety of conditions. To flourish in these different niches, children must adopt different strategies. Thus, educators should beware of advice that one "royal road" leads to anything. There are numerous roads.

Bibliography

Blurton Jones, N. (1972). Categories of child interaction. In N. Blurton Jones (Ed.), *Ethological studies in child behavior* (pp. 92–129). Cambridge: Cambridge University Press.

Bredekamp, S. (1987). *Developmentally appropriate practice in early childhood programs serving children from birth through age 8.* Washington, DC: National Association for the Education of Young Children.

Bruner, J., Jolly, A., & Sylva, K. (Eds.). (1976). *Play: Its role in development and evolution.* New York: Basic Books.

Burns, S., & Brainerd, C. (1979). Effects of constructive and dramatic play on perspective taking in young children. *Developmental Psychology, 15,* 512–521.

Coie, J., & Koeppl, G. (1990). Adapting intervention to the problems of aggressive and disturbed rejected children. In S. Asher & J. Coie (Eds.), *Peer rejection in childhood* (pp. 309–337). New York: Cambridge University Press.

Costabile, A., Smith, P. K., Matheson, L., Aston, J., Hunter, T., & Boulton, M. (1991). Cross-national comparisons of how children distinguish play from serious fighting. *Developmental Psychology, 27,* 881–887.

DeRossier, M., Cillessen, T., Coie, J., & Dodge, K. (1994). Group social context and children's aggressive behavior. *Child Development, 65,* 1068–1079.

Dodge, K., & Frame, C. (1982). Social cognitive deficits and biases in aggressive boys. *Child Development, 53,* 620–635.

Fagen, R. (1981). *Animal play.* New York: Oxford University Press.

Garvey, C. (1990). *Play.* Cambridge, MA: Harvard University Press.

Hartup, W. W. (1983). Peer relations. In E. M. Hetherington (Ed.), *Handbook of child psychology* (Vol. 4, pp. 103–196). New York: John Wiley.

Humphreys, A., & Smith, P. K. (1984). Rough-and-tumble play in preschool and the playground. In P. K. Smith (Ed.), *Play in animals and humans* (pp. 241–266). Oxford: Basil Blackwell.

Maccoby, E. E. (1986). Social groupings in childhood: Their relationship to prosocial and antisocial behavior in boys and girls. In D. Olweus, J. Block, & M. Radkye-Yarrow (Eds.), *Development of antisocial and prosocial behavior* (pp. 263–284). New York: Academic.

Maccoby, E. E., & Jacklin, C. N. (1974). *The psychology of sex differences*. Stanford: Stanford University Press.

Olweus, D. (1979). Stability and aggressive patterns in males: A review. *Psychological Bulletin, 86,* 852–875.

Olweus, D. (1993). Bullies on playgrounds. In C. Hart (Ed.), *Children on playgrounds* (pp. 85–128). Albany: State University of New York Press.

Parker, J., & Asher, S. (1987). Personal relations and later social adjustment: Are low-accepted children at-risk? *Psychological Bulletin, 102,* 357–382.

Pellegrini, A. D. (1988). Elementary school children's rough-and-tumble play and social competence. *Developmental Psychology, 24,* 802–806.

Pellegrini, A. D. (1989a). Elementary school children's rough-and-tumble play. *Early Childhood Research Quarterly, 4,* 245–260.

Pellegrini, A. D. (1989b). What is a category? The case of rough-and-tumble play. *Ethology and Sociobiology, 10,* 331–341.

Pellegrini, A. D. (1991). A longitudinal study of popular and rejected children's rough-and-tumble play. *Early Education and Development, 2,* 205–213.

Pellegrini, A. D. (1993). Boys' rough-and-tumble play, social competence, and group composition. *British Journal of Developmental Psychology, 11,* 237–248.

Pellegrini, A. D. (1995). *The developmental and educational roles of children's playground behavior*. Albany: State University of New York Press.

Pellegrini, A. D., & Galda, L. (1993). Ten years after: A re-examination of the relations between symbolic play and literacy. *Reading Research Quarterly, 28*(2), 162–175.

Pellegrini, A. D., & Horvat, M. (1995). A developmental contextual critique of attention deficit hyperactivity disorder. *Educational Researcher, 24*(1), 13–20.

Pellegrini, A. D., Huberty, P. D., & Jones, I. (1995). The effects of recess timing on children's playground and classroom behavior. *American Educational Research Journal.*

Pellegrini, A. D., & Smith, P. K. (1993). School recess: Implications for education and development. *Review of Educational Research, 63,* 51–68.

Smith, P. K. (1982). Does play matter? Functional and evolutionary aspects of animal and human play. *The Behavioral and Brain Sciences, 5,* 139–184.

Smith, P. K. (1988). Children's play and its role in early development: A re-evaluation of the "play ethos." In A. D. Pellegrini (Ed.), *Psychological bases for early education* (pp. 229–244) Chichester, UK: John Wiley.

Smith, P. K. (1994). The war play debate. In J. Goldstein (Ed.), *Toys, play, and child development* (pp. 67–84). New York: Cambridge University Press.

Smith , P. K., & Connolly, K. (1972). Patterns of play and social interaction in preschool children. In N. Blurton Jones (Ed.), *Ethological studies in child behavior* (pp. 65–96). Cambridge: Cambridge University Press.

Smith, P. K., & Connolly, K. (1980). *The ecology of preschool behavior*. Cambridge: Cambridge University Press.

Smith, P. K., Smees, R., Pellegrini, A. D., & Menesini, E. (1993, July). *Play fighting and serious fighting: Perspectives on their relationships*. Paper presented at the biennial meeting of the International Society for the Study of Behavioral Development, Recife, Brazil.

Smith, P. K., & Thompson, D. (Eds.). (1991). *Practical approaches to bullying*. London: David Fulton.

Sutton-Smith, B. (1988). War toys and childhood aggression. *Play and Culture, 1,* 57–69.

Wegener-Spohring, G. (1994). War toys and

aggressive play scenes. In J. Goldstein (Ed.), *Toys, play, and child development* (pp. 85–109). New York: Cambridge University Press.

Whiting, B., & Edwards, C. (1973). A cross-cultural analysis of sex differences in behavior of children age 3 through 11. *Journal of Social Psychology, 91*, 171–188.

Games with Rules

Rheta DeVries

Games with rules are a form of play involving competitive interindividual relationships in the context of regulations as to possibilities and prohibitions, with sanctions for violations. While various writers (Baldwin, 1897/1973; Mead, 1934/1962) have considered the role of games with rules in psychological development, it is to Piaget that we owe the greatest debt for elaborating their psychological significance in the child's development. In his book, *La formation du symbole chez l'enfant: Imitation, jeu and reve, image et representation* (published in English as *Play, Dreams, and Imitation in Childhood*) Piaget (1945/1963) discussed games with rules as the third in a succession of types of structure in children's activities. Let us consider the developmental context of group games according to Piaget.

The Developmental Context of Group Games

The first structure, practice play, appears in the first months of life as the infant continues to exercise actions already mastered simply for pleasure. Examples in later childhood include throwing pebbles in a lake, throwing a ball, lacing and unlacing shoes, and jumping back and forth over a puddle. While such practice play diminishes in frequency over childhood, it reappears whenever there is a new acquisition, even in adulthood. Practice play begins to evolve into symbolic play during the second year of life when the infant loses interest in practicing something already mastered and becomes interested in imitating the content of actions. Examples include imitation of one's own familiar actions out of context, such as sleeping or

eating, and extends eventually to exact imitations of reality, for example, instead of simply using a piece of wood for a boat, really making a boat with a hollowed-out space, masts, sails, and seats. Practice play declines after the age of four years when the child becomes more interested in activities involving adaptation to reality. It does not disappear altogether, however, and continues into adult activities of fantasies and dramatic productions.

Both practice play and symbolic play evolve into games with rules, beginning between ages four and seven years and especially belonging to ages seven to eleven years. In the case of practice play, actions are socialized. Piaget (1945/1963, p. 143) gives the example of three five-year-olds whose play at jumping from stairs evolves into rules as they agree to try to jump as far as they can from the same step, and decide that anyone who falls loses.

In the case of symbolic play, symbols can be socialized into a system of rules. Piaget (1945/1963, pp. 143–144) gives the example of some shepherd boys who cut hazel branches in a Y shape and pretended these were cows, with the two tips of the Y representing horns and the lower part the body, with spots on top and loosened bark on bottom for the belly. This symbolism evolved into a game with rules: the cows had to be balanced horn to horn, after which the competition was to push them by the base of the Y to see which one fell on its back and therefore lost.

Piaget (1932/1965) developed in much more detail the evolution of games with rules in his book, *The Moral Judgment of the Child*. His description of stages in the practice of rules and consciousness of rules in the game of marbles provides an account of development that is still important and applicable to children's play more than sixty years later.

Stages in the Game of Marbles

Piaget's approach was to pretend he had forgotten how to play marbles and to ask children (ages approximately six to fourteen years) to instruct him so that he could play with them. In this way, he was able to learn children's conceptions of the rules. He brought pairs of children together to play the game by themselves in order further to observe their practice of rules with one another, and he then interviewed children as to their consciousness about various aspects of rules, for example, whether they could invent rules, the origin of the rules, and so forth. He also observed younger children with marbles.

Let us consider the results with regard to the practice of rules. Piaget found four stages or levels in children's play. The first stage is *motor and individual play*, occurring before the age of two years, when the child simply uses the marbles to explore their properties (for example, by dropping them one by one onto a carpet) or in symbolic play (for example, "cooking" them in a toy saucepan). While the child in these activities imposes some regularities on the marbles, these cannot be called rules because they are asocial and entail no obligation to engage in these actions.

The second stage is *egocentric play*, occurring between about two and five years of age, when the child tries to learn other people's rules and submits to their authority. While social in intent, the child's rules are not thoroughly social in action. That is, the child imitates observable actions of players but cannot at first think about the opposed intentions of players. Play is thus not competitive, and the child at this stage often says that everybody won. While children play side by side, they do not unify their rules and often play by different rules, without noticing or without considering this important.

The third stage is *incipient cooperation*, appearing between seven and eight years of age (although we certainly observe this much earlier, even in some four-year-olds, among children with considerable experience in playing games). The hallmark of this stage is, paradoxically, the emergence of a competitive attitude. Rules now rest on mutual agreement and reciprocity. The desire to unify rules leads children to see the necessity of coordinating with others

in deciding on what the rules are to be, following them, and agreeing on their consequences. At the beginning of this stage, children still may have incomplete rule systems and cooperation may exist more in intention than successful action. What is important is that children are consciously trying to coordinate with others. At the end of this stage, the child understands fully the necessity of rules as the basis for agreement on how to play. When asked, for example, why there are rules in the game of marbles, one eleven-year-old answered, "So as not to be always quarrelling you must have rules, and then play properly [stick to them]" (Piaget, 1932/ 1965, pp. 66, 71). Thus, the feeling of obligation to obey rules is motivated not by external coercion, as in the second stage, but by self-regulated cooperation.

The fourth stage is *codification of rules*, beginning at eleven to twelve years of age among Piaget's subjects (although we observe this stage much earlier among children experienced with games). At this stage, children are not only interested in cooperation but also in anticipating all possible instances of conflict of interest, and providing a codified set of rules to regulate play. Children elaborate the game in a very complex way and, when disagreements arise about rules, players know how to come to agreement. One thirteen-year-old acknowledged that people sometimes play differently, but said that when there are conflicting ideas, "You ask each other what you want to do." Asked what happens if they cannot agree, he said, "We scrap for a bit and then we fix things up" (Piaget, 1932/1965, p. 49). At this stage, the relation to others is autonomous, since the regulation by rules is mutual self-regulation. (See Piaget, 1932/1965, for further details on this research on marbles.)

This general outline of progress in the practice of rules in marbles has parallels in all other games with rules.

Stages in Playing Guess-Which-Hand-the-Penny-Is-In

Another game studied systematically is guess-which-hand-the-penny-is-in (where one player puts his or her hands behind his or her back, grasps a penny in one fist, and presents both fists for the opponent to guess which hand it is in). Working with children ages three to seven, the researcher found it easy to engage them immediately simply by showing them a penny and inviting them to guess which hand the penny was in. With a penny in both hands (so children were always successful for about ten guesses), the researcher was able to observe children's spontaneous approaches to finding the penny, especially with regard to whether they guessed the same hand each time, alternated from left to right, or shifted their guesses in an irregular way. After about ten guesses, the researcher left the pennies on the floor behind her and continued to play with both fists empty, enabling her to observe the child's reactions to not finding the penny. Taking up both pennies again, she guaranteed that the child's last guess was successful. She then gave a penny to the child and invited him or her to hide it so the researcher could guess.

This game is especially good for assessing whether, or to what degree, a child is able to take the perspective of the other in the game. As Piaget found with marbles, young children at first only imitate what is observable to them in others' physical actions. Not yet aware of the possibility of deceptiveness and secrecy (requiring the ability to think about others' intentions), some see the game as one in which one person simply gives the penny to another. With this idea of the game, they enact the hider's role by simply holding out a palm with the penny. Others see the game as one in which one person puts the penny in a fist, with the object being for the other to find the penny; with this conception of the game, the young child may offer only one fist, or hold one fist forward suggestively, even becoming irritated if the other does not point to the fist with the penny. Clearly, a competitive attitude is missing. When a competitive attitude emerges, the child still does not necessarily take adequately into account the other's perspective. For example, while not wanting the other to find the penny, the child may unconsciously provide clues to the location of the penny by presenting a limp empty fist, changing the location of the penny before putting hands behind the back, bringing out fists while obviously still getting a good grip on the penny, and so forth. Earlier levels of play of this game involve perseverating in guessing or hiding in the same hand or, at a somewhat more advanced level, moving or guessing the location in a regular left-right-left-right alternation. More advanced play is characterized by irregular shifting in guessing and hiding. (For a more detailed discussion of the systematic study of this game, see DeVries, 1970; summarized in DeVries & Kohlberg, 1990; and Kamii & DeVries, 1980).

Stages in Playing Tic-Tac-Toe

Similarly, DeVries and Fernie (1990) recount the results of systematic study of the videotaped play of tic-tac-toe among children three to nine years of age. Using a board and movable plastic Xs and Os, and working with children one at a time, Fernie asked children if they knew how to play and learned their conceptions of the game. If they did not know how to play, he explained the rules. After playing a series of about ten games, Fernie then interviewed the children as to their conceptions of the game and what would be "good moves" in several standard situations. An observer made a record of the exact sequence of plays in each game, and children's play was analyzed in detail with regard to whether they followed the rules, used blocking or two-way strategies, and so forth. An assessment from verbal and nonverbal behaviors was made as to whether the child had a competitive attitude.

Findings in this study parallel those of Piaget. Level 1 of motor and individual play was observed when children simply stack Xs and Os, throw them, and use them as props for pretense. Three sublevels of level 1 egocentric play are described, from 1A, schematic imitation of some aspects of the game (simply putting pieces in spaces without taking turns), to 1B, taking turns (and no longer going out of turn to complete a line), to 1C, knowing that the goal of the game is a straight line (and no longer believing a crooked line is adequate). Level 2 of cooperative play has three sublevels, with level 2A signaled by the emergence of a competitive attitude, although children do not yet think of logical strategies by which to try to win. Level 2B emerges with the strategy of blocking used only some of the time when necessary (by playing in a space that, if filled by the opponent's piece, would complete a line, as a means to trying to win). Preoccupied with this newly invented strategy, however, the child blocks at times without noticing the possibility of a win by playing a different space. Level 3A involves the consolidation of defensive strategies that include blocking most of the time when necessary in order to avoid losing. At level 3B, the child constructs the temporal aspect of the game, reflected in recognizing that the first line wins without attempting to continue playing when the opponent completes a line. At level 4A, the child coordinates an advanced offensive strategy through using two-way setups, trying to guarantee a win by setting up the situation so that the possibility to make three in a line exists in two directions at the same time. The child sometimes loses sight, however, of a possibility to win when preoccupied with how to arrange a two-way setup. Finally, at level 4B, the child coordinates strategies by shifting flexibly, when necessary, between two-way setups and blocking. (For a more detailed presentation of the systematic study of this game, see DeVries & Fernie, 1990; summarized in DeVries & Kohlberg, 1990).

Education through Games with Rules

Kamii and DeVries (1980) took seriously Piaget's work on games with rules and proposed the inclusion of group games in constructivist programs of early education that aim to promote children's development. In their book, *Group Games in Early Education: Implications of Piaget's Theory,* they (Kamii & DeVries, 1980; also, DeVries & Kohlberg, 1990) discuss the educational rationale for games with rules as educational activities.

Games with rules can be justified as educational because they promote children's sociomoral and intellectual development.

Sociomoral Development in Games with Rules

The sociomoral objective of constructivist teaching is long-term progress in the structure or stage of moral reasoning, not just in the specific content of moral rules or even behavior conforming to moral rules. That is, as Kohlberg (1987) has argued, our aim should focus not in an isolated way just on teaching moral rules or moral behaviors but on facilitating the construction of inner moral convictions about what is good and necessary in one's relations with others. If one focuses only on promoting conformity to heteronomous rules given ready-made to children, conforming behavior may reflect only superficial knowledge of social expectation without personal commitment to the moral value itself.

The broad constructivist sociomoral goal is for children to develop autonomous feelings of obligation (or moral necessity) about relations with others that are not just dictates accepted from adults. Rather, a feeling of moral necessity reflects an internal system of personal convic-

tions. Such a personal system is autonomous insofar as it leads to beliefs and behavior that are self-regulated rather than other-regulated. It is cooperative insofar as it reflects a view of the self as part of a system of reciprocal social relations.

From the point of view of promoting children's autonomy, group games contribute by providing a context in which children can voluntarily accept and submit themselves to rules. Children are free to exercise their autonomy by choosing to play and choosing to follow rules. Rules in games are different from the set of obligations adults must impose in daily living, such as eating certain foods, going to bed at a certain time, and not playing with certain delicate objects. Rules in everyday living are fully formed and given to the child ready-made. The child usually cannot understand the reasons for these rules and thus can only abide by them out of obedience to the authority of adults. That is, he or she cannot follow them out of an internal feeling of commitment to their necessity.

Autonomous adoption of sociomoral rules is prevented to the extent that the child is bound by a heteronomous attitude. That is, when children think and act in terms of what they perceive to be the requirements of others, they are not likely to submit these to the reflection that leads to understood and self-accepted values. The loosening of the heteronomous attitude requires experiences in which children can exercise autonomy by choosing to follow or not follow rules, reflecting on the consequences, and gradually growing to understand the reasons for rules that are rooted in maintaining desired relations with others.

In a game with rules, the adult authority and system of rules is temporarily suspended. Players can practice cooperation among equals when adult authority is put aside in favor of rules to which adults, too, must conform. When the adult participates as one player among others, adult authority can be more easily suspended in the minds of children, and this opportunity for interacting with the adult on a more equal basis is particularly good for the loosening of children's heteronomous attitudes. In daily living, it is difficult for the adult to tolerate a child's breaking a rule. In games, however, rules are not so sacred. In games, adult authority can decrease while children's power increases. When power is equalized, coercion ceases to be the regulating force, and autonomous cooperation can begin.

In games, therefore, children find conditions in which they can willingly adapt to society. Children thus have the opportunity to exercise autonomy in freely regulating their actions with others in relation to rules. They experience the consequences of failing to follow a rule when others protest and the game comes to a halt; they can then decide whether to change their behavior or, with the help of the teacher or another child, change the rule. This leads to dawning awareness of the necessity of collective agreement to the continuation of a mutually satisfying experience. In a game, children thus have the possibility of creating, in part, the rules and values by which they regulate their behavior.

In a game with rules, society intervenes in the experience of the individual, offering a situation in which the child can adapt to external social rules and construct feelings of obligation to them. From the point of view of promoting children's cooperation, games with rules contribute by providing a context, a minisociety, in which children can autonomously relate to others according to rules. Interest in the game leads to interest in others. Interest in playing with others according to the rules leads to efforts to coordinate individual actions with those of others. Self-regulation thus evolves into mutual adaptation, that is, the mutual accommodation and mutual adjustment of cooperation. Interest in the end, playing the game, brings an interest in the means, cooperation, by which to have fun in the game.

Games uniquely promote attitudes of reciprocity that lead to feelings of moral necessity, which is the core of sociomoral development. These feelings of obligation arise not out of obedience, but out of a feeling of personal necessity. Feelings of moral necessity about relations with others develop in games as children confront issues of fairness, individual rights, and the reasons for rules. They can practice mutual respect, which is a defining characteristic of cooperation and democratic principles.

A competitive game is especially conducive to moral development because opposed intentions must be coordinated within a broader context of cooperation. That is, competition can only exist when players cooperate in agreeing on the rules, enforcing them, abiding by them, and accepting their consequences even when unfavorable to themselves. The game cannot occur unless players cooperate by coordinating their points of view. When players have different conceptions of how a game should be played, the game may stop; this creates a situation in which children have the opportunity to confront the different perspective of someone else, decenter, and negotiate an agreement. Seen in this light, the competitive aspect is, in fact, subordinate to the cooperative aspect. Following mutually agreed-upon rules puts everyone on an equal basis in a social system regulated by the players themselves. Playing a group game is thus a useful point of departure for promoting children's sociomoral progress. (See DeVries & Zan, 1994, for elaboration of the constructivist sociomoral atmosphere of which playing games with rules is only one part. See also DeVries & Kohlberg, 1990, for a discussion of the contribution of games with rules to children's personality development.)

Research on Children's Sociomoral Development in the Context of a Game

In a comparative study of three kindergarten classrooms reflecting different educational paradigms (constructivist, behaviorist, and eclectic), I used the context of a game to assess children's sociomoral development. A teacher-made board game was used in which players rolled a die to determine how many spaces to move along a path from start to finish. Pairs of children were taught to play this simple game with its rules for turn-taking, going back to the nearest picture of a haunted house upon landing on a ghost, and going back to start when the opponent lands on the space one occupies. During the teaching session, the experimenter played alongside the children. Several days later, the same pair of children was invited to play the game again, but this time without the adult's participation. The goal was to learn how children engage and negotiate with each other (self-regulate) when no adult controls or influences them. Microanalysis of videotapes utilized Selman's (Selman & Schultz, 1990) conceptualization of developmental levels of interpersonal understanding.

Briefly, to summarize the results, children from the constructivist program were more actively engaged with one another. They had more friendly, shared experiences with each other and not only negotiated more but negotiated more successfully. They used significantly more strategies reflecting consideration for the other's point of view and made efforts to achieve mutually satisfactory interaction. In harmonious interactions, these children were also more reciprocal, for example, sharing secrets and recalling past shared experiences, than children from the other two classrooms (who engaged in much more impulsive silliness). Children from the constructivist classroom also used a greater variety of different strategies and resolved more conflicts than children from the behaviorist and eclectic classrooms. Children from the behaviorist classroom tended to try to resolve conflicts by overwhelming the other person physically or emotionally and, in general, related in less complex ways. (See DeVries, Reese-Learned, & Morgan, 1991, for details of this study; and see DeVries, Haney, & Zan, 1991, for a description of the study of the sociomoral atmosphere of these three classrooms.)

Intellectual Development in Games with Rules

Descriptions of stages given above reflect intellectual development in children's play of games as studied systematically by researchers. Kamii and DeVries (1980) studied how children play games in constructivist classrooms where teachers facilitated children's play. Working with teachers to develop an approach to using games with rules, they videotaped instances of games and analyzed what children and teachers did. This work led to the conclusion that the cognitive advantages of games with rules vary, depending on the type of game, its idiosyncratic characteristics, and the ways in which children use it.

Kamii and DeVries (1980) categorize group games into eight types (aiming, racing, chasing, hiding, guessing, games involving verbal commands, card games, and board games), giving many examples of each of these types with cognitive rationales. Aiming games, for example, are good for the structuring of space because children think about spatial relationships when they try to figure out how to hit a target.

Not all games with rules are educational. Recreational games include those that provide no intellectual challenge to children. A particular game may be educational for some children but not others. Kamii and DeVries (1980) discuss criteria for educational games and present principles of teaching group games. Detailed accounts of how teachers use seven specific games are provided, with comments on teachers' strategies.

Children's play of games with rules is important for their intellectual, sociomoral, and personality development. Psychological research reveals stages in play that signal developmental progress. Educational research reveals how teachers can use games with rules as an important component of constructivist education that aims to promote children's development. Program comparison research reveals that young children in constructivist classrooms who play games on a regular basis are more advanced in their interpersonal understanding and ability to negotiate and resolve conflicts with peers. These findings suggest that games with rules should be seriously considered an important part of early education.

Bibliography

Baldwin, J. M. (1973). *Social and ethical interpretations in mental development.* New York: Arno. (Original work published 1897)

DeVries, R. (1970). The development of role-taking in young, bright, average, and retarded children as reflected in social guessing game behavior. *Child Development, 41* (3), 759–770.

DeVries, R., & Fernie, D. (1990). Stages in children's play of tic tac toe. *Journal of Research in Childhood Education, 4* (2), 98–111.

DeVries, R., Haney, J., & Zan, B. (1991). Sociomoral atmosphere in direct-instruction, eclectic, and constructivist kindergartens: A study of teachers' interpersonal understanding. *Early Childhood Research Quarterly, 6,* 449–471.

DeVries, R., & Kohlberg, L. (1990). *Constructivist early education: Overview and comparison with other programs.* 2nd Ed. Washington, DC: National Association for the Education of Young Children.

DeVries, R., Reese-Learned, H., & Morgan, P. (1991). Sociomoral development in direct-instruction, eclectic, and constructivist kindergartens: A study of children's enacted interpersonal understanding. *Early Childhood Research Quarterly, 6,* 473–517.

DeVries, R., & Zan, B. (1994). *Moral classrooms, moral children: Creating a constructivist atmosphere in early education.* New York: Teachers College Press.

Kamii, C., & DeVries, R. (1980). *Group games in early education: Implications of Piaget's theory.* Washington, DC: National Association for the Education of Young Children.

Kohlberg, L. (1987). *Child psychology and childhood education: A cognitive-developmental view.* New York: Longman.

Mead, G. H. (1962). *Mind, self, and society.* Chicago: University of Chicago Press. (Original work published 1934)

Piaget, J. (1963). *Play, dreams, and imitation in childhood.* New York: Norton. (First published as *La formation du symbol chez l'enfant: Imitation, jeu et reve, image et representation.* Delachaux et Niestle, 1945.

Piaget, J. (1965). *The moral judgment of the child.* New York: Basic Books. (Original work published 1932)

Selman, R., & Shultz, L. (1990). *Making a friend in youth.* Chicago: University of Chicago Press.

Sport as Play (and Work)

Dan C. Hilliard

Whether sport as a form of social activity is more like work or play is a question that emerged in the beginnings of the sociology of sport and has not yet been resolved. Empirical studies of youth sport and of adult recreational sport find elements of work and play in each. In recent years, there has been a tendency for sport sociologists to emphasize the worklike characteristics of sport and to deemphasize its playful elements. What is needed is a conception of sport that recognizes the coexistence of play and work elements in the sport experience.

Perspectives on Sport as Play (and Work)

In his seminal article "American Sports: Play and Display," Gregory P. Stone (1973) explores the relationship of sport and play, claiming that "sport and play are fraught with anomalies" (Stone, 1973, p. 68). One anomaly is the confusion of the play and work dimensions within sport. Popular sports, for example, are "played" by professional "players," thus becoming work (Stone, 1973, p. 75). As the discipline of sport sociology has developed in the twenty-plus years since Stone's article, the relative roles of play and work in our understandings of sport have remained, at least implicitly, a major issue for scholars in the field.

Pioneers in sport sociology borrowed heavily from the works of Huizinga (1955) and Caillois (1961) and therefore included the element of play in their understandings of sport. Loy (1969) applies Caillois's characteristics of play to sport and concludes that sport contains most of the elements of play. He notes that the free nature of play is common to some forms of amateur sport but certainly not to professional sport; that spatial and temporal separateness definitely characterize sport; that there is an attempt in sport to ensure uncertainty of outcome; that sport is unproductive in the sense that no new material goods are produced; that sports are governed by extensive rules; and that sport stands outside ordinary or real life. One early leader in the field of sport sociology strongly disagrees, however, claiming that play and sport are mutually exclusive categories (Edwards, 1973). He proposes a four-fold classification of play, contest, game, and sport. This view defines play by the intrinsic pleasures it produces and has "no seriousness, purpose, meaning, or goals for the actor beyond those emerging within the boundaries and context of the play act itself" (p. 49). In contrast, sport is defined by the presence of an external reward structure and is "carried out by actors who represent or who are part of formally organized associations having the goal of achieving valued tangibles or intangibles through defeating opposing groups" (pp. 57–58).

Implicit in this definitional struggle are assumptions about whether or not intrinsic and extrinsic rewards can occur through the same activity. Another approach to this problem would be to define sport in terms of features of the activity per se, namely, as a competitive activity based on physical skills, and to pose the issue of satisfactions as an empirical question (Hilliard, 1977, pp. 8–9). The following review will focus on the experience of sport participation, looking first at youth sport and then contrasting it with adult sport.

Studies of Youth Sport

An important early formulation on youth sport by Webb (1968) posited a process of "professionalization" of attitudes toward play during child development, such that an early emphasis on fairness in play eventually gives way to an emphasis on skill and victory. Researchers who tested this hypothesis with a sample of ten-and eleven-year-old boys found that those who participated in any form of organized sport placed a greater emphasis on skill and victory than did those boys not participating in organized sport (Mantel & Vander Velden, 1974). These and similar results may be interpreted as evidence for a socialization effect of youth sport participation. This interpretation, however, is limited by two significant methodological problems.

First, in cross-sectional studies, differences between subsamples may be antecedent to sport participation and may thus reflect a self-selection process (Du Bois, 1986). A cross-sectional study used a thirteen-item fixed response measure of attitudes toward participation among children in two soccer leagues, an "instructional league" and a "competitive league" (Du Bois, 1986). Subjects were tested multiple times over the course of two sport seasons. The results of this study support both a social selection and a social interaction interpretation. Social selection is supported by the fact that there were initial differences in attitudes between the instructional and competitive league participants. A social interaction model is supported by the finding that attitudes among both subsamples changed over the course of the study.

Second, the "professionalization" measure (Webb, 1968), which requires that respondents rank the importance of fairness, skill, and winning, may artificially create distinctions that participants do not make (Knoppers, Zuidema, & Meyer, 1989). Researchers developed the Game Orientation Scale (GOS) (Knoppers, Schuiteman, & Love, 1986) to alleviate problems inherent in ranking as a methodology, allowing for two separate orientations to emerge: a play orientation and a professional orientation. A subsequent use of this instrument with a sample of youth soccer and basketball camp participants found that there was a very weak correlation between the play and professional orientations of their subjects; that is, the data suggest that the play orientation and the professional orientation are *not* opposite ends of a continuum (Knoppers, Zuidema, & Meyer, 1989).

Greer and Lacy (1989) disputed Knopper's contention that the GOS is an improvement over the Webb scale. They employed a Context Modified Webb scale (CMW) to assess the attitudes of a sample of fourth- and fifth-graders (Lacy & Greer, 1992). They found that results on the GOS and the CMW were very similar.

Despite the large number of studies conducted on children's attitudes toward sport participation and despite the serious attention given to measurement issues in this area of research, few generalizations can be made. Older children and children with more extensive sport experience generally express more "professionalized" attitudes than younger children and those with less extensive sport experience. Girls generally express less professionalized attitudes than boys; however, when age and sport experience are carefully controlled, this difference may disappear.

Two major questions are still unanswered: First, do the play orientation and the professional orientation form a unidimensional continuum, or are they independent orientations? Second, are observed differences in orientation toward sport a function of social selection or social causation?

If sport experience influences attitudes, the structure of that sport experience affects the development of particular attitudes. Coakley (1980, 1983, 1986) compared informal, player-controlled games with formal, adult-controlled games. Informal games occurred in backyards and on playgrounds; players chose their own teams, devised their own handicapping systems and local rules modifications, and mediated their own disputes. In formal games, adults scheduled practices and games, adults directed the actions of players, and adults agreed upon rules and mediated disputes.

Coakley (1986) found that while informal games were oriented around action, formal games were oriented around rules. Participants in informal games valued action, personal involvement, a close score, and opportunities to be with friends. Participants in formal, adult-controlled games also emphasized action and personal involvement, especially by identifying their role in the game with the position they played. They were more likely to be "serious" about the game and to be concerned with game outcome than participants in informal games. Intrinsic rewards, however, still outweighed winning in importance, even among formal game participants.

Coakley (1986) questioned the impact of formal, adult-controlled sport on the developmental experience of youth by raising a number of questions: Does formal, adult-organized sport crowd informal, youth-controlled sport out of children's lives? What effect does participation in formal, adult-controlled sport have on the child's relationship with his or her family? Does emphasis on formal, adult-controlled sport produce burnout among young athletes? To date, none of these questions has been fully answered by empirical analysis.

An observational study of Little League baseball provides insight into the intersection of youth and adult worlds through formal, adult-controlled sport (Fine, 1987). The researcher discovered that while adults did try to use Little League baseball to teach "lessons for life" and to communicate an adult-imposed moral agenda, they were not totally successful. The players had their own concerns, and they expressed both sport-related concerns and broader cultural concerns in the context of interaction with coaches and teammates. Regarding the game itself, the boys seemed to combine a play frame with a more "serious" orientation. They were concerned about opportunities to enjoy the company of friends, to exchange gossip and banter, and to display their toughness and "coolness"; however, they were also interested in winning, and looked down on teammates and coaches whom they perceived as not making an appropriate effort to win.

Participation in Little League baseball, however, is also an opportunity for preadolescent boys to express nonsport concerns, particularly sexual and aggressive themes. Boys spend much time talking about sex, engaging in pranks aimed at girls and low-status boys, and trading insults and sexual banter. Through these activities, the boys create a subculture of preadolescence, quite apart from the moral socialization intended by the adult organizers of Little League. While the sexist and homophobic themes evident in this culture might be disturbing, the existence of the culture is proof of the failure of adult-directed sport to dominate the lives of youth. Also, much of the boys' activity is both physically and verbally playful. Thus, the experience of Little League baseball contains both elements of sport as a context for play and sport as preparation for the world of work.

Because adult-directed and even some informal youth sport is modeled on adult sport,

conceptions of adult sport have an indirect effect on the sport experiences of children. The following sections, therefore, explore the play and work elements of adult sport.

Related Perspectives in Adult Sport as Recreation

While studies of youth sport focus on sport as part of the developmental process, a related perspective to adult sport participation defines sport as a voluntarily enacted recreational or leisure activity. The question of what social and psychological satisfactions adults obtain through sport participation, and how those satisfactions relate to dominant social roles, has been an important question in the sociology of sport, as in the sociology of leisure. Kenyon (1970) developed a scale measuring six dimensions of satisfaction from sport participation, which included general social satisfactions such as opportunity for affiliation; activity-specific satisfactions such as catharsis; the opportunity to experience risk; feelings of vertigo; and beneficial consequences of participation, such as improved physical fitness. Using a methodology similar to Kenyon's, Hilliard and Zurcher (1978) found that participants in adult sports leagues were able to obtain simultaneously a variety of satisfactions, from interacting with friends and "having fun," to enjoying the "immediate gratification" of a successfully executed skill, to receiving awards and status from sport success. In other words, they were able to enjoy both the "playful" and the "serious" elements of sport, and they avoided conflict between these two sport frames through techniques of physical and temporal segregation.

An important research tradition in the sociology of leisure attempts to link such satisfactions to characteristics of dominant roles through the compensatory and spillover hypotheses of leisure activity choice (Burch, 1969; Wilensky, 1960). The compensatory hypothesis suggests that individuals choose recreational activities substantially different from their ordinary routines, whereas the spillover hypothesis suggests that persons choose leisure activities that are similar in many ways to their dominant role activities. Steele and Zurcher (1973) argue for a compensatory interpretation of leisure activity choice in their study of bowlers. Mitchell (1983) implicitly does the same in his study of mountain climbers.

The compensatory and spillover hypotheses, however, present a host of problems. First, one must distinguish between patterns of participation per se and the meanings associated with participation. For example, direct comparisons of rates of participation in physical activity—male versus female, younger versus older adult, working class versus professional class, and so forth—may lend support for the spillover hypothesis, even as the study of meanings suggests a compensatory interpretation. Persons with active, demanding jobs may engage in active, demanding leisure activities, but they may claim they are doing so because their leisure activities meet needs unfulfilled by their work roles. A second, related, problem has to do with defining the dimensions along which compensation or extension occur. There are multiple dimensions to both work roles and leisure roles, and one may find patterns of compensation along one dimension combined with extension along another. In summary, a long research tradition extending back at least to the 1950s (Havighurst, 1957; Havighurst & Feigenbaum, 1959) has failed to demonstrate the superiority of either the compensatory or the spillover hypothesis.

A potentially more fruitful approach is to consider the leisure activity as a social context in its own right. Zurcher (1970) applies his concept of the "ephemeral role" to a "friendly poker game"; Steele and Zurcher (1973) apply the same concept to bowlers across a range of skill levels. Drawing upon Huizinga's (1955) ideas about play, the ephemeral role concept emphasizes the separateness of the leisure scene and the temporary suspension of ordinary roles and statuses. This idea of the leisure scene as a world unto itself is developed in two important bodies of literatures, one on "flow" and the other on sport subcultures.

In *Beyond Boredom and Anxiety,* Csikszentmihalyi (1985) discusses the concept of "flow," a physical and mental state of unity and focus accomplished through immersion in the intrinsic satisfactions of a challenging activity: "Flow is potentially the most creative, the most fulfilling kind of experience, because it is free of phylogenetic and historical constraints and hence allows people to experiment with new actions and new challenges" (p. 185).

The subtitle of his study, *The Experience of Play in Work and Games,* is significant. Flow may be achieved through work, as a chapter on surgery illustrates. Sport or demanding physical activity, such as rock climbing, may also produce flow (MacAloon & Csikszentmihalyi, 1985). The structure of sport, however, and particularly its rules and its emphasis on extrinsic rewards, may limit participants' opportunities to achieve flow. Competition in sport, in particular, may result in levels of concentration and focus that produce flow, but it may also paralyze participants in the following way: "the merging of action and awareness which typifies the flow state does not allow for the intrusion of an outside perspective with such worries as 'How am I doing?' or 'Why am I doing this?' or even 'What is happening to me?' (MacAloon & Csikszentmihalyi, 1985, p. 90). More recently, Csikszentmihalyi (1990) has investigated the broader range of conditions under which flow may be achieved, including bodily movement, and other physical sensations such as sex, music, and taste.

Thus sport as a separate sphere of life that presents the opportunity to engage in challenging physical activity may encourage the attainment of flow. Sport as a structure emphasizing performance norms, rules, and extrinsic measures of success, however, may discourage the attainment of the flow state.

Closely related to the idea of flow is the study of the experience of emotion in sport. The sociology of emotions is a relatively new field, beginning with a study on "emotion work" among airline attendants (Hochschild, 1983). Zurcher (1982) developed the notion of "the staging of emotion" and applied it to the experience of college football players. Researchers later applied the concept to minor league hockey players (Gallmeier, 1987) and to recreational triathletes (Hilliard, 1986). In the staging of emotion, various sensory stimuli combine with expectations expressed by coaches, team leaders, and peers to divide the athletic event into a sequence of stages, during each of which participants may, and indeed are expected to, express certain emotions in socially acceptable ways. While the concept of flow emphasizes individual experience and the personal construction of meaning, the staging of emotion emphasizes public expression of feelings within a socially constructed environment. Nevertheless, the emotions expressed are "real" and in some cases intrinsically satisfying, for example, the shared expression of elation following a team victory.

More recently a researcher used a photo elicitation methodology to study emotions among collegiate women gymnasts (Snyder, 1990). He found that participants expressed both negative emotions (fear of injury and failure, frustration, and disappointment) and positive emotions (happiness and joy) in this demanding individual sport. The gymnasts expressed emotions according to "feeling rules" that were part of the subculture of the sport.

The work on the sociology of emotion in sport suggests the importance of sport subcultures in providing and affirming meanings that produce satisfactions among participants. A useful model of subcultural influence that can be applied to the world of sport is the processual model (Becker, 1953), originally used to explain continuing marijuana use. This model contends that experienced participants teach novice participants in any culture both skills and techniques and meaning systems. Continued participation is contingent, therefore, on the novice's being able to accept and internalize the proffered meanings. In this sense, satisfaction with a leisure activity is socially constructed. Applying this notion to sport participation, other researchers argue that social or affiliational satisfactions predominate in the early stages of involvement in a sport subculture, and that skill-specific and status-affirming satisfactions are layered onto the affiliation satisfactions over time as participants develop skills (Hilliard & Zurcher, 1978).

A relevant study addresses an important aspect of the development of commitment to a sports subculture (Donnelly & Young, 1988). The researchers note that every sport subculture contains inherent contradictions that are only discovered after the novice gets beyond the mythical image of the sport created for public consumption. Rock climbers, for example, generally claim that rock climbing is neither extremely dangerous nor highly competitive. But novice climbers soon discover that climbing is very dangerous; they also discover that there is much more competition within the subculture of climbing than they had originally anticipated. Persons who cannot come to grips with this disjunction between prior perception and "reality" will discontinue participation. Those who can resolve or tolerate these apparent contradictions will go on to incorporate participation in the subculture into their identity and use this identity in their public presentation of self.

Finally, recent work within the cultural studies paradigm has emphasized adolescent and adult sport subcultures as important sites

of resistance to hegemonic ideology. Beal (1995) shows how skateboarders collectively resist the competitive structure of sport that mimics the work setting. Granskog (1992) has demonstrated that triathlon participation is a liberating experience for women who had little opportunity during adolescence to explore their interests and abilities in sports. Guthrie and Castelnuovo (1995) found the potential for personal liberation and social transformation in the activities of elite female bodybuilders. All of these studies point to the personal and political potential of playful physical activity, but in every case there are both social structural and cultural constraints that limit the transformative power of the activity.

In summary, there exists a substantial literature on the social psychology of adult recreational sport. This literature emphasizes the satisfactions obtained through participation in an activity that is separate from one's dominant social roles and their attendant obligations. There is strong evidence in this literature that a play element exists in adult sport.

Paradigm Shift in Sport Sociology

Thorne (1994) claims that the emerging specialty area in the sociology of childhood is granted low prestige within sociology in the United States because the prevailing socialization model assumes that children are simply in the process of developing into adults. If play is associated with childhood and work with adulthood, one would expect a sociology of sport that emphasized sport's playful qualities to suffer low prestige as well. Indeed, this seems to be the case. The sociology of sport, which began in the United States and Canada in the mid-1960s, has emerged as a serious specialty area within the past thirty years, in kinesiology if not in sociology. The legitimation of this new specialty area has been accompanied by a paradigm shift, the result of which has been to de-emphasize the link between sport and play and to emphasize the link between sport and work.

Hemphill (1992) argues that two major views of sport exist: (1) a "traditional" conception of sport as an extension of play, and (2) a contemporary conception of sport as an extension of alienated capitalist labor. The work of U.S. sport historian Allen Guttmann (1978) represents the former category, while European philosophers of sport (Brohm, 1978; Rigauer, 1982) best exemplify the latter.

This reconceptualization of sport as work is related to a broader paradigm shift in sociology generally and in the sociology of sport in particular, in which the traditional sociological paradigms—functionalism, Marxism, and symbolic interactionism—have been superseded by new perspectives, such as critical theory, cultural studies, and postmodernist social criticism. Whereas the functionalist paradigm generally treats sport as an institution reflecting the characteristics of the larger society (see Eitzen & Sage, 1982, for an example of a text using such an approach), the cultural studies paradigm treats sport as a crucial cultural institution that serves to reproduce the social relations of late capitalist societies (see Sage, 1990, for an example of a text using this approach). In communicating an ideology that supports these stratified social relations, sport adopts a worklike, "no pain, no gain" philosophy. Hoberman (1988) refers to this emphasis in modern sport as the "performance principle," in which the human body is objectified and is subjected to highly technologized training techniques in a search for ever better sport performance. Thus, sport can easily be used to illustrate *The McDonaldization of Society* (Ritzer, 1993), characterized by efficiency, calculability, predictability, and increased control through the substitution of nonhuman technology for human activity.

The cultural studies paradigm also emphasizes the study of mediated sport as mass entertainment, thus shifting attention away from recreational athletes to professional and quasi-professional athletes (such as intercollegiate and amateur Olympic athletes). This is consistent with the reconceptualization of sport as an extension of alienated capitalist labor (Hemphill, 1992). The problem with this perspective is that the athletes themselves rarely complain about this exploitation. While their lack of complaint may be evidence of false consciousness and the effectiveness of sport as ideology, it is also likely that athletes experience intrinsic satisfactions through sport, even those who are most subjected to rationalized training techniques and to the pressures of high-profile athletic performance. The challenge is to produce a conceptualization of sport that avoids the dichotomization of sport as *either* work *or* play, moving toward a more complex understanding of how play and work elements "play" upon one another in this complex human institution.

Both children's sport and adult sport contain elements of play as well as elements of work. The increasing commodification and professionalization of adult sport in the late twentieth century and the shift toward new paradigms in the social sciences have led to a cultural emphasis on the work elements of adult sport. This has consequences for children's sport, too, since adult-directed children's sport is modeled on adult sport. Perhaps a return to the serious study of children's sport would serve to remind sport scholars of the importance of play in sport.

Bibliography

Beal, B. (1995). Disqualifying the official: An exploration of social resistance through the subculture of skateboarding. *Sociology of Sport Journal*, 12, 252–267.

Becker, H. (1953). On becoming a marihuana user. *American Journal of Sociology, 59*, 235–242.

Brohm, J. M. (1978). *Sport: A prison of measured time.* London: Inks Links.

Burch, W. (1969). The social circles of leisure: Competing explanations. *Journal of Leisure Research, 1*, 125–148.

Caillois, R. (1961). *Man, play, and games.* New York: Free Press.

Coakley, J. (1980). Play, games and sport: Developmental implications for young people. *Journal of Sport Behavior, 3,* 99–118.

Coakley, J. (1983). Play, games and sports: developmental implications for young people. In J. C. Harris & R. J. Parks (Eds.), *Play, games, and sports in cultural contexts* (pp. 431–450). Champaign, IL: Human Kinetics.

Coakley, J. (1986). *Sport in society: Issues and controversies.* St. Louis: Times Mirror-Mosby.

Csikszentmihalyi, M. (1985). *Beyond boredom and anxiety.* San Francisco: Jossey-Bass.

Csikszentmihalyi, M. (1990). *Flow: The psychology of optimal experience.* New York: Harper & Row.

Donnelly, P., & Young, K. (1988). The construction and confirmation of identity in sport subcultures. *Sociology of Sport Journal, 5,* 223–240.

Du Bois, P. (1986). The effect of participation in sport on the value orientations of young athletes. *Sociology of Sport Journal, 3,* 29–42.

Edwards, H. (1973). *Sociology of sport.* Homewood, IL: Dorsey.

Eitzen, S., & Sage, G. (1982). *Sociology of North American sport.* Dubuque, IA: Wm. C. Brown.

Fine, G. (1987). *With the boys: Little League baseball and preadolescent culture.* Chicago: University of Chicago Press.

Gallmeier, C. (1987). Putting on the game face: The staging of emotions in professional hockey. *Sociology of Sport Journal, 4,* 347–362.

Granskog, J. (1992). Tri-ing together: An exploratory analysis of the social networks of female and male triathletes. *Play & Culture, 5,* 76–91.

Greer, D., & Lacy, M. (1989). On the conceptualization and measurement of attitudes toward play: The Webb scale and the GOS. *Sociology of Sport Journal, 6,* 380–390.

Guthrie, S., & Castelnuovo, S. (1995). Elite women bodybuilders: Models of resistance or compliance? *Play & Culture, 5,* 401–408.

Guttmann, A. (1978). *From ritual to record.* New York: Columbia University Press.

Havighurst, R. (1957). The leisure activities of the middle-aged. *American Journal of Sociology, 63,* 152–162.

Havighurst, R., & Feigenbaum, K. (1959). Leisure and life-style. *American Journal of Sociology, 64,* 396–404.

Hemphill, D. (1992). Sport, political ideology and freedom. *Journal of Sport and Social Issues, 16,* 15–33.

Hilliard, D. (1977). *Adult participation in organized leisure sports activities.* Unpublished doctoral dissertation, University of Texas at Austin.

Hilliard, D. (1986). *The staging of emotions in endurance athletic competitions.* Paper presented at the Western Social Science Association, Reno, NV.

Hilliard, D., & Zurcher, L. (1978). The temporal segregation of activities and their meanings in leisure sports settings. *Leisure Today, 26,* 58–62.

Hoberman, J. (1988). Sport and the technological image of man. In W. Morgan & K. Meier (Eds.), *Philosophic inquiry in sports* (pp. 319–328). Champaign, IL: Human Kinetics.

Hochschild, A. (1983). *The managed heart.* Berkeley: University of California Press.

Huizinga, J. (1955). *Homo ludens: The study of the play element in culture.* Boston: Beacon.

Kenyon, G. (1970). Six scales for assessing attitudes toward physical activity. In W. Morgan (Ed.), *Contemporary readings in sport psychology* (pp. 83–94). Springfield, IL: Charles C. Thomas.

Knoppers, A., Schuiteman, J., & Love, B. (1986). Winning is not the only thing. *Sociology of Sport Journal, 3,* 43–56.

Knoppers, A., Zuidema, M., & Meyer, B. (1989). Playing to win or playing to play? *Sociology of Sport Journal, 6,* 70–76.

Lacy, M., & Greer, D. (1992). Conceptualizing attitudes toward play: The game orientation scale and the context modified Webb scale. *Sociology of Sport Journal, 9,* 286–294.

Loy, J. (1969). The nature of sport: A definitional effort. In G. Kenyon & J. Loy (Eds.), *Sport, culture, and society* (pp. 56–71). London: Collier-Macmillan.

MacAloon, J., & Csikszentmihalyi, M. (1983). Deep play and the flow experience in rock climbing. In J. C. Harrins & R. J. Park (Eds.), *Play, games and sports in cultural contexts* (pp. 361–384). Champaign, IL: Human Kinetics.

Mantel, R., & Vander Velden, L. (1974). The relationship between the professionalization of attitude toward play of preadolescent boys and participation in organized sport. In G. Sage (Ed.), *Sport and American society: Selected readings* (pp. 172–179). Reading, MA: Addison-Wesley.

Mitchell, R. (1983). *Mountain experience.* Chicago: University of Chicago Press.

Rigauer, B. (1982). *Sport and work.* New York: Columbia University Press.

Ritzer, G. (1993). *The McDonaldization of society.* Thousand Oaks, CA: Pine Forge Press.

Sage, G. (1990). *Power and ideology in American sport.* Champaign, IL: Human Kinetics.

Snyder, E. (1990). Emotion and sport: A case study of collegiate women gymnasts. *Sociology of Sport Journal, 7,* 254–270.

Steele, P., & Zurcher, L. (1973). Leisure

sports as "ephemeral roles": An exploratory study. *Pacific Sociological Review, 16,* 345–356.

Stone, G. (1973). American sports: Play and display. In J. Talamini & C. Page (Eds.), *Sport and society: An anthology* (pp. 65–84). Boston: Little Brown.

Thorne, B. (1994). *Gender play.* Address given to the North American Society for the Sociology of Sport.

Webb, H. (1968). Professionalization of attitudes toward play among adolescents. In G. Kenyon (Ed.), *Aspects of contemporary sport sociology* (pp. 161–178). Chicago: Athletic Institute.

Wilensky, H. (1960). Work, careers, and social integration. *International Social Science Journal, 12,* 543–560.

Zurcher, L. (1970). The friendly poker game: A study of an ephemeral role. *Social Forces, 49,* 173–186.

Zurcher, L. (1982). The staging of emotions: A dramaturgical analysis. *Symbolic Interaction, 5,* 1–19.

Play in the Disciplines and Professions

Introduction

Play begins within the first year of life and continues throughout life in different forms that are more or less socially acceptable in particular contexts. Play also pervades most fields of study and work in some form, although often at a tacit rather than articulated level. There is playfulness, for example, in generating new knowledge within the multiple methods of inquiry in different fields of study. One might playfully ask: How does this canon play? (*Canon* refers to the generally accepted ways of studying and structuring knowledge and practice within the recognized disciplines and ways of knowing of a particular culture.) One might ask: Should there be a canon? What political forces influence the decisions and priorities? To what extent does play exist as a featured way of knowing? How might people become more aware of the assumptions that guide their playful or non-playful behavior?

That adults in the United States have not typically categorized their work activities as playful may lead to a general devaluing of play, even for children. Even when playfulness is not tolerated within the canon and scope of a field, it is possible to imagine that there is a body of expression in literature or behavior that transforms disciplinary knowledge, the workplace, and tasks within the discipline, through playful ways of knowing.

In this section specialists from an array of disciplines and professions tell about how they play as adults within their respective fields. Their views provide additional insight into the power of play to enrich human experience even in the workplace. Representatives from the arts and humanities, the natural and social sciences, and the professions that variously draw upon their respective disciplines have met the challenge of self-reflection and explored the potential of multiple ways of knowing through viewing playfulness within their adult conceptions of disciplinary knowledge. They have shared the playful experiences that take place within their respective fields of specialization and conveyed lucidly the ways in which their playful selves fit into the contexts of their chosen life's work. Their observations and insights can help to illuminate our perspectives about play in childhood.

Different fields encompass a different balance between work as playful in itself and work in an environment that might facilitate or generate playfulness. There is a distinction in this sense between the relative focus on content and the contextual balance of playfulness and nonplay. Preparing for work in medicine, for example, entails challenges and risk-taking; an environment that can be overwhelming might be survivable at some moments by humor, such as joking about a "cadaver ball" held in many medical schools after students complete a year's work in the anatomy laboratory.

Play across the disciplines, therefore, provides for the participating adults the experiences of relief, community, satisfaction, humor, friendly mischief, and, occasionally, new connections. Their playful experiences at work (as well as at leisure) can create contextual forces that might affect a societal and cultural climate for play in childhood. It is also worthwhile, therefore, to consider what the multiple forms of adult play within their professional fields tell us about what adults need to do with children in terms of tolerating, sanctioning, valuing, soliciting, facilitating, and encouraging play and playfulness.

These particular contributions also highlight the value of retaining, rather than extinguishing, the kind of play in which children can express their power to self-organize and be self-directed learners and community members. The essays also underscore the importance of balance and having enough time to explore as well as to play, to fool around and tinker with the physical world, and to daydream.

The Arts and Humanities

Transcendence in the Play of Remembrance

William R. Myers

To play is to participate in the creation of the human being in its fullest context. This is a task of meaning and hence of religion. And yet religion, when defined as beliefs and practices regarding ultimacy held in common by persons in a formal tradition, rarely is helpful in discussing play. For example, in what is only a slight oversimplification, the Protestant tradition came to believe that hard work was indicative of good moral character and therefore was rewarded with material success. Given this view, coupled with the belief that the child was predisposed to ignorance and sin, play was devalued to be at best a distraction for the child and at worst a sign of how far the child had strayed from the will of God.

As an ordained minister working within the Protestant tradition, the author inherited (and was socialized into) this viewpoint. He might read how theological giants like Aquinas and Augustine once claimed play as a necessary virtue for being more fully human (Rahner, 1967), but as a Protestant he avoids play. His work, on the other hand, consumes a lot of his energy and time. Some might say that while he works too hard, his satisfaction in that role is born of work's righteousness. In any case, he tends to fill his spare time apart from work with useful "projects," a euphemism for still more work.

It seems to me that he has come to embody what the Victorians set out to achieve; that is, by turning almost every natural activity into a utilitarian task, he has set work *against* play (Cohen, 1987). Play then becomes an illicit reward for work, so that even on those rare occasions when he does play, afterward he experiences guilt at his so doing, because he could have used that time to complete a work task.

Others have similar perspectives. The cartoon character Calvin of *Calvin and Hobbes*

fame, for example, confronts his father one day with a question: "How come grown-ups don't go out to play?" A good question, and Calvin's father lets him in on the adult secret: "Grown-ups can only justify playing outside by calling it exercise, doing it when they'd rather not, and keeping records to quantify their performance." Calvin exclaims: "That sounds like a job." To which his father responds: ". . . except that you don't get paid." Then Calvin asks a follow-up question: "So play is worse than work?" His father concludes, "Being a grown-up is tough" (Watterson, 1995).

As text, this cartoon expresses the adult dilemma regarding work and play. That Calvin, the child protagonist of the comic strip, shares the name of a major Protestant founder, John Calvin, only makes the cartoon more pointed. That Calvin's father responds to Calvin's question with how adults "justify" playing out of a product-oriented, work's righteousness position can only be meant to stand in contrast with the Protestant Reformation's concept of justification *by faith alone*. Making play "worse than work" is the ironic conclusion drawn by Calvin during this exchange, and whether or not Calvin's father is exacting his own peculiar revenge on Calvin for his being a rambunctious child (willfully ignorant and prone to sin) does not make much difference here, because being a grown-up *is* tough, particularly when people are trying to understand what it means to be human in a rapidly changing technological world.

Renewing Playfulness

When an infant takes a first step, is this "work" or is it "play"? This may be a false polarity, because to the infant it clearly is both things. Thus, one perspective contends that play is children's work; for adults, play is not work, again using the false polarity. But then, the childlike comingling of work and play becomes lost to adulthood. This dilemma underlies the *Calvin and Hobbes* cartoon cited above, and while the reader may laugh at Calvin, it is laughter born of recognition.

How do human beings come to play, anyway? One important view is that play initially emerges in the relational interplay of mother and child (Erikson, 1976). Both mother and child arrive at such relational interplay with "the joint need . . . for a mutuality of recognition, by face and by name" (Erikson, 1994, p. 44). This view contends that we transfer some of our earliest forms of "I" and "you" from this maternal relationship to other relationships, including "a divine thou" (Erikson, 1981, pp. 330–331). Clearly this line of thought resonates with stories such as those contained in Genesis, the initial book of the Torah. In that book, Adam and Eve are at play in the mythical garden of Eden and have every need fulfilled except their desire to be like God. Their pursuit of this desire results in extraction from the garden and introduces them into a world filled with work and pain. Work, therefore, becomes the punishment for the Fall from the garden. The relationship of Adam and Eve to God is that of children to parent: the child is known face-to-face and by name; the child plays, grows up, becomes adult, and enters the world of work to play no more.

But is this every adult's fate? Here the epigenetic stance of Erikson offers a counterpoint. Quoting Jesus' saying, "whoever does not receive the Kingdom of God like a child shall not enter it" (Mark 10:14–16), Erikson postulates "an adult condition in which childlikeness has not been destroyed, and in which a potential return to childlike trust has not been forestalled" (1994, p. 349). Jesus' saying "unless you turn and become like children" (Matthew 18:3) mandates a return by all adults to such childlikeness via "a positive 'metanoia'" (Erikson, 1994, p. 348). Erikson concludes that, for adults, "what is suggested, then, is a preservation and reenactment of the wonder of childhood: the innocent eye and ear" (1994, p. 349). Thus in Erikson's view: "the adult was once a child and a youth. He [*sic*] will never be either again: but neither will he ever be without the heritage of those former states. In fact, I would

postulate that, in order to be truly adult, he must on each level renew some of the playfulness of childhood and some of the sportiveness of the young" (1976, p. 701).

Ritualization and Transcendence

But what are we "renewing"? For Erikson, human beings come to play in the way(s) they do, both as children and as adults, in large part because the relational interplay of child and mother is not only mutual and playful, but also because it is formalized. *Ritualization* is the positive term used by Erikson (1994) to describe this regularized and recurring kind of interplay. An example of this ritualization is the behavior of the author's sixteen-month-old daughter, Michal, who became so adept at inventing ways of playing peekaboo that her father called her "the tiny peekaboo-er." She would crawl, dragging a diaper, into her mother's lap. Sitting upright, she would drape the diaper over her head. After waiting for a few moments, she would jerk the diaper away, shrieking with delight. As she continued to grow, much of her play would center on placing her teddy bear in a clothes closet, banging the door shut, saying, "Bye, bye, bear," and then quickly opening the door again. Still later, one of her favorite games was to ask her mother for a key. After receiving the key, she would open the front door, toddle through the doorway, and slam the door behind her while saying, "I goin' bye bye, Mommy." Holding her key, she would play at locking the door and then knock on it. If her knocking did not result in her mother's immediately opening the door, she would call, "I home, Mommy." We can see that Michal was playing through a very real question: What happens when Mommy or Daddy go to work? (Myers & Myers, 1992).

Erikson's idea of ritualization is helpful in contemplating Michal and her play. Indeed, without such ritualizations, Michal would have been metaphorically at sea when the door closed and a parent left. Without the abstracting capability of adults, children need consistent object relations. In such relationship lies the core of basic trust and the initiation of "I," "you," and "thou" (Erikson, 1981). There is a lag between "object permanence," which is the understanding that objects continue to exist even when they are out of sight (Piaget, 1952), and the understanding that the most important persons in our lives continue to love us (Mahler,

1968). Children must develop this latter type of "object permanence" even while they experience the fact that adults often must leave children. Of key concern is that those who care for the child during such an absence can also be trusted. The third time a familiar babysitter, Meredith, arrived at our home, Michal began to chant, "No moy Meredith, no moy Meredith." She had figured out that when Meredith arrived, her parents left. Having heard Michal's chant, we would say goodbye, leave the house, walk around a nearby corner, wait a few moments, and then return to listen at the door to see how it was going. And when we did this, we were able to hear Michal and Meredith happily playing. Michal had made her complaint, but she was able to move beyond the pain of our leaving because she was within the safe caregiving of familiar and trusted Meredith.

This, then, is an example of *transcendence*. The word transcend comes from *transcendere*, which literally means "to climb over" (McKechnie, [*Webster's*] 1983, p. 1937). Transcendence points at the process of moving over, going beyond, across, or through real or imagined limits, obstacles, or boundaries. Young children are continuously issued invitations to transcendence by the contexts in which they live. Families, other adults, and communal institutions implicitly anchor such invitations within cultural and religious value systems. In the United States autonomy is highly prized and children are given ample early opportunities to play through, that is, to engage actively in transcending the scary occasions when parents leave and children may feel lonely, even when a trusted babysitter provides an anchor.

In similar fashion, persons of all ages continually choose to engage actively in (or reject) the possibilities of transcendence presented to them in the circumstances of their daily living. Walking to lunch one day in my urban, university neighborhood, for example, I met a person I had not seen for a long time. Explaining to me that she was "playing," she said that "the kids are grown now" and that she was "tired of the humdrum, quiet, suburban lifestyle." She was spending much of her time attending lectures and walking in the university neighborhood while "asking myself if I could live here." As we walked and talked, I realized how invested she was in negotiating this major life change. She had come to suburban living as a young wife and mother. Her corporate husband, whose ample earnings had supported her at home, demanded a divorce after fifteen years of marriage. She had then taken a job, kept the house, raised the children, and never remarried. Now she saw life presenting her with an invitation that might mean positive change as well as potential loss, and she found herself wondering whether she could leave suburbia and step out in a new way to live within this interesting yet scary urban terrain. She knew that she wanted to grow beyond her suburban world, but she was fearful that her concerns about moving would make her "chicken out." Thus, she has been "playing" at what such a move might be like for her, just as Michal played out her life transitions. This experience is an invitation of transcendence for this adult on her own.

Transcendence can be said to be the central process defining us both as human and as beings connected to a supreme being, God, ultimate other, or thou (Phenix, 1974). Transcendence is the inescapable reality of our existence and can be more easily understood as "the experience of limitless going beyond any given state or realization of being" (Phenix, 1974, p. 118). This possibility of "going beyond" means that the material certainties of my life as well as who I am are always open, never final, and continually exist within a context of ever wider relationships and possibilities. A closer look at these things uncovers their impermanence; that is, nothing, including who we are, is "just what it appears to be here and now without any further prospects or associations" (p. 118). Further, "it is phenomenologically not the case that some persons, called 'religious' or 'spiritual' types, experience [transcendence] while others do not" (p. 118). In that every human experience "is rooted in transcendence . . . analysis of all human consciousness discloses the reality of transcendence as a fundamental presupposition of the human condition" (p. 122).

Spirit, Hope, and World

Spirit becomes the word for naming "the property of limitless going beyond" (Phenix, 1974, p. 119). When a child like Michal is said to "have spirit," we mean that she is expressing "perennial discomfort and dissatisfaction with any and every finite realization" (p. 119). *Hope* is the sense that one can experience transcendence. However, certain cultures are only capable of generating themes of silence, and then hope has been cut out, spirit crushed, and transcendence shut down in that culture (Freire, 1968). Even under such conditions, however, the simple act—yet at the same time, complex, mysterious, and brave—of naming this culture's "theme of silence" gives voice to a hoped-for future, a *world-yet-to-come* that will be born of such spirit.

Alternatively, when I, as a middle-class theologian located in the United States, consider the world, I wonder if my interest in play is not conditioned by, and also a direct result of, my affluence; that is, the ways we have adapted in this country to manage our free time seem to me to reveal cultural patterns of alienation. "Having fun" often becomes our escape from moral sensitivity to those world concerns we want to avoid as well as their implications for our own middle-class existence. In this sense, play becomes a dodge and just one more commodified form linked with our self-serving interest to turn away from the problems of our globe. Recognition of these issues could tempt the theologian into making moral pronouncements; however, such a path often moves us back into a work's-righteousness orientation (where everything, including play, is judged according to its usefulness and "worth").

Sacred Play

Perhaps theologians would do better to reflect upon God's participation in creation, which participation involved meaningful (and useful) action, but which was not in any way a *necessary* action. God's activity in creation therefore often is likened to *play*, in that it is meaningful but not necessary. Created in the image of God, human beings also are called to be engaged (with God) in the ongoing creation of the universe. There is, however, one central difference, in that God's creation (God's play) is out of nothing; human creation (their play) is bracketed by what has been given (they are not God). Nevertheless, human beings are called to cocreate; that is, they are, with God, to engage playfully and spiritedly in their relational and hopeful future. Thus, when they play, they and all that has been given them, are at stake.

Play therefore anticipates liberation. A theologian suggests that "in playing we anticipate our liberation and with laughing rid ourselves of the bonds which alienate us from real life" (Moltman, 1972). Because true play (not the escape of "having fun") is the human vocation, it begins with relationship and is an ex-

pression of freedom and joyful participation in God's own transcendent process. In play human beings experience being *in* God's grace; they are created in the image of God, and despite their expulsion from the garden of Eden, continue to remain in relationship with God down through history. Thus, for human beings, there is deep longing "to play" in the creative activity of transcendence, almost as if they recognize in such play their beginning and their loss. In play, they can reconstruct their world; that is, participate in the creation (and the re-creation) of the human being in its fullest context. In adult play (comingling with work), we move from the known into the unknown. Thus humans spiritedly engage in the process of transcendence through playing.

Because the conditions of life often drive people into a purely utilitarian view of life—one that separates work from play, avoids the possibility of transcendence, and exists without much hope—religion often provides (at its best) a "counter-play of liturgy and sacrament" (Rahner, 1967, p. 10).

The Play of Remembrance

Echoing God's pleasure in creation (the initiation of human history), relational play is immune to the threats and rewards provided by a culture that defines worth in terms of commodity. Such freedom must be celebrated. Worship is often, but not always, an occasion for such celebration. In worship, a "play of remembrance" connects the past in the present even as participants hopefully embrace the future. The discursive gestures of a community at such play embody, surround, and immerse the players within the transcendent process of a relational image of a God who is both creator and liberator.

Such play is multivocal; it occurs in relational activity as dissimilar as prayer and protest. To play in the midst of other competing cultural discourses is often perceived to be a deadly serious activity for those who are thus confronted. To play may also, in similar circumstances, appear to be useless dithering, an irrational response to circumstances that demand something more forceful, such as intentional communal action or the straitjacket of enlightenment, rationality, or managerial control. Such play, for those within the play of remembrance, however, is a spirited relational embodiment of what it means to be fully human.

The events of an extended bike-hike trip provides an example of such play from the author's experience. Bike hikes are occasions when clusters of youth and adults spend up to two weeks in cross-country journeys of five to eight hundred miles. On one bike hike, tensions emerged when some experienced bikers who had wanted to ride one hundred miles per day were opposed by other riders for whom that distance was too long; three other youths felt isolated by the group and others pointed out that a number of cliques were being formed. Because of these tensions, any sense of a growing community trust was rapidly falling apart. At this point the planned celebration of Communion, a ritual of importance to this group, seemed to become a distant possibility. Because the minister needed to leave for an errand, the group decided to postpone Communion until his return.

After his departure, the fragmented group quickly tired of exploring the area and found itself in the church sanctuary discussing the trip. As they reviewed the week, they concluded that things were not going well; in fact, the evening, in the words of one group member, was "blah." The youth ministry senior staff member, sensing the group's low morale, took a chance. She suggested that everyone become involved in a mock funeral, pointedly connected to the events of the week, to be followed by a mock wedding. The role-play became elaborate, with forays into the church schoolrooms for costumes, and both youth and adults participated.

When the minister arrived back after midnight, he imagined that all the bikers would be asleep and Communion would not be held that night. Instead, he was greeted by a unified group who applauded his arrival, shouting, "We want Communion!" After singing songs, symbols of the week's ride were presented. One participant brought a water bottle, representing life and survival, from which all partook. Another held up a bike flag that represented his link with the rest of the group when his riding lagged behind. Everyone touched the flag and waved it at one another. Standing in a circle, group members reflected on their playing out their story, which was marked both by wilderness and promise. The minister realized that, within the "sacred space" of the church basement, realities had been fractured and altered through the play of remembrance. He felt changed as a result of this experience, having entered the play of remembrance as part of a mixed and hurting collection of individuals but leaving as a member of a tested community. He knew the next day's biking would be a moveable feast (and it was) (Myers, 1987).

There are many occasions when such plays of remembrance burst forth exuberantly. They are, in one moment, the liminal deconstruction and reconstruction of person and social worlds; that is, they embody relational participation in the transcendent process (Turner, 1969). Unfortunately, occasions for worship too frequently are culturally accommodated, ceremonial, stereotypical, and meaningless repetitions of ritual that has lost this playful, transcendent quality. Indeed, some traditions assert that the play of remembrance only occurs through the sermon; that is, through wordplay alone. While other traditions remain open to the inclusion of all five senses as gateways to remembrance, it is not sufficient to assume that such inclusion automatically guarantees the play of remembrance. What is needed is someone who knows the story and who understands how to steward the boundaries of such space so that those gathered can, together, become the play of remembrance.

As a theologian, the author believes that human beings are connected to God by what might be termed an *adult-God interplay* marked by God's certain presence and by humans' inborn ability to transcend. It is in the communal play of remembrance that believers come to invoke the presence of God (the one who limitlessly transcends) and to celebrate this interplay. The shape of the communal play of remembrance is therefore anchored by the believers' memories of mother-child interplay as well as by their adult conceptions of God's relationship with them (adult-God interplay) down through history.

Both the individual and the community engage in sacred play to the degree that they embrace the process of transcendence. While this is neither guaranteed nor the special property of participation in organized religions, the "playful cocreative work" of believers, and of their community, calls on the remembered past in the transcending present. With spirit, the gathered community expectantly begins to embody a future marked not with despair, but with hope.

Bibliography
Cohen, D. (1987). *The development of play.* New York: Routledge.

Erikson, E. H. (1976). Play and actuality. In J. S. Bruner, A. Jolly, & K. Sylva (Eds.), *Play: Its role in development and evolution* (pp. 688–704). New York: Basic Books.

Erikson, E. H. (1981). The Galilean sayings and the sense of "I." *Yale Review, 70*(3), 330–331.

Erikson, E. H. (1994). *The life cycle completed.* New York: Norton.

Freire, P. (1968). *The pedagogy of the oppressed.* New York: Seaburg.

Mahler, M. (1968). *On human symbiosis and the vicissitudes of individuation. Vol. 1.* New York: International Universities Press.

McKechnie, J. L. (Ed.) (1983). *Webster's New Universal Unabridged Dictionary* (2nd ed.). New York: Simon & Schuster.

Moltman, J. (1972). *Theology of play.* New York: Harper & Row.

Myers, B. K., and Myers, W. R. (1992). *Engaging in transcendence: The church's ministry and covenant with young children.* Cleveland: Pilgrim.

Myers, W. R. (1987). *Theological themes of youth ministry.* New York: Pilgrim.

Phenix, P. H. (1974). Transcendence and the curriculum. In E. W. Eisner & E. Vallance (Eds.), *Conflicting conceptions of curriculum* (pp. 117–133). Berkeley: McCutchan.

Piaget, J. (1952). *The origins of intelligence in children* (D. E. Berlyne, Trans.). New York: International Universities Press.

Rahner, H. (1967). *Man at play.* New York: Herder and Herder.

Turner, V. W. (1969). *The ritual process: Structure and anti-structure.* Chicago: Aldine.

Watterson, W. (1995). Calvin and Hobbes. *Chicago Tribune,* May 9, Sec. 5, p. 7.

Play in the Visual Arts

One Photographer's Way-of-Working

Hilary A. Johnson

Visual art is a practical activity in which elements such as skill, intention, problem solving, and meaning are all part of an artist's work. In this context, play in the arts is both creative and risky: creative because it helps provide the individual variation and unpredictable results that are critical to artistic activity, and risky because it may divert artists from their original intention. An example of how one photographer engages in playful activity can serve to illustrate these ideas.

Practical Creativity, Spontaneity, and Risk: An Artist's Play

Visual artists at work are much like people at work in other disciplines: they have skills to employ, intentions to achieve, media to work with that both constrain and provide opportunities, problems to solve, and criteria to judge the quality of the products of their efforts. Ultimately, they are looking for ways to discover, identify, clarify, elaborate, and express what they find meaningful.

While many people typically think of the visual arts as a creative discipline in which playful exploration is a natural part of the process, much of the work artists do is practical: they need to perfect techniques and skills, develop perception, master materials and equipment, and produce results while they work on a particular piece. In the visual arts, as in all the disciplines, individuals must make choices about where to invest their time and attention, about which direction to follow and which to forsake, and about the merit of the work they produce.

When the visual arts are viewed in this pragmatic way, the notion of play as an element of serious disciplinary work may seem out of place. Playfulness may lead people away from their intended direction. "Playing around," after all, can be uncontrolled and unskilled. Acts of playfulness may seem not to make sense because they are not grounded in concerns about reasoned choice and accepted standards of merit. In the context of the unpredictable nature of playful activity, the discussion that follows considers the meaning of playful activity in disciplinary work and its functional importance to the visual arts.

Play in the visual arts is immediate and responsive rather than planned out and goal-directed. Play is inventive and divergent rather than repetitive. The results of play are surprising and uncertain rather than predictable. Because play has all these dynamic qualities, engaging in it may make it difficult for artists to accomplish the practical work involved in a production-oriented discipline like the visual arts. Playful activity, for instance, may distract artists from their original intentions, or it may lead them to experiment with new, unreliable techniques. Despite these risky qualities, the ability to play is often a fruitful and crucial part of a visual artist's repertoire.

It would be nice at this point to be able to generalize about play and how it is exhibited by visual artists; however, the forms play can take and what these forms afford different artists are idiosyncratic: different artists play in different ways. It is, in part, the personalized ways that visual artists play that lends uniqueness to their use of the techniques and media they share in common. Ten painters with the same brushes, paper, and colors will find ten different ways to put imagery into form. In the arts, variation is critical, and play is one of the ways that artists create variation.

The major portion of this essay describes how one visual artist, a photographer, engages in playful activities. His playfulness is an integral part of his personal way-of-working, that is, it allows him to take advantage of unexpected photographic opportunities, to find images others might not see, and create new experimental ways-of-working others might not think of trying. At the same time, this same playfulness may divert this artist's attention away from the subject themes, primary goals, and intentions that make up his work. The ability to play can lead to new discoveries and new ideas, but not all new discoveries and ideas are fruitful ones. As it is discussed here, play can be both exciting in its potential for creativity and risky in its potential to take up precious time and attention with no guarantee of useful results.

The artist whose approach to photography will be described here is both a fine art photographer and a teacher of photography. He has generously allowed the author of this essay to join him in the field as well as in his studio to watch him work, and he has spent many hours reflecting out loud about his personal ways-of-working in the visual arts.

One Artist's Playful Way-of-Working

Steven Dzerigian is an artist of Armenian descent, with a full black beard, a curling mustache, sparkling coal-black eyes, a prominent nose, and an endless smile. His studio reflects his personality in its surprising combination of chaos and organization. Cluttered shelves, from ceiling to floor, are filled with collected shells, bones, and broken antique toys. Rusting road signs are nailed to the wall. A life-size mannequin stands in one corner dressed in an old jacket and a Skycap's patent leather visored hat. In another corner, a metallic gold, full-size drum set sits quietly waiting to be played.

In the midst of the eclectic and colorful mix of oddments, his work tables and materials are precisely laid out, the table surfaces clean and ordered. His tools, colored pencils, mat cutters, and the like are each given a specific place. His darkroom is small and efficient, personally designed and arranged to his taste. Slide trays and print drawers are neatly and precisely labeled. This studio has been long and well used; it has just what this artist needs and no extra space.

The lack of extensive studio space fits Steve's approach—he is not a studio photographer. This artist finds his images in the natural and human worlds around him. Being connected and involved in the "goings-on of the world" is of primary interest to him as a person and as an artist. Some critics have described photography as a medium that allows visual artists to distance themselves and objectify their subjects. However, in this case, the artist's excitement about the medium springs from the intimacy of both physical and visual involvement that his work engenders.

Searching for images is a constant activity for this photographer. Rather than planning ahead or working with preconceived ideas, Steve will often, as he puts it, "stalk" images. He goes into the world looking for the unexpected. In the following passage, he describes learning his approach to finding images during his early childhood from a remarkable source:

> One of my teachers had [a] great influence, and that was my dog, Namer. We were living in the country, and Namer would chase the neighbor's cattle into the fences, so we had to keep her roped up. I thought that was really a horrible thing to have to do, but it was necessary. I used to take her for walks on our triangular piece of property.
>
> All of a sudden I thought, "Why am I forcing her to go on my little path?" So I decided from that point on that I would follow her [path instead]. I would never let the lead get tight, so if she ran, I ran; if she stopped, I stopped: if she sniffed out something, I would follow. So I would follow her and she became a teacher.
>
> I basically learned my stalking techniques from this dog. I move quickly without thinking too much. If I suspect something, I kind of sniff it out and see what is happening. If it excites me, if it means something, then I will make an image. And then something else will get my attention, and it just happened by chance.

The process of stalking images to imprint on film, looking for images by lingering at one place and scrambling to the next, sniffing out the unexpected, savoring what you find, and wandering spontaneously while leaving your path to chance is an inherently playful approach. This photographer creates found, rather than planned, images.

He describes himself as working "intuitively." He says, "For me to meander about and to get there 'the long way' is more interesting. There is a variety, and I feel a freedom." It is feeling that guides him, excitement that motivates him, and his spontaneous response to the world he encounters that leads him to make the image he makes. In this way, playing and working merge in his search for images.

The photographic medium brings with it many technical constraints, such as the optic qualities of cameras and lenses, the limits of film and paper, and the processing and chemistry of development. At the same time, this medium is sensitive to the often illusive qualities of color, light, and contrast and is able to capture equally illusive events in time. Relying on the strengths of this medium, this photographer has developed a way-of-working within it that allows him to take advantage of the luck of discovery, the excitement of the unpredictable, fleeting moments, and his own spontaneous response to his world. He knows how to use his medium to record what captures his eye.

The spontaneity is an iconoclastic way of working in an art form historically dominated by what he calls the "previsualization tradition." He says of this tradition, "To visualize something ahead of time and then to make [the image] perfectly to match your visualization [was] the intended goal." He sees things differently:

> There is a loss every time you try to predict something photographically. There is a gain because you have control, but there is also a loss. Because I am making something quite different than it was in the real world, I don't hold on very dearly to what I think it should look like, or what it is supposed to look like. I like to give reality some room. I like to leave my preconceptions behind. I like to be surprised.

Other photographers can certainly work quite differently within this same medium. Where another artist might plan content and composition, Steve wants to take advantage of the unexpected. Where another artist might go looking for a particular subject, this artist likes to be "seized" and surprised by what he finds. Where another artist might work for a lifetime in one photographic format, on one theme, this artist works with many photographic techniques and with several themes simultaneously.

He describes what it feels like to be exploring all the "different possibilities" of his work by using the metaphor of the turbulent flow of a river. He says, "I will be floating around for a while going with the current. All of a sudden I will hit a spot and there will be a fork, and then all of a sudden I am in some rapids going in a [new] direction. It is still the same river, but I have flowed into a different realm because all of a sudden something else is exciting me. So I can't, I won't struggle to stay on that one calm part of the river. That would be exhausting." He is "seized" by "an idea or a feeling" as he would be seized by the "irresistible force of the rapids."

The urge to play—which in this case means to explore, to take chances, and to respond to the world in unpredictable ways—is as strong for this photographer as the force of the rapids in his metaphor. In these moments, Steve faces the potential risks and dangers of the playful activity he relies upon in his way-of-working. The joy of playful exploration may sometimes lead him away from the direction he has set for his work. The risk, he admits, "of always staying open to discovery" is that often he can be "pulled too soon out of an ongoing project" he has been working long and hard to develop. "We can cultivate variations and that it is exciting. The price for that is of course that you may vary off the path. The end result is you only have so much time, and the more time you spend in a variation the less time you may have with a primary theme."

The excitement of play, chance, and discovery, as well as the "satisfaction of building a coherent body of work in a particular theme" are critical to this photographer's "path" as an artist. To balance these two elements in his work, Steve is constantly thoughtful about the trade-offs he must make between enticing, playful diversions, and the developing themes he has in progress. He says: "At a certain point a choice has to be made, weighing the importance of following a diversion or working toward completion on a particular project. When I am interested in so many things I could easily just wibble-wobble off the path. So I maintain enough discipline to stay with something, to finish a project. On the other hand, willingness to experiment and play I think is always crucial."

To give an example of how he keeps his attention on both play and thematic progress, he refers to a current series of anthropomor-

Figure 1. Anthropomorphism, Death Valley, California. *Black and white print, hand colored with pencil. This image is part of the artist's anthropomorphism series and depicts a humanlike form discovered in the landscape of Death Valley.*

phic images displayed around his studio (see Figure 1).

> Oftentimes I'll be working on a project like this, but I am always out to discover. I am always ready to see more than the literal reality.
>
> That is what this anthropomorphism series touches on. It goes back to when my mother wanted me to eat scrambled eggs and I didn't want to eat them. As soon as she said, "Oh, see there, it looks like an elephant" or "That looks like a little bear," then I would eat it.
>
> And so I started seeing this animation in supposedly inanimate objects. Now I have given into that, instead of neglecting them I really look for them even more. . . . On the

other hand, while I may have a keen eye on finding anthropomorphisms, I try to stay open for other new discoveries.

This kind of dual attention allows him to "cultivate accidents that work, without succumbing to the whim of distraction."

Another way Steve works that allows him to keep the level of playfulness high in his way-of-working is by allowing many parallel themes to continue over time. Using another playful metaphor he describes how he manages these parallel themes. "So," he says, "I am juggling several themes at once. I am not looking for them to develop totally at one particular moment. I think they may be lifelong pursuits." He has confidence that, over time, "The larger body of work will surface in the process."

These larger bodies of work are both numerous and varied, including, among others, a landscape series, several different kinds of portrait series, a Polaroid found-object series, a computer-enhanced series, a hand-colored series, and a series depicting Mayan ruins. One theme in particular, which he has nicknamed "Little Ironies," consists of images that represent the ironic, humorous, and sometimes macabre side of humanity and nature. Some lighthearted, some filled with black humor, these images are explicitly playful in content.

Playfulness exists in both the working process of this artist and the subject themes he wishes to capture. On the one hand, while his technical proficiency is high, he allows, even depends on playful working methods to find and capture his images. On the other hand, even where he does rely on traditional uses of camera and film, the content of his images can take a playful turn, as in the anthropomorphism and "Little Ironies" series.

In one body of work, this artist has combined playfulness in technique and in content to create a series where play both creates and expresses. This group of unpredictable images springs solely from his enjoyment of spontaneity and play. He calls this way-of-working and its products "Choreophotography" (see Figure 2). This series combines a playful working process; it is spontaneous and unpredictable, with playful content. The subjects of the images are captured in surprising ways, with a playful technique; the images are printed from negatives, which creates a color reversal in the displayed images.

The title of this series comes from the dynamic way Steve uses the camera to make these images. He "dances" with his camera while taking the picture of the subject. In more traditional forms of photography, the camera is fixed, or at least still. The photographic images this traditional approach produces speak well about such qualities as "reality," "place," and "event." In "Choreophotography," the camera is moving; the images this technique produces thus address "movement," "time," "energy," and "chance." He describes the physical freedom he experiences and the quality of energy captured in these images in the following way:

Part of the reason for working this way was to have a sense of freedom—no tripod, not

Figure 2. Lunar Equilibrium. *Color negative print. This image (an example of "choreophotography") was achieved through the use of a very long exposure, camera movement, and flash lighting at night. The dark curving lines were drawn on the film by the artist pointing the camera at the moon and then moving the camera. The trees were captured with the illumination of photographic flash. The expected darks and lights are reversed in the image because it is a print of the film negative.*

even putting the camera up to the eye. Then I am just allowing the camera to move. I move the camera to mirror my response or feeling toward the situation. I might take something in the scene as a cue and then work with it. I don't think, I just respond. I move very quickly with this series.

Working this way produced images that revealed a different kind of energy, an energy that I could feel but I could not see when I took the picture.

In this series, with all the "jumping around, dancing, bouncing around, splashing in water or what have you, there is a lot of invested energy," and not a lot of control. Having worked on this theme for years and having "burned" many rolls of film, only thirty images have survived his demanding editing process to become part of the printed series. Shot mainly at night, with long exposure times that allow the camera to record movement through time, these images capture swirling carnival lights, street musicians in multiple echoing positions as they move while playing their instrument, and unusual views of nature made dynamic through the movement of the camera. It is a risky way to work, but that riskiness is part of what makes the finished images expressive.

These playfully created images depict a different kind of energy, energy that viewers can "feel" in the photographic images, but not necessarily "see" in the original subject. The representation in these images of this illusive quality of energy was an unpredictable surprise, a chance outcome rising out of an experimental way-of-working. Dancing with the camera, a playful uncontrollable activity, allows this "felt" quality of energy to manifest in the images. The essence of this photographer's approach to his work is to make room for this kind of unexpected result. He says, "If I get a handful of these images that really speak, that are genuinely on, it is enough. It is worth taking all the risks. To me that is really satisfying."

The Playful Path to Self-Expression

The preceding pages have been devoted to the description of how one particular kind of playful activity operates in one particular visual artist's approach. As previously discussed, not all artists play in the same way for the same reasons: it is this unpredictable nature of play that makes it a critical element of artistic practice. Play is one way variation and personal self-expression are achieved in the artistic professions.

Visual artists, like other professionals, can be educated in the techniques and procedures that are associated with their chosen media. Self-expression, that is, the compression of personal meaning into an artistic form, is more difficult to achieve. Each artist's path of self-expression is his or her own. Self-expression is not teachable in the traditional sense; it is not something that can be passed from teacher to student. Each artist must take the techniques they learn and invent a personal way-of-working. Because of the variation, surprise, unexpected results, new ways-of-seeing, and diversions play provides, it is one of the primary avenues for the discovery of personal self-expression in the visual arts.

Play in the visual arts can take as many forms as there are artists to create them. This essay has described the playful way-of-working of one visual artist, a photographer. In the work of this artist, his playful approach produces both his working process and the content of many of the images he creates. It allows him to take advantage of unexpected photographic opportunities, find images others might not see, and create new experimental ways-of-working others might not think of trying. However, this same playfulness is risky for two reasons: First, it may divert this artist's attention away from making headway on the major bodies of work he has in progress; second, play leads the artist to experiment with technical uncertainties that can produce unexpected, uncontrollable results.

The photographer described here uses a playful approach that allows him to work spontaneously, to stay open to discovery, to enjoy the unexpected, and to follow his personal excitement. He uses these playful ways-of-working in concert with discipline and a strong desire to build a coherent body of work to produce his personal forms of self-expression in the visual arts. Despite the risks involved in being diverted from his primary themes and intentions, it is acts of playfulness that allow this artist to produce work that is personal, genuine, and "really satisfying."

Further Reading

Bayles, D., & Orland, T. (1993). Art and fear: Observations on the perils (and rewards) of ARTMAKING. Santa Barbara: Capra.

Bruner, J. (1986). *Actual minds, possible worlds*. Cambridge, MA: Harvard University Press.

Dewey, J. (1934). *Art as experience*. New York: Wideview/Perigee.

Ecker, D. (1993). The artistic process as qualitative problem-solving. *Journal of Aesthetics and Art Criticism, 21*(3), 283–290.

Eisner, E. (1991). *The enlightened eye: Qualitative inquiry and the enhancement of educational practice*. New York: Macmillan.

Howard, V. A. (1982). *Artistry: The work of artists*. Cambridge, MA: Hackett.

Mintzberg, H. (1987, July/August). Crafting strategy. *Harvard Business Review, 65*(4), 66–75.

Nachmanovitch, S. (1990). *Free play: Improvisation in life and art*. Los Angeles: Jeremy P. Tarcher.

Sudnow, D. (1978). *Ways of the hand: The organization of improvised conduct*. Cambridge, MA: MIT Press.

The Playful Ways
of the Performing Artist

Anne L. Wennerstrand

According to Jung (1923, 1974), "The creation of something new is not accomplished by the intellect but by the play instinct acting from inner necessity. The creative mind plays with the objects it loves" (p. 123).

Elements of Dance

In its freest sense, play is doing for its own sake. Play is embodied behavior, and through playing with the elements he or she loves, the performing artist creates the vital essence of live performance. Playfulness, as both a spirit and a way of seeing, provides the energy at the heart of performing. Play is a way of perceiving. In dance, theater and music, play provides the means to explore and communicate in a flexible way. Choreographers, theater makers, and composers often use play and game structures both as modes of exploration and to generate material. Modern dance, in particular, which had its beginnings around the turn of the century, has evolved rapidly as a form. It owes some aspects of its evolution to the innovative use of basic locomotor movement, sports imagery, play, and game structures.

Since its inception, the genres of dance known as modern and postmodern have seen a great number of changes and variations. In the United States, modern dance began with the playful images of performing artist Isadora Duncan, a turn-of-the-century dancer, who was inspired by nature and the natural movement expression of the human body. Duncan built her dances by using the most basic movements inspired by child's play, such as skips, jumps, walks, runs, and hops. Her movement vocabulary, which she developed in opposition to the peripherally initiated movements of ballet, involved the use of the whole body. She advocated movement that was initiated from the center of the body outward. Considered outrageous at the time, her style was a rejection of the academic approaches to movement then being practiced. Her playful attitudes have survived and continue to inspire modern-day performers (Banes, 1980).

There has always been an emphasis on the personal in the development of modern dance in the United States. There also has been a rapid development of movement styles that express not only the particular physicality of a given choreographer but also his or her theories of movement as well as political and cultural concerns (Banes, 1980). As performers "revolt" against current style and theory, new forms rapidly emerge. This has made the history of modern dance cyclical; there are revolutions that become institutions, which are rejected and then adapted with variation. This rapid cycling has formed what we call modern and postmodern dance and fueled their eclectic development. Maintaining a playful attitude toward the development of form is meaningful as well as practical for artists who are breaking new ground in modern dance. The whole notion of art as a form of liberated play was an integral part of the performing arts community of the sixties' avant-garde movement (Banes, 1993). The evolution of modern dance during this century reflects the use of play and games, radical juxtapositions of disparate elements, indeterminacy, and chance. More recently, extreme play and appropriation of games from other cultures have become formative concerns for performers.

Improvisation

A central aspect of play is the ability to improvise. Like play, the act of improvising generates contexts that are in a state of transformation requiring moment-to-moment responses from the participants. Possibilities emerge during these transformations from which movement and movement relationships evolve.

Improvisation is that aspect of play which simultaneously involves inner and outer perceiving. To improvise, the performer composes randomly in the moment and in a spontaneous way. Actors, dancers, and musicians utilize improvisation for its own sake, or for generating material for performance. Thus it is both a device and a process. The instantaneous nature of improvisation is precisely what makes it so compelling.

In improvising, the performing artist develops and relies on a type of concentration that is wholly internal and subjective. This intrinsic subjectivity both inspires the performer and simultaneously provides a source of information. In the emptiness and potential of any given moment, the performer responds from this state of subjectivity. The subjective experience may be made up of beliefs, fantasies, expectations, and theories about what the performer is doing. An interface transpires with real conditions or that which is objectively perceived. In a live rehearsal or performance situation, objective reality includes not only other performers or collaborators who may be involved, but takes into consideration a constantly shifting scene of space and time.

Spatial Dimension

Play, too, is an experience that occurs in the space-time continuum (Winnicott, 1971). Spatial awareness includes a sensitivity to what is in front of you, behind you, above you, below you, and at your sides at any given moment. This may also involve knowledge of inner landscapes, including breath, musculoskeletal action, and glandular response. This kind of spatial awareness both senses and knows how the body spontaneously coordinates its systems in relation to spatial planes and how much emphasis takes place in an action (dynamics). The performer constantly fluctuates between states of motion, stillness, and potential motion. The dancer thus develops a keen awareness of space while simultaneously testing, manipulating, and investigating its qualities.

Temporal Dimension

There is also a temporal aspect to performing, the forward movement of time itself. Perception of time includes taking into account variables such as music or sound scores, silences, rhythms, and length of phrasing. Dance, as a temporal art, occurs over time; its nature is ephemeral and fleeting. The human body in motion plays around with time and in doing so steps outside of time. Time may be compressed or concentrated, or expanded upon, such as when a gesture is performed extremely slowly. Both ways of manipulating time have the effect of making action more readable and intense (Brook, 1995). When a rhythm or pulse is introduced, the effect is a compression or expansion of action as perceived by the audience. A director describes this act of compressing time as a "removal of everything that is not strictly necessary and [an] intensification of what is there" (Brook, 1995, p. 12). This leads to the creation of make-believe and exaggerated worlds. When time and space are compressed in this way, observers are drawn into an "as-if" existence that is like life but in a more concentrated form.

Taking all of these conditions into account, dance (like play) has a somewhat precarious nature. The precariousness of play, according to one theory, is due to this interplay between inner and outer states (Winnicott, 1971). That which is subjective and that which is actual or shared objectively contribute to what we call "play" (Winnicott, 1971).

Through development of this subjective concentration, a performing artist may strive to draw upon the playfulness from which creativity flows. When a trained and skilled performer is able to tap this source, there is a particular feeling that is instinctively recognizable. A type of spontaneous ability develops through experience that is like learning to ride a bicycle, which requires continuous adjustment to changing conditions through play with weight, time, rhythm, space, balance, and geometry (Nachmanovitch, 1990). The rider physically senses speed as well as potential and actual motion. The performing artist, especially the dancer, makes a similar kind of continual adjustment to constantly fluctuating conditions. Using the body as a mode of expression, the dancer communicates impulses within the conditions and laws of the physical universe that present the constantly shifting scene. Adjustments become intuitive through ritual and repetition; they are gradually transformed into skills that become more complex or are experienced for their own sake.

Children at play similarly use "practice games" whose function is to practice a behavior for pleasure or for the pleasure obtained from mastery of new behaviors: "For instance, when a child jumps over a stream for the fun of jumping, jumps back and begins again, he goes through the same actions as when he jumps because he wants to go to the other side, but he does so for pleasure, not of necessity or in order to learn a new behavior" (Piaget, 1951, p. 110). Actions that at first may serve a functional purpose, therefore, can evolve into actions done for their own nonutilitarian sake.

Physical Dimension

The most fundamental element of dance is the body, which becomes the primary medium for communication. Play is enacted through the physical form. People play with and through the body. The playing experience lives within the body, looking outward as a moving forward experience (Denzin, 1982). While playing, the individual engages the entire personality and draws on deep resources of creativity; it is through this creativity that the individual discovers the self (Winnicott, 1971). So in dance, the self is revealed and communicated through the medium of movement interfacing with space, time, and dynamics. If play is a "condition" (among others) for learning (Fromberg, 1995), then dance, like play, is a condition for learning about how this embodied self responds to the shifting demands of the environment. Dance, as the most obviously kinetic and ephemeral of the performing arts, not only embodies play but cultivates playfulness.

Social Dimension

Like play, development in the performing arts involves social processes. Other people are part of objective reality that the performer responds to in the dance milieu. Even a soloist practicing in the rehearsal studio usually works with a choreographer or a director. Dance involves interactive social processes, making it a medium for learning about oneself in relationship to others. Creating a context of dance and theater implies the addition of an observer. "I once claimed that theater begins when two people meet. If one person stands up and another watches him, this is already a start. For there to be a development, a third person is needed for an encounter to take place—then life takes over and it is possible to go very far" (Brook, 1995, p. 16).

Experiences are constructed through play and dance in the potentiality of an empty and clear space. This empty space gives rise to new experience. As the performer's imagination unfolds into this space, a set of rules evolves and a symbolic dance language is simultaneously constructed and revealed. This language is immediately understandable and meaningful on many levels. An observer viscerally feels dance movement without actually performing it. This is due to its kinetic and, usually, nonverbal aspect.

Human beings have the early experience of movement that is the precursor to verbal symbol formation. Human representation of thought, from a psychological perspective, develops on a continuum from physical movement and sound (Piaget, 1951). Symbols are created as children internalize their sensorimotor activities (Piaget, 1951). Movement and sound become internalized as images before humans attach words or symbols. Thus, movement, which we feel in our bones, is meaningful expression. In this context, "Action is the basis for all knowing, and thinking is internalized acting" (Stinson, 1985, p. 14).

For children, developmental changes in motor skills come about through repetition, variation, and practice. They must master gravity, which presents a major obstacle during the first year of life. While exploring gravity and the physical world through movement, the child learns to crawl, creep, walk, run, jump, and leap. By doing so, children gradually gain mastery over the environment and their own movement. During the toddler years, children are in almost constant motion. As they master new movement behaviors, they incresingly gain control over the environment (Piaget, 1951). Children, through improvisation and play, therefore, use their bodies to "poke" at the world, learning how both they and it respond.

Perhaps the form of improvisation that is most like social play, and can be experienced the most viscerally by observers and participants, is the form known as "contact" improvisation. In the mid-seventies, performing artist and dancer Steve Paxton was instrumental in disseminating a new dance form that continues to grow as an exploration of space, time, and interactive social processes. Contact improvisation is a model that incorporates aspects of martial arts, social dancing, and child's play. *Contact Quarterly,* the official publication for the discipline of contact improvisation, defines contact improvisation as: "a movement form, improvisational by nature, involving two or more bodies in contact. Impulses, weight and momentum are communicated through a point of physical contact that continually rolls across and around the bodies of the dancers. . . . Like bolos, fluid and eccentrically weighted, the dancing bodies swing, bounce, roll, and fly through and with a common center" (Siddall, 1980, p. 42).

Participants transmit information to each other about their particular dancing relationship through touch and balance, remaining aware of gravity through contact with surfaces such as the floor and other bodies. Improvisers do not use their hands, but maintain contact through a point that is sensed and shared kinesthetically. Dancers doing contact improvisation maintain an internal, almost meditative, awareness that translates a concentration throughout the entire body. Balance in this system relates to the supporting part of the body, which might be a foot, head, shoulder, or back. In contact improvisation, the floor is an ally (Banes, 1980). Contact improvisation aids in the development of principles that are analogous to those of play. These include orienting oneself in the space-time continuum, adjusting to shifting goals and demands in the improvisation environment, and spontaneously interpreting symbolic language and signals that are continually generated.

In contact improvisation, no one moment is more significant than the other; rather, a shifting flow of time develops between dancers which is shared with the audience or observers. Within this flow, however, there is an undeniable edge which makes contact improvisation very exciting to observe and do. Bodies might sail into amazing juxtaposition while moving around the vertical, horizontal, and sagittal spatial planes. Moments of flight are commonplace. Dancers tumble and spill over, under, and through one another. There is no attempt to cover over "mistakes" because the nature of the form is to include everything that happens as valid. The process of improvising in this way generates a metaphorical movement language that creates multiple layers of meaning for participants and observers. In contact improvisation, performers take physical and emotional risks to become exhilarated and to experience giving and taking. This involves moving in relationship to other people, while at the same time maintaining an awareness of self. In experiencing the self in this way, one loses self-consciousness and merges with an expanded feeling not unlike the experience of concentrated play.

Context Defines Dance and Play

There is an infinite variety of actions that could be called play, as there are infinite possibilities for what is called a performance. Context determines how one identifies play as opposed to dance or theater. In play, acts are pulled from their normal context into the special context of play. The context is marked by the message, "this is play" (Nachmanovitch, 1990). Play has been described by Bateson as "the name of a frame for action" (1979, p. 153). He describes play as a patterned interaction that may be situationally free but serves the purpose of binding participants together. People play when they know they are playing, and play is made possible by the concept of play itself (Csikszentmihalyi, 1979). Likewise, one knows when one is dancing. These perceptions are ultimately dependent upon how one interprets and represents one's actions to oneself. In viewing theatrical dancing, the borders between sports, play, and dance may be ambiguous. It may be hard, beyond context, to say exactly what defines one or the other: "When a baseball team plays the game sans ball, has the performance become a dance? When we decide to pay attention to the movement of the players even as they use the ball, have we turned the game into a piece of choreography?" (Banes, 1983, p. 277).

These questions of context as well as the blurred boundaries between nondance movement forms and dance itself led in part to artists such as choreographer Merce Cunningham developing work that departed radically from what traditionalists claim to be the narrative concern in modern dance. This departure/revolution set a new trend in motion for the performing arts community. Cunningham and his collaborator John Cage regarded music and movement as inherently meaningful. At least since 1951, Cunningham created dances that incorporated the chance method of choreography. This included using methods such as charts, the tossing of coins, and the use of divination tools such as the *I Ching* to select elements in order to predetermine movement sequences, body parts, or use of space. Using games of chance not only helped to generate movement material, but also let the choreographer give up a certain measure of control, thus making the creative process more democratic and less hierarchical. Cunningham and Cage's explorations with these procedures paved the way for a new and influential wave of dance and theater making that emerged during the early sixties.

The Judson Dance Theater, which came into being during the early sixties, personified ideals of community, freedom, and art as play (Banes, 1994). The Judson Church, in New York's Greenwich Village, became the site for the series of dance concerts that was to influence the modern dance movement for the next three decades. The Judson was a collective of young artists who radically changed the course of modern dance, in part by rejecting the choreographic methods of the prior generation and infusing their work with the spirit of play and community. An early press release describes their mission:

> The Judson Church will periodically present the work of dancers, composers, and various non-dancers working with ideas related to dance. The methods of composition of the works in this series range from the traditional ones which predetermine all elements of a piece to those which establish a situation, environment, or basic set of instructions governing one or more aspects of a work—thus allowing details and continuity to become manifest in a spontaneous or indeterminate manner. It is hoped that the contents of this series will not so much reflect a single point of view as convey a spirit of inquiry into the nature of new possibilities. (Cited in Banes, 1983, p. 82)

The Judson Dance Theater changed the nature of dance performance by embracing the energy and creativity of youth. Members of the Judson Dance Theater, including Simone Forti, Steve Paxton, Yvonne Rainer, and Trisha Brown, prominently used games and play in their choreography. Making play into art was part of the rejection of both mainstream culture and the pomposity of the previous generation of avant-garde artists who viewed high art as very serious business (Banes, 1993). Notions of spontaneity, antivirtuosity, democracy, the naturalness of children, and the radical juxtaposition of dance elements all contributed to creating the Judson aesthetic, which tolerated invention and valued change.

The dance construction called "Huddle," for example, was created by Judson member Simone Forti in 1961. "Huddle" is a cooperative game that lasts for about ten minutes and is examined by the audience like a piece of moving and evolving human sculpture. In the dance, six or seven people form a strong base by facing each other and bending forward, putting their arms around each other's waists and shoulders. One person (the climber) separates from the group as the rest of the performers move closer together to fill the gap. The climber moves over the huddle, slowly finding available hand- and footholds that emerge from the underlying moving structure. "Huddle" requires performers to formulate intuitive and consensual rules in order that the individual plans progress smoothly. Laughter is permitted (Banes, 1980).

The play aesthetic developed by the Judson group continues to influence new work in dance today, but with different implications. The eighties and nineties have returned to virtuosity and an extreme intensity of physicality as well as a noticeable return to the hierarchical nature of dance making. In the eighties, according to one commentator, the "ordinary" body was no longer the simple body with which we were born (Banes, 1994). With the rise in jogging, body-building machines, and the cultural obsession with ambition and control, our culture demands physical appearance that is fully "constructed" (Banes, 1994). The current culture, therefore, requires that the average person become some kind of athlete.

The Extreme Dimension

Since the late seventies there has been a notable rise in the fascination with extremely risky sports. These sports, usually requiring elaborate equipment, include hang gliding, bungy jumping, parachuting, and rock climbing. The change in attitude toward rock climbing, for instance, which used to be practiced only by mountaineers, reflects a general change in society: "A game activity which until a generation ago was performed leisurely, with a complex logico-meaningful framework of experiences is now becoming a calculated, precise, expert enterprise within a much narrower framework of experiences" (Csikszentmihalyi, in Cohen, 1993, p. 158).

The popularization of extreme forms of play and sport also has had an influence on dance making. Elizabeth Streb, for example, a choreographer whose work has been gaining popularity during the eighties and nineties, makes performances that embody extreme play. Her dance company, known as Ringside, plays with the physicality, strength, and vulnerability of the human form itself. Although she has developed a specific technique for her gladiatorlike performers, Streb's dancers risk real physical injury during their performances. Her dancers slam, fall, crash, and hurl themselves into the floors, walls, and ceilings of the sets constructed for her dances. Her dances have an urgency, speed, and sound that is similar to hockey players checking each other on the boards. Her dances are not done to music, but are rather like sporting events in which the audience can hear the loud grunts and moans of her performers (augmented by microphones) taking their "hits" and sometimes missing. In her view, dance celebrates not only direction and purpose but also the "miss," which is the element of human error. Streb's work does not camouflage gravity and force. Other forms of dance emphasize the techniques of the legs, pelvis, and spine, which vertically absorb the shock of gravity. Streb describes her dancers taking a "hit": "I'm talking specifically about falling from ten feet up and taking the hit horizontally. I'm not talking about anything but really taking the hit. OK, in boxing they take the hit. But I'm talking about high velocity, high impact, physical, taking the hit. As a choice" (Streb & Greenberg, 1995, p. 16). A comparison of this kind of extreme play with the playful attitudes of Isadora Duncan's work at the turn of the century indicates just how far play has come in influencing the evolution and development of contemporary performance.

Play has always strongly influenced performing artists. Performers also draw upon and learn from the special qualities that play develops, including inner sensing, negotiation of the outside world, and strengthening of interactive social processes. Play in this context develops spontaneity and decision making. Performing artists also have used play to inspire important new forms in the evolution of their art. This is especially true in modern dance, which has developed rapidly during this century and has been greatly influenced by the use of play and game-like structures. It was the use of the chance techniques of Merce Cunningham and John Cage, for example, which really provided a context in which the sixties' avant-garde could emerge. The performances of those times, which were influenced and structured by play, have been important in shaping the aesthetic that one finds in contemporary performing arts.

Play begins in the body. It is very important in educational work with children and adults to keep connected to a sense of play and movement. Through movement, people tap into their innate potential for playful attitudes, which, in turn, develop and further their ability to learn in any discipline. Like play, movement facilitates learning and movement action is the basis for knowing.

Bibliography

Banes, S. (1980). *Terpsichore in sneakers*. Boston: Houghton Mifflin.

Banes, S. (1983). *Democracy's body: Judson DanceTheater 1962–1964*. Ann Arbor: University of Michigan Research Press.

Banes, S. (1993). *Greenwich Village 1963: Avant-garde performance and the effervescent body*. Durham: Duke University Press.

Banes, S. (1994). *Writing dancing in the age of postmodernism*. Hanover, NH: University Press of New England.

Bateson, G. (1979). *Mind and nature*. New York: Dutton.

Brook, P. (1995). *The open door*. New York: Theater Communications Group.

Cohen, D. (1993). *The development of play*. London: Routledge.

Csikszentmihalyi, M. (1979). Some paradoxes in the definition of play. In A. T. Cheska (Ed.), *Play as context* (pp. 14–25). West Point: Leisure Press.

Denzin, N. K. (1982). The paradoxes of play. In J. W. Loy (Ed.), *The paradoxes of play* (pp. 13–24). West Point: Leisure Press.

Fromberg, D. P. (1995). *The full-day kindergarten* (2nd ed.). New York: Teachers College Press.

Jung, C. (1974). Psychological types. In H. Read, G. Adler, & W. McGuire (Eds.), *Collected Works of C. G. Jung* (Vol. 6, p. 123). Princeton, NJ: Princeton University Press.

Nachmanovitch, S. (1990). *Freeplay.* New York: G. P. Putnam's Sons.

Piaget, J. (1951). *Play, dreams and imitation in childhood.* New York: Norton.

Siddall, C. (1980, Spring/Summer). A definition. *Contact Quarterly, 5,* 3–4.

Stinson, S. (1985). Piaget for dance educators. *Dance Research Journal, 17*(1), 9–15.

Streb, E., & Greenberg, N. (1995). Neil Greenberg talks to Elizabeth Streb about subjectivity and objectivity in art but discussion turns to life and death. *Movement Research Peformance Journal, 11,* 10, 15.

Winnicott, D. W. (1971). *Playing and reality.* New York: Basic Books.

The Natural and Social Sciences

At Play in the Field of Archaeology

Susan S. Lukesh

One could characterize an archaeologist as an adult who has managed to turn the child's most entertaining forms of play into a lifetime pursuit. Children build fantasy worlds and find them real; archaeologists reconstruct past worlds and make them real to others. Children visit houses under construction and imagine how they would furnish them and who would live in them; archaeologists study the extant foundation walls and imagine how the buildings were completed; they study the artifacts and try to imagine how they were used in the context of the buildings. Children build sand castles, vying with each other for the biggest and best; archaeologists recreate past castles, vying with each other for the most important, the most complex, or simply the oldest.

Children collect stamps, fascinated by what they tell about the countries of origin and the dates of manufacture, immensely enjoying the business of cataloguing. Archaeologists record the events of an excavation, take photographs, make drawings, and compile computer records, subsequently poring over these records and imagining their contexts.

Children complete jigsaw puzzles, struggling to finish the edges and fill in the interior. Archaeologists routinely find themselves faced with a jigsaw puzzle, without a picture to follow and lacking all the pieces, whose outline they can only imagine.

Just as children take incidental objects such as discarded toilet paper rolls and make them into exotic objects such as telescopes and megaphones, archaeologists take odd and unknown objects and attempt to understand what they once were and what they might represent. Children organize and arrange tea parties, setting out cups and saucers, determining what vessels to use for what function. Archaeologists identify and classify ceramic vessels, generally the single most plentiful type of object recovered, and attempt to determine what they were used for and how and where they were made. Children build villages outdoors and amuse themselves by peopling them with stores and customers. Archaeologists study the extant walls and imagine how the buildings and rooms were used. Children create their own scripts when they play and might pretend to develop another or secret encoded language; archaeologists study decorative patterns on pots or syllabic graffiti and attempt to interpret what such patterns and symbols meant. Finally, the child's desire to hear bedtime stories of people long ago and far away becomes the archaeologist's desire to verify those stories (as Schliemann did with Troy) or to write new stories (as Evans did with the Minoan civilization).

The effort of archaeologists is divided between intense fieldwork on the one hand, and, on the other, more leisurely reflection on the excavated materials. During fieldwork, archaeologists routinely work long hours under adverse conditions, and when the time comes for a break, it is well appreciated. Jokes and laughter provide excuses to sit back and enjoy each other's company, and visitors and newcomers are pressed for news from home, an old newspaper, and even current jokes. Close collaboration during the fieldwork, often carried out by a few who are responsible for special activities such as recordkeeping, may lead to friendships for life. The almost private world these collaborators work in, the intensity of the effort, and certainly the excitement of the possible outcome mimic the best worlds of children's play.

Similarly, one member of the excavation

may undertake additional tasks alone. During a recent excavation at I Faraglioni, Ustica, the author's undergraduate assistant supported her in the recordkeeping and, as happens to all who work with sherds, became enamored of those that fit together and the potential for reconstruction that lay before us. He subsequently took on as a task the reconstruction of as much of the pottery as was possible. His efforts with one pithos (a large water-storage vessel) stand out especially (see Figure 1). We pulled all the possible sherds together and he began the reconstruction, a true three-dimensional picture puzzle. Day after day he became engrossed in the work and, like the child oblivious to the setting sun, had to be reminded of the time and told to come in for dinner. The pithos stands complete today, and photographs of him laboring over it are displayed in my office.

Collaborative brainstorming may arise at any moment. My colleagues and I recently spent part of an afternoon puzzling over an odd object of which at least thirteen examples have been recovered from the site (see Figure 2). Previously suggested examples of use (as a cooking stand or as an object to assist in spinning) cannot be supported. For well over an hour we tossed out ideas, following wild thoughts and imaginative reconstructions. We are left with an object that must have had some real practical function, and although our efforts were to no avail this time,

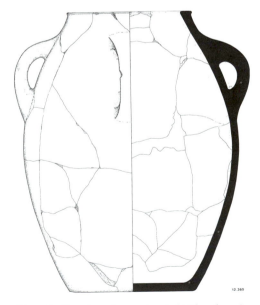

Figure 1. *Drawing of reconstructed pithos from I Faraglioni, Ustica, Sicily (height approximately 50 cm)*

the enjoyment of this session remains.

Archaeology is an especially satisfying discipline, as the problems, skills, and enjoyments derived from play seem equally embedded in this work. Many people tell me today that, when young, they had wanted to become an archaeologist, yet this choice had not occurred to me when I was a child. The idea formed late for me, although, having been admonished not to touch a pithos in a museum, I distinctly remember vowing to "have all the pots I want to touch someday." A few years later I turned to archaeology, when I discovered that people other than Heinrich Schliemann and Arthur Evans (with their wealth) could and did practice archaeology, and, more importantly, when I realized that if I were to spend my life doing something, it should be something that was fun and that I wanted to do.

Although as a child I never thought of archaeology, still I was a child who organized and arranged tea parties, who with my brothers built a village in our backyard, who surreptitiously visited houses under construction in the neighborhood, and who collected stamps. Jigsaw puzzles filled many rainy days, and mystery books then and now are distinct pleasures.

Is it any wonder that many children aspire to be archaeologists and many adults recall such a desire? The archaeologist has transformed some elements of children's play into an adult's lifework.

Archaeology takes many forms. There are field archaeologists, who excavate and then study what they have found, putting the remains into the larger context of the known world; there are the armchair archaeologists, whose main passion is studying the remains of antiquity that others have recovered. Then there are field archaeologists whose work takes them to different countries for extended but not permanent periods of time. There are also archaeologists who live at home and practice daily in their own countries. In the United States these archaeologists are often connected with the U.S. Forest Service or contract archaeology firms; in Italy, for example, they are connected with the government superintendencies that oversee all excavations in the country.

It is the field archaeologist who practices on foreign shores who thrills the layperson and attracts the new recruits. However, an excavation is not summer camp. Indeed, it has been likened to boot camp: early hours, long days working hard in the sun, evenings spent preparing for the next day, combined with camaraderie and a shared sense of purpose. While not summer camp, field excavation and the world of the archaeologist encompass many of the same skills and characteristics of summer camp: exploring the world, creativity, fantasy and imagination, challenge and risk-taking, and even skill mastery and achievement.

An excavation is often short term, intense, taking place at a great distance from the home of the players—a situation ripe for technical, practical, and even social problems to occur. Skills that are used when things run well (creativity, problem solving, and interactive social skills) are doubly needed when equipment fails, food supplies are limited, tempers are short, or staff become ill. I recall one particularly trying time when new equipment lacked a crucial cable. The developer of this equipment was in Tennessee, and we were on a small island off the coast of Sicily. Telephones were available along the country roads, but without phone booths, traffic (e.g., earth movers, motorbikes) made any conversation difficult. Before we resorted to that option, we attempted our own repairs, and only when this failed did we call Tennessee to request a new cable. That came, fortunately with another colleague who had yet to leave the States. We continued to have problems and one day found ourselves in the local bar, setting up the computer beside the telephone in order to better speak with the developers, the only solution we could imagine.

Every member of an excavation team is actively involved in finding a solution to problems, however odd the implementation might be. On excavations, as in most situations, there is a real need for all to work together for the common good (whether making up for the cook who has come down with chicken pox, splicing a cable, or filling in for the sherd washers). Routine group discussions consider not only immediate problems and possible solutions but interpretations of material recovered and stratigraphy revealed, as well as future strategies for excavation. Imagination based on knowledge is critical to the ultimate interpretation of the site as well as to daily efforts and routine problem solving. Just as sports teach children a team approach to winning, multidisciplinary colleagues must work together to interpret the remains of a site into a unified whole.

The tools of excavation range from picks and shovels, brushes and glue, to high-tech equipment, often the same tools that a child has in the sandbox and art room. Many of today's archaeologists as children did not have comput-

Figure 2. Black and white photograph of an alare from I Faraglioni, Ustica, Sicily (height with handle approximately 27.5 cm)

ers to play with; they learn now as adults. This learning often takes the form of games or play, albeit under somewhat different conditions than children experience. Tomorrow's archaeologists will have become acquainted with the model-building, simulation capabilities of computers as part of their play and will more readily incorporate them into their professional work.

Every toystore is filled with picture puzzles and model-building kits of cars and airplanes, castles, fortresses, and bridges, and today, of course, computer versions of the same. Other computer games allow children to walk into worlds long past, and some even simulate archaeological excavations. Some kits available to children present a pot to be reconstructed. The adult who has become an archaeologist continues to create models, models of history that are more challenging than the model kits because there is no set of instructions, no real idea of what the model represents, and, most difficult, no certain knowledge that all the pieces are present. As we excavate new areas and create or refine our models, changing the parameters as new evidence presents itself, there is no doubt that many characteristics of play such as imagination, creativity, problem solving, risk-taking, challenge, construction of meaning, and flexibility of thought are fundamental to the discipline. What delighted us in the many and elaborate games we played as children continues to captivate us as adults.

Bibliography

Fitton, J. L. (1996). *The discovery of bronze-age Greece*. Cambridge, MA: Harvard University Press. (For additional information about Heinrich Schliemann and Arthur Evans)

Holloway, R. R., & Lukesh, S. S. (1995). *Ustica I, excavations of 1990 and 1991. Archaeologia Transatlantica XIV*. (For additional information about the first two seasons of excavation of I Faraglioni, Ustica)

Playfulness in the Biological Sciences

Roger Ganschow with Leonore Ganschow

In 1951 a pair of scientists, James Watson and Francis Crick, together made an important discovery that had a profound influence on the direction that the biological sciences were to take over the next half century (Watson, 1968; Watson & Crick, 1958). They discovered the structure of the DNA molecule, the molecule of heredity. At the time, Crick was an Englishman working toward his Ph.D. and Watson an American postdoctoral trainee in England to gain expertise in biochemistry. Their discovery was highly unusual in that it was not based on their own experimentation or direct observation. Rather, they gathered data accumulated by others, drew inferences, and formulated the first plausible model for the molecular basis of inheritance.

What was unique about their relationship was their ability to play with others' research findings by bouncing them off one another. For example, Watson mentions "the fun of talking to Francis Crick" and his unconcealed amusement at "the idea of Francis and me dirtying our own hands with experiments" (Watson, 1968, p. 37).

The time was ripe for their discovery. Although other, more prominent scientists were pursuing the molecular basis of heredity, it was Watson and Crick who had the persistence, the competitive spirit, the right connections, and the creativity to develop a plausible model of DNA structure that explained the molecular basis of inheritance. Playful persistence was necessary because both were supposed to be working on other projects. Watson, for example, was threatened with loss of financial support from the National Institutes of Health because he was spending most of his time on a nonfunded project.

Competition lent a game-like atmosphere to their discussions. A big competitor in this game was the Nobel laureate, Linus Pauling, whose son was studying in the same department at Cambridge as these collaborators. They also needed the right connections to obtain the data to generate their hypothesis. Crick, for example, had access to data on molecular measurements of the DNA molecule from an X-ray crystallography lab at the University of London, information that at the time was unavailable to Pauling. Most important, however, was the manner in which Watson and Crick played with the data. These neophyte scientists combined their brilliance and creative skills with a deep passion for uncovering the mystery of DNA's structure. Despite numerous efforts, both direct and indirect, to break up these intellectual playmates, their passion for this "holy grail" could not be dampened and their belief that success was just a few calculations away could not be shaken.

Their example leads to reflections on how their discovery shaped the career of the first author and how and when playfulness occurs during the scientific method. The major emphasis in this essay is how scientific method and strong inference tie into the role of playfulness in the biological sciences. Before examining these relationships, though, the first author reflects on his early training.[1]

The Early Training of a Scientist

When he left college to become a high school biology teacher in 1960, the first author was fascinated with the recent discovery that essentially all cells of a living organism contained identical DNA molecules and, therefore, identical genetic information. Thus, to arrive at the variety of cell types, such as liver, brain, and skin cells, which comprise a human organism, precise mechanisms had to exist during the development of the fertilized egg into an adult that would result in the differential expression of genes among various kinds of cells. The issue of what this mechanism might be so intrigued the first author at the time that he stopped teaching after two years and decided to try to find a solution as a graduate student.

He was fortunate to come into contact with a professor who was also keenly interested in this idea. He had enrolled in the graduate course, Molecular Aspects of Developmental Biology, taught by this professor. At that time little was known about this subject since virtually all of molecular biolgy research was focused on simple living systems such as bacteria and their viruses, systems that were essentially unicellular, with little, if any, differential gene expression. Clearly, the time in the history of biology was right for a "pure play" of ideas on the subject matter of this course rather than a direct experimental attack. The first author remembers his graduate training days as being very playful because of this unique opportunity to brainstorm freely about a central question in biology, which had its seeds in Watson and Crick's discovery. He vividly recalls the excitement of devouring the results reported in each month's issue of the *Proceedings of the National Academy of Science USA*. In the early sixties, this was the leading scientific journal in the burgeoning field of molecular biology. The science librarian considered him a nuisance since, around the time of the journal's arrival each month, he would call her repeatedly until it appeared.

Since Ph.D.s in biological science are generally awarded for hypothesis testing rather than hypothesis generation, he reined in his speculative energies regarding this burning issue and focused his predoctoral laboratory research on understanding functional classes of genes in the laboratory mouse. But he wanted to begin to try to understand mechanisms of differential gene expression in mice, to establish a link between present molecular knowledge of simple bacterial systems and the highly complex mammalian system. It was clearly the next level to which scientists had to go to begin to answer the burning question. Again he was fortunate to find an outstanding laboratory for postdoctoral training that at that time was dealing as directly

as one could with the issue and which allowed him to begin to pursue his ideas experimentally.

Looking back on these years of pre- and postdoctoral training, the first author sees them as exceedingly playful, because there were infinite possibilities and little was actually known about the subject of the control of differential gene expression in higher organisms. Because everyone understood that these issues were very complex, they could speculate about general answers without having data to confuse them; that is, they had a lot of ideas without a lot of information. It all went back to Watson and Crick, for it was they who got molecular genetics started; others then carried molecular genetics very slowly into the mammalian system. It is only since the 1970s that scientists have been able to do critical experiments that address this issue, utilizing the now famous tools of recombinant DNA technology. Even in 1996, many of the answers to how differential gene expression is achieved remain obscure.

It should be pointed out, however, that it is not only historical timing that permits playfulness to be interjected into the process of scientific inquiry. Other elements also open the process to playfulness, and these will now be considered.

The Scientific Method and Strong Inference

The exploration of playfulness begins with a description of the scientific method and an important related concept, strong inference. The scientific method is a formal structure for answering questions; it is a system for establishing knowledge in the sciences. One formulates an explanation of some natural phenomenon (the hypothesis), makes predictions based upon this hypothesis, and then tests these predictions through experiments and observations. Last, one draws inferences or conclusions based on the information gathered. In brief, the major components of the scientific method are the development of hypotheses, the experimentation/observations, and finally, the drawing of inferences or conclusions from the observations.

The strong inference approach to scientific thinking, first proposed by Platt (1964), is simply the traditional method of inductive inference as an approach to truth seeking. This approach, which is one form of the scientific method, attempts to rule out all but a single hypothesis, to arrive at an unambiguous answer to a question. Rigorously applying the scientific method, the scientist recycles through the steps of the procedure, generating subhypotheses or a series of sequential hypotheses, to rule out experimentally as many of those hypotheses as possible. This approach to creative experimental design results in a situation in which, when the scientist has completed the experimental phase of the scientific method, he or she is left with a single hypothesis (the answer to the question), which is the strong inference. It is only through the development of strong inference that scientific knowledge can truly progress. Playfulness has a role in some steps in the scientific method leading to strong inference, but not in others.

Speculations about Playfulness in the Scientific Method

The steps of the scientific method can be categorized into playful and nonplayful aspects, with the beginning and ending steps in the sequence being the ones that provide multiple opportunities for playfulness and are enhanced by such playfulness. The intervening steps, however, afford little opportunity for playfulness, and, in fact, cannot tolerate it. Why is this so and what does it mean?

Hypothesis Development

Hypothesis development involves formulating a wide range of possible answers to a question. In the biological sciences, the answers generated pertain to explanations of the structures and functions of living things. This first phase of the scientific method is perhaps the most playful step because it provides considerable opportunity (and often takes an extensive amount of time) for the exploration of ideas. Obviously, in order to generate ideas, the experimenter must draw upon previous knowledge. In the field of developmental biology, for example, a critical research question that has engaged hundreds of scientists for the past thirty-five years stems to some extent from Watson and Crick's discovery. Several cycles of hypothesis development relating to this question and an estimated time frame over which the hypothesis generation has taken place are shown in Figure 1.

One can see from the figure what the elements of playfulness might be during the hypothesis-generation stage:

- These playful periods can be lengthy, lasting years
- Playful periods are interspersed with nonplayful periods where hypotheses are

Question (1950s)	Does the structure of the DNA molecule have the characteristics expected for biological inheritance?
Hypothesis	Structural features of DNA are those of a self-reproducing molecule necessary for biological inheritance (Watson & Crick, 1958). *Hypothesis supported*
A Subsequent Question (1960s)	If genes (regions along the length of the DNA molecule) and their expression account for the unique characteristics of each cell type, how can one account for differences between cell types, for example, between nerve cells and muscle cells?
Alternative Hypotheses	1. Cells have different sets of genes; different genes are passed on to different cells during the development of organisms; different cell types have unique sets of genes. *Hypothesis refuted*
	2. All cells have the same genes, but only unique sets of genes are expressed in each cell type, giving each its unique structure and function. *Hypothesis supported*
A Subsequent Question (1960s to present)	What is the mechanism that turns genes on and off in particular cell types in a manner that is predictable in time and space?
Hypotheses	A,B,C,D,E, etc., being tested.

Figure 1. Chain of Questions and Hypotheses Stemming from Watson and Crick's Discovery

rigorously tested by experiment and/or observation

- These research questions and hypotheses are the basis of scientific creativity; they provide the opportunity to formulate new questions, thus generating new opportunities for playfulness.

Experimentation/Observation Phase

Once questions are generated and turned into hypotheses, the scientist enters the experimental design/implementation phase, in which there is little room for play. Often at this stage of implementing the experimental plan, the biological scientist turns the detailed plan over to a technician and then returns to the "playground" of hypothesis development. One might say that playfulness ends when the scientific team moves to the lab bench or into the field for observation. Here the hypotheses are translated into feasible experiments, where every detail is carefully considered and constructed. Decisions must be made as to what data to collect and how to collect them. The researcher generally follows a scripted experimental plan and carefully attends to all details. It would be inappropriate and downright dangerous, for example, to take a playful attitude toward the handling of radioactive substances and harsh chemicals that are often a part of the biologist's experimental arsenal. Likewise, strict rules and regulations exist governing animal care and use. The work of a scientist who fails to attend to these regulations would be quickly halted by numerous institutional oversight committees and governmental agencies.

In the implementation phase the researcher carries out the detailed experimental/observational plan. Depending on the nature of the experiment and its outcomes, this stage could take months and even years. Again, careful attention to implementing the design is critical; thus, this is not the time for playfulness. If the scientist becomes too playful during this period, he or she could diminish the interpretability of the experiment by not attending critically to design and procedural issues. Although the scientist might need to alter and modify the initial plan of action, it is critical that scientific energies be focused on careful planning and detailed observation.

Drawing Inferences

The final phase of the scientific method requires careful examination of the results of experimentation/observation to determine whether or not the tested hypotheses are supported. The results may support the tested hypothesis, but leave untested other possible answers to the question. This is the point where a commitment to strong inference is essential; it is necessary to determine whether other possible answers (hypotheses) should be tested and, if so, whether such tests are experimentally feasible.

While clearly not as unstructured as initial hypothesis development, the success of this phase nevertheless is similar in that once scientists have drawn their inferences from the data and ascertain the strength of such inferences, they have come full circle in the process. If they judge the inference to be strong and no other answers to the question seem possible, they can move on to other hypotheses and possible answers. On the other hand, if the inference is not strong (i.e., an ambiguous answer results), then they must either test alternative hypotheses or leave the question with an ambiguous answer.

The phase of drawing inferences is generally enhanced by a relaxed and interactive approach to the analysis of observations. It is often the case that the researcher is so close to the problem being examined that aspects of the process take on a level of unjustified importance. Sometimes the researcher's emotional involvement in the outcomes overpowers good judgment. It is therefore very helpful to step back and share this important part of the process with others, such as colleagues in the same field with whom one feels a comfortable level of trust. Such interaction is enhanced by a freewheeling spirit in which both the researcher and the interacting colleague feel free to be honest without getting personal.

The biologist author of this article, for example, for the past twelve years has participated in a group that was formed specifically for this purpose. Approximately ten colleagues at the same institution in the common area of molecular biology meet one evening a month to focus on the host's recent research efforts. The format of these meetings is purposefully kept playful. The meetings provide important feedback to most of the members, who over the past twelve years have maintained productive and well-funded research programs. Members in the group are invited based to some extent on their desire and ability to receive honest criticism of their own research program and to provide criticism of others' programs without getting personal. This setting has proven to be a playful and productive experience for the biological scientists. There are other play-enhancing settings as well.

Settings Where Playfulness Is Most Likely to Occur

Scientific meetings often provide a similar playful environment for interactive inference drawing, although it is not as easy to select those with whom one will interact. Ideas usually have the opportunity to flower at scientific meetings, however. Many such meetings are specifically contrived settings meant to strengthen the knowledge base efficiently by bringing together a limited number of scientists with similar interests and providing them with the time to ponder, gather, and integrate new ideas and develop new hypotheses. One might call the scientific meeting an opportunity for "structured play."

Scientific meetings during the winter season often provide interaction opportunities in play-encouraging environments such as Caribbean islands, Rocky Mountain ski resorts, or Florida coastal resorts. Not only are recreational opportunities available, but also a playful setting for the informal interchange of ideas is provided. In summer, each of the many Gordon Conferences (discussed in *Science*, 1996) draws the best researchers to small New England academies for a week of platform and poster presentations on highly specific subjects in the biological and chemical sciences. Examples of such subjects include steroid hormone mechanisms, the genetics of cancer, and transcriptional regulation of gene expression. The Gordon Conferences encourage researchers to present even their most preliminary results and speculations by prohibiting formal referencing of presented research data and ideas. At all of these meetings, the mornings and evenings are devoted to formal presentations. Afternoons are unstructured but generally include relaxed and playful interchange among the participants. Thus, scientific experts in a field have the opportunity to churn novel ideas and establish new connections and collaborations in these semistructured and play-encouraging environments.

Playfulness as the Satisfaction of Curiosity

Few scientists can be successful without going through all of the steps in the scientific method. Interestingly, Watson and Crick were among those special few who never really made experimental contributions to the historic model they developed. Rather, they drew upon the observations of others to construct their model of DNA structure. Brought together by chance, each pursuing formal research training in very different areas, their collective and creative genius blossomed from a common and passionate desire to discover a plausible model for the structure of the DNA molecule. Watson's (1968) description of the events that led to this discovery makes it very clear that the long hours of discussion and argument over many months were enhanced by the shared spirit of playfulness each was able to engender in himself and accept in the other. This spirit permeated their creative process, allowing and encouraging intellectual honesty and criticism while minimizing the involvement of interpersonal animosity and competitiveness.

Perhaps each discipline has its own kind of playfulness and its own unique places where play does and does not occur. In the biological sciences, ultimately, playfulness promotes the satisfaction of one's curiosity about the chemical and physical mechanisms that underlie life processes. Science is about asking questions, and playfulness facilitates this process at the proper place and time. Best of all, engaging in scientific discovery is something that scientists enjoy doing. What could be more playful than having fun?

Note

1. The first author, a scientist, was inclined to consider the writing of an essay on playfulness to be a frivolous activity and, though fun to talk about, impossible to translate into anything resembling the writing that accompanies scientific experiments. In his words, "This is the most unplayful thing I've ever done." Therefore, he engaged the assistance of a second author, an educator, who is accustomed to playing with ideas. In her view, generating this essay was one of the *most* playful things she had ever done. Thus, this effort represents a collaboration from the perspectives of two very different disciplines.

Bibliography

Gordon Conferences. (1996). *Science, 271,* 826–847.

Platt, J. R. (1964). Strong inference. *Science, 146,* 347–353.

Watson, J. D. (1968). *The double helix.* New York: New American Library.

Watson, J. D., & Crick, F. H. C. (1958). Molecular structure of nucleic acids. *Nature, 171,* 737–738.

Sociologists and Play Research

Donald E. Lytle

Play is implicit in, if not foundational to, many sociological investigations. Yet it has been exceedingly rare for sociologists to consider the phenomenon of human playful enterprise. Even sport sociologists do not focus on play per se. From the beginnings of the young science of sociology, adults and adult institutions, organizations, and groups were the focus of inquiry. Play, viewed as the primary activity of children, was incompatible with the traditional macrosociological perspectives of Marxism, functionalism, and conflict theory. Exceptions were born out of the Chicago school of sociology and included George Herbert Mead's analysis of self, Herbert Blumer's social movement concepts, and Erving Goffman's dramaturgical focus of human behavior.

There are several parallels, however, between sociology and play, which some scholars have viewed negatively. Some in the natural science disciplines, for example, find sociology lacking in importance; others, in the general public, view play as unimportant and unproductive. Many people also believe that they understand both playful phenomena and the foundations of empirical sociological study. Despite these assumptions, both fields of study are intimately involved with fundamental social behavior.

Although there is a definite void in sociologists' pursuit of play research, their unique interests and methods are examples of how researchers employ creative, imaginative, and playful ideas. Often, their scientific zeal has a curious, exuberant, tinkering, and playful style. In effect, there are parallels between sociology and play, as well as how sociologists engage in playful behavior.

A contemporary text introducing the discipline of sociology says, "A sociologist is a person who goes to a football game and watches the crowd" (Landis, 1992, p. 11). This statement is both ironic and revealing. It is ironic because the formal relationship of play to the discipline of sociology is relatively nonexistent. There are, nevertheless, sociology of leisure texts (e.g., Godbey & Kelly, 1992), over thirty journals that publish articles relative to sociology of sport, and well over one hundred sport sociologists throughout the world; yet there have been only a few sociologists who have even modestly dealt with the concept of play.

It is curious that play has been given such short shrift in the literature, because sociology is based upon such strong play-related parameters as social processes, group interaction, role-playing, personal influence, and cultural considerations. In a classic underpinning of play research, Dutch culture historian Johan Huizinga (1955) attributed a lofty and significant role to play in providing social order, promoting social grouping, and founding human culture. Referring to social scientists in general, some sociologists state, "seldom have analysts attempted to bridge the gaps between play and seriousness by demonstrating the similarity of activity in these two spheres" (Ducharme & Fine, 1994, p. 89). Only a few sociologists are represented in the numerous publications that deal with play.

Why has the study of play been given such scant attention within the discipline of sociology? Part of the answer lies in the fact that sociologists most often consider play within the traditional context of childhood as part of Huizinga's romanticism of playful behavior that pervades the Western tradition. This developmental emphasis and positive socialization perspective is a biased orientation, ultimately fostering an adult view of children as innocent, uncorrupted noble savages. This ideology has allowed little room for the realization of adult play as a possible area of sociological study. Nevertheless, there have been sociologists who have participated openly in play theory and research.

Parallels: Sociology and Play

Some academicians have viewed neither sociological inquiry nor play as academically credible subjects of valid scientific inquiry. More subtly, sociologists confronted humans with the assumptions of their social selves, often with threatening and fearful results. Similar portrayals of the worst cases of human lives now seem to be present in popular print materials and on television. These popular, representational forms touch the expressive core of human beings in dynamic action with others, thereby transforming difficult emotions through playful media.

There is also a parallel in how individuals believe they understand play and the tenets of sociology. One view holds that, even beyond empirical research, sociological concepts and theorizing can become so much a part of one's everyday repertoire as to appear "just common sense" (Berger, 1992, p. 12). People similarly view play as commonplace and obvious. The more closely examined reality, however, is that its processes are not easily understood or fully defined. A play theorist takes the position that play is order out of disorder in the subjunctive mood (Sutton-Smith, 1991). It is a "labile entity" (Sutton-Smith, 1993, p. 248) that lends itself to rhetorical uses that do not do justice to the uniqueness and broadness of play behaviors and possibilities. The numerous attempts at defining play, and the plentiful theoretical play constructions result in contradictions that underscore the paradoxical nature of play. One book alone deals with fifteen theories of play (Ellis, 1973). Humans have a universal capacity to play, and sociologists as important social science researchers study the multidimensional and complex nature of Homo ludens. They are facing potential ridicule, however, as well as treading on ambiguous territory, if they advertise their goals as the *study* of play.

Sociologists have studied the meaning of the term *deviance*, and some have explained behavior in terms of people who could not or would not adjust to norms (Durkheim, 1972).

In the twentieth century, this approach to sociology became commonplace. Sociologists of the Chicago school, for example, studied hoboes and other products of urban displacement. With examples such as mental institutions, juvenile delinquency, tattoo parlors, funeral homes, and prostitution, the unconventional or exotic (i.e., the deviant) has been the major focus of study from the perspective of symbolic interactionism. It is possible to infer a similar denigration of play (i.e., as deviant) in *Webster's Third New International Dictionary,* which contains such phrases as "playing fast and loose," "playing around," "being a playfellow, a play actor, or a play maker," and "playing the fool" (1976, pp. 1736–1738). From the perspective of common language use, playing and the player often appear to be dangerous, devious, and deceitful, as shown in the following everyday constructions: "plays both ends against the middle"; "plays tricks"; "play on words"; "play hob"; "play havoc"; "play one against the other"; "make a play for"; "play up to"; "play into your hands"; and "play upon one's feelings." The layperson's view that play is dangerous and deceitful, even involving "lies," contrasts with the fact that playing often is fun. Similiarly, the sociology "of the different" also interests people, for it *is* fun to study and read about.

Theory and Theorists: Play and Sociology

Even though most sociologists have not articulated how the role of play has informed their discipline, there have been and continue to be some notable exceptions. The manifest complex relationships of self to groups and society is difficult enough without having to include the elusive and dynamic qualities of play, yet those of the Chicago school seemed to "play" with that notion. George Herbert Mead was the founder of that sociological perspective. He began teaching social psychological theory and principles in 1900 at the University of Chicago and, although his death occurred in 1934, his influence has spread within social psychology and sociology.

Instead of emphasizing the macrolevel standard of understanding society via social patterns, Mead "played up" the individual's experiencing of society on a microlevel. This significant departure from traditional sociological theory came to be called symbolic interactionism. He conceptualized the relation-ship between self and society as a dynamic pro-cess involving many interacting elements. His theory of symbolic interactionism sees the gen-esis of self occurring in a process of play and game, in which play involves the child's dy-namic imagination: "When a child plays they [sic] play at something" (Mead, 1934, p. 150). Play involves taking on the role of another, through which the child acquires significant societal symbols and through conscious self-indication forms a conception that is differen-tiating and relational: "In the play period the child utilizes his own responses to these stimuli which he makes use of in building a self. The responses which he has a tendency to make to these stimuli organizes them. . . . He has a set of stimuli which call out in himself the sort of responses they call out in others. Such is the simplest form of being another to one's self" (Mead, 1934, p. 151).

Thus, when a child plays he or she is pre-paring for future social challenges. Imagine playing a position on a team, which is socially differentiated and organized collectively to en-gage in some common action. This team is Mead's metaphor for community, and orga-nized games prepare the child to take the atti-tude of all the other people in the game. At the same time it includes playing all the roles within the context of an organized set of rules. With-out being able to take all the different roles, the child cannot successfully participate in the game. "The game represents the passage in the life of the child from taking the role of others in play to the organized part that is essential to self consciousness" (Mead, 1934, p. 152). This is an explanation of how the playfully action-oriented members of society account for the growth of mind and the life-minded self of the playful individual.

Herbert Blumer (1969), the other pioneer-ing member of the University of Chicago's so-ciology department, provides an overview of symbolic interactionism by postulating three key elements:

1. Humans act toward things on the basis of meanings, which then guide and shape their behavior and that of others.
2. Meanings of people, places, and things emerge through social interaction.
3. Meanings are dynamically negotiated through an interpretive process of the self-reflexive playful human.

Erving Goffman maintained the rich socio-logical tradition of the University of Chicago ever since he completed graduate studies there in the late 1940s and early 1950s. Although his sociology was unique, he was influenced by Mead and Blumer's symbolic interaction para-digm and also the ethnographic social science methods of others. Goffman saw that the regu-lation and maintenance of the flow of social action paralleled human play and the action of games (Ducharme & Fine, 1994; Goffman, 1961, 1974). To him, play represents an ab-stract/ideal type of endeavor (Goffman, 1961) that is freely chosen, autotelic, and risk-taking (Goffman, 1967). Play "activity is defined as an end in itself, sought out, embraced, and utterly [the player's] own" (Goffman, 1967, p. 185). To Goffman, the player can be one who "thinks and acts" as an agent of play, or one who takes responsibility for defining given situations to "something without flesh or blood that profits by the outcome of the game" (1967, p. 34). He describes the simple rituals of the "actors" in their normative behavior of reciprocity accom-panying social interaction (Goffman, 1963, 1967, 1971).

Other sociologists also assume a frame-work of play that takes into account both the similarities and differences of play and ritual: Play identified with ritual "accents the plastic-ity of ideation" and surrounds itself with "meta-messages about the ordering of social reality"; it is "expressive of social order" and "com-ments on the immediate on-going fragments of social reality" (Handelman, 1976, p. 190). The qualities of plasticity, social order expression, and immediate social reality commentary are contrasted negatively with ritual and thus con-firm paradox, for play is unable to affirm or change the social order.

It may well be, as one sociologist states, that a single reality of play does not exist, "only techniques for ordering the way in which we choose to view it" (Fine, 1988, p. 44). Maybe this is why Goffman alludes to play and illus-trates but does not analyze it per se.

Similar to Mead, Goffman relates the ac-tion and importance of social intercourse to games largely metaphorically. For example, gaming represents meanings that people put into the games and gaming process and are thus "world-building activities" (Goffman, 1961, p. 27). In similar fashion, he uses play illustra-tively to see "how far one can go by treating fun seriously" (p. 17). These discussions of play and human presentations allude to a hidden thesis that play underscores human dramaturgical interpersonal and intrapsychic interactions, for "Such productive performances are always instances of play, in Goffman's analysis, and in many important cases they are best understood as games, which Goffman treats as a subset of play" (Bogue & Spariosu, 1994, p. x).

Nonetheless, the premise of this essay is that academically trained sociologists have not studied play structures, theory, or actions per se. Ironically, however, many *are* studying playful human action within sociological specialties and interdisciplinary subdisciplines, such as "cultural psychology" and social psychology; however, they typically would not acknowledge the relation of their work to play scholarship. These researchers publish articles in a variety of journals, and their specializations range from sociology of science, medicine, sociolinguistics, social psychology, popular culture, and media studies, to environmental, clinical, educational, industrial, and occupational sociology. Clinical sociologists, for example, analyze the appearance of human bodies (Glassner, 1988) and the adolescent drug world (Glassner & Loughlin, 1987). Based largely on existential sociology theory, a medical sociologist reports on chronic pain (Kotarba, 1983).

Contemporary Sociologists' Playing against the Grain: What They Have Learned about Play

Sociologists and educational sociology researchers produce theory and research relative to ethnographies of children and play groups. For example, a researcher who studied preschool peer environments cautioned researchers to suspend the usual "adult interpretations and assumptions about children's behavior," such as the "tendency to view children's play as practice at being an adult" (Corsaro, 1985, p. 3). An ethnographic study of children's play focuses on how gender is socially constructed by children as "social actors" (Thorne, 1993, p. 157).

Writing extensively on the "sociology of everyday life" from a symbolic interactionist perspective, a sociologist has focused on professionals and amateurs in art, science, sports, and entertainment (Stebbins, 1993, p. ix). Although reporting on the collective amateurism of adult players within theater, archeology, and softball (Stebbins, 1979), this sociologist prefers the connotation of serious leisure instead of play (Stebbins, 1992).

Another significant body of sociological research deals with fantasy games, Little League baseball (Fine, 1987a), contemporary legends (Fine, 1992b), and the scandals of Hollywood and Washington, DC (Fine, 1992a). Gary Alan Fine is a sociologist who playfully engages in the art and craft, and fun, of skilled creative research and imaginative analysis. In his three-year study of the sport experiences of ten- to twelve-year-old boys on ten teams in five different baseball leagues, he became a participant-observer (Fine, 1987a). He conducted interviews, took field notes, and participated in informal conversations. He also investigated such diverse subjects as the strategic play of high school debaters to the fun exhibited by mushroom hunters (Fine, 1987b). Examining young boys' baseball leagues (Fine, 1987a) and the "dirty play" of preadolescent children (Fine, 1986), he details the "fun" of players involved in, and their underlying reasons for, the aggressive pranks and sexual, sexist, and racist talk. He labels as "idiocultures" the systems of meanings guiding the boys' interactions with their friends. These are used as "experience filters" through which the boys redefine the idealized morals and rules of significant adults such as parents and coaches. One conclusion is that this enterprise involves both work and play. As with many other contemporary sociologists, he states that he is not studying play (G. A. Fine, personal communication, September 15, 1995). However, his various studies have analyzed and documented playful behaviors exhibited by playful humans.

Almost all sociologists view their "work" as serious and not related to play. There are other sociologists, however, who view their "work" as both "serious" and related to play. Richard Mitchell refers to the play of mountain climbers as they undertake the "climbing game: For them, strenuous effort becomes fun, necessity offers opportunity, labor is leisure" (1983, p. 207). He draws heavily on the conception of flow popularized by Mihalyi Csikszentmihalyi (1975). Flow occurs when a challenging task is matched by appropriate skill. The concept of flow is often mistakenly thought to be a model of play. It does little, however, to explain play as socially constructed, but Mitchell (1983) is correct in observing that nonextrinsically motivated rewards are overlooked in social science research. Another example of play within the sociological literature is the study of adults' and children's collecting behavior (Danet & Katriel, 1989).

Five broad qualities comprising playfulness have been identified: physical spontaneity, social spontaneity, cognitive spontaneity, manifest joy, and sense of humor (Lieberman, 1977). This author would add a sixth: the playfulness characteristic of the empowerment brought about through the personal control and choice of the player. In play's repeatability and freedom-affirming and personally powerful effects, one can gain increased knowledge, physical, social, and cognitive skills, and thus a more favorable view of oneself. In the process, humans become mirrors in which others might appraise their self-esteem and self-concept. One writer considers play, games, and sports "all features of our social being and as such [they] cannot be conceived of independently of the organizing principles, expectations and disappointments which define lived social experience at any given historical moment" (Gruneau, 1980, p. 83).

Methods and Research Practices

The joy with which Fine engages in his research is apparent in the following statement: "I confess: I love political scandals. I pawed over the *Star*. I devoured every moment of the Clarence Thomas hearings. I remember the details of Gary Hart's farewell press conference. I reveled in John Tower's alcoholic stupors. I still have a fondness in my heart for Fanne Foxe and Elizabeth Ray and their erstwhile congressional friends, Wilbur Mills and Wayne Hays" (Fine, 1992a, p. 2).

There are many other sociologists, however, who do not share this playful spirit, for they "take pride in the abstract, antiseptic quality of their work" (Berger, 1992, p. 12), a perspective that contrasts with the belief that research does not and cannot remain separate from the world it describes. Part of that social world, according to the author of this essay, includes the playful potential and behaviors of researchers.

For instance, a manuscript, originally published in the *Journal of Communications* as the work of "Murdock Pencil, Professor of Social Darwinism," entitled, "PLEASE PASS THE SALT: Examining the Motivational Variables, Idiosyncratic Dynamics and Historic Precedents Associated With the Utterance," has circulated. In the essay, actually written by Michael Pacanowsky (1978), the fictitious social science author presents the results of a "scientific experiment" that delineates the behavioral and sociological/psychological theoretical referents of passing salt. This author once assigned it as a reading in a social psychology class and not one of thirty-five students initially viewed it as a clever parody. It is all the more humorous, and deceptive, for it reads as a typical experimental study and parodies many famous sociologists, such as Philip Zimbardo (1971), Stanley Milgram (1974), Soloman Asch (1952), and Leon Festinger (1957).

Such exhibitions of playfulness, however, are not an acknowledged part of sociological inquiry. More typically, social science scholars exhibit their ludic nature in exploration of topics, concepts, and creative experimentation. In fact, the foregoing listed researchers serve as wonderful examples of scientists who employed imaginative protocols and even "pretend." From Asch's conformity studies to Milgram's obedience study and Festinger's cognitive dissonance studies, their experiments are classics in the literature and among the most replicated experimentally; in other words, the most played with theoretically and actually by other researchers.

Philip Zimbardo's (1971) prison experiment, focusing on "pretend" roles, serves as a double example. He was so immersed in playing the role of "prison warden" in his mock prison in the basement of the psychology building at Stanford University that he got caught up in a rumor of a "prison revolt" and escape attempt. He waited up one night in the "prison" hallway, thinking the "prisoners" were going to try an escape; he was there to prevent the escape, playing the role of warden instead of being the experimenter in charge of this volatile project concerning deindividuation. The project had to be stopped after six days, a week earlier than planned. This classic experiment exhibited a creative enactment that showed the terrifying consequences for college students playing the roles of guards and prisoners, and also showed the fertile imagination of a social science researcher who took on a role counter to his professional role.

Ethnographic methods in social research have been and continue to be a mainstay and derive their strength from their detailed description. This fact has not gone unnoticed by sociologists, and many have employed the method that once was the distinct domain of anthropologists. As Clifford Geertz's (1973) well-known argument suggests, "thick description" captures aspects of social reality, especially the symbolic meaning of acts to those who participate in them, that would be lost under more superficial methods of gathering data. Playful behavior is best seen through the lens of ethnographic description. It is why Geertz (1972) refers to thick description as "deep play."

Through these processes a subtle reality and hidden perspective is evident. Contemporary sociologists studying the myriad dimensions of social human behavior are specialists investigating education, family, law, youth, elders, gangs, sex, politics, religion, industry, art, language, science, medicine, and the city. Although most sociologists follow a tradition of quantitative methods, there is a minority who engage in qualitative studies that employ documentary historical research and ethnographic methods. These methods focus on common life experiences and are presented in understandable language. Instead of detailing highly abstract theoretical schemata, their research is akin to play, for hermeneutical understanding is seen throughout the life span in the persuasiveness, consistency, and naturalness of the playful action itself.

Unlike many other disciplines, it is commonplace for sociologists to hold other degrees and academic appointments. It is not unusual for them also to teach and engage in research related to women's and men's studies, sport/human movement, social work, political science, law, history, anthropology, economics, and psychology. Thus sociology, with its wide reach and the possible latitude of sociological inquiry, as well as the nature of the discipline, lends itself to the study of human playful behaviors and relationships.

The field of sociology may also be related to play in that it is often viewed as a declining field with a confusing academic scope. This view is similar to the position that disdains playful practices and the multidimensional nature of play. Even contemporary culture is manifesting this conventional and stereotypic sense of play in what some have called the dumbing-down effect. This concept even has its own verb, *to dumb down,* meaning to make more stupid or juvenile. It is exhibited in media presentations and popular films, such as *Forrest Gump* and *Dumb and Dumber.*

However, the amplitude and depth of individual and group social investigations under the rubric of sociology parallels the expansiveness of playful manifestations. There is much to be done pertaining to the sociology of play, particularly concerning how groups are formed, maintained, and discontinued through playful interactions. The excellent research of early childhood educators, psychologists, and linguists may provide insights concerning these dynamics, including the rhythmicity of playful interactions and the construction of speech acts in play. On a broader front are questions that still need answers: What is transpiring relative to play within families, education, law, government, and industry? How does play relate to cultures and cultural transmissions, deviance, and subcultures? What role does play have in the interplay of individuals and groups and their patterns of enactment of festivals, celebrations, rituals and rites, and everyday "get-togethers"? The questions for sociologists, like play, are open-ended and important.

Bibliography

Asch, S. (1952). *Social psychology.* Englewood Cliffs, NJ: Prentice-Hall.

Berger, P. L. (1992, November/December). A disinvitation? *Society, 30*(1), 12–18.

Blumer, H. (1969). *Symbolic interactionism: Perspective and method.* Englewood Cliffs, NJ: Prentice-Hall.

Bogue, R., & Spariosu, M. I. (Eds.). (1994). Editors' foreword. In R. Bogue & M. I. Spariosu (Eds.), *The play of the self* (p. x). Albany: State University of New York Press.

Corsaro, W. A. (1985). *Friendship and peer culture in the early years.* Norwood, NJ: Ablex.

Csikszentmihalyi, M. (1975). *Beyond boredom and anxiety.* San Francisco: Jossey-Bass.

Danet, B., & Katriel, T. (1989, August). No two alike: Play and aesthetics in collecting. *Play and Culture, 2*(3), 223–227.

Ducharme, L. J., & Fine, G. A. (1994). No escaping obligation in the play of the self: Erving Goffman on the demands and constraints of play. In J. R. Bogue & M. K. Spariosu (Eds.), *In the play of the self* (pp. 89–111). Albany: State University of New York Press.

Durkheim, E. (1972). *Selected Writings* (A.

Giddens, Ed. & Trans.). Cambridge: Cambridge University Press.

Ellis, M. J. (1973). *Why people play.* Englewood Cliffs, NJ: Prentice-Hall.

Festinger, L. (1957). *A theory of cognitive dissonance.* Stanford: Stanford University Press.

Fine, G. A. (1986). The dirty play of little boys. *Society, 24*(1), 63–67.

Fine, G. A. (1987a). *With the boys: Little League baseball and preadolescent culture.* Chicago: University of Chicago Press.

Fine, G. A. (1987b). Community and boundary: Personal experience stories of mushroom collectors. *Journal of Folklore Research, 24,* 223–240.

Fine, G. A. (1988). Good children and dirty play. *Play and Culture, 1*(1) 43–56.

Fine, G. A. (1992a, February 16). Americans should admit it: We love a good scandal. *Atlanta Journal and Constitution.* p. F2.

Fine, G. A. (1992b). *Manufacturing tales: Sex and money in contemporary legends.* Chicago: University of Chicago Press.

Geertz, C. (1972). Deep play: Notes on the Balinese cockfight. *Daedalus, 101*(1), 1–37.

Geertz, C. (1973). Thick description: Toward an interpretive theory of culture. In C. Geertz (Ed.), *The interpretation of cultures* (pp. 3–30). New York: Basic Books.

Glassner, B. (1988). *Bodies: Why we look the way we do (and how we feel about it).* New York: Putnam.

Glassner, B., & Loughlin, J. (1987). *Drugs in adolescent worlds: Burnouts to straights.* New York: St. Martin's.

Godbey, G., & Kelly, J. R. (1992). *The sociology of leisure.* State College, PA: Venture.

Goffman, E. (1961). *Encounters.* New York: Bobbs-Merrill.

Goffman, E. (1963). *Behavior in public places.* New York: Free Press.

Goffman, E. (1967). Where the action is. In E. Goffman (Ed.), *Interaction ritual: Essays on face-to-face behavior* (pp. 149–270). New York: Doubleday Anchor.

Goffman, E. (1969). *Strategic interaction.* Philadelphia: University of Pennsylvania Press.

Goffman, E. (1971). *Relations in public.* New York: Basic Books.

Goffman, E. (1974). *Frame analysis.* New York: Harper & Row.

Gruneau, R. S. (1980). Freedom and constraint: The paradoxes of play, games, and sports. *Journal of Sport History, 7*(3), 68–86.

Handelman, D. (1976). Re-thinking banana time. *Urban Life, 4*(4), 33–48.

Huizinga, J. (1955). *Homo ludens: The play element in culture.* Boston: Beacon.

Kotarba, J. A. (1983). *Chronic pain: Its social dimensions.* Beverly Hills, CA: Sage.

Landis, J. R. (1992). *Sociology: Concepts and characteristics* 8th ed. Belmont, CA: Wadsworth.

Lieberman, J. N. (1977). *Playfulness: Its relationship to imagination and creativity.* New York: Academic.

Mead, G. H. (1934). *Mind, self and society.* Chicago: University of Chicago Press.

Milgrim, S. (1974). *Obedience to authority.* New York: Harper & Row.

Mitchell, R. G. (1983). *Mountain experience: The psychology and sociology of adventure.* Chicago: University of Chicago Press.

Pacanowsky, M. (1978, April 9). Please pass the salt: Examining the motivational variable, idiosyncratic dynamics and historic precedents associated with the utterance. *Washington Post,* p. C1.

Stebbins, R. A. (1979). *Amateurs: On the margin between work and leisure.* Beverly Hills, CA: Sage.

Stebbins, R. A. (1992). *Amateurs, professionals, and serious leisure.* Montreal: McGill-Queens University Press.

Stebbins, R. A. (1993). *Predicaments: Moral difficulty in everyday life.* Lanham, MD: University Press of America.

Sutton-Smith, B. (1991, March 14). Issues in the interpretation of play . . . A personal chronology. Paper presented at the Association for the Study of Play Conference. Charleston, SC.

Sutton-Smith, B. (1993). Play rhetorics and toy rhetorics. *Journal of Play Theory and Research, 1*(4), 239–248.

Thorne, B. (1993). *Gender play: Girls and boys in school.* Brunswick, NJ: Rutgers University Press.

Webster's Third New International Dictionary of the English Language. (1976). Unabridged. Springfield, MA: G. C. Merriam.

Zimbardo, P. G. (1971). *The Stanford prison experiment.* Slide/tape presentation. Palo Alto, CA: Stanford University.

Chemists and Play

Elizabeth Kean

At different ages, play with chemistry takes different forms. Very young children wonder at the "magic" of sudden transformations of chemicals. Through the grades, children move from hands-on manipulations of household materials to more abstract symbolic manipulations, with test- and lecture-driven teaching eventually predominating as the learning mode. Recent innovations, such as thematic, activity-based learning and computer simulations, hold promise for more playful learning processes at intermediate, secondary, and college levels. Chemists share their craft through demonstrations in public and academic settings, and devise a creative, often competitive culture that has distinct appeal for diverse segments of the population.

There has always been a playful component in chemistry that has often been exhibited in "public play" as well as in science play at home and in the elementary school. This playfulness, however, has not always carried over into the teaching of chemistry to elementary, high school, and college students, even though most professional chemists retain a playful element in their work. This essay discusses public, school, and professional play in the discipline of chemistry.

Public Play and Home Play with Chemistry

Many people encounter chemistry as a formalized discipline in their local shopping mall. For more than a dozen years, chemists and chemistry students have set up minilabs in malls and other public places, where they have performed "gee-whiz" demonstrations while touting the idea that "Chemistry is fun!" In these events, chemists show amazing and mystifying reactions. They mix together chemicals that oscillate between two or three colors with clocklike regularity. They perform astounding tricks, such as inserting a skewer into a balloon without breaking it (a little oil helps, as does knowing where the rubber in the balloon is the thickest). They explode things such as soap bubbles filled with mixtures of hydrogen and oxygen, to the delight of children and adults alike, although girls are often less excited by this than boys. What is the reason behind all of this public play? It is to introduce chemistry as an exciting and interesting occupation, and one that is worthy of consideration as a career. Who would not want to spend their lives playing with all those things?

The introduction of the shopping mall chemist is the current generation's answer to the old Gilbert Chemistry Kit. Popular in the 1940s to 1960s, these kits provided many a boy (and they usually were boys) with the experience of investigating the world of chemicals. Filled with small vials of chemicals that were supplemented with common household chemicals, children mixed, heated, cooled, and decanted—playing with the stuff of chemistry. When instructions were followed, children obtained and rationalized predictable results. The young experimenters learned that chemical behavior was predictable and that there were regularities in how the world worked. Such things seemed to encourage those children to learn chemistry. There was also an element of danger in those simple experiments, because things could go wrong. Many adult chemists have stories about working on their kits when parents were not around and filling the house with smoke and smells or otherwise creating havoc. The resulting trouble was worth it for the excitement of doing something for which the result was not predictable. These venerable sets can still be found in antique shops and flea markets, looking quaint and simple. Today's generations, raised on video and computer games, seem to have less interest in chemistry play at home.

The old chemistry kits and the shopping mall exhibits have similar purposes: to get children to see the subject matter of the world as interesting and fun. Chemistry can show them the excitement and the satisfaction of being able to control and manipulate a part of their surroundings. Moreover, these experiences heighten chances that these children might go on to further study of chemistry. Another purpose for emphasizing the enjoyable aspects of chemistry, however, may be because in recent times chemistry has had some bad press. People often think of chemicals as substances that damage the environment and kill people and animals. Because of such incidents as the use of napalm in Vietnam and the industrial chemical deaths in India, the image of chemistry is not often associated with social benefits and health. Chemists, therefore, willingly present public displays to put a kinder and gentler face on the field and those who practice it.

Chemistry in the Elementary School: Sometimes Play

The image of chemistry as a playful and enjoyable activity changes once students begin to study chemistry formally in schools. In the elementary school, teachers include little chemistry in the curriculum because science is still not one of the major areas of study. Reading and mathematics take up most of the students' time, with the teachers often relegating the study of science to Friday afternoon at 2:30, unless something better comes along. Although the recent emphasis on encouraging students to study more science (along with mathematics) has changed this schedule somewhat, science still tends to be a minor part of most students' elementary experience. In the best of circumstances, when teachers have sufficient support and training, thematically based science taught in a "hands-on, minds-on" manner can engage students in a study of their surroundings. In such cases, students can often engage in manipulating common household chemicals, experimenting with mixing, testing (e.g., for acid-

ity by putting a strip of paper with acid-sensitive dyes impregnated on it), and otherwise playing around with the ordinary chemicals in their surroundings. There are many elements of play in such work, as students try one thing and another and also, at times, pretend to be scientists at work. In some classes, students wear lab coats and otherwise assume the role of scientists. These can be playful and fun-filled activities.

In most cases, unfortunately, science in the elementary school is taught with textbooks. In the early 1990s, as part of a team of chemists, physicists, science educators, and elementary teachers, the author examined the most commonly used elementary textbooks to look at their treatment of some typical physical science concepts. One of the more striking features was that the texts for kindergarten through grade two had a number of activities for students to do, many of which involved manipulating common chemicals. These activities became the chemistry curriculum and often included some of the elements of play. Even in these cases, however, there was always a specific correct answer to be obtained, rather than the experimentation that is often so interesting and fun for students.

For more literate students, in grades three to six, the tenor of the science texts usually changed. If experiments were suggested, they were not included within the main text, but were set off in little boxes. The job of learning chemistry with the text materials was now the task of learning to read about aspects of chemistry and to learn the names of the chemicals. The play aspects largely disappeared, replaced by the familiar and dreary worksheets and word tasks of conventional schooling.

The most defeating aspect of this transition comes from the early deemphasis on real chemicals and their transmutation into the symbolic aspects of the objects. Students at unreasonably early ages may be required to learn the definitions of atoms and ions, elements and compounds, and to write largely incomprehensible symbolic representations for chemicals (e.g., $NaCl$). The more inventive teachers make these activities into play by setting them up as games with internally consistent rules; for example: "So if you want to write the correct formula of a compound from an element in the first column of the periodic chart with an element in the next to last column, you know that you have one of each. Let's try some of them now and see who can get the formula first."

Children differ in their willingness to play such word/symbolic games, particularly since these words have no concrete referent in their lives or for any other purpose except a school exercise.

Chemistry in the Middle School: Let Me Tell You About . . .

The transition to chemistry learning in middle school is again one that can be accomplished in different ways. In the worst-case scenario, the classroom becomes the forerunner of the most common high school instructional pattern, in which *teacher telling* is the usual activity. Teachers expect students to copy down and repeat teacher-given information about chemicals and their behavior. Often this material is presented without a stated purpose or a context.

In more inventive and positive ways, some middle school teachers have begun to center their chemistry activities around the lives of their students. These students engage in studying the chemicals that are in their lives, using a phenomenological as well as a symbolic approach. One rather extreme example of this is found in a Pennsylvania middle school in which a group of students and teachers spend the entire year studying a watershed (Springer, 1994). Students learn chemistry integrated with geology, physics, biology, social studies, communication, and art. While this is beyond most school settings at the present time, it does illustrate how such activity-based learning of chemistry can accommodate aspects of role-playing. As another middle school teacher recently put it, "I want my students to become scientists, working the way scientists work, not merely to study science." Such activities, in which students take the role of chemists and engage in the work of chemists (e.g., making materials, predicting products, and learning how to dispose of chemicals properly), is also a form of role-playing.

Views from the Lecture Hall: High School and Beyond

Because chemistry is not a required subject at most high schools, only the volunteers are present. Students may enroll not because they want to learn chemistry, however, but rather because they are intending to go to college and major in subjects that require college chemistry.

Thus, many high school chemistry teachers choose to model the type of instruction they know their students will experience in college, which is the lecture. One high school chemistry teacher opened his desk drawer to show the author the many letters he had received from former students thanking him for preparing them so well for college chemistry. In truth, few of these teachers have ever experienced as learners themselves a science course taught in any other way except lecture, and so they teach the way they were taught. Given the similarities between high school and college chemistry teaching, therefore, these two levels are treated together in this essay.

At these advanced levels, the student is now in the full realm of decontextualized chemistry. Not only is lecturing the major mode of information transmission, laboratory experiences are typically "cookbook labs," in which the experiences serve to confirm what has been taught in the lecture. As the head of the National Academy of Sciences said recently at a national meeting, "When I studied chemistry at college, I studied cooking" (Albers, 1995).

So where is play in such experiences? Besides the humor that a good lecturer often uses, there are also the demonstrations that are intended to startle and entertain. These are similar to shopping mall chemistry, although they also intend to illustrate chemical concepts and principles; however, their success in doing so has been questioned (Kaplan, 1993). Play with symbols has also become part of the folklore of some high school and college introductory courses. Many beginning students, for example, are confronted with questions such as, "What is the name of this compound: HIOAg?" Students scratch their heads trying to use their chemical naming rules for this compound, which would contain hydrogen (H), iodine (I), oxygen (O), and silver (Ag). The smarter students (or those with older siblings who had previously been in the professor's class) realize that this is not a compound at all, but really stands for "Hiyo, Silver," the Lone Ranger's trademark incantation. (This example probably dates me; I do not know how much longer generations of students will find the Lone Ranger a part of their cultural heritage.) Another symbol play example is the presentation of a wheel-like arrangement in which each of the spokes of the wheel terminates in the chemical symbol Fe++, the ferrous ion. This is, of course, a "Ferris wheel."

Aside from these plays on symbols and words in traditional courses, there is little room for anything other than the business of accumulating the required knowledge base. If most students are asked about their high school or college chemistry courses, they would agree that *play* is not a word that comes readily to their minds to describe the experience.

Chemical Computer Play: On the Horizon

The growing influence of computer games and simulations may change the traditional picture of chemistry teaching. Nearly a decade ago there began to be a series of computer simulations that allowed the student to do chemical manipulations. For example, the student could control the amounts of chemicals and the environmental conditions for the manufacture of certain chemicals (e.g., NH_3). Using too much of one chemical, too much pressure, or a higher temperature might create a (simulated) explosion. As the student learned to manipulate things to keep parameters under control, more and more chemical product could be obtained at different levels of cost. Students could compete in these simulations to see who could make the most product or the most money. Competitions like these are not equally appealing to all chemistry students. Boys seem to enjoy them more than girls, although girls will often participate for the pleasure of working with another person on a team. Teachers, however, have not generally introduced even computer programs such as these as an important part of the chemistry curriculum.

A new generation of multimedia problem-oriented computer programs, in which students solve multifaceted problems that require the use of specific chemistry knowledge, are now providing a hopeful possibility for reducing the tedium of learning the many facts, concepts, principles, and typical solutions associated with introductory chemistry. One team of chemists (Middlecamp & Rose, 1994) is working on a project for a publisher to create a year-long chemistry course that consists of a number of problem modules. One module, for example, is organized around a space shuttle launch that is aborted at the last minute. The students must find out why this has occurred, investigating such questions as whether there is too little of one of the fuels or whether a gauge is malfunctioning. Another problem concerns designing a

new oil-based pharmaceutical product and developing its flavor and packaging material. To complete such modules, students must select relevant parts of the knowledge base and understand important chemical ideas that permit appropriate choices to be made.

Such innovative curricula are part of a larger set of changes under way in chemistry curriculum reform for high school and college. The National Science Foundation has given four major awards of $5 million each to consortia of universities and colleges to help them develop curricula that include more hands-on, open-ended activities within the chemistry learning process. These innovations hold promise that the inventiveness and enjoyment so characteristic of play will become a more visible part of the chemistry learning scene.

Professional Chemists at Work and at Play

The preceding sections of this essay focused on the interface between chemistry instructor and chemistry student, in particular, ways that teachers introduce students to the subject. This section focuses on the professional chemists themselves. Is play a part of their role?

In addition to gaining pleasure by introducing students to the enjoyment of chemistry, many chemists continue to have fun with chemistry throughout their careers. As one chemist recently said, "I still like to blow things up!" Others talk about the toys they get to play with and the interesting reactions that often have powerful visual effects, such as color changes or precipitate formation and dissolution. These are often the chemists who seek out opportunities to share their excitement about chemistry with young children and the general public. The development of sophisticated ways of presenting the material and making sense of the phenomena to nonspecialists is a creative outlet for them.

Still others gain personal satisfaction in continuing to make discoveries about how the physical world works. They enjoy their physical manipulation of equipment and their ability to transform materials. This author was excited as a graduate student to synthesize a new material—one that, as far as anyone knew, had never existed anywhere in the universe! This level of creativity, which includes developing new theories, designing new laboratory processes, and observing new transformations of substances, often has a joyfulness, a playfulness, and the satisfaction of intellectual games that keep most chemists engaged and involved in their work. This is true in spite of the fact that most of the discoveries today involve less direct interaction with phenomena and more interpretation of molecular events based on second- or third-hand evidence (e.g., putting a sample of a chemical into a machine and obtaining spectra from which one can deduce some property of the chemical).

Chemists also occasionally play in their print communication. One paper published in a chemistry journal, for example, was written in blank verse (Bunnett & Keapley, 1971). Although the editors agreed to its publication, they did warn others in a footnote that this would not be a regular occurrence in that journal. Only a few especially talented people, however, seem able to combine successfully their talents in such diverse fields as organic chemistry and poetry.

Within the chemical culture, there is also a sense of community that often has a playful element. At the annual or semiannual meetings, friends and colleagues discuss new results, gossip, and tell (tall?) stories of their students and research projects. This community also indulges in gamesmanship. It can be intensely competitive, exemplified in races to see who can be first to solve a hot problem and in passionate attacks and defenses in person or in print when others propose alternative solutions. For many chemists, as is true for other scientists, there is also the satisfaction that comes from participating in a culture that is not accessible to everyone. Some chemists seem to enjoy this secret club feeling that not everyone is smart enough to be a chemist. How else is it possible to explain the willingness of chemistry faculty to let their courses be the "gatekeeping" courses for so many professional majors? For example, students wishing to become doctors, nurses, or engineers must first take general chemistry (and perhaps organic chemistry). With failure rates often in the 25 to 50 percent range, this barrier keeps many from advancing to the major of their choice. Chemists often express pride in these failure rates and seem unaware that many smart people choose not to become chemists for reasons other than lack of success in taking chemistry.

This portrait of the chemical culture may help to explain why the field is predominantly a white male occupation. It is a field in which overcoming the limitations and mysteries of nature, creating new materials, explaining how things work, and making Mother Nature do one's bidding hold appeal for those who seek that sense of power. It is not an especially welcoming field for women and people of color, who may feel welcome only to the extent that they enjoy the challenge of beating down the barriers to the profession. If they enjoy the challenge of demonstrating that they are better at chemistry than many other people and enjoy competition and gamesmanship in general, they will do well in the field. While no study of chemists' childhood play is in the literature, it may be that competitive games as well as creative play with scientific materials are important parts of their early play experiences.

For those persons who manage to overcome (or even thrive on) the obstacles on the way to a chemistry career, they have a professional field that is often visually interesting, explosive with promise, filled with intriguing problems, and challenging to creative talent. Chemistry has a fascination and appeal both to the youngest observer in the shopping mall and to the chemist who has seen a particular chemical reaction hundreds of times. It seems magical and, with its ability to explain the invisible world of atoms and molecules and to transform experience, perhaps it is.

Bibliography

Albers, B. (1995). *President's address*. Presented at annual meeting of the American Association for the Advancement of Science, Atlanta, GA.

Bunnett, J. F., & Keapley, F., Jr. (1971). Comparative mobility of halogens in reaction of dihalobenzenes with potassium amide in ammonia. *Journal of Organic Chemistry, 36,* 184–186.

Kaplan, C. (1993). *Students' perception of chemistry lecture demonstrations*. Unpublished master's thesis, University of Nebraska-Lincoln.

Middlecamp, C., & Rose, N. (1994). *Goal-oriented, problem-based, multimedia software*. Paper presented at the annual meeting of the American Chemical Society, Washington, DC.

Springer, M. (1994). *Watershed: A successful voyage into integrative learning*. Washington, DC: National Middle School Association.

The Playful Ways
of Mathematicians' Work

Sharon Whitton

Play has a role both in the work of mathematicians and in the evolution of mathematics. Although play is not often acknowledged as a major contributing factor in mathematicians' work, their methods of inquiry resemble many of the behaviors of children involved in meaningful play. Illustrations of such play exist in the areas of arithmetic, algebra, geometry, and contemporary mathematics. To glean a historical perspective on the role of play in the evolution of mathematics, readers are invited to use these illustrations in designing exploratory activities for children. The goal is to provide environments in which children, through meaningful play, will have opportunities to construct their own knowledge and appreciation of mathematics.

Mathematics as a Playful Endeavor

"Math is my favorite sport. It's the game I play best." This was the author's response when friends questioned her enjoyment of mathematics and why she had chosen it as a profession. With this statement, she was trying to convey her attitude toward the subject, that there is a game-like quality about mathematics. Nevertheless, the reply startled people because this discipline is not usually coupled with terms like *games, sports,* and *play.* These are words usually reserved for recreation and leisure—not mathematics.

The recreations of mathematicians usually involve topics such as number puzzles, magic squares, and a multitude of games of strategy. In their work, however, mathematicians seldom acknowledge the role of play as a major contributing factor. They view their work in far more serious terms. After all, mathematics is the language that people use to communicate intelligently about the forces that shape their lives, forces such as nuclear power that depends on sophisticated mathematical calculations; space explorations that require immense mathematical expertise; or policies made by governmental agencies based on interpretations of statistical data. These are the applications of mathematics that contribute directly to the well-being of society.

Mathematicians consider their work to be the creation of new mathematics and the adaptation of existing mathematics to meet society's needs. Coincidentally, these endeavors call for imagination, risk-taking, creativity, and flexibility of thought—all characteristics associated with children involved in meaningful play (Sponseller, 1976; Weininger, 1979).

A renowned eighteenth-century mathematician, Felix Klein (1849–1928), identified imagination as a major factor in mathematicians' work. He explained that even though the hallmark of mathematics is deductive logic, the work of mathematicians is seldom orderly. The finished product of an elegant proof rarely reveals the serendipitous, sometimes disorderly, process of discovery. According to Klein, "The mathematician . . . does not work in a rigorous, deductive manner, but rather uses fantasy" (cited in Steen, 1989, p. 83). Thus, mathematical discoveries are achieved frequently through playful means, with numerous false starts, beginning in the middle, or even working backwards; and sometimes the whole idea is born of fantasy.

Another mathematician, writing about mathematics and imagination (Kasner & Newman, 1940), alludes to the work of mathematicians as a type of playfulness, similar to that of a child solving puzzles: "Puzzles are made of the things that the mathematician, no less than the child, plays with, and dreams and wonders about, for they are made of the things and circumstances of the world he [sic] lives in" (p. 188). The analogy of mathematics and puzzles is consistent with the perspective in this essay. While recognizing the utilitarian aspects of mathematics and its contribution to society, the author has always approached mathematical tasks as tantalizing puzzles, waiting to be solved.

This view of mathematics is not unusual. It goes back to ancient Greece when mathematicians played with mathematics as people play with crossword puzzles and chess today. Plato himself taught that mathematics is "the highest exercise to which human leisure could be devoted" (Hogben, 1971, p. 15).

History has revealed that numerous mathematical discoveries and applications are the products of mathematicians' playfulness. For example, Archimedes (287–212 B.C.), the greatest mathematician of ancient times, attributed his mechanical inventions (the pulley and lever, catapulting war machines, and the water-drilling screw) to his "diversions of geometry at play" (Edwards, 1979, p. 29).

Mathematicians often use methods of inquiry that are consonant with children's behaviors during play. These methods are action-oriented and include some combination of the following:

- Constructing a model
- Extending a pattern and making conjectures
- Organizing information
- Developing a method
- Discovering relationships
- Justifying a conclusion

Mathematical behaviors, therefore, include thinking, figuring things out, and reasoning—behaviors that children exhibit while engaged in meaningful play. Thus, even though most mathematicians do not formally acknowledge the role of play in their work, the characteristics of playfulness are ubiquitous and inseparable from their methods of inquiry.

Redefining Mathematics

It is difficult to describe mathematicians' work without addressing the definition of math-ematics. Recent surveys (National Research Council, 1989) indicate that people in the United States have numerous misconceptions about mathematics. This is due to a variety of factors stemming from outmoded teaching methodologies and the very fact that mathematics has undergone significant changes in the last half century.

If you ask people to define mathematics, the typical response of many is that it concerns numbers and computation. While mathematics often involves numerical data, its primary focus is not on computation per se, but rather on reasoning, problem solving, and pattern recognition. It may seem incongruous, but mathematicians do not consider arithmetical computation to be a major component of their work. Instead, they view it as a tool for solving certain types of problems, never as an end in itself.

The *Curriculum and Evaluation Standards for School Mathematics* (National Council of Teachers of Mathematics [NCTM], 1989a) identifies the major foci of the school curriculum in broad terms such as problem solving, reasoning, communicating, and building connections with the real world. The NCTM, does acknowledge the relative importance of arithmetic computation in the development of number sense in young children. It is quick to emphasize, however, that such computation should arise from relevant problem situations and should not be taught in isolation.

Perhaps more illuminating is the recent definition of mathematics given by the National Research Council (NRC) in its publication, *Everybody Counts* (1989). Specifically, "Mathematics is a science of pattern and order" (p. 31), concerned with ideas of dimension, quantity, uncertainty, shape, and change.

To enhance mathematics education, the NRC recommends that children at the youngest ages, when their "unfettered curiosity remains high" (Steen, 1990, p. 5), be introduced to a rich variety of patterns for exploration. Moreover, children should engage in activities that are alive with action, such as playing with pendulums to explore dynamics, pouring water to compare volume, and constructing kaleidoscopes to discover properties of symmetry. With these informal play activities, children will gain markedly in their mathematical reasoning facility long before they are introduced to the abstractions of higher mathematics.

This essay contends that educators should exploit the similarities between meaningful play and the genuine work of mathematicians as they create learning experiences and curricula for the elementary student. Teachers should seek out ways for infusing play into the teaching and learning of mathematics.

Play Encounters in Mathematical History

Given this redefinition of mathematics as "a science of pattern and order" and that many of the behaviors of mathematicians are like those of children at play, it may be beneficial to look at how certain mathematical concepts actually evolved. For example, the bulk of Archimedes' discoveries were made during playful explorations (described in his treatise on the subject, *The Method*). The merit of hands-on explorations is underscored by his statement, "Certain things first became clear to me by a mechanical method" (cited in Edwards, 1979, p. 68). Information of this type could inform the teaching of mathematics in elementary schools. Teachers and children could design similar activities to foster children's own construction of mathematical concepts.

The following sections illustrate hands-on explorations that teachers could include in children's play. Such explorations may be beneficial in guiding children to develop an understanding of fundamental mathematical concepts.

Playful Activities in Arithmetic

People sometimes discover mathematics by deliberately seeking out patterns. More frequently, the discovery arises naturally by observing regularities occurring during play or in everyday life.

Early history indicates that people found numbers themselves to be of special interest. The ancient Greeks (ca. 500 B.C.), for example, were doing mathematics centuries before arithmetic existed as we know it today. The earliest recorded civilizations were interested in number patterns and connected them with patterns of stones in the sand. Although numerical symbols were not yet invented, they used physical models to represent quantities and to organize ideas in ways that led to the discovery of many numerical properties.

The set of natural (or counting) numbers was of special interest to the Greeks. The simple act of playing with stones in the sand resulted in their construction of this number system. The subsequent constructions of the integers, rationals, irrationals, and real numbers came from these initial constructions.

The designs that follow in Figures 1–4 were created by the ancient Greeks (ca. 500 B.C.) to represent natural numbers and their related properties. Adults can invite children today to create similar patterns through play, even before they begin to count or learn addition facts.

1. *Natural Numbers.* The Pythagoreans (ca. 500 B.C.) used stones to construct the natural numbers. They represented numbers as physical models, as illustrated in Figure 1.

Figure 1.

Each succeeding number was formed by duplicating the previous column and extending its length by one stone.

2. *Even Numbers.* They formed even numbers by pairing the stones, as shown in Figure 2.

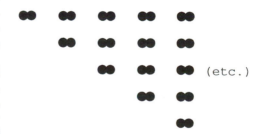

3. *Odd Numbers.* Odd numbers were similar to even numbers, except that they had a single stone extending beyond each pair (see Figure 3). This led to the currently used phrase, "odd man out."

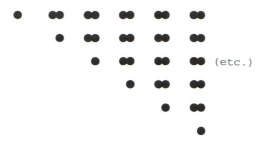

Figure 3.

4. *Perfect Square Numbers.* Perfect square numbers were created by arranging stones in arrays in the shape of a square, as in Figure 4. The Greeks called a square formed by three rows, each consisting of three stones each, "three squared" or nine. Note that today we still refer to a number n raised to the power of two as "n squared."

Number Relationships

Children need to know that people of all races, from many different nationalities, both male and female, have contributed significantly to the field of mathematics. Hypatia, an Egyptian woman born in A.D. 370, for example, made original contributions to the fields of number theory, geometry, and algebra. She discovered number relationships by partitioning groups of stones in a variety of ways.

The activity in Figure 5 illustrates a concept discussed by this first female mathematician on record. Children delight in discovering for themselves the relationship between the sum of the odd numbers and perfect squares. Notice the pattern revealed when you partition consecutive perfect squares, as shown in Figure 5. This arrangement shows that the sum of n consecutive odd natural numbers is equivalent to $n2$.

The activity illustrated in Figure 6 demonstrates how to construct all the possible number pairs that produce a given sum. Begin by creating a rectangular array of stones with dimension n by $n+1$. Figure 6, for example, shows a rectangle of the dimensions 10 by 11. If you partition the rectangle stepwise, you see all of

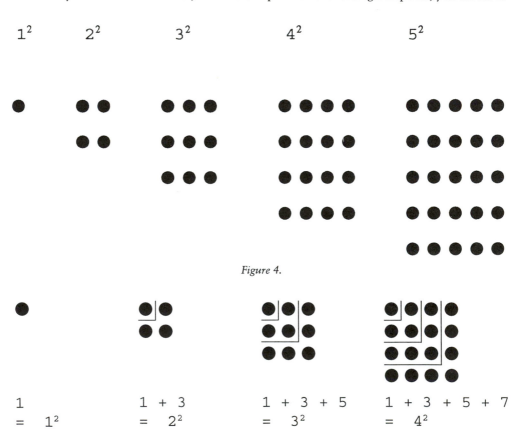

Figure 4.

Figure 5.

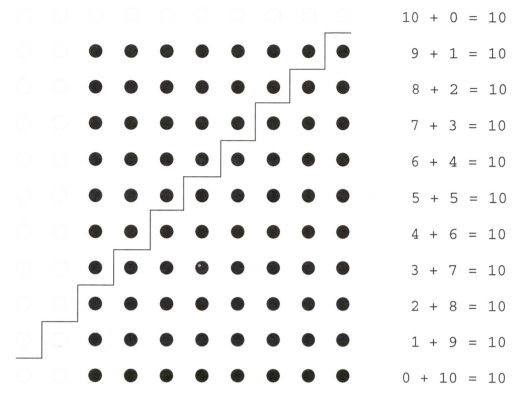

$$10 + 0 = 10$$
$$9 + 1 = 10$$
$$8 + 2 = 10$$
$$7 + 3 = 10$$
$$6 + 4 = 10$$
$$5 + 5 = 10$$
$$4 + 6 = 10$$
$$3 + 7 = 10$$
$$2 + 8 = 10$$
$$1 + 9 = 10$$
$$0 + 10 = 10$$

Figure 6.

the pairs of natural numbers (including zero) that form the sum *n*. For the number 10, for example, you see all of the possible number pairs whose sum is 10.

Fifth-grade children meet the challenge of looking at the pattern created by the steps and finding the sum of the natural numbers from 1 to 10 without adding or counting the stones. Since the sum is represented by one half of the design, most students conclude that the answer is found by multiplying 10 by 11 and then dividing the product by 2 to get 55.

Next, they meet the challenge of imagining a similar rectangular array of stones that is 100 by 101. Then they are able to find the sum of the natural numbers from 1 to 100. Nearly everyone arrives at the correct answer of 5050, quite a formidable feat for fifth-graders. Karl Gauss (1777–1855) was called a "child prodigy" for doing a similar problem at age eleven.

Teachers can use similar hands-on activities to discover many other properties of natural numbers, including the identification of primes; the binary operations of +, -, x, and <<division symbol>>; and factoring. The ancient Chinese were also fascinated with numerical and spatial

patterns. Like the Greeks, their approach was to manipulate physical models to discover patterns and make generalizations about their world. One of the mathematical entities that appears to be of Chinese origin is magic squares. The one shown in Figure 7 is attributed to Yu the Great (2200 B.C.). The square array was presented by means of knots of strings. This array represents the magic square:

8	3	4
1	5	9
6	7	2

It is "magic" because the sum of each row, column, and diagonal is the same. The challenge is to create other magic squares.

Magic squares are relevant today because they are still popular entities in recreational mathematics for solving problems in probability. More recently, they have been applied in Latin Square experimental research designs (National Council of Teachers of Mathematics, 1989b).

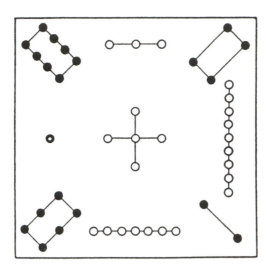

Figure 7. Chinese Representation of a Magic Square

Playful Activities in Algebra

The ancient Greeks, using mechanical devices, solved problems classified as riddles. These riddles today would fall under the rubric of algebra. In solving the riddles, the Greeks made use of Archimedes' law of the lever and other geometric models. In general, the Greeks' solutions to all mathematical problems were geometric and rhetorical in nature rather than numerical and symbolic. Modern algebra took many centuries to evolve.

Al-Khowarizmi, an Arab, wrote the first algebra book, *Al-jabr w'al mugabalah,* about A.D. 825. The word *algebra* comes from its title, as the spelling of *al-jabr* eventually became *algebra*. The chief merit of this work was the use of numeric symbols instead of geometric models and the solution of equations by operational procedures, although Al-Khowarizmi does verify his procedures by means of geometric models that reflected the earlier Greek influence. François Viete (1540–1603), a Frenchman, contributed the idea of variables, and the Englishman Robert Recorde in 1557 made use of the equal sign (=). The transition to a fully symbolic algebraic nota-tion, however, took place in the seventeenth century.

The teaching of algebra benefits from an understanding of how algebra has evolved from ancient to modern times. From this knowledge, the essay author created a game to provide an advance organizer for students' formal introduction to the subject. Within this game format and with very little assistance, children are able to discover the fundamental properties for solving first-degree equations in one variable. Reminiscent of Archimedes' *law of the lever,* the game requires that children solve riddles by manipulating objects on both ends of small balance beams or seesaws. Unappreciated by many people, a balanced seesaw is a physical model for an equation. The seesaw model can create infinite riddles for the game. A standard example is illustrated in Figure 8.

To balance a small seesaw, objects of equal weight are placed an equal distance from each end. The objects consist of bags with an equal number of cookies in each bag and some loose cookies that are not in bags. The goal of the riddle is to find the number of cookies in each bag without looking into the bags.

The method of manipulation is to remove objects from both sides of the seesaw to maintain the balance. (Moving objects closer to the center is disallowed in this game.) Eventually, the player can find the number of cookies that balance with a single bag, thus solving the riddle.

In Figure 8, the steps for solving the riddle are shown pictorially in the left-hand column. Symbols that represent these actions appear in the right-hand column.

Figure 8, depicting manipulations with balanced seesaws, shows the actual emergence of the laws for solving equations. Since the unknown quantity is the number of cookies in each bag, variable B symbolizes this amount. While solving the riddle, the players discover that it is necessary to isolate the variable on one side of the equation. Moreover, if the seesaw is to remain balanced, it is essential to do the same thing to both sides of the seesaw; that is, they must apply the same action to both sides of the equation.

Playful Activities in Geometry

This rich combination of mathematical ingredients—Archimedean problems, algebraic computational techniques, and a predisposition to play freely with physical models—produced a

It is clear that manipulating physical models and arranging them into patterns has led to some major developments in mathematics. Effective teachers of young children provide opportunities to construct these same models and guide children, through play, to make similar discoveries.

Four bags and one cookie will balance with two bags and seven cookies. How many cookies are in each bag?

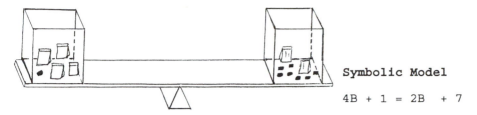

Symbolic Model

4B + 1 = 2B + 7

Activities

Remove 1 cookie from each side.

4B + 1 - 1 = 2B + 7 - 1

4B = 2B + 6

Remove 2 bags from each side.

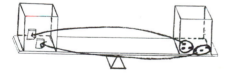

4B - 2B = 2B - 2B + 6

2B = 6

Divide 6 cookies into 2 equal parts.   (2B)/2 = 6/2

B = 3

Figure 8. Hands-on algebraic equations

profusion of powerful methods. People used these methods to solve area and volume problems of geometry long before the invention of the calculus by Newton and Leibniz. Johann Kepler (1571–1630) made significant contributions to the field of geometry that led eventually to the development of calculus.

Specifically, Kepler created an ingenious method for finding the area and volume of shapes with curved sides. He imagined a given geometric figure composed of infinitely many puzzle pieces. He would rearrange these area or volume pieces and then add them up to obtain the area or volume of the given curved region. Kepler's method for finding the area of a circle, for example, was to cut a circle into many congruent sectors and to rearrange them into the shape of a rectangle (see Figure 9).

This rectangle has the same area as the circle. Notice that the base of the rectangle is equal to half the circumference of the circle $(2\pi r/2 = \pi r)$ and the height is the same as the radius r of the circle. Since we find the area of any rectangle by multiplying the base by the height, the area of this rectangle, and also the circle, is found by $(\pi r)(r) = \pi r^2$.

A circle is divided into congruent sectors.

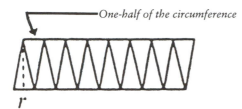

The sectors fit together to form a rectangular shape like this.

Figure 9. The Area of a Circle

Children can make this discovery also when they cut paper circles in a similar fashion, then rearrange them into rectangles. They enjoy using pizza pies and giant cookies, however, much more than paper.

**Playful Investigations
in Contemporary Mathematics**

The devices for playful investigations in contemporary mathematics have expanded to include electronic calculators and computers. These machines allow people to test conjectures and do investigations at a remarkably rapid pace, in fractions of a nanosecond (one billionth of a second). Among the newest areas, evolving as a direct result of these tools, are the fields of chaos theory and fractal geometry. Many of the underlying principles in these fields were discovered through free play with computers and computer-generated games (Peitgen, Jurgens, & Saupe, 1992, p. 35).

Chaos theory and fractal geometry provide a rich environment for exploring and modeling the complexity of nature. They offer ways to see patterns and order where formerly only the erratic and unpredictable were observed. Chaos theory, for example, can explain the formation of mountain ranges and the growth patterns of trees. Fractal geometry is closely linked to chaos theory in that it provides the structures that give order to chaos. Fractal geometry and chaos theory are also

linked by the fact that many contemporary pacesetting discoveries in these fields only became possible by using computers.

Intuitively speaking, a fractal is a repetitive, self-similar, geometric pattern of fractional dimension. Computer software exists for generating fractals with beautiful color and exciting structure. In particular, Microsoft's interactive encyclopedia, *Encarta '95,* permits the user to play with its fractal program to create an array of computer-generated fractals. Computers, therefore, extend the possibilities for mathematical play.

The characteristics of meaningful play are pervasive in mathematicians' work. It is a fact that many mathematical discoveries were born of playful activities involving hands-on explorations and puzzles of varied types. The above illustrations of actual activities that brought about the emergence of specific areas of mathematics might encourage readers to use them to engage children in meaningful play. Within such an exploratory environment, children may be invited to make their own mathematical discoveries and thereby construct their own knowledge and appreciation of mathematical logic.

Bibliography

Edwards, C. (1979). *Historical development of the calculus.* New York: Springer-Verlag.

Hogben, L. (1971). *Mathematics for the million.* New York: Norton.

Kasner, E., & Newman, J. (1940). *Mathematics and imagination.* New York: Simon and Schuster.

National Council of Teachers of Mathematics. (1989a). *Curriculum and evaluation standards for school mathematics.* Reston: Author.

National Council of Teachers of Mathematics. (1989b). *Historical topics for the mathematics classroom.* Reston: Author.

National Research Council, Mathematical Sciences Education Board (1989). *Everybody counts: A report to the nation on the future of mathematics education.* Washington, DC: National Academy Press.

Peitgen, H., Jurgens, J., & Saupe, D. (1992). *Chaos and fractals.* New York: Springer-Verlag.

Sponseller, D. (Ed.). (1976). *Play as a learn-*

ing medium. Washington, DC: National Association for the Education of Young Children.

Steen, L. (Ed.). (1990). *On the shoulders of giants.* Washington, DC: National Academy Press.

Weininger, O. (1979). *Play and education.* Springfield: Charles C. Thomas.

Business, Education, Journalism, the Law, and Medicine

Mixing Business with Pleasure

Play in the World of Work

Lynette Unger

The study of play in business appears at first glance to be a contradiction in terms. The business world often views play as the antithesis of work. Economic and management theories have long embraced a work-play dichotomy, compartmentalizing life into work and leisure/play[1] time and differentiating the two domains in terms of the psychological satisfactions they deliver. Work is the central, controlling element, and leisure is the time we have left for self-actualization and fun.

The separation of work and play also shapes our thinking in the workplace. Work should be free of play; playing at work is unprofessional. Promotion and salary are much more likely to reward normative compliance than risky or playful behavior. The literature on creativity consistently excludes the business world as an arena for creative expression (Blowhowiak, 1992). Unfortunately, limitations on play in much of the American workplace exist at a time when innovation is critical to the growth of global business.

The first part of this essay criticizes the theoretical separation of work and play in terms of geography, time, and psychological satisfactions. The second half explores the current U.S. workplace and the growing need for playfulness at work. It first investigates how the corporate structure and business education limit play, then discusses playfulness as a contributor to job performance.

Geographical Boundaries of Work and Play

Changes in the workplace underscore the permeability of the psychological boundary between work and play and the satisfactions they provide. The arenas of work and play are growing more similar. Researchers have focused on three areas: playful activities at work, worklike activities at play, and the convergence of work and play venues.

Play at Work

Leisure episodes within work time have come increasingly under study. Traditional researchers have focused on situational variables such as physical and social surroundings that create the leisure scenario (Chase & Cheek, 1979). Recent study, however, defines leisure episodes as more spontaneous. Leisure episodes, for example, can happen at work or in other situations not generally identified as leisure. One can experience leisure in many places and situations, including the workplace (Samdahl, 1992).

Beyond these spontaneous leisure episodes, researchers have recognized work-related leisure activities, which may not be play in the subjective sense. Many employees, for example, play golf with customers, attend the office or plant Christmas party, and share business lunches and other social occasions for reasons other than personal fulfillment. While these are identified as leisure activities, they comply with the dictates of role expectations. Personal play may or may not be a part of the experience (J. R. Kelly, 1972).

Work at Play

Conversely, play and leisure can be a means to build human capital or develop one's value in the workplace. Often people seek to strengthen their abilities and skills through leisure activities (J. Kelly 1983, 1987). Leisure is key to feelings of competency; like-minded participants have built personal identity and communities through long-term leisure activities (Freidson, 1990; Stebbins, 1979). The effort on the part of major corporations to increase their employees' health and wellness by maintaining fitness centers and programs is testimony. Such human-capital-building programs typically focus on leisure and sport facilities. Voluntarism also often appears to be a leisure or nonwork activity (Olson, 1973).

Convergence of the Work and Play Arenas

Technology has enabled decompartmentalization of leisure. We may see it as contained, but leisure is leaking into the rest of our time in the form of multitiered activities and innovations in the work venue. We listen to books on tape while commuting, we play with "Gameboy" waiting for our plane, we listen to the radio at work or chores, and some 34 percent of out-of-home television viewing takes place at work (Mandese, 1992). Home computers, faxes, and copiers further blur the geographic lines between work and play. Finally, the work, chore, and play arenas are converging, as employees become cocooners, telecommuters, job sharers, and mommy- and daddy-trackers.

The Work-Play Dichotomy: Time

Economists historically have defined leisure as time free from paid work, a viewpoint rooted in traditional microeconomic labor-leisure analysis (Henderson & Quandt, 1971). Even today, trends in aggregate working conditions such as average work week or length of average working life are routinely used to trace the amount of aggregate leisure available. The labor-leisure dichotomy has been extended more recently to a tripartite model of time: total time is comprised of work, chore/family, and leisure components. Leisure is again seen as residual, that which is left when work time and chore/family time have been subtracted from total time available (Becker, 1965).

The notion of leisure as a residual raises two issues. First, some researchers maintain that work is central to life and a joyless, unsatisfying necessity (Anthony, 1977; Freidson, 1990). Second, work and occupational status may have such a strong influence on life that they dictate the type of play one enjoys.

Is Work Central and Leisure Residual?

While it is clear that work time is often a constraint that prevents participation in leisure (Jackson & Witt, 1994), the work-play duality is an oversimplification of reality. Research over the past two decades has questioned the operationalization of leisure as residual time, and there is clear evidence that family time and/or leisure are more central to life than work (Gorz, 1982; Kelly & Kelly, 1994; Loscocco, 1989). Moreover, it is also clear that work can be playful and fun (Freidson, 1990).

Researchers identify two conceptual problems with limiting leisure to residual time. First, a "more is better" normative stance is implied, when quite the opposite may be true, as is the situation among the unemployed or elderly (Freidson, 1990). Second, the objective definition of leisure as time, while easy to operationalize, has always suffered from its forced compartmentalization. How do we categorize an hour spent chatting on the phone with a friend while washing dishes? How should weeding a garden or caring for a child be categorized if we really enjoy these "chores"? How might we categorize gambling or volunteer work?

Does Our Work Influence Our Play?

While earlier research shows a relationship between occupational status and roles and leisure activity choice (Clarke, 1956; Reissman, 1954), more recent studies indicate that play is unrelated to work activities. Earlier researchers compared the compensatory and spillover hypotheses (Wilensky, 1961). Compensatory leisure is when an activity is sought that is different from and compensates for something lacking in the work routine; an alienated worker, for example, who has a boring job might engage in drag racing or brawling when at leisure. In comparison, the spillover hypothesis maintains that there is a tendency toward consistency in leisure behavior, that familiar routines at work carry over into leisure behavior choice; the same person with a boring line job, for example, might also come home, drink beer all night, and stare at the dog. But recent research across different occupational categories provides little support for either hypothesis (Kelly & Kelly, 1994): satisfaction at work was not correlated with family or leisure satisfaction, demonstrating little spillover; there was also no support for the compensatory hypothesis because work satisfaction was not related to family or leisure disengagement.

The Work-Play Dichotomy: Psychological Aspects

The Subjective Experience of Play

Research has long addressed the presence of subjective qualities in the leisure experience, regardless of the activity being pursued. Studies focus primarily on three dimensions of leisure and play: intrinsic satisfaction, perceived freedom, and involvement (Unger & Kernan 1983). These dimensions have also been shown to be part of the work experience.

Leisure is often seen as *intrinsically motivated* and as an end in itself rather than a utilitarian means to an end (Dumazedier, 1974). Many researchers have noted leisure's pleasurable and satisfying nature (Berlyne, 1969; Mannell, Zuzanek, & Larson, 1988; Samdahl, 1987). A number of empirical studies substantiate the presence of intrinsic satisfaction in subjective play across many different situations (Iso-Ahola, 1979; Mannell, 1989; Unger & Kernan, 1983). Interestingly, some researchers distinguish leisure from work in the sense that work is extrinsically motivated because it is pursued largely for financial gains (Freidson, 1990).

Perceived freedom appears to be consistently present in the leisure experience. Leisure is often perceived as free, voluntary, and without coercion or obligation (Dumazedier, 1974). Some researchers have identified perceived freedom as the single precondition of the leisure experience (Ingham, 1986). Again, researchers have often used an obligatory-discretionary continuum to segregate leisure and play from other activities. Many studies have demonstrated the presence of perceived freedom in play (Iso-Ahola, 1979; Mannell, 1978; Unger & Kernan, 1983).

Researchers suggest that play means *high involvement* or total absorption in an activity. At play, we enter a world distinct from daily life, described by some as a fantastic escape from reality or simply just an interlude that is separate from the ordinary (Berlyne, 1969; Samdahl & Kleiber, 1988). Recent research has generated considerable support for this dimension as well (Csikszentmihalyi, 1990; Havitz & Dimanche, 1990).

Yet there is considerable evidence that many leisure activities may often be nondiscretionary or otherwise constrained. Leisure researchers who study constraints and activity termination have identified many factors that encroach on the true freedom and intrinsic satisfaction play provides (Jackson & Witt, 1994). These include intrapersonal factors (physical limitations), interpersonal factors (lack of partners), and structural factors (crowding, limited facilities). In a more general sense, cultural anthropologists have pointed out that leisure experiences may be tainted by the same alienation felt at work under a repressive social system (Allison & Duncan, 1987; J. Kelly, 1992). For example, leisure can be reduced to mere consumption, a reward for suffering the drudgery of alienated work. It is often limited by socioeconomic resources.

Are Work and Play Really So Different?

Work often takes on the same characteristics as leisure. The subjective experiences that have been identified as unique to the leisure or play experience—intrinsic satisfaction, perceived freedom and involvement—often are experienced at work as well.

There is evidence that, even beyond compensation received, work often offers *intrinsic satisfaction* (Yankelovich, 1983). Freidson (1990) distinguishes labors of love from alienated labor in a Marxist sense. Labors of love are creative and offer gratifications independent of economic necessity and conventional material rewards. While Freidson identifies voluntarism, amateurism and under- or unpaid artistic work as true labors of love, other researchers indicate that paid work also offers experiences of intrinsic satisfaction (Csikszentmihalyi, 1975; Schwalbe, 1986). In a recent study, two hundred workers engaged in a variety of occupations rated work higher than average on satisfaction, although significantly lower than the leisure and family domains (Kelly & Kelly, 1994). In earlier studies, the intrinsically satisfying experiences of work appear to be limited more to white-collar workers (Noe, 1971; Spreitzer & Snyder, 1974).

There is clear evidence that *perceived freedom* is important in the workplace. One researcher identifies self-determination—the use of initiative, thought, and independent judgment—as a primary factor in work satisfaction (Kohn, 1990). Other research underscores the importance of autonomy on the job (Becherer, Morgan, & Richard, 1982; Dubinsky & Hartley, 1984).

Similarly, *involvement* appears to be present in the work as well as play experience. Csikszentmihalyi (1975, 1990) has found "flow," similar to involvement, more often in work than in leisure situations. Others, however, found significantly less experience/involvement and disengagement (opportunity for rest and relaxation, peaceful environment) in work than in family and leisure activities (Kelly & Kelly, 1994). Still other recent studies on work satisfaction have found involvement to have a positive correlation with job satisfaction (Becherer, Morgan, & Richard, 1982; Brown & Peterson, 1993).

Beyond the fact that intrinsic satisfaction, perceived freedom, and involvement appear to be common experiences in both leisure and work, social interaction is also important in both domains. Social interaction is an important reason for leisure activity participation (Crandall, 1979). Researchers often define social contact (such as visiting friends or talking on the phone) as a leisure activity itself or an innate element of certain activities such as sports (McKechnie, 1974). Some researchers have extended this thinking to define leisure as a group activity, in contrast to work, which is an individual activity (Chase & Cheek, 1979).

Recent research finds social interaction also salient in the workplace. Employees of all types, for example, appreciate informal relationships in the workplace (Epstein, 1990; Granovetter, 1985; Kelly & Kelly, 1994).

The Need for Playfulness at Work

There are enormous pressures to innovate in the global marketplace. While the U.S. trade deficit continues to grow, Americans enjoy a trade surplus in high-technology industries such as software, telecommunications, and many services. Export growth among small, innovative companies in the past five years has grown eight to ten times faster than U.S. exports overall. Trade negotiation efforts have focused often on intellectual property protection to shelter American innovation worldwide. Corporate growth relies on new products, new services, and new systems, yet new product failure rates continue to run at 80 to 90 percent. Corporations must successfully innovate and commercialize as rapidly as possible.

An exhaustive analysis of studies on innovation at work identifies three streams of research (Wolfe, 1994). The first, on the *diffusion of innovation,* focuses on the marketing function and how it can encourage the spread of innovation through targeted populations. The

second area studies what determines organizational innovativeness; here, the level of analysis is the organization, and the *number of successful innovations* typically is the dependent variable. The third area investigates the *process* that organizations use to implement innovation and bring new products and services to market. It focuses on stages of development from idea conception to commercialization; again, the level of analysis is the firm.

What is striking in these findings is the lack of focus on the individual innovator (Wolfe, 1994). Even research that studies stages of innovation development pays much less attention to idea generation than to subsequent developmental stages. Similarly in studies of entrepreneurship, the emphasis is on commercialization of an innovation, rather than the creation of the innovation. Management research appears to focus on creating a corporate structure that encourages bringing innovation to market, but shies away from research at the inventor level.

Because U.S. citizens have always been seen as leaders in innovation, industry may take this playfulness for granted (Rostow, 1993). Perhaps words like *creative* or *free spirit* are not considered businesslike, or possibly the structural impediments and stereotyping of older hierarchical organizational models still remain. It is clear that individual creativity is often mismanaged. Business leaders often lack understanding of the role of creativity, and estimates indicate that only 5 percent of executives ever have formal training in creativity (Blowhowiak, 1992). It seems that business sees play, the essence and beginning of creativity at the individual level, as unprofessional; yet it is the very thing that business in the United States needs to stimulate to capitalize on its competitive advantage.

Structural Problems That Hamper Innovation

Recognizing the need to stimulate innovation in the workplace, companies have designed "the new workplace" to accommodate the economic necessity for innovation as well as the changing demographics and expectations of the workforce (Kanter, 1978). It is clear that all organizational functions, not just research and development, should be geared toward innovation. While larger companies cannot return to their more freewheeling entrepreneurial days, they can incorporate structural changes that enhance creativity and risk-taking and encourage rapid commercialization of innovation. Many firms have incorporated structures such as project teams, increased employee involvement, independent business units, elimination of middle-management layers, entrepreneurship programs, and versatile work scheduling (e.g., job sharing and flex time) (Kanter, 1990).

Yet there are clear barriers, both structural and attitudinal, which often prevent innovative thinking. Kanter (1990) identifies three areas where new workplace practices and configurations strain the hierarchical structure on which most corporations rest. First, reward systems based on employee participation threaten the traditional hierarchy, as innovative participants may get paid more than the boss.

Second, the very structure of a large corporation encourages stability and maintenance of the status quo. Historically, workers were paid to work and managers were paid to innovate, think, and direct (Blowhowiak, 1992). The management of innovation is difficult for the large corporation because it is difficult to forecast and assign time tables, and organizations need to predict outcomes with reasonable confidence (Quinn, 1985). Innovation requires stability in leadership, championing, and personal commitment to development, often impossible in larger corporations where employees are tracked for promotion and where reliable outcomes lead to upward mobility. Finally, innovation involves bringing together different parts of the organization that may sooner or later be affected in corporations that are structured around functions (e.g., marketing, product development, manufacturing). In a smaller business, the entrepreneur must, similarly, wrestle with the provision of these functions through hiring or outside services.

Third, there is a need to expand work hours to nurture an innovation (Kanter, 1990). The "new workplace increases the absorptiveness of work" (p. 298), and, consequently, workers with outside commitments may have less time to champion the innovation. Women, who shoulder most of the burden of family management, may be particularly at the mercy of this situation.

Creativity in Business Training

Graduate business schools and corporations have only begun to address the need for creative management training. Over the last century,

formal business education has evolved through three stages: schools of commerce, which train for a particular trade such as bookkeeping; schools of management, which prepare people to manage in large corporations; and now "new" schools of management, which train managers to creatively address unknown problems and demands (Ruefli, 1985). These new schools of management are not yet a reality, but there is a great deal of dialogue concerning what is needed from modern business education. Some experts urge more business-academic interface and legitimization of creative management. Others insist that a paucity of communication and interpersonal skills exacerbate a lack of creative approach, and that business students need to learn self-motivation and initiative (Dowd & Liedtka, 1994).

In the business world, creativity is often recast as "problem-solving" ability. Skills of problem solving are enhanced by developing expertise, the ability to identify important cues in the environment (Simon, 1985). Business schools, particularly leading schools in graduate business education, have incorporated a variety of methods to compress the time needed to acquire expertise. Case methods, business games, computer simulations, and learning from experts' presentations have all been important methods to encourage creative problem solving. Hands-on experience, such as internships, project classes, and advertising campaign courses also have been used to expand didactic learning. Courses in entrepreneurism, always recognized as a bastion for the mavericks of business, are becoming increasingly popular in response to student demand.

In recent years, the value of a liberal arts underpinning has increasingly been recognized in graduate business schools' admissions policies and in course development. Courses in oral and written communication as well as interpersonal skill development have been incorporated into many business curricula, and these are often taught by interdisciplinary teams. In some programs, students take courses in political science, history, or literature. In schools stressing international business education, courses in foreign language and cultural proficiency, as well as field studies abroad, are often included.

While formal business education has made some strides toward preparing students for the more freewheeling, downsized business enterprise, it has not been sufficient. Companies find it necessary to conduct in-house training in creative management and countless books and formalized programs for generating creativity have appeared in the past decade (VanGundy, 1992). While most of these approaches are not labeled "play" training, they do incorporate the features that often distinguish play, such as creativity, risk-taking, challenge, and innovation.

Playfulness and Job Performance

In an era of downsizing and increased worldwide competition, worker productivity becomes very important. There is evidence that playfulness may have a positive impact on job performance. While acknowledging a historically questionable relationship between personality variables and job performance in the management literature, Barrick and Mount (1991) correlated the "big five" personality factors with job performance across five occupations. In their meta-analysis of 117 studies, they found that openness of experience, a dimension that has been described as imaginative, curious, original, and broad-minded, was a valid predictor of training proficiency. Persons scoring high on this characteristic may be more motivated to learn and consequently benefit more from training. Openness to experience may also correlate positively with ability to learn (Barrick & Mount, 1991; Hunter, 1983).

Another recent study of salesperson performance studied four groups of variables and their correlations with job satisfaction, which was also shown to be an effective predictor of sales performance (Brown & Peterson, 1993). This meta-analysis also found that individual differences, which included demographic and socioeconomic factors along with measures of work motivation, were associated with job satisfaction. Work motivation in this case bears similarities to intrinsic satisfaction, a finding that is also consistent with earlier studies (Bagozzi, 1980; Hafer & McCuen, 1985; Kohli, 1985). Job/task characteristics also were frequently correlated with job satisfaction. Play-related characteristics of job satisfaction included the amount of autonomy, which is similar to perceived freedom on the job, the degree of innovativeness required, and the kind of job involvement (Becherer, Morgan, & Richard, 1982).

Downsizing and restructuring have forced corporations to regroup employees. Innovations in work groups have mandated particular attention to the cultivation of teamwork.

Changes in corporate structure such as mergers, joint ventures, and strategic alliances, involving different corporate cultures and procedures and often different national cultures as well, underscore the importance of team building. While the research generally focuses on knowledge, skills, and abilities because they can be taught (Stevens & Campion, 1994), there is some evidence for personality-based selection of teams, and playfulness may be one characteristic of a good team player. Researchers identify qualities such as initiative, trust, openness, helpfulness, flexibility, and supportiveness (Stevens & Campion, 1994). Openness and flexibility in these workplace contexts appear to be similar to playfulness.

While they are typically seen as opposites, the distinction between work and play is blurred. Their geographical boundaries are lessened by technological advances and social change. Viewed as different components of time, work and play often overlap or are difficult to separate. The satisfactions provided by both life domains are similar, and they often suffer similar constraints. Maintaining the distinctions between work and play threatens global business development. While play is necessary to spark the innovation that fuels corporate growth, old and new corporate structures often discourage its presence and training for creative management is only in its early stages. Playfulness may also play an important role in effective job performance.

Note

1. In this essay, the terms *leisure* and *play* are used synonymously.

Bibliography

Allison, M., & Duncan, M. (1987). Women, work and leisure: The days of our lives. *Leisure Sciences, 9,* 143–162.

Anthony, P. D. (1977). *The ideology of work.* London: Tavistock.

Bagozzi, R. P. (1980). Performance and satisfaction in an industrial sales force: An examination of their antecedents and simultaneity. *Journal of Marketing, 44,* 65–67.

Barrick, M. P., & Mount, M. K. (1991). The big five personality dimensions and job performance: A meta-analysis. *Personnel Psychology, 44,* 1–26.

Becerer, R. C., Morgan, F. W., & Richard, L. M. (1982). The job characteristics of industrial salespersons: Relationship to motivation and satisfaction. *Journal of Marketing, 46,* 125–135.

Becker, G. S. (1965). A theory of the allocation of time. *Economic Journal, 75,* 493–517.

Berlyne, D. E. (1969). Laughter, humor and play. In G. Lindzey and E. Aronson (Eds.), *The handbook of social psychology* (Vol. 2, pp. 795–852). Reading, MA: Addison Wesley.

Blowhowiak, D. W. (1992). *Mavericks!* Homewood, IL: Irwin.

Brown, S. P., & Peterson, R. A. (1993). Antecedents and consequences of salesperson job satisfaction: Meta-analysis and assessment of causal effects. *Journal of Marketing Research, 30,* 63–77.

Chase, D. R., & Cheek, N. H. (1979). Activity preferences and participation: Conclusions from a factor analysis study. *Journal of Leisure Research, 11,* 92–101.

Clarke, A. C. (1956). The use of leisure and its relation to levels of occupational prestige. *American Sociological Review, 21,* 301–307.

Crandall, R. (1979). Social interaction, affect and leisure. *Journal of Leisure Research, 11,* 165–181.

Csikszentmihalyi, M. (1975). *Beyond boredom and anxiety.* San Francisco: Jossey-Bass.

Csikszentmihalyi, M. (1990). *Flow: The psychology of optimal experience.* New York: Harper & Row.

Dowd, K. O., & Liedtka, J. (1994). What corporations seek in MBA hires: A survey. *Selections, 10*(2), 34–39.

Dubinsky, A. J., & Hartley, S. W. (1984). A path-analytic study of a model of salesperson performance. *Journal of the Academy of Marketing Science, 14,* 36–46.

Dumazedier, J. (1974). *Sociology of leisure.* Amsterdam: Elsevier.

Epstein, C. (1990). The cultural perspective and the study of work. In K. Erikson & S. P. Vallas (Eds.), *The nature of work* (pp. 88–98). New Haven: Yale University Press.

Freidson, E. (1990). Labors of love in theory and practice: A prospectus. In K. Erikson & S. P. Vallas (Eds.), *The nature of work* (pp. 149–161).

New Haven: Yale University Press.

Gorz, A. (1982). *Farewell to the working class: An essay in post-industrial socialism.* Boston: South End.

Granovetter, M. (1985). Economic action, social structure, and embeddedness. *American Journal of Sociology, 19,* 481–510.

Hafer, J., & McCuen, B. A. (1985). Antecedents of performance and satisfaction in a service sales force as compared to an industrial sales force. *Journal of Personal Selling and Sales Management, 5,* 7–17.

Havitz, M. E., & Dimanche, F. (1990). Propositions for testing the involvement construct in recreational and tourism contexts. *Leisure Sciences, 12,* 179–195.

Henderson, J. M., & Quandt, R. E. (1971). *Microeconomic theory: Mathematical approach.* New York: McGraw-Hill.

Hunter, J. E. (1983). A causal analysis of cognitive ability, job knowledge, job performance and supervisory ratings. In F. Landy, S. Zedeck & J. Cleveland (Eds.), *Performance measurement and theory* (pp. 257–266). Hillsdale, NJ: Lawrence Erlbaum.

Ingham, R. (1986). Psychological contributions to the study of leisure. Part 1. *Leisure Studies, 5,* 255–279.

Iso-Ahola, S. E. (1979). Basic dimensions of definitions of leisure. *Journal of Leisure Research, 2*(1), 28–39.

Jackson, E. L., & Witt, P. A. (1994). Change and stability in leisure constraints: A comparison of two surveys conducted four years apart. *Journal of Leisure Research, 26,* 250–274.

Kanter, R. M. (1978). Work in a new America. *Daedalus, 107,* 47–48.

Kanter, R. M. (1990). The new work force meets the changing workplace. In K. Erikson & S. P. Vallas (Eds.), *The nature of work* (pp. 279–303). New Havens: Yale University Press.

Kelly, J. (1983). *Leisure identities and interactions.* London: Allen and Unwin.

Kelly, J. (1987). *Freedom to be: A new sociology of leisure.* New York: Macmillan.

Kelly, J. (1992). Leisure. In E. Borgatta (Ed.), *The encyclopedia of sociology* (Vol. 3, pp. 1099–1107). New York: Macmillan.

Kelly, J. R. (1972). Work and leisure: A simplified paradigm. *Journal of Leisure Research, 4,* 50–62.

Kelly, John R., & Kelly, Janice R. (1994). Multiple dimensions of meaning in the domains of work, family and leisure. *Journal of Leisure Research, 26,* 250–274.

Kohli, A. K. (1985). Some unexplored supervisory behaviors and their influence on salespeople's role clarity, specific self-esteem, job satisfaction and motivation. *Journal of Marketing Research, 22,* 424–433.

Kohn, M. (1990). Unresolved issues in work/personality. In K. Erikson & S. P. Vallas (Eds.), *The nature of work* (pp. 36–68). New Haven: Yale University Press.

Loscocco, K. (1989). The instrumentally oriented factory worker: Myth or reality? *Work and Occupations, 16,* 3–25.

Mandese, J. (1992). Network study tracks out-of-home viewing. *Advertising Age, 40,* 38.

Mannell, R. C. (1989). Leisure satisfaction. In E. L. Jackson & T. L. Burton (Eds.), *Understanding leisure and recreation: Mapping the past, charting the future* (pp. 281–302). State College, PA: Venture.

Mannell, R. C., Zuzanek, J., & Larson, R. (1988). Leisure states and "flow" experiences: Testing perceived freedom and intrinsic motivation hypotheses. *Journal of Leisure Research, 20,* 289–304.

McKechnie, G. (1974). The psychological structure of leisure: Past behavior. *Journal of Leisure Research, 6,* 27–45.

Noe, F. P. (1971). Autonomous spheres of leisure activity for the industrial executive and blue collarite. *Journal of Leisure Research, 3,* 220–227.

Olson, M. (1973). *The logic of collective action: Public goods and the theory of groups.* Cambridge, MA: Harvard University Press.

Quinn, J. B. (1985). Managing innovation: Controlled chaos. *Harvard Business Review, 67,* 73–84.

Reissman, L. (1954). Class, leisure and social participation. *American Sociological Review, 19,* 76–84.

Rostow, W. W. (1993). The American administrative style: A costly inheritance. In R. L. Kuhn (Ed.), *Generating creativity and innovation in large bureaucracies* (pp. 21–50). Westport, CT: Quorum.

Ruefli, T. W. (1985). Creative and innovative management: A manifesto for academia. In R. L. Kuhn (Ed.), *Frontiers in creative and innovative management* (pp. 277–293). Cambridge, MA: Ballinger.

Samdahl, D. M. (1987). A symbolic interactionist model of leisure, theory and empirical support. *Leisure Sciences, 10,* 27–39.

Samdahl, D. M. (1992). Leisure in our lives: Exploring the common leisure occasion. *Journal of Leisure Research, 24,* 19–32.

Samdahl, D. M., & Kleiber, D. A. (1988). Self-awareness and leisure experience. *Leisure Sciences, 11,* 1–10.

Schwalbe, M. L. (1986). *The psychosocial consequences of natural and alienated labor.* Albany: State University of New York Press.

Simon, H. A. (1985). What we know about the creative process. In R. L. Kuhn (Ed.), *Frontiers in creative and innovative management* (pp. 3–20). Cambridge, MA: Ballinger.

Spreitzer, E., & Snyder, E. (1974). Work orientation, meaning of leisure and mental health. *Journal of Leisure Research, 6,* 207–212.

Stebbins, R. A. (1979). *Amateurs: On the margins between work and leisure.* Newbury Park, CA: Sage.

Stevens, M. J., & Campion, M. A. (1994). The knowledge, skill and ability requirements for teamwork. *Journal of Management, 20,* 503–553.

Unger, L. S., & Kernan, J. B. (1983). On the meaning of leisure: An investigation of some determinants of the subjective experience. *Journal of Consumer Research, 9,* 381–392.

VanGundy, A. B. (1992). *Idea power.* New York: American Management Association Committee.

Wilensky, H. (1961). The uneven distribution of leisure: The impact of economic growth on free time. *Social Problems, 1,* 32–38.

Wolfe, R. A. (1994). Organizational innovation: Review, critique and suggested research directions. *Journal of Management Studies, 3,* 405–431.

Yankelovich, D. (1983). *Work and human values: An international report on jobs in the 1980s and 1990s.* New York: Aspen Institute for Humanistic Studies.

Play among Education Professionals

Joan P. Isenberg

Conversations and anecdotal evidence about play in the lives of educators indicate that play is often implicit in the way these professionals think about problems and solutions, create new pathways and ideas, and make decisions when facing the unexpected. These perspectives suggest some thoughts on the role of play among educators for the future.

Although there are many theories, definitions, and reasons advanced for why play is important, none has been devoted explicitly to explaining the role of play in the development of mentally healthy and creative professionals (Blatner & Blatner, 1988). In particular, play experts have not discussed how play influences the mental as well as physical life of education professionals or its relationship to these adults' work-related creativity and imagination. As the context for a discussion of play among education professionals, a definition of play and playfulness is provided.

Definition of Play and Playfulness

Although those who study play have not always agreed on a definition of play, most experts do agree that there are some characteristics that distinguish play from other forms of human behavior (Bretherton, 1984; Fromberg, 1992, 1995). Similarly, although experts have varied definitions of a professional, they do concede that the characteristic hallmarks of a professional include "acquiring more specialized knowledge, gaining greater insights about responsible practice, learning to function as decision-makers, and earning more prestige in the larger community" (Jalongo & Isenberg, 1995, p. 129). Fromberg's (1992) definition of play

identifies seven characteristics that can be used to draw interesting parallels between play and the playful behaviors seen among diverse education professionals. Play is:

1. *Symbolic,* in that it represents reality with "as-if" and "what-if" attitudes. One author describes using imagination as "what-if" behavior, which enables one to think through solutions to problems either in one's head or aloud (Weininger, 1988). The "as-if" attitude is the activity that facilitates the further thinking of ideas (the play). For a child pretending to be an alien, the "what-if" behavior is the imagination or "thinking through" of the roles and feelings of an alien, while the "as-if" behavior is the play itself that enables the child to experience particular attributes and feelings.

   This process, however, is not reserved for children. A classroom teacher uses a similar thinking method in lesson planning and unit building. Teachers engage in "what-if" behavior when they mentally invent procedures that help children access their prior knowledge or determine appropriate forms of assessment. Similarly, they take an "as-if" attitude in implementing and modifying procedures, providing experiences, and monitoring pacing throughout the teaching/learning process.

2. *Meaningful,* in that it connects or relates experiences. Play, for children, has meaning because it is integrally connected to their everyday experiences. Educators are concerned with a similar issue of meaning when they provide student experiences.

To provoke and broaden prospective teachers' perspectives, for example, teacher educators take into account how the circumstances of simulated teaching dilemmas can connect with students' life situations and experiences and with broader historical and philosophical patterns. Whether the topic is classroom management, sensitivity to diverse families and cultures, or responses to specific ethical dilemmas, meaningful play with the topic helps students examine it from multiple perspectives.

3. *Active,* in that individuals are doing things. Play of children is always an active process. Activity is also essential for adult thinking. Stories about famous scientists such as Albert Einstein, James Watt, and James Watson describe how they were actively involved in explorations and inventions. Each of them became "unusually engrossed in playing with concrete physical objects, mechanical models, geometrical puzzles, . . . wooden cubes" (Shepard, 1988, p. 173) as they pursued their inventions. Similarly, school counselors and lead teachers often experience actively, concretely, and engrossingly the intervention or teaching strategy they wish to employ prior to helping novice students and peers learn it.

4. *Pleasurable,* even when the activity is serious. Children focus on their play very intently and enjoy that intensity of involvement. The notion that enjoyment can enhance one's work and activity is often difficult for Western cultures to grasp, yet it is an important part of education. Educators who have been struggling with teaching a particular skill or concept, for example, are likely to continue to seek advice and counsel from colleagues and other sources until they experience a breakthrough with the students. Although the task of helping others learn is extremely serious work, the pleasure that most educators gain from exploring alternative teaching/learning methods and participating in their students' "ah ha" experiences makes their effort very worthwhile.

5. *Voluntary and intrinsically motivating,* whether the motivation is curiosity, mastery, or financial. Children's curiosity and mastery motivations are clearly evi-

dent in their play. Educators also show the ability to choose activities that are important to achieving their motivational goals. The building principal who has been transferred to a school explicitly to change the school climate, for example, may have inherited an angry, resistant staff who wish to keep the status quo. To create a climate for change, the principal must choose alternative ways to empower current staff and select new staff who will be open to change. The principal and staff must be highly motivated to make the changes needed for a more comfortable school climate. These voluntary and intrinsically motivating aspects that propel such change parallel this aspect of play behavior.

6. *Rule-governed,* whether implicitly or explicitly expressed. Children's play is often highly rule-governed, although this is not always apparent to the casual observer because the rules are usually child-imposed. Similarly, educators both follow established teaching and learning rules and procedures and develop great variety and autonomy in their rule-governed behavior. Although common rules serve to inform teaching and learning, the way a particular educator chooses to present and represent the facts and information within those constraints is the prerogative of the educator's creative, unique, and exploratory terrain.

7. *Episodic,* in that there is evidence of emerging and shifting goals that develop throughout the experience. As children play, their goals develop in various ways; in fact, a hallmark of play is that of goal flexibility. Similarly, a director of a child care program might find that, in explaining the curriculum to a group of parents, the parents raise unexpected questions or concerns. As the director provides information, other parents may ask related and probing questions, which may cause the director to shift responses, consider new ways of sharing information, connect differently with the particular group, and generate new or modified goals from the session input.

As these examples show, each of these seven behaviors that characterize play is also present in the work life of educational professionals.

These elements also ignite other play-related behaviors such as imagination, creativity, innovative problem solving, risk-taking, challenge, construction of meaning, flexibility of thought, and interactive social processes. Because few connections between play and the education professions have been previously explored, the next section focuses on ways to extend the exploration of these connections.

Playful Characteristics in the Education Profession

The characteristics of play and playful behavior appear intuitively or implicitly both in the modus operandi and typical methodologies of most professionals. Conversations with and observations of educators in a variety of roles, however, have revealed that few of these professionals ever consider that playful ways of knowing hold a central place in their professional lives. Their view of play is often limited to children's physical recess play and adults' playing of games. Thus, they do not connect their concerns about responsible practice, specialized knowledge, and good decision-making practice with the characteristics of play previously discussed. There are, nevertheless, many playful characteristics that permeate educators' behavior and thinking.

Pleasurable and Flexible Thought

Most professionals fantasize about assuming different roles within their profession. Playing with these roles in one's mind enhances mental health, strengthens understanding of the elements of the role, and stimulates thinking about that role (Blatner & Blatner, 1988). These characteristics are evident in many curriculum redesign efforts. Teachers, principals, specialists, and central office personnel, for example, may collaboratively design an assessment tool to be piloted and evaluated. In such a districtwide revamping of an assessment measure, characteristics of playfulness are often needed. When there are many players on a project, each must understand how differing roles and responsibilities affect each other. Being able to imagine the roles of these different team members is crucial to the project's success. Their experience is similar to that of scientists on a space shuttle, in which team members must combine their specialized knowledge with flexible thinking to engage in decision making and problem solving.

Voluntary Participation

Play requires a choice of participation or nonparticipation in an activity. In childhood, invitations to "come play" represent happy times. Here, children are free to enter or not enter the play world of others, to assume different roles, to exercise their imaginations, and to distance themselves from current pressures or self-conscious experiences (Blatner & Blatner, 1988, p. 9). In a similar fashion, professionals experience rewards from voluntary participation in professional activity. The design team members discussed earlier, for example, receive satisfaction from participating in this creative endeavor, assuming the imagined and real roles and responsibilities of the teachers, parents, administrators, and students who are stakeholders, and being relieved from humdrum and routine work by engagement in this project. Voluntary behavior of this type increases educators' vitality, creativity, and power.

Active and Innovative Problem Solving

There are many ways educators are actively involved in problem-solving activities. Learning to play with ideas and models or negotiate roles requires a realignment of the mental orientation to book learning. Educators learning in social contexts must have not only specialized knowledge of developmental principles, content fields, and pedagogy, but also the capacity to face novelty and take risks as they plan new approaches to teaching. They must often incorporate the elements of play that are necessary for visionary, creative, and nontraditional ways of thinking.

Episodic, Spontaneous Thinking

Educators need to employ episodic characteristics when goals or strategies must be shifted to meet changing situations that require flexible and spontaneous thinking. Spontaneity is the opposite of habitual, routine ways of thinking about people, events, problems, or materials. Because spontaneity is a quality of mind, it generates new thinking and new frames of reference by "thinking afresh . . . balancing impulse and restraint, and integrating imagination, reason, and intuition. [It is] . . . more than impulsivity because it requires some intention to achieve an aesthetic or constructive effect" (Blatner & Blatner, 1988, p. 23).

Environments must have a moderate level of structure to capitalize on spontaneous thinking in both the physical and human workplace. With too little structure, professional roles and responsibilities are not clear and do not allow for flexible thinking. Too much structure, however, impedes the development of new ideas, new solutions, and new ways of operating. When members of an educational intervention team, charged with evaluating a child's placement and progress, negotiate and demonstrate episodic and spontaneous characteristics to make difficult but appropriate decisions, they are engaging in these play-related behaviors.

Methodologies of Inquiry

Even as educators have not considered play part of their modus operandi, neither have they regarded their methods of inquiry as having playful elements. Two inquiry methods that especially lend themselves to playful ways of knowing, however, are experiential learning/ role-play and case methods. Each of these methodologies depends on playful characteristics to maximize the amount of learning and foster student identification with the complex aspects of their profession.

Experiential Learning/Role-Playing
Experiential learning, in particular role-playing, enables prospective education professionals to find solutions and answer questions that fit their own styles. This may occur when a prospective teacher learns about handling a classroom through a simulated teaching experience, the principal discovers ways to interact with diverse families by taking a role in a case study, or a school counselor learns particular counseling skills and practices through video analysis of his or her role playing (Blatner & Blatner, 1988). Role-playing enables participants to move beyond "knowing about" the kinds of information that can be communicated by books or lectures, and to begin to "understand," which involves the active integration of the imaginative and emotional dimensions of the mind. Experiential learning develops professionals who not only *know about* but also *know how* and *know why* to provide particular experiences. "Learning by doing" supports the creative and playful aspects of professional behavior and illustrates the old proverb that you can give a person a fish or teach that person to fish: the first condition leads to dependence, the sec-

ond to self-sufficiency. The future of the profession rests on the preparation and retraining of education professionals who will exercise sound, theory-based, research-based, and practice-tested judgment (Isenberg & Jalongo, 1993).

In role-playing situations, students engage in role reversals. For prospective educators, assuming the role of others (e.g., client, student, parent, principal, school board member, legislator) can assist students in understanding the "emotional needs and subtleties of interactions . . . to try out constructive strategies and refine and practice skills" (Blatner & Blatner, 1988, p. 149). In this way, professionals become "more aware of the impact of their own repertoire of behaviors on clients or co-workers, and then go on to learn what actions or kinds of statements are likely to confuse, mystify, or subtly humiliate" (p. 144).

Case Method
Case methodology, which is the use of authentic, professional dilemmas to gain deeper insights into the complexities of a particular field, has been a prime teaching technique in business, law, and nursing. Cases provide a common mode of inquiry that enables professionals to play with ideas, roles, and situations. By focusing on complex problem-solving situations, requiring participants to recognize the multiple possibilities and layers situated in professional dilemmas, and provoking the application of understandings rather than the passive acceptance of ideas, they force students to wrestle with the real-world problems of their respective fields (Christensen, 1990; Merseth, 1991; Silverman, Welty, & Lyon, 1992). Case use in education is a very recent phenomenon; it is an important one because those who work in all interactive professions need the flexibility to negotiate the shared script building with colleagues that evolves out of professional knowledge development. These processes of negotiation parallel the sociodramatic script building of children. There are other characteristics of the case method that require both the participants and facilitators to demonstrate playful behaviors:

- *Risk-taking behavior.* For the case leader in particular, this may be a new form of teaching or training; leaders must entail risk by exposing their teaching skills, sense of control, and ability to manage open-ended discussion to a new methodology.

- *Innovative problem solving.* Participants seek possible solutions after examining the perspectives of stakeholders they usually ignore and hearing views that may be in conflict with their own.
- *Flexible thinking.* Participants reorganize data to explore different solutions.
- *Construction of meaning.* Participants figure out new ways of relating to constituents.
- *Interactive social processes.* Participants confront the differing views of other case discussants.

When used as part of teacher preparation programs, cases can help students understand strategies for working with children who have special learning needs, grapple with issues generated by changing viewpoints of families in education, and struggle with difficult issues of school finance or school law. Moreover, the case method can be an effective learning tool for practicing teachers who are asked to write cases about the teaching dilemmas they have encountered (National Association of Early Childhood Teacher Educators, 1991).

Thus, using these two methodologies, which require the development of playful characteristics, also promotes professional growth. Although such playful simulated experiences are very useful, however, probably the easiest connection to play for laypersons to see is the typical preparation requirement of actual practice in a "real-life" educational setting (student teaching or internship) before complete professional status is awarded.

Role of Practice/Technique

Specialized skills and techniques are particular to every profession, and educators must learn many of these. Nachmanovitch (1990) suggests there is also a kind of metalearning (or a metadoing) that overarches the practice of specific techniques that has its roots in play: "Technique itself springs from play, because we can acquire technique only by practice of practice, by persistently experimenting and playing with our tools and testing their limits and resistances. Creative work is play; it is free speculation using materials of one's chosen form" (p. 42).

The school counselor who uses reflective listening, the principal who designs and monitors budgets, and the classroom teacher who adapts curriculum to teach learners with diverse abilities will have achieved their expertise through systematic, elaborated practice of the specific skills needed for their position. Practice of such specialized skills is essential if professionals are to avoid rigid thinking and stereotypic ways of performing their work.

This practice provides the momentum and confidence that professionals need to confront the unexpected surprises in daily work. Educators who have had the opportunity to practice their skills draw upon them when dealing with varied situations, refine them in real situations, and add embellishments to them in order to increase their repertoire of responses. There is a big difference between imagining roles—a school superintendent, a children's rights advocate, a teacher in an inclusive classroom, or a designer of a new school—and actually practicing the skills required to perform them. New professionals may "have great creative proclivities, glorious inspirations, and exalted feelings, . . . [but] there is no creativity unless creations actually come into existence" (Nachmanovitch, 1990, p. 66).

Clearly, the practice that prospective counselors and principals gain from internships, that teachers gain from student teaching, and that teacher educators glean from peer evaluation of their use of case methods provides the arena for mastery of technical skill: "Mastery comes from practice; practice comes from playful, compulsive experimentation and from the sense of wonder. In practice, work is play, intrinsically rewarding. It is that feeling of our inner child wanting to play for just five minutes more" (Nachmanovitch, 1990, p. 73). Indeed, mastery of the education profession comes in part from the play of the professionals-in-training.

For the Future

Playful behaviors in the education profession are clearly related to using creativity and innovative thinking, finding new solutions to old problems, and mastering specialized knowledge. Play is a critical link with the effective social interaction and problem generating and solving that future educators need. Educational practice certainly entails risk, but a playful approach to practice can lead to a feeling of mastery.

The needs of the global marketplace of the twenty-first century will require human and technical resources from education professionals that are different from those used in the past. They must lead beyond the thinking of the industrial age and into the thinking of the next century, which entails a respect and understanding for the skills of "open-mindedness, intuition, independence of thought" (Blatner & Blatner, 1988, p. 41). If educators can engage in break-the-mold thinking even as they possess the specialized skills and responsible practices associated with their profession, they will be able to meet the challenges of the future.

The appropriate education of children for future society requires rethinking educational practice from birth through adulthood. Tomorrow's workers will need resilient and flexible thinking; risk-taking powers; autonomy in trying out, testing, and experimenting with ideas and materials; the ability to adapt quickly to produce innovative solutions to problems; and a breadth of expertise. They will also need to possess the basic skills of reading, writing, and computing at high levels to make decisions and become active team members (Isenberg & Jalongo, 1993).

Schools of the future must educate children who know how to learn, cope with change, adapt to a changing work environment, and think critically (Haycock, 1991; Tetenbaum & Mulkeen, 1986). They will be educating children for a rapidly changing workforce in which success will depend greatly upon the ability to think flexibly, divergently, and innovatively while functioning with autonomy and a level of risk taking (Haycock, 1991).

Education professionals have an important role in opening the conversations about the role of play and playful ways of knowing among and within every profession. First, however, they must view play and its attendant playful characteristics as essential behaviors needed by educational professionals in the twenty-first century. New ways of thinking and doing business will be the norm—and play has a role in the new professional outlook.

Bibliography

Blatner, A., & Blatner, A. (1988). *The art of play: An adult's guide to reclaiming imagination and spontaneity.* New York: Human Sciences.

Bretherton, I. (Ed.). (1984). *Symbolic play: The development of social understanding.* New York: Academic.

Chistensen, C. R. (1990, May). *Teaching a case.* Paper presented at Case Methods Conference, Commonwealth Center for the Education of Teachers, Charlottesville, VA.

Fromberg, D. P. (1992). Play. In C. Seefeldt (Ed.), *The early childhood curriculum: A review of current research* (pp. 42–84). New York: Teachers College Press.

Fromberg, D. P. (1995). *The full-day kindergarten: Planning and practicing a dynamic themes curriculum* (2nd ed.). New York: Teachers College Press.

Haycock, K. (1991). Reaching for the year 2000. *Childhood Education, 67*(5), 276–279.

Isenberg, J. P., & Jalongo, M. R. (1993). *Creative expression and play in the early childhood curriculum.* New York: Macmillan.

Jalongo, M. R., Isenberg, J. P. (1995). *Teachers' Stories: From personal narrative to professional insight.* San Francisco: Jossey-Bass.

Merseth, K. (1991). *The case for cases in teacher education.* Washington, DC: American Association of Higher Education and the American Association of Colleges of Teacher Education.

Nachmanovitch, S. (1990). *Free play: The power of improvisation in life and the arts.* New York: Putnam.

National Association of Early Childhood Teacher Educators. (1991). *The case writing manual.* Centenary College, Hackettstown, NJ: Author.

Shepard, R. (1988). The imagination of the scientist. In K. Egan & D. Nadaner (Eds.), *Imagination and education* (pp. 153–185). New York: Teachers College Press.

Silverman, R., Welty, W., & Lyon, S. (1992). *Case studies for teacher problem-solving.* New York: McGraw-Hill.

Tetenbaum, T. J., & Mulkeen, T. A. (1986). Computers as an agent for educational change. *Computers in the Schools, 2*(4), 91–103.

Weininger, O. (1988). "What if" and "as if" imagination and pretend play in early childhood. In K. Egan & D. Nadaner (Eds.), *Imagination and education* (pp. 141–149). New York: Teachers College Press.

Play by Newspaper Journalists and Editors

Ellen C. Creager

When Col. Harlan Sanders, founder of Kentucky Fried Chicken, died, the editors on the copy desk at the *Ann Arbor News* had to come up with a headline for his obituary, and quickly: they were five minutes from deadline. The pressure was mounting.

"I know!" shouted one editor. "I've got it: 'Colonel Sanders Kicks the Bucket.'"

The entire office staff collapsed in laughter. Was the headline unusable? Yes. Was it ridiculous? Yes. But two minutes later, they had a more appropriate headline, and the paper met its deadline again.

Newspaper journalists "play" all the time as a method of inspiring creative and innovative stories and headlines. As children, they probably especially liked word games such as Scrabble, scavenger hunts, cracking the Big Boy secret code, running races, and being first to tell their parents what they saw on the way home from school. As adults, newspaper reporters "play" at work in similar ways to relieve stress, spur creativity, keep morale up, and compete for stories.

From the perspective of this author's former occupation as a feature writer for the *Detroit Free Press*,[1] play is an integral part of being a writer. The job was to write feature articles for the nation's ninth largest newspaper. The *Free Press* gave great latitude to its employees in dress and approach to work, as long as the newspaper benefited from this freedom.

At their best, journalists employ what a newspaper historian calls "the journalistic method . . . a product of the same spirit that spawned the techniques of historical research and intelligence gathering, the same spirit that gave birth to the scientific method. All such activities are motivated by a belief that the

world has something to teach the mind, that rumination will be unproductive without the opportunity to graze on fresh information" (Stephens, 1988, p. 228). "Sit down before a fact as a little child," commanded the nineteenth-century English biologist Thomas Henry Huxley, "be prepared to give up every preconceived notion, follow humbly wherever and to whatever abyss nature leads, or you shall learn nothing" (in Stephens, 1988, p. 229). In the pursuit of their craft, therefore, newspaper journalists employ various types of play.

A Competition to Win and Be First

One of the most satisfying experiences for newspaper reporters is the race to be first with an important story, to "break" a story, beating the newspaper across town. Traditionally, this competition spurred newspapers to work very hard to produce high-quality stories. Today, however, nearly every big city in America has only one newspaper left, so there is no cross-town competition. This lack leaves many newspaper reporters feeling as though they are children running the 50-yard dash against themselves.

Today, much of the "race" for news is between traditional newspapers and more sensational TV and radio reports. On the one hand, newspaper journalists sometimes complain that television reporters (and tabloid newspaper reporters) do not "play fair" because they buy stories, barge uninvited into people's homes, or make up sensational stories. On the other hand, traditional newspaper reporters believe that in the end they will "win" because the public trusts their accounts far more than other media's, and they play by the rules. Sometimes, their idealism is rewarded. A tabloid paper, *The National Enquirer,* and the television show *A Current Affair* in 1995 published many sensationalized stories on the O. J. Simpson murder trial, paying millions of dollars for exclusive interviews with various figures in the drama. When it was time for the judge to choose one reporter to sit in the courtroom and cover the trial, however, he chose Linda Deutsch, a reporter from the Associated Press, a respected news wire service. Thus, in the race for respect, traditional newspaper people believe they are still winners.

Wordplay

In the race for stories, newspaper reporters have to hustle and outdo their competitors, real or imagined. They must do it with the only weapon they possess, their way with words.

Wordplay is the purest form of play among journalists. Feature writers and sports writers constantly search for unusual and creative ways of expressing themselves. Headline and caption writers, too, need a finely honed sense of wordplay. This facility with words is critical to both the product and the workplace environment; it takes several forms.

Pure Word Play
It is not unusual for a writer to ask aloud in the office questions that would be regarded as bizarre in any other office. The amazing thing is that other writers calmly answer the questions! Recently in the features department, someone asked, "What rhymes with Roger Wilko?" "Stephen Bilko," someone shot back.

One day, someone complained that another reporter had created file names for twenty-five separate stories using every single letter of the alphabet except *K.* He had *A,* he had *B,* and so on. Why no *K?* Because another reporter was hoarding *K* to prevent him from getting a monopoly on the alphabet!

In a newspaper office, people will look up words just for pleasure. Instead of saying they have writer's block, reporters will say, "I used up all the words in my computer." They describe their jobs as "working at the paragraph factory." A newspaper is the only place, with the exception perhaps of a library, where people think it is fun to stump coworkers on the spelling of *anomalous,* or argue over the first name

of Dobie Gillis's girlfriend. (It was Zelda.)

On a daily basis, headline writers in particular have to play with words so they will fit into limited spaces and still be accurate. Even their mistakes are fertile grounds for wordplay appreciation. The respected *Columbia Journalism Review* collects published headline mistakes every month. Books of these mistakes give clear indication that some journalists did not think about their wordplay quite long enough. The *Buffalo News* in 1983 ran this headline: "Jerk Injures Neck; Wins Award." Even the respected *International Herald Tribune* is not exempt from mistakes. In 1986, it ran this alarming headline: "Police Discover Crack in Australia" (Cooper, 1987, p. 67).

A Social Yardstick
Journalists measure each other by the quality of their wordplay. A person who is clever with words and banter is esteemed among colleagues, especially when it translates into his or her writing or editing.

A Creative Association of Ideas
Unlike some corporate meetings where a written agenda stifles creativity, story meetings in newspaper features departments encourage leaps of thinking to come up with fresh ideas for newspaper articles. Once, *Detroit Free Press* editors wanted some kind of story about the gigantic $43 million lottery prize in Michigan. Should reporters interview previous winners? Should they talk to lottery officials?

Instead, a group of feature writers and editors spun a creative web around the question of what one could buy with $43 million. One reporter actually discovered that someone could buy four Cedar Point roller coasters—or pay the national debt for one minute.

A Way to Invent Quizzes, Games, or Contests for Readers
Newspapers often seek to be "interactive" and engage readers in thinking about a topic or event. The *Detroit Free Press,* as part of a series on average salaries, once created a quiz about salaries that got readers thinking about whether they were really rich or poor in the greater scheme of things. This type of writing takes a free-form creativity that actually requires great discipline.

A Way to Poke Fun at Management

Signs about policies or procedures posted around the *Free Press* are always altered by staff members, proving that no matter whether you are five or fifty, the pen is mightier than the sword. Other signs are also altered, for example, the sign on the office refrigerator says "Abandon Hope All Ye Who Enter Here."

Actual "Toys" and Playthings in the Office

Newspapers that have remodeled their offices often try to force editors and reporters to keep things clean and uncluttered, but they are rarely successful. Most reporters have strange collections of toys at their desks, acquired over the years of reporting. Among the clutter on this author's desk, beneath the poster of a blue-haired Marge Simpson, was a 1959 replica Barbie doll (the *Free Press* did a story on her once), four rocks from Lake Huron (courtesy of a story about why there are no seashells in the Great Lakes), and a K'nex building blocks motorcycle (left over from a press kit). The reporter at the next desk had a giant water gun in his bottom drawer, a kazoo, and various noisemakers that he used at appropriate moments. A newsroom editor displayed a huge collection of little wind-up toys with which she played when she was thinking (or trying to think).

Once, as a protest of bad lighting, all the reporters on the city desk at the *Free Press* brought in hideous lamps for their desks, which remained for several years, much to the chagrin of management.

Playing Jokes or Thinking of Jokes

Jokes are an imperative in a newspaper office. This is for two reasons. One, just as in an elementary school class of children, everyone wants to know if you are smart enough to "get" the joke. Irony is especially prized. Journalists quickly weed out those who cannot keep up; those left behind are widely derided or ignored.

Two, joking is a way of coping. Just like the struggling student joking around in the back of math class, journalists joke as a way of relieving tension. As with doctors or police officers, joking is an inside method of dealing with horrors. In the early 1980s, when iron-fisted Yugoslav dictator General Tito went through a long illness and finally died, the copy desk toyed with running a series of headlines in the same place every day: "Tito Still Alive," "Tito Not Dead Yet," "Tito Dies"—and the kicker—"Tito Still Dead."

The *Detroit Free Press's* European correspondent recently was trapped in Sarajevo, Bosnia-Herzogovenia, in a very dangerous spot. He could not get out of the hotel, and enemy soldiers were shooting at the building. He could send messages back to the office at $24 a minute, and editors could send to him. What did he want? Jokes. One editor sent him this message: "Dolly Parton says she's not offended about dumb blonde jokes. 'I know I'm not dumb,' she says. 'I'm also not blonde.'" His spirits boosted, the reporter finally was smuggled out of Sarajevo in an armored personnel carrier, whistling like a child going past the graveyard.

Gamesmanship

To get a story, journalists sometimes must play a game of getting the confidence of a source. Doing this requires following certain rules: reporters need to know what to say, what not to say, what to promise, and what not to promise. Many journalists have been in trouble for promising confidentiality and then not giving it. Still others have ended up in jail for contempt because they would not reveal a source's name. Many green journalists have trouble because nobody has taught them the "game" yet. It takes months or years to learn the game and learn how to play it.

Anne Hull, an award-winning feature writer for the *St. Petersburg Times,* told an interviewer in 1994 how she played the game when interviewing a reticent police officer who had been shot: "I didn't really play reporter with her too much. I just was there with my notebook. I stopped the, 'how do you feel about . . .?' The good stuff never comes that way, never, ever. . . . The story was so little about actual questions and answers. It was more about hanging out with people. It's observing" (Scanlan, 1994, pp. 76–77). The interviewer asked Hull what "playing reporter" meant. Hull replied: "I think of the people on the courtroom steps holding a microphone and their blank note pad. . . . I freeze in those situations. I don't ask the right questions. But in the company of someone, I'm just very comfortable."

New reporters sent out to cover the police, city council, or the mayor often feel as though they are on a playground, and none of the other children will tell them the rules. Until you figure them out for yourself, or until someone takes pity on you and helps you, you cannot play—or get the story.

In some competitive newsrooms, journalists must learn a game of office politics. One magazine asked five journalists what they most disliked about their jobs. It was not the writing. It was not the beat they covered; in fact, they all loved that part of the work. It was the new bottom-line mentality of corporate newspaper owners clashing with long, individualistic traditions of journalism. Today, reporters who do not understand the new "rules" of journalism risk being thrown out on the street. However, not without protest! For example, Carol Horner, a reporter for the *Philadelphia Inquirer* explained, "I think journalism serves an important role in this culture and democracy despite the new wave of business people running newspapers who promulgate and push the idea that newspapers are widgets. They can call our work 'product' until hell freezes over but we are not widgets and never will be!" (Rockmore, 1994, p. 34).

Discovering Secrets and Telling Secrets

Like the old circle game of "telephone," newspaper reporters spend a lot of time hearing stories, rumors, and tips, then trying to find out if they are true, and if so, what it means for the public. As wanderers on a treasure hunt, they must follow the clues. A newspaper historian says, "The journalistic method is the pursuit of independently verifiable facts about current events through enterprise, observation and investigation" (Stephens, 1988, p. 229). That is more easily said than done.

When journalist Anne Hull was asked to pick a metaphor to express her view of herself as a writer, she replied, "A detective" (Scanlon, 1994, p. 86). Often, journalists are required to solve puzzles and unravel mysteries. Whether one is covering Watergate or unexplained expenses at the mayor's office, the job requires analytical skill and creative thinking, the same skills first employed back at the puzzle table in preschool.

What Journalists Do Not Do: Pretend

By its very nature, journalism is about real life. In college newspaper writing courses, students often are asked to go out and find a real subject about which to write for a class assignment, rather than making up a story. In professional training sessions, reporters and editors squirm if forced to play-act or pretend. Many corporate consultants find their seminars fall dead flat when they try to train editors and reporters with zippy role-playing games. Why? Journalism and fiction are incompatible.

When reporters play pretend in their work, they are usually in trouble. At the *Detroit Free Press,* for example, reporters are not allowed to misrepresent themselves, pretend to be someone they are not, or even use unnamed sources except in rare circumstances. Further, if they make up quotes or facts, they will be fired.

The most famous example of a journalist playing pretend at a high level is Janet Cooke. She was a feature writer for the *Washington Post.* In 1980, she won the Pulitzer Prize for her vivid series about an eleven-year-old cocaine addict. The trouble was, the story turned out to be fabricated. Cooke's prize was yanked and she was fired. Yet the damage to the whole industry was done. If journalists can fool the Pulitzer committee, could they not fool the public with other false stories? The Cooke incident was an embarrassing watershed for journalists everywhere. Pretending is for the theater or Halloween, not the newspaper office.

At *The State,* a newspaper in Columbia, South Carolina, managers reorganized the newsroom. Why? One of the biggest drawbacks to working there, managers admitted, was that "Ideas were limited by who you are and what you do [and] politeness and conformity were placed above helpful and creative confrontation" (Johnson, 1993, p. 28). Under the new rules drawn up by the editor, "Talent, energy, creativity and innovation are valued and rewarded" The other new rule? "People have fun."

Does the bottom-line world of newspapers still have room for journalists to play? They must, if the companies value creativity and originality. Despite the pressures of earning a living as an adult, many reporters feel their jobs to be intrinsic to who they are; if they had to, they would do it for free. If they seem cynical, it is only because they cling to an easily bruised idealism and sense of fairness. If they are earnest, it is only because they have never lost a curiosity about the world and what is happening around them. If they seem to probe too much, it is only because they have never lost the child's urge to know, then tell, then know some more.

Note

1. Ironically, shortly after the author wrote this essay, the Knight Ridder Corporation's newspaper was engulfed in a bitter labor dispute that decimated the staff and killed the genial newsroom atmosphere she describes. When permanent replacement workers were hired by the company, many of the creative employees described in this article fled to other work places. The company is presently apealing an NLRB ruling of unfair labor practices.

Bibliography

Cooper, G. (1987). Red tape holds up new bridge. In G. Cooper (Ed.), *Columbia Journalism Review* (p. 67). New York: Perigee.

Johnson, S. (1993). Newsroom circles. *Quill, 81*(2), 28.

Rockmore, M. (1994). Job dissatisfaction among journalists. *Editor and Publisher, 127*(17), 34.

Scanlan, C. (1994). *1994 best newspaper writing*. New York: Bonus.

Stephens, M. (1988). *A history of news: From the drum to the satellite*. New York: Penguin.

Use of Play in the Law

Christopher E. Mengel

The Law Firm as "The Team"

When we were very young, every child on the block wanted to be chosen to play in pick-up games in the neighborhood. It did not matter if it was baseball, basketball, or Red Rover; each of us wanted to be chosen for the team first. Inevitably, the two oldest children, usually boys, got to choose the sides. Just as inevitably, the youngest, weakest, and most inexperienced child was the last person picked.

The hierarchy of most law firms is very similar to the "team on the block." Most major law firms in the United States are run by those with the most seniority. Usually they are men. The senior partners, in turn, get to choose which associates will get to play on their team. In most instances, the person lowest on the legal totem pole is the youngest and most inexperienced attorney, usually the young person fresh out of law school. Although there are many exceptions, most major law firms are run by elderly men who have paid their dues and possess the skills. Children's neighborhood games are the same. The message is "Pay your dues and satisfy the older children, and some day you will be the person who will run the game and pick the players, too." As more women enter the profession and move slowly up the legal totem pole, a few are reaching the top and get to make the rules for their firms. However, as in children's games, girls must fight to be the team leaders.

Litigation as the Playing Field

Litigation is the area most fertile to draw comparisons between play and the law profession. It involves playacting, pretend, war games, storytelling, organized sports, and gamesmanship.

Play-Acting

Litigation is not unlike the neighborhood plays or skits that children put on in someone's basement for the benefit of their parents. Children write dialogue, assign parts, borrow their mother's or father's clothes for costumes, and then perform. They try to be credible and believable to their audience, which is usually their parents. Litigation has many of the same elements. Initially, lawyers carefully prepare the story that is to be "played." They take depositions, send interrogatories, sign afffidavits, and interview witnesses (who will have "parts" in the play). Of particular importance is planning the nonverbal signs and messages that the players will give to the audience. Gestures, posture, hand movements, and a "balanced stance," just as in hitting a baseball, are all important factors that reinforce or damage the players' credibility (Bernstein, 1994).

The preparation also includes devising props and securing costumes. Lawyers consider questions such as "Is the client's haircut short enough? Should he wear his glasses?" The important thing is to get the jury to empathize with the lawyer's client. If he is on trial for drug dealing, for example, he must at least look like a model, upstanding citizen. He should remove his gold chains and rings, take off his earring, and hide his tattoo. As one scholar indicates, the last thing a trial attorney wants to do is spend needless energy or time trying to overcome an initial bad impression occasioned by a client's poor appearance (Lane, 1994, p. 17).

There is also a theory that attorneys should wear dark suits as their "costume" at the beginning of a trial and wear lighter suits as the trial progresses. The reason is that, initially, the attorney shows the jury the importance of his client's case by dressing respectably and conservatively. As the trial goes on, however, and the jury begins to empathize with the client, the lighter color contributes to less formality and a greater comfort level with the jury (Lane, 1994, p. 17).

Playacting ability is a great benefit in the law. It is not surprising that Geoffrey Fieger, the colorful and successful attorney for assisted suicide advocate Dr. Jack Kevorkian, has his undergraduate degree in theater arts from the University of Michigan. It also is not surprising that some of the most successful and long-lasting dramatic productions, such as *Inherit the Wind*, have been based on legal cases or that long-running popular television shows such as *L.A. Law* are set in dramatic courtrooms.

Pretend

Pretense is playacting taken even further. Pretending is a valuable tool in the preparation of attorneys. In law school, most students participate in various moot court programs which allow them to represent make-believe clients in mock trials. Students take the part of defense or prosecuting attorneys, with other students acting as witnesses and jurors. This method often also is used by practicing attorneys. Some sizable law firms continue to sharpen their attorneys' skills or prepare for big cases by conducting mock trials with witnesses who are actually actors in front of pretend jurors who are members of the community.

War Games

When boys are growing up, their neighborhood play often centers on war games. With sticks for guns, they hide behind trees, crawl under bushes, and then leap out at each other. Their play goal is to annihilate and destroy their opponent. The goal of litigation is not dissimilar. Many firms have special rooms designated as "war rooms" in which they stockpile their arsenal of exhibits, research reports, and discovery materials. These rooms are used solely for the preparation of major cases for trial. The strategy of war play in litigation is the same as that of children's war games: Assess one's own strengths and utilize those strengths to exploit the weaknesses of the opponent. The recent O. J. Simpson murder trial, for instance, was classic modern gladiatorial combat. There was no blood, but both sides tried to annihilate and destroy the opponent. As with war games, surprises are allowed within the confines of specific and well-delineated rules of evidence. The goal is not necessarily to play "fair," but to stretch the rules as much as you can to win.

Big companies and corporations do particularly well in winning major litigation because they have an arsenal of resources at their disposal that they can use to exploit the weaknesses of those less able to afford numerous investigators, computerized legal research, jury selection polls, and other costly techniques of trial preparation. In some megafirms, as many as thirty partners and associates may join forces (the team!) on a single major case (Samuelson, 1990). In childhood, there are always those who, seeing other children brandish dinky squirt guns, suddenly bring out the giant water balloons. The same thing occurs in the war games of the courtroom.

Storytelling

One of the most well-respected attorneys in the United States, Gerry Spence (1995), says that a trial is like a story. In order to effectively represent a client, the attorney's story must have a theme, plot, interesting characters, and copious, detailed description (p. 113). Above all else, the story must be credible to the listener. Spence's "down-home" folksy manner and his persona as a cowboy from Wyoming charms jurors into believing his story. Ultimately, if a story is credible, interesting, and well told, jurors will sit in their seats with the rapt attention of children listening to ghost stories around a campfire. The importance of persuasive storytelling in a courtroom cannot be underestimated. As one leading lawyer recently stated, "Storytelling should play a part in every aspect of every case" (Ogborn, 1995, p. 64). Ultimately, the purpose of storytelling in trials, unlike nursery rhymes, fairy tales, or novels, is to "incite listeners to act," to find in favor of the lawyer's client (p. 65).

How do lawyers know if their stories are credible? The jury's reaction will tell the lawyer that. Once, at the end of a trial, the author's law partner asked a jury to award the client a significant amount of money. The opposing attorney, who was bald, began his closing argument by telling the jury that he was so taken aback by the amount of money requested by the partner that it "almost put hair on my head." Although the partner thought that the opposing counsel's attempt at humor was hysterically funny, not a single juror cracked a smile. At that moment, the partner knew he had won his case.

Organized Sports

As in basketball and other organized sports, there are certain well-defined rules and procedures in the law that attorneys must follow. If either side commits a "foul," they will get penalized. It is the judge's function to "referee" the action and be the final arbiter of disputes between the players. For example, in the courtroom, an attorney who speaks out of turn will risk a contempt charge. An attorney who does not have correct papers prepared and witnesses available or who fails legally to protect his or her client's interest can be slapped with sanctions, charged with malpractice, or have the case thrown out of court. Unlike a penalty in a basketball game, a penalty in a courtroom can affect attorneys' and clients' lives forever.

Gamesmanship

In law, most disputes never get to trial. Instead, skills of gamesmanship come into play in negotiation. Both sides know that the first offer is not the "real" offer that the party will ultimately accept. Both sides secretly have what they call a "go-to-hell" figure, which is their bottom line for settling the case before trial. The attorney knows that the risk of losing is outweighed by the chance at victory if negotiations fall below the "go-to-hell" figure. Gamesmanship is the adversary's method of getting to a cooperative solution. Many children find this type of gamesmanship a lot of fun, whether they are seeing if they can best their parents in a dispute over what time to go to bed or their playmates in who gets to be soccer goalie. Some children seem to be natural-born negotiators!

Playacting, pretense, war games, storytelling, organized sports, and gamesmanship all are valuable aspects of childhood play which, when performed skillfully by an adult, can assure a successful career as an attorney. The stakes, of course, are higher in the courtroom than in a childhood game of Red Rover or pick-up basketball, but the same strategic skills are required. The most successful lawyers, no matter what their age, never forget that using the leadership learned in childhood play is a winning strategy.

Bibliography

Bernstein, C. (1994). Winning trials nonverbally: Six ways to establish control in the courtroom. *Trial, 30,* 61–65.

Lane, F. (1994). *Lane's Goldstein trial technique* (3rd ed., Vol. 1A). Deerfield, IL: Clark Boardman Callaghan.

Ogborn, M. (1995). Storytelling throughout trial. *Trial, 31*(8), 64–65.

Samuelson, S. S. (1990). The organizational structure of law firms: Lessons from management theory. *Ohio State Law Journal, 51*(1), 647–651.

Spence, G. (1995). *How to argue and win every time.* New York: St. Martin's.

Playfulness in Medicine

A Pediatric Perspective

Debra Esernio-Jenssen
Victor Turow

Serious Medicine

Playfulness is not taught in medical school. In fact, physicians are taught to take themselves very seriously. From the first day, however, medical students are instructed to wear starched white jackets and address themselves as "Doctor," a form of pretense. The first two years of medical school are primarily devoted to the basic sciences, including anatomy, histology, biochemistry, pathology, physiology, and so forth. "Playful" pranks, such as dressing up or posing cadavers, reflect a need to obscure the reality of dissecting a human being and help cope with the first months of medical school. Such acts are, of course, seen by some as disrespectful and met with disapproval. Yet, except for play therapy, a specific treatment modality taught in child psychiatry, the formal medical school curriculum does not address play. It is as if play is presumed to be an inherent, individual, variable, and unteachable part of human nature.

After the basic sciences, medical students learn interviewing skills and physical diagnosis prior to entering the patient wards. The clinical rotations, often solemn, intimidating experiences, are designed to give the student exposure to the various medical professions: surgery, obstetrics and gynecology, internal medicine, psychiatry, pediatrics, and family medicine or community medicine. From their ward experiences, which range from six to twelve weeks per rotation, students are expected to choose their ultimate medical career. A research study found that certain medical student characteristics are associated with choosing a career in primary care (family practice, general internal medicine, or general pediatrics) (Bland, 1995). Those who choose primary care are more likely to be female, older, and married; have a diverse undergraduate background; have nonphysician parents; have lower income expectations; are more interested in a heterogeneous patient population with a variety of health problems; and have less interest in prestige, high technology, and surgery. Also, students tend to playfully stereotype each other in terms of choosing a medical field: the "nerds" choose residencies in internal medicine; "arrogant, self-confident" individuals become surgeons; "jocks" enter orthopedics; and the "narcissists" become plastic surgeons. Those students who are "different" or somewhat "weird" become psychiatrists, and "normal, nice guys" choose obstetrics and gynecology if they are insomniacs or pediatrics if they need more sleep.

A Dose of Laughter

Pediatrics is one medical specialty that encourages play, and pediatricians tend to be very playful by nature. Most individuals who choose to enter pediatrics love children. Most are optimists; even the sickest child usually has a favorable outcome. Most believe that "an ounce of prevention is worth a pound of cure." Most believe that anticipating parental concerns with regard to developmental and health issues of the child, and discussing these issues before they arise, is effective. This upbeat nature typically permeates a pediatrician's office. Pediatricians' waiting rooms are usually brightly illuminated with walls covered with photographs of children or wallpapered in a child's motif. Examination rooms are similarly designed to create a more comfortable and friendly environment for the often frightened child. Toys, books, music, interactive games, and movie videos are commonly found. The atmosphere is relaxed and cheerful. Attire is informal. In fact, most pediatricians or residents do not wear white jackets. Residents in the authors' office-based clinic are expected to be well-kempt, and hospital "scrubs" are forbidden. Even though ties are optional, most men choose to wear them; for many, their playful nature is expressed through their ties. One of the authors' associates, whose nickname is "Dr. Mickey," has a fabulous assortment of Mickey Mouse ties. A resident who has been playfully labeled by his peers as "the absent-minded professor" loves to wear Looney Tune character ties. The women usually dress casually and comfortably. Unlike corporate attire, jumpsuits, dress shorts, and pants predominate. Clothing accessories add flavor to their outfits. Purple dinosaur pins, banana-shaped earrings, and tiny stuffed animals attached to the ubiquitous necklace and the stethoscope, are some examples. "Dr. Debbie's" favorite accessory is a Star Trek communications button given to her by an aspiring Trekkie. Not only does it complement her wardrobe, it is very versatile. The noise generated by tapping the button is a great distraction for her patients and, when in a difficult situation with a parent, she can be "beamed up" to safety.

Each new season or holiday is a welcome opportunity to redecorate the office. Halloween is especially fun because the doctors, nurses, and other office staff dress in costume. Snow White and the Seven Dwarves are often represented, as is Mickey Mouse (guess who?) and his friends. And of course, Big Bird and the other Sesame Street characters make their appearance. The parents and the patients, even the adolescents, enjoy the professionals' frivolousness. No one, however, enjoys it more than the physicians. Imagine painting your face white, adding a big black nose and then proceeding in earnest to diagnose tonsillitis and ear infections! The Christmas season is truly joyous. The office walls are covered with holiday pictures of patients. Christmas trees, Hanukkah menorahs, wreaths, and mistletoe are strategically placed. Parents bear gifts of baked goods, nuts, candy, and more baked goods. The office Muzak is changed to Christmas carols and the staff wear candy-cane earrings. This festive environment is conducive to play.

Play as a Diagnostic Aid

The real art of pediatrics is performing a thorough physical examination on an uncooperative child. Standard textbooks on pediatric examination include lengthy descriptions of maneuvering the otoscope to accommodate a child's ear anatomy and positioning the child to get the best view of the perineum. Methods employed to make an examination fun are often not discussed. Medical students begin to acquire these skills by modeling the behaviors of residents and faculty pediatricians. Different pediatricians use various play techniques that they adjust to accommodate the age and maturity of their patients. Each individual develops his or her own style. Some common techniques include explaining to a child that you need to look in his or her ear to find some favorite cartoon or storybook character, or singing familiar tunes to distract a crying infant. They may not listen, but the physicians enjoy it. A twenty-four- to thirty-six-month-old child usually dreads the doctor's office. By redressing the body part that was already examined, the pediatrician not only actively plays with the child but, at the same time, reassures the child that the visit will be completed shortly, once the child is fully dressed. When examining young school-aged children, "Dr. Vic" adds the same silly suffix to every anatomical part ("earskis," "noseskis"). Amazingly, many children laugh.

The art of play is also used to evaluate a child developmentally or to assess the extent of an injury or illness. Children are often seen—sometimes scantily clad—crawling, hopping, skipping, or running through the examination corridors. One of our patients demonstrated her newly acquired gymnastic skill of a back handspring; everyone watched in awe, but we knew that the left wrist she hurt the day before could not be significantly injured. The child with fever and abdominal pain who, if challenged, will repeatedly jump higher than the pediatrician is unlikely to have appendicitis.

Assessing the growth and development of a child is fundamental to pediatrics. Although child development is a pediatric subspecialty, general pediatricians must be well trained in normal development to adequately detect any delays or deviations. Various components of the standard developmental screening tests, such as the Denver II (Denver Developmental Screening Test), CLAMS (Clinical Linguistic and Auditory Milestone Scale), and CAT (Clinical Adaptive

Test) are incorporated into the routine health maintenance visits (Johnson, 1993). A quick developmental assessment usually involves an evaluation of a child's gross motor, fine motor, social, and language skills. It is within these specific developmental guidelines that physicians explicitly integrate play. A four-month-old grasps a toy rattle; an eight-month-old plays pat-a-cake; a twelve-month-old throws a ball; an eighteen-month-old feeds a doll; a twenty-four-month-old turns pages in a book one at a time and plays in parallel with other children; a thirty-six-month-old pedals a tricycle, builds a tower of eight cubes, and plays in groups; a forty-eight-month-old hops, draws a person with three body parts, and knows four colors; and a sixty-month-old skips and plays competitive games.

Routine screening tests have also been adapted to incorporate play. Instead of figuring out which way an *E* is pointing, children can now choose from a cake, equestrian, jeep, and telephone in the Allen Preschool Picture Test, and a bird, rabbit, boy, or girl in the Michigan Preschool Test when using the Titmus II Vision Tester (Titmus II, 1985). Pulmonary function testing utilized to evaluate restrictive or obstructive lung disease has a program geared for children. A child exhales as quickly and forcefully as possible into a mouthpiece, which drives a sailboat farther than the control "challenger" and at the same time assesses lung function. Even obtaining a throat culture can be made "fun" by offering a choice of grape - or cherry-flavored tongue blades.

At North Shore Hospital in Manhasset, New York, pediatric residents may gain further exposure to the art of play by observing the Child Life Program at work. Such programs incorporate music, art, massage, and the work of play therapists in treating or entertaining patients on the hospital wards. The playroom, staffed by volunteers, provides a social environment for noncritical, noninfectious children, reinforcing the "We're sick but we're kids and we're getting better" theme. Visits by entertainers, clowns, and sports figures (and Santa at Christmas time) elevate the spirits of staff and patients alike.

People often say, "Work hard and play hard." Yet many people actually play as they work. In striving to put patients at ease, pediatricians are allowed the luxury of expressing the child or adolescent in themselves without feeling self-conscious. The nature of practicing pediatrics encourages various, often individualized, forms of play.

In spite of a medical curriculum lacking in play training, students who are children at heart discover pediatrics. And pediatricians have mastered the art of play.

Bibliography

Bland, C. J. (1995). Determinants of primary care specialty choice: A non-statistical meta-analysis of the literature. *Academic Medicine, 70*(7), 620–641.

Johnson, K. B. (1993). *The Harriet Lane handbook* (13th ed.). St. Louis: Mosby-Year Book.

Titmus II. (1985). *Training manual*. Petersburg, VA: Titmus Optical.

The Present and Future of Play

Introduction

At one time in her life Doris Bergen was a member of the World Future Society, attending conferences and avidly reading the organization's journal. She has remained very interested in predictions about the future even though her professional responsibilities no longer give her time to be active in future forecasting. The most important thing she learned when she was involved in trying to answer such questions as "How do you think children will be playing in the year 2050?" was that there are numerous factors existing at any one time that have the potential to affect the future and that the weight given to these factors by various future forecasters differed greatly.

Futurists take the trends that appear to be evident at one particular time and project them into future years to decide what their eventual impact may be. What appears as only a slight trend, if projected using existing probability formulas, may be predicted as a major influence on future conditions. (This slight-into-massive transformation parallels the chaos theory concept of sensitive dependence on initial conditions.) What was most intriguing to Bergen about the programs of future-oriented conferences was that the presentations seemed to be evenly distributed between those that predicted dire consequences and those that envisioned glowing possibilities. Many times the futurists were using similar present-day data to make these negative or positive predictions!

What does this mean for those persons who are trying to predict the future of play? While many factors that may affect play remain to be identified, two present trends can be cited that have the potential to be major influences in the future. One is the increase in sophisticated technology, which is making it possible for human beings to have more leisure (either chosen or forced by economic change), communicate more intensely with others throughout the world (through computers and television), travel more widely (through faster transportation options), and expand the possibilities of action and thinking (with CD-ROM, virtual reality, and video games). The other is the explosion of knowledge in psychobiology, which is opening up windows of opportunity in health (genetic evaluation and repairs, as well as new medications), cognitive science (understanding, memory, and other information-processing domains), and social-personality psychology (enhancing mental health, understanding social attraction, and conflict). Each of these trends, if carried forward, enables us to make either a very positive or a very negative prediction about the future of children's play.

First, the positive: Play will become so valued by adults, who will have the leisure, health, and technological resources to engage in more play themselves, that the value of play for children will be more widely recognized. Children will be encouraged to play with all aspects of their learning, to use new play materials and processes, and to interact regularly with adults in intergenerational and intercultural play. Both males and females will be encouraged to play with many media and in cooperative as well as competitive ways. Instead of having actual warring conflicts, disagreements will be handled in symbolic games and conflict resolution will be managed in a low-risk context; thus children will learn through their play to resolve social as well as cognitive problems. Health will improve, the value of play for information processing will be recognized, and technologically enhanced creative thinking will be promoted.

Now, the negative: Play will be taken over by adults, who will appropriate for themselves all of the growth-enhancing value of play. These adults will require children to earn the right to play, after they have mastered some authoritatively determined body of knowledge. Because the population as a whole will be older, the needs of adults will be even more preeminent than they are now; thus children's ideas and actions will seem less important and their need to play will not be considered of great importance. The gender divisions seen presently in children's play will continue to be encouraged by the media, resulting in even greater competitive, adult-directed, sports-games demands, especially on boys. Technological development will not lead to the resolution of conflict through symbolic games but rather will result in more sophisticated methods of destroying other cultures and races. The children's play that is permitted will increasingly mirror a violent society, with the toys that now provide these models becoming pervasive.

The most important point to remember in predicting the future is that the actions taken in the present can promote or diminish the trends that will affect the future. If policymakers decide what should be the play opportunities for children in the future and they act to influence the present society in ways that strengthen the trends that can lead to these outcomes, then it is possible to envision a positive future in which play will be recognized as important for all people, and children will be encouraged to reach their full play potential. To create these conditions, adults need to realize that the future of children's play depends on everyone.

The essayists within this section have considered the impact of technology on play and schooling. They have also raised important questions concerning issues of children's power as players and the impact of violent themes on their play behavior as well as their actual relationships with others. There is also discussion of some strategies that committed adults might employ in advocating for children's right to play in the contemporary world. The section concludes with a last look at the contexts, perspectives, and meanings of play now and to come.

Electronically Mediated Playscapes

Eugene F. Provenzo Jr.

Play has always been closely linked to the idea of simulation. When a preschooler builds a block city she is constructing a simulation of buildings, people, and roadways. When a kindergartner plays house with a doll or stuffed animal, he is creating a simulation of a household or family.

Historically, simulated play environments have been tactile and object-oriented. Toys, combined with the active imagination of the child, have been the main vehicle for creating these simulations. For the English novelist Charlotte Brontë, for example, a set of wooden toy soldiers were props with which she and her sisters, Emily and Anne, and their brother Branwell created a series of games in which the toy soldiers became "young men" who were publishers, authors, and antiquarians who then used the soldiers to populate an imaginary island with characters who were given names such as Boaster, Hayman, Clown, and Hunter (Singer & Singer, 1990).

We can wonder about the extent to which simulated playscapes like those created by the Brontë children are responsible for, or at least contribute to, the direction people take in their adult lives. In the case of Winston Churchill, for example, it is clear that his military career was directly related to his play experience as a child. As an adult he recalled that his decision to pursue a military career

was entirely due to my collection of soldiers. I had ultimately nearly fifteen hundred. They were all of one size, all British, and organized as an infantry division with a cavalry brigade. My brother Jack commanded the hostile army. . . . The day came when my father himself paid a for-

mal visit of inspection. All the troops were arranged in the correct formation of attack. He spent twenty minutes studying the scene—which was really impressive. . . . At the end he asked me if I would like to go into the Army. I thought it would be splendid to command an Army, so I said "Yes" at once: and immediately I was taken at my word . . . the toy soldiers turned the current of my life. Henceforward all my education was directed to passing into Sandhurst [officer training school]. (1944, pp. 19–20)

Television and the Playscape of Children

Throughout the late nineteenth and early twentieth centuries, toys and games were sold primarily through shop displays, newspaper advertisements, and catalogues. Those being targeted to purchase the products were almost always adult consumers who would buy the toys for children (Jackson, 1994).

With the introduction of commercial television in the late 1940s and early 1950s, however, toy manufacturers discovered a totally new means by which to communicate directly with child consumers. Although early commercial television initially involved the entire family sharing in its viewing, those marketing children's goods such as cereal, candy, and toys gradually began to direct their message directly at children. In doing so, they asserted "the market's right of place within the matrix of socialization" (Kline, 1993, p. viii).

In the U.S. toy industry, the Mattel Corporation was the first to take full advantage of television to advertise its toys. In 1955, they invested $500,000 an amount equal to the total value of the company, to sponsor Walt Disney's new program, *The Mickey Mouse Club*. *The Mickey Mouse Club*, combined with Mattel's marketing program, proved to be an enormous success and immediately ensured that Mattel would become one of the most successful toy companies in the United States (Jackson, 1994).

Because of child-focused advertising, toys like the talking doll Chatty Cathy became enormously profitable. In 1961, for example, a year after the introduction of the Chatty Cathy doll, Mattel's profits rose to $4 million, a 73 percent increase over the previous year (Jackson, 1994).

As a child in elementary school during the mid- and late-1950s, the author clearly remembers the Mattel Chatty Cathy doll advertisements. They were quite compelling. These advertisements, however, did not shape his play. Other advertisements did, and he clearly remembers incorporating scenes from them into his play, even when his toys did not match those being advertised.

He had received a toy called the Yankee Doodle Missile Launcher for Christmas when he was in fourth grade. It was totally unexpected, not at all the sort of practical thing or educational toy he normally got from his parents. He absolutely loved it! His greatest triumph was the successful launching of a missile attack on the Russians (this was the era of the cold war and *Sputnik*, after all), while he simultaneously watched the advertisement for the toy on a Saturday morning television program. He vividly recalls playing with the missile launcher just as he had seen it played with in the television advertisement. This phenomenon represents perhaps the most disturbing aspect of the relationship between television advertising and programming, and the play experience of children: the scripting of the play of children by television. It is a phenomenon analyzed with considerable insight by Stephen Kline (1993) after having watched Daniel, the little boy with whom he lived, construct endless imaginary battles using character toys promoted on television. In observing him, Kline began to wonder about the extent to which Daniel's "imaginative play was being framed by television" (p. viii).

In some ways, Daniel's experience was similar to this essay's author; in other ways, it was significantly different. Advertising and programming models directed toward children have become considerably more sophisticated since the time the author regularly watched Saturday morning television over thirty-five years ago. Daniel's toys, unlike his, were action characters around whom entire programs were developed. This marketing phenomenon began in 1969, when Mattel tried to launch a half-hour television program based on its Hot Wheels toys. Not only would there be advertisements for Hot Wheels, but the basic story line of the program would be based around the Hot Wheels racing characters.

The Federal Trade Commission blocked television stations from showing the Hot Wheels programs, arguing that programming and advertising for children should be kept separate. This policy, however, was eventually reversed. As part of the more open business and regulatory climate of the early 1980s during the Reagan administration, the Federal Trade Commission and the Federal Communication Commission stopped blocking children's programming with licensed toy character tie-ins (Kline, 1993, 138–139). Beginning in 1983, U.S. toy manufacturers started sponsoring television programs whose characters were based on different lines of character and action toys. This was a remarkable change from previous marketing strategies. Toy companies were creating action toys and then building television programs around them. In this way, programs for children became half-hour advertisements for specific lines of toys.

The first program whose content was based on a toy product was Mattel's *He Man and the Masters of the Universe*. By 1986, there were over sixty children's shows whose content was based on toy product lines. These included Kenner's *Care Bears* and *Strawberry Shortcake*, Hasbro-Bradley's *The Transformers* and *G.I. Joe*, Tonka's *Gobots*, and Mattel's *Rainbow Bright* (Clark, 1988).

The success of this strategy was overwhelming. In three years Mattel sold over 70 million *He Man* plastic figures. The *He Man* programs were so successful for Mattel that the company decided to introduce a companion series, *She-Ra, Princess of Power*. Hasbro-Bradley used program/commericals to market their Transformer toys and sold $100 million worth of their product line in their first year, making it the most successful toy introduced up until that time (Clark, 1988).

The significance of massive toy advertising, and even more importantly, product-line programming based around action figures, is that it created a highly mediated electronic play environment for children. Rather than drawing on their own imaginations for play, children began relying on the scripts provided by television advertising and programming. One need only visit an elementary school, talk to the children, and watch them play to realize the extent to which this is true.

No product or program, however, goes on forever. *He Man* and *She-Ra* were succeeded by the *Mutant Ninja Turtles,* whose ultimate origins lay in comic books, and more recently, by the *Mighty Morphin Power Rangers.* In fact, new characters create the demand for new products, new programming, and in turn, generate even greater profits. In this context, since most children's television is being funded by the marketplace, the question arises: To what extent are manufacturers and programmers interested in developing healthy play experiences for children? Or, are they simply interested in selling their product? As Kline (1993) argues: "autonomy and innocence seem antithetical to the current practices of our cultural industries as they struggle ceaselessly to increase their hold over our children's imaginations. We cannot lose sight of the question of quality when the cultural products delivered by the market are ultimately motivated not by an interest in the desire to enlighten, integrate, or even educate the child, but by economic considerations" (pp. 19–20).

Present-day U.S. culture, therefore, is faced with a situation in which the experience of children's play is being significantly mediated by television and advertising. Play becomes scripted by the media. The child draws on television programming and advertising for his or her play, rather than drawing on self-generated schemata or simulations collaboratively constructed with other children. This situation becomes even more problematic as the culture increasingly involves itself in new media forms such as video games.

Video Games as Impoverished Rule-Driven Simulations

Currently, the single most common playscape for children in the United States is the video game. Video games have become an enormous business. At the present, video game systems are in over a third of all households. In 1992, the video game industry grossed $5.3 billion. This represents more money than all of the ticket sales at movie theaters for the same period. Some analysts estimate that by the end of the century, interactive entertainment software could be a $35 billion industry (Provenzo, 1995).

The meaning and social content of video games, particularly those produced by the Nintendo Corporation, have been analyzed by this author (Provenzo, 1991). Video games are highly sexist, racist, and violent. They are also extremely limiting, in that they program children in specific ways to construct the world around them.

Video games are like blocks or toy soldiers, in that they are a type of simulation. Unlike blocks and toy soldiers, however, they are electronically mediated. Video games, like television, function in a tactually impoverished, two-dimensional environment. Most video games are highly circumscribed: because of programming limitations and the speed of most machines, players view the game characters from above or from the side, not from the perspective of the character in the game.

Although current video games are graphically limited, they are rapidly evolving toward the same visual standards as those found in commercial television. In fact, the newest wave of video games is much more like film and television than older and more traditional animated video games such as "Pac-Man" or "Super Mario Bros. 2." CD-ROM technology now makes it possible to insert movie or video footage directly into games. The results are increasingly realistic and offer the sense of viewing television or film.

The importance of this point is that video games, as simulations, are becoming increasingly realistic. In doing so, they almost certainly become more influential in teaching children and shaping their behavior. This is disturbing in light of the fact that video games, besides often being sexist, violent, and racist, provide children with few choices and little opportunity to use their imagination: "when you play a video game you are a player in a game programmed by someone else" (Turkle, 1984, p. 92).

Games like "Mortal Kombat" or "Doom," for example, allow a very limited number of programmed responses. The possibilities for using different strategies are extremely limited. There are relatively few combinatorial possibilities. Creative solutions simply do not exist. When, as a child, the author played war with the neighborhood children, for example, they made up the game as they went along. Defections to the other side were frequent and modifications of weapons were an ongoing and complex process; strategy and negotiations were important components of the game. This simply cannot happen in the physically impoverished and tightly rule-bound universe of video games.

Video games are, in fact, highly limiting, rule-bound systems. They discourage originality and the creation of alternative rules and scenarios. To win most video games, for example, players must follow a complex series of instructions according to a very carefully defined set of rules. If they do not, they lose the game. The master video game player not only has highly developed eye-hand coordination, but the ability and willingness to follow the precise and limiting rules built into any game.

Video games do not have to program children. They can be designed so that players can make choices, more than one person can play at a time, and so on. The reality is, however, that very few games operate in this way. Like television, they create a socially isolated experience for the child.

Video Games as Socially Isolating

Although some of the early research on video games suggests that children can share their video game playing experience with one another, the fact remains that the nature of computer and video game technology is such that it tends to isolate individuals from one another. In the current design of video games, one plays by oneself. Unlike rough-and-tumble play, young children do not discuss and negotiate what goes on in the playscape. The game player responds to a scenario on the screen and plays the game alone. There is no social mediation or discussion of whether or not an action is good or bad, right or wrong, fair or unjust.

Most video games present a significantly impoverished playscape for children, when compared with other more socially focused settings that require children to interact with one another. This does not need to be the case. Video games can be designed so that social interaction is automatically built in. An example of this is visible in some of the video games/simulations that amusement park activity companies, such as Evans and Sutherland, are developing.

Evans and Sutherland, an early developer of flight simulators, has recently marketed a program called "The Loch Ness Adventure." The adventure takes place inside a command vehicle, in this case, a submarine on the famous Loch Ness in Scotland. In the adventure scenario, eight people sit in the command vehicle and attempt to save the recently discovered Loch Ness monster from extinction, by protecting its eggs from evil bounty hunters.

Two players pilot and operate the submarine through the water. They view what is going on through polarized glasses on a large viewing screen or "window" at the front of the command module. The commander of the submarine gives orders to his or her crew, which includes a navigator and a periscope operator.

"The Loch Ness Adventure" is appealing as an interactive and participatory adventure. It has a nonviolent design and appeals to people who are interested in sharing a gaming activity and adventure. Unlike more traditional video game scenarios, it does not socially isolate the player, but provides the opportunity for cooperative gaming and interaction. While the game is rule-driven, it provides for the players a wide range of choices, many more than traditional video games.

Other electronic gaming models also suggest the possibilities of an expanded playscape. Multi-user dungeons or MUDs are imaginary adventure games created in online computer databases, which trace their roots back to participatory adventure games like "Dungeons and Dragons." MUDs are "imaginary worlds in computer databases where people use words and programming languages to improvise melodramas, build worlds and all the objects in them, solve puzzles, invent amusements and tools, compete for prestige and power, gain wisdom, seek revenge, indulge greed and lust and violent impulses" (Rheingold, 1993, p. 145). MUDs were introduced in England in 1980. By the early 1990s there were nearly two hundred MUD-type games underway on the Internet based on nineteen different programming languages (Rheingold, 1993).

Essentially, MUDs allow users to enter into a highly complex gaming scenario, to define a character for themselves, and to endow their character with specific characteristics and powers. A chair can talk, a wall when touched might release the solution to a puzzle, and a tree can have consciousness. Other players participating in the game can also explore the objects that a player creates in a MUD, such as castles, dungeons, and spaceships.

MUDs, and games like "The Loch Ness Adventure," suggest a very different type of playscape and gaming experience than more traditional video games. To what extent these games will become popular remains to be seen. A critical factor in the development of new types of playscapes will involve the extent to which virtual reality technology becomes more realistic and gaming systems become even more interactive.

Virtual Reality and Interactive Technologies

Video games are also becoming increasingly interactive and physical. New virtual reality technologies already on the market make it possible to participate physically in what takes place on a television or computer screen. In Sega's "Activator!," for example, the play lays a track of sensors in a circle around one's feet: when one jumps, one's character jumps; when one punches, one's character punches; and when one kicks, one's character kicks. Nintendo has just introduced a new system of video 3-D "eyephones" for their gaming system "Virtual Boy," the first of many such virtual reality devices that are likely to come onto the market in the near future.

Researchers believe that CD-ROM-based video games, particularly when combined with new types of virtual reality devices, are a new type of television (see Provenzo, 1995). It will be television that allows the viewer to participate in, and not just view, a program. This is a new medium. This author is convinced that the new types of media will create a new type of play and thus represent another example of a radically redefined playscape for children. What happens when a child can watch a television program or movie and then enter a simulation/game in which he or she can assume the role of a character seen in the program? This is being done on a very crude level right now when a child watches a RoboCop film or cartoon and then plays the "RoboCop" video game. Some questions that arise are: What will it be like when children can receive sensory feedback and literally feel a punch or a hit? How will advertisers manipulate this new medium? Answers are likely to become apparent as the playscape of interactive media becomes increasingly accessible. The merging of video games into television programming seems inevitable, as the difference between televisions and computers becomes less and less clear.

Contemporary culture is a turning point in the history of play. Electronically mediated playscapes shaped by television, video games, and new technologies such as virtual reality are drawing children away from more traditional and tactually oriented models of play.

What has drawn many researchers and educators to play as a topic for study is its potential to allow the child to be a creator, an animator of ideas and actions. When a child plays with a set of building blocks, "the actions he performs are not those of a user but those of a demiurge. He creates forms which walk, which roll, he creates life, not property: objects now act by themselves, they are no longer an inert and complicated material in the palm of his hand" (Barthes, 1972, p. 54). To what extent is this type of play possible in the mediated electronic playscapes that new technologies are creating for children? To what extent is the child an animator of play or being programmed to play?

As new models of play are increasingly linked to the electronically mediated culture, the answer seems to be that children's play is becoming less animated, more programmed, and more limiting. This is a sad development and bodes ill for the future of play. But this does not need to be the case. It is critical, however, to understand the limitations imposed on play by the proliferation of electronically mediated and simulated playscapes, and provide children with meaningful alternatives.

Bibliography

Barthes, R. (1972). Toys. In R. Barthes (Ed.), *Mythologies* (A. Lavers, Ed. and Trans.), (pp. 53–55). Boston: Hill and Wang.

Churchill, W. (1944). *A roving commission: The story of my early life.* New York: Scribner's.

Clark, E. (1988). *The want makers: Inside the world of advertising.* New York: Penguin.

Jackson, K. M. (1994). Targeting babyboom children as consumers: Mattel uses television to sell talking dolls. In H. Eiss (Ed.), *Images of the child* (pp. 187–197). Bowling Green, OH: Bowling Green State University Popular Press.

Kline, S. (1993). The making of children's

culture. In S. Kline (Ed.), *Out of the garden: Toys, TV, and children's culture in the age of marketing* (pp. 44–76). London: Verso.

Provenzo, E. F., Jr. (1991). *Video kids: Making sense of Nintendo.* Cambridge, MA: Harvard University Press.

Provenzo, E. F., Jr. (1995, Spring). Brave new video: Video games and the emergence of interactive television for children. *Taboo: The Journal of Culture and Education, 1,* 153–154.

Rheingold, H. (1993). *The virtual community: Homesteading on the electronic frontier.* Reading, MA: Addison-Wesley.

Singer, D. G., & Singer, J. L. (1990). *The house of make-believe: Children's play and the developing imagination.* Cambridge, MA: Harvard University Press.

Turkle, S. (1984). *The second self: Computers and the human spirit.* New York: Simon and Schuster.

Advocacy for the Child's Right to Play

Marcy Guddemi
Tom Jambor
Robin Moore

For more than three and a half decades the Declaration on the Rights of the Child has confirmed that children have the right to food and survival, to shelter and protection, to development and education, to freedom and participation—and the right to leisure and play. It states "Mankind [*sic*] owes the child the best it has to give" (United Nations Declaration on the Rights of the Child, 1959). This 1959 United Nations document has been a strong force behind many educational reforms and social legislation for children in the United States, such as PL 94–142 and Chapter I and II legislation. Ironically, despite the widespread influence of this 1959 document, the United States has specifically ignored the section on the child's *right to play* (Article 7, paragraph 3), as evidenced by the decreasing natural play spaces available to today's preschool and school-age children, the lack of legislation and programs ensuring and providing for the child's right to play, and the blatant disregard of the United Nations 1989 document, the Convention on the Rights of the Child.[1] Since young children cannot be advocates for their own rights, the responsibility is bestowed upon all concerned, especially informed adults, to speak out on issues concerning the importance of play for young children. Although children's right to play is being threatened at the present time, there are some current and proposed efforts to advocate for these rights.

Current Status of Play in the United States

To discuss the status of play in the United States, it is useful to introduce three contemporary play forms: informal, nonformal, and formal.

Informal play is a universal form, genetically programmed in each individual in what some scholars assume to be a biological drive of curiosity. This form of play stimulates children's capacity to learn, and to develop basic skills and competencies, through exploration and engagement with the world around them. In free play children activate their genetic inheritance as part of the Earth's biosystem—the play environment of air, water, soil, vegetation, animals, and gravity.

Nonformal play includes programmed forms where children work with trained play professionals in playful settings. The adult role is to work alongside children, to facilitate rather than direct activity, to help create the "potential" space where playful engagement from within the child can live in the world (Winnicott, 1971). In some countries, this form is well developed. In Europe, nonformal play innovations were driven by the demographic and social changes that arose at the end of World War II (Bengtsson, 1972; Brett, Moore, & Provenzo, 1993; Hurtwood, 1968).

Traditional games such as jump rope, stickball, chanting games, and chasing games serve as a bridge between the informal and nonformal domains of play. Children are constantly influencing and adapting these forms of play to the changing cultural context of childhood. Traditional games are one means available to children for adapting themselves creatively to situations where play opportunities are limited, for instance, in the difficult environment of inner-city neighborhoods. Traditional games also provide a vehicle for practicing and perfecting play skills. Traditional games can also provide a starting point or cultural frame of reference in the programming of nonformal play.

An interesting case of nonformal play is the children's museum, an institution that has seen such phenomenal growth in recent years. Many museums are excellent examples of nonformal education centers. Many offer playful settings and activities, especially for young children. The main emphasis of most children's museums, however, is education rather than play, since the learning objectives are preset by the design as one-way relationships with stand-alone exhibits. Although exhibits are often fashionably "interactive," in reality the range, degree, and depth of interactivity bears little comparison to manipulative, free play environments where children are in control of their own behavior (especially those providing natural materials). The second generation of children's museums now emerging (perhaps with more appropriate names) will provide more engaging, truly interactive, playful learning environments with outdoor as well as indoor settings.

What is *formal play,* then? Like formal education it is the sector of play that is highly directed by adults. It certainly includes competitive sports and games of the physical education/Little League variety, where attitudes of "winning at all costs" have been severely criticized in recent years (Elkind, 1981). Formal play can also include children's theater and the more recent indoor commercial play developments such as Kids Sports and Discovery Zone. These settings usually limit their offerings within a narrow range of gross motor play in fixed environments that in fact leave very little for children to manipulate (except for the ubiquitous ball pits).

One cannot dispute that all types of play are important. Informal play, however, is an essential need for children's healthy development. Unfortunately, daily informal play is disappearing from the lives of children in the United States. Thus, they are losing one of their United Nations' guaranteed rights. Several factors are evident in today's society that affect the future of informal play and necessitate far stronger advocacy for play.

Factors Discouraging Informal Play

Continuing Poverty
More than one out of five children in the United States are living with inadequate provision for their development and even survival because of poverty and substandard living conditions (Newsweek, 1992). In inner cities of the United States, conditions are often similar to those of third world economies. Older children are rearing younger children, performing manual labor (or sexual activities) for drug money, and even begging for food rather than playing. Many children are forced to work at life-sustaining chores as soon as they are old enough to follow directions and to understand that if they do not work they will be punished. Poverty often forces children to be miniature adults during their early years. It robs them of their right to informal play and also presents a barrier to nonformal and formal play opportunities.

Changing Cultural Values
While there is no place or time for any type of play in poverty settings, in more affluent neighborhoods there is often an indifference toward the importance of informal play. Whereas children traditionally have been shielded from adult responsibilities and encouraged to play into their teen years, play is now increasingly frowned on by parents who want their children to "learn," rather than play, at the earliest possible age (Elkind, 1987). "Learning," to such parents, means academics or perhaps music or sports skills. Those parents, however, overlook the social and emotional learning that comes through play. Many people in this society believe that play is frivolous, while "work," especially schoolwork, is productive.

Today, children are also being thrust into adulthood by being encouraged to wear adult (often sexually provocative) clothes, by being constantly exposed to sexual and violent situations on television and radio, and by being forced to handle adult-initiated stresses, such as divorce, unemployment, war, and racial oppression. Premature exposure to adult issues is exacerbated by children's increased dependence on television and on their use of video/computer games as part of their daily routine. Preschool children watch an average of 4.5 hours of television each day without adult supervision (Guddemi, 1986). Passive viewing of television and use of other media/technology act as a double negation of the child's right to play. Not only can children be adversely affected by what they view and hear, but the time spent watching television and playing video games is taken from time that could be spent in more active, creative, informal play (Guddemi, 1986).

Inadequate Time for Play

According to contemporary observers, childhood and play are rapidly disappearing in the United States and other Western nations (Elkind, 1987; Postman, 1982). Children's weekly itineraries are jammed with a progression of lessons and formal play opportunities such as music lessons, Scout meetings, Little League, soccer, and dance lessons. There is not sufficient time to allow children to play informally or to just let them be children in their own space and time.

Inadequate Space for Play

Consider an educator's comment, that "Children give life to neighborhoods," yet neighborhoods are giving nothing back to children (Boyer, 1992, p. 91). Children need safe spaces close to home in which to play together and to use their creativity. Their needs have not received sufficient priority in the development and redevelopment of urban neighborhoods. Children growing up in high-density cities in apartment complexes have as little as four square meters of living and playing space per family (Ebenson, 1979; Moore, 1990). Research shows that the higher the floor of residential occupancy, the less children play (Moore, 1990). In their rush to build banks, hotels, malls, and suburbs, city planners have forgotten the play needs of their children. Thus they provide developers no incentives to build play spaces into their designs (Moore, 1990).

Internationally, nine countries have some form of national standards for children's play spaces in residential environments, but the United States is not one of them (Ebenson, 1979; Moore, 1990). Even in the suburbs, touted as the answer to crime-ridden and crowded inner cities, there are few sidewalks and few play spaces devoted to children. For many children, walking or riding bikes to a friend's house to play is hazardous. Parents complain that all play experiences require a chauffeur and must be prearranged. Community developments that do plan for a play or recreation space cater mainly to adults' needs, with clubhouses, tennis, and exercise rooms, but not to the child's needs.

Changing School Agendas

Play opportunities have also fallen on hard times for children at many elementary schools across the nation. Recesses and the lunch time free period are being sacrificed for increased academic content (Jambor, 1994). Administrators and teachers, pressured to exhibit high standardized test scores, in many cases have eliminated the playground time cherished by children in the past. Diminished are opportunities for children to develop and nurture social and physical skills, as well as opportunities to work out emotional responses in a setting with few adult restrictions. Lost are the outdoor play periods that produced and preserved childhood games and rituals passed on from older to younger children.

Today's elementary schools and many preschools overemphasize work and underemphasize play indoors. Many schools and learning settings force young children to sit for hours with dittos, paper, and pencils, working on rote memorization exercises (Elkind, 1987). Children, however, learn best through play. For optimal intellectual growth, they need to explore and play with their environment by touching and manipulating objects and materials to test their developing cognitive constructs against reality. These developmental opportunities, however, are disappearing as indoor play, as well as outdoor recess play periods, are squeezed out of the curriculum in all too many schools.

Play in its fullest potential not only helps children grow and learn intellectual skills, but also enhances social skills by stimulating children to interact creatively, to settle differences through sharing, cooperating, and taking turns. Societywide, play integrates genders, ages, and ethnic backgrounds. Children grow emotionally, learn, and gain confidence and self-respect through their successful play activities. Play also helps children grow physically as they gain coordination, strength, agility, and other basic physical skills. Play, in fact, is one of the most important requirements for developing a healthy child. To eliminate school recess and indoor play periods is thus counterproductive to all areas of children's development.

Decline of Child Fitness

With play disappearing in the lives of today's children, they face much higher health and fitness risks throughout life than children of past generations. The American Academy of Pediatrics (The American Academy of Pediatrics, 1988) reports that 50 percent of children in the United States are not getting enough exercise to develop healthy hearts and lungs; 40 percent of five- to eight-year-old children show at least one risk factor for heart disease, such as high blood pressure, high cholesterol, or low physical activity. Low physical activity also means children will be more susceptible to other serious health problems such as hypertension, diabetes, psychological disorders, and impaired heart tolerance (Dennison, 1988). Sedentary behavior has put children's health and fitness in jeopardy. Between 1970 and 1992, obesity had increased 54 percent among children in the United States between the ages of six and eleven; 15–20 percent of children were fat; 55 percent of girls and 25 percent of boys between ages six and eleven could not do even one push-up (U.S. Center for Disease Control, 1992).

By removing play opportunities indoors and outdoors we are taking away the child's right to grow up as healthy individuals. The solution to these health and fitness problems is simple: Increase play opportunities for children, which will increase their physical activity and, thus, their physical ability and health.

Few educators realize, however, the vast importance of a curriculum that provides a balance between mind and body. Physical exercise shapes the bones, muscles, heart, and lungs, but it also fuels the brain with a better blood supply, feeds brain cells with a healthier supply of natural substances that enhance their growth, and helps the brain to provide a greater number of connections between its neurons (Brink, 1995). Vigorous physical play makes the brain better able to process all kinds of information. Liberal doses of play might even raise those all-important test scores.

Increased Playground Safety Guidelines

From the first outdoor gymnasium at the Salem, Massachusetts, Latin School, to the first park playground in Chicago, to today's multitude of slick contemporary playground designs, playgrounds are an icon for childhood. Although playground designs have changed over the years, children have not and neither have their play needs. Children continue to seek out challenges within their play environments and reach out for new levels of excitement once skills are mastered. The play value of any playground can be judged by the interactions of the children using it. As children seek new challenges, however, some bumps and scratches are likely to occur. Minor injuries are the inevitable consequence of playful interactions and the accompanying judgments that are the essence of learning by doing (or learning by trial and error).

The main purpose of safety standards should be not *to avoid* the inevitable minor hurts, but *to protect* children from more serious injury. During 1990, approximately 150,000 children were injured seriously enough on playgrounds to warrant hospital treatment (American Society for Testing and Materials, 1993). These statistics have prompted the Consumer Product Safety Commission (1991) and the American Society for Testing Materials (1993) to develop guidelines for playgrounds in the United States. Besides providing standards for equipment design, surfaces, and installation, these guidelines are now used in courts of law as a standard to judge liability in an injury case.

The encouraging news is that, as awareness of playground hazards and poorly designed features grows, these are being eliminated. The discouraging news is that playgrounds have become ever more boring and sterile environments, creating a double bind for playground designers and manufactures.

In the United States, the word *playground* has become almost synonymous with *liability* and *litigation*. In the name of safety, and burdened by the fear of lawsuits, challenge and risk-taking adventure have been factored out of playgrounds. Without challenge children often do not return, or, if they do, they find ways to take risks, to get thrills, and find adventure by using equipment in ways the designer had not intended. The relationship seems clear: when "play value" is reduced, children find ways to factor it back in, usually in the form of undesirable risk-taking. Creating "safe" playgrounds with high "play value" has become a most difficult task.

While the problem appears complex, one answer may actually be quite simple. Adults could dismantle the playgrounds developed in the past one hundred years and let children have their open land back. Then children could return to their natural play environment, the one that originally existed before the neighborhood existed. Playground designers could move beyond an excessive focus on equipment and replant the forests and fields that once were there as "natural play preserves." They could produce designs that compact these natural elements to fit into neighborhood and school sites. Children's original outdoor playgrounds were nature itself (Froebel, 1887). Children should be allowed to return to the playground of nature, creating dams, canals, and bridges in natural streams; nurturing gardens of flowers, plants, and trees; exploring boulders, ridges, and tree limbs; raising and caring for animals; and running and playing games in open fields. Children have not changed: they are still looking for places to climb trees, to build forts, to play childhood games, and to just lie back and watch the clouds roll by; they want places where they can just be children and do childlike things.

Current Efforts to Advocate for the Child's Right to Play

The Convention on the Rights of the Child

The updated United Nations document on children's rights, the Convention on the Rights of the Child, is a critically important legal document. It was adopted by the United Nations General Assembly on November 20, 1989, and came into force on September 2, 1990. The Convention covers comprehensively the human and civil rights of children everywhere, including the right to play, specifically addressed in Article 31. The Convention connects all persons and groups who work with or on behalf of children.

While the "right to play" first appeared in the 1959 United Nations Declaration on the Rights of the Child, it is now superseded by this more powerful, legally binding Article 31 of the Convention. Article 31 not only addresses the right to play but also, appropriately, the right to cultural development and participation in the arts. In other words, play, culture, and the arts are closely linked, interwoven aspects of child and community development. Specifically, Article 31 states:

> States Parties recognize the right of the child to rest and leisure, to engage in play and recreational activities appropriate to the age of the child and to participate freely in cultural life and the arts.
>
> States Parties shall respect and promote the right of the child to participate fully in cultural and artistic life and shall encourage the provision of appropriate and equal opportunities for cultural, artistic, recreational and leisure activity.

The United States, however, chose not to sign the Convention in a timely fashion, making it the only Western country, in company with several small or recently formed countries, that had not taken action on the Convention. On February 16, 1995, six years after the United Nations'

adoption, President Clinton signed the Convention and sent it to the Senate for ratification. As of this writing, the Senate has not yet ratified his signature. The three main arguments that have been expressed at various times to justify the lack of U.S. involvement and the responses to those arguments are:

1. *Federal versus State Rights.* The Convention is not a federal matter, since the states have laws that cover all of the issues addressed by the Convention. *Response.* Many other countries with both states and a strong federal system of government (Canada and Australia, in particular) have ratified the Convention. The United Nations intended the Convention to be a matter for national policy.

2. *Abortion.* The Convention does not address abortion. Since the Convention does not take a stand for or against, the argument is that the Convention tacitly supports abortion. *Response.* Since even the Vatican has ratified the Convention, this argument seems extremely weak.

3. *Capital Punishment.* The Convention says that no one can be punished for capital crimes committed before the age of eighteen. Several states have laws that contravene this right; therefore, if the United States took action on the Convention it would contravene established law in some states. *Response.* The U.S. government has made no effort to bring state governors together to urge them to bring their state laws in line with the Convention's statement that children under 18 years of age should not be punished for capital crimes. It represents as excellent opportunity to rid the nation of laws that every other Western industrial nation has abolished.

As of May 1995, the latest information on the status of the Convention obtained from the UNICEF Office on Children's Rights in New York follows. Of the 191 member countries:

- 174 countries had *ratified* the Convention and thereby become States Parties to the Convention. They must abide by its conditions and must adhere to a reporting schedule to the United Nations Human Rights Commission in Geneva.

- 6 additional countries, including the United States, had *signed* the Convention, thereby making a moral commitment to proceed with ratification.
- 11 countries had *done nothing.*

In response to the lack of commitment of many countries, across three decades, to uphold children's rights, in particular the right to play, an organized international effort initiated in 1961 continues to be a voice for children.

International Association for the Child's Right to Play

The International Association for the Child's Right to Play (IPA) was founded in 1961 to be a voice for the child's right to play and to support and uphold the original 1959 United Nations Declaration of Rights of the Child and the subsequent 1989 Convention on the Rights of the Child. IPA is a professional organization with members from a variety of backgrounds, including architects, landscape architects, physical educators, art educators, teachers, child care givers, city planners, pediatricians, parents, and park and recreation professionals. IPA members understand that the United Nations' *granting* to children the right to food and survival, shelter and protection, development and education, freedom and participation, and the right to leisure and play is the easy part. *Guaranteeing* children those same rights is much more difficult and is the ultimate mission of IPA.

IPA actively promotes the child's right to play in many ways. In 1977, as a lead-in to the 1979 International Year of the Child, IPA published the Declaration on the Child's Right to Play (1979/1990). The updated document (1990) explains Article 31 of the Convention and the IPA mission as advocacy tools to promote the child's right to play. It states that children are the foundation of the world's future and that play is an integral part of this foundation:

Children have played at all times throughout history and in all cultures.
Play, along with the basic needs of nutrition, health, shelter and education, is vital to develop the potential of all children.
Play is communication and expression, combining thought and action; it gives satisfaction and a feeling of achievement.
Play is instinctive, voluntary, and spontaneous.
Play helps children develop physically, mentally, emotionally and socially.
Play is a means of learning to live, not a mere passing of time. (p. 2)

Other IPA projects include publication of a quarterly magazine, *Playrights,* sponsorship and participation in triennial world play conferences and annual regional conferences; membership on the Non-Government Organizations/UNESCO Council; serving as official spokesperson for play issues in the media; and encouraging various play-related projects in developing nations. Currently, the most important agenda item for IPA/USA (the U.S. affiliate of IPA) is to promote the Convention on the Rights of the Child, specifically Article 31 (1989), and to support the U.S. Senates ratification of the Convention.

International Initiatives Promoting Children's Right to Play

Several other countries began promoting children's right to play many decades ago. Adventure playgrounds, for example, were developed in Denmark more than fifty years ago, as were the Swedish playparks (Bengtsson, 1970; Brett et al., 1993). Germany has been creatively addressing the play needs of its children for more than twenty-five years (Moore, 1993). The history of the right to play in the United Kingdom matches that of Scandinavia (National Play Information Centre, 1994; Birch, 1995). Because of the early start by these and other European countries, these countries have maintained their position as innovative leaders in responding to the more recent new "call" to address the right to play.

Sweden has been particularly active. In 1992 IPA-Sweden received a grant from the Swedish government to cooperate with other national bodies to hold a series of six Article 31 study conferences around the country for adults working with children. On the recommendation of the cooperating partners to give the conferences high status, the meetings were held in conference hotels and town halls. The participants raised questions from a child's perspective, including: Why does the child's environment have to be so neat and tidy all the time? What do we do with children who cannot play? What about the right of all children (regardless of ability, ethnic background, or gender) to participate in the decisions affecting their environment? Key issues included the planning and design of school facilities with regard to play needs, the need for a stimulating outdoor environment, and the need to upgrade the quality of school yards (Moore & Wong, 1997; Titman, 1994).

Unga Örnar (Young Eagles), a Swedish national organization of children and youth, implemented an impressive participatory project with young people concerning the complete Convention on the Rights of the Child soon after it was ratified. In the first phase of the project, a working group of adolescents and consulting adult professionals produced a "Convention Pack" for dissemination to school children. The information pack was used as a vehicle for a series of seminars and training sessions with local study groups held around the country. Local politicians and offices were often involved and had to sit in the Childhood Chair (or *Barndomstolen*). Children invited them to answer questions and discuss the implementation of the Convention. Although this project applied to the whole Convention, it provided an excellent model for engaging children and youth directly in the issues raised by the Convention, including play. At the same time, it provided a vehicle for training in democratic processes.

Another Swedish innovation that preceded the Convention-related efforts was the idea of developing a Play Political Program to engage political representatives in the development of a policy document in relation to play, with recommendations directed to each of the responsible governmental sectors—in essence, a localized version of the IPA Declaration on the Child's Right to Play. This concept was subsequently implemented in various forms in New Zealand, Scotland (Clydesdale), Northern Ireland, Wales, and England (Avon, Bristol, and Leicester).

The United Kingdom has possibly the largest number of organizations in the world dealing with children's play, producing a constant stream of publications, initiatives, conferences, and innovations (see IPA under Resources at end of essay). The early support of Article 31 produced separate initiatives in England, Northern Ireland, and Scotland. Each country has explicated Article 31 with respect to its local institutional, cultural, political, and economic environment (see Play-Train under Resources). The Children's Rights Development Unit in London, for example, has pushed Article 31 along with other initiatives. The Lothian Regional Council, through its Children's Family Charter and other policy initiatives, promotes play on the political front in partnership with the Lothian Play Forum, a voluntary organization that supports approximately two hundred play programs in the region. The Playboard in Northern Ireland has been equally active, particularly promoting play as a means of communication to break down long-standing religious strife (see Playboard under Resources).

In the United Kingdom, the National Play Information Center is the current version of a government-sponsored series of national programs or centers that have been on the British scene since the early 1980s. The National Playing Fields Association (1991), a private advocacy and technical assistance organization, has been active for a much longer period, and is still addressing play needs. Therefore, an important part of its broad agenda was the purchase of space that was threatened by development.

Most of the prominent British organizations, including Kids Clubs Network, City Farms, Adventure Playgrounds, Playgrounds for Children with Special Needs, and Handicapped Adventure Playground Association (HAPA), advocate and develop to varying degrees four essential components to implement the Child's Right to Play: place, program, management, and training. After many years of intense discussion about the issue of the "professionalization" of play, the United Kingdom has been implementing *playwork* training initiatives at a national level for several years. The British invented the term *playwork* to define the broad range of professionals involved in the field of play (Shier, 1994).

Since 1990, the United Kingdom has promoted PlayDay, a national day of community-based play for all ages, families, play organizations, and others. This proved so successful that two years later it broadened to a European PlayDay. At the same time, the PlayDay concept was adapted in 1992 by IPA/USA.

Since the early 1980s IPA has been broadening its focus to embrace all regions of the world and to develop a network of two-way (and even multidirectional) cooperative relationships between Europe, where the play movement started, and countries looking for professional, technical assistance. Japan is an example of this IPA "technology transfer": due to the energy and enthusiasm of a dedicated group of

IPA-Japan playworkers, and an enlightened and supportive local government in one of the Tokyo wards, Hanegi Playpark opened in Setagaya Ward in the 1980s. Since then, initiatives have spread to other areas of Tokyo and other Japanese cities. The group is very active in using Article 31 to draw attention to the harmful effects on Japanese youth of the "pressure cooker" system of education (Okuda, 1995).

Other parts of Asia that have moved ahead in promoting play include Hong Kong and India. India has been particularly successful in building IPA "professional bridges" with the Netherlands and Sweden. Technical delegations from both countries have spent time in India engaged in community projects, professional training activities, and lobby work to help play policy, training, and play space development move forward.

South America is another part of the world where, for many years, interesting things have occurred in relation to play. Increased communications have led to greater sharing. Politically speaking, Argentina has the unique distinction of integrating the Child's Right to Play into their national constitution, newly adopted in 1994. Argentina has the longest IPA track record in Latin America and has been able to benefit from IPA technical delegations and bridges to the United States and Sweden in recent years. Swedish professionals involved in international work in children's rights, in turn, have found opportunities through IPA-Argentina to work directly with children and professionals in a variety of institutions, and gain professional exposure to the long-standing play field in Argentina, where the field of "animation" is well developed, as it is in neighboring Uruguay and Brazil (Moore, 1994, 1995). During "animation," adults take leadership roles to play with children and enrich their play experiences, for example, dressing up in funny costumes to play with children and make them laugh.

Each of these countries has much to offer the United States, especially through sharing information about their encouragement of play in the nonformal sector, which offers children alternative, playful, educative leisure experiences that are quite different from the offerings in the formal educational system, still traditional and rigid in many of these countries. Some countries still offer children many places for safe, informal play, something that appears to be disappearing from childhood in the United States (Rivkin, 1995). In the cities of many countries, for example, children can play in the streets and small plazas, safe from other people—although not from traffic, which is often horrendous and oblivious to pedestrian rights.

In summary, the countries that took an early lead in advocacy and community programs for children's play, before the end of World War II in some cases, have been joined by many countries in other regions of the world. Some of the more recent adherents adapted European models to local conditions or have developed their own innovative models.

Barometers of the Future

Children's natural, free, informal play and how and where it happens are a clear measure of the health of a society. On the one hand, the evolution of children's play in the United States during the past few years may reflect and predict the future of play. On the other hand, the current situation could be changed through efforts to uphold children's right to play. Two basic measures by which to evaluate the status of play in the United States are time and space.

Time

Play needs time that is less bounded by pressures of functional living. As time pressures intrude, play diminishes in quality; if they become too dominant, play ceases altogether. One way to document change in play time is to ask children themselves: Are they spending more or less time playing now than in the past?

How will these trends develop in the future? Commentators have presented anecdotal evidence in recent years about the loss of play time or its formalization. As discussed above, children seem to be spending more time engaged in formal play activities outside of school that are just one step removed from the classroom, including music lessons, sports activities, and extra tutoring in academic subjects. Reliable data on these trends, however, are difficult to come by.

Many more children, certainly, are spending more hours in after-school care programs. These programs offer children whose families can afford them, a wide range of recreational opportunities, some of which may preserve playfulness. But what do children from low-income families do with their leisure time? Are they staying at home watching television in cramped domestic spaces lacking play facilities, playing in unsafe on-the-street settings, or participating in formal play opportunities? Answers to these questions can provide the type of information that can support policies encouraging more time for play.

Space

As time is reduced and restricted, so is space. The problem is that viable, protected, secure spaces, offering adequate diversity of play settings and therefore play choices, are not available, even though the number of commercialized play spaces has increased. Parents at all income levels perceive that streets are more dangerous than they used to be, that children playing in the street or local park or playground run a risk of being physically harmed in some way. In some communities these concerns have reached levels of unreasonable paranoia.

Playgrounds, where they exist, still usually focus on manufactured, fixed equipment. In addition to playgrounds that can support gross motor play, children need opportunities to stimulate their fine motor skills, social development, negotiation skills, creativity, problem-solving skills, imagination, and emotional skills, as well as direct experience with their inherited world. Furthermore, these dimensions of development tend to have a low priority in the formal curriculum of school. How can children access spaces that stimulate these dimensions, now that neighborhood streets, vacant lots, and open fields are not available? It appears that a growing number of children lack these opportunities in the United States. This information needs to be collected, however, to inform public policy.

Political Standing of Play in the United States

A major problem in advancing the play political agenda in the United States is the weak political power and status of children. Children are a politically silent, defenseless group whose rights are rarely considered separately from that of their families or the rest of society. Symptomatic of the political problem is the substantial (or at least vocal) number of adults who state that young people do not have rights apart from their family. Disregard of children's rights and a lack of visibility of their needs in political agendas trickles down and causes exclusion from all manner of initiatives where they should be included. In the latest trend in urban planning toward a so-called new urbanism, for example, which introduces higher-density neighborhoods with more focus on social relations among residents, children are hardly ever mentioned as bona fide residents with particular needs like everyone else. A review of the recent volumes published in this field revealed only one that included the word *children* in the index. Are these the throes of a new Victorian era where children should not be heard or seen? Who will speak for children?

The following suggestions are provided as a plan of action for promoting children's right to play in the United States, inspired by similar actions in other parts of the world:

Plan of Action: A Play Political Program for the United States

- Ratify the Convention on the Rights of the Child and engage young people in national, nonformal education programs to understand their rights.
- Create legislation for minimum provision of play spaces in new and rehabilitated residential areas.
- Develop guidelines and standards for the conservation of natural features and areas in land-use planning and residential subdivisions to serve children's need for informal free play.
- Promote traffic-calming designs on residential streets to make them available for children's play and create a community pedestrian zone for all residents.
- Advocate and develop play programs for after school and during school vacations.
- Develop safe-haven play and learning centers on school sites and other suitable community locations easily accessible to children, providing nonformal educational opportunities focused on domains of child development that typically are not receiving sufficient attention in the formal educational program, for example, the arts (also a focus of Article 31).
- Make recess and extended play time at lunch mandatory in public schools.

- Work with schools of education and teacher-training programs to establish a full understanding of "learning through play."
- Work with schools of education and teacher-training programs to establish credentialed programs in playwork and animation. Promote the professional status of these new professionals who are trained specifically to work with children through play.
- Replace passive television viewing with active, informal play opportunities.

If the future of play for children is to be assured and play considered a guaranteed right of every child, there is much work to be done. In the next millennium, society owes children "the best it has to give," which includes the right to play.

Note
1. In contrast, many countries have embraced the United Nations Convention as a key instrument and critical opportunity to readdress children's civil rights.

Bibliography

American Academy of Pediatrics. (1988). Physical fitness facts. *Young Children, 43*(2), 23.

American Society for Testing and Materials. (1993). *Standard consumer safety performance specifications for playground equipment for public use. Designation: F 1487–93.* Philadelphia: Author.

Bengtsson, A. (1970). *Environmental planning for children's play.* New York: Praeger.

Bengtsson, A. (Ed.). (1972). *Adventure playgrounds.* New York: Praeger.

Birch, T. (1995). Initiative in Sweden: Grassroots project on the Convention on the Rights of the Child. *PlayRights, 17*(1), 26–28.

Boyer, E. L. (1991). *Ready to learn.* Princeton, NJ: Carnegie Foundation for the Advancement of Teaching.

Brett, A., Moore, R., & Provenzo, E. (1993). *The complete playground book.* Syracuse, NY: Syracuse University Press.

Brink, S. (1995, May 15). Health guide, 1995: Smart moves. *U.S. News and World Report,* 76–83.

Consumer Product Safety Commission. (1991). *Handbook for public playground safety.* Washington, DC: Author.

Dennison, B. (1988). Childhood physical fitness tests: Predictor of adult physical activity levels? *Pediatrics, 82,* 3.

Ebensen, S. B. (1979). *An international inventory and comparative study of legislation and guidelines for children's play spaces in the residential environment.* Ottawa: Canada Mortgage and Housing Corporation.

Elkind, D. (1981). *The hurried child.* Reading, MA: Addison-Wesley.

Elkind, D. (1987). *Miseducation: Preschoolers at risk.* New York: Knopf.

Froebel, F. (1887). *The education of man* (W. N. Hailman, Trans.). New York: D. Appleton.

Guddemi, M. P. (1986). Television and young children. (ERIC Document No. ED 267 929)

Hurtwood, Lady Allen. (1968). *Planning for play.* London: Thames and Hudson/Evergreen Foundation.

International Association for the Child's Right to Play. (1990). *IPA declaration of the child's right to play* (Rev. ed.). IPA Malta Consultation for the International Year of the Child (1979).

Jambor, T. (1994, Fall). School recess and social development. *Dimensions, 23*(1), 17–20.

Moore, R. (1993). Deutches Kinderhilfswerk. *PlayRights, 15*(4), 7.

Moore, R. (1994). Reintroducing Uruguay. *PlayRights, 16*(1), 18.

Moore, R. (1995). Commercialized play in São Paulo Shopping Centre. *PlayRights, 17*(1), 11–12.

Moore, R. (1996). *Natural learning: The story of the Washington School environmental yard.* Berkeley, CA: MIG Communications.

Moore, R., & Wong, H. (1997). *Natural learning: The life history of an environmental schoolyard.* Berkeley, CA: MIG Communication.

Moore, R. C. (1990, November 21–22). *International approaches to planning for children's playspace.* Presentation for National Playing Fields Association Conference, Action for Play: Planning for the twenty-first century, London, England.

National Play Information Centre. (1994). What is Playday?—U.K. version.

PlayRights, 16(2), 4–5.

National Playing Fields Association. (1991). *A place to play* (Annual report). London: Author.

Newsweek, (1992, May 4). Slavery. *119,* 30–32.

Okuda, R. (1995). Children's spirit of play and creativity being withered by adults' management: Appeal to child's right to play. *PlayRights, 17*(3), 29.

Playboard. (1990). *Play without frontiers: A policy document on community relations in children's play.* Belfast: Author.

Play-Train. (1995). *Article 31 Action Pack: Children's rights and children's play.* Birmingham, UK: Author.

Postman, N. (1982). *The disappearance of childhood.* New York: Delacorte.

Rivkin, M. (1995). *The great outdoors: Restoring children's right to play outside.* Washington, DC: National Association for the Education of Young Children.

Shier, H. (1994). *Getting recognition: Report of the national consultation on getting national recognition for playwork training and qualifications.* London: National Play Information Centre/IPA Resources.

Titman, W. (1994). *Special places; special people: The hidden curriculum of school grounds.* Godalming, Surrey, UK: World Wildlife Fund/Learning Landscapes Trust.

United Nations. (1989). *The Convention on the Rights of the Child.* New York: Author.

U.S. Centre for Disease Control. (1992). Teens don't exercise enough, survey says. *Birmingham News,* January 24.

Winnicott, D. (1971). *Playing and reality.* New York: Basic Books.

Resources

Evergreen Foundation, 24 Mercer Street, Toronto, Ontario, Canada M5V 1H3. Tel: 1 416 596 1495. Fax: 1 416 596 1443.

IPA Nation Play Information Centre, 359–361 Euston Road, London NW1 3AL, UK. Tel: 44 171 383 5455. Fax: 44 171 387 3152.

Learning Through Landscapes Trust, Southside Offices, the Law Courts, Winchester SO23 9Dl, UK. Tel: 44 1962 84658. Fax: 44 1962 869099.

National Playing Fields Association, 25 Ovington Square, London SW3 1LQ. Tel: 171 584 6445. Fax: 171 581 2402.

Playboard, 253 Lisburn Road, Belfast BT9 7EM, Northern Ireland. Tel: 44 1232 382633.

Play Train, 31 Farm Road, Sparkbrook, Birmingham, B11 1LS, UK. Tel: 44 121 766 8446. Fax: 44 121 766 8889.

UNICEF Office on Children's Rights, United Nations, New York, New York 10017. Tel: 212-326-7307.

Educational Implications of Play with Computers

Steven B. Silvern

Research on play as well as research on children's use of computers explore play in a variety of forms and from differing perspectives. Thus, any examination of the implications of play with computers requires specifying the meaning of the term *play* and describing what children typically do with computers. Those who have studied and theorized about play have conceived of it as being anything from dark, messy, and barbaric (Sutton-Smith, 1981) to a beneficial, voluntary match between challenge and skills unrelated to real-life consequences (Csikszentmihalyi, 1979). Within this range of perspectives, there is an increasing debate about the advisability of certain kinds of computer play for children.

Scientists who believe that media strongly influence children's actions warn that play with violent computer or video games can increase children's tendencies toward violence. It is possible, however, to imagine that children will be drawn toward other ideas within the context of games that seem to be barbaric. The dark, more complex levels of the adventure game "Zelda," for example, require clever solutions rather than use of brute force. Similarly, the game "Adventure" requires planning and use of caution instead of fighting skill. Researchers interested in studying the phenomenon of play with computers usually focus more on this "play as challenge" motive rather than the "play as barbaric" motive.

Examination of children's use of computers may entail studying their exploration (Hutt, 1979) rather than their play (Escobedo, 1992). Exploration can be included within a concept of play: in exploration children attempt to find out what an object or material does, whereas in play they attempt to find out what they can do

with the object or material (Bergen, 1988). The distinction is primarily temporal because exploration occurs before play (Hutt, 1979). During observations of children's play, however, it is extremely difficult to draw a temporal dividing line between exploration and play. Therefore, knowing that some, though not all, scholars may disagree, this essay defines play with computers as the players' attempts to find out both what the computers can do and what the players can do with the computers. When children are engaged in computer play, there is a match between challenge and skills that may or may not relate to real-life consequences. Play with computers also may involve play in both antiseptic, socially acceptable environments and in environments that offer darker, more aggressive simulations.

Play in Microworlds

The computer provides a microworld in which children can both imitate and play, for, despite Piaget's (1976) classifications, imitation occurs within a playful frame and observers easily categorize these actions as play behaviors. Microworlds provide a context that challenges children's skills and thoughts. The children might be trying to hit a target, design a pleasing representation, or accomplish a self-imposed task. Early researchers studying the effects of the computer program Logo (Papert, 1980) recognized self-imposed activity in children's attempts to change the color of the screen by filling it up with hundreds of lines (Silvern, 1988). No one observing the laughter and joy exuded by successful children could conclude that the activity was anything other than play. At the same time, no one observing the intense concentration children exhibited as they matched their thoughts to the problem posed could conclude that the children were not learning during their playful interaction with the computer and with each other.

Although one might discuss the characteristics of good microworlds, such a discussion goes beyond the scope of this essay. Suffice it to say that children are drawn to a microworld by the playful challenge that it presents. The question that must be answered, however, is what kinds of microworlds will children be playing with in the future? A seminal thinker in the computer field went so far as to suggest that computers would make schools obsolete (Papert, 1980). Fifteen years later, this statement still appears to be an extremely radical prediction. That is because, not only has there not been the dramatic race to computers that he foresaw, there has even been a retrenching in teaching that has focused on the use of computers primarily for practice of didactic materials. There are, however, a number of ways that schools are presently encouraging children to enter such computer microworlds as computer games, the computer as a tool, and the Internet.

Play with Computer Games

Many educators have suggested that electronic games can provide ideal microworlds for children's learning in school (Baird & Silvern, 1990; Silvern, 1985). Computer games challenge the player's abilities to reason, provide nonthreatening environments to encourage exploration, support academic risk-taking, and create a demand to learn how to apply school learning. To advance to the next level of play in "The King's Rule" (O'Brien, 1984), for example, the player must supply the guard with the general rule of problem solving being applied at that level. Adventure games like "Winnie the Pooh in the Hundred Acre Wood" and "Mickey's Space Adventure" (Walt Disney Personal Computer Software, 1984) encourage map making as well as solving relational problems. They also expect children to join together to use their combined understandings to try to solve problems.

Even though the prediction that computer games will play a substantive role in children's learning and provide many excellent learning opportunities is a modest one, such games are not now widely used in classrooms, and there

is some doubt that they ever will be. Early theorists and later researchers both have recommended that children's learning be based in play and games (Dewey, 1900; Kamii & DeVries, 1980); yet schools are still adamantly resistant to having play as a major component in classrooms (Block & King, 1987). There remains within school an ethic that identifies the appropriate activity for learning as work, hard work, and asserts that children may play games only after work is done, especially as a reward for good work. Within school there is also a dichotomy between play and work, and the majority of classroom activity planners perceive that games are too enjoyable to use as real classroom experiences (Sutton-Smith, 1987).

Play with Computing Tools

Children can also experience computer play in schools by receiving opportunities to use tool applications in playful ways (Henninger, 1994). Within this vision, children use drawing or word processing programs for their own ends. In a kindergarten classroom, for example, children can use "Kid Pix 2" to generate pictures that they will write about in their journals (Broderbund, 1994). The creation of the pictures is fanciful and most often demonstrates the playful manipulation of a particular kind of instrument. Children might use word processing programs to experiment and play with writing or use spatial design programs to create structures.

An eight-year-old and her friends, for example, used the word processor to create a school newspaper, greeting cards, and advertisements for a scheme to make money. The children even composed a song on the computer that was later used in a school presentation on intercultural relations. These children successfully negotiated with the teacher to engage in these playful literacy creations in place of their typical literacy-related school work. In the same vein, Israeli kindergartners write stories and keep records on the computers in their classrooms as a part of their play activity (Silvern & Levita, 1994). This playful use of computers is certainly being adopted in classrooms and appears to be a dominating function of computers, especially in early childhood classrooms. The challenge for teachers is to keep the computer as a playful instrument and not to use it only as a machine that involves children's doing drill activities.

The Internet as a Microworld Playground

Perhaps the most innovative current play with computers is *surfing* the Internet computer network (note that even the verb is playful). The Internet is a connection of thousands of public and private computers crisscrossing the globe. Anyone with a computer can be a "site" on the Internet. Internet sites contain computer files and applications that are available for users regardless of location. Some of these applications are free (freeware) and some require a small fee from the user (shareware). The University of Michigan, for example, maintains such a site (www.umich.edu/nsdamask/umich. mirrors1). Located at this site is a compilation of files and applications for both Macintosh and DOS (IBM-type) computers as well as other computer platforms. Teachers and children from a school or from one classroom who wish to use a particular application can "visit" (connect to) the University of Michigan via the Internet and download (obtain) some files and applications that are appropriate for their use.

Sites may contain everything from games to articles that explain how to make bombs (the horror of the Internet). They may also contain pictures, movies, and music and other sounds. The Internet provides opportunities for both a "challenge" use (at the game, simulation, and word processing or design level) and a "barbaric" use (finding access to dark, dangerous, and mischief-making information). Thus, children can challenge themselves to find useful and enjoyable information and activities as well as engage in illicit dark imaginings. As yet adults have not found a good solution to alleviate their concerns about these darker possibilities.

The Internet can certainly serve as an essential research tool for both children and adults and it certainly does serve this purpose. The Internet is also a playground, however, because it fits precisely into the concept of play, answering questions such as What is this? What can I make it do? What will I find at a particular site? What will be new or surprising? and What will I be able to do with it? Children can think of the Internet as a toybox in which the games and toys inside are concealed by cryptic names. They might ask, for example, "What is in 'Susan' or in 'MacTrek'?" Then the children can download applications that have interesting names, to see what is in these various "toyboxes" and to find out what they can do with them. Of course, teachers will want to monitor this play activity closely while still allowing for reasonable exploration. One might imagine children searching for one piece of information and becoming sidetracked by something more interesting, similar to looking for one word in the dictionary and having one's attention diverted by other words. Just as in other forms of play, the "product" may be of less interest than the "process" of exploring, manipulating, and expanding on the activities in the electronic playground of ideas, images, sounds, and games.

Accessing the Internet Playground

There are various tools for accessing data on the Internet, but the most promising tool for young children is a World Wide Web (WWW) browser. Two popular browsers that are free to educational institutions are Netscape Navigator TM (Netscape Communications Corporation, 1995) and NCSA Mosaic (University of Illinois, 1994). Browsers use text, pictures, and icons to help the user "navigate" the Internet. Specific items in the browser point to other sites on the Internet; thus, the user can travel to another Internet site by using the mouse to click on a picture or icon. Each user may custom-design a "home page" that "points" to different Internet locations. It is possible, therefore, for teachers to create an interface that allows children selected access to the Internet. Because the WWW browser can use icons and pictures as "pointers," children who cannot yet read or who do not know English (the lingua franca of the Internet) can use the Internet. This means that users may access data from a huge variety of sources without using memory on the home computer. It also means that data can be readily available for children's play and learning. Text can also be stored as sound, so that by clicking on an icon children can hear the text as they read it or listen instead of reading it. There is a dinosaur museum on the Internet, for example, that displays pictures and information about a dig; the text is available to be heard as well as read.

There are so much data available on the Internet that it is difficult to imagine what a child might access. A kindergarten teacher whose class was doing a theme on the arts, for example, "went," with one of the five-year-olds in the class, to visit the Louvre (an Internet site). Although they never left the classroom, by using the WWW browser, they found the paintings of Monet in the Louvre site. The paintings were conveniently catalogued as early and late, so they did not have to search among the other works to find the paintings they wanted to see. Once they found those paintings, they were able to download them, print them, and save them on disk for later use. The five-year-old selected the paintings she preferred and talked with other children about the aspects of the paintings that made them attractive to her. She particularly liked *La Promenade* because of the sky. This is but one example of potential play material available in cyberspace; there are samples of art, music, photographs, games, and movies about almost every subject one might imagine. The Internet is a manipulative center (microworld) that contains a vast number of items with which children can play and from which they can learn.

Playing in the Internet Playground

The informational items that have been described might also be found in a book or on a tape, filmstrip, or movie. The distinction between these media and the Internet is that the items are permanent and static in traditional media; that is, the information from these media does not lend itself to playful exploration. Although the teacher and child easily could have found the same Monet paintings in library books that reprint his work, once they had found out the characteristics of the painting reproductions, what else could they have done with them? Could they have rearranged them to explore a particular theme? Could they have changed the colors in them to see if the mood or idea of the painting changed? Could they have found a pattern, copied it, and compared it to other patterns in other paintings, or even repeated the pattern in the same picture? In other words, they could not have manipulated the static media in a playful way to generate new ideas or meanings. The computer clearly allows children to manipulate data in ways that are not possible using other media.

The Internet, in particular, provides a host of data for the user to manipulate. Users, for example, can reproduce, rotate, reverse, and change the colors of pictures. How might Monet's *La Promenade* be different if it contained several figures instead of just two? With the computer, children can play with art in ways that are impossible with books, films, or slides. Similarly, users can playfully manipulate sounds, movies/videos, and text. One attribute of the Internet, therefore, is that it can provide source material for playful manipulation.

Using the WWW, adults can structure the environment so that children can easily access the kind of data with which they wish to play. They can create a page that takes them to museums or one that permits them to visit other schools (there are approximately three hundred elementary schools registered on the Internet). They can create a page that takes them to virtual reality sites, in which they create a nonreal environment that simulates a form of reality (i.e., pretend play!). One such site is "Addventure," where children follow and add to an endless adventure story. Children can find "Addventure" on the Internet by using the Web browser (http://www.addventure.com/addventure/). A single home page provides access by use of icons or pictures.

Children can experience another aspect of play by "traveling" from site to site. Without leaving the classroom, they can find out what other places are like. If they "visit" another school, they can see what projects those children are working on and try to find ways to be involved in the distant projects. It is possible for children to store their ideas on the WWW so that other children can access those ideas and make suggestions. These forms offer the possibility of children's playing with each other's ideas. Imagine how the culture of one child might influence another child several thousand miles away! The examples show that the Internet provides many ways in which children and adults can enrich their play.

The Down Side of Computer Play

The positive aspects of play with computers have been presented in detail. Computers themselves are not good or bad, however, but how humans choose to use them might be. Adults may encourage inappropriate as well as appropriate uses of computers in classrooms. It is inappropriate, for example, for teachers to require children to use the computer as an electronic worksheet and then call that activity play. Some software requires children to type in the completion to repetitive, meaningless equations that then blow up space monsters. There are also "run-and-jump" games that require nothing more from children than a facility with pushing buttons. Naturally, adults concerned with appropriate educational activities will avoid using such software, just as they avoid trite books and meaningless drill and practice worksheets.

Another inappropriate use of technology is when teachers isolate children and arrange for computer interactions solely with the machine. While there are times when individual challenge can be fun, this should not be the only domain of human-computer interface. Playing games, solving problems, and searching for new and interesting interactions are all social endeavors, and adults need to arrange for children to engage socially around the technology.

Rather than using poor technology, or using technology poorly, it would be better not to have children using the technology at all. Adults can choose the way they use technology with children. They need to select software and activities that playfully challenge children's skills. They can arrange for telecommunications events that take children far beyond the here and now into a world of imagination and action that makes other media pale in comparison.

Occasionally, one reads or hears horror stories about children accessing data that they should not access. There is now software available on the Internet, however, that effectively blocks children from inappropriate sites. Adults can arrange their telecommunications interfaces so that exploration can occur within fairly safe parameters. Adult involvement and interest in what children are doing and their occasional collaboration with children in computer play are also helpful ways to assure that children's computer play will be appropriate.

The Future of Play

Given the potential that this technology offers, educators now must consider how the computer can enhance school learning and how to use play effectively in schools in the future. Unlike the predictions of theorists described earlier, this author does not see schools becoming obsolete. It is likely, however, that teachers will begin to realize more fully the rich learning that can occur when children and adults play together in cyberspace. With that recognition, there is a possibility that teachers will make significant changes in the content and activity emphases of their classrooms and give more credence to the role of play in learning. A number of changes may occur, including a change in the boundaries of school, a move from individual learning to cooperative learning, and opportunity to play with forms and ideas that were not accessible before.

Boundary Changes

There are two ways that school boundaries may change. First, the physical boundaries of school can be transformed as children gain access to the WWW from home and school. Imagine parents and children accessing the school's WWW page from their home. The following scenario might occur:

Dad: What did you do in school today?
Bud: Come on, Dad, turn on the computer and I'll show you. OK, first click on Cyber Elementary School. There, set the pointer to Miss Electra's class. Click on it. See my picture? Click on it.
Dad: Whoa! How many projects did you work on today?
Bud: Three. See, I've got three things on my page. This one's really neat. A school in France is doing a project on cleaning up the environment. They've asked us for pictures that show what kinds of things we are doing. I took a video of our nature trail before we started our pick-up project, while we were cleaning up, and after we finished the project. Click on the nature trail sign and you can see the video. I sent them the video by e-mail today. I hope they like it. Maybe I'll get a message back tomorrow.
Dad: Good idea. What else can we do?
Bud: Well, we can look at the projects of Leslie, Tracey, Shasta, and Yoni. Let's go to their pages and see what they've done.
Dad: Look, this icon here shows that you have mail waiting for you. Hey, the school from France has sent you a message already. Let's see what it says . . .

Home access to school through the WWW would give parents a more intimate role in their child's school activities. Not only could parents have access to what their child has done, but the parents also could have access to information that teachers, counselors, and administrators might supply. Children and parents could work on projects and play together while enhancing what the child is doing at school.

The second way boundaries will change was also illustrated in the conversation between

Dad and Bud. Children will now have access to environments that go beyond the school walls. They will be able to play with the Internet at home as well as at school and to "travel" around the globe searching for new ideas or challenges. There is no longer the need to be limited to the thoughts and actions of those in the immediate environment: it is possible to share in the thoughts of others on the planet and to cooperatively engage them in games or other activities.

Cooperative Learning

The Internet is based on the idea of communication; it goes against the popularly held assumption that each person has to learn a defined set of "facts" in a completely individual way. This isolated learning style is challenged when, every day, individuals can read e-mail and see questions posed and answered by a diverse group of individuals in various parts of the globe. This cooperative learning model can easily find its way into the classroom. Learning can then be based on the playful manipulation of problems shared with other learners on the Internet. Such a model works on the assumption that problems have multiple possible solutions and that each solution should be evaluated for its worthiness. For example, a child, may become enamored of a book of arithmetic puzzles that could have multiple answers. It would be fun for the child to post these puzzles on the WWW page and see the kinds of answers other people provide. Making puzzles for others is another form of play that works well on the Internet. One example of this is the "Great Internet Hunt," only one of many puzzles found on various WWW pages.

Play with Forms

This type of play entails the manipulation of graphic or other media data that have never been available for manipulation before. Children can paint a mustache on the Mona Lisa, for example, or put additional figures in the painting *La Promenade*. These changes are not permanent, so this play with forms is not harmful. Being able to manipulate that which was once inaccessible opens up whole new realms of play. Imagine using a video image and creating a new soundtrack for it! The possibilities for play with forms are bounded only by the child's imagination and the adult's willingness to let

formerly static, sometimes sacred, forms be manipulated in play.

Schools of the future, therefore, may change not only in place or time but also in content, impact, and reach. Adults and children can adapt the topics and manner of study. The types of learners who are involved together can expand. The overall scope of study can extend throughout the world.

More than a dozen years ago a colleague raised the objection, "I don't see how playing with a turtle is going to change children's thinking." (The "turtle" is used in LOGO programming.) The reply to that objection was a chapter on how thinking differently will change thinking (Silvern & McCary, 1986). A similar question can be posed now: How will play with computers, especially play with the Internet, change children's play and how they learn through play? Will playing differently change playing? Will learning differently change learning?

Having different play "materials" may or may not change the way one thinks (although it would appear that the world would be quite different today if children had not had toy chariots to play with thousands of years ago). Having items to play with that *require* a different way of thinking, however, can change one's thoughts. Sixty years ago few people ever dreamed of leaving New York, say, or using the telephone to talk to someone outside of the city because communicating with people in other places was the purpose of the mail. Forty years ago most individuals considered flying to a destination a big event and used long-distance telephone calling sparingly. Today, the majority of people in technologized countries think it is normal to fly to other continents and to contact people throughout the world by telephone. How people think and behave is affected by what tools they have to think with.

Today there is the Internet, a thinking tool that is new for the present generation. It appears to be shrinking the world. The messages that used to be sent by mailed letters no longer take weeks to get to a destination; they take seconds. Responses are equally quick. The Internet is expanding people's imagination because images, sounds, and ideas are no longer set in stone; people can adapt and try them in different environments with different people. Play is not limited to the games and players who are immediately present; rather, play can include actions in an imaginary place that exists only in cyberspace with people who are far away. It is possible to play with games that go beyond what is available at the local department store. Unlike chess-by-mail, for example, where each move took days or weeks to complete, one can play with another person thousands of miles away in real time.

The Internet encourages the manipulation of possibilities so that one can find out what the Internet can do and what one can do with the Internet (taking Hutt's [1979] definition into cyberspace). It allows players to test the limits of their capabilities in a match between challenge and skill within a nonthreatening environment, removed from most of the dangers of the real world. Play will lead human beings into the twenty-first century.

Bibliography

Baird, W. E., & Silvern, S. B. (1990). Electronic games: Children controlling the cognitive environment. *Early Child Development and Care, 61,* 43–49.

Bergen, D. (1988). Stages of play development. In D. Bergen (Ed.), *Play as a medium for learning and development: A handbook of theory and practice* (pp. 49–67). Portsmouth, NH: Heinemann.

Block, J. H., & King, N. R. (Eds.). (1987). *School play: A source book.* New York: Garland.

Broderbund Software. (1994). Kid Pix [Computer software]. Novato, CA: Author.

Csikszentmihalyi, M. (1979). The concept of flow. In B. Sutton-Smith (Ed.), *Play and learning* (pp. 257–274). New York: Gardner.

Dewey, J. (1900). Froebel's educational principles. *Elementary School Record, l,* 143–151.

Escobedo, T. H. (1992). Play in a new medium: Children's talk and graphics at computers. *Play and Culture, 5,* 120–140.

Henninger, M. L. (1994). Computers and preschool children's play: Are they compatible? *Journal of Computing in Childhood Education, 5,* 231–239.

Hutt, C. (1979). Exploration and play (#2). In B. Sutton-Smith (Ed.), *Play and learning* (pp. 175–194). New York: Gardner.

Kamii, C., & DeVries, R. (1980). *Group games in early education: Implications of Piaget's theory.* Washington, DC: National Association for the Education of Young Children.

Netscape Communications Corporation. (1995). Netscape Navigator TM [Computer software]. Mountain View, CA: Author.

O'Brien, T. C. (1984). The King's Rule [Computer software]. Pleasantville, NY: Sunburst Communications.

Papert, S. (1980). *Mindstorms: Children, computers, and powerful ideas.* New York: Basic Books.

Piaget, J. (1976). *The grasp of consciousness* (S. Wedgwood, Trans.) Cambridge, MA: Harvard University Press.

Silvern, S. B. (1985). Classroom use of video games. *Educational Research Quarterly, 112,* 10–16.

Silvern, S. B. (1988). Creativity through play with LOGO. *Childhood Education, 64,* 220–224.

Silvern, S. B., & Levita, A. (1994). Wordprocessing in the kindergarten. *Kindergarten Echos, 59,* 147–154.

Silvern, S. B., & McCary, J. C. (1986). Computers in the educational lives of children: Developmental issues. In J. L. Hoot (Ed.), *Computers in early childhood education: Issues and practices* (pp. 6–21). Englewood Cliffs, NJ: Prentice Hall.

Sutton-Smith, B. (1981). *A history of children's play: The New Zealand playground 1840–1950.* Philadelphia: University of Pennsylvania Press.

Sutton-Smith, B. (1987). School play: A commentary. In J. H. Block & N. R. King (Eds.), *School play: A source book* (pp. 277–289). New York: Garland.

University of Illinois. (1994). NCSA Mosaic [Computer software]. Champaign, IL: Author.

Walt Disney Personal Computer Software. (1984). Mickey's Space Adventure [Computer Software]. Anaheim, CA: Author.

Walt Disney Personal Computer Software. (1984). Winnie the Pooh in the Hundred Acre Wood [Computer Software]. Anaheim, CA: Author.

Emerging and Future Contexts, Perspectives, and Meanings of Play

Doris Bergen
Doris Pronin Fromberg

The contexts, perspectives, and meanings of play will continue to be influenced by a postmodern world. Readers may take up the issues as well as the conclusions regarding play raised in this book as a basis for many future discussions.

New Contexts for Play in a Postmodern World

During an era that is both rooted in the hierarchical linear determinism of the factory model and in transition to an emerging postmodern, self-organizing system, play is in a paradoxical position. This paradox is confounded by the impact of technology through the mass media, such as television and computer communication. Technology has created two major accessibility dichotomies, one of which is seen in the contrast between the general access to varied technologies by the "haves" and the lack of access to most technologies because of the daily economic realities of the "have-nots." The other dichotomy exists in the knowledge gap between the same mass media messages presented on television, the most commonly accessible technology to people of all cultures in the United States, and the specific nontechnical event knowledge beyond the media that is multicultural and individualistic. These accessibility differences create a dynamic that cuts across most general trends cited as indicative of postmodern social systems.

Influences of Technologically Based Play

The influence of a postmodern world in which roles, agents, relationships, functions, materials, lifestyles, and advocates may become delineated in fresh ways is not likely to repress children's play, although these influences may suggest different directions and opportunities, especially for children with more or less access to technology. The play of children whose technology access is limited to television has already been greatly affected by that medium of information. With the advent of these new media and the mediation of direct experiences that they bring, a shift in forms of play has begun for those children with access to these technologies.

Computer Networks and Games

There is increasing access to the Internet in elementary schools and homes. Although at the present time this access is unequally distributed, the potential that all children and adults in the technologized world will eventually have access is likely. The Internet, with its various "rooms" and specialized subjects, can be the social approximation of "hanging out" with friends. The Internet also has been used for quilting (Louie, 1995), formerly a social leisure activity for older girls and women that had its historical roots in practical necessity. At the same time, "[h]omemade goods, which involved play and imagination as well as hard work, were 'inefficient' in the modern era but are being rediscovered in the post-modern era" (Elkind, 1991, p. 9). On the one hand, the capacity of networking with computers, when freely chosen, can feel playful and can add to the possibility for children to engage in cooperative and constructive projects. On the other hand, beyond entertainment, the freewheeling industry that communicates through computer networks raises the issue of children's exploitation by adults, whether for extended commercial gain, prurient interests, sexual abuse, or exposure to extreme violence.

Computerized games have replicated some aspects of board games or games that engage physical skills with balls, sticks, blocks, or balance. The technology offers increasingly accurate voice recognition and realistic voice synthesis that provides additional feedback and "friendly" use. In such tranformations, there is a redistribution of physical involvement and social contact, as well as different levels of access for people of varying ages and abilities.

To the extent that children can enter into play frames that contain the potential for them to ask "What if . . .?" and behave "as if . . . ," play is possible. It is apparent that the computer offers some parallels with play that can be seductive because it is intrinsically motivating, usually basically risk-free, empowering, and satisfying. The boundaries of play or the playground, however, exist in a different medium. The issues to raise in the face of electronic frames and toys is the degree to which direct experience and child empowerment trade off for varied implementations. For the physically challenged child, for example, finger or voice control through a computer becomes empowering.

Virtual Reality

A power shift takes place, however, when virtual reality laboratories and playgrounds program their simulated range of play opportunities. "Instead of using screens and keyboards, people can put displays over their eyes, gloves on their hands, and headphones on their ears. A computer controls what they sense; and they, in turn, can control the computer" (Aukstakalnis & Blatner, 1992, p. 7). Participants can feel, smell, see, hear, zap, and experience velocity changes. For example, the participant can recreate some of the vicissitudes of watching a slapstick comedy or horror film, in watching either film, there is a thrill of suspense, relief, and sense of empowerment in risking the adrenalin rush without danger of humiliation, damage, or destruction.

The multisensory nature and three-dimensionality of virtual reality technology can affect tacitly held assumptions about play and learning. Public school education in the United States, for example, affords primacy to the two-dimensional visual domain by emphasizing written skills. By marginalizing the strong oral skills in which children are competent before they begin formal education, many children become immediately handicapped. The strong heuristics in the oral tradition of human beings offer valuable ways of encoding and retrieving experiences (Egan, 1988). Sociodramatic play, in particular, rests heavily on oral skills. By marginalizing these skills, therefore, schools may contribute to the disempowerment of children in additional ways that subtly influence their creative and social competence as well as their capacity to play. It is possible that virtual reality technology can "readjust the ratio, moving the auditory back into parity with the visual . . . and potentially all other modes of sensation as well" (Moulthrop, 1993, p. 80). To the extent that this readjustment occurs, it is possible that such technology can provide a better balance in schools than is currently the case.

Regardless of the range of options, *virtual* is still not *real*: the impressive array of options has limits. The consumer can construct and create only information that programmers can translate into digital form (Wexelblat, 1993). The programmers' imaginations, connection-making options, and aesthetic sensibilities may also close down children's unique connection-making and problem-solving processes before they have a chance to become engaged. Television programming, in itself, markets particular ideologies and attitudes toward people based upon gender, class, race, and abilities. By reaching more deeply into and touching human sensory experiences, it is certainly possible that, as access to virtual reality technology expands, it can become equally influential. Of course, influence has the potential to broaden as well as narrow one's social perspectives and personal possibilities. Now that there is a recursive relationship among toys, television, and stories in books, with commercial interests transforming any one medium into the others, the notion of immersing children in the simulated three-dimensional environments of virtual reality technology invites speculation concerning both the best and worst case scenarios that might result.

At the same time, it is apparent that among the services of virtual reality technology are the possibilities to entertain, educate, and empower (Moulthrop, 1993). The capacity of human beings to entertain multiple mental models helps to make virtual reality possible. As another mental model, virtual reality builds on the shared awareness that makes scripted play possible. As is the case within the play continuum, the stages of virtual reality include passivity (person cannot control), exploration (person attempts to find out how things work), and interaction (person can interact and change events) (Wexelblat, 1993, p. 23): "[T]he technology is simply a tool" (p. 14). As with any tool or medium, providing balance in children's access and use of time becomes an important consideration. Perhaps it is helpful to consider computers, CD-ROM (voice and motion picture synthesized), and virtual reality technologies as additional playground sites. Virtual reality technology may develop into the broadly available, ultimate, mediated experience that can transport participants into sensing other times, places, and physical experiences.

The process of balancing simulation with real experience remains the challenge of the future. To maintain this balance, children need to have opportunities for authentic play experiences. There have been many voices raised to promote attention to "real-life" experiences for children, even as the virtual world becomes more prominent. There also are signs that adults are attempting to balance their vicarious experiences with more authentic pastimes. If the current surge of interest in pursuing more and varied authentic activities—ranging, for example, from pick-your-own apples to climbing real rocks, hiking through and clogging national parks—is a prologue to the future, then it is possible to be optimistic about meeting the challenge of a balanced life. The postmodern world is, after all, focused on the situation-specific, individual perspective and experience. Such a focus coalesces with the nature of play as a context-based pastime that can empower the player. It will be very important, however, for advocates of play to monitor the contexts that children will inhabit in the future so they can assure that the balance of real and virtually real is a healthy one for children.

Influences of Psychobiologically Based Play

In the world of the next century, technology will continue to develop, whereas the biology of the human brain will not be much changed. Because biological evolution is much slower than cultural evolution, humans are "forced to grapple with current social and environmental issues using a brain that biological evolution has tuned to the far different cognitive challenges of 30,000 years ago" (Sylwester, 1995, p. 21).

Humans have designed technological innovations to serve as another layer of brain, a "technological brain" that senses what humans cannot directly sense, moves bodies through the air in ways that humans cannot move, and infuses into the human brain unhumanlike experiences for which meaning must be sought by the brain's existing emotional and cognitive processes. Sometimes, human coping with these technologically induced experiences is breathtakingly positive, but, more often, technological innovation creates new problems that require creative and flexible uses of human biological and psychological capacities. Fortunately, one part of the human brain, the frontal lobe, has evolved with the "extra power" to enable humans to cope with situations requiring such problem solving and critical thinking.

These capacities of the brain, which have always been needed to cope with environmental and creature-induced crises, enabling humans to figure out ways to survive in emergency situations, are available for other uses when survival issues are not prominent. To keep these abilities functioning optimally, humans have "invented social and cultural problems to keep them continually stimulated and alert. The arts, games, and social organization provide pleasant metaphoric settings that help to develop and maintain our brain's problem-solving mechanisms. They are not trivial activities" (Sylwester, 1995, p. 53). Rather, they enhance the brain's effectiveness in rapid processing of "ambiguities, metaphors, abstractions, patterns, and changes" (p. 53). In particular, the prefrontal cortex, which is the last part of the brain to mature in adolescence, enables humans to "plan and rehearse future actions, to take risks in our brain's mental world rather than in the real world" (p. 54); that is, it is the site of the human capacity to play with ideas. It is conceivable that, in the future, the technological brain will take over many more of the mundane aspects of human thought, thus releasing an even greater portion of the higher brain centers for playful activity and "music, art, drama, invention, and a host of other human experiences that open us to the broad exploration of our complex world" (p. 54). Virtual reality and other recent technological innovations also point to the possibility of finding other worlds of presently unperceived sensory experiences for human exploration. If this seems an impossible dream, it is only necessary to remember a time when such phenomena as radio waves and

X-rays did not exist in human thought or experience. It may be that the human capacity to play is only beginning to be demonstrated!

This playful brain power, which has been present in humans for centuries, also results in "behavioral plasticity . . . which is the . . . ability to change at a faster rate than can be driven by the gradual evolution of the gene pool" (Ellis, 1988, p. 24). It is likely that rigid predictability of behavior, which prevents adapting to changing conditions, is not a major quality of human behavior because over the course of many centuries those individuals who could adapt to new situations, learn quickly, demonstrate flexible actions, and meet challenges by using risky new behaviors were more likely to be the ones who survived. From this perspective, "Whenever the environment is changing it selects for playful individuals. . . . Playfulness is thus stabilized and enhanced from generation to generation by the genes. . . . [Therefore,] . . . play is never 'just play' . . . it is during play that humans are most human. They learn to extend the limits of human experience and to develop the capability to deal with the unknown. . . . [Therefore, play] . . . will be the basis for our future adaptation to the unpredictable future" (Ellis, 1988, p. 25).

When looking at the future of play from a psychobiological perspective, consider the distinction between what defines an Olympic sport and what is "just a game." As a spectator at the 1996 Olympic Games in Atlanta, Doris Bergen was able to admire the marvelous human physical and emotional feats displayed in Olympic events while admiring the human species as a whole. Humans have invented so many other play/game/sport activities that could conceivably be included as Olympic events in the future. In 1996, beach volleyball and mountain biking made the list; perhaps next time Frisbee or bowling or golf or line dancing or ballroom dancing or Roller Blading might be included. The human capacity to invent and play games is phenomenal, as is the human capacity to accept challenge, risk failure, and strive for excellent performance. If the plethora of "new" play/game/sport activities evident in present culture is any indication, the future of physical and game play is very healthy.

A *Star Trek* museum exhibit that Doris Bergen visited represented an interesting intermingling of the "real" and "could-be-real." The exhibit showed artifacts from some actual space adventures and from episodes of this popular television adventure show, and it predicted which of the "pretend" artifacts used so convincingly on the television screen might eventually be "real" artifacts used in space or even in everyday life. It described the world of four hundred years ago, when Galileo created a sensation with playfully serious ideas that subsequently changed the view of humans' play in the universe. In contrast, it speculated that the world of four hundred years in the future might be even more unusual than that of the world portrayed by the imagination of *Star Trek* writers. The "as-if" mode of space adventure holds a very powerful attraction for humankind. It does not seem to be very different from the "as-if" mode of five-year-olds' pretend and, indeed, it may serve very similar purposes. "In the same way that play provided a medium for invention in other centuries, it encourages the thinking and dreaming that are needed for survival now" (Bergen, 1988, p. 301). From the vantage point of the year 2000, those who hope that pretend play will continue to be valued in the future seem to have little to worry about.

Although the technology shown in many fictional space epics is very advanced, the human interactions are still very primitive. Such behaviors as war, rivalry, and deceit are portrayed as central human behaviors that have not changed at all; they are merely more likely to be demonstrated through powerful technological means. Similarly, such emotions as greed, hatred, and jealousy are as likely to be the motivators of these behaviors as they are in present life. Because "our prefrontal cortex (with its strong limbic system connections) also regulates important elements of our emotional life—feelings of empathy, compassion, altruism, and parenting" (Sylwester, 1995, p. 53)—it may be that, as technology takes on more of the mundane parts of our planning, predicting, and worrying, our brain will be able to play with ideas that envision a new world of motive and behavior as well. "Perhaps, in the future, war games will be played on a computer or in a stadium with symbolic weapons so that we can even leave the crazy 'reality' of war's pain and destruction behind us" (Bergen, 1988, p. 301) and perhaps replace war itself. More importantly, if adults of all ages, within many contexts, embracing differing perspectives, and realizing varied meanings, can "convey to children our knowledge that a life playfully and actively lived is worth the risk" (p. 301), then the future of play is secure. As adults play more, when freed by expanded technology from the tedium of daily survival, children also can continue to imagine the possible and use play to engage in social negotiation, self-empowerment, and the unalloyed joy of a transcendent experience.

Bibliography

Aukstakalnis, S., & Blatner, D. (1992). *Silicon mirage: The art and science of virtual reality* (E. Ross, Ed.). Berkeley, CA: Peachpit.

Bergen, D. (1988). Play, technology, and the authentic self. In D. Bergen (Ed.), *Play as a medium for learning and development* (pp. 299–301). Portsmouth, NH: Heinemann.

Egan, K. (1988). *Primary understanding.* New York: Routledge.

Elkind, D. (1991, June). Postmodern play. *Readings,* 8–11.

Ellis, M. J. (1988). Play and the origin of species. In D. Bergen (Ed.), *Play as a medium for learning and development* (pp. 23–25). Portsmouth, NH: Heinemann.

Louie, E. (1995, May 11). Quilting: Artistry over the Internet. *New York Times,* C1.

Moulthrop, S. (1993). Writing cyberspace: Literacy in the age of simulacra. In A. Wexelblat (Ed.), *Virtual reality: Applications and explorations* (pp. 77–90). Cambridge, MA: Academic.

Sylwester, R. (1995). *A celebration of neurons: An educator's guide to the human brain.* Alexandria, VA: Association for Supervision and Curriculum Development.

Wexelblat, A. (Ed.). (1993). *Virtual reality: Applications and explorations.* Cambridge, MA: Academic.

Contributors

Myrdene Anderson is an associate professor and an anthropologist who studies the geographic foci of high latitudes and altitudes, especially the Saami people of Lapland. She received her doctorate from Yale. Her publications include work on semiotics modeling, stereotypes, and ethnicity issues. As an only child for six years, her play included wandering in the Pacific Northwest woods, climbing trees, sitting on ant-hills, and taming forest creatures. Then she had a period of indulging two younger half-sisters in play. A favorite indoor pastime was when her sisters would give her several unlikely story characters, for which she would ad lib for a long time, making a slice of bacon, a whistle, and a throw rug cavort about in a design-it-yourself fable.

Donna R. Barnes, a historian and philosopher of education at Hofstra University, is fascinated with the ways children have always learned eventually to take on adult roles in their communities and societies. She sees play, games, and toys as important building blocks for developing children, and later adults, blessed with imagination knowledge, skills, and values. With interests that are historical, aesthetic, culinary, artistic, and multicultural, she plays at re-creating food, meals, and menus from around the world. Other adult play activities include travel, reading, word games, gardening, photography, and attending musical concerts, ballets, and theater performances.

Doris Bergen (coeditor) is professor of educational psychology at Miami University, where she serves as department chair and director of the Center for Human Development, Learning, and Teaching. She is a past president of the National Association of Early Childhood Teacher Educators and editor of the *Journal for Research in Childhood Education.* For most of her academic career she has studied and written about children's development and especially about play as a medium for development and learning. Of late, she has been looking at the way children's sense of humor develops. Although, as a lover of play, she has chosen scholarly interests that are fun to explore, most of her life is spent working. Even then, however, during much of her work time she experiences the "flow" that is really like play. Her most recent "work as play" activity has been serving as a consultant in the production of a children's television series. Her "official" play activities as an adult are reading, theatergoing, and gardening. She also runs, but that is definitely work!

Elena Bodrova received her Ph.D. from the Russian Academy of Education and conducted research at the Institute for Preschool Education, which has implemented Vygotskian ideas in the early childhood classroom for over thirty years. She currently teaches at Metropolitan State College of Denver. She and Dr. Deborah Leong have written a book, *Tools of the Mind: The Vygotskian Approach to Early Childhood Education* (Merrill/Prentice-Hall, 1996) and a film on the Vygotskian approach for early childhood educators. Dr. Bodrova enjoys playing with her five-year-old son, Andrei.

James F. Christie is a professor at Arizona State University, where he teaches courses in reading and early childhood education. He is the author of numerous books and articles on play, especially on how play can function as a medium for emerging literacy development. His favorite play pursuits include growing arid-climate plants in his garden (it must be play because there are few tangible outcomes) and messing around with computers.

Robert J. Coplan is assistant professor of psychology at Carleton University, Ottawa, Ontario. His doctorate is in developmental psychology from the University of Waterloo and his research is in social development and peer relations. He has studied the development of shyness and social withdrawal in early childhood and the factors that influence social and academic adjustment in preschool and kindergarten. His research interests include the study of social development and preschool adjustment. When not working, he plays piano in a local blues band.

Ellen C. Creager has been a journalist since 1977 and was a feature writer and reporter for the *Detroit Free Press*. Her journalism degree is from Michigan State. Her work has been published in *Publisher's Weekly*, the *Wall Street Journal*, *Newsday*, and *New York Daily News*. She also writes for a variety of corporate clients such as Compuserve, and for hospitals and universities. Creager now makes her living as a book author and freelance writer. As a child, she was the first one to find all the Easter eggs every year, but she could never keep a secret.

R. Hays Cummins received his Ph.D. in oceanography from Texas A and M. He is a professor of interdisciplinary studies at Miami University, director of Discovery-Oriented Science Instruction in the School of Interdisciplinary Studies, and science editor for *Dragonfly*. Most of his research is in the areas of ecology and paleoecology, and he teaches a wide variety of subjects, including field courses in tropical ecology in Costa Rica and the Bahamas. Dr. Cummins plays sports with his friends and children, especially basketball and racquetball. He enjoys all outdoor pursuits and explorations on land and sea. He also plays a mean game of poker.

Amanda Dargan is director of the Center for Folk Arts and Education at the Bank Street College of Education in New York City. For thirteen years, she served as folk arts program director for the Queens Council on the Arts. Among her publications is *City Play* (with Steve Zeitlin), which won the 1992 American Folklore Society Opie Award for the best book on children's folklore. She earned her Ph.D. in folk-

lore and folklife from the University of Pennsylvania. When she is not working, she plays with her two children, Ben and Eliza.

Jane Ilene Freeman Davidson is a master teacher at the University of Delaware Laboratory Preschool and a lecturer in the Department of Individual and Family Studies. She is the author of two books, *Children and Computers Together in the Early Childhood Classroom* (1989) and *Emergent Literacy and Dramatic Play in Early Education* (1996). Teaching four-year-olds allows her to play even as she works. She particularly enjoys the pretend play of young children and its more adult version, the theater. When playing without children she does puzzles, logic games, and other forms of play that require the manipulation of language and ideas. She enjoys playing at Torch Lake with her children, Lily and Michael, and her husband, Jeff.

Rheta DeVries is director of the Regents' Center for Early Developmental Education and professor of curriculum and instruction at the University of Northern Iowa. A former public school teacher, she received her Ph.D. in psychology from the University of Chicago and did postdoctoral work at the University of Geneva, Switzerland. Previous publications include *Constructivist Early Education: Overview and Comparisons with Other Programs* (coauthored with Lawrence Kohlberg) and and *Group Games in Early Education* (both coauthored with Constance Kamii). She enjoys playing the piano, and playing flute with anyone who will play with her.

Debra Esernio-Jenssen is the associate chief of pediatrics at North Shore University Hospital in Manhasset, New York, and an assistant professor in clinical pediatrics at New York University Medical School. She also directs the Lead Poisoning Prevention Program and chairs the Child Protection Committee at North Shore. She received her medical degree from the University of Rochester School of Medicine and Dentistry. In her free time, she is a vice president and co-chair of the Medical Advisory Committee of the Child Care Council of Nassau County. She enjoys most sports. She runs, swims, cycles, and plays volleyball, softball, golf, and tennis. If she is not training with her husband for a triathlon then she is off at some park playing freeze tag with her two sons (of course, she's always "it") or spending time with nieces and nephews. She always wanted to be a physician but she really envisioned herself as a spaceship doctor traveling throughout the galaxy. In addition to science fiction, she loves cartoons and thinks that watching them helps her relate better to her patients.

Beverly I. Fagot is professor of psychology at the University of Oregon and a research scientist at Oregon Social Learning Center in Eugene. Her research interests in child development focus on gender role development and she is the author of numerous publications on the play and gender role connection. For her own play, she enjoys outdoor activities and likes to hike and to drift on Northwest rivers.

Greta G. Fein is a professor of education and psychology at the University of Maryland. She has been a student of play since the early 1970s, making her debut with the chapter on play that appeared in *Day Care in Context,* her first book on early child care. This interest has continued uninterrupted to the present. Her own play takes two forms: one is on the tennis court, playing a game to which she is addicted; another is playing with one or both of her grandsons, another addiction that yields many hours of pleasure.

Rebecca Fewell received a B.A. from Agnes Scott College in 1958, and M.A. and Ph.D. degrees in 1969 and 1972 from Peabody College and Vanderbilt University. She was an elementary teacher prior to entering graduate school in special education. She has taught at Vanderbilt, the University of Washington, and Tulane University, and is currently professor of pediatrics and psychology at the University of Miami. She has written extensively on issues of assessment in young children with disabilities. Her favorite play activities are computerized stock investing, biking, and bridge.

George Forman earned his Ph.D. in 1967 in developmental psychology from the University of Alabama. He has studied children at play since 1968, when he left the university laboratory for the playground. He has studied children putting together jigsaw puzzles, building with geometric blocks, and drawing with markers. He has watched children use computer animation to make their own stories and microworlds. He has videotaped children in India, Japan, Korea, and especially in Italy, as they built designs using many different art and construction media. He has published books on the use of play in early education, the use of blocks in the curriculum, and the educational use of video replay. He has invented toys, puzzles, the Gravity Wall, and, most recently, a water works exhibit at the Kohl Children's Museum in Chicago. His own playground is his digital video editing suite, where he produces educational videotapes to explain the competence children express when they play.

Peter J. Freitag is associate professor of sociology at Clarkson University, where he teaches courses in work and play, culture and society, and interdisciplinary humanities. His publications and presentations include studies of the relationship between business and government, the American labor movement, and the transmission of cultural values through children's games. He has been playing board games since he first received a copy of Candyland in the mid-1950s. For the past twenty years he has collected games and currently serves as vice president of the American Game Collectors Association.

Valeria J. Freysinger is an associate professor of leisure studies and lifespan development in the Department of Physical Education, Health, and Sport Studies at Miami University. She received her doctorate from the University of Wisconsin, Madison. Her research interests include leisure as a context for and means of development and the impact of gender on experiences of leisure, work, and family. When she was a child, seven siblings provided ready-made playmates for physical and outdoor activities; a love of reading and baking was picked up from her mother and great-aunt. Hiking, camping, reading, and ethnic cooking continue to be favorite leisure pursuits today.

Doris Pronin Fromberg (coeditor) is a professor of education and past chairperson of the Department of Curriculum and Teaching, Hofstra University. She has served as a teacher and administrator in public and private schools, as well as director of Teacher Corps projects. She is past president of the National Association of Early Childhood Teacher Educators (NAECTE) and chair of the Special Interest Group on Early Education and Child Development of the American Educational Research Association. She was recipient of the 1996 Early Childhood

Teacher Educator of the Year Award from NAECTE/Allyn & Bacon. Among her publications are *The Full-Day Kindergarten: Planning and Practicing a Dynamic Themes Curriculum* (Teachers College Press, 2nd ed., 1995) and *The Encyclopedia of Early Childhood Education* (coedited with L. R. Williams, Garland, 1992). When not working playfully, she enjoys romping with the family dog, jogging, rock climbing, folk dancing, and imagining novels with alternative nonarchetypical heroines.

Joe L. Frost spent his childhood on a small farm in the Ouachita Mountains of central Arkansas. He enjoyed working and playing with animals, tending gardens and farm crops, and swimming in the beautiful Fourche River. Presently, he continues to make regular visits to this area while serving as Parker Centennial Professor in the program of early childhood education at the University of Texas at Austin. He has directed a major play and playground research project for the past two decades, writes extensively on this subject, and lectures and conducts workshops throughout the United States and in various countries.

Leonore Ganschow is a professor of special education in the Department of Educational Psychology at Miami University. Her doctorate is from the University of Cincinnati. She often structures her play as she does her life, by building in relaxation time. During these play periods, she takes walks, plays tennis, learns German by reading the German version of mysteries that she has already read in English, reads escape fiction, sings in a choir, and plays the piano by ear. Her favorite play activity, however, is to brainstorm ideas with her students and colleagues.

Roger Ganschow is professor emeritus of pediatrics at the University of Cincinnati College of Medicine and a staff scientist at the Children's Hospital Research Foundation. His research focus is on the regulation of gene expression in mammalian systems. He received his Ph.D. from the State University of New York at Buffalo and his postdoctoral training at the Stanford University School of Medicine. As he approached retirement, he found himself increasingly involved in play away from work. This play includes singing in a choir, perusing stock news in America Online's "Motley Fool" area, computer monitoring of personal finances,

planning travel, reading sailing literature, and, best of all, skippering a thirty-five-foot sailboat.

Barbara P. Garner is an assistant professor at Louisiana Tech University. Her doctorate in child development is from the University of North Carolina at Greensboro. She has been a director of a program for infants and toddlers, a teacher, and a supervisor of teachers, and has designed an infant and toddler caregiver training institute that has been presented throughout the southeastern United States. As a child, Dr. Garner's favorite play activity was with baby dolls; as an adult, her interest has developed into play with babies, especially her grandbabies.

Laura Gaynard received her doctorate from the University of Pennsylvania. She has done research and published works on child hospital play. She is currently child life manager at Primary Children's Medical Center in Salt Lake City and an adjunct faculty member at the University of Utah. Downhill skiing is her favorite form of play and the reason she moved to Salt Lake City. Other play that she enjoys includes camping, hiking, tennis, and just hanging out with good friends. Of course, she also plays at work with young patients and their siblings (which is also great fun).

Karen Gitlin-Weiner is a licensed psychologist who currently works with emotionally troubled adolescent girls and maintains a private practice focused on children, adolescents, and their families. Dr. Gitlin-Weiner has conducted many training seminars on play assessment and play therapy and worked as a special educator, consultant, and psychologist for emotionally, behaviorally, and learning-disabled youngsters. She is coeditor of the book *Play Diagnosis and Assessment*. In her childhood she enjoyed both solitary and interactional play activities and appreciates her family's influence in showing her the various roles that play can have. She learned from them that a sense of playfulness can infuse any situation, even very difficult and potentially conflictual ones, and that commercial play materials are not necessary to engage in playful behaviors. She believes that it is within the power of our own minds to use the world of play and playfulness in our own best interest.

Michelle Glick received her B.A. from Tulane University in 1992 and an M.S. in applied developmental psychology in 1994 from the University of Miami. She is completing her work as a doctoral student in applied developmental psychology at the University of Miami. Presently she serves as a research assistant in an early intervention program. As a graduate student with little free time, she notes that her current play skills would benefit from intervention. However, her favorite play activities include long walks on the beach, listening to Blues with her husband, and spending time with her nephew Mitchell.

Marcy Guddemi is the vice president of education and research for KinderCare Learning Centers, Inc., in Montgomery, Alabama. She is the secretary of the International Association for the Child's Right to Play and past president of the American Association for the Child's Right to Play, which are advocacy organizations promoting the child's right to play as guaranteed by the United Nations. Dr. Guddemi received her undergraduate and master's degrees from Ohio State University and her doctorate in early childhood education from the University of Texas at Austin. She is a national and international consultant in the field of play and play environments and author of numerous academic articles and books. When not "working" she enjoys various sports and "playing" with her twelve-year-old daughter and artist husband.

Wendy Haight is a visiting assistant professor in the School of Social Work at the University of Illinois, Urbana-Champaign. Her doctorate in developmental psychology is from the University of Chicago. She has done much of her research on adult-child interactions in pretend play and on sociocultural issues in child development. Her two children, ages eight and three, keep her pretend play skills honed and her interest high.

Jennifer A. Hall completed her undergraduate work at Trinity College in Hartford, Connecticut, and a Ph.D. in clinical psychology at the University of Connecticut. She is an assistant professor at Eckerd College in St. Petersburg, Florida. Her research is published in the *Journal of Personality and Psychology, Child Development*, and the *Journal of Interpersonal Violence*. As a child, Jennifer loved to play with her friends from the neighborhood and school and, in a pinch, would even play with her older brother Keith.

Dan C. Hilliard is professor of sociology at Southwestern University in Georgetown, Texas. He received his Ph.D. in sociology from the University of Texas–Austin. His research is on adult recreation and sport; he has studied bowling, tennis, soccer, softball, rugby, triathlon, and ultradistance running, as well as how the media represents athletes. A lifelong wannabe athlete, he has participated in basketball, tennis, and rugby, as well as distance running and triathlons. He has maintained an interest in research on adult recreational sport for over twenty years. His current research is on images of race and gender in mediated sport.

Linda Homeyer is an assistant professor in the Counseling and Guidance Program of the Department of Educational Administration and Psychological Services at Southwest Texas State University, San Marcus. She is a registered play therapy supervisor and is actively involved in play therapy relationships with children. Her research on the play behaviors of sexually abused children is extensive and resulted in a unique instrument for assessing sexually abused children. Dr. Homeyer is the recipient of the 1995 Graduate School award for Who's Who in American Universities.

Alice Sterling Honig is professor emerita of child development at Syracuse University. Her numerous articles, chapters, and books focus particularly on caregiving, teaching, and parenting young children. For twenty years, Dr. Honig has directed the annual Quality Infant/Toddler Caregiving workshop at Syracuse University. As a licensed clinician, she works with families to help them resolve child-rearing problems. Dr. Honig serves as North American editor for the British journal, *Early Child Development and Care*. When not working, Dr. Honig's play preferences are eclectic: they include solving double-acrostic puzzles, giving folk song concerts in many languages, reading stories to grandchildren, writing poetry, exploring neolithic cave art, gardening, avid museum visiting, and e-mail exchange with friends across the world.

Joan P. Isenberg is a teacher educator, author, and consultant in early childhood education and early childhood teacher education. She is a professor at George Mason University, where she recently received the distinguished faculty award for teaching excellence. She has published extensively on play, early childhood education, and teacher education. Integral to her professional approach is the use of play to enable teachers to make meaning of their teaching, of children's learning, and of the education profession at large. She is past president of the National Association of Early Childhood Teacher Educators. Her personal play and interests include her family, bridge, reading, the arts, and the ocean.

Tom Jambor is an associate professor of early childhood development at the University of Alabama at Birmingham, an international playground designer, lecturer on children's development through play, and author of articles and texts related to children's outdoor play needs and safe environments. He is currently vice president for North America for the International Association of the Child's Right to Play (IPA) and past president of IPA's U.S. affiliate. His philosophy of life has evolved around a quote from George Bernard Shaw: "Man [*sic*] does not cease to play because he grows old; Man grows old because he ceases to play!" Thus, after "work" there is always a daily dose of social and physical interaction with friends and family. There is always time to play.

Ranald H. Jarrell, after earning two law degrees and practicing law for ten years, received a doctorate in early childhood from Teachers College. He is now at Arizona State University West, teaching child development and math and science instructional methods, and conducting research on the influences of family dynamics on children's mathematical self-perceptions. As a child in rural West Virginia, he experimented with centrifugal force by slinging buckeyes from increasingly longer wires made of coat hangers. His eventual achievement of slinging buckeyes over a hundred yards was not appreciated by the school principal, who called it "mischievous playing around" when one of the buckeyes hit him (the principal) in the head. Ran, however, now considers it to have been experimentation with manipulation of independent variables, with a careful effort to measure the resultant change in the dependent variable, that is, mathematical playing around.

Hilary A. Johnson is currently finishing her doctoral work at Stanford University's School of Education. She has spent the past fifteen years working as a consultant to organizations, helping them to build their internal learning capabilities. Her motivation for returning to

school was to investigate how artistic forms of thought might play a role within different professional domains. Her play time is filled with watercolor painting, photography, and two (very playful) West Highland terriers.

James E. Johnson has been, since 1988, professor of education and in charge of early childhood education in the Department of Curriculum and Instruction in the College of Education at Pennsylvania State University. He coauthored *Play and Early Childhood Development* (with James Christie and Thomas Yawkey) and coedited *Play in Diverse Cultures* (with Jaipaul Roopnarine and Frank Hooper), among numerous publications in the areas of socialization, early education, and children's play. He grew up in Warren, Michigan, and remembers war and adventure play in natural environments near his home, where he later organized baseball, football, and hockey teams. He was Michigan's Junior Chess Champion one year in the 1960s, and he remains an avid chess enthusiast.

Yasmin Bettina Kafai is an assistant professor at the UCLA Graduate School of Education and Information Studies. For over ten years, she has conducted research projects at the forefront of children's interactive media. She worked for five years with Seymour Papert and Idit Harel at the MIT Media Laboratory, exploring young children's computational design environments, children's thinking and learning in mathematics, gender differences, and their collaborative interactions with and without technological support. She recently published works including *Minds in Play: Computer Game Design as a Context for Children's Learning* and *Constructionism in Practice: Designing, Thinking, and Learning in a Digital World.* Currently, she and her research team at UCLA are investigating the potential of game-making activities in mathematics and science, and researching prototypes of collaborative Internet activities. She has studied in France, Germany, and the United States, and holds a doctorate from Harvard University. When she is not working, she likes to go to the movies and play card games on the computer.

Elizabeth Kean is a recovering chemist who, after many years of supporting student learning in chemistry at the University of Wisconsin-Madison, is currently a professor of education and associate chair of the Department of

Teacher Education at California State University, Sacramento. She spends her time encouraging the use of technology among faculty, writing grants to support innovative work by faculty that has a direct impact on the education of young urban children, and finding new ways to create partnerships among the science community, teacher educators, and practicing teachers. As a child, she spent much time in athletic competition, recognizing she would never be a professional basketball player because of her five-foot stature and lack of Title IX protection. Play these days includes time in San Francisco, at the Pacific Ocean and coastal redwoods, and in the Sierra Nevada Mountains.

Garry Landreth is a Regents professor in the Department of Counselor Education and director of the Center for Play Therapy at the University of North Texas, Denton. He is a registered play therapy supervisor and is actively involved in play therapy relationships with children. He trains parents to be therapeutic agents in the lives of their children by using child-centered play therapy procedures in structured play sessions in their own homes. Dr. Landreth has published sixty-five journal articles and seven books, including *Play Therapy: The Art of Relationship*. He is chair of the board of directors of the International Association for Play Therapy and has conducted training workshops on play therapy throughout the United States and Europe and in Canada and China. He is the recipient of the 1995 Virginia Axline Award for Professional Contributions. He notes that experiencing a child's play is a wonderful time of relationship building and discovery: a time of *being with* that transcends the limits of time and space. It is a time to experience being fully accepted and to make exciting discoveries. He believes such times for him are among the most meaningful of his life.

Deborah J. Leong received her Ph.D. from Stanford University and teaches courses in child development and educational psychology at Metropolitan State College of Denver. She and Dr. Elena Bodrova have written a book, *Tools of the Mind: The Vygotskian Approach to Early Childhood Education* (Merrill/Prentice-Hall, 1996) and a film on the Vygotskian approach for early childhood educators. Jeremy, Dr. Leong's nine-year-old son, has been the inspiration for many of her anecdotes on the play of young children.

Leslie Leve recently received her Ph.D. from the University of Oregon in developmental psychology. She is a research associate at the Oregon Social Learning Center, currently coordinating a large project on twins and peers.

Diane Levin is professor of education at Wheelock College in Boston, where she teaches courses on play, violence, media, and early childhood education. She has written four books and numerous articles on how violence in society affects children's play, learning, and behavior. She is project leader of the Early Childhood Peaceable Classroom Project at Educators for Social Responsibility in Cambridge and has served on the Panel on Violence in the Lives of Children of the National Association for the Education of Young Children. Many of her most important lessons about play have come from living and playing with her thirteen-year-old son, Eli.

Susan S. Lukesh is an archaeologist, adjunct associate professor, and associate provost for planning and budget at Hofstra University in Hempstead, New York. Her doctorate, in computers and archaelogy, is from Brown University. She conducts her research at prehistoric excavation sites in Southern Italy and Sicily. Although as a child she had not thought about becoming an archaeologist, she loved reading mysteries, a relaxing habit she keeps today.

Donald E. Lytle teaches upper-division and graduate courses in physical education and sociology at California State University, Chico. He is a former president of the Association for the Study of Play (TASP). When not playing with creating puzzles and problems for the readers of his column, *Dr. Play,* for the TASP newsletter, he enjoys playing with his daughter, Kelsey (four), and son, Sean (one). He also finds time for wallyball and gardening in his busy ludic life.

M. Lee Manning teaches in the Department of Educational Curriculum and Instruction, Darden College of Education, Old Dominion University, Norfolk, Virginia. His doctorate is from the University of South Carolina. As a child, when he lived around other children, he skated and rode bikes and pretended to be cars or planes; when he lived several miles from others, he played alone as he roamed creeks, gullies, and hills pretending to be an explorer. Whether playing alone or with other children, he usually had a "secret lab" where he conducted experiments and thought of inventions. Today, similar to previous "exploring," his play includes roaming and exploring beaches.

Christopher E. Mengel is an attorney and partner with the law offices of Berkley, Mengel, and Vining, P. C., in Detroit, Michigan. He is an appellate specialist who litigates in business, probate, criminal, and family law. He attended Notre Dame, Holy Cross, and the Detroit College of Law and was a teaching fellow at the law college. Recently he was honored for gaving the best appellate brief submitted to the Michigan Supreme Court in its 1996 term. He spent his childhood playing shortstop. Even then, he hated to lose.

Gayle Mindes is professor of education and associate dean at DePaul University. She is a graduate of Loyola University of Chicago with a major concentration in early childhood completed at the Erikson Institute. During the past seventeen years she has taught courses in early childhood at the graduate and undergraduate level. Dr. Mindes served in a variety of leadership capacities in the field of early childhood education in Illinois. She also has served as a consultant for Head Start, child care agencies, public schools, and state agencies. She is coauthor of *Planning a Theme-Based Curriculum* (with Carla Berry, Delmar, 1993) and *Assessing Young Children* (with Harold Ireton and Carol Mardell-Czudnowski, Delmar, 1996). Gayle enjoys playing with recipes and viewing movies, plays, and contemporary art. More actively, she walks and enjoys travel.

Robin Moore grew up in the woods and fields of southern England. He has degrees in architecture from London University, and city and regional planning from MIT, where he first became interested in how to design the physical environment in order to support child development. Pursuing this interest, he has conducted a series of action research projects in North and South America and England. He is president of the International Association for the Child's Right to Play (IPA), former chair of the Environmental Design Research Association, a principal in the design and planning firm of Moore Iacofano Goltsman, and professor of landscape architecture in the School of Design at North Carolina State University, Raleigh. He has

taught at the University of California, Berkeley, and Stanford University. He is author of *Plants for Play, Childhood's Domain: Play and Place in Child Development,* and coauthor of *Complete Playground Book, Play for All Guidelines,* the *Play for All CD,* and *Natural Learning.* He still likes goofing off in the woods, fields, lakes, streams, and beaches wherever and whenever he can—which is never enough.

Shirley K. Morgenthaler is a professor of education and coordinator of graduate studies in early childhood education at Concordia University. Her doctorate is in early childhood education and curriculum development, and she teaches courses in those areas. She serves as the director of the local Child Care Resource and Referral Services satellite office and of the Dedicated Early Support for Children at Risk National Clearinghouse, an operation that focuses on providing information to churches about children's programs and children at risk. Her own favorite play with objects involves the challenge of riding the movement of water and tube behind a speeding boat. Her continuing play with objects also involves doing crossword puzzles and fishing. The challenges of cognitive play, strategy play, and pragmatic play are well represented in her life.

Stephen R. Morris is an assistant professor of philosophy at Central Connecticut State University. He is currently on leave from that position to pursue a law degree at New York University School of Law, and he will receive his JD degree in 1998. His Ph.D. is from the University of Pennsylvania. He most loves the play of world-creation, the play of ideas, and the play of words in ancient texts.

Christopher A. Myers received his Ph.D. in ecology and now teaches courses on ecology-related themes, information technology, and the imagination in the School of Interdisciplinary Studies at Miami University. As a director of Project Dragonfly, he is trying to prove that scientists and kids can actually have fun together. His personal play life includes visiting ecosystems with his wife, Lynne Born Myers, and four-year-old daughter, Mickey; writing stories for children; as well as general shenanigans, monkeyshines, and tomfooleries.

William R. Myers is an ordained Presbyterian (USA) minister, professor of religious education, and academic dean at the Chicago Theological Seminary. He has authored numerous books and articles in the areas of research in ministry, religious education, and youth ministry including one written about his daughter. He is at play in a canoe, on a bike, or in church.

Patricia Monighan Nourot is associate professor of education and coordinator of early childhood education programs and graduate programs in the School of Education at Sonoma State University, Rohnert Park, California. She is the coauthor of two books on play in childhood, *Looking at Children's Play: A Bridge between Theory and Practice* (1987) and *Play at the Center of the Curriculum* (1993). She is principal author of *California's Guide to Early Primary Education* (1996) and has written several articles and chapters concerning the role of play in learning and development. When "at play" Nourot is cooking, hiking in the Napa Valley, or reading detective novels.

Sherri Oden is a senior research associate at the High/Scope Educational Research Foundation in Ypsilanti, Michigan, where she directs research on child and youth development in educational programs such as Head Start. She received a Ph.D. in human development and educational psychology from the University of Illinois, was a professor at several colleges and universities, and published research in numerous journals and books on child and youth development and education. She has been particularly interested in the development of children's social skills. She enjoys many activities with her nieces, Kirsty and Rebecca, and her nephew, Mathew, who are helping her to rediscover the joy of true play.

Mary Martin Patton is an assistant professor of early childhood education at Texas Christian University. She received her doctorate from the University of Texas at Austin. Play is central to her teaching, research, and family life. She is the eighth child in a family of thirteen children, and her fondest memories of play center around days of creating elaborate environments out of large furniture boxes with her brothers and sisters. She also remembers spending Sundays during the summer swimming and picnicking at a park on Lake Austin. Her own three children are master players who enjoy family camping, biking, swimming, picnicking, and hours of unstructured play time at the creek and in the

neighborhood. Only now that she has her own children can she appreciate the efforts of her parents to make family time happen.

Anthony D. Pellegrini received his Ph.D. from Ohio State University in 1978 and works at the University of Georgia as a professor of early childhood education. He has studied many aspects of children's and adolescents' play, including symbolic play and rough-and-tumble play and has authored numerous articles, book chapters, and books on these topics. He is currently working on a project examining the role of recess in the primary school curriculum. In the middle of most work days, he takes a play break to swim or run.

Eugene F. Provenzo Jr. is a professor of education at the University of Miami. He is the author of numerous books and articles on education and social policy and the history of education in the United States. He is the author of *Video Kids: Making Sense of Nintendo* (Harvard University Press, 1991) and is currently working on a book entitled *Toys, Creativity, and Culture*. An award-winning toy designer, he spends his time at play writing novels and creating surrealist sculptures.

Patricia G. Ramsey is a professor of psychology and education at Mount Holyoke College in South Hadley, Massachusetts. She has published a number of articles and chapters reporting her research on children's early attitude development and their friendship patterns. She is the author of two books, *Teaching and Learning in a Diverse World: Multicultural Education for Young Children* and *Making Friends in School: Promoting Peer Relationships in Early Childhood* (both published by Teachers College Press). She loves to play: sports (for fun), day dreaming, writing silly poems, telling funny stories, and, most of all, games, fantasies, and general hilarity with her children.

Mary S. Rivkin is a professor in the early childhood education program at the University of Maryland, Baltimore County. She received her Ph.D. from the University of Maryland. She has taught in inner-city and suburban classes of three-year-olds through graduate school. She is the author of *The Great Outdoors: Restoring Children's Right to Play Outside*. Observations as a mother, teacher, and urban/suburban householder inspired her research into the changing outdoor environment for children. She grew up in a small city in the Pacific Northwest, playing outside as much as possible, particularly liking to climb trees, make mudpies, explore flowers and bushes, and simply mess around.

Kenneth H. Rubin is coach of the Reston Raiders Midget (15–18 years) travel hockey club, and a center on the Potomac Oldtimers men's hockey team. When not playing, he is professor of human development and director of the Center for Children, Relationships, and Culture at the University of Maryland. He is the author of many books and articles on play and social development and the designer of an observational instrument used extensively in research on play.

Carol Seefeldt is professor of human development at the Institute for Child Study, University of Maryland, where she teaches graduate classes. She received the 1983–1984 Distinguished Scholar-Teacher Award from the university. During her forty years in the field of early childhood education she has taught from two-year-old nursery school through third grade. She directed a church-related kindergarten and served as regional training officer for Project Head Start, conducted educational programs for Head Start teachers and teachers of migrant children in the United States, and provided training for teachers in Japan and Ukraine. Her research interests are in curriculum development and program evaluation as well as intergenerational attitudes. She is evaluator of the Montgomery County Head Start–Public School Transition Demonstration, following former Head Start children and their families through grade three. Her love of horses has included being a rider and cheering her son and daughter in their work and play with horses.

Cecilia Shore is associate professor of psychology at Miami University. Her doctoral work was done at the University of Colorado. Her research involves cognitive and language development in infants and toddlers, specifically concerning relationships between language and play, individual differences in language, and situational effects of parent-child speech interactions. Her play as a child included making stone houses furnished with natural objects for imaginary elves to live in. As an adult she does essentially the same thing by playing SimCity.

Steven B. Silvern is a professor of early childhood education at Auburn University. His doctorate is in child development from the University of Wisconsin–Madison. He teaches introductory and advanced courses on Piaget, as well as language development, construction of number, early childhood curriculum, and program evaluation courses. He has been studying children's play and learning for twenty-one years and is the author of multiple articles and chapters on the subject. When not playing with words or heads, Steven plays at golf.

Dorothy G. Singer is codirector of the Yale University Family Television Research and Consulting Center. She is also a research scientist in the Department of Psychology at Yale and an affiliate of the Yale Child Study Center. She received her doctorate in psychology from Columbia University. Her interests include research on the effects of television on children's cognitive, social, and emotional development. She has authored over 120 articles and ten books. She coauthored *The House of Make-Believe: Play and the Developing Imagination.* Her most recent book is *Playing for Their Lives: Helping Troubled Children through Play Therapy.* Play means horseback riding, cooking, and walking in the woods. She is an exceptionally playful grandparent.

Jerome L. Singer received his doctorate in clinical psychology from the University of Pennsylvania. He is professor of psychology at Yale University, where he served as director of the graduate program in clinical psychology and director of graduate studies in psychology. He is codirector, with Dr. Dorothy G. Singer, of the Yale University Family Television Research and Consultation Center. He is a specialist in research on the psychology of imagination and daydreaming. Dr. Singer has authored more than two-hundred technical articles on thought processes, imagery, personality, and psychotherapy as well as on children's play and the effects of television. He has written or edited more than fifteen books, including *The Inner World of Daydreaming; The Power of Human Imagination; Television, Imagination and Aggression: A Study of Preschoolers; The House of Make-Believe: Children's Play and the Developing Imagination; The Parents' Guide: Use TV to Your Child's Advantage;* and *Imagery Methods in Psychotherapy and Behavior Modification.* Tennis, bird watching, and listening to opera are Dr. Singer's main modes of "play." He is an exceptionally playful grandparent.

Jeffrey Trawick-Smith is a professor of education at Eastern Connecticut State University and has conducted and published research on young children's play. He received his doctorate from Indiana University. This research interest did not emerge by accident: he has been an expert player from his earliest days. Among his more impressive make-believe roles of childhood were The Wolverine, a role he invented while browsing pictures in an encyclopedia and one he enacted with all of the ferocity that he lacked in real life; The Flying, Invisible Minister, a role that blended the spiritual qualities of a religious leader with the more practical crime-fighting talents of Superman; and The Groom, a role he played reluctantly with his older sister, who as The Bride never tired of formal weddings. As an adult he engages in utter, unbound silliness with his two sons and writes novels. He also writes playful and controversial chapters about play.

Victor Turow is an associate in the Division of General Pediatrics at North Shore University Hospital in Manhasset, New York, and an assistant professor in clinical pediatrics at Cornell University Medical College. He received his medical degree from the State University of New York–Downstate Medical School and completed a pediatric residency at Long Island Jewish Hospital. He worked as a general pediatrician in private practice on Long Island's south shore for eight years prior to joining the North Shore faculty in 1990. Except for a great outside jump shot, he is more cerebral than athletic. He is an avid reader, classic movie watcher, and a sometimes computer game addict. Although initially he never desired to be a physician, he found his niche in pediatrics. He lives with his wife, their two children, and their cat in Sea Cliff, New York.

Lynette Unger is a professor of marketing at Miami University. Her doctorate, in marketing, is from the University of Cincinnati. She teaches promotion management and international marketing and is presently serving as associate dean of the R.T. Farmer School of Business. She enjoys playing with her three children and also devotes leisure hours to masters swimming and has competed in pool and outwater events in local, national, and international meets. She experiences leisure while reading, singing, walking, watching movies, traveling, and napping. "Sometimes I sits and thinks and sometimes I just sits" (Satchel Paige).

Karen VanderVen is coordinator and professor of child development and child care in the School of Social Work at the University of Pittsburgh and a 1995–1996 visiting scholar at Harvard University Graduate School of Education. Her special interests include play and activity, professionalization of early childhood education, and human service applications of chaos theory. She is editor of the *Journal of Child and Youth Care Work,* on the editorial board of five other journals, and author of over 150 publications. She is a frequent presenter on play topics at the annual conferences of the National Association for the Education of Young Children. In her "spare" time, she is a certified scuba diver, dives for new additions to her extensive collection of Florida and Caribbean seashells, plays basketball, watches birds, enjoys her cats, collects Florida mystery books, and practices juggling. She is interested in innovation and invention, and utilizes her shelf of varied toys and playthings to generate new ideas.

Anne L. Wennerstrand is coordinator of undergraduate dance education at New York University, where she teaches modern dance technique, composition, and pedagogical methods especially with children. As a performer, she was most notably a member of Laura Dean Dancers and Musicians from 1986 to 1994, touring throughout the United States and Europe. Wennerstrand holds masters degrees in social work and dance/movement therapy and combines these modalities with her passion for body-based systems of knowledge, including yoga, meditation, martial arts, and contact improvisation. She is a therapist at the Post Graduate Center for Mental Health in Manhattan. She is most playful with her dog, Lola, cat, Josie, and partner, Doug Elkins, with whom she resides on the Upper West Side of Manhattan. She also enjoys roller coasters.

Sharon Whitton is a professor of mathematics education and chairperson of the Department of Curriculum and Teaching at Hofstra University, Hempstead, New York. She concedes that it is difficult in her line of work to distinguish work from play. However, when she is not doing mathematics or teaching someone something about mathematics, she enjoys solving puzzles of all sorts, working with computers, reading, and attending musical and dramatic performances.

Nancy W. Wiltz received her Ph.D. in curriculum and instruction from University of Maryland. She teaches courses in human development, and supervises student teachers in early childhood education. She also serves as the early childhood liaison between the Department of Human Development and the Office of Laboratory Experiences. As a former preschool teacher and the mother of two, she intuitively knew that children loved to play, but she did not become a "student of play" until she became a graduate student and discovered the magnitude and depth of play as a serious research topic. In her spare time, she enjoys playing with her husband. This is her first publication.

Christopher R. Wolfe holds a Ph.D. in learning, developmental, and cognitive psychology from the University of Pittsburgh, where he worked in the Learning Research and Development Center. He is an associate professor of interdisciplinary studies at Miami University, director of Quantitative Reasoning and Instructional Computing for the Western College Program, and on-line editor of *Dragonfly*. In addition to playing with blocks and little vehicles with his four-year-old son, Michael, he enjoys reading, fishing, camping, snorkeling, gardening, jazz, rock 'n' roll, and watching sports on the tube. Go Cleveland!

Irma C. Woods grew up in the hot, humid, but breezy climate of a coastal South Texas town; trees were a luxury, and as a child she delighted in playing in their cool, cozy shade. Today, she continues to enjoy the outdoors, particularly canoeing, camping, and gardening. She is a former first grade teacher and social worker of a state agency and teaches in the Early Childhood Department at Del Mar College in Corpus Christi, Texas. Her doctoral work at the University of Texas focuses on the influence of culture on play and developmentally appropriate practice in the care of young children.

Steve Zeitlin received his Ph.D. in folklore from the University of Pennsylvania. He is the director and cofounder of City Lore, an organization dedicated to the preservation of New York City's living cultural heritage. Zeitlin served as a regular commentator for the nationally syndicated public radio show, *Crossroads* (frequently rebroadcast on *Morning Edition*). Prior to arriving in New York, he served for eight years as a folklorist at the Smithsonian Institution in Washington, D.C., and taught at George Washington University and American University. He is coauthor of a number of books on American folk culture, including *A Celebration of American Family Folklore; The Grand Generation: Memory, Mastery and Legacy;* and *City Play*. He is currently completing a book on Jewish stories for Simon and Schuster. He has also coproduced a number of award-winning film documentaries, including *Free Show Tonite* on the traveling medicine shows of the 1920s and 1930s. He considers all of his work a form of play.

Index

Abelson, R. P., 38, 49
Abraham, R., 130, 131, 249, 255
Abuse, 85, 194, 197, 211, 352
Academic work, 39, 155, 159, 213, 244, 272, 395, 511, 520, 521, 526
Access, 210, 235, 237, 538
Achievement, 284, 303–312
Adams, D. W., 304, 311
Adams, J., 226, 231
Aday, R. H., 283, 287
Adler, A., 83, 89
Administrators, 130. *See also* Teachers, influence of
Adolescence, 6, 12, 14, 21, 28, 59, 66, 72–73, 190, 191, 228, 267, 292, 296, 308, 316, 325, 373, 374, 379, 404, 420, 470, 508, 509, 539
Adulthood, 14, 16, 21, 113, 127, 409, 416, 420
Adults, influence of, 1, 5, 29, 47, 54, 62, 64–65, 82, 84, 95, 106, 117, 131, 133, 140, 142, 143, 152, 154, 156, 158, 159, 166, 170, 179, 188, 196, 197, 203, 205, 208, 210, 211, 212, 215, 229, 237–238, 243, 244, 252–255, 259–265, 267, 272, 273, 277–282, 283, 284, 286, 301, 302, 303, 315, 316, 317, 320, 322, 323, 324, 328, 329, 330, 333–334, 340–345, 349, 353–355, 359, 361, 362, 363–366, 372, 392, 394, 401–403, 404, 418, 425, 473, 474, 494, 511, 534–535, 537–538
Adventure playgrounds, 229, 233–234, 238, 525
Advocacy, 154, 157, 159–160, 229, 230, 235, 262, 284, 287, 355, 512, 524, 528, 537, 538, 539
Aesthetics, 12, 62, 149, 154, 227, 228, 237, 392–393, 419, 446, 447, 495, 519–529
Affection, 254. *See also* Emotions
African American, 26, 222, 226
After-school activities, 25, 238, 283, 521, 526–527
Age segregation, 283. *See also* Teachers, influence of
Aggression, 120, 143, 151, 155, 159, 188, 189, 190, 191, 195, 196, 197, 210, 213, 242, 243, 260, 266, 269, 270, 281, 284, 301, 309, 327, 329, 344, 353, 355, 370, 372, 373, 386, 402, 403, 404, 405
Ahlgren, A., 74, 76
AIDS, 292
Aimard, P., 325, 334
Albers, B., 470, 472
Alger, H., 304
Al-Khowarizmi, 478
Allan, F., 83, 89, 197
Allan, J., 250, 255
Allen, J., 84, 89
Allen, L. E., 59, 67
Allen Preschool Picture Test, 509
Allison, M., 487, 490
Allman, T., 204, 206
Almy, M., 160, 360, 366, 381, 384, 390
Alward, K., 345, 347, 379, 386, 390
Amarel, M., 170, 172
America-Israel Foundation, 11, 13
American Academy of Pediatrics, 521
American Alliance for Health, Physical Education, Recreation, and Dance, 235, 236
American Association of Retired Persons, 293, 297
American Folklore Society, 220
American Society of Testing Materials, 235, 323
Americans with Disabilities Act of 1990 (PL 101–336), 235, 237
Amir, T., 294, 297
Amos, P.T., 296, 297
Anderson, M., 103–108, 543
Andronico, M., 85, 90
Andrus, R., 368, 374
Angier, N., 228, 230
Animals, xiv, 5, 6, 8, 9, 10, 11, 72–73, 106, 177, 181, 182, 195, 227, 229, 230, 234, 249, 250, 380, 385
Animation, 96, 438. *See also* Computers, animation
Anthony, P. D., 486, 490
Anthropological theory, 330
Anthropology, 5
Anthropomorphism, 438
Apple, M., 47

Aquinas, T., 429
Archaeology, 5, 451–454, 464
Archer, J., 339, 345
Archimbault, J., 180, 183
Archimedes, 474, 475, 478
Ariel, S., 86, 87, 90
Aries, P., 104
Armstrong, H.F., 222, 224
Armstrong, J., 41, 47
Arnoff, F.N., 296, 298
Arouitt, G.E., 283, 288
Arroyo, F., 237, 238
Arth, 219, 224
Arts, 8, 11, 12, 50, 61, 96, 109, 127, 139, 140,
        143, 147, 149, 150, 151, 195, 208, 209,
        244, 251–252, 268, 271, 294, 297, 315,
        353, 360, 362, 393, 425, 435–448, 451,
        453, 464, 470, 487, 509, 523, 531, 532–
        533, 539
Asch, S., 465, 466
Asher, S. R., 24, 33, 244, 247, 269, 270, 271, 273,
        275, 276, 279, 404, 407
Ashmead, D. H., 315, 317
Assessment, 54, 59, 74, 77, 80, 81, 82, 86, 110,
        133, 159, 170, 191, 193, 196, 201–207,
        211, 212, 219, 259, 269, 301, 313, 315–
        316, 342, 351, 352, 357, 360, 361, 363,
        365, 366, 378, 386, 393, 394, 398, 411,
        508–509
Assessment, Evaluation, and Programming System
        Measurement for Birth to Three Years,
        204
Aston, J., 405, 406
Atchley, R.C., 15, 21
Athletics. See Sports
Attachment, 89, 142, 261, 279, 372
Attention, 203, 210, 228, 253, 284, 291, 314, 328,
        361, 436
Attention deficit disorders, 80, 230, 246, 403.
        See also Disabilities
Attitudes, 24
Attractors, 121, 122, 123, 124, 130
Audiotape, 486, 533
Audiovisual equipment, 149
Auditory learning, 313. See also Styles
Augustine, St., 429
Aukstakalnis, S., 538, 541
Autonomy, 43, 126, 210, 220, 410, 412, 413, 430,
        487, 490, 494, 498, 515
Axline, V., 82–83, 90, 195, 197, 236, 238, 250,
        255, 361, 364, 366
Ayers, D., 271, 274

Baer, J., 124, 131
Bagozzi, R. P., 490
Baillargeon, R., 315, 317
Bainum, C. K., 327, 328, 334
Baird, W. E., 531, 536
Bakhtin, M., 383, 387

Balance, 425, 445, 539
Baldwin, D. A., 138, 144
Baldwin, J. A., 409, 414
Bandura, A., 83, 90, 342, 345
Banes, S., 442, 445, 446, 447
Bariaud, F., 329, 333
Barnes, D. R., 5–13, 543–544
Barnes, H., 170, 173
Barnet, D., 237, 238
Barnett, L. A., 16, 21, 327, 334
Barnett, M. A., 327, 334
Baroody, A., 57, 59, 67
Barret, A. M., 33, 314, 317
Barrick, M. P., 490
Barthes, R., 517
Baruch, D. W., 349–355
Bates, E., 166, 168, 169, 170, 172, 173
Bates, J. E., 370, 376
Bateson, G. A., 46, 47, 379, 387, 445, 447
Baudonniere, P. M., 370, 373
Baumrind, D., 372, 374
Baumwell, L., 166, 173
Bayles, D., 440
Beal, B., 420, 421
Beane, J., 123, 129, 131
Beardsall, L., 267, 268, 274
Becherer, R. C., 487, 488, 490, 491
Beck, A., 83, 90
Beck, L. E., 71, 75
Beck, M., 291, 298
Becker, G. S., 486, 491
Becker, H., 420, 421
Beckwith, J., 237, 238
Beeghley, J., 142, 144, 166, 173, 201, 205
Behaviorism, 121, 413, 414, 419
Beizer, L., 170, 172, 260, 263
Belsky, J., 141, 145, 165, 172, 202, 203, 206, 373,
        375
Bengtsson, A., 234, 238, 519, 524, 528
Benton, A. L., 316, 317
Beresin, A. R., 25, 31
Bergen, D. M., xiv–xv, 70, 72, 75, 133, 134, 143,
        144, 146, 153, 157, 158, 159, 160, 181,
        183, 204, 206, 209, 248, 254, 255, 269,
        271, 273, 283, 287, 288, 319, 323, 324–
        337, 338, 345, 363, 366, 379, 387, 511,
        530, 536, 537–541, 543
Berger, A. R., 42, 48
Berger, P. L., 462, 465, 466
Berk, L. E., 124, 126, 131, 236, 239, 278, 282,
        283, 288, 349, 355, 380, 387
Berlyne, D. E., 37, 47, 487, 491
Bernstein, C., 504, 506
Bernstein, D., 325, 335
Bettelheim, B., 287, 288, 349, 355, 383, 387
Beuf, A., 248, 255
Bias, 23
Biber, B., 193, 197, 220, 224
Biblow, E., 197
Bifurcations, 121, 123, 124, 125, 128, 130, 131

Bilingual. *See* Linguistically different
Biology, 14, 21, 403, 480
Birch, T., 524, 528
Birth order, 267. *See also* Siblings
Biting, 195, 211
Bixler, R., 84, 90
Bjarkman, P. C., 107, 108
Bjorck-Akesson, E., 285, 288
Black, B., 242, 247, 379, 380, 384, 387
Black, J., 259, 260, 261, 262, 263
Bland, C.J., 507, 509
Blatner, A., 493, 495, 496, 498
Blatner, D., 538, 541
Bloch, M. N., 26, 31
Block, J. H., 189–190, 191, 341, 345, 531, 536
Blocks, xv, 28, 29, 38, 39, 60, 61, 62, 93, 98, 125, 126, 127, 139, 142, 143, 148, 149, 150, 151, 165, 170, 195, 196 209, 210, 244, 271, 320, 338, 342, 348, 350, 360, 361, 362, 380, 386, 392, 396, 399, 501, 513, 515. *See also* Construction
Bloom, L., 167, 172
Blowhowiak, D. W., 485, 488, 489, 491
Bluestone, J., 194, 197
Blumer, H., 461, 463, 466
Blurton Jones, N., 401, 406
Boals, B. M., 154, 160
Boder, E., 170, 172
Bodrova, E., 277–282
Boer, F., 267, 273
Bogue, R., 464, 466
Bohannon, P., 47
Bohm, D., 383, 397
Bohr, N., 66
Bolig, R., 248, 255
Bolton, N., 59, 67
Bond, L. A., 268, 276
Bonny, H., 316, 317
Books, 28, 30, 131, 151, 179, 180, 204, 228, 229, 284, 295, 344, 360, 533, 538
Booth, C. L., 372, 373, 374, 377
Boredom, 248. *See also* Emotions
Bornstein, M. H., 140, 145, 166, 173
Bossert, S. T., 272, 274
Both L., 373, 376
Bott, H., 368, 374
Botwin, G. J., 38, 47
Boulton, M. J., 24, 25, 31, 405, 406
Bowers, L., 235, 236, 240
Bowes, J., 325, 335, 326
Bowker, A., 373, 374, 376
Bowlby, J., 251, 255
Bowman, J., 46, 47
Boyatis, C., 165, 172
Boyer, E. L., 284, 285, 286, 288, 521, 528
Boys. *See* Gender
Brackett, C. W., 324, 325, 335
Brady, M., 310, 311
Brain, 251, 321, 372
Brainerd, C. J., 71, 75, 76, 402, 406

Brannon, C., 94, 99
Bransford, J., 392, 399
Bredekamp, S., 37, 47, 290, 291, 292, 298, 401, 406
Bretherton, I., 142, 144, 166, 168, 169, 170, 172, 173, 260, 264, 283, 288, 379, 387, 493, 498
Brett, A., 234, 238, 239, 519, 528
Bricker, D., 204, 206
Brickman, H., 313, 317
Briley, S., 38, 39, 40, 48
Brink, S., 319, 320, 321, 322, 323, 522, 528
Brirenfeld, M., personal communication, 221
Brock, B. J., 285, 288
Broderbund Software, 531, 536
Brodin, J., 285, 288
Brody, G. H., 267, 276
Brodzinsky, D. M., 327, 335
Brohm, J. M., 421
Bronfenbrenner, U., 121, 129, 131, 385, 387
Bronson, M. B., 147, 148, 153
Bronson, W. C., 371, 374
Bronte, C., 513
Brook, P., 443, 444, 447
Brooks, J. G., 74, 75
Brooks, M. G., 74, 75
Brooks-Gunn, J., 292, 298
Brown, G. E., 327, 335
Brown, I. C., 12, 13
Brown, J., 325, 328, 329, 335
Brown, M. W., 179, 183
Brown, S. P., 488, 490, 491
Brown, T., 446
Bruce, T., 154, 160
Bruegel, P., 12
Bruner, J. S., 71, 75, 154, 160, 170, 172, 313, 314, 317, 383, 387, 401, 406, 441
Bruya, L. D., 235, 259
Buchsbaum, M., 321, 323
Buckholdt, D. R., 213, 214
Bunnett, J. F., 472
Burch, W., 418, 421
Burchardt, C. J., 341, 347
Burlingham, D. T., 349, 355
Burns, S., 402, 406
Burts, D. C., 370, 372, 375
Busch, R. R., 219, 224
Business, 10, 287, 485–492
Business persons' play, 485–492
Bussis, A. M., 170, 172
Butcher, J., 204, 206

Cadaco, 309
Cage, J., 445, 446
Caillois, R., 219, 224
Cajete, B., 74, 75
Caldera, Y. M., 143, 144
Calkins, S. D., 368, 369, 370, 372, 375, 376
Callois, B., 372, 374, 416, 421
Calvin, J., 429

Campion, M. A., 490, 492
Canary, R. H., 303, 311
Cangelosi, D., 82, 90
Canning, S., 237, 239
Canon, 425. *See also* Disciplines; Methods of inquiry
Cantrell, M. L., 271, 273
Canzler, L., 325, 327, 335
Caplan, F., 196, 197
Caplan, T., 196, 197
Capuano, F., 369, 375
Career models, 341, 468, 671. *See also* Gender;
    Adults, influence of
Carey, L., 86, 91
Carlsson-Paige, N., 342–346, 348, 349, 350, 351,
    352, 353, 354, 381, 384, 387
Carroll, K. A., 142, 145
Carson, D. K., 327, 335
Carson, R., 10, 13, 75
Carter, A. S., 81, 91, 139, 145
Carter, D. B., 340, 345
Cartoons, 429–430, 508, 517, 518
Casby, M. H., 201, 206
Cash, M., 327, 335
Cass, J. E., 194, 197
Castelnuovo, S., 420, 422
Caster, T. R., 201, 206
Cattanach, A., 77, 80, 90
Cavallo, D., 232, 233, 239
Cavanaugh, J. C., 14, 22
CD-ROM, 315, 511, 515, 517, 539. *See also*
    Computers
Celebrations, 5, 11, 12, 17, 210, 509. *See also*
    Festivals; Holidays
Chadwick, E., 285, 288
Chaffee, H. B., 304
Chaille, C., 94, 99, 379, 390
Challenge, 301, 319–323, 361, 362, 363, 453. *See
    also* Risk-taking; Scaffolding; Self-concept
Chalmers D., 320, 323
Chamberlain, V.M., 283, 288
Chants, 179, 182, 220, 221, 249, 431, 519. *See also*
    Language play
Chaos theory, 1, 119–132, 170, 480
Chapman, A. J., 327, 335
Chapman, W. A., 327, 335
Char, 396, 399
Chard, S. C., 271, 274
Chase, D. R., 485, 488, 491
Chase, J. E., 11, 13
Chase-Lansdale, P. L., 292, 298
Chawla, L., 228, 230
Cheek, N. H., 485, 488, 491
Chemists' play, 468–472
Chen, X., 373, 374, 376
Cherfas, J., 311
Cherry, F., 341, 347
Child care centers, 284, 295
Child, E., 27, 31
Child labor, 520
Child Life Council, 248

Child life specialists, 248, 252–255
Children's Defense Fund, 352, 355
Chittenden, E. A., 170, 172
Choreophotography, 439–440
Christensen, C. R., 496, 498
Christie, J. F., 50–55, 146, 153, 201, 204, 206,
    244, 246, 247, 284, 288, 338, 346, 363,
    366, 386, 387
Christman, M., 27, 32
Christoffel, K. K., 226, 230
Chukovsky, K., 176, 183, 331, 335
Churchill, W., 513
Cicchetti, D., 201, 205
Cielinski, 140, 144
Cillessen, T., 402, 406
Citron, C. C., 341, 347
City play. *See* Urban play
Clark, D., 211, 214
Clark, E., 514, 517
Clark, E. O., 311
Clarke, A. C., 486, 491
Clark-Stewart, K. A., 140, 144
Class, social. *See* Socioeconomic status
Classification, 61, 62
Classroom organization, 50, 52, 53, 63
Clay, 60, 63, 126, 127, 140, 360
Clements, R., 285, 288
Client-centered therapy, 82–83
Clinical Adaptive Test, 508
Clinical Linguistic and Auditory Milestone Scale,
    508–509
Clinical perspectives, 77–92
Coakley, J., 417, 418, 421
Cochran, M., 24, 31
Cognitive-behavior therapy, 83–84
Cognitive development, 71, 94, 137, 140, 141,
    144, 146, 150–151, 154, 158, 187, 190,
    201, 202, 203, 204, 209, 210, 211, 228,
    234, 236, 268, 277, 279, 281, 284, 287,
    314, 324, 325, 326, 331, 332, 333, 334,
    339–340, 359, 361, 382, 393, 395, 401,
    414, 539
Cognitive science, 511
Cognitive theory, 330–333, 360, 361
Cohen, D., 81, 91, 194, 196, 197, 198, 429, 433,
    447
Cohen, J., 321, 323
Coherent curriculum, 129
Cohn, J., 262, 263
Coie, J. D., 270, 274, 402, 404, 406
Cole, D. A., 373, 374
Collecting, 147, 149, 451, 452
Colorado Child Temperament Inventory, 369
Commercial playgrounds. *See* Playgrounds,
    pay-to-play
Commission for Racial Justice, 226, 230
Communication, 87, 88, 89, 105, 157, 169, 177,
    188, 190, 193, 195, 196, 204, 209, 210,
    211, 273, 290, 313, 327, 382, 470, 473,
    474, 489, 524, 535, 538

nonverbal, 155, 165, 166, 202, 211, 301, 327, 330, 331, 379, 380, 411, 504
physical, 444, 445. *See also* Dance
theory, 330
Community, 146, 222, 285, 297
Compensatory theory, 418, 419, 486
Competition, xv, 5, 6, 95, 107, 125, 126, 150, 156, 157, 177, 221, 267, 272, 305, 308, 309–310, 317, 371, 410, 411, 416, 418, 419, 420, 453, 455, 468, 471, 488, 490, 499, 500, 502, 504–506, 511, 512, 540. *See also* Games
Complexity theory. *See* Chaos theory
Computer, 147, 222, 277, 293, 395, 396, 399, 451, 453, 486, 498, 500, 511, 530–536
animation, 392, 393
games, 29, 93–99, 151, 158, 284, 291, 297, 310, 315, 360, 393
simulations, 150, 313, 314, 362, 468, 471, 489, 515
See also Games; Video games
Conceptual learning, 1
Conflict resolution, 242, 271, 272, 273. *See also* Social competence
Conn, C., 98, 99
Connolly, J. A., 380, 387
Connolly, K., 401, 402, 407
Connor, J. A., 341, 347
Connor, J. M., 190, 191
Conservation, concept of, 326, 327
Construction play, 9, 39, 62, 93, 95–96, 97, 99, 125, 126, 147–148, 149–150, 152, 189, 233–234, 235, 236, 267, 271, 277, 285, 320, 357, 360, 368, 370, 392–400, 451, 452, 453, 466, 474, 475, 578, 539. *See also* Blocks; Spatial learning
Constructivist learning, 57, 71–72, 93, 122, 123, 124, 176, 272, 320, 394, 413, 473, 478
Consumer Federation of America, 235
Consumer Products Safety Commission, 147, 153, 522, 528
Contact Quarterly, 445
Continuity, 15–17, 19–21, 268–269
Contresas, J., 140, 144
Convention on the Rights of the Child, 519, 522, 524, 527, 528
Cook, K. V., 143, 145
Cooke, J., 502
Cook-Gumperz, J., 340, 345, 384, 390
Cooking, 291
Coolahan, K. C., 237, 239
Cooper, G., 500, 503
Cooper, M., 221
Cooper, S. E., 68, 75
Cooperative play, 95, 371, 395, 396, 402, 424, 410, 413, 446, 453, 458, 489, 495, 504, 511, 516, 531, 534, 535. *See also* Social Competence; Sociodramatic play
Copeland, R. W., 57, 58, 60, 63, 67
Coplan, R. J., 143, 161, 368–377

Corsaro, W. A., 26, 31, 32, 40, 47, 241, 246, 271, 274, 379, 380, 383, 386, 387, 464, 466
Corte, M. D., 201, 206
Costabile, A., 405, 406
Cox, M., 268, 274
Cox, R., 268, 274
Crafts. *See* Arts
Crandall, R., 488, 491
Creager, E. C., 499–503, 544
Creativity, 3, 68, 69, 74, 88, 123, 125, 128, 149, 150, 152, 190, 212, 221, 222, 223, 235, 236, 259, 273, 287, 301, 315, 316, 328, 342, 353, 381, 383, 419, 435, 442, 443, 446, 453, 455, 461, 465, 470, 473, 485, 487, 489, 490, 493, 495, 497, 499, 500, 502, 511, 521. *See also* Imagination
Crick, F. H. C., 455, 456, 457, 459, 460
Crick, N. R., 245, 246
Critical theory, 50, 51
Croll, S., 319, 323
Cross-cultural, 5, 6, 7, 8, 9, 10, 11, 12, 13, 25, 26, 28, 29, 30, 41, 106, 109, 152, 155, 158, 159, 170, 176, 179, 182, 187, 189, 190, 213, 226, 228, 229, 230, 232, 233, 238, 249, 252, 261, 262, 277, 293, 294, 303, 319, 321, 322, 339, 383, 388, 403, 404, 442, 474, 475, 476, 478, 511, 519, 521, 523–526, 531
Csikszentmihalyi, I. S., 106, 108
Csikszentmihalyi, M., 18, 22, 70, 72, 75, 106, 108, 209, 214, 321, 323, 383, 387, 419, 421, 422, 445, 447, 464, 466, 487, 491, 530, 536
Cuisenaire rods, 246
Cullen, J., 43, 47
Cultural context, 1, 5, 74, 189, 213. *See also* Sociocultural context
Cummins, R. H., 68–76, 544
Cunningham, M., 445, 446, 447
Curiosity, 343, 344, 459, 461, 474, 490, 503
Curriculum design, 271. *See also* Teachers, influence of
Curtis, P., 98, 99
Custer, W. L., 44, 46, 47
Customs, 270, 340

Daglish, L., 340, 347, 402, 407
Daiute, C., 154, 155, 158, 160
Daly, P. F., 33, 314, 317
Damast, A. M., 140, 145, 166, 173
Damon, W., 28, 31, 340, 346
Dance, 147, 222, 223, 230, 283, 294, 439–440
Dancers' play, 442–448
Danet, B., 465, 466
Daniels, D., 371, 376
Dargan, A., 219, 244, 544
Darling, D., 127, 131
Darwin, C., 7, 13, 227
Davidson, D., 321, 323
Davidson, J. I. F., 175–183, 544

Daydreaming, 155, 316. *See also* Imagination
Death, 194, 226, 249, 293, 304, 348, 350, 501
de Beauvoir, S., 292, 298
Debnam, D., 237, 239
Deception, 411, 540. *See also* Moral development
DeDomenico, G., 84, 90
Defense mechanisms, 81, 82, 89, 249, 255
De Groot, E. B., 223, 239
DeMaria, M., 77, 90
de Mause, L., 107, 108
De Mille, R., 316, 317
Dennis, J. M., 9, 13
Dennison, B., 522, 528
Denver Developmental Screening Test, 508
Denzin, N. K., 46, 47, 444, 447
Derossier, M., 402, 406
Desmond, R., 142, 145
Desrosiers, M., 370, 376
Development, life-span. *See* Life-span
Developmental-cognitive theory, 360, 361
Developmental delays, 80, 95, 197. *See also*
        Disabilities
Developmentally Appropriate Practice, 37, 236–
        237, 253
Devlin, J., 249, 255
DeVries, R., 271, 274, 409–415, 531, 536 544
Dewey, J., 156, 160, 233, 361, 366, 441, 531, 536
DeWolf, M., 370, 372, 375
Diamant, A., 352, 355
Dickson, L., 259, 260, 261, 262, 263
Diepold, J. H., 341, 347
Dierking, L. D., 285, 288
Dimanche, F., 487, 491
Ding, G. F., 324, 335
Disabilities, 77–87, 133, 134, 151, 166, 170, 172,
        191, 203, 204, 205, 208–214, 228, 236,
        237, 238, 246–256, 259, 262, 270–271,
        285, 295, 313, 319, 320, 374, 538
Disequilibrium, 121, 122, 123, 127
Dishion, T. J., 372, 375
Disruption, 28, 47, 87, 210, 228, 277, 286
Dissanayake, E., 249, 250, 251, 252, 254, 255
Divergent thinking. *See* Creativity
Diversity, 23–33. *See also* Cross-cultural; Disabili-
        ties; Gender; Socioeconomic class
Division for Early Childhood, 212, 214
Divorce, 85, 268, 291, 292, 339, 430, 520. *See*
        also Families
Dixon, W. E., Jr., 168, 169, 172
DNA molecules. *See also* Genetics
Dodge, K., 402, 405, 406
Dombrowski, J., 27, 33
Donahue, P., 321, 323
Donnelly, P., 420, 421
Dornbusch, S. M., 372, 376
Doubleday,C., 170, 172
Dovey, K., 228, 231
Dowd, K. O., 489, 491
Downey, T., 77, 78, 91
Downs, A. G., 340, 346

Doyle, A. B., 25, 31, 270, 274, 380, 387
Dragonfly, 68, 70, 74
Dragonfly project, 73–75
Drama, 6, 11, 17, 409, 520, 539
Dreams, 474
Drug abuse. *See* Substance abuse
Dryfoos, J., 130, 131
Dubeau, D., 369, 375
Dubinsky, A. J., 487, 491
DuBois, P., 417, 421
Dubrow, N., 352, 356, 372, 375
Ducharme, L. J., 461, 463, 466
Duckworth, E., 129, 131
Duffy, A., personal communication, 220
Dumas, J. E., 369, 375
Dumazedier, J., 487, 491
Duncan, I., 442, 447, 487, 491
Duncan, M., 487, 490
Dunlop, K. H.., 271, 273
Dunn, J., 142, 145, 260, 261, 263, 267, 268, 273,
        274, 275
Dunn, K. J., 365, 366
Dunn, R. S., 365, 366
Dunning, E., 16, 17, 21
Dupuis, S. L., 20, 22
Durkheim, E., 462, 466
Dutton, S., 68, 76
Dyson, A. H., 1, 2, 354, 355, 381, 383, 388
Dzerigian, S., 436–440
Dzewaltowski, D.A., 18, 22

Ebbeson, E. B., 313, 314, 317
Ebensen, S. B., 157, 160, 237, 238, 239, 521, 528
Ecker, D., 441
Eckerman, C. O., 141, 144
Eckler, J. A., 381, 388
Ecological theory, 121, 129
Economics, 15, 119, 130. *See also* Socioeconomic
        status
Edelbrock, C., 188, 191
Edelman, M. W., 223, 224, 226, 231
Edmonds, V., 304, 311
Education, 6, 37, 466
Educators' play, 493–498
Edwards, C. P., 187, 190, 192, 225, 231, 260, 261,
        262, 263, 265, 339, 347 474, 475, 480
Edwards, H., 416, 422
Egan, K., 379, 382, 383, 384, 385, 388
Eiffermann, R., 321, 323
Einon, D., 308, 311
Einslein, J., 370, 375
Einstein, A., 71, 494
Eisenberg, N., 143, 144
Eisner, E., 441
Eitzen, S., 421, 422
Ekstein, R., 78, 79, 90
Elder, G. H., 15, 21
Electronic toys, 221, 513–518. *See also* Video games
Elementary school age, 43. *See also* Primary;
        Middle elementary age

Elgas, P., 271, 274, 380, 386, 388, 389
Elias, N., 16, 17, 21
Elkind, D., 119, 131, 284, 288, 521, 521, 528, 537, 541
Elkonin, D., 277, 279, 282
Ellis, A., 83, 90
Ellis, M. J., 157, 160, 357, 462, 467, 540, 541
Emergent literacy. *See* Literacy
Emery, G., 83, 90
Emotional development, 77–78, 242, 334
Emotions, xiv, 17–19, 41, 78, 80–89, 111, 115, 146, 152, 154, 155, 191, 193–198, 209, 210, 223, 236, 244, 245, 246, 248–256, 259, 262, 266, 269, 270, 277, 290, 292–297, 316, 319, 320, 322, 330, 334, 338, 339, 340–344, 345, 360, 361, 363, 365, 370, 371, 374, 378, 382, 383, 402, 419, 420, 430, 436, 455, 496, 538, 539
Ensher, G., 211, 214
Ensminger, M. E., 292, 298
Entertainment, 121, 125, 130, 464, 537
Entertainment centers, 234–235. *See also* Playgrounds, pay-for-play
Entrainment, 121, 122, 123, 129, 130
Entrepreneurship, 489
Environmental education, 229, 230
Enz, B., 50, 52, 53, 54, 55
Epstein, C., 488, 491
Epstein, J. L., 24, 28, 31
Erikson, E. H., 18, 21,78, 79, 90, 133, 134, 147, 152, 153, 209, 214, 236, 239, 250, 255, 338, 346, 360, 366, 378, 388, 429, 434
Erodynamics, 130
Eron, L., 316
Ershler, J., 370, 375, 381, 388
Ervin-Tripp, S., 341, 346
Escalona, S., 141, 144, 283, 288
Escobedo, T. H., 530, 536
Esernio-Jenssen, D., 507–509, 544
Esman, A., 250, 255
Etaugh, C., 159, 160, 340, 346
Ethics, 531
Ethnicity, 21, 23–32, 151, 213, 215, 213, 259–260, 272, 273
Eubank-Ahrens, B., 230, 231
Euripides, 110
Evaluation. *See* Assessment
Evans, A., 451, 452
Evans, E., 283, 287
Event knowledge, 360, 537. *See also* Scripts; Themes
Event representation, 38. *See also* Scripts
Evergreen Foundation, 230, 529
Ewen, S., 304, 311
Exercise, 232, 236, 237. *See also* Physical development
Exploration, 64, 68–76, 94, 125, 137, 138, 139, 140, 142, 143, 146, 147, 149, 152, 155, 165, 166, 168, 188, 202, 285, 286, 301, 343, 368, 370, 383, 394, 425, 437, 444,

465, 475, 480, 494, 519, 530, 533, 534, 536, 539
Exploratory Representational Play, 68–76
Extreme play, 442, 446–447

Fabrizi, M. S., 325, 327, 335
Fagen, R., 403, 404, 406
Fagot, B. I., 143, 144, 187–192, 205, 206, 338, 340, 341, 346, 544
Faith, 429ff.
Falk, J. H., 285, 288
Fall, M., 80, 90
Family, 199, 208, 228, 235, 250, 254, 283, 285–286, 287, 296, 345
    context, 15, 106, 146
    literacy, 50, 283, 287
    therapy, 69, 86
Fantuzzo, J., 237, 239
Farah, M. J., 313, 317
Farver, J. M., 31, 32, 261, 262, 263, 380, 388
Featherman, D., 14, 21
Federal Communications Commission, 352
Federal Trade Commission, 514
Fegenbaum, K., 419, 422
Fein, G. G., 42, 46, 47, 48, 69, 76, 105, 108, 133, 134, 141, 144, 148, 153, 155, 161, 165, 172, 181, 183, 209, 214, 236, 240, 259, 263, 339, 340, 346, 370, 371, 375, 376, 379, 380, 381, 384, 388, 390, 545
Feng, J., 159, 160
Fensen, L., 142, 144
Fenson, L., 202, 206, 359, 362, 366
Ferguson, C., 165, 172
Fernie, D. E., 39, 43, 47, 48, 271, 274, 380, 386, 388, 389, 411, 412, 414
Ferrarese, M., 373, 375
Festinger, L., 465, 466
Festivals, 111, 295, 466, 485. *See also* Celebrations; Holidays
Fewell, R. R., 201–207, 545
Feynman, R. P., 70, 75
Fieger, G., 505
Field, T. M., 372, 375
Fiese, B., 260, 263
Film, 95, 212, 293, 345, 352, 439, 466, 515, 517, 533
Fine, E. H., 69, 75
Fine, G., 418, 422
Fine, G. A., 461, 463, 464, 465, 466, 467
Finke, R. A., 315, 317
Finkelstein, N. W., 24, 34, 270, 274
Fintushel, N., 292, 298
Fischella, J., 327, 334
Fischer, K. S., 139, 144
Fise, M. E., 235, 240
Fisher, R., 385, 388
Fivush, R., 38, 39, 40, 47, 341, 346
Flannery, D., 20, 21
Flavell, J. H., 361, 366
Fleming-Johnson, F., 242, 247

Flexner, S., 249, 255
Flow theory, 72, 75, 419, 488
Fogel, A., 141, 144, 259, 263
Foley, G. M., 202, 204, 207, 259, 262, 264
Foley, J., 248, 256
Folklore, 5, 220–221, 470
Foner, A., 18, 22
Foot, T., 12, 13
Forbes, D. L., 244, 247
Forman, G.,392–400, 545
Forsyth, S., 292, 298
Forti, S., 446
Fosnot, C., 395, 399
Foster grandparents, 295. *See also* Intergenera-
    tional activity
Foucault, M., 16, 21
Fouts, G. T., 268, 274
Fowell, N., 37, 48
Fox, D. J., 24, 32
Fox, N. A., 369, 370, 372, 375
FOXFIRE, 294. *See also* Intergenerational activity
Fractals, 121, 122, 123 127, 129, 130, 480.
    See also Chaos theory; Geometry
Fraiberg, S., 378, 388 Frame, C., 405, 406
Francis, M., 230, 231
Frank, L., 193, 195, 198, 378, 388
Franklin, M. B., 281, 282, 393, 400
Freedman, D., 130, 131
Freedman, D. G., 372, 375
Freeman, E. B., 244, 247
Freidson, E., 486, 487, 491
Freire, P., 434, 432
Freitag, P. J., 303–312, 545
French, D. C., 242, 243, 247
Freud, A., 78, 79, 81, 209, 214, 251, 255, 349,
    355
Freud, S., 16, 21, 81, 90, 151, 153, 193, 198, 314,
    317, 328, 335
Freysinger, V. J., 14–22, 133, 134, 545
Fried, E., 170, 172
Friedlander, P., 109, 116, 117
Friedman, L., 381, 388
Friendships, xv, 1, 26, 28, 141, 146, 149, 157, 190,
    242, 243, 266, 269, 272, 273, 280, 291,
    295, 296, 308, 371, 382, 386, 405, 417,
    451
Froebel, F., 98, 156, 233, 399, 493, 498, 522, 528
Fromberg, D. P., xiii-xiv, 1, 2, 120, 121, 122, 125,
    127, 131, 137, 144, 282, 288, 342, 346,
    379, 388, 394, 395, 399, 444, 447, 537–
    541, 545
Frost, J. L., 46, 48, 204, 206, 232–240, 283, 288
Fuchs, V., 284, 288
Fulghum, R., 213, 214
Functionalism, 104, 421, 461
Functional play. See Exploration
Fung, H., 261, 262, 263
Furuno, S., 204, 206
Future, 1, 67, 119, 127, 130, 131, 155, 157, 170,
    221, 232, 287, 297, 310, 345, 382, 497–

498, 511–512, 517, 526–527, 531, 534–
535, 537–541
Fuzzy logic, 70, 71, 121, 122, 125, 129, 130

Gagnon, D., 94, 99
Gailey, C., 94, 99
Gaitz, C. M., 17, 18, 22
Galda, L., 154, 159, 160
Galileo, 540
Gallmeier, C., 419, 422
Galper, A., 293, 294, 298
Gambling, 104, 238, 315, 446, 486
Games, xiii, xv, 5, 9, 12, 13, 15, 25, 28, 39, 43, 44,
    45, 52, 58, 62, 63, 65–66, 68, 69, 78,
    85, 89, 95, 96, 98, 103, 104, 109, 110,
    116, 117, 125, 126, 127, 140, 146, 147,
    150–151, 152, 156, 157–158, 165, 170,
    181, 202, 208, 209, 210, 219, 220, 221,
    222, 223, 225, 227, 232, 234, 237, 242,
    266, 267, 284, 287, 291, 292, 303–312,
    313, 321, 334, 357, 359, 360, 361, 362,
    365, 396, 397–398, 403, 404–415, 430,
    442, 444, 445, 446, 463, 465, 470, 471,
    473, 474, 478, 485, 486, 489, 495, 499–
    502, 504–506, 511, 512, 513–518, 519,
    521, 523, 535–536, 539, 540
Ganschow, L., 455–460, 546
Ganschow, R., 455–460, 546
Garbarino, J., 352, 356, 372, 375
Garcia, R. L., 25, 32
Garcia-Coll, C., 372, 375
Gardening, 236, 237, 238
Gardner, H., 166, 167–170, 173, 174
Garmezy, N., 373, 375
Garner, B. P., 137–145, 546
Garvey, C., 77, 90, 142, 145, 155, 158, 159, 160,
    198, 241, 244, 247, 259, 261, 263, 264,
    379, 381, 383, 388
Garza, M., 38, 39, 40, 48
Gaskins, S., 379, 388
Gauss, C., 476
Gauthier, R., 189, 192
Gaynard, L., 248–256
Gays, 292
Geertz, C., 466, 467
Gehlbach, R. D., 237, 239
Geller, L., 177, 178, 183
Gell-Man, M., 121, 131
Gender, xiv, 5, 7, 12, 15, 18–19, 21, 23–33, 40, 69,
    84, 95, 96, 97, 105, 106, 117, 143, 147,
    151, 154, 155ff, 187–192, 212, 213,
    266, 267, 269, 270, 270, 272, 273, 291,
    296, 297, 304, 307–308, 309, 314, 325,
    327, 328, 329, 334, 338–347, 360, 362,
    370, 379, 384–385, 401, 403, 406, 417,
    418, 419, 464, 466, 468, 471, 489, 504,
    507, 511, 512, 519, 521, 537, 538
Genetics, 321, 339, 371–372, 445–457, 540
Generation Day Care, 294. *See also* Intergenera-
    tional activity

Genishi, C., 382, 389
Geology, 470
Geometry, 127. *See also* Spatial learning
George, H., 306
Giannino, S., 18, 22
Gibbons, J., 269, 274, 372, 375
Gibbs, E. D., 268, 276
Gibbs, J. T., 24, 32
Giele, J. Z., 15, 21
Giffin, H., 165, 172, 180, 183, 380, 381, 388
GIFT, 295
Gil, E., 80, 86, 90
Gilbert Chemistry Kit, 468
Ginnot, H., 84, 90
Ginsberg, H. P., 58, 60, 67
Girls. See Gender
Gitlin-Weiner, K., 77–92, 546
Glassner, B., 464, 467
Gleick, J., 120, 121, 122, 131
Gleidman, J., 213, 214
Glick, M., 201–207, 546
Global issues, 119, 485, 488, 497–498, 535
Godbey, G., 16, 19, 22, 462, 467
Goerner, S., 119, 120, 121, 122, 124, 131
Goffman, E., 219, 223, 224, 248, 256
Goldberger, J., 252, 253, 255, 256
Golden, 308
Goldenson, R. M., 195, 198, 378, 389
Goldfield, B ., 168–169, 170, 172
Goldhaber, J., 71, 76, 395, 399
Goldman, J., 379, 390
Goldstein, J. H., 107, 108, 340, 346, 349, 355
Golomb, C., 381, 388
Golombok, S., 341, 346
Goltsman, S. M., 237, 239
Goncu, A., 261, 262, 263, 379, 380, 388
Goodenough, F., 189, 192
Goodfellow, C., 303, 312
Goodman, H., 270, 274
Goodson, B. D., 147, 148, 153
Goossens, M., 166, 173
Gordon Conferences, 460, 459
Gordon, C., 17, 18, 22
Gordon, J., 344, 346
Gordon, S., 344, 346
Gorz, A., 486, 491
Gossip, 113, 418, 465, 471
Gottman, J. M., 191, 192
Gould, R., 378, 388
Gowen, J. W., 203, 206
Gowing, E. D., 381, 388
Goyer, A., 294, 298
Gracey, H. L., 46, 47, 48
Graef, R., 18, 20
Graffiti, 222, 451
Grandparents. *See* Intergenerational activities
Granott, N., 393, 399
Granovetter, M., 488, 491
Granskog, J., 420, 422
Graul, S. K., 284, 288

Green, R., 191, 192
Greenacre, P., 82, 90
Greenberg, N., 447, 448
Greenberg, S., 7, 13
Greenfield, P. M., 94, 98, 99, 393, 400
Greensite,M., 170, 172
Greer, D., 417, 422
Gregg, A., 324, 335
Griesler, P. C., 27, 32
Griffin, E., 378, 388
Groch, A. S., 325, 328, 335
Grollman, S., 166, 174
Groom, J. M., 370, 375
Groos, K., 154, 160
Grottlieb, J., 270, 274
Groves, B. M., 349, 355
Gruendel, J., 38, 39, 40, 48
Gruneau, R. S., 465, 467
Gubrium, J. F., 213, 214
Guddemi, M., 284, 288, 519–529, 546–547
Guerney, B., 85, 86, 90
Guerney, L., 85, 90
Gulko, J., 189, 192
Guralnick, M. H., 370, 375
Guthrie, S., 420, 422
Guthrie, W. K. C., 110, 117
Guttmann, A., 420, 422
Gymnasiums, 232
Gymnastics, 15, 222, 508. *See also* Sports

Habits, 107, 110, 116
Hafer, J., 490, 491
Hagan, R., 143, 144, 187, 189, 192, 205, 206
Haier, R., 321, 323
Haight, W., 259–265, 384, 388
Hale, E., 221, 224
Hale, J. E., 213, 214
Hale, O., 221, 224
Hall, G. S., 233
Hall, J. A., 266–276, 547
Hall, N., 50, 54
Halliday, J., 379, 384, 388
Hals, D., 84, 90
Hambridge, B., 84, 90
Hamilton-Speer, P., 61, 67
Hampson, P. J., 314, 317
Handelman, D., 463, 467
Handicapped Adventure Playground Association,
            319, 320, 323, 525
Handy, C., 119, 131
Haney, J. P., 271, 274, 411, 412, 414
Hanrahan, A., 201, 205
Hardy-Brown, K., 169–172
Harel, I., 392–399
Hargreaves, A., 129, 131
Harkness, S., 262, 263
Harrell, S., 296, 297
Harris, A. R., 19, 21
Harrison, R. H., 270, 274
Harrist, A. W., 370, 376

Hart, C. H., 370, 372, 375
Hart, R., 228, 231
Harter, S., 19, 21
Hartley, R. E., 195, 198, 378, 388
Hartley, S. W., 487, 491
Hartrup, W. W., 371, 375, 405, 407
Hartup, W. W., 242, 243, 247
Harvey, M. R., 228, 231
Hasbro-Bradley, 308, 309, 514
Haskins, R., 24, 34, 270, 274
Hasselbring, T., 392, 399
Hatch, J. A., 244, 247
Hausslein, E., 248, 255
Havighurst, R., 419, 421
Havitz, M. E., 487, 491
Hawaii Early Learning Profile, 204
Hawes, B. L., 223, 224
Haycock, K., 498
Haymes, S. N., 213, 214
Hazeltine, P., 320, 323
Hazen, N., 142, 144, 242, 247
Head Start, 26, 295
Health, 27, 85, 197, 226, 296, 507
Health care settings, 248–256, 294, 295, 511, 520,
        521–522, 539. See also Hospitals
Helbing, N., 189, 192
Hellendoorn, J., 80, 90, 259, 263
Heller, H. B., 271, 274
Helms, D. B., 156, 157, 161
Hemphill, D., 420, 421, 422
Henderson, J. M., 486, 491
Hendricks, C., 235, 239
Hennessey, B. A., 42, 48
Henniger, M. L., 69, 71, 75, 157, 160, 236, 239,
        531, 536
Henry, J., 381, 389
Hensel, R., 321, 323
Heraclitus, 109
Hermeneutics, 112
Hernandez, R., 143, 144
Herrnstein, R., 286, 289
Herzberger, S. D., 268, 274
Hesketh, G. L., 106, 108
Hess, B., 296, 298
Heterogeneous grouping, 272. See also Interage
Hetherington, E. M., 268, 274
Hewes, J., 320, 323
High/Scope, 271
Hill, F., 394, 399
Hill, R. M., 202, 296
Hilliard, D. C., 416–423, 547
Hillman, M., 226, 231
Hirsch, B., 142, 145
Hirsch, E. S., 360, 366
History, 14, 15, 56, 107, 110–111, 290, 297
History of play, 5–13, 155–156, 232–233 ff., 277,
        303, 304
Hobbies, 149, 151
Hoberman, J., 421, 422
Hochschild, A., 419, 422

Hodd, L., 167, 172
Hofstadter, D. R., 123, 131
Hogan, A. E., 139, 144
Hogben, L., 474, 480
Hohmann, M., 271, 274
Holidays, 12, 151,292, 502, 508. See also Festivals
Holistic theory, 84. See also Integrative learning
Holland, V., 261
Holloway, R. R., 454
Holstein, J. A., 213, 214
Homans, G., 249, 256
Homework, 287
Homeyer, L., 193–198, 236, 239, 549
Homogeneous grouping, 296. See also Teachers,
        influence of
Honig, A. S., 327, 336, 338–347, 547
Hooper, F. H., 370, 376
Hope-Graff, S., 166, 172
Horibe, F., 177, 183, 325, 336
Horna, J. L., 20, 22
Horner, C., 502
Hornung, M., 27, 33, 203, 207, 369, 399
Horowitz, M. J., 313, 314, 317
Hort, B., 190, 192
Horvat, M., 403, 407
Hosaka, C. M., 204, 206
Hospitalization, 195, 245
Hospitals, 215, 238, 248–256
Housekeeping, 28, 29, 38
Houston Adventure Play Association, 238
Howard, J. A., 203, 206
Howard, V. A., 441
Howe, C. Z., 19, 22
Howes, C., 24, 32, 141, 142, 144, 149, 153, 155,
        203, 206, 259, 263, 269, 274, 370, 375,
        379, 381, 384, 388
Hoyenga, K. B., 339–346
Hoyenga, K. T., 339–346
Huang, L. N., 24, 32
Huberty, P. D., 403, 407
Huckeby, E., 259, 260, 261, 262, 263
Hudson, S., 233, 239
Huesmann, L. R., 316
Hufford, M., personal communication, 222
Hughes, F. P., 140, 142, 144, 196, 198, 209, 214,
        356, 361, 363, 364, 366
Huizinga, J., 12, 13, 109, 112, 117, 380, 382, 388,
        416, 419, 422, 461, 467
Hull, A., 501
Human services, 127, 130
Humor, 11, 43, 103, 112, 114, 151, 155, 156, 158,
        175, 176, 177, 179, 180, 182, 193, 197,
        208, 211, 221, 237, 297, 301, 339, 379,
        382, 425, 439, 451, 465, 470, 500–501,
        505, 506, 507–508
    definition, 333
    development, 324–337
    purposes, 191, 212, 329, 334
Humphreys A., 402, 403, 405, 407
Humphries, S., 230, 231

Hunt, J. M., 138, 145
Hunter, A. G., 292, 298
Hunter, J. E., 490, 491
Hunter, T., 405, 406
Hurtwood, Lady A., 319, 428, 519
Huston, A. C., 143, 144, 340, 346
Hutt, C., 139, 144, 301, 302, 394, 400, 530, 536
Huxley, T. H., 499
Hymel, S., 270, 275, 373, 375, 377
Hypatia, 476

Iacofano, D. S., 237, 239
Iacuzzi, J. Q., 285, 288
Iano, R. P., 271, 274
I Ching, 445
Igoa, C., 27, 32
Illicit play, 43
Imagery, 436, 439, 440, 442, 444, 452, 478
    eidetic, 314, 333
Imagination, xv, 5, 9, 11, 51, 69, 78, 82, 88, 89,
        95, 96, 97, 98, 117, 128, 142, 148, 149,
        152, 159, 177, 190, 191, 193, 220, 234,
        244, 261, 272, 279, 284, 286, 313–318,
        359, 362–363, 378, 379, 382, 386, 401,
        402, 425, 443, 444, 453, 461, 464, 465,
        490, 493, 495, 496, 513, 514–515, 534,
        535, 537
Imitation, 6, 7, 8, 106, 110, 112, 113, 114, 137,
        140, 141, 168, 179, 190, 209, 211, 219,
        223, 328, 351, 353, 354, 359, 379, 380,
        409, 411, 508
Immigrants, 27
Immorlica, A. C., 295, 298
Improvisation, 114, 221, 223, 379. *See also* Role
        play; Sociodramatic play
Inatsuka, T. T., 204, 206
Inclusion, 152, 208, 212, 237, 270, 285–286. *See
        also* Teachers, influence of
Independence, 152, 226, 281, 296
Individual differences. *See* Styles
Individuality, 26
Infants and toddlers, 50, 79, 93, 125, 137–145,
        166, 167, 168, 170, 175, 187, 188, 190,
        204, 209, 237, 251, 260, 262, 267, 279–
        280, 283–284, 314, 315, 320, 329, 330,
        338, 330, 340, 341, 342–343, 359, 363,
        365, 371, 509
Inferences, 457. *See also* Research methodology
Ingham, R., 487, 491
Inhelder, B., 353, 356
Insults, 177, 301
Integrated studies, 74, 82, 127, 131, 204, 205,
        372, 464, 470, 474, 489
Integrative learning, 97, 133, 134, 137, 151, 158,
        165, 168, 170, 176, 187, 190, 191, 201,
        228, 379, 383
Intellectual competence, 37. *See also* Cognitive
        development
Intergenerational activities, 106, 130, 283–289,
        338–339, 344, 379, 511, 525. *See also*

Heterogeneous grouping; Play, interage
Intermediate-age children, 130, 154–161. *See also*
        Middle-school- years
International Association for the Child's Right to
        Play (IPA), 425–525, 528
International Play Journal, 524
Internet, 532–533, 535–536, 537
Intimacy, 190–191, 219, 436
Intuitions, 71
Ireton, H., 212, 214
Irwin, T. H., 111, 117
Isaacs, S., 378, 389
Isabella, R. A., 373, 375
Isenberg, J. P., 493–498, 547
Isenberg, J. P., 386, 389, 493, 496, 498
Iso-Ahola, S. E., 487, 491

Jacklin, C., 189, 190, 192, 339, 346
Jackson, E. L., 486, 487, 491
Jackson, K. M., 513, 514, 517
Jackson, S., 285, 288
Jacobs, P. J., 234, 239
Jacobson, J. L., 141, 145
Jaeger, W., 6, 13
Jahn, F., 232
Jalongo, M. R., 386, 388, 493, 496, 498
Jambor, T. W., 189, 192, 202, 207, 284, 288, 319–
        323, 369, 370, 377, 519–529, 547
James, B., 248, 256
Jantz, R. K., 290, 291, 292, 293, 294, 298
Jarrell, R. H., 56–67, 547–548
Jendreck, M. P., 292, 298
Jennings, S., 78, 80, 90
Jensen, M., 319, 323
Jernberg, A., 85, 91
Jernberg, E., 85, 91
Jersild, A. L., 324, 335
Jesus, 430
Johnson, H. A., 435–441, 548
Johnson, J. E., 28, 33, 107, 108, 146–153, 189, 192,
        201, 204, 206, 247, 284, 288, 338, 346,
        363, 366, 370, 376, 375, 381, 388, 548
Johnson, K. B., 509
Johnson, M., 18, 22
Johnson, S., 502, 503
Johnston, M. K., 242, 243, 247
Jolly, A., 401, 406
Jones, E., 53, 54, 211, 214, 354, 355, 379, 381,
        383, 386, 389
Jones, I., 403, 407
Jones, M. C., 324, 336
Jordan, V. B., 24, 32
Josephson, J. P., 69, 75
Journalism, 465
Journalists' play, 499–503
Judson Dance Theater, 446
Jung, C., 84 442, 447
Jurgens, J., 480
Justice, 146, 213, 382, 413
Justin, F., 324, 325, 336

Kafai, Y. B., 93–99, 548
Kagan, J., 269, 274, 371, 372, 375
Kahana-Kalman, R., 166, 173
Kahn, C. H., 109, 111, 117
Kahn, L., 341, 347
Kaku, M., 383, 389
Kamii, C. K., 60, 67, 62, 411, 412, 414, 531, 536
Kanter, R. M., 489, 491
Kantor, R., 38, 39, 48, 271, 274, 380, 386, 388, 389
Kaplan, B., 169, 174
Kaplan, C., 470, 472
Karns, J., 259, 263
Kasner, E., 473, 480
Katriel, T., 465, 466
Katz, L. G., 271, 274
Katz, M. M., 244, 247
Katz, P. A., 24, 32
Kean, E., 468, 472, 548
Keapley, F., Jr., 472
Kegan, R., 124, 125, 131
Kellam, S. G., 292, 298
Kellert, S. R., 227, 231
Kelley, M. F., 147, 153
Kelly, G., 83, 91
Kelly, J. R., 16, 19, 20, 22, 462, 467, 485, 486, 487, 488, 491, 492
Kenner, 514
Kenyon, G., 418, 422
Kepler, J., 479
Kerferd, G. B., 110, 117
Kernan, J. B., 487, 492
Kessel, F., 379, 380, 389
Kids Clubs Network, 525
Kier, C. A., 268, 274
Kimmerle, M., 138, 144
Kinder, M., 94, 99
Kindergarten, 29, 31, 41, 42, 68, 69, 178, 181, 232, 237, 243, 244, 342, 383, 386
King, C. E., 6, 7, 8, 9, 13
King, J. F., 327, 336
King, N. R., 38, 39, 41, 42, 43, 47, 48, 55, 106, 147, 153, 155, 156, 160, 316, 317, 382, 389, 384, 531, 536
King, P. F., 327, 336
Kingsley, C., 6, 13
Kirk, S. A., 213, 214
Kirshenblatt-Gimblett, B., 220, 223, 224, 326, 336
Kitto, H. D., 6, 13
Klausner, E., 170, 172
Kleiber, D. A., 17, 18, 19, 22, 327, 334, 487, 492
Klein, A. J., 327, 336
Klein, B. L., 46, 48
Klein, E., 38, 39, 40, 41, 43, 48, 49, 382, 389
Klein, F., 473
Klein, M., 81, 91
Kline, S., 513, 514, 515, 517
Klineberg, O., 25, 32
Knell, S. M., 78, 80, 83, 91
Knoppers, A., 417, 422
Koeppl, G., 404, 406

Kohl, D., personal communication, 397
Kohlberg, L., 380, 381, 384, 395, 399, 412, 414, 415
Kohli, A. K., 482, 490
Kohn, M., 487, 492
Kokoski, T. M., 287, 288
Korn, E. R., 317, 318
Kornhaber, A., 292, 298
Kosko, B., 122, 131
Kosslyn, S. M., 313, 314, 317
Koste, V. G., 362, 366
Kostelny, K., 320, 321, 323, 349, 352, 355, 356, 372, 375
Kozelka, R. M., 16, 22
Kotarba, J. A., 464, 467
Kottman, T., 84, 91
Kozol, J., 226, 231
Kramer, J. T., 235, 240
Krantz, P., 83, 91, 255, 256
Kronsberg, S., 143, 144
Kupersmidt, J. B., 27, 32, 270, 274
Kuschner, D. S., 58, 672
Kutchins, H., 213, 214
Kuykendall, J., 349, 355

Lacy, M., 417, 422
Ladd, G., 245, 246, 275, 370, 375
LaFreniere, J., 189, 192, 369, 375
Laidley, L. N., 248, 252, 253, 254, 255
Lambert, J., 234, 238, 239
Lambert, W. E., 25, 32
Lamborn, S. D., 372, 376
Landau, G. M., 195–196, 198
Landis, J. R., 461, 467
Landreth, G., 193–198, 236, 239, 548
Lane, F., 504, 505, 506
Langendorfer, S.J., 235, 239
Langer, J., 393, 400
Langlois, J. H., 340, 346
Language, 105, 204, 261, 325, 328, 385
    delays, 166, 210
    development, 140, 141, 142, 149, 150, 156, 157, 163–183, 197, 203, 211, 241, 260, 266, 284, 329, 381, 383, 531
    play, 114, 155, 156, 158, 175–183, 222, 331, 332–333, 334, 433, 451, 464, 500, 508, 531. See also Humor
Larcarda, M. E., xv
Largo, R. H., 203, 206
Larson, R., 487, 492
Larsson, L., 238, 239
Laughlin, C. D., 107, 108
Laughlin, F., 393, 399
Laughter, 446, 451, 508–509
Laursen, B., 242, 243, 247
Law, 113, 130, 226, 227, 235, 466
Lawsuits, 235, 319, 323
Lawton, J., 37, 48, 381, 388
Lawyers' play, 504–506
Leaper, C., 191, 192

Learning Through Landscapes, 529. *See also*
    Natural habitats
Leavitt, L. A., 267, 275, 283–284, 289
LeCompte, M. D., 41, 42, 46, 48
Lee, F., 292, 298
Lee, S., 260, 264
Leeb-Lundberg, K., 61, 67
Leibniz, J., 479
Leinbach, M. D., 143, 144, 187, 188, 189, 192,
    340, 346
Leisure, 16, 21, 116, 133, 155, 224, 416, 418, 419,
    420, 425, 461, 464, 477, 485, 486, 488,
    511, 523, 537
LeMare, L., 372, 373, 375, 376
Leon, H. V., 296, 298
Leonard, L., 166, 172
Leong, D. J., 277–282, 548–549
Lepper, M. R., 94, 97, 99
Lesbians, 292
Leve, L., 187–192, 549
Levenson, S., 220, 224
Levenstein, P., 263, 264, 283, 284, 288
Lever, J., 303, 312
Levin, D. E., 348–356, 381, 384, 387 , 549
Levin, S., 84, 89
Levine, J., 197, 198
Levita, A., 531, 536
Levy, C. J., 226, 231
Levy, D., 226, 231
Lewis, J. M., 78, 91
Lezine, I., 393, 400
Li, A. K. F., 68, 75
Libraries, 229, 244, 285, 286, 294, 500
Liddell, H. G., 109, 110, 117
Lieberman, J. N., 327, 336, 465, 467
Liedtka, J., 489, 491
Lieven, E., 170, 173
Life-span development, 14–22, 77, 103, 124, 133,
    144, 189, 311, 321, 466
Lifton, T., 119, 131
Light, P., 38, 48
Lightbown, P., 167, 172
Lightfoot, C., 260, 264
Lillard, A. S., 44, 46, 48
Linder, T. W., 204, 204, 205, 206, 211, 214
Linguistically different, 25, 273, 285
Linguistics, 56
Lisosky, J. M., 352, 256
Liss, M. B., 24, 32, 159, 160, 270, 275, 340, 346,
    356, 379, 384, 389
Literacy, 10–11, 139, 146, 244, 277
    development, 1, 50–55, 151, 154, 160, 165,
      324
    family, 50, 283, 287
Literature, children's, 10
Little League, 222. *See also* After-school activities
Littman, I., 190, 192
Liu, W., 133, 134, 158, 160
Lloyd, S., 325, 336
Loc Kits, Inc., 397, 398

Lockman, J. J., 138, 140, 145
Loftus, E. F., 94, 99, 315, 317
Loftus, G. R., 94, 99, 315, 317
LOGO, 397, 530, 535
Lohr, D., 94, 99
Lollis, S., 372, 373, 376
London Handicapped Adventure Playground
    Association, 238
Long, J. M., 372, 375
Lopreato, J., 249, 256
Lorge, I., 296, 298
Loscocco, K., 486, 492
Lothian Play Forum, 525
Loughlin, J., 464, 467
Louie, E., 537, 541
Lounsbury, K. R., 327, 328, 334
Louv, R., 227, 231
Love, B., 417, 422
Lowenfeld, M., 82, 91
Low-income, 226, 232. *See also* Socioeconomic status
Loy, J. W., 106, 108, 416, 422
Lubin, D., 244, 247
Lucas, B., 229, 231
Lukesh, S. S., 451–454, 549
Lund, N. L., 83, 91, 255, 256
Lunzer, E. A., 203, 206
Luria, A. S., 315. 317
Lusk, A., 230, 231
Luske, B., 213, 214
Lyon, S., 496, 498
Lytle, D. E., 461–467, 549

MacAloon, J., 419, 422
Maccoby, E. E., 28, 32, 187, 189, 190, 192, 269,
    273, 339, 340, 342, 346, 403
MacDonald, K., 261, 264
Macken, M., 165, 172
MacKinnon, C. E., 267, 268, 275, 276
MacKinnon, J., 373, 374, 376
Maehr, M. L., 19, 22, 468, 471
Magic, 112, 151, 382, 383
Magie, L. J., 306
Mahler, M., 430, 434
Mainstreaming. *See* Inclusion
Maioni, T. L., 27, 33, 203, 207, 369, 399
Malapropisms, 176. *See also* Language, play
Malinowski, B., 249, 250, 256
Mallory, B., 212, 213
Malone, T. W., 94, 97, 99
Mandese, J., 486, 492
Mandler, J. M., 38, 48, 315, 317
Mann, B. L., 379, 389
Mannell, R. D., 487, 492
Manning, M. L., 154–161, 544
Mantel, R., 417, 422
Manz, P. H., 237, 239
Mapping, 124, 228
Mardell-Czudnowski, C., 212, 214
Margolis, J. A., 33, 314, 317
Markell, R. A., 244, 247

Markman, E. M., 138, 144
Marks, D. F., 313, 317
Marrou, H. I., 6, 13
Marshall, T. R., 372, 375
Martin, B., 180, 183
Martin, D., 227, 231
Marxism, 421, 461, 487
Masiello, T., 259, 260, 261, 262, 263
Masten, A. S., 327, 336, 369, 373, 375, 376
Match, 213
Mathematical development, xv, 56–67, 182, 190, 246, 287, 361, 393, 395, 396. *See also* Number relationships
Mathematicians' play, 473–481
Matheny, A. P., 371, 376
Matheson, C. C., 141, 144, 149, 153, 379, 381, 384, 388
Matheson, L., 405, 406
Mathews, W. S., 342, 346
Matillo, G., 165, 172
Mattel, 308, 514
Matthews, W., 379, 389
Maturation, 15
Mayes, L. C., 81, 91, 139, 145
Mazur, S., 349, 355
McArthur, M., 20, 22
McCalla, C. L., 84, 91
McCary, J. C., 531, 535
McCaslin, N., 316, 317
McClurg, P. A., 94, 99
McCollum, A. T., 248, 256
McCool, D. E., 142, 145
McCuen, B. A., 490, 491
McCune-Nicolich, L., 166, 173, 202, 203, 206
McDougall, P., 373, 374, 376
McDuffie, W., 283, 287
McFarland, P., 306, 312
McGettigan, F. J., 271, 274
McGhee, P. E., 327, 335
McGhee, P., 177, 183, 325, 326, 328, 330, 331, 332, 333, 336
McHale, J. P., 138, 140, 145
McIlwraith, R. D., 316
McKechnie, G., 488, 492
McKechnie, J. L., 431, 434
McKinnon, J., 372, 374
McLoughlin Brothers, 311
McLoyd, V. C., 27, 32, 155, 160
McNaughton, S., 379, 384, 388
Mead, G. H., 371, 376, 381, 384, 389, 409, 414, 461, 462–463, 467
Mead, M., 290, 298
Meaning, 1, 5, 15–16, 20, 37, 51, 54, 69, 73, 81, 84, 96, 101–108, 112, 122, 155, 159, 176, 197, 208, 219, 222, 227, 241, 244, 259, 260, 301–302, 303, 316, 325, 326, 328, 332, 341, 350–354, 360–365, 370, 379, 383–385, 393, 395, 401, 405, 419–420, 432, 435, 436, 445, 453, 463, 474, 493, 495, 497, 540

Media, 24, 111, 130, 221, 283, 350, 379, 421, 429, 464, 466, 512, 517, 520, 530, 533, 537, 539. *See also* Television
Medicine, 425, 464, 507–509
Melartin, R. L., 138, 144
Meltzoff, A., 315, 317
Menesini, E., 405, 407
Mengel, C. E., 505–506, 549
Mental health, 495
Mergen, B., 107, 108, 311, 312, 360, 362
Mero, E. B., 232, 233, 239
Merseth, K., 496, 498
Metacognition, 127, 131, 279, 380, 394, 395
Metacommunication, 180, 181, 379, 381–382, 384, 386
Metaphor, 86, 89, 98, 109, 383, 438, 445, 502, 539
Metaphysics, 109, 115, 116
Methods of inquiry, 425, 436, 470, 473, 474, 495. *See also* Research methodology
Metz, K., 383, 400
Meyer, B., 417, 422
Meyer, C., 382, 390
Meyrowitz, J., 106
Michel, G. F., 138, 144
Michigan Preschool Test, 509
Mick, L. A., 138, 144
Middle elementary age, 66, 69, 154–161, 246, 269, 271, 294, 316, 320, 326, 329, 332, 360, 362, 363, 365, 371, 372, 384, 395, 403, 469, 470. *See also* Intermediate age children
Middle school, 28, 328
Miedzian, M., 349, 355, 356
Milgrim, S., 465, 467
Miller, B., 58, 67
Miller, M. H., 115, 117
Miller, P., 142, 145, 259, 260, 261, 262, 264, 379, 384, 388, 389
Miller, T. E., 24, 33
Mills, R. S. L., 270, 275, 373, 377
Milne, A. A., 261
Milton Bradley, 304, 307, 308, 309, 311
Mindes, G., 208–214, 549
Minkler, M., 292, 298
Minsky, M., 399, 400
Mintz, J., 261, 262, 263
Mintzberg, H., 441
Miracle, A., 249, 256
Mischel, W., 313, 314, 317
Mitchell, E. D., 232, 240
Mitchell, R., 418, 422
Mitchell, R. G., 465, 467
Mixed-age. *See* Interage
Mize, J., 270, 275
Mobius strip, 127
Modell, J., 15, 21
Models, 14, 71, 94, 150, 152, 211, 244, 271, 272, 284, 292, 304–306, 310, 342, 352, 453, 474, 475, 477, 478, 488, 494, 495, 512, 514, 517, 526, 538

Moller, L., 189, 192

Moltman, J., 432, 434

Monighan-Nourot, P., 360, 366, 381, 384, 388

Montessori, M., 46, 48, 271, 361, 366

Moore, M. K., 315, 317

Moore, R. C., 225, 228, 229, 231, 234, 237, 238,
239, 319–323, 519–529, 549–550

Moore, S. G., 242, 247

Moral development, 96, 232, 271, 303, 305, 307–310,
324, 340, 378, 409, 412–414, 418, 464

Morgan, E., 338, 347

Morgan, F. W., 487, 488, 490, 491

Morgan, P., 414

Morgenthaler, S.K., 359–367, 550

Morison, P., 369, 376

Morris, P. E., 314, 317

Morris, S. R., 109–118, 550

Morrison, M. L., 235, 240

Morrow, L. M., 51, 52, 54, 55

Mosier, C., 261, 262, 263

Moss, H. A., 371, 375

Most, R. K., 165, 172, 202, 203, 206

Motivation, 16, 19, 41, 69, 70, 74, 79, 103, 137,
147, 155, 167, 168–169, 194, 203, 222,
281, 327, 368

intrinsic, 73, 416, 419, 420, 421, 487, 494

Motor skills, 362. *See also* Physical development

Moulthrop, S., 538, 541

Mount, M. K., 490

Mounts, N. S., 372, 376

Moustakas, C., 83, 91, 195, 198

Meuller, E. C., 141, 145

Mulkeen, T. A., 498

Mullan, M. R., 201, 206

Multicultural, 301, 476, 537. *See also* Cross-
cultural; Sociocultural

Multi-user dungeons, 98, 516–517

Munn, P., 267, 268, 275

Museum of International Folk Art, 8

Museums, 6, 7, 11, 238, 285, 291, 294, 392, 397–
398, 452, 520, 531, 532

Music, xiv, 8, 17, 39, 139, 149, 159, 202, 209,
213, 220, 222, 230, 251, 269, 291, 313,
316, 317, 319, 393, 419, 442, 445, 509,
526, 532, 533, 539

Myers, B. K., 430, 434

Myers, C. A., 68–76

Myers, L. C., 24, 32, 270, 275

Myers, W. R., 429–434, 550

Myths, 116, 260, 379, 382

Nabhan, G. P., 228, 229, 231

Nachmanovitch, S., 122, 131, 383, 389, 441, 443,
445, 497, 498

Naimark, H., 27, 32

Naisbitt, J., 119, 131

NALPAC Corp., 309

National Academy of Sciences, 470

National Association for the Education of Young
Children, 37

National Association of Early Childhood Teacher
Educators, 497

National Council of Teachers of Mathematics, 474,
477, 480

National Institutes of Health, 455

National Play Information Center, 524, 525, 528

National Playing Fields Association, 525, 528

National Research Council, 474

National Science Foundation, 471

National Science Teachers Association, 74

Natural habitats, 12, 225–231, 320. *See also* Outdoor play

Nature-nurture, 143

Negotiation, 143, 280, 361, 362, 380, 382. *See
also* Play, dynamics; Scaffolding

Nehamas, A., 111, 117

Neighborhood, 25, 219, 220, 225, 226, 228, 234,
241, 242, 243, 245, 266, 269, 283, 285–
286, 519, 520, 521, 527

Nelson, K., 38, 39, 40, 48, 49, 165, 167, 170, 173,
379, 389

Nesbitt, K., 353, 355

Netscape Communications Corp., 532, 536

Neubauer, P. D., 78, 91, 194, 196, 198

Neugarten, B., 19, 22, 290, 292, 298

Neulinger, J. C., 16, 22

Neuman, S. B., 51, 52, 54, 55

New, R., 212, 214, 220, 224

Newberry, E., 303

Newman, J., 473, 480

Newman, M. A., 24, 32, 270, 275

Newmann, S., 295, 298

Newson, E., 261, 264

Newson, J., 261, 264

Newsweek, 520, 529

Newton, I., 479

Nicolich, L., 203, 206

Nicolopoulou, A., 379, 384, 389

Nintendo Corp., 515, 517

Nobel prize, 131

Nocol, A., 142, 145

Noe, F. P., 487, 492

Nonlinear dynamical systems theory, 170. *See also*
Chaos theory

Norbeck, E., 249, 256

Nordstrom, L., 373, 375

Nourot, P. M., 345, 347, 378–390, 550

Novelty, 121

Nucci, L., 340, 346

Nucci, M. S., 340, 346

Nutrition, 27

Nwokah, E., 259, 263

Oaklander, V., 83, 91, 195, 198

Object permanence, 431. *See also* Cognitive
development

Objects, 137, 138–140, 141, 146, 147, 166, 167,
261, 279, 359–367, 378. *See also* Toys

O'Brien, M., 143, 144

O'Brien, T. C., 531, 536

Ocko, S., 97, 99, 395, 400
O'Connell, B., 166, 173
O'Connor, K., 78, 80, 85, 86, 91, 260, 264
Oden, S., 266–276, 550
Ogawa, J. R., 242, 243, 247
Ogburn, M., 505, 506
Ogbu, J. U., 23, 24, 27, 32
Ogura, T., 203, 206
O'Hara, J., 263, 264, 283, 284, 288
Okuda, R., 526, 529
Oldfather, P., 379, 389
Olds, A., 228, 231
Olson, M., 486, 492
Olweus, D., 402, 403, 407
O'Neill, D., 320, 323
Opie, I., 179, 183, 326, 336
Opie, P., 179, 183, 326, 336
Opper, S., 60, 67
Oral culture, 228, 295
O'Reilly, A., 166, 173
O'Reilly, K. A., 204, 206
Orellana, M., 382, 384, 389
Orland, T., 440
Osgood, N. J., 19, 22
Ostrow, A. C., 18, 22
Ostwald, M., 113, 115, 117
Otto, K., 261, 264
Outdoor play, 10, 11, 13, 39, 43, 133, 158, 221,
        225–231, 246, 266, 269, 319, 320, 361.
        See also Natural habitats; Playgrounds

Pacanowsky, M., 465, 467
Paideia, 109–118
Paidia, 109–118
Painter, M., 202, 207
Paley, V. G., 28, 32, 149, 153, 244, 247, 342, 346,
        378, 382, 383, 384, 386, 389
Palkovitz, R., 327, 335
Papert, S., 94, 99, 392–399, 530, 531, 536
Papousek, H., 140, 145
Papousek, M., 140, 145
Paratore, J. R., 283, 288
Pardo, C., 352, 356
Parents, 5, 15, 41, 79, 86, 283–289
        influence of. *See* Adults, influence of
Parke, R. D., 15, 21, 259, 260, 261, 262, 263, 283,
        288
Parker, J., 370, 375
Parker, J. G., 269, 275, 404, 407
Parker Brothers, 306, 308, 311
Parks, 226, 286
Parsons, M., 272, 276
Parten, M. B., 133, 134, 203, 206, 280, 282, 339,
        346, 368, 376–377
Pasternak, J. F., 143, 144
Pathology, 15. *See also* Disabilities
Patterson, C. J., 27, 32, 340, 345
Patton, M. M., 283–289, 550
Paul, B., 244, 247
Paxton, S., 444, 446

Pea, R. D., 396, 400
Pearson, J. L., 292, 298
Peers, influence of, 266–276
Peitgen, H., 480
Pellegrini, A. D., 151, 154, 157, 159, 160, 161,
        271, 275, 373, 376, 384, 394, 400, 401–
        408, 551
Pellegrini, D. S., 369, 376
Peller, L. E., 78, 79, 91
Penrose, R., 120, 127, 131
Pepler, D. M., 68, 76, 142, 145
Perception, 16, 24
Perkins, D., 127, 128, 132
Perlmutter, M., 157, 161, 315, 317
Perrin, J., 365, 366
Perry, S., 287, 288
Perseverance, 242. *See also* Styles; Teachers,
        influence of
Personality, 151, 153, 170, 193, 197, 268, 273,
        369, 371, 372, 444, 490
Perspective-taking, 44. *See also* Intellectual/Social
        competence
Peters, A., 167, 173
Peterson, R. A., 488, 490, 491
Petrillo, M., 248, 256
Pettit, G. S., 370, 376
Phase portraits, 121, 122, 124
Phase transitions, 301. *See also* Chaos theory
Phenix, P. H., 430, 434
Philosophers' play, 109–118
Philosophy, 5
Phinney, J. S., 28, 32
Photographers' way-of-working, 435–441
Photographs, 30, 221, 295, 315, 438, 439, 451,
        452, 453, 507
Physical
        activity, 234, 402
        development, 15, 137, 139–140, 147, 149,
                151, 156–157, 176, 187, 203, 204, 209,
                210–211, 212, 226, 234, 236, 237, 266,
                268, 270, 314, 319, 324, 328, 418, 444.
                See also Motor development
        dynamics, 444
        fitness, 233, 236, 486, 521–522. *See also*
                Exercise
        play, 43, 156, 202, 261, 267, 520
        science, 469, 470
Physicians' play, 507–509
Piaget, J., 25, 32, 43, 48, 56, 57, 60, 67, 70, 78,
        79, 91, 93, 95, 133, 134, 138, 139, 145,
        154, 161, 165, 169, 173, 190, 201, 206,
        259, 263, 281, 282, 315, 328, 330, 331,
        335, 340, 353, 356, 361, 362, 366, 368,
        370–371, 376, 378, 390, 395, 396, 400,
        409, 410, 415, 430, 444, 447, 530, 536
Pien, D., 325, 330, 336
Piers, M. W., 195–196, 198
Pilon, R., 177, 183
Pinderhughes, E. E., 327, 336
Pine, J., 170, 173

Pippin, E. A., 142, 145
Pizzini, E. L., 69, 76
Plato, 113–118, 474
Platt, J. R., 460, 456
Plaut, E. A., 80, 91
Play
        definitions, xiv, 1, 37, 42, 46, 68, 70, 77–78,
                81, 82, 83, 103, 107, 109, 112, 114,
                115, 116, 121, 122, 125, 137, 148, 154,
                155, 159, 176, 208, 211, 212, 241, 250,
                252, 278, 294, 297, 319, 321, 328, 333,
                357, 368, 378–379, 393, 394, 395, 401–
                403, 416, 425, 429, 433, 435, 440, 443,
                445, 451, 452, 459, 466, 473, 486, 487,
                488, 490, 493–494, 524, 530, 533, 538,
                539, 540
        Development Progress Scale, 204
        duration, 244, 246, 254, 260, 272, 281, 292,
                392, 395, 398, 402, 521, 526
        dynamics, 14, 122, 169, 359, 383, 394–395
        environmental design, 188, 244, 246, 271,
                285–286
        influences of, 46, 133, 134, 159, 160, 201,
                203, 209, 236, 238, 241, 268, 272, 277,
                283, 284, 287, 303, 306–310, 322, 324,
                338, 357, 365, 366, 374, 381–382, 383,
                386, 387, 396, 398, 401, 403, 405, 435,
                444, 471, 521, 522, 524, 531, 540
        interage, 188, 223, 236, 269, 272, 278, 280,
                281, 290–299, 521
        Observation Scale, 370
        purposes, 5, 78, 80, 105, 110, 126, 127, 144,
                149, 156, 176–183, 193, 194, 195, 196,
                197, 221, 248, 250, 252, 259, 277, 334,
                418, 425, 432, 440, 461, 527, 541
        rural, xiv
        sexual, 301, 342–345, 418
        therapy, 77–87, 133, 172, 194, 234, 255,
                259, 316, 361
        Train, 525, 529
        types, 26, 370. See also Rough-and-tumble play
Playboard, 525, 529
Playfulness, 327, 393, 395, 425, 429–430, 435,
                436, 438ff, 442, 455ff, 461ff, 468, 470,
                474, 485, 498
Playground Association of America, 233
Playgrounds, 5, 25, 27, 95, 149, 152, 179, 203–
                204, 215, 219, 227, 229, 232–240, 241,
                266, 284, 324, 328, 362, 402, 522–523,
                525, 538, 539
        for children with special needs, 235, 237, 238,
                319, 320, 525
        pay-to-play, 234–235, 238, 285, 292, 294,
                321, 516, 520, 527
Playrights, 524
Plomin, R., 369, 371, 376
Poetry, 112, 151, 176, 179, 180, 181, 211, 220,
                221, 223, 270, 326, 383, 471
Policy, 21, 304, 403, 473, 512, 527. See also
        Advocacy

Political education, 304–305
Polizzi, R., 308, 311, 312
Pollio, H., 325, 327, 328, 334,325
Pollution, 226
Poole, B. L., 238, 239
Poole, G. S., 238, 239
Pope, K. S., 313, 318
Popenoe, D., 286, 288
Porges, W. S., 372, 375
Postman, N., 106, 108, 521, 529
Postmodern, 107, 119
Powell, J. A., 283, 288
Power, T. G., 283, 288
Powlishta, K., 189, 192
Practice, 94, 105, 137, 138, 139, 142, 176, 179,
                180, 190, 194, 277, 320, 409, 412, 417,
                444, 464, 497
Pragmatic theory, 360, 361, 366
Predictability, 16
Predispositions, 170. See also Styles
Prekindergarten age, 359–360, 374
Prentice, N. M., 327, 337
Preschool age, 137–145, 280–281, 320, 362, 363
Preschool Play Behavior Scale, 369
Preschool SocioAffective Profile, 369
Pretense, 1, 10, 38, 39, 43–45, 46, 51, 78, 80, 83,
                87, 89, 93, 94, 125, 128, 133, 141, 142,
                143, 144, 146, 148–149, 152, 158, 159,
                165, 168, 169, 170, 177, 180, 181, 182,
                190, 193, 194, 202, 230, 234, 241, 242,
                244, 245, 254, 259, 260, 262, 266, 267,
                269, 280, 281, 308, 315, 316, 317, 324,
                328, 330–331, 334, 345, 359ff, 378,
                409, 469, 502, 504–505, 533. See also
                Sociodramatic play
Price, J. M., 370, 375, 376
Primary grades, 27, 58, 146–153, 243, 246, 320–
                321, 342, 360, 362, 403, 404
Print culture, 95
Privacy, 156
Prizant, B. M., 205, 206
Problem solving, 60, 65, 69, 74, 78, 82, 88, 168,
                190, 194, 196, 203, 211,245, 268, 271,
                360, 361, 394, 395, 398, 404, 435, 474,
                477, 489, 493, 495, 496, 497, 498, 531,
                534, 535, 538, 539
Professional associations, 154
Professionalism, 129, 425, 488, 493, 496, 498
Project approach, 125, 271. See also Curriculum
                design
Props, 28, 31, 52, 53, 141, 142, 148, 170, 195,
                219, 245, 246, 279, 281, 316, 360, 361,
                362, 504
Provenzo, E. F., Jr., 94, 99, 234, 238, 239, 513–
                518, 519, 528, 551
Psychoanalytic/psychodynamic theory, 81–82, 194,
                338, 360–361, 378
Psychological development, 77–92
Psychology, 5, 14, 21
Puppets, 11, 82, 83, 149, 194, 295, 316

Putnam, S., 260, 264
Pythagoreans. *See* Number relationships

Quandt, R. E., 486, 491
Quantum theory, 120
Questions, 63, 64–65, 69, 74, 291, 363, 382, 392, 457, 500, 501
Quilting, 532
Quinn, J. B., 489, 492
Quisenberry, N., 27, 32

Race 21, 23–33, 213, 269–270, 273, 471, 538. *See also* Ethnicity
Radcliffe-Brown, A. R., 249, 256
Radio, 210, 222, 520, 539
Radlinski, S. H., 202, 207, 259, 262, 264
Rahner, H., 432, 434
Rainer, Y., 429, 434, 446
Ramm, J. F., 961
Ramsey, P. G., 23–33, 269, 331, 336, 269, 270, 271, 273, 275, 551
Rand, M. K., 52, 55
Ransbury, M. K., 156, 161
Rapping, 179, 222. *See also* Chants; Poetry
Rau, S. R., 12, 13
Ray, R. O., 20, 22
Rayna, S., 393, 400
Reading, 50, 277, 284, 317, 469, 488. *See also* Literacy
Recess, xiv, 28, 40, 43, 152, 157, 175, 246, 402, 521, 528
Recorde, R., 478
Recreation, 233. *See also* Leisure
Recreation specialists, 285
Recursion, 121, 122, 123, 130
Redburn, L., 248, 252, 254, 255
Reese-Learned, H., 414
Reeve, C. D. C., 113, 117
Reid, S., 89, 91, 331, 336
Reifel, S., 39, 40, 48, 393, 400
Reissman, L., 486, 492
Rejection, 272, 405
Religion, 11, 12, 215, 249, 250, 266, 290, 304, 429–434
Repetition, 249, 251–253, 328, 353, 354, 444, 533. *See also* Practice; Rituals
Representation, 11, 44, 46, 78, 87, 94, 95, 122, 126, 138, 148–149, 166, 168, 169, 193, 194, 195, 197, 202, 222, 241, 255, 277, 278, 279, 281, 301, 303, 313, 353, 359, 362, 378, 379, 381, 393, 396, 409, 433, 439, 440, 443, 444, 478
Rescorla, L., 168, 173
Research methodology, 21, 47, 169, 201–205, 297, 316, 324, 327, 357, 363–366, 368–370, 395–396, 398, 404–406, 409–410, 413–414, 417, 418, 419–420, 436, 456–459, 464, 465, 496–497
Resnick, L. B., 71, 76
Resnick, M., 97, 99, 395, 400

Retirement. *See* Intergenerational activity
Revenson, T., 315, 318
Reville, S., 296, 299
Revised Class Play, 369
Reyna, V. F., 71, 75, 76
Reynolds, E., 53, 54, 211, 214, 321, 323, 354, 355, 379, 381, 383, 386, 389
Reznick, J. S., 372, 375
Rheingold, H., 71, 76, 516, 518
Rhodes, R., 67
Rhymes, 178, 221, 224, 505. *See also* Chants; Poetry
Rhythm, 176, 249, 251–252, 253, 443, 466
Richard, L. M., 487, 488, 490, 491
Richardson, J. G., 340, 346
Riddles, 325–326, 327, 329, 378. *See also* Language play
Riegel, K., 15, 22
Riemann, S., 261, 264
Rigauer, B., 421, 422
Rightmyer, J., 327, 335
Riley, D., 24, 31
Riley, M. W., 18, 20
Risk-taking, 51, 128, 301, 319–323, 392, 395, 418, 425, 436, 437, 440, 453, 473, 485, 489, 495, 496, 498, 522, 531, 539, 540. *See also* Challenge; Gambling
Rites, 249, 301
Rituals, 12, 23, 25, 28, 30, 141, 182, 211, 213, 248–256, 393, 430, 443, 463, 521
Ritz, K., 385, 390
Ritzer, G., 421, 422
Rivkin, M. S., 225–231, 364, 366, 526, 529, 551
Rizzo, T. A., 271, 272, 275
Rizzo, W., 26, 32
Roach, M. A., 267, 275, 283–284, 289
Roberts, J. M., 219, 224
Roberts, J. S., 16, 22
Robertson, J., 251, 255
Robertson-Beckley, R., 292, 298
Robey, L., 285, 288
Robinson, C., 27, 32
Robinson, D. A. G., 68, 75
Robinson, R., 116, 118
Rocissano, L., 362, 366
Rockmore, M., 502, 503
Rogers, C., 82, 91
Rogers, C. R., 316, 318
Rogers, C. S., 181, 183
Rogers, P. J., 58, 59, 67
Rogers, S. J., 203, 207
Roggman, L. A., 142
Rojek, C., 16, 22
Role play, 11, 45, 80, 83, 85, 88, 89, 94, 98, 107, 189, 196, 210, 253, 303, 378, 433, 461, 470, 495, 502, 505
Romero, M., 41, 42, 43, 48
Roopnarine, J. L., 107, 108, 189, 192, 370, 376
Root, M. P., 23, 33
Rose, K., 292, 298

Rose-Krasnor, L., 372, 373, 374, 377
Rosen, C. E., 361, 366
Rosenberg, B. G., 338, 347
Rosenberg, H. S., 316, 318
Rosenblatt, D., 168, 174
Rosenbluth, D., 251, 255
Rosenfeld, E., 316
Roskos, K., 50, 51, 52, 54, 55
Ross, D., 342, 345
Ross, H. S., 68, 76, 142, 145
Ross, J., 59, 67
Ross, S. S., 342, 345
Rostow, W. W., 488, 492
Roth, W., 213, 214
Rothbart, M. K., 325, 330, 336
Rothenberg, L., 85, 91
Rotheram, M. J., 28, 32
Rouard, M., 234, 239
Rough-and-tumble play, 28, 140, 147, 151, 159,
        170, 189, 209, 211, 213, 269, 339, 357,
        370, 373, 401–408, 516
Routines, 210. See also Environmental design
Rowden, L., 373, 375
Rowe, D. C., 369, 376
Rowe, S., 230, 231
Roy, C., 202, 207
Rubin, K. H., 27, 33, 46, 48, 69, 76, 133, 134,
        143, 147, 148, 153, 155, 161, 189, 192,
        202, 203, 207, 209, 214, 241, 247, 259,
        264, 270, 271, 275, 363, 367, 368–377,
        390, 551
Ruch, W., 333, 336
Ruefli, T. W., 489, 492
Rules, 42. See also Games
Rush, A. J., 83, 90
Russ, S., 124, 132
Rutherford F. J., 74, 76

Sachs, J., 379, 390
Sachs, K., 260, 263
Safety, 103, 147, 193ff, 211, 223, 224ff, 232ff,
        252, 272, 285, 297, 301, 316, 319, 320,
        322, 323, 334, 343, 350, 398, 468, 508,
        521, 522–523, 527
Sage, G., 421, 422
Sahm, W. B., 189, 192
Saki, 349, 355
Salthe, S. N., 103, 104, 108
Saltz, T., 295, 298
Samdahl, D. M., 16, 17, 22, 485, 487, 492
Samuelson, S. S., 505, 506
Sancilio, M. F., 242, 247
Sand play, 63, 195, 232, 236, 237, 238, 320, 363
Sanford, G., 248, 256
Sanger, S., 248, 256
Sapon-Shevin, M., 272, 275
Sapora, A. V., 232, 240
Saracho, O. N., 69, 76
Sargent, J. R., 97, 99
Saupe, D., 480

Savary, L., 316, 317
Sawyers, J. K., 181, 183
Scaffolding, 71–71, 124, 140, 150, 152, 280, 281,
        283, 345, 381, 384, 394. See also
        Adults, influence; Teachers, influence;
        Vygotsky
Scales, B., 345, 347, 360, 366, 379, 381, 384, 386,
        389, 390
Scanlan, C., 501, 503
Scarr, S., 371, 377
Scatalogical language, 177, 179, 329, 332. See also
        Language play
Schackman, M., 191
Schaefer, C. E., 77, 86, 87, 88, 89, 91, 92, 195,
        198, 361, 367
Schaefer, F., 308, 311, 312
Schaie, K. W., 14, 22
Schallow, J. R., 316
Schan, C. G., 341, 347
Schank, R. C., 38, 49
Schedule, 271–272. See also Play, duration
Schiffer, M., 85, 91
Schliemann, H., 451, 452
Schneekloth, L. H., 237, 240
Schoen, D., 203, 206
Schofield, J., 25, 33
School climate, 241–247, 494
School reform, 129
Schrader, C. T., 51, 53, 55
Schreck, M. A., 20, 22
Schuiteman, J., 417, 422
Schulman, J., 248, 256
Schultz, N. W., 487, 492
Schwalbe, M. L., 487, 492
Schwartz, J., 397
Schwartz, S. S., 241, 246
Schwartzman, H. B., 42, 46, 47, 49, 165, 173, 259,
        264, 379, 382, 291
Schwarz, K., 26, 31
Schwedes, H., 69, 76
Science, 116, 151, 155, 190, 464, 474, 508
        study, 315
Scientific development, 68–76
Scientists' play, 70–71, 455–460
Scripts, 1, 38, 39, 40, 81, 104, 105, 106, 141, 142,
        149, 170, 177, 180, 181, 212, 250, 255,
        301, 315, 345, 350, 351, 353, 360, 362,
        378–391, 451, 458, 496, 504, 514, 515,
        538. See also Themes
Scott, J., 17, 18, 22
Scott, R., 109, 110, 117
Secrets, 269, 411, 413, 417
Security, 196. See also Attachment
Seefeldt, C., 120, 132, 290–299, 398
Sega, 517
Segregation, 23, 152. See also Inclusion
Seidman, S., 165, 173, 379, 390
Seidner, L. B., 141, 142, 144
Seifer, R., 140, 144
Selchow & Righter, 308

Self-concept, 15, 64, 78, 82, 88, 126, 144, 146, 194, 196, 248, 270, 319, 373, 383, 385, 387, 444, 463, 465, 485
Self-organization, 121, 122, 123, 128
Seligmann, J., 292, 299
Selman, R., 413–415
Semonsky, C., 85, 92
Sena, R., 166, 173
Senge, P., 131, 132
Senhouse, L., personal communication, 221
Senior citizens, 202
Sensitive dependence on initial conditions, 121, 122, 123, 124, 127
Serbin, L. A., 189, 190, 191, 192, 269, 275, 341, 347
Serock, K., 293, 294, 298
Severeide, R. C., 69, 76
Sewing, 149, 291. See also Crafts
Sexuality, 182, 301, 308, 329, 338–347, 404, 418, 419, 520
Sexual language, 178
Shade, D. D., 235, 236, 240
Shaffer, D. R., 338, 347
Shakespeare, W., 109, 118
Shannon, P., 50, 55
Shaw, B. F., 83, 90
Shefataya, L., 342, 347, 353, 356
Sheik, A. A., 317, 318
Sheingold, K., 396, 400
Sheldon, A., 382, 385, 390
Shell, E. R., 234, 240
Shepard, R., 494, 498
Sheridan, M. K., 202, 207, 259, 262, 264
Sherman, F., 24, 32, 270, 275
Sherman, L. S., 327, 328, 336
Sherwood, R., 392, 399
Shier, H., 525, 529
Shopping malls, 310, 468, 469,471. See also Community; Playgrounds
Shore, C., 165–174, 551
Shotwell, J. M., 170, 173
Show, C., 170, 173
Shultz, L., 413–415
Shultz, T. R., 173, 177, 183, 325, 330, 336
Siblings, xv, 12, 84, 106, 190, 195, 210, 211, 215, 243, 254, 259, 266–276, 277, 280, 341, 361, 379
Siddall, C., 445, 448
Sies, A. C., 362, 367
Sigel, I., 41, 49
Sigelman, C. K., 24, 33, 338, 347
Sigman, M., 166, 173
Sigmund, K., 126, 127, 132
Sign language, 315
Sikes, L., 235, 240
Silverman, R., 496, 498
Silvern, S. B., 530–536, 551
Silvey, A., 291, 199
Simon, H. A., 489, 492
Simon, J., 234, 240

Simpson, C. H., 340, 346
Sims, C. R., 283, 287
Sin, 429ff. See also Moral development
Sinclair, H., 393, 400
Singer, D. G., 142, 145, 196, 198, 259, 261, 264, 284, 289, 313–318, 349, 356, 360, 362, 363, 367, 513, 518, 551–552
Singer, J. L., 142, 145, 196, 197, 198, 245, 261, 264, 284, 289, 313–318, 330–331, 333, 336, 337, 360, 362, 367, 513, 518, 552
Singing, 195, 270, 294, 326, 334, 384, 508. See also Chants; Music; Poetry
Singleton, L. C., 24, 33, 275, 279
Sipowicz, R., 248, 256
Skarpness, L. R., 487, 492
Skinner, B. F., 83, 92
Slade, A., 260, 264, 338, 347
Slang, 178
Slaughter, D. Y., 27, 33
Slavin, R. E., 29, 33, 272, 275
Slavson, S., 85, 92
Slomkowski, C., 267, 268, 274
Smale, B. J. A., 20, 22
Smedley, A., 23, 33
Smees, R., 405, 407
Smilansky, S., 27, 33, 58, 119, 121, 123, 124, 125, 132, 148, 152, 153, 188, 192, 196, 202, 207, 245, 247, 284, 289, 342, 347, 353, 356, 368, 377, 378, 379, 386, 390
Smith, J., 281, 282, 393, 400
Smith, P. K., 24, 25, 31, 37, 49, 68, 76, 260, 340, 347, 364, 401, 402, 403, 405, 406, 407
Snacks, 204, 287
Snidman, N., 372, 275
Snow, C., 172
Snyder, E., 420, 422, 487, 492
Snyder, L., 168, 169, 170, 172
Sobel, D., 228, 231
Social competence, 85, 146, 155, 157, 167, 189, 203, 208, 209, 210, 241–242, 245, 246, 269, 270, 277, 284, 303–312, 324, 327, 333, 334, 341, 349, 353, 368–377, 383, 385, 386, 402, 404, 405, 413–414, 453, 497, 538
Social development, 1, 140, 141, 149, 176, 183, 202, 234, 242, 266, 268, 281, 319, 340, 368–377, 396, 401, 405, 521
Social-interactionist theories, 170
Socialization, 16, 42, 368–377
Social learning, 62, 152
Social sciences, 470
Sociocultural context, 23–33, 39, 42, 50, 69, 84, 95, 103, 105–106, 113, 119, 120, 133, 151, 152, 158, 208, 209, 212, 215, 225, 249, 261, 269–270, 281, 290, 294, 301, 303, 311, 330, 352, 354, 355, 357, 360, 361–362, 368, 379, 382, 383, 385, 418, 421, 429, 442, 446, 456, 459, 461, 465, 468, 471, 487, 494, 515, 519, 537, 539
Sociocultural influences, 14, 21, 260, 270

Sociodramatic play, 1, 11, 27, 51, 54, 58, 124, 125, 142, 148–149, 150, 152, 165, 166, 170, 175, 180, 181, 189, 196, 204, 210, 229, 244, 277ff, 285, 301, 338, 341, 342, 344, 345, 350–351, 353, 354, 357, 360, 361–362, 368, 370, 378–391, 402, 404, 405, 420, 421, 425, 465, 496, 538. *See also* Pretend play; Pretense

Socioeconomic status, 5, 8, 21, 23–33, 151, 152, 154, 155, 156, 226, 262, 268, 269, 273, 291, 293, 294, 296, 306, 310, 419, 486, 487, 490, 520, 526–527, 537, 538

Sociologists' play, 461–467

Sociology, 5, 330

Sociopolitical context, 349, 350, 351

Socrates, 65, 110, 111, 112, 113, 114, 115, 117

Soderman, A., 320, 321, 323

Software, 397, 515. *See also* Computers

Solnit, A., 194, 196, 198

Solomon, J., 84, 92

Solsken, J., 50, 55

Sophocles, 110

Sorenson, C. T., 233, 234, 240

Spariosu, M. I., 112, 118, 464, 466

Spatial learning, xv, 94, 95, 190, 210, 222, 228, 340, 345, 362, 393, 414, 443, 473, 531

Special needs. *See* Disabilities; Styles

Spence, G., 505

Spencer, H., 154, 161

Spieker, S. J., 373, 377

Spillover theory, 418, 419, 486

Spitzer, S., 39, 49

Spodek, B., 69, 76

Sponseller, D., 473, 480

Sports, 15, 17, 45, 69, 96, 103, 104, 105, 125, 147, 151, 155, 156–157, 182, 204, 208, 209, 212, 213, 220, 222, 225, 226, 227, 269, 281, 285, 291, 297, 309, 315, 317, 321, 357, 363, 433, 442, 443, 445, 446, 453, 463ff, 473, 506, 507, 512, 521, 526. *See also* Games

Sport sociology, 416–423

Spreitzer E., 487, 492

Springer, M., 470, 472

Sroufe, L. A., 330, 336, 372, 377

St. Antoine, S., 228, 229, 231

Stahl, A., 293, 299

Stambak, M., 393, 400

Standardized tests, 203, 315, 316, 521. *See also* Assessment

Stebbins, R. A., 464, 467, 486

Steele, C., 327, 377

Steele, P., 418, 419, 422

Steen, L., 473, 474, 481

Stein, J., 249, 255

Stein, L. C., 320, 321, 323, 349, 355

Steinberg, L., 372, 376

Steinberg, R., 12, 13

Steinkamp, M. W., 16, 19, 22

Stephens, M., 502, 503

Stereotypes, 69, 95, 143, 189, 190, 212, 267, 283, 294, 296, 297, 310, 311, 338, 340–341, 345, 433, 466, 488, 491, 499, 508

Stern, D. N., 330, 336

Stern, V., 196, 198

Sternglanz, S. H., 269, 275

Stevens, M. J., 490, 492

Stevens, P., 42, 46, 49

Stevenson, M. B., 267, 275, 283–284, 289

Stewart, S. L., 369, 370, 372, 375, 377

Stinson, S., 444, 448

Stone, G., 416, 423

Stone, I. F., 113, 118

Stoneman, Z., 267, 271, 273, 276

Stork, L., 27, 32

Storytelling, 11, 31, 65, 83, 93, 96, 142, 177, 180, 182, 210, 250, 284, 316, 326, 334, 353, 381, 382, 383, 505, 506

Strasser, S., 7, 13

Strayer, F. F., 189, 192

Streb, E., 446, 447

Stress, 195, 211

Struntz, K. A., 296, 299

Stubbe, D., 81, 91, 139, 145

Styles, 23, 152, 165–174, 189, 191, 212, 270, 273, 321, 327, 338–339, 362, 364–365, 370, 371, 372, 384–386, 403, 404, 405, 470, 496, 508, 537

Su, P., 249, 255, 339, 346

Subrahmanyan, K., 94, 99

Substance abuse, 285, 292, 296, 374, 464, 465, 502, 504

Suchar, C. S., 213, 214

Sudnow, D., 441

Sugawara, A. I., 41, 47, 188, 191

Sullivan, H. S., 371, 377

Sulzby, E., 50, 55

Super, C., 262, 263

Supersymmetry, 119–132

Suppes, P., 321, 323

Surprise, 121, 435

Survival instinct, 249. *See also* Emotions; Health care settings

Sutton-Smith, B., 16, 22, 37, 38, 43, 47, 49, 80, 90, 94, 99, 107, 142, 145, 155, 161, 222, 223, 224, 237, 239, 244, 247, 259, 260, 261, 262, 263, 264, 284, 289, 303, 312, 322, 323, 330, 337, 338, 347, 349, 356, 357, 383, 390, 401, 405, 407, 462, 467, 530, 531, 536

Swadener, E. B., 28, 33

Sweeney, M., 393, 399

Swick, K. J., 283, 289

Sylva, K., 202, 207, 401, 406

Sylwester, R., 539, 540, 541

Symbolic. *See* Representation

Symbolic interactionism, 421, 462–463

Tafoya, E., 292, 293, 298

Taft, J., 83, 92

Takanishi, R., 39, 49
Takeuchi, M., 262, 264
Talbot, J., 237, 240
Tamis-LeMonda, C., 140, 145, 166, 173
Tanguay, P., 170, 172
Taylor, A. R., 271, 276
Teachers, influence of, 37, 39, 40, 41, 47, 51, 52–
        53, 56, 69, 71, 73, 110, 113, 114, 119,
        120, 123, 124, 126, 128, 129, 152, 154,
        158, 159, 190, 191, 203, 215, 223, 230,
        241, 242, 243, 244, 245–246, 269, 271,
        273, 277, 280, 281, 287, 334, 341, 345,
        352–355, 386, 387, 395, 402, 412, 414,
        468, 469, 470, 471, 475, 476, 480, 494,
        521
Teale, W., 50, 55
Teasing, 5, 179, 267, 272, 316, 327
Technology, 1, 9, 13, 14, 15, 93–99, 158, 211,
        226, 227, 277, 284, 290, 293, 295, 310,
        421, 429, 486, 488, 507, 511, 512, 537–
        539
Tegano, D., 272, 276
Television, 5, 10, 20, 25, 50, 95, 106, 142, 181,
        209, 222, 234, 284, 285, 287, 291, 293,
        317, 341–342, 345, 348–358, 360, 379,
        486, 499, 504, 511, 513, 514
Tests. See Assessment
Tetenbaum, J., 498
Teti, D. M., 268, 276
Tew, J. D., 327, 335
Textbooks, 469
Theater, 444, 464
Thelen, E., 124, 132, 170, 174
Themes, 6, 7, 23, 24, 29, 30, 31, 38, 39, 45, 46,
        51, 52, 53–54, 81, 82, 84ff, 94, 96, 97,
        122, 123, 125, 129, 141–142, 147, 148,
        150, 151, 152, 157, 158, 159, 166, 167,
        168, 170, 175, 177, 179, 180, 181, 182,
        189, 190, 194–195, 196, 202, 209, 210,
        213, 219, 220, 221, 234, 236, 241, 242,
        243, 244–245, 246, 249, 252, 253, 254,
        259, 260, 270, 277, 278, 279, 280, 281,
        286, 301, 303–306, 308, 309, 311, 315,
        321–322, 327, 329, 331, 332, 333, 339,
        340, 341–342, 343, 344, 345, 348–356,
        359–363, 378–391, 409, 410, 418, 431,
        433, 436, 437, 438, 439, 440, 451, 452,
        468, 469, 501, 505, 509, 512, 513–517,
        520, 531, 532–533, 540
Theokas, C., 29, 33, 269, 275
Theology, 5, 429–434
Theory of mind, 44
Thomas, L., 230, 231
Thompson, D., 235, 236, 240, 402, 407
Thompson, R., 248, 251, 252, 253, 254, 256
Thompson, R. H., 267, 275, 283–284, 289
Thorne, B., 28, 29, 33, 420, 423, 464
Time. See Play, duration
Tinsworth, D. E., 235, 240
Title IX, 15

Titman, W., 525, 529
Titmus II Vision Tester, 509
Toddlers. See Infants and toddlers
Toileting, 250, 343
Tonick, I. J., 269, 275
Tonka, 514
Torney-Puta, J. V., 316
Torrance, E. P., 301, 302
Tower, R. B., 197, 198, 330–331, 337
Toy libraries. See Libraries
Toys, 5, 6, 7, 9, 10, 15, 29, 31, 38, 39, 41, 42, 79,
        82, 83, 84, 89, 93, 94, 95, 96, 97, 105,
        106, 116, 138–140, 141, 142, 143, 147,
        148, 150, 151, 152, 158, 159, 166, 168,
        170, 181, 187, 202, 203, 209, 212, 219,
        220, 221, 223, 230, 245, 254, 255, 261,
        266, 279, 284, 285, 286, 303, 308, 341,
        348–356, 362ff, 380, 393, 401, 402,
        403, 410, 471, 475, 478, 501, 538
    media-linked, 345, 348–355, 513–518
Tracy, D. M., 69, 76
Transcendence, 429–434
Transdisciplinary, 211
    play-based assessment, 204, 205. See also
        Integrative study
Transogram, 307, 308
Trauma, 194, 215, 249, 254, 334. See also Health
        care settings
Trautner, H. M., 189, 192
Trawick-Smith, J., 241–247, 386, 390, 522
Trudye, J., 260, 264
Trumbull, D., 71, 76
Turkle, S., 94, 99, 395, 396, 400, 515, 518
Turner, J. S., 156, 157, 161
Turner, V. W., 433, 434
Turow, V., 507–509, 552
Twins, 371–372
Tyler, L., 39, 49

Unga Ornar, 525
Unger, E., 141, 142, 144, 149, 153, 379, 381, 384,
        388
Unger, L., 485–492, 552
UNICEF Office on Children's Rights, 523–524,
        529
United Games, 311
United Nations, 520
United Nations Declaration on the Rights of the
        Child, 519, 523
United States Center for Disease Control, 522, 529
United States Consumer Product Safety Commission,
        235, 322
Unkel, M., 19, 22
Urban play, xiii, xiv, 213, 219–224, 234, 235, 286,
        519, 520, 521, 527
Ury, W., 385, 388
Uzgiris, I., 138, 145

Vacation schools, 232. See also After-school activities
Vaden, N. A., 27, 32

Valsiner, J., 260, 264
Van de Putte, S., 11, 13, 85, 92
van der Kooij, R., 80, 90, 259, 263
Van Fleet, R., 86, 92
Van Hoorn, J., 345, 347, 360, 366, 379, 381, 386,
    389, 391
Vance, B., 233, 237, 240
Vandalism, 238
Vandell, D. L., 141, 145
Vanderberg, B.,46, 48, 69, 76, 133, 134, 147, 148,
    153, 155, 161, 209, 214, 236, 240, 259,
    260, 263, 265, 271, 276, 339, 340, 346,
    371, 376, 379, 390
Vander Velden, L., 417, 422
VanderVen, K., 119–132, 552–523
VanGundy, A. B., 490, 492
Vaughn, B. E., 140, 144
Verba, M., 393, 400
Vernon, D., 248, 256
Verry, E. E., 367, 377
Video games, 93–97, 151, 158, 222, 234, 235,
    284, 310, 315, 352, 468, 511, 513–518,
    520, 530. See also Computer, games
Viete, F., 478
Violence, 151, 159, 234, 235, 238, 244, 286, 385,
    386, 530. See also Play themes
Violent play, 342, 348–356, 401, 512, 516
    developmental perspective, 350, 351, 353–355
    functions, 351–352
    sociopolitical perspective, 349, 350, 353–355
    See also Rough-and-tumble play
Virtual playgrounds, 93, 150, 396–397
Virtual reality, 93, 150, 396–397, 511, 517, 538–
    539
Visintainer, M., 252, 253, 256
Vlastos, G., 113, 118
Vollstedt, R., 37, 49
Voluntarism, 294, 486, 487, 509
von Aufshnaiter, S., 69, 76
Vondra, J., 141, 145
von Glasersfeld, E., 147, 153
Vukelich, C., 52, 54, 55, 158, 161
Vygotsky, L. S., 51, 55, 63, 70, 71–72, 76, 124,
    259, 265, 260, 277–282, 382, 383, 384,
    390, 394

Wachs, T. C., 167, 170, 174, 361, 367
Waelder, R.,82, 92
Walker, V. S., 271, 274
Wallach, F., 236, 240, 322, 323
Wallis, J., 303
Walt Disney Personal Computer Software, 531
Wang, X., 261, 262, 263
Ward, A., 235, 240
Wardle, F., 52, 54, 386, 387
Warman, B., 293, 398
Wassermann, S., 69, 76
Waterloo Longitudinal Project, 373
Water play, 60, 63, 65, 126, 139, 195, 236, 237,
    238, 320, 394, 505

Watjust, M., 285, 288
Watley, J. L., 141, 144
Watson, J. D., 455, 456, 457, 459, 460, 494
Watson, K. S., 189, 192, 202, 207, 369, 370, 377
Watson, M., 165, 166, 172, 174
Watt, J., 494
Watterson, W., 434
Wearing, B., 20, 21, 22, 23
Webb, H., 417, 423
Webbing, 124
Webster, D., 462, 467
Weeks, T. E., 165, 174
Wegener-Spohring, G., 401, 407
Weil, A. M.,25, 32
Weinberg, S., 130, 131, 132
Weininger, O., 381, 388, 473, 481, 493, 498
Weinstein, J., 290, 292, 298
Weinstein, R. S., 39, 49
Weintraub, J., 379, 384, 389
Weiss, B. W., 201, 205
Welsh, A., 86, 90
Welty, W., 496, 498
Wennerstrand, A. L., 442–448, 553
Werner, H., 169, 174
West, J., 379, 389
Westby, C. E., 203, 207
Wetherby, A. M., 205, 206
Wexelblat, A., 538, 541
Wheatley, M., 121, 132
Wheelchairs. See Access
Wheeler, K. J., 327, 335
Wheeler, V. A., 270, 273
Whiren, A. P., 320, 321, 323, 349, 355
Whitelegg, J., 226, 231
Whiting, B. B., 187, 190, 192, 225, 231, 260, 261,
    262, 263, 265, 339, 347
Whitt, J. K., 327, 337
Whitton, S., 473–481, 553
Whitworth, L. A., 24, 33
Wigington, H., 286, 289
Wilde, O., 261
Wilensky, H., 418, 423, 486, 492
Wilkinson, C. D., 9, 13
Williams, G. A., 271, 276
Williams, K., 261, 262, 263
Wilson, E. O., 227, 231
Wilson, J., 286, 289
Wiltz, N. W., 37–49, 553
Wimbarti, S., 261, 263
Wing, L. A., 42, 49
Winnicott, D. W., 82, 92, 360, 367, 443, 448, 519,
    529
Winsler, A., 124, 126, 131, 278, 282, 283, 288
Witt, P. A., 486, 487, 491
Wittmer, D. S., 341, 347
Wolchick, S. A., 143, 144
Wolf, D., 166, 167–170, 173, 174
Wolfe, C. R., 68–76
Wolfe, D. P., 260, 264, 338, 347
Wolfe, R. A., 488, 492

Wolfenstein, M., 329, 333, 337
Wolfer, J., 248, 252, 253, 254, 255, 256
Wong, H., 229, 231
Wood, B., 235, 240
Wooding, C., 260, 261, 263
Woods, I. C., 232–240, 553
Work, 38, 42–43, 77, 103, 105, 106, 116, 119,
        128, 130, 137, 147, 155, 159, 212, 224,
        254, 262, 284, 293, 306, 322, 416–423,
        425, 429, 430, 435, 440, 451, 458, 464,
        470, 485–492, 494, 497, 499, 509, 531,
        537
Wortham, S. C., 235, 236, 240
Wright, D. S., 327, 335
Wright, F. L., 399
Wright, J. L., 235, 236, 240
Writing, 11, 50, 54, 115, 116, 140, 160, 193, 244,
        301, 315, 353, 498, 500, 502, 531
Wu, F., 24, 32
Wunsch, J. P., 330, 336

Yankelovich, D., 487, 492
Yasilove, D., 326, 337
Yawkey, T. D., 58, 67, 146, 153, 201, 204, 206,
        244, 247, 284, 288, 338, 346, 363, 366

Young, K., 420, 421
Youngblade, L. M., 142, 145
Yu the Great, 476

Zakrzewska, M., 232
Zamarelli, J., 59, 67
Zamsky, E. S., 292, 298
Zan, B., 271, 274, 411, 412, 413, 414
Zeece, P. D., 284, 288
Zeisloft-Falbey, B., 204, 206
Zeiss, A. R., 313, 314, 317
Zeitlin, S., 219–224, 553
Zhang, X., 41, 49
Zicht, G., 85, 92
Zigler, E., 327, 336
Zimbardo, P. G., 465, 467
Zirpoli, T. J., 201, 214
Zone of proximal development, 71–72. *See also*
        Scaffolding; Vygotsky
Zoo, 11, 291
Zucker, K. M., 191, 192
Zuidema, M., 417, 422
Zukav, G., 383, 391
Zurcher, L., 418, 419, 420, 422
Zuzanek, J., 487, 492